C0-ALK-141

THE OFFICIAL®

1993 PRICE GUIDE TO

FOOTBALL CARDS

BY
DR. JAMES BECKETT

TWELFTH EDITION

HOUSE OF COLLECTIBLES ● NEW YORK

Important Notice. All of the information, including valuations, in this book has been compiled from the most reliable sources, and every effort has been made to eliminate errors and questionable data. Nevertheless, the possibility of error in a work of such immense scope, always exists. The publisher will not be held responsible for losses which may occur in the purchase, sale, or other transaction of items because of information contained herein. Readers who feel they have discovered errors are invited to write and inform us, so they may be corrected in subsequent editions. Those seeking further information on the topics covered in this book are advised to refer to the complete line of *Official Price Guides* published by the House of Collectibles.

© 1992 by James Beckett III

HC This is a registered trademark of Random House, Inc.

All rights reserved under International and Pan-American Copyright Conventions.

Published by:
House of Collectibles
201 East 50th Street
New York, New York 10022

Distributed by Ballantine Books, a division of Random House, Inc., New York and simultaneously in Canada by Random House of Canada Limited, Toronto.

Manufactured in the United States of America

Library of Congress Catalog Card Number: 81-86222

ISBN: 0-876-37897-1

Twelfth Edition: September 1992

10 9 8 7 6 5 4 3 2 1

Table of Contents

Preface

Isn't it great? Every year this book gets bigger and bigger, packed with all the new sets coming out. But even more exciting is that every year there are more collectors, more shows, more stores, and more interest in the cards we love so much. This edition has been enhanced and expanded from the previous edition. The cards you collect — who they depict, what they look like, where they are from, and (most important to many of you) what their current values are — are enumerated within. Many of the features contained in the other Beckett Price Guides have been incorporated into this volume since condition grading, nomenclature, and many other aspects of collecting are common to the card hobby in general. We hope you find the book both interesting and useful in your collecting pursuits.

While football cards once were considered inferior to baseball cards in the eyes of many card collectors, the fantastic growth of the sports memorabilia collecting hobby over the past few years has given rise to an ever-increasing number of collectors who are giving football another look. The reason for the emergence of football cards in particular is due largely to the continuing and increasing popularity of the sport itself. This surge in interest has made the stars and superstars of the NFL well known to millions of fans who watch them during the fall and read about them all year. Not only have the NFL's standout quarterbacks and running backs become household names, but the wide receivers, defensive linemen, defensive backs, head coaches and even the kickers are justifiably receiving a great deal of media coverage. Finally, the comparatively high cost of quality baseball cards has diverted many card collectors to other sports. Today, as you can see from this Price Guide, football cards are valuable, too.

Also, football cards typically are produced in smaller sets, making it easier for collectors to complete them. For example, from 1983 through 1989, Topps' NFL sets were issued in sets of 396 — half as many as the Topps baseball sets. Only recently has the tremendous growth in the football card market finally spawned sets that approach the size of baseball card sets. Generally, football sets concentrate on each team's "name" players; therefore, there are fewer commons. Obviously, purchasers pull more superstars and Rookie Cards per pack, making these cards even more attractive to collectors. Of course, the debuts of Action Packed, Fleer, Pacific, Pro Set, Pro Line, Score, Upper Deck and Wild Card football sets have changed the market drastically. In other words, baseball cards still are No. 1 — but football isn't far behind.

The Beckett Guide has been successful where other attempts have failed because it is complete, current, and valid. This Price Guide contains not just one, but three prices by condition for all the football cards listed. These account for almost every football card in existence. The prices were added to the card lists just prior to printing and reflect not the author's opinions or desires but the going retail prices for each card, based on the marketplace (sports memorabilia conventions and shows, sports card shops, hobby papers, current mail-order catalogs, computer trading networks, auction results, and other firsthand reportings of actual realized prices).

What is the best price guide on the market today? Of course card sellers will consider the price guide with the highest prices as the best — while card buyers will naturally prefer the one with the lowest prices. Accuracy, however, is the true test. Use the price guide used by more collectors and dealers than all the others combined. Look for the Beckett name. I won't put my name on anything I won't stake my reputation on. Not the lowest and not the highest — but the most accurate, with integrity.

To facilitate your use of this book, read the complete introductory section in the pages following before going to the pricing pages. Every collectible field has its own terminology; we've tried to capture most of these terms and definitions in our glossary. Please read carefully the section on grading and the condition of your cards, as you will not be able to determine which price column is appropriate for a given card without first assessing its condition.

Welcome to the world of football cards.

Sincerely, Dr. James Beckett

Acknowledgments

A great deal of diligence, hard work, and dedicated effort went into this year's volume. However, the high standards to which we hold ourselves could not have been met without the expert input and generous time contributed by many people. Our sincere thanks are extended to each and every one of you.

I believe this year's Price Guide is our best yet. For that, you can thank all of the contributors nationwide (listed below) as well as our staff here in Dallas. Our company now boasts a substantial Technical Services team which has made (and is continuing to make) direct and important contributions to this work. Technical Services capably handled numerous technical details and provided able assistance in pricing for this edition of the annual guide. That effort was directed by Technical Services manager Pepper Hastings. He was assisted by Technical Services coordinator Mary Gregory, Price Guide analysts Theo Chen, Mike Hersh, Dan Hitt, Mary Huston, Rich Klein, Tom Layberger, Allan Muir, Grant Sandground and Dave Sliepka. Also contributing to our Technical Services functions were Jana Threatt, Wendy Jewell, Margaret Mall, Peter Tepp, and Scott Layton. The price gathering and analytical talents of this fine group of hobbyists has helped make our Beckett team stronger, while making this guide and its companion monthly Price Guides more widely recognized as the hobby's most reliable and relied upon sources of pricing information.

Granted, the production of any book is a total staff effort. However, I owe special thanks to the members of our Book Team who demonstrated extraordinary contributions to this football book.

Scott Layton, our research associate, served as point man in the demanding area of new set entry and was a key person in the organization of both technological and people resources for the book. Margaret Mall and Kent Lawrence ensured the proper administration of our contributor price guide surveys. Pricing analysts Theo Chen, Dan Hitt and Rich Klein track the football card market year-round, and their baseline analysis and careful proofreading were key contributions to the accuracy of this annual.

Airey Baringer spent many late-night hours paginating and typesetting the text layout. Gayla Newberry was responsible for many of the card photos you see throughout the book. Maria Gonzalez-Davis again was meticulous in her work on the paste-up table. Wendy Kizer spent tireless hours on the phone attending to the wishes of our dealer advertisers. Once the ad specifications were delivered to our offices, John Marshall used his computer skills to turn raw copy into attractive display advertisements that were carefully proofed by Bruce Felps. Finally, Managing Editor of Special Projects, Susan K. Elliott, set up initial schedules and ensured that all deadlines were met.

My sincere thanks to everyone on our Book Team and to all at Beckett Publications for another job well done.

It is very difficult to be "accurate" — one can only do one's best. But this job is especially difficult since we're shooting at a moving target: Prices are fluctuating all the time. Having several full-time pricing experts has definitely proven to be better than just one, and I thank all of them for working together to provide you, our readers, with the most accurate prices possible.

Those who have worked closely with us on this and many other books, have again proven themselves invaluable — Mike Aronstein, Baseball Hobby News (Frank and Vivian Barning), Jerry Bell, Chris Benjamin, Sy Berger (Topps Chewing Gum), Mike Blaisdell, Bill Bossert (Mid-Atlantic Sports Cards), John Bradley (JOGO), Cartophilium (Andrew Pywowarczuk), Ralph Ciarlo, Mike Cramer (Pacific Trading Cards), Alan Custer, Robert Der, Bill and Diane Dodge, John Douglas, John Durkos, Gervise Ford, Steve Freedman, Larry and Jeff Fritsch, Mike Gallella, Steven Galletta, Tony Galovich, Jim Galusha, Steve Gold (AU Sports), Mike and Howard Gordon, George Grauer, John Greenwald, Wayne Grove, Bill Haber, Jerry and Etta Hersh, Gary Hlady, Wayne Kleman, Lesnik Public Relations (Timm Boyle and Bob Ibach), Lew Lipset, Jim Macie, Paul Marchant, Michael McDonald (The Sports Page), Dick Millerd, Michael Moretto, Brian Morris, Don Niemi, Mike O'Brien, Richard Ochoa, Oldies and Goodies (Nigel Spill), Michael Perrotta, Steve Peters, Jack Pollard, Tom Reid, Gavin Riley, Mark Rose, Alan Rosen (Mr. Mint), Rotman Productions (Andy Rapoza and Steve Rotman), John Rumierz, San Diego Sport Collectibles (Bill Goepner and Nacho Arredondo), Kevin Savage (Sports Gallery), Mike Schechter (MSA), Bob Smith, Eric A. Smith, John Spalding, Sports Collectors Store (Pat Quinn and Don Steinbach), Frank Steele, Murvin Sterling, Paul S. Taylor, Lee Temanson, Bill Wesslund, Kit Young, and Robert Zanze. Finally we give a special acknowledgment to Dennis W. Eckes, "Mr. Sport Americana," whose untimely passing last year was a real loss to the hobby and to me personally. The success of the Beckett Price Guides has always been the result of a team effort.

Many people have provided price input, illustrative material, checklist verifications, errata, and/or background information. At the risk of inadvertently overlooking or omitting these many contributors, we would like to individually thank Carl Abrams (Phoenix Coins), Jerry Adamic, Ken Adams, George Ahlsen, Dan Ainsworth, Ryan Akiyama, Aliso Hills Stamp and Coin, All-Pro Cards, John Alutto, Richard Ames (Pacific Coast Sporting Goods), Dennis Anderson, Mark Anderson, Dan Armstrong, Neil Armstrong (World Series Cards), Athleticards (Richard Tattoli), Joe Avirett, Rod Bain, Darryl Baker, Richard Balinao, Bankston's, Tom Barborich, Clark Barlow, Kevin Barnes, William E. Baxendale, Bay State Cards (Lenny DeAngelico), Rick Bayles, B's Gifts & Gadgets II, Bellevue Ballcards (Robert Shevlin), Patrick Benes, Skip Bertman, Beulah Sports (Jeff Blatt), Brian L. Bigelow, Robert Bignell, David Bitar, Jeff Bland, John Bolduc,

Jason Bolinger, Matt Bonner, Guy Bostock, Rob Boyhan, Bill Brandt, Patrick Brinkman, Robert Brown, Duane Bruce, Dan Bruner (The Card King), Don Buck, Jordan Burchette, V.E. Burgess, Eric Burgoyne, Charles Busch, Jason A. Bush, Ed Cain, Terry Cannon, Danny Cariseo, Eddie Carlson, Dennis Carney, Jack Carpenter, Bud Carter, Terry Castle, Central Collectible Corner, Dwight Chapin, Marques Chitison, Dennis Christensen, Orr Cihlar, Ryan Coffey, Matt Collett, Bob Collins, Tim Collins, Michael Cooper, Taylor Crane, Tim Crawford, Peter Cylvick, Chad Czerwinski, Brian Davis, Samuel Davis, Aaron Day, Dick Dietzel, Rich Digiammo, Mark Dinger, Marc A. Dixon, Mike Diyorio, Payton Dobbs, J.M. Doidge, Edward Donahue, Double "J" Cards, Jeff Dundale, Andrew Dupuy, David Dyal, Gail Edwards, Dennis Egolf, Billy Ellis, Mike Ellis, Stephen Elwell, Robin Emmerling, Ed Emmitt, Doak Ewing, Bob Faber, Bob Farmer, Scott Farmer, Jim Ferguson, G. Florence, David Fortner, Richard Freiburghouse, Doug French, Anthony Fresciano, Brian Froehlich, Jim Freund, Dan Fridley, Gallagher Archives, Juven Garcia, Gregg Gardner, Scott Gerace, Tom Giacchino, Marvin Gifford, Dick Gilkeson, Teran Gillins, Michael R. Gionet, Timothy Golden, Shane Goldsmith, Jeff Goldstein, Ray Gomez, Joseph Gong, Dan Goodwin, Gregg Gornes, Christopher Graeff, Rosa Green, Matt Gresman, Michael Grimshaw, Mike Gruszecki, John Gullo, Eric Gunderson, Steve Haefling, Hall's Nostalgia, Bill Hansen, G.W. Hanson, Richard Hapach, Phil Harrell, Mike Harrilla, Chris Harvey, Scott Hatfield, James Head, Howard Hecht, John Heil, Jeff Hein, Davin Hensrud, Dave Hermann, Chad Herr, Howard Herrington, Clay Hill, David Hill, K. Hisatomi, Michael Hobgood, Chris Holcombe, Jason Holldorf, Chris Homblen, Russ Hoover, Ed Hosch, D.J. Hunter, Dean Hybl, Daniel Ignatuk, Lawrence Irving, Bob Ivanjack, Jason Jackson, Robert Jackson, Larry James, Dan Jaskula, Joe Jeffcoat, Jim Jirasek, Keith Johnsen, Chris Johnson, Michael Johnson, Terry Johnson, Stewart Jones, Larry Jordon, Nathan Joyce, Steven L. Judd, Joe Kacz, John Kanach, Jay and Mary Kasper, Frank Katen, Donna Kehl, Rick Keplinger, Kris Keyes, Wayne Kleman, Michael Klug, Charles Kook, John Kranz, Terry Kreider, Joe R. Kuba, Thomas Kunnecke, Keith Laber, Tom C. Lalli, Mike Landolina, Ted Larkins (Card Clubhouse), Dan Lavin, Randy Law, Walter Ledzki, Michael Lee, Marc Lefkowitz (Baseball Card Baron), Paul Lehotsky, Tom Leon (Unisource Collectibles), Irv Lerner, Howie Levy of Blue Chip, Teresa Lewis, Chris Litcher, David Lomba, Keith Lorenz, Joe Lunsford, Dennis Lusk, Kevin Lynch, Michael MacDonald, Jay MacEachern, Gary Marley, Steve Marson, Don Masline, Chris Mauro, Bronson Mathis, Patrick May, Mike McCann, Jason McConnell, Michael McDonald (The Sports Page), Patrick McGinn, Glenn McIntosh, Matt McPherson, Harvey Medlin, Anthony Mendiola, Blake Meyer, David R. Mica, Lee Milazzo, Danny Miller, Jake Miller, Jay Miller, Patrick Mills, Shawn Minnick, Kenny Mitchell, Ron Moermond, Adam Mohr, John Montgomery, Chas Moore, Frank B. Moore, Zach Moore, Joe Morano, Koi Morford, Rusty Morse, Adam Moseley, Chuck Mounts, Dick Mueller, Matt Mullikin, Alexander Munroe, Dave Murray, A.C. Naylor, Craig A. Nelson, Mark Nelson, Charles New,

Toby Newbanks, Robert Norman, Vic Noto, Michael Odom, John O'Hara, Nicholas Onaindia, Roger Oiler, Bobby Orr, Mike Orth, Matt Oster, Kevin Padget, Andrew Pak, Vern Page, Clay Pasternack, Douglas Pawson, John D. Peterson Jr., Ira Petsrillo, Gary Pettett, Tom Pfirrmann, Hoa Pham, Alan Phillips, Clint Pollard, Chris Pomerleau, Michael Potter, Mike Powell, Randy Proctor, James G. Pugh, Jonathan Pullano, Steve Raab, Paul M. Realini, Red River Coins & Cards, Steve Reeves, Phil Regli, Bob Regoli, O.W. Reinholt, Scott Rewak, Tim Reynolds, Ann Rhea, Dave Richardson, Owen Ricker, Evelyn Roberts, Jim Roberts, Terry Roberts, Steve Rodgers, Chris Rogissart, Robert Ronke, Chip Rosenberg, Eric Rosenfield, Michael Rosentreter, Brian A. Ross, Ryan Rowan, Eugene Rudnick, George Rusnak, Ryan Ruston, Alan Ryan, Terry Sack, Troy Saechao, Joe Sak, Mark Salmon, Terry Sample, Carole Say, Nathan Schank, Steve Schlichter, Kurt Schlichting, R.J. Schulhof, Patrick W. Scoggin, Jeb Scolman, John Scott, Peter Scott, C. Serpa, Rick Seykoski, Tom Shadden, Travis L. Sheldon, Eddie Shelton, Stacy Sigman, Jed Slaughter, Jim Smith, Levi Smith, Mike Snow, Steve F. Soter, Carl Specht, Alan Steger, Sean Stegmaier, Cary Stephenson, Dan Stickney, Bob Stobaugh Jr., The Stonebaughs, Jack Stowe, Del Stracke, Richard Strobino, Andy Studie, John Stufflebeam, William Taylor, Thomas Terebesi, Artie Terry, Danny Tharp, Gerald Thomas, Stephen Thomas, D.W. Thompson, Thunderbird Cards, Dan Tisdale, Dan Todd, Jim Trinidad, Darius Trunk, Ralph Tschabold, John Tumazos, Adam J. Ullery, Eric Unglaub, Carson Van Lindt, Nate VandenLangenburg, Kevin M. Vanderkelen, Sam Varnado, Jesse Vickey, Michelle Villeneuve, Vance Villanueva, Ed Ward, Reuben Ward, Scott Ward, Brandt Warder, David Walter, Jim Watkins, Greg Weeks, Michael Werneke, Jim Wheaton, Richard White, C.B. Wickett, William Wicksnin, Lee Wigmore, Gerald Wiles, Bob Wilke (The Shoe Box), Donny Wilkinson, Ed Willett, Wesley A. Williams, John E. Wilson, Joe Winnett, David Wood, Chris Wozniak, Grant Wright, Michel Wyczynski, Dennis Yareszko, and Chad Zezula.

Every year, we make active solicitations for expert input. We are particularly appreciative of help (however extensive or cursory) provided for this volume. We receive many inquiries, comments and questions regarding material within this book. In fact, each and every one is read and digested. Time constraints, however, prevent us from personally replying. But keep sharing your knowledge. Your letters and input are part of the "big picture" of hobby information we can pass along to readers in our books and magazines. Even though we cannot respond to each letter, you are making significant contributions to the hobby through your interest and comments.

In the years since this guide debuted, Beckett Publications has grown beyond any rational expectation. A great many talented and hard working individuals have been instrumental in this growth and success. Our whole team is to be congratulated for what we together have accomplished.

Our Beckett Publications team is led by Associate Publisher Claire Backus, Vice Presidents Joe Galindo and Fred Reed, and Director of Marketing Jeff

Amano. They are ably assisted by Fernando Albieri, Theresa Anderson, Gena Andrews, Jeff Anthony, Airey Baringer II, Barbara Barry, Nancy Bassi, Therese Bellar, Louise Bird, Wendy Bird, Cathryn Black, Terry Bloom, Lisa Borden, Dianne Boudreaux, Amy Brougher, Anthony Brown, Chris Calandro, Emily Camp, Mary Campana, Renata Campos, Beckie Cann, Sammy Cantrell, Susan Catka, Jose Chavez, Theo Chen, Lynne Chinn, Tommy Collins, Belinda Cross, Billy Culbert, Randy Cummings, Patrick Cunningham, Gail Docekal, Andrew Drago, Louise Ebaugh, Alejandro Egusquiza, Mila Egusquiza, Susan Elliott, Daniel Evans, Bruce Felps, Jorge Field, Sara Field, Jean Paul Figari, Jeany Finch, Robson Fonseca, Kim Ford, Jeannie Fulbright, Gayle Gasperin, Anita Gonzalez, Mary Gonzalez-Davis, Jeff Greer, Mary Gregory, Julie Grove, Marcio Guimaraes, Karen Hall, Carmen Hand, Sabrina Harbour, Lori Harmeyer, Vivian Harmon, Beth Harwell, Jenny Harwell, Mark Harwell, Pepper Hastings, Joanna Hayden, Cindy Herbert, Mike Hersh, Barbara Hinkle, Tracy Hinton, Dan Hitt, Heather Holland, E.J. Hradek, Rex Hudson, Mary Huston, Don James, Sara Jenks, Julia Jernigan, Wendy Jewell, Jay Johnson, Fran Keng, Monte King, Debbie Kingsbury, Amy Kirk, Sheri Kirk, Rudy Klancnik, Rich Klein, Frances Knight, John Knotts, Kent Lawrence, Tom Layberger, Jane Ann Layton, Scott Layton, Lori Lindsey, Cheryl Lingenfelter, Margaret Mall, Mark Manning, Louis Marroquin, John Marshall, Laura Massey, Kaki Matheson, Teri McGahey, Kirk McKinney, Mary McNertney, Omar Mediano, Edras Mendez, Sherry Monday, Robert Montenegro, Stephen Moore, Glen Morante, Elizabeth Morris, Daniel Moscoso, Daniel Moscoso Jr., Mike Moss, Randy Mosty, Allan Muir, Hugh Murphy, Shawn Murphy, Marie Neubauer, Wendy Neumann, Allen Neumann, Gayla Newberry, Rosanna Olaechea, Lisa O'Neill, Rich Olivieri, Abraham Pacheco, Guillermo Pacheco, Michael Patton, Mike Payne, Suzee Payton, Ronda Pearson, Julie Polomis, Reed Poole, Linda Rainwater, Roberto Ramirez, Roger Randall, Nikki Renshaw, Patrick Richard, Cristina Riojas, Jamile Romero, Stephen Rueckhaus, Grant Sandground, Gary Santaniello, Gabriel Santos, Manuel Santos, Stacy Schreiner, Maggie Seward, Elaine Simmons, Carol Slawson, Steve Slawson, Dave Sliepka, Judi Smalling, Steven Smith, Lisa Spaight, Margaret Steele, Mark Stokes, Jason Stone, Cindy Struble, Doree Tate, Peter Tepp, Jim Tereschuk, Christiann Thomas, Becky Thompson, Jana Threatt, Jason Todd, Valerie Voigt, Steve Wilson, Carol Ann Wurster, and Robert Yearby. In addition, our consultants James and Sandi Beane and Dan Swanson performed several major system programming jobs for us again this year, to help us accomplish our work faster and more accurately. The whole Beckett Publications team has my thanks for jobs well done. Thank you, everyone.

I also thank my family, especially my wife, Patti, and daughters, Christina, Rebecca, and Melissa, for putting up with me again.

Introduction

Welcome to the exciting world of sports card collecting, America's fastest-growing avocation. You have made a good choice in buying this book, since it will open up to you the entire panorama of this field in the simplest, most concise way. Hundreds of thousands of different sports cards have been issued during the past century. And the number of total sports cards produced by all manufacturers last year has been estimated at several billion, with an initial wholesale value of more than $1 billion. Sales of older cards by dealers may account for an equal or greater amount. With all that cardboard available in the marketplace, it should be no surprise that several million sports fans like you collect sports cards today, and that number is growing each year.

The growth of *Beckett Baseball Card Monthly, Beckett Basketball Monthly, Beckett Football Card Monthly, Beckett Hockey Monthly,* and *Beckett Focus on Future Stars* is another indication of this rising crescendo of popularity for sports cards. Founded in 1984 by Dr. James Beckett, the author of this Price Guide, *Beckett Baseball Card Monthly* has reached the pinnacle of the sports card hobby, with nearly 2 million readers anxiously awaiting each enjoyable and informative issue. The other four magazines have met similar success, with hundreds of thousands of readers devoted to each publication.

So collecting sports cards — while still pursued as a hobby with youthful exuberance by kids in your neighborhood — has also taken on the trappings of an industry, with thousands of full- and part-time card dealers, as well as vendors of supplies, clubs and conventions. In fact, each year since 1980, thousands of hobbyists have assembled for a National Sports Collectors Convention, at which hundreds of dealers have displayed their wares, seminars have been conducted, autographs penned by sports notables, and millions of cards changed hands. These colossal affairs have been staged in Los Angeles, Detroit, St. Louis, Chicago, New York, Anaheim, Arlington (Texas), San Francisco, Atlantic City, and this year in Atlanta. So sports card collecting really is national in scope!

This increasing interest is reflected in card values. As more collectors compete for available supplies, card prices rise (especially for older premium-grade cards). A perusal of the prices in this book, compared to the figures in earlier editions of this Price Guide, will quickly confirm this. Which brings us back around to the book you have in your hands. It is the best guide available to the exciting world of your favorite sport's cards. Read it and use it. May your enjoyment and your card collection increase in the coming months and years.

About the Author

Dr. Jim Beckett, the leading authority on sport card values in the United States, maintains a wide range of activities in the world of sports. He possesses one of the finest collections of sports cards and autographs in the world, has made numerous appearances on radio and television, and frequently has been cited in many national publications. He was awarded the first "Special Achievement Award" for Contributions to the Hobby by the National Sports Collectors Convention in 1980, the "Jock-Jasperson Award" for Hobby Dedication in 1983, and the "Buck Barker, Spirit of the Hobby" Award in 1991.

Dr. Beckett is the author of *The Sport Americana Baseball Card Price Guide, The Official Price Guide to Baseball Cards, The Sport Americana Price Guide to Baseball Collectibles, The Sport Americana Baseball Memorabilia and Autograph Price Guide, The Sport Americana Football Card Price Guide, The Official Price Guide to Football Cards, The Sport Americana Hockey Card Price Guide, The Official Price Guide to Hockey Cards, The Sport Americana Basketball Card Price Guide and Alphabetical Checklist, The Official Price Guide to Basketball Cards,* and *The Sport Americana Baseball Card Alphabetical Checklist.* In addition, he is the founder, publisher, and editor of *Beckett Baseball Card Monthly, Beckett Basketball Monthly, Beckett Football Card Monthly, Beckett Hockey Monthly,* and *Beckett Focus on Future Stars,* magazines dedicated to advancing the card collecting hobby.

Jim Beckett received his Ph.D. in Statistics from Southern Methodist University in 1975. Prior to starting Beckett Publications in 1984, Dr. Beckett served as an Associate Professor of Statistics at Bowling Green State University and as a Vice President of a consulting firm in Dallas, Texas. He currently resides in Dallas with his wife Patti and their daughters, Christina, Rebecca, and Melissa.

How to Collect

Each collection is personal and reflects the individuality of its owner. There are no set rules on how to collect cards. Since card collecting is a hobby or leisure pastime, what you collect, how much you collect, and how much time and money you spend collecting, are entirely up to you. The funds you have available for collecting and your own personal taste should determine how you collect. Information and ideas presented here are intended to help you get the most enjoyment from this hobby.

It is impossible to collect every card ever produced. Therefore, beginners as well as intermediate and advanced collectors usually specialize in some way. One of the most popular aspects of this hobby is that individual collectors can define and tailor their collecting methods to match their own tastes. To give you some ideas of the various approaches to collecting, we will list some of the more popular areas of specialization.

Many collectors select complete sets from particular years. For example, they may concentrate on assembling complete sets from all the years since their birth or since they became avid sports fans. They may try to collect a card for every player during that specified period of time. Many others wish to acquire only certain players. Usually such players are the superstars of the sport, but occasionally collectors will specialize in all the cards of players who attended a particular college or came from a certain town. Some collectors are only interested in the first cards or Rookie Cards of certain players.

Another fun way to collect cards is by team. Most fans have a favorite team, and it is natural for that loyalty to be translated into a desire for cards of the players on that favorite team. For most of the recent years, team sets (all the cards from a given team for that year) are readily available at a reasonable price. This concept can also be applied to your favorite college's products. For instance, University of Maryland collectors would pursue cards of Randy White, Boomer Esiason, Ferrell Edmunds, etc.

Obtaining Cards

Several avenues are open to card collectors to seek their favorite issues. Cards can be purchased in the traditional way at the local candy, grocery, or drug stores, with the bubble gum or other products included. For many years, it has been possible to purchase complete sets of cards through mail-order advertisers found in traditional sports media publications, such as *The Sporting News, Football Digest, Street & Smith* yearbooks, and others. These sets are also advertised in card collecting periodicals. Many collectors will begin by subscribing to at least one of the hobby periodicals. In fact, subscription offers can be found in the advertising section of this book. In addition, a great variety of cards (typically from all eras and all sports) are available through the growing number of hobby retail stores dedicated to sports cards and memorabilia around the country.

Most serious card collectors obtain old (and new) cards from one or more of several main sources: (1) trading or buying from other collectors or dealers; (2) responding to buy, sell or auction ads in hobby publications; (3) buying at a local hobby store; and/or (4) attending sports collectibles shows or conventions.

We advise that you try all four methods since each has its own distinct advantages: (1) trading is a great way to make new friends; (2) hobby periodicals help you keep up with what's going on in the hobby (including when and where the conventions are happening); (3) stores provide the opportunity for considering (any day of the week) a great diversity of material in a relaxed sports-oriented atmosphere most fans love; and (4) shows provide enjoyment and the opportunity to view millions of collectibles under one roof, in addition to meeting some of the hundreds or even thousands of other collectors with similar interests, who also attend the shows.

Preserving Your Cards

Cards are fragile. They must be handled properly in order to retain their value. Careless handling can easily result in creased or bent cards. It is, however, not recommended that tweezers or tongs be used to pick up your cards since such utensils might mar or indent card surfaces and thus reduce those cards' conditions and values. In general, your cards should be handled directly as little as possible. This is sometimes easier to say than to do. Although there are many who use custom boxes, storage trays, or even shoe boxes, plastic sheets represent an inexpensive method to store and display cards. A collection stored in plastic pages in a three-ring album allows you to view your collection at any time without the need to touch the card itself. Cards also can be kept in single holders (of various types and thickness) designed for the enjoyment of each card individually. Most experienced collectors use a combination of the above methods. When purchasing plastic sheets for your cards, be sure that you find the pocket size that fits the cards snugly. Don't put your 1950 Bowmans in a sheet designed to fit 1980 Topps. Most hobby and collectibles shops and virtually all collectors conventions will have these plastic pages available in quantity, or you can purchase them directly from the advertisers in this book. Also remember that pocket size isn't the only factor to consider when looking for plastic sheets. Some collectors concerned with long-term storage of their cards in plastic sheets are cautious to avoid sheets containing PVC and request non-PVC sheets from their dealer.

Damp, sunny and/or hot conditions — no, this is not a weather forecast — are three elements to avoid in extremes if you are interested in preserving your collection. Too much (or too little) humidity can cause gradual deterioration of a card. Direct sunlight (or fluorescent light) will bleach out the color of a card. Extreme heat accelerates the decomposition of the card. On the other hand, many cards have lasted more than 50 years with minimal scientific intervention. So be cautious, even if the above factors typically present a problem only when present in the extreme. It never hurts to be prudent.

Collecting/Investing

Collecting individual players and collecting complete sets are both popular vehicles for investment and speculation. Most investors and speculators stock up on complete sets or on quantities of players they think have good investment potential.

There is obviously no guarantee in this book, or anywhere else for that matter, that cards will outperform the stock market or other investment alternatives in the future. After all, sports cards do not pay quarterly dividends, and cards cannot be sold at their "current values" as easily as stocks or bonds.

Nevertheless, investors have noticed a favorable long-term trend in the past performance of many sports collectibles, and certain cards and sets have outperformed just about any other investment in some years. Many hobbyists maintain that the best investment is, and always will be, the building of a collection, which traditionally has held up better than outright speculation.

Some of the obvious questions are: Which cards? When do I buy? When do I sell? The best investment you can make is in your own education. The more you know about your collection, the hobby and the players depicted on the cards, the more informed the decisions you will be able to make. We're not selling investment tips. We're selling information about the current value of sports cards. It's up to you to use that information to your best advantage.

Nomenclature

Each hobby has its own language to describe its area of interest. The nomenclature traditionally used for trading cards is derived from the American Card Catalog (frequently referenced to as ACC), published in 1960 by Nostalgia Press. That catalog, written by Jefferson Burdick (who is called the father of card collecting for his pioneering work), uses letter and number designations for each separate set of cards.

The letter used in the ACC designation refers to a generic type of card. While both sport and non-sport issues are classified in the ACC, we shall confine ourselves to the sport issues. The following list defines the letters and their meanings as used by the American Card Catalog, as applied to football cards:

F - Food Inserts
H - Advertising
M - Periodicals
N - 19th Century U.S. Tobacco
PC - Postcards
R - Recent Candy and Gum Cards, 1930 to Present
UO - Gas and Oil Inserts
V - Canadian Candy
W - Exhibits, Strip Cards, Team Cards

Following the letter prefix and an optional hyphen are one-, two-, or three-digit numbers, R(-)999. These typically represent the company or entity issuing the cards. In several cases, the ACC number is extended by an additional hyphen and another one- or two-digit numerical suffix. For example, the 1957 Topps regular series football card issue carries an ACC designation of R415-5. The "R" indicates a Candy or Gum Card produced since 1930. The "415" is the ACC designation for Topps Chewing Gum football card issues and the "5" is the ACC designation for the 1957 regular issue (Topps' fifth football set).

Like other traditional methods of identification, this system provides order to the process of cataloging cards; however, most serious collectors learn the ACC designation of the popular sets by repetition and familiarity, rather than by attempting to "figure out" what they might or should be.

From 1948 forward, collectors and dealers commonly refer to all sets by their year, maker, type of issue, and any other distinguishing characteristic. For example, such a characteristic could be an unusual issue, or one of several regular issues put out by a specific maker in a single year. Regional issues are usually referred to by year, maker, and sometimes, by set title or theme.

Glossary/Legend

Our glossary defines terms frequently used in the football card collecting hobby. Many of these terms are also common to other types of sports memorabilia collecting. Some terms may have several meanings, depending on use and context.

ACC - Acronym for American Card Catalog.

AFC - American Football Conference.

AFL - American Football League.

AP - All-Pro card. A card that portrays an All-Pro player of the previous year, that says "All Pro" on its face. "AP" also is an abbreviation for Associated Press.

ALPH - Alphabetical.

AR - Archrivals (1991 Upper Deck).

AS - Abbreviation for All-Star (card).

AT - Aerial Threats (1991 Upper Deck).

ATG - All-Time Great card.

INSERT - A special card or other collectible (often a poster or sticker) contained in the same package along with cards of a major set. Sometimes called a BONUS CARD.

BOX - Card issued on a box.

BRICK - A group or "lot" of cards, usually 50 or more having common characteristics, that is intended to be bought, sold, or traded as a unit.

C - Center.

C90 - Class of 1990 (1990 Score).

CB - Cornerback.

CC - Crunch Crew (1990 Score and 1991 Score).

CFL - Abbreviation for Canadian Football League.

CHECKLIST - A list of the cards contained in a particular set. The list is always in numerical order if the cards are numbered. Some unnumbered sets are artificially numbered in alphabetical order, or by team and alphabetically within the team for convenience.

CL - Checklist card. A card that lists in order the cards and players in the set or series. Older checklist cards in Mint condition that have not been checked off are very desirable and command large premiums.

CO - Coach card.

COIN - A small disc of metal or plastic portraying a player in its center.

COLLECTOR - A person who engages in the hobby of collecting cards primarily for his own enjoyment, with any profit motive being secondary.

COLLECTOR ISSUE - A set produced for the sake of the card itself, with no product or service sponsor. It derives its name from the fact that most of these sets are produced for sale directly to the hobby market.

COMBINATION CARD - A single card depicting two or more players (not including team cards).

COMMON CARD - The typical card of any set; it has no premium value accruing from subject matter, numerical scarcity, popular demand, or anomaly.

CONVENTION - A large gathering of dealers and collectors at a single location for the purpose of buying, selling, and sometimes, trading sports memorabilia items. Conventions are open to the public and sometimes also feature autograph guests, door prizes, films, contests, etc. More commonly called "shows."

COR - Corrected card. A version of an error card that was fixed by the manufacturer.

COUPON - See Tab.

CREASE - A wrinkle on the card, usually caused by bending the card. Creases are common defects resulting from careless handling. Also see the Condition Guide.

DB - Defensive back.

DEALER - A person who engages in buying, selling and trading sports collectibles or supplies. A dealer may also be a collector, but as a dealer, he anticipates a profit.

DIE-CUT - A card with part of its stock partially cut, allowing one or more parts to be folded or removed. After removal or appropriate folding, the remaining part of the card can frequently be made to stand up.

DISC - A circular-shaped card.

DISPLAY SHEET - A clear, plastic page that is punched for insertion into a binder (with standard three-ring spacing) containing pockets for displaying cards. Many different styles of sheets exist with pockets of varying sizes to hold the many differing card formats. The vast majority of current cards measure 2-1/2 by 3-1/2 inches and fit in nine-pocket sheets.

DP - Double Print. A card that was printed in approximately double the quantity compared to other cards in the same series, or draft picks card.

DT - Defensive tackle or Dream Team subset (1991 Score).

ERR - Error card. A card with erroneous information, spelling, or depiction on either side of the card. Most errors are never corrected by the producing card company.

ERROR CARD - A card with erroneous information, spelling, or depiction on either side of the card. Most errors are never corrected by the producing card company.

EXHIBIT - The generic name given to thick stock, postcard-size cards with single-color, obverse pictures. The name is derived from the Exhibit Supply Co. of Chicago, the principal manufacturer of this type of card. These are also known as Arcade cards since they were found in many arcades.

FB - Fullback.

FG - Field goal.

FOIL - A special type of sticker with a metallic-looking surface.

FULL SHEET - A complete sheet of cards that has not been cut into individual cards by the manufacturer. Also called an uncut sheet.

G - Guard.

GF - Ground Force (1990 Score).

GW - Game Winners (1991 Score Pinnacle).

HG - Hot Gun (1990 Score).

HH - Head to Head (1991 Score Pinnacle).

HIGH NUMBER - The cards in the last series of number, in a year in which such higher-numbered cards were printed or distributed in significantly lesser amount than the lower-numbered cards. The high-number designation refers to a scarcity of the high-numbered cards. Many older football card sets have high numbers in terms of this definition.

HL - Highlight card, for example, from the 1978 Topps subset.

HOF - Hall of Fame, or Hall of Famer (also abbreviated HOFer).

HOR - Horizontal pose on a card as opposed to the standard vertical orientation found on most cards.

IA - In Action card. A special type of card depicting a player in an action photo, such as the 1982 Topps cards.

ID - Idols (1991 Score Pinnacle).

INSERT - A card of a different type, e.g., a poster, or any other sports collectible contained and sold in the same package along with a card or cards of a major set.

IR - Instant Replay card. Similar to In Action and Super Action cards. Found only in the 1984 Topps football set.

ISSUE - Synonymous with set, but usually used in conjunction with a manufacturer, e.g., a Topps issue.

KP - Kid Picture card (the 1973 Topps subset).

LAYERING - The separation or peeling of one or more layers of the card stock, usually at the corner of the card. Also see the Condition Guide.

LB - Linebacker.

LEGITIMATE ISSUE - A set produced to promote or boost sales of a product or service, e.g., bubble gum, cereal, cigarettes, etc. Most collector issues are not legitimate issues in this sense.

LID - A circular-shaped card (possibly with tab) that forms the top of the container for the product being promoted.

LL - League leader card. A card depicting the leader or leaders in a specific statistical category from the previous season. Not to be confused with team leader (TL).

MAJOR SET - A set produced by a national manufacturer of cards, containing a large number of cards. Usually 100 or more different cards comprise a major set.

MINI - A small card or stamp (specifically the 1969 Topps Four-in-One football inserts or the 1987 Topps mini football set issued for the United Kingdom).

MVP - Most Valuable Player.

NEW - Newsreel cards (1991 Pro Set).

NOTCHING - The grooving of a card, usually caused by fingernails, rubber bands, or bumping card edges against other objects, which reduces the condition and value of the card. Also see the Condition Guide.

NY - New York.

OBVERSE - The front, face, or pictured side of the card.

OFF - Officials cards (1991 Pro Set).

OT - Offensive tackle.

P1 - First Printing.

P2 - Second Printing.

PANEL - An extended card that is composed of multiple individual cards.

PB - Pro Bowl.

PERIPHERAL SET - A loosely defined term that applies to any non-regular issue set. This term most often is used to describe food issue, giveaway, regional or sendaway sets that contain a fairly small number of cards and are not accepted by the hobby as major sets.

PP - Platinum Performer (1991 Pro Set Platinum).

PRED - Predator (1989 Score subset).

PREMIUM CARDS - A class of products introduced recently, intended to have higher quality card stock and photography than regular cards, but more limited production and higher cost. Defining what is and isn't a premium card is somewhat subjective.

PREMIUM - A card, sometimes on photographic stock, that is purchased or obtained in conjunction with (or redeemed for) another card or product. This term applies mainly to older products, as newer cards distributed in this manner are generally lumped together as peripheral sets.

PROMOTIONAL SET - A set, usually containing a small number of cards, issued by a national card producer and distributed in limited quantities or to a select group of people, such as major show attendees or dealers with wholesale accounts. Presumably, the purpose of a promo set is to stir up demand for an upcoming set. Also called a preview, prototype or test set.

QB - Quarterback.

RARE - A card or series of cards of very limited availability. Unfortunately, "rare" is a subjective term sometimes used indiscriminately. Using the strict definitions, rare cards are harder to obtain than scarce cards.

RB - Record Breaker card or running back.

RC - Rookie Card. A player's first appearance on a regular-issue card from one of the major card companies. Each company has only one regular-issue set per season, and that is the widely available traditional set. With a few exceptions, each player has only one RC in any given set. A Rookie Card cannot be an All-Star, Highlight, In Action, league leader, Super Action or team leader card. It can, however, be a coach card or draft picks card.

REGIONAL - A card issued and distributed only in a limited geographical area of the country. The producer may or may not be a major, national producer of trading cards. The key is whether the set was distributed nationally in any form or not.

REP - Replay cards (1991 Pro Set).

REVERSE - The back or narrative side of the card.

REV NEG - Reversed or flopped photo side of the card. This is a major type of error card, but only some are corrected.

RM - Rocket Man (1990 Score).

ROY - Rookie of the Year.

S - Safety.

SA - Super Action card. Similar to an In Action card.

SACK - Sack Attack (1991 Score).

SASE - Self-addressed, stamped envelope.

SCARCE - A card or series of cards of limited availability. This subjective term is sometimes used indiscriminately to promote or hype value. Using strict definitions, scarce cards are easier to obtain as rare cards.

SEMI-HIGH - A card from the next-to-last series of a sequentially issued set. It has more value than an average card and generally less value than a high number. A card is not called a semi-high unless its next-to-last series has an additional premium attached to it.

SERIES - The entire set of cards issued by a particular producer in a particular year, e.g., the 1978 Topps series. Also, within a particular set, series can refer to a group of (consecutively numbered) cards printed at the same time, e.g., the first series of the 1948 Leaf set (#'s 1 to 49).

SET - One each of an entire run of cards of the same type, produced by a particular manufacturer during a single season. In other words, if you have a complete set of 1975 Topps football cards, then you have every card from #1 up to and including #528; i.e., all the different cards that were produced.

SHOW - A large gathering of dealers and collectors at a single location for the purpose of buying, selling and trading sports cards and memorabilia. Conventions are open to the public and sometimes also feature autograph guests, door prizes, films, contests, etc.

SKIP-NUMBERED - A set that has many unissued card numbers between the lowest number in the set and the highest number in the set, e.g., the 1949 Leaf football set contains 49 cards skip-numbered from #'s 1-144. A major set in which a few numbers were not printed is not considered to be skip-numbered.

SL - Sidelines (1991 Score Pinnacle) or Season Leaders (1991 Upper Deck).

SP - Single or Short Print. A card which was printed in lesser quantity compared to the other cards in the same series (also see DP). This term only can be used in a relative sense and in reference to one particular set. For instance, the 1989 Pro Set Pete Rozelle SP is less common than the other cards in that set, but it isn't necessarily scarcer than regular cards of any other set.

SPD - Speedburner (1989 Score subset).

SPECIAL CARD - A card that portrays something other than a single player or team; for example, the 1990 Fleer Joe Montana/Jerry Rice Super Bowl MVPs card #397.

SR - Super Rookie (1987, 1988 and 1989 Topps).

STAMP - Adhesive-backed papers depicting a player. The stamp may be individual or in a sheet of many stamps. Moisture must be applied to the adhesive in order for the stamp to be attached to another surface.

STAR CARD - A card that portrays a player of some repute, usually determined by his ability, but sometimes referring to popularity.

STICKER - A card-like item with a removable layer that can be affixed to another surface. Example: 1983 Topps inserts.

STOCK - The cardboard or paper on which the card is printed.

SUPER ACTION - A card type similar to In Action. Abbreviated in the Price Guide as SA.

SUPERSTAR CARD - A card that portrays a superstar, e.g., a Hall of Fame member or a player whose current performance eventually may warrant serious Hall of Fame consideration.

TAB - A card portion set off from the rest of the card, usually with perforations, that may be removed without damaging the central character or event depicted by the card.

TC - Team card or team checklist card.

TEAM CARD - A card that depicts an entire team.

TECH - Technicians (1991 Score Pinnacle).

TL - Team leader card or Top Leader (1991 Score).

TM - Team MVPs (1991 Score and 1991 Upper Deck).

TR - Traded card.

TRIMMED - A card cut down from its original size. Trimmed cards are undesirable to most collectors, and are therefore less valuable than otherwise identical, untrimmed cards. Also see the Condition Guide.

TSN - The Sporting News.

UER - Uncorrected error card.

UPI - United Press International.

USFL - United States Football League.

VARIATION - One of two or more cards from the same series, with the same card number (or player with identical pose, if the series is unnumbered) differing from one another in some aspect, from the printing, stock or other feature of the card. This is often caused when the manufacturer of the cards notices an error in a particular card, corrects the error and then resumes the print run. In this case there will be two versions or variations of the same card. Sometimes one of the variations is relatively scarce. Variations also can result from accidental or deliberate design changes, information updates, photo substitutions, etc.

VERT - Vertical pose on a card.

WFL - World Football League.

WLAF - World League of American Football.

XRC - Extended Rookie Card. A player's first appearance on a card, but issued in a set that was not distributed nationally nor in packs. In football sets, this term generally refers to the 1984 and 1985 Topps USFL sets.

90 - Ninety-plus (1991 Score).

History of Football Cards

Until the 1930s, the first and only set which featured football players was the Mayo N302 set. The first bubblegum issue dedicated entirely to football players did not appear until the National Chicle issue of 1935. Before this, athletes from several sports were pictured in the multi-sport Goudey Sport Kings issue of 1933. In that set, football was represented by three legends whose fame has not diminished through the years: Red Grange, Knute Rockne and Jim Thorpe. But it was not until 1948, and the post-war bubblegum boom, that the next football issues appeared. Bowman and Leaf Gum companies both issued football card sets in that year. From this point on, football cards have been issued annually by one company or another up to the present time, with Topps being the only major card producer until 1989, when Pro Set and Score debuted and sparked a football card boom.

Football cards depicting players from the Canadian Football League (CFL) did not appear until Parkhurst issued a 100-card set in 1952. Four years later, Parkhurst issued another CFL set with 50 small cards this time. Topps began issuing CFL sets in 1958 and continued annually until 1965, although from 1961 to 1965 these cards were printed in Canada by O-Pee-Chee. Post Cereal issued two CFL sets in 1962 and 1963; these cards formed the backs of boxes of Post Cereals distributed in Canada. The O-Pee-Chee company, which has maintained a working relationship with the Topps Gum Company, issued four CFL sets in the years 1968, 1970, 1971 and 1972. Since 1981, the JOGO Novelties Company has been producing a number of CFL sets depicting past and present players. Returning to American football issues, Bowman resumed its football cards (by then with full-color fronts) from 1950 to 1955. The company twice increased the size of its card during that period. Bowman was unopposed during most of the early 1950s as the sole producer of cards featuring pro football players.

Topps issued its first football card set in 1950 with a group of very small, felt-back cards. In 1951 Topps issued what is referred to as the Magic Football Card set. This set of 75 has a scratch-off section on the back which answers a football quiz. Topps did not issue another football set until 1955 when its All-American Football set paid tribute to past college football greats. In January 1956, Topps Gum Company (of Brooklyn) purchased the Bowman Company (of Philadelphia). After the purchase, Topps issued sets of National Football League (NFL) players up until 1963. The 1961 Topps football set also included American Football League (AFL) players in the high-number series (#'s 133-198). Topps sets from 1964 to 1967 contained AFL players only. From 1968 to the present, Topps has issued a major set of football cards each year.

When the AFL was founded in 1960, Fleer produced a 132-card set of AFL players and coaches. In 1961, Fleer issued a 220-card set (even larger than the

Topps issue of that year) featuring players from both the NFL and AFL. Apparently, for that one year, Topps and Fleer tested a reciprocal arrangement, trading the card printing rights to each other's contracted players. The 1962 and 1963 Fleer sets feature only AFL players. Both sets are relatively small at 88 cards each.

Post Cereal issued a 200-card set of National League football players in 1962, which contains numerous scarcities, namely those players appearing on unpopular varieties of Post Cereal. From 1964 to 1967, the Philadelphia Gum company issued four 198-card NFL player sets.

In 1984 and 1985, Topps produced a set for the now defunct United States Football League, in addition to its annual NFL set. The 1984 set in particular is quite scarce, due to both low distribution and the high demand for the extended Rookie Cards of current NFL superstars Jim Kelly and Reggie White, among others.

In 1986, the McDonald's fast-food chain generated the most excitement in football cards in many years. McDonald's created a nationwide football card promotion in which customers could receive a card or two per food purchase, upon request. However, the cards distributed were only of the local team, or of the McDonald's All-Stars for areas not near NFL cities. Also, each set was produced with four possible color tabs: blue, black, gold and green. The tab color distributed depended on the week of the promotion. In general, cards with blue tabs are the scarcest, although for some teams the cards with black tabs are the hardest to find. The tabs were intended to be scratched off and removed by customers to be redeemed for food and other prizes, but among collectors, cards with scratched or removed tabs are categorized as having a major defect, and therefore are valued considerably less.

The entire set, including four color tabs for all 29 subsets, totals over 2,800 different cards. The hoopla over the McDonald's cards fell off precipitously after 1988, as collector interest shifted to the new 1989 Score and Pro Set issues. The popularity of football cards has continued to grow since 1986. Topps introduced Super Rookie cards in 1987. Card companies other than Topps noticed the burgeoning interest in football cards, resulting in the two landmark 1989 football sets: a 330-card Score issue, and a 440-card Pro Set release. Score later produced a self-contained 110-card supplemental set, while Pro Set printed 100 Series II cards and a 21-card Final Update set. Topps, Pro Set and Score all improved card quality and increased the size of their sets for 1990. That season also marked Fleer's return to football cards and Action Packed's first major set.

In 1991, Pacific, Pro Line, Upper Deck and Wild Card joined a market that is now at least as competitive as the baseball card market. And the premium card trend that began in baseball cards spilled over to the gridiron in the form of Fleer Ultra, Pro Set Platinum, Score Pinnacle and Topps Stadium Club sets.

This is but a thumbnail sketch of football card issues from their inception to the present. It is difficult to tell the whole story in just a few paragraphs. There are several other good sources of information. Serious collectors should subscribe to at least one of the excellent hobby magazines or papers. We also suggest that you try to attend a sports collectibles convention or visit a store in your area. Card collecting is still a young and informal hobby, and there is a chance you will run into one or more of the "experts" in this field, who are usually more than happy to share their knowledge with you.

Business of Sports Card Collecting

Determining Value

Why are some cards more valuable than others? Obviously, the economic law of supply and demand is applicable to sports card collecting, just as it is to any other field where a commodity is bought, sold, or traded in a free, unregulated market.

Supply (the number of cards available on the market) is less than the total number of cards originally produced, since attrition diminishes that original quantity. Each year a percentage of cards is typically thrown away, destroyed, or otherwise lost to collectors. This percentage is much smaller today than it was in the past because more and more people have become increasingly aware of the value of sports cards.

For those who collect only Mint condition cards, the supply of older cards can be quite small indeed. Until recently, collectors were not so conscious of the need to preserve the condition of their cards. For this reason, it is difficult to know exactly how many 1953 Bowman football cards are currently available, Mint or otherwise. It is generally accepted that there are fewer 1953 Bowmans available than 1963, 1973, or 1983 Topps football cards. If demand were equal for each of these sets, the law of supply and demand would increase the price for the least available sets. Demand, however, is never equal for all sets, so price correlations can be complicated.

The total number of cards produced for any given issue can only be approximated, as compared to other collectibles such as coins and stamps. The reason is simple: Card manufacturers are predominantly private companies, which are not required to reveal such internal information, while governments are required to release figures regarding currency and postage stamp production. The demand for any given card is influenced by many factors. These include: (1) the age of the card; (2) the number of cards printed; (3) the player(s) portrayed on the card; (4) the attractiveness and popularity of the set; and perhaps most importantly, (5) the physical condition of the card.

In general, (1) the older the card, (2) the fewer the number of the cards printed, (3) the more famous the player, (4) the more attractive and popular the set, or (5) the better the condition of the card, the higher the value of the card will be. There are exceptions to all but one of these factors: the condition of the card. Given two cards similar in all respects except condition, the one in the best condition will always be valued higher.

While there are certain guidelines that help to establish the value of a card, the numerous exceptions and peculiarities make any simple, direct mathematical formula to determine card values impossible.

One certainty in the sports card hobby is the high demand for Rookie Cards, specifically for RCs of superstar players. A Rookie Card is defined as the first card from a major set of a particular player. Because minor league baseball players have signed contracts and are therefore professionals, baseball Rookie Cards often are issued before or during a player's first major league season. These cards usually are designated "Future Stars," "Major League Prospects," "Rated Rookies," or something similar on the front.

Football Rookie Cards, on the other hand, are printed only after a player has renounced his collegiate eligibility. Pro Set's 1991 issue created an exception to that rule, however, with a card for Heisman Trophy winner Ty Detmer (#37), who was heading into his senior season. Until recently, most football Rookie Cards were released one or two years after the player's first professional season. But beginning with the 1989 efforts of Pro Set and Score, RCs of prominent players now are more likely to be printed during or before their rookie years.

Before 1987, the fronts of football Rookie Cards did not have any special notation. But on 1987 and later sets, Topps has printed "Topps Super Rookie" on the card fronts of certain players who had outstanding rookie seasons the previous year. Newer football card manufacturers have created many similar rookie-related subsets, designated as such on the fronts.

Regional Variation

Two types of price variations exist among the sections of the country where a card is bought or sold. The first is the general price variation on all cards bought and sold in one geographical area as compared to another. Card prices are slightly higher on the East and West coasts, and slightly lower in the middle of the country. Although prices may vary from the East to the West, or from the Southwest to the Midwest, the prices listed in this guide are nonetheless presented as a consensus of all sections of this large and diverse country.

Still, prices for a particular player's cards may well be higher in his home team's area than in other regions. This represents the second type of regional price variation, in which local players are favored over those from distant areas. For example, a Terry Bradshaw card is valued higher in Pittsburgh than in San Diego because Bradshaw played in Pittsburgh; therefore, the demand there for Terry Bradshaw cards is higher than it is in San Diego. On the other hand, a Dan Fouts card is priced higher in San Diego where he played, than in Pittsburgh, for similar reasons. Frequently, even common player cards (particularly pre-1980) command such a premium from hometown collectors.

Set Prices

A somewhat paradoxical situation exists in the price of a complete set vs. the combined cost of the individual cards in the set. In nearly every case, the sum of the prices for the individual cards is higher than the cost for the complete set. This is especially prevalent in the cards of the past few years. The reasons for this apparent anomaly stem from the habits of collectors, and from the carrying costs to dealers. Today, each card in a set is normally produced in the same quantity as all others in its set.

However, many collectors pick up only stars, superstars and particular teams. As a result, the dealer is left with a shortage of certain player cards and an abundance of others. He therefore incurs an expense in simply "carrying" these less desirable cards in stock. On the other hand, if he sells a complete set, he gets rid of large numbers of cards at one time. For this reason, he is generally willing to receive less money for a complete set. By doing this, he recovers all of his costs and also makes a profit.

The disparity between the price of the complete set and that for the sum of the individual cards also has been influenced by the fact that major manufacturers are now precollating card sets. Since "pulling" individual cards from sets involves a specific type of labor (and cost), the singles or star card market is not affected significantly by precollation.

Set prices also do not include rare card varieties, unless specifically stated. Of course, the prices for sets do include one example of each type for the given set, but this is the least expensive variety.

Scarce Series

Scarce series occur because Topps cards issued before 1973 were made available to the public each year in several series of finite numbers of cards, as opposed to all cards of the set being available for purchase at one time. At some point during the season, interest in the current year cards usually waned. Consequently, the manufacturers produced smaller numbers of these later series cards. Nearly all nationwide issues from post-World War II manufacturers (1948 to 1972) exhibit these series variations.

In the past, Topps, for example, has issued sports card series consisting of many different number of cards, including 55, 66, 80, 88, 110, and others. However, after 1968, the sheet size generally has been 132. Despite Topps' standardization of the sheet size, the company double printed one sheet in 1983 and possibly in 1984 and 1985, too. This was apparently an effort to induce collectors to buy more packs.

We are always looking for information about or photographs of full uncut sheets of cards for research. Each year we try to update the hobby's knowledge of distribution anomalies. Please let us know us at the address in this book if you have first hand knowledge that would be helpful in this pursuit.

Grading Your Cards

Each hobby has its own grading terminology — stamps, coins, comic books, beer cans, right down the line. Collectors of sports cards are no exception. The one invariable criterion for determining the value of a card is its condition. The better the condition of the card, the more valuable it is. However, condition grading is very subjective. Individual card dealers and collectors differ in the strictness of their grading, but the stated condition of a card should be determined without regard to whether it is being bought or sold.

The physical defects that lower the condition of a card are usually quite apparent, but each individual places his own estimation (negative value, in this case) on these defects. We present the condition guide for use in determining values listed in this Price Guide in the hopes that excess subjectivity can be minimized.

The defects listed in the condition guide below are those either created at the time of printing, such as uneven borders, or those defects that occur to a card under normal handling — corner sharpness, gloss, edge wear, light creases — and finally, environmental conditions, such as browning. Other defects to cards are caused by human carelessness, and in all cases should be noted separately and in addition to the condition grade. Among the more common alterations are tape, tape stains, heavy creases, rubber band marks, water damage, smoke damage, trimming, paste, tears, writing, pin or tack holes, any back damage, and missing parts (tabs, tops, coupons, backgrounds).

Centering

It is important to define in words and pictures what is meant by frequently used hobby terms relating to grading cards. The adjacent pictures portray various stages of centering. Centering can range from well-centered to slightly off-center to off-center to badly off-center to miscut.

Slightly Off-Center (60/40): A slightly off-center card is one which is found to have one border bigger than the opposite border. This degree once was only offensive to purists, but now some hobbyists try to avoid cards that are anything other than perfectly centered.

Off-Center (70/30): An off-center card has one border which is noticeably more than twice as wide as the opposite border.

Badly Off-Center (80/20 or worse): A badly off-center card has virtually no border on one side of the card.

Miscut: A miscut card actually shows part of the adjacent card in its larger border and consequently a corresponding amount of its card is cut off.

CENTERING

Slightly Off-Centered

Off-Centered

Badly Off-Centered

Miscut

Corner Wear

Degrees of corner wear generate several common terms used to facilitate accurate grading. The wear on card corners can be expressed as fuzzy corners, corner wear or slightly rounded corners, rounded corners, or badly rounded corners.

Fuzzy Corners: Fuzzy corners still come to a right angle (to a point) but the point has begun to fray slightly.

Corner Wear or Slightly Rounded Corners: The slight fraying of corners has increased to where there is no longer a point to the corner. Nevertheless, the corner is still reasonably sharp. There may be evidence of some slight loss of color in the corner also.

Rounded Corners: The corner is no longer sharp but is not badly rounded.

Badly Rounded Corners: The corner is rounded to an objectionable degree. Excessive wear and rough handling are evident.

Creases

A third common defect is the crease. The degree of creasing in a card is very difficult to show in a drawing or picture. On giving the specific condition of an expensive card for sale, the seller should note any creases additionally. Creases can be categorized as to severity according to the following scale.

Light Crease: A light crease is a crease which is barely noticeable on close inspection. In fact when cards are in plastic sheets or holders, a light crease may not be seen (until the card is taken out of the holder). A light crease on the front is much more serious than a light crease on the card back only.

Medium Crease: A medium crease is noticeable when held and studied at arm's length by the naked eye, but does not overly detract from the appearance of the card. It is an obvious crease, but not one that breaks the picture surface of the card.

Heavy Crease: A heavy crease is one which has torn or broken through the card's picture surface, e.g., puts a tear in the photo surface.

Alterations

Deceptive Trimming: This occurs when someone alters the card in order (1) to shave off edge wear, (2) to improve the sharpness of the corners, or (3) to improve centering — obviously their objective is to falsely increase the perceived value of the card to an unsuspecting buyer. The shrinkage is usually only evident if the trimmed card is compared to an adjacent full-sized card or if the trimmed card itself is measured.

Obvious Trimming: Obvious trimming is noticeable and unfortunate. It is usually performed by non-collectors who give no thought to the present or future value of their cards.

Deceptively Retouched Borders: This occurs when the borders (especially on those cards with dark borders) are touched up on the edges and corners with magic marker of appropriate color in order to make the card appear to be Mint.

Categorization of Defects

A "Micro Defect" would be fuzzy corners, slight off-centering, printers' lines, printers' spots, slightly out of focus, or slight loss of original gloss. A NrMt card may have one micro defect. An ExMt card may have two or more micro defects.

A "Minor Defect" would be corner wear or slight rounding, off-centering, light crease on back, wax or gum stains on reverse, loss of original gloss, writing or tape marks on back, or rubber band marks. An Excellent card may have minor defects.

A "Major Defect" would be rounded corner(s), badly off-centering, crease(s), deceptive trimming, deceptively retouched borders, pin hole, staple hole, incidental writing or tape marks on front, severe warping, water stains, medium crease(s), or sun fading. A VG card may have one major defect. A Good card may have two or more major defects.

A "Catastrophic Defect" is the worst kind of defect and would include such defects as badly rounded corner(s), miscutting, heavy crease(s), obvious trimming, punch hole, tack hole, tear(s), corner missing or clipped, destructive writing on front. A Fair card may have one catastrophic defect. A Poor card has two or more catastrophic defects.

Condition Guide

Mint (Mt) - A card with no defects. The card has sharp corners, even borders, original gloss or shine on the surface, sharp focus of the picture, smooth edges, no signs of wear and white borders. A Mint card does NOT have printers' lines or other printing defects, or other serious quality control problems that should have been discovered by the card company before distribution. Note also that there is no allowance made for the age of the card.

Near Mint (NrMt) - A card with a micro defect. Any of the following would be sufficient to lower the grade of a card from Mint to the Near Mint category: layering at some of the corners (fuzzy corners), a very small amount of the original gloss lost, very minor wear on the edges, slightly off-center borders, slight wear visible only on close inspection, slight off-whiteness of the borders.

Excellent to Mint (ExMt) - A card with micro defects, but no minor defects. Two or three of the following would be sufficient to lower the grade of a card from Mint to the ExMt category: layering at some of the corners (fuzzy corners), a very small amount of the original gloss lost, minor wear on the edges, slightly off-center borders, slight wear visible only on close inspection, slight off-whiteness of the borders.

Excellent (Ex) - A card with minor defects. Any of the following would be sufficient to lower the grade of a card from Mint to the Excellent category: slight rounding at some of the corners, a small amount of the original gloss lost, minor wear on the edges, off-center borders, wear visible only on close inspection, off-whiteness of the borders.

Very Good (VG) - A card that has been handled but not abused. Some rounding at all corners, slight layering or scuffing at one or two corners, slight notching on edges, gloss lost from the surface but not scuffed, borders might be somewhat uneven but some white is visible on all borders, noticeable yellowing or browning of borders, light crease(s), pictures may be slightly off focus.

Good (G) - A well-handled card, rounding and some layering at the corners, scuffing at the corners and minor scuffing on the face, borders noticeably uneven and browning, loss of gloss on the face, medium crease(s), notching on the edges.

Fair (F) - Round and layering corners, brown and dirty borders, frayed edges, noticeable scuffing on the face, white not visible on one or more borders, medium to heavy creases, cloudy focus.

Poor (P) - An abused card: The lowest grade of card, frequently some major physical alteration has been performed on the card, collectible only as a filler until a better-condition replacement can be obtained.

Categories between these major condition grades are frequently used, such as Very Good to Excellent (VG-Ex), Fair to Good (F-G), etc. Such grades indicate a card with all qualities at least in the lower of the two categories, but with several qualities in the higher of the two categories. In the case of ExMt, it essentially refers to a card which is halfway between Excellent and Mint.

Unopened packs, boxes and factory-collated sets are considered Mint in their unknown (and presumed perfect) state. However, once opened or broken out, each of these cards is graded (and valued) in its own right by taking into account any quality control defects (such as off-centering, printers' lines, machine creases, or gum stains) present in spite of the fact that the card has never been handled.

Cards before 1980 that are priced in the Price Guide in top condition of NrMt are obviously worth an additional premium when offered in strict Mint condition. This additional premium increases relative to the age and scarcity of the card. For example, Mint cards from the late 1970s may bring only a 10 percent premium for Mint (above NrMt), whereas high demand (or condition rarity) cards from early vintage sets can be sold for as much as double (and occasionally even more) the NrMt price when offered in strict Mint condition.

Cards before 1946 which are priced in the Price Guide in a top condition of ExMt, obviously are worth an additional premium when offered in strict Near Mint or better condition. This additional premium increases relative to the age and scarcity of the card.

Selling Your Cards

Just about every collector sells cards or will sell cards eventually. Someday you may be interested in selling your duplicates or maybe even your whole collection. You may sell to other collectors, friends, or dealers. You may even sell cards you purchased from a certain dealer back to that same dealer. In any event, it helps to know some of the mechanics of the typical transaction between buyer and seller.

Dealers will buy cards in order to resell them to other collectors who are interested in the cards. Dealers will always pay a higher percentage for items which (in their opinion) can be resold quickly, and a much lower percentage for those items which are perceived as having low demand and hence are slow moving. In either case, dealers must buy at a price that allows for the expense of doing business and a margin for profit.

If you have cards for sale, the best advice we can give is that you get several offers for your cards — either from card shops or at a card show — and take the best offer, all things considered. Note, the "best" offer may not be the one for the highest amount. And remember, if a dealer really wants your cards, he won't let you get away without making his best competitive offer. Another alternative is to place your cards in an auction as one or several lots.

Many people think nothing of going into a department store and paying $15 for an item of clothing the store paid $5. But, if you were selling your $15 card to a dealer and he offered you only $5 for it, you might think his markup unreasonable. To complete the analogy: most department stores (and card dealers) that consistently pay $10 for $15 items eventually go out of business. An exception is when the dealer has a willing buyer for the item(s) you are attempting to sell lined up, or if the cards are so Hot that it's likely he'll only have to hold the cards for a short period of time.

In those cases, an offer of up to 75 percent of book value will still allow the dealer to make a reasonable profit considering the short time he will need to hold the merchandise. In general, however, most cards and collections will bring offers in the range of 25 percent to 50 percent of retail price. Also consider that most material from the past five to 10 years is very plentiful. If that's what you're selling, expect even less or no offer at all unless you have Hot cards that the dealer can move easily.

Interesting Notes

The numerically first card of an issue is the single card most likely to obtain excessive wear. Consequently, you typically will find the price on the No. 1 card (in NrMt or Mint condition) somewhat higher than might otherwise be the case. Similarly, but to a lesser extent (because normally the less important, reverse side of the card is the one exposed), the numerically last card in an issue is also prone to abnormal wear. This extra wear and tear occurs because the first and last cards are exposed to the elements (human element included) more than any other cards. They are generally end cards in any brick formations, rubber bandings, stackings on wet surfaces, and like activities.

Sports cards have no intrinsic value. The value of a card, like the value of other collectibles, can only be determined by you and your enjoyment in viewing and possessing these cardboard swatches.

Remember, the buyer ultimately determines the price of each baseball card. You are the determining price factor because you have the ability to say no to the price of any card by not exchanging your hard-earned money for a given card. When the cost of a trading card exceeds the enjoyment you will receive from it, your answer should be no. We assess and report the prices. You set them!

We are always interested in receiving the price input of collectors and dealers from around the country. We happily credit major contributors. We welcome your opinions, since your contributions assist us in ensuring a better guide each year. If you would like to join our survey list for the next editions of this book and others authored by Dr. Beckett, please send your name and address to Dr. James Beckett, 4887 Alpha Road, Suite 200, Dallas, Texas 75244.

Advertising

Within this guide you will find advertisements for sports memorabilia material, mail order, and retail sports collectibles establishments. All advertisements were accepted in good faith based on the reputation of the advertiser; however, neither the author, the publisher, the distributors, nor the other advertisers in the Price Guide accept any responsibility for any particular advertiser not complying with the terms of his or her ad.

Readers should also be aware that prices in advertisements are subject to change throughout the annual period before a new edition of this volume is issued each fall. When replying to an advertisement late in the sporting year following the fall release of this volume, the reader should take this into account, and contact the dealer by phone or in writing for up-to-date price quotes and availability. Should you come into contact with any of the advertisers in this guide as a result of their advertisement herein, please mention to them this source as your contact.

Recommended Reading

With the increase in popularity of the hobby in recent years, there has been a corresponding increase in available literature. Below is a list of the books and periodicals that receive our highest recommendation and that we hope will further your knowledge and enjoyment of our great hobby.

The Sport Americana Baseball Card Price Guide by Dr. James Beckett (No. 14, $15.95, released 1992, published by Edgewater Book Company) — the most informative, up-to-date, and reliable price guide/checklist on its subject matter ever compiled. No serious hobbyist should be without it.

The Official Price Guide to Baseball Cards by Dr. James Beckett (No. 12, $5.99, released 1992, published by The House of Collectibles) — this work is essentially an abridgment of *The Sport Americana Baseball Card Price Guide* immediately above, published in a convenient and economical pocket-size format and provides Dr. Beckett's pricing of the major baseball sets since 1948.

The Sport Americana Football Card Price Guide by Dr. James Beckett (No. 8, $14.95, released 1991, published by Edgewater Book Company) — the most comprehensive price guide/checklist ever issued on football cards. No serious football card hobbyist should be without it.

The Official Price Guide to Football Cards by Dr. James Beckett (No. 10, $5.95, released 1991, published by The House of Collectibles) — essentially an abridgment of *The Sport Americana Football Card Price Guide* listed above in a convenient and economical pocket-size format providing Dr. Beckett's pricing of the major football sets since 1948.

The Sport Americana Hockey Card Price Guide by Dr. James Beckett (No. 1, $12.95, released 1991, published by Edgewater Book Company) — the most informative, up-to-date, and reliable price guide/checklist on its subject matter ever compiled. No serious hobbyist should be without it.

The Official Price Guide to Hockey Cards by Dr. James Beckett (No. 1, $5.99, released 1991, published by The House of Collectibles) — this work is essentially an abridgment of *The Sport Americana Hockey Card Price Guide* immediately above, published in a convenient and economical pocket-size format and provides Dr. Beckett's pricing of the major hockey sets since 1951.

The Sport Americana Basketball Card Price Guide and Alphabetical Checklist by Dr. James Beckett (No. 1, $12.95, released 1991, published by Edgewater

Book Company) — the most informative, up-to-date, and reliable price guide/ checklist on its subject matter ever compiled. No serious hobbyist should be without it.

The Official Price Guide to Basketball Cards by Dr. James Beckett (No. 1, $5.99, released 1991, published by The House of Collectibles) — this work is essentially an abridgment of *The Sport Americana Basketball Card Price Guide and Alphabetical Checklist* immediately above, published in a convenient and economical pocket-size format and provides Dr. Beckett's pricing of the major basketball sets since 1948.

The Sport Americana Price Guide to Baseball Collectibles by Dr. James Beckett (No. 2, $12.95, released 1988, published by Edgewater Book Company) — the complete guide and checklist with up-to-date values for box cards, coins, decals, R-cards, bread labels, exhibits, discs, lids, fabric, pins, Canadian cards, stamps, stickers, and miscellaneous Topps issues.

The Sport Americana Baseball Card Alphabetical Checklist by Dr. James Beckett (No. 5, $14.95, released 1992, published by Edgewater Book Company) — an alphabetical listing, by the last name of the player portrayed on the card. Virtually all major and minor league baseball cards produced through the 1991 major sets are listed.

The Sport Americana Price Guide to the Non-Sports Cards 1930-1960 by Christopher Benjamin and Dennis W. Eckes ($14.95, released 1991, published by Edgewater Book Company) — the definitive guide to virtually all popular non-sports American tobacco and bubblegum cards issued between 1930 and 1960. In addition to cards, illustrations and prices for wrappers are also included.

The Sport Americana Price Guide to the Non-Sports Cards by Christopher Benjamin and Dennis W. Eckes (No. 3, Part Two, $12.95, released 1988, co-published by Den's Collector's Den and Edgewater Book Company) — the definitive guide to all popular non-sports American tobacco and bubblegum cards. In addition to cards, illustrations and prices for wrappers are also included. Part Two covers non-sports cards from 1961 to 1987.

The Sport Americana Baseball Address List by Jack Smalling and Dennis W. Eckes (No. 6, $12.95, released 1990, published by Edgewater Book Company) — the definitive guide for autograph hunters, giving addresses and deceased information for virtually all major league baseball players, managers, and even umpires, past and present.

The Sport Americana Team Baseball Card Checklist by Jeff Fritsch (No. 6, $12.95, released 1992, published by Edgewater Book Company) — includes all Topps, Bowman, Fleer, Play Ball, Goudey, Upper Deck and Donruss cards, with the players portrayed on the cards listed by their team. The book is invaluable to the collector who specializes in an individual team because it is the most complete baseball card team checklist available.

The Sport Americana Team Football and Basketball Card Checklist by Jane Fritsch, Jeff Fritsch, and Dennis W. Eckes (No. 1, $10.95, released 1990, published by Edgewater Book Company) — The book is invaluable to the collector who specializes in an individual team because it is the most complete football and basketball card team checklist available.

Beckett Baseball Card Monthly, published and edited by Dr. James Beckett — contains the most extensive and accepted monthly Price Guide, collectible glossy superstar covers, colorful feature articles, "who's Hot and who's not" section, Convention Calendar, tips for beginners, "Readers Write" letters to and responses from the editor, information on errors and varieties, autograph collecting tips, and profiles of the sport's Hottest stars. Published every month, *BBCM* is the hobby's largest paid circulation periodical.

Beckett Football Card Monthly, *Beckett Basketball Monthly*, *Beckett Hockey Monthly*, and *Beckett Focus on Future Stars* were built on the success of *BBCM*. These other publications contain many of the same features as I, and contain the most relied upon Price Guides to their respective segments of the sports card hobby.

Prices in this Guide

Prices found in this guide reflect current retail rates just prior to the printing of this book. They do not reflect the FOR SALE prices of the author, the publisher, the distributors, the advertisers, or any card dealers associated with this guide. No one is obligated in any way to buy, sell, or trade his or her cards based on these prices. The price listings were compiled by the author from actual buy/sell transactions at sports conventions, buy/sell advertisements in the hobby papers, for sale prices from dealer catalogs and price lists, and discussions with leading hobbyists in the U.S. and Canada. All prices are in U.S. dollars.

Errata

There are thousands of names, more than 100,000 prices and untold other words in this book. There are going to be a few typographical errors, a few misspellings and possibly a number or two out of place. If you catch a blooper, drop me a note directly or in care of the publisher, and we will fix it in the next year's edition.

1989 Action Packed Test

The 1989 Action Packed Football Test set contains 30 standard-size (2 1/2" by 3 1/2") cards. The cards have rounded corners and gold borders. The fronts have "raised" color action shots, and the horizontally-oriented backs feature mug shots and complete stats. The set, which includes 10 players each from the Chicago Bears, New York Giants, and Washington Redskins, was packaged in six-card poly packs. These cards were not packaged very well, many cards come creased or bent out of packs, and a typical box will yield quite a few duplicates. Although this was supposed to be a limited test issue, the test apparently was successful as there were reports that more than 4300 cases were produced of these cards. Factory sets packaged in small dull-gold colored boxes were also available on a limited basis. The cards are copyrighted by Hi-Pro Marketing of Northbrook, Illinois and the packs are labeled "Action Packed." On the card back of number 6 Dan Hampton it lists his uniform number as 95 which is actually Richard Dent's number; Hampton wears 99 for the Bears. The cards are numbered in alphabetical order within teams, Chicago Bears (1-10), New York Giants (11-20), and Washington Redskins (21-30). Since this set was a test issue, the cards of Dave Meggett and Mark Rypien are not considered true rookie cards.

		MINT	EXC	G-VG
COMPLETE SET (30)		25.00	12.50	2.50
COMMON PLAYER (1-30)		.50	.25	.05

☐ 1	Neal Anderson	4.00	2.00	.40
☐ 2	Trace Armstrong	.60	.30	.06
☐ 3	Kevin Butler	.50	.25	.05
☐ 4	Richard Dent	.75	.35	.07
☐ 5	Dennis Gentry	.50	.25	.05
☐ 6	Dan Hampton UER	.75	.35	.07
	(wrong uniform number on back)			
☐ 7	Jay Hilgenberg	.60	.30	.06
☐ 8	Thomas Sanders	.60	.30	.06
☐ 9	Mike Singletary	.75	.35	.07
☐ 10	Mike Tomczak	.75	.35	.07
☐ 11	Raul Allegre	.50	.25	.05
☐ 12	Ottis Anderson	.75	.35	.07
☐ 13	Mark Bavaro	.60	.30	.06
☐ 14	Terry Kinard	.50	.25	.05
☐ 15	Lionel Manuel	.50	.25	.05
☐ 16	Leonard Marshall	.60	.30	.06
☐ 17	Dave Meggett	4.50	2.25	.45
☐ 18	Joe Morris	.75	.35	.07
☐ 19	Phil Simms	1.00	.50	.10
☐ 20	Lawrence Taylor	1.75	.85	.17
☐ 21	Kelvin Bryant	.75	.35	.07
☐ 22	Darrell Green	1.00	.50	.10
☐ 23	Dexter Manley	.60	.30	.06
☐ 24	Charles Mann	.60	.30	.06
☐ 25	Wilber Marshall	.60	.30	.06
☐ 26	Art Monk	1.50	.75	.15
☐ 27	Jamie Morris	.60	.30	.06
☐ 28	Tracy Rocker	.60	.30	.06
☐ 29	Mark Rypien UER	12.00	6.00	1.20
	(Born 10/2/52, should be 10/2/62)			
☐ 30	Ricky Sanders	1.00	.50	.10

1990 Action Packed

This 280-card set was issued in two skip-numbered series. The cards are the same style as previous year's "test" issue and are standard size, 2 1/2" by 3 1/2". The set is organized numerically within team and teams themselves are in alphabetical order by city name, Atlanta Falcons (1-10), Buffalo Bills (11-20), Chicago Bears (21-30), Cincinnati Bengals (31-40), Cleveland Browns (41-50), Dallas Cowboys (51-60), Denver Broncos (61-70), Detroit Lions (71-80), Green Bay Packers (81-90), Houston Oilers (91-100), Indianapolis Colts (101-110), Kansas City Chiefs (111-120), Los Angeles Raiders (121-130), Los Angeles Rams (131-

140), Miami Dolphins (141-150), Minnesota Vikings (151-160), New England Patriots (161-170), New Orleans Saints (171-180), New York Giants (181-190), New York Jets (191-200), Philadelphia Eagles (201-210), Phoenix Cardinals (211-220), Pittsburgh Steelers (221-230), San Diego Chargers (231-240), San Francisco 49ers (241-250), Seattle Seahawks (251-260), Tampa Bay Buccaneers (261-270), and Washington Redskins (271-280). For cards numbered 3, 26, 193, and 222, the action note on the card back does not correspond with the picture on the front. Later in the year Action Packed released these cards in the form of pre-packed ten-card complete team sets.

	MINT	EXC	G-VG
COMPLETE SET (280)	70.00	35.00	7.00
COMMON PLAYER (1-280)	.20	.10	.02
☐ 1 Aundray Bruce UER	.30	.15	.03
(Andre on back)			
☐ 2 Scott Case	.30	.15	.03
☐ 3 Tony Casillas	.30	.15	.03
☐ 4 Shawn Collins	.30	.15	.03
☐ 5 Marcus Cotton	.20	.10	.02
☐ 6 Bill Fralic	.20	.10	.02
☐ 7 Tim Green	.40	.20	.04
☐ 8 Chris Miller	1.25	.60	.12
☐ 9 Deion Sanders	1.50	.75	.15
☐ 10 John Settle	.30	.15	.03
☐ 11 Cornelius Bennett	.40	.20	.04
☐ 12 Shane Conlan	.30	.15	.03
☐ 13 Kent Hill	.20	.10	.02
☐ 14 Jim Kelly	2.25	1.10	.22
☐ 15 Mark Kelso	.20	.10	.02
☐ 16 Scott Norwood	.20	.10	.02
☐ 17 Andre Reed	.60	.30	.06
☐ 18 Fred Smerlas	.20	.10	.02
☐ 19 Bruce Smith	.50	.25	.05
☐ 20 Thurman Thomas	2.50	1.25	.25
☐ 21 Neal Anderson UER	.65	.30	.06
(Action note begins, "Neil ...")			
☐ 22 Kevin Butler	.20	.10	.02
☐ 23 Richard Dent	.30	.15	.03
☐ 24 Dennis Gentry	.20	.10	.02
☐ 25 Dan Hampton	.30	.15	.03
☐ 26 Jay Hilgenberg	.30	.15	.03
☐ 27 Steve McMichael	.30	.15	.03
☐ 28 Brad Muster	.30	.15	.03
☐ 29 Mike Singletary	.30	.15	.03
☐ 30 Mike Tomczak	.30	.15	.03
☐ 31 James Brooks	.30	.15	.03
☐ 32 Rickey Dixon	.40	.20	.04
☐ 33 Boomer Esiason	.50	.25	.05
☐ 34 David Fulcher	.20	.10	.02
☐ 35 Rodney Holman	.30	.15	.03
☐ 36 Tim Krumrie	.20	.10	.02
☐ 37 Tim McGee	.30	.15	.03
☐ 38 Anthony Munoz UER	.30	.15	.03
(Action note says he's blocking Howie Long, but jersey begins with a nine)			
☐ 39 Reggie Williams	.30	.15	.03
☐ 40 Ickey Woods	.30	.15	.03
☐ 41 Thane Gash	.30	.15	.03
☐ 42 Mike Johnson	.20	.10	.02
☐ 43 Bernie Kosar	.50	.25	.05
☐ 44 Reggie Langhorne	.20	.10	.02
☐ 45 Clay Matthews	.20	.10	.02
☐ 46 Eric Metcalf	.50	.25	.05
☐ 47 Frank Minnifield	.20	.10	.02
☐ 48 Ozzie Newsome	.40	.20	.04
☐ 49 Webster Slaughter	.20	.10	.02
☐ 50 Felix Wright	.20	.10	.02
☐ 51 Troy Aikman	3.00	1.50	.30
☐ 52 James Dixon	.30	.15	.03
☐ 53 Michael Irvin	1.00	.50	.10
☐ 54 Jim Jeffcoat	.20	.10	.02
☐ 55 Ed Too Tall Jones	.30	.15	.03
☐ 56 Eugene Lockhart	.20	.10	.02
☐ 57 Danny Noonan	.20	.10	.02
☐ 58 Paul Palmer	.20	.10	.02
☐ 59 Everson Walls	.30	.15	.03
☐ 60 Steve Walsh	.40	.20	.04
☐ 61 Steve Atwater	.30	.15	.03
☐ 62 Tyrone Braxton	.30	.15	.03
☐ 63 John Elway	.90	.45	.09
☐ 64 Bobby Humphrey	.60	.30	.06
☐ 65 Mark Jackson	.30	.15	.03
☐ 66 Vance Johnson	.30	.15	.03
☐ 67 Greg Kragen	.20	.10	.02
☐ 68 Karl Mecklenburg	.30	.15	.03
☐ 69 Dennis Smith	.30	.15	.03
☐ 70 David Treadwell	.30	.15	.03
☐ 71 Jim Arnold	.20	.10	.02

☐ 72	Jerry Ball	.30	.15	.03
☐ 73	Bennie Blades	.30	.15	.03
☐ 74	Mel Gray	.30	.15	.03
☐ 75	Richard Johnson	.30	.15	.03
☐ 76	Eddie Murray	.30	.15	.03
☐ 77	Rodney Peete UER	.40	.20	.04
	(On back, squeaker misspelled as squeeker)			
☐ 78	Barry Sanders	6.00	3.00	.60
☐ 79	Chris Spielman	.30	.15	.03
☐ 80	Walter Stanley	.20	.10	.02
☐ 81	Dave Brown	.20	.10	.02
☐ 82	Brent Fullwood	.20	.10	.02
☐ 83	Tim Harris	.30	.15	.03
☐ 84	Johnny Holland	.20	.10	.02
☐ 85	Don Majkowski	.60	.30	.06
☐ 86	Tony Mandarich	.30	.15	.03
☐ 87	Mark Murphy	.20	.10	.02
☐ 88	Brian Noble UER	.20	.10	.02
	(Fumble recovery stats show 9 instead of 7)			
☐ 89	Ken Ruettgers	.30	.15	.03
☐ 90	Sterling Sharpe UER	.90	.45	.09
	(Born Glenville, Ga., should be Chicago)			
☐ 91	Ray Childress	.30	.15	.03
☐ 92	Ernest Givins	.30	.15	.03
☐ 93	Alonzo Highsmith	.30	.15	.03
☐ 94	Drew Hill	.30	.15	.03
☐ 95	Bruce Matthews	.20	.10	.02
☐ 96	Bubba McDowell	.30	.15	.03
☐ 97	Warren Moon	1.00	.50	.10
☐ 98	Mike Munchak	.30	.15	.03
☐ 99	Allen Pinkett	.30	.15	.03
☐ 100	Mike Rozier	.30	.15	.03
☐ 101	Albert Bentley	.30	.15	.03
☐ 102	Duane Bickett	.20	.10	.02
☐ 103	Bill Brooks	.20	.10	.02
☐ 104	Chris Chandler	.30	.15	.03
☐ 105	Ray Donaldson	.20	.10	.02
☐ 106	Chris Hinton	.30	.15	.03
☐ 107	Andre Rison	1.25	.60	.12
☐ 108	Keith Taylor	.30	.15	.03
☐ 109	Clarence Verdin	.30	.15	.03
☐ 110	Fredd Young	.20	.10	.02
☐ 111	Deron Cherry	.30	.15	.03
☐ 112	Steve DeBerg	.30	.15	.03
☐ 113	Dino Hackett	.20	.10	.02
☐ 114	Albert Lewis	.30	.15	.03
☐ 115	Nick Lowery	.30	.15	.03
☐ 116	Christian Okoye	.75	.35	.07
☐ 117	Stephone Paige	.30	.15	.03
☐ 118	Kevin Ross	.30	.15	.03
☐ 119	Derrick Thomas	1.25	.60	.12
☐ 120	Mike Webster	.30	.15	.03
☐ 121	Marcus Allen	.40	.20	.04
☐ 122	Eddie Anderson	.30	.15	.03
☐ 123	Steve Beuerlein	.40	.20	.04
☐ 124	Tim Brown	.40	.20	.04
☐ 125	Mervyn Fernandez	.40	.20	.04
☐ 126	Willie Gault	.30	.15	.03
☐ 127	Bob Golic	.20	.10	.02
☐ 128	Bo Jackson UER	1.50	.75	.15
	(Final column in stats has LG, should be TD)			
☐ 129	Howie Long	.30	.15	.03
☐ 130	Greg Townsend	.30	.15	.03
☐ 131	Flipper Anderson	.40	.20	.04
☐ 132	Greg Bell	.30	.15	.03
☐ 133	Robert Delpino	.40	.20	.04
☐ 134	Henry Ellard	.30	.15	.03
☐ 135	Jim Everett	.60	.30	.06
☐ 136	Jerry Gray	.20	.10	.02
☐ 137	Kevin Greene	.20	.10	.02
☐ 138	Tom Newberry	.20	.10	.02
☐ 139	Jackie Slater	.30	.15	.03
☐ 140	Doug Smith	.20	.10	.02
☐ 141	Mark Clayton	.30	.15	.03
☐ 142	Jeff Cross	.30	.15	.03
☐ 143	Mark Duper	.30	.15	.03
☐ 144	Ferrell Edmunds	.30	.15	.03
☐ 145	Jim C.Jensen	.20	.10	.02
☐ 146	Dan Marino	1.50	.75	.15
☐ 147	John Offerdahl	.30	.15	.03
☐ 148	Louis Oliver	.30	.15	.03
☐ 149	Reggie Roby	.30	.15	.03
☐ 150	Sammie Smith	.40	.20	.04
☐ 151	Joey Browner	.30	.15	.03
☐ 152	Anthony Carter	.30	.15	.03
☐ 153	Chris Doleman	.30	.15	.03
☐ 154	Steve Jordan	.30	.15	.03
☐ 155	Carl Lee	.30	.15	.03
☐ 156	Randall McDaniel	.30	.15	.03
☐ 157	Keith Millard	.30	.15	.03
☐ 158	Herschel Walker	.60	.30	.06
☐ 159	Wade Wilson	.30	.15	.03
☐ 160	Gary Zimmerman	.20	.10	.02
☐ 161	Hart Lee Dykes	.30	.15	.03
☐ 162	Irving Fryar	.30	.15	.03
☐ 163	Steve Grogan	.30	.15	.03
☐ 164	Maurice Hurst	.30	.15	.03
☐ 165	Fred Marion	.20	.10	.02
☐ 166	Stanley Morgan	.30	.15	.03
☐ 167	Robert Perryman	.30	.15	.03
☐ 168	John Stephens UER	.30	.15	.03
	(Taking handoff from Eason, not Grogan)			
☐ 169	Andre Tippett	.30	.15	.03
☐ 170	Brent Williams	.20	.10	.03
☐ 171	John Fourcade	.30	.15	.03
☐ 172	Bobby Hebert	.30	.15	.03
☐ 173	Dalton Hilliard	.30	.15	.03
☐ 174	Rickey Jackson	.30	.15	.03
☐ 175	Vaughan Johnson	.30	.15	.03

☐ 176 Eric Martin	.30	.15	.03
☐ 177 Robert Massey	.20	.10	.02
☐ 178 Rueben Mayes UER	.20	.10	.02
(Final column in stats			
has LG, should be TD)			
☐ 179 Sam Mills	.30	.15	.03
☐ 180 Pat Swilling	.40	.20	.04
☐ 181 Ottis Anderson	.30	.15	.03
☐ 182 Carl Banks	.30	.15	.03
☐ 183 Mark Bavaro	.30	.15	.03
☐ 184 Mark Collins	.30	.15	.03
☐ 185 Leonard Marshall	.30	.15	.03
☐ 186 Dave Meggett	.90	.45	.09
☐ 187 Gary Reasons	.20	.10	.02
☐ 188 Phil Simms	.40	.20	.04
☐ 189 Lawrence Taylor	.80	.40	.08
☐ 190 Odessa Turner	.50	.25	.05
☐ 191 Kyle Clifton	.30	.15	.03
☐ 192 James Hasty	.30	.15	.03
☐ 193 Johnny Hector	.30	.15	.03
☐ 194 Jeff Lageman	.30	.15	.03
☐ 195 Pat Leahy	.30	.15	.03
☐ 196 Erik McMillan	.30	.15	.03
☐ 197 Ken O'Brien	.30	.15	.03
☐ 198 Mickey Shuler	.20	.10	.02
☐ 199 Al Toon	.30	.15	.03
☐ 200 Jo Jo Townsell	.30	.15	.03
☐ 201 Eric Allen UER	.30	.15	.03
(Card has 24 passes de-			
fended, Eagles say 25)			
☐ 202 Jerome Brown	.30	.15	.03
☐ 203 Keith Byars UER	.30	.15	.03
(LG column shows TD's,			
not longest run)			
☐ 204 Cris Carter	.30	.15	.03
☐ 205 Wes Hopkins	.20	.10	.02
(Photo from 1985 season)			
☐ 206 Keith Jackson UER	.40	.20	.04
(Born AK, should be AR)			
☐ 207 Seth Joyner	.30	.15	.03
(Photo not from an			
Eagle home game)			
☐ 208 Mike Quick	.30	.15	.03
(Photo is from a			
pre-1985 game)			
☐ 209 Andre Waters	.20	.10	.02
☐ 210 Reggie White	.50	.25	.05
☐ 211 Rich Camarillo	.20	.10	.02
☐ 212 Roy Green	.30	.15	.03
☐ 213 Ken Harvey	.50	.25	.05
☐ 214 Gary Hogeboom	.30	.15	.03
☐ 215 Tim McDonald	.30	.15	.03
☐ 216 Stump Mitchell	.30	.15	.03
☐ 217 Luis Sharpe	.20	.10	.02
☐ 218 Vai Sikahema	.30	.15	.03
☐ 219 J.T. Smith	.30	.15	.03
☐ 220 Ron Wolfley	.20	.10	.02

☐ 221 Gary Anderson	.20	.10	.02
☐ 222 Bubby Brister UER	.30	.15	.03
(Stats say 0 TD passes			
in 1989, should be 9)			
☐ 223 Merril Hoge	.30	.15	.03
☐ 224 Tunch Ilkin	.20	.10	.02
☐ 225 Louis Lipps	.30	.15	.03
☐ 226 David Little	.20	.10	.02
☐ 227 Greg Lloyd	.30	.15	.03
☐ 228 Dwayne Woodruff	.20	.10	.02
☐ 229 Rod Woodson	.30	.15	.03
(AJR patch is from			
1988 season, not 1989)			
☐ 230 Tim Worley	.30	.15	.03
☐ 231 Marion Butts	.80	.40	.08
☐ 232 Gill Byrd	.30	.15	.03
☐ 233 Burt Grossman	.30	.15	.03
☐ 234 Jim McMahon	.30	.15	.03
☐ 235 Anthony Miller UER	.40	.20	.04
(Text says 76 catches,			
stats say 75)			
☐ 236 Leslie O'Neal UER	.30	.15	.03
(Born AK, should be AR)			
☐ 237 Gary Plummer	.20	.10	.02
☐ 238 Billy Ray Smith	.30	.15	.03
(Action note begins,			
"Billy Ray ...")			
☐ 239 Tim Spencer	.20	.10	.02
☐ 240 Lee Williams	.30	.15	.03
☐ 241 Mike Cofer	.20	.10	.02
☐ 242 Roger Craig	.40	.20	.04
☐ 243 Charles Haley	.30	.15	.03
☐ 244 Ronnie Lott	.50	.25	.05
☐ 245 Guy McIntyre	.20	.10	.02
☐ 246 Joe Montana	2.00	1.00	.20
☐ 247 Tom Rathman	.30	.15	.03
☐ 248 Jerry Rice	1.25	.60	.12
☐ 249 John Taylor	.80	.40	.08
☐ 250 Michael Walter	.20	.10	.02
☐ 251 Brian Blades	.50	.25	.05
☐ 252 Jacob Green	.30	.15	.03
☐ 253 Dave Krieg	.30	.15	.03
☐ 254 Steve Largent	1.25	.60	.12
☐ 255 Joe Nash	.20	.10	.02
☐ 256 Rufus Porter	.30	.15	.03
☐ 257 Eugene Robinson	.20	.10	.02
☐ 258 Paul Skansi	.30	.15	.03
☐ 259 Curt Warner UER	.30	.15	.03
(Yards and attempts			
are reversed in text)			
☐ 260 John L. Williams	.30	.15	.03
☐ 261 Mark Carrier	.30	.15	.03
☐ 262 Reuben Davis	.30	.15	.03
☐ 263 Harry Hamilton	.20	.10	.02
☐ 264 Bruce Hill	.30	.15	.03
☐ 265 Donald Igwebuike	.20	.10	.02
☐ 266 Eugene Marve	.20	.10	.02

☐ 267 Kevin Murphy	.30	.15	.03
☐ 268 Mark Robinson	.20	.10	.02
☐ 269 Lars Tate	.30	.15	.03
☐ 270 Vinny Testaverde	.30	.15	.03
☐ 271 Gary Clark	.50	.25	.05
☐ 272 Monte Coleman	.20	.10	.02
☐ 273 Darrell Green	.50	.25	.05
☐ 274 Charles Mann UER	.30	.15	.03
(CA is not alpha-			
betized on back)			
☐ 275 Wilber Marshall	.30	.15	.03
☐ 276 Art Monk	.50	.25	.05
☐ 277 Gerald Riggs	.30	.15	.03
☐ 278 Mark Rypien	2.00	1.00	.20
☐ 279 Ricky Sanders	.40	.20	.04
☐ 280 Alvin Walton	.30	.15	.03
☐ xx Jim Plunkett	10.00	5.00	1.00
(Unnumbered; Braille			
on card back)			

1990 Action Packed Rookies

This 84-card standard size set (2 1/2" by 3 1/2") was issued to feature most of the rookies who made an impact in the 1990 season that Action Packed did not issue in their regular set. The first 64 cards in the set are 1990 rookies while the last 20 cards are either players who were traded during the off-season or players such as Randall Cunningham who were not included in the regular set. The key rookies in the set are Jeff George, Rodney Hampton, Johnny Johnson, Rob Moore, Emmitt Smith, and Blair Thomas. The set was released through both the Action Packed dealer

network and via traditional retail outlets and was available both in wax packs and as collated factory sets.

	MINT	EXC	G-VG
COMPLETE SET (84)	35.00	17.50	3.50
COMMON PLAYER (1-64)	.20	.10	.02
COMMON PLAYER (65-84)	.20	.10	.02
☐ 1 Jeff George	3.50	1.75	.35
Indianapolis Colts			
☐ 2 Richmond Webb	.60	.30	.06
Miami Dolphins			
☐ 3 James Williams	.30	.15	.03
Buffalo Bills			
☐ 4 Tony Bennett	.60	.30	.06
Green Bay Packers			
☐ 5 Darrell Thompson	.90	.45	.09
Green Bay Packers			
☐ 6 Steve Broussard	.80	.40	.08
Atlanta Falcons			
☐ 7 Rodney Hampton	3.25	1.60	.32
New York Giants			
☐ 8 Rob Moore	2.50	1.25	.25
New York Jets			
☐ 9 Alton Montgomery	.30	.15	.03
Denver Broncos			
☐ 10 LeRoy Butler	.30	.15	.03
Green Bay Packers			
☐ 11 Anthony Johnson	.40	.20	.04
Indianapolis Colts			
☐ 12 Scott Mitchell	.60	.30	.06
Miami Dolphins			
☐ 13 Mike Fox	.30	.15	.03
New York Giants			
☐ 14 Robert Blackmon	.30	.15	.03
Seattle Seahawks			
☐ 15 Blair Thomas	2.75	1.35	.27
New York Jets			
☐ 16 Tony Stargell	.40	.20	.04
New York Jets			
☐ 17 Peter Tom Willis	.80	.40	.08
Chicago Bears			
☐ 18 Harold Green	1.25	.60	.12
Cincinnati Bengals			
☐ 19 Bernard Clark	.30	.15	.03
Cincinnati Bengals			
☐ 20 Aaron Wallace	.40	.20	.04
Los Angeles Raiders			
☐ 21 Dennis Brown	.30	.15	.03
San Francisco 49ers			
☐ 22 Johnny Johnson	2.50	1.25	.25
Phoenix Cardinals			
☐ 23 Chris Calloway	.30	.15	.03
Pittsburgh Steelers			
☐ 24 Walter Wilson	.30	.15	.03
San Diego Chargers			

☐ 25 Dexter Carter 80	.40	.08
San Francisco 49ers		
☐ 26 Percy Snow 60	.30	.06
Kansas City Chiefs		
☐ 27 Johnny Bailey 50	.25	.05
Chicago Bears		
☐ 28 Mike Bellamy 30	.15	.03
Philadelphia Eagles		
☐ 29 Ben Smith 30	.15	.03
Philadelphia Eagles		
☐ 30 Mark Carrier UER 1.00	.50	.10
Chicago Bears		
(stats say 54 yards		
in '89, text has 58)		
☐ 31 James Francis 80	.40	.08
Cincinnati Bengals		
☐ 32 Lamar Lathon 50	.25	.05
Houston Oilers		
☐ 33 Bern Brostek 30	.15	.03
Los Angeles Rams		
☐ 34 Emmitt Smith UER 15.00	7.50	1.50
Dallas Cowboys		
(Career yardage on		
back is 4232,		
should be 3928)		
☐ 35 Andre Collins UER 40	.20	.04
Washington Redskins		
(born '86, should		
be '66)		
☐ 36 Alexander Wright 80	.40	.08
Dallas Cowboys		
☐ 37 Fred Barnett 1.00	.50	.10
Philadelphia Eagles		
☐ 38 Junior Seau 75	.35	.07
San Diego Chargers		
☐ 39 Cortez Kennedy 75	.35	.07
Seattle Seahawks		
☐ 40 Terry Wooden 30	.15	.03
Seattle Seahawks		
☐ 41 Eric Davis 30	.15	.03
San Francisco 49ers		
☐ 42 Fred Washington 20	.10	.02
Chicago Bears		
☐ 43 Reggie Cobb 1.25	.60	.12
Tampa Bay Buccaneers		
☐ 44 Andre Ware 1.00	.50	.10
Detroit Lions		
☐ 45 Anthony Smith 30	.15	.03
Los Angeles Raiders		
☐ 46 Shannon Sharpe 40	.20	.04
Denver Broncos		
☐ 47 Harlon Barnett 30	.15	.03
Cleveland Browns		
☐ 48 Greg McMurtry 60	.30	.06
New England Patriots		
☐ 49 Stacey Simmons 30	.15	.03
Indianapolis Colts		
☐ 50 Calvin Williams 60	.30	.06
Philadelphia Eagles		
☐ 51 Anthony Thompson 1.25	.60	.12
Phoenix Cardinals		
☐ 52 Ricky Proehl 80	.40	.08
Phoenix Cardinals		
☐ 53 Tony Jones 50	.25	.05
Houston Oilers		
☐ 54 Ray Agnew 30	.15	.03
New England Patriots		
☐ 55 Tommy Hodson 60	.30	.06
New England Patriots		
☐ 56 Ron Cox 30	.15	.03
Chicago Bears		
☐ 57 Leroy Hoard 80	.40	.08
Cleveland Browns		
☐ 58 Eric Green UER 1.50	.75	.15
Pittsburgh Steelers		
(back photo reversed)		
☐ 59 Barry Foster 1.25	.60	.12
Pittsburgh Steelers		
☐ 60 Keith McCants 80	.40	.08
Tampa Bay Buccaneers		
☐ 61 Oliver Barnett 30	.15	.03
Atlanta Falcons		
☐ 62 Chris Warren 40	.20	.04
Seattle Seahawks		
☐ 63 Pat Terrell 30	.15	.03
Los Angeles Rams		
☐ 64 Renaldo Turnbull 40	.20	.04
New Orleans Saints		
☐ 65 Chris Chandler 30	.15	.03
Tampa Bay Buccaneers		
☐ 66 Everson Walls 20	.10	.02
New York Giants		
☐ 67 Alonzo Highsmith 20	.10	.02
Dallas Cowboys		
☐ 68 Gary Anderson 30	.15	.03
Tampa Bay Buccaneers		
☐ 69 Fred Smerlas 20	.10	.02
San Francisco 49ers		
☐ 70 Jim McMahon 30	.15	.03
Philadelphia Eagles		
☐ 71 Curt Warner 30	.15	.03
Los Angeles Rams		
☐ 72 Stanley Morgan 30	.15	.03
Indianapolis Colts		
☐ 73 Dave Waymer 20	.10	.02
San Francisco 49ers		
☐ 74 Billy Joe Tolliver 30	.15	.03
San Diego Chargers		
☐ 75 Tony Eason 30	.15	.03
New York Jets		
☐ 76 Max Montoya 20	.10	.02
Los Angeles Raiders		
☐ 77 Greg Bell 20	.10	.02
Los Angeles Raiders		

☐ 78 Dennis McKinnon	.20	.10	.02
Dallas Cowboys			
☐ 79 Raymond Clayborn	.20	.10	.02
Cleveland Browns			
☐ 80 Broderick Thomas	.40	.20	.04
Tampa Bay Buccaneers			
☐ 81 Timm Rosenbach	.30	.15	.03
Phoenix Cardinals			
☐ 82 Tim McKyer	.20	.10	.02
Miami Dolphins			
☐ 83 Andre Rison	.60	.30	.06
Atlanta Falcons			
☐ 84 Randall Cunningham	.60	.30	.06
Philadelphia Eagles			

1991 Action Packed

This 280-card standard size set (2 1/2" by 3 1/2") marked the third year Action Packed issued football cards. This set is basically arranged by alphabetical order within alphabetical team order. The set looks as if there is less relief on the card as in previous years and the action photos on the front of the cards are framed in gold along the left side and on the bottom of the card. The cards feature sharp photography on the front while the backs feature complete biographical information, a portrait shot of the player as well as the last five seasons stats and some career highlights. There is also a small space on the bottom for the players signature. The differences between the regular issue and the unnumbered Randall Cunningham prototype is a black border around the gold strip, the Action Packed logo no longer has the football player above it. The back of the card has a gold border with black highlighting the gold around the photo. The

Cunningham prototype is not included as part of the complete set. The cards are arranged by teams: Atlanta Falcons (1-10), Buffalo Bills (11-20), Chicago Bears (21-30), Cincinnati Bengals (31-40), Cleveland Browns (41-50), Dallas Cowboys (51-60), Denver Broncos (61-70), Detroit Lions (71-80), Green Bay Packers (81-90), Houston Oilers (91-100), Indianapolis Colts (101-110), Kansas City Chiefs (111-120), Los Angeles Raiders (121-130), Los Angeles Rams (131-140), Miami Dolphins (141-150), Minnesota Vikings (151-160), New England Patriots (161-170), New Orleans Saints (171-180), New York Giants (181-190), New York Jets (191-200), Philadelphia Eagles (201-210), Phoenix Cardinals (211-220), Pittsburgh Steelers (221-230), San Diego Chargers (231-240), San Francisco 49ers (241-250), Seattle Seahawks (251-260), Tampa Bay Buccaneers (261-270), Washington Redskins (271-280). The 1991 Action Packed factory sets also included an 11-card braille subset which is separately listed below for clarity.

	MINT	EXC	G-VG
COMPLETE SET (280)	67.00	30.00	7.00
COMMON PLAYER (1-280)	.20	.10	.02

☐ 1 Steve Broussard	.45	.22	.04
☐ 2 Scott Case	.20	.10	.02
☐ 3 Brian Jordan	.60	.30	.06
☐ 4 Darion Conner	.30	.15	.03
☐ 5 Tim Green	.20	.10	.02
☐ 6 Chris Miller	.50	.25	.05
☐ 7 Andre Rison	.60	.30	.06
☐ 8 Mike Rozier	.20	.10	.02
☐ 9 Deion Sanders	.75	.35	.07
☐ 10 Jessie Tuggle	.20	.10	.02
☐ 11 Leonard Smith	.20	.10	.02
☐ 12 Shane Conlan	.30	.15	.03
☐ 13 Kent Hull	.20	.10	.02
☐ 14 Keith McKeller	.30	.15	.03
☐ 15 James Lofton	.50	.25	.05
☐ 16 Andre Reed	.50	.25	.05
☐ 17 Bruce Smith	.40	.20	.04
☐ 18 Darryl Talley	.30	.15	.03
☐ 19 Steve Tasker	.20	.10	.02
☐ 20 Thurman Thomas	1.50	.75	.15
☐ 21 Neal Anderson	.50	.25	.05
☐ 22 Trace Armstrong	.20	.10	.02
☐ 23 Mark Bortz	.20	.10	.02
☐ 24 Mark Carrier	.40	.20	.04
☐ 25 Wendell Davis	.75	.35	.07
☐ 26 Richard Dent	.30	.15	.03
☐ 27 Jim Harbaugh	.40	.20	.04
☐ 28 Jay Hilgenberg	.20	.10	.02
☐ 29 Brad Muster	.30	.15	.03

☐ 30 Mike Singletary	.30	.15	.03
☐ 31 Harold Green	.60	.30	.06
☐ 32 James Brooks	.30	.15	.03
☐ 33 Eddie Brown	.30	.15	.03
☐ 34 Boomer Esiason	.40	.20	.04
☐ 35 James Francis	.30	.15	.03
☐ 36 David Fulcher	.20	.10	.02
☐ 37 Rodney Holman	.20	.10	.02
☐ 38 Tim McGee	.30	.15	.03
☐ 39 Anthony Munoz	.30	.15	.03
☐ 40 Ickey Woods	.30	.15	.03
☐ 41 Rob Burnett	.40	.20	.04
☐ 42 Thane Gash	.20	.10	.02
☐ 43 Mike Johnson	.20	.10	.02
☐ 44 Brian Brennan	.20	.10	.02
☐ 45 Reggie Langhorne	.20	.10	.02
☐ 46 Kevin Mack	.30	.15	.03
☐ 47 Clay Matthews	.20	.10	.02
☐ 48 Eric Metcalf	.30	.15	.03
☐ 49 Anthony Pleasant	.20	.10	.02
☐ 50 Ozzie Newsome	.30	.15	.03
☐ 51 Troy Aikman	1.50	.75	.15
☐ 52 Issiac Holt	.20	.10	.02
☐ 53 Michael Irvin	.60	.30	.06
☐ 54 Jimmie Jones	.20	.10	.02
☐ 55 Eugene Lockhart	.20	.10	.02
☐ 56 Kelvin Martin	.20	.10	.02
☐ 57 Ken Norton Jr.	.20	.10	.02
☐ 58 Jay Novacek	.40	.20	.04
☐ 59 Emmitt Smith	5.00	2.50	.50
☐ 60 Daniel Stubbs	.20	.10	.02
☐ 61 Steve Atwater	.30	.15	.03
☐ 62 Michael Brooks	.20	.10	.02
☐ 63 John Elway	.50	.25	.05
☐ 64 Simon Fletcher	.20	.10	.02
☐ 65 Bobby Humphrey	.40	.20	.04
☐ 66 Mark Jackson	.30	.15	.03
☐ 67 Vance Johnson	.30	.15	.03
☐ 68 Karl Mecklenburg	.30	.15	.03
☐ 69 Dennis Smith	.20	.10	.02
☐ 70 Greg Kragen	.20	.10	.02
☐ 71 Jerry Ball	.20	.10	.02
☐ 72 Lomas Brown	.20	.10	.02
☐ 73 Robert Clark	.30	.15	.03
☐ 74 Michael Cofer	.20	.10	.02
☐ 75 Mel Gray	.20	.10	.02
☐ 76 Richard Johnson	.20	.10	.02
☐ 77 Rodney Peete	.40	.20	.04
☐ 78 Barry Sanders	3.00	1.50	.30
☐ 79 Chris Spielman	.30	.15	.03
☐ 80 Andre Ware	.50	.25	.05
☐ 81 Matt Brock	.40	.20	.04
☐ 82 LeRoy Butler	.20	.10	.02
☐ 83 Tim Harris	.30	.15	.03
☐ 84 Perry Kemp	.20	.10	.02
☐ 85 Don Majkowski	.40	.20	.04
☐ 86 Mark Murphy	.20	.10	.02
☐ 87 Brian Noble	.20	.10	.02
☐ 88 Sterling Sharpe	.40	.20	.04
☐ 89 Darrell Thompson	.50	.25	.05
☐ 90 Ed West	.20	.10	.02
☐ 91 Ray Childress	.30	.15	.03
☐ 92 Ernest Givins	.40	.20	.04
☐ 93 Drew Hill	.30	.15	.03
☐ 94 Haywood Jeffires	.75	.35	.07
☐ 95 Richard Johnson	.30	.15	.03
☐ 96 Sean Jones	.20	.10	.02
☐ 97 Bruce Matthews	.20	.10	.02
☐ 98 Warren Moon	.75	.35	.07
☐ 99 Mike Munchak	.30	.15	.03
☐ 100 Lorenzo White	.30	.15	.03
☐ 101 Albert Bentley	.30	.15	.03
☐ 102 Duane Bickett	.20	.10	.02
☐ 103 Bill Brooks	.20	.10	.02
☐ 104 Jeff George	.75	.35	.07
☐ 105 Jon Hand	.20	.10	.02
☐ 106 Jeff Herrod	.20	.10	.02
☐ 107 Jessie Hester	.30	.15	.03
☐ 108 Mike Prior	.20	.10	.02
☐ 109 Rohn Stark	.20	.10	.02
☐ 110 Clarence Verdin	.20	.10	.02
☐ 111 Steve DeBerg	.30	.15	.03
☐ 112 Dan Saleaumua	.20	.10	.02
☐ 113 Albert Lewis	.30	.15	.03
☐ 114 Nick Lowery	.30	.15	.03
☐ 115 Christian Okoye	.40	.20	.04
☐ 116 Stephone Paige	.30	.15	.03
☐ 117 Kevin Ross	.20	.10	.02
☐ 118 Dino Hackett	.20	.10	.02
☐ 119 Derrick Thomas UER	.75	.35	.07
(Drafted in '89,			
not '90)			
☐ 120 Barry Word UER	1.25	.60	.12
(Bio says 1105 yards,			
stats say 1015)			
☐ 121 Marcus Allen	.40	.20	.04
☐ 122 Mervyn Fernandez	.30	.15	.03
☐ 123 Willie Gault	.30	.15	.03
☐ 124 Bo Jackson	.90	.45	.09
☐ 125 Terry McDaniel	.20	.10	.02
☐ 126 Don Mosebar	.20	.10	.02
☐ 127 Jay Schroeder	.30	.15	.03
☐ 128 Greg Townsend	.30	.15	.03
☐ 129 Aaron Wallace	.30	.15	.03
☐ 130 Steve Wisniewski	.20	.10	.02
☐ 131 Flipper Anderson	.30	.15	.03
☐ 132 Henry Ellard	.30	.15	.03
☐ 133 Jim Everett	.30	.15	.03
☐ 134 Cleveland Gary	.30	.15	.03
☐ 135 Jerry Gray	.30	.15	.03
☐ 136 Kevin Greene	.30	.15	.03
☐ 137 Buford McGee	.20	.10	.02
☐ 138 Vince Newsome	.20	.10	.02
☐ 139 Jackie Slater	.30	.15	.03
☐ 140 Frank Stams	.20	.10	.02
☐ 141 Jeff Cross	.20	.10	.02

☐ 142 Mark Duper	.30	.15	.03
☐ 143 Ferrell Edmunds	.20	.10	.02
☐ 144 Dan Marino	1.00	.50	.10
☐ 145 Louis Oliver	.30	.15	.03
☐ 146 John Offerdahl	.20	.10	.02
☐ 147 Tony Paige	.20	.10	.02
☐ 148 Sammie Smith	.40	.20	.04
☐ 149 Richmond Webb	.30	.15	.03
☐ 150 Jarvis Williams	.20	.10	.02
☐ 151 Joey Browner	.30	.15	.03
☐ 152 Anthony Carter	.30	.15	.03
☐ 153 Chris Doleman	.30	.15	.03
☐ 154 Hassan Jones	.20	.10	.02
☐ 155 Steve Jordan	.30	.15	.03
☐ 156 Carl Lee	.20	.10	.02
☐ 157 Randall McDaniel	.20	.10	.02
☐ 158 Mike Merriweather	.20	.10	.02
☐ 159 Herschel Walker	.40	.20	.04
☐ 160 Wade Wilson	.30	.15	.03
☐ 161 Ray Agnew	.20	.10	.02
☐ 162 Bruce Armstrong	.20	.10	.02
☐ 163 Marv Cook	.30	.15	.03
☐ 164 Hart Lee Dykes	.30	.15	.03
☐ 165 Irving Fryar	.30	.15	.03
☐ 166 Tommy Hodson	.30	.15	.03
☐ 167 Ronnie Lippett	.20	.10	.02
☐ 168 Fred Marion	.20	.10	.02
☐ 169 John Stephens	.30	.15	.03
☐ 170 Brent Williams	.20	.10	.02
☐ 171A Morten Andersen ERR	.30	.15	.03
(Back photo has white emblem, should be black)			
☐ 171B Morten Andersen COR	.30	.15	.03
☐ 172A Gene Atkins ERR	.20	.10	.02
(Back photo has white emblem, should be black)			
☐ 172B Gene Atkins COR	.20	.10	.02
☐ 173A Craig Heyward ERR	.30	.15	.03
(Back photo has white emblem, should be black)			
☐ 173B Craig Heyward COR	.30	.15	.03
☐ 174A Rickey Jackson ERR	.30	.15	.03
(Back photo has white emblem, should be black)			
☐ 174B Rickey Jackson COR	.30	.15	.03
☐ 175A Vaughan Johnson ERR	.30	.15	.03
(Back photo has white emblem, should be black)			
☐ 175B Vaughan Johnson COR	.30	.15	.03
☐ 176A Eric Martin ERR	.30	.15	.03
(Back photo has white emblem, should be black)			
☐ 176B Eric Martin COR	.30	.15	.03
☐ 177A Rueben Mayes ERR	.30	.15	.03
(Back photo has white emblem, should be black)			
☐ 177B Rueben Mayes COR	.30	.15	.03
☐ 178A Pat Swilling ERR	.30	.15	.03
(Back photo has white emblem, should be black)			
☐ 178B Pat Swilling COR	.30	.15	.03
☐ 179A Renaldo Turnbull ERR	.30	.15	.03
(Back photo has white emblem, should be black)			
☐ 179B Renaldo Turnbull COR	.30	.15	.03
☐ 180A Steve Walsh ERR	.30	.15	.03
(Back photo has white emblem, should be black)			
☐ 180B Steve Walsh COR	.30	.15	.03
☐ 181 Ottis Anderson	.30	.15	.03
☐ 182 Rodney Hampton	1.25	.60	.12
☐ 183 Jeff Hostetler	.75	.35	.07
☐ 184 Pepper Johnson	.30	.15	.03
☐ 185 Sean Landeta	.20	.10	.02
☐ 186 Dave Meggett	.40	.20	.04
☐ 187 Bart Oates	.20	.10	.02
☐ 188 Phil Simms	.30	.15	.03
☐ 189 Lawrence Taylor	.40	.20	.04
☐ 190 Reyna Thompson	.30	.15	.03
☐ 191 Brad Baxter	.40	.20	.04
☐ 192 Dennis Byrd	.30	.15	.03
☐ 193 Kyle Clifton	.20	.10	.02
☐ 194 James Hasty	.20	.10	.02
☐ 195 Pat Leahy	.30	.15	.03
☐ 196 Erik McMillan	.30	.15	.03
☐ 197 Rob Moore	1.25	.60	.12
☐ 198 Ken O'Brien	.30	.15	.03
☐ 199 Mark Boyer	.20	.10	.02
☐ 200 Al Toon	.30	.15	.03
☐ 201 Fred Barnett	.50	.25	.05
☐ 202 Jerome Brown	.30	.15	.03
☐ 203 Keith Byars	.30	.15	.03
☐ 204 Randall Cunningham	.50	.25	.05
☐ 205 Wes Hopkins	.20	.10	.02
☐ 206 Keith Jackson	.30	.15	.03
☐ 207 Seth Joyner	.30	.15	.03
☐ 208 Heath Sherman	.30	.15	.03
☐ 209 Reggie White	.40	.20	.04
☐ 210 Calvin Williams	.30	.15	.03
☐ 211 Roy Green	.30	.15	.03
☐ 212 Ken Harvey	.20	.10	.02
☐ 213 Luis Sharpe	.20	.10	.02
☐ 214 Ernie Jones	.30	.15	.03
☐ 215 Tim McDonald	.30	.15	.03
☐ 216 Freddie Joe Nunn	.20	.10	.02
☐ 217 Ricky Proehl	.30	.15	.03
☐ 218 Timm Rosenbach	.40	.20	.04
☐ 219 Anthony Thompson	.40	.20	.04
☐ 220 Lonnie Young	.20	.10	.02
☐ 221 Gary Anderson	.20	.10	.02
☐ 222 Bubby Brister	.30	.15	.03
☐ 223 Eric Green	.50	.25	.05
☐ 224 Merril Hoge	.30	.15	.03
☐ 225 Carnell Lake	.20	.10	.02

☐ 226 Louis Lipps	.30	.15	.03
☐ 227 David Little	.20	.10	.02
☐ 228 Greg Lloyd	.20	.10	.02
☐ 229 Gerald Williams	.20	.10	.02
☐ 230 Rod Woodson	.30	.15	.03
☐ 231 Marion Butts	.40	.20	.04
☐ 232 Gill Byrd	.30	.15	.03
☐ 233 Burt Grossman	.30	.15	.03
☐ 234 Courtney Hall	.20	.10	.02
☐ 235 Ronnie Harmon	.30	.15	.03
☐ 236 Anthony Miller	.30	.15	.03
☐ 237 Leslie O'Neal	.30	.15	.03
☐ 238 Junior Seau	.30	.15	.03
☐ 239 Billy Joe Tolliver	.30	.15	.03
☐ 240 Lee Williams	.30	.15	.03
☐ 241 Dexter Carter	.30	.15	.03
☐ 242 Kevin Fagan	.20	.10	.02
☐ 243 Charles Haley	.30	.15	.03
☐ 244 Brent Jones	.30	.15	.03
☐ 245 Ronnie Lott	.40	.20	.04
☐ 246 Guy McIntyre	.20	.10	.02
☐ 247 Joe Montana	1.00	.50	.10
☐ 248 Jerry Rice	.90	.45	.09
☐ 249 John Taylor	.40	.20	.04
☐ 250 Roger Craig	.30	.15	.03
☐ 251 Brian Blades	.30	.15	.03
☐ 252 Derrick Fenner	.60	.30	.06
☐ 253 Nesby Glasgow	.20	.10	.02
☐ 254 Jacob Green	.30	.15	.03
☐ 255 Tommy Kane	.30	.15	.03
☐ 256 Dave Krieg	.30	.15	.03
☐ 257 Rufus Porter	.20	.10	.02
☐ 258 Eugene Robinson	.20	.10	.02
☐ 259 Cortez Kennedy	.30	.15	.03
☐ 260 John L. Williams	.30	.15	.03
☐ 261 Gary Anderson	.30	.15	.03
☐ 262 Mark Carrier	.30	.15	.03
☐ 263 Steve Christie	.20	.10	.02
☐ 264 Reggie Cobb	.50	.25	.05
☐ 265 Paul Gruber	.30	.15	.03
☐ 266 Wayne Haddix	.30	.15	.03
☐ 267 Bruce Hill	.20	.10	.02
☐ 268 Keith McCants	.30	.15	.03
☐ 269 Vinny Testaverde	.30	.15	.03
☐ 270 Broderick Thomas	.30	.15	.03
☐ 271 Earnest Byner	.30	.15	.03
☐ 272 Gary Clark	.50	.25	.05
☐ 273 Darrell Green	.40	.20	.04
☐ 274 Jim Lachey	.30	.15	.03
☐ 275 Chip Lohmiller	.20	.10	.02
☐ 276 Charles Mann	.30	.15	.03
☐ 277 Wilber Marshall	.30	.15	.03
☐ 278 Art Monk	.50	.25	.05
☐ 279 Mark Rypien	.80	.40	.08
☐ 280 Alvin Walton	.20	.10	.02
☐ xx Randall Cunningham	10.00	5.00	1.00
Philadelphia Eagles			

(Unnumbered prototype; front design similar to All-Madden Team cards)

1991 Action Packed Braille

These eleven cards are included only in the factory sets of 1991 Action Packed. Card numbers 281-288 feature the category leaders of the AFC and NFC. They have the same front design as the regular issue, but different borderless embossed color player photos. The player cards have horizontally oriented backs written in Braille. Two logo cards and a checklist card complete the set. The cards are numbered on the back.

	MINT	EXC	G-VG
COMPLETE SET (11)	15.00	6.00	1.00
COMMON PLAYER (281-288)	1.25	.60	.12
COMMON PLAYER (289-291)	.35	.17	.03
☐ 281 NFC Passing Leader Randall Cunningham Philadelphia Eagles	2.25	1.10	.22
☐ 282 AFC Passing Leader Warren Moon Houston Oilers	2.25	1.10	.22
☐ 283 NFC Rushing Leader Barry Sanders Detroit Lions	8.00	4.00	.80
☐ 284 AFC Rushing Leader Thurman Thomas Buffalo Bills	6.50	3.25	.65

		MINT	EXC	G-VG
☐ 285	NFC Receiving Leader . 3.25		1.60	.32
	Jerry Rice			
	San Francisco 49ers			
☐ 286	AFC Receiving Leader . 2.25		1.10	.22
	Haywood Jeffires			
	Houston Oilers			
☐ 287	NFC Sack Leader 1.25		.60	.12
	Charles Haley			
	San Francisco 49ers			
☐ 288	AFC Sack Leader 1.75		.85	.17
	Derrick Thomas			
	Kansas City Chiefs			
☐ 289	NFC Logo Card .... .35		.17	.03
☐ 290	AFC Logo Card .... .35		.17	.03
☐ 291	Checklist Card .... .50		.15	.03

1991 Action Packed Rookie/Update

This 84-card standard size (2 1/2" by 3 1/2") set marks the second year that Action Packed has issued a Rookie/Update set. Cards were issued in foil packs as well as in collated factory sets. The set contains 74 rookie cards (including the 26 1st round draft picks) plus 10 traded and update cards. The front design consists of embossed color player photos, with an embossed red helmet with a white "R". The gold indicia and logo are bordered in red instead of black as on the regular set. In red print, the horizontally oriented backs have the player's college regular season and career statistics. The Emmitt Smith rookie prototype card was included as a bonus with each case of 1991 Action Packed Rookie/Update foil or sets ordered. The Emmitt Smith prototype is

not included in the complete set price. The cards are numbered on the back. The key rookie cards in this set are Nick Bell, Ricky Ervins, Todd Marinovich, Dan McGwire, Leonard Russell, and Harvey Williams.

		MINT	EXC	G-VG
	COMPLETE SET (84)	25.00	10.00	2.00
	COMMON PLAYER (1-84) .... .20		.10	.02
☐ 1	Herman Moore 1.25		.50	.10
	Detroit Lions			
☐ 2	Eric Turner 1.00		.50	.10
	Cleveland Browns			
☐ 3	Mike Croel 1.50		.75	.15
	Denver Broncos			
☐ 4	Alfred Williams .... .40		.20	.04
	Cincinnati Bengals			
☐ 5	Stanley Richard .... .50		.20	.04
	San Diego Chargers			
☐ 6	Russell Maryland 1.00		.50	.10
	Dallas Cowboys			
☐ 7	Pat Harlow .... .40		.20	.04
	New England Patriots			
☐ 8	Alvin Harper 1.25		.50	.10
	Dallas Cowboys			
☐ 9	Mike Pritchard 1.50		.75	.15
	Atlanta Falcons			
☐ 10	Leonard Russell 2.50		1.25	.25
	New England Patriots			
☐ 11	Jarrod Bunch .... .30		.15	.03
	New York Giants			
☐ 12	Dan McGwire 2.00		1.00	.20
	Seattle Seahawks			
☐ 13	Bobby Wilson .... .30		.15	.03
	Washington Redskins			
☐ 14	Vinnie Clark .... .30		.15	.03
	Green Bay Packers			
☐ 15	Kelvin Pritchett .... .30		.15	.03
	Detroit Lions			
☐ 16	Harvey Williams 2.00		1.00	.20
	Kansas City Chiefs			
☐ 17	Stan Thomas .... .30		.15	.03
	Chicago Bears			
☐ 18	Todd Marinovich 2.50		1.25	.25
	Los Angeles Raiders			
☐ 19	Antone Davis .... .30		.15	.03
	Philadelphia Eagles			
☐ 20	Greg Lewis .... .75		.30	.06
	Denver Broncos			
☐ 21	Brett Favre 1.25		.50	.10
	Atlanta Falcons			
☐ 22	Wesley Carroll 1.00		.50	.10
	New Orleans Saints			
☐ 23	Ed McCaffrey .... .60		.30	.06
	New York Giants			
☐ 24	Reggie Barrett .... .40		.20	.04

	Detroit Lions			
☐ 25	Chris Zorich .... .60	.30	.06	
	Chicago Bears			
☐ 26	Kenny Walker 1.00	.50	.10	
	Denver Broncos			
☐ 27	Aaron Craver .... .50	.20	.04	
	Miami Dolphins			
☐ 28	Browning Nagle 1.25	.50	.10	
	New York Jets			
☐ 29	Nick Bell 2.00	1.00	.20	
	Los Angeles Raiders			
☐ 30	Anthony Morgan .... .50	.20	.04	
	Chicago Bears			
☐ 31	Jesse Campbell .... .30	.15	.03	
	Philadelphia Eagles			
☐ 32	Eric Bieniemy .... .75	.30	.06	
	San Diego Chargers			
☐ 33	Ricky Ervins UER 4.00	2.00	.40	
	Washington Redskins			
	(Totals don't add up)			
☐ 34	Kanavis McGhee .... .40	.20	.04	
	New York Giants			
☐ 35	Shawn Moore .... .30	.15	.03	
	Denver Broncos			
☐ 36	Todd Lyght .... .75	.30	.06	
	Los Angeles Rams			
☐ 37	Eric Swann .... .40	.20	.04	
	Phoenix Cardinals			
☐ 38	Henry Jones .... .30	.15	.03	
	Buffalo Bills			
☐ 39	Ted Washington .... .30	.15	.03	
	San Francisco 49ers			
☐ 40	Charles McRae .... .40	.20	.04	
	Tampa Bay Buccaneers			
☐ 41	Randal Hill 1.25	.50	.10	
	Phoenix Cardinals			
☐ 42	Huey Richardson .... .40	.20	.04	
	Pittsburgh Steelers			
☐ 43	Roman Phifer .... .30	.15	.03	
	Los Angeles Rams			
☐ 44	Ricky Watters .... .75	.30	.06	
	San Francisco 49ers			
☐ 45	Esera Tuaolo .... .30	.15	.03	
	Green Bay Packers			
☐ 46	Michael Jackson .... .75	.30	.06	
	Cleveland Browns			
☐ 47	Shawn Jefferson .... .30	.15	.03	
	San Diego Chargers			
☐ 48	Tim Barnett .... .50	.20	.04	
	Kansas City Chiefs			
☐ 49	Chuck Webb .... .50	.20	.04	
	Green Bay Packers			
☐ 50	Moe Gardner .... .50	.20	.04	
	Atlanta Falcons			
☐ 51	Mo Lewis .... .40	.20	.04	
	New York Jets			
☐ 52	Mike Dumas .... .30	.15	.03	

	Houston Oilers			
☐ 53	Jon Vaughn 1.00	.50	.10	
	New England Patriots			
☐ 54	Jerome Henderson .... .30	.15	.03	
	New England Patriots			
☐ 55	Harry Colon .... .30	.15	.03	
	New England Patriots			
☐ 56	David Daniels .... .30	.15	.03	
	Seattle Seahawks			
☐ 57	Phil Hansen .... .30	.15	.03	
	Buffalo Bills			
☐ 58	Ernie Mills .... .40	.20	.04	
	Pittsburgh Steelers			
☐ 59	John Kasay .... .30	.15	.03	
	Seattle Seahawks			
☐ 60	Darren Lewis .... .60	.30	.06	
	Chicago Bears			
☐ 61	James Joseph .... .75	.30	.06	
	Philadelphia Eagles			
☐ 62	Robert Wilson .... .40	.20	.04	
	Tampa Bay Buccaneers			
☐ 63	Lawrence Dawsey 1.00	.50	.10	
	Tampa Bay Buccaneers			
☐ 64	Mike Jones .... .30	.15	.03	
	Phoenix Cardinals			
☐ 65	Dave McCloughan .... .30	.15	.03	
	Indianapolis Colts			
☐ 66	Erric Pegram .... .60	.30	.06	
	Atlanta Falcons			
☐ 67	Aeneas Williams .... .40	.20	.04	
	Phoenix Cardinals			
☐ 68	Reggie Johnson .... .50	.20	.04	
	Denver Broncos			
☐ 69	Todd Scott .... .30	.15	.03	
	Minnesota Vikings			
☐ 70	James Jones .... .30	.15	.03	
	Cleveland Browns			
☐ 71	Lamar Rogers .... .30	.15	.03	
	Cincinnati Bengals			
☐ 72	Darryll Lewis .... .40	.20	.04	
	Houston Oilers			
☐ 73	Bryan Cox .... .30	.15	.03	
	Miami Dolphins			
☐ 74	Leroy Thompson .... .30	.15	.03	
	Pittsburgh Steelers			
☐ 75	Mark Higgs 1.25	.50	.10	
	Miami Dolphins			
☐ 76	John Friesz .... .75	.30	.06	
	San Diego Chargers			
☐ 77	Tim McKyer .... .20	.10	.02	
	Atlanta Falcons			
☐ 78	Roger Craig .... .30	.15	.03	
	Los Angeles Raiders			
☐ 79	Ronnie Lott .... .30	.15	.03	
	Los Angeles Raiders			
☐ 80	Steve Young .... .30	.15	.03	
	San Francisco 49ers			

☐ 81	Percy Snow	.20	.10	.02
	Kansas City Chiefs			
☐ 82	Cornelius Bennett	.30	.15	.03
	Buffalo Bills			
☐ 83	Johnny Johnson	.60	.30	.06
	Phoenix Cardinals			
☐ 84	Blair Thomas	.90	.45	.09
	New York Jets			
☐ xx	Emmitt Smith	10.00	4.00	.75
	Dallas Cowboys			
	(Unnumbered rookie			
	prototype)			

1992 Action Packed

The 1992 Action Packed football set contains 280 cards measuring the standard size (2 1/2" by 3 1/2"). The fronts feature borderless embossed color player photos, accented by either gold and aqua (NFC) or gold and red (AFC) border stripes, running down either the left or right side of the card face. The team helmet appears in the lower left or right corner, with the player's name and position printed at the card bottom. The horizontally oriented backs carry biography, player profile, a color head shot, and an "Action Note" in the form of an extended caption to the photo on the front. The cards are numbered on the back and checklisted below alphabetically according to teams as follows: Atlanta Falcons (1-10), Buffalo Bills (11-20), Chicago Bears (21-30), Cincinnati Bengals (31-40), Cleveland Browns (41-50), Dallas Cowboys (51-60), Denver Broncos (61-70), Detroit Lions (71-80), Green Bay Packers (81-90), Houston Oilers (91-100), Indianapolis Colts (101-110), Kansas City

Chiefs (111-120), Los Angeles Raiders (121-130), Los Angeles Rams (131-140), Miami Dolphins (141-150), Minnesota Vikings (151-160), New England Patriots (161-170), New Orleans Saints (171-180), New York Giants (181-190), New York Jets (191-200), Philadelphia Eagles (201-210), Phoenix Cardinals (211-220), Pittsburgh Steelers (221-230), San Diego Chargers (231-240), San Francisco 49ers (241-250), Seattle Seahawks (251-260), Tampa Bay Buccaneers (261-270), and Washington Redskins (271-280). To show support for their injured teammate, a special "thumbs up" logo with Mike Utley's number 60 was placed on the back of all Detroit Lions' cards. The set closes with a Braille subset (281-288) and Logo cards (289-290). The eight Braille cards, available this year in foil packs as well as factory sets, feature category leaders in their division. Action Packed also made one each of 26 18K solid gold Tiffany-designed cards, and certificates for a chance to win these cards were randomly inserted in the regular series foil packs.

	MINT	EXC	G-VG
COMPLETE SET (280)	75.00	37.50	7.50
COMMON PLAYER (1-280)	.20	.10	.02
COMMON PLAYER (281-288)	1.25	.60	.12
COMMON LOGO (289-290)	.35	.17	.03

☐ 1	Steve Broussard	.30	.15	.03
☐ 2	Michael Haynes	.60	.30	.06
☐ 3	Tim McKyer	.20	.10	.02
☐ 4	Chris Miller	.50	.25	.05
☐ 5	Andre Rison	.50	.25	.05
☐ 6	Jessie Tuggle	.20	.10	.02
☐ 7	Mike Pritchard	.75	.35	.07
☐ 8	Moe Gardner	.25	.12	.02
☐ 9	Brian Jordan	.50	.25	.05
☐ 10	Mike Kenn and	.25	.12	.02
	Chris Hinton			
☐ 11	Steve Tasker	.20	.10	.02
☐ 12	Cornelius Bennett	.25	.12	.02
☐ 13	Shane Conlan	.25	.12	.02
☐ 14	Darryl Talley	.25	.12	.02
☐ 15	Thurman Thomas	1.50	.75	.15
☐ 16	James Lofton	.50	.25	.05
☐ 17	Don Beebe	.25	.12	.02
☐ 18	Jim Ritcher	.20	.10	.02
☐ 19	Keith McKeller	.20	.10	.02
☐ 20	Nate Odomes	.20	.10	.02
☐ 21	Mark Carrier USC	.25	.12	.02
☐ 22	Wendell Davis	.50	.25	.05
☐ 23	Richard Dent	.25	.12	.02
☐ 24	Jim Harbaugh	.25	.12	.02
☐ 25	Jay Hilgenberg	.25	.12	.02

□				
26	Steve McMichael	.25	.12	.02
27	Tom Waddle	.60	.30	.06
28	Neal Anderson	.25	.12	.02
29	Brad Muster	.25	.12	.02
30	Shaun Gayle	.20	.10	.02
31	Jim Breech	.20	.10	.02
32	James Brooks	.25	.12	.02
33	James Francis	.25	.12	.02
34	David Fulcher	.20	.10	.02
35	Harold Green	.50	.25	.05
36	Rodney Holman	.20	.10	.02
37	Anthony Munoz	.25	.12	.02
38	Tim Krumrie	.20	.10	.02
39	Tim McGee	.20	.10	.02
40	Eddie Brown	.25	.12	.02
41	Kevin Mack	.25	.12	.02
42	James Jones	.20	.10	.02
43	Vince Newsome	.20	.10	.02
44	Ed King	.20	.10	.02
45	Eric Metcalf	.25	.12	.02
46	Leroy Hoard	.25	.12	.02
47	Stephen Braggs	.20	.10	.02
48	Clay Matthews	.20	.10	.02
49	David Brandon	.40	.20	.04
50	Rob Burnett	.20	.10	.02
51	Larry Brown	.20	.10	.02
52	Alvin Harper	.50	.25	.05
53	Michael Irvin	.60	.30	.06
54	Ken Norton Jr.	.20	.10	.02
55	Jay Novacek	.30	.15	.03
56	Emmitt Smith	4.50	2.25	.45
57	Tony Tolbert	.20	.10	.02
58	Nate Newton	.20	.10	.02
59	Steve Beuerlein	.35	.17	.03
60	Tony Casillas	.25	.12	.02
61	Steve Atwater	.25	.12	.02
62	Mike Croel	.75	.35	.07
63	Gaston Green	.50	.25	.05
64	Mark Jackson	.25	.12	.02
65	Greg Kragen	.20	.10	.02
66	Karl Mecklenburg	.25	.12	.02
67	Dennis Smith	.20	.10	.02
68	Steve Sewell	.20	.10	.02
69	John Elway	.60	.30	.06
70	Simon Fletcher	.25	.12	.02
71	Mel Gray	.20	.10	.02
72	Barry Sanders	3.00	1.50	.30
73	Jerry Ball	.25	.12	.02
74	Bennie Blades	.25	.12	.02
75	Lomas Brown	.20	.10	.02
76	Erik Kramer	1.50	.75	.15
77	Chris Spielman	.25	.12	.02
78	Ray Crockett	.20	.10	.02
79	Willie Green	.50	.25	.05
80	Rodney Peete	.25	.12	.02
81	Sterling Sharpe	.30	.15	.03
82	Tony Bennett	.20	.10	.02
83	Chuck Cecil	.20	.10	.02
84	Perry Kemp	.20	.10	.02
85	Brian Noble	.20	.10	.02
86	Darrell Thompson	.25	.12	.02
87	Mike Tomczak	.25	.12	.02
88	Vince Workman	.40	.20	.04
89	Esera Tuaolo	.20	.10	.02
90	Mark Murphy	.20	.10	.02
91	William Fuller	.20	.10	.02
92	Ernest Givins	.30	.15	.03
93	Drew Hill	.25	.12	.02
94	Al Smith	.20	.10	.02
95	Ray Childress	.25	.12	.02
96	Haywood Jeffires	.75	.35	.07
97	Cris Dishman	.25	.12	.02
98	Warren Moon	.75	.35	.07
99	Lamar Lathon	.25	.12	.02
100	Mike Munchak and Bruce Matthews	.25	.12	.02
101	Bill Brooks	.20	.10	.02
102	Duane Bickett	.20	.10	.02
103	Eugene Daniel	.20	.10	.02
104	Jeff Herrod	.20	.10	.02
105	Jessie Hester	.20	.10	.02
106	Donnell Thompson	.20	.10	.02
107	Anthony Johnson	.20	.10	.02
108	Jon Hand	.20	.10	.02
109	Rohn Stark	.20	.10	.02
110	Clarence Verdin	.20	.10	.02
111	Derrick Thomas	.75	.35	.07
112	Steve DeBerg	.25	.12	.02
113	Deron Cherry	.20	.10	.02
114	Chris Martin	.20	.10	.02
115	Christian Okoye	.30	.15	.03
116	Dan Saleaumua	.20	.10	.02
117	Neil Smith	.20	.10	.02
118	Barry Word	.60	.30	.06
119	Tim Barnett	.35	.17	.03
120	Albert Lewis	.25	.12	.02
121	Ronnie Lott	.30	.15	.03
122	Marcus Allen	.30	.15	.03
123	Todd Marinovich	1.50	.75	.15
124	Nick Bell	1.00	.50	.10
125	Tim Brown	.25	.12	.02
126	Ethan Horton	.25	.12	.02
127	Greg Townsend	.20	.10	.02
128	Jeff Gossett and Jeff Jaeger	.20	.10	.02
129	Scott Davis	.20	.10	.02
130	Steve Wisniewski and Don Mosebar	.20	.10	.02
131	Kevin Greene	.25	.12	.02
132	Roman Phifer	.20	.10	.02
133	Tony Zendejas	.20	.10	.02
134	Pat Terrell	.20	.10	.02
135	Flipper Anderson	.25	.12	.02
136	Robert Delpino	.25	.12	.02

☐ 137 Jim Everett	.30	.15	.03
☐ 138 Larry Kelm	.20	.10	.02
☐ 139 Todd Lyght	.50	.25	.05
☐ 140 Henry Ellard	.25	.12	.02
☐ 141 Mark Clayton	.25	.12	.02
☐ 142 Jeff Cross	.20	.10	.02
☐ 143 Mark Duper	.25	.12	.02
☐ 144 John Offerdahl	.20	.10	.02
☐ 145 Louis Oliver	.20	.10	.02
☐ 146 Pete Stoyanovich	.20	.10	.02
☐ 147 Richmond Webb	.20	.10	.02
☐ 148 Mark Higgs	.75	.35	.07
☐ 149 Tony Paige	.20	.10	.02
☐ 150 Bryan Cox	.20	.10	.02
☐ 151 Anthony Carter	.30	.15	.03
☐ 152 Cris Carter	.25	.12	.02
☐ 153 Rich Gannon	.25	.12	.02
☐ 154 Steve Jordan	.25	.12	.02
☐ 155 Mike Merriweather	.20	.10	.02
☐ 156 Henry Thomas	.20	.10	.02
☐ 157 Herschel Walker	.30	.15	.03
☐ 158 Randall McDaniel	.20	.10	.02
☐ 159 Terry Allen	.75	.35	.07
☐ 160 Joey Browner	.25	.12	.02
☐ 161 Leonard Russell	1.50	.75	.15
☐ 162 Bruce Armstrong	.20	.10	.02
☐ 163 Vincent Brown	.20	.10	.02
☐ 164 Hugh Millen	1.25	.60	.12
☐ 165 Andre Tippett	.25	.12	.02
☐ 166 Jon Vaughn	.90	.45	.09
☐ 167 Pat Harlow	.25	.12	.02
☐ 168 Marv Cook	.25	.12	.02
☐ 169 Irving Fryar	.25	.12	.02
☐ 170 Maurice Hurst	.20	.10	.02
☐ 171 Pat Swilling	.25	.12	.02
☐ 172 Vince Buck	.20	.10	.02
☐ 173 Rickey Jackson	.25	.12	.02
☐ 174 Sam Mills	.20	.10	.02
☐ 175 Bobby Hebert	.25	.12	.02
☐ 176 Vaughan Johnson	.20	.10	.02
☐ 177 Floyd Turner	.20	.10	.02
☐ 178 Fred McAfee	.40	.20	.04
☐ 179 Morten Andersen	.25	.12	.02
☐ 180 Eric Martin	.20	.10	.02
☐ 181 Rodney Hampton	.60	.30	.06
☐ 182 Pepper Johnson	.20	.10	.02
☐ 183 Leonard Marshall	.20	.10	.02
☐ 184 Stephen Baker	.20	.10	.02
☐ 185 Mark Ingram	.20	.10	.02
☐ 186 Dave Meggett	.30	.15	.03
☐ 187 Bart Oates	.20	.10	.02
☐ 188 Mark Collins	.20	.10	.02
☐ 189 Myron Guyton	.20	.10	.02
☐ 190 Jeff Hostetler	.50	.25	.05
☐ 191 Jeff Lageman	.25	.12	.02
☐ 192 Brad Baxter	.25	.12	.02
☐ 193 Mo Lewis	.25	.12	.02
☐ 194 Chris Burkett	.20	.10	.02
☐ 195 James Hasty	.20	.10	.02
☐ 196 Rob Moore	.75	.35	.07
☐ 197 Kyle Clifton	.20	.10	.02
☐ 198 Terance Mathis	.25	.12	.02
☐ 199 Marvin Washington	.20	.10	.02
☐ 200 Lonnie Young	.20	.10	.02
☐ 201 Reggie White	.25	.12	.02
☐ 202 Eric Allen	.20	.10	.02
☐ 203 Fred Barnett	.35	.17	.03
☐ 204 Keith Byars	.25	.12	.02
☐ 205 Seth Joyner	.25	.12	.02
☐ 206 Clyde Simmons	.25	.12	.02
☐ 207 Jerome Brown	.25	.12	.02
☐ 208 Wes Hopkins	.20	.10	.02
☐ 209 Keith Jackson	.25	.12	.02
☐ 210 Calvin Williams	.20	.10	.02
☐ 211 Aeneas Williams	.20	.10	.02
☐ 212 Ken Harvey	.20	.10	.02
☐ 213 Ernie Jones	.20	.10	.02
☐ 214 Freddie Joe Nunn	.20	.10	.02
☐ 215 Rich Camarillo	.20	.10	.02
☐ 216 Johnny Johnson	.40	.20	.04
☐ 217 Tim McDonald	.20	.10	.02
☐ 218 Eric Swann	.25	.12	.02
☐ 219 Eric Hill	.20	.10	.02
☐ 220 Anthony Thompson	.25	.12	.02
☐ 221 Hardy Nickerson	.20	.10	.02
☐ 222 Barry Foster	.30	.15	.03
☐ 223 Louis Lipps	.25	.12	.02
☐ 224 Greg Lloyd	.20	.10	.02
☐ 225 Neil O'Donnell	1.25	.60	.12
☐ 226 Jerrol Williams	.20	.10	.02
☐ 227 Eric Green	.40	.20	.04
☐ 228 Rod Woodson	.25	.12	.02
☐ 229 Carnell Lake	.20	.10	.02
☐ 230 Dwight Stone	.20	.10	.02
☐ 231 Marion Butts	.30	.15	.03
☐ 232 John Friesz	.60	.30	.06
☐ 233 Burt Grossman	.25	.12	.02
☐ 234 Ronnie Harmon	.20	.10	.02
☐ 235 Gill Byrd	.20	.10	.02
☐ 236 Rod Bernstine	.25	.12	.02
☐ 237 Courtney Hall	.20	.10	.02
☐ 238 Nate Lewis	.20	.10	.02
☐ 239 Joe Phillips	.20	.10	.02
☐ 240 Henry Rolling	.20	.10	.02
☐ 241 Keith Henderson	.35	.17	.03
☐ 242 Guy McIntyre	.20	.10	.02
☐ 243 Bill Romanowski	.20	.10	.02
☐ 244 Don Griffin	.20	.10	.02
☐ 245 Dexter Carter	.25	.12	.02
☐ 246 Charles Haley	.25	.12	.02
☐ 247 Brent Jones	.25	.12	.02
☐ 248 John Taylor	.30	.15	.03
☐ 249 Steve Young	.40	.20	.04
☐ 250 Larry Roberts	.20	.10	.02

☐ 251	Brian Blades	.25	.12	.02
☐ 252	Jacob Green	.25	.12	.02
☐ 253	John Kasay	.20	.10	.02
☐ 254	Cortéz Kennedy	.25	.12	.02
☐ 255	Rufus Porter	.20	.10	.02
☐ 256	John L. Williams	.25	.12	.02
☐ 257	Tommy Kane	.30	.15	.03
☐ 258	Eugene Robinson	.20	.10	.02
☐ 259	Terry Wooden	.20	.10	.02
☐ 260	Chris Warren	.25	.12	.02
☐ 261	Lawrence Dawsey	.40	.20	.04
☐ 262	Mark Carrier	.25	.12	.02
☐ 263	Keith McCants	.25	.12	.02
☐ 264	Jesse Solomon	.20	.10	.02
☐ 265	Vinny Testaverde	.25	.12	.02
☐ 266	Ricky Reynolds	.20	.10	.02
☐ 267	Broderick Thomas	.25	.12	.02
☐ 268	Gary Anderson	.25	.12	.02
☐ 269	Reggie Cobb	.35	.17	.03
☐ 270	Tony Covington	.20	.10	.02
☐ 271	Darrell Green	.35	.17	.03
☐ 272	Charles Mann	.25	.12	.02
☐ 273	Wilber Marshall	.25	.12	.02
☐ 274	Gary Clark	.40	.20	.04
☐ 275	Chip Lohmiller	.20	.10	.02
☐ 276	Earnest Byner	.25	.12	.02
☐ 277	Jim Lachey	.25	.12	.02
☐ 278	Art Monk	.40	.20	.04
☐ 279	Mark Rypien	.75	.35	.07
☐ 280	Mark Schlereth	.35	.17	.03
☐ 281	Mark Rypien BR	2.50	1.25	.25
	Washington Redskins			
	'91 NFC Passing Yardage			
	Leader			
☐ 282	Warren Moon BR	2.25	1.10	.22
	Houston Oilers			
	'91 AFC Passing Yardage			
	Leader			
☐ 283	Emmitt Smith BR	9.00	4.50	.90
	Dallas Cowboys			
	'91 NFC Rushing Leader			
☐ 284	Thurman Thomas BR	5.00	2.50	.50
	Buffalo Bills			
	'91 AFC Rushing Leader			
☐ 285	Michael Irvin BR	2.50	1.25	.25
	Dallas Cowboys			
	'91 NFC Receiving Leader			
☐ 286	Haywood Jeffires BR	2.25	1.10	.22
	Houston Oilers			
	'91 AFC Receiving Leader			
☐ 287	Pat Swilling BR	1.25	.60	.12
	New Orleans Saints			
	'91 NFC Sack Leader			
☐ 288	Ronnie Lott BR	1.50	.75	.15
	Los Angeles Raiders			
	'91 AFC Interception			
	Leader			

☐ 289	NFC Logo	.35	.17	.03
☐ 290	AFC Logo	.35	.17	.03

1948 Bowman

The 1948 Bowman set is considered the first football set of the modern era. The set is complete at 108 cards; each measures 2 1/16" by 2 1/2". The cards were printed in three sheets; the third sheet (containing all the card numbers divisible by three, i.e., 3, 6, 9, 12, 15, etc.) being printed in much lesser quantities. Hence, cards with numbers divisible by three are substantially more valuable than the other cards in the set. The second sheet (numbers 2, 5, 8, 11, 14, etc.) is also regarded as slightly tougher to obtain than the first sheet (numbers 1, 4, 7, 10, 13, etc.) which contains the most plentiful cards. The key rookie cards in this set are Sammy Baugh, Charley Conerly, Sid Luckman, Johnny Lujack, Steve Van Buren, and Bob Waterfield.

	NRMT	VG-E	GOOD
COMPLETE SET (108)	6200.00	2650.00	850.00
COMMON 1/4/7/10/13	15.00	7.50	1.50
COMMON 3/5/8/11/14	18.00	9.00	1.80
COMMON 3/6/9/12/15	90.00	45.00	9.00
☐ 1 Joe Tereshinski	150.00	15.00	3.00
Washington Redskins			
☐ 2 Larry Olsonoski	18.00	9.00	1.80
Green Bay Packers			
☐ 3 John Lujack	225.00	110.00	22.00
Chicago Bears			
☐ 4 Ray Poole	15.00	7.50	1.50
New York Giants			
☐ 5 Bill DeCorrevont	18.00	9.00	1.80
Chicago Cardinals			

☐ 6 Paul Briggs	90.00	45.00	9.00
Detroit Lions			
☐ 7 Steve Van Buren	125.00	60.00	12.50
Philadelphia Eagles			
☐ 8 Kenny Washington	42.00	20.00	4.00
Los Angeles Rams			
☐ 9 Nolan Luhn	90.00	45.00	9.00
Green Bay Packers			
☐ 10 Chris Iversen	15.00	7.50	1.50
New York Giants			
☐ 11 Jack Wiley	18.00	9.00	1.80
Pittsburgh Steelers			
☐ 12 Charley Conerly	225.00	110.00	22.00
New York Giants			
☐ 13 Hugh Taylor	25.00	12.50	2.50
Washington Redskins			
☐ 14 Frank Seno	18.00	9.00	1.80
Boston Yanks			
☐ 15 Gil Bouley	90.00	45.00	9.00
Los Angeles Rams			
☐ 16 Tommy Thompson	35.00	17.50	3.50
Philadelphia Eagles			
☐ 17 Charlie Trippi	100.00	50.00	10.00
Chicago Cardinals			
☐ 18 Vince Banonis	90.00	45.00	9.00
Chicago Cardinals			
☐ 19 Art Faircloth	15.00	7.50	1.50
New York Giants			
☐ 20 Clyde Goodnight	18.00	9.00	1.80
Green Bay Packers			
☐ 21 Bill Chipley	90.00	45.00	9.00
Boston Yanks			
☐ 22 Sammy Baugh	325.00	160.00	32.00
Washington Redskins			
☐ 23 Don Kindt	18.00	9.00	1.80
Chicago Bears			
☐ 24 John Koniszewski	90.00	45.00	9.00
Washington Redskins			
☐ 25 Pat McHugh	15.00	7.50	1.50
Philadelphia Eagles			
☐ 26 Bob Waterfield	165.00	80.00	16.00
Los Angeles Rams			
☐ 27 Tony Compagno	90.00	45.00	9.00
Pittsburgh Steelers			
☐ 28 Paul Governali	15.00	7.50	1.50
New York Giants			
☐ 29 Pat Harder	40.00	20.00	4.00
Chicago Cardinals			
☐ 30 Vic Lindskog	90.00	45.00	9.00
Philadelphia Eagles			
☐ 31 Salvatore Rosato	15.00	7.50	1.50
Washington Redskins			
☐ 32 John Mastrangelo	18.00	9.00	1.80
Pittsburgh Steelers			
☐ 33 Fred Gehrke	90.00	45.00	9.00
Los Angeles Rams			
☐ 34 Bosh Pritchard	15.00	7.50	1.50

Philadelphia Eagles			
☐ 35 Mike Micka	18.00	9.00	1.80
Boston Yanks			
☐ 36 Bulldog Turner	180.00	90.00	18.00
Chicago Bears			
☐ 37 Len Younce	15.00	7.50	1.50
New York Giants			
☐ 38 Pat West	18.00	9.00	1.80
Los Angeles Rams			
☐ 39 Russ Thomas	100.00	50.00	10.00
Detroit Lions			
☐ 40 James Peebles	15.00	7.50	1.50
Washington Redskins			
☐ 41 Bob Skoglund	18.00	9.00	1.80
Green Bay Packers			
☐ 42 Walt Stickle	90.00	45.00	9.00
Chicago Bears			
☐ 43 Whitey Wistert	22.00	11.00	2.20
Philadelphia Eagles			
☐ 44 Paul Christman	45.00	22.50	4.50
Chicago Cardinals			
☐ 45 Jay Rhodemyre	90.00	45.00	9.00
Green Bay Packers			
☐ 46 Skip Minisi	15.00	7.50	1.50
New York Giants			
☐ 47 Bob Mann	18.00	9.00	1.80
Detroit Lions			
☐ 48 Mal Kutner	90.00	45.00	9.00
Chicago Cardinals			
☐ 49 Dick Poillon	15.00	7.50	1.50
Washington Redskins			
☐ 50 Charles Cherundolo	18.00	9.00	1.80
Pittsburgh Steelers			
☐ 51 Gerald Cowhig	90.00	45.00	9.00
Los Angeles Rams			
☐ 52 Neil Armstrong	27.00	13.50	2.70
Philadelphia Eagles			
☐ 53 Frank Maznicki	18.00	9.00	1.80
Boston Yanks			
☐ 54 John Sanchez	90.00	45.00	9.00
Washington Redskins			
☐ 55 Frank Reagan	15.00	7.50	1.50
New York Giants			
☐ 56 Jim Hardy	18.00	9.00	1.80
Los Angeles Rams			
☐ 57 John Badaczewski	90.00	45.00	9.00
Boston Yanks			
☐ 58 Robert Nussbaumer	15.00	7.50	1.50
Washington Redskins			
☐ 59 Marvin Pregulman	18.00	9.00	1.80
Detroit Lions			
☐ 60 Elbert Nickel	100.00	50.00	10.00
Pittsburgh Steelers			
☐ 61 Alex Wojciechowicz	80.00	40.00	8.00
Philadelphia Eagles			
☐ 62 Walt Schlinkman	18.00	9.00	1.80
Green Bay Packers			

☐ 63	Pete Pihos 180.00	90.00	18.00
	Philadelphia Eagles		
☐ 64	Joseph Sulaitis 15.00	7.50	1.50
	New York Giants		
☐ 65	Mike Holovak 40.00	20.00	4.00
	Chicago Bears		
☐ 66	Cecil Souders 90.00	45.00	9.00
	Detroit Lions		
☐ 67	Paul McKee 15.00	7.50	1.50
	Washington Redskins		
☐ 68	Bill Moore 18.00	9.00	1.80
	Pittsburgh Steelers		
☐ 69	Frank Minini 90.00	45.00	9.00
	Chicago Bears		
☐ 70	Jack Ferrante 15.00	7.50	1.50
	Philadelphia Eagles		
☐ 71	Leslie Horvath 40.00	20.00	4.00
	Los Angeles Rams		
☐ 72	Ted Fritsch Sr. 100.00	50.00	10.00
	Green Bay Packers		
☐ 73	Tex Coulter 15.00	7.50	1.50
	New York Giants		
☐ 74	Boley Dancewicz 18.00	9.00	1.80
	Boston Yanks		
☐ 75	Dante Mangani 90.00	45.00	9.00
	Los Angeles Rams		
☐ 76	James Hefti 15.00	7.50	1.50
	Washington Redskins		
☐ 77	Paul Sarringhaus 18.00	9.00	1.80
	Detroit Lions		
☐ 78	Joe Scott 90.00	45.00	9.00
	New York Giants		
☐ 79	Bucko Kilroy 27.00	13.50	2.70
	Philadelphia Eagles		
☐ 80	Bill Dudley 100.00	50.00	10.00
	Detroit Lions		
☐ 81	Marshall Goldberg 100.00	50.00	10.00
	Chicago Cardinals		
☐ 82	John Cannady 15.00	7.50	1.50
	New York Giants		
☐ 83	Perry Moss 18.00	9.00	1.80
	Green Bay Packers		
☐ 84	Harold Crisler 90.00	45.00	9.00
	Boston Yanks		
☐ 85	Bill Gray 15.00	7.50	1.50
	Washington Redskins		
☐ 86	John Clement 18.00	9.00	1.80
	Pittsburgh Steelers		
☐ 87	Dan Sandifer 90.00	45.00	9.00
	Washington Redskins		
☐ 88	Ben Kish 15.00	7.50	1.50
	Philadelphia Eagles		
☐ 89	Herbert Banta 18.00	9.00	1.80
	Los Angeles Rams		
☐ 90	Bill Garnaas 90.00	45.00	9.00
	Pittsburgh Steelers		
☐ 91	Jim White 15.00	7.50	1.50

	New York Giants		
☐ 92	Frank Barzilauskas 18.00	9.00	1.80
	Boston Yanks		
☐ 93	Vic Sears 90.00	45.00	9.00
	Philadelphia Eagles		
☐ 94	John Adams 15.00	7.50	1.50
	Washington Redskins		
☐ 95	George McAfee 100.00	50.00	10.00
	Chicago Bears		
☐ 96	Ralph Heywood 90.00	45.00	9.00
	Detroit Lions		
☐ 97	Joe Muha 15.00	7.50	1.50
	Philadelphia Eagles		
☐ 98	Fred Enke 18.00	9.00	1.80
	Detroit Lions		
☐ 99	Harry Gilmer 120.00	60.00	12.00
	Washington Redskins		
☐ 100	Bill Miklich 15.00	7.50	1.50
	New York Giants		
☐ 101	Joe Gottlieb 18.00	9.00	1.80
	Pittsburgh Steelers		
☐ 102	Bud Angsman 90.00	45.00	9.00
	Chicago Cardinals		
☐ 103	Tom Farmer 15.00	7.50	1.50
	Washington Redskins		
☐ 104	Bruce Smith 40.00	20.00	4.00
	Green Bay Packers		
☐ 105	Bob Cifers 90.00	45.00	9.00
	Pittsburgh Steelers		
☐ 106	Ernie Steele 15.00	7.50	1.50
	Philadelphia Eagles		
☐ 107	Sid Luckman 175.00	85.00	18.00
	Chicago Bears		
☐ 108	Buford Ray 350.00	60.00	12.00
	Green Bay Packers		

1950 Bowman

The 1950 Bowman set is Bowman's first color football set. The color quality on the cards is superior to previous Bowman sports' issues. The set is complete at 144 cards; the cards measure approximately 2 1/16" by 2 1/2". The card backs feature black printing except for the player's name and the logo for the "5-Star Bowman Picture Card Collectors Club" which are in red. The set features the football "Rookie cards" of Tony Canadeo, Tom Fears, Otto Graham, Lou Groza, Elroy Hirsch, Dante Lavelli, Marion Motley, Joe Perry, and Y.A. Tittle. With a few exceptions the set numbering

is arranged so that trios of players from the same team are numbered together in sequence.

	NRMT	VG-E	GOOD
COMPLETE SET (144)	3600.00	1650.00	450.00
COMMON PLAYER (1-36)	15.00	7.50	1.50
COMMON PLAYER (37-72)	15.00	7.50	1.50
COMMON PLAYER (73-108)	15.00	7.50	1.50
COMMON PLAYER (109-144)	15.00	7.50	1.50

		NRMT	VG-E	GOOD
☐ 1	Doak Walker Detroit Lions	110.00	30.00	6.00
☐ 2	John Greene Detroit Lions	15.00	7.50	1.50
☐ 3	Bob Nowasky Baltimore Colts	15.00	7.50	1.50
☐ 4	Jonathan Jenkins Baltimore Colts	15.00	7.50	1.50
☐ 5	Y.A. Tittle Baltimore Colts	250.00	125.00	25.00
☐ 6	Lou Groza Cleveland Browns	150.00	75.00	15.00
☐ 7	Alex Agase Cleveland Browns	21.00	10.50	2.10
☐ 8	Mac Speedie Cleveland Browns	25.00	12.50	2.50
☐ 9	Tony Canadeo Green Bay Packers	40.00	20.00	4.00
☐ 10	Larry Craig Green Bay Packers	15.00	7.50	1.50
☐ 11	Ted Fritsch Sr. Green Bay Packers	18.00	9.00	1.80
☐ 12	Joe Goldring New York Yanks	15.00	7.50	1.50
☐ 13	Martin Ruby New York Yanks	18.00	9.00	1.80
☐ 14	George Taliaferro New York Yanks	21.00	10.50	2.10
☐ 15	Tank Younger Los Angeles Rams	25.00	12.50	2.50
☐ 16	Glenn Army Davis Los Angeles Rams	110.00	55.00	11.00
☐ 17	Bob Waterfield Los Angeles Rams	50.00	25.00	5.00
☐ 18	Val Jansante Pittsburgh Steelers	15.00	7.50	1.50
☐ 19	Joe Geri Pittsburgh Steelers	15.00	7.50	1.50
☐ 20	Jerry Nuzum Pittsburgh Steelers	15.00	7.50	1.50
☐ 21	Elmer Angsman Chicago Cardinals	15.00	7.50	1.50
☐ 22	Billy Dewell Chicago Cardinals	15.00	7.50	1.50
☐ 23	Steve Van Buren Philadelphia Eagles	45.00	22.50	4.50
☐ 24	Cliff Patton Philadelphia Eagles	15.00	7.50	1.50
☐ 25	Bosh Pritchard Philadelphia Eagles	15.00	7.50	1.50
☐ 26	John Lujack Chicago Bears	50.00	25.00	5.00
☐ 27	Sid Luckman Chicago Bears	55.00	27.50	5.50
☐ 28	Bulldog Turner Chicago Bears	36.00	18.00	3.60
☐ 29	Bill Dudley Washington Redskins	30.00	15.00	3.00
☐ 30	Hugh Taylor Washington Redskins	18.00	9.00	1.80
☐ 31	George Thomas Washington Redskins	15.00	7.50	1.50
☐ 32	Ray Poole New York Giants	15.00	7.50	1.50
☐ 33	Travis Tidwell New York Giants	15.00	7.50	1.50
☐ 34	Gail Bruce San Francisco 49ers	15.00	7.50	1.50
☐ 35	Joe Perry San Francisco 49ers	110.00	55.00	11.00
☐ 36	Frankie Albert San Francisco 49ers	30.00	15.00	3.00
☐ 37	Bobby Layne Detroit Lions	100.00	50.00	10.00
☐ 38	Leon Hart Detroit Lions	27.00	13.50	2.70
☐ 39	Bob Hoernschemeyer Detroit Lions	15.00	7.50	1.50
☐ 40	Dick Barwegan Baltimore Colts	15.00	7.50	1.50
☐ 41	Adrian Burk Baltimore Colts	20.00	10.00	2.00
☐ 42	Barry French Baltimore Colts	15.00	7.50	1.50
☐ 43	Marion Motley Cleveland Browns	70.00	35.00	7.00
☐ 44	Jim Martin Cleveland Browns	20.00	10.00	2.00
☐ 45	Otto Graham	400.00	200.00	40.00

	Cleveland Browns			
☐ 46	Al Baldwin	15.00	7.50	1.50
	Green Bay Packers			
☐ 47	Larry Coutre	15.00	7.50	1.50
	Green Bay Packers			
☐ 48	John Rauch	15.00	7.50	1.50
	New York Yanks			
☐ 49	Sam Tamburo	15.00	7.50	1.50
	New York Yanks			
☐ 50	Mike Swistowicz	15.00	7.50	1.50
	New York Yanks			
☐ 51	Tom Fears	70.00	35.00	7.00
	Los Angeles Rams			
☐ 52	Elroy Hirsch	110.00	55.00	11.00
	Los Angeles Rams			
☐ 53	Dick Huffman	15.00	7.50	1.50
	Los Angeles Rams			
☐ 54	Bob Gage	15.00	7.50	1.50
	Pittsburgh Steelers			
☐ 55	Bob Tinsley	15.00	7.50	1.50
	Los Angeles Rams			
☐ 56	Bill Blackburn	15.00	7.50	1.50
	Chicago Cardinals			
☐ 57	John Cochran	15.00	7.50	1.50
	Chicago Cardinals			
☐ 58	Bill Fischer	15.00	7.50	1.50
	Chicago Cardinals			
☐ 59	Whitey Wistert	18.00	9.00	1.80
	Philadelphia Eagles			
☐ 60	Clyde Scott	15.00	7.50	1.50
	Philadelphia Eagles			
☐ 61	Walter Barnes	15.00	7.50	1.50
	Philadelphia Eagles			
☐ 62	Bob Perina	15.00	7.50	1.50
	Baltimore Colts			
☐ 63	Bill Wightkin	15.00	7.50	1.50
	Chicago Bears			
☐ 64	Bob Goode	15.00	7.50	1.50
	Washington Redskins			
☐ 65	Al Demao	15.00	7.50	1.50
	Washington Redskins			
☐ 66	Harry Gilmer	18.00	9.00	1.80
	Washington Redskins			
☐ 67	Bill Austin	15.00	7.50	1.50
	New York Giants			
☐ 68	Joe Scott	15.00	7.50	1.50
	New York Giants			
☐ 69	Tex Coulter	18.00	9.00	1.80
	New York Giants			
☐ 70	Paul Salata	15.00	7.50	1.50
	San Francisco 49ers			
☐ 71	Emil Sitko	15.00	7.50	1.50
	San Francisco 49ers			
☐ 72	Bill Johnson	15.00	7.50	1.50
	San Francisco 49ers			
☐ 73	Don Doll	20.00	10.00	2.00
	Detroit Lions			
☐ 74	Dan Sandifer	15.00	7.50	1.50
	Detroit Lions			
☐ 75	John Panelli	15.00	7.50	1.50
	Detroit Lions			
☐ 76	Bill Leonard	15.00	7.50	1.50
	Baltimore Colts			
☐ 77	Bob Kelly	15.00	7.50	1.50
	Baltimore Colts			
☐ 78	Dante Lavelli	50.00	25.00	5.00
	Cleveland Browns			
☐ 79	Tony Adamle	18.00	9.00	1.80
	Cleveland Browns			
☐ 80	Dick Wildung	15.00	7.50	1.50
	Green Bay Packers			
☐ 81	Tobin Rote	25.00	12.50	2.50
	Green Bay Packers			
☐ 82	Paul Burris	15.00	7.50	1.50
	Green Bay Packers			
☐ 83	Lowell Tew	15.00	7.50	1.50
	New York Yanks			
☐ 84	Barney Poole	15.00	7.50	1.50
	New York Yanks			
☐ 85	Fred Naumetz	15.00	7.50	1.50
	Los Angeles Rams			
☐ 86	Dick Hoerner	15.00	7.50	1.50
	Los Angeles Rams			
☐ 87	Bob Reinhard	15.00	7.50	1.50
	Los Angeles Rams			
☐ 88	Howard Hartley	15.00	7.50	1.50
	Pittsburgh Steelers			
☐ 89	Darrell Hogan	15.00	7.50	1.50
	Pittsburgh Steelers			
☐ 90	Jerry Shipkey	15.00	7.50	1.50
	Pittsburgh Steelers			
☐ 91	Frank Tripucka	24.00	12.00	2.40
	Chicago Cardinals			
☐ 92	Garrard Ramsey	15.00	7.50	1.50
	Chicago Cardinals			
☐ 93	Pat Harder	20.00	10.00	2.00
	Chicago Cardinals			
☐ 94	Vic Sears	15.00	7.50	1.50
	Philadelphia Eagles			
☐ 95	Tommy Thompson	20.00	10.00	2.00
	Philadelphia Eagles			
☐ 96	Bucko Kilroy	18.00	9.00	1.80
	Philadelphia Eagles			
☐ 97	George Connor	30.00	15.00	3.00
	Chicago Bears			
☐ 98	Fred Morrison	15.00	7.50	1.50
	Chicago Bears			
☐ 99	Jim Keane	15.00	7.50	1.50
	Chicago Bears			
☐ 100	Sammy Baugh	125.00	60.00	12.50
	Washington Redskins			
☐ 101	Harry Ulinski	15.00	7.50	1.50
	Washington Redskins			
☐ 102	Frank Spaniel	15.00	7.50	1.50

Baltimore Colts
- [ ] 103 Charley Conerly 50.00 25.00 5.00
  New York Giants
- [ ] 104 Dick Hensley 15.00 7.50 1.50
  New York Giants
- [ ] 105 Eddie Price 18.00 9.00 1.80
  New York Giants
- [ ] 106 Ed Carr 15.00 7.50 1.50
  San Francisco 49ers
- [ ] 107 Leo Nomellini 40.00 20.00 4.00
  San Francisco 49ers
- [ ] 108 Verl Lillywhite 15.00 7.50 1.50
  San Francisco 49ers
- [ ] 109 Wallace Triplett 15.00 7.50 1.50
  Detroit Lions
- [ ] 110 Joe Watson 15.00 7.50 1.50
  Detroit Lions
- [ ] 111 Cloyce Box 18.00 9.00 1.80
  Detroit Lions
- [ ] 112 Billy Stone 15.00 7.50 1.50
  Baltimore Colts
- [ ] 113 Earl Murray 15.00 7.50 1.50
  Baltimore Colts
- [ ] 114 Chet Mutryn 18.00 9.00 1.80
  Baltimore Colts
- [ ] 115 Ken Carpenter 15.00 7.50 1.50
  Cleveland Browns
- [ ] 116 Lou Rymkus 20.00 10.00 2.00
  Cleveland Browns
- [ ] 117 Dub Jones 25.00 12.50 2.50
  Cleveland Browns
- [ ] 118 Clayton Tonnemaker . 15.00 7.50 1.50
  Green Bay Packers
- [ ] 119 Walt Schlinkman 15.00 7.50 1.50
  Green Bay Packers
- [ ] 120 Billy Grimes 15.00 7.50 1.50
  Green Bay Packers
- [ ] 121 George Ratterman 22.00 11.00 2.20
  New York Yanks
- [ ] 122 Bob Mann 15.00 7.50 1.50
  New York Yanks
- [ ] 123 Buddy Young 27.00 13.50 2.70
  New York Yanks
- [ ] 124 Jack Zilly 15.00 7.50 1.50
  Los Angeles Rams
- [ ] 125 Tom Kalmanir 15.00 7.50 1.50
  Los Angeles Rams
- [ ] 126 Frank Sinkovitz 15.00 7.50 1.50
  Pittsburgh Steelers
- [ ] 127 Elbert Nickel 15.00 7.50 1.50
  Pittsburgh Steelers
- [ ] 128 Jim Finks 25.00 12.50 2.50
  Pittsburgh Steelers
- [ ] 129 Charlie Trippi 28.00 14.00 2.80
  Chicago Cardinals
- [ ] 130 Tom Wham 15.00 7.50 1.50
  Chicago Cardinals

- [ ] 131 Ventan Yablonski 15.00 7.50 1.50
  Chicago Cardinals
- [ ] 132 Chuck Bednarik 45.00 22.50 4.50
  Philadelphia Eagles
- [ ] 133 Joe Muha 15.00 7.50 1.50
  Philadelphia Eagles
- [ ] 134 Pete Pihos 28.00 14.00 2.80
  Philadelphia Eagles
- [ ] 135 Washington Serini 15.00 7.50 1.50
  Chicago Bears
- [ ] 136 George Gulyanics 15.00 7.50 1.50
  Chicago Bears
- [ ] 137 Ken Kavanaugh 25.00 12.50 2.50
  Chicago Bears
- [ ] 138 Howie Livingston 15.00 7.50 1.50
  Washington Redskins
- [ ] 139 Joe Tereshinski 15.00 7.50 1.50
  Washington Redskins
- [ ] 140 Jim White 15.00 7.50 1.50
  New York Giants
- [ ] 141 Gene Roberts 15.00 7.50 1.50
  New York Giants
- [ ] 142 William Swiacki 18.00 9.00 1.80
  New York Giants
- [ ] 143 Norm Standlee 18.00 9.00 1.80
  San Francisco 49ers
- [ ] 144 Knox Ramsey 42.00 12.00 2.50
  Chicago Cardinals

1951 Bowman

The 1951 Bowman set of 144 numbered cards witnessed an increase in card size from previous Bowman football sets. The cards were enlarged from the previous year to 2 1/16" by 3 1/8". The 144-card set is very similar

in format to the baseball card set of that year. The card backs are printed in maroon and blue on gray card stock. The set features the football "Rookie cards" of Tom Landry, Emlen Tunnell, and Norm Van Brocklin. The Bill Walsh in this set went to Notre Dame and is not the Bill Walsh who coached the San Francisco 49ers in the 1980s. The set numbering is arranged so that two, three, or four players from the same team are numbered together in sequence.

	NRMT	VG-E	GOOD
COMPLETE SET (144)	3000.00	1400.00	375.00
COMMON PLAYER (1-144)	12.50	6.25	1.25
☐ 1 Weldon Humble Cleveland Browns	40.00	10.00	2.00
☐ 2 Otto Graham Cleveland Browns	125.00	60.00	12.50
☐ 3 Mac Speedie Cleveland Browns	18.00	9.00	1.80
☐ 4 Norm Van Brocklin Los Angeles Rams	165.00	80.00	16.00
☐ 5 Woodley Lewis Los Angeles Rams	15.00	7.50	1.50
☐ 6 Tom Fears Los Angeles Rams	30.00	15.00	3.00
☐ 7 George Musacco New York Yanks	12.50	6.25	1.25
☐ 8 George Taliaferro New York Yanks	15.00	7.50	1.50
☐ 9 Barney Poole New York Yanks	12.50	6.25	1.25
☐ 10 Steve Van Buren Philadelphia Eagles	32.00	16.00	3.20
☐ 11 Whitey Wistert Philadelphia Eagles	15.00	7.50	1.50
☐ 12 Chuck Bednarik Philadelphia Eagles	34.00	17.00	3.20
☐ 13 Bulldog Turner Chicago Bears	32.00	16.00	3.20
☐ 14 Bob Williams Chicago Bears	12.50	6.25	1.25
☐ 15 John Lujack Chicago Bears	32.00	16.00	3.20
☐ 16 Roy Rebel Steiner Green Bay Packers	12.50	6.25	1.25
☐ 17 Earl Jug Girard Green Bay Packers	12.50	6.25	1.25
☐ 18 Bill Neal Green Bay Packers	12.50	6.25	1.25
☐ 19 Travis Tidwell New York Giants	12.50	6.25	1.25
☐ 20 Tom Landry New York Giants	450.00	225.00	45.00
☐ 21 Arnie Weinmeister New York Giants	36.00	18.00	3.60
☐ 22 Joe Geri Pittsburgh Steelers	12.50	6.25	1.25
☐ 23 Bill Walsh Pittsburgh Steelers	15.00	7.50	1.50
☐ 24 Fran Rogel Pittsburgh Steelers	12.50	6.25	1.25
☐ 25 Doak Walker Detroit Lions	30.00	15.00	3.00
☐ 26 Leon Hart Detroit Lions	18.00	9.00	1.80
☐ 27 Thurman McGraw Detroit Lions	12.50	6.25	1.25
☐ 28 Buster Ramsey Chicago Cardinals	12.50	6.25	1.25
☐ 29 Frank Tripucka Chicago Cardinals	20.00	10.00	2.00
☐ 30 Don Paul Chicago Cardinals	12.50	6.25	1.25
☐ 31 Alex Loyd San Francisco 49ers	12.50	6.25	1.25
☐ 32 Y.A. Tittle San Francisco 49ers	90.00	45.00	9.00
☐ 33 Verl Lillywhite San Francisco 49ers	12.50	6.25	1.25
☐ 34 Sammy Baugh Washington Redskins	100.00	50.00	10.00
☐ 35 Chuck Drazenovich Washington Redskins	12.50	6.25	1.25
☐ 36 Bob Goode Washington Redskins	12.50	6.25	1.25
☐ 37 Horace Gillom Cleveland Browns	12.50	6.25	1.25
☐ 38 Lou Rymkus Cleveland Browns	15.00	7.50	1.50
☐ 39 Ken Carpenter Cleveland Browns	12.50	6.25	1.25
☐ 40 Bob Waterfield Los Angeles Rams	36.00	18.00	3.60
☐ 41 Vitamin Smith Los Angeles Rams	12.50	6.25	1.25
☐ 42 Glenn Army Davis Los Angeles Rams	32.00	16.00	3.20
☐ 43 Dan Edwards New York Yanks	12.50	6.25	1.25
☐ 44 John Rauch New York Yanks	12.50	6.25	1.25
☐ 45 Zollie Toth New York Yanks	12.50	6.25	1.25
☐ 46 Pete Pihos Philadelphia Eagles	25.00	12.50	2.50
☐ 47 Russ Craft Philadelphia Eagles	12.50	6.25	1.25
☐ 48 Walter Barnes Philadelphia Eagles	12.50	6.25	1.25
☐ 49 Fred Morrison Chicago Bears	12.50	6.25	1.25

☐ 50 Ray Bray 12.50   6.25   1.25
    Chicago Bears
☐ 51 Ed Sprinkle 15.00   7.50   1.50
    Chicago Bears
☐ 52 Floyd Reid 12.50   6.25   1.25
    Green Bay Packers
☐ 53 Billy Grimes 12.50   6.25   1.25
    Green Bay Packers
☐ 54 Ted Fritsch Sr. 15.00   7.50   1.50
    Green Bay Packers
☐ 55 Al DeRogatis 15.00   7.50   1.50
    New York Giants
☐ 56 Charley Conerly 36.00   18.00 3.60
    New York Giants
☐ 57 Jon Baker 12.50   6.25   1.25
    New York Giants
☐ 58 Tom McWilliams 12.50   6.25   1.25
    Pittsburgh Steelers
☐ 59 Jerry Shipkey 12.50   6.25   1.25
    Pittsburgh Steelers
☐ 60 Lynn Chandnois 12.50   6.25   1.25
    Pittsburgh Steelers
☐ 61 Don Doll 12.50   6.25   1.25
    Detroit Lions
☐ 62 Lou Creekmur 15.00   7.50   1.50
    Detroit Lions
☐ 63 Bob Hoernschemeyer 12.50   6.25   1.25
    Detroit Lions
☐ 64 Tom Wham 12.50   6.25   1.25
    Chicago Cardinals
☐ 65 Bill Fischer 12.50   6.25   1.25
    Chicago Cardinals
☐ 66 Robert Nussbaumer .. 12.50   6.25   1.25
    Green Bay Packers
☐ 67 Gordon Soltau 12.50   6.25   1.25
    San Francisco 49ers
☐ 68 Visco Grgich 12.50   6.25   1.25
    San Francisco 49ers
☐ 69 John Strzykalski 15.00   7.50   1.50
    San Francisco 49ers
☐ 70 Pete Stout 12.50   6.25   1.25
    Washington Redskins
☐ 71 Paul Lipscomb 12.50   6.25   1.25
    Washington Redskins
☐ 72 Harry Gilmer 15.00   7.50   1.50
    Washington Redskins
☐ 73 Dante Lavelli 30.00   15.00 3.00
    Cleveland Browns
☐ 74 Dub Jones 18.00   9.00   1.80
    Cleveland Browns
☐ 75 Lou Groza 60.00   30.00 6.00
    Cleveland Browns
☐ 76 Elroy Hirsch 35.00   17.50 3.50
    Los Angeles Rams
☐ 77 Tom Kalmanir 12.50   6.25   1.25
    Los Angeles Rams
☐ 78 Jack Zilly 12.50   6.25   1.25
    Los Angeles Rams
☐ 79 Bruce Alford 15.00   7.50   1.50
    New York Yanks
☐ 80 Art Weiner 12.50   6.25   1.25
    New York Yanks
☐ 81 Brad Ecklund 12.50   6.25   1.25
    New York Yanks
☐ 82 Bosh Pritchard 12.50   6.25   1.25
    Philadelphia Eagles
☐ 83 John Green 12.50   6.25   1.25
    Philadelphia Eagles
☐ 84 H. Ebert Van Buren . 12.50   6.25   1.25
    Philadelphia Eagles
☐ 85 Julie Rykovich 12.50   6.25   1.25
    Chicago Bears
☐ 86 Fred Davis 12.50   6.25   1.25
    Chicago Bears
☐ 87 John Hoffman 12.50   6.25   1.25
    Chicago Bears
☐ 88 Tobin Rote 18.00   9.00   1.80
    Green Bay Packers
☐ 89 Paul Burris 12.50   6.25   1.25
    Green Bay Packers
☐ 90 Tony Canadeo 25.00   12.50 2.50
    Green Bay Packers
☐ 91 Emlen Tunnell 70.00   35.00 7.00
    New York Giants
☐ 92 Otto Schnellbacher . 12.50   6.25   1.25
    New York Giants
☐ 93 Ray Poole 12.50   6.25   1.25
    New York Giants
☐ 94 Darrell Hogan 12.50   6.25   1.25
    Pittsburgh Steelers
☐ 95 Frank Sinkovitz 12.50   6.25   1.25
    Pittsburgh Steelers
☐ 96 Ernie Stautner 70.00   35.00 7.00
    Pittsburgh Steelers
☐ 97 Elmer Angsman 12.50   6.25   1.25
    Chicago Cardinals
☐ 98 Jack Jennings 12.50   6.25   1.25
    Chicago Cardinals
☐ 99 Jerry Groom 12.50   6.25   1.25
    Chicago Cardinals
☐ 100 John Prchlik 12.50   6.25   1.25
    Detroit Lions
☐ 101 J. Robert Smith 12.50   6.25   1.25
    Detroit Lions
☐ 102 Bobby Layne 70.00   35.00 7.00
    Detroit Lions
☐ 103 Frankie Albert 20.00   10.00 2.00
    San Francisco 49ers
☐ 104 Gail Bruce 12.50   6.25   1.25
    San Francisco 49ers
☐ 105 Joe Perry 35.00   17.50 3.50
    San Francisco 49ers
☐ 106 Leon Heath 12.50   6.25   1.25
    Washington Redskins

☐ 107	Ed Quirk .... Washington Redskins	12.50	6.25	1.25
☐ 108	Hugh Taylor .... Washington Redskins	15.00	7.50	1.50
☐ 109	Marion Motley .... Cleveland Browns	30.00	15.00	3.00
☐ 110	Tony Adamle .... Cleveland Browns	15.00	7.50	1.50
☐ 111	Alex Agase .... Cleveland Browns	15.00	7.50	1.50
☐ 112	Tank Younger .... Los Angeles Rams	18.00	9.00	1.80
☐ 113	Bob Boyd .... Los Angeles Rams	12.50	6.25	1.25
☐ 114	Jerry Williams .... Los Angeles Rams	12.50	6.25	1.25
☐ 115	Joe Golding .... New York Yanks	12.50	6.25	1.25
☐ 116	Sherman Howard .... New York Yanks	12.50	6.25	1.25
☐ 117	John Wozniak .... New York Yanks	12.50	6.25.	1.25
☐ 118	Frank Reagan .... Philadelphia Eagles	12.50	6.25	1.25
☐ 119	Vic Sears .... Philadelphia Eagles	12.50	6.25	1.25
☐ 120	Clyde Scott .... Philadelphia Eagles	12.50	6.25	1.25
☐ 121	George Gulyanics ...... Chicago Bears	12.50	6.25	1.25
☐ 122	Bill Wightkin .... Chicago Bears	12.50	6.25	1.25
☐ 123	Chuck Hunsinger ...... Chicago Bears	12.50	6.25	1.25
☐ 124	Jack Cloud .... Green Bay Packers	12.50	6.25	1.25
☐ 125	Abner Wimberly .... Green Bay Packers	12.50	6.25	1.25
☐ 126	Dick Wildung .... Green Bay Packers	12.50	6.25	1.25
☐ 127	Eddie Price .... New York Giants	15.00	7.50	1.50
☐ 128	Joe Scott .... New York Giants	12.50	6.25	1.25
☐ 129	Jerry Nuzum .... Pittsburgh Steelers	12.50	6.25	1.25
☐ 130	Jim Finks .... Pittsburgh Steelers	18.00	9.00	1.80
☐ 131	Bob Gage .... Pittsburgh Steelers	12.50	6.25	1.25
☐ 132	William Swiacki .... Detroit Lions	15.00	7.50	1.50
☐ 133	Joe Watson .... Detroit Lions	12.50	6.25	1.25
☐ 134	Ollie Cline .... Detroit Lions	12.50	6.25	1.25
☐ 135	Jack Lininger	12.50	6.25	1.25

☐ 136	Detroit Lions Fran Polsfoot .... Chicago Cardinals	12.50	6.25	1.25
☐ 137	Charlie Trippi .... Chicago Cardinals	25.00	12.50	2.50
☐ 138	Ventan Yablonski ...... Chicago Cardinals	12.50	6.25	1.25
☐ 139	Emil Sitko .... Chicago Cardinals	12.50	6.25	1.25
☐ 140	Leo Nomellini .... San Francisco 49ers	30.00	15.00	3.00
☐ 141	Norm Standlee .... San Francisco 49ers	15.00	7.50	1.50
☐ 142	Eddie Saenz .... Washington Redskins	12.50	6.25	1.25
☐ 143	Al Demao .... Washington Redskins	12.50	6.25	1.25
☐ 144	Bill Dudley .... Washington Redskins	55.00	17.50	3.50

1952 Bowman Large

The 1952 Bowman set contains 144 numbered cards, each of both a small and large size. The small cards measure 2 1/16" by 3 1/8" whereas the large cards measure 2 1/2" by 3 3/4". The fronts and backs of both sets are identical except for size. The checklist below lists prices for the "large" set. Certain numbers were systematically printed in lesser quantities due to the fact that Bowman apparently could not fit all the cards in the series (of 72) on one sheet; the affected numbers are those which are divisible by nine and those which are "one more" than those divisible by nine. These shorter-printed (lesser quantity produced)

cards are marked in the checklist below by SP. The set features the football "Rookie cards" of Paul Brown, Jack Christiansen, Art Donovan, Frank Gifford, George Halas, Yale Lary, Gino Marchetti, Ollie Matson, Hugh McElhenny, and Andy Robustelli.

	NRMT	VG-E	GOOD
COMPLETE SET (144)	11000.00	4500.00	1350.00
COMMON PLAYER (1-72)	21.00	10.50	2.10
COMMON PLAYER (73-144)	32.00	16.00	3.20

		NRMT	VG-E	GOOD
☐ 1	Norm Van Brocklin Los Angeles Rams	300.00	75.00	15.00
☐ 2	Otto Graham Cleveland Browns	165.00	80.00	16.00
☐ 3	Doak Walker Detroit Lions	45.00	22.50	4.50
☐ 4	Steve Owen CO New York Giants	45.00	22.50	4.50
☐ 5	Frankie Albert San Francisco 49ers	27.00	13.50	2.70
☐ 6	Laurie Niemi Washington Redskins	21.00	10.50	2.10
☐ 7	Chuck Hunsinger Chicago Bears	21.00	10.50	2.10
☐ 8	Ed Modzelewski Pittsburgh Steelers	24.00	12.00	2.40
☐ 9	Joe Spencer SP Green Bay Packers	50.00	25.00	5.00
☐ 10	Chuck Bednarik SP Philadelphia Eagles	80.00	40.00	8.00
☐ 11	Barney Poole Dallas Texans	21.00	10.50	2.10
☐ 12	Charlie Trippi Chicago Cardinals	45.00	22.50	4.50
☐ 13	Tom Fears Los Angeles Rams	45.00	22.50	4.50
☐ 14	Paul Brown CO Cleveland Browns	110.00	55.00	11.00
☐ 15	Leon Hart Detroit Lions	27.00	13.50	2.70
☐ 16	Frank Gifford New York Giants	575.00	250.00	50.00
☐ 17	Y.A. Tittle San Francisco 49ers	120.00	60.00	12.00
☐ 18	Charlie Justice SP Washington Redskins	100.00	50.00	10.00
☐ 19	George Connor SP Chicago Bears	80.00	40.00	8.00
☐ 20	Lynn Chandnois Pittsburgh Steelers	21.00	10.50	2.10
☐ 21	Bill Howton Green Bay Packers	33.00	16.00	3.00
☐ 22	Kenneth Snyder Philadelphia Eagles	21.00	10.50	2.10
☐ 23	Gino Marchetti Dallas Texans	110.00	55.00	11.00
☐ 24	John Karras Chicago Cardinals	21.00	10.50	2.10
☐ 25	Tank Younger Los Angeles Rams	27.00	13.50	2.70
☐ 26	Tommy Thompson Cleveland Browns	27.00	13.50	2.70
☐ 27	Bob Miller SP Detroit Lions	200.00	100.00	20.00
☐ 28	Kyle Rote SP New York Giants	90.00	45.00	9.00
☐ 29	Hugh McElhenny San Francisco 49ers	150.00	75.00	15.00
☐ 30	Sammy Baugh Washington Redskins	250.00	125.00	25.00
☐ 31	Jim Dooley Chicago Bears	27.00	13.50	2.70
☐ 32	Ray Mathews Pittsburgh Steelers	21.00	10.50	2.10
☐ 33	Fred Cone Green Bay Packers	21.00	10.50	2.10
☐ 34	Al Pollard Philadelphia Eagles	21.00	10.50	2.10
☐ 35	Brad Ecklund Dallas Texans	21.00	10.50	2.10
☐ 36	John Lee Hancock SP Chicago Cardinals	225.00	110.00	22.00
☐ 37	Elroy Hirsch SP Los Angeles Rams	80.00	40.00	8.00
☐ 38	Keever Jankovich Cleveland Browns	21.00	10.50	2.10
☐ 39	Emlen Tunnell New York Giants	50.00	25.00	5.00
☐ 40	Steve Dowden Green Bay Packers	21.00	10.50	2.10
☐ 41	Claude Hipps Pittsburgh Steelers	21.00	10.50	2.10
☐ 42	Norm Standlee San Francisco 49ers	21.00	10.50	2.10
☐ 43	Dick Todd CO Washington Redskins	21.00	10.50	2.10
☐ 44	Babe Parilli Green Bay Packers	30.00	15.00	3.00
☐ 45	Steve Van Buren SP Philadelphia Eagles	135.00	65.00	13.50
☐ 46	Art Donovan SP Dallas Texans	165.00	80.00	16.00
☐ 47	Bill Fischer Chicago Cardinals	21.00	10.50	2.10
☐ 48	George Halas CO Chicago Bears	150.00	75.00	15.00
☐ 49	Jerell Price Chicago Cardinals	21.00	10.50	2.10
☐ 50	John Sandusky Cleveland Browns	27.00	13.50	2.70
☐ 51	Ray Beck New York Giants	21.00	10.50	2.10

☐ 52	Jim Martin 24.00	12.00	2.40
	Detroit Lions		
☐ 53	Joe Bach CO UER 21.00	10.50	2.10
	(Misspelled Back)		
	Pittsburgh Steelers		
☐ 54	Glen Christian SP 50.00	25.00	5.00
	San Francisco 49ers		
☐ 55	Andy Davis SP 50.00	25.00	5.00
	Washington Redskins		
☐ 56	Tobin Rote 27.00	13.50	2.70
	Green Bay Packers		
☐ 57	Wayne Millner CO 65.00	32.50	6.50
	Philadelphia Eagles		
☐ 58	Zollie Toth 21.00	10.50	2.10
	Dallas Texans		
☐ 59	Jack Jennings 21.00	10.50	2.10
	Chicago Cardinals		
☐ 60	Bill McColl 21.00	10.50	2.10
	Chicago Bears		
☐ 61	Les Richter 30.00	15.00	3.00
	Los Angeles Rams		
☐ 62	Walt Michaels 32.00	16.00	3.20
	Cleveland Browns		
☐ 63	Charley Conerly SP ... 350.00	175.00	35.00
	New York Giants		
☐ 64	Howard Hartley SP 50.00	25.00	5.00
	Pittsburgh Steelers		
☐ 65	Jerome Smith 21.00	10.50	2.10
	San Francisco 49ers		
☐ 66	James Clark 21.00	10.50	2.10
	Washington Redskins		
☐ 67	Dick Logan 21.00	10.50	2.10
	Cleveland Browns		
☐ 68	Wayne Robinson 21.00	10.50	2.10
	Philadelphia Eagles		
☐ 69	James Hammond 21.00	10.50	2.10
	Dallas Texans		
☐ 70	Gene Schroeder 21.00	10.50	2.10
	Chicago Bears		
☐ 71	Tex Coulter 24.00	12.00	2.40
	New York Giants		
☐ 72	John Schweder SP ... 300.00	150.00	30.00
	Pittsburgh Steelers		
☐ 73	Vitamin Smith SP 80.00	40.00	8.00
	Los Angeles Rams		
☐ 74	Joe Campanella 32.00	16.00	3.20
	Cleveland Browns		
☐ 75	Joe Kuharich CO 35.00	17.50	3.50
	Chicago Cardinals		
☐ 76	Herman Clark 32.00	16.00	3.20
	Chicago Bears		
☐ 77	Dan Edwards 32.00	16.00	3.20
	Dallas Texans		
☐ 78	Bobby Layne 135.00	65.00	13.50
	Detroit Lions		
☐ 79	Bob Hoernschemeyer .. 32.00	16.00	3.20
	Detroit Lions		
☐ 80	John Carr Blount 32.00	16.00	3.20
	Philadelphia Eagles		
☐ 81	John Kastan SP 80.00	40.00	8.00
	New York Giants		
☐ 82	Harry Minarik SP 100.00	50.00	10.00
	Pittsburgh Steelers		
☐ 83	Joe Perry 70.00	35.00	7.00
	San Francisco 49ers		
☐ 84	Ray Parker CO 32.00	16.00	3.20
	Detroit Lions		
☐ 85	Andy Robustelli 140.00	70.00	14.00
	Los Angeles Rams		
☐ 86	Dub Jones 35.00	17.50	3.50
	Cleveland Browns		
☐ 87	Mal Cook 32.00	16.00	3.20
	Chicago Cardinals		
☐ 88	Billy Stone 32.00	16.00	3.20
	Chicago Bears		
☐ 89	George Taliaferro 35.00	17.50	3.50
	Dallas Texans		
☐ 90	Thomas Johnson SP 80.00	40.00	8.00
	Green Bay Packers		
☐ 91	Leon Heath SP 70.00	35.00	7.00
	Washington Redskins		
☐ 92	Pete Pihos 50.00	25.00	5.00
	Philadelphia Eagles		
☐ 93	Fred Benners 32.00	16.00	3.20
	New York Giants		
☐ 94	George Tarasovic 32.00	16.00	3.20
	Pittsburgh Steelers		
☐ 95	Lawrence Shaw CO 32.00	16.00	3.20
	San Francisco 49ers		
☐ 96	Bill Wightkin 32.00	16.00	3.20
	Chicago Bears		
☐ 97	John Wozniak 32.00	16.00	3.20
	Dallas Texans		
☐ 98	Bobby Dillon 35.00	17.50	3.50
	Green Bay Packers		
☐ 99	Joe Stydahar CO SP ... 450.00	225.00	45.00
	Los Angeles Rams		
☐ 100	Dick Alban SP 80.00	40.00	8.00
	Washington Redskins		
☐ 101	Arnie Weinmeister 50.00	25.00	5.00
	New York Giants		
☐ 102	Robert Joe Cross 32.00	16.00	3.20
	Chicago Bears		
☐ 103	Don Paul 32.00	16.00	3.20
	Chicago Cardinals		
☐ 104	Buddy Young 35.00	17.50	3.50
	Dallas Texans		
☐ 105	Lou Groza 90.00	45.00	9.00
	Cleveland Browns		
☐ 106	Ray Pelfrey 32.00	16.00	3.20
	Green Bay Packers		
☐ 107	Maurice Nipp 32.00	16.00	3.20
	Philadelphia Eagles		
☐ 108	Hubert Johnston SP ... 350.00	175.00	35.00

Washington Redskins
- [ ] 109 Volney Quinlan SP 70.00   35.00   7.00
Los Angeles Rams
- [ ] 110 Jack Simmons 32.00   16.00   3.20
Chicago Cardinals
- [ ] 111 George Ratterman 35.00   17.50   3.50
Cleveland Browns
- [ ] 112 John Badaczewski 32.00   16.00   3.20
Washington Redskins
- [ ] 113 Bill Reichardt 32.00   16.00   3.20
Green Bay Packers
- [ ] 114 Art Weiner 32.00   16.00   3.20
Dallas Texans
- [ ] 115 Keith Flowers 32.00   16.00   3.20
Detroit Lions
- [ ] 116 Russ Craft 32.00   16.00   3.20
Philadelphia Eagles
- [ ] 117 Jim O'Donahue SP 80.00   40.00   8.00
San Francisco 49ers
- [ ] 118 Darrell Hogan SP 70.00   35.00   7.00
Pittsburgh Steelers
- [ ] 119 Frank Ziegler 32.00   16.00   3.20
Philadelphia Eagles
- [ ] 120 Deacon Dan Towler 36.00   18.00   3.60
Los Angeles Rams
- [ ] 121 Fred Williams 32.00   16.00   3.20
Chicago Bears
- [ ] 122 Jimmy Phelan CO 32.00   16.00   3.20
Dallas Texans
- [ ] 123 Eddie Price 35.00   17.50   3.50
New York Giants
- [ ] 124 Chet Ostrowski 32.00   16.00   3.20
Washington Redskins
- [ ] 125 Leo Nomellini 55.00   27.50   5.50
San Francisco 49ers
- [ ] 126 Steve Romanik SP 275.00   135.00   27.00
Chicago Bears
- [ ] 127 Ollie Matson SP 200.00   100.00   20.00
Chicago Cardinals
- [ ] 128 Dante Lavelli 50.00   25.00   5.00
Cleveland Browns
- [ ] 129 Jack Christiansen 110.00   55.00   11.00
Detroit Lions
- [ ] 130 Dom Moselle 32.00   16.00   3.20
Green Bay Packers
- [ ] 131 John Rapacz 32.00   16.00   3.20
New York Giants
- [ ] 132 Chuck Ortman 32.00   16.00   3.20
Pittsburgh Steelers
- [ ] 133 Bob Williams 32.00   16.00   3.20
Chicago Bears
- [ ] 134 Chuck Ulrich 32.00   16.00   3.20
Chicago Cardinals
- [ ] 135 Gene Ronzani CO SP 400.00   200.00   40.00
Green Bay Packers
- [ ] 136 Bert Rechichar SP 70.00   35.00   7.00
Cleveland Browns

- [ ] 137 Bob Waterfield 85.00   42.50   8.50
Los Angeles Rams
- [ ] 138 Bobby Walston 36.00   18.00   3.60
Philadelphia Eagles
- [ ] 139 Jerry Shipkey 32.00   16.00   3.20
Pittsburgh Steelers
- [ ] 140 Yale Lary 115.00   55.00   11.00
Detroit Lions
- [ ] 141 Gordon Soltau 32.00   16.00   3.20
San Francisco 49ers
- [ ] 142 Tom Landry 475.00   225.00   47.00
New York Giants
- [ ] 143 John Papit 32.00   16.00   3.20
Washington Redskins
- [ ] 144 Jim Lansford SP ... 2000.00   350.00   75.00
Dallas Texans

1952 Bowman Small

The 1952 Bowman set contains 144 numbered cards, each of both a small and large size. The small cards measure approximately 2 1/16" by 3 1/8" whereas the large cards measure 2 1/2" by 3 3/4". The fronts and backs of both sets are identical except for size. The checklist below lists prices for the "small" set. The set features the football "Rookie cards" of Paul Brown, Jack Christiansen, Art Donovan, Frank Gifford, George Halas, Yale Lary, Gino Marchetti, Ollie Matson, Hugh McElhenny, and Andy Robustelli.

	NRMT	VG-E	GOOD
COMPLETE SET (144)	4300.00	2050.00	550.00
COMMON PLAYER (1-72)	15.00	7.50	1.50
COMMON PLAYER (73-144) .	20.00	10.00	2.00

☐ 1 Norm Van Brocklin 150.00	50.00	10.00	
Los Angeles Rams			
☐ 2 Otto Graham 120.00	60.00	12.00	
Cleveland Browns			
☐ 3 Doak Walker 28.00	14.00	2.80	
Detroit Lions			
☐ 4 Steve Owen CO 28.00	14.00	2.80	
New York Giants			
☐ 5 Frankie Albert 21.00	10.50	2.10	
San Francisco 49ers			
☐ 6 Laurie Niemi 15.00	7.50	1.50	
Washington Redskins			
☐ 7 Chuck Hunsinger 15.00	7.50	1.50	
Chicago Bears			
☐ 8 Ed Modzelewski 18.00	9.00	1.80	
Pittsburgh Steelers			
☐ 9 Joe Spencer 15.00	7.50	1.50	
Green Bay Packers			
☐ 10 Chuck Bednarik 30.00	15.00	3.00	
Philadelphia Eagles			
☐ 11 Barney Poole 15.00	7.50	1.50	
Dallas Texans			
☐ 12 Charlie Trippi 28.00	14.00	2.80	
Chicago Cardinals			
☐ 13 Tom Fears 28.00	14.00	2.80	
Los Angeles Rams			
☐ 14 Paul Brown CO 65.00	32.50	6.50	
Cleveland Browns			
☐ 15 Leon Hart 21.00	10.50	2.10	
Detroit Lions			
☐ 16 Frank Gifford 425.00	200.00	42.00	
New York Giants			
☐ 17 Y.A. Tittle 80.00	40.00	8.00	
San Francisco 49ers			
☐ 18 Charlie Justice 25.00	12.50	2.50	
Washington Redskins			
☐ 19 George Connor 25.00	12.50	2.50	
Chicago Bears			
☐ 20 Lynn Chandnois 15.00	7.50	1.50	
Pittsburgh Steelers			
☐ 21 Bill Howton 25.00	12.50	2.50	
Green Bay Packers			
☐ 22 Kenneth Snyder 15.00	7.50	1.50	
Philadelphia Eagles			
☐ 23 Gino Marchetti 75.00	37.50	7.50	
Dallas Texans			
☐ 24 John Karras 15.00	7.50	1.50	
Chicago Cardinals			
☐ 25 Tank Younger 21.00	10.50	2.10	
Los Angeles Rams			
☐ 26 Tommy Thompson 21.00	10.50	2.10	
Cleveland Browns			
☐ 27 Bob Miller 15.00	7.50	1.50	
Detroit Lions			
☐ 28 Kyle Rote 40.00	20.00	4.00	
New York Giants			

☐ 29 Hugh McElhenny 85.00	42.50	8.50	
San Francisco 49ers			
☐ 30 Sammy Baugh 125.00	60.00	12.50	
Washington Redskins			
☐ 31 Jim Dooley 21.00	10.50	2.10	
Chicago Bears			
☐ 32 Ray Mathews 15.00	7.50	1.50	
Pittsburgh Steelers			
☐ 33 Fred Cone 15.00	7.50	1.50	
Green Bay Packers			
☐ 34 Al Pollard 15.00	7.50	1.50	
Philadelphia Eagles			
☐ 35 Brad Ecklund 15.00	7.50	1.50	
Dallas Texans			
☐ 36 John Lee Hancock 15.00	7.50	1.50	
Chicago Cardinals			
☐ 37 Elroy Hirsch 32.00	16.00	3.20	
Los Angeles Rams			
☐ 38 Keever Jankovich 15.00	7.50	1.50	
Cleveland Browns			
☐ 39 Emlen Tunnell 32.00	16.00	3.20	
New York Giants			
☐ 40 Steve Dowden 15.00	7.50	1.50	
Green Bay Packers			
☐ 41 Claude Hipps 15.00	7.50	1.50	
Pittsburgh Steelers			
☐ 42 Norm Standlee 15.00	7.50	1.50	
San Francisco 49ers			
☐ 43 Dick Todd CO 15.00	7.50	1.50	
Washington Redskins			
☐ 44 Babe Parilli 25.00	12.50	2.50	
Green Bay Packers			
☐ 45 Steve Van Buren 32.00	16.00	3.20	
Philadelphia Eagles			
☐ 46 Art Donovan 75.00	37.50	7.50	
Dallas Texans			
☐ 47 Bill Fischer 15.00	7.50	1.50	
Chicago Cardinals			
☐ 48 George Halas CO 75.00	37.50	7.50	
Chicago Bears			
☐ 49 Jerrell Price 15.00	7.50	1.50	
Chicago Cardinals			
☐ 50 John Sandusky 20.00	10.00	2.00	
Cleveland Browns			
☐ 51 Ray Beck 15.00	7.50	1.50	
New York Giants			
☐ 52 Jim Martin 18.00	9.00	1.80	
Detroit Lions			
☐ 53 Joe Bach CO UER 15.00	7.50	1.50	
(Misspelled Back)			
Pittsburgh Steelers			
☐ 54 Glen Christian 15.00	7.50	1.50	
San Francisco 49ers			
☐ 55 Andy Davis 15.00	7.50	1.50	
Washington Redskins			
☐ 56 Tobin Rote 21.00	10.50	2.10	
Green Bay Packers			

☐ 57 Wayne Millner CO 36.00   18.00   3.60
       Philadelphia Eagles
☐ 58 Zollie Toth 15.00   7.50   1.50
       Dallas Texans
☐ 59 Jack Jennings 15.00   7.50   1.50
       Chicago Cardinals
☐ 60 Bill McColl 15.00   7.50   1.50
       Chicago Bears
☐ 61 Les Richter 21.00   10.50   2.10
       Los Angeles Rams
☐ 62 Walt Michaels 22.00   11.00   2.20
       Cleveland Browns
☐ 63 Charley Conerly 38.00   18.00   3.75
       New York Giants
☐ 64 Howard Hartley 15.00   7.50   1.50
       Pittsburgh Steelers
☐ 65 Jerome Smith 15.00   7.50   1.50
       San Francisco 49ers
☐ 66 James Clark 15.00   7.50   1.50
       Washington Redskins
☐ 67 Dick Logan 15.00   7.50   1.50
       Cleveland Browns
☐ 68 Wayne Robinson 15.00   7.50   1.50
       Philadelphia Eagles
☐ 69 James Hammond 15.00   7.50   1.50
       Dallas Texans
☐ 70 Gene Schroeder 15.00   7.50   1.50
       Chicago Bears
☐ 71 Tex Coulter 18.00   9.00   1.80
       New York Giants
☐ 72 John Schweder 15.00   7.50   1.50
       Pittsburgh Steelers
☐ 73 Vitamin Smith 20.00   10.00   2.00
       Los Angeles Rams
☐ 74 Joe Campanella 20.00   10.00   2.00
       Cleveland Browns
☐ 75 Joe Kuharich CO 24.00   12.00   2.40
       Chicago Cardinals
☐ 76 Herman Clark 20.00   10.00   2.00
       Chicago Bears
☐ 77 Dan Edwards 20.00   10.00   2.00
       Dallas Texans
☐ 78 Bobby Layne 85.00   42.50   8.50
       Detroit Lions
☐ 79 Bob Hoernschemeyer .. 20.00   10.00   2.00
       Detroit Lions
☐ 80 John Carr Blount 20.00   10.00   2.00
       Philadelphia Eagles
☐ 81 John Kastan 20.00   10.00   2.00
       New York Giants
☐ 82 Harry Minarik 20.00   10.00   2.00
       Pittsburgh Steelers
☐ 83 Joe Perry 38.00   18.00   3.50
       San Francisco 49ers
☐ 84 Ray Parker CO 20.00   10.00   2.00
       Detroit Lions
☐ 85 Andy Robustelli 75.00   37.50   7.50

       Los Angeles Rams
☐ 86 Dub Jones 24.00   12.00   2.40
       Cleveland Browns
☐ 87 Mal Cook 20.00   10.00   2.00
       Chicago Cardinals
☐ 88 Billy Stone 20.00   10.00   2.00
       Chicago Bears
☐ 89 George Taliaferro 24.00   12.00   2.40
       Dallas Texans
☐ 90 Thomas Johnson 20.00   10.00   2.00
       Green Bay Packers
☐ 91 Leon Heath 20.00   10.00   2.00
       Washington Redskins
☐ 92 Pete Pihos 32.00   16.00   3.20
       Philadelphia Eagles
☐ 93 Fred Benners 20.00   10.00   2.00
       New York Giants
☐ 94 George Tarasovic 20.00   10.00   2.00
       Pittsburgh Steelers
☐ 95 Lawrence Shaw CO 20.00   10.00   2.00
       San Francisco 49ers
☐ 96 Bill Wightkin 20.00   10.00   2.00
       Chicago Bears
☐ 97 John Wozniak 20.00   10.00   2.00
       Dallas Texans
☐ 98 Bobby Dillon 24.00   12.00   2.40
       Green Bay Packers
☐ 99 Joe Stydahar CO 38.00   18.00   3.50
       Los Angeles Rams
☐ 100 Dick Alban 20.00   10.00   2.00
       Washington Redskins
☐ 101 Arnie Weinmeister 32.00   16.00   3.20
       New York Giants
☐ 102 Robert Joe Cross 20.00   10.00   2.00
       Chicago Bears
☐ 103 Don Paul 20.00   10.00   2.00
       Chicago Cardinals
☐ 104 Buddy Young 24.00   12.00   2.40
       Dallas Texans
☐ 105 Lou Groza 45.00   22.50   4.50
       Cleveland Browns
☐ 106 Ray Pelfrey 20.00   10.00   2.00
       Green Bay Packers
☐ 107 Maurice Nipp 20.00   10.00   2.00
       Philadelphia Eagles
☐ 108 Hubert Johnston 20.00   10.00   2.00
       Washington Redskins
☐ 109 Volney Quinlan 20.00   10.00   2.00
       Los Angeles Rams
☐ 110 Jack Simmons 20.00   10.00   2.00
       Chicago Cardinals
☐ 111 George Ratterman 24.00   12.00   2.40
       Cleveland Browns
☐ 112 John Badaczewski 20.00   10.00   2.00
       Washington Redskins
☐ 113 Bill Reichardt 20.00   10.00   2.00
       Green Bay Packers

☐ 114	Art Weiner 20.00	10.00	2.00
	Dallas Texans		
☐ 115	Keith Flowers 20.00	10.00	2.00
	Detroit Lions		
☐ 116	Russ Craft 20.00	10.00	2.00
	Philadelphia Eagles		
☐ 117	Jim O'Donahue 20.00	10.00	2.00
	San Francisco 49ers		
☐ 118	Darrell Hogan 20.00	10.00	2.00
	Pittsburgh Steelers		
☐ 119	Frank Ziegler 20.00	10.00	2.00
	Philadelphia Eagles		
☐ 120	Deacon Dan Towler ... 25.00	12.50	2.50
	Los Angeles Rams		
☐ 121	Fred Williams 20.00	10.00	2.00
	Chicago Bears		
☐ 122	Jimmy Phelan CO 20.00	10.00	2.00
	Dallas Texans		
☐ 123	Eddie Price 24.00	12.00	2.40
	New York Giants		
☐ 124	Chet Ostrowski 20.00	10.00	2.00
	Washington Redskins		
☐ 125	Leo Nomellini 33.00	16.00	3.25
	San Francisco 49ers		
☐ 126	Steve Romanik 20.00	10.00	2.00
	Chicago Bears		
☐ 127	Ollie Matson 75.00	37.50	7.50
	Chicago Cardinals		
☐ 128	Dante Lavelli 33.00	16.00	3.25
	Cleveland Browns		
☐ 129	Jack Christiansen 65.00	32.50	6.50
	Detroit Lions		
☐ 130	Dom Moselle 20.00	10.00	2.00
	Green Bay Packers		
☐ 131	John Rapacz 20.00	10.00	2.00
	New York Giants		
☐ 132	Chuck Ortman 20.00	10.00	2.00
	Pittsburgh Steelers		
☐ 133	Bob Williams 20.00	10.00	2.00
	Chicago Bears		
☐ 134	Chuck Ulrich 20.00	10.00	2.00
	Chicago Cardinals		
☐ 135	Gene Ronzani CO 20.00	10.00	2.00
	Green Bay Packers		
☐ 136	Bert Rechichar 20.00	10.00	2.00
	Cleveland Browns		
☐ 137	Bob Waterfield 40.00	20.00	4.00
	Los Angeles Rams		
☐ 138	Bobby Walston 27.00	13.50	2.70
	Philadelphia Eagles		
☐ 139	Jerry Shipkey 20.00	10.00	2.00
	Pittsburgh Steelers		
☐ 140	Yale Lary 65.00	32.50	6.50
	Detroit Lions		
☐ 141	Gordon Soltau 20.00	10.00	2.00
	San Francisco 49ers		
☐ 142	Tom Landry 250.00	125.00	25.00

	New York Giants		
☐ 143	John Papit 20.00	10.00	2.00
	Washington Redskins		
☐ 144	Jim Lansford 100.00	17.50	3.50
	Dallas Texans		

1953 Bowman

The 1953 Bowman set of 96 cards continued the new, larger card size. The cards measure approximately 2 1/2" by 3 3/4". The set is somewhat smaller in number than would be thought since Bowman was the only major producer of football cards during this year. There are 24 cards marked SP in the checklist below which are considered in shorter supply than the other cards in the set. The Bill Walsh in this set went to Notre Dame and is not the Bill Walsh who coached the San Francisco 49ers in the 1980s. The most notable rookie card in this set is Eddie LeBaron.

	NRMT	VG-E	GOOD
COMPLETE SET (96) 2400.00	1100.00	300.00
COMMON PLAYER (1-96) 15.00	7.50	1.50
COMMON PLAYER SP 21.00	10.50	2.10
☐ 1 Eddie LeBaron 110.00	20.00	4.00
Washington Redskins		
☐ 2 John Dottley 15.00	7.50	1.50
Chicago Bears		
☐ 3 Babe Parilli 21.00	10.50	2.10
Green Bay Packers		
☐ 4 Bucko Kilroy 18.00	9.00	1.80
Philadelphia Eagles		
☐ 5 Joe Tereshinski 15.00	7.50	1.50

☐ 6	Doak Walker	27.00	13.50	2.70
	Washington Redskins			
☐ 7	Fran Polsfoot	15.00	7.50	1.50
	Detroit Lions			
☐ 8	Sisto Averno	15.00	7.50	1.50
	Chicago Cardinals			
☐ 9	Marion Motley	28.00	14.00	2.80
	Baltimore Colts			
☐ 10	Pat Brady	15.00	7.50	1.50
	Cleveland Browns			
☐ 11	Norm Van Brocklin	65.00	32.50	6.50
	Pittsburgh Steelers			
☐ 12	Bill McColl	15.00	7.50	1.50
	Los Angeles Rams			
☐ 13	Jerry Groom	15.00	7.50	1.50
	Chicago Bears			
☐ 14	Al Pollard	15.00	7.50	1.50
	Chicago Cardinals			
☐ 15	Dante Lavelli	27.00	13.50	2.70
	Philadelphia Eagles			
☐ 16	Eddie Price	18.00	9.00	1.80
	Cleveland Browns			
☐ 17	Charlie Trippi	27.00	13.50	2.70
	New York Giants			
☐ 18	Elbert Nickel	15.00	7.50	1.50
	Chicago Cardinals			
☐ 19	George Taliaferro	18.00	9.00	1.80
	Pittsburgh Steelers			
☐ 20	Charley Conerly	38.00	18.00	3.50
	Baltimore Colts			
☐ 21	Bobby Layne	65.00	32.50	6.50
	New York Giants			
☐ 22	Elroy Hirsch	32.00	16.00	3.20
	Detroit Lions			
☐ 23	Jim Finks	22.00	11.00	2.20
	Los Angeles Rams			
☐ 24	Chuck Bednarik	32.00	16.00	3.20
	Pittsburgh Steelers			
☐ 25	Kyle Rote	25.00	12.50	2.50
	Philadelphia Eagles			
☐ 26	Otto Graham	125.00	60.00	12.50
	New York Giants			
☐ 27	Harry Gilmer	18.00	9.00	1.80
	Cleveland Browns			
☐ 28	Tobin Rote	22.00	11.00	2.20
	Washington Redskins			
☐ 29	Billy Stone	15.00	7.50	1.50
	Green Bay Packers			
☐ 30	Buddy Young	21.00	10.50	2.10
	Chicago Bears			
☐ 31	Leon Hart	22.00	11.00	2.20
	Baltimore Colts			
☐ 32	Hugh McElhenny	33.00	16.00	3.20
	Detroit Lions			
☐ 33	Dale Samuels	15.00	7.50	1.50
	San Francisco 49ers			
	Chicago Cardinals			

☐ 34	Lou Creekmur	18.00	9.00	1.80
	Detroit Lions			
☐ 35	Tom Catlin	15.00	7.50	1.50
	Cleveland Browns			
☐ 36	Tom Fears	28.00	14.00	2.80
	Los Angeles Rams			
☐ 37	George Connor	27.00	13.50	2.70
	Chicago Bears			
☐ 38	Bill Walsh	18.00	9.00	1.80
	Pittsburgh Steelers			
☐ 39	Leo Sanford	21.00	10.50	2.10
	Chicago Cardinals			
☐ 40	Horace Gillom	15.00	7.50	1.50
	Cleveland Browns			
☐ 41	John Schweder SP	21.00	10.50	2.10
	Pittsburgh Steelers			
☐ 42	Tom O'Connell	15.00	7.50	1.50
	Chicago Bears			
☐ 43	Frank Gifford SP	300.00	150.00	30.00
	New York Giants			
☐ 44	Frank Continetti SP	21.00	10.50	2.10
	Baltimore Colts			
☐ 45	John Olszewski SP	21.00	10.50	2.10
	Chicago Cardinals			
☐ 46	Dub Jones	21.00	10.50	2.10
	Cleveland Browns			
☐ 47	Don Paul SP	21.00	10.50	2.10
	Los Angeles Rams			
☐ 48	Gerald Weatherly	15.00	7.50	1.50
	Chicago Bears			
☐ 49	Fred Bruney SP	21.00	10.50	2.10
	San Francisco 49ers			
☐ 50	Jack Scarbath	15.00	7.50	1.50
	Washington Redskins			
☐ 51	John Karras	15.00	7.50	1.50
	Chicago Cardinals			
☐ 52	Al Conway	15.00	7.50	1.50
	Philadelphia Eagles			
☐ 53	Emlen Tunnell SP	50.00	25.00	5.00
	New York Giants			
☐ 54	Gern Nagler SP	21.00	10.50	2.10
	Baltimore Colts			
☐ 55	Kenneth Snyder SP	21.00	10.50	2.10
	Philadelphia Eagles			
☐ 56	Y.A. Tittle	70.00	35.00	7.00
	San Francisco 49ers			
☐ 57	John Rapacz SP	21.00	10.50	2.10
	New York Giants			
☐ 58	Harley Sewell SP	21.00	10.50	2.10
	Detroit Lions			
☐ 59	Don Bingham	15.00	7.50	1.50
	Chicago Bears			
☐ 60	Darrell Hogan	15.00	7.50	1.50
	Pittsburgh Steelers			
☐ 61	Tony Curcillo	15.00	7.50	1.50
	Chicago Cardinals			
☐ 62	Ray Renfro SP	28.00	14.00	2.80

Cleveland Browns
☐ 63 Leon Heath 15.00   7.50   1.50
Washington Redskins
☐ 64 Tex Coulter SP 21.00 10.50   2.10
New York Giants
☐ 65 Dewayne Douglas 15.00   7.50   1.50
New York Giants
☐ 66 J. Robert Smith SP 21.00 10.50   2.10
Detroit Lions
☐ 67 Bob McChesney SP 21.00 10.50   2.10
New York Giants
☐ 68 Dick Alban SP 21.00 10.50   2.10
Washington Redskins
☐ 69 Andy Kozar 15.00   7.50   1.50
Chicago Bears
☐ 70 Merwin Hodel SP 21.00 10.50   2.10
New York Giants
☐ 71 Thurman McGraw 15.00   7.50   1.50
Detroit Lions
☐ 72 Cliff Anderson 15.00   7.50   1.50
Chicago Cardinals
☐ 73 Pete Pihos 25.00 12.50   2.50
Philadelphia Eagles
☐ 74 Julie Rykovich 15.00   7.50   1.50
Washington Redskins
☐ 75 John Kreamcheck SP .. 21.00 10.50   2.10
Chicago Bears
☐ 76 Lynn Chandnois 15.00   7.50   1.50
Pittsburgh Steelers
☐ 77 Cloyce Box SP 25.00 12.50   2.50
Detroit Lions
☐ 78 Ray Mathews 15.00   7.50   1.50
Pittsburgh Steelers
☐ 79 Bobby Walston 15.00   7.50   1.50
Philadelphia Eagles
☐ 80 Jim Dooley 18.00   9.00   1.80
Chicago Bears
☐ 81 Pat Harder SP 25.00 12.50   2.50
Detroit Lions
☐ 82 Jerry Shipkey 15.00   7.50   1.50
Pittsburgh Steelers
☐ 83 Bobby Thomason 18.00   9.00   1.80
Philadelphia Eagles
☐ 84 Hugh Taylor 18.00   9.00   1.80
Washington Redskins
☐ 85 George Ratterman 18.00   9.00   1.80
Cleveland Browns
☐ 86 Don Stonesifer 15.00   7.50   1.50
Chicago Cardinals
☐ 87 John Williams SP 21.00 10.50   2.10
Washington Redskins
☐ 88 Leo Nomellini 28.00 14.00   2.80
San Francisco 49ers
☐ 89 Frank Ziegler 15.00   7.50   1.50
Philadelphia Eagles
☐ 90 Don Paul 15.00   7.50   1.50
Chicago Cardinals

☐ 91 Tom Dublinski 15.00   7.50   1.50
Baltimore Colts
☐ 92 Ken Carpenter 15.00   7.50   1.50
Cleveland Browns
☐ 93 Ted Marchibroda 27.00 13.50   2.70
Pittsburgh Steelers
☐ 94 Chuck Drazenovich 15.00   7.50   1.50
Washington Redskins
☐ 95 Lou Groza SP 60.00 30.00   6.00
Cleveland Browns
☐ 96 William Cross SP 60.00 15.00   3.00
Chicago Cardinals

1954 Bowman

The 1954 Bowman set of 128 cards was produced in four series of 32; the third series (65-96) being somewhat more difficult to obtain. The cards measure 2 1/2" by 3 3/4". The card backs feature the player's name in black print inside a red outline of a football. A "football quiz" question with upside-down answer is also given on the back. The player's statistical information from the previous season is summarized on the right-hand side of the back of the card. The "Whizzer" White in the set (125) is not Byron White, the Supreme Court Justice, but Wilford White, the father of Dallas Cowboys' quarterback, Danny White. The Bill Walsh in this set went to Notre Dame and is not the Bill Walsh who coached the San Francisco 49ers in the 1980s. Prominent football "rookie cards" included in this set are Doug Atkins and George Blanda.

	NRMT	VG-E	GOOD
COMPLETE SET (128)	1600.00	750.00	200.00
COMMON PLAYER (1-64)	6.00	3.00	.60
COMMON PLAYER (65-96)	12.00	6.00	1.20
COMMON PLAYER (97-128)	6.00	3.00	.60

☐ 1 Ray Mathews 22.00 5.00 1.00
Pittsburgh Steelers
☐ 2 John Huzvar .... 6.00 3.00 .60
Baltimore Colts
☐ 3 Jack Scarbath .... 6.00 3.00 .60
Washington Redskins
☐ 4 Doug Atkins 35.00 17.50 3.50
Cleveland Browns
☐ 5 Bill Stits .... 6.00 3.00 .60
Detroit Lions
☐ 6 Joe Perry 18.00 9.00 1.80
San Francisco 49ers
☐ 7 Kyle Rote 13.50 6.50 1.25
New York Giants
☐ 8 Norm Van Brocklin ... 33.00 16.00 3.25
Los Angeles Rams
☐ 9 Pete Pihos 16.00 8.00 1.60
Philadelphia Eagles
☐ 10 Babe Parilli 12.00 6.00 1.20
Green Bay Packers
☐ 11 Zeke Bratkowski 20.00 10.00 2.00
Chicago Bears
☐ 12 Ollie Matson 20.00 10.00 2.00
Chicago Cardinals
☐ 13 Pat Brady .... 6.00 3.00 .60
Pittsburgh Steelers
☐ 14 Fred Enke .... 6.00 3.00 .60
Baltimore Colts
☐ 15 Harry Ulinski .... 6.00 3.00 .60
Washington Redskins
☐ 16 Bobby Garrett .... 6.00 3.00 .60
Cleveland Browns
☐ 17 Bill Bowman .... 6.00 3.00 .60
Detroit Lions
☐ 18 Leo Rucka .... 6.00 3.00 .60
San Francisco 49ers
☐ 19 John Cannady .... 6.00 3.00 .60
New York Giants
☐ 20 Tom Fears 17.00 8.50 1.70
Los Angeles Rams
☐ 21 Norm Willey .... 6.00 3.00 .60
Philadelphia Eagles
☐ 22 Floyd Reid .... 6.00 3.00 .60
Green Bay Packers
☐ 23 George Blanda 250.00 125.00 25.00
Chicago Bears
☐ 24 Don Doheney .... 6.00 3.00 .60
Chicago Cardinals
☐ 25 John Schweder .... 6.00 3.00 .60
Pittsburgh Steelers
☐ 26 Bert Rechichar .... 6.00 3.00 .60

☐ 27 Harry Dowda .... 6.00 3.00 .60
Philadelphia Eagles
☐ 28 John Sandusky .... 7.50 3.75 .75
Cleveland Browns
☐ 29 Les Bingaman .... 9.00 4.50 .90
Detroit Lions
☐ 30 Joe Arenas .... 6.00 3.00 .60
San Francisco 49ers
☐ 31 Ray Wietecha .... 6.00 3.00 .60
New York Giants
☐ 32 Elroy Hirsch 20.00 10.00 2.00
Los Angeles Rams
☐ 33 Harold Giancanelli .... 6.00 3.00 .60
Philadelphia Eagles
☐ 34 Bill Howton 10.00 5.00 1.00
Green Bay Packers
☐ 35 Fred Morrison .... 6.00 3.00 .60
Chicago Bears
☐ 36 Bobby Cavazos .... 6.00 3.00 .60
Chicago Cardinals
☐ 37 Darrell Hogan .... 6.00 3.00 .60
Pittsburgh Steelers
☐ 38 Buddy Young .... 7.50 3.75 .75
Baltimore Colts
☐ 39 Charlie Justice 12.00 6.00 1.20
Washington Redskins
☐ 40 Otto Graham 65.00 32.50 6.50
Cleveland Browns
☐ 41 Doak Walker 17.00 8.50 1.70
Detroit Lions
☐ 42 Y.A. Tittle 45.00 22.50 4.50
San Francisco 49ers
☐ 43 Buford Long .... 6.00 3.00 .60
New York Giants
☐ 44 Volney Quinlan .... 6.00 3.00 .60
Los Angeles Rams
☐ 45 Bobby Thomason .... 7.50 3.75 .75
Philadelphia Eagles
☐ 46 Fred Cone .... 6.00 3.00 .60
Green Bay Packers
☐ 47 Gerald Weatherly .... 6.00 3.00 .60
Chicago Bears
☐ 48 Don Stonesifer .... 6.00 3.00 .60
Chicago Cardinals
☐ 49 Lynn Chandnois .... 6.00 3.00 .60
Pittsburgh Steelers
☐ 50 George Taliaferro .... 7.50 3.75 .75
Baltimore Colts
☐ 51 Dick Alban .... 6.00 3.00 .60
Washington Redskins
☐ 52 Lou Groza 27.00 13.50 2.70
Cleveland Browns
☐ 53 Bobby Layne 40.00 20.00 4.00
Detroit Lions
☐ 54 Hugh McElhenny 22.00 11.00 2.20
San Francisco 49ers

☐ 55 Frank Gifford	125.00	60.00	12.50
New York Giants			
☐ 56 Leon McLaughlin	6.00	3.00	.60
Los Angeles Rams			
☐ 57 Chuck Bednarik	20.00	10.00	2.00
Philadelphia Eagles			
☐ 58 Art Hunter	6.00	3.00	.60
Green Bay Packers			
☐ 59 Bill McColl	6.00	3.00	.60
Chicago Bears			
☐ 60 Charlie Trippi	16.00	8.00	1.60
Chicago Cardinals			
☐ 61 Jim Finks	10.00	5.00	1.00
Pittsburgh Steelers			
☐ 62 Bill Lange	6.00	3.00	.60
Baltimore Colts			
☐ 63 Laurie Niemi	6.00	3.00	.60
Washington Redskins			
☐ 64 Ray Renfro	7.50	3.75	.75
Cleveland Browns			
☐ 65 Dick Chapman	12.00	6.00	1.20
Detroit Lions			
☐ 66 Bob Hantla	12.00	6.00	1.20
San Francisco 49ers			
☐ 67 Ralph Starkey	12.00	6.00	1.20
New York Giants			
☐ 68 Don Paul	12.00	6.00	1.20
Los Angeles Rams			
☐ 69 Kenneth Snyder	12.00	6.00	1.20
Philadelphia Eagles			
☐ 70 Tobin Rote	16.00	8.00	1.60
Green Bay Packers			
☐ 71 Arthur DeCarlo	12.00	6.00	1.20
Pittsburgh Steelers			
☐ 72 Tom Keane	12.00	6.00	1.20
Baltimore Colts			
☐ 73 Hugh Taylor	14.00	7.00	1.40
Washington Redskins			
☐ 74 Warren Lahr	15.00	7.50	1.50
Cleveland Browns			
☐ 75 Jim Neal	12.00	6.00	1.20
Detroit Lions			
☐ 76 Leo Nomellini	33.00	16.00	3.25
San Francisco 49ers			
☐ 77 Dick Yelvington	12.00	6.00	1.20
New York Giants			
☐ 78 Les Richter	14.00	7.00	1.40
Los Angeles Rams			
☐ 79 Bucko Kilroy	14.00	7.00	1.40
Philadelphia Eagles			
☐ 80 John Martinkovic	12.00	6.00	1.20
Green Bay Packers			
☐ 81 Dale Dodrill	14.00	7.00	1.40
Pittsburgh Steelers			
☐ 82 Ken Jackson	12.00	6.00	1.20
Baltimore Colts			
☐ 83 Paul Lipscomb	12.00	6.00	1.20
Washington Redskins			
☐ 84 John Bauer	12.00	6.00	1.20
Cleveland Browns			
☐ 85 Lou Creekmur	14.00	7.00	1.40
Detroit Lions			
☐ 86 Eddie Price	14.00	7.00	1.40
New York Giants			
☐ 87 Kenneth Farragut	12.00	6.00	1.20
Philadelphia Eagles			
☐ 88 Dave Hanner	16.00	8.00	1.60
Green Bay Packers			
☐ 89 Don Boll	12.00	6.00	1.20
Washington Redskins			
☐ 90 Chet Hanulak	12.00	6.00	1.20
Cleveland Browns			
☐ 91 Thurman McGraw	12.00	6.00	1.20
Detroit Lions			
☐ 92 Don Heinrich	16.00	8.00	1.60
New York Giants			
☐ 93 Dan McKown	12.00	6.00	1.20
Philadelphia Eagles			
☐ 94 Bob Fleck	12.00	6.00	1.20
Green Bay Packers			
☐ 95 Jerry Hilgenberg	12.00	6.00	1.20
Cleveland Browns			
☐ 96 Bill Walsh	14.00	7.00	1.40
Pittsburgh Steelers			
☐ 97A Tom Finnin ERR	24.00	12.00	2.40
Baltimore Colts			
☐ 97B Tom Finnan COR	6.00	3.00	.60
Baltimore Colts			
☐ 98 Paul Barry	6.00	3.00	.60
Washington Redskins			
☐ 99 Harry Jagade	6.00	3.00	.60
Cleveland Browns			
☐ 100 Jack Christiansen	18.00	9.00	1.80
Detroit Lions			
☐ 101 Gordon Soltau	6.00	3.00	.60
San Francisco 49ers			
☐ 102 Emlen Tunnell	18.00	9.00	1.80
New York Giants			
☐ 103 Stan West	6.00	3.00	.60
Los Angeles Rams			
☐ 104 Jerry Williams	6.00	3.00	.60
Philadelphia Eagles			
☐ 105 Veryl Switzer	6.00	3.00	.60
Green Bay Packers			
☐ 106 Billy Stone	6.00	3.00	.60
Chicago Bears			
☐ 107 Jerry Watford	6.00	3.00	.60
Chicago Cardinals			
☐ 108 Elbert Nickel	6.00	3.00	.60
Pittsburgh Steelers			
☐ 109 Ed Sharkey	6.00	3.00	.60
Baltimore Colts			
☐ 110 Steve Meilinger	6.00	3.00	.60
Washington Redskins			

□ 111	Dante Lavelli	16.00	8.00	1.60
	Cleveland Browns			
□ 112	Leon Hart	11.00	5.50	1.10
	Detroit Lions			
□ 113	Charley Conerly	25.00	12.50	2.50
	New York Giants			
□ 114	Richard Lemmon	6.00	3.00	.60
	Philadelphia Eagles			
□ 115	Al Carmichael	6.00	3.00	.60
	Green Bay Packers			
□ 116	George Connor	16.00	8.00	1.60
	Chicago Bears			
□ 117	John Olszewski	6.00	3.00	.60
	Chicago Cardinals			
□ 118	Ernie Stautner	18.00	9.00	1.80
	Pittsburgh Steelers			
□ 119	Ray Smith	6.00	3.00	.60
	Chicago Bears			
□ 120	Neil Worden	6.00	3.00	.60
	Philadelphia Eagles			
□ 121	Jim Dooley	7.50	3.75	.75
	Chicago Bears			
□ 122	Arnold Galiffa	10.00	5.00	1.00
	San Francisco 49ers			
□ 123	Kline Gilbert	6.00	3.00	.60
	Chicago Bears			
□ 124	Bob Hoernschemeyer	6.00	3.00	.60
	Detroit Lions			
□ 125	Whizzer White	12.00	6.00	1.20
	Chicago Bears			
□ 126	Art Spinney	6.00	3.00	.60
	Baltimore Colts			
□ 127	Joe Koch	6.00	3.00	.60
	Chicago Bears			
□ 128	John Lattner	55.00	12.50	2.50
	Pittsburgh Steelers			

1955 Bowman

The 1955 Bowman set of 160 cards was Bowman's last sports issue before the company was purchased by Topps in January of 1956. Numbers above 64 are somewhat more difficult to obtain. The cards measure approximately 2 1/2" by 3 3/4". On the bottom of the card back is found a play diagram. Card backs are printed in red and blue on gray card stock. The notable rookie cards in this set are Len Ford, Frank Gatski, John Henry Johnson, Mike McCormick, Jim Ringo, Bob St. Clair, and Pat Summerall.

		NRMT	VG-E	GOOD
COMPLETE SET (160)		1450.00	675.00	175.00
COMMON PLAYER (1-64)		4.00	2.00	.40
COMMON PLAYER (65-160)		5.00	2.50	.50
□ 1	Doak Walker	42.00	10.00	2.00
	Detroit Lions			
□ 2	Mike McCormack	28.00	14.00	2.80
	Cleveland Browns			
□ 3	John Olszewski	4.00	2.00	.40
	Chicago Cardinals			
□ 4	Dorne Dibble	4.00	2.00	.40
	Detroit Lions			
□ 5	Lindon Crow	4.00	2.00	.40
	Chicago Cardinals			
□ 6	Hugh Taylor UER	5.00	2.50	.50
	(First word in bio should be Bones)			
	Washington Redskins			
□ 7	Frank Gifford	100.00	50.00	10.00
	New York Giants			
□ 8	Alan Ameche	25.00	12.50	2.50
	Baltimore Colts			
□ 9	Don Stonesifer	4.00	2.00	.40
	Chicago Cardinals			
□ 10	Pete Pihos	11.00	5.50	1.10
	Philadelphia Eagles			
□ 11	Bill Austin	4.00	2.00	.40
	New York Giants			
□ 12	Dick Alban	4.00	2.00	.40
	Washington Redskins			
□ 13	Bobby Walston	4.00	2.00	.40
	Philadelphia Eagles			
□ 14	Len Ford	30.00	15.00	3.00
	Cleveland Browns			
□ 15	Jug Girard	4.00	2.00	.40
	Detroit Lions			
□ 16	Charley Conerly	24.00	12.00	2.40
	New York Giants			
□ 17	Volney Peters	4.00	2.00	.40

Washington Redskins			
☐ 18 Max Boydston 4.00	2.00	.40
Chicago Cardinals			
☐ 19 Leon Hart 8.00	4.00	.80
Detroit Lions			
☐ 20 Bert Rechichar 4.00	2.00	.40
Baltimore Colts			
☐ 21 Lee Riley 4.00	2.00	.40
Detroit Lions			
☐ 22 Johnny Carson 4.00	2.00	.40
Washington Redskins			
☐ 23 Harry Thompson 4.00	2.00	.40
Los Angeles Rams			
☐ 24 Ray Wietecha 4.00	2.00	.40
New York Giants			
☐ 25 Ollie Matson 16.00	8.00	1.60
Chicago Cardinals –			
☐ 26 Eddie LeBaron 8.00	4.00	.80
Washington Redskins			
☐ 27 Jack Simmons 4.00	2.00	.40
Chicago Cardinals			
☐ 28 Jack Christiansen 11.00	5.50	1.10
Detroit Lions			
☐ 29 Bucko Kilroy 5.00	2.50	.50
Philadelphia Eagles			
☐ 30 Tom Keane 4.00	2.00	.40
Chicago Cardinals			
☐ 31 Dave Leggett 4.00	2.00	.40
Chicago Cardinals			
☐ 32 Norm Van Brocklin 25.00	12.50	2.50
Los Angeles Rams			
☐ 33 Harlon Hill 8.00	4.00	.80
Chicago Bears			
☐ 34 Robert Haner 4.00	2.00	.40
Washington Redskins			
☐ 35 Veryl Switzer 4.00	2.00	.40
Green Bay Packers			
☐ 36 Dick Stanfel 6.00	3.00	.60
Detroit Lions			
☐ 37 Lou Groza 24.00	12.00	2.40
Cleveland Browns			
☐ 38 Tank Younger 6.00	3.00	.60
Los Angeles Rams			
☐ 39 Dick Flanagan 4.00	2.00	.40
Pittsburgh Steelers			
☐ 40 Jim Dooley 5.00	2.50	.50
Chicago Bears			
☐ 41 Ray Collins 4.00	2.00	.40
New York Giants			
☐ 42 John Henry Johnson ... 38.00	18.00	3.50
San Francisco 49ers			
☐ 43 Tom Fears 11.00	5.50	1.10
Los Angeles Rams			
☐ 44 Joe Perry 18.00	9.00	1.80
San Francisco 49ers			
☐ 45 Gene Brito 6.00	3.00	.60
Washington Redskins			

☐ 46 Bill Johnson 4.00	2.00	.40
San Francisco 49ers			
☐ 47 Deacon Dan Towler 6.00	3.00	.60
Los Angeles Rams			
☐ 48 Dick Moegle 5.00	2.50	.50
San Francisco 49ers			
☐ 49 Kline Gilbert 4.00	2.00	.40
Chicago Bears			
☐ 50 Les Gobel 4.00	2.00	.40
Chicago Cardinals			
☐ 51 Ray Krouse 4.00	2.00	.40
New York Giants			
☐ 52 Pat Summerall 45.00	22.50	4.50
Chicago Cardinals			
☐ 53 Ed Brown 8.00	4.00	.80
Chicago Bears			
☐ 54 Lynn Chandnois 4.00	2.00	.40
Pittsburgh Steelers			
☐ 55 Joe Heap 4.00	2.00	.40
New York Giants			
☐ 56 John Hoffman 4.00	2.00	.40
Chicago Bears			
☐ 57 Howard Ferguson 4.00	2.00	.40
Green Bay Packers			
☐ 58 Bobby Watkins 4.00	2.00	.40
Chicago Bears			
☐ 59 Charlie Ane 4.00	2.00	.40
Detroit Lions			
☐ 60 Ken MacAfee 7.00	3.50	.70
New York Giants			
☐ 61 Ralph Guglielmi 7.00	3.50	.70
Washington Redskins			
☐ 62 George Blanda 85.00	42.50	8.50
Chicago Bears			
☐ 63 Kenneth Snyder 4.00	2.00	.40
Philadelphia Eagles			
☐ 64 Chet Ostrowski 4.00	2.00	.40
Washington Redskins			
☐ 65 Buddy Young 6.00	3.00	.60
Baltimore Colts			
☐ 66 Gordon Soltau 5.00	2.50	.50
San Francisco 49ers			
☐ 67 Eddie Bell 5.00	2.50	.50
Philadelphia Eagles			
☐ 68 Ben Agajanian 8.00	4.00	.80
New York Giants			
☐ 69 Tom Dahms 5.00	2.50	.50
Los Angeles Rams			
☐ 70 Jim Ringo 38.00	18.00	3.50
Green Bay Packers			
☐ 71 Bobby Layne 35.00	17.50	3.50
Detroit Lions			
☐ 72 Y.A. Tittle 40.00	20.00	4.00
San Francisco 49ers			
☐ 73 Bob Gaona 5.00	2.50	.50
Pittsburgh Steelers			
☐ 74 Tobin Rote 8.00	4.00	.80

	Green Bay Packers			
☐ 75	Hugh McElhenny	18.00	9.00	1.80
	San Francisco 49ers			
☐ 76	John Kreamcheck	5.00	2.50	.50
	Chicago Bears			
☐ 77	Al Dorow	5.00	2.50	.50
	Washington Redskins			
☐ 78	Bill Wade	8.50	4.25	.85
	Los Angeles Rams			
☐ 79	Dale Dodrill	5.00	2.50	.50
	Pittsburgh Steelers			
☐ 80	Chuck Drazenovich	5.00	2.50	.50
	Washington Redskins			
☐ 81	Billy Wilson	8.50	4.25	.85
	San Francisco 49ers			
☐ 82	Les Richter	6.00	3.00	.60
	Los Angeles Rams			
☐ 83	Pat Brady	5.00	2.50	.50
	Pittsburgh Steelers			
☐ 84	Bob Hoernschemeyer ...	5.00	2.50	.50
	Detroit Lions			
☐ 85	Joe Arenas	5.00	2.50	.50
	San Francisco 49ers			
☐ 86	Len Szafaryn UER	5.00	2.50	.50
	Green Bay Packers			
	(Listed as Ben on front)			
☐ 87	Rick Casares	12.00	6.00	1.20
	Chicago Bears			
☐ 88	Leon McLaughlin	5.00	2.50	.50
	Los Angeles Rams			
☐ 89	Charley Toogood	5.00	2.50	.50
	Los Angeles Rams			
☐ 90	Tom Bettis	5.00	2.50	.50
	Green Bay Packers			
☐ 91	John Sandusky	6.00	3.00	.60
	Cleveland Browns			
☐ 92	Bill Wightkin	5.00	2.50	.50
	Chicago Bears			
☐ 93	Darrell Brewster	5.00	2.50	.50
	Cleveland Browns			
☐ 94	Marion Campbell	9.00	4.50	.90
	San Francisco 49ers			
☐ 95	Floyd Reid	5.00	2.50	.50
	Green Bay Packers			
☐ 96	Harry Jagade	5.00	2.50	.50
	Chicago Bears			
☐ 97	George Taliaferro	6.00	3.00	.60
	Philadelphia Eagles			
☐ 98	Carleton Massey	5.00	2.50	.50
	Cleveland Browns			
☐ 99	Fran Rogel	5.00	2.50	.50
	Pittsburgh Steelers			
☐ 100	Alex Sandusky	5.00	2.50	.50
	Baltimore Colts			
☐ 101	Bob St. Clair	28.00	14.00	2.80
	San Francisco 49ers			
☐ 102	Al Carmichael	5.00	2.50	.50
	Green Bay Packers			
☐ 103	Carl Taseff	7.50	3.75	.75
	Baltimore Colts			
☐ 104	Leo Nomellini	15.00	7.50	1.50
	San Francisco 49ers			
☐ 105	Tom Scott	5.00	2.50	.50
	Philadelphia Eagles			
☐ 106	Ted Marchibroda	8.00	4.00	.80
	Pittsburgh Steelers			
☐ 107	Art Spinney	5.00	2.50	.50
	Baltimore Colts			
☐ 108	Wayne Robinson	5.00	2.50	.50
	Philadelphia Eagles			
☐ 109	Jim Ricca	5.00	2.50	.50
	Detroit Lions			
☐ 110	Lou Ferry	5.00	2.50	.50
	Pittsburgh Steelers			
☐ 111	Roger Zatkoff	5.00	2.50	.50
	Green Bay Packers			
☐ 112	Lou Creekmur	6.00	3.00	.60
	Detroit Lions			
☐ 113	Kenny Konz	5.00	2.50	.50
	Cleveland Browns			
☐ 114	Doug Eggers	5.00	2.50	.50
	Baltimore Colts			
☐ 115	Bobby Thomason	6.00	3.00	.60
	Philadelphia Eagles			
☐ 116	Bill McPeak	5.00	2.50	.50
	Pittsburgh Steelers			
☐ 117	William Brown	5.00	2.50	.50
	Green Bay Packers			
☐ 118	Royce Womble	5.00	2.50	.50
	Baltimore Colts			
☐ 119	Frank Gatski	28.00	14.00	2.80
	Cleveland Browns			
☐ 120	Jim Finks	8.00	4.00	.80
	Pittsburgh Steelers			
☐ 121	Andy Robustelli	15.00	7.50	1.50
	Los Angeles Rams			
☐ 122	Bobby Dillon	6.00	3.00	.60
	Green Bay Packers			
☐ 123	Leo Sanford	5.00	2.50	.50
	Chicago Cardinals			
☐ 124	Elbert Nickel	5.00	2.50	.50
	Pittsburgh Steelers			
☐ 125	Wayne Hansen	5.00	2.50	.50
	Chicago Bears			
☐ 126	Buck Lansford	5.00	2.50	.50
	Philadelphia Eagles			
☐ 127	Gern Nagler	5.00	2.50	.50
	Chicago Cardinals			
☐ 128	Jim Salsbury	5.00	2.50	.50
	Detroit Lions			
☐ 129	Dale Atkeson	5.00	2.50	.50
	Washington Redskins			
☐ 130	John Schweder	5.00	2.50	.50
	Pittsburgh Steelers			

☐ 131	Dave Hanner 6.00	3.00	.60
	Green Bay Packers		
☐ 132	Eddie Price 6.00	3.00	.60
	New York Giants		
☐ 133	Vic Janowicz 12.00	6.00	1.20
	Washington Redskins		
☐ 134	Ernie Stautner 16.00	8.00	1.60
	Pittsburgh Steelers		
☐ 135	James Parmer 5.00	2.50	.50
	Philadelphia Eagles		
☐ 136	Emlen Tunnell UER ... 16.00	8.00	1.60
	New York Giants		
	(Misspelled Tunnel		
	on card front)		
☐ 137	Kyle Rote 11.00	5.50	1.10
	New York Giants		
☐ 138	Norm Willey 5.00	2.50	.50
	Philadelphia Eagles		
☐ 139	Charlie Trippi 14.00	7.00	1.40
	Chicago Cardinals		
☐ 140	Bill Howton 8.00	4.00	.80
	Green Bay Packers		
☐ 141	Bobby Clatterbuck 6.00	3.00	.60
	New York Giants		
☐ 142	Bob Boyd 5.00	2.50	.50
	Los Angeles Rams		
☐ 143	Bob Toneff 6.50	3.25	.65
	San Francisco 49ers		
☐ 144	Jerry Helluin 5.00	2.50	.50
	Green Bay Packers		
☐ 145	Adrian Burk 5.00	2.50	.50
	Philadelphia Eagles		
☐ 146	Walt Michaels 8.50	4.25	.85
	Cleveland Browns		
☐ 147	Zollie Toth 5.00	2.50	.50
	Baltimore Colts		
☐ 148	Frank Varrichione 8.50	4.25	.85
	Pittsburgh Steelers		
☐ 149	Dick Bielski 5.00	2.50	.50
	Philadelphia Eagles		
☐ 150	George Ratterman 6.00	3.00	.60
	Cleveland Browns		
☐ 151	Mike Jarmoluk 5.00	2.50	.50
	Philadelphia Eagles		
☐ 152	Tom Landry 180.00	90.00	18.00
	New York Giants		
☐ 153	Ray Renfro 6.00	3.00	.60
	Cleveland Browns		
☐ 154	Zeke Bratkowski 8.50	4.25	.85
	Chicago Bears		
☐ 155	Jerry Norton 6.00	3.00	.60
	Philadelphia Eagles		
☐ 156	Maurice Bassett 5.00	2.50	.50
	Cleveland Browns		
☐ 157	Volney Quinlan 5.00	2.50	.50
	Los Angeles Rams		
☐ 158	Chuck Bednarik 18.00	9.00	1.80

	Philadelphia Eagles		
☐ 159	Don Colo 5.00	2.50	.50
	Cleveland Browns		
☐ 160	L.G. Dupre 30.00	6.00	1.25
	Baltimore Colts		

1991 Bowman

The premier edition of the 1991 Bowman Football set was produced by Topps and contains 561 cards. The cards measure the standard size (2 1/2" by 3 1/2"). The fronts feature color player photos, with blue and orange borders on a white card face. The player's name appears in white lettering on a purple stripe below the picture. The backs are printed in black and green on gray and present biography, player profile, and last season's statistics. The cards are numbered on the back and checklisted below alphabetically according to teams as follows: Atlanta Falcons (12-29), Buffalo Bills (30-50), Chicago Bears (51-71), Cincinnati Bengals (72-88), Cleveland Browns (89-103), Dallas Cowboys (104-122), Denver Broncos (123-142), Detroit Lions (143-158), Green Bay Packers (159-178), Houston Oilers (179-197), Indianapolis Colts (198-214), Kansas City Chiefs (215-234), Los Angeles Raiders (235-253), Los Angeles Rams (254-283), Miami Dolphins (284-302), Minnesota Vikings (303-320), New England Patriots (321-336), New Orleans Saints (337-355), New York Giants (356-375), New York Jets (376-394), Philadelphia Eagles (395-413), Phoenix Cardinals (414-431), Pittsburgh Steelers (432-449), San Diego Chargers (450-468), San Francisco 49ers (469-490), Seattle Seahawks

(491-509), Tampa Bay Buccaneers (510-527), and Washington Redskins (528-546). Subsets within this set include Rookie Superstars (1-11), League Leaders (273-283), and Road to Super Bowl XXV (547-557). These 33 cards are gold foil embossed, and, supposedly, each pack contains one of these foil cards. The cards are numbered on the back. The key rookie cards in this set are Nick Bell, Mike Croel, Ricky Ervins, Todd Marinovich, Dan McGwire, Browning Nagle, Mike Pritchard, and Harvey Williams.

	MINT	EXC	G-VG
COMPLETE SET (561)	15.00	7.50	1.50
COMMON PLAYER (1-561)	.03	.01	.00

☐ 1 Jeff George RS	.15	.07	.01
☐ 2 Richmond Webb RS	.06	.03	.00
☐ 3 Emmitt Smith RS	.60	.30	.06
☐ 4 Mark Carrier RS UER	.06	.03	.00
(Chambers was rookie			
in '74, not '73)			
☐ 5 Steve Christie RS	.03	.01	.00
☐ 6 Keith Sims RS	.03	.01	.00
☐ 7 Rob Moore RS UER	.25	.12	.02
(Yards misspelled as			
yarders on back)			
☐ 8 Johnny Johnson RS	.12	.06	.01
☐ 9 Eric Green RS	.10	.05	.01
☐ 10 Ben Smith RS	.06	.03	.00
☐ 11 Tory Epps RS	.03	.01	.00
☐ 12 Andre Rison	.15	.07	.01
☐ 13 Shawn Collins	.03	.01	.00
☐ 14 Chris Hinton	.06	.03	.00
☐ 15 Deion Sanders	.20	.10	.02
☐ 16 Darion Conner	.06	.03	.00
☐ 17 Michael Haynes	.20	.10	.02
☐ 18 Chris Miller	.15	.07	.01
☐ 19 Jessie Tuggle	.03	.01	.00
☐ 20 Scott Fulhage	.03	.01	.00
☐ 21 Bill Fralic	.06	.03	.00
☐ 22 Floyd Dixon	.03	.01	.00
☐ 23 Oliver Barnett	.03	.01	.00
☐ 24 Mike Rozier	.06	.03	.00
☐ 25 Tory Epps	.03	.01	.00
☐ 26 Tim Green	.03	.01	.00
☐ 27 Steve Broussard	.10	.05	.01
☐ 28 Bruce Pickens	.20	.10	.02
☐ 29 Mike Pritchard	.60	.30	.06
☐ 30 Andre Reed	.10	.05	.01
☐ 31 Darryl Talley	.06	.03	.00
☐ 32 Nate Odomes	.03	.01	.00
☐ 33 Jamie Mueller	.03	.01	.00
☐ 34 Leon Seals	.03	.01	.00
☐ 35 Keith McKeller	.08	.04	.01
☐ 36 Al Edwards	.08	.04	.01
☐ 37 Butch Rolle	.03	.01	.00
☐ 38 Jeff Wright	.08	.04	.01
☐ 39 Will Wolford	.03	.01	.00
☐ 40 James Williams	.03	.01	.00
☐ 41 Kent Hull	.03	.01	.00
☐ 42 James Lofton	.15	.07	.01
☐ 43 Frank Reich	.06	.03	.00
☐ 44 Bruce Smith	.08	.04	.01
☐ 45 Thurman Thomas	.50	.25	.05
☐ 46 Leonard Smith	.03	.01	.00
☐ 47 Shane Conlan	.06	.03	.00
☐ 48 Steve Tasker	.03	.01	.00
☐ 49 Ray Bentley	.03	.01	.00
☐ 50 Cornelius Bennett	.08	.04	.01
☐ 51 Stan Thomas	.08	.04	.01
☐ 52 Shaun Gayle	.03	.01	.00
☐ 53 Wendell Davis	.12	.06	.01
☐ 54 James Thornton	.03	.01	.00
☐ 55 Mark Carrier	.08	.04	.01
☐ 56 Richard Dent	.08	.04	.01
☐ 57 Ron Morris	.03	.01	.00
☐ 58 Mike Singletary	.08	.04	.01
☐ 59 Jay Hilgenberg	.06	.03	.00
☐ 60 Donnell Woolford	.03	.01	.00
☐ 61 Jim Covert	.06	.03	.00
☐ 62 Jim Harbaugh	.10	.05	.01
☐ 63 Neal Anderson	.15	.07	.01
☐ 64 Brad Muster	.06	.03	.00
☐ 65 Kevin Butler	.03	.01	.00
☐ 66 Trace Armstrong UER	.03	.01	.00
(Bio says 80 tackles			
in '90, stats say 82)			
☐ 67 Ron Cox	.03	.01	.00
☐ 68 Peter Tom Willis	.10	.05	.01
☐ 69 Johnny Bailey	.08	.04	.01
☐ 70 Mark Bortz UER	.03	.01	.00
(Bio has 6th round,			
but was 8th round)			
☐ 71 Chris Zorich	.25	.12	.02
☐ 72 Lamar Rogers	.15	.07	.01
☐ 73 David Grant UER	.03	.01	.00
(Listed as DE, but			
should be NT)			
☐ 74 Lewis Billups	.03	.01	.00
☐ 75 Harold Green	.15	.07	.01
☐ 76 Ickey Woods	.08	.04	.01
☐ 77 Eddie Brown	.06	.03	.00
☐ 78 David Fulcher	.03	.01	.00
☐ 79 Anthony Munoz	.08	.04	.01
☐ 80 Carl Zander	.03	.01	.00
☐ 81 Rodney Holman	.03	.01	.00
☐ 82 James Brooks	.08	.04	.01
☐ 83 Tim McGee	.06	.03	.00
☐ 84 Boomer Esiason	.10	.05	.01
☐ 85 Leon White	.03	.01	.00
☐ 86 James Francis UER	.08	.04	.01
(Ron is CB, card			

says he's LB)				
☐ 87 Mitchell Price	.10	.05	.01	
☐ 88 Ed King	.15	.07	.01	
☐ 89 Eric Turner	.50	.25	.05	
☐ 90 Rob Burnett	.08	.04	.01	
☐ 91 Leroy Hoard	.15	.07	.01	
☐ 92 Kevin Mack UER	.06	.03	.00	
(Height 6-2, should be 6-0)				
☐ 93 Thane Gash UER	.03	.01	.00	
(Comma omitted after name in bio)				
☐ 94 Gregg Rakoczy	.03	.01	.00	
☐ 95 Clay Matthews	.03	.01	.00	
☐ 96 Eric Metcalf	.06	.03	.00	
☐ 97 Stephen Braggs	.03	.01	.00	
☐ 98 Frank Minnifield	.03	.01	.00	
☐ 99 Reggie Langhorne	.03	.01	.00	
☐ 100 Mike Johnson	.03	.01	.00	
☐ 101 Brian Brennan	.03	.01	.00	
☐ 102 Anthony Pleasant	.03	.01	.00	
☐ 103 Godfrey Myles UER	.08	.04	.01	
(Vertical misspelled as verticle)				
☐ 104 Russell Maryland	.45	.22	.04	
☐ 105 James Washington	.08	.04	.01	
☐ 106 Nate Newton	.03	.01	.00	
☐ 107 Jimmie Jones	.03	.01	.00	
☐ 108 Jay Novacek	.10	.05	.01	
☐ 109 Alexander Wright	.15	.07	.01	
☐ 110 Jack Del Rio	.03	.01	.00	
☐ 111 Jim Jeffcoat	.03	.01	.00	
☐ 112 Mike Saxon	.03	.01	.00	
☐ 113 Troy Aikman	.35	.17	.03	
☐ 114 Issiac Holt	.03	.01	.00	
☐ 115 Ken Norton	.03	.01	.00	
☐ 116 Kelvin Martin	.06	.03	.00	
☐ 117 Emmitt Smith	1.25	.60	.12	
☐ 118 Ken Willis	.03	.01	.00	
☐ 119 Daniel Stubbs	.03	.01	.00	
☐ 120 Michael Irvin	.20	.10	.02	
☐ 121 Danny Noonan	.03	.01	.00	
☐ 122 Alvin Harper	.50	.25	.05	
☐ 123 Reggie Johnson	.25	.12	.02	
☐ 124 Vance Johnson	.06	.03	.00	
☐ 125 Steve Atwater	.06	.03	.00	
☐ 126 Greg Kragen	.03	.01	.00	
☐ 127 John Elway	.15	.07	.01	
☐ 128 Simon Fletcher	.03	.01	.00	
☐ 129 Wymon Henderson	.03	.01	.00	
☐ 130 Ricky Nattiel	.06	.03	.00	
☐ 131 Shannon Sharpe	.08	.04	.01	
☐ 132 Ron Holmes	.03	.01	.00	
☐ 133 Karl Mecklenburg	.06	.03	.00	
☐ 134 Bobby Humphrey	.08	.04	.01	
☐ 135 Clarence Kay	.03	.01	.00	
☐ 136 Dennis Smith	.03	.01	.00	
☐ 137 Jim Juriga	.03	.01	.0	
☐ 138 Melvin Bratton	.06	.03	.0	
☐ 139 Mark Jackson UER	.06	.03	.0	
(Apostrophe placed in front of longest)				
☐ 140 Michael Brooks	.03	.01	.0	
☐ 141 Alton Montgomery	.03	.01	.00	
☐ 142 Mike Croel	.75	.35	.0	
☐ 143 Mel Gray	.03	.01	.0	
☐ 144 Michael Cofer	.03	.01	.0	
☐ 145 Jeff Campbell	.06	.03	.0	
☐ 146 Dan Owens	.03	.01	.0	
☐ 147 Robert Clark UER	.06	.03	.0	
(Drafted in '87, not '89)				
☐ 148 Jim Arnold	.03	.01	.0	
☐ 149 William White	.03	.01	.0	
☐ 150 Rodney Peete	.08	.04	.0	
☐ 151 Jerry Ball	.03	.01	.0	
☐ 152 Bennie Blades	.06	.03	.0	
☐ 153 Barry Sanders UER	.75	.35	.0	
(Drafted in '89, not '88)				
☐ 154 Andre Ware	.12	.06	.0	
☐ 155 Lomas Brown	.03	.01	.0	
☐ 156 Chris Spielman	.06	.03	.0	
☐ 157 Kelvin Pritchett	.15	.07	.0	
☐ 158 Herman Moore	.60	.30	.0	
☐ 159 Chris Jacke	.03	.01	.0	
☐ 160 Tony Mandarich	.06	.03	.0	
☐ 161 Perry Kemp	.03	.01	.0	
☐ 162 Johnny Holland	.03	.01	.0	
☐ 163 Mark Lee	.03	.01	.0	
☐ 164 Anthony Dilweg	.06	.03	.0	
☐ 165 Scott Stephen	.08	.04	.0	
☐ 166 Ed West	.03	.01	.0	
☐ 167 Mark Murphy	.03	.01	.0	
☐ 168 Darrell Thompson	.12	.06	.0	
☐ 169 James Campen	.08	.04	.0	
☐ 170 Jeff Query	.03	.01	.0	
☐ 171 Brian Noble	.03	.01	.0	
☐ 172 Sterling Sharpe UER	.10	.05	.0	
(Card says he gained 3314 yards in 1990)				
☐ 173 Robert Brown	.03	.01	.0	
☐ 174 Tim Harris	.06	.03	.0	
☐ 175 LeRoy Butler	.03	.01	.0	
☐ 176 Don Majkowski	.08	.04	.0	
☐ 177 Vinnie Clark	.12	.06	.0	
☐ 178 Esera Tuaolo	.10	.05	.0	
☐ 179 Lorenzo White UER	.06	.03	.0	
(Bio says 3rd year, actually 4th year)				
☐ 180 Warren Moon	.20	.10	.0	
☐ 181 Sean Jones	.03	.01	.0	
☐ 182 Curtis Duncan	.03	.01	.0	
☐ 183 Al Smith	.03	.01	.0	

184 Richard Johnson	.10	.05	.01
185 Tony Jones	.06	.03	.00
186 Bubba McDowell	.03	.01	.00
187 Bruce Matthews	.03	.01	.00
188 Ray Childress	.06	.03	.00
189 Haywood Jeffires	.20	.10	.02
190 Ernest Givins	.10	.05	.01
191 Mike Munchak	.06	.03	.00
192 Greg Montgomery	.03	.01	.00
193 Cody Carlson	.12	.06	.01
194 Johnny Meads	.03	.01	.00
195 Drew Hill UER	.08	.04	.01
(Age listed as 24,			
should be 34)			
196 Mike Dumas	.15	.07	.01
197 Darryll Lewis	.15	.07	.01
198 Rohn Stark	.03	.01	.00
199 Clarence Verdin UER	.06	.03	.00
(Played 2 seasons in			
USFL, not one)			
200 Mike Prior	.03	.01	.00
201 Eugene Daniel	.03	.01	.00
202 Dean Biasucci	.03	.01	.00
203 Jeff Herrod	.03	.01	.00
204 Keith Taylor	.03	.01	.00
205 Jon Hand	.03	.01	.00
206 Pat Beach	.03	.01	.00
207 Duane Bickett	.03	.01	.00
208 Jessie Hester UER	.08	.04	.01
(Bio confuses Hester's			
NFL history)			
209 Chip Banks	.06	.03	.00
210 Ray Donaldson	.03	.01	.00
211 Bill Brooks	.06	.03	.00
212 Jeff George	.35	.17	.03
213 Tony Siragusa	.08	.04	.01
214 Albert Bentley	.06	.03	.00
215 Joe Valerio	.10	.05	.01
216 Chris Martin	.06	.03	.00
217 Christian Okoye	.08	.04	.01
218 Stephone Paige	.06	.03	.00
219 Percy Snow	.06	.03	.00
220 David Szott	.08	.04	.01
221 Derrick Thomas	.15	.07	.01
222 Todd McNair	.03	.01	.00
223 Albert Lewis	.06	.03	.00
224 Neil Smith	.06	.03	.00
225 Barry Word	.25	.12	.02
226 Robb Thomas	.08	.04	.01
227 John Alt	.03	.01	.00
228 Jonathan Hayes	.03	.01	.00
229 Kevin Ross	.03	.01	.00
230 Nick Lowery	.06	.03	.00
231 Tim Grunhard	.03	.01	.00
232 Dan Saleaumua	.03	.01	.00
233 Steve DeBerg	.08	.04	.01
234 Harvey Williams	.75	.35	.07

235 Nick Bell UER	.75	.35	.07
(Lives in Nevada,			
not California)			
236 Mervyn Fernandez UER	.08	.04	.01
(Drafted in '83, not			
FA '87 as on card)			
237 Howie Long	.06	.03	.00
238 Marcus Allen	.10	.05	.01
239 Eddie Anderson	.03	.01	.00
240 Ethan Horton	.03	.01	.00
241 Lionel Washington	.03	.01	.00
242 Steve Wisniewski UER	.03	.01	.00
(Drafted, should			
be traded to)			
243 Bo Jackson UER	.35	.17	.03
(Drafted by Raiders,			
should say drafted by			
Tampa Bay in '86)			
244 Greg Townsend	.03	.01	.00
245 Jeff Jaeger	.03	.01	.00
246 Aaron Wallace	.06	.03	.00
247 Garry Lewis	.03	.01	.00
248 Steve Smith	.03	.01	.00
249 Willie Gault UER	.06	.03	.00
('90 stats 839 yards,			
should be 985)			
250 Scott Davis	.03	.01	.00
251 Jay Schroeder	.08	.04	.01
252 Don Mosebar	.03	.01	.00
253 Todd Marinovich	1.50	.75	.15
254 Irv Pankey	.03	.01	.00
255 Flipper Anderson	.06	.03	.00
256 Tom Newberry	.06	.03	.00
257 Kevin Greene	.06	.03	.00
258 Mike Wilcher	.03	.01	.00
259 Bern Brostek	.03	.01	.00
260 Buford McGee	.03	.01	.00
261 Cleveland Gary	.06	.03	.00
262 Jackie Slater	.06	.03	.00
263 Henry Ellard	.08	.04	.01
264 Alvin Wright	.03	.01	.00
265 Darryl Henley	.15	.07	.01
266 Damone Johnson	.10	.05	.01
267 Frank Stams	.03	.01	.00
268 Jerry Gray	.06	.03	.00
269 Jim Everett	.10	.05	.01
270 Pat Terrell	.03	.01	.00
271 Todd Lyght	.40	.20	.04
272 Aaron Cox	.03	.01	.00
273 Barry Sanders LL	.25	.12	.02
Rushing Leader			
274 Jerry Rice LL	.15	.07	.01
Receiving Leader			
275 Derrick Thomas LL	.08	.04	.01
Sack Leader			
276 Mark Carrier LL	.06	.03	.00
Interception Leader			

☐ 277 Warren Moon LL .... .12	.06	.01	
Passing Yardage Leader			
☐ 278 Randall Cunningham LL .08	.04	.01	
Rushing Average Leader			
☐ 279 Nick Lowery LL .... .06	.03	.00	
Scoring Leader			
☐ 280 Clarence Verdin LL .... .06	.03	.00	
Punt Return Leader			
☐ 281 Thurman Thomas LL ...... .15	.07	.01	
Yards From Scrimmage			
Leader			
☐ 282 Mike Horan LL .... .06	.03	.00	
Punting Average Leader			
☐ 283 Flipper Anderson LL .... .06	.03	.00	
Receiving Average Leader			
☐ 284 John Offerdahl .... .06	.03	.00	
☐ 285 Dan Marino UER .... .25	.12	.02	
(2637 yards gained,			
should be 3563)			
☐ 286 Mark Clayton .... .08	.04	.01	
☐ 287 Tony Paige .... .03	.01	.00	
☐ 288 Keith Sims .... .03	.01	.00	
☐ 289 Jeff Cross .... .03	.01	.00	
☐ 290 Pete Stoyanovich .... .03	.01	.00	
☐ 291 Ferrell Edmunds .... .03	.01	.00	
☐ 292 Reggie Roby .... .03	.01	.00	
☐ 293 Louis Oliver .... .03	.01	.00	
☐ 294 Jarvis Williams .... .03	.01	.00	
☐ 295 Sammie Smith .... .08	.04	.01	
☐ 296 Richmond Webb .... .06	.03	.00	
☐ 297 J.B. Brown .... .03	.01	.00	
☐ 298 Jim Jensen .... .03	.01	.00	
☐ 299 Mark Duper .... .06	.03	.00	
☐ 300 David Griggs .... .03	.01	.00	
☐ 301 Randal Hill .... .60	.30	.06	
☐ 302 Aaron Craver .... .20	.10	.02	
(See also 320)			
☐ 303 Keith Millard .... .06	.03	.00	
☐ 304 Steve Jordan .... .06	.03	.00	
☐ 305 Anthony Carter .... .08	.04	.01	
☐ 306 Mike Merriweather .... .03	.01	.00	
☐ 307 Audray McMillian UER ... .10	.05	.01	
(Front Audray,			
back Audrey)			
☐ 308 Randall McDaniel .... .03	.01	.00	
☐ 309 Gary Zimmerman .... .03	.01	.00	
☐ 310 Carl Lee .... .03	.01	.00	
☐ 311 Reggie Rutland .... .03	.01	.00	
☐ 312 Hassan Jones .... .03	.01	.00	
☐ 313 Kirk Lowdermilk UER ..... .03	.01	.00	
(Reversed negative)			
☐ 314 Herschel Walker .... .12	.06	.01	
☐ 315 Chris Doleman .... .06	.03	.00	
☐ 316 Joey Browner .... .06	.03	.00	
☐ 317 Wade Wilson .... .06	.03	.00	
☐ 318 Henry Thomas .... .03	.01	.00	
☐ 319 Rich Gannon .... .08	.04	.01	
☐ 320 Al Noga UER .... .03	.01	.00	
(Numbered incorrectly			
as 302 on card)			
☐ 321 Pat Harlow .... .15	.07	.01	
☐ 322 Bruce Armstrong .... .03	.01	.00	
☐ 323 Maurice Hurst .... .03	.01	.00	
☐ 324 Brent Williams .... .03	.01	.00	
☐ 325 Chris Singleton .... .06	.03	.00	
☐ 326 Jason Staurovsky .... .03	.01	.00	
☐ 327 Marvin Allen .... .03	.01	.00	
☐ 328 Hart Lee Dykes .... .03	.01	.00	
☐ 329 Johnny Rembert .... .06	.03	.00	
☐ 330 Andre Tippett .... .06	.03	.00	
☐ 331 Greg McMurtry .... .08	.04	.01	
☐ 332 John Stephens .... .08	.04	.01	
☐ 333 Ray Agnew .... .03	.01	.00	
☐ 334 Tommy Hodson .... .08	.04	.01	
☐ 335 Ronnie Lippett .... .03	.01	.00	
☐ 336 Marv Cook .... .10	.05	.01	
☐ 337 Tommy Barnhardt .... .08	.04	.01	
☐ 338 Dalton Hilliard .... .06	.03	.00	
☐ 339 Sam Mills .... .06	.03	.00	
☐ 340 Morten Andersen .... .06	.03	.00	
☐ 341 Stan Brock .... .03	.01	.00	
☐ 342 Brett Maxie .... .08	.04	.01	
☐ 343 Steve Walsh .... .08	.04	.01	
☐ 344 Vaughan Johnson .... .06	.03	.00	
☐ 345 Rickey Jackson .... .06	.03	.00	
☐ 346 Renaldo Turnbull .... .06	.03	.00	
☐ 347 Joel Hilgenberg .... .03	.01	.00	
☐ 348 Toi Cook .... .08	.04	.01	
☐ 349 Robert Massey .... .03	.01	.00	
☐ 350 Pat Swilling .... .10	.05	.01	
☐ 351 Eric Martin .... .06	.03	.00	
☐ 352 Rueben Mayes UER .... .06	.03	.00	
(Bio says 2nd round,			
should be 3rd)			
☐ 353 Vince Buck .... .06	.03	.00	
☐ 354 Brett Perriman .... .06	.03	.00	
☐ 355 Wesley Carroll .... .40	.20	.04	
☐ 356 Jarrod Bunch .... .15	.07	.01	
☐ 357 Pepper Johnson .... .06	.03	.00	
☐ 358 Dave Meggett .... .10	.05	.01	
☐ 359 Mark Collins .... .06	.03	.00	
☐ 360 Sean Landeta .... .03	.01	.00	
☐ 361 Maurice Carthon .... .03	.01	.00	
☐ 362 Mike Fox UER .... .06	.03	.00	
(Listed as DE,			
should say DT)			
☐ 363 Jeff Hostetler .... .20	.10	.02	
☐ 364 Phil Simms .... .08	.04	.01	
☐ 365 Leonard Marshall .... .06	.03	.00	
☐ 366 Gary Reasons .... .03	.01	.00	
☐ 367 Rodney Hampton .... .40	.20	.04	
☐ 368 Greg Jackson .... .08	.04	.01	
☐ 369 Jumbo Elliott .... .03	.01	.00	
☐ 370 Bob Kratch .... .08	.04	.01	

☐ 371 Lawrence Taylor	.10	.05	.01
☐ 372 Erik Howard	.03	.01	.00
☐ 373 Carl Banks	.06	.03	.00
☐ 374 Stephen Baker	.06	.03	.00
☐ 375 Mark Ingram	.06	.03	.00
☐ 376 Browning Nagle	.75	.35	.07
☐ 377 Jeff Lageman	.06	.03	.00
☐ 378 Ken O'Brien	.08	.04	.01
☐ 379 Al Toon	.08	.04	.01
☐ 380 Joe Prokop	.03	.01	.00
☐ 381 Tony Stargell	.06	.03	.00
☐ 382 Blair Thomas	.45	.22	.04
☐ 383 Erik McMillan	.06	.03	.00
☐ 384 Dennis Byrd	.06	.03	.00
☐ 385 Freeman McNeil	.08	.04	.01
☐ 386 Brad Baxter	.10	.05	.01
☐ 387 Mark Boyer	.03	.01	.00
☐ 388 Terance Mathis	.15	.07	.01
☐ 389 Jim Sweeney	.06	.03	.00
☐ 390 Kyle Clifton	.03	.01	.00
☐ 391 Pat Leahy	.06	.03	.00
☐ 392 Rob Moore	.50	.25	.05
☐ 393 James Hasty	.03	.01	.00
☐ 394 Blaise Bryant	.10	.05	.01
☐ 395A Jesse Campbell ERR	1.50	.75	.15
(Photo actually			
Dan McGwire; see 509)			
☐ 395B Jesse Campbell COR	.12	.06	.01
☐ 396 Keith Jackson	.06	.03	.00
☐ 397 Jerome Brown	.06	.03	.00
☐ 398 Keith Byars	.06	.03	.00
☐ 399 Seth Joyner	.06	.03	.00
☐ 400 Mike Bellamy	.06	.03	.00
☐ 401 Fred Barnett	.15	.07	.01
☐ 402 Reggie Singletary	.10	.05	.01
☐ 403 Reggie White	.08	.04	.01
☐ 404 Randall Cunningham	.15	.07	.01
☐ 405 Byron Evans	.03	.01	.00
☐ 406 Wes Hopkins	.03	.01	.00
☐ 407 Ben Smith	.03	.01	.00
☐ 408 Roger Ruzek	.03	.01	.00
☐ 409 Eric Allen UER	.03	.01	.00
(Comparative misspelled			
as comparate)			
☐ 410 Anthony Toney UER	.03	.01	.00
(Heath Sherman was			
rookie in '89, not '90)			
☐ 411 Clyde Simmons	.06	.03	.00
☐ 412 Andre Waters	.03	.01	.00
☐ 413 Calvin Williams	.08	.04	.01
☐ 414 Eric Swann	.20	.10	.02
☐ 415 Eric Hill	.06	.03	.00
☐ 416 Tim McDonald	.06	.03	.00
☐ 417 Luis Sharpe	.03	.01	.00
☐ 418 Ernie Jones UER	.06	.03	.00
(Photo actually			
Steve Jordan)			
☐ 419 Ken Harvey	.03	.01	.00
☐ 420 Ricky Proehl	.10	.05	.01
☐ 421 Johnny Johnson	.25	.12	.02
☐ 422 Anthony Bell	.03	.01	.00
☐ 423 Timm Rosenbach	.10	.05	.01
☐ 424 Rich Camarillo	.03	.01	.00
☐ 425 Walter Reeves	.03	.01	.00
☐ 426 Freddie Joe Nunn	.03	.01	.00
☐ 427 Anthony Thompson UER	.08	.04	.01
(40 touchdowns, sic)			
☐ 428 Bill Lewis	.03	.01	.00
☐ 429 Jim Wahler	.08	.04	.01
☐ 430 Cedric Mack	.03	.01	.00
☐ 431 Michael Jones	.10	.05	.01
☐ 432 Ernie Mills	.20	.10	.02
☐ 433 Tim Worley	.06	.03	.00
☐ 434 Greg Lloyd	.03	.01	.00
☐ 435 Dermontti Dawson	.03	.01	.00
☐ 436 Louis Lipps	.06	.03	.00
☐ 437 Eric Green	.15	.07	.01
☐ 438 Donald Evans	.03	.01	.00
☐ 439 David Johnson	.08	.04	.01
☐ 440 Tunch Ilkin	.03	.01	.00
☐ 441 Bubby Brister	.08	.04	.01
☐ 442 Chris Calloway	.03	.01	.00
☐ 443 David Little	.03	.01	.00
☐ 444 Thomas Everett	.03	.01	.00
☐ 445 Carnell Lake	.03	.01	.00
☐ 446 Rod Woodson	.06	.03	.00
☐ 447 Gary Anderson	.03	.01	.00
☐ 448 Merril Hoge	.06	.03	.00
☐ 449 Gerald Williams	.03	.01	.00
☐ 450 Eric Moten	.15	.07	.01
☐ 451 Marion Butts	.10	.05	.01
☐ 452 Leslie O'Neal	.06	.03	.00
☐ 453 Ronnie Harmon	.06	.03	.00
☐ 454 Gill Byrd	.06	.03	.00
☐ 455 Junior Seau	.10	.05	.01
☐ 456 Nate Lewis	.15	.07	.01
☐ 457 Leo Goeas	.03	.01	.00
☐ 458 Burt Grossman	.06	.03	.00
☐ 459 Courtney Hall	.03	.01	.00
☐ 460 Anthony Miller	.08	.04	.01
☐ 461 Gary Plummer	.03	.01	.00
☐ 462 Billy Joe Tolliver	.08	.04	.01
☐ 463 Lee Williams	.06	.03	.00
☐ 464 Arthur Cox	.03	.01	.00
☐ 465 John Kidd UER	.03	.01	.00
(Stron gleg, sic)			
☐ 466 Frank Cornish	.03	.01	.00
☐ 467 John Carney	.03	.01	.00
☐ 468 Eric Bieniemy	.30	.15	.03
☐ 469 Don Griffin	.03	.01	.00
☐ 470 Jerry Rice	.35	.17	.03
☐ 471 Keith DeLong	.03	.01	.00
☐ 472 John Taylor	.12	.06	.01
☐ 473 Brent Jones	.06	.03	.00

☐ 474 Pierce Holt	.03	.01	.00
☐ 475 Kevin Fagan	.03	.01	.00
☐ 476 Bill Romanowski	.03	.01	.00
☐ 477 Dexter Carter	.08	.04	.01
☐ 478 Guy McIntyre	.03	.01	.00
☐ 479 Joe Montana	.45	.22	.04
☐ 480 Charles Haley	.06	.03	.00
☐ 481 Mike Cofer	.03	.01	.00
☐ 482 Jesse Sapolu	.03	.01	.00
☐ 483 Eric Davis	.03	.01	.00
☐ 484 Mike Sherrard	.06	.03	.00
☐ 485 Steve Young	.12	.06	.01
☐ 486 Darryl Pollard	.03	.01	.00
☐ 487 Tom Rathman	.06	.03	.00
☐ 488 Michael Carter	.06	.03	.00
☐ 489 Ricky Watters	.35	.17	.03
☐ 490 John Johnson	.08	.04	.01
☐ 491 Eugene Robinson	.03	.01	.00
☐ 492 Andy Heck	.03	.01	.00
☐ 493 John L. Williams	.08	.04	.01
☐ 494 Norm Johnson	.03	.01	.00
☐ 495 David Wyman	.03	.01	.00
☐ 496 Derrick Fenner UER	.12	.06	.01
(Drafted in '88,			
should be '89)			
☐ 497 Rick Donnelly	.03	.01	.00
☐ 498 Tony Woods	.06	.03	.00
☐ 499 Derek Loville UER	.08	.04	.01
(Ahmad Rashad is			
misspelled Ahmed)			
☐ 500 Dave Krieg	.08	.04	.01
☐ 501 Joe Nash	.03	.01	.00
☐ 502 Brian Blades	.08	.04	.01
☐ 503 Cortez Kennedy	.10	.05	.01
☐ 504 Jeff Bryant	.03	.01	.00
☐ 505 Tommy-Kane	.12	.06	.01
☐ 506 Travis McNeal	.03	.01	.00
☐ 507 Terry Wooden	.06	.03	.00
☐ 508 Chris Warren	.06	.03	.00
☐ 509A Dan McGwire ERR	3.00	1.50	.30
(Photo actually Jesse			
Campbell; see 395)			
☐ 509B Dan McGwire COR	2.00	1.00	.20
☐ 510 Mark Robinson	.03	.01	.00
☐ 511 Ron Hall	.03	.01	.00
☐ 512 Paul Gruber	.06	.03	.00
☐ 513 Harry Hamilton	.03	.01	.00
☐ 514 Keith McCants	.08	.04	.01
☐ 515 Reggie Cobb	.15	.07	.01
☐ 516 Steve Christie UER	.03	.01	.00
(Listed as Californian,			
should be Canadian)			
☐ 517 Broderick Thomas	.06	.03	.00
☐ 518 Mark Carrier	.06	.03	.00
☐ 519 Vinny Testaverde	.08	.04	.01
☐ 520 Ricky Reynolds	.03	.01	.00
☐ 521 Jesse Anderson	.03	.01	.00
☐ 522 Reuben Davis	.03	.01	.00
☐ 523 Wayne Haddix	.06	.03	.00
☐ 524 Gary Anderson UER	.08	.04	.01
(Photo actually			
Don Mosebar)			
☐ 525 Bruce Hill	.03	.01	.00
☐ 526 Kevin Murphy	.03	.01	.00
☐ 527 Lawrence Dawsey	.40	.20	.04
☐ 528 Ricky Ervins	1.75	.85	.17
☐ 529 Charles Mann	.06	.03	.00
☐ 530 Jim Lachey	.06	.03	.00
☐ 531 Mark Rypien UER	.20	.10	.02
(No stat for percentage;			
2,0703 yards, sic)			
☐ 532 Darrell Green	.10	.05	.01
☐ 533 Stan Humphries	.08	.04	.01
☐ 534 Jeff Bostic UER	.06	.03	.00
(Age listed as 32 in			
stats and 33 in bio)			
☐ 535 Earnest Byner	.08	.04	.01
☐ 536 Art Monk UER	.12	.06	.01
(Bio says 718 recep-			
tions, should be 730)			
☐ 537 Don Warren	.06	.03	.00
☐ 538 Darryl Grant	.03	.01	.00
☐ 539 Wilber Marshall	.06	.03	.00
☐ 540 Kurt Gouveia	.08	.04	.01
☐ 541 Markus Koch	.08	.04	.01
☐ 542 Andre Collins	.03	.01	.00
☐ 543 Chip Lohmiller	.03	.01	.00
☐ 544 Alvin Walton	.03	.01	.00
☐ 545 Gary Clark	.15	.07	.01
☐ 546 Ricky Sanders	.08	.04	.01
☐ 547 Redskins vs. Eagles	.08	.04	.01
(Gary Clark)			
☐ 548 Bengals vs. Oilers	.06	.03	.00
(Cody Carlson)			
☐ 549 Dolphins vs. Chiefs	.06	.03	.00
(Mark Clayton)			
☐ 550 Bears vs. Saints UER	.06	.03	.00
(Neal Anderson;			
Name misspelled			
Andersen on back)			
☐ 551 Bills vs. Dolphins	.12	.06	.01
(Thurman Thomas)			
☐ 552 49ers vs. Redskins	.06	.03	.00
(Line play)			
☐ 553 Giants vs. Bears	.06	.03	.00
(Ottis Anderson)			
☐ 554 Raiders vs. Bengals	.15	.07	.01
(Bo Jackson)			
☐ 555 AFC Championship	.06	.03	.00
(Andre Reed)			
☐ 556 NFC Championship	.06	.03	.00
(Jeff Hostetler)			
☐ 557 Super Bowl XXV	.06	.03	.00
(Ottis Anderson)			

☐ 558 Checklist 1-140	.06	.01	.00
☐ 559 Checklist 141-280	.06	.01	.00
☐ 560 Checklist 281-420 UER	.06	.01	.00
(301 Randall Hill)			
☐ 561 Checklist 421-561	.06	.01	.00

1991 Classic Draft Picks

This 50-card standard size, 2 1/2" by 3 1/2", set was issued by Classic Cards and featured most of the early picks of the 1991 National Football League draft. Among the players in the set are number one pick Russell Maryland and Raghib Ismail. The set has a grey wallpaper type border which surrounds a small photo of the player.

	MINT	EXC	G-VG
COMPLETE SET (50)	10.00	5.00	1.00
COMMON PLAYER (1-50)	.07	.03	.01

☐ 1 Raghib (Rocket) Ismail	3.00	1.50	.30
☐ 2 Russell Maryland	1.00	.50	.10
☐ 3 Eric Turner	.50	.25	.05
☐ 4 Bruce Pickens	.20	.10	.02
☐ 5 Mike Croel	.90	.45	.09
☐ 6 Todd Lyght	.50	.25	.05
☐ 7 Eric Swann	.35	.17	.03
☐ 8 Antone Davis	.20	.10	.02
☐ 9 Stanley Richard	.30	.15	.03
☐ 10 Pat Harlow	.20	.10	.02
☐ 11 Alvin Harper	.60	.30	.06
☐ 12 Mike Pritchard	.90	.45	.09
☐ 13 Leonard Russell	1.25	.60	.12
☐ 14 Dan McGwire	1.00	.50	.10

☐ 15 Bobby Wilson	.25	.12	.02
☐ 16 Alfred Williams	.25	.12	.02
☐ 17 Vinnie Clark	.20	.10	.02
☐ 18 Kelvin Pritchett	.20	.10	.02
☐ 19 Harvey Williams	1.25	.60	.12
☐ 20 Stan Thomas	.10	.05	.01
☐ 21 Randal Hill	.75	.35	.07
☐ 22 Todd Marinovich	1.25	.60	.12
☐ 23 Henry Jones	.10	.05	.01
☐ 24 Jarrod Bunch	.20	.10	.02
☐ 25 Mike Dumas	.20	.10	.02
☐ 26 Ed King	.15	.07	.01
☐ 27 Reggie Johnson	.20	.10	.02
☐ 28 Roman Phifer	.20	.10	.02
☐ 29 Mike Jones	.10	.05	.01
☐ 30 Brett Favre	.60	.30	.06
☐ 31 Browning Nagle	.75	.35	.07
☐ 32 Esera Tuaolo	.15	.07	.01
☐ 33 George Thornton	.10	.05	.01
☐ 34 Dixon Edwards	.20	.10	.02
☐ 35 Darryll Lewis UER	.25	.12	.02
(Misspelled Darryl)			
☐ 36 Eric Bieniemy	.35	.17	.03
☐ 37 Shane Curry	.07	.03	.01
☐ 38 Jerome Henderson	.10	.05	.01
☐ 39 Wesley Carroll	.35	.17	.03
☐ 40 Nick Bell	.75	.35	.07
☐ 41 John Flannery	.10	.05	.01
☐ 42 Ricky Watters	.25	.12	.02
☐ 43 Jeff Graham	.20	.10	.02
☐ 44 Eric Moten	.10	.05	.01
☐ 45 Jesse Campbell	.10	.05	.01
☐ 46 Chris Zorich	.50	.25	.05
☐ 47 Doug Thomas	.10	.05	.01
☐ 48 Phil Hansen	.10	.05	.01
☐ 49 Kanavis McGhee	.20	.10	.02
☐ 50 Reggie Barrett	.25	.12	.02

1992 Classic Draft Picks

The 1992 Classic Draft Picks set contains 100 cards featuring the highest rated football players eligible for the 1992 NFL draft. Cards 1-60 were available in blister packs bearing unique set numbers, with a production run reportedly of 300,000 sets. The foil included an additional 40 cards; cards 61-100 were

exclusive to the hobby set. The production run of the foil was limited to 14,000, ten-box cases, and to 40,000 of each bonus card. The cards measure the standard size (2 1/2" by 3 1/2"). The fronts have glossy color player photos enclosed by thin black borders. A Classic logo in the lower left corner is superimposed over a blue bottom stripe that includes player information. Against the background of an unfocused image of a ball carrier breaking through the line, the backs have biography, college statistics, and career summary, with a color head shot in the lower left corner. The cards are numbered on the back.

	MINT	EXC	G-VG
COMPLETE SET (100)	15.00	7.50	1.50
COMMON PLAYER (1-60)	.07	.03	.01
COMMON PLAYER (61-100)	.07	.03	.01

		MINT	EXC	G-VG
☐ 1	Desmond Howard Michigan	1.75	.85	.17
☐ 2	David Klingler Houston	1.50	.75	.15
☐ 3	Quentin Coryatt Texas A and M	.75	.35	.07
☐ 4	Bill Johnson Michigan State	.15	.07	.01
☐ 5	Eugene Chung Virginia Tech	.15	.07	.01
☐ 6	Derek Brown Notre Dame	.75	.35	.07
☐ 7	Carl Pickens Tennessee	.60	.30	.06
☐ 8	Chris Mims Tennessee	.15	.07	.01
☐ 9	Charles Davenport North Carolina State	.20	.10	.02
☐ 10	Ray Roberts Virginia	.15	.07	.01
☐ 11	Chuck Smith Tennessee	.15	.07	.01
☐ 12	Joe Bowden Oklahoma	.10	.05	.01
☐ 13	Mirko Jurkovic Notre Dame	.12	.06	.01
☐ 14	Tony Smith Southern Mississippi	.35	.17	.03
☐ 15	Ken Swilling Georgia Tech	.20	.10	.02
☐ 16	Greg Skrepenak Michigan	.20	.10	.02
☐ 17	Phillippi Sparks Arizona State	.15	.07	.01
☐ 18	Alonzo Spellman Ohio State	.30	.15	.03
☐ 19	Bernard Dafney Tennessee	.10	.05	.01
☐ 20	Edgar Bennett Florida State	.50	.25	.05
☐ 21	Shane Dronett Texas	.15	.07	.01
☐ 22	Jeremy Lincoln Tennessee	.12	.06	.01
☐ 23	Dion Lambert UCLA	.10	.05	.01
☐ 24	Siran Stacy Alabama	.35	.17	.03
☐ 25	Tony Sacca Penn State	.60	.30	.06
☐ 26	Sean Lumpkin Minnesota	.10	.05	.01
☐ 27	Tommy Vardell Stanford	.60	.30	.06
☐ 28	Keith Hamilton Pittsburgh	.12	.06	.01
☐ 29	Ashley Ambrose Mississippi Valley	.15	.07	.01
☐ 30	Sean Gilbert Pittsburgh	.40	.20	.04
☐ 31	Casey Weldon Florida State	.75	.35	.07
☐ 32	Marc Boutte LSU	.12	.06	.01
☐ 33	Santana Dotson Baylor	.10	.05	.01
☐ 34	Ronnie West Pittsburgh State	.12	.06	.01
☐ 35	Michael Bankston Sam Houston	.10	.05	.01
☐ 36	Mike Pawlawski California	.25	.12	.02
☐ 37	Dale Carter Tennessee	.25	.12	.02
☐ 38	Carlos Snow Ohio State	.07	.03	.01
☐ 39	Corey Barlow Auburn	.10	.05	.01

☐ 40	Mark D'Onofrio	.20	.10	.02
	Penn State			
☐ 41	Matt Blundin	.60	.30	.06
	Virginia			
☐ 42	George Rooks	.10	.05	.01
	Syracuse			
☐ 43	Patrick Rowe	.25	.12	.02
	San Diego State			
☐ 44	Dwight Hollier	.10	.05	.01
	North Carolina			
☐ 45	Joel Steed	.12	.06	.01
	Colorado			
☐ 46	Erick Anderson	.25	.12	.02
	Michigan			
☐ 47	Rodney Culver	.25	.12	.02
	Notre Dame			
☐ 48	Chris Hakel	.20	.10	.02
	William and Mary			
☐ 49	Luke Fisher	.12	.06	.01
	East Carolina			
☐ 50	Kevin Smith	.20	.10	.02
	Texas A and M			
☐ 51	Robert Brooks	.20	.10	.02
	South Carolina			
☐ 52	Bucky Richardson	.15	.07	.01
	Texas A and M			
☐ 53	Steve Israel	.15	.07	.01
	Pittsburgh			
☐ 54	Marco Coleman	.35	.17	.03
	Georgia Tech			
☐ 55	Johnny Mitchell	.30	.15	.03
	Nebraska			
☐ 56	Scottie Graham	.20	.10	.02
	Ohio State			
☐ 57	Keith Goganious	.15	.07	.01
	Penn State			
☐ 58	Tommy Maddox	.60	.30	.06
	UCLA			
☐ 59	Terrell Buckley	.75	.35	.07
	Florida State			
☐ 60	Dana Hall	.20	.10	.02
	Washington			
☐ 61	Ty Detmer	.50	.25	.05
☐ 62	Darryl Williams	.25	.12	.02
☐ 63	Jason Hanson	.12	.06	.01
☐ 64	Leon Searcy	.15	.07	.01
☐ 65	Gene McGuire	.10	.05	.01
☐ 66	Will Furrer	.40	.20	.04
☐ 67	Darren Woodson	.15	.07	.01
☐ 68	Tracy Scroggins	.15	.07	.01
☐ 69	Corey Widmer	.10	.05	.01
☐ 70	Robert Harris	.15	.07	.01
☐ 71	Larry Tharpe	.10	.05	.01
☐ 72	Lance Olberding	.10	.05	.01
☐ 73	Stacey Dillard	.10	.05	.01
☐ 74	Anthony Hamlet	.10	.05	.01
☐ 75	Tommy Jeter	.12	.06	.01

☐ 76	Mike Evans	.12	.06	.01
☐ 77	Shane Collins	.15	.07	.01
☐ 78	Mark Thomas	.12	.06	.01
☐ 79	Chester McGlockton	.15	.07	.01
☐ 80	Robert Porcher	.20	.10	.02
☐ 81	Marquez Pope	.15	.07	.01
☐ 82	Rico Smith	.15	.07	.01
☐ 83	Tyrone Williams	.12	.06	.01
☐ 84	Rod Smith	.15	.07	.01
☐ 85	Tyrone Legette	.15	.07	.01
☐ 86	Wayne Hawkins	.15	.07	.01
☐ 87	Derrick Moore	.15	.07	.01
☐ 88	Tim Lester	.12	.06	.01
☐ 89	Calvin Holmes	.10	.05	.01
☐ 90	Reggie Dwight	.12	.06	.01
☐ 91	Eddie Robinson	.15	.07	.01
☐ 92	Robert Jones	.20	.10	.02
☐ 93	Ricardo McDonald	.15	.07	.01
☐ 94	Howard Dinkins	.12	.06	.01
☐ 95	Todd Collins	.12	.06	.01
☐ 96	Eddie Blake	.10	.05	.01
☐ 97	Classic Quarterbacks	.50	.25	.05
☐ 98	Back to Back	.50	.25	.05
☐ 99	Checklist	.07	.03	.01
☐ 100	Checklist	.07	.03	.01

1992 Collector's Edge

This 175-card football set was produced by Collector's Edge. The cards are printed on plastic stock and production quantities are limited to 100,000 of each card, with every card individually numbered. Two thousand five hundred cards autographed by John Elway were randomly inserted in foil packs and factory

sets. The standard-size (2 1/2" by 3 1/2") cards
feature on the fronts color action photos
bordered in black. The team helmet appears in
the lower right corner. Inside a dark green
border, the backs have a head shot, biography,
and statistics against a ghosted reproduction
of the front photo. The cards have a removable
paper backing to discourage intermediate
purchasers from looking at the serial number.
The cards are numbered on the back and
checklisted below alphabetically according to
teams as follows: Atlanta Falcons (1-6), Buffalo
Bills (7-12), Chicago Bears (13-18), Cincinnati
Bengals (19-24), Cleveland Browns (25-30),
Dallas Cowboys (31-36), Denver Broncos (37-
43), Detroit Lions (44-49), Green Bay Packers
(50-55), Houston Oilers (56-62), Indianapolis
Colts (63-69), Kansas City Chiefs (70-76), Los
Angeles Raiders (77-83), Los Angeles Rams
(84-89), Miami Dolphins (90-96), Minnesota
Vikings (97-102), New England Patriots (103-
109), New Orleans Saints (110-115), New
York Giants (116-121), New York Jets (122-
127), Philadelphia Eagles (128-133), Phoenix
Cardinals (134-139), Pittsburgh Steelers (140-
145), San Diego Chargers (146-151), San
Francisco 49ers (152-157), Seattle Seahawks
(158-163), Tampa Bay Buccaneers (164-169),
and Washington Redskins (170-175).

	MINT	EXC	G-VG
COMPLETE SET (175)	65.00	30.00	6.00
COMMON PLAYER (1-175)	.30	.15	.03

☐ 1	Chris Miller	.75	.35	.07
☐ 2	Steve Broussard	.50	.25	.05
☐ 3	Mike Pritchard	1.25	.60	.12
☐ 4	Tim Green	.30	.15	.03
☐ 5	Andre Rison	.75	.35	.07
☐ 6	Deion Sanders	.90	.45	.09
☐ 7	Jim Kelly	1.50	.75	.15
☐ 8	James Lofton	.75	.35	.07
☐ 9	Andre Reed	.60	.30	.06
☐ 10	Bruce Smith	.45	.22	.04
☐ 11	Thurman Thomas	1.75	.85	.17
☐ 12	Cornelius Bennett	.50	.25	.05
☐ 13	Jim Harbaugh	.45	.22	.04
☐ 14	William Perry	.35	.17	.03
☐ 15	Mike Singletary	.45	.22	.04
☐ 16	Mark Carrier	.35	.17	.03
☐ 17	Kevin Butler	.30	.15	.03
☐ 18	Tom Waddle	.75	.35	.07
☐ 19	Boomer Esiason	.60	.30	.06
☐ 20	David Fulcher	.30	.15	.03
☐ 21	Anthony Munoz	.45	.22	.04
☐ 22	Tim McGee	.30	.15	.03
☐ 23	Harold Green	.75	.35	.07
☐ 24	Rickey Dixon	.30	.15	.03
☐ 25	Bernie Kosar	.60	.30	.06
☐ 26	Michael Dean Perry	.60	.30	.06
☐ 27	Mike Baab	.30	.15	.03
☐ 28	Brian Brennan	.30	.15	.03
☐ 29	Michael Jackson	.75	.35	.07
☐ 30	Eric Metcalf	.35	.17	.03
☐ 31	Troy Aikman	1.50	.75	.15
☐ 32	Emmitt Smith	6.00	3.00	.60
☐ 33	Michael Irvin	1.00	.50	.10
☐ 34	Jay Novacek	.50	.25	.05
☐ 35	Issiac Holt	.30	.15	.03
☐ 36	Ken Norton	.30	.15	.03
☐ 37	John Elway	.75	.35	.07
☐ 38	Gaston Green	.90	.45	.09
☐ 39	Charles Dimry	.30	.15	.03
☐ 40	Vance Johnson	.35	.17	.03
☐ 41	Dennis Smith	.30	.15	.03
☐ 42	David Treadwell	.30	.15	.03
☐ 43	Michael Young	.30	.15	.03
☐ 44	Bennie Blades	.35	.17	.03
☐ 45	Mel Gray	.30	.15	.03
☐ 46	Andre Ware	.35	.17	.03
☐ 47	Rodney Peete	.40	.20	.04
☐ 48	Toby Caston	.45	.22	.04
☐ 49	Herman Moore	1.25	.60	.12
☐ 50	Brian Noble	.30	.15	.03
☐ 51	Sterling Sharpe	.50	.25	.05
☐ 52	Mike Tomczak	.40	.20	.04
☐ 53	Vinnie Clark	.30	.15	.03
☐ 54	Tony Mandarich	.35	.17	.03
☐ 55	Ed West	.30	.15	.03
☐ 56	Warren Moon	.90	.45	.09
☐ 57	Ray Childress	.35	.17	.03
☐ 58	Haywood Jeffires	.75	.35	.07
☐ 59	Al Smith	.30	.15	.03
☐ 60	Cris Dishman	.45	.22	.04
☐ 61	Ernest Givins	.50	.25	.05
☐ 62	Richard Johnson	.30	.15	.03
☐ 63	Eric Dickerson	1.00	.50	.10
☐ 64	Jessie Hester	.30	.15	.03
☐ 65	Rohn Stark	.30	.15	.03
☐ 66	Clarence Verdin	.30	.15	.03
☐ 67	Dean Biasucci	.30	.15	.03
☐ 68	Duane Bickett	.30	.15	.03
☐ 69	Jeff George	1.00	.50	.10
☐ 70	Christian Okoye	.50	.25	.05
☐ 71	Derrick Thomas	.90	.45	.09
☐ 72	Stephone Paige	.35	.17	.03
☐ 73	Dan Saleaumua	.30	.15	.03
☐ 74	Deron Cherry	.30	.15	.03
☐ 75	Kevin Ross	.30	.15	.03
☐ 76	Barry Word	.90	.45	.09
☐ 77	Ronnie Lott	.60	.30	.06
☐ 78	Greg Townsend	.30	.15	.03
☐ 79	Willie Gault	.35	.17	.03
☐ 80	Howie Long	.35	.17	.03

☐ 81	Winston Moss	.30	.15	.03	☐ 138	Timm Rosenbach	.45	.22	.04
☐ 82	Steve Smith	.30	.15	.03	☐ 139	Anthony Thompson	.40	.20	.04
☐ 83	Jay Schroeder	.45	.22	.04	☐ 140	Bubby Brister	.45	.22	.04
☐ 84	Jim Everett	.50	.25	.05	☐ 141	Merril Hoge	.35	.17	.03
☐ 85	Flipper Anderson	.35	.17	.03	☐ 142	Louis Lipps	.35	.17	.03
☐ 86	Henry Ellard	.35	.17	.03	☐ 143	Eric Green	.60	.30	.06
☐ 87	Tony Zendejas	.30	.15	.03	☐ 144	Gary Anderson	.30	.15	.03
☐ 88	Robert Delpino	.35	.17	.03	☐ 145	Neil O'Donnell	1.50	.75	.15
☐ 89	Pat Terrell	.30	.15	.03	☐ 146	Rod Bernstine	.35	.17	.03
☐ 90	Dan Marino	1.00	.50	.10	☐ 147	John Friesz	.75	.35	.07
☐ 91	Mark Clayton	.45	.22	.04	☐ 148	Anthony Miller	.35	.17	.03
☐ 92	Jim Jensen	.30	.15	.03	☐ 149	Junior Seau	.35	.17	.03
☐ 93	Reggie Roby	.30	.15	.03	☐ 150	Leslie O'Neal	.35	.17	.03
☐ 94	Sammie Smith	.45	.22	.04	☐ 151	Nate Lewis	.30	.15	.03
☐ 95	Tony Martin	.30	.15	.03	☐ 152	Steve Young	.60	.30	.06
☐ 96	Jeff Cross	.30	.15	.03	☐ 153	Kevin Fagan	.30	.15	.03
☐ 97	Anthony Carter	.35	.17	.03	☐ 154	Charles Haley	.35	.17	.03
☐ 98	Chris Doleman	.35	.17	.03	☐ 155	Tom Rathman	.35	.17	.03
☐ 99	Wade Wilson	.35	.17	.03	☐ 156	Jerry Rice	1.50	.75	.15
☐ 100	Cris Carter	.35	.17	.03	☐ 157	John Taylor	.45	.22	.04
☐ 101	Mike Merriweather	.30	.15	.03	☐ 158	Brian Blades	.35	.17	.03
☐ 102	Gary Zimmerman	.30	.15	.03	☐ 159	Patrick Hunter	.30	.15	.03
☐ 103	Chris Singleton	.30	.15	.03	☐ 160	Cortez Kennedy	.35	.17	.03
☐ 104	Bruce Armstrong	.30	.15	.03	☐ 161	Vann McElroy	.30	.15	.03
☐ 105	Marv Cook	.45	.22	.04	☐ 162	Dan McGwire	2.25	1.10	.22
☐ 106	Andre Tippett	.35	.17	.03	☐ 163	John L. Williams	.35	.17	.03
☐ 107	Tommy Hodson	.45	.22	.04	☐ 164	Gary Anderson	.35	.17	.03
☐ 108	Greg McMurtry	.35	.17	.03	☐ 165	Broderick Thomas	.35	.17	.03
☐ 109	Jon Vaughn	.90	.45	.09	☐ 166	Vinny Testaverde	.45	.22	.04
☐ 110	Vaughan Johnson	.30	.15	.03	☐ 167	Lawrence Dawsey	.60	.30	.06
☐ 111	Craig Heyward	.35	.17	.03	☐ 168	Paul Gruber	.35	.17	.03
☐ 112	Floyd Turner	.30	.15	.03	☐ 169	Keith McCants	.35	.17	.03
☐ 113	Pat Swilling	.50	.25	.05	☐ 170	Mark Rypien	1.00	.50	.10
☐ 114	Rickey Jackson	.35	.17	.03	☐ 171	Gary Clark	.60	.30	.06
☐ 115	Steve Walsh	.45	.22	.04	☐ 172	Earnest Byner	.45	.22	.04
☐ 116	Phil Simms	.50	.25	.05	☐ 173	Brian Mitchell	.50	.25	.05
☐ 117	Carl Banks	.35	.17	.03	☐ 174	Monte Coleman	.30	.15	.03
☐ 118	Mark Ingram	.30	.15	.03	☐ 175	Joe Jacoby	.30	.15	.03
☐ 119	Bart Oates	.30	.15	.03					
☐ 120	Lawrence Taylor	.60	.30	.06					
☐ 121	Jeff Hostetler	.90	.45	.09					
☐ 122	Rob Moore	1.00	.50	.10					
☐ 123	Ken O'Brien	.45	.22	.04					
☐ 124	Bill Pickel	.30	.15	.03					
☐ 125	Irv Eatman	.30	.15	.03					
☐ 126	Browning Nagle	1.25	.60	.12					
☐ 127	Al Toon	.45	.22	.04					
☐ 128	Randall Cunningham	.75	.35	.07					
☐ 129	Eric Allen	.30	.15	.03					
☐ 130	Mike Golic	.30	.15	.03					
☐ 131	Fred Barnett	.60	.30	.06					
☐ 132	Keith Byars	.35	.17	.03					
☐ 133	Calvin Williams	.30	.15	.03					
☐ 134	Randal Hill	1.25	.60	.12					
☐ 135	Ricky Proehl	.40	.20	.04					
☐ 136	Lance Smith	.30	.15	.03					
☐ 137	Ernie Jones	.30	.15	.03					

1992 Courtside Draft Pix

The 1992 Courtside Draft Pix football set contains 140 player cards. Ten short printed insert cards (five Award Winner and five All-America) were randomly inserted in the foil packs. This set also includes a foilgram card featuring Steve Emtman. Fifty thousand foilgram cards were printed, and collectors could receive one by sending in ten foil pack

wrappers. Moreover, one set of foilgram cards and 20 free promo cards were offered to dealers for each case order. It has been reported that the production run was limited to 7,500 numbered cases, and that no factory sets were issued. Gold, silver, and bronze foil versions of the regular cards were randomly inserted within the foil cases in quantities of 1,000, 2,000, and 3,000 respectively. Moreover, it is claimed that over 70,000 autographed cards were inserted. The standard-size (2 1/2" by 3 1/2") card feature on the fronts glossy color action photos bordered in white (some of the cards are oriented horizontally). The player's name and position appear in a gold stripe cutting across the bottom. On the backs, the upper half has a color close-up photo, with biography and collegiate statistics below. The cards are numbered on the back.

	MINT	EXC	G-VG
COMPLETE SET (140)	14.00	7.00	1.40
COMMON PLAYER (1-140)	.07	.03	.01
☐ 1 Steve Emtman	1.25	.60	.12
Washington			
☐ 2 Quentin Coryatt	.75	.35	.07
Texas A and M			
☐ 3 Ken Swilling	.20	.10	.02
Georgia Tech			
☐ 4 Jay Leeuwenburg	.10	.05	.01
Colorado			
☐ 5 Mazio Royster	.20	.10	.02
Southern California			
☐ 6 Matt Veatch	.07	.03	.01
San Diego State			
☐ 7 Scott Lockwood	.12	.06	.01
Southern California			
☐ 8 Todd Collins	.12	.06	.01
Carson-Newman			
☐ 9 Gene McGuire	.12	.06	.01
Notre Dame			
☐ 10 Dale Carter	.25	.12	.02
Tennessee			
☐ 11 Michael Bankston	.10	.05	.01
Sam Houston			
☐ 12 Jeremy Lincoln	.12	.06	.01
Tennessee			
☐ 13 Troy Auzenne	.10	.05	.01
California			
☐ 14 Rod Smith	.15	.07	.01
Notre Dame			
☐ 15 Andy Kelly	.10	.05	.01
Tennessee			
☐ 16 Chris Holder	.10	.05	.01
Tuskegee			
☐ 17 Rico Smith	.15	.07	.01
Colorado			
☐ 18 Chris Pedersen	.07	.03	.01
Iowa State			
☐ 19 Brian Treggs	.07	.03	.01
California			
☐ 20 Eugene Chung	.15	.07	.01
Virginia Tech			
☐ 21 Joel Steed	.12	.06	.01
Colorado			
☐ 22 Ricardo McDonald	.15	.07	.01
Pittsburgh			
☐ 23 Nate Turner	.12	.06	.01
Nebraska			
☐ 24 Sean Lumpkin	.10	.05	.01
Minnesota			
☐ 25 Ty Detmer	.50	.25	.05
BYU			
☐ 26 Matt Darby	.10	.05	.01
UCLA			
☐ 27 Michael Warfield	.07	.03	.01
Catawba			
☐ 28 Tracy Scroggins	.15	.07	.01
Tulsa			
☐ 29 Carl Pickens	.60	.30	.06
Tennessee			
☐ 30 Chris Mims	.15	.07	.01
Tennessee			
☐ 31 Mark D'Onofrio	.20	.10	.02
Penn State			
☐ 32 Dwight Hollier	.10	.05	.01
North Carolina			
☐ 33 Siupeli Malamala	.15	.07	.01
Washington			
☐ 34 Mark Barsotti	.12	.06	.01
Fresno State			
☐ 35 Charles Davenport	.20	.10	.02
North Carolina State			
☐ 36 Brian Bollinger	.10	.05	.01
North Carolina			
☐ 37 Willie McClendon	.10	.05	.01

	Florida			
☐ 38	Calvin Holmes	.10	.05	.01
	Southern California			
☐ 39	Phillippi Sparks	.15	.07	.01
	Arizona State			
☐ 40	Darryl Williams	.25	.12	.02
	Miami			
☐ 41	Greg Skrepenak	.20	.10	.02
	Michigan			
☐ 42	Larry Webster	.15	.07	.01
	Maryland			
☐ 43	Dion Lambert	.10	.05	.01
	UCLA			
☐ 44	Sam Gash	.15	.07	.01
	Penn State			
☐ 45	Patrick Rowe	.25	.12	.02
	San Diego State			
☐ 46	Scottie Graham	.20	.10	.02
	Ohio State			
☐ 47	Darian Hagan	.30	.15	.03
	Colorado			
☐ 48	Arthur Marshall	.07	.03	.01
	Georgia			
☐ 49	Amp Lee	.75	.35	.07
	Florida State			
☐ 50	Tommy Vardell	.60	.30	.06
	Stanford			
☐ 51	Robert Porcher	.20	.10	.02
	South Carolina State			
☐ 52	Reggie Dwight	.12	.06	.01
	Troy State			
☐ 53	Torrance Small	.15	.07	.01
	Alcorn State			
☐ 54	Ronnie West	.12	.06	.01
	Pittsburgh State			
☐ 55	Tony Brooks	.25	.12	.02
	Notre Dame			
☐ 56	Anthony McDowell	.12	.06	.01
	Texas Tech			
☐ 57	Chris Hakel	.25	.12	.02
	William and Mary			
☐ 58	Ed Cunningham	.10	.05	.01
	Washington			
☐ 59	Ashley Ambrose	.15	.07	.01
	Mississippi Valley St.			
☐ 60	Alonzo Spellman	.30	.15	.03
	Ohio State			
☐ 61	Harold Heath	.07	.03	.01
	Jackson State			
☐ 62	Ron Lopez	.07	.03	.01
	Utah State			
☐ 63	Bill Johnson	.15	.07	.01
	Michigan State			
☐ 64	Kent Graham	.12	.06	.01
	Ohio State			
☐ 65	Aaron Pierce	.20	.10	.02
	Washington			
☐ 66	Bucky Richardson	.15	.07	.01
	Texas A and M			
☐ 67	Todd Kinchen	.15	.07	.01
	Louisiana State			
☐ 68	Ken Ealy	.07	.03	.01
	Central Michigan			
☐ 69	Carlos Snow	.07	.03	.01
	Ohio State			
☐ 70	Dana Hall	.20	.10	.02
	Washington			
☐ 71	Matt Rodgers	.25	.12	.02
	Iowa			
☐ 72	Howard Dinkins	.12	.06	.01
	Florida State			
☐ 73	Tim Lester	.12	.06	.01
	Eastern Kentucky			
☐ 74	Mark Chmura	.15	.07	.01
	Boston College			
☐ 75	Johnny Mitchell	.35	.17	.03
	Nebraska			
☐ 76	Mirko Jurkovic	.12	.06	.01
	Notre Dame			
☐ 77	Anthony Lynn	.07	.03	.01
	Texas Tech			
☐ 78	Roosevelt Collins	.10	.05	.01
	Texas Christian			
☐ 79	Tony Sands	.07	.03	.01
	Kansas			
☐ 80	Kevin Smith	.20	.10	.02
	Texas A and M			
☐ 81	Tony Brown	.10	.05	.01
	Fresno State			
☐ 82	Bobby Fuller	.07	.03	.01
	South Carolina			
☐ 83	Darryl Ashmore	.10	.05	.01
	Northwestern			
☐ 84	Tyrone Legette	.15	.07	.01
	Nebraska			
☐ 85	Mike Gaddis	.25	.12	.02
	Oklahoma			
☐ 86	Gerald Dixon	.12	.06	.01
	South Carolina			
☐ 87	T.J. Rubley	.15	.07	.01
	Tulsa			
☐ 88	Mark Thomas	.12	.06	.01
	North Carolina State			
☐ 89	Corey Widmer	.10	.05	.01
	Montana State			
☐ 90	Robert Jones	.20	.10	.02
	East Carolina			
☐ 91	Eddie Robinson	.15	.07	.01
	Alabama State			
☐ 92	Rob Tomlinson	.07	.03	.01
	Cal State-Chico			
☐ 93	Russ Campbell	.12	.06	.01
	Kansas State			
☐ 94	Keith Goganious	.15	.07	.01

	Penn State		
☐ 95	Rod Moore 07	.03	.01
	Utah State		
☐ 96	Jerry Ostroski 10	.05	.01
	Tulsa		
☐ 97	Tyji Armstrong 15	.07	.01
	Mississippi		
☐ 98	Ronald Humphrey 12	.06	.01
	Mississippi Valley St.		
☐ 99	Corey Harris 20	.10	.02
	Vanderbilt		
☐ 100	Terrell Buckley 75	.35	.07
	Florida State		
☐ 101	Cal Dixon 10	.05	.01
	Florida		
☐ 102	Tyrone Williams 12	.06	.01
	Western Ontario		
☐ 103	Joe Bowden 10	.05	.01
	Oklahoma		
☐ 104	Santana Dotson 10	.05	.01
	Baylor		
☐ 105	Jeff Blake 25	.12	.02
	East Carolina		
☐ 106	Erick Anderson 25	.12	.02
	Michigan		
☐ 107	Steve Israel 15	.07	.01
	Pittsburgh		
☐ 108	Chad Roghair 07	.03	.01
	Princeton		
☐ 109	Todd Harrison 15	.07	.01
	North Carolina State		
☐ 110	Chester McGlockton 15	.07	.01
	Clemson		
☐ 111	Marquez Pope 15	.07	.01
	Fresno State		
☐ 112	George Rooks 10	.05	.01
	Syracuse		
☐ 113	Dion Johnson 10	.05	.01
	East Carolina		
☐ 114	Tim Simpson 10	.05	.01
	Illinois		
☐ 115	Chris Walsh 10	.05	.01
	Stanford		
☐ 116	Marc Boutte 12	.06	.01
	LSU		
☐ 117	Jamie Gill 07	.03	.01
	Texas Tech		
☐ 118	Willie Clay 10	.05	.01
	Georgia Tech		
☐ 119	Tim Paulk 10	.05	.01
	Florida		
☐ 120	Ray Roberts 15	.07	.01
	Virginia		
☐ 121	Jeff Thomason 07	.03	.01
	Oregon		
☐ 122	Leodis Flowers 10	.05	.01
	Nebraska		

☐ 123	Robert Brooks 20	.10	.02
	South Carolina		
☐ 124	Jeff Ellis 07	.03	.01
	Ohio State		
☐ 125	John Fina 15	.07	.01
	Arizona		
☐ 126	Michael Smith 07	.03	.01
	Kansas State		
☐ 127	Mike Saunders 15	.07	.01
	Iowa		
☐ 128	John Brown III 12	.06	.01
	Houston		
☐ 129	Reggie Yarbrough 12	.06	.01
	Cal State-Fullerton		
☐ 130	Leon Searcy 20	.10	.02
	Miami		
☐ 131	Marcus Woods 07	.03	.01
	Oregon		
☐ 132	Shane Collins 15	.07	.01
	Arizona State		
☐ 133	Chuck Smith 15	.07	.01
	Tennessee		
☐ 134	Keith Hamilton 12	.06	.01
	Pittsburgh		
☐ 135	Rodney Blackshear 10	.05	.01
	Texas Tech		
☐ 136	Corey Barlow 10	.05	.01
	Auburn		
☐ 137	Robert Harris 15	.07	.01
	Southern-Baton Rouge		
☐ 138	Tony Smith 35	.17	.03
	Southern Mississippi		
☐ 139	Checklist 1 07	.03	.01
☐ 140	Checklist 2 07	.03	.01

1960 Fleer

The 1960 Fleer set of 132 cards was Fleer's first venture into football card production. The cards measure the standard 2 1/2" by 3 1/2". American Football League players only are included in this set. This set was issued during the American Football League's first season. Several well-known coaches are featured in the set. The card backs are printed in red and black. The key card in the set is Jack Kemp's rookie card. The cards are frequently found off-centered as Fleer's first effort into the football card market left much to be desired in the area of quality control.

	NRMT	VG-E	GOOD
COMPLETE SET (132)	625.00	300.00	75.00
COMMON PLAYER (1-132)	2.00	1.00	.20

☐ 1 Harvey White	16.00	2.50	.50
Boston Patriots			
☐ 2 Tom"Corky" Tharp	2.00	1.00	.20
New York Titans			
☐ 3 Dan McGrew	2.00	1.00	.20
Buffalo Bills			
☐ 4 Bob White	3.00	1.50	.30
Houston Oilers			
☐ 5 Dick Jamieson	2.00	1.00	.20
Dallas Texans			
☐ 6 Sam Salerno	2.00	1.00	.20
Denver Broncos			
☐ 7 Sid Gillman CO	11.00	5.50	1.10
Los Angeles Chargers			
☐ 8 Ben Preston	2.00	1.00	.20
Los Angeles Chargers			
☐ 9 George Blanch	2.00	1.00	.20
Oakland Raiders			
☐ 10 Bob Stransky	2.00	1.00	.20
Denver Broncos			
☐ 11 Fran Curci	2.50	1.25	.25
Dallas Texans			
☐ 12 George Shirkey	2.00	1.00	.20
Houston Oilers			
☐ 13 Paul Larson	2.00	1.00	.20
Oakland Raiders			
☐ 14 John Stolte	2.00	1.00	.20
Los Angeles Chargers			
☐ 15 Serafino Fazio	3.00	1.50	.30
Boston Patriots			
☐ 16 Tom Dimitroff	2.00	1.00	.20
Boston Patriots			
☐ 17 Elbert Dubenion	6.00	3.00	.60
Buffalo Bills			
☐ 18 Hogan Wharton	2.00	1.00	.20
Houston Oilers			
☐ 19 Tom O'Connell	2.00	1.00	.20
Buffalo Bills			
☐ 20 Sammy Baugh CO	33.00	16.50	3.30
New York Titans			
☐ 21 Tony Sardisco	2.00	1.00	.20
Boston Patriots			
☐ 22 Alan Cann	2.00	1.00	.20
Boston Patriots			
☐ 23 Mike Hudock	2.00	1.00	.20
New York Titans			
☐ 24 Bill Atkins	2.00	1.00	.20
Buffalo Bills			
☐ 25 Charlie Jackson	2.00	1.00	.20
Dallas Texans			
☐ 26 Frank Tripucka	4.50	2.25	.45
Denver Broncos			
☐ 27 Tony Teresa	2.00	1.00	.20
Oakland Raiders			
☐ 28 Joe Amstutz	2.00	1.00	.20
Oakland Raiders			
☐ 29 Bob Fee	2.00	1.00	.20
Boston Patriots			
☐ 30 Jim Baldwin	2.00	1.00	.20
New York Titans			
☐ 31 Jim Yates	2.00	1.00	.20
Houston Oilers			
☐ 32 Don Flynn	2.00	1.00	.20
Dallas Texans			
☐ 33 Ken Adamson	2.00	1.00	.20
Denver Broncos			
☐ 34 Ron Drzewiecki	2.00	1.00	.20
Oakland Raiders			
☐ 35 J.W. Slack	2.00	1.00	.20
Los Angeles Chargers			
☐ 36 Bob Yates	2.00	1.00	.20
Boston Patriots			
☐ 37 Gary Cobb	2.00	1.00	.20
Buffalo Bills			
☐ 38 Jacky Lee	3.00	1.50	.30
Houston Oilers			
☐ 39 Jack Spikes	3.00	1.50	.30
Dallas Texans			
☐ 40 Jim Padgett	2.00	1.00	.20
Denver Broncos			
☐ 41 Jack Larsheid	2.00	1.00	.20
Oakland Raiders			
☐ 42 Bob Reifsnyder	3.00	1.50	.30
Los Angeles Chargers			
☐ 43 Fran Rogel	2.00	1.00	.20
New York Titans			
☐ 44 Ray Moss	2.00	1.00	.20
Buffalo Bills			
☐ 45 Tony Banfield	2.50	1.25	.25
Houston Oilers			
☐ 46 George Herring	2.00	1.00	.20
Denver Broncos			
☐ 47 Willie Smith	2.00	1.00	.20
Denver Broncos			

☐ 48 Buddy Allen 2.00	1.00	.20
Oakland Raiders		
☐ 49 Bill Brown 2.00	1.00	.20
Boston Patriots		
☐ 50 Ken Ford 2.00	1.00	.20
New York Titans		
☐ 51 Billy Kinard 2.00	1.00	.20
Buffalo Bills		
☐ 52 Buddy Mayfield 2.00	1.00	.20
Houston Oilers		
☐ 53 Bill Krisher 2.50	1.25	.25
Dallas Texans		
☐ 54 Frank Bernardi 2.00	1.00	.20
Denver Broncos		
☐ 55 Lou Saban CO 3.50	1.75	.35
Boston Patriots		
☐ 56 Gene Cockrell 2.00	1.00	.20
New York Titans		
☐ 57 Sam Sanders 2.00	1.00	.20
Buffalo Bills		
☐ 58 George Blanda 33.00	16.00	3.00
Houston Oilers		
☐ 59 Sherrill Headrick 3.50	1.75	.35
Dallas Texans		
☐ 60 Carl Larpenter 2.00	1.00	.20
Denver Broncos		
☐ 61 Gene Prebola 2.00	1.00	.20
Oakland Raiders		
☐ 62 Dick Chorovich 2.00	1.00	.20
Los Angeles Chargers		
☐ 63 Bob McNamara 2.00	1.00	.20
Boston Patriots		
☐ 64 Tom Saidock 2.00	1.00	.20
New York Titans		
☐ 65 Willie Evans 2.00	1.00	.20
Buffalo Bills		
☐ 66 Billy Cannon UER 12.50	6.25	1.25
Houston Oilers		
(Hometown: Istruma,		
should be Istrouma)		
☐ 67 Sam McCord 2.00	1.00	.20
Oakland Raiders		
☐ 68 Mike Simmons 2.00	1.00	.20
New York Titans		
☐ 69 Jim Swink 3.00	1.50	.30
Dallas Texans		
☐ 70 Don Hitt 2.00	1.00	.20
Houston Oilers		
☐ 71 Gerhard Schwedes 2.50	1.25	.25
Boston Patriots		
☐ 72 Thurlow Cooper 2.00	1.00	.20
New York Titans		
☐ 73 Abner Haynes 12.50	6.25	1.25
Dallas Texans		
☐ 74 Billy Shoemake 2.00	1.00	.20
Denver Broncos		
☐ 75 Marv Lasater 2.00	1.00	.20

Oakland Raiders		
☐ 76 Paul Lowe 12.00	6.00	1.20
Los Angeles Chargers		
☐ 77 Bruce Hartman 2.00	1.00	.20
Boston Patriots		
☐ 78 Blanche Martin 2.00	1.00	.20
New York Titans		
☐ 79 Gene Grabosky 2.00	1.00	.20
Buffalo Bills		
☐ 80 Lou Rymkus CO 2.50	1.25	.25
Houston Oilers		
☐ 81 Chris Burford 4.50	2.25	.45
Dallas Texans		
☐ 82 Don Allen 2.00	1.00	.20
Denver Broncos		
☐ 83 Bob Nelson 2.00	1.00	.20
Oakland Raiders		
☐ 84 Jim Woodard 2.00	1.00	.20
Oakland Raiders		
☐ 85 Tom Rychlec 2.00	1.00	.20
Buffalo Bills		
☐ 86 Bob Cox 2.00	1.00	.20
Boston Patriots		
☐ 87 Jerry Cornelison 2.00	1.00	.20
Dallas Texans		
☐ 88 Jack Work 2.00	1.00	.20
Denver Broncos		
☐ 89 Sam DeLuca 2.00	1.00	.20
Los Angeles Chargers		
☐ 90 Rommie Loudd 2.00	1.00	.20
Los Angeles Chargers		
☐ 91 Teddy Edmondson 2.00	1.00	.20
New York Titans		
☐ 92 Buster Ramsey CO 2.50	1.25	.25
Buffalo Bills		
☐ 93 Doug Asad 2.00	1.00	.20
Houston Oilers		
☐ 94 Jimmy Harris 2.00	1.00	.20
Dallas Texans		
☐ 95 Larry Cundiff 2.00	1.00	.20
Denver Broncos		
☐ 96 Richie Lucas 3.50	1.75	.35
Buffalo Bills		
☐ 97 Don Norwood 2.00	1.00	.20
Boston Patriots		
☐ 98 Larry Grantham 3.50	1.75	.35
New York Titans		
☐ 99 Bill Mathis 3.00	1.50	.30
Houston Oilers		
☐ 100 Mel Branch 4.00	2.00	.40
Dallas Texans		
☐ 101 Marvin Terrell 2.00	1.00	.20
Dallas Texans		
☐ 102 Charlie Flowers 3.00	1.50	.30
Los Angeles Chargers		
☐ 103 John McMullan 2.00	1.00	.20
New York Titans		

☐ 104 Charlie Kaaihue .... 2.00 ... 1.00 ...... .20
      Oakland Raiders
☐ 105 Joe Schaffer .... 2.00 ... 1.00 ...... .20
      Buffalo Bills
☐ 106 Al Day .... 2.00 ... 1.00 ...... .20
      Denver Broncos
☐ 107 Johnny Carson .... 2.00 ... 1.00 ...... .20
      Houston Oilers
☐ 108 Alan Goldstein .... 2.00 ... 1.00 ...... .20
      Oakland Raiders
☐ 109 Doug Cline .... 2.00 ... 1.00 ...... .20
      Houston Oilers
☐ 110 Al Carmichael .... 2.00 ... 1.00 ...... .20
      Denver Broncos
☐ 111 Bob Dee .... 2.00 ... 1.00 ...... .20
      Boston Patriots
☐ 112 John Bredice .... 2.00 ... 1.00 ...... .20
      New York Titans
☐ 113 Don Floyd .... 2.50 ... 1.25 ...... .25
      Houston Oilers
☐ 114 Ronnie Cain .... 2.00 ... 1.00 ...... .20
      Denver Broncos
☐ 115 Stan Flowers .... 2.00 ... 1.00 ...... .20
      Boston Patriots
☐ 116 Hank Stram CO .... 16.00 .. 8.00 .... 1.60
      Dallas Texans
☐ 117 Bob Dougherty .... 2.00 ... 1.00 ...... .20
      Oakland Raiders
☐ 118 Ron Mix .... 32.00 . 16.00 .... 3.20
      Los Angeles Chargers
☐ 119 Roger Ellis .... 2.00 ... 1.00 ...... .20
      New York Titans
☐ 120 Elvin Caldwell .... 2.00 ... 1.00 ...... .20
      Boston Patriots
☐ 121 Bill Kimber .... 2.00 ... 1.00 ...... .20
      Los Angeles Chargers
☐ 122 Jim Matheny .... 2.00 ... 1.00 ...... .20
      Houston Oilers
☐ 123 Curley Johnson .... 2.50 ... 1.25 ...... .25
      Dallas Texans
☐ 124 Jack Kemp .... 275.00 135.00 .. 27.00
      Los Angeles Chargers
☐ 125 Ed Denk .... 2.00 ... 1.00 ...... .20
      Boston Patriots
☐ 126 Jerry McFarland .... 2.00 ... 1.00 ...... .20
      New York Titans
☐ 127 Dan Lanphear .... 2.00 ... 1.00 ...... .20
      Houston Oilers
☐ 128 Paul Maguire .... 11.00 .. 5.50 .... 1.10
      Los Angeles Chargers
☐ 129 Ray Collins .... 2.00 ... 1.00 ...... .20
      Dallas Texans
☐ 130 Ron Burton .... 3.50 ... 1.75 ...... .35
      Boston Patriots
☐ 131 Eddie Erdelatz CO ..... 2.50 ... 1.25 ...... .25
      Oakland Raiders
☐ 132 Ron Beagle .... 16.00 .. 3.00 ...... .60
      Oakland Raiders

1961 Fleer

The 1961 Fleer football set contains 220 cards. The cards measure 2 1/2" by 3 1/2". Most of the players are pictured in action with a background. The set contains NFL (1-132) and AFL (133-220) players. The cards are grouped alphabetically by team nicknames within league, e.g., Chicago Bears (1-9), Cleveland Browns (10-19), St. Louis Cardinals (20-29), Baltimore Colts (30-39), Dallas Cowboys (40-48), Philadelphia Eagles (49-58), San Francisco 49ers (59-67), New York Giants (68-77), Detroit Lions (78-87), Green Bay Packers (88-97), Los Angeles Rams (98-107), Washington Redskins (108-116), Pittsburgh Steelers (117-125), Minnesota Vikings (126-132), Buffalo Bills (133-143), Denver Broncos (144-154), Los Angeles Chargers (155-165), Houston Oilers (166-176), Boston Patriots (177-187), Oakland Raiders (188-198), Dallas Texans (199-209), and New York Titans (210-220). The backs are printed in black and lime green on a white card stock. The key rookies in this set are John Brodie, Don Maynard, Don Meredith, and Jim Otto.

	NRMT	VG-E	GOOD
COMPLETE SET (220)	1350.00	600.00	175.00
COMMON PLAYER (1-132)	2.00	1.00	.20
COMMON PLAYER (133-220) .	3.50	1.75	.35

☐ 1 Ed Brown .... 10.00 ... 2.00 ...... .40
☐ 2 Rick Casares .... 3.00 ... 1.50 ...... .30
☐ 3 Willie Galimore .... 3.00 ... 1.50 ...... .30
☐ 4 Jim Dooley .... 2.50 ... 1.25 ...... .25
☐ 5 Harlon Hill .... 2.50 ... 1.25 ...... .25
☐ 6 Stan Jones .... 4.50 ... 2.25 ...... .45
☐ 7 J.C. Caroline .... 2.00 ... 1.00 ...... .20
☐ 8 Joe Fortunato .... 2.50 ... 1.25 ...... .25

☐ 9	Doug Atkins	5.25	2.60	.50
☐ 10	Milt Plum	3.00	1.50	.30
☐ 11	Jim Brown	120.00	60.00	12.00
☐ 12	Bobby Mitchell	6.50	3.25	.65
☐ 13	Ray Renfro	2.50	1.25	.25
☐ 14	Gern Nagler	2.00	1.00	.20
☐ 15	Jim Shofner	2.50	1.25	.25
☐ 16	Vince Costello	2.00	1.00	.20
☐ 17	Galen Fiss	2.00	1.00	.20
☐ 18	Walt Michaels	2.50	1.25	.25
☐ 19	Bob Gain	2.00	1.00	.20
☐ 20	Mal Hammack	2.00	1.00	.20
☐ 21	Frank Mestnick	2.00	1.00	.20
☐ 22	Bobby Joe Conrad	2.50	1.25	.25
☐ 23	John David Crow	3.00	1.50	.30
☐ 24	Sonny Randle	3.00	1.50	.30
☐ 25	Don Gillis	2.00	1.00	.20
☐ 26	Jerry Norton	2.00	1.00	.20
☐ 27	Bill Stacy	2.00	1.00	.20
☐ 28	Leo Sugar	2.00	1.00	.20
☐ 29	Frank Fuller	2.00	1.00	.20
☐ 30	John Unitas	55.00	27.50	5.50
☐ 31	Alan Ameche	3.50	1.75	.35
☐ 32	Lenny Moore	7.00	3.50	.70
☐ 33	Raymond Berry	7.00	3.50	.70
☐ 34	Jim Mutscheller	2.00	1.00	.20
☐ 35	Jim Parker	5.00	2.50	.50
☐ 36	Bill Pellington	2.00	1.00	.20
☐ 37	Gino Marchetti	5.50	2.75	.55
☐ 38	Gene Lipscomb	3.25	1.60	.32
☐ 39	Art Donovan	5.00	2.50	.50
☐ 40	Eddie LeBaron	3.25	1.60	.32
☐ 41	Don Meredith	180.00	90.00	18.00
☐ 42	Don McIlhenny	2.50	1.25	.25
☐ 43	L.G. Dupre	2.50	1.25	.25
☐ 44	Fred Dugan	2.00	1.00	.20
☐ 45	Bill Howton	2.75	1.35	.27
☐ 46	Duane Putnam	2.00	1.00	.20
☐ 47	Gene Cronin	2.00	1.00	.20
☐ 48	Jerry Tubbs	2.50	1.25	.25
☐ 49	Clarence Peaks	2.00	1.00	.20
☐ 50	Ted Dean	2.50	1.25	.25
☐ 51	Tommy McDonald	2.75	1.35	.27
☐ 52	Bill Barnes	2.00	1.00	.20
☐ 53	Pete Retzlaff	2.50	1.25	.25
☐ 54	Bobby Walston	2.00	1.00	.20
☐ 55	Chuck Bednarik	5.50	2.75	.55
☐ 56	Maxie Baughan	6.00	3.00	.60
☐ 57	Bob Pellegrini	2.00	1.00	.20
☐ 58	Jesse Richardson	2.00	1.00	.20
☐ 59	John Brodie	65.00	32.50	6.50
☐ 60	J.D. Smith	2.50	1.25	.25
☐ 61	Ray Norton	2.50	1.25	.25
☐ 62	Monty Stickles	2.75	1.35	.27
☐ 63	Bob St. Clair	4.25	2.10	.42
☐ 64	Dave Baker	2.00	1.00	.20
☐ 65	Abe Woodson	2.50	1.25	.25
☐ 66	Matt Hazeltine	2.00	1.00	.20
☐ 67	Leo Nomellini	4.50	2.25	.45
☐ 68	Charley Conerly	12.00	6.00	1.20
☐ 69	Kyle Rote	4.00	2.00	.40
☐ 70	Jack Stroud	2.00	1.00	.20
☐ 71	Roosevelt Brown	5.00	2.50	.50
☐ 72	Jim Patton	2.50	1.25	.25
☐ 73	Erich Barnes	2.50	1.25	.25
☐ 74	Sam Huff	8.50	4.25	.85
☐ 75	Andy Robustelli	5.00	2.50	.50
☐ 76	Dick Modzelewski	2.50	1.25	.25
☐ 77	Roosevelt Grier	4.00	2.00	.40
☐ 78	Earl Morrall	3.75	1.85	.37
☐ 79	Jim Ninowski	2.50	1.25	.25
☐ 80	Nick Pietrosante	4.00	2.00	.40
☐ 81	Howard Cassady	2.75	1.35	.27
☐ 82	Jim Gibbons	2.00	1.00	.20
☐ 83	Gail Cogdill	3.00	1.50	.30
☐ 84	Dick Lane	5.00	2.50	.50
☐ 85	Yale Lary	5.00	2.50	.50
☐ 86	Joe Schmidt	5.25	2.60	.50
☐ 87	Darris McCord	2.00	1.00	.20
☐ 88	Bart Starr	36.00	18.00	3.60
☐ 89	Jim Taylor	30.00	15.00	3.00
☐ 90	Paul Hornung	33.00	16.00	3.00
☐ 91	Tom Moore	5.00	2.50	.50
☐ 92	Boyd Dowler	5.50	2.75	.55
☐ 93	Max McGee	3.00	1.50	.30
☐ 94	Forrest Gregg	6.00	3.00	.60
☐ 95	Jerry Kramer	5.00	2.50	.50
☐ 96	Jim Ringo	4.50	2.25	.45
☐ 97	Bill Forester	2.50	1.25	.25
☐ 98	Frank Ryan	3.00	1.50	.30
☐ 99	Ollie Matson	6.50	3.25	.65
☐ 100	Jon Arnett	2.50	1.25	.25
☐ 101	Dick Bass	3.50	1.75	.35
☐ 102	Jim Phillips	2.50	1.25	.25
☐ 103	Del Shofner	3.00	1.50	.30
☐ 104	Art Hunter	2.00	1.00	.20
☐ 105	Lindon Crow	2.00	1.00	.20
☐ 106	Les Richter	2.50	1.25	.25
☐ 107	Lou Michaels	2.50	1.25	.25
☐ 108	Ralph Guglielmi	2.50	1.25	.25
☐ 109	Don Bosseler	2.00	1.00	.20
☐ 110	John Olszewski	2.00	1.00	.20
☐ 111	Bill Anderson	2.00	1.00	.20
☐ 112	Joe Walton	2.50	1.25	.25
☐ 113	Jim Schrader	2.00	1.00	.20
☐ 114	Gary Glick	2.00	1.00	.20
☐ 115	Ralph Felton	2.00	1.00	.20
☐ 116	Bob Toneff	2.00	1.00	.20
☐ 117	Bobby Layne	20.00	10.00	2.00
☐ 118	John Henry Johnson	5.50	2.75	.55
☐ 119	Tom Tracy	2.50	1.25	.25
☐ 120	Jimmy Orr	3.50	1.75	.35
☐ 121	John Nisby	2.00	1.00	.20
☐ 122	Dean Derby	2.00	1.00	.20

☐ 123	John Reger	2.00	1.00	.20
☐ 124	George Tarasovic	2.00	1.00	.20
☐ 125	Ernie Stautner	5.00	2.50	.50
☐ 126	George Shaw	2.50	1.25	.25
☐ 127	Hugh McElhenny	6.00	3.00	.60
☐ 128	Dick Haley	2.00	1.00	.20
☐ 129	Dave Middleton	2.00	1.00	.20
☐ 130	Perry Richards	2.00	1.00	.20
☐ 131	Gene Johnson	2.00	1.00	.20
☐ 132	Don Joyce	2.00	1.00	.20
☐ 133	John(Chuck) Green	3.50	1.75	.35
☐ 134	Wray Carlton	4.50	2.25	.45
☐ 135	Richie Lucas	4.50	2.25	.45
☐ 136	Elbert Dubenion	4.50	2.25	.45
☐ 137	Tom Rychlec	3.50	1.75	.35
☐ 138	Mack Yoho	3.50	1.75	.35
☐ 139	Phil Blazer	3.50	1.75	.35
☐ 140	Dan McGrew	3.50	1.75	.35
☐ 141	Bill Atkins	3.50	1.75	.35
☐ 142	Archie Matsos	4.00	2.00	.40
☐ 143	Gene Grabosky	3.50	1.75	.35
☐ 144	Frank Tripucka	4.50	2.25	.45
☐ 145	Al Carmichael	3.50	1.75	.35
☐ 146	Bob McNamara	3.50	1.75	.35
☐ 147	Lionel Taylor	9.00	4.50	.90
☐ 148	Eldon Danenhauer	4.50	2.25	.45
☐ 149	Willie Smith	3.50	1.75	.35
☐ 150	Carl Larpenter	3.50	1.75	.35
☐ 151	Ken Adamson	3.50	1.75	.35
☐ 152	Goose Gonsoulin	5.50	2.75	.55
☐ 153	Joe Young	3.50	1.75	.35
☐ 154	Gordy Molz	3.50	1.75	.35
☐ 155	Jack Kemp	150.00	75.00	15.00
☐ 156	Charlie Flowers	4.50	2.25	.45
☐ 157	Paul Lowe	5.50	2.75	.55
☐ 158	Don Norton	3.50	1.75	.35
☐ 159	Howard Clark	3.50	1.75	.35
☐ 160	Paul Maguire	5.00	2.50	.50
☐ 161	Ernie Wright	4.50	2.25	.45
☐ 162	Ron Mix	12.50	6.25	1.25
☐ 163	Fred Cole	3.50	1.75	.35
☐ 164	Jim Sears	3.50	1.75	.35
☐ 165	Volney Peters	3.50	1.75	.35
☐ 166	George Blanda	32.00	16.00	3.20
☐ 167	Jacky Lee	4.50	2.25	.45
☐ 168	Bob White	4.00	2.00	.40
☐ 169	Doug Cline	3.50	1.75	.35
☐ 170	Dave Smith	3.50	1.75	.35
☐ 171	Billy Cannon	6.50	3.25	.65
☐ 172	Bill Groman	4.50	2.25	.45
☐ 173	Al Jamison	3.50	1.75	.35
☐ 174	Jim Norton	3.50	1.75	.35
☐ 175	Dennit Morris	3.50	1.75	.35
☐ 176	Don Floyd	4.50	2.25	.45
☐ 177	Butch Songin	3.50	1.75	.35
☐ 178	Billy Lott	4.50	2.25	.45
☐ 179	Ron Burton	4.50	2.25	.45
☐ 180	Jim Colclough	3.50	1.75	.35
☐ 181	Charley Leo	3.50	1.75	.35
☐ 182	Walt Cudzik	3.50	1.75	.35
☐ 183	Fred Bruney	3.50	1.75	.35
☐ 184	Ross O'Hanley	3.50	1.75	.35
☐ 185	Tony Sardisco	3.50	1.75	.35
☐ 186	Harry Jacobs	3.50	1.75	.35
☐ 187	Bob Dee	3.50	1.75	.35
☐ 188	Tom Flores	16.00	8.00	1.60
☐ 189	Jack Larsheid	3.50	1.75	.35
☐ 190	Dick Christy	3.50	1.75	.35
☐ 191	Alan Miller	3.50	1.75	.35
☐ 192	Jim Smith	3.50	1.75	.35
☐ 193	Gerald Burch	3.50	1.75	.35
☐ 194	Gene Prebola	3.50	1.75	.35
☐ 195	Alan Goldstein	3.50	1.75	.35
☐ 196	Don Manoukian	3.50	1.75	.35
☐ 197	Jim Otto	45.00	22.50	4.50
☐ 198	Wayne Crow	3.50	1.75	.35
☐ 199	Cotton Davidson	4.50	2.25	.45
☐ 200	Randy Duncan	4.50	2.25	.45
☐ 201	Jack Spikes	4.50	2.25	.45
☐ 202	Johnny Robinson	7.50	3.75	.75
☐ 203	Abner Haynes	6.00	3.00	.60
☐ 204	Chris Burford	4.50	2.25	.45
☐ 205	Bill Krisher	4.50	2.25	.45
☐ 206	Marvin Terrell	3.50	1.75	.35
☐ 207	Jimmy Harris	3.50	1.75	.35
☐ 208	Mel Branch	4.50	2.25	.45
☐ 209	Paul Miller	3.50	1.75	.35
☐ 210	Al Dorow	3.50	1.75	.35
☐ 211	Dick Jamieson	3.50	1.75	.35
☐ 212	Pete Hart	3.50	1.75	.35
☐ 213	Bill Shockley	3.50	1.75	.35
☐ 214	Dewey Bohling	3.50	1.75	.35
☐ 215	Don Maynard	65.00	32.50	6.50
☐ 216	Bob Mischak	3.50	1.75	.35
☐ 217	Mike Hudock	3.50	1.75	.35
☐ 218	Bob Reifsnyder	4.50	2.25	.45
☐ 219	Tom Saidock	3.50	1.75	.35
☐ 220	Sid Youngelman	20.00	3.50	.75

1962 Fleer

The 1962 Fleer football set contains 88 cards featuring AFL players only. Card numbering is by team city name order, e.g., Boston Patriots (1-11), Buffalo Bills (12-22), Dallas Texans (23-33), Denver Broncos (34-44), Houston Oilers (45-55), New York Titans (56-66), Oakland Raiders (67-77), and San Diego

Chargers (78-88). The cards measure 2 1/2"
by 3 1/2". The card backs are printed in black
and blue on a white card stock. The key
rookies in this set are Ernie Ladd and Fred
Williamson.

	NRMT	VG-E	GOOD
COMPLETE SET (88)	600.00	300.00	60.00
COMMON PLAYER (1-88)	4.50	2.25	.45

		NRMT	VG-E	GOOD
☐ 1	Billy Lott	15.00	3.50	.75
☐ 2	Ron Burton	5.50	2.75	.55
☐ 3	Gino Cappelletti	12.00	6.00	1.20
☐ 4	Babe Parilli	5.50	2.75	.55
☐ 5	Jim Colclough	4.50	2.25	.45
☐ 6	Tony Sardisco	4.50	2.25	.45
☐ 7	Walt Cudzik	4.50	2.25	.45
☐ 8	Bob Dee	4.50	2.25	.45
☐ 9	Tommy Addison	4.50	2.25	.45
☐ 10	Harry Jacobs	4.50	2.25	.45
☐ 11	Ross O'Hanley	4.50	2.25	.45
☐ 12	Art Baker	4.50	2.25	.45
☐ 13	John"Chuck" Green	4.50	2.25	.45
☐ 14	Elbert Dubenion	5.50	2.75	.55
☐ 15	Tom Rychlec	4.50	2.25	.45
☐ 16	Billy Shaw	5.50	2.75	.55
☐ 17	Ken Rice	4.50	2.25	.45
☐ 18	Bill Atkins	4.50	2.25	.45
☐ 19	Richie Lucas	5.50	2.75	.55
☐ 20	Archie Matsos	5.00	2.50	.50
☐ 21	Laverne Torczon	4.50	2.25	.45
☐ 22	Warren Rabb	4.50	2.25	.45
☐ 23	Jack Spikes	5.00	2.50	.50
☐ 24	Cotton Davidson	5.50	2.75	.55
☐ 25	Abner Haynes	7.50	3.75	.75
☐ 26	Jimmy Saxton	5.50	2.75	.55
☐ 27	Chris Burford	5.50	2.75	.55
☐ 28	Bill Miller	4.50	2.25	.45
☐ 29	Sherrill Headrick	5.50	2.75	.55
☐ 30	E.J. Holub	8.00	4.00	.80
☐ 31	Jerry Mays	8.00	4.00	.80
☐ 32	Mel Branch	5.50	2.75	.55
☐ 33	Paul Rochester	4.50	2.25	.45
☐ 34	Frank Tripucka	5.50	2.75	.55
☐ 35	Gene Mingo	4.50	2.25	.45
☐ 36	Lionel Taylor	6.00	3.00	.60
☐ 37	Ken Adamson	4.50	2.25	.45
☐ 38	Eldon Danenhauer	5.00	2.50	.50
☐ 39	Goose Gonsoulin	5.50	2.75	.55
☐ 40	Gordy Holz	4.50	2.25	.45
☐ 41	Bud McFadin	4.50	2.25	.45
☐ 42	Jim Stinnette	4.50	2.25	.45
☐ 43	Bob Hudson	4.50	2.25	.45
☐ 44	George Herring	4.50	2.25	.45
☐ 45	Charley Tolar	5.50	2.75	.55
☐ 46	George Blanda	45.00	22.50	4.50
☐ 47	Billy Cannon	7.50	3.75	.75
☐ 48	Charlie Hennigan	9.00	4.50	.90
☐ 49	Bill Groman	5.00	2.50	.50
☐ 50	Al Jamison	4.50	2.25	.45
☐ 51	Tony Banfield	5.00	2.50	.50
☐ 52	Jim Norton	4.50	2.25	.45
☐ 53	Dennit Morris	4.50	2.25	.45
☐ 54	Don Floyd	5.00	2.50	.50
☐ 55	Ed Husmann UER	4.50	2.25	.45
	(Misspelled Hussman on both sides)			
☐ 56	Robert Brooks	4.50	2.25	.45
☐ 57	Al Dorow	4.50	2.25	.45
☐ 58	Dick Christy	4.50	2.25	.45
☐ 59	Don Maynard	25.00	12.50	2.50
☐ 60	Art Powell	6.50	3.25	.65
☐ 61	Mike Hudock	4.50	2.25	.45
☐ 62	Bill Mathis	5.00	2.50	.50
☐ 63	Butch Songin	5.00	2.50	.50
☐ 64	Larry Grantham	5.50	2.75	.55
☐ 65	Nick Mumley	4.50	2.25	.45
☐ 66	Tom Saidock	4.50	2.25	.45
☐ 67	Alan Miller	4.50	2.25	.45
☐ 68	Tom Flores	8.50	4.25	.85
☐ 69	Bob Coolbaugh	4.50	2.25	.45
☐ 70	George Fleming	4.50	2.25	.45
☐ 71	Wayne Hawkins	4.50	2.25	.45
☐ 72	Jim Otto	15.00	7.50	1.50
☐ 73	Wayne Crow	4.50	2.25	.45
☐ 74	Fred Williamson	12.00	6.00	1.20
☐ 75	Tom Louderback	4.50	2.25	.45
☐ 76	Volney Peters	4.50	2.25	.45
☐ 77	Charley Powell	4.50	2.25	.45
☐ 78	Don Norton	4.50	2.25	.45
☐ 79	Jack Kemp	140.00	70.00	14.00
☐ 80	Paul Lowe	6.50	3.25	.65
☐ 81	Dave Kocourek	5.00	2.50	.50
☐ 82	Ron Mix	11.00	5.50	1.10
☐ 83	Ernie Wright	4.50	2.25	.45
☐ 84	Dick Harris	4.50	2.25	.45
☐ 85	Bill Hudson	4.50	2.25	.45
☐ 86	Ernie Ladd	18.00	9.00	1.80

☐ 87 Earl Faison	5.50	2.75	.55
☐ 88 Ron Nery	12.00	3.00	.60

1963 Fleer

LANCE ALWORTH

The 1963 Fleer football set of 88 cards features AFL players only. Card numbers follow team order, Boston Patriots (1-11), New York Titans (12-22), Buffalo Bills (23-33), Houston Oilers (34-44), Kansas City Chiefs (45-55), Oakland Raiders (56-66), San Diego Chargers (67-77), and Denver Broncos (78-88). Card numbers 6 and 64 are more difficult to obtain than the other cards in the set; their shortage is believed to be attributable to their possible replacement on the printing sheet by the unnumbered checklist. The cards measure 2 1/2" by 3 1/2". The card backs are printed in red and black on a white card stock. The set price below does include the checklist card. Cards with numbers divisible by 4 can be found with or without a red stripe on the bottom of the card back; it is thought that those without the red stripe are in lesser supply. The key rookie cards in this set are Lance Alworth, Nick Buoniconti, and Len Dawson.

	NRMT	VG-E	GOOD
COMPLETE SET (89)	1650.00	750.00	200.00
COMMON PLAYER (1-88)	6.00	3.00	.60
☐ 1 Larry Garron	16.50	5.00	1.00
☐ 2 Babe Parilli	8.50	4.25	.85
☐ 3 Ron Burton	7.50	3.75	.75
☐ 4 Jim Colclough	6.00	3.00	.60
☐ 5 Gino Cappelletti	9.00	4.50	.90
☐ 6 Charles Long SP	210.00	100.00	20.00

☐ 7 Bill Neighbors	9.00	4.50	.90
☐ 8 Dick Felt	6.00	3.00	.60
☐ 9 Tommy Addison	6.00	3.00	.60
☐ 10 Nick Buoniconti	50.00	25.00	5.00
☐ 11 Larry Eisenhauer	9.00	4.50	.90
☐ 12 Bill Mathis	7.50	3.75	.75
☐ 13 Lee Grosscup	10.00	5.00	1.00
☐ 14 Dick Christy	6.00	3.00	.60
☐ 15 Don Maynard	36.00	18.00	3.60
☐ 16 Alex Kroll	8.00	4.00	.80
☐ 17 Bob Mischak	6.00	3.00	.60
☐ 18 Dainard Paulson	6.00	3.00	.60
☐ 19 Lee Riley	6.00	3.00	.60
☐ 20 Larry Grantham	7.50	3.75	.75
☐ 21 Hubert Bobo	6.00	3.00	.60
☐ 22 Nick Mumley	6.00	3.00	.60
☐ 23 Cookie Gilchrist	16.00	8.00	1.60
☐ 24 Jack Kemp	150.00	75.00	15.00
☐ 25 Wray Carlton	7.50	3.75	.75
☐ 26 Elbert Dubenion	8.00	4.00	.80
☐ 27 Ernie Warlick	7.50	3.75	.75
☐ 28 Billy Shaw	6.00	3.00	.60
☐ 29 Ken Rice	6.00	3.00	.60
☐ 30 Booker Edgerson	6.00	3.00	.60
☐ 31 Ray Abbruzzese	6.00	3.00	.60
☐ 32 Mike Stratton	9.00	4.50	.90
☐ 33 Tom Sestak	8.00	4.00	.80
☐ 34 Charley Tolar	7.00	3.50	.70
☐ 35 Dave Smith	6.00	3.00	.60
☐ 36 George Blanda	50.00	25.00	5.00
☐ 37 Billy Cannon	10.00	5.00	1.00
☐ 38 Charlie Hennigan	8.50	4.25	.85
☐ 39 Bob Talamini	7.00	3.50	.70
☐ 40 Jim Norton	6.00	3.00	.60
☐ 41 Tony Banfield	6.00	3.00	.60
☐ 42 Doug Cline	6.00	3.00	.60
☐ 43 Don Floyd	7.00	3.50	.70
☐ 44 Ed Husmann	6.00	3.00	.60
☐ 45 Curtis McClinton	10.00	5.00	1.00
☐ 46 Jack Spikes	7.50	3.75	.75
☐ 47 Len Dawson	150.00	75.00	15.00
☐ 48 Abner Haynes	10.00	5.00	1.00
☐ 49 Chris Burford	7.50	3.75	.75
☐ 50 Fred Arbanas	9.00	4.50	.90
☐ 51 Johnny Robinson	8.00	4.00	.80
☐ 52 E.J. Holub	8.00	4.00	.80
☐ 53 Sherrill Headrick	8.00	4.00	.80
☐ 54 Mel Branch	7.50	3.75	.75
☐ 55 Jerry Mays	8.00	4.00	.80
☐ 56 Cotton Davidson	7.50	3.75	.75
☐ 57 Clem Daniels	11.00	5.50	1.10
☐ 58 Bo Roberson	6.00	3.00	.60
☐ 59 Art Powell	8.50	4.25	.85
☐ 60 Bob Coolbaugh	6.00	3.00	.60
☐ 61 Wayne Hawkins	6.00	3.00	.60
☐ 62 Jim Otto	24.00	12.00	2.40
☐ 63 Fred Williamson	10.00	5.00	1.00

☐ 64	Bob Dougherty SP	210.00	100.00	20.00
☐ 65	Dalva Allen	6.00	3.00	.60
☐ 66	Chuck McMutry	6.00	3.00	.60
☐ 67	Gerry McDougall	6.00	3.00	.60
☐ 68	Tobin Rote	8.50	4.25	.85
☐ 69	Paul Lowe	8.50	4.25	.85
☐ 70	Keith Lincoln	16.00	8.00	1.60
☐ 71	Dave Kocourek	7.00	3.50	.70
☐ 72	Lance Alworth	150.00	75.00	15.00
☐ 73	Ron Mix	16.00	8.00	1.60
☐ 74	Charles McNeil	9.00	4.50	.90
☐ 75	Emil Karas	6.00	3.00	.60
☐ 76	Ernie Ladd	13.00	6.50	1.30
☐ 77	Earl Faison	7.50	3.75	.75
☐ 78	Jim Stinnette	6.00	3.00	.60
☐ 79	Frank Tripucka	9.00	4.50	.90
☐ 80	Don Stone	6.00	3.00	.60
☐ 81	Bob Scarpitto	6.00	3.00	.60
☐ 82	Lionel Taylor	9.00	4.50	.90
☐ 83	Jerry Tarr	6.00	3.00	.60
☐ 84	Eldon Danenhauer	7.00	3.50	.70
☐ 85	Goose Gonsoulin	7.50	3.75	.75
☐ 86	Jim Fraser	6.00	3.00	.60
☐ 87	Chuck Gavin	6.00	3.00	.60
☐ 88	Bud McFadin	12.00	4.00	.80
☐ xx	Checklist Card SP (unnumbered)	350.00	60.00	12.00

1990 Fleer Have These

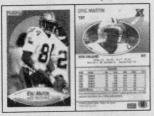

The 1990 Fleer set contains 400 standard-size (2 1/2" by 3 1/2") cards. The fronts have color action photos and team colored inner borders with white outer borders. The vertically oriented backs are multicolored and have stats and color mug shots. The set numbering is according to teams and alphabetical within teams as is the Fleer custom, San Francisco

49ers (1-17), Denver Broncos (18-32), Los Angeles Rams (33-46), Cleveland Browns (47-60), New York Giants (61-77), Philadelphia Eagles (78-93), Minnesota Vikings (94-109), Buffalo Bills (110-124), Houston Oilers (125-138), Pittsburgh Steelers (139-153), Washington Redskins (154-168), Green Bay Packers (169-182), New Orleans Saints (183-196), Kansas City Chiefs (197-209), Cincinnati Bengals (210-223), Indianapolis Colts (224-235), Miami Dolphins (236-248), Los Angeles Raiders (249-262), Seattle Seahawks (263-274), Detroit Lions (275-287), Chicago Bears (288-302), San Diego Chargers (303-316), New England Patriots (317-329), Phoenix Cardinals (330-342), Tampa Bay Buccaneers (343-357), New York Jets (358-370), Atlanta Falcons (371-383), and Dallas Cowboys (384-396). The teams are essentially ordered by their respective order of finish during the 1989 season. The following cards have AFC logo location variations: 18, 20-22, 24, 27-30, 32, 49-56, 58, 60, 110-111, 113-117, 119, 122, 124, 198, 200-211, 213-217, and 221-223. Jim Covert (290) and Mark May (162) can be found with or without a thin line just above the text on the back. The key rookies in this set are Jeff George, Jeff Hostetler, and Blair Thomas.

	MINT	EXC	G-VG
COMPLETE SET (400)	12.00	6.00	1.20
COMMON PLAYER (1-400)	.03	.01	.00
☐ 1 Harris Barton	.06	.03	.00
☐ 2 Chet Brooks	.08	.04	.01
☐ 3 Michael Carter	.06	.03	.00
☐ 4 Mike Cofer UER (FGA and FGM columns switched)	.06	.03	.00
☐ 5 Roger Craig	.10	.05	.01
☐ 6 Kevin Fagan	.08	.04	.01
☐ 7 Charles Haley UER (Fumble recoveries should be 2 in '86 and 5 career, card says 1 and 4)	.06	.03	.00
☐ 8 Pierce Holt	.08	.04	.01
☐ 9 Ronnie Lott	.10	.05	.01
☐ 10A Joe Montana ERR (31,054 TD's)	.90	.45	.09
☐ 10B Joe Montana COR (216 TD's)	.50	.25	.05
☐ 11 Bubba Paris	.06	.03	.00
☐ 12 Tom Rathman	.08	.04	.01
☐ 13 Jerry Rice	.45	.22	.04
☐ 14 John Taylor	.15	.07	.01
☐ 15 Keena Turner	.03	.01	.00

☐ 16 Mike Walter	.03	.01	.00
☐ 17 Steve Young	.10	.05	.01
☐ 18 Steve Atwater	.10	.05	.01
☐ 19 Tyrone Braxton	.06	.03	.00
☐ 20 Michael Brooks	.10	.05	.01
☐ 21 John Elway	.20	.10	.02
☐ 22 Simon Fletcher	.06	.03	.00
☐ 23 Bobby Humphrey	.12	.06	.01
☐ 24 Mark Jackson	.06	.03	.00
☐ 25 Vance Johnson	.06	.03	.00
☐ 26 Greg Kragen	.06	.03	.00
☐ 27 Ken Lanier	.10	.05	.01
☐ 28 Karl Mecklenburg	.06	.03	.00
☐ 29 Orson Mobley	.12	.06	.01
☐ 30 Steve Sewell	.06	.03	.00
☐ 31 Dennis Smith	.06	.03	.00
☐ 32 David Treadwell	.03	.03	.00
☐ 33 Flipper Anderson	.10	.05	.01
☐ 34 Greg Bell	.06	.03	.00
☐ 35 Henry Ellard	.08	.04	.01
☐ 36 Jim Everett	.12	.06	.01
☐ 37 Jerry Gray	.06	.03	.00
☐ 38 Kevin Greene	.06	.03	.00
☐ 39 Pete Holohan	.03	.01	.00
☐ 40 LeRoy Irvin	.03	.01	.00
☐ 41 Mike Lansford	.03	.01	.00
☐ 42 Buford McGee	.15	.07	.01
☐ 43 Tom Newberry	.03	.01	.00
☐ 44 Vince Newsome	.10	.05	.01
☐ 45 Jackie Slater	.06	.03	.00
☐ 46 Mike Wilcher	.03	.01	.00
☐ 47 Matt Bahr	.03	.01	.00
☐ 48 Brian Brennan	.03	.01	.00
☐ 49 Thane Gash	.08	.04	.01
☐ 50 Mike Johnson	.03	.01	.00
☐ 51 Bernie Kosar	.15	.07	.01
☐ 52 Reggie Langhorne	.03	.01	.00
☐ 53 Tim Manoa	.08	.04	.01
☐ 54 Clay Matthews	.03	.01	.00
☐ 55 Eric Metcalf	.08	.04	.01
☐ 56 Frank Minnifield	.03	.01	.00
☐ 57 Gregg Rakoczy UER	.08	.04	.01
(First line of text calls him Greg)			
☐ 58 Webster Slaughter	.06	.03	.00
☐ 59 Bryan Wagner	.03	.01	.00
☐ 60 Felix Wright	.03	.01	.00
☐ 61 Raul Allegre	.03	.01	.00
☐ 62 Ottis Anderson UER	.08	.04	.01
(Stats say 9,317 yards, should be 9,317)			
☐ 63 Carl Banks	.08	.04	.01
☐ 64 Mark Bavaro	.06	.03	.00
☐ 65 Maurice Carthon	.03	.01	.00
☐ 66 Mark Collins UER	.06	.03	.00
(Total fumble recoveries should be 5, not 3)			

☐ 67 Jeff Hostetler	.50	.25	.05
☐ 68 Erik Howard	.03	.01	.00
☐ 69 Pepper Johnson	.06	.03	.00
☐ 70 Sean Landeta	.03	.01	.00
☐ 71 Lionel Manuel	.06	.03	.00
☐ 72 Leonard Marshall	.06	.03	.00
☐ 73 Dave Meggett	.15	.07	.01
☐ 74 Bart Oates	.03	.01	.00
☐ 75 Doug Riesenberg	.10	.05	.01
☐ 76 Phil Simms	.10	.05	.01
☐ 77 Lawrence Taylor	.10	.05	.01
☐ 78 Eric Allen	.06	.03	.00
☐ 79 Jerome Brown	.06	.03	.00
☐ 80 Keith Byars	.06	.03	.00
☐ 81 Cris Carter	.06	.03	.00
☐ 82A Byron Evans ERR	.20	.10	.02
(should be 83 according to checklist)			
☐ 82B Randall Cunningham	.15	.07	.01
☐ 83A Ron Heller ERR	.25	.12	.02
(should be 84 according to checklist)			
☐ 83B Byron Evans COR	.15	.07	.01
☐ 84 Ron Heller	.15	.07	.01
☐ 85 Terry Hoage	.12	.06	.01
☐ 86 Keith Jackson	.10	.05	.01
☐ 87 Seth Joyner	.06	.03	.00
☐ 88 Mike Quick	.06	.03	.00
☐ 89 Mike Schad	.10	.05	.01
☐ 90 Clyde Simmons	.06	.03	.00
☐ 91 John Teltschik	.03	.01	.00
☐ 92 Anthony Toney	.03	.01	.00
☐ 93 Reggie White	.08	.04	.01
☐ 94 Ray Berry	.06	.03	.00
☐ 95 Joey Browner	.06	.03	.00
☐ 96 Anthony Carter	.08	.04	.01
☐ 97 Chris Doleman	.06	.03	.00
☐ 98 Rick Fenney	.08	.04	.01
☐ 99 Rich Gannon	.25	.12	.02
☐ 100 Hassan Jones	.08	.04	.01
☐ 101 Steve Jordan	.06	.03	.00
☐ 102 Rich Karlis	.03	.01	.00
☐ 103 Andre Ware	.35	.17	.03
☐ 104 Kirk Lowdermilk	.06	.03	.00
☐ 105 Keith Millard	.08	.04	.01
☐ 106 Scott Studwell	.03	.01	.00
☐ 107 Herschel Walker	.15	.07	.01
☐ 108 Wade Wilson	.08	.04	.01
☐ 109 Gary Zimmerman	.06	.03	.00
☐ 110 Don Beebe	.12	.06	.01
☐ 111 Cornelius Bennett	.12	.06	.01
☐ 112 Shane Conlan	.08	.04	.01
☐ 113 Jim Kelly	.35	.17	.03
☐ 114 Scott Norwood UER	.03	.01	.00
(FGA and FGM columns switched)			
☐ 115 Mark Kelso UER	.03	.01	.00

(Some stats added wrong
on back)

☐ 116	Larry Kinnebrew	.03	.01	.00
☐ 117	Pete Metzelaars	.03	.01	.00
☐ 118	Scott Radecic	.06	.03	.00
☐ 119	Andre Reed	.10	.05	.01
☐ 120	Jim Ritcher	.10	.05	.01
☐ 121	Bruce Smith	.08	.04	.01
☐ 122	Leonard Smith	.03	.01	.00
☐ 123	Art Still	.06	.03	.00
☐ 124	Thurman Thomas	.60	.30	.06
☐ 125	Steve Brown	.03	.01	.00
☐ 126	Ray Childress	.06	.03	.00
☐ 127	Ernest Givins	.10	.05	.01
☐ 128	John Grimsley	.03	.01	.00
☐ 129	Alonzo Highsmith	.06	.03	.00
☐ 130	Drew Hill	.08	.04	.01
☐ 131	Bruce Matthews	.03	.01	.00
☐ 132	Johnny Meads	.06	.03	.00
☐ 133	Warren Moon UER	.25	.12	.02

(186 completions in '87
and 1341 career, should
be 184 and 1339)

☐ 134	Mike Munchak	.06	.03	.00
☐ 135	Mike Rozier	.06	.03	.00
☐ 136	Dean Steinkuhler	.06	.03	.00
☐ 137	Lorenzo White	.10	.05	.01
☐ 138	Tony Zendejas	.03	.01	.00
☐ 139	Gary Anderson	.03	.01	.00
☐ 140	Bubby Brister	.10	.05	.01
☐ 141	Thomas Everett	.06	.03	.00
☐ 142	Derek Hill	.10	.05	.01
☐ 143	Merril Hoge	.06	.03	.00
☐ 144	Tim Johnson	.06	.03	.00
☐ 145	Louis Lipps	.08	.04	.01
☐ 146	David Little	.03	.01	.00
☐ 147	Greg Lloyd	.06	.03	.00
☐ 148	Mike Mularkey	.10	.05	.01
☐ 149	John Rienstra	.10	.05	.01
☐ 150	Gerald Williams UER	.10	.05	.01

(Tackles and fumble
recovery headers
are switched)

☐ 151	Keith Willis UER	.03	.01	.00

(Tackles and fumble
recovery headers
are switched)

☐ 152	Rod Woodson	.08	.04	.01
☐ 153	Tim Worley	.06	.03	.00
☐ 154	Gary Clark	.15	.07	.01
☐ 155	Darryl Grant	.06	.03	.00
☐ 156	Darrell Green	.15	.07	.01
☐ 157	Joe Jacoby	.06	.03	.00
☐ 158	Jim Lachey	.06	.03	.00
☐ 159	Chip Lohmiller	.06	.03	.00
☐ 160	Charles Mann	.06	.03	.00
☐ 161	Wilber Marshall	.06	.03	.00

☐ 162	Mark May	.03	.01	.00
☐ 163	Ralf Mojsiejenko	.03	.01	.00
☐ 164	Art Monk UER	.15	.07	.01

(No explanation of
How Acquired)

☐ 165	Gerald Riggs	.08	.04	.01
☐ 166	Mark Rypien	.35	.17	.03
☐ 167	Ricky Sanders	.10	.05	.01
☐ 168	Don Warren	.06	.03	.00
☐ 169	Robert Brown	.10	.05	.01
☐ 170	Blair Bush	.03	.01	.00
☐ 171	Brent Fullwood	.06	.03	.00
☐ 172	Tim Harris	.06	.03	.00
☐ 173	Chris Jacke	.06	.03	.00
☐ 174	Perry Kemp	.06	.03	.00
☐ 175	Don Majkowski	.10	.05	.01
☐ 176	Tony Mandarich	.08	.04	.01
☐ 177	Mark Murphy	.03	.01	.00
☐ 178	Brian Noble	.03	.01	.00
☐ 179	Ken Ruettgers	.06	.03	.00
☐ 180	Sterling Sharpe	.15	.07	.01
☐ 181	Ed West	.08	.04	.01
☐ 182	Keith Woodside	.06	.03	.00
☐ 183	Morten Andersen	.06	.03	.00
☐ 184	Stan Brock	.03	.01	.00
☐ 185	Jim Dombrowski	.10	.05	.01
☐ 186	John Fourcade	.08	.04	.01
☐ 187	Bobby Hebert	.10	.05	.01
☐ 188	Craig Heyward	.06	.03	.00
☐ 189	Dalton Hilliard	.06	.03	.00
☐ 190	Rickey Jackson	.06	.03	.00
☐ 191	Buford Jordan	.10	.05	.01
☐ 192	Eric Martin	.06	.03	.00
☐ 193	Robert Massey	.06	.03	.00
☐ 194	Sam Mills	.08	.04	.01
☐ 195	Pat Swilling	.12	.06	.01
☐ 196	Jim Wilks	.03	.01	.00
☐ 197	John Alt	.10	.05	.01
☐ 198	Walker Lee Ashley	.06	.03	.00
☐ 199	Steve DeBerg	.10	.05	.01
☐ 200	Leonard Griffin	.10	.05	.01
☐ 201	Albert Lewis	.08	.04	.01
☐ 202	Nick Lowery	.06	.03	.00
☐ 203	Bill Maas	.06	.03	.00
☐ 204	Pete Mandley	.03	.01	.00
☐ 205	Chris Martin	.08	.04	.01
☐ 206	Christian Okoye	.10	.05	.01
☐ 207	Stephone Paige	.06	.03	.00
☐ 208	Kevin Porter	.10	.05	.01
☐ 209	Derrick Thomas	.25	.12	.02
☐ 210	Lewis Billups	.06	.03	.00
☐ 211	James Brooks	.08	.04	.01
☐ 212	Jason Buck	.06	.03	.00
☐ 213	Rickey Dixon	.15	.07	.01
☐ 214	Boomer Esiason	.10	.05	.01
☐ 215	David Fulcher	.06	.03	.00
☐ 216	Rodney Holman	.06	.03	.00

□ 217 Lee Johnson	.03	.01	.00
□ 218 Tim Krumrie	.03	.01	.00
□ 219 Tim McGee	.08	.04	.00
□ 220 Anthony Munoz	.10	.05	.01
□ 221 Bruce Reimers	.10	.05	.01
□ 222 Leon White	.06	.03	.00
□ 223 Ickey Woods	.08	.04	.01
□ 224 Harvey Armstrong	.12	.06	.01
□ 225 Michael Ball	.10	.05	.01
□ 226 Chip Banks	.06	.03	.00
□ 227 Pat Beach	.03	.01	.00
□ 228 Duane Bickett	.06	.03	.00
□ 229 Bill Brooks	.06	.03	.00
□ 230 Jon Hand	.06	.03	.00
□ 231 Andre Rison	.20	.10	.02
□ 232 Rohn Stark	.03	.01	.00
□ 233 Donnell Thompson	.03	.01	.00
□ 234 Jack Trudeau	.06	.03	.00
□ 235 Clarence Verdin	.06	.03	.00
□ 236 Mark Clayton	.10	.05	.01
□ 237 Jeff Cross	.06	.03	.00
□ 238 Jeff Dellenbach	.08	.04	.01
□ 239 Mark Duper	.08	.04	.01
□ 240 Ferrell Edmunds	.06	.03	.00
□ 241 Hugh Green UER	.06	.03	.00
(Back says Traded '86, should be '85)			
□ 242 E.J. Junior	.06	.03	.00
□ 243 Marc Logan	.06	.03	.00
□ 244 Dan Marino	.30	.15	.03
□ 245 John Offerdahl	.06	.03	.00
□ 246 Reggie Roby	.03	.01	.00
□ 247 Sammie Smith	.10	.05	.01
□ 248 Pete Stoyanovich	.06	.03	.00
□ 249 Marcus Allen	.10	.05	.01
□ 250 Eddie Anderson	.10	.05	.01
□ 251 Steve Beuerlein	.15	.07	.01
□ 252 Mike Dyal	.10	.05	.01
□ 253 Mervyn Fernandez	.10	.05	.01
□ 254 Bob Golic	.06	.03	.00
□ 255 Mike Harden	.03	.01	.00
□ 256 Bo Jackson	.40	.20	.04
□ 257 Howie Long UER	.06	.03	.00
(Born Sommerville, should be Somerville)			
□ 258 Don Mosebar	.06	.03	.00
□ 259 Jay Schroeder	.10	.05	.01
□ 260 Steve Smith	.06	.03	.00
□ 261 Greg Townsend	.06	.03	.00
□ 262 Lionel Washington	.03	.01	.00
□ 263 Brian Blades	.10	.05	.01
□ 264 Jeff Bryant	.03	.01	.00
□ 265 Grant Feasel	.08	.04	.01
□ 266 Jacob Green	.06	.03	.00
□ 267 James Jefferson	.06	.03	.00
□ 268 Norm Johnson	.03	.01	.00
□ 269 Dave Krieg UER	.08	.04	.01

(Misspelled Kreig on card front)			
□ 270 Travis McNeal	.08	.04	.01
□ 271 Joe Nash	.03	.01	.00
□ 272 Rufus Porter	.06	.03	.00
□ 273 Kelly Stouffer	.08	.04	.01
□ 274 John L. Williams	.08	.04	.01
□ 275 Jim Arnold	.03	.01	.00
□ 276 Jerry Ball	.06	.03	.00
□ 277 Bennie Blades	.06	.03	.00
□ 278 Lomas Brown	.03	.01	.00
□ 279 Michael Cofer	.03	.01	.00
□ 280 Bob Gagliano	.08	.04	.01
□ 281 Richard Johnson	.06	.03	.00
□ 282 Eddie Murray	.06	.03	.00
□ 283 Rodney Peete	.12	.06	.01
□ 284 Barry Sanders	.90	.45	.09
□ 285 Eric Sanders	.10	.05	.01
□ 286 Chris Spielman	.08	.04	.01
□ 287 Eric Williams	.10	.05	.01
□ 288 Neal Anderson	.15	.07	.01
□ 289A Kevin Butler ERR/ERR	.25	.12	.02
(Listed as Punter on front and back)			
□ 289B Kevin Butler COR/ERR	.65	.30	.06
(Listed as Placekicker on front and Punter on back)			
□ 289C Kevin Butler ERR/COR	.65	.30	.06
(Listed as Punter on front and Placekicker on back)			
□ 289D Kevin Butler COR/COR	.08	.04	.01
(Listed as Placekicker on front and back)			
□ 290 Jim Covert	.06	.03	.00
□ 291 Richard Dent	.08	.04	.01
□ 292 Dennis Gentry	.03	.01	.00
□ 293 Jim Harbaugh	.20	.10	.02
□ 294 Jay Hilgenberg	.06	.03	.00
□ 295 Vestee Jackson	.06	.03	.00
□ 296 Steve McMichael	.06	.03	.00
□ 297 Ron Morris	.06	.03	.00
□ 298 Brad Muster	.08	.04	.01
□ 299 Mike Singletary	.08	.04	.01
□ 300 James Thornton UER	.06	.03	.00
(Missing birthdate)			
□ 301 Mike Tomczak	.08	.04	.01
□ 302 Keith Van Horne	.06	.03	.00
□ 303 Chris Bahr UER	.03	.01	.00
('86 FGA and FGM stats are reversed)			
□ 304 Martin Bayless	.10	.05	.01
□ 305 Marion Butts	.15	.07	.01
□ 306 Gill Byrd	.06	.03	.00
□ 307 Arthur Cox	.06	.03	.00
□ 308 Burt Grossman	.06	.03	.00

☐ 309 Jamie Holland	.03	.01	.00
☐ 310 Jim McMahon	.08	.04	.01
☐ 311 Anthony Miller	.10	.05	.01
☐ 312 Leslie O'Neal	.06	.03	.00
☐ 313 Billy Ray Smith	.06	.03	.00
☐ 314 Tim Spencer	.03	.01	.00
☐ 315 Broderick Thompson	.08	.04	.01
☐ 316 Lee Williams	.06	.03	.00
☐ 317 Bruce Armstrong	.06	.03	.00
☐ 318 Tim Goad	.08	.04	.01
☐ 319 Steve Grogan	.08	.04	.01
☐ 320 Roland James	.03	.01	.00
☐ 321 Cedric Jones	.10	.05	.01
☐ 322 Fred Marion	.03	.01	.00
☐ 323 Stanley Morgan	.08	.04	.01
☐ 324 Robert Perryman	.06	.03	.00
(Back says Robert, front says Bob)			
☐ 325 Johnny Rembert	.06	.03	.00
☐ 326 Ed Reynolds	.08	.04	.01
☐ 327 Kenneth Sims	.03	.01	.00
☐ 328 John Stephens	.08	.04	.01
☐ 329 Danny Villa	.08	.04	.01
☐ 330 Robert Awalt	.03	.01	.00
☐ 331 Anthony Bell	.06	.03	.00
☐ 332 Rich Camarillo	.03	.01	.00
☐ 333 Earl Ferrell	.03	.01	.00
☐ 334 Roy Green	.08	.04	.01
☐ 335 Gary Hogeboom	.06	.03	.00
☐ 336 Cedric Mack	.03	.01	.00
☐ 337 Freddie Joe Nunn	.03	.01	.00
☐ 338 Luis Sharpe	.03	.01	.00
☐ 339 Vai Sikahema	.03	.01	.00
☐ 340 J.T. Smith	.06	.03	.00
☐ 341 Tom Tupa	.15	.07	.01
☐ 342 Percy Snow	.15	.07	.01
☐ 343 Mark Carrier	.08	.04	.01
☐ 344 Randy Grimes	.06	.03	.00
☐ 345 Paul Gruber	.06	.03	.00
☐ 346 Ron Hall	.06	.03	.00
☐ 347 Jeff George	.80	.40	.08
☐ 348 Bruce Hill UER	.06	.03	.00
(Photo on back is actually Jerry Bell)			
☐ 349 William Howard UER	.10	.05	.01
(Yards rec. says 284, should be 285)			
☐ 350 Donald Igwebuike	.03	.01	.00
☐ 351 Chris Mohr	.10	.05	.01
☐ 352 Winston Moss	.10	.05	.01
☐ 353 Ricky Reynolds	.06	.03	.00
☐ 354 Mark Robinson	.06	.03	.00
☐ 355 Lars Tate	.06	.03	.00
☐ 356 Vinny Testaverde	.08	.04	.01
☐ 357 Broderick Thomas	.10	.05	.01
☐ 358 Troy Benson	.03	.01	.00
☐ 359 Jeff Criswell	.10	.05	.01

☐ 360 Tony Eason	.08	.04	.01
☐ 361 James Hasty	.06	.03	.00
☐ 362 Johnny Hector	.06	.03	.00
☐ 363 Bobby Humphery UER	.06	.03	.00
(Photo on back is act- ually Bobby Humphrey)			
☐ 364 Pat Leahy	.06	.03	.00
☐ 365 Erik McMillan	.06	.03	.00
☐ 366 Freeman McNeil	.08	.04	.01
☐ 367 Ken O'Brien	.08	.04	.01
☐ 368 Ron Stallworth	.08	.04	.01
☐ 369 Al Toon	.08	.04	.01
☐ 370 Blair Thomas	.70	.35	.07
☐ 371 Aundray Bruce	.08	.04	.01
☐ 372 Tony Casillas	.06	.03	.00
☐ 373 Shawn Collins	.06	.03	.00
☐ 374 Evan Cooper	.06	.03	.00
☐ 375 Bill Fralic	.06	.03	.00
☐ 376 Scott Funhage	.03	.01	.00
☐ 377 Mike Gann	.03	.01	.00
☐ 378 Ron Heller	.03	.01	.00
☐ 379 Keith Jones	.06	.03	.00
☐ 380 Mike Kenn	.06	.03	.00
☐ 381 Chris Miller	.20	.10	.02
☐ 382 Deion Sanders UER	.30	.15	.03
(Stats say no '89 fumble recoveries, should be 1)			
☐ 383 John Settle	.06	.03	.00
☐ 384 Troy Aikman	.60	.30	.06
☐ 385 Bill Bates	.06	.03	.00
☐ 386 Willie Broughton	.06	.03	.00
☐ 387 Steve Folsom	.06	.03	.00
☐ 388 Ray Horton UER	.03	.01	.00
(Extra line after career totals)			
☐ 389 Michael Irvin	.30	.15	.03
☐ 390 Jim Jeffcoat	.03	.01	.00
☐ 391 Eugene Lockhart	.06	.03	.00
☐ 392 Kelvin Martin	.10	.05	.01
☐ 393 Nate Newton	.06	.03	.00
☐ 394 Mike Saxon UER	.06	.03	.00
(6 career blocked kicks, stats add up to 4)			
☐ 395 Derrick Shepard	.06	.03	.00
☐ 396 Steve Walsh UER	.10	.05	.01
(Yards Passing 50.2; Percentage and yards data are switched)			
☐ 397 Super Bowl MVP's	.20	.10	.02
(Jerry Rice and Joe Montana) HOR			
☐ 398 Checklist Card UER	.06	.01	.00
(Card 103 not listed)			
☐ 399 Checklist Card UER	.06	.01	.00
(Bengals misspelled)			
☐ 400 Checklist Card	.07	.01	.00

1990 Fleer All-Pro

The 1990 Fleer All-Pro set contains 25 standard-size (2 1/2" by 3 1/2") cards. The fronts are silver with a portrait and an action photo. The vertically oriented backs have detailed career information. These cards were randomly distributed in Fleer poly packs, approximately five per box.

	MINT	EXC	G-VG
COMPLETE SET (25)	14.00	7.00	1.40
COMMON PLAYER (1-25)	.25	.12	.02
☐ 1 Joe Montana	2.50	1.25	.25
San Francisco 49ers			
☐ 2 Jerry Rice UER	1.50	.75	.15
San Francisco 49ers			
(photo on front is			
actually John Taylor)			
☐ 3 Keith Jackson	.50	.25	.05
Philadelphia Eagles			
☐ 4 Barry Sanders	3.00	1.50	.30
Detroit Lions			
☐ 5 Christian Okoye	.60	.30	.06
Kansas City Chiefs			
☐ 6 Tom Newberry	.25	.12	.02
Los Angeles Rams			
☐ 7 Jim Covert	.25	.12	.02
Chicago Bears			
☐ 8 Anthony Munoz	.35	.17	.03
Cincinnati Bengals			
☐ 9 Mike Munchak	.25	.12	.02
Houston Oilers			
☐ 10 Jay Hilgenberg	.25	.12	.02
Chicago Bears			
☐ 11 Chris Doleman	.35	.17	.03
Minnesota Vikings			
☐ 12 Keith Millard	.35	.17	.03
Minnesota Vikings			
☐ 13 Derrick Thomas	.75	.35	.07
Kansas City Chiefs			
☐ 14 Lawrence Taylor	.60	.30	.06
New York Giants			
☐ 15 Karl Mecklenburg	.35	.17	.03
Denver Broncos			
☐ 16 Reggie White	.60	.30	.06
Philadelphia Eagles			
☐ 17 Tim Harris	.35	.17	.03
Green Bay Packers			
☐ 18 David Fulcher	.25	.12	.02
Cincinnati Bengals			
☐ 19 Ronnie Lott	.75	.35	.07
San Francisco 49ers			
☐ 20 Eric Allen	.25	.12	.02
Philadelphia Eagles			
☐ 21 Steve Atwater	.35	.17	.03
Denver Broncos			
☐ 22 Rich Camarillo	.25	.12	.02
Phoenix Cardinals			
☐ 23 Morten Andersen	.35	.17	.03
New Orleans Saints			
☐ 24 Andre Reed	.75	.35	.07
Buffalo Bills			
☐ 25 Rod Woodson	.50	.25	.05
Pittsburgh Steelers			

1990 Fleer Update

This 120-card standard size set (2 1/2" by 3 1/2") was produced and released by Fleer and featured some of the leading rookies and players who switched franchises for the 1990 season. The set was issued in its own box and was distributed through the Fleer dealers. The set is in the same design as the regular issue. The key rookies in this set are Mark Carrier,

Derrick Fenner, Eric Green, Haywood Jeffires, Rob Moore, Rodney Hampton, Johnny Johnson, and Emmitt Smith. The set is arranged in team order: Indianapolis Colts (1-4), New England Patriots (5-7), Cincinnati Bengals (8-9), New York Giants (10-14), Philadelphia Eagles (15-19), Washington Redskins (20-24), Pittsburgh Steelers (25-29), Cleveland Browns (30-32), Houston Oilers (33-36), Dallas Cowboys (37-41), Phoenix Cardinals (42-45), San Francisco 49ers (46-51), Los Angeles Rams (52-56), Atlanta Falcons (57-60), New Orleans Saints (61-63), Los Angeles Raiders (64-69), Buffalo Bills (70-73), New York Jets (74-78), Miami Dolphins (79-81), Seattle Seahawks (82-86), Kansas City Chiefs (87-91), Detroit Lions (92), Minnesota Vikings (93-95), Green Bay Packers (96-100), San Diego Chargers (101-104), Tampa Bay Buccaneers (105-108), Chicago Bears (109-115), and Denver Broncos (116-119).

	MINT	EXC	G-VG
COMPLETE SET (120)	30.00	12.00	2.50
COMMON PLAYER (U1-U120)	.05	.02	.00

☐ U1 Albert Bentley	.10	.05	.01
☐ U2 Dean Biasucci	.05	.02	.00
☐ U3 Ray Donaldson	.05	.02	.00
☐ U4 Jeff George	2.00	1.00	.20
☐ U5 Ray Agnew	.15	.07	.01
☐ U6 Greg McMurtry	.60	.30	.06
☐ U7 Chris Singleton	.30	.15	.03
☐ U8 James Francis	.70	.35	.07
☐ U9 Harold Green	1.25	.60	.12
☐ U10 John Elliott	.10	.05	.01
☐ U11 Rodney Hampton	3.00	1.50	.30
☐ U12 Gary Reasons	.08	.04	.01
☐ U13 Lewis Tillman	.10	.05	.01
☐ U14 Everson Walls	.08	.04	.01
☐ U15 David Alexander	.10	.05	.01
☐ U16 Jim McMahon	.10	.05	.01
☐ U17 Ben Smith	.15	.07	.01
☐ U18 Andre Waters	.05	.02	.00
☐ U19 Calvin Williams	.50	.25	.05
☐ U20 Earnest Byner	.10	.05	.01
☐ U21 Andre Collins	.20	.10	.02
☐ U22 Russ Grimm	.08	.04	.01
☐ U23 Stan Humphries	.15	.07	.01
☐ U24 Martin Mayhew	.15	.07	.01
☐ U25 Barry Foster	.75	.35	.07
☐ U26 Eric Green	1.50	.75	.15
☐ U27 Tunch Ilkin	.05	.02	.00
☐ U28 Hardy Nickerson	.05	.02	.00
☐ U29 Jerrol Williams	.08	.04	.01
☐ U30 Mike Baab	.05	.02	.00
☐ U31 Leroy Hoard	.60	.30	.06
☐ U32 Eddie Johnson	.10	.05	.01
☐ U33 William Fuller	.08	.04	.01
☐ U34 Haywood Jeffires	4.00	2.00	.40
☐ U35 Don Maggs	.10	.05	.01
☐ U36 Allen Pinkett	.10	.05	.01
☐ U37 Robert Awalt	.05	.02	.00
☐ U38 Dennis McKinnon	.05	.02	.00
☐ U39 Ken Norton	.30	.15	.03
☐ U40 Emmitt Smith	20.00	10.00	2.00
☐ U41 Alexander Wright	.75	.35	.07
☐ U42 Eric Hill	.10	.05	.01
☐ U43 Johnny Johnson	1.75	.85	.17
☐ U44 Timm Rosenbach	.12	.06	.01
☐ U45 Anthony Thompson	.75	.35	.07
☐ U46 Dexter Carter	.75	.35	.07
☐ U47 Eric Davis UER	.25	.12	.02
(Listed as WR on front, DB on back)			
☐ U48 Keith DeLong	.10	.05	.01
☐ U49 Brent Jones	.30	.15	.03
☐ U50 Darryl Pollard	.10	.05	.01
☐ U51 Steve Wallace	.10	.05	.01
☐ U52 Bern Brostek	.10	.05	.01
☐ U53 Aaron Cox	.10	.05	.01
☐ U54 Cleveland Gary	.15	.07	.01
☐ U55 Fred Strickland	.15	.07	.01
☐ U56 Pat Terrell	.15	.07	.01
☐ U57 Steve Broussard	.60	.30	.06
☐ U58 Scott Case	.08	.04	.01
☐ U59 Brian Jordan	1.00	.50	.10
☐ U60 Andre Rison	.60	.30	.06
☐ U61 Kevin Haverdink	.12	.06	.01
☐ U62 Rueben Mayes	.08	.04	.01
☐ U63 Steve Walsh	.15	.07	.01
☐ U64 Greg Bell	.08	.04	.01
☐ U65 Tim Brown	.12	.06	.01
☐ U66 Willie Gault	.08	.04	.01
☐ U67 Vance Mueller	.15	.07	.01
☐ U68 Bill Pickel	.05	.02	.00
☐ U69 Aaron Wallace	.30	.15	.03
☐ U70 Glenn Parker	.10	.05	.01
☐ U71 Frank Reich	.12	.06	.01
☐ U72 Leon Seals	.15	.07	.01
☐ U73 Darryl Talley	.12	.06	.01
☐ U74 Brad Baxter	.45	.22	.04
☐ U75 Jeff Criswell	.05	.02	.00
☐ U76 Jeff Lageman	.10	.05	.01
☐ U77 Rob Moore	3.25	1.60	.32
☐ U78 Blair Thomas	3.75	1.85	.37
☐ U79 Louis Oliver	.10	.05	.01
☐ U80 Tony Paige	.08	.04	.01
☐ U81 Richmond Webb	.35	.17	.03
☐ U82 Robert Blackmon	.12	.06	.01
☐ U83 Derrick Fenner	1.00	.50	.10
☐ U84 Andy Heck	.08	.04	.01
☐ U85 Cortez Kennedy	.75	.35	.07

☐ U86 Terry Wooden	.20	.10	.02
☐ U87 Jeff Donaldson	.05	.02	.00
☐ U88 Tim Grunhard	.15	.07	.01
☐ U89 Emile Harry	.15	.07	.01
☐ U90 Dan Saleaumua	.10	.05	.01
☐ U91 Percy Snow	.15	.07	.01
☐ U92 Andre Ware	.50	.25	.05
☐ U93 Darrell Fullington	.10	.05	.01
☐ U94 Mike Merriweather	.08	.04	.01
☐ U95 Henry Thomas	.05	.02	.01
☐ U96 Robert Brown	.05	.02	.00
☐ U97 LeRoy Butler	.12	.06	.01
☐ U98 Anthony Dilweg	.15	.07	.01
☐ U99 Darrell Thompson	.75	.35	.07
☐ U100 Keith Woodside	.08	.04	.01
☐ U101 Gary Plummer	.05	.02	.00
☐ U102 Junior Seau	.60	.30	.06
☐ U103 Billy Joe Tolliver	.15	.07	.01
☐ U104 Mark Vlasic	.20	.10	.02
☐ U105 Gary Anderson	.10	.05	.01
☐ U106 Ian Beckles	.15	.07	.01
☐ U107 Reggie Cobb	1.25	.60	.12
☐ U108 Keith McCants	.35	.17	.03
☐ U109 Mark Bortz	.15	.07	.01
☐ U110 Maury Buford	.05	.02	.00
☐ U111 Mark Carrier	.80	.40	.08
☐ U112 Dan Hampton	.10	.05	.01
☐ U113 William Perry	.10	.05	.01
☐ U114 Ron Rivera	.05	.02	.00
☐ U115 Lemuel Stinson	.12	.06	.01
☐ U116 Melvin Bratton	.15	.07	.01
☐ U117 Gary Kubiak	.20	.10	.02
☐ U118 Alton Montgomery	.12	.06	.01
☐ U119 Ricky Nattiel	.08	.04	.01
☐ U120 Checklist Card	.08	.01	.00

1991 Fleer

This 432-card standard size (2 1/2" by 3 1/2") set marked Fleer's second year of football sets featuring named players (not including the older AFL/NFL sets they produced between 1960 and 1963). The player cards feature a full-color action shot on the front and the back has a full-color shot along with complete statistics about the player involved. The cards have green borders on both the front and the back. Among the special subsets in the set are NFL Hitters, NFL League Leaders, and a Rookie Subset. The card numbering is alphabetical by player within teams, which are arranged

themselves in alphabetical order by conference as follows, Buffalo Bills (1-14), Cincinnati Bengals (15-29), Cleveland Browns (30-42), Denver Broncos (43-57), Houston Oilers (58-73), Indianapolis Colts (74-87), Kansas City Chiefs (88-101), Los Angeles Raiders (102-117), Miami Dolphins (118-133), New England Patriots (134-146), New York Jets (147-154), Pittsburgh Steelers (155-169), San Diego Chargers (170-182), Seattle Seahawks (183-195), Atlanta Falcons (196-211), Chicago Bears (212-226), Dallas Cowboys (227-238), Detroit Lions (239-248), Green Bay Packers (249-263), Los Angeles Rams (264-276), Minnesota Vikings (277-290), New Orleans Saints (291-304), New York Giants (305-321), Philadelphia Eagles (322-337), Phoenix Cardinals (338-351), San Francisco 49ers (352-367), Tampa Bay Buccaneers (368-381), Washington Redskins (382-395), Hot Hitters (396-407), League Leaders (408-419), Rookie Prospects (420-428), and Checklists (429-432). The key rookie cards in this set are Nick Bell, Russell Maryland, and Kenny Walker.

	MINT	EXC	G-VG
COMPLETE SET (432)	10.00	5.00	1.00
COMMON PLAYER (1-432)	.03	.01	.00

☐ 1 Shane Conlan	.06	.03	.00
☐ 2 John Davis	.12	.06	.01
☐ 3 Kent Hull	.03	.01	.00
☐ 4 James Lofton	.15	.07	.01
☐ 5 Keith McKeller	.08	.04	.01
☐ 6 Scott Norwood	.03	.01	.00
☐ 7 Nate Odomes	.06	.03	.00
☐ 8 Andre Reed	.10	.05	.01
☐ 9 Jim Ritcher	.03	.01	.00
☐ 10 Leon Seals	.03	.01	.00
☐ 11 Bruce Smith	.08	.04	.01
☐ 12 Leonard Smith	.03	.01	.00

☐ 13 Steve Tasker	.03	.01	.00
☐ 14 Thurman Thomas	.45	.22	.04
☐ 15 Lewis Billups	.03	.01	.00
☐ 16 James Brooks	.08	.04	.01
☐ 17 Eddie Brown	.08	.04	.01
☐ 18 Carl Carter	.08	.04	.01
☐ 19 Boomer Esiason	.10	.05	.01
☐ 20 James Francis	.08	.04	.01
☐ 21 David Fulcher	.03	.01	.00
☐ 22 Harold Green	.15	.07	.01
☐ 23 Rodney Holman	.03	.01	.00
☐ 24 Bruce Kozerski	.03	.01	.00
☐ 25 Tim McGee	.06	.03	.00
☐ 26 Anthony Munoz	.08	.04	.01
☐ 27 Bruce Reimers	.03	.01	.00
☐ 28 Ickey Woods	.06	.03	.00
☐ 29 Carl Zander	.03	.01	.00
☐ 30 Mike Baab	.03	.01	.00
☐ 31 Brian Brennan	.03	.01	.00
☐ 32 Rob Burnett	.08	.04	.01
☐ 33 Paul Farren	.06	.03	.00
☐ 34 Thane Gash	.03	.01	.00
☐ 35 David Grayson	.03	.01	.00
☐ 36 Mike Johnson	.03	.01	.00
☐ 37 Reggie Langhorne	.03	.01	.00
☐ 38 Kevin Mack	.06	.03	.00
☐ 39 Eric Metcalf	.06	.03	.00
☐ 40 Frank Minnifield	.03	.01	.00
☐ 41 Gregg Rakoczy	.03	.01	.00
☐ 42 Felix Wright	.03	.01	.00
☐ 43 Steve Atwater	.06	.03	.00
☐ 44 Michael Brooks	.03	.01	.00
☐ 45 John Elway	.15	.07	.01
☐ 46 Simon Fletcher	.03	.01	.00
☐ 47 Bobby Humphrey	.10	.05	.01
☐ 48 Mark Jackson	.06	.03	.00
☐ 49 Keith Kartz	.08	.04	.01
☐ 50 Clarence Kay	.03	.01	.00
☐ 51 Greg Kragen	.03	.01	.00
☐ 52 Karl Mecklenburg	.06	.03	.00
☐ 53 Warren Powers	.06	.03	.00
☐ 54 Dennis Smith	.03	.01	.00
☐ 55 Jim Szymanski	.08	.04	.01
☐ 56 David Treadwell	.03	.01	.00
☐ 57 Michael Young	.06	.03	.00
☐ 58 Ray Childress	.06	.03	.00
☐ 59 Curtis Duncan	.06	.03	.00
☐ 60 William Fuller	.06	.03	.00
☐ 61 Ernest Givins	.08	.04	.01
☐ 62 Drew Hill	.08	.04	.01
☐ 63 Haywood Jeffires	.20	.10	.02
☐ 64 Richard Johnson	.06	.03	.00
☐ 65 Sean Jones	.03	.01	.00
☐ 66 Don Maggs	.03	.01	.00
☐ 67 Bruce Matthews	.03	.01	.00
☐ 68 Johnny Meads	.03	.01	.00
☐ 69 Greg Montgomery	.06	.03	.00
☐ 70 Warren Moon	.20	.10	.02
☐ 71 Mike Munchak	.06	.03	.00
☐ 72 Allen Pinkett	.06	.03	.00
☐ 73 Lorenzo White	.06	.03	.00
☐ 74 Pat Beach	.03	.01	.00
☐ 75 Albert Bentley	.06	.03	.00
☐ 76 Dean Biasucci	.03	.01	.00
☐ 77 Duane Bickett	.03	.01	.00
☐ 78 Bill Brooks	.03	.01	.00
☐ 79 Sam Clancy	.03	.01	.00
☐ 80 Ray Donaldson	.03	.01	.00
☐ 81 Jeff George	.35	.17	.03
☐ 82 Alan Grant	.06	.03	.00
☐ 83 Jessie Hester	.10	.05	.01
☐ 84 Jeff Herrod	.06	.03	.00
☐ 85 Rohn Stark	.03	.01	.00
☐ 86 Jack Trudeau	.03	.01	.00
☐ 87 Clarence Verdin	.06	.03	.00
☐ 88 John Alt	.03	.01	.00
☐ 89 Steve DeBerg	.08	.04	.01
☐ 90 Tim Grunhard	.03	.01	.00
☐ 91 Dino Hackett	.03	.01	.00
☐ 92 Jonathan Hayes	.03	.01	.00
☐ 93 Albert Lewis	.06	.03	.00
☐ 94 Nick Lowery	.06	.03	.00
☐ 95 Bill Maas UER	.03	.01	.00
(Back photo actually			
David Szott)			
☐ 96 Christian Okoye	.08	.04	.01
☐ 97 Stephone Paige	.06	.03	.00
☐ 98 Kevin Porter	.03	.01	.00
☐ 99 David Szott	.08	.04	.01
☐ 100 Derrick Thomas	.15	.07	.01
☐ 101 Barry Word	.25	.12	.02
☐ 102 Marcus Allen	.10	.05	.01
☐ 103 Tom Benson	.06	.03	.00
☐ 104 Tim Brown	.10	.05	.01
☐ 105 Riki Ellison	.03	.01	.00
☐ 106 Mervyn Fernandez	.06	.03	.00
☐ 107 Willie Gault	.06	.03	.00
☐ 108 Bob Golic	.03	.01	.00
☐ 109 Ethan Horton	.10	.05	.01
☐ 110 Bo Jackson	.35	.17	.03
☐ 111 Howie Long	.06	.03	.00
☐ 112 Don Mosebar	.03	.01	.00
☐ 113 Jerry Robinson	.03	.01	.00
☐ 114 Jay Schroeder	.08	.04	.01
☐ 115 Steve Smith	.03	.01	.00
☐ 116 Greg Townsend	.03	.01	.00
☐ 117 Steve Wisniewski	.03	.01	.00
☐ 118 Mark Clayton	.08	.04	.01
☐ 119 Mark Duper	.06	.03	.00
☐ 120 Ferrell Edmunds	.03	.01	.00
☐ 121 Hugh Green	.06	.03	.00
☐ 122 David Griggs	.06	.03	.00
☐ 123 Jim C. Jensen	.03	.01	.00
☐ 124 Dan Marino	.25	.12	.02

☐ 125	Tim McKyer	.03	.01	.00
☐ 126	John Offerdahl	.03	.01	.00
☐ 127	Louis Oliver	.03	.01	.00
☐ 128	Tony Paige	.03	.01	.00
☐ 129	Reggie Roby	.03	.01	.00
☐ 130	Keith Sims	.06	.03	.00
☐ 131	Sammie Smith	.08	.04	.01
☐ 132	Pete Stoyanovich	.03	.01	.00
☐ 133	Richmond Webb	.06	.03	.00
☐ 134	Bruce Armstrong	.03	.01	.00
☐ 135	Vincent Brown	.06	.03	.00
☐ 136	Hart Lee Dykes	.03	.01	.00
☐ 137	Irving Fryar	.06	.03	.00
☐ 138	Tim Goad	.03	.01	.00
☐ 139	Tommy Hodson	.08	.04	.01
☐ 140	Maurice Hurst	.06	.03	.00
☐ 141	Ronnie Lippett	.03	.01	.00
☐ 142	Greg McMurtry	.08	.04	.01
☐ 143	Ed Reynolds	.03	.01	.00
☐ 144	John Stephens	.08	.04	.01
☐ 145	Andre Tippett	.06	.03	.00
☐ 146	Danny Villa	.03	.01	.00
	(Old photo wearing			
	retired number)			
☐ 147	Brad Baxter	.10	.05	.01
☐ 148	Kyle Clifton	.03	.01	.00
☐ 149	Jeff Criswell	.03	.01	.00
☐ 150	James Hasty	.03	.01	.00
☐ 151	Jeff Lageman	.06	.03	.00
☐ 152	Pat Leahy	.06	.03	.00
☐ 153	Rob Moore	.50	.25	.05
☐ 154	Al Toon	.08	.04	.01
☐ 155	Gary Anderson	.03	.01	.00
☐ 156	Bubby Brister	.08	.04	.01
☐ 157	Chris Calloway	.06	.03	.00
☐ 158	Donald Evans	.06	.03	.00
☐ 159	Eric Green	.15	.07	.01
☐ 160	Bryan Hinkle	.03	.01	.00
☐ 161	Merril Hoge	.06	.03	.00
☐ 162	Tunch Ilkin	.03	.01	.00
☐ 163	Louis Lipps	.06	.03	.00
☐ 164	David Little	.03	.01	.00
☐ 165	Mike Mularkey	.03	.01	.00
☐ 166	Gerald Williams	.03	.01	.00
☐ 167	Warren Williams	.03	.01	.00
☐ 168	Rod Woodson	.08	.04	.01
☐ 169	Tim Worley	.06	.03	.00
☐ 170	Martin Bayless	.03	.01	.00
☐ 171	Marion Butts	.10	.05	.01
☐ 172	Gill Byrd	.06	.03	.00
☐ 173	Frank Cornish	.06	.03	.00
☐ 174	Arthur Cox	.03	.01	.00
☐ 175	Burt Grossman	.06	.03	.00
☐ 176	Anthony Miller	.08	.04	.01
☐ 177	Leslie O'Neal	.06	.03	.00
☐ 178	Gary Plummer	.03	.01	.00
☐ 179	Junior Seau	.10	.05	.01
☐ 180	Billy Joe Tolliver	.08	.04	.01
☐ 181	Derrick Walker	.10	.05	.01
☐ 182	Lee Williams	.06	.03	.00
☐ 183	Robert Blackmon	.03	.01	.00
☐ 184	Brian Blades	.08	.04	.01
☐ 185	Grant Feasel	.03	.01	.00
☐ 186	Derrick Fenner	.12	.06	.01
☐ 187	Andy Heck	.03	.01	.00
☐ 188	Norm Johnson	.03	.01	.00
☐ 189	Tommy Kane	.12	.06	.01
☐ 190	Cortez Kennedy	.08	.04	.01
☐ 191	Dave Krieg	.08	.04	.01
☐ 192	Travis McNeal	.03	.01	.00
☐ 193	Eugene Robinson	.03	.01	.00
☐ 194	Chris Warren	.08	.04	.01
☐ 195	John L. Williams	.08	.04	.01
☐ 196	Steve Broussard	.10	.05	.01
☐ 197	Scott Case	.03	.01	.00
☐ 198	Shawn Collins	.06	.03	.00
☐ 199	Darion Conner UER	.08	.04	.01
	(Player on back 8			
	is not Conner 56)			
☐ 200	Tory Epps	.06	.03	.00
☐ 201	Bill Fralic	.06	.03	.00
☐ 202	Michael Haynes	.25	.12	.02
☐ 203	Chris Hinton	.06	.03	.00
☐ 204	Keith Jones	.03	.01	.00
☐ 205	Brian Jordan	.20	.10	.02
☐ 206	Mike Kenn	.03	.01	.00
☐ 207	Chris Miller	.15	.07	.01
☐ 208	Andre Rison	.15	.07	.01
☐ 209	Mike Rozier	.06	.03	.00
☐ 210	Deion Sanders	.20	.10	.02
☐ 211	Gary Wilkins	.10	.05	.01
☐ 212	Neal Anderson	.15	.07	.01
☐ 213	Trace Armstrong	.03	.01	.00
☐ 214	Mark Bortz	.03	.01	.00
☐ 215	Kevin Butler	.03	.01	.00
☐ 216	Mark Carrier	.08	.04	.01
☐ 217	Wendell Davis	.15	.07	.01
☐ 218	Richard Dent	.08	.04	.01
☐ 219	Dennis Gentry	.03	.01	.00
☐ 220	Jim Harbaugh	.10	.05	.01
☐ 221	Jay Hilgenberg	.06	.03	.00
☐ 222	Steve McMichael	.06	.03	.00
☐ 223	Ron Morris	.03	.01	.00
☐ 224	Brad Muster	.06	.03	.00
☐ 225	Mike Singletary	.08	.04	.01
☐ 226	James Thornton	.03	.01	.00
☐ 227	Tommie Agee	.06	.03	.00
☐ 228	Troy Aikman	.35	.17	.03
☐ 229	Jack Del Rio	.03	.01	.00
☐ 230	Issiac Holt	.03	.01	.00
☐ 231	Ray Horton	.03	.01	.00
☐ 232	Jim Jeffcoat	.03	.01	.00
☐ 233	Eugene Lockhart	.03	.01	.00
☐ 234	Kelvin Martin	.06	.03	.00

☐ 235 Nate Newton	.03	.01	.00
☐ 236 Mike Saxon	.03	.01	.00
☐ 237 Emmitt Smith	1.25	.60	.12
☐ 238A Danny Stubbs (Danny on back)	.10	.05	.01
☐ 238B Danny Stubbs (Daniel on back)	.10	.05	.01
☐ 239 Jim Arnold	.03	.01	.00
☐ 240 Jerry Ball	.06	.03	.00
☐ 241 Bennie Blades	.06	.03	.00
☐ 242 Lomas Brown	.03	.01	.00
☐ 243 Robert Clark	.06	.03	.00
☐ 244 Mike Cofer	.03	.01	.00
☐ 245 Mel Gray	.03	.01	.00
☐ 246 Rodney Peete	.08	.04	.01
☐ 247 Barry Sanders	.75	.35	.07
☐ 248 Andre Ware	.12	.06	.01
☐ 249 Matt Brock	.10	.05	.01
☐ 250 Robert Brown	.03	.01	.00
☐ 251 Anthony Dilweg	.08	.04	.01
☐ 252 Johnny Holland	.03	.01	.00
☐ 253 Tim Harris	.06	.03	.00
☐ 254 Chris Jacke	.03	.01	.00
☐ 255 Perry Kemp	.03	.01	.00
☐ 256 Don Majkowski UER (1990 attempts should be 264, not 265)	.08	.04	.01
☐ 257 Tony Mandarich	.06	.03	.00
☐ 258 Mark Murphy	.03	.01	.00
☐ 259 Brian Noble	.03	.01	.00
☐ 260 Jeff Query	.03	.01	.00
☐ 261 Sterling Sharpe	.10	.05	.01
☐ 262 Ed West	.03	.01	.00
☐ 263 Keith Woodside	.06	.03	.00
☐ 264 Flipper Anderson	.06	.03	.00
☐ 265 Aaron Cox	.03	.01	.00
☐ 266 Henry Ellard	.08	.04	.01
☐ 267 Jim Everett	.10	.05	.01
☐ 268 Cleveland Gary	.08	.04	.01
☐ 269 Kevin Greene	.06	.03	.00
☐ 270 Pete Holohan	.03	.01	.00
☐ 271 Mike Lansford	.03	.01	.00
☐ 272 Duval Love	.08	.04	.01
☐ 273 Buford McGee	.03	.01	.00
☐ 274 Tom Newberry	.03	.01	.00
☐ 275 Jackie Slater	.06	.03	.00
☐ 276 Frank Stams	.03	.01	.00
☐ 277 Alfred Anderson	.03	.01	.00
☐ 278 Joey Browner	.06	.03	.00
☐ 279 Anthony Carter	.08	.04	.01
☐ 280 Chris Doleman	.06	.03	.00
☐ 281 Rick Fenney	.03	.01	.00
☐ 282 Rich Gannon	.08	.04	.01
☐ 283 Hassan Jones	.06	.03	.00
☐ 284 Steve Jordan	.06	.03	.00
☐ 285 Carl Lee	.03	.01	.00
☐ 286 Randall McDaniel	.03	.01	.00
☐ 287 Keith Millard	.06	.03	.00
☐ 288 Herschel Walker	.12	.06	.01
☐ 289 Wade Wilson	.08	.04	.01
☐ 290 Gary Zimmerman	.03	.01	.00
☐ 291 Morten Andersen	.06	.03	.00
☐ 292 Jim Dombrowski	.03	.01	.00
☐ 293 Gill Fenerty	.08	.04	.01
☐ 294 Craig Heyward	.08	.04	.01
☐ 295 Dalton Hilliard	.06	.03	.00
☐ 296 Rickey Jackson	.06	.03	.00
☐ 297 Vaughan Johnson	.06	.03	.00
☐ 298 Eric Martin	.06	.03	.00
☐ 299 Robert Massey	.03	.01	.00
☐ 300 Rueben Mayes	.06	.03	.00
☐ 301 Sam Mills	.06	.03	.00
☐ 302 Brett Perriman	.06	.03	.00
☐ 303 Pat Swilling	.10	.05	.01
☐ 304 Steve Walsh	.08	.04	.01
☐ 305 Ottis Anderson	.08	.04	.01
☐ 306 Matt Bahr	.03	.01	.00
☐ 307 Mark Bavaro	.06	.03	.00
☐ 308 Maurice Carthon	.03	.01	.00
☐ 309 Mark Collins	.03	.01	.00
☐ 310 John Elliott	.03	.01	.00
☐ 311 Rodney Hampton	.40	.20	.04
☐ 312 Jeff Hostetler	.20	.10	.02
☐ 313 Erik Howard	.03	.01	.00
☐ 314 Pepper Johnson	.06	.03	.00
☐ 315 Sean Landeta	.03	.01	.00
☐ 316 Dave Meggett	.10	.05	.01
☐ 317 Bart Oates	.03	.01	.00
☐ 318 Phil Simms	.08	.04	.01
☐ 319 Lawrence Taylor	.10	.05	.01
☐ 320 Reyna Thompson	.06	.03	.00
☐ 321 Everson Walls	.03	.01	.00
☐ 322 Eric Allen	.03	.01	.00
☐ 323 Fred Barnett	.15	.07	.01
☐ 324 Jerome Brown	.06	.03	.00
☐ 325 Keith Byars	.06	.03	.00
☐ 326 Randall Cunningham	.15	.07	.01
☐ 327 Byron Evans	.03	.01	.00
☐ 328 Ron Heller	.03	.01	.00
☐ 329 Keith Jackson	.08	.04	.01
☐ 330 Seth Joyner	.06	.03	.00
☐ 331 Heath Sherman	.08	.04	.01
☐ 332 Clyde Simmons	.06	.03	.00
☐ 333 Ben Smith	.03	.01	.00
☐ 334 Anthony Toney	.03	.01	.00
☐ 335 Andre Waters	.03	.01	.00
☐ 336 Reggie White	.08	.04	.01
☐ 337 Calvin Williams	.08	.04	.01
☐ 338 Anthony Bell	.03	.01	.00
☐ 339 Rich Camarillo	.03	.01	.00
☐ 340 Roy Green	.08	.04	.01
☐ 341 Tim Jorden	.08	.04	.01
☐ 342 Cedric Mack	.03	.01	.00
☐ 343 Dexter Manley	.03	.01	.00

☐ 344 Freddie Joe Nunn	.03	.01	.00	
☐ 345 Ricky Proehl	.10	.05	.01	
☐ 346 Tootie Robbins	.03	.01	.00	
☐ 347 Timm Rosenbach	.10	.05	.01	
☐ 348 Luis Sharpe	.03	.01	.00	
☐ 349 Vai Sikahema	.03	.01	.00	
☐ 350 Anthony Thompson	.08	.04	.01	
☐ 351 Lonnie Young	.03	.01	.00	
☐ 352 Dexter Carter	.08	.04	.01	
☐ 353 Mike Cofer	.03	.01	.00	
☐ 354 Kevin Fagan	.03	.01	.00	
☐ 355 Don Griffin	.03	.01	.00	
☐ 356 Charles Haley UER	.06	.03	.00	
(Total fumbles should				
be 6, not 5)				
☐ 357 Pierce Holt	.03	.01	.00	
☐ 358 Brent Jones	.06	.03	.00	
☐ 359 Guy McIntyre	.03	.01	.00	
☐ 360 Joe Montana	.45	.22	.04	
☐ 361 Darryl Pollard	.03	.01	.00	
☐ 362 Tom Rathman	.06	.03	.00	
☐ 363 Jerry Rice	.35	.17	.03	
☐ 364 Bill Romanowski	.06	.03	.00	
☐ 365 John Taylor	.12	.06	.01	
☐ 366 Steve Wallace	.03	.01	.00	
☐ 367 Steve Young	.12	.06	.01	
☐ 368 Gary Anderson	.08	.04	.01	
☐ 369 Ian Beckles	.03	.01	.00	
☐ 370 Mark Carrier	.08	.04	.01	
☐ 371 Reggie Cobb	.15	.07	.01	
☐ 372 Reuben Davis	.06	.03	.00	
☐ 373 Randy Grimes	.03	.01	.00	
☐ 374 Wayne Haddix	.06	.03	.00	
☐ 375 Ron Hall	.03	.01	.00	
☐ 376 Harry Hamilton	.03	.01	.00	
☐ 377 Bruce Hill	.03	.01	.00	
☐ 378 Keith McCants	.08	.04	.01	
☐ 379 Bruce Perkins	.08	.04	.01	
☐ 380 Vinny Testaverde UER	.08	.04	.01	
(Misspelled Vinnie				
on card front)				
☐ 381 Broderick Thomas	.06	.03	.00	
☐ 382 Jeff Bostic	.06	.03	.00	
☐ 383 Earnest Byner	.08	.04	.01	
☐ 384 Gary Clark	.12	.06	.01	
☐ 385 Darryl Grant	.03	.01	.00	
☐ 386 Darrell Green	.10	.05	.01	
☐ 387 Stan Humphries	.08	.04	.01	
☐ 388 Jim Lachey	.06	.03	.00	
☐ 389 Charles Mann	.06	.03	.00	
☐ 390 Wilber Marshall	.06	.03	.00	
☐ 391 Art Monk	.12	.06	.01	
☐ 392 Gerald Riggs	.06	.03	.00	
☐ 393 Mark Rypien	.20	.10	.02	
☐ 394 Ricky Sanders	.08	.04	.01	
☐ 395 Don Warren	.03	.01	.00	
☐ 396 Bruce Smith HIT	.06	.03	.00	
☐ 397 Reggie White HIT	.08	.04	.01	
☐ 398 Lawrence Taylor HIT	.08	.04	.01	
☐ 399 David Fulcher HIT	.06	.03	.00	
☐ 400 Derrick Thomas HIT	.08	.04	.01	
☐ 401 Mark Carrier HIT	.08	.04	.01	
☐ 402 Mike Singletary HIT	.08	.04	.01	
☐ 403 Charles Haley HIT	.06	.03	.00	
☐ 404 Jeff Cross HIT	.06	.03	.00	
☐ 405 Leslie O'Neal HIT	.06	.03	.00	
☐ 406 Tim Harris HIT	.06	.03	.00	
☐ 407 Steve Atwater HIT	.06	.03	.00	
☐ 408 Joe Montana LL UER	.20	.10	.02	
(4th on yardage				
list, not 3rd)				
☐ 409 Randall Cunningham LL	.08	.04	.01	
☐ 410 Warren Moon LL	.10	.05	.01	
☐ 411 Andre Rison LL UER	.10	.05	.01	
(Card incorrectly				
numbered as 412 and				
Michigan State mis-				
spelled as Stage)				
☐ 412 Haywood Jeffires LL	.06	.03	.00	
(See number 411)				
☐ 413 Stephone Paige LL	.06	.03	.00	
☐ 414 Phil Simms LL	.06	.03	.00	
☐ 415 Barry Sanders LL	.25	.12	.02	
☐ 416 Bo Jackson LL	.15	.07	.01	
☐ 417 Thurman Thomas LL	.15	.07	.01	
☐ 418 Emmitt Smith LL	.50	.25	.05	
☐ 419 John L. Williams LL	.06	.03	.00	
☐ 420 Nick Bell RP	.75	.35	.07	
☐ 421 Eric Bieniemy RP	.30	.15	.03	
☐ 422 Mike Dumas RP UER	.15	.07	.01	
(Returned interception				
vs. Purdue, not				
Michigan State)				
☐ 423 Russell Maryland RP	.45	.22	.04	
☐ 424 Derek Russell RP	.25	.12	.02	
☐ 425 Chris Smith RP UER	.10	.05	.01	
(Bengals misspelled				
as Begals)				
☐ 426 Mike Stonebreaker RP	.10	.05	.01	
☐ 427 Patrick Tyrance RP	.10	.05	.01	
☐ 428 Kenny Walker RP	.45	.22	.04	
(How Acquired has a				
different style)				
☐ 429 Checklist 1 UER	.06	.01	.00	
(David Grayson mis-				
spelled as Graysor)				
☐ 430 Checklist 2	.06	.01	.00	
☐ 431 Checklist 3	.06	.01	.00	
☐ 432 Checklist 4	.07	.01	.00	

		MINT	EXC	G-VG
☐ 24	Jim Lachey UER ....15 (Acquired by trade in '87, not '88)	.15	.07	.01
☐ 25	Anthony Munoz 30	.30	.15	.03
☐ 26	Thurman Thomas 1.50	1.50	.75	.15

1991 Fleer All-Pro

This 26-card standard size (2 1/2" by 3 1/2")
set was issued by Fleer as an insert in their
1991 Football packs. The set features attractive
full-color photography.

		MINT	EXC	G-VG
	COMPLETE SET (26) 7.50	7.50	3.75	.75
	COMMON PLAYER (1-26) 15	.15	.07	.01
☐ 1	Andre Reed UER ....50 (Caught 81 passes in '89, should be 88)	.50	.25	.05
☐ 2	Bobby Humphrey 30	.30	.15	.03
☐ 3	Kent Hull 15	.15	.07	.01
☐ 4	Mark Bortz 15	.15	.07	.01
☐ 5	Bruce Smith 30	.30	.15	.03
☐ 6	Greg Townsend 15	.15	.07	.01
☐ 7	Ray Childress 15	.15	.07	.01
☐ 8	Andre Rison 60	.60	.30	.06
☐ 9	Barry Sanders 1.75	1.75	.85	.17
☐ 10	Bo Jackson 1.00	1.00	.50	.10
☐ 11	Neal Anderson 50	.50	.25	.05
☐ 12	Keith Jackson 30	.30	.15	.03
☐ 13	Derrick Thomas 50	.50	.25	.05
☐ 14	John Offerdahl 15	.15	.07	.01
☐ 15	Lawrence Taylor 50	.50	.25	.05
☐ 16	Darrell Green 30	.30	.15	.03
☐ 17	Mark Carrier UER ....30 (No period in last sentence of bio)	.30	.15	.03
☐ 18	David Fulcher UER ....15 (Bill Wyche, should be Sam)	.15	.07	.01
☐ 19	Joe Montana 1.00	1.00	.50	.10
☐ 20	Jerry Rice 90	.90	.45	.09
☐ 21	Charles Haley 15	.15	.07	.01
☐ 22	Mike Singletary 30	.30	.15	.03
☐ 23	Nick Lowery 15	.15	.07	.01

1991 Fleer Pro-Visions

This ten-card standard size (2 1/2" by 3 1/2")
set was issued by Fleer as an insert to their
1991 Football packs. The set is in the same
basic, attractive design as the Pro-Vision
baseball subset. The cards were drawn by
artist Terry Smith.

		MINT	EXC	G-VG
	COMPLETE SET (10) 6.50	6.50	3.25	.65
	COMMON PLAYER (1-10) 40	.40	.20	.04
☐ 1	Joe Montana 1.25	1.25	.60	.12
☐ 2	Barry Sanders 2.50	2.50	1.25	.25
☐ 3	Lawrence Taylor 60	.60	.30	.06
☐ 4	Mike Singletary 40	.40	.20	.04
☐ 5	Dan Marino 1.25	1.25	.60	.12
☐ 6	Bo Jackson 1.00	1.00	.50	.10
☐ 7	Randall Cunningham 60	.60	.30	.06
☐ 8	Bruce Smith 40	.40	.20	.04
☐ 9	Derrick Thomas 90	.90	.45	.04
☐ 10	Howie Long 40	.40	.20	.04

1991 Fleer Ultra

The 1991 Fleer Ultra football set contains 300 cards measuring the standard size (2 1/2" by 3 1/2"). The front design has a color action player photo, bleeding to the card sides but with silver borders above and beneath the picture. Player information is given in white lettering in the bottom silver border. The backs have a yellow fading to orange and green background, with the same silver borders as on the fronts. A color head shot of the player in a shield format is sandwiched between two smaller action shots of the player. Brief biographical information and statistics appear at the bottom of the back. The cards are numbered on the back and checklisted below alphabetically within and according to teams in the AFC and NFC as follows: Buffalo Bills (1-10), Cincinnati Bengals (11-24), Cleveland Browns, (25-32), Denver Broncos (33-43), Houston Oilers (44-55), Indianapolis Colts (56-63), Kansas City Chiefs (64-74), Los Angeles Raiders (75-85), Miami Dolphins (86-93), New England Patriots (94-99), New York Jets (100-108), Pittsburgh Steelers (109-118), San Diego Chargers (119-131), Seattle Seahawks (132-142), Atlanta Falcons (143-150), Chicago Bears (151-161), Dallas Cowboys (162-165), Detroit Lions (166-169), Green Bay Packers (170-180), Los Angeles Rams (181-190), Minnesota Vikings (191-203), New Orleans Saints (204-213), New York Giants (214-226), Philadelphia Eagles (227-236), Phoenix Cardinals (237-244), San Francisco 49ers (245-256), Tampa Bay Buccaneers (257-267), and Washington Redskins (268-278). The last subset included in this set was Rookie Prospects (279-298). The key rookie cards in this set are Nick Bell, Mike Croel, Todd Marinovich, Russell Maryland, Dan McGwire, and Mike Pritchard.

	MINT	EXC	G-VG
COMPLETE SET (300)	14.00	7.00	1.40
COMMON PLAYER (1-300)	.05	.02	.00

		MINT	EXC	G-VG
☐ 1	Don Beebe	.10	.05	.01
☐ 2	Shane Conlan	.08	.04	.01
☐ 3	Pete Metzelaars	.05	.02	.00
☐ 4	Jamie Mueller	.08	.04	.01
☐ 5	Scott Norwood	.05	.02	.00
☐ 6	Andre Reed	.10	.05	.01
☐ 7	Leon Seals	.05	.02	.00
☐ 8	Bruce Smith	.08	.04	.01
☐ 9	Leonard Smith	.05	.02	.00
☐ 10	Thurman Thomas	.50	.25	.05
☐ 11	Lewis Billups	.05	.02	.00
☐ 12	Jim Breech	.05	.02	.00
☐ 13	James Brooks	.08	.04	.01
☐ 14	Eddie Brown	.08	.04	.01
☐ 15	Boomer Esiason	.10	.05	.01
☐ 16	David Fulcher	.05	.02	.00
☐ 17	Rodney Holman	.05	.02	.00
☐ 18	Bruce Kozerski	.05	.02	.00
☐ 19	Tim Krumrie	.05	.02	.00
☐ 20	Tim McGee	.08	.04	.01
☐ 21	Anthony Munoz	.10	.05	.01
☐ 22	Leon White	.05	.02	.00
☐ 23	Ickey Woods	.08	.04	.01
☐ 24	Carl Zander	.05	.02	.00
☐ 25	Brian Brennan	.05	.02	.00
☐ 26	Thane Gash	.05	.02	.00
☐ 27	Leroy Hoard	.15	.07	.01
☐ 28	Mike Johnson	.05	.02	.00
☐ 29	Reggie Langhorne	.05	.02	.00
☐ 30	Kevin Mack	.08	.04	.01
☐ 31	Clay Matthews	.05	.02	.00
☐ 32	Eric Metcalf	.08	.04	.01
☐ 33	Steve Atwater	.08	.04	.01
☐ 34	Melvin Bratton	.05	.02	.00
☐ 35	John Elway	.15	.07	.01
☐ 36	Bobby Humphrey	.10	.05	.01
☐ 37	Mark Jackson	.08	.04	.01
☐ 38	Vance Johnson	.08	.04	.01
☐ 39	Ricky Nattiel	.05	.02	.00
☐ 40	Steve Sewell	.08	.04	.01
☐ 41	Dennis Smith	.05	.02	.00
☐ 42	David Treadwell	.05	.02	.00
☐ 43	Mike Young	.08	.04	.01
☐ 44	Ray Childress	.08	.04	.01
☐ 45	Cris Dishman	.20	.10	.02
☐ 46	William Fuller	.08	.04	.01
☐ 47	Ernest Givins	.10	.05	.01
☐ 48	John Grimsley UER	.05	.02	.00
	(Acquired line should be Trade '91, not			

Draft 6-'84)

☐ 49 Drew Hill	.08	.04	.01
☐ 50 Haywood Jeffires	.20	.10	.02
☐ 51 Sean Jones	.05	.02	.00
☐ 52 Johnny Meads	.05	.02	.00
☐ 53 Warren Moon	.20	.10	.02
☐ 54 Al Smith	.05	.02	.00
☐ 55 Lorenzo White	.08	.04	.01
☐ 56 Albert Bentley	.08	.04	.01
☐ 57 Duane Bickett	.05	.02	.00
☐ 58 Bill Brooks	.08	.04	.01
☐ 59 Jeff George	.35	.17	.03
☐ 60 Mike Prior	.05	.02	.00
☐ 61 Rohn Stark	.05	.02	.00
☐ 62 Jack Trudeau	.05	.02	.00
☐ 63 Clarence Verdin	.08	.04	.01
☐ 64 Steve DeBerg	.08	.04	.01
☐ 65 Emile Harry	.05	.02	.00
☐ 66 Albert Lewis	.08	.04	.01
☐ 67 Nick Lowery UER	.08	.04	.01

(NFL Exp. has 12
years, should be 13)

☐ 68 Todd McNair	.05	.02	.00
☐ 69 Christian Okoye	.08	.04	.01
☐ 70 Stephone Paige	.08	.04	.01
☐ 71 Kevin Porter UER	.05	.02	.00

(Front has traded
logo, but he has been
a Chief all career)

☐ 72 Derrick Thomas	.15	.07	.01
☐ 73 Robb Thomas	.08	.04	.01
☐ 74 Barry Word	.25	.12	.02
☐ 75 Marcus Allen	.10	.05	.01
☐ 76 Eddie Anderson	.05	.02	.00
☐ 77 Tim Brown	.10	.05	.01
☐ 78 Mervyn Fernandez	.08	.04	.01
☐ 79 Willie Gault	.08	.04	.01
☐ 80 Ethan Horton	.05	.02	.00
☐ 81 Howie Long	.08	.04	.01
☐ 82 Vance Mueller	.05	.02	.00
☐ 83 Jay Schroeder	.08	.04	.01
☐ 84 Steve Smith	.05	.02	.00
☐ 85 Greg Townsend	.05	.02	.00
☐ 86 Mark Clayton	.08	.04	.01
☐ 87 Jim C. Jensen	.05	.02	.00
☐ 88 Dan Marino	.25	.12	.02
☐ 89 Tim McKyer UER	.05	.02	.00

(Acquired line should
be Trade '91, not
Trade '90)

☐ 90 John Offerdahl	.08	.04	.01
☐ 91 Louis Oliver	.08	.04	.01
☐ 92 Reggie Roby	.05	.02	.00
☐ 93 Sammie Smith	.08	.04	.01
☐ 94 Hart Lee Dykes	.05	.02	.00
☐ 95 Irving Fryar	.08	.04	.01
☐ 96 Tommy Hodson	.08	.04	.01
☐ 97 Maurice Hurst	.05	.02	.00
☐ 98 John Stephens	.08	.04	.01
☐ 99 Andre Tippett	.08	.04	.01
☐ 100 Mark Boyer	.05	.02	.00
☐ 101 Kyle Clifton	.05	.02	.00
☐ 102 James Hasty	.05	.02	.00
☐ 103 Erik McMillan	.08	.04	.01
☐ 104 Rob Moore	.50	.25	.05
☐ 105 Joe Mott	.10	.05	.01
☐ 106 Ken O'Brien	.08	.04	.01
☐ 107 Ron Stallworth UER	.05	.02	.00

(Acquired line should
be Trade '91, not
Draft 4-'89)

☐ 108 Al Toon	.08	.04	.01
☐ 109 Gary Anderson	.05	.02	.00
☐ 110 Bubby Brister	.08	.04	.01
☐ 111 Thomas Everett	.05	.02	.00
☐ 112 Merril Hoge	.08	.04	.01
☐ 113 Louis Lipps	.08	.04	.01
☐ 114 Greg Lloyd	.05	.02	.00
☐ 115 Hardy Nickerson	.05	.02	.00
☐ 116 Dwight Stone	.05	.02	.00
☐ 117 Rod Woodson	.08	.04	.01
☐ 118 Tim Worley	.08	.04	.01
☐ 119 Rod Bernstine	.08	.04	.01
☐ 120 Marion Butts	.10	.05	.01
☐ 121 Gill Byrd	.08	.04	.01
☐ 122 Arthur Cox	.05	.02	.00
☐ 123 Burt Grossman	.05	.02	.00
☐ 124 Ronnie Harmon	.05	.02	.00
☐ 125 Anthony Miller	.08	.04	.01
☐ 126 Leslie O'Neal	.08	.04	.01
☐ 127 Gary Plummer	.05	.02	.00
☐ 128 Sam Seale	.10	.05	.01
☐ 129 Junior Seau	.10	.05	.01
☐ 130 Broderick Thompson	.05	.02	.00
☐ 131 Billy Joe Tolliver	.08	.04	.01
☐ 132 Brian Blades	.08	.04	.01
☐ 133 Jeff Bryant	.05	.02	.00
☐ 134 Derrick Fenner	.12	.06	.01
☐ 135 Jacob Green	.08	.04	.01
☐ 136 Andy Heck	.05	.02	.00
☐ 137 Patrick Hunter UER	.12	.06	.01

(Photos on back
show 23 and 27)

☐ 138 Norm Johnson	.05	.02	.00
☐ 139 Tommy Kane	.15	.07	.01
☐ 140 Dave Krieg	.08	.04	.01
☐ 141 John L. Williams	.08	.04	.01
☐ 142 Terry Wooden	.08	.04	.01
☐ 143 Steve Broussard	.10	.05	.01
☐ 144 Keith Jones	.05	.02	.00
☐ 145 Brian Jordan	.20	.10	.02
☐ 146 Chris Miller	.15	.07	.01
☐ 147 John Rade	.05	.02	.00
☐ 148 Andre Rison	.15	.07	.01

☐ 149 Mike Rozier	.08	.04	.01
☐ 150 Deion Sanders	.20	.10	.02
☐ 151 Neal Anderson	.15	.07	.01
☐ 152 Trace Armstrong	.05	.02	.00
☐ 153 Kevin Butler	.05	.02	.00
☐ 154 Mark Carrier	.08	.04	.01
☐ 155 Richard Dent	.08	.04	.01
☐ 156 Dennis Gentry	.05	.02	.00
☐ 157 Jim Harbaugh	.10	.05	.01
☐ 158 Brad Muster	.08	.04	.01
☐ 159 William Perry	.08	.04	.01
☐ 160 Mike Singletary	.08	.04	.01
☐ 161 Lemuel Stinson	.05	.02	.00
☐ 162 Troy Aikman	.35	.17	.03
☐ 163 Michael Irvin	.20	.10	.02
☐ 164 Mike Saxon	.05	.02	.00
☐ 165 Emmitt Smith	1.25	.60	.12
☐ 166 Jerry Ball	.05	.02	.00
☐ 167 Michael Cofer	.05	.02	.00
☐ 168 Rodney Peete	.08	.04	.01
☐ 169 Barry Sanders	.75	.35	.07
☐ 170 Robert Brown	.05	.02	.00
☐ 171 Anthony Dilweg	.08	.04	.01
☐ 172 Tim Harris	.08	.04	.01
☐ 173 Johnny Holland	.05	.02	.00
☐ 174 Perry Kemp	.05	.02	.00
☐ 175 Don Majkowski	.08	.04	.01
☐ 176 Brian Noble	.05	.02	.00
☐ 177 Jeff Query	.05	.02	.00
☐ 178 Sterling Sharpe	.12	.06	.01
☐ 179 Charles Wilson	.05	.02	.00
☐ 180 Keith Woodside	.05	.02	.00
☐ 181 Flipper Anderson	.08	.04	.01
☐ 182 Bern Brostek	.05	.02	.00
☐ 183 Pat Carter	.15	.07	.01
☐ 184 Aaron Cox	.05	.02	.00
☐ 185 Henry Ellard	.08	.04	.01
☐ 186 Jim Everett	.10	.05	.01
☐ 187 Cleveland Gary	.08	.04	.01
☐ 188 Jerry Gray	.08	.04	.01
☐ 189 Kevin Greene	.08	.04	.01
☐ 190 Mike Wilcher	.05	.02	.00
☐ 191 Alfred Anderson	.05	.02	.00
☐ 192 Joey Browner	.08	.04	.01
☐ 193 Anthony Carter	.08	.04	.01
☐ 194 Chris Doleman	.08	.04	.01
☐ 195 Rick Fenney	.05	.02	.00
☐ 196 Darrell Fullington	.05	.02	.00
☐ 197 Rich Gannon	.08	.04	.01
☐ 198 Hassan Jones	.05	.02	.00
☐ 199 Steve Jordan	.08	.04	.01
☐ 200 Mike Merriweather	.05	.02	.00
☐ 201 Al Noga	.05	.02	.00
☐ 202 Herschel Walker	.12	.06	.01
☐ 203 Wade Wilson	.08	.04	.01
☐ 204 Morten Andersen	.08	.04	.01
☐ 205 Gene Atkins	.05	.02	.00
☐ 206 Toi Cook	.10	.05	.01
☐ 207 Craig Heyward	.08	.04	.01
☐ 208 Dalton Hilliard	.08	.04	.01
☐ 209 Vaughan Johnson	.08	.04	.01
☐ 210 Eric Martin	.08	.04	.01
☐ 211 Brett Perriman	.08	.04	.01
☐ 212 Pat Swilling	.10	.05	.01
☐ 213 Steve Walsh	.08	.04	.01
☐ 214 Ottis Anderson	.08	.04	.01
☐ 215 Carl Banks	.08	.04	.01
☐ 216 Maurice Carthon	.05	.02	.00
☐ 217 Mark Collins	.05	.02	.00
☐ 218 Rodney Hampton	.40	.20	.04
☐ 219 Erik Howard	.05	.02	.00
☐ 220 Mark Ingram	.08	.04	.01
☐ 221 Pepper Johnson	.08	.04	.01
☐ 222 Dave Meggett	.10	.05	.01
☐ 223 Phil Simms	.08	.04	.01
☐ 224 Lawrence Taylor	.10	.05	.01
☐ 225 Lewis Tillman	.05	.02	.00
☐ 226 Everson Walls	.05	.02	.00
☐ 227 Fred Barnett	.15	.07	.01
☐ 228 Jerome Brown	.08	.04	.01
☐ 229 Keith Byars	.08	.04	.01
☐ 230 Randall Cunningham	.15	.07	.01
☐ 231 Byron Evans	.05	.02	.00
☐ 232 Wes Hopkins	.05	.02	.00
☐ 233 Keith Jackson	.08	.04	.01
☐ 234 Heath Sherman	.08	.04	.01
☐ 235 Anthony Toney	.05	.02	.00
☐ 236 Reggie White	.08	.04	.01
☐ 237 Rich Camarillo	.05	.02	.00
☐ 238 Ken Harvey	.05	.02	.00
☐ 239 Eric Hill	.05	.02	.00
☐ 240 Johnny Johnson	.25	.12	.02
☐ 241 Ernie Jones	.08	.04	.01
☐ 242 Tim McDonald	.08	.04	.01
☐ 243 Timm Rosenbach	.10	.05	.01
☐ 244 Jay Taylor	.10	.05	.01
☐ 245 Dexter Carter	.08	.04	.01
☐ 246 Mike Cofer	.05	.02	.00
☐ 247 Kevin Fagan	.05	.02	.00
☐ 248 Don Griffin	.05	.02	.00
☐ 249 Charles Haley	.08	.04	.01
☐ 250 Brent Jones	.08	.04	.01
☐ 251 Joe Montana UER	.45	.22	.04
(Born: Monongahela, not New Eagle)			
☐ 252 Darryl Pollard	.05	.02	.00
☐ 253 Tom Rathman	.08	.04	.01
☐ 254 Jerry Rice	.35	.17	.03
☐ 255 John Taylor	.12	.06	.01
☐ 256 Steve Young	.12	.06	.01
☐ 257 Gary Anderson	.08	.04	.01
☐ 258 Mark Carrier	.08	.04	.01
☐ 259 Chris Chandler	.08	.04	.01
☐ 260 Reggie Cobb	.15	.07	.01

□ 261 Reuben Davis	.05	.02	.00
□ 262 Willie Drewrey	.05	.02	.00
□ 263 Ron Hall	.05	.02	.00
□ 264 Eugene Marve	.05	.02	.00
□ 265 Winston Moss UER	.05	.02	.00
(Acquired line should be Trade '91, not Draft 2-'87)			
□ 266 Vinny Testaverde	.08	.04	.01
□ 267 Broderick Thomas	.08	.04	.01
□ 268 Jeff Bostic	.08	.04	.01
□ 269 Earnest Byner	.08	.04	.01
□ 270 Gary Clark	.15	.07	.01
□ 271 Darrell Green	.10	.05	.01
□ 272 Jim Lachey	.08	.04	.01
□ 273 Wilber Marshall	.08	.04	.01
□ 274 Art Monk	.12	.06	.01
□ 275 Gerald Riggs	.08	.04	.01
□ 276 Mark Rypien	.20	.10	.02
□ 277 Ricky Sanders	.08	.04	.01
□ 278 Alvin Walton	.05	.02	.00
□ 279 Nick Bell	.75	.35	.07
□ 280 Eric Bieniemy	.30	.15	.03
□ 281 Jarrod Bunch	.15	.07	.01
□ 282 Mike Croel	.75	.35	.07
□ 283 Brett Favre	.75	.35	.07
□ 284 Moe Gardner	.20	.10	.02
□ 285 Pat Harlow	.15	.07	.01
□ 286 Randal Hill	.60	.30	.06
□ 287 Todd Marinovich	1.50	.75	.15
□ 288 Russell Maryland	.45	.22	.04
□ 289 Dan McGwire	1.25	.60	.12
□ 290 Ernie Mills UER	.20	.10	.02
(Patterns misspelled as pattersn in first sentence)			
□ 291 Herman Moore	.60	.30	.06
□ 292 Godfrey Myles	.08	.04	.01
□ 293 Browning Nagle	.75	.35	.07
□ 294 Mike Pritchard	.60	.30	.06
□ 295 Esera Tuaolo	.10	.05	.01
□ 296 Mark Vander Poel	.12	.06	.01
□ 297 Ricky Watters UER	.35	.17	.03
(Photo on back actually Ray Griggs)			
□ 298 Chris Zorich	.25	.12	.02
□ 299 Checklist Card	.12	.04	.01
(Randall Cunningham and Emmitt Smith)			
□ 300 Checklist Card	.12	.04	.01
(Randall Cunningham and Emmitt Smith)			

1991 Fleer Ultra All-Stars

The 1991 Fleer Ultra All-Stars set consists of 10 standard-size (2 1/2" by 3 1/2") cards. On the fronts, a color head shot of the player in a shield format is sandwiched between two smaller action shots of the player. The card face is gold, with player information provided in a green stripe at the bottom. Within a gold border on a white background, the backs present player profile. The cards are numbered on the back and were issued as inserts into the regular 1991 Fleer Ultra packs that were sold in black boxes.

	MINT	EXC	G-VG
COMPLETE SET (10)	10.00	5.00	1.00
COMMON PLAYER (1-10)	.75	.35	.07
□ 1 Barry Sanders	3.50	1.75	.35
Detroit Lions			
□ 2 Keith Jackson	.75	.35	.07
Philadelphia Eagles			
□ 3 Bruce Smith	.90	.45	.09
Buffalo Bills			
□ 4 Randall Cunningham	1.25	.60	.12
Philadelphia Eagles			
□ 5 Dan Marino	2.00	1.00	.20
Miami Dolphins			
□ 6 Charles Haley	.75	.35	.07
San Francisco 49ers			
□ 7 John L. Williams	.75	.35	.07
Seattle Seahawks			
□ 8 Darrell Green	1.00	.50	.10
Washington Redskins			
□ 9 Stephone Paige	.75	.35	.07
Kansas City Chiefs			
□ 10 Kevin Greene	.75	.35	.07
Los Angeles Rams			

1991 Fleer Ultra Performances

This ten-card standard-size (2 1/2" by 3 1/2") set was produced by Fleer to showcase outstanding NFL football players. The front features a color action player photo, banded above and below by silver stripes but bleeding to the edge of the card on the sides. To highlight the featured player, the background and other players in the picture are washed out. Inside black and silver borders, the back presents player profile. The cards are numbered on the back and were issued as inserts into the regular 1991 Fleer Ultra packs that were sold in green boxes.

	MINT	EXC	G-VG
COMPLETE SET (10)	12.00	6.00	1.20
COMMON PLAYER (1-10)	.75	.35	.07
☐ 1 Emmitt Smith	3.75	1.85	.37
Dallas Cowboys			
☐ 2 Andre Rison	1.50	.75	.15
Atlanta Falcons			
☐ 3 Derrick Thomas	1.00	.50	.10
Kansas City Chiefs			
☐ 4 Joe Montana	2.00	1.00	.20
San Francisco 49ers			
☐ 5 Warren Moon	2.00	1.00	.20
Houston Oilers			
☐ 6 Mike Singletary	.75	.35	.07
Chicago Bears			
☐ 7 Thurman Thomas	3.25	1.60	.32
Buffalo Bills			
☐ 8 Rod Woodson	.75	.35	.07
Pittsburgh Steelers			
☐ 9 Jerry Rice	2.00	1.00	.20
San Francisco 49ers			
☐ 10 Reggie White	.90	.45	.09
Philadelphia Eagles			

1991 Fleer Ultra Update

This 100-card set was produced by Fleer and featured some of the leading rookies and players who switched franchises during the 1991 season. The front design has a color action player photo, bleeding to the card sides but with silver borders above and beneath the picture. On the backs, a color head shot of the player in a shield format is sandwiched between two smaller action shots of the player. The backs are accented in blue and green, with biography and statistics (1990 and career) at the bottom. The cards are numbered on the back and checklisted below alphabetically according to and within teams as follows: Atlanta Falcons (1-5), Buffalo Bills (6-10), Chicago Bears (11-13), Cincinnati Bengals (14-15), Cleveland Browns (16-19), Dallas Cowboys (20-22), Denver Broncos (23-25), Detroit Lions (26-29), Green Bay Packers (30-33), Houston Oilers (34-36), Kansas City Chiefs (37-39), Los Angeles Raiders (40-43), Los Angeles Rams (44-46), Miami Dolphins (47-49), Minnesota Vikings (50-51), New England Patriots (52-57), New Orleans Saints (58-61), New York Giants (62-66), New York Jets (67-69), Philadelphia Eagles (70-73), Phoenix Cardinals (74-76), Pittsburgh Steelers (77-80), San Diego Chargers (81-84), San Francisco 49ers (85-89), Seattle Seahawks (90-91), Tampa Bay Buccaneers (92-95), and

Washington Redskins (96-98). The key rookie cards in this set are Ricky Ervins, Mark Higgs, Hugh Millen, Leonard Russell, and Harvey Williams.

	MINT	EXC	G-VG
COMPLETE SET (100)	22.00	11.00	2.20
COMMON PLAYER (U1-U100)	.05	.02	.00

☐ U1 Brett Favre	.75	.35	.07
☐ U2 Moe Gardner	.20	.10	.02
☐ U3 Tim McKyer	.05	.02	.00
☐ U4 Bruce Pickens	.35	.17	.03
☐ U5 Mike Pritchard	.75	.35	.07
☐ U6 Cornelius Bennett	.12	.06	.01
☐ U7 Phil Hansen	.20	.10	.02
☐ U8 Henry Jones	.20	.10	.02
☐ U9 Mark Kelso	.05	.02	.00
☐ U10 James Lofton	.15	.07	.01
☐ U11 Anthony Morgan	.35	.17	.03
☐ U12 Stan Thomas	.12	.06	.01
☐ U13 Chris Zorich	.25	.12	.02
☐ U14 Reggie Rembert	.10	.05	.01
☐ U15 Alfred Williams	.35	.17	.03
☐ U16 Michael Jackson	.50	.25	.05
☐ U17 Ed King	.20	.10	.02
☐ U18 Joe Morris	.08	.04	.01
☐ U19 Vince Newsome	.05	.02	.00
☐ U20 Tony Casillas	.08	.04	.01
☐ U21 Russell Maryland	.50	.25	.05
☐ U22 Jay Novacek	.12	.06	.01
☐ U23 Mike Croel	.75	.35	.07
☐ U24 Gaston Green	.30	.15	.03
☐ U25 Kenny Walker	.60	.30	.06
☐ U26 Melvin Jenkins	.15	.07	.01
☐ U27 Herman Moore	.75	.35	.07
☐ U28 Kelvin Pritchett	.15	.07	.01
☐ U29 Chris Spielman	.08	.04	.01
☐ U30 Vinnie Clark	.15	.07	.01
☐ U31 Allen Rice	.05	.02	.00
☐ U32 Vai Sikahema	.05	.02	.00
☐ U33 Esera Tuaolo	.10	.05	.01
☐ U34 Mike Dumas	.20	.10	.02
☐ U35 John Flannery	.15	.07	.01
☐ U36 Allen Pinkett	.08	.04	.01
☐ U37 Tim Barnett	.30	.15	.03
☐ U38 Dan Saleaumua	.05	.02	.00
☐ U39 Harvey Williams	1.25	.60	.12
☐ U40 Nick Bell	1.25	.60	.12
☐ U41 Roger Craig	.10	.05	.01
☐ U42 Ronnie Lott	.12	.06	.01
☐ U43 Todd Marinovich	1.50	.75	.15
☐ U44 Robert Delpino	.10	.05	.01
☐ U45 Todd Lyght	.50	.25	.05
☐ U46 Robert Young	.15	.07	.01
☐ U47 Aaron Craver	.30	.15	.03
☐ U48 Mark Higgs	1.00	.50	.10
☐ U49 Vestee Jackson	.05	.02	.00
☐ U50 Carl Lee	.05	.02	.00
☐ U51 Felix Wright	.05	.02	.00
☐ U52 Darrell Fullington	.05	.02	.00
☐ U53 Pat Harlow	.08	.04	.01
☐ U54 Eugene Lockhart	.05	.02	.00
☐ U55 Hugh Millen	1.00	.50	.10
☐ U56 Leonard Russell	2.00	1.00	.20
☐ U57 Jon Vaughn	.75	.35	.07
☐ U58 Quinn Early	.05	.02	.00
☐ U59 Bobby Hebert	.12	.06	.01
☐ U60 Rickey Jackson	.08	.04	.01
☐ U61 Sam Mills	.08	.04	.01
☐ U62 Jarrod Bunch	.15	.07	.01
☐ U63 John Elliott	.05	.02	.00
☐ U64 Jeff Hostetler	.25	.12	.02
☐ U65 Ed McCaffrey	.40	.20	.04
☐ U66 Kanavis McGhee	.30	.15	.03
☐ U67 Mo Lewis	.25	.12	.02
☐ U68 Browning Nagle	.75	.35	.07
☐ U69 Blair Thomas	.75	.35	.07
☐ U70 Antone Davis	.20	.10	.02
☐ U71 Brad Goebel	.30	.15	.03
(See card U74)			
☐ U72 Jim McMahon	.10	.05	.01
☐ U73 Clyde Simmons	.08	.04	.01
☐ U74 Randal Hill UER	.45	.22	.04
(Card number on back U71 instead of U74)			
☐ U75 Eric Swann	.35	.17	.03
☐ U76 Tom Tupa	.15	.07	.01
☐ U77 Jeff Graham	.30	.15	.03
☐ U78 Eric Green	.20	.10	.02
☐ U79 Neil O'Donnell	1.25	.60	.12
☐ U80 Huey Richardson	.35	.17	.03
☐ U81 Eric Bieniemy	.25	.12	.02
☐ U82 John Friesz	.45	.22	.04
☐ U83 Eric Moten	.15	.07	.01
☐ U84 Stanley Richard	.30	.15	.03
☐ U85 Todd Bowles	.08	.04	.01
☐ U86 Merton Hanks	.12	.06	.01
☐ U87 Tim Harris	.08	.04	.01
☐ U88 Pierce Holt	.05	.02	.00
☐ U89 Ted Washington	.20	.10	.02
☐ U90 John Kasay	.20	.10	.02
☐ U91 Dan McGwire	1.25	.60	.12
☐ U92 Lawrence Dawsey	.50	.25	.05
☐ U93 Charles McRae	.30	.15	.03
☐ U94 Jesse Solomon	.05	.02	.00
☐ U95 Robert Wilson	.20	.10	.02
☐ U96 Ricky Ervins	3.50	1.75	.35
☐ U97 Charles Mann	.08	.04	.01
☐ U98 Bobby Wilson	.12	.06	.01
☐ U99 Jerry Rice	.40	.20	.04
Pro-Visions			
☐ U100 Checklist Card	.15	.05	.01
(Nick Bell and Jim McMahon)			

1992 Fleer

The 1992 Fleer football set contains 480 cards measuring the standard size (2 1/2" by 3 1/2"). The cards were available in 17-card wax packs, 42-card rack packs, and 32-card cello packs. The fronts display glossy color action photos bordered in white. The player's name appears in a color stripe at the bottom of the picture, with the team logo in a shield icon at the lower right corner. The backs carry a close-up color photo, with biography and career statistics in a box on the lower portion of the card. The cards are numbered on the back and checklisted below alphabetically according to teams as follows: Atlanta Falcons (1-16), Buffalo Bills (17-34), Chicago Bears (35-52), Cincinnati Bengals (53-62), Cleveland Browns (63-76), Dallas Cowboys (77-91), Denver Broncos (92-108), Detroit Lions (109-125), Green Bay Packers (126-140), Houston Oilers (141-157), Indianapolis Colts (158-168), Kansas City Chiefs (169-187), Los Angeles Raiders (188-206), Los Angeles Rams (207-221), Miami Dolphins (222-237), Minnesota Vikings (238-253), New England Patriots (254-268), New Orleans Saints (269-286), New York Giants (287-302), New York Jets (303-314), Philadelphia Eagles (315-328), Phoenix Cardinals (329-339), Pittsburgh Steelers (340-353), San Diego Chargers (354-369), San Francisco 49ers (370-386), Seattle Seahawks (387-399), Tampa Bay Buccaneers (400-412), and Washington Redskins (413-431). Other subsets included are Prospects (432-451), League Leaders (452-470), Pro-Visions (471-476), and Checklists (477-480).

	MINT	EXC	G-VG
COMPLETE SET (480)	17.00	8.50	1.70

COMMON PLAYER (1-480)	.03	.01	.00
☐ 1 Steve Broussard	.10	.05	.01
☐ 2 Rick Bryan	.03	.01	.00
☐ 3 Scott Case	.03	.01	.00
☐ 4 Tory Epps	.03	.01	.00
☐ 5 Bill Fralic	.06	.03	.00
☐ 6 Moe Gardner	.08	.04	.01
☐ 7 Michael Haynes	.20	.10	.02
☐ 8 Chris Hinton	.06	.03	.00
☐ 9 Brian Jordan	.15	.07	.01
☐ 10 Mike Kenn	.06	.03	.00
☐ 11 Tim McKyer	.06	.03	.00
☐ 12 Chris Miller	.15	.07	.01
☐ 13 Erric Pegram	.12	.06	.01
☐ 14 Mike Pritchard	.30	.15	.03
☐ 15 Andre Rison	.15	.07	.01
☐ 16 Jessie Tuggle	.03	.01	.00
☐ 17 Carlton Bailey	.12	.06	.01
☐ 18 Howard Ballard	.03	.01	.00
☐ 19 Don Beebe	.06	.03	.00
☐ 20 Cornelius Bennett	.10	.05	.01
☐ 21 Shane Conlan	.06	.03	.00
☐ 22 Kent Hull	.03	.01	.00
☐ 23 Mark Kelso	.03	.01	.00
☐ 24 James Lofton	.15	.07	.01
☐ 25 Keith McKeller	.06	.03	.00
☐ 26 Scott Norwood	.03	.01	.00
☐ 27 Nate Odomes	.03	.01	.00
☐ 28 Frank Reich	.08	.04	.01
☐ 29 Jim Ritcher	.03	.01	.00
☐ 30 Leon Seals	.03	.01	.00
☐ 31 Darryl Talley	.06	.03	.00
☐ 32 Steve Tasker	.03	.01	.00
☐ 33 Thurman Thomas	.40	.20	.04
☐ 34 Will Wolford	.03	.01	.00
☐ 35 Neal Anderson	.12	.06	.01
☐ 36 Trace Armstrong	.03	.01	.00
☐ 37 Mark Carrier	.06	.03	.00
☐ 38 Richard Dent	.08	.04	.01
☐ 39 Shaun Gayle	.03	.01	.00
☐ 40 Jim Harbaugh	.08	.04	.01
☐ 41 Jay Hilgenberg	.06	.03	.00
☐ 42 Darren Lewis	.15	.07	.01
☐ 43 Steve McMichael	.06	.03	.00
☐ 44 Brad Muster	.06	.03	.00
☐ 45 William Perry	.06	.03	.00
☐ 46 John Roper	.03	.01	.00
☐ 47 Lemuel Stinson	.03	.01	.00
☐ 48 Stan Thomas	.03	.01	.00
☐ 49 Keith Van Horne	.03	.01	.00
☐ 50 Tom Waddle	.15	.07	.01
☐ 51 Donnell Woolford	.03	.01	.00
☐ 52 Chris Zorich	.10	.05	.01
☐ 53 Eddie Brown	.06	.03	.00
☐ 54 James Francis	.06	.03	.00
☐ 55 David Fulcher	.03	.01	.00

☐ 56	David Grant	.03	.01	.00	☐ 113	Ray Crockett	.03	.01	.00
☐ 57	Harold Green	.15	.07	.01	☐ 114	Mike Farr	.03	.01	.00
☐ 58	Rodney Holman	.03	.01	.00	☐ 115	Mel Gray	.03	.01	.00
☐ 59	Lee Johnson	.03	.01	.00	☐ 116	Willie Green	.15	.07	.01
☐ 60	Tim Krumrie	.03	.01	.00	☐ 117	Tracy Hayworth	.10	.05	.01
☐ 61	Anthony Munoz	.10	.05	.01	☐ 118	Erik Kramer	.40	.20	.04
☐ 62	Joe Walter	.08	.04	.01	☐ 119	Herman Moore	.30	.15	.03
☐ 63	Mike Baab	.03	.01	.00	☐ 120	Dan Owens	.03	.01	.00
☐ 64	Stephen Braggs	.03	.01	.00	☐ 121	Rodney Peete	.08	.04	.01
☐ 65	Richard Brown	.10	.05	.01	☐ 122	Brett Perriman	.03	.01	.00
☐ 66	Dan Fike	.03	.01	.00	☐ 123	Barry Sanders	.75	.35	.07
☐ 67	Scott Galbraith	.12	.06	.01	☐ 124	Chris Spielman	.06	.03	.00
☐ 68	Randy Hilliard	.10	.05	.01	☐ 125	Marc Spindler	.03	.01	.00
☐ 69	Michael Jackson	.15	.07	.01	☐ 126	Tony Bennett	.03	.01	.00
☐ 70	Tony Jones	.03	.01	.00	☐ 127	Matt Brock	.03	.01	.00
☐ 71	Ed King	.03	.01	.00	☐ 128	LeRoy Butler	.03	.01	.00
☐ 72	Kevin Mack	.06	.03	.00	☐ 129	Johnny Holland	.03	.01	.00
☐ 73	Clay Matthews	.03	.01	.00	☐ 130	Perry Kemp	.03	.01	.00
☐ 74	Eric Metcalf	.06	.03	.00	☐ 131	Don Majkowski	.08	.04	.01
☐ 75	Vince Newsome	.03	.01	.00	☐ 132	Mark Murphy	.03	.01	.00
☐ 76	John Rienstra	.03	.01	.00	☐ 133	Brian Noble	.03	.01	.00
☐ 77	Steve Beuerlein	.12	.06	.01	☐ 134	Bryce Paup	.03	.01	.00
☐ 78	Larry Brown	.03	.01	.00	☐ 135	Sterling Sharpe	.10	.05	.01
☐ 79	Tony Casillas	.03	.01	.00	☐ 136	Scott Stephen	.03	.01	.00
☐ 80	Alvin Harper	.20	.10	.02	☐ 137	Darrell Thompson	.08	.04	.01
☐ 81	Issiac Holt	.03	.01	.00	☐ 138	Mike Tomczak	.08	.04	.01
☐ 82	Ray Horton	.03	.01	.00	☐ 139	Esera Tuaolo	.03	.01	.00
☐ 83	Michael Irvin	.20	.10	.02	☐ 140	Keith Woodside	.06	.03	.00
☐ 84	Daryl Johnston	.03	.01	.00	☐ 141	Ray Childress	.06	.03	.00
☐ 85	Kelvin Martin	.03	.01	.00	☐ 142	Cris Dishman	.08	.04	.01
☐ 86	Nate Newton	.03	.01	.00	☐ 143	Curtis Duncan	.03	.01	.00
☐ 87	Ken Norton	.03	.01	.00	☐ 144	John Flannery	.03	.01	.00
☐ 88	Jay Novacek	.10	.05	.01	☐ 145	William Fuller	.03	.01	.00
☐ 89	Emmitt Smith	1.25	.60	.12	☐ 146	Ernest Givins	.10	.05	.01
☐ 90	Vinson Smith	.03	.01	.00	☐ 147	Haywood Jeffires	.15	.07	.01
☐ 91	Mark Stepnoski	.03	.01	.00	☐ 148	Sean Jones	.03	.01	.00
☐ 92	Steve Atwater	.06	.03	.00	☐ 149	Lamar Lathon	.06	.03	.00
☐ 93	Mike Croel	.25	.12	.02	☐ 150	Bruce Matthews	.03	.01	.00
☐ 94	John Elway	.15	.07	.01	☐ 151	Bubba McDowell	.03	.01	.00
☐ 95	Simon Fletcher	.06	.03	.00	☐ 152	Johnny Meads	.03	.01	.00
☐ 96	Gaston Green	.20	.10	.02	☐ 153	Warren Moon	.20	.10	.02
☐ 97	Mark Jackson	.06	.03	.00	☐ 154	Mike Munchak	.06	.03	.00
☐ 98	Keith Kartz	.03	.01	.00	☐ 155	Al Smith	.03	.01	.00
☐ 99	Greg Kragen	.03	.01	.00	☐ 156	Doug Smith	.03	.01	.00
☐ 100	Greg Lewis	.15	.07	.01	☐ 157	Lorenzo White	.06	.03	.00
☐ 101	Karl Mecklenburg	.06	.03	.00	☐ 158	Michael Ball	.03	.01	.00
☐ 102	Derek Russell	.10	.05	.01	☐ 159	Chip Banks	.03	.01	.00
☐ 103	Steve Sewell	.03	.01	.00	☐ 160	Duane Bickett	.03	.01	.00
☐ 104	Dennis Smith	.03	.01	.00	☐ 161	Bill Brooks	.03	.01	.00
☐ 105	David Treadwell	.03	.01	.00	☐ 162	Ken Clark	.03	.01	.00
☐ 106	Kenny Walker	.20	.10	.02	☐ 163	Jon Hand	.03	.01	.00
☐ 107	Doug Widell	.03	.01	.00	☐ 164	Jeff Herrod	.03	.01	.00
☐ 108	Michael Young	.03	.01	.00	☐ 165	Jessie Hester	.03	.01	.00
☐ 109	Jerry Ball	.06	.03	.00	☐ 166	Scott Radecic	.03	.01	.00
☐ 110	Bennie Blades	.03	.01	.00	☐ 167	Rohn Stark	.03	.01	.00
☐ 111	Lomas Brown	.03	.01	.00	☐ 168	Clarence Verdin	.03	.01	.00
☐ 112	Scott Conover	.10	.05	.01	☐ 169	John Alt	.03	.01	.00

□ 170	Tim Barnett	.12	.06	.01	□ 227	Harry Galbreath	.03	.01	.00
□ 171	Tim Grunhard	.03	.01	.00	□ 228	David Griggs	.03	.01	.00
□ 172	Dino Hackett	.03	.01	.00	□ 229	Mark Higgs	.25	.12	.02
□ 173	Jonathan Hayes	.03	.01	.00	□ 230	Vestee Jackson	.03	.01	.00
□ 174	Bill Maas	.03	.01	.00	□ 231	John Offerdahl	.06	.03	.00
□ 175	Chris Martin	.03	.01	.00	□ 232	Louis Oliver	.03	.01	.00
□ 176	Christian Okoye	.10	.05	.01	□ 233	Tony Paige	.03	.01	.00
□ 177	Stephone Paige	.06	.03	.00	□ 234	Reggie Roby	.03	.01	.00
□ 178	Jayice Pearson	.10	.05	.01	□ 235	Sammie Smith	.08	.04	.01
□ 179	Kevin Porter	.03	.01	.00	□ 236	Pete Stoyanovich	.03	.01	.00
□ 180	Kevin Ross	.03	.01	.00	□ 237	Richmond Webb	.06	.03	.00
□ 181	Dan Saleaumua	.03	.01	.00	□ 238	Terry Allen	.30	.15	.03
□ 182	Tracy Simien	.10	.05	.01	□ 239	Ray Berry	.03	.01	.00
□ 183	Neil Smith	.03	.01	.00	□ 240	Joey Browner	.06	.03	.00
□ 184	Derrick Thomas	.15	.07	.01	□ 241	Anthony Carter	.08	.04	.01
□ 185	Robb Thomas	.06	.03	.00	□ 242	Cris Carter	.06	.03	.00
□ 186	Mark Vlasic	.08	.04	.01	□ 243	Chris Doleman	.06	.03	.00
□ 187	Barry Word	.15	.07	.01	□ 244	Rich Gannon	.06	.03	.00
□ 188	Marcus Allen	.10	.05	.01	□ 245	Tim Irwin	.03	.01	.00
□ 189	Eddie Anderson	.03	.01	.00	□ 246	Steve Jordan	.06	.03	.00
□ 190	Nick Bell	.35	.17	.03	□ 247	Carl Lee	.03	.01	.00
□ 191	Tim Brown	.06	.03	.00	□ 248	Randall McDaniel	.03	.01	.00
□ 192	Scott Davis	.03	.01	.00	□ 249	Mike Merriweather	.03	.01	.00
□ 193	Riki Ellison	.03	.01	.00	□ 250	Harry Newsome	.03	.01	.00
□ 194	Mervyn Fernandez	.06	.03	.00	□ 251	John Randle	.03	.01	.00
□ 195	Willie Gault	.06	.03	.00	□ 252	Henry Thomas	.03	.01	.00
□ 196	Jeff Gossett	.03	.01	.00	□ 253	Herschel Walker	.10	.05	.01
□ 197	Ethan Horton	.06	.03	.00	□ 254	Ray Agnew	.03	.01	.00
□ 198	Jeff Jaeger	.03	.01	.00	□ 255	Bruce Armstrong	.03	.01	.00
□ 199	Howie Long	.06	.03	.00	□ 256	Vincent Brown	.03	.01	.00
□ 200	Ronnie Lott	.10	.05	.01	□ 257	Marv Cook	.08	.04	.01
□ 201	Todd Marinovich	.60	.30	.06	□ 258	Irving Fryar	.06	.03	.00
□ 202	Don Mosebar	.03	.01	.00	□ 259	Pat Harlow	.03	.01	.00
□ 203	Jay Schroeder	.08	.04	.01	□ 260	Tommy Hodson	.08	.04	.01
□ 204	Greg Townsend	.03	.01	.00	□ 261	Maurice Hurst	.03	.01	.00
□ 205	Lionel Washington	.03	.01	.00	□ 262	Ronnie Lippett	.03	.01	.00
□ 206	Steve Wisniewski	.03	.01	.00	□ 263	Eugene Lockhart	.03	.01	.00
□ 207	Flipper Anderson	.06	.03	.00	□ 264	Greg McMurtry	.06	.03	.00
□ 208	Bern Brostek	.03	.01	.00	□ 265	Hugh Millen	.40	.20	.04
□ 209	Robert Delpino	.08	.04	.01	□ 266	Leonard Russell	.60	.30	.06
□ 210	Henry Ellard	.06	.03	.00	□ 267	Andre Tippett	.06	.03	.00
□ 211	Jim Everett	.10	.05	.01	□ 268	Brent Williams	.03	.01	.00
□ 212	Cleveland Gary	.06	.03	.00	□ 269	Morten Andersen	.06	.03	.00
□ 213	Kevin Greene	.06	.03	.00	□ 270	Gene Atkins	.03	.01	.00
□ 214	Darryl Henley	.06	.03	.00	□ 271	Wesley Carroll	.20	.10	.02
□ 215	Damone Johnson	.03	.01	.00	□ 272	Jim Dombrowski	.03	.01	.00
□ 216	Larry Kelm	.03	.01	.00	□ 273	Quinn Early	.03	.01	.00
□ 217	Todd Lyght	.15	.07	.01	□ 274	Gill Fenerty	.06	.03	.00
□ 218	Jackie Slater	.06	.03	.00	□ 275	Bobby Hebert	.08	.04	.01
□ 219	Michael Stewart	.03	.01	.00	□ 276	Joel Hilgenberg	.03	.01	.00
□ 220	Pat Terrell	.03	.01	.00	□ 277	Rickey Jackson	.06	.03	.00
□ 221	Robert Young	.03	.01	.00	□ 278	Vaughan Johnson	.03	.01	.00
□ 222	Mark Clayton	.08	.04	.01	□ 279	Eric Martin	.03	.01	.00
□ 223	Bryan Cox	.03	.01	.00	□ 280	Brett Maxie	.03	.01	.00
□ 224	Aaron Craver	.06	.03	.00	□ 281	Fred McAfee	.15	.07	.01
□ 225	Jeff Cross	.03	.01	.00	□ 282	Sam Mills	.03	.01	.00
□ 226	Mark Duper	.06	.03	.00	□ 283	Pat Swilling	.08	.04	.01

☐ 284 Floyd Turner	.03	.01	.00
☐ 285 Steve Walsh	.08	.04	.01
☐ 286 Frank Warren	.03	.01	.00
☐ 287 Stephen Baker	.06	.03	.00
☐ 288 Maurice Carthon	.03	.01	.00
☐ 289 Mark Collins	.03	.01	.00
☐ 290 John Elliott	.03	.01	.00
☐ 291 Myron Guyton	.03	.01	.00
☐ 292 Rodney Hampton	.20	.10	.02
☐ 293 Jeff Hostetler	.15	.07	.01
☐ 294 Mark Ingram	.03	.01	.00
☐ 295 Pepper Johnson	.03	.01	.00
☐ 296 Sean Landeta	.03	.01	.00
☐ 297 Leonard Marshall	.03	.01	.00
☐ 298 Dave Meggett	.08	.04	.01
☐ 299 Bart Oates	.03	.01	.00
☐ 300 Phil Simms	.10	.05	.01
☐ 301 Reyna Thompson	.03	.01	.00
☐ 302 Lewis Tillman	.06	.03	.00
☐ 303 Brad Baxter	.06	.03	.00
☐ 304 Kyle Clifton	.03	.01	.00
☐ 305 James Hasty	.03	.01	.00
☐ 306 Joe Kelly	.03	.01	.00
☐ 307 Jeff Lageman	.06	.03	.00
☐ 308 Mo Lewis	.08	.04	.01
☐ 309 Erik McMillan	.06	.03	.00
☐ 310 Rob Moore	.25	.12	.02
☐ 311 Tony Stargell	.03	.01	.00
☐ 312 Jim Sweeney	.03	.01	.00
☐ 313 Marvin Washington	.03	.01	.00
☐ 314 Lonnie Young	.03	.01	.00
☐ 315 Eric Allen	.03	.01	.00
☐ 316 Fred Barnett	.12	.06	.01
☐ 317 Jerome Brown	.06	.03	.00
☐ 318 Keith Byars	.06	.03	.00
☐ 319 Wes Hopkins	.03	.01	.00
☐ 320 Keith Jackson	.08	.04	.01
☐ 321 James Joseph	.20	.10	.02
☐ 322 Seth Joyner	.06	.03	.00
☐ 323 Jeff Kemp	.03	.01	.00
☐ 324 Roger Ruzek	.03	.01	.00
☐ 325 Clyde Simmons	.06	.03	.00
☐ 326 William Thomas	.03	.01	.00
☐ 327 Reggie White	.08	.04	.01
☐ 328 Calvin Williams	.03	.01	.00
☐ 329 Rich Camarillo	.03	.01	.00
☐ 330 Ken Harvey	.03	.01	.00
☐ 331 Eric Hill	.03	.01	.00
☐ 332 Johnny Johnson	.15	.07	.01
☐ 333 Ernie Jones	.03	.01	.00
☐ 334 Tim Jorden	.03	.01	.00
☐ 335 Tim McDonald	.03	.01	.00
☐ 336 Freddie Joe Nunn	.03	.01	.00
☐ 337 Luis Sharpe	.03	.01	.00
☐ 338 Eric Swann	.08	.04	.01
☐ 339 Aeneas Williams	.03	.01	.00
☐ 340 Gary Anderson	.03	.01	.00
☐ 341 Bubby Brister	.08	.04	.01
☐ 342 Adrian Cooper	.03	.01	.00
☐ 343 Barry Foster	.10	.05	.01
☐ 344 Eric Green	.12	.06	.01
☐ 345 Bryan Hinkle	.03	.01	.00
☐ 346 Tunch Ilkin	.03	.01	.00
☐ 347 Carnell Lake	.03	.01	.00
☐ 348 Louis Lipps	.06	.03	.00
☐ 349 David Little	.03	.01	.00
☐ 350 Greg Lloyd	.03	.01	.00
☐ 351 Neil O'Donnell	.35	.17	.03
☐ 352 Dwight Stone	.03	.01	.00
☐ 353 Rod Woodson	.06	.03	.00
☐ 354 Rod Bernstine	.06	.03	.00
☐ 355 Eric Bieniemy	.12	.06	.01
☐ 356 Marion Butts	.10	.05	.01
☐ 357 Gill Byrd	.06	.03	.00
☐ 358 John Friesz	.15	.07	.01
☐ 359 Burt Grossman	.06	.03	.00
☐ 360 Courtney Hall	.03	.01	.00
☐ 361 Ronnie Harmon	.03	.01	.00
☐ 362 Shawn Jefferson	.03	.01	.00
☐ 363 Nate Lewis	.03	.01	.00
☐ 364 Craig McEwen	.12	.06	.01
☐ 365 Eric Moten	.03	.01	.00
☐ 366 Joe Phillips	.03	.01	.00
☐ 367 Gary Plummer	.03	.01	.00
☐ 368 Henry Rolling	.03	.01	.00
☐ 369 Broderick Thompson	.03	.01	.00
☐ 370 Harris Barton	.03	.01	.00
☐ 371 Steve Bono	.40	.20	.04
☐ 372 Todd Bowles	.03	.01	.00
☐ 373 Dexter Carter	.06	.03	.00
☐ 374 Michael Carter	.06	.03	.00
☐ 375 Mike Cofer	.03	.01	.00
☐ 376 Keith DeLong	.03	.01	.00
☐ 377 Charles Haley	.06	.03	.00
☐ 378 Merton Hanks	.03	.01	.00
☐ 379 Tim Harris	.06	.03	.00
☐ 380 Brent Jones	.06	.03	.00
☐ 381 Guy McIntyre	.03	.01	.00
☐ 382 Tom Rathman	.06	.03	.00
☐ 383 Bill Romanowski	.03	.01	.00
☐ 384 Jesse Sapolu	.03	.01	.00
☐ 385 John Taylor	.10	.05	.01
☐ 386 Steve Young	.12	.06	.01
☐ 387 Robert Blackmon	.03	.01	.00
☐ 388 Brian Blades	.06	.03	.00
☐ 389 Jacob Green	.03	.01	.00
☐ 390 Dwayne Harper	.06	.03	.00
☐ 391 Andy Heck	.03	.01	.00
☐ 392 Tommy Kane	.10	.05	.01
☐ 393 John Kasay	.03	.01	.00
☐ 394 Cortez Kennedy	.06	.03	.00
☐ 395 Bryan Millard	.03	.01	.00
☐ 396 Rufus Porter	.03	.01	.00
☐ 397 Eugene Robinson	.03	.01	.00

☐ 398 John L. Williams	.06	.03	.00
☐ 399 Terry Wooden	.03	.01	.00
☐ 400 Gary Anderson	.06	.03	.00
☐ 401 Ian Beckles	.03	.01	.00
☐ 402 Mark Carrier	.06	.03	.00
☐ 403 Reggie Cobb	.12	.06	.01
☐ 404 Lawrence Dawsey	.12	.06	.01
☐ 405 Ron Hall	.03	.01	.00
☐ 406 Keith McCants	.06	.03	.00
☐ 407 Charles McRae	.03	.01	.00
☐ 408 Tim Newton	.03	.01	.00
☐ 409 Jesse Solomon	.03	.01	.00
☐ 410 Vinny Testaverde	.08	.04	.01
☐ 411 Broderick Thomas	.06	.03	.00
☐ 412 Robert Wilson	.06	.03	.00
☐ 413 Jeff Bostic	.03	.01	.00
☐ 414 Earnest Byner	.08	.04	.01
☐ 415 Gary Clark	.12	.06	.01
☐ 416 Andre Collins	.06	.03	.00
☐ 417 Brad Edwards	.03	.01	.00
☐ 418 Kurt Gouveia	.03	.01	.00
☐ 419 Darrell Green	.10	.05	.01
☐ 420 Joe Jacoby	.03	.01	.00
☐ 421 Jim Lachey	.06	.03	.00
☐ 422 Chip Lohmiller	.03	.01	.00
☐ 423 Charles Mann	.06	.03	.00
☐ 424 Wilber Marshall	.06	.03	.00
☐ 425 Ron Middleton	.10	.05	.01
☐ 426 Brian Mitchell	.12	.06	.01
☐ 427 Art Monk	.12	.06	.01
☐ 428 Mark Rypien	.20	.10	.02
☐ 429 Ricky Sanders	.06	.03	.00
☐ 430 Mark Schlereth	.12	.06	.01
☐ 431 Fred Stokes	.03	.01	.00
☐ 432 Edgar Bennett	.25	.12	.02
Green Bay Packers			
☐ 433 Brian Bollinger	.10	.05	.01
San Francisco 49ers			
☐ 434 Joe Bowden	.10	.05	.01
Houston Oilers			
☐ 435 Terrell Buckley	.75	.35	.07
Green Bay Packers			
☐ 436 Willie Clay	.15	.07	.01
Detroit Lions			
☐ 437 Steve Gordon	.08	.04	.01
New England Patriots			
☐ 438 Keith Hamilton	.10	.05	.01
New York Giants			
☐ 439 Carlos Huerta	.10	.05	.01
San Diego Chargers			
☐ 440 Matt LaBounty	.08	.04	.01
San Francisco 49ers			
☐ 441 Amp Lee	.35	.17	.03
San Francisco 49ers			
☐ 442 Ricardo McDonald	.10	.05	.01
Cincinnati Bengals			
☐ 443 Chris Mims	.15	.07	.01
San Diego Chargers			
☐ 444 Michael Mooney	.10	.05	.01
Houston Oilers			
☐ 445 Patrick Rowe	.20	.10	.02
Cleveland Browns			
☐ 446 Leon Searcy	.15	.07	.01
Pittsburgh Steelers			
☐ 447 Siran Stacy	.35	.17	.03
Philadelphia Eagles			
☐ 448 Kevin Turner	.15	.07	.01
New England Patriots			
☐ 449 Tommy Vardell	.60	.30	.06
Cleveland Browns			
☐ 450 Bob Whitfield	.15	.07	.01
Atlanta Falcons			
☐ 451 Darryl Williams	.15	.07	.01
Cincinnati Bengals			
☐ 452 Thurman Thomas LL	.17	.08	.01
Buffalo Bills			
☐ 453 Emmitt Smith LL	.50	.25	.05
Dallas Cowboys			
☐ 454 Haywood Jeffires LL	.08	.04	.01
Houston Oilers			
☐ 455 Michael Irvin LL	.10	.05	.01
Dallas Cowboys			
☐ 456 Mark Clayton LL	.06	.03	.00
Miami Dolphins			
☐ 457 Barry Sanders LL	.25	.12	.02
Detroit Lions			
☐ 458 Pete Stoyanovich LL	.03	.01	.00
Miami Dolphins			
☐ 459 Chip Lohmiller LL	.03	.01	.00
Washington Redskins			
☐ 460 William Fuller LL	.03	.01	.00
Houston Oilers			
☐ 461 Pat Swilling LL	.06	.03	.00
New Orleans Saints			
☐ 462 Ronnie Lott LL	.06	.03	.00
Los Angeles Raiders			
☐ 463 Ray Crockett LL	.03	.01	.00
Detroit Lions			
☐ 464 Tim McKyer LL	.03	.01	.00
Atlanta Falcons			
☐ 465 Aeneas Williams LL	.03	.01	.00
Phoenix Cardinals			
☐ 466 Rod Woodson LL	.06	.03	.00
Pittsburgh Steelers			
☐ 467 Mel Gray LL	.03	.01	.00
Detroit Lions			
☐ 468 Nate Lewis LL	.03	.01	.00
San Diego Chargers			
☐ 469 Steve Young LL	.08	.04	.01
San Francisco 49ers			
☐ 470 Reggie Roby LL	.03	.01	.00
Miami Dolphins			
☐ 471 John Elway PV	.10	.05	.01
Denver Broncos			

		MINT	EXC	G-VG
☐ 472	Ronnie Lott PV	.08	.04	.01
	Los Angeles Raiders			
☐ 473	Art Monk PV	.08	.04	.01
	Washington Redskins			
☐ 474	Warren Moon PV	.12	.06	.01
	Houston Oilers			
☐ 475	Emmitt Smith PV	.50	.25	.05
	Dallas Cowboys			
☐ 476	Thurman Thomas PV	.17	.08	.01
	Buffalo Bills			
☐ 477	Checklist Card	.06	.01	.00
☐ 478	Checklist Card	.06	.01	.00
☐ 479	Checklist Card	.06	.01	.00
☐ 480	Checklist Card	.06	.01	.00

1992 Fleer All-Pro

This 24-card subset was available in Fleer's wax packs. The cards measure the standard size (2 1/2" by 3 1/2"). On a dark blue card face, the fronts feature color player cut outs superimposed on a red, white, and blue NFL logo emblem. The player's name and position appear in gold foil lettering at the lower left corner. The backs carry a color head shot and player profile on a pink background. The cards are numbered on the back.

		MINT	EXC	G-VG
COMPLETE SET (24)		22.00	11.00	2.20
COMMON PLAYER (1-24)		.75	.35	.07
☐ 1	Marv Cook	1.00	.50	.10
	New England Patriots			
☐ 2	Mike Kenn	.75	.35	.07
	Atlanta Falcons			
☐ 3	Steve Wisniewski	.75	.35	.07
	Los Angeles Raiders			
☐ 4	Jim Ritcher	.75	.35	.07
	Buffalo Bills			
☐ 5	Jim Lachey	.75	.35	.07
	Washington Redskins			
☐ 6	Michael Irvin	2.00	1.00	.20
	Dallas Cowboys			
☐ 7	Andre Rison	1.50	.75	.15
	Dallas Cowboys			
☐ 8	Thurman Thomas	4.00	2.00	.40
	Buffalo Bills			
☐ 9	Barry Sanders	5.50	2.75	.55
	Detroit Lions			
☐ 10	Bruce Matthews	.75	.35	.07
	Houston Oilers			
☐ 11	Mark Rypien	2.00	1.00	.20
	Washington Redskins			
☐ 12	Jeff Jaeger	.75	.35	.07
	Los Angeles Raiders			
☐ 13	Reggie White	1.00	.50	.10
	Philadelphia Eagles			
☐ 14	Clyde Simmons	.75	.35	.07
	Philadelphia Eagles			
☐ 15	Pat Swilling	1.00	.50	.10
	New Orleans Saints			
☐ 16	Sam Mills	.75	.35	.07
	New Orleans Saints			
☐ 17	Ray Childress	.75	.35	.07
	Houston Oilers			
☐ 18	Jerry Ball	.75	.35	.07
	Detroit Lions			
☐ 19	Derrick Thomas	1.75	.85	.17
	Kansas City Chiefs			
☐ 20	Darrell Green	1.00	.50	.10
	Washington Redskins			
☐ 21	Ronnie Lott	1.25	.60	.12
	Los Angeles Raiders			
☐ 22	Steve Atwater	.75	.35	.07
	Denver Broncos			
☐ 23	Mark Carrier	1.00	.50	.10
	Chicago Bears			
☐ 24	Jeff Gossett	.75	.35	.07
	Los Angeles Raiders			

1992 Fleer Mark Rypien

This 12-card "Performance Highlights" subset chronicles the career of Mark Rypien, Super Bowl XXVI's Most Valuable Player. Each card

is gold-foil stamped. Rypien autographed over 2,000 of his cards, which were randomly inserted in wax, rack, and cello packs. Moreover, collectors could obtain three additional cards of him by mailing in 10 Fleer pack proofs of purchase. The cards measure the standard size (2 1/2" by 3 1/2"). On a dark blue card face, the fronts feature color action photos outlined in the team's colors. The words "Mark Rypien Performance Highlights" appear in gold lettering above the picture. The backs carry capsule summaries of different phases of Rypien's career. The cards are numbered on the back.

	MINT	EXC	G-VG
COMPLETE SET (12)	10.00	5.00	1.00
COMMON PLAYER (1-12)	1.00	.50	.10
□ 1 A Matter of Faith	1.00	.50	.10
□ 2 Mr. Everything	1.00	.50	.10
□ 3 Great Expectations	1.00	.50	.10
□ 4 Hills and Valleys	1.00	.50	.10
□ 5 Breakout Season	1.00	.50	.10
□ 6 The End of the Beginning	1.00	.50	.10
□ 7 Bowled Over	1.00	.50	.10
□ 8 Watching and Waiting	1.00	.50	.10
□ 9 QB Controversy	1.00	.50	.10
□ 10 Redemption	1.00	.50	.10
□ 11 Pain and Pressure	1.00	.50	.10
□ 12 Jubilation	1.00	.50	.10

1992 Fleer Rookie Sensations

This 20-card subset was inserted in 1992 Fleer cello packs. The cards measure the standard size (2 1/2" by 3 1/2"). The color action player photos on the fronts are slightly tilted to the left and have shadow borders on the left and bottom. The card face is designed like a football field, with a green background sectioned off by white yard line markers. At the card top, the words "Rookie Sensations" are accented by gold foil stripes representing the flight of a football, while the player's name appears in gold foil lettering below the picture. The backs have a similar design to the fronts and present career summary. The cards are numbered on the back.

	MINT	EXC	G-VG
COMPLETE SET (20)	100.00	50.00	10.00
COMMON PLAYER (1-20)	4.50	2.25	.45
□ 1 Moe Gardner Atlanta Falcons	5.00	2.50	.50
□ 2 Mike Pritchard Atlanta Falcons	9.00	4.50	.90
□ 3 Stan Thomas Chicago Bears	4.50	2.25	.45
□ 4 Larry Brown Dallas Cowboys	4.50	2.25	.45
□ 5 Todd Lyght Los Angeles Rams	6.00	3.00	.60
□ 6 James Joseph Philadelphia Eagles	7.00	3.50	.70
□ 7 Aeneas Williams Phoenix Cardinals	5.00	2.50	.50
□ 8 Michael Jackson Cleveland Browns	6.00	3.00	.60

☐ 9 Ed King	4.50	2.25	.45
Cleveland Browns			
☐ 10 Mike Croel	8.00	4.00	.80
Denver Broncos			
☐ 11 Kenny Walker	8.00	4.00	.80
Denver Broncos			
☐ 12 Tim Barnett	5.00	2.50	.50
Kansas City Chiefs			
☐ 13 Nick Bell	10.00	5.00	1.00
Los Angeles Raiders			
☐ 14 Todd Marinovich	12.00	6.00	1.20
Los Angeles Raiders			
☐ 15 Leonard Russell	12.00	6.00	1.20
New England Patriots			
☐ 16 Pat Harlow	4.50	2.25	.45
New England Patriots			
☐ 17 Mo Lewis	5.00	2.50	.50
New York Jets			
☐ 18 John Kasay	4.50	2.25	.45
Seattle Seahawks			
☐ 19 Lawrence Dawsey	6.00	3.00	.60
Tampa Bay Buccaneers			
☐ 20 Charles McRae	4.50	2.25	.45
Tampa Bay Buccaneers			

1992 Fleer Team Leaders

This 24-card subset was inserted in 1992 Fleer rack packs. The cards measure the standard size (2 1/2" by 3 1/2"). The color action player photos on the fronts are bordered in black. The player's name, team, position, and a "Team Leader" logo appear in gold foil lettering toward the bottom of the card face. On a light grayish-blue background, the backs

feature a color head shot in an oval frame and present career summary. The cards are numbered on the back.

	MINT	EXC	G-VG
COMPLETE SET (24)	30.00	15.00	3.00
COMMON PLAYER (1-24)	1.00	.50	.10
☐ 1 Chris Miller	2.00	1.00	.20
Atlanta Falcons			
☐ 2 Neal Anderson	2.00	1.00	.20
Chicago Bears			
☐ 3 Emmitt Smith	6.00	3.00	.60
Dallas Cowboys			
☐ 4 Chris Spielman	1.00	.50	.10
Detroit Lions			
☐ 5 Brian Noble	1.00	.50	.10
Green Bay Packers			
☐ 6 Jim Everett	1.50	.75	.15
Los Angeles Rams			
☐ 7 Joey Browner	1.25	.60	.12
Minnesota Vikings			
☐ 8 Sam Mills	1.00	.50	.10
New Orleans Saints			
☐ 9 Rodney Hampton	2.50	1.25	.25
New York Giants			
☐ 10 Reggie White	1.50	.75	.15
Philadelphia Eagles			
☐ 11 Tim McDonald	1.00	.50	.10
Phoenix Cardinals			
☐ 12 Charles Haley	1.25	.60	.12
San Francisco 49ers			
☐ 13 Mark Rypien	2.50	1.25	.25
Washington Redskins			
☐ 14 Cornelius Bennett	1.50	.75	.15
Buffalo Bills			
☐ 15 Clay Matthews	1.00	.50	.10
Cleveland Browns			
☐ 16 John Elway	2.00	1.00	.20
Denver Broncos			
☐ 17 Warren Moon	2.50	1.25	.25
Houston Oilers			
☐ 18 Derrick Thomas	2.00	1.00	.20
Kansas City Chiefs			
☐ 19 Greg Townsend	1.00	.50	.10
Los Angeles Raiders			
☐ 20 Bruce Armstrong	1.00	.50	.10
New England Patriots			
☐ 21 Brad Baxter	1.25	.60	.12
New York Jets			
☐ 22 Rod Woodson	1.25	.60	.12
Pittsburgh Steelers			
☐ 23 Marion Butts	1.50	.75	.15
San Diego Chargers			
☐ 24 Rufus Porter	1.00	.50	.10
Seattle Seahawks			

1948 Leaf

The 1948 Leaf set of 98 cards features black and white flesh areas and solid color backgrounds. The cards measure approximately 2 3/8" by 2 7/8". The cards can be found on either gray or cream colored card stock. The second 49 cards of this set are more difficult to obtain than the first 49 cards. This set features the Rookie Cards of many football stars since it was, along with the 1948 Bowman set, the first major post-war set of football cards. The first cards of Sammy Baugh, Chuck Bednarik, Charlie Conerly, Jackie Jensen, Bobby Layne, Sid Luckman, Leo Nomellini, Steve Van Buren, Doak Walker, and Bob Waterfield, among others, are featured in this set. The card backs say "Copyright 1948".

	NRMT	VG-E	GOOD
COMPLETE SET (98)	5600.00	2650.00	850.00
COMMON PLAYER (1-49)	15.00	7.50	1.50
COMMON PLAYER (50-98)	75.00	37.50	7.50
☐ 1 Sid Luckman	225.00	75.00	15.00
Chicago Bears			
☐ 2 Steve Suhey	18.00	9.00	1.80
Pittsburgh Steelers			
☐ 3A Bulldog Turner	85.00	42.50	8.50
Chicago Bears			
(reddish background)			
☐ 3B Bulldog Turner	85.00	42.50	8.50
Chicago Bears			
(white background)			
☐ 4 Doak Walker	90.00	45.00	9.00
Southern Methodist			
☐ 5 Levi Jackson	18.00	9.00	1.80
Yale			
☐ 6 Bobby Layne	200.00	100.00	20.00
Chicago Bears			
☐ 7 Bill Fischer	15.00	7.50	1.50
Notre Dame			
☐ 8A Vince Banonis	18.00	9.00	1.80
Chicago Cardinals			
(white name on front)			
☐ 8B Vince Banonis	18.00	9.00	1.80
Chicago Cardinals			
(black name on front)			
☐ 9 Tommy Thompson	30.00	15.00	3.00
Philadelphia Eagles			
☐ 10 Perry Moss	15.00	7.50	1.50
Green Bay Packers			
☐ 11 Terry Brennan	22.00	11.00	2.20
Notre Dame			
☐ 12A William Swiacki	18.00	9.00	1.80
New York Giants			
(white name on front)			
☐ 12B William Swiacki	18.00	9.00	1.80
New York Giants			
(black name on front)			
☐ 13 Johnny Lujack	90.00	45.00	9.00
Chicago Bears			
☐ 14A Mal Kutner	18.00	9.00	1.80
Chicago Cardinals			
(white name on front)			
☐ 14B Mal Kutner	18.00	9.00	1.80
Chicago Cardinals			
(black name on front)			
☐ 15 Charlie Justice	50.00	25.00	5.00
North Carolina			
☐ 16 Pete Pihos	60.00	30.00	6.00
Philadelphia Eagles			
☐ 17A Kenny Washington	27.00	13.50	2.70
Los Angeles Rams			
(white name on front)			
☐ 17B Kenny Washington	27.00	13.50	2.70
Los Angeles Rams			
(black name on front)			
☐ 18 Harry Gilmer	24.00	12.00	2.40
Washington Redskins			
☐ 19A George McAfee ERR	100.00	50.00	10.00
(listed as Gorgeous			
George on front)			
Chicago Bears			
☐ 19B George McAfee COR	65.00	32.50	6.50
Chicago Bears			
☐ 20 George Taliaferro	24.00	12.00	2.40
Indiana			
☐ 21 Paul Christman	35.00	17.50	3.50
Chicago Cardinals			
☐ 22 Steve Van Buren	100.00	50.00	10.00
Philadelphia Eagles			
☐ 23 Ken Kavanaugh	27.00	13.50	2.70
Chicago Bears			
☐ 24 Jim Martin	25.00	12.50	2.50
Notre Dame			
☐ 25 Bud Angsman	15.00	7.50	1.50
Chicago Cardinals			

☐ 26 Bob Waterfield 120.00   60.00   12.00
Los Angeles Rams
☐ 27A Fred Davis 15.00   7.50   1.50
Chicago Bears
(yellow background)
☐ 27B Fred Davis 15.00   7.50   1.50
Chicago Bears
(white background)
☐ 28 Whitey Wistert 18.00   9.00   1.80
Philadelphia Eagles
☐ 29 Charlie Trippi 65.00   32.50   6.50
Chicago Cardinals
☐ 30 Paul Governali 15.00   7.50   1.50
New York Giants
☐ 31 Tom McWilliams 15.00   7.50   1.50
Mississippi State
☐ 32 Larry Zimmerman 15.00   7.50   1.50
Boston Yanks
☐ 33 Pat Harder UER 24.00   12.00   2.40
Chicago Cardinals
☐ 34 Sammy Baugh 275.00   135.00   27.00
Washington Redskins
☐ 35 Ted Fritsch Sr. 18.00   9.00   1.80
Green Bay Packers
☐ 36 Bill Dudley 60.00   30.00   6.00
Detroit Lions
☐ 37 George Connor 60.00   30.00   6.00
Chicago Bears
☐ 38 Frank Dancewicz 15.00   7.50   1.50
Boston Yanks
☐ 39 Billy Dewell 15.00   7.50   1.50
Chicago Cardinals
☐ 40 John Nolan 15.00   7.50   1.50
Boston Yanks
☐ 41A Harry Szulborski 15.00   7.50   1.50
Purdue
(yellow jersey)
☐ 41B Harry Szulborski 15.00   7.50   1.50
Purdue
(orange jersey)
☐ 42 Tex Coulter 18.00   9.00   1.80
New York Giants
☐ 43 Robert Nussbaumer 15.00   7.50   1.50
Washington Redskins
☐ 44 Bob Mann 15.00   7.50   1.50
Detroit Lions
☐ 45 Jim White 15.00   7.50   1.50
New York Giants
☐ 46 Jack Jacobs 18.00   9.00   1.80
Green Bay Packers
☐ 47 John Clement 15.00   7.50   1.50
Pittsburgh Steelers
☐ 48 Frank Reagan 15.00   7.50   1.50
New York Giants
☐ 49 Frank Tripucka 40.00   20.00   4.00
Notre Dame
☐ 50 John Rauch 75.00   37.50   7.50
Georgia
☐ 51 Mike Dimitro 75.00   37.50   7.50
UCLA
☐ 52 Leo Nomellini 200.00   100.00   20.00
Minnesota
☐ 53 Charley Conerly 225.00   110.00   22.00
New York Giants
☐ 54 Chuck Bednarik 225.00   110.00   22.00
Pennsylvania
☐ 55 Chick Jagade 75.00   37.50   7.50
Indiana
☐ 56 Bob Folsom 75.00   37.50   7.50
SMU
☐ 57 Eugene Rossides 75.00   37.50   7.50
Columbia
☐ 58 Art Weiner 75.00   37.50   7.50
No. Carolina
☐ 59 Alex Sarkistian 75.00   37.50   7.50
Northwestern
☐ 60 Dick Harris 75.00   37.50   7.50
University of Texas
☐ 61 Len Younce 75.00   37.50   7.50
New York Giants
☐ 62 Gene Derricotte 75.00   37.50   7.50
Michigan
☐ 63 Roy Steiner 75.00   37.50   7.50
Alabama
☐ 64 Frank Seno 75.00   37.50   7.50
Boston Yanks
☐ 65 Bob Hendren 75.00   37.50   7.50
USC
☐ 66 Jack Cloud 75.00   37.50   7.50
William and Mary
☐ 67 Harrell Collins 75.00   37.50   7.50
Louisiana State U.
☐ 68 Clyde LeForce 75.00   37.50   7.50
Detroit Lions
☐ 69 Larry Joe 75.00   37.50   7.50
Penn State
☐ 70 Phil O'Reilly 75.00   37.50   7.50
Purdue
☐ 71 Paul Campbell 75.00   37.50   7.50
Texas
☐ 72 Ray Evans 75.00   37.50   7.50
Pittsburgh Steelers
☐ 73 Jackie Jensen 225.00   110.00   22.00
California
☐ 74 Russ Steger 75.00   37.50   7.50
Illinois
☐ 75 Tony Minisi 75.00   37.50   7.50
New York Giants
☐ 76 Clayton Tonnemaker ... 75.00   37.50   7.50
Minnesota
☐ 77 George Savitsky 75.00   37.50   7.50
Philadelphia Eagles
☐ 78 Clarence Self 75.00   37.50   7.50
Wisconsin

☐ 79	Rod Franz .... California	75.00	37.50	7.50
☐ 80	Jim Youle .... Boston Yanks	75.00	37.50	7.50
☐ 81	Billy Bye .... Minnesota	75.00	37.50	7.50
☐ 82	Fred Enke .... Detroit Lions	75.00	37.50	7.50
☐ 83	Fred Folger .... Duke	75.00	37.50	7.50
☐ 84	Jug Girard .... Green Bay Packers	75.00	37.50	7.50
☐ 85	Joe Scott .... New York Giants	75.00	37.50	7.50
☐ 86	Bob Demoss .... Purdue	75.00	37.50	7.50
☐ 87	Dave Templeton .... Ohio State	75.00	37.50	7.50
☐ 88	Herb Siegert .... Illinois	75.00	37.50	7.50
☐ 89	Bucky O'Conner .... Los Angeles Rams	75.00	37.50	7.50
☐ 90	Joe Whisler .... Ohio State	75.00	37.50	7.50
☐ 91	Leon Hart .... Notre Dame	120.00	60.00	12.00
☐ 92	Earl Banks .... Iowa	75.00	37.50	7.50
☐ 93	Frank Aschenbrenner .. Northwestern	75.00	37.50	7.50
☐ 94	John Goldsberry .... Indiana	75.00	37.50	7.50
☐ 95	Porter Payne .... Georgia	75.00	37.50	7.50
☐ 96	Pete Perini .... Ohio State	75.00	37.50	7.50
☐ 97	Jay Rhodemyre .... Green Bay Packers	75.00	37.50	7.50
☐ 98	Al DiMarco .... Iowa	135.00	45.00	9.00

1949 Leaf

The 1949 Leaf set is skip-numbered from number 1 to number 150. The set contains 49 cards. The set is styled very similarly to the other Leaf sets of the 1948-49 era. The cards measure approximately 2 3/8" by 2 7/8". The cards can be found on either gray or cream colored card stock. The card backs detail an offer to send in five wrappers and a dime for a

12" by 6" felt pennant of one of the teams listed on the different card backs including college and pro teams. There are no key rookie cards in this set as virtually all of the players in the 1949 set were also in the 1948 Leaf set as well. The card backs say "Copyright 1949".

	NRMT	VG-E	GOOD
COMPLETE SET (49)	1500.00	650.00	175.00
COMMON PLAYER (1-150) ...	16.00	8.00	1.60
☐ 1 Bob Hendren .... Washington Redskins	60.00	10.00	2.00
☐ 2 Joe Scott .... New York Giants	16.00	8.00	1.60
☐ 3 Frank Reagan .... Philadelphia Eagles	16.00	8.00	1.60
☐ 4 John Rauch .... New York Bulldogs	16.00	8.00	1.60
☐ 7 Bill Fischer .... Chicago Cardinals	16.00	8.00	1.60
☐ 9 Bud Angsman .... Chicago Cardinals	16.00	8.00	1.60
☐ 10 Billy Dewell .... Chicago Cardinals	16.00	8.00	1.60
☐ 13 Tommy Thompson .... Philadelphia Eagles	25.00	12.50	2.50
☐ 15 Sid Luckman .... Chicago Bears	90.00	45.00	9.00
☐ 16 Charlie Trippi .... Chicago Cardinals	32.00	16.00	3.20
☐ 17 Bob Mann .... Detroit Lions	16.00	8.00	1.60
☐ 19 Paul Christman .... Chicago Cardinals	25.00	12.50	2.50
☐ 22 Bill Dudley .... Detroit Lions	32.00	16.00	3.20
☐ 23 Clyde LeForce .... Detroit Lions	16.00	8.00	1.60
☐ 26 Sammy Baugh .... Washington Redskins	150.00	75.00	15.00
☐ 28 Pete Pihos .... Philadelphia Eagles	32.00	16.00	3.20

☐ 31 Tex Coulter 18.00   9.00   1.80
     New York Giants

☐ 32 Mal Kutner 18.00   9.00   1.80
     Chicago Cardinals

☐ 35 Whitey Wistert 18.00   9.00   1.80
     Philadelphia Eagles

☐ 37 Ted Fritsch Sr. 18.00   9.00   1.80
     Green Bay Packers

☐ 38 Vince Banonis 16.00   8.00   1.60
     Chicago Cardinals

☐ 39 Jim White 16.00   8.00   1.60
     New York Giants

☐ 40 George Connor 34.00   16.00   3.00
     Chicago Bears

☐ 41 George McAfee 34.00   16.00   3.00
     Chicago Bears

☐ 43 Frank Tripucka 25.00   12.50   2.50
     Philadelphia Eagles

☐ 47 Fred Enke 16.00   8.00   1.60
     Detroit Lions

☐ 49 Charley Conerly 60.00   30.00   6.00
     New York Giants

☐ 51 Ken Kavanaugh 25.00   12.50   2.50
     Chicago Bears

☐ 52 Bob Demoss 16.00   8.00   1.60
     New York Bulldogs

☐ 56 John Lujack 55.00   27.50   5.50
     Chicago Bears

☐ 57 Jim Youle 16.00   8.00   1.60
     Detroit Lions

☐ 62 Harry Gilmer 20.00   10.00   2.00
     Washington Redskins

☐ 65 Robert Nussbaumer 16.00   8.00   1.60
     Chicago Cardinals

☐ 67 Bobby Layne 100.00   50.00   10.00
     New York Bulldogs

☐ 70 Herb Siegert 16.00   8.00   1.60
     Washington Redskins

☐ 74 Tony Minisi 16.00   8.00   1.60
     New York Giants

☐ 79 Steve Van Buren 55.00   27.50   5.50
     Philadelphia Eagles

☐ 81 Perry Moss 16.00   8.00   1.60
     Green Bay Packers

☐ 89 Bob Waterfield 60.00   30.00   6.00
     Los Angeles Rams

☐ 90 Jack Jacobs 18.00   9.00   1.80
     Green Bay Packers

☐ 95 Kenny Washington 25.00   12.50   2.50
     Los Angeles Rams

☐ 101 Pat Harder UER 22.00   11.00   2.20
     (Misspelled Harber
     on card front)
     Chicago Cardinals

☐ 110 William Swiacki 20.00   10.00   2.00
     New York Giants

☐ 118 Fred Davis 16.00   8.00   1.60

     Chicago Bears

☐ 126 Jay Rhodemyre 16.00   8.00   1.60
     Green Bay Packers

☐ 127 Frank Seno 16.00   8.00   1.60
     New York Bulldogs

☐ 134 Chuck Bednarik 65.00   32.50   6.50
     Philadelphia Eagles

☐ 144 George Savitsky 16.00   8.00   1.60
     Philadelphia Eagles

☐ 150 Bulldog Turner 80.00   30.00   6.00
     Chicago Bears

1991 Pacific Plus I

This 550-card standard size (2 1/2" by 3 1/2") set was the first full football set issued by Pacific Trading Cards. This set was issued in alphabetical order by teams, which were also in alphabetical order. There were a few exceptions with regard to players Pacific could not get permission from the National Football League Players Association to print. The sets feature a full-color glossy front with the name on the left hand side of the card. The left border of the card is in the same colors as the teams helmet. In the lower left hand corner of the card there is a Pacific pennant. The team identity and player's position is under the player's picture. The back of the card has an approximate 45 degree tilt to it and includes a full-color portrait of the player, complete biographical information, and interesting facts about the players. The order in which the cards appear are Atlanta Falcons (1-19), Buffalo Bills (20-37), Chicago Bears (38-56), Cincinnati Bengals (57-74), Cleveland Browns (75-91), Dallas Cowboys (92-110), Denver Broncos (111-129), Detroit Lions (130-148), Green Bay

Packers (149-168), Houston Oilers (169-186), Indianapolis Colts (187-204), Kansas City Chiefs (205-224), Los Angeles Raiders (225-244), Los Angeles Rams (245-262), Miami Dolphins (263-282), Minnesota Vikings (283-302), New England Patriots (303-319), New Orleans Saints (320-339), New York Giants (340-342 and 344-360), New York Jets (361-380), Philadelphia Eagles (381-399), Phoenix Cardinals (400-418), Pittsburgh Steelers (419-436), San Diego Chargers (437 and 439-455), San Francisco 49ers (456-474), Seattle Seahawks (475-494), Tampa Bay Buccaneers (495-514), Washington Redskins (515-518 and 520-533), and Rookie Cards (534-550). The key rookie cards in this set are Mike Croel, Todd Marinovich, and Dan McGwire.

	MINT	EXC	G-VG
COMPLETE SET (550)	16.00	8.00	1.60
COMMON PLAYER (1-550)	.03	.01	.00

☐ 1 Deion Sanders	.20	.10	.02
☐ 2 Steve Broussard	.10	.05	.01
☐ 3 Aundray Bruce	.06	.03	.00
☐ 4 Rick Bryan	.06	.03	.00
☐ 5 John Rade	.03	.01	.00
☐ 6 Scott Case	.03	.01	.00
☐ 7 Tony Casillas	.06	.03	.00
☐ 8 Shawn Collins	.06	.03	.00
☐ 9 Darion Conner	.08	.04	.01
☐ 10 Tory Epps	.06	.03	.00
☐ 11 Bill Fralic	.06	.03	.00
☐ 12 Mike Gann	.03	.01	.00
☐ 13 Tim Green UER	.06	.03	.00
(Listed as DT, should say DE)			
☐ 14 Chris Hinton	.06	.03	.00
☐ 15 Houston Hoover UER	.06	.03	.00
(Deion misspelled as Deon on card back)			
☐ 16 Chris Miller	.15	.07	.01
☐ 17 Andre Rison	.15	.07	.01
☐ 18 Mike Rozier	.06	.03	.00
☐ 19 Jessie Tuggle	.06	.03	.00
☐ 20 Don Beebe	.08	.04	.00
☐ 21 Ray Bentley	.03	.01	.00
☐ 22 Shane Conlan	.06	.03	.00
☐ 23 Kent Hull	.03	.01	.00
☐ 24 Mark Kelso	.03	.01	.00
☐ 25 James Lofton UER	.12	.06	.01
(Photo on front actually Flip Johnson)			
☐ 26 Scott Norwood	.03	.01	.00
☐ 27 Andre Reed	.10	.05	.01
☐ 28 Leonard Smith	.03	.01	.00
☐ 29 Bruce Smith	.08	.04	.01
☐ 30 Leon Seals	.03	.01	.00
☐ 31 Darryl Talley	.06	.03	.00
☐ 32 Steve Tasker	.03	.01	.00
☐ 33 Thurman Thomas	.45	.22	.04
☐ 34 James Williams	.03	.01	.00
☐ 35 Will Wolford	.03	.01	.00
☐ 36 Frank Reich	.08	.04	.01
☐ 37 Jeff Wright	.08	.04	.01
☐ 38 Neal Anderson	.15	.07	.01
☐ 39 Trace Armstrong	.03	.01	.00
☐ 40 Johnny Bailey UER	.08	.04	.01
(Gained 5320 yards in college, should be 6320)			
☐ 41 Mark Bortz UER	.03	.01	.00
(Johnny Bailey misspelled as Johnny on card back)			
☐ 42 Cap Boso	.08	.04	.01
☐ 43 Kevin Butler	.03	.01	.00
☐ 44 Mark Carrier	.08	.04	.01
☐ 45 Jim Covert	.06	.03	.00
☐ 46 Wendell Davis	.12	.06	.01
☐ 47 Richard Dent	.08	.04	.01
☐ 48 Shaun Gayle	.03	.01	.00
☐ 49 Jim Harbaugh	.10	.05	.01
☐ 50 Jay Hilgenberg	.06	.03	.00
☐ 51 Brad Muster	.08	.04	.01
☐ 52 William Perry	.08	.04	.01
☐ 53 Mike Singletary UER	.08	.04	.01
(No College listed, should say Baylor)			
☐ 54 Peter Tom Willis	.10	.05	.01
☐ 55 Donnell Woolford	.03	.01	.00
☐ 56 Steve McMichael	.06	.03	.00
☐ 57 Eric Ball	.03	.01	.00
☐ 58 Lewis Billups	.03	.01	.00
☐ 59 Jim Breech	.03	.01	.00
☐ 60 James Brooks	.08	.04	.01
☐ 61 Eddie Brown	.08	.04	.01
☐ 62 Rickey Dixon	.06	.03	.00
☐ 63 Boomer Esiason	.10	.05	.01
☐ 64 James Francis	.08	.04	.01
☐ 65 David Fulcher	.03	.01	.00
☐ 66 David Grant	.03	.01	.00
☐ 67 Harold Green UER	.15	.07	.01
(Misplaced apostrophe in Gamecocks)			
☐ 68 Rodney Holman	.06	.03	.00
☐ 69 Stanford Jennings	.03	.01	.00
☐ 70A Tim Krumrie ERR	.12	.06	.01
(Misspelled Krumprie on card front)			
☐ 70B Tim Krumrie COR	.12	.06	.01
☐ 71 Tim McGee	.06	.03	.00
☐ 72 Anthony Munoz	.08	.04	.01
☐ 73 Mitchell Price	.10	.05	.01
☐ 74 Eric Thomas	.03	.01	.00

☐ 75 Ickey Woods	.06	.03	.00
☐ 76 Mike Baab	.03	.01	.00
☐ 77 Thane Gash	.03	.01	.00
☐ 78 David Grayson	.03	.01	.00
☐ 79 Mike Johnson	.03	.01	.00
☐ 80 Reggie Langhorne	.03	.01	.00
☐ 81 Kevin Mack	.06	.03	.00
☐ 82 Clay Matthews	.03	.01	.00
☐ 83A Eric Metcalf ERR	.12	.06	.01
("Terry is the son of Terry")			
☐ 83B Eric Metcalf COR	.12	.06	.01
("Eric is the son of Terry")			
☐ 84 Frank Minnifield	.03	.01	.00
☐ 85 Mike Oliphant	.03	.01	.00
☐ 86 Mike Pagel	.03	.01	.00
☐ 87 John Talley	.10	.05	.01
☐ 88 Lawyer Tillman	.06	.03	.00
☐ 89 Gregg Rakoczy UER	.03	.01	.00
(Misspelled Greg on both sides of card)			
☐ 90 Bryan Wagner	.03	.01	.00
☐ 91 Rob Burnett	.08	.04	.01
☐ 92 Tommie Agee	.06	.03	.00
☐ 93 Troy Aikman UER	.35	.17	.03
(4328 yards is career total not season; text has him breaking passing record which is not true)			
☐ 94A Bill Bates ERR	.12	.06	.01
(Black line on card front)			
☐ 94B Bill Bates COR	.12	.06	.01
(No black line on card front)			
☐ 95 Jack Del Rio	.03	.01	.00
☐ 96 Issiac Holt UER	.03	.01	.00
(Photo on back actually Timmy Newsome)			
☐ 97 Michael Irvin	.20	.10	.02
☐ 98 Jim Jeffcoat UER	.03	.01	.00
(On back, red line has Jeff not Jim)			
☐ 99 Jimmy Jones	.06	.03	.00
☐ 100 Kelvin Martin	.06	.03	.00
☐ 101 Nate Newton	.03	.01	.00
☐ 102 Danny Noonan	.03	.01	.00
☐ 103 Ken Norton	.06	.03	.00
☐ 104 Jay Novacek	.10	.05	.01
☐ 105 Mike Saxon	.03	.01	.00
☐ 106 Derrick Sheppard	.06	.03	.00
☐ 107 Emmitt Smith	1.25	.60	.12
☐ 108 Daniel Stubbs	.03	.01	.00
☐ 109 Tony Tolbert	.03	.01	.00
☐ 110 Alexander Wright	.15	.07	.01
☐ 111 Steve Atwater	.06	.03	.00

☐ 112 Melvin Bratton	.06	.03	.00
☐ 113 Tyrone Braxton UER	.06	.03	.00
(Went to North Dakota State, not South Dakota)			
☐ 114 Alphonso Carreker	.03	.01	.00
☐ 115 John Elway	.15	.07	.01
☐ 116 Simon Fletcher	.03	.01	.00
☐ 117 Bobby Humphrey	.10	.05	.01
☐ 118 Mark Jackson	.06	.03	.00
☐ 119 Vance Johnson	.06	.03	.00
☐ 120 Greg Kragen UER	.03	.01	.00
(Recovered 20 fumbles in '89, yet 11 in career)			
☐ 121 Karl Mecklenburg UER	.06	.03	.00
(Misspelled Mecklenberg on card front)			
☐ 122A Orson Mobley ERR	.50	.25	.05
(Misspelled Orsen)			
☐ 122B Orson Mobley COR	.08	.04	.01
☐ 123 Alton Montgomery	.03	.01	.00
☐ 124 Ricky Nattiel	.06	.03	.00
☐ 125 Steve Sewell	.06	.03	.00
☐ 126 Shannon Sharpe	.10	.05	.01
☐ 127 Dennis Smith	.03	.01	.00
☐ 128A Andre Townsend ERR	.60	.30	.06
(Misspelled Andie on card front)			
☐ 128B Andre Townsend COR	.12	.06	.01
☐ 129 Mike Horan	.03	.01	.00
☐ 130 Jerry Ball	.06	.03	.00
☐ 131 Bennie Blades	.06	.03	.00
☐ 132 Lomas Brown	.03	.01	.00
☐ 133 Jeff Campbell UER	.08	.04	.01
(No NFL totals line)			
☐ 134 Robert Clark	.06	.03	.00
☐ 135 Michael Cofer	.03	.01	.00
☐ 136 Dennis Gibson	.03	.01	.00
☐ 137 Mel Gray	.03	.01	.00
☐ 138 LeRoy Irvin UER	.03	.01	.00
(Misspelled LEROY; spent 10 years with Rams, not 11)			
☐ 139 George Jamison	.08	.04	.01
☐ 140 Richard Johnson	.03	.01	.00
☐ 141 Eddie Murray	.06	.03	.00
☐ 142 Dan Owens	.03	.01	.00
☐ 143 Rodney Peete	.08	.04	.01
☐ 144 Barry Sanders	.75	.35	.07
☐ 145 Chris Spielman	.06	.03	.00
☐ 146 Mark Spindler	.03	.01	.00
☐ 147 Andre Ware	.12	.06	.01
☐ 148 William White	.06	.03	.00
☐ 149 Tony Bennett	.06	.03	.00
☐ 150 Robert Brown	.03	.01	.00
☐ 151 LeRoy Butler	.03	.01	.00
☐ 152 Anthony Dilweg	.08	.04	.01
☐ 153 Michael Haddix	.03	.01	.00

☐ 154 Ron Hallstrom	.03	.01	.00
☐ 155 Tim Harris	.06	.03	.00
☐ 156 Johnny Holland	.03	.01	.00
☐ 157 Chris Jacke	.03	.01	.00
☐ 158 Perry Kemp	.03	.01	.00
☐ 159 Mark Lee	.03	.01	.00
☐ 160 Don Majkowski	.08	.04	.01
☐ 161 Tony Mandarich UER	.06	.03	.00
(United Stated)			
☐ 162 Mark Murphy	.03	.01	.00
☐ 163 Brian Noble	.03	.01	.00
☐ 164 Shawn Patterson	.12	.06	.01
☐ 165 Jeff Query	.03	.01	.00
☐ 166 Sterling Sharpe	.10	.05	.01
☐ 167 Darrell Thompson	.12	.06	.01
☐ 168 Ed West	.03	.01	.00
☐ 169 Ray Childress UER	.06	.03	.00
(Front DE, back DT)			
☐ 170A Cris Dishman ERR	.25	.12	.02
(Misspelled Chris on both sides)			
☐ 170B Cris Dishman COR/ERR	1.00	.50	.10
(Misspelled Chris on back only)			
☐ 170C Cris Dishman COR	.20	.10	.02
☐ 171 Curtis Duncan	.06	.03	.00
☐ 172 William Fuller	.06	.03	.00
☐ 173 Ernest Givins UER	.10	.05	.01
(Missing a highlight line on back)			
☐ 174 Drew Hill	.08	.04	.01
☐ 175A Haywood Jeffires ERR	.25	.12	.02
(Misspelled Jeffries on both sides of card)			
☐ 175B Haywood Jeffires COR	.25	.12	.02
☐ 176 Sean Jones	.03	.01	.00
☐ 177 Lamar Lathon	.06	.03	.00
☐ 178 Bruce Matthews	.03	.01	.00
☐ 179 Bubba McDowell	.03	.01	.00
☐ 180 Johnny Meads	.03	.01	.00
☐ 181 Warren Moon UER	.20	.10	.02
(Birth listed as '65, should be '56)			
☐ 182 Mike Munchak	.06	.03	.00
☐ 183 Allen Pinkett	.06	.03	.00
☐ 184 Dean Steinkuhler UER	.06	.03	.00
(Oakland, should be Outland)			
☐ 185 Lorenzo White UER	.06	.03	.00
(Rout misspelled as route on card back)			
☐ 186A John Grimsley ERR	.12	.06	.01
(Misspelled Grimsby)			
☐ 186B John Grimsley COR	.12	.06	.01
☐ 187 Pat Beach	.03	.01	.00
☐ 188 Albert Bentley	.06	.03	.00
☐ 189 Dean Biasucci	.03	.01	.00

☐ 190 Duane Bickett	.03	.01	.00
☐ 191 Bill Brooks	.03	.01	.00
☐ 192 Eugene Daniel	.03	.01	.00
☐ 193 Jeff George	.35	.17	.03
☐ 194 Jon Hand	.03	.01	.00
☐ 195 Jeff Herrod	.03	.01	.00
☐ 196A Jessie Hester ERR	.50	.25	.05
(Misspelled Jesse)			
☐ 196B Jessie Hester COR	.12	.06	.01
☐ 197 Mike Prior	.03	.01	.00
☐ 198 Stacey Simmons	.06	.03	.00
☐ 199 Rohn Stark	.03	.01	.00
☐ 200 Pat Tomberlin	.08	.04	.01
☐ 201 Clarence Verdin	.06	.03	.00
☐ 202 Keith Taylor	.06	.03	.00
☐ 203 Jack Trudeau	.03	.01	.00
☐ 204 Chip Banks	.03	.01	.00
☐ 205 John Alt	.03	.01	.00
☐ 206 Deron Cherry	.06	.03	.00
☐ 207 Steve DeBerg	.08	.04	.01
☐ 208 Tim Grunhard	.03	.01	.00
☐ 209 Albert Lewis	.06	.03	.00
☐ 210 Nick Lowery UER	.06	.03	.00
(12 years NFL exp., should be 13)			
☐ 211 Bill Maas	.03	.01	.00
☐ 212 Chris Martin	.03	.01	.00
☐ 213 Todd McNair	.03	.01	.00
☐ 214 Christian Okoye	.08	.04	.01
☐ 215 Stephone Paige	.06	.03	.00
☐ 216 Steve Pelluer	.06	.03	.00
☐ 217 Kevin Porter	.03	.01	.00
☐ 218 Kevin Ross	.03	.01	.00
☐ 219 Dan Saleaumua	.03	.01	.00
☐ 220 Neil Smith	.06	.03	.00
☐ 221 David Szott UER	.08	.04	.01
(Listed as Off. Guard)			
☐ 222 Derrick Thomas	.15	.07	.01
☐ 223 Barry Word	.50	.25	.05
☐ 224 Percy Snow	.08	.04	.01
☐ 225 Marcus Allen	.10	.05	.01
☐ 226 Eddie Anderson UER	.03	.01	.00
(Began career with Sea- hawks, not Raiders)			
☐ 227 Steve Beuerlein UER	.10	.05	.01
(Not injured during '90 season, but was inactive)			
☐ 228A Tim Brown ERR	.15	.07	.01
(No position on card)			
☐ 228B Tim Brown COR	.15	.07	.01
☐ 229 Scott Davis	.03	.01	.00
☐ 230 Mike Dyal	.03	.01	.00
☐ 231 Mervyn Fernandez UER	.03	.01	.00
(Card says free agent in '87, but was drafted in '83)			
☐ 232 Willie Gault UER	.06	.03	.00

(Text says 60 catches
in '90, stats say 50)

☐ 233 Ethan Horton UER	.10	.05	.01
(No height and weight listings)			
☐ 234 Bo Jackson UER	.35	.17	.03
(Drafted in '87, not '86)			
☐ 235 Howie Long	.06	.03	.00
☐ 236 Terry McDaniel	.03	.01	.00
☐ 237 Max Montoya	.03	.01	.00
☐ 238 Don Mosebar	.03	.01	.00
☐ 239 Jay Schroeder	.08	.04	.01
☐ 240 Steve Smith	.03	.01	.00
☐ 241 Greg Townsend	.03	.01	.00
☐ 242 Aaron Wallace	.08	.04	.01
☐ 243 Lionel Washington	.03	.01	.00
☐ 244A Steve Wisniewski ERR	.12	.06	.01
(Misspelled Winsniewski on both sides; Drafted, should say traded to)			
☐ 244B Steve Wisniewski ERR	.75	.35	.07
(Misspelled Winsniewski on card back)			
☐ 244C Steve Wisniewski COR	.12	.06	.01
☐ 245 Flipper Anderson	.06	.03	.00
☐ 246 Latin Berry	.15	.07	.01
☐ 247 Robert Delpino	.06	.03	.00
☐ 248 Marcus Dupree	.06	.03	.00
☐ 249 Henry Ellard	.08	.04	.01
☐ 250 Jim Everett	.10	.05	.01
☐ 251 Cleveland Gary	.06	.03	.00
☐ 252 Jerry Gray	.06	.03	.00
☐ 253 Kevin Greene	.06	.03	.00
☐ 254 Pete Holohan UER	.03	.01	.00
(Photo on back actually Kevin Greene)			
☐ 255 Buford McGee	.03	.01	.00
☐ 256 Tom Newberry	.03	.01	.00
☐ 257A Irv Pankey ERR	.12	.06	.01
(Misspelled as Panky on both sides of card)			
☐ 257B Irv Pankey COR	.12	.06	.01
☐ 258 Jackie Slater	.06	.03	.00
☐ 259 Doug Smith	.03	.01	.00
☐ 260 Frank Stams	.03	.01	.00
☐ 261 Michael Stewart	.03	.01	.00
☐ 262 Fred Strickland	.03	.01	.00
☐ 263 J.B. Brown UER	.03	.01	.00
(No periods after initials on card front)			
☐ 264 Mark Clayton	.08	.04	.01
☐ 265 Jeff Cross	.03	.01	.00
☐ 266 Mark Dennis	.08	.04	.01
☐ 267 Mark Duper	.06	.03	.00
☐ 268 Ferrell Edmunds	.03	.01	.00
☐ 269 Dan Marino	.25	.12	.02
☐ 270 John Offerdahl	.06	.03	.00
☐ 271 Louis Oliver	.03	.01	.00
☐ 272 Tony Paige	.03	.01	.00
☐ 273 Reggie Roby	.03	.01	.00
☐ 274 Sammie Smith	.08	.04	.01
(Picture is sideways on the card)			
☐ 275 Keith Sims	.06	.03	.00
☐ 276 Brian Sochia	.03	.01	.00
☐ 277 Pete Stoyanovich	.03	.01	.00
☐ 278 Richmond Webb	.06	.03	.00
☐ 279 Jarvis Williams	.03	.01	.00
☐ 280 Tim McKyer	.03	.01	.00
☐ 281A Jim C. Jensen ERR	.12	.06	.01
(Misspelled Jenson on card back)			
☐ 281B Jim C. Jensen COR	.12	.06	.01
☐ 282 Scott Secules	.08	.04	.01
☐ 283 Ray Berry	.03	.01	.00
☐ 284 Joey Browner UER	.06	.03	.00
(Safetys, sic)			
☐ 285 Anthony Carter	.08	.04	.01
☐ 286A Cris Carter ERR	.20	.10	.02
(Misspelled Chris on both sides)			
☐ 286B Cris Carter COR/ERR	.50	.25	.05
(Misspelled Chris on card back)			
☐ 286C Cris Carter COR	.20	.10	.02
☐ 287 Chris Doleman	.06	.03	.00
☐ 288 Mark Dusbabek UER	.08	.04	.01
(Front DT, back LB)			
☐ 289 Hassan Jones	.06	.03	.00
☐ 290 Steve Jordan	.06	.03	.00
☐ 291 Carl Lee	.03	.01	.00
☐ 292 Kirk Lowdermilk	.03	.01	.00
☐ 293 Randall McDaniel	.03	.01	.00
☐ 294 Mike Merriweather	.03	.01	.00
☐ 295A Keith Millard UER	.12	.06	.01
(No position on card)			
☐ 295B Keith Millard COR	.12	.06	.01
☐ 296 Al Noga UER	.03	.01	.00
(Card says DT, should say DE)			
☐ 297 Scott Studwell UER	.03	.01	.00
(83 career tackles, but bio says 156 tackles in '81 season)			
☐ 298 Henry Thomas	.03	.01	.00
☐ 299 Herschel Walker	.10	.05	.01
☐ 300 Gary Zimmerman	.03	.01	.00
☐ 301 Rick Gannon	.08	.04	.01
☐ 302 Wade Wilson UER	.08	.04	.01
(Led AFC, should say led NFC)			
☐ 303 Vincent Brown	.03	.01	.00

☐ 304	Marv Cook	.03	.01	.00
☐ 305	Hart Lee Dykes	.06	.03	.00
☐ 306	Irving Fryar	.06	.03	.00
☐ 307	Tommy Hodson UER (No NFL totals line)	.08	.04	.01
☐ 308	Maurice Hurst	.03	.01	.00
☐ 309	Ronnie Lippett UER (On back, reserves should be reserve)	.03	.01	.00
☐ 310	Fred Marion	.03	.01	.00
☐ 311	Greg McMurtry	.08	.04	.01
☐ 312	Johnny Rembert	.03	.01	.00
☐ 313	Chris Singleton	.06	.03	.00
☐ 314	Ed Reynolds	.03	.01	.00
☐ 315	Andre Tippett	.06	.03	.00
☐ 316	Garin Veris	.03	.01	.00
☐ 317	Brent Williams	.03	.01	.00
☐ 318A	John Stephens ERR (Misspelled Stevens on both sides of card)	.15	.07	.01
☐ 318B	John Stephens COR/ERR (Misspelled Stevens on card back)	.75	.35	.07
☐ 318C	John Stephens COR	.15	.07	.01
☐ 319	Sammy Martin	.06	.03	.00
☐ 320	Bruce Armstrong	.03	.01	.00
☐ 321A	Morten Andersen ERR (Misspelled Anderson on both sides of card)	.60	.30	.06
☐ 321B	Morten Andersen COR/ERR (Misspelled Anderson on card back)	.60	.30	.06
☐ 321C	Morten Andersen COR	.08	.04	.01
☐ 322	Gene Atkins UER (No NFL Exp. line)	.03	.01	.00
☐ 323	Vince Buck	.06	.03	.00
☐ 324	John Fourcade	.06	.03	.00
☐ 325	Kevin Haverdink	.03	.01	.00
☐ 326	Bobby Hebert	.08	.04	.01
☐ 327	Craig Heyward	.08	.04	.01
☐ 328	Dalton Hilliard	.06	.03	.00
☐ 329	Rickey Jackson	.06	.03	.00
☐ 330A	Vaughan Johnson ERR (Misspelled Vaughn)	.12	.06	.01
☐ 330B	Vaughan Johnson COR	.12	.06	.01
☐ 331	Eric Martin	.06	.03	.00
☐ 332	Wayne Martin	.03	.01	.00
☐ 333	Reuben Mayes UER (Misspelled Rueben on both sides of card)	.06	.03	.00
☐ 334	Sam Mills	.06	.03	.00
☐ 335	Brett Perriman	.06	.03	.00
☐ 336	Pat Swilling	.08	.04	.01
☐ 337	Renaldo Turnbull	.06	.03	.00
☐ 338	Lonzell Hill	.03	.01	.00
☐ 339	Steve Walsh UER (19 of 20 for 70.3, should be 95 percent)	.08	.04	.01
☐ 340	Carl Banks UER (Led defensive in tackles, should say defense)	.06	.03	.00
☐ 341	Mark Bavaro UER (Weight on back 145, should say 245)	.06	.03	.00
☐ 342	Maurice Carthon	.03	.01	.00
☐ 343	Pat Harlow	.15	.07	.01
☐ 344	Eric Dorsey	.03	.01	.00
☐ 345	John Elliott	.03	.01	.00
☐ 346	Rodney Hampton	.40	.20	.04
☐ 347	Jeff Hostetler	.20	.10	.02
☐ 348	Erik Howard UER (Listed as DT, should be NT)	.03	.01	.00
☐ 349	Pepper Johnson	.06	.03	.00
☐ 350A	Sean Landeta ERR (Misspelled Landetta on both sides of card)	.12	.06	.01
☐ 350B	Sean Landeta COR	.50	.25	.05
☐ 351	Leonard Marshall	.06	.03	.00
☐ 352	David Meggett	.10	.05	.01
☐ 353A	Bart Oates ERR (Misspelled Oats on both sides)	.12	.06	.01
☐ 353A	Bart Oates COR/ERR (Misspelled Oats on card back)	.75	.35	.07
☐ 353C	Bart Oates COR	.12	.06	.01
☐ 354	Gary Reasons	.03	.01	.00
☐ 355	Phil Simms	.08	.04	.01
☐ 356	Lawrence Taylor	.10	.05	.01
☐ 357	Reyna Thompson	.06	.03	.00
☐ 358	Brian Williams UER (Front C-G, back G)	.03	.01	.00
☐ 359	Matt Bahr	.03	.01	.00
☐ 360	Mark Ingram	.06	.03	.00
☐ 361	Brad Baxter	.10	.05	.01
☐ 362	Mark Boyer	.06	.03	.00
☐ 363	Dennis Byrd	.06	.03	.00
☐ 364	Dave Cadigan UER (Terance misspelled as Terrance on back)	.03	.01	.00
☐ 365	Kyle Clifton	.03	.01	.00
☐ 366	James Hasty	.03	.01	.00
☐ 367	Joe Kelly UER (Front 50, back 58)	.03	.01	.00
☐ 368	Jeff Lageman	.06	.03	.00
☐ 369	Pat Leahy UER (Career-best FG in '65, should say '85)	.06	.03	.00
☐ 370	Terance Mathis	.12	.06	.01
☐ 371	Erik McMillan	.06	.03	.00

☐ 372	Rob Moore	.50	.25	.05
☐ 373	Ken O'Brien	.08	.04	.01
☐ 374	Tony Stargell	.06	.03	.00
☐ 375	Jim Sweeney UER	.03	.01	.00
	(Landetta, sic)			
☐ 376	Al Toon	.08	.04	.01
☐ 377	Johnny Hector	.06	.03	.00
☐ 378	Jeff Criswell	.03	.01	.00
☐ 379	Mike Haight	.08	.04	.01
☐ 380	Troy Benson	.03	.01	.00
☐ 381	Eric Allen	.03	.01	.00
☐ 382	Fred Barnett	.15	.07	.01
☐ 383	Jerome Brown	.06	.03	.00
☐ 384	Keith Byars	.06	.03	.00
☐ 385	Randall Cunningham	.15	.07	.01
☐ 386	Byron Evans	.03	.01	.00
☐ 387	Wes Hopkins	.03	.01	.00
☐ 388	Keith Jackson	.08	.04	.01
☐ 389	Seth Joyner UER	.06	.03	.00
	(Fumble recovery line not aligned)			
☐ 390	Bobby Wilson	.08	.04	.01
☐ 391	Heath Sherman	.08	.04	.01
☐ 392	Clyde Simmons UER	.06	.03	.00
	(Listed as DT, should say DE)			
☐ 393	Ben Smith	.03	.01	.00
☐ 394	Andre Waters	.03	.01	.00
☐ 395	Reggie White UER	.08	.04	.01
	(Derrick Thomas holds NFL record with 7 sacks)			
☐ 396	Calvin Williams	.08	.04	.01
☐ 397	Al Harris	.03	.01	.00
☐ 398	Anthony Toney	.03	.01	.00
☐ 399	Mike Quick	.06	.03	.00
☐ 400	Anthony Bell	.03	.01	.00
☐ 401	Rich Camarillo	.03	.01	.00
☐ 402	Roy Green	.08	.04	.01
☐ 403	Ken Harvey	.03	.01	.00
☐ 404	Eric Hill	.03	.01	.00
☐ 405	Garth Jax UER	.08	.04	.01
	(Should have comma before "the" on card back)			
☐ 406	Ernie Jones	.08	.04	.01
☐407A	Cedric Mack ERR	.12	.06	.01
	(Misspelled Cedrick on card front)			
☐407B	Cedric Mack COR	.12	.06	.01
☐ 408	Dexter Manley	.03	.01	.00
☐ 409	Tim McDonald	.06	.03	.00
☐ 410	Freddie Joe Nunn	.03	.01	.00
☐ 411	Ricky Proehl	.10	.05	.01
☐ 412	Moe Gardner	.15	.07	.01
☐ 413	Timm Rosenbach	.10	.05	.01
☐ 414	Luis Sharpe UER	.03	.01	.00
	(Lomiller, sic)			
☐ 415	Vai Sikahema UER	.03	.01	.00

	(Front RB, back PR)			
☐ 416	Anthony Thompson	.08	.04	.01
☐ 417	Ron Wolfley UER	.03	.01	.00
	(Missing NFL fact line under vital stats)			
☐ 418	Lonnie Young	.03	.01	.00
☐ 419	Gary Anderson	.03	.01	.00
☐ 420	Bubby Brister	.08	.04	.01
☐ 421	Thomas Everett	.03	.01	.00
☐ 422	Eric Green	.15	.07	.01
☐ 423	Delton Hall	.03	.01	.00
☐ 424	Bryan Hinkle	.03	.01	.00
☐ 425	Merril Hoge	.06	.03	.00
☐ 426	Carnell Lake	.03	.01	.00
☐ 427	Louis Lipps	.06	.03	.00
☐ 428	David Little	.03	.01	.00
☐ 429	Greg Lloyd	.03	.01	.00
☐ 430	Mike Mularkey	.03	.01	.00
☐ 431	Keith Willis UER	.03	.01	.00
	(No period after C in L.C. Greenwood on back)			
☐ 432	Dwayne Woodruff	.03	.01	.00
☐ 433	Rod Woodson UER	.08	.04	.01
	(No NFL experience listed on card)			
☐ 434	Tim Worley	.06	.03	.00
☐ 435	Warren Williams	.03	.01	.00
☐ 436	Terry Long UER	.03	.01	.00
	(Not 5th NFL team, tied for 7th)			
☐ 437	Martin Bayless	.03	.01	.00
☐ 438	Jarrod Bunch	.15	.07	.01
☐ 439	Marion Butts	.10	.05	.01
☐ 440	Gill Byrd UER	.06	.03	.00
	(Pickoffs misspelled as two words)			
☐ 441	Arthur Cox	.03	.01	.00
☐ 442	John Friesz	.35	.17	.03
☐ 443	Leo Goeas	.03	.01	.00
☐ 444	Burt Grossman	.06	.03	.00
☐ 445	Courtney Hall UER	.03	.01	.00
	(In DYK section, is should be in)			
☐ 446	Ronnie Harmon	.06	.03	.00
☐ 447	Nate Lewis	.12	.06	.01
☐ 448	Anthony Miller	.08	.04	.01
☐ 449	Leslie O'Neal	.06	.03	.00
☐ 450	Gary Plummer	.03	.01	.00
☐ 451	Junior Seau	.10	.05	.01
☐ 452	Billy Ray Smith	.06	.03	.00
☐ 453	Billy Joe Tolliver	.08	.04	.01
☐ 454	Broderick Thompson	.03	.01	.00
☐ 455	Lee Williams	.06	.03	.00
☐ 456	Michael Carter	.06	.03	.00
☐ 457	Mike Cofer	.03	.01	.00
☐ 458	Kevin Fagan	.03	.01	.00
☐ 459	Charles Haley	.06	.03	.00

☐ 460 Pierce Holt	.03	.01	.00
☐ 461 Johnny Jackson	.10	.05	.01
☐ 462 Brent Jones	.06	.03	.00
☐ 463 Guy McIntyre	.03	.01	.00
☐ 464 Joe Montana	.45	.22	.04
☐ 465A Bubba Paris ERR	.12	.06	.01
(Misspelled Parris;			
reversed negative)			
☐ 465B Bubba Paris ERR	.60	.30	.06
(Misspelled Parris)			
☐ 465C Bubba Paris COR	.10	.05	.01
☐ 466 Tom Rathman UER	.06	.03	.00
(Born 10/7/62,			
not 11/7/62)			
☐ 467 Jerry Rice UER	.35	.17	.03
(4th to catch 100,			
should say 2nd)			
☐ 468 Mike Sherrard	.06	.03	.00
☐ 469 John Taylor UER	.12	.06	.01
(AL1-Time, sic)			
☐ 470 Steve Young	.10	.05	.01
☐ 471 Dennis Brown	.03	.01	.00
☐ 472 Dexter Carter	.08	.04	.01
☐ 473 Bill Romanowski	.06	.03	.00
☐ 474 Dave Waymer	.03	.01	.00
☐ 475 Robert Blackmon	.03	.01	.00
☐ 476 Derrick Fenner	.12	.06	.01
☐ 477 Nesby Glasgow UER	.03	.01	.00
(Missing total line			
for fumbles)			
☐ 478 Jacob Green	.06	.03	.00
☐ 479 Andy Heck	.03	.01	.00
☐ 480 Norm Johnson UER	.03	.01	.00
(They own and operate			
card store, not run)			
☐ 481 Tommy Kane	.12	.06	.01
☐ 482 Cortez Kennedy	.08	.04	.01
☐ 483A Dave Krieg ERR	.12	.06	.01
(Misspelled Kreig			
on both sides)			
☐ 483B Dave Krieg COR	.12	.06	.01
☐ 484 Bryan Millard	.03	.01	.00
☐ 485 Joe Nash	.03	.01	.00
☐ 486 Rufus Porter	.03	.01	.00
☐ 487 Eugene Robinson	.03	.01	.00
☐ 488 Mike Tice	.08	.04	.01
☐ 489 Chris Warren	.08	.04	.01
☐ 490 John L. Williams	.08	.04	.01
(No period after L			
on card front)			
☐ 491 Terry Wooden	.06	.03	.00
☐ 492 Tony Woods	.06	.03	.00
☐ 493 Brian Blades	.08	.04	.01
☐ 494 Paul Skansi	.06	.03	.00
☐ 495 Gary Anderson	.08	.04	.01
☐ 496 Mark Carrier	.08	.04	.01
☐ 497 Chris Chandler	.08	.04	.01
☐ 498 Steve Christie	.06	.03	.00
☐ 499 Reggie Cobb	.15	.07	.01
☐ 500 Reuben Davis	.03	.01	.00
☐ 501 Willie Drewrey UER	.03	.01	.00
(Misspelled Drewery on			
both sides of card)			
☐ 502 Randy Grimes	.03	.01	.00
☐ 503 Paul Gruber	.06	.03	.00
☐ 504 Wayne Haddix	.06	.03	.00
☐ 505 Ron Hall	.03	.01	.00
☐ 506 Harry Hamilton	.03	.01	.00
☐ 507 Bruce Hill	.03	.01	.00
☐ 508 Eugene Marve	.03	.01	.00
☐ 509 Keith McCants	.08	.04	.01
☐ 510 Winston Moss	.03	.01	.00
☐ 511 Kevin Murphy	.03	.01	.00
☐ 512 Mark Robinson	.03	.01	.00
☐ 513 Vinny Testaverde	.08	.04	.01
☐ 514 Broderick Thomas	.06	.03	.00
☐ 515 Jeff Bostic UER	.06	.03	.00
(Lomiller, sic)			
☐ 516 Todd Bowles	.06	.03	.00
☐ 517 Earnest Byner	.08	.04	.01
☐ 518 Gary Clark	.12	.06	.01
☐ 519 Craig Erickson	.40	.20	.04
☐ 520 Darryl Grant	.03	.01	.00
☐ 521 Darrell Green	.10	.05	.01
☐ 522 Russ Grimm	.03	.01	.00
☐ 523 Stan Humphries	.08	.04	.01
☐ 524 Joe Jacoby UER	.06	.03	.00
(Lomiller, sic)			
☐ 525 Jim Lachey	.06	.03	.00
☐ 526 Chip Lohmiller	.03	.01	.00
☐ 527 Charles Mann	.06	.03	.00
☐ 528 Wilber Marshall	.06	.03	.00
☐ 529 Art Monk	.12	.06	.01
☐ 530 Tracy Rocker	.03	.01	.00
☐ 531 Mark Rypien	.20	.10	.02
☐ 532 Ricky Sanders UER	.08	.04	.01
(Stats say caught 56,			
text says 57)			
☐ 533 Alvin Walton UER	.03	.01	.00
(Listed as WR,			
should be S)			
☐ 534 Todd Marinovich UER	1.50	.75	.15
(17 percent, should			
be 71 percent)			
☐ 535 Mike Dumas	.15	.07	.01
☐ 536A Russell Maryland ERR	.45	.22	.04
(No highlight line)			
☐ 536B Russell Maryland COR	.45	.22	.04
(Highlight line added)			
☐ 537 Eric Turner UER	.45	.22	.04
(Don Rogers misspelled			
as Rodgers)			
☐ 538 Ernie Mills	.20	.10	.02
☐ 539 Ed King	.15	.07	.01

		MINT	EXC	G-VG
☐ 540	Michael Stonebreaker 10	.05	.01
☐ 541	Chris Zorich 25	.12	.02
☐ 542	Mike Croel UER 75	.35	.07
	(Missing highlight		
	line under bio notes)		
☐ 543	Eric Moten 15	.07	.01
☐ 544	Dan McGwire 1.25	.60	.12
☐ 545	Keith Cash 08	.04	.01
☐ 546	Kenny Walker UER 45	.22	.04
	(Drafted 8th round,		
	not 7th)		
☐ 547	Leroy Hoard UER 15	.07	.01
	(LeROY on card)		
☐ 548	Luis Chrisobol UER 08	.04	.01
	(Should should be		
	showed; front LB,		
	back G)		
☐ 549	Stacy Danley 15	.07	.01
☐ 550	Todd Lyght 40	.20	.04

☐ 2	Checklist 2 ....1.50	.50	.10
☐ 3	Checklist 3 ....1.50	.50	.10
☐ 4	Checklist 4 ....1.50	.50	.10
☐ 5	Checklist 5 ....1.50	.50	.10

1991 Pacific Plus II

1991 Pacific Plus Checklists

Upon request from collectors, Pacific produced checklist cards. These checklist cards were numbered 1-5 and were randomly inserted into the late-run foil and wax packs. The cards are standard size, 2 1/2" by 3 1/2". According to Pacific, only 10,000 checklist sets were produced.

	MINT	EXC	G-VG
COMPLETE SET (5) 6.00	2.00	.40
COMMON PLAYER (1-5) 1.50	.50	.10
☐ 1 Checklist 1 ....1.50	.50	.10

The second series of the 1991 Pacific Plus set contains 110 cards measuring the standard size (2 1/2" by 3 1/2"). The fronts feature glossy color action player photos with white borders. In addition, two different color stripes per team accentuate the pictures and add color to the fronts. The player's name is printed vertically in the colored stripe on the left side of the picture. The horizontally oriented backs present biography, statistics, and career summary in a diagonal format on a background consisting of alternating white and (various) color stripes. The cards are numbered on the back and checklisted below alphabetically according to teams as follows: Atlanta Falcons (551-557), Buffalo Bills (558-560), Chicago Bears (561-565), Cincinnati Bengals (566-568), Cleveland Browns (569-571), Dallas Cowboys (572-575), Denver Broncos (576-579), Detroit Lions (580-582), Green Bay Packers (583-586), Houston Oilers (587-590), Indianapolis Colts (591-595), Kansas City Chiefs (596-598), Los Angeles Raiders (599-603), Los Angeles Rams (604-606), Miami Dolphins (607-609), Minnesota Vikings (610), New England Patriots (611-616), New Orleans Saints (617-619), New York Giants (620-622), New York Jets (623-625), Philadelphia Eagles (626-630), Phoenix Cardinals (631-637), Pittsburgh Steelers (638-640), San Diego

Chargers (641-644), San Francisco 49ers (645-646), Seattle Seahawks (647-651), Tampa Bay Buccaneers (652-657), and Washington Redskins (658-660). The key rookie cards in this set are Nick Bell, Ricky Ervins, Mark Higgs, Browning Nagle, Mike Pritchard, Leonard Russell, and Harvey Williams. Pacific claimed that their production run for this second series was limited to 5,894 foil cases.

	MINT	EXC	G-VG
COMPLETE SET (110)	12.00	6.00	1.20
COMMON PLAYER (551-660)	.05	.02	.00

☐ 551 Brett Favre	.75	.35	.07
☐ 552 Mike Pritchard	.60	.30	.06
☐ 553 Moe Gardner	.12	.06	.01
☐ 554 Tim McKyer	.05	.02	.00
☐ 555 Erric Pegram	.25	.12	.02
☐ 556 Norm Johnson	.05	.02	.00
☐ 557 Bruce Pickens	.20	.10	.02
☐ 558 Henry Jones	.15	.07	.01
☐ 559 Phil Hansen	.15	.07	.01
☐ 560 Cornelius Bennett	.08	.04	.01
☐ 561 Stan Thomas	.10	.05	.01
☐ 562 Chris Zorich	.12	.06	.01
☐ 563 Anthony Morgan	.25	.12	.02
☐ 564 Darren Lewis	.30	.15	.03
☐ 565 Mike Stonebreaker	.08	.04	.01
☐ 566 Alfred Williams	.15	.07	.01
☐ 567 Lamar Rogers	.15	.07	.01
☐ 568 Erik Wilhelm UER	.60	.30	.06
(No NFL Experience			
line on card back)			
☐ 569 Ed King	.08	.04	.01
☐ 570 Michael Jackson	.35	.17	.03
☐ 571 James Jones	.10	.05	.01
☐ 572 Russell Maryland	.25	.12	.02
☐ 573 Dixon Edwards	.10	.05	.01
☐ 574 Darrick Brownlow	.10	.05	.01
☐ 575 Larry Brown	.12	.06	.01
☐ 576 Mike Croel	.50	.25	.05
☐ 577 Keith Traylor	.12	.06	.01
☐ 578 Kenny Walker	.35	.17	.03
☐ 579 Reggie Johnson	.25	.12	.02
☐ 580 Herman Moore	.60	.30	.06
☐ 581 Kelvin Pritchett	.15	.07	.01
☐ 582 Kevin Scott	.15	.07	.01
☐ 583 Vinnie Clark	.12	.06	.01
☐ 584 Esera Tuaolo	.10	.05	.01
☐ 585 Don Davey	.15	.07	.01
☐ 586 Blair Kiel	.30	.15	.03
☐ 587 Mike Dumas	.10	.05	.01
☐ 588 Darryll Lewis	.15	.07	.01
☐ 589 John Flannery	.15	.07	.01
☐ 590 Kevin Donnally	.10	.05	.01
☐ 591 Shane Curry	.08	.04	.01

☐ 592 Mark Vander Poel	.12	.06	.01
☐ 593 Dave McCloughan	.15	.07	.01
☐ 594 Mel Agee	.10	.05	.01
☐ 595 Kerry Cash	.12	.06	.01
☐ 596 Harvey Williams	.75	.35	.07
☐ 597 Joe Valerio	.10	.05	.01
☐ 598 Tim Barnett UER	.30	.15	.03
(Harvey Williams			
pictured on front)			
☐ 599 Todd Marinovich	.90	.45	.09
☐ 600 Nick Bell	.75	.35	.07
☐ 601 Roger Craig	.10	.05	.01
☐ 602 Ronnie Lott	.10	.05	.01
☐ 603 Mike Jones	.15	.07	.01
☐ 604 Todd Lyght	.20	.10	.02
☐ 605 Roman Phifer	.15	.07	.01
☐ 606 David Lang	.15	.07	.01
☐ 607 Aaron Craver	.20	.10	.02
☐ 608 Mark Higgs	.60	.30	.06
☐ 609 Chris Green	.15	.07	.01
☐ 610 Randy Baldwin	.15	.07	.01
☐ 611 Pat Harlow	.10	.05	.01
☐ 612 Leonard Russell	1.25	.60	.12
☐ 613 Jerome Henderson	.15	.07	.01
☐ 614 Scott Zolak	.15	.07	.01
☐ 615 Jon Vaughn	.60	.30	.06
☐ 616 Harry Colon	.15	.07	.01
☐ 617 Wesley Carroll	.40	.20	.04
☐ 618 Quinn Early	.08	.04	.01
☐ 619 Reggie Jones	.15	.07	.01
☐ 620 Jarrod Bunch	.12	.06	.01
☐ 621 Kanavis McGhee	.20	.10	.02
☐ 622 Ed McCaffrey	.30	.15	.03
☐ 623 Browning Nagle	.75	.35	.07
☐ 624 Mo Lewis	.15	.07	.01
☐ 625 Blair Thomas	.45	.22	.04
☐ 626 Antone Davis	.12	.06	.01
☐ 627 Jim McMahon	.10	.05	.01
☐ 628 Scott Kowalkowski	.15	.07	.01
☐ 629 Brad Goebel	.25	.12	.02
☐ 630 William Thomas	.10	.05	.01
☐ 631 Eric Swann	.20	.10	.02
☐ 632 Mike Jones	.10	.05	.01
☐ 633 Aeneas Williams	.15	.07	.01
☐ 634 Dexter Davis	.10	.05	.01
☐ 635 Tom Tupa UER	.10	.05	.01
(Did play in 1990,			
but not as QB)			
☐ 636 Johnny Johnson	.25	.12	.02
☐ 637 Randal Hill	.60	.30	.06
☐ 638 Jeff Graham	.25	.12	.02
☐ 639 Ernie Mills	.10	.05	.01
☐ 640 Adrian Cooper	.15	.07	.01
☐ 641 Stanley Richard	.20	.10	.02
☐ 642 Eric Bieniemy	.30	.15	.03
☐ 643 Eric Moten	.08	.04	.01
☐ 644 Shawn Jefferson	.15	.07	.01

☐ 645	Ted Washington	.15	.07	.01
☐ 646	John Johnson	.08	.04	.01
☐ 647	Dan McGwire	.90	.45	.09
☐ 648	Doug Thomas	.15	.07	.01
☐ 649	David Daniels	.15	.07	.01
☐ 650	John Kasay	.12	.06	.01
☐ 651	Jeff Kemp	.08	.04	.01
☐ 652	Charles McRae	.15	.07	.01
☐ 653	Lawrence Dawsey	.40	.20	.04
☐ 654	Robert Wilson	.20	.10	.02
☐ 655	Dexter Manley	.05	.02	.00
☐ 656	Chuck Weatherspoon	.15	.07	.01
☐ 657	Tim Ryan	.10	.05	.01
☐ 658	Bobby Wilson	.08	.04	.01
☐ 659	Ricky Ervins	1.75	.85	.17
☐ 660	Matt Millen	.08	.04	.01

1992 Pacific Plus I

The 1992 Pacific Plus I set consists of 330 cards measuring the standard size (2 1/2" by 3 1/2"). The fronts feature glossy color action player photos enclosed by white borders. The player's name is printed vertically in a color stripe running down the left side of the picture, with the team helmet in the lower left corner. In a horizontal format, the backs have a second color photo and player profile. The cards are numbered on the back and checklisted below alphabetically according to teams as follows: Atlanta Falcons (1-13), Buffalo Bills (14-26), Chicago Bears (27-39), Cincinnati Bengals (40-51), Cleveland Browns (52-61), Dallas Cowboys (62-72), Denver Broncos (73-86), Detroit Lions (87-97), Green Bay Packers (98-108), Houston Oilers (109-119), Indianapolis Colts (120-130), Kansas City Chiefs (131-

143), Los Angeles Raiders (144-154), Los Angeles Rams (155-165), Miami Dolphins (166-176), Minnesota Vikings (177-187), New England Patriots (188-198), New Orleans Saints (199-209), New York Giants (210-220), New York Jets (221-231), Philadelphia Eagles (232-242), Phoenix Cardinals (243-253), Pittsburgh Steelers (254-264), San Diego Chargers (265-275), San Francisco 49ers (276-286), Seattle Seahawks (287-297), Tampa Bay Buccaneers (298-308), and Washington Redskins (309-319). The set closes with Draft Picks (320-330).

	MINT	EXC	G-VG
COMPLETE SET (330)	14.00	7.00	1.40
COMMON PLAYER (1-330)	.03	.01	.00

☐ 1	Steve Broussard	.10	.05	.01
☐ 2	Darion Conner	.06	.03	.00
☐ 3	Tory Epps	.03	.01	.00
☐ 4	Michael Haynes	.20	.10	.02
☐ 5	Chris Hinton	.06	.03	.00
☐ 6	Mike Kenn	.06	.03	.00
☐ 7	Tim McKyer	.06	.03	.00
☐ 8	Chris Miller	.15	.07	.01
☐ 9	Erric Pegram	.12	.06	.01
☐ 10	Mike Pritchard	.30	.15	.03
☐ 11	Moe Gardner	.08	.04	.01
☐ 12	Tim Green	.03	.01	.00
☐ 13	Norm Johnson	.03	.01	.00
☐ 14	Don Beebe	.06	.03	.00
☐ 15	Cornelius Bennett	.10	.05	.01
☐ 16	Al Edwards	.03	.01	.00
☐ 17	Mark Kelso	.03	.01	.00
☐ 18	James Lofton	.12	.06	.01
☐ 19	Frank Reich	.06	.03	.00
☐ 20	Leon Seals	.03	.01	.00
☐ 21	Darryl Talley	.06	.03	.00
☐ 22	Thurman Thomas	.40	.20	.04
☐ 23	Kent Hull	.03	.01	.00
☐ 24	Jeff Wright	.03	.01	.00
☐ 25	Nate Odomes	.03	.01	.00
☐ 26	Carwell Gardner	.03	.01	.00
☐ 27	Neal Anderson	.12	.06	.01
☐ 28	Mark Carrier	.06	.03	.00
☐ 29	Johnny Bailey	.06	.03	.00
☐ 30	Jim Harbaugh	.08	.04	.01
☐ 31	Jay Hilgenberg	.06	.03	.00
☐ 32	William Perry	.06	.03	.00
☐ 33	Wendell Davis	.12	.06	.01
☐ 34	Donnell Woolford	.03	.01	.00
☐ 35	Keith Van Horne	.03	.01	.00
☐ 36	Shaun Gayle	.03	.01	.00
☐ 37	Tom Waddle	.15	.07	.01
☐ 38	Chris Zorich	.10	.05	.01
☐ 39	Tom Thayer	.03	.01	.00

□				
□ 40	Rickey Dixon	.03	.01	.00
□ 41	James Francis	.06	.03	.00
□ 42	David Fulcher	.03	.01	.00
□ 43	Reggie Rembert	.06	.03	.00
□ 44	Anthony Munoz	.10	.05	.01
□ 45	Harold Green	.15	.07	.01
□ 46	Mitchell Price	.03	.01	.00
□ 47	Rodney Holman	.03	.01	.00
□ 48	Bruce Kozerski	.03	.01	.00
□ 49	Bruce Reimers	.03	.01	.00
□ 50	Erik Wilhelm	.30	.15	.03
□ 51	Harlon Barnett	.03	.01	.00
□ 52	Mike Johnson	.03	.01	.00
□ 53	Brian Brennan	.03	.01	.00
□ 54	Ed King	.03	.01	.00
□ 55	Reggie Langhorne	.03	.01	.00
□ 56	James Jones	.03	.01	.00
□ 57	Mike Baab	.03	.01	.00
□ 58	Dan Fike	.03	.01	.00
□ 59	Frank Minnifield	.03	.01	.00
□ 60	Clay Matthews	.03	.01	.00
□ 61	Kevin Mack	.06	.03	.00
□ 62	Tony Casillas	.03	.01	.00
□ 63	Jay Novacek	.10	.05	.01
□ 64	Larry Brown	.03	.01	.00
□ 65	Michael Irvin	.20	.10	.02
□ 66	Jack Del Rio	.03	.01	.00
□ 67	Ken Willis	.03	.01	.00
□ 68	Emmitt Smith	1.25	.60	.12
□ 69	Alan Veingrad	.03	.01	.00
□ 70	John Gesek	.03	.01	.00
□ 71	Steve Beuerlein	.12	.06	.01
□ 72	Vinson Smith	.10	.05	.01
□ 73	Steve Atwater	.06	.03	.00
□ 74	Mike Croel	.25	.12	.02
□ 75	John Elway	.15	.07	.01
□ 76	Gaston Green	.20	.10	.02
□ 77	Mike Horan	.03	.01	.00
□ 78	Vance Johnson	.06	.03	.00
□ 79	Karl Mecklenburg	.06	.03	.00
□ 80	Shannon Sharpe	.03	.01	.00
□ 81	David Treadwell	.03	.01	.00
□ 82	Kenny Walker	.20	.10	.02
□ 83	Greg Lewis	.15	.07	.01
□ 84	Shawn Moore	.08	.04	.01
□ 85	Alton Montgomery	.03	.01	.00
□ 86	Michael Young	.03	.01	.00
□ 87	Jerry Ball	.06	.03	.00
□ 88	Bennie Blades	.06	.03	.00
□ 89	Mel Gray	.03	.01	.00
□ 90	Herman Moore	.30	.15	.03
□ 91	Erik Kramer	.40	.20	.04
□ 92	Willie Green	.15	.07	.01
□ 93	George Jamison	.03	.01	.00
□ 94	Chris Spielman	.06	.03	.00
□ 95	Kelvin Pritchett	.03	.01	.00
□ 96	William White	.03	.01	.00

□				
□ 97	Mike Utley	.12	.06	.01
□ 98	Tony Bennett	.03	.01	.00
□ 99	LeRoy Butler	.03	.01	.00
□ 100	Vinnie Clark	.03	.01	.00
□ 101	Ron Hallstrom	.03	.01	.00
□ 102	Chris Jacke	.03	.01	.00
□ 103	Tony Mandarich	.06	.03	.00
□ 104	Sterling Sharpe	.10	.05	.01
□ 105	Don Majkowski	.08	.04	.01
□ 106	Johnny Holland	.03	.01	.00
□ 107	Esera Tuaolo	.03	.01	.00
□ 108	Darrell Thompson	.08	.04	.01
□ 109	Bubba McDowell	.03	.01	.00
□ 110	Curtis Duncan	.03	.01	.00
□ 111	Lamar Lathon	.06	.03	.00
□ 112	Drew Hill	.08	.04	.01
□ 113	Bruce Matthews	.03	.01	.00
□ 114	Bo Orlando	.20	.10	.02
□ 115	Don Maggs	.03	.01	.00
□ 116	Lorenzo White	.06	.03	.00
□ 117	Ernest Givins	.10	.05	.01
□ 118	Tony Jones	.06	.03	.00
□ 119	Dean Steinkuhler	.03	.01	.00
□ 120	Dean Biasucci	.03	.01	.00
□ 121	Duane Bickett	.03	.01	.00
□ 122	Bill Brooks	.03	.01	.00
□ 123	Ken Clark	.03	.01	.00
□ 124	Jessie Hester	.03	.01	.00
□ 125	Anthony Johnson	.03	.01	.00
□ 126	Chip Banks	.03	.01	.00
□ 127	Mike Prior	.03	.01	.00
□ 128	Rohn Stark	.03	.01	.00
□ 129	Jeff Herrod	.03	.01	.00
□ 130	Clarence Verdin	.03	.01	.00
□ 131	Tim Manoa	.03	.01	.00
□ 132	Brian Baldinger	.08	.04	.01
□ 133	Tim Barnett	.12	.06	.01
□ 134	J.J. Birden	.06	.03	.00
□ 135	Deron Cherry	.03	.01	.00
□ 136	Steve DeBerg	.08	.04	.01
□ 137	Nick Lowery	.06	.03	.00
□ 138	Todd McNair	.03	.01	.00
□ 139	Christian Okoye	.10	.05	.01
□ 140	Mark Vlasic	.08	.04	.01
□ 141	Dan Saleaumua	.03	.01	.00
□ 142	Neil Smith	.03	.01	.00
□ 143	Robb Thomas	.06	.03	.00
□ 144	Eddie Anderson	.03	.01	.00
□ 145	Nick Bell	.35	.17	.03
□ 146	Tim Brown	.08	.04	.01
□ 147	Roger Craig	.10	.05	.01
□ 148	Jeff Gossett	.03	.01	.00
□ 149	Ethan Horton	.06	.03	.00
□ 150	Jamie Holland	.03	.01	.00
□ 151	Jeff Jaeger	.03	.01	.00
□ 152	Todd Marinovich	.60	.30	.06
□ 153	Marcus Allen	.10	.05	.01

☐ 154	Steve Smith	.03	.01	.00	☐ 211	Rodney Hampton	.20	.10	.02
☐ 155	Flipper Anderson	.06	.03	.00	☐ 212	Jeff Hostetler	.15	.07	.01
☐ 156	Robert Delpino	.06	.03	.00	☐ 213	Pepper Johnson	.03	.01	.00
☐ 157	Cleveland Gary	.06	.03	.00	☐ 214	Leonard Marshall	.03	.01	.00
☐ 158	Kevin Greene	.06	.03	.00	☐ 215	Doug Riesenberg	.03	.01	.00
☐ 159	Dale Hatcher	.03	.01	.00	☐ 216	Stephen Baker	.06	.03	.00
☐ 160	Duval Love	.03	.01	.00	☐ 217	Mike Fox	.03	.01	.00
☐ 161	Ron Brown	.03	.01	.00	☐ 218	Bart Oates	.03	.01	.00
☐ 162	Jackie Slater	.06	.03	.00	☐ 219	Everson Walls	.03	.01	.00
☐ 163	Doug Smith	.03	.01	.00	☐ 220	Gary Reasons	.03	.01	.00
☐ 164	Aaron Cox	.03	.01	.00	☐ 221	Jeff Lageman	.06	.03	.00
☐ 165	Larry Kelm	.03	.01	.00	☐ 222	Joe Kelly	.03	.01	.00
☐ 166	Mark Clayton	.08	.04	.01	☐ 223	Mo Lewis	.08	.04	.01
☐ 167	Louis Oliver	.03	.01	.00	☐ 224	Tony Stargell	.03	.01	.00
☐ 168	Mark Higgs	.25	.12	.02	☐ 225	Jim Sweeney	.03	.01	.00
☐ 169	Aaron Craver	.06	.03	.00	☐ 226	Freeman McNeil	.08	.04	.01
☐ 170	Sammie Smith	.08	.04	.01	☐ 227	Brian Washington	.03	.01	.00
☐ 171	Tony Paige	.03	.01	.00	☐ 228	Johnny Hector	.06	.03	.00
☐ 172	Jeff Cross	.03	.01	.00	☐ 229	Terance Mathis	.08	.04	.01
☐ 173	David Griggs	.03	.01	.00	☐ 230	Rob Moore	.25	.12	.02
☐ 174	Richmond Webb	.06	.03	.00	☐ 231	Brad Baxter	.06	.03	.00
☐ 175	Vestee Jackson	.03	.01	.00	☐ 232	Eric Allen	.03	.01	.00
☐ 176	Jim C. Jensen	.03	.01	.00	☐ 233	Fred Barnett	.12	.06	.01
☐ 177	Anthony Carter	.06	.03	.00	☐ 234	Jerome Brown	.06	.03	.00
☐ 178	Cris Carter	.06	.03	.00	☐ 235	Keith Byars	.06	.03	.00
☐ 179	Chris Doleman	.06	.03	.00	☐ 236	William Thomas	.03	.01	.00
☐ 180	Rich Gannon	.06	.03	.00	☐ 237	Jessie Small	.03	.01	.00
☐ 181	Al Noga	.03	.01	.00	☐ 238	Robert Drummond	.03	.01	.00
☐ 182	Randall McDaniel	.03	.01	.00	☐ 239	Reggie White	.08	.04	.01
☐ 183	Todd Scott	.03	.01	.00	☐ 240	James Joseph	.20	.10	.02
☐ 184	Henry Thomas	.03	.01	.00	☐ 241	Brad Goebel	.10	.05	.01
☐ 185	Felix Wright	.03	.01	.00	☐ 242	Clyde Simmons	.06	.03	.00
☐ 186	Gary Zimmerman	.03	.01	.00	☐ 243	Rich Camarillo	.03	.01	.00
☐ 187	Herschel Walker	.10	.05	.01	☐ 244	Ken Harvey	.03	.01	.00
☐ 188	Vincent Brown	.03	.01	.00	☐ 245	Garth Jax	.03	.01	.00
☐ 189	Harry Colon	.03	.01	.00	☐ 246	Johnny Johnson	.15	.07	.01
☐ 190	Irving Fryar	.06	.03	.00	☐ 247	Mike Jones	.03	.01	.00
☐ 191	Marv Cook	.10	.05	.01	☐ 248	Ernie Jones	.03	.01	.00
☐ 192	Leonard Russell	.60	.30	.06	☐ 249	Tom Tupa	.06	.03	.00
☐ 193	Hugh Millen	.40	.20	.04	☐ 250	Ron Wolfley	.03	.01	.00
☐ 194	Pat Harlow	.06	.03	.00	☐ 251	Luis Sharpe	.03	.01	.00
☐ 195	Jon Vaughn	.25	.12	.02	☐ 252	Eric Swann	.08	.04	.01
☐ 196	Ben Coates	.15	.07	.01	☐ 253	Anthony Thompson	.08	.04	.01
☐ 197	Johnny Rembert	.03	.01	.00	☐ 254	Gary Anderson	.03	.01	.00
☐ 198	Greg McMurtry	.06	.03	.00	☐ 255	Dermontti Dawson	.03	.01	.00
☐ 199	Morten Andersen	.06	.03	.00	☐ 256	Jeff Graham	.10	.05	.01
☐ 200	Tommy Barnhardt	.03	.01	.00	☐ 257	Eric Green	.12	.06	.01
☐ 201	Bobby Hebert	.08	.04	.01	☐ 258	Louis Lipps	.06	.03	.00
☐ 202	Dalton Hilliard	.06	.03	.00	☐ 259	Neil O'Donnell	.40	.20	.04
☐ 203	Sam Mills	.03	.01	.00	☐ 260	Rod Woodson	.06	.03	.00
☐ 204	Pat Swilling	.08	.04	.01	☐ 261	Dwight Stone	.03	.01	.00
☐ 205	Rickey Jackson	.06	.03	.00	☐ 262	Aaron Jones	.03	.01	.00
☐ 206	Stan Brock	.03	.01	.00	☐ 263	Keith Willis	.03	.01	.00
☐ 207	Reggie Jones	.03	.01	.00	☐ 264	Ernie Mills	.08	.04	.01
☐ 208	Gill Fenerty	.06	.03	.00	☐ 265	Martin Bayless	.03	.01	.00
☐ 209	Eric Martin	.03	.01	.00	☐ 266	Rod Bernstine	.06	.03	.00
☐ 210	Matt Bahr	.03	.01	.00	☐ 267	John Carney	.03	.01	.00

☐ 268 John Friesz	.15	.07	.01
☐ 269 Nate Lewis	.03	.01	.00
☐ 270 Shawn Jefferson	.03	.01	.00
☐ 271 Burt Grossman	.06	.03	.00
☐ 272 Eric Moten	.03	.01	.00
☐ 273 Gary Plummer	.03	.01	.00
☐ 274 Henry Rolling	.03	.01	.00
☐ 275 Steve Hendrickson	.12	.06	.01
☐ 276 Michael Carter	.06	.03	.00
☐ 277 Steve Bono	.40	.20	.04
☐ 278 Dexter Carter	.06	.03	.00
☐ 279 Mike Cofer	.03	.01	.00
☐ 280 Charles Haley	.06	.03	.00
☐ 281 Tom Rathman	.06	.03	.00
☐ 282 Guy McIntyre	.03	.01	.00
☐ 283 John Taylor	.10	.05	.01
☐ 284 Dave Waymer	.03	.01	.00
☐ 285 Steve Wallace	.03	.01	.00
☐ 286 Jamie Williams	.03	.01	.00
☐ 287 Brian Blades	.06	.03	.00
☐ 288 Jeff Bryant	.03	.01	.00
☐ 289 Grant Feasel	.03	.01	.00
☐ 290 Jacob Green	.03	.01	.00
☐ 291 Andy Heck	.03	.01	.00
☐ 292 Kelly Stouffer	.08	.04	.01
☐ 293 John Kasay	.03	.01	.00
☐ 294 Cortez Kennedy	.06	.03	.00
☐ 295 Bryan Millard	.03	.01	.00
☐ 296 Eugene Robinson	.03	.01	.00
☐ 297 Tony Woods	.03	.01	.00
☐ 298 Jesse Anderson	.03	.01	.00
☐ 299 Gary Anderson	.06	.03	.00
☐ 300 Mark Carrier	.06	.03	.00
☐ 301 Reggie Cobb	.12	.06	.01
☐ 302 Robert Wilson	.10	.05	.01
☐ 303 Jesse Solomon	.03	.01	.00
☐ 304 Broderick Thomas	.06	.03	.00
☐ 305 Lawrence Dawsey	.12	.06	.01
☐ 306 Charles McRae	.03	.01	.00
☐ 307 Paul Gruber	.03	.01	.00
☐ 308 Vinny Testaverde	.08	.04	.01
☐ 309 Brian Mitchell	.12	.06	.01
☐ 310 Darrell Green	.10	.05	.01
☐ 311 Art Monk	.12	.06	.01
☐ 312 Russ Grimm	.03	.01	.00
☐ 313 Mark Rypien	.20	.10	.02
☐ 314 Bobby Wilson	.03	.01	.00
☐ 315 Wilber Marshall	.06	.03	.00
☐ 316 Gerald Riggs	.06	.03	.00
☐ 317 Chip Lohmiller	.03	.01	.00
☐ 318 Joe Jacoby	.03	.01	.00
☐ 319 Martin Mayhew	.03	.01	.00
☐ 320 Amp Lee	.35	.17	.03
☐ 321 Terrell Buckley	.75	.35	.07
☐ 322 Tommy Vardell	.60	.30	.06
☐ 323 Ricardo McDonald	.10	.05	.01
☐ 324 Joe Bowden	.10	.05	.01

☐ 325 Darryl Williams	.15	.07	.01
☐ 326 Carlos Huerta	.10	.05	.01
☐ 327 Patrick Rowe	.20	.10	.02
☐ 328 Siran Stacy	.35	.17	.03
☐ 329 Dexter McNabb	.15	.07	.01
☐ 330 Willie Clay	.15	.07	.01

1992 Pacific Legends of the Game Steve Largent

This nine-card set captures highlights from the career of future Hall of Famer Steve Largent. The standard-size (2 1/2" by 3 1/2") cards were randomly inserted in first series foil packs and jumbo packs; Largent personally autographed 1,000 cards. The color action photos on the fronts have white borders, with the player's name and a caption in a multicolored stripe cutting across the bottom of the picture. In a horizontal format, the backs carry another color photo and career summary. The cards are numbered on the back.

	MINT	EXC	G-VG
COMPLETE SET (9)	12.50	6.25	1.25
COMMON PLAYER (1-9)	1.50	.75	.15

☐ 1 Great Rookie Start	1.50	.75	.15
☐ 2 Largent Leads NFL	1.50	.75	.15
☐ 3 Hi-Steppin'	1.50	.75	.15
☐ 4 NFL Leader	1.50	.75	.15
☐ 5 Team Captain	1.50	.75	.15
☐ 6 Pro Bowl	1.50	.75	.15

☐ 7	Man of the Year 1.50	.75	.15
☐ 8	The Final Season 1.50	.75	.15
☐ 9	Retirement Celebration ... 1.50	.75	.15

1992 Pacific Statistical Leaders

*This 30-card standard-size (2 1/2" by 3 1/2")
set features the team statistical leaders from
the 28 NFL teams, plus two cards devoted to
the AFC and NFC rushing leaders. The cards
were randomly inserted into series I foil packs.
The fronts display glossy color action photos
bordered in white. At the bottom of the picture,
the player's name and accomplishment appear
in a multi-colored stripe. The backs reflect the
team's colors and have mini-photos of three
other team leaders. The cards are numbered
on the back and the team leader cards are
checklisted alphabetically according to team
name.*

	MINT	EXC	G-VG
COMPLETE SET (30)	25.00	12.50	2.50
COMMON PLAYER (1-30)	.50	.25	.05

☐ 1	Chris Miller 1.00	.50	.10
	Atlanta Falcons		
☐ 2	Thurman Thomas 3.00	1.50	.30
	Buffalo Bills		
☐ 3	Jim Harbaugh .... .75	.35	.07
	Chicago Bears		
☐ 4	Jim Breech .... .50	.25	.05
	Cincinnati Bengals		
☐ 5	Kevin Mack .... .60	.30	.06
	Cleveland Browns		

☐ 6	Emmitt Smith 5.00	2.50	.50
	Dallas Cowboys		
☐ 7	Gaston Green 1.00	.50	.10
	Denver Broncos		
☐ 8	Barry Sanders 4.00	2.00	.40
	Detroit Lions		
☐ 9	Tony Bennett .... .60	.30	.06
	Green Bay Packers		
☐ 10	Warren Moon 1.00	.50	.10
	Houston Oilers		
☐ 11	Bill Brooks .... .50	.25	.05
	Indianapolis Colts		
☐ 12	Christian Okoye .... .75	.35	.07
	Kansas City Chiefs		
☐ 13	Jay Schroeder .... .60	.30	.06
	Los Angeles Raiders		
☐ 14	Robert Delpino .... .60	.30	.06
	Los Angeles Rams		
☐ 15	Mark Higgs .... .75	.35	.07
	Miami Dolphins		
☐ 16	John Randle .... .50	.25	.05
	Minnesota Vikings		
☐ 17	Leonard Russell 2.00	1.00	.20
	New England Patriots		
☐ 18	Pat Swilling .... .60	.30	.06
	New Orleans Saints		
☐ 19	Rodney Hampton 1.50	.75	.15
	New York Giants		
☐ 20	Terance Mathis .... .60	.30	.06
	New York Jets		
☐ 21	Fred Barnett .... .75	.35	.07
	Philadelphia Eagles		
☐ 22	Aeneas Williams .... .60	.30	.06
	Phoenix Cardinals		
☐ 23	Neil O'Donnell 1.00	.50	.10
	Pittsburgh Steelers		
☐ 24	Marion Butts .... .75	.35	.07
	San Diego Chargers		
☐ 25	Steve Young .... .75	.35	.07
	San Francisco 49ers		
☐ 26	John L. Williams .... .60	.30	.06
	Seattle Seahawks		
☐ 27	Reggie Cobb .... .60	.30	.06
	Tampa Bay Buccaneers		
☐ 28	Mark Rypien 1.50	.75	.15
	Washington Redskins		
☐ 29	Thurman Thomas 2.50	1.25	.25
	Buffalo Bills		
	AFC Rushing Leaders		
☐ 30	Emmitt Smith 4.00	2.00	.40
	Dallas Cowboys		
	NFC Rushing Leaders		

1992 Pacific Plus I Checklists

These checklist cards were randomly inserted in first series foil and jumbo packs. They are numbered on the back "X of 8," apparently in anticipation of the four checklist cards that were to be issued with the second series. The cards are standard size, 2 1/2" by 3 1/2".

	MINT	EXC	G-VG
COMPLETE SET (4)	3.00	1.50	.30
COMMON PLAYER (1-4)	1.00	.50	.30
☐ 1 Checklist 1 (1-110)	1.00	.50	.10
☐ 2 Checklist 2 (111-220)	1.00	.50	.10
☐ 3 Checklist 3 (221-330)	1.00	.50	.10
☐ 4 Checklist 4	1.00	.50	.10
(Highlight Cards)			

1964 Philadelphia

The 1964 Philadelphia Gum set of 198 football cards, featuring National Football League players, is the first of four annual issues released by the company. The cards measure 2 1/2" by 3 1/2". Each player has a question about that player in a cartoon at the bottom of the reverse; the answer is given upside down in blue ink. Each team has a team picture card as well as a card diagramming one of the team's plays; this "play card" shows a small black and white picture of the team's coach on the front of the card. The card backs are printed in blue and black on a gray card stock. The cards are numbered within team, i.e., Baltimore Colts (1-14), Chicago Bears (15-28), Cleveland Browns (29-42), Dallas Cowboys (43-56), Detroit Lions (57-70), Green Bay Packers (71-84), Los Angeles Rams (85-98), Minnesota Vikings (99-112), New York Giants (113-126), Philadelphia Eagles (127-140), Pittsburgh Steelers (141-154), San Francisco 49ers (155-168), St. Louis Cardinals (169-182), Washington Redskins (183-196), and Checklists (197-198). Within each team group the players are arranged alphabetically by last name. The two checklist cards say "Official 1963 Checklist" at the top; one collector speculates that this "uncorrected error" may be an additional explanation as to their scarcity in that confused collectors in back 1964 may have discarded them. The key rookie cards in this set are Herb Adderley, Willie Davis, John Mackey, Merlin Olsen, and Jack Pardee.

	NRMT	VG-E	GOOD
COMPLETE SET (198)	850.00	425.00	85.00
COMMON PLAYER (1-198)	1.35	.65	.13
☐ 1 Raymond Berry	20.00	5.00	1.00
☐ 2 Tom Gilburg	1.35	.65	.13
☐ 3 John Mackey	20.00	10.00	2.00
☐ 4 Gino Marchetti	4.00	2.00	.40
☐ 5 Jim Martin	1.35	.65	.13
☐ 6 Tom Matte	4.50	2.25	.45
☐ 7 Jimmy Orr	1.75	.85	.17
☐ 8 Jim Parker	4.00	2.00	.40
☐ 9 Bill Pellington	1.35	.65	.13
☐ 10 Alex Sandusky	1.35	.65	.13
☐ 11 Dick Szymanski	1.35	.65	.13
☐ 12 John Unitas	45.00	22.50	4.50
☐ 13 Baltimore Colts	3.25	1.60	.32
Team Card			

☐ 14	Baltimore Colts 14.00	7.00	1.40
	Play Card		
	(Don Shula)		
☐ 15	Doug Atkins 4.00	2.00	.40
☐ 16	Ron Bull 1.75	.85	.17
☐ 17	Mike Ditka 25.00	12.50	2.50
☐ 18	Joe Fortunato 1.75	.85	.17
☐ 19	Willie Galimore 1.75	.85	.17
☐ 20	Joe Marconi 1.35	.65	.13
☐ 21	Bennie McRae 2.50	1.25	.25
☐ 22	Johnny Morris 2.00	1.00	.20
☐ 23	Richie Petitbon 2.00	1.00	.20
☐ 24	Mike Pyle 1.35	.65	.13
☐ 25	Roosevelt Taylor 4.00	2.00	.40
☐ 26	Bill Wade 1.75	.85	.17
☐ 27	Chicago Bears 3.25	1.60	.32
	Team Card		
☐ 28	Chicago Bears 11.00	5.50	1.10
	Play Card		
	(George Halas)		
☐ 29	Johnny Brewer 1.35	.65	.13
☐ 30	Jim Brown 70.00	35.00	7.00
☐ 31	Gary Collins 5.00	2.50	.50
☐ 32	Vince Costello 1.35	.65	.13
☐ 33	Galen Fiss 1.35	.65	.13
☐ 34	Bill Glass 1.75	.85	.17
☐ 35	Ernie Green 3.50	1.75	.35
☐ 36	Rich Kreitling 1.35	.65	.13
☐ 37	John Morrow 1.35	.65	.13
☐ 38	Frank Ryan 2.00	1.00	.20
☐ 39	Charlie Scales 2.00	1.00	.20
☐ 40	Dick Schafrath 3.00	1.50	.30
☐ 41	Cleveland Browns 3.25	1.60	.32
	Team Card		
☐ 42	Cleveland Browns 2.00	1.00	.20
	Play Card		
	(Blanton Collier)		
☐ 43	Don Bishop 1.35	.65	.13
☐ 44	Frank Clarke 3.50	1.75	.35
☐ 45	Mike Connelly 1.35	.65	.13
☐ 46	Lee Folkins 1.35	.65	.13
☐ 47	Cornell Green 4.25	2.10	.42
☐ 48	Bob Lilly 21.00	10.50	2.10
☐ 49	Amos Marsh 1.35	.65	.13
☐ 50	Tommy McDonald 2.00	1.00	.20
☐ 51	Don Meredith 30.00	15.00	3.00
☐ 52	Pettis Norman 2.50	1.25	.25
☐ 53	Don Perkins 2.75	1.35	.27
☐ 54	Guy Reese 1.35	.65	.13
☐ 55	Dallas Cowboys 3.25	1.60	.32
	Team Card		
☐ 56	Dallas Cowboys 14.00	7.00	1.40
	Play Card		
	(Tom Landry)		
☐ 57	Terry Barr 1.35	.65	.13
☐ 58	Roger Brown 1.75	.85	.17
☐ 59	Gail Cogdill 1.35	.65	.13

☐ 60	John Gordy 1.35	.65	.13
☐ 61	Dick Lane 3.75	1.85	.37
☐ 62	Yale Lary 3.75	1.85	.37
☐ 63	Dan Lewis 1.35	.65	.13
☐ 64	Darris McCord 1.35	.65	.13
☐ 65	Earl Morrall 2.75	1.35	.27
☐ 66	Joe Schmidt 4.00	2.00	.40
☐ 67	Pat Studstill 3.75	1.85	.37
☐ 68	Wayne Walker 3.75	1.85	.37
☐ 69	Detroit Lions 3.25	1.60	.32
	Team Card		
☐ 70	Detroit Lions 2.00	1.00	.20
	Play Card		
	(George Wilson)		
☐ 71	Herb Adderley 30.00	15.00	3.00
☐ 72	Willie Davis 30.00	15.00	3.00
☐ 73	Forrest Gregg 4.00	2.00	.40
☐ 74	Paul Hornung 22.00	11.00	2.20
☐ 75	Henry Jordan 1.75	.85	.17
☐ 76	Jerry Kramer 3.50	1.75	.35
☐ 77	Tom Moore 1.75	.85	.17
☐ 78	Jim Ringo 3.75	1.85	.37
☐ 79	Bart Starr 28.00	14.00	2.80
☐ 80	Jim Taylor 12.00	6.00	1.20
☐ 81	Jesse Whittenton 3.00	1.50	.30
☐ 82	Willie Wood 7.00	3.50	.70
☐ 83	Green Bay Packers 3.25	1.60	.32
	Team Card		
☐ 84	Green Bay Packers 25.00	12.50	2.50
	Play Card		
	(Vince Lombardi)		
☐ 85	Jon Arnett 1.75	.85	.17
☐ 86	Pervis Atkins 2.00	1.00	.20
☐ 87	Dick Bass 1.75	.85	.17
☐ 88	Carroll Dale 1.35	.65	.13
☐ 89	Roman Gabriel 4.50	2.25	.45
☐ 90	Ed Meador 1.75	.85	.17
☐ 91	Merlin Olsen 70.00	35.00	7.00
☐ 92	Jack Pardee 10.00	5.00	1.00
☐ 93	Jim Phillips 1.35	.65	.13
☐ 94	Carver Shannon 1.35	.65	.13
☐ 95	Frank Varrichione 1.35	.65	.13
☐ 96	Danny Villanueva 1.35	.65	.13
☐ 97	Los Angeles Rams 3.25	1.60	.32
	Team Card		
☐ 98	Los Angeles Rams 2.00	1.00	.20
	Play Card		
	(Harland Svare)		
☐ 99	Grady Alderman 2.75	1.35	.27
☐ 100	Larry Bowie 1.35	.65	.13
☐ 101	Bill Brown 4.00	2.00	.40
☐ 102	Paul Flatley 2.50	1.25	.25
☐ 103	Rip Hawkins 1.35	.65	.13
☐ 104	Jim Marshall 4.50	2.25	.45
☐ 105	Tommy Mason 1.75	.85	.17
☐ 106	Jim Prestel 1.35	.65	.13
☐ 107	Jerry Reichow 1.35	.65	.13

☐ 108	Ed Sharockman 1.35	.65	.13
☐ 109	Fran Tarkenton 40.00	20.00	4.00
☐ 110	Mick Tingelhoff 6.00	3.00	.60
☐ 111	Minnesota Vikings 3.25	1.60	.32
	Team Card		
☐ 112	Minnesota Vikings 3.75	1.85	.37
	Play Card		
	(Norm Van Brocklin)		
☐ 113	Erich Barnes 1.75	.85	.17
☐ 114	Roosevelt Brown 4.00	2.00	.40
☐ 115	Don Chandler 1.75	.85	.17
☐ 116	Darrell Dess 1.35	.65	.13
☐ 117	Frank Gifford 45.00	22.50	4.50
☐ 118	Dick James 1.35	.65	.13
☐ 119	Jim Katcavage 1.75	.85	.17
☐ 120	John Lovetere 1.35	.65	.13
☐ 121	Dick Lynch 3.50	1.75	.35
☐ 122	Jim Patton 1.75	.85	.17
☐ 123	Del Shofner 1.75	.85	.17
☐ 124	Y.A. Tittle 18.00	9.00	1.80
☐ 125	New York Giants 3.25	1.60	.32
	Team Card		
☐ 126	New York Giants 2.00	1.00	.20
	Play Card		
	(Allie Sherman)		
☐ 127	Sam Baker 1.35	.65	.13
☐ 128	Maxie Baughan 2.00	1.00	.20
☐ 129	Timmy Brown 2.00	1.00	.20
☐ 130	Mike Clark 1.35	.65	.13
☐ 131	Irv Cross 6.00	3.00	.60
☐ 132	Ted Dean 1.35	.65	.13
☐ 133	Ron Goodwin 1.35	.65	.13
☐ 134	King Hill 1.75	.85	.17
☐ 135	Clarence Peaks 1.35	.65	.13
☐ 136	Pete Retzlaff 1.35	.65	.13
☐ 137	Jim Schrader 1.35	.65	.13
☐ 138	Norm Snead 2.50	1.25	.25
☐ 139	Philadelphia Eagles 3.25	1.60	.32
	Team Card		
☐ 140	Philadelphia Eagles 2.00	1.00	.20
	Play Card		
	(Nick Skorich)		
☐ 141	Gary Ballman 2.50	1.25	.25
☐ 142	Charley Bradshaw 1.35	.65	.13
☐ 143	Ed Brown 1.75	.85	.17
☐ 144	John Henry Johnson 4.00	2.00	.40
☐ 145	Joe Krupa 1.35	.65	.13
☐ 146	Bill Mack 1.35	.65	.13
☐ 147	Lou Michaels 1.35	.65	.13
☐ 148	Buzz Nutter 1.35	.65	.13
☐ 149	Myron Pottios 1.35	.65	.13
☐ 150	John Reger 1.35	.65	.13
☐ 151	Mike Sandusky 1.35	.65	.13
☐ 152	Clendon Thomas 1.35	.65	.13
☐ 153	Pittsburgh Steelers 3.25	1.60	.32
	Team Card		
☐ 154	Pittsburgh Steelers 2.00	1.00	.20

	Play Card		
	(Buddy Parker)		
☐ 155	Kermit Alexander 4.25	2.10	.42
☐ 156	Bernie Casey 1.75	.85	.17
☐ 157	Dan Colchico 1.35	.65	.13
☐ 158	Clyde Conner 1.35	.65	.13
☐ 159	Tommy Davis 1.35	.65	.13
☐ 160	Matt Hazeltine 1.35	.65	.13
☐ 161	Jim Johnson 4.25	2.10	.42
☐ 162	Don Lisbon 1.35	.65	.13
☐ 163	Lamar McHan 1.35	.65	.13
☐ 164	Bob St. Clair 3.50	1.75	.35
☐ 165	J.D. Smith 1.75	.85	.17
☐ 166	Abe Woodson 1.75	.85	.17
☐ 167	San Francisco 49ers 3.25	1.60	.32
	Team Card		
☐ 168	San Francisco 49ers 2.00	1.00	.20
	Play Card		
	(Red Hickey)		
☐ 169	Garland Boyette UER ... 1.75	.85	.17
	(Photo on front		
	is not Boyette)		
☐ 170	Bobby Joe Conrad 1.75	.85	.17
☐ 171	Bob DeMarco 2.50	1.25	.25
☐ 172	Ken Gray 2.50	1.25	.25
☐ 173	Jimmy Hill 1.35	.65	.13
☐ 174	Charlie Johnson 2.75	1.35	.27
☐ 175	Ernie McMillan 1.75	.85	.17
☐ 176	Dale Meinert 1.35	.65	.13
☐ 177	Luke Owens 1.35	.65	.13
☐ 178	Sonny Randle 1.75	.85	.17
☐ 179	Joe Robb 1.35	.65	.13
☐ 180	Bill Stacy 1.35	.65	.13
☐ 181	St. Louis Cardinals 3.25	1.60	.32
	Team Card		
☐ 182	St. Louis Cardinals 2.00	1.00	.20
	Play Card		
	(Wally Lemm)		
☐ 183	Bill Barnes 1.35	.65	.13
☐ 184	Don Bosseler 1.35	.65	.13
☐ 185	Sam Huff 5.00	2.50	.50
☐ 186	Sonny Jurgensen 18.00	9.00	1.80
☐ 187	Bob Khayat 1.35	.65	.13
☐ 188	Riley Mattson 1.35	.65	.13
☐ 189	Bobby Mitchell 5.00	2.50	.50
☐ 190	John Nisby 1.35	.65	.13
☐ 191	Vince Promuto 1.35	.65	.13
☐ 192	Joe Rutgens 1.35	.65	.13
☐ 193	Lonnie Sanders 1.35	.65	.13
☐ 194	Jim Steffen 1.35	.65	.13
☐ 195	Washington Redskins 3.25	1.60	.32
	Team Card		
☐ 196	Washington Redskins 2.00	1.00	.20
	Play Card		
	(Bill McPeak)		
☐ 197	Checklist 1 UER 25.00	3.00	.60
☐ 198	Checklist 2 UER 45.00	4.50	.90

1965 Philadelphia

The 1965 Philadelphia Gum set of NFL players is complete at 198 cards. The cards measure the standard 2 1/2" by 3 1/2". The card backs show (when rubbed with a coin) a question and answer interrelated to other cards. Each team has a team picture card as well as a card featuring a diagram of one of the team's plays; this play card shows a small coach's picture in black and white on the front of the card. The card backs are printed in maroon on a gray card stock. The cards are numbered within team, i.e., Baltimore Colts (1-14), Chicago Bears (15-28), Cleveland Browns (29-42), Dallas Cowboys (43-56), Detroit Lions (57-70), Green Bay Packers (71-84), Los Angeles Rams (85-98), Minnesota Vikings (99-112), New York Giants (113-126), Philadelphia Eagles (127-140), Pittsburgh Steelers (141-154), St. Louis Cardinals (155-168), San Francisco 49ers (169-182), Washington Redskins (183-196), and Checklists (197-198). Within each team group the players are arranged alphabetically by last name. The key rookie cards in this set are Carl Eller, Paul Krause, Mel Renfro, Charley Taylor and Paul Warfield.

	NRMT	VG-E	GOOD
COMPLETE SET (198)	725.00	350.00	80.00
COMMON PLAYER (1-198)	1.25	.60	.12
☐ 1 Baltimore Colts Team Card	8.50	2.00	.40
☐ 2 Raymond Berry	5.00	2.50	.50
☐ 3 Bob Boyd	1.25	.60	.12
☐ 4 Wendell Harris	1.25	.60	.12
☐ 5 Jerry Logan	1.25	.60	.12
☐ 6 Tony Lorick	1.25	.60	.12
☐ 7 Lou Michaels	1.25	.60	.12
☐ 8 Lenny Moore	5.00	2.50	.50
☐ 9 Jimmy Orr	1.75	.85	.17
☐ 10 Jim Parker	3.75	1.85	.37
☐ 11 Dick Szymanski	1.25	.60	.12
☐ 12 John Unitas	34.00	15.00	3.00
☐ 13 Bob Vogel	2.00	1.00	.20
☐ 14 Baltimore Colts Play Card (Don Shula)	6.50	3.25	.65
☐ 15 Chicago Bears Team Card	3.25	1.60	.32
☐ 16 Jon Arnett	1.75	.85	.17
☐ 17 Doug Atkins	3.75	1.85	.37
☐ 18 Rudy Bukich	2.25	1.10	.22
☐ 19 Mike Ditka	15.00	7.50	1.50
☐ 20 Dick Evey	1.25	.60	.12
☐ 21 Joe Fortunato	1.75	.85	.17
☐ 22 Bobby Joe Green	2.50	1.25	.25
☐ 23 Johnny Morris	1.75	.85	.17
☐ 24 Mike Pyle	1.25	.60	.12
☐ 25 Roosevelt Taylor	1.75	.85	.17
☐ 26 Bill Wade	1.75	.85	.17
☐ 27 Bob Wetoska	1.25	.60	.12
☐ 28 Chicago Bears Play Card (George Halas)	5.00	2.50	.50
☐ 29 Cleveland Browns Team Card	3.25	1.60	.32
☐ 30 Walter Beach	1.25	.60	.12
☐ 31 Jim Brown	60.00	30.00	6.00
☐ 32 Gary Collins	2.25	1.10	.22
☐ 33 Bill Glass	1.75	.85	.17
☐ 34 Ernie Green	1.75	.85	.17
☐ 35 Jim Houston	2.50	1.25	.25
☐ 36 Dick Modzelewski	1.75	.85	.17
☐ 37 Bernie Parrish	1.25	.60	.12
☐ 38 Walter Roberts	1.25	.60	.12
☐ 39 Frank Ryan	2.25	1.10	.22
☐ 40 Dick Schafrath	1.75	.85	.17
☐ 41 Paul Warfield	70.00	35.00	7.00
☐ 42 Cleveland Browns Play Card (Blanton Collier)	1.75	.85	.17
☐ 43 Dallas Cowboys Team Card	3.25	1.60	.32
☐ 44 Frank Clarke	1.75	.85	.17
☐ 45 Mike Connelly	1.25	.60	.12
☐ 46 Buddy Dial	1.75	.85	.17
☐ 47 Bob Lilly	11.00	5.50	1.10
☐ 48 Tony Liscio	1.25	.60	.12
☐ 49 Tommy McDonald	2.00	1.00	.20
☐ 50 Don Meredith	25.00	12.50	2.50
☐ 51 Pettis Norman	1.75	.85	.17
☐ 52 Don Perkins	2.50	1.25	.25
☐ 53 Mel Renfro	10.00	5.00	1.00
☐ 54 Jim Ridlon	1.25	.60	.12

☐ 55	Jerry Tubbs 1.75	.85	.17
☐ 56	Dallas Cowboys 7.00	3.50	.70
	Play Card		
	(Tom Landry)		
☐ 57	Detroit Lions 3.25	1.60	.32
	Team Card		
☐ 58	Terry Barr 1.25	.60	.12
☐ 59	Roger Brown 1.75	.85	.17
☐ 60	Gail Cogdill 1.25	.60	.12
☐ 61	Jim Gibbons 1.25	.60	.12
☐ 62	John Gordy 1.25	.60	.12
☐ 63	Yale Lary 3.50	1.75	.35
☐ 64	Dick LeBeau 3.00	1.50	.30
☐ 65	Earl Morrall 2.50	1.25	.25
☐ 66	Nick Pietrosante 2.00	1.00	.20
☐ 67	Pat Studstill 1.75	.85	.17
☐ 68	Wayne Walker 1.75	.85	.17
☐ 69	Tom Watkins 1.25	.60	.12
☐ 70	Detroit Lions 1.75	.85	.17
	Play Card		
	(George Wilson)		
☐ 71	Green Bay Packers 3.25	1.60	.32
	Team Card		
☐ 72	Herb Adderley 7.00	3.50	.70
☐ 73	Willie Davis 7.00	3.50	.70
☐ 74	Boyd Dowler 2.00	1.00	.20
☐ 75	Forrest Gregg 4.00	2.00	.40
☐ 76	Paul Hornung 20.00	10.00	2.00
☐ 77	Henry Jordan 1.75	.85	.17
☐ 78	Tom Moore 1.75	.85	.17
☐ 79	Ray Nitschke 10.00	5.00	1.00
☐ 80	Elijah Pitts 3.50	1.75	.35
☐ 81	Bart Starr 25.00	12.50	2.50
☐ 82	Jim Taylor 9.00	4.50	.90
☐ 83	Willie Wood 6.50	3.25	.65
☐ 84	Green Bay Packers 10.00	5.00	1.00
	Play Card		
	(Vince Lombardi)		
☐ 85	Los Angeles Rams 3.25	1.60	.32
	Team Card		
☐ 86	Dick Bass 1.75	.85	.17
☐ 87	Roman Gabriel 4.25	2.10	.42
☐ 88	Roosevelt Grier 3.50	1.75	.35
☐ 89	Deacon Jones 7.00	3.50	.70
☐ 90	Lamar Lundy 4.00	2.00	.40
☐ 91	Marlin McKeever 1.75	.85	.17
☐ 92	Ed Meador 1.75	.85	.17
☐ 93	Bill Munson 3.50	1.75	.35
☐ 94	Merlin Olsen 20.00	10.00	2.00
☐ 95	Bobby Smith 1.25	.60	.12
☐ 96	Frank Varrichione 1.25	.60	.12
☐ 97	Ben Wilson 1.25	.60	.12
☐ 98	Los Angeles Rams 1.75	.85	.17
	Play Card		
	(Harland Svare)		
☐ 99	Minnesota Vikings 3.25	1.60	.32
	Team Card		

☐ 100	Grady Alderman 1.75	.85	.17
☐ 101	Hal Bedsole 2.50	1.25	.25
☐ 102	Bill Brown 2.00	1.00	.20
☐ 103	Bill Butler 1.25	.60	.12
☐ 104	Fred Cox 2.75	1.35	.27
☐ 105	Carl Eller 15.00	7.50	1.50
☐ 106	Paul Flatley 1.75	.85	.17
☐ 107	Jim Marshall 3.50	1.75	.35
☐ 108	Tommy Mason 1.75	.85	.17
☐ 109	George Rose 1.25	.60	.12
☐ 110	Fran Tarkenton 30.00	15.00	3.00
☐ 111	Mick Tingelhoff 2.50	1.25	.25
☐ 112	Minnesota Vikings 3.00	1.50	.30
	Play Card		
	(Norm Van Brocklin)		
☐ 113	New York Giants 3.25	1.60	.32
	Team Card		
☐ 114	Erich Barnes 1.75	.85	.17
☐ 115	Roosevelt Brown 3.75	1.85	.37
☐ 116	Clarence Childs 1.25	.60	.12
☐ 117	Jerry Hillebrand 1.25	.60	.12
☐ 118	Greg Larson 3.00	1.50	.30
☐ 119	Dick Lynch 1.75	.85	.17
☐ 120	Joe Morrison 3.25	1.60	.32
☐ 121	Lou Slaby 1.25	.60	.12
☐ 122	Aaron Thomas 3.00	1.50	.30
☐ 123	Steve Thurlow 1.25	.60	.12
☐ 124	Ernie Wheelwright 1.25	.60	.12
☐ 125	Gary Wood 2.25	1.10	.22
☐ 126	New York Giants 1.75	.85	.17
	Play Card		
	(Allie Sherman)		
☐ 127	Philadelphia Eagles 3.25	1.60	.32
	Team Card		
☐ 128	Sam Baker 1.75	.85	.17
☐ 129	Maxie Baughan 2.25	1.10	.22
☐ 130	Timmy Brown 2.00	1.00	.20
☐ 131	Jack Concannon 3.50	1.75	.35
☐ 132	Irv Cross 3.00	1.50	.30
☐ 133	Earl Gros 1.25	.60	.12
☐ 134	Dave Lloyd 1.25	.60	.12
☐ 135	Floyd Peters 3.50	1.75	.35
☐ 136	Nate Ramsey 1.25	.60	.12
☐ 137	Pete Retzlaff 1.75	.85	.17
☐ 138	Jim Ringo 3.50	1.75	.35
☐ 139	Norm Snead 2.50	1.25	.25
☐ 140	Philadelphia Eagles 1.75	.85	.17
	Play Card		
	(Joe Kuharich)		
☐ 141	Pittsburgh Steelers 3.25	1.60	.32
	Team Card		
☐ 142	John Baker 1.25	.60	.12
☐ 143	Gary Ballman 1.75	.85	.17
☐ 144	Charley Bradshaw 1.25	.60	.12
☐ 145	Ed Brown 1.75	.85	.17
☐ 146	Dick Haley 1.25	.60	.12
☐ 147	John Henry Johnson ... 4.00	2.00	.40

☐ 148 Brady Keys	1.25	.60	.12
☐ 149 Ray Lemek	1.25	.60	.12
☐ 150 Ben McGee	1.25	.60	.12
☐ 151 Clarence Peaks	1.25	.60	.12
☐ 152 Myron Pottios	1.25	.60	.12
☐ 153 Clendon Thomas	1.25	.60	.12
☐ 154 Pittsburgh Steelers	1.75	.85	.17
Play Card			
(Buddy Parker)			
☐ 155 St. Louis Cardinals	3.25	1.60	.32
Team Card			
☐ 156 Jim Bakken	3.75	1.85	.37
☐ 157 Joe Childress	1.25	.60	.12
☐ 158 Bobby Joe Conrad	1.75	.85	.17
☐ 159 Bob DeMarco	1.25	.60	.12
☐ 160 Pat Fischer	4.25	2.10	.42
☐ 161 Irv Goode	1.25	.60	.12
☐ 162 Ken Gray	1.75	.85	.17
☐ 163 Charlie Johnson	2.50	1.25	.25
☐ 164 Bill Koman	1.25	.60	.12
☐ 165 Dale Meinert	1.25	.60	.12
☐ 166 Jerry Stovall	3.00	1.50	.30
☐ 167 Abe Woodson	1.75	.85	.17
☐ 168 St. Louis Cardinals	1.75	.85	.17
Play Card			
(Wally Lemm)			
☐ 169 San Francisco 49ers	3.25	1.60	.32
Team Card			
☐ 170 Kermit Alexander	2.00	1.00	.20
☐ 171 John Brodie	9.00	4.50	.90
☐ 172 Bernie Casey	2.00	1.00	.20
☐ 173 John David Crow	2.25	1.10	.22
☐ 174 Tommy Davis	1.25	.60	.12
☐ 175 Matt Hazeltine	1.25	.60	.12
☐ 176 Jim Johnson	2.00	1.00	.20
☐ 177 Charlie Krueger	3.00	1.50	.30
☐ 178 Roland Lakes	1.25	.60	.12
☐ 179 George Mira	3.50	1.75	.35
☐ 180 Dave Parks	4.00	2.00	.40
☐ 181 John Thomas	1.25	.60	.12
☐ 182 San Francisco 49ers	2.50	1.25	.25
Play Card			
(Jack Christiansen)			
☐ 183 Washington Redskins	3.25	1.60	.32
Team Card			
☐ 184 Pervis Atkins	1.75	.85	.17
☐ 185 Preston Carpenter	1.25	.60	.12
☐ 186 Angelo Coia	1.25	.60	.12
☐ 187 Sam Huff	5.00	2.50	.50
☐ 188 Sonny Jurgensen	15.00	7.50	1.50
☐ 189 Paul Krause	10.00	5.00	1.00
☐ 190 Jim Martin	1.25	.60	.12
☐ 191 Bobby Mitchell	5.00	2.50	.50
☐ 192 John Nisby	1.25	.60	.12
☐ 193 John Paluck	1.25	.60	.12
☐ 194 Vince Promuto	1.25	.60	.12
☐ 195 Charley Taylor	45.00	22.50	4.50

☐ 196 Washington Redskins	1.75	.85	.17
Play Card			
(Bill McPeak)			
☐ 197 Checklist 1	22.00	2.50	.50
☐ 198 Checklist 2	44.00	4.50	.90

1966 Philadelphia

The 1966 Philadelphia Gum football card set contains 198 cards featuring NFL players. The cards measure the standard 2 1/2" by 3 1/2". The backs contain the player's name, a card number, a short biography, and a "Guess Who" quiz. The quiz answer is found on another card. The last two cards in the set are checklist cards. Each team's "play card" shows a color photo of actual game action, described on the back. The card backs are printed in green and black on a white card stock. The cards are numbered within team, i.e., Atlanta Falcons (1-13), Baltimore Colts (14-26), Chicago Bears (27-39), Cleveland Browns (40-52), Dallas Cowboys (53-65), Detroit Lions (66-78), Green Bay Packers (79-91), Los Angeles Rams (92-104), Minnesota Vikings (105-117), New York Giants (118-130), Philadelphia Eagles (131-143), Pittsburgh Steelers (144-156), St. Louis Cardinals (157-169), San Francisco 49ers (170-182), Washington Redskins (183-195), Referee Signals (196), and Checklists (197-198). Within each team group the players are arranged alphabetically by last name. The set features the debut of Chicago Bears' greats, Dick Butkus and Gale Sayers.

	NRMT	VG-E	GOOD
COMPLETE SET (198)	850.00	425.00	85.00

COMMON PLAYER (1-198)	1.25	.60	.12
☐ 1 Atlanta Falcons Insignia	8.00	1.50	.30
☐ 2 Larry Benz	1.25	.60	.12
☐ 3 Dennis Claridge	1.25	.60	.12
☐ 4 Perry Lee Dunn	1.25	.60	.12
☐ 5 Dan Grimm	1.25	.60	.12
☐ 6 Alex Hawkins	1.75	.85	.17
☐ 7 Ralph Heck	1.25	.60	.12
☐ 8 Frank Lasky	1.25	.60	.12
☐ 9 Guy Reese	1.25	.60	.12
☐ 10 Bob Richards	1.25	.60	.12
☐ 11 Ron Smith	2.00	1.00	.20
☐ 12 Ernie Wheelwright	1.25	.60	.12
☐ 13 Atlanta Falcons Roster	2.00	1.00	.20
☐ 14 Baltimore Colts Team Card	3.00	1.50	.30
☐ 15 Raymond Berry	5.00	2.50	.50
☐ 16 Bob Boyd	1.25	.60	.12
☐ 17 Jerry Logan	1.25	.60	.12
☐ 18 John Mackey	4.50	2.25	.45
☐ 19 Tom Matte	2.00	1.00	.20
☐ 20 Lou Michaels	1.25	.60	.12
☐ 21 Lenny Moore	5.00	2.50	.50
☐ 22 Jimmy Orr	1.75	.85	.17
☐ 23 Jim Parker	3.50	1.75	.35
☐ 24 John Unitas	28.00	14.00	2.80
☐ 25 Bob Vogel	1.25	.60	.12
☐ 26 Baltimore Colts Play Card (Moore/Parker)	2.50	1.25	.25
☐ 27 Chicago Bears Team Card	3.00	1.50	.30
☐ 28 Doug Atkins	3.50	1.75	.35
☐ 29 Rudy Bukich	1.75	.85	.17
☐ 30 Ron Bull	1.75	.85	.17
☐ 31 Dick Butkus	165.00	80.00	16.00
☐ 32 Mike Ditka	12.50	6.25	1.25
☐ 33 Joe Fortunato	1.75	.85	.17
☐ 34 Bobby Joe Green	1.25	.60	.12
☐ 35 Roger LeClerc	1.25	.60	.12
☐ 36 Johnny Morris	1.75	.85	.17
☐ 37 Mike Pyle	1.25	.60	.12
☐ 38 Gale Sayers	200.00	100.00	20.00
☐ 39 Chicago Bears Play Card (Gale Sayers)	5.00	2.50	.50
☐ 40 Cleveland Browns Team Card	3.00	1.50	.30
☐ 41 Jim Brown	55.00	27.50	5.50
☐ 42 Gary Collins	1.75	.85	.17
☐ 43 Ross Fichtner	1.25	.60	.12
☐ 44 Ernie Green	1.75	.85	.17
☐ 45 Gene Hickerson	2.50	1.25	.25
☐ 46 Jim Houston	1.75	.85	.17
☐ 47 John Morrow	1.25	.60	.12
☐ 48 Walter Roberts	1.25	.60	.12
☐ 49 Frank Ryan	2.00	1.00	.20
☐ 50 Dick Schafrath	1.75	.85	.17
☐ 51 Paul Wiggin	2.00	1.00	.20
☐ 52 Cleveland Browns Play Card (Ernie Green sweep)	1.75	.85	.17
☐ 53 Dallas Cowboys Team Card	3.00	1.50	.30
☐ 54 George Andrie UER (text says startling, should be starting)	2.25	1.10	.22
☐ 55 Frank Clarke	1.75	.85	.17
☐ 56 Mike Connelly	1.25	.60	.12
☐ 57 Cornell Green	2.00	1.00	.20
☐ 58 Bob Hayes	9.00	4.50	.90
☐ 59 Chuck Howley	5.00	2.50	.50
☐ 60 Bob Lilly	8.00	4.00	.80
☐ 61 Don Meredith	22.00	11.00	2.20
☐ 62 Don Perkins	2.00	1.00	.20
☐ 63 Mel Renfro	3.25	1.60	.32
☐ 64 Danny Villanueva	1.25	.60	.12
☐ 65 Dallas Cowboys Play Card	1.75	.85	.17
☐ 66 Detroit Lions Team Card	3.00	1.50	.30
☐ 67 Roger Brown	1.75	.85	.17
☐ 68 John Gordy	1.25	.60	.12
☐ 69 Alex Karras	8.00	4.00	.80
☐ 70 Dick LeBeau	1.75	.85	.17
☐ 71 Amos Marsh	1.25	.60	.12
☐ 72 Milt Plum	1.75	.85	.17
☐ 73 Bobby Smith	1.25	.60	.12
☐ 74 Wayne Rasmussen	1.25	.60	.12
☐ 75 Pat Studstill	1.75	.85	.17
☐ 76 Wayne Walker	1.75	.85	.17
☐ 77 Tom Watkins	1.25	.60	.12
☐ 78 Detroit Lions Play Card (George Izo pass)	1.75	.85	.17
☐ 79 Green Bay Packers Team Card	3.00	1.50	.30
☐ 80 Herb Adderley UER (Adderly on back)	5.00	2.50	.50
☐ 81 Lee Roy Caffey	2.25	1.10	.22
☐ 82 Don Chandler	1.75	.85	.17
☐ 83 Willie Davis	5.00	2.50	.50
☐ 84 Boyd Dowler	1.75	.85	.17
☐ 85 Forrest Gregg	3.75	1.85	.37
☐ 86 Tom Moore	1.75	.85	.17
☐ 87 Ray Nitschke	6.50	3.25	.65
☐ 88 Bart Starr	22.00	11.00	2.20
☐ 89 Jim Taylor	8.00	4.00	.80
☐ 90 Willie Wood	4.50	2.25	.45
☐ 91 Green Bay Packers Play Card	1.75	.85	.17

(Don Chandler FG)

☐ 92	Los Angeles Rams .... 3.00 Team Card	1.50	.30
☐ 93	Willie Brown .... 1.75 (flanker)	.85	.17
☐ 94	Dick Bass and .... 3.00 Roman Gabriel	1.50	.30
☐ 95	Bruce Gossett 2.00	1.00	.20
☐ 96	Deacon Jones 5.00	2.50	.50
☐ 97	Tommy McDonald 1.75	.85	.17
☐ 98	Marlin McKeever 1.25	.60	.12
☐ 99	Aaron Martin 1.25	.60	.12
☐ 100	Ed Meador 1.75	.85	.17
☐ 101	Bill Munson 2.00	1.00	.20
☐ 102	Merlin Olsen 9.00	4.50	.90
☐ 103	Jim Stiger 1.25	.60	.12
☐ 104	Los Angeles Rams .... 1.75 Play Card	.85	.17
	(Willie Brown run)		
☐ 105	Minnesota Vikings .... 3.00 Team Card	1.50	.30
☐ 106	Grady Alderman 1.75	.85	.17
☐ 107	Bill Brown 1.75	.85	.17
☐ 108	Fred Cox 1.75	.85	.17
☐ 109	Paul Flatley 1.75	.85	.17
☐ 110	Rip Hawkins 1.25	.60	.12
☐ 111	Tommy Mason 1.75	.85	.17
☐ 112	Ed Sharockman 1.25	.60	.12
☐ 113	Gordon Smith 1.25	.60	.12
☐ 114	Fran Tarkenton 30.00	15.00	3.00
☐ 115	Mick Tingelhoff 2.25	1.10	.22
☐ 116	Bobby Walden 2.00	1.00	.20
☐ 117	Minnesota Vikings .... 1.75 Play Card	.85	.17
	(Bill Brown run)		
☐ 118	New York Giants .... 3.00 Team Card	1.50	.30
☐ 119	Roosevelt Brown 3.50	1.75	.35
☐ 120	Henry Carr 2.50	1.25	.25
☐ 121	Clarence Childs 1.25	.60	.12
☐ 122	Tucker Frederickson 3.00	1.50	.30
☐ 123	Jerry Hillebrand 1.25	.60	.12
☐ 124	Greg Larson 1.25	.60	.12
☐ 125	Spider Lockhart 2.75	1.35	.27
☐ 126	Dick Lynch 1.75	.85	.17
☐ 127	Earl Morrall and .... 2.00 Bob Scholtz	1.00	.20
☐ 128	Joe Morrison 1.75	.85	.17
☐ 129	Steve Thurlow 1.25	.60	.12
☐ 130	New York Giants .... 1.75 Play Card	.85	.17
	(Chuck Mercein over)		
☐ 131	Philadelphia Eagles .... 3.00 Team Card	1.50	.30
☐ 132	Sam Baker 1.75	.85	.17
☐ 133	Maxie Baughan 2.00	1.00	.20
☐ 134	Bob Brown 4.50	2.25	.45

☐ 135	Timmy Brown 1.75	.85	.17
☐ 136	Irv Cross 2.50	1.25	.25
☐ 137	Earl Gros 1.25	.60	.12
☐ 138	Ray Poage 1.25	.60	.12
☐ 139	Nate Ramsey 1.25	.60	.12
☐ 140	Pete Retzlaff 1.25	.60	.12
☐ 141	Jim Ringo 3.50	1.75	.35
☐ 142	Norm Snead 2.25	1.10	.22
☐ 143	Philadelphia Eagles .... 1.75 Play Card	.85	.17
	(Earl Gros tackled)		
☐ 144	Pittsburgh Steelers .... 3.00 Team Card	1.50	.30
☐ 145	Gary Ballman 1.75	.85	.17
☐ 146	Charley Bradshaw 1.25	.60	.12
☐ 147	Jim Butler 1.25	.60	.12
☐ 148	Mike Clark 1.25	.60	.12
☐ 149	Dick Hoak 2.00	1.00	.20
☐ 150	Roy Jefferson 3.00	1.50	.30
☐ 151	Frank Lambert 1.25	.60	.12
☐ 152	Mike Lind 1.25	.60	.12
☐ 153	Bill Nelsen 3.75	1.85	.37
☐ 154	Clarence Peaks 1.25	.60	.12
☐ 155	Clendon Thomas 1.25	.60	.12
☐ 156	Pittsburgh Steelers .... 1.75 Play Card	.85	.17
	(Gary Ballman scores)		
☐ 157	St. Louis Cardinals .... 3.00 Team Card	1.50	.30
☐ 158	Jim Bakken 1.75	.85	.17
☐ 159	Bobby Joe Conrad 1.75	.85	.17
☐ 160	Willis Crenshaw 2.50	1.25	.25
☐ 161	Bob DeMarco 1.25	.60	.12
☐ 162	Pat Fischer 2.00	1.00	.20
☐ 163	Charlie Johnson 2.00	1.00	.20
☐ 164	Dale Meinert 1.25	.60	.12
☐ 165	Sonny Randle 1.75	.85	.17
☐ 166	Sam Silas 2.00	1.00	.20
☐ 167	Bill Triplett 1.25	.60	.12
☐ 168	Larry Wilson 4.50	2.25	.45
☐ 169	St. Louis Cardinals .... 1.75 Play Card	.85	.17
☐ 170	San Francisco 49ers ...3.00 Team Card	1.50	.30
☐ 171	Kermit Alexander 1.75	.85	.17
☐ 172	Bruce Bosley 1.25	.60	.12
☐ 173	John Brodie 7.50	3.75	.75
☐ 174	Bernie Casey 1.75	.85	.17
☐ 175	John David Crow 1.75	.85	.17
☐ 176	Tommy Davis 1.25	.60	.12
☐ 177	Jim Johnson 1.75	.85	.17
☐ 178	Gary Lewis 1.25	.60	.12
☐ 179	Dave Parks 1.75	.85	.17
☐ 180	Walter Rock 1.25	.60	.12
☐ 181	Ken Willard 4.25	2.10	.42
☐ 182	San Francisco 49ers ... 1.75 Play Card	.85	.17

(Tommy Davis FG)

		NRMT	VG-E	GOOD
☐ 183	Washington Redskins Team Card	3.00	1.50	.30
☐ 184	Rickie Harris	1.25	.60	.12
☐ 185	Sonny Jurgensen	10.00	5.00	1.00
☐ 186	Paul Krause	3.25	1.60	.32
☐ 187	Bobby Mitchell	5.00	2.50	.50
☐ 188	Vince Promuto	1.25	.60	.12
☐ 189	Pat Richter	2.25	1.10	.22
☐ 190	Joe Rutgens	1.25	.60	.12
☐ 191	John Sample	1.75	.85	.17
☐ 192	Lonnie Sanders	1.25	.60	.12
☐ 193	Jim Steffen	1.25	.60	.12
☐ 194	Charley Taylor UER (Called Charley and Charlie on card back)	12.00	6.00	1.20
☐ 195	Washington Redskins Play Card	1.75	.85	.17
☐ 196	Referee Signals	3.00	1.50	.30
☐ 197	Checklist 1	20.00	2.00	.40
☐ 198	Checklist 2	40.00	4.00	.80

1967 Philadelphia

JOHNNY UNITAS

The 1967 Philadelphia Gum set of NFL players is complete at 198 cards and was Philadelphia Gum's last issue. This set is easily distinguished from the other Philadelphia football sets by its yellow border on the fronts of the cards. The cards measure 2 1/2" by 3 1/2". The card backs are printed in brown on a white card stock. The cards are numbered within team, i.e., Atlanta Falcons (1-12), Baltimore Colts (13-24), Chicago Bears (25-36), Cleveland Browns (37-48), Dallas Cowboys (49-60), Detroit Lions (61-72), Green Bay Packers (73-84), Los Angeles Rams (85-96), Minnesota

Vikings (97-108), New York Giants (109-120), New Orleans Saints (121-132), Philadelphia Eagles (133-144), Pittsburgh Steelers (145-156), St. Louis Cardinals (157-168), San Francisco 49ers (169-180), Washington Redskins (181-192), Play Cards (193-195), Referee Signals (196), and Checklists (197-198). Within each team group the players are arranged alphabetically by last name. The key rookie cards in this set are Lee Roy Jordan, Leroy Kelly, Tommy Nobis, Dan Reeves.

		NRMT	VG-E	GOOD
COMPLETE SET (198)		600.00	300.00	60.00
COMMON PLAYER (1-198)		1.25	.60	.12
☐ 1	Atlanta Falcons Team Card	6.00	1.50	.30
☐ 2	Junior Coffey	2.00	1.00	.20
☐ 3	Alex Hawkins	1.75	.85	.17
☐ 4	Randy Johnson	2.25	1.10	.22
☐ 5	Lou Kirouac	1.25	.60	.12
☐ 6	Billy Martin	1.25	.60	.12
☐ 7	Tommy Nobis	12.00	6.00	1.20
☐ 8	Jerry Richardson	2.00	1.00	.20
☐ 9	Marion Rushing	1.25	.60	.12
☐ 10	Ron Smith	1.25	.60	.12
☐ 11	Ernie Wheelwright	1.25	.60	.12
☐ 12	Atlanta Falcons Insignia	1.75	.85	.17
☐ 13	Baltimore Colts Team Card	3.00	1.50	.30
☐ 14	Raymond Berry UER (photo actually Bob Boyd)	4.00	2.00	.40
☐ 15	Bob Boyd	1.25	.60	.12
☐ 16	Ordell Braase	1.25	.60	.12
☐ 17	Alvin Haymond	1.25	.60	.12
☐ 18	Tony Lorick	1.25	.60	.12
☐ 19	Lenny Lyles	1.25	.60	.12
☐ 20	John Mackey	4.00	2.00	.40
☐ 21	Tom Matte	1.75	.85	.17
☐ 22	Lou Michaels	1.25	.60	.12
☐ 23	John Unitas	28.00	14.00	2.80
☐ 24	Baltimore Colts Insignia	1.75	.85	.17
☐ 25	Chicago Bears : Team Card	3.00	1.50	.30
☐ 26	Rudy Bukich UER (misspelled Buckich on card back)	1.75	.85	.17
☐ 27	Ron Bull	1.75	.85	.17
☐ 28	Dick Butkus	45.00	22.50	4.50
☐ 29	Mike Ditka	7.50	3.75	.75
☐ 30	Dick Gordon	2.50	1.25	.25
☐ 31	Roger LeClerc	1.25	.60	.12
☐ 32	Bennie McRae	1.25	.60	.12

☐ 33	Richie Petitbon	1.75	.85	.17
☐ 34	Mike Pyle	1.25	.60	.12
☐ 35	Gale Sayers	80.00	40.00	8.00
☐ 36	Chicago Bears Insignia	1.75	.85	.17
☐ 37	Cleveland Browns Team Card	3.00	1.50	.30
☐ 38	Johnny Brewer	1.25	.60	.12
☐ 39	Gary Collins	1.75	.85	.17
☐ 40	Ross Fichtner	1.25	.60	.12
☐ 41	Ernie Green	1.75	.85	.17
☐ 42	Gene Hickerson	1.25	.60	.12
☐ 43	Leroy Kelly	15.00	7.50	1.50
☐ 44	Frank Ryan	2.00	1.00	.20
☐ 45	Dick Schafrath	1.75	.85	.17
☐ 46	Paul Warfield	15.00	7.50	1.50
☐ 47	John Wooten	1.25	.60	.12
☐ 48	Cleveland Browns Insignia	1.75	.85	.17
☐ 49	Dallas Cowboys Team Card	3.00	1.50	.30
☐ 50	George Andrie	1.75	.85	.17
☐ 51	Cornell Green	1.75	.85	.17
☐ 52	Bob Hayes	3.50	1.75	.35
☐ 53	Chuck Howley	2.25	1.10	.22
☐ 54	Lee Roy Jordan	17.00	8.50	1.70
☐ 55	Bob Lilly	6.00	3.00	.60
☐ 56	Dave Manders	2.00	1.00	.20
☐ 57	Don Meredith	21.00	10.50	2.10
☐ 58	Dan Reeves	14.00	7.00	1.40
☐ 59	Mel Renfro	2.50	1.25	.25
☐ 60	Dallas Cowboys Insignia	1.75	.85	.17
☐ 61	Detroit Lions Team Card	3.00	1.50	.30
☐ 62	Roger Brown	1.75	.85	.17
☐ 63	Gail Cogdill	1.25	.60	.12
☐ 64	John Gordy	1.25	.60	.12
☐ 65	Ron Kramer	1.75	.85	.17
☐ 66	Dick LeBeau	1.75	.85	.17
☐ 67	Mike Lucci	4.25	2.10	.42
☐ 68	Amos Marsh	1.25	.60	.12
☐ 69	Tom Nowatzke	1.25	.60	.12
☐ 70	Pat Studstill	1.75	.85	.17
☐ 71	Karl Sweetan	1.75	.85	.17
☐ 72	Detroit Lions Insignia	1.75	.85	.17
☐ 73	Green Bay Packers Team Card	3.00	1.50	.30
☐ 74	Herb Adderley UER (Adderly on back)	3.50	1.75	.35
☐ 75	Lee Roy Caffey	1.25	.60	.12
☐ 76	Willie Davis	3.50	1.75	.35
☐ 77	Forrest Gregg	3.50	1.75	.35
☐ 78	Henry Jordan	1.75	.85	.17
☐ 79	Ray Nitschke	5.00	2.50	.50
☐ 80	Dave Robinson	4.50	2.25	.45
☐ 81	Bob Skoronski	1.25	.60	.12
☐ 82	Bart Starr	21.00	10.50	2.10
☐ 83	Willie Wood	3.50	1.75	.35
☐ 84	Green Bay Packers Insignia	1.75	.85	.17
☐ 85	Los Angeles Rams Team Card	3.00	1.50	.30
☐ 86	Dick Bass	1.75	.85	.17
☐ 87	Maxie Baughan	1.75	.85	.17
☐ 88	Roman Gabriel	3.25	1.60	.32
☐ 89	Bruce Gossett	1.25	.60	.12
☐ 90	Deacon Jones	4.50	2.25	.45
☐ 91	Tommy McDonald	1.75	.85	.17
☐ 92	Marlin McKeever	1.25	.60	.12
☐ 93	Tom Moore	1.75	.85	.17
☐ 94	Merlin Olsen	6.50	3.25	.65
☐ 95	Clancy Williams	1.25	.60	.12
☐ 96	Los Angeles Rams Insignia	1.75	.85	.17
☐ 97	Minnesota Vikings Team Card	3.00	1.50	.30
☐ 98	Grady Alderman	1.25	.60	.12
☐ 99	Bill Brown	1.75	.85	.17
☐ 100	Fred Cox	1.75	.85	.17
☐ 101	Paul Flatley	1.75	.85	.17
☐ 102	Dale Hackbart	2.00	1.00	.20
☐ 103	Jim Marshall	3.00	1.50	.30
☐ 104	Tommy Mason	1.75	.85	.17
☐ 105	Milt Sunde	2.00	1.00	.20
☐ 106	Fran Tarkenton	25.00	12.50	2.50
☐ 107	Mick Tingelhoff	2.00	1.00	.20
☐ 108	Minnesota Vikings Insignia	1.75	.85	.17
☐ 109	New York Giants Team Card	3.00	1.50	.30
☐ 110	Henry Carr	1.75	.85	.17
☐ 111	Clarence Childs	1.25	.60	.12
☐ 112	Allen Jacobs	1.25	.60	.12
☐ 113	Homer Jones	2.50	1.25	.25
☐ 114	Tom Kennedy	1.75	.85	.17
☐ 115	Spider Lockhart	1.75	.85	.17
☐ 116	Joe Morrison	1.75	.85	.17
☐ 117	Francis Peay	1.75	.85	.17
☐ 118	Jeff Smith	1.25	.60	.12
☐ 119	Aaron Thomas	1.75	.85	.17
☐ 120	New York Giants Insignia	1.75	.85	.17
☐ 121	New Orleans Saints Insignia (see also card 132)	2.25	1.10	.22
☐ 122	Charley Bradshaw	1.25	.60	.12
☐ 123	Paul Hornung	15.00	7.50	1.50
☐ 124	Elbert Kimbrough	1.25	.60	.12
☐ 125	Earl Leggett	1.25	.60	.12
☐ 126	Obert Logan	1.25	.60	.12
☐ 127	Riley Mattson	1.25	.60	.12
☐ 128	John Morrow	1.25	.60	.12

☐ 129	Bob Scholtz	1.25	.60	.12
☐ 130	Dave Whitsell	1.25	.60	.12
☐ 131	Gary Wood	1.75	.85	.17
☐ 132	New Orleans Saints	2.25	1.10	.22
	Roster UER			
	(121 on back)			
☐ 133	Philadelphia Eagles	3.00	1.50	.30
	Team Card			
☐ 134	Sam Baker	1.75	.85	.17
☐ 135	Bob Brown	2.00	1.00	.20
☐ 136	Timmy Brown	1.75	.85	.17
☐ 137	Earl Gros	1.25	.60	.12
☐ 138	Dave Lloyd	1.25	.60	.12
☐ 139	Floyd Peters	1.75	.85	.17
☐ 140	Pete Retzlaff	1.25	.60	.12
☐ 141	Joe Scarpati	1.25	.60	.12
☐ 142	Norm Snead	2.00	1.00	.20
☐ 143	Jim Skaggs	1.25	.60	.12
☐ 144	Philadelphia Eagles	1.75	.85	.17
	Insignia			
☐ 145	Pittsburgh Steelers	3.00	1.50	.30
	Team Card			
☐ 146	Bill Asbury	1.25	.60	.12
☐ 147	John Baker	1.25	.60	.12
☐ 148	Gary Ballman	1.75	.85	.17
☐ 149	Mike Clark	1.25	.60	.12
☐ 150	Riley Gunnels	1.25	.60	.12
☐ 151	John Hilton	1.25	.60	.12
☐ 152	Roy Jefferson	1.75	.85	.17
☐ 153	Brady Keys	1.25	.60	.12
☐ 154	Ben McGee	1.25	.60	.12
☐ 155	Bill Nelsen	2.00	1.00	.20
☐ 156	Pittsburgh Steelers	1.75	.85	.17
	Insignia			
☐ 157	St. Louis Cardinals	3.00	1.50	.30
	Team Card			
☐ 158	Jim Bakken	1.75	.85	.17
☐ 159	Bobby Joe Conrad	1.75	.85	.17
☐ 160	Ken Gray	1.75	.85	.17
☐ 161	Charlie Johnson	2.00	1.00	.20
☐ 162	Joe Robb	1.25	.60	.12
☐ 163	Johnny Roland	3.50	1.75	.35
☐ 164	Roy Shivers	1.75	.85	.17
☐ 165	Jackie Smith	5.50	2.75	.55
☐ 166	Jerry Stovall	2.00	1.00	.20
☐ 167	Larry Wilson	3.75	1.85	.37
☐ 168	St. Louis Cardinals	1.75	.85	.17
	Insignia			
☐ 169	San Francisco 49ers	3.00	1.50	.30
	Team Card			
☐ 170	Kermit Alexander	1.75	.85	.17
☐ 171	Bruce Bosley	1.25	.60	.12
☐ 172	John Brodie	6.00	3.00	.60
☐ 173	Bernie Casey	1.75	.85	.17
☐ 174	Tommy Davis	1.25	.60	.12
☐ 175	Howard Mudd	1.25	.60	.12
☐ 176	Dave Parks	1.75	.85	.17

☐ 177	John Thomas	1.25	.60	.12
☐ 178	Dave Wilcox	4.50	2.25	.45
☐ 179	Ken Willard	2.00	1.00	.20
☐ 180	San Francisco 49ers	1.75	.85	.17
	Insignia			
☐ 181	Washington Redskins	3.00	1.50	.30
	Team Card			
☐ 182	Charlie Gogolak	2.00	1.00	.20
☐ 183	Chris Hanburger	5.50	2.75	.55
☐ 184	Len Hauss	3.50	1.75	.35
☐ 185	Sonny Jurgensen	8.00	4.00	.80
☐ 186	Bobby Mitchell	4.50	2.25	.45
☐ 187	Brig Owens	1.25	.60	.12
☐ 188	Jim Shorter	1.25	.60	.12
☐ 189	Jerry Smith	2.25	1.10	.22
☐ 190	Charley Taylor	6.50	3.25	.65
☐ 191	A.D. Whitfield	1.25	.60	.12
☐ 192	Washington Redskins	1.75	.85	.17
	Insignia			
☐ 193	Cleveland Browns	2.50	1.25	.25
	Play Card			
	(Leroy Kelly)			
☐ 194	New York Giants	1.75	.85	.17
	Play Card			
	(Joe Morrison)			
☐ 195	Atlanta Falcons	1.75	.85	.17
	Play Card			
	(Ernie Wheelright)			
☐ 196	Referee Signals	2.25	1.10	.22
☐ 197	Checklist 1	20.00	2.00	.40
☐ 198	Checklist 2	36.00	3.50	.70

1991 Pro Line Portraits

This 300-card standard-size (2 1/2" by 3 1/2") set features some of the NFL's most popular players in non-game shots. The players and coaches are posed wearing their team's colors. The fronts are beautiful full-color borderless shots of the players, while the backs feature a quote from the player and a portrait pose of the player. The cards were available in wax packs. Essentially the whole set was available individually autographed; these certified autographed cards randomly included in packs were unnumbered cards. The key rookie cards in this set are Nick Bell, Dan McGwire, Browning

Nagle, and Mike Pritchard. The cards are numbered on the back.

	MINT	EXC	G-VG
COMPLETE SET (300)	10.00	5.00	1.00
COMMON PLAYER (1-300)	.03	.01	.00

☐ 1 Jim Kelly	.35	.17	.03
Buffalo Bills			
☐ 2 Carl Banks	.06	.03	.00
New York Giants			
☐ 3 Neal Anderson	.15	.07	.01
Chicago Bears			
☐ 4 James Brooks	.08	.04	.01
Cincinnati Bengals			
☐ 5 Reggie Langhorne	.03	.01	.00
Cleveland Browns			
☐ 6 Robert Awalt	.03	.01	.00
Dallas Cowboys			
☐ 7 Greg Kragen	.03	.01	.00
Denver Broncos			
☐ 8 Steve Young	.10	.05	.01
San Francisco 49ers			
☐ 9 Nick Bell	.75	.35	.07
Los Angeles Raiders			
☐ 10 Ray Childress	.06	.03	.00
Houston Oilers			
☐ 11 Albert Bentley	.06	.03	.00
Indianapolis Colts			
☐ 12 Albert Lewis	.06	.03	.00
Kansas City Chiefs			
☐ 13 Howie Long	.06	.03	.00
Los Angeles Raiders			
☐ 14 Flipper Anderson	.06	.03	.00
Los Angeles Rams			
☐ 15 Mark Clayton	.08	.04	.01
Miami Dolphins			
☐ 16 Jarrod Bunch	.15	.07	.01
New York Giants			
☐ 17 Bruce Armstrong	.03	.01	.00
New England Patriots			
☐ 18 Vinnie Clark	.10	.05	.01
Green Bay Packers			
☐ 19 Rob Moore	.50	.25	.05
New York Jets			
☐ 20 Eric Allen	.03	.01	.00
Philadelphia Eagles			
☐ 21 Timm Rosenbach	.10	.05	.01
Phoenix Cardinals			
☐ 22 Gary Anderson	.03	.01	.00
Pittsburgh Steelers			
☐ 23 Martin Bayless	.03	.01	.00
San Diego Chargers			
☐ 24 Kevin Fagan	.03	.01	.00
San Francisco 49ers			
☐ 25 Brian Blades	.08	.04	.01
Seattle Seahawks			
☐ 26 Gary Anderson	.08	.04	.01
Tampa Bay Buccaneers			
☐ 27 Earnest Byner	.08	.04	.01
Washington Redskins			
☐ 28 O.J. Simpson RET	.12	.06	.01
Buffalo Bills			
☐ 29 Dan Henning CO	.03	.01	.00
San Diego Chargers			
☐ 30 Sean Landeta	.03	.01	.00
New York Giants			
☐ 31 James Lofton	.15	.07	.01
Buffalo Bills			
☐ 32 Mike Singletary	.08	.04	.01
Chicago Bears			
☐ 33 David Fulcher	.03	.01	.00
Cincinnati Bengals			
☐ 34 Mark Murphy	.03	.01	.00
Green Bay Packers			
☐ 35 Issiac Holt	.03	.01	.00
Dallas Cowboys			
☐ 36 Dennis Smith	.03	.01	.00
Denver Broncos			
☐ 37 Lomas Brown	.03	.01	.00
Detroit Lions			
☐ 38 Ernest Givins	.08	.04	.01
Houston Oilers			
☐ 39 Duane Bickett	.03	.01	.00
Indianapolis Colts			
☐ 40 Barry Word	.25	.12	.02
Kansas City Chiefs			
☐ 41 Tony Mandarich	.06	.03	.00
Green Bay Packers			
☐ 42 Cleveland Gary	.06	.03	.00
Los Angeles Rams			
☐ 43 Ferrell Edmunds	.03	.01	.00
Miami Dolphins			
☐ 44 Randal Hill	.60	.30	.06
Miami Dolphins			
☐ 45 Irving Fryar	.06	.03	.00
New England Patriots			
☐ 46 Henry Jones	.15	.07	.01

Buffalo Bills			
☐ 47 Blair Thomas 40	.20	.04	
New York Jets			
☐ 48 Andre Waters 03	.01	.00	
Philadelphia Eagles			
☐ 49 J.T. Smith 06	.03	.00	
Phoenix Cardinals			
☐ 50 Thomas Everett 03	.01	.00	
Pittsburgh Steelers			
☐ 51 Marion Butts 10	.05	.01	
San Diego Chargers			
☐ 52 Tom Rathman 06	.03	.00	
San Francisco 49ers			
☐ 53 Vann McElroy 03	.01	.00	
Seattle Seahawks			
☐ 54 Mark Carrier 08	.04	.01	
Tampa Bay Buccaneers			
☐ 55 Jim Lachey 06	.03	.00	
Washington Redskins			
☐ 56 Joe Theismann RET 08	.04	.01	
Washington Redskins			
☐ 57 Jerry Glanville CO 03	.01	.00	
Atlanta Falcons			
☐ 58 Doug Riesenberg 03	.01	.00	
New York Giants			
☐ 59 Cornelius Bennett 08	.04	.01	
Buffalo Bills			
☐ 60 Mark Carrier 08	.04	.01	
Chicago Bears			
☐ 61 Rodney Holman 03	.01	.00	
Cincinnati Bengals			
☐ 62 Leroy Hoard 15	.07	.01	
Cleveland Browns			
☐ 63 Michael Irvin 20	.10	.02	
Dallas Cowboys			
☐ 64 Bobby Humphrey 10	.05	.01	
Denver Broncos			
☐ 65 Mel Gray 03	.01	.00	
Detroit Lions			
☐ 66 Brian Noble 03	.01	.00	
Green Bay Packers			
☐ 67 Al Smith 03	.01	.00	
Houston Oilers			
☐ 68 Eric Dickerson 25	.12	.02	
Indianapolis Colts			
☐ 69 Steve DeBerg 08	.04	.01	
Kansas City Chiefs			
☐ 70 Jay Schroeder 08	.04	.01	
Los Angeles Raiders			
☐ 71 Irv Pankey 03	.01	.00	
Los Angeles Rams			
☐ 72 Reggie Roby 03	.01	.00	
Miami Dolphins			
☐ 73 Wade Wilson 08	.04	.01	
Minnesota Vikings			
☐ 74 Johnny Rembert 03	.01	.00	
New England Patriots			

☐ 75 Russell Maryland 45	.22	.04	
Dallas Cowboys			
☐ 76 Al Toon 08	.04	.01	
New York Jets			
☐ 77 Randall Cunningham 15	.07	.01	
Philadelphia Eagles			
☐ 78 Lonnie Young 03	.01	.00	
New York Jets			
☐ 79 Carnell Lake 03	.01	.00	
Pittsburgh Steelers			
☐ 80 Burt Grossman 06	.03	.00	
San Diego Chargers			
☐ 81 Jim Mora CO 03	.01	.00	
New Orleans Saints			
☐ 82 Dave Krieg 08	.04	.01	
Seattle Seahawks			
☐ 83 Bruce Hill 03	.01	.00	
Tampa Bay Buccaneers			
☐ 84 Ricky Sanders 08	.04	.01	
Washington Redskins			
☐ 85 Roger Staubach RET 10	.05	.01	
Dallas Cowboys			
☐ 86 Richard Williamson CO 03	.01	.00	
Tampa Bay Buccaneers			
☐ 87 Everson Walls 03	.01	.00	
New York Giants			
☐ 88 Shane Conlan 06	.03	.00	
Buffalo Bills			
☐ 89 Mike Ditka CO 06	.03	.00	
Chicago Bears			
☐ 90 Mark Bortz 03	.01	.00	
Chicago Bears			
☐ 91 Tim McGee 06	.03	.00	
Cincinnati Bengals			
☐ 92 Michael Dean Perry 25	.12	.02	
Cleveland Browns			
☐ 93 Danny Noonan 03	.01	.00	
Dallas Cowboys			
☐ 94 Mark Jackson 06	.03	.00	
Denver Broncos			
☐ 95 Chris Miller 15	.07	.01	
Atlanta Falcons			
☐ 96 Ed McCaffrey 30	.15	.03	
New York Giants			
☐ 97 Lorenzo White 06	.03	.00	
Houston Oilers			
☐ 98 Ray Donaldson 03	.01	.00	
Indianapolis Colts			
☐ 99 Nick Lowery 06	.03	.00	
Kansas City Chiefs			
☐ 100 Steve Smith 03	.01	.00	
Los Angeles Raiders			
☐ 101 Jackie Slater 06	.03	.00	
Los Angeles Rams			
☐ 102 Louis Oliver 06	.03	.00	
Miami Dolphins			
☐ 103 Kanavis McGhee 25	.12	.02	

	New York Giants		
☐ 104	Ray Agnew 03	.01	.00
	New England Patriots		
☐ 105	Sam Mills 06	.03	.00
	New Orleans Saints		
☐ 106	Bill Pickel 03	.01	.00
	New York Jets		
☐ 107	Keith Byars 06	.03	.00
	Philadelphia Eagles		
☐ 108	Ricky Proehl 10	.05	.01
	Phoenix Cardinals		
☐ 109	Merril Hoge 06	.03	.00
	Pittsburgh Steelers		
☐ 110	Rod Bernstine 06	.03	.00
	San Diego Chargers		
☐ 111	Andy Heck 03	.01	.00
	Seattle Seahawks		
☐ 112	Broderick Thomas 06	.03	.00
	Tampa Bay Buccaneers		
☐ 113	Andre Collins 03	.01	.00
	Washington Redskins		
☐ 114	Paul Warfield RET 08	.04	.01
	Cleveland Browns		
☐ 115	Bill Belichick CO 03	.01	.00
	Cleveland Browns		
☐ 116	Ottis Anderson 08	.04	.01
	New York Giants		
☐ 117	Andre Reed 10	.05	.01
	Buffalo Bills		
☐ 118	Andre Rison 15	.07	.01
	Atlanta Falcons		
☐ 119	Dexter Carter 08	.04	.01
	San Francisco 49ers		
☐ 120	Anthony Munoz 08	.04	.01
	Cincinnati Bengals		
☐ 121	Bernie Kosar 10	.05	.01
	Cleveland Browns		
☐ 122	Alonzo Highsmith 06	.03	.00
	Dallas Cowboys		
☐ 123	David Treadwell 03	.01	.00
	Denver Broncos		
☐ 124	Rodney Peete 08	.04	.01
	Detroit Lions		
☐ 125	Haywood Jeffires 20	.10	.02
	Houston Oilers		
☐ 126	Clarence Verdin 06	.03	.00
	Indianapolis Colts		
☐ 127	Christian Okoye 08	.04	.01
	Kansas City Chiefs		
☐ 128	Greg Townsend 03	.01	.00
	Los Angeles Raiders		
☐ 129	Tom Newberry 03	.01	.00
	Los Angeles Rams		
☐ 130	Keith Sims 03	.01	.00
	Miami Dolphins		
☐ 131	Myron Guyton 03	.01	.00
	New York Giants		

☐ 132	Andre Tippett 06	.03	.00
	New England Patriots		
☐ 133	Steve Walsh 08	.04	.01
	New Orleans Saints		
☐ 134	Erik McMillan 06	.03	.00
	New York Jets		
☐ 135	Jim McMahon 08	.04	.01
	Philadelphia Eagles		
☐ 136	Derek Hill 03	.01	.00
	Phoenix Cardinals		
☐ 137	David Johnson 08	.04	.01
	Pittsburgh Steelers		
☐ 138	Leslie O'Neal 06	.03	.00
	San Diego Chargers		
☐ 139	Pierce Holt 03	.01	.00
	San Francisco 49ers		
☐ 140	Cortez Kennedy 08	.04	.01
	Seattle Seahawks		
☐ 141	Danny Peebles 03	.01	.00
	Tampa Bay Buccaneers		
☐ 142	Alvin Walton 03	.01	.00
	Washington Redskins		
☐ 143	Drew Pearson RET 06	.03	.00
	Dallas Cowboys		
☐ 144	Dick MacPherson CO 03	.01	.00
	New England Patriots		
☐ 145	Erik Howard 03	.01	.00
	New York Giants		
☐ 146	Steve Tasker 03	.01	.00
	Buffalo Bills		
☐ 147	Bill Fralic 06	.03	.00
	Atlanta Falcons		
☐ 148	Don Warren 06	.03	.00
	Washington Redskins		
☐ 149	Eric Thomas 03	.01	.00
	Cincinnati Bengals		
☐ 150	Jack Pardee CO 03	.01	.00
	Houston Oilers		
☐ 151	Gary Zimmerman 03	.01	.00
	Minnesota Vikings		
☐ 152	Leonard Marshall 06	.03	.00
	New York Giants		
☐ 153	Chris Spielman 06	.03	.00
	Detroit Lions		
☐ 154	Sam Wyche CO 03	.01	.00
	Cincinnati Bengals		
☐ 155	Rohn Stark 03	.01	.00
	Indianapolis Colts		
☐ 156	Stephone Paige 06	.03	.00
	Kansas City Chiefs		
☐ 157	Lionel Washington 03	.01	.00
	Los Angeles Raiders		
☐ 158	Henry Ellard 08	.04	.01
	Los Angeles Rams		
☐ 159	Dan Marino 25	.12	.02
	Miami Dolphins		
☐ 160	Lindy Infante CO 03	.01	.00

Green Bay Packers			
☐ 161 Dan McGwire	1.25	.60	.12
Seattle Seahawks			
☐ 162 Ken O'Brien	.08	.04	.01
New York Jets			
☐ 163 Tim McDonald	.06	.03	.00
Phoenix Cardinals			
☐ 164 Louis Lipps	.06	.03	.00
Pittsburgh Steelers			
☐ 165 Billy Joe Tolliver	.08	.04	.01
San Diego Chargers			
☐ 166 Harris Barton	.03	.01	.00
San Francisco 49ers			
☐ 167 Tony Woods	.06	.03	.00
Seattle Seahawks			
☐ 168 Matt Millen	.03	.01	.00
Washington Redskins			
☐ 169 Gale Sayers RET	.10	.05	.01
Chicago Bears			
☐ 170 Ron Meyer CO	.03	.01	.00
Indianapolis Colts			
☐ 171 William Roberts	.03	.01	.00
New York Giants			
☐ 172 Thurman Thomas	.45	.22	.04
Buffalo Bills			
☐ 173 Steve McMichael	.06	.03	.00
Chicago Bears			
☐ 174 Ickey Woods	.06	.03	.00
Cincinnati Bengals			
☐ 175 Eugene Lockhart	.03	.01	.00
New England Patriots			
☐ 176 George Seifert CO	.03	.01	.00
San Francisco 49ers			
☐ 177 Keith Jones	.06	.03	.00
Atlanta Falcons			
☐ 178 Jack Trudeau	.03	.01	.00
Indianapolis Colts			
☐ 179 Kevin Porter	.03	.01	.00
Kansas City Chiefs			
☐ 180 Ronnie Lott	.10	.05	.01
Los Angeles Raiders			
☐ 181 M. Schottenheimer CO	.03	.01	.00
Kansas City Chiefs			
☐ 182 Morten Andersen	.06	.03	.00
New Orleans Saints			
☐ 183 Anthony Thompson	.08	.04	.01
Phoenix Cardinals			
☐ 184 Tim Worley	.06	.03	.00
Pittsburgh Steelers			
☐ 185 Billy Ray Smith	.06	.03	.00
San Diego Chargers			
☐ 186 David Whitmore	.08	.04	.01
San Francisco 49ers			
☐ 187 Jacob Green	.06	.03	.00
Seattle Seahawks			
☐ 188 Browning Nagle	.75	.35	.07
New York Jets			
☐ 189 Franco Harris RET	.08	.04	.01
Pittsburgh Steelers			
☐ 190 Art Shell CO	.06	.03	.00
Los Angeles Raiders			
☐ 191 Bart Oates	.03	.01	.00
New York Giants			
☐ 192 William Perry	.08	.04	.01
Chicago Bears			
☐ 193 Chuck Noll CO	.03	.01	.00
Pittsburgh Steelers			
☐ 194 Troy Aikman	.35	.17	.03
Dallas Cowboys			
☐ 195 Jeff George	.35	.17	.03
Indianapolis Colts			
☐ 196 Derrick Thomas	.15	.07	.01
Kansas City Chiefs			
☐ 197 Roger Craig	.10	.05	.01
Los Angeles Raiders			
☐ 198 John Fourcade	.06	.03	.00
New Orleans Saints			
☐ 199 Rod Woodson	.08	.04	.01
Pittsburgh Steelers			
☐ 200 Anthony Miller	.08	.04	.01
San Diego Chargers			
☐ 201 Jerry Rice	.35	.17	.03
San Francisco 49ers			
☐ 202 Eugene Robinson	.03	.01	.00
Seattle Seahawks			
☐ 203 Charles Mann	.06	.03	.00
Washington Redskins			
☐ 204 Mel Blount RET	.06	.03	.00
Pittsburgh Steelers			
☐ 205 Don Shula CO	.06	.03	.00
Miami Dolphins			
☐ 206 Jumbo Elliott	.03	.01	.00
New York Giants			
☐ 207 Jay Hilgenberg	.06	.03	.00
Chicago Bears			
☐ 208 Deron Cherry	.06	.03	.00
Kansas City Chiefs			
☐ 209 Dan Reeves CO	.03	.01	.00
Denver Broncos			
☐ 210 Roman Phifer	.12	.06	.01
Los Angeles Rams			
☐ 211 David Little	.03	.01	.00
Pittsburgh Steelers			
☐ 212 Lee Williams	.06	.03	.00
San Diego Chargers			
☐ 213 John Taylor	.12	.06	.01
San Francisco 49ers			
☐ 214 Monte Coleman	.03	.01	.00
Washington Redskins			
☐ 215 Walter Payton RET	.15	.07	.01
Chicago Bears			
☐ 216 John Robinson CO	.03	.01	.00
Los Angeles Rams			
☐ 217 Pepper Johnson	.06	.03	.00

	New York Giants			
☐ 218	Tom Thayer	.03	.01	.00
	Chicago Bears			
☐ 219	Dan Saleaumua	.03	.01	.00
	Kansas City Chiefs			
☐ 220	Ernest Spears	.10	.05	.01
	New Orleans Saints			
☐ 221	Bubby Brister	.08	.04	.01
	Pittsburgh Steelers			
☐ 222	Junior Seau	.10	.05	.01
	San Diego Chargers			
☐ 223	Brent Jones	.06	.03	.00
	San Francisco 49ers			
☐ 224	Rufus Porter	.03	.01	.00
	Seattle Seahawks			
☐ 225	Jack Kemp RET	.10	.05	.01
	Buffalo Bills			
☐ 226	Wayne Fontes CO	.03	.01	.00
	Detroit Lions			
☐ 227	Phil Simms	.08	.04	.01
	New York Giants			
☐ 228	Shaun Gayle	.03	.01	.00
	Chicago Bears			
☐ 229	Bill Maas	.03	.01	.00
	Kansas City Chiefs			
☐ 230	Renaldo Turnbull	.03	.01	.00
	New Orleans Saints			
☐ 231	Bryan Hinkle	.03	.01	.00
	Pittsburgh Steelers			
☐ 232	Gary Plummer	.03	.01	.00
	San Diego Chargers			
☐ 233	Jerry Burns CO	.03	.01	.00
	Minnesota Vikings			
☐ 234	Lawrence Taylor	.10	.05	.01
	New York Giants			
☐ 235	Joe Gibbs CO	.03	.01	.00
	Washington Redskins			
☐ 236	Neil Smith	.06	.03	.00
	Kansas City Chiefs			
☐ 237	Rich Kotite CO	.06	.03	.00
	Philadelphia Eagles			
☐ 238	Jim Covert	.06	.03	.00
	Chicago Bears			
☐ 239	Tim Grunhard	.03	.01	.00
	Kansas City Chiefs			
☐ 240	Joe Bugel CO	.03	.01	.00
	Phoenix Cardinals			
☐ 241	Dave Wyman	.03	.01	.00
	Seattle Seahawks			
☐ 242	Maury Buford	.03	.01	.00
	Chicago Bears			
☐ 243	Kevin Ross	.03	.01	.00
	Kansas City Chiefs			
☐ 244	Jimmy Johnson CO	.03	.01	.00
	Dallas Cowboys			
☐ 245	Jim Morrissey	.10	.05	.01
	Chicago Bears			

☐ 246	Jeff Hostetler	.20	.10	.02
	New York Giants			
☐ 247	Andre Ware	.12	.06	.01
	Houston Oilers			
☐ 248	Steve Largent RET	.10	.05	.01
	Seattle Seahawks			
☐ 249	Chuck Knox CO	.03	.01	.00
	Seattle Seahawks			
☐ 250	Boomer Esiason	.10	.05	.01
	Cincinnati Bengals			
☐ 251	Kevin Butler	.03	.01	.00
	Chicago Bears			
☐ 252	Bruce Smith	.08	.04	.01
	Buffalo Bills			
☐ 253	Webster Slaughter	.06	.03	.00
	Cleveland Browns			
☐ 254	Mike Sherrard	.06	.03	.00
	San Francisco 49ers			
☐ 255	Steve Broussard	.10	.05	.01
	Atlanta Falcons			
☐ 256	Warren Moon	.20	.10	.02
	Houston Oilers			
☐ 257	John Elway	.15	.07	.01
	Denver Broncos			
☐ 258	Bob Golic	.03	.01	.00
	Los Angeles Raiders			
☐ 259	Jim Everett	.10	.05	.01
	Los Angeles Rams			
☐ 260	Bruce Coslet CO	.06	.03	.00
	New York Jets			
☐ 261	James Francis	.08	.04	.01
	Cincinnati Bengals			
☐ 262	Eric Dorsey	.03	.01	.00
	New York Giants			
☐ 263	Marcus Dupree	.06	.03	.00
	Los Angeles Rams			
☐ 264	Hart Lee Dykes	.06	.03	.00
	New England Patriots			
☐ 265	Vinny Testaverde	.08	.04	.01
	Tampa Bay Buccaneers			
☐ 266	Chip Lohmiller	.03	.01	.00
	Washington Redskins			
☐ 267	John Riggins RET	.08	.04	.01
	Washington Redskins			
☐ 268	Mike Schad	.03	.01	.00
	Philadelphia Eagles			
☐ 269	Kevin Greene	.06	.03	.00
	Los Angeles Rams			
☐ 270	Dean Biasucci	.03	.01	.00
	Indianapolis Colts			
☐ 271	Mike Pritchard	.60	.30	.06
	Atlanta Falcons			
☐ 272	Ted Washington	.15	.07	.01
	San Francisco 49ers			
☐ 273	Alfred Williams	.15	.07	.01
	Cincinnati Bengals			
☐ 274	Chris Zorich	.25	.12	.02

Chicago Bears
☐ 275	Reggie Barrett	.20	.10	.02
Detroit Lions
☐ 276	Chris Hinton	.06	.03	.00
Atlanta Falcons
☐ 277	Tracy Johnson	.10	.05	.01
Atlanta Falcons
☐ 278	Jim Harbaugh	.10	.05	.01
Chicago Bears
☐ 279	John Roper	.06	.03	.00
Chicago Bears
☐ 280	Mike Dumas	.15	.07	.01
Houston Oilers
☐ 281	Herman Moore	.60	.30	.06
Detroit Lions
☐ 282	Eric Turner	.50	.25	.05
Cleveland Browns
☐ 283	Steve Atwater	.06	.03	.00
Denver Broncos
☐ 284	Michael Cofer	.03	.01	.00
Detroit Lions
☐ 285	Darion Conner	.06	.03	.00
Atlanta Falcons
☐ 286	Darryl Talley	.06	.03	.00
Buffalo Bills
☐ 287	Donnell Woolford	.03	.01	.00
Chicago Bears
☐ 288	Keith McCants	.08	.04	.01
Tampa Bay Buccaneers
☐ 289	Ray Handley CO	.06	.03	.00
New York Giants
☐ 290	Ahmad Rashad RET	.06	.03	.00
Minnesota Vikings
☐ 291	Eric Swann	.20	.10	.02
Phoenix Cardinals
☐ 292	Dalton Hilliard	.06	.03	.00
New Orleans Saints
☐ 293	Rickey Jackson	.06	.03	.00
New Orleans Saints
☐ 294	Vaughan Johnson	.06	.03	.00
New Orleans Saints
☐ 295	Eric Martin	.06	.03	.00
New Orleans Saints
☐ 296	Pat Swilling	.08	.04	.01
New Orleans Saints
☐ 297	Anthony Carter	.08	.04	.01
Minnesota Vikings
☐ 298	Guy McIntyre	.03	.01	.00
San Francisco 49ers
☐ 299	Bennie Blades	.06	.03	.00
Detroit Lions
☐ 300	Paul Farren	.06	.03	.00
Cleveland Browns

1991 Pro Line Wives

This seven-card standard size (2 1/2" by 3 1/2") set was included in the 1991 Pro Line Portraits set. These seven cards feature wives of some of the NFL's most popular personalities, including former television actress Jennifer Montana and star of the Cosby show, Phylicia Rashad. The cards are numbered on the back.

		MINT	EXC	G-VG
COMPLETE SET (7)		1.00	.50	.10
COMMON PLAYER (SC1-SC7)		.15	.07	.01
☐ SC1	Jennifer Montana	.40	.20	.04
☐ SC2	Babette Kosar	.15	.07	.01
☐ SC3	Janet Elway	.15	.07	.01
☐ SC4	Michelle Oates	.15	.07	.01
☐ SC5	Toni Lipps	.15	.07	.01
☐ SC6	Stacy O'Brien	.15	.07	.01
☐ SC7	Phylicia Rashad	.20	.10	.02

1989 Pro Set

Pro Set's 1989 football set was produced in series. The cards are standard size, 2 1/2" by 3 1/2", and feature full-color photos on both the card front and back. The first series of 440 cards is ordered numerically by teams and alphabetically within teams, e.g., Atlanta Falcons (1-16), Buffalo Bills (17-34), Chicago Bears (35-53), Cincinnati Bengals (54-72), Cleveland Browns (73-86), Dallas Cowboys

Barry Sanders, Deion Sanders, Sammie Smith, Derrick Thomas, and Steve Walsh.

(87-98), Denver Broncos (99-114), Detroit Lions (115-127), Green Bay Packers (128-139), Houston Oilers (140-154), Indianapolis Colts (155-166), Kansas City Chiefs (167-181), Los Angeles Raiders (182-194), Los Angeles Rams (195-210), Miami Dolphins (211-225), Minnesota Vikings (226-243), New England Patriots (244-260), New Orleans Saints (261-278), New York Giants (279-293), New York Jets (294-311), Philadelphia Eagles (312-327), Phoenix Cardinals (328-341), Pittsburgh Steelers (342-355), San Diego Chargers (356-368), San Francisco 49ers (369-389), Seattle Seahawks (390-408), Tampa Bay Buccaneers (409-421), Washington Redskins (422-440). The William Perry card number 47 was supposedly a mistake in that it was apparently printed and released briefly before appropriate permissions had been granted. The Pete Rozelle commemorative card was expressly intended to be scarce as it was supposed to be placed randomly in one out of every 200 first seies wax packs. The set is considered complete without either the Perry or the Rozelle cards. The key rookies in the first series set are Brian Blades, Bubby Brister, Michael Irvin, Don Majkowski, Anthony Miller, Chris Miller, Mark Rypien, John Stephens, John Taylor and Thurman Thomas. The second series contains 100 cards. The fronts of the second series cards have color action photos bordered in red; otherwise, they are similar in appearance to the first series. Cards numbered 485-515 feature the 1989 first-round draft picks from the previous spring's college draft and cards numbered 516-540 are "Pro Set Prospects". These cards were distributed only in Series II packs, usually three to five per pack. The key rookie cards in the second series are Troy Aikman, Bobby Humphrey, Eric Metcalf, Rodney Peete, Andre Rison,

	MINT	EXC	G-VG
COMPLETE SET (540)	32.00	16.00	3.20
COMMON PLAYER (1-440)	.03	.01	.00
COMMON PLAYER (441-540)	.03	.01	.00
☐ 1 Stacey Bailey	.06	.03	.01
☐ 2 Aundray Bruce	.08	.04	.01
☐ 3 Rick Bryan	.03	.01	.00
☐ 4 Bobby Butler	.03	.01	.00
☐ 5 Scott Case	.12	.06	.01
☐ 6 Tony Casillas	.08	.04	.01
☐ 7 Floyd Dixon	.06	.03	.00
☐ 8 Rick Donnelly	.03	.01	.00
☐ 9 Bill Fralic	.06	.03	.00
☐ 10 Mike Gann	.03	.01	.00
☐ 11 Mike Kenn	.06	.03	.00
☐ 12 Chris Miller	1.25	.60	.12
☐ 13 John Rade	.03	.01	.00
☐ 14 Gerald Riggs UER	.10	.05	.01
(uniform number is 42 but 43 on back)			
☐ 15 John Settle	.20	.10	.02
☐ 16 Marion Campbell CO	.03	.01	.00
☐ 17 Cornelius Bennett	.30	.15	.03
☐ 18 Derrick Burroughs	.03	.01	.00
☐ 19 Shane Conlan	.10	.05	.01
☐ 20 Ronnie Harmon	.06	.03	.00
☐ 21 Kent Hull	.10	.05	.01
☐ 22 Jim Kelly	.60	.30	.06
☐ 23 Mark Kelso	.06	.03	.00
☐ 24 Pete Metzelaars	.03	.01	.00
☐ 25 Scott Norwood	.08	.04	.01
☐ 26 Andre Reed	.20	.10	.02
☐ 27 Fred Smerlas	.06	.03	.00
☐ 28 Bruce Smith	.12	.06	.01
☐ 29 Leonard Smith	.03	.01	.00
☐ 30 Art Still	.06	.03	.00
☐ 31 Darryl Talley	.08	.04	.01
☐ 32 Thurman Thomas	3.50	1.75	.35
☐ 33 Will Wolford	.12	.06	.01
☐ 34 Marv Levy CO	.03	.01	.00
☐ 35 Neal Anderson	.40	.20	.04
☐ 36 Kevin Butler	.03	.01	.00
☐ 37 Jim Covert	.06	.03	.00
☐ 38 Richard Dent	.10	.05	.01
☐ 39 Dave Duerson	.03	.01	.00
☐ 40 Dennis Gentry	.03	.01	.00
☐ 41 Dan Hampton	.08	.04	.01
☐ 42 Jay Hilgenberg	.06	.03	.00
☐ 43 Dennis McKinnon UER	.06	.03	.00
(caught 20 or 21 passes as a rookie)			
☐ 44 Jim McMahon	.08	.04	.01
☐ 45 Steve McMichael	.06	.03	.00

☐ 46 Brad Muster	.25	.12	.02
☐ 47A William Perry SP	10.00	5.00	1.00
☐ 47B Ron Morris	.15	.07	.01
☐ 48 Ron Rivera	.03	.01	.00
☐ 49 Vestee Jackson	.10	.05	.01
☐ 50 Mike Singletary	.12	.06	.01
☐ 51 Mike Tomczak	.08	.04	.01
☐ 52 Keith Van Horne	.10	.05	.01
☐ 53A Mike Ditka CO	.08	.04	.01
(no HOF mention			
on card front)			
☐ 53B Mike Ditka CO	.50	.25	.05
(HOF banner on front)			
☐ 54 Lewis Billups	.08	.04	.01
☐ 55 James Brooks	.10	.05	.01
☐ 56 Eddie Brown	.10	.05	.01
☐ 57 Jason Buck	.10	.05	.01
☐ 58 Boomer Esiason	.20	.10	.02
☐ 59 David Fulcher	.06	.03	.00
☐ 60A Rodney Holman	.35	.17	.03
(BENGALS on front)			
☐ 60B Rodney Holman	2.00	1.00	.20
(Bengals on front)			
☐ 61 Reggie Williams	.06	.03	.00
☐ 62 Joe Kelly	.10	.05	.01
☐ 63 Tim Krumrie	.03	.01	.00
☐ 64 Tim McGee	.10	.05	.01
☐ 65 Max Montoya	.06	.03	.00
☐ 66 Anthony Munoz	.10	.05	.01
☐ 67 Jim Skow	.03	.01	.00
☐ 68 Eric Thomas	.15	.07	.01
☐ 69 Leon White	.10	.05	.01
☐ 70 Ickey Woods	.25	.12	.02
☐ 71 Carl Zander	.03	.01	.00
☐ 72 Sam Wyche CO	.06	.03	.00
☐ 73 Brian Brennan	.03	.01	.00
☐ 74 Earnest Byner	.12	.06	.01
☐ 75 Hanford Dixon	.03	.01	.00
☐ 76 Mike Pagel	.06	.03	.00
☐ 77 Bernie Kosar	.15	.07	.01
☐ 78 Reggie Langhorne	.20	.10	.02
☐ 79 Kevin Mack	.06	.03	.00
☐ 80 Clay Matthews	.06	.03	.00
☐ 81 Gerald McNeil	.06	.03	.00
☐ 82 Frank Minnifield	.06	.03	.00
☐ 83 Cody Risien	.03	.01	.00
☐ 84 Webster Slaughter	.12	.06	.01
☐ 85 Felix Wright	.03	.01	.00
☐ 86 Bud Carson CO	.03	.01	.00
☐ 87 Bill Bates	.06	.03	.00
☐ 88 Kevin Brooks	.08	.04	.01
☐ 89 Michael Irvin	2.00	1.00	.20
☐ 90 Jim Jeffcoat	.03	.01	.00
☐ 91 Ed Too Tall Jones	.10	.05	.01
☐ 92 Eugene Lockhart	.08	.04	.01
☐ 93 Nate Newton	.08	.04	.01
☐ 94 Danny Noonan	.08	.04	.01
☐ 95 Steve Pelluer	.06	.03	.00
☐ 96 Herschel Walker	.35	.17	.03
☐ 97 Everson Walls	.06	.03	.00
☐ 98 Jimmy Johnson CO	.08	.04	.01
☐ 99 Keith Bishop	.03	.01	.00
☐ 100A John Elway ERR	6.00	3.00	.60
(Drafted 1st Round)			
☐ 100B John Elway COR	.35	.17	.03
(Acquired Trade)			
☐ 101 Simon Fletcher	.20	.10	.02
☐ 102 Mike Harden	.03	.01	.00
☐ 103 Mike Horan	.03	.01	.00
☐ 104 Mark Jackson	.08	.04	.01
☐ 105 Vance Johnson	.08	.04	.01
☐ 106 Rulon Jones	.06	.03	.00
☐ 107 Clarence Kay	.03	.01	.00
☐ 108 Karl Mecklenburg	.08	.04	.01
☐ 109 Ricky Nattiel	.06	.03	.00
☐ 110 Steve Sewell	.20	.10	.02
☐ 111 Dennis Smith	.06	.03	.00
☐ 112 Gerald Willhite	.03	.01	.00
☐ 113 Sammy Winder	.06	.03	.00
☐ 114 Dan Reeves CO	.06	.03	.00
☐ 115 Jim Arnold	.03	.01	.00
☐ 116 Jerry Ball	.15	.07	.01
☐ 117 Bennie Blades	.30	.15	.03
☐ 118 Lomas Brown	.06	.03	.00
☐ 119 Mike Cofer	.06	.03	.00
☐ 120 Garry James	.06	.03	.00
☐ 121 James Jones	.06	.03	.00
☐ 122 Chuck Long	.06	.03	.00
☐ 123 Pete Mandley	.03	.01	.00
☐ 124 Ed Murray	.06	.03	.00
☐ 125 Chris Spielman	.30	.15	.03
☐ 126 Dennis Gibson	.06	.03	.00
☐ 127 Wayne Fontes CO	.06	.03	.00
☐ 128 John Anderson	.03	.01	.00
☐ 129 Brent Fullwood	.10	.05	.01
☐ 130 Mark Cannon	.03	.01	.00
☐ 131 Tim Harris	.08	.04	.01
☐ 132 Mark Lee	.06	.03	.00
☐ 133 Don Majkowski	.60	.30	.06
☐ 134 Mark Murphy	.06	.03	.00
☐ 135 Brian Noble	.06	.03	.00
☐ 136 Ken Ruettgers	.15	.07	.01
☐ 137 Johnny Holland	.06	.03	.00
☐ 138 Randy Wright	.06	.03	.00
☐ 139 Lindy Infante CO	.06	.03	.00
☐ 140 Steve Brown	.03	.01	.00
☐ 141 Ray Childress	.06	.03	.00
☐ 142 Jeff Donaldson	.03	.01	.00
☐ 143 Ernest Givins	.12	.06	.01
☐ 144 John Grimsley	.03	.01	.00
☐ 145 Alonzo Highsmith	.08	.04	.01
☐ 146 Drew Hill	.12	.06	.01
☐ 147 Robert Lyles	.08	.04	.01
☐ 148 Bruce Matthews	.15	.07	.01

☐ 149 Warren Moon	.50	.25	.05
☐ 150 Mike Munchak	.06	.03	.00
☐ 151 Allen Pinkett	.20	.10	.02
☐ 152 Mike Rozier	.08	.04	.01
☐ 153 Tony Zendejas	.06	.03	.00
☐ 154 Jerry Glanville CO	.06	.03	.00
☐ 155 Albert Bentley	.06	.03	.00
☐ 156 Dean Biasucci	.03	.01	.00
☐ 157 Duane Bickett	.06	.03	.00
☐ 158 Bill Brooks	.03	.01	.00
☐ 159 Chris Chandler	.15	.07	.01
☐ 160 Pat Beach	.03	.01	.00
☐ 161 Ray Donaldson	.03	.01	.00
☐ 162 Jon Hand	.06	.03	.00
☐ 163 Chris Hinton	.06	.03	.00
☐ 164 Rohn Stark	.03	.01	.00
☐ 165 Fredd Young	.06	.03	.00
☐ 166 Ron Meyer CO	.03	.01	.00
☐ 167 Lloyd Burruss	.03	.01	.00
☐ 168 Carlos Carson	.06	.03	.00
☐ 169 Deron Cherry	.06	.03	.00
☐ 170 Irv Eatman	.03	.01	.00
☐ 171 Dino Hackett	.06	.03	.00
☐ 172 Steve DeBerg	.10	.05	.01
☐ 173 Albert Lewis	.08	.04	.01
☐ 174 Nick Lowery	.06	.03	.00
☐ 175 Bill Maas	.06	.03	.00
☐ 176 Christian Okoye	.25	.12	.02
☐ 177 Stephone Paige	.06	.03	.00
☐ 178 Mark Adickes	.03	.01	.00
(Out of alphabetical sequence for his team)			
☐ 179 Kevin Ross	.15	.07	.01
☐ 180 Neil Smith	.15	.07	.01
☐ 181 Marty Schottenheimer CO	.06	.03	.00
☐ 182 Marcus Allen	.10	.05	.01
☐ 183 Tim Brown	.50	.25	.05
☐ 184 Willie Gault	.08	.04	.01
☐ 185 Bo Jackson	.70	.35	.07
☐ 186 Howie Long	.08	.04	.01
☐ 187 Vann McElroy	.03	.01	.00
☐ 188 Matt Millen	.06	.03	.00
☐ 189 Don Mosebar	.12	.06	.01
☐ 190 Bill Pickel	.03	.01	.00
☐ 191 Jerry Robinson UER	.03	.01	.00
(Stats show 1 TD, but text says 2 TD's)			
☐ 192 Jay Schroeder	.12	.06	.01
☐ 193A Stacey Toran	.06	.03	.00
(No mention of death on card front)			
☐ 193B Stacey Toran	.50	.25	.05
(1961-1989 banner on card front)			
☐ 194 Mike Shanahan CO	.06	.03	.00
☐ 195 Greg Bell	.06	.03	.00
☐ 196 Ron Brown	.06	.03	.00
☐ 197 Aaron Cox	.15	.07	.01
☐ 198 Henry Ellard	.08	.04	.01
☐ 199 Jim Everett	.15	.07	.01
☐ 200 Jerry Gray	.06	.03	.00
☐ 201 Kevin Greene	.08	.04	.01
☐ 202 Pete Holohan	.03	.01	.00
☐ 203 LeRoy Irvin	.06	.03	.00
☐ 204 Mike Lansford	.03	.01	.00
☐ 205 Tom Newberry	.12	.06	.01
☐ 206 Mel Owens	.10	.05	.01
☐ 207 Jackie Slater	.06	.03	.00
☐ 208 Doug Smith	.03	.01	.00
☐ 209 Mike Wilcher	.03	.01	.00
☐ 210 John Robinson CO	.06	.03	.00
☐ 211 John Bosa	.06	.03	.00
☐ 212 Mark Brown	.03	.01	.00
☐ 213 Mark Clayton	.12	.06	.01
☐ 214A Ferrell Edmunds ERR	.50	.25	.05
(Misspelled Edmonds on front and back)			
☐ 214B Ferrell Edmunds COR	.15	.07	.01
☐ 215 Roy Foster	.03	.01	.00
☐ 216 Lorenzo Hampton	.03	.01	.00
☐ 217 Jim C. Jensen UER	.10	.05	.01
(Born Albington, should be Abington)			
☐ 218 William Judson	.03	.01	.00
☐ 219 Eric Kumerow	.10	.05	.01
☐ 220 Dan Marino	.50	.25	.05
☐ 221 John Offerdahl	.06	.03	.00
☐ 222 Fuad Reveiz	.03	.01	.00
☐ 223 Reggie Roby	.06	.03	.00
☐ 224 Brian Sochia	.08	.04	.01
☐ 225 Don Shula CO	.08	.04	.01
☐ 226 Alfred Anderson	.06	.03	.00
☐ 227 Joey Browner	.10	.05	.01
☐ 228 Anthony Carter	.08	.04	.01
☐ 229 Chris Doleman	.10	.05	.01
☐ 230 Hassan Jones	.15	.07	.01
☐ 231 Steve Jordan	.08	.04	.01
☐ 232 Tommy Kramer	.08	.04	.01
☐ 233 Carl Lee	.10	.05	.01
☐ 234 Kirk Lowdermilk	.10	.05	.01
☐ 235 Randall McDaniel	.12	.06	.01
☐ 236 Doug Martin	.03	.01	.00
☐ 237 Keith Millard	.06	.03	.00
☐ 238 Darrin Nelson	.06	.03	.00
☐ 239 Jesse Solomon	.03	.01	.00
☐ 240 Scott Studwell	.03	.01	.00
☐ 241 Wade Wilson	.10	.05	.01
☐ 242 Gary Zimmerman	.06	.03	.00
☐ 243 Jerry Burns CO	.03	.01	.00
☐ 244 Bruce Armstrong	.10	.05	.01
☐ 245 Raymond Clayborn	.03	.01	.00
☐ 246 Reggie Dupard	.10	.05	.01
☐ 247 Tony Eason	.08	.04	.01

248	Sean Farrell	.03	.01	.00
249	Doug Flutie	.20	.10	.02
250	Brent Williams	.10	.05	.01
251	Roland James	.03	.01	.00
252	Ronnie Lippett	.03	.01	.00
253	Fred Marion	.03	.01	.00
254	Larry McGrew	.03	.01	.00
255	Stanley Morgan	.08	.04	.01
256	Johnny Rembert	.12	.06	.01
257	John Stephens	.50	.25	.05
258	Andre Tippett	.06	.03	.00
259	Garin Veris	.03	.01	.00
260A	Raymond Berry CO (No HOF mention on card front)	.10	.05	.01
260B	Raymond Berry CO (HOF banner on card front)	.30	.15	.03
261	Morten Andersen	.06	.03	.00
262	Hoby Brenner	.03	.01	.00
263	Stan Brock	.03	.01	.00
264	Brad Edelman	.03	.01	.00
265	James Geathers	.03	.01	.00
266A	Bobby Hebert ERR ("passers" in 42-0)	.50	.25	.05
266B	Bobby Hebert COR ("passes" in 42-0)	.12	.06	.01
267	Craig Heyward	.15	.07	.01
268	Lonzell Hill	.12	.06	.01
269	Dalton Hilliard	.08	.04	.01
270	Rickey Jackson	.08	.04	.01
271	Steve Korte	.08	.04	.01
272	Eric Martin	.08	.04	.01
273	Rueben Mayes	.08	.04	.01
274	Sam Mills	.08	.04	.01
275	Brett Perriman	.15	.07	.01
276	Pat Swilling	.20	.10	.02
277	John Tice	.03	.01	.00
278	Jim Mora CO	.06	.03	.00
279	Eric Moore	.10	.05	.01
280	Carl Banks	.06	.03	.00
281	Mark Bavaro	.06	.03	.00
282	Maurice Carthon	.03	.01	.00
283	Mark Collins	.15	.07	.01
284	Erik Howard	.03	.01	.00
285	Terry Kinard	.03	.01	.00
286	Sean Landeta	.03	.01	.00
287	Lionel Manuel	.06	.03	.00
288	Leonard Marshall	.06	.03	.00
289	Joe Morris	.08	.04	.00
290	Bart Oates	.03	.01	.00
291	Phil Simms	.15	.07	.01
292	Lawrence Taylor	.15	.07	.01
293	Bill Parcells CO	.08	.04	.01
294	Dave Cadigan	.08	.04	.01
295	Kyle Clifton	.15	.07	.01
296	Alex Gordon	.03	.01	.00
297	James Hasty	.12	.06	.01
298	Johnny Hector	.06	.03	.00
299	Bobby Humphery	.03	.01	.00
300	Pat Leahy	.06	.03	.00
301	Marty Lyons	.06	.03	.00
302	Reggie McElroy	.10	.05	.01
303	Erik McMillan	.25	.12	.02
304	Freeman McNeil	.08	.04	.01
305	Ken O'Brien	.10	.05	.01
306	Pat Ryan	.03	.01	.00
307	Mickey Shuler	.03	.01	.00
308	Al Toon	.12	.06	.01
309	Jo Jo Townsell	.06	.03	.00
310	Roger Vick	.06	.03	.00
311	Joe Walton CO	.03	.01	.00
312	Jerome Brown	.08	.04	.01
313	Keith Byars	.08	.04	.01
314	Cris Carter	.45	.22	.04
315	Randall Cunningham	.30	.15	.03
316	Terry Hoage	.03	.01	.00
317	Wes Hopkins	.03	.01	.00
318	Keith Jackson	.50	.25	.05
319	Mike Quick	.06	.03	.00
320	Mike Reichenbach	.03	.01	.00
321	Dave Rimington	.08	.04	.01
322	John Teltschik	.03	.01	.00
323	Anthony Toney	.06	.03	.00
324	Andre Waters	.06	.03	.00
325	Reggie White	.15	.07	.01
326	Luis Zendejas	.03	.01	.00
327	Buddy Ryan CO	.08	.04	.01
328	Robert Awalt	.03	.01	.00
329	Tim McDonald	.15	.07	.01
330	Roy Green	.08	.04	.01
331	Neil Lomax	.08	.04	.01
332	Cedric Mack	.03	.01	.00
333	Stump Mitchell	.06	.03	.00
334	Niko Noga	.08	.04	.01
335	Jay Novacek	.50	.25	.05
336	Freddie Joe Nunn	.03	.01	.00
337	Luis Sharpe	.03	.01	.00
338	Vai Sikahema	.06	.03	.00
339	J.T. Smith	.06	.03	.00
340	Ron Wolfley	.03	.01	.00
341	Gene Stallings CO	.03	.01	.00
342	Gary Anderson	.03	.01	.00
343	Bubby Brister	.35	.17	.03
344	Dermontti Dawson	.10	.05	.01
345	Thomas Everett	.12	.06	.01
346	Delton Hall	.10	.05	.01
347	Bryan Hinkle	.08	.04	.01
348	Merril Hoge	.20	.10	.02
349	Tunch Ilkin	.10	.05	.01
350	Aaron Jones	.10	.05	.01
351	Louis Lipps	.08	.04	.01
352	David Little	.03	.01	.00
353	Hardy Nickerson	.10	.05	.01

☐ 354 Rod Woodson	.25	.12	.02	☐ 401 Eugene Robinson	.08	.04	.01
☐ 355A Chuck Noll CO ERR ("one of only three")	.15	.07	.01	☐ 402 Bruce Scholtz	.03	.01	.00
☐ 355B Chuck Noll CO COR ("one of only two")	.15	.07	.01	☐ 403 Kelly Stouffer	.20	.10	.02
☐ 356 Gary Anderson	.08	.04	.01	☐ 404A Curt Warner ERR ("yards (1,455) ...")	2.50	1.25	.25
☐ 357 Rod Bernstine	.25	.12	.02	☐ 404B Curt Warner COR ("yards (6,074) ...")	.10	.05	.01
☐ 358 Gill Byrd	.06	.03	.00	☐ 405 John L. Williams	.12	.06	.01
☐ 359 Vencie Glenn	.06	.03	.00	☐ 406 Tony Woods	.15	.07	.01
☐ 360 Dennis McKnight	.08	.04	.00	☐ 407 David Wyman	.10	.05	.01
☐ 361 Lionel James	.06	.03	.00	☐ 408 Chuck Knox CO	.06	.03	.00
☐ 362 Mark Malone	.06	.03	.00	☐ 409 Mark Carrier	.35	.17	.03
☐ 363A Anthony Miller ERR (TD total 14.8)	1.50	.75	.15	☐ 410 Randy Grimes	.08	.04	.01
☐ 363B Anthony Miller COR (TD total 3)	.60	.30	.06	☐ 411 Paul Gruber	.15	.07	.01
☐ 364 Ralf Mojsiejenko	.03	.01	.00	☐ 412 Harry Hamilton	.03	.01	.00
☐ 365 Leslie O'Neal	.08	.04	.01	☐ 413 Ron Holmes	.06	.03	.00
☐ 366 Jamie Holland	.10	.05	.01	☐ 414 Donald Igwebuike	.03	.01	.00
☐ 367 Lee Williams	.06	.03	.00	☐ 415 Dan Turk	.08	.04	.01
☐ 368 Dan Henning CO	.03	.01	.00	☐ 416 Ricky Reynolds	.10	.05	.01
☐ 369 Harris Barton	.08	.04	.01	☐ 417 Bruce Hill	.25	.12	.02
☐ 370 Michael Carter	.06	.03	.00	☐ 418 Lars Tate	.15	.07	.01
☐ 371 Mike Cofer	.08	.04	.01	☐ 419 Vinny Testaverde	.10	.05	.01
☐ 372 Roger Craig	.12	.06	.01	☐ 420 James Wilder	.06	.03	.00
☐ 373 Riki Ellison	.15	.07	.01	☐ 421 Ray Perkins CO	.06	.03	.00
☐ 374 Jim Fahnhorst	.08	.04	.01	☐ 422 Jeff Bostic	.03	.01	.00
☐ 375 John Frank	.12	.06	.01	☐ 423 Kelvin Bryant	.06	.03	.00
☐ 376 Jeff Fuller	.08	.04	.01	☐ 424 Gary Clark	.20	.10	.02
☐ 377 Don Griffin	.03	.01	.00	☐ 425 Monte Coleman	.03	.01	.00
☐ 378 Charles Haley	.08	.04	.01	☐ 426 Darrell Green	.20	.10	.02
☐ 379 Ronnie Lott	.15	.07	.01	☐ 427 Joe Jacoby	.03	.01	.00
☐ 380 Tim McKyer	.08	.04	.01	☐ 428 Jim Lachey	.06	.03	.00
☐ 381 Joe Montana	.75	.35	.07	☐ 429 Charles Mann	.06	.03	.00
☐ 382 Tom Rathman	.08	.04	.01	☐ 430 Dexter Manley	.06	.03	.00
☐ 383 Jerry Rice	.75	.35	.07	☐ 431 Darryl Grant	.10	.05	.01
☐ 384 John Taylor	.90	.45	.09	☐ 432 Mark May	.10	.05	.01
☐ 385 Keena Turner	.03	.01	.00	☐ 433 Art Monk	.20	.10	.02
☐ 386 Michael Walter	.03	.01	.00	☐ 434 Mark Rypien	2.00	1.00	.20
☐ 387 Bubba Paris	.08	.04	.01	☐ 435 Ricky Sanders	.12	.06	.01
☐ 388 Steve Young	.20	.10	.02	☐ 436 Alvin Walton	.08	.04	.01
☐ 389 George Seifert CO	.06	.03	.00	☐ 437 Don Warren	.06	.03	.00
☐ 390 Brian Blades	.90	.45	.09	☐ 438 Jamie Morris	.08	.04	.01
☐ 391A Brian Bosworth ERR (Seattle on front)	.50	.25	.05	☐ 439 Doug Williams	.08	.04	.01
☐ 391B Brian Bosworth COR (Listed by team nick-name on front)	.15	.07	.01	☐ 440 Joe Gibbs CO	.08	.04	.01
☐ 392 Jeff Bryant	.03	.01	.00	☐ 441 Marcus Cotton Atlanta Falcons	.10	.05	.01
☐ 393 Jacob Green	.06	.03	.00	☐ 442 Joel Williams Atlanta Falcons	.08	.04	.01
☐ 394 Norm Johnson	.03	.01	.00	☐ 443 Joe Devlin Buffalo Bills	.08	.04	.01
☐ 395 Dave Krieg	.10	.05	.01	☐ 444 Robb Riddick Buffalo Bills	.03	.01	.00
☐ 396 Steve Largent	.25	.12	.02	☐ 445 William Perry Chicago Bears	.08	.04	.01
☐ 397 Bryan Millard	.08	.04	.01	☐ 446 Thomas Sanders Chicago Bears	.12	.06	.01
☐ 398 Paul Moyer	.08	.04	.01	☐ 447 Brian Blados Cincinnati Bengals	.10	.05	.01
☐ 399 Joe Nash	.03	.01	.00				
☐ 400 Rufus Porter	.12	.06	.01				

☐ 448 Cris Collinsworth .... .06 .03 .00
Cincinnati Bengals
☐ 449 Stanford Jennings .... .03 .01 .00
Cincinnati Bengals
☐ 450 Barry Krauss UER .... .03 .01 .00
(Listed as playing for
Indianapolis 1979-88)
Cleveland Browns
☐ 451 Ozzie Newsome .... .10 .05 .01
Cleveland Browns
☐ 452 Mike Oliphant .... .10 .05 .01
Cleveland Browns
☐ 453 Tony Dorsett .... .15 .07 .01
Denver Broncos
☐ 454 Bruce McNorton .... .03 .01 .00
Detroit Lions
☐ 455 Eric Dickerson .... .35 .17 .03
Indianapolis Colts
☐ 456 Keith Bostic .... .03 .01 .00
Indianapolis Colts
☐ 457 Sam Clancy .... .08 .04 .01
Indianapolis Colts
☐ 458 Jack Del Rio .... .08 .04 .01
Kansas City Chiefs
☐ 459 Mike Webster .... .06 .03 .00
Kansas City Chiefs
☐ 460 Bob Golic .... .06 .03 .00
Los Angeles Raiders
☐ 461 Otis Wilson .... .06 .03 .00
Los Angeles Raiders
☐ 462 Mike Haynes .... .06 .03 .00
Los Angeles Raiders
☐ 463 Greg Townsend .... .06 .03 .00
Los Angeles Raiders
☐ 464 Mark Duper .... .08 .04 .01
Miami Dolphins
☐ 465 E.J. Junior .... .06 .03 .00
Miami Dolphins
☐ 466 Troy Stradford .... .06 .03 .00
Miami Dolphins
☐ 467 Mike Merriweather .... .06 .03 .00
Minnesota Vikings
☐ 468 Irving Fryar .... .06 .03 .00
New England Patriots
☐ 469 Vaughan Johnson .... .25 .12 .02
New Orleans Saints
☐ 470 Pepper Johnson .... .06 .03 .00
New York Giants
☐ 471 Gary Reasons .... .12 .06 .01
New York Giants
☐ 472 Perry Williams .... .08 .04 .01
New York Giants
☐ 473 Wesley Walker .... .08 .04 .01
New York Jets
☐ 474 Anthony Bell .... .10 .05 .01
Phoenix Cardinals
☐ 475 Earl Ferrell .... .03 .01 .00

Phoenix Cardinals
☐ 476 Craig Wolfley .... .08 .04 .01
Pittsburgh Steelers
☐ 477 Billy Ray Smith .... .06 .03 .00
San Diego Chargers
☐ 478A Jim McMahon .... .10 .05 .01
(No mention of trade
on card front)
San Diego Chargers
☐ 478B Jim McMahon .... .45 .22 .04
(Traded banner
on card front)
San Diego Chargers
☐ 478C Jim McMahon 100.00 50.00 10.00
(Traded banner
on card front but no
line on back saying
also see card 44)
San Diego Chargers
☐ 479 Eric Wright .... .03 .01 .00
San Francisco 49ers
☐ 480A Earnest Byner .... .12 .06 .01
(No mention of trade
on card front)
Washington Redskins
☐ 480B Earnest Byner .... .45 .22 .04
(Traded banner
on card front)
Washington Redskins
☐ 480C Earnest Byner 100.00 50.00 10.00
(Traded banner
on card front but no
line on back saying
also see card 74)
Washington Redskins
☐ 481 Russ Grimm .... .03 .01 .00
Washington Redskins
☐ 482 Wilber Marshall .... .06 .03 .00
Washington Redskins
☐ 483A Gerald Riggs .... .10 .05 .01
(No mention of trade
on card front)
Washington Redskins
☐ 483B Gerald Riggs .... .45 .22 .04
(Traded banner
on card front)
Washington Redskins
☐ 483C Gerald Riggs 100.00 50.00 10.00
(Traded banner
on card front but no
line on back saying
also see card 14)
Washington Redskins
☐ 484 Brian Davis .... .10 .05 .01
Washington Redskins
☐ 485 Shawn Collins .... .15 .07 .01
Atlanta Falcons

☐ 486 Deion Sanders 1.75	.85	.17
Atlanta Falcons		
☐ 487 Trace Armstrong .... .12	.06	.01
Chicago Bears		
☐ 488 Donnell Woolford .... .15	.07	.01
Chicago Bears		
☐ 489 Eric Metcalf .... .25	.12	.02
Cleveland Browns		
☐ 490 Troy Aikman 2.50	1.25	.25
Dallas Cowboys		
☐ 491 Steve Walsh .... .40	.20	.04
Dallas Cowboys		
☐ 492 Steve Atwater .... .30	.15	.03
Denver Broncos		
☐ 493 Bobby Humphrey UER .. .75	.35	.07
Denver Broncos		
(Jersey 41 on back,		
should be 26)		
☐ 494 Barry Sanders 7.50	3.75	.75
Detroit Lions		
☐ 495 Tony Mandarich .... .15	.07	.01
Green Bay Packers		
☐ 496 David Williams .... .08	.04	.01
Houston Oilers		
☐ 497 Andre Rison UER 1.50	.75	.15
(Jersey number not		
listed on back)		
Indianapolis Colts		
☐ 498 Derrick Thomas 1.50	.75	.15
Kansas City Chiefs		
☐ 499 Cleveland Gary .... .30	.15	.03
Los Angeles Rams		
☐ 500 Bill Hawkins .... .08	.04	.01
Los Angeles Rams		
☐ 501 Louis Oliver .... .12	.06	.01
Miami Dolphins		
☐ 502 Sammie Smith .... .60	.30	.06
Miami Dolphins		
☐ 503 Hart Lee Dykes .... .15	.07	.01
New England Patriots		
☐ 504 Wayne Martin .... .10	.05	.01
New Orleans Saints		
☐ 505 Brian Williams .... .08	.04	.01
New York Giants		
☐ 506 Jeff Lageman .... .25	.12	.02
New York Jets		
☐ 507 Eric Hill .... .12	.06	.01
Phoenix Cardinals		
☐ 508 Joe Wolf .... .10	.05	.01
Phoenix Cardinals		
☐ 509 Timm Rosenbach .... .35	.17	.03
Phoenix Cardinals		
☐ 510 Tom Ricketts .... .10	.05	.01
Pittsburgh Steelers		
☐ 511 Tim Worley .... .10	.05	.01
Pittsburgh Steelers		
☐ 512 Burt Grossman .... .15	.07	.01

San Diego Chargers		
☐ 513 Keith DeLong .... .15	.07	.01
San Francisco 49ers		
☐ 514 Andy Heck .... .10	.05	.01
Seattle Seahawks		
☐ 515 Broderick Thomas .... .50	.25	.05
Tampa Bay Buccaneers		
☐ 516 Don Beebe .... .40	.20	.04
Buffalo Bills		
☐ 517 James Thornton .... .20	.10	.02
Chicago Bears		
☐ 518 Eric Kattus .... .10	.05	.01
Cincinnati Bengals		
☐ 519 Bruce Kozerski .... .08	.04	.01
Cincinnati Bengals		
☐ 520 Brian Washington .... .10	.05	.01
Cleveland Browns		
☐ 521 Rodney Peete UER .... .50	.25	.05
Detroit Lions		
(Jersey 19 on back,		
should be 9)		
☐ 522 Erik Affholter .... .15	.07	.01
Green Bay Packers		
☐ 523 Anthony Dilweg .... .20	.10	.02
Green Bay Packers		
☐ 524 O'Brien Alston .... .08	.04	.01
Indianapolis Colts		
☐ 525 Mike Elkins .... .10	.05	.01
Kansas City Chiefs		
☐ 526 Jonathan Hayes .... .10	.05	.01
Kansas City Chiefs		
☐ 527 Terry McDaniel .... .12	.06	.01
Los Angeles Raiders		
☐ 528 Frank Stams .... .15	.07	.01
Los Angeles Rams		
☐ 529 Darryl Ingram .... .12	.06	.01
Minnesota Vikings		
☐ 530 Henry Thomas .... .06	.03	.00
Minnesota Vikings		
☐ 531 Eric Coleman .... .10	.05	.01
New England Patriots		
☐ 532 Sheldon White .... .10	.05	.01
New York Giants		
☐ 533 Eric Allen .... .15	.07	.01
Philadelphia Eagles		
☐ 534 Robert Drummond .... .10	.05	.01
Philadelphia Eagles		
☐ 535A Gizmo Williams 50.00	25.00	5.00
(Without Scouting Photo		
on front and "Footbal"		
misspelled on back)		
Philadelphia Eagles		
☐ 535B Gizmo Williams .... .25	.12	.02
(Without Scouting Photo		
on front but "Canadian		
Football" on back)		
Philadelphia Eagles		

☐ 535C	Gizmo Williams ....20 (With Scouting Photo on card front) Philadelphia Eagles	.10	.02
☐ 536	Billy Joe Tolliver ....20 San Diego Chargers	.10	.02
☐ 537	Danny Stubbs ....08 San Francisco 49ers	.04	.01
☐ 538	Wesley Walls ....12 San Francisco 49ers	.06	.01
☐ 539A	James Jefferson ERR ..65 (No Prospect banner on card front) Seattle Seahawks	.30	.06
☐ 539B	James Jefferson COR ..15 (Prospect banner on card front) Seattle Seahawks	.07	.01
☐ 540	Tracy Rocker ....12 Washington Redskins	.06	.01
☐ CC1	Pete Rozelle SP ....2.00 (Commissioner)	1.00	.20

1989 Pro Set Final Update

The 1989 Pro Set Final Update contains 21 standard-size (2 1/2" by 3 1/2") cards. The fronts have color action photos which are similar in appearance to the regular 1989 Pro Set cards. Cards numbered 542-549 are Pro Set Prospects, 550-555 have no special stripe, and cards 556-561 are designated as "Traded". These cards were distributed in Final Series II packs as well as being offered direct from Pro Set as a shrink-wrapped set for 2.00 plus 50

Pro Set Play Book points. The key rookie cards in this final update set are Marion Butts, Dave Meggett, and Sterling Sharpe.

	MINT	EXC	G-VG
COMPLETE SET (21) 3.00		1.50	.30
COMMON PLAYER (541-561) 03		.01	.00
☐ 541 Art Shell CO ....12 Los Angeles Raiders		.06	.01
☐ 542 Lemuel Stinson ....12 Chicago Bears		.06	.01
☐ 543 Tyrone Braxton UER ......12 Denver Broncos (back photo actually Ken Bell)		.06	.01
☐ 544 David Treadwell ....08 Denver Broncos		.04	.01
☐ 545 Flipper Anderson ....30 Los Angeles Rams		.15	.03
☐ 546 Dave Meggett ....60 New York Giants		.30	.06
☐ 547 Lewis Tillman ....12 New York Giants		.06	.01
☐ 548 Carnell Lake ....12 Pittsburgh Steelers		.06	.01
☐ 549 Marion Butts ....90 San Diego Chargers		.45	.09
☐ 550 Sterling Sharpe ....1.50 Green Bay Packers		.75	.15
☐ 551 Ezra Johnson ....03 Indianapolis Colts		.01	.00
☐ 552 Clarence Verdin ....08 Indianapolis Colts		.04	.01
☐ 553 Mervyn Fernandez ....20 Los Angeles Raiders		.10	.02
☐ 554 Ottis Anderson ....10 New York Giants		.05	.01
☐ 555 Gary Hogeboom ....08 Kansas City Chiefs		.04	.01
☐ 556 Paul Palmer TR ....06 Dallas Cowboys		.03	.00
☐ 557 Jesse Solomon TR ....03 Dallas Cowboys		.01	.00
☐ 558 Chip Banks TR ....06 Indianapolis Colts		.03	.00
☐ 559 Steve Pelluer TR ....06 Kansas City Chiefs		.03	.00
☐ 560 Darrin Nelson TR ....06 San Diego Chargers		.03	.00
☐ 561 Herschel Walker TR ......30 Minnesota Vikings		.15	.03

1990 Pro Set I

The 1990 Pro Set Series I issue contains 377 standard-size (2 1/2" by 3 1/2") cards. The fronts have striking color action photos and team colored borders on the top and bottom edges; there are no borders on the sides. The horizontally oriented backs have stats and color mug shots. Cards 1-29 are special selections from Pro Set commemorating events or leaders from the previous year. The cards in the set are numbered by teams, Atlanta Falcons (30-38), Buffalo Bills (39-48), Chicago Bears (49-59), Cincinnati Bengals (60-68), Cleveland Browns (69-77), Dallas Cowboys (78-85), Denver Broncos (86-94), Detroit Lions (95-106), Green Bay Packers (107-116), Houston Oilers (117-127), Indianapolis Colts (128-139), Kansas City Chiefs (140-148), Los Angeles Raiders (149-161), Los Angeles Rams (162-176), Miami Dolphins (177-185), Minnesota Vikings (186-200), New England Patriots (201-209), New Orleans Saints (210-221), New York Giants (222-232), New York Jets (233-242), Philadelphia Eagles (243-253), Phoenix Cardinals (254-265), Pittsburgh Steelers (266-275), San Diego Chargers (276-283), San Francisco 49ers (284-299), Seattle Seahawks (300-308), Tampa Bay Buccaneers (309-319), Washington Redskins (320-333), and Pro Bowl Selections (334-378). Pro Set also produced and randomly inserted 10,000 Lombardi Trophy hologram cards; speculation is that there is one special Lombardi card in every tenth case. These attractive "Lombardi" cards are hand numbered "x" of 10,000 and are highly sought after. The best rookie cards in this set are Percy Snow, Anthony Thompson, and Andre Ware; most of the rookies apparently were "saved" for Pro Set Series II. The

(withdrawn) Eric Dickerson card is not included in the complete set price below. Similarly, the set price below does not include any of the scarce variation cards, e.g., 1A, 75A, etc.

	MINT	EXC	G-VG
COMPLETE SET (377)	9.00	4.50	.90
COMMON PLAYER (1-378)	.03	.01	.00
☐ 1A Barry Sanders ROY	100.00	40.00	7.50
(Distributed to dealers at the Hawaii trade show in February 1990; distinguished from the regular card by profile head shot photo without ROY trophy on on card back)			
☐ 1B Barry Sanders UER	.60	.30	.06
Rookie of the Year (TD total says 14, but adds up to 11)			
☐ 2A Joe Montana ERR	.35	.17	.03
Player of the Year (Jim Kelly's stats in text)			
☐ 2B Joe Montana COR	.35	.17	.03
Player of the Year (Corrected from 3521 yards to 3130)			
☐ 3 Lindy Infante UER	.03	.01	.00
Coach of the Year (missing Coach next to Packers)			
☐ 4 Warren Moon UER	.12	.06	.01
Man of the Year (missing R symbol)			
☐ 5 Keith Millard	.06	.03	.00
Defensive Player of the Year			
☐ 6 Derrick Thomas UER	.10	.05	.01
Defensive Rookie of the Year (no 1989 on front banner of card)			
☐ 7 Ottis Anderson	.06	.03	.00
Comeback Player of the Year			
☐ 8 Joe Montana	.25	.12	.02
Passing Leader			
☐ 9 Christian Okoye	.08	.04	.01
Rushing Leader			
☐ 10 Thurman Thomas	.20	.10	.02
Total Yardage Leader			
☐ 11 Mike Cofer	.03	.01	.00
Kick Scoring Leader			
☐ 12 Dalton Hilliard UER	.06	.03	.00

TD Scoring Leader
(O.J. Simpson not
listed in stats, but
is mentioned in text)

☐ 13 Sterling Sharpe	.08	.04	.01
Receiving Leader			
☐ 14 Rich Camarillo	.03	.01	.00
Punting Leader			
✓☐ 15A Walter Stanley ERR	1.25	.60	.12
Punt Return Leader.			
(jersey on front reads			
87, back says 8 or 86)			
☐ 15B Walter Stanley COR	.10	.05	.01
Punt Return Leader			
✓☐ 16 Rod Woodson	.06	.03	.00
Kickoff Return Leader			
✓☐ 17 Felix Wright	.03	.01	.00
Interception Leader			
☐ 18A Chris Doleman ERR	.08	.04	.01
Sack Leader			
(Townsent, Jeffcoact)			
☐ 18B Chris Doleman COR	.08	.04	.01
Sack Leader			
(Townsend, Jeffcoat)			
✓☐ 19A Andre Ware	.35	.17	.03
Heisman Trophy			
(no drafted stripe			
on card front)			
☐ 19B Andre Ware	.35	.17	.03
Heisman Trophy			
(drafted stripe			
on card front)			
☐ 20A Mohammed Elewonibi	.08	.04	.01
Outland Trophy			
(no drafted stripe			
on card front)			
✓☐ 20B Mohammed Elewonibi	.08	.04	.01
Outland Trophy			
(drafted stripe			
on card front)			
☐ 21A Percy Snow	.15	.07	.01
Lombardi Award			
(no drafted stripe			
on card front)			
✓☐ 21B Percy Snow	.15	.07	.01
Lombardi Award			
(drafted stripe			
on card front)			
✓☐ 22A Anthony Thompson	.30	.15	.03
Maxwell Award			
(no drafted stripe			
on card front)			
☐ 22B Anthony Thompson	.30	.15	.03
Maxwell Award			
(drafted stripe			
on card front)			
☐ 23 Buck Buchanan	.06	.03	.00

	1990 HOF Selection			
✓☐ 24 Bob Griese	.06	.03	.00
	1990 HOF Selection			
✓☐ 25A Franco Harris ERR	.08	.04	.01
	1990 HOF Selection			
	(Born 2/7/50)			
☐ 25B Franco Harris COR	.08	.04	.01
	1990 HOF Selection			
	(Born 3/7/50)			
✓☐ 26 Ted Hendricks	.06	.03	.00
	1990 HOF Selection			
✓☐ 27A Jack Lambert ERR	.08	.04	.01
	1990 HOF Selection			
	(Born 7/2/52)			
☐ 27B Jack Lambert COR	.08	.04	.01
	1990 HOF Selection			
	(Born 7/8/52)			
✓☐ 28 Tom Landry	.08	.04	.01
	1990 HOF Selection			
☐ 29 Bob St.Clair	.06	.03	.00
	1990 HOF Selection			
✓☐ 30 Aundray Bruce UER	.06	.03	.00
	(Stats say Falcons)			
✓☐ 31 Tony Casillas UER	.06	.03	.00
	(Stats say Falcons)			
✓☐ 32 Shawn Collins	.06	.03	.00
✓☐ 33 Marcus Cotton	.03	.01	.00
☐ 34 Bill Fralic	.06	.03	.00
☐ 35 Chris Miller	.20	.10	.02
☐ 36 Deion Sanders UER	.30	.15	.03
	(Stats say Falcons)			
✓☐ 37 John Settle	.06	.03	.00
✓☐ 38 Jerry Glanville CO	.03	.01	.00
☐ 39 Cornelius Bennett	.10	.05	.01
✓☐ 40 Jim Kelly	.35	.17	.03
✓☐ 41 Mark Kelso UER	.03	.01	.00
	(No fumble rec. in '88;			
	mentioned in '89)			
✓☐ 42 Scott Norwood	.03	.01	.00
✓☐ 43 Nate Odomes	.10	.05	.01
✓☐ 44 Scott Radecic	.06	.03	.00
✓☐ 45 Jim Ritcher	.10	.05	.01
✓☐ 46 Leonard Smith	.03	.01	.00
✓☐ 47 Darryl Talley	.08	.04	.01
✓☐ 48 Marv Levy CO	.03	.01	.00
☐ 49 Neal Anderson	.15	.07	.01
✓☐ 50 Kevin Butler	.03	.01	.00
✓☐ 51 Jim Covert	.06	.03	.00
✓☐ 52 Richard Dent	.08	.04	.01
✓☐ 53 Jay Hilgenberg	.06	.03	.00
✓☐ 54 Steve McMichael	.06	.03	.00
✓☐ 55 Ron Morris	.06	.03	.00
✓☐ 56 John Roper	.10	.05	.01
✓☐ 57 Mike Singletary	.08	.04	.01
✓☐ 58 Keith Van Horne	.03	.01	.00
☐ 59 Mike Ditka CO	.06	.03	.00
☐ 60 Lewis Billups	.03	.01	.00

✓ ☐ 61 Eddie Brown	.08	.04	.01
✓ ☐ 62 Jason Buck	.03	.01	.00
✓ ☐ 63A Rickey Dixon ERR	.75	.35	.07
(Info missing under bio notes)			
☐ 63B Rickey Dixon COR	.20	.10	.02
☐ 64 Tim McGee	.08	.04	.01
✓ ☐ 65 Eric Thomas	.06	.03	.00
☐ 66 Ickey Woods	.06	.03	.00
☐ 67 Carl Zander	.03	.01	.00
☐ 68A Sam Wyche CO ERR	.50	.25	.05
(Info missing under bio notes)			
☐ 68B Sam Wyche CO COR	.08	.04	.01
☐ 69 Paul Farren	.08	.04	.01
☐ 70 Thane Gash	.08	.04	.01
☐ 71 David Grayson	.06	.03	.01
☐ 72 Bernie Kosar	.15	.07	.01
☐ 73 Reggie Langhorne	.03	.01	.00
✓ ☐ 74 Eric Metcalf	.08	.04	.01
☐ 75A Cody Risien SP	10.00	5.00	1.00
(withdrawn)			
☐ 75B Ozzie Newsome ERR	.10	.05	.01
(Born Little Rock)			
☐ 75C Ozzie Newsome COR	.10	.05	.01
(Born Muscle Shoals)			
☐ 76 Felix Wright	.03	.01	.00
☐ 77 Bud Carson CO	.03	.01	.00
☐ 78 Troy Aikman	.60	.30	.06
☐ 79 Michael Irvin	.30	.15	.03
☐ 80 Jim Jeffcoat	.03	.01	.00
☐ 81 Crawford Ker	.08	.04	.01
☐ 82 Eugene Lockhart	.03	.01	.00
☐ 83 Kelvin Martin	.10	.05	.01
☐ 84 Ken Norton	.15	.07	.01
☐ 85 Jimmy Johnson CO	.06	.03	.00
☐ 86 Steve Atwater	.08	.04	.01
☐ 87 Tyrone Braxton	.06	.03	.00
☐ 88 John Elway	.20	.10	.02
☐ 89 Simon Fletcher	.03	.01	.00
☐ 90 Ron Holmes	.03	.01	.00
☐ 91 Bobby Humphrey	.12	.06	.01
☐ 92 Vance Johnson	.06	.03	.00
☐ 93 Ricky Nattiel	.06	.03	.00
☐ 94 Dan Reeves CO	.06	.03	.00
☐ 95 Jim Arnold	.03	.01	.00
☐ 96 Jerry Ball	.03	.01	.00
☐ 97 Bennie Blades	.06	.03	.00
☐ 98 Lomas Brown	.03	.01	.00
☐ 99 Michael Cofer	.03	.01	.00
☐ 100 Richard Johnson	.06	.03	.00
☐ 101 Eddie Murray	.06	.03	.00
☐ 102 Barry Sanders	.90	.45	.09
☐ 103 Chris Spielman	.06	.03	.00
☐ 104 William White	.15	.07	.01
☐ 105 Eric Williams	.10	.05	.01
☐ 106 Wayne Fontes CO UER	.03	.01	.00
(Says born in MO, actually born in MA)			
☐ 107 Brent Fullwood	.06	.03	.00
☐ 108 Ron Hallstrom	.10	.05	.01
☐ 109 Tim Harris	.06	.03	.00
☐ 110A Johnny Holland ERR	1.25	.60	.12
(No name or position at top of reverse)			
☐ 110B Johnny Holland COR	.08	.04	.01
☐ 111A Perry Kemp ERR	1.00	.50	.10
(Photo on back is actually Ken Stiles, wearing gray shirt)			
☐ 111B Perry Kemp COR	.08	.04	.01
(Wearing green shirt)			
☐ 112 Don Majkowski	.10	.05	.01
☐ 113 Mark Murphy	.03	.01	.00
☐ 114A Sterling Sharpe ERR	.20	.10	.02
(Born Glenville, Ga.)			
☐ 114B Sterling Sharpe COR	1.50	.75	.15
(Born Chicago)			
☐ 115 Ed West	.08	.04	.01
☐ 116 Lindy Infante CO	.03	.01	.00
☐ 117 Steve Brown	.03	.01	.00
☐ 118 Ray Childress	.06	.03	.00
☐ 119 Ernest Givins	.10	.05	.01
☐ 120 John Grimsley	.03	.01	.00
☐ 121 Alonzo Highsmith	.06	.03	.00
☐ 122 Drew Hill	.08	.04	.01
☐ 123 Bubba McDowell	.10	.05	.01
☐ 124 Dean Steinkuhler	.06	.03	.00
☐ 125 Lorenzo White	.10	.05	.01
☐ 126 Tony Zendejas	.03	.01	.00
☐ 127 Jack Pardee CO	.03	.01	.00
☐ 128 Albert Bentley	.06	.03	.00
☐ 129 Dean Biasucci	.03	.01	.00
☐ 130 Duane Bickett	.06	.03	.00
☐ 131 Bill Brooks	.06	.03	.00
☐ 132 Jon Hand	.06	.03	.00
☐ 133 Mike Prior	.03	.01	.00
☐ 134A Andre Rison	.25	.12	.02
(No mention of trade on card front)			
☐ 134B Andre Rison	.60	.30	.06
(Traded banner on card front; also reissued with Final Update)			
☐ 134C Andre Rison	.40	.20	.04
(Traded banner on card front; message from Lud Denny on back)			
☐ 135 Rohn Stark	.03	.01	.00
☐ 136 Donnell Thompson	.03	.01	.00
☐ 137 Clarence Verdin	.06	.03	.00
☐ 138 Fredd Young	.03	.01	.00
☐ 139 Ron Meyer CO	.03	.01	.00
☐ 140 John Alt	.10	.05	.01

☐ 141 Steve DeBerg	.10	.05	
☐ 142 Irv Eatman	.03	.01	.00
☐ 143 Dino Hackett	.03	.01	.00
☐ 144 Nick Lowery	.06	.03	.00
☐ 145 Bill Maas	.06	.03	.00
☐ 146 Stephone Paige	.06	.03	.00
☐ 147 Neil Smith	.06	.03	.00
☐ 148 Marty Schottenheimer CO	.03	.01	.00
☐ 149 Steve Beuerlein	.15	.07	.01
☐ 150 Tim Brown	.10	.05	.01
☐ 151 Mike Dyal	.10	.05	.01
☐ 152A Mervyn Fernandez ERR (Acquired: Free Agent '87)	.10	.05	
☐ 152B Mervyn Fernandez COR (Acquired: Drafted 10th Round, 1983)	.10	.05	.01
☐ 153 Willie Gault	.06	.03	.00
☐ 154 Bob Golic	.03	.01	.00
☐ 155 Bo Jackson	.40	.20	.04
☐ 156 Don Mosebar	.03	.01	.00
☐ 157 Steve Smith	.06	.03	.00
☐ 158 Greg Townsend	.06	.03	.00
☐ 159 Bruce Wilkerson	.08	.04	.01
☐ 160 Steve Wisniewski	.06	.03	.00
☐ 161A Art Shell CO ERR (Born 11/25/46)	.08	.04	.01
☐ 161B Art Shell CO COR (Born 11/26/46)	.75	.35	.07
☐ 162 Flipper Anderson	.10	.05	.01
☐ 163 Greg Bell UER (Stats have 5 catches, should be 9)	.06	.03	.00
☐ 164 Henry Ellard	.08	.04	.01
☐ 165 Jim Everett	.12	.06	.01
☐ 166 Jerry Gray	.06	.03	.00
☐ 167 Kevin Greene	.06	.03	.00
☐ 168 Pete Holohan	.03	.01	.00
☐ 169 Larry Kelm	.08	.04	.01
☐ 170 Tom Newberry	.03	.01	.00
☐ 171 Vince Newsome	.10	.05	.01
☐ 172 Irv Pankey	.03	.01	.00
☐ 173 Jackie Slater	.06	.03	.00
☐ 174 Fred Strickland	.08	.04	.01
☐ 175 Mike Wilcher UER (Fumble rec. number different from 1989 Pro Set card)	.03	.01	.00
☐ 176 John Robinson CO UER (Stats say Rams, should say L.A. Rams)	.03	.01	.00
☐ 177 Mark Clayton	.10	.05	.01
☐ 178 Roy Foster	.03	.01	.00
☐ 179 Harry Galbreath	.08	.04	.01
☐ 180 Jim C. Jensen	.03	.01	.00
☐ 181 Dan Marino	.30	.15	.03
☐ 182 Louis Oliver	.06	.03	.00
☐ 183 Sammie Smith	.10	.05	.01
☐ 184 Brian Sochia	.03	.01	.00
☐ 185 Don Shula CO	.06	.03	.00
☐ 186 Joey Browner	.06	.03	.00
☐ 187 Anthony Carter	.08	.04	.01
☐ 188 Chris Doleman	.06	.03	.00
☐ 189 Steve Jordan	.06	.03	.00
☐ 190 Carl Lee	.06	.03	.00
☐ 191 Randall McDaniel	.06	.03	.00
☐ 192 Mike Merriweather	.06	.03	.00
☐ 193 Keith Millard	.06	.03	.00
☐ 194 Al Noga	.06	.03	.00
☐ 195 Scott Studwell	.03	.01	.00
☐ 196 Henry Thomas	.03	.01	.00
☐ 197 Herschel Walker	.15	.07	.01
☐ 198 Wade Wilson	.08	.04	.01
☐ 199 Gary Zimmerman	.06	.03	.00
☐ 200 Jerry Burns CO	.03	.01	.00
☐ 201 Vincent Brown	.10	.05	.01
☐ 202 Hart Lee Dykes	.06	.03	.00
☐ 203 Sean Farrell	.03	.01	.00
☐ 204A Fred Marion (Belt visible on John Taylor)	.25	.12	.02
☐ 204B Fred Marion (Belt not visible)	.06	.03	.00
☐ 205 Stanley Morgan UER (Text says he reached 10,000 yards fastest; 3 players did it in 10 seasons)	.08	.04	.01
☐ 206 Eric Sievers	.10	.05	.01
☐ 207 John Stephens	.08	.04	.01
☐ 208 Andre Tippett	.06	.03	.00
☐ 209 Rod Rust CO	.03	.01	.00
☐ 210A Morten Andersen ERR (Card number and name on back in white)	.50	.25	.05
☐ 210B Morten Andersen COR (Card number and name on back in black)	.06	.03	.00
☐ 211 Brad Edelman	.03	.01	.00
☐ 212 John Fourcade	.08	.04	.01
☐ 213 Dalton Hilliard	.10	.05	.01
☐ 214 Rickey Jackson	.06	.03	.00
☐ 215 Vaughan Johnson	.06	.03	.00
☐ 216A Eric Martin ERR (Card number and name on back in white)	.50	.25	.05
☐ 216B Eric Martin COR (Card number and name on back in black)	.06	.03	.00
☐ 217 Sam Mills	.06	.03	.00
☐ 218 Pat Swilling UER (Total fumble recoveries listed	.10	.05	.01

as 4, should be 5)

219 Frank Warren	.12	.06	.01
220 Jim Wilks	.03	.01	.00
221A Jim Mora CO ERR	.50	.25	.05
(Card number and name on back in white)			
221B Jim Mora CO COR	.06	.03	.00
(Card number and name on back in black)			
222 Raul Allegre	.03	.01	.00
223 Carl Banks	.06	.03	.00
224 John Elliott	.06	.03	.00
225 Erik Howard	.03	.01	.00
226 Pepper Johnson	.06	.03	.00
227 Leonard Marshall UER	.06	.03	.00
(In Super Bowl XXI, George Martin had the safety)			
228 David Meggett	.15	.07	.01
229 Bart Oates	.03	.01	.00
230 Phil Simms	.10	.05	.01
231 Lawrence Taylor	.10	.05	.01
232 Bill Parcells CO	.06	.03	.00
233 Troy Benson	.03	.01	.00
234 Kyle Clifton UER	.03	.01	.00
(Born: Onley, should be Olney)			
235 Johnny Hector	.06	.03	.00
236 Jeff Lageman	.06	.03	.00
237 Pat Leahy	.06	.03	.00
238 Freeman McNeil	.08	.04	.01
239 Ken O'Brien	.08	.04	.01
240 Al Toon	.08	.04	.01
241 Jo Jo Townsell	.06	.03	.00
242 Bruce Coslet CO	.06	.03	.00
243 Eric Allen	.06	.03	.00
244 Jerome Brown	.06	.03	.00
245 Keith Byars	.06	.03	.00
246 Cris Carter	.08	.04	.01
247 Randall Cunningham	.15	.07	.01
248 Keith Jackson	.10	.05	.01
249 Mike Quick	.06	.03	.00
250 Clyde Simmons	.06	.03	.00
251 Andre Waters	.03	.01	.00
252 Reggie White	.08	.04	.01
253 Buddy Ryan CO	.03	.01	.00
254 Rich Camarillo	.03	.01	.00
255 Earl Ferrell	.03	.01	.00
(No mention of retirement on card front)			
256 Roy Green	.08	.04	.01
257 Ken Harvey	.12	.06	.01
258 Ernie Jones	.20	.10	.02
259 Tim McDonald	.06	.03	.00
260 Timm Rosenbach UER	.10	.05	.01
(Born '67, should be '66)			
261 Luis Sharpe	.03	.01	.00

262 Vai Sikahema	.03	.01	.00
263 J.T. Smith	.06	.03	.00
264 Ron Wolfley UER	.03	.01	.00
(Born Blaisdel, should be Blasdel)			
265 Joe Bugel CO	.06	.03	.00
266 Gary Anderson	.03	.01	.00
267 Bubby Brister	.10	.05	.01
268 Merril Hoge	.06	.03	.00
269 Carnell Lake	.03	.01	.00
270 Louis Lipps	.08	.04	.01
271 David Little	.03	.01	.00
272 Greg Lloyd	.06	.03	.00
273 Keith Willis	.03	.01	.00
274 Tim Worley	.06	.03	.00
275 Chuck Noll CO	.03	.01	.00
276 Marion Butts	.15	.07	.01
277 Gill Byrd	.06	.03	.00
278 Vencie Glenn UER	.03	.01	.00
(Sack total should be 2, not 2.5)			
279 Burt Grossman	.06	.03	.00
280 Gary Plummer	.03	.01	.00
281 Billy Ray Smith	.06	.03	.00
282 Billy Joe Tolliver	.08	.04	.01
283 Dan Henning CO	.03	.01	.00
284 Harris Barton	.03	.01	.00
285 Michael Carter	.06	.03	.00
286 Mike Cofer	.03	.01	.00
287 Roger Craig	.10	.05	.01
288 Don Griffin	.03	.01	.00
289A Charles Haley ERR	.08	.04	.01
(Fumble recoveries 1 in '86 and 4 total)			
289B Charles Haley COR	.80	.40	.08
(Fumble recoveries 2 in '86 and 5 total)			
290 Pierce Holt	.08	.04	.01
291 Ronnie Lott	.10	.05	.01
292 Guy McIntyre	.06	.03	.00
293 Joe Montana	.50	.25	.05
294 Tom Rathman	.06	.03	.00
295 Jerry Rice	.45	.22	.04
296 Jesse Sapolu	.03	.01	.00
297 John Taylor	.15	.07	.01
298 Michael Walter	.03	.01	.00
299 George Seifert CO	.03	.01	.00
300 Jeff Bryant	.03	.01	.00
301 Jacob Green	.06	.03	.00
302 Norm Johnson UER	.06	.03	.00
(Card shop not in Garden Grove, should say Fullerton)			
303 Bryan Millard	.03	.01	.00
304 Joe Nash	.03	.01	.00
305 Eugene Robinson	.03	.01	.00
306 John L. Williams	.08	.04	.01

307 Dave Wyman ....03 .01 .00 (NFL EXP is in caps, inconsistent with rest of the set)		
308 Chuck Knox CO ....03 .01 .00		
309 Mark Carrier ....08 .04 .01		
310 Paul Gruber ....03 .01 .00		
311 Harry Hamilton ....03 .01 .00		
312 Bruce Hill ....03 .01 .00		
313 Donald Igwebuike ....03 .01 .00		
314 Kevin Murphy ....06 .03 .00		
315 Ervin Randle ....03 .01 .00		
316 Mark Robinson ....06 .03 .00		
317 Lars Tate ....06 .03 .00		
318 Vinny Testaverde ....08 .04 .01		
319A Ray Perkins CO ERR . 1.50 .75 .15 (No name or title at top of reverse)		
319B Ray Perkins CO COR ...06 .03 .00		
320 Earnest Byner ....08 .04 .01		
321 Gary Clark ....15 .07 .01		
322 Darryl Grant ....06 .03 .00		
323 Darrell Green ....15 .07 .01		
324 Jim Lachey ....06 .03 .00		
325 Charles Mann ....06 .03 .00		
326 Wilber Marshall ....06 .03 .00		
327 Ralf Mojsiejenko ....03 .01 .00		
328 Art Monk ....15 .07 .01		
329 Gerald Riggs ....08 .04 .01		
330 Mark Rypien ....35 .17 .03		
331 Ricky Sanders ....10 .05 .01		
332 Alvin Walton ....06 .03 .00		
333 Joe Gibbs CO ....03 .01 .00		
334 Aloha Stadium ....03 .01 .00 Site of Pro Bowl		
335 Brian Blades PB ....06 .03 .00		
336 James Brooks PB ....06 .03 .00		
337 Shane Conlan PB ....06 .03 .00		
338 Eric Dickerson PB SP 10.00 5.00 1.00 (Card withdrawn)		
339 Ray Donaldson PB ....03 .01 .00		
340 Ferrell Edmunds PB .....06 .03 .00		
341 Boomer Esiason PB ......08 .04 .01		
342 David Fulcher PB ....03 .01 .00		
343A Chris Hinton PB ....75 .35 .07 (No mention of trade on card front)		
343B Chris Hinton PB ....08 .04 .01 (Traded banner on card front)		
344 Rodney Holman PB ....06 .03 .00		
345 Kent Hull PB ....03 .01 .00		
346 Tunch Ilkin PB ....03 .01 .00		
347 Mike Johnson PB ....03 .01 .00		
348 Greg Kragen PB ....03 .01 .00		
349 Dave Krieg PB ....06 .03 .00		
350 Albert Lewis PB ....06 .03 .00		

351 Howie Long PB ....06 .03 .00		
352 Bruce Matthews PB ....03 .01 .00		
353 Clay Matthews PB ....03 .01 .00		
354 Erik McMillan PB ....06 .03 .00		
355 Karl Mecklenburg PB .....06 .03 .00		
356 Anthony Miller PB ....06 .03 .00		
357 Frank Minnifield PB ....03 .01 .00		
358 Max Montoya PB ....03 .01 .00		
359 Warren Moon PB ....12 .06 .01		
360 Mike Munchak PB ....06 .03 .00		
361 Anthony Munoz PB ....08 .04 .01		
362 John Offerdahl PB ....03 .01 .00		
363 Christian Okoye PB ....08 .04 .01		
364 Leslie O'Neal PB ....06 .03 .00		
365 Rufus Porter PB UER ....03 .01 .00 (TM logo missing)		
366 Andre Reed PB ....08 .04 .01		
367 Johnny Rembert PB ......03 .01 .00		
368 Reggie Roby PB ....03 .01 .00		
369 Kevin Ross PB ....03 .01 .00		
370 Webster Slaughter PB ...06 .03 .00		
371 Bruce Smith PB ....08 .04 .01		
372 Dennis Smith PB ....03 .01 .00		
373 Derrick Thomas PB ....10 .05 .01		
374 Thurman Thomas PB .....20 .10 .02		
375 David Treadwell PB ....03 .01 .00		
376 Lee Williams PB ....03 .01 .00		
377 Rod Woodson PB ....06 .03 .00		
378 Bud Carson CO PB ....03 .01 .00		

1990 Pro Set II

The second series of Pro Set football features cards in the same style and size (2 1/2" by 3 1/2") as the first series. The set is somewhat skip-numbered in that some numbers were saved for inclusion in Pro Set's Final Update.

The key rookies in this set are Jeff George, Rodney Hampton, Jeff Hostetler, Rob Moore, Emmitt Smith, and Blair Thomas. Cards 796-798 are black and white photos. Pro Set issued their AFC Pro Bowl series at the end of Series I and their NFC Pro Bowl series to open Series II. AFC Pro Bowlers have their regular cards in Series II and the NFC Pro bowlers in Series I. The only exceptions to this rule are AFC coach Bud Carson (all coaches are in Series I) and Chris Hinton, who doesn't have a regular card. Draft cards found near the end of the set are sequenced by draft order.

	MINT	EXC	G-VG
COMPLETE SET	11.00	5.50	1.10
COMMON PLAYER (379-798)	.03	.01	.00
☐ 379 Eric Allen PB	.06	.03	.00
Philadelphia Eagles			
☐ 380 Neal Anderson PB	.08	.04	.01
Chicago Bears			
☐ 381 Jerry Ball PB	.03	.01	.00
Detroit Lions			
☐ 382 Joey Browner PB	.06	.03	.00
Minnesota Vikings			
☐ 383 Rich Camarillo PB	.03	.01	.00
Phoenix Cardinals			
☐ 384 Mark Carrier PB	.06	.03	.00
Tampa Bay Buccaneers			
☐ 385 Roger Craig PB	.08	.04	.01
San Francisco 49ers			
☐ 386 Randall Cunningham PB	.08	.04	.01
Philadelphia Eagles			
☐ 387 Chris Doleman PB	.06	.03	.00
Minnesota Vikings			
☐ 388 Henry Ellard PB	.06	.03	.00
Los Angeles Rams			
☐ 389 Bill Fralic PB	.06	.03	.00
Atlanta Falcons			
☐ 390 Brent Fullwood PB	.06	.03	.00
Green Bay Packers			
☐ 391 Jerry Gray PB	.03	.01	.00
Los Angeles Rams			
☐ 392 Kevin Greene PB	.06	.03	.00
Los Angeles Rams			
☐ 393 Tim Harris PB	.06	.03	.00
Green Bay Packers			
☐ 394 Jay Hilgenberg PB	.06	.03	.00
Chicago Bears			
☐ 395 Dalton Hilliard PB	.03	.01	.00
New Orleans Saints			
☐ 396 Keith Jackson PB	.08	.04	.01
Philadelphia Eagles			
☐ 397 Vaughan Johnson PB	.06	.03	.00
New Orleans Saints			
☐ 398 Steve Jordan PB	.03	.01	.00
Minnesota Vikings			
☐ 399 Carl Lee PB	.03	.01	.00
Minnesota Vikings			
☐ 400 Ronnie Lott PB	.08	.04	.01
San Francisco 49ers			
☐ 401 Don Majkowski PB	.08	.04	.01
Green Bay Packers			
(Not pictured in Pro			
Bowl uniform)			
☐ 402 Charles Mann PB	.03	.01	.00
Washington Redskins			
☐ 403 Randall McDaniel PB	.03	.01	.00
Minnesota Vikings			
☐ 404 Tim McDonald PB	.03	.01	.00
Phoenix Cardinals			
☐ 405 Guy McIntyre PB	.03	.01	.00
San Francisco 49ers			
☐ 406 David Meggett PB	.08	.04	.01
New York Giants			
☐ 407 Keith Millard PB	.03	.01	.00
Minnesota Vikings			
☐ 408 Joe Montana PB	.15	.07	.01
San Francisco 49ers			
(not pictured in Pro			
Bowl uniform)			
☐ 409 Eddie Murray PB	.03	.01	.00
Detroit Lions			
☐ 410 Tom Newberry PB	.03	.01	.00
Los Angeles Rams			
☐ 411 Jerry Rice PB	.15	.07	.01
San Francisco 49ers			
☐ 412 Mark Rypien PB	.10	.05	.01
Washington Redskins			
☐ 413 Barry Sanders PB	.35	.17	.03
Detroit Lions			
☐ 414 Luis Sharpe PB	.03	.01	.00
Phoenix Cardinals			
☐ 415 Sterling Sharpe PB	.08	.04	.01
Green Bay Packers			
☐ 416 Mike Singletary PB	.06	.03	.00
Chicago Bears			
☐ 417 Jackie Slater PB	.03	.01	.00
Los Angeles Rams			
☐ 418 Doug Smith PB	.03	.01	.00
Los Angeles Rams			
☐ 419 Chris Spielman PB	.06	.03	.00
Detroit Lions			
☐ 420 Pat Swilling PB	.06	.03	.00
New Orleans Saints			
☐ 421 John Taylor PB	.08	.04	.01
San Francisco 49ers			
☐ 422 Lawrence Taylor PB	.08	.04	.01
New York Giants			
☐ 423 Reggie White PB	.08	.04	.01
Philadelphia Eagles			
☐ 424 Ron Wolfley PB	.03	.01	.00
Phoenix Cardinals			

425 Gary Zimmerman PB 03	.01	.00	
Minnesota Vikings			
426 John Robinson CO PB ...03	.01	.00	
Los Angeles Rams			
427 Scott Case UER 03	.01	.00	
Atlanta Falcons			
(front CB, back S)			
428 Mike Kenn 03	.01	.00	
Atlanta Falcons			
429 Mike Gann 03	.01	.00	
Atlanta Falcons			
430 Tim Green 12	.06	.01	
Atlanta Falcons			
431 Michael Haynes 50	.25	.05	
Atlanta Falcons			
432 Jessie Tuggle UER 12	.06	.01	
Atlanta Falcons			
(Front Jessie,			
back Jessie)			
433 John Rade 03	.01	.00	
Atlanta Falcons			
434 Andre Rison 15	.07	.01	
Atlanta Falcons			
435 Don Beebe 08	.04	.01	
Buffalo Bills			
436 Ray Bentley 06	.03	.00	
Buffalo Bills			
437 Shane Conlan 08	.04	.01	
Buffalo Bills			
438 Kent Hull 03	.01	.00	
Buffalo Bills			
439 Pete Metzelaars 03	.01	.00	
Buffalo Bills			
440 Andre Reed UER 10	.05	.01	
Buffalo Bills			
(Vance Johnson also had			
more catches in '85)			
441 Frank Reich 08	.04	.01	
Buffalo Bills			
442 Leon Seals 10	.05	.01	
Buffalo Bills			
443 Bruce Smith 08	.04	.01	
Buffalo Bills			
444 Thurman Thomas 60	.30	.06	
Buffalo Bills			
445 Will Wolford 03	.01	.00	
Buffalo Bills			
446 Trace Armstrong 03	.01	.00	
Chicago Bears			
447 Mark Bortz 10	.05	.01	
Chicago Bears			
448 Tom Thayer 10	.05	.01	
Chicago Bears			
449A Dan Hampton ERR 60	.30	.06	
Chicago Bears			
(Card back says DE)			
449B Dan Hampton COR 08	.04	.01	

Chicago Bears			
(Card back says DT)			
450 Shaun Gayle 10	.05	.01	
Chicago Bears			
451 Dennis Gentry 03	.01	.00	
Chicago Bears			
452 Jim Harbaugh 20	.10	.02	
Chicago Bears			
453 Vestee Jackson 03	.01	.00	
Chicago Bears			
454 Brad Muster 08	.04	.01	
Chicago Bears			
455 William Perry 08	.04	.01	
Chicago Bears			
456 Ron Rivera 03	.01	.00	
Chicago Bears			
457 James Thornton 03	.01	.00	
Chicago Bears			
458 Mike Tomczak 08	.04	.01	
Chicago Bears			
459 Donnell Woolford 03	.01	.00	
Chicago Bears			
460 Eric Ball 06	.03	.00	
Cincinnati Bengals			
461 James Brooks 08	.04	.01	
Cincinnati Bengals			
462 David Fulcher 03	.01	.00	
Cincinnati Bengals			
463 Boomer Esiason 10	.05	.01	
Cincinnati Bengals			
464 Rodney Holman 06	.03	.00	
Cincinnati Bengals			
465 Bruce Kozerski 03	.01	.00	
Cincinnati Bengals			
466 Tim Krumrie 03	.01	.00	
Cincinnati Bengals			
467 Anthony Munoz 08	.04	.01	
Cincinnati Bengals			
(Type on front smaller			
compared to other cards)			
468 Brian Blados 03	.01	.00	
Cincinnati Bengals			
469 Mike Baab 03	.01	.00	
Cleveland Browns			
470 Brian Brennan 03	.01	.00	
Cleveland Browns			
471 Raymond Clayborn 03	.01	.00	
Cleveland Browns			
472 Mike Johnson 03	.01	.00	
Cleveland Browns			
473 Kevin Mack 06	.03	.00	
Cleveland Browns			
474 Clay Matthews 03	.01	.00	
Cleveland Browns			
475 Frank Minnifield 03	.01	.00	
Cleveland Browns			
476 Gregg Rakoczy 08	.04	.01	

Cleveland Browns					Green Bay Packers			
□ 477 Webster Slaughter	.06	.03	.00	□ 502 Alan Veingrad	.08	.04	.01
Cleveland Browns					Green Bay Packers			
□ 478 James Dixon	.08	.04	.01	□ 503 Mark Lee	.03	.01	.00
Dallas Cowboys					Green Bay Packers			
□ 479 Robert Awalt UER	.03	.01	.00	□ 504 Tony Mandarich	.06	.03	.00
Dallas Cowboys					Green Bay Packers			
(front 89, back 46)					□ 505 Brian Noble	.03	.01	.00
□ 480 Dennis McKinnon UER	.03	.01	.00	Green Bay Packers			
Dallas Cowboys					□ 506 Jeff Query	.08	.04	.01
(front 81, back 85)					Green Bay Packers			
□ 481 Danny Noonan	.03	.01	.00	□ 507 Ken Ruettgers	.06	.03	.00
Dallas Cowboys					Green Bay Packers			
□ 482 Jesse Solomon	.03	.01	.00	□ 508 Patrick Allen	.10	.05	.01
Dallas Cowboys					Houston Oilers			
□ 483 Danny Stubbs UER	.03	.01	.00	□ 509 Curtis Duncan	.06	.03	.00
Dallas Cowboys					Houston Oilers			
(front 66, back 96)					□ 510 William Fuller	.06	.03	.00
□ 484 Steve Walsh	.10	.05	.01	Houston Oilers			
Dallas Cowboys					□ 511 Haywood Jeffires	.60	.30	.06
□ 485 Michael Brooks	.10	.05	.01	Houston Oilers			
Denver Broncos					□ 512 Sean Jones	.03	.01	.00
□ 486 Mark Jackson	.06	.03	.00	Houston Oilers			
Denver Broncos					□ 513 Terry Kinard	.03	.01	.00
□ 487 Greg Kragen	.06	.03	.00	Houston Oilers			
Denver Broncos					□ 514 Bruce Matthews	.03	.01	.00
□ 488 Ken Lanier	.10	.05	.01	Houston Oilers			
Denver Broncos					□ 515 Gerald McNeil	.06	.03	.00
□ 489 Karl Mecklenburg	.06	.03	.00	Houston Oilers			
Denver Broncos					□ 516 Greg Montgomery	.10	.05	.01
□ 490 Steve Sewell	.06	.03	.00	Houston Oilers			
Denver Broncos					□ 517 Warren Moon	.25	.12	.02
□ 491 Dennis Smith	.06	.03	.00	Houston Oilers			
Denver Broncos					□ 518 Mike Munchak	.06	.03	.00
□ 492 David Treadwell	.03	.01	.00	Houston Oilers			
Denver Broncos					□ 519 Allen Pinkett	.08	.04	.01
□ 493 Michael Young	.20	.10	.02	Houston Oilers			
Denver Broncos					□ 520 Pat Beach	.03	.01	.00
□ 494 Robert Clark	.20	.10	.02	Indianapolis Colts			
Detroit Lions					□ 521 Eugene Daniel	.03	.01	.00
□ 495 Dennis Gibson	.03	.01	.00	Indianapolis Colts			
Detroit Lions					□ 522 Kevin Call	.08	.04	.01
□ 496A Kevin Glover ERR	.35	.17	.03	Indianapolis Colts			
Detroit Lions					□ 523 Ray Donaldson	.03	.01	.00
(Card back says C/G)					Indianapolis Colts			
□ 496B Kevin Glover COR	.10	.05	.01	□ 524 Jeff Herrod	.08	.04	.01
Detroit Lions					Indianapolis Colts			
(Card back says C)					□ 525 Keith Taylor	.06	.03	.00
□ 497 Mel Gray	.06	.03	.00	Indianapolis Colts			
Detroit Lions					□ 526 Jack Trudeau	.06	.03	.00
□ 498 Rodney Peete	.12	.06	.01	Indianapolis Colts			
Detroit Lions					□ 527 Deron Cherry	.06	.03	.00
□ 499 Dave Brown	.03	.01	.00	Kansas City Chiefs			
Green Bay Packers					□ 528 Jeff Donaldson	.03	.01	.00
□ 500 Jerry Holmes	.06	.03	.00	Kansas City Chiefs			
Green Bay Packers					□ 529 Albert Lewis	.08	.04	.01
□ 501 Chris Jacke	.03	.01	.00	Kansas City Chiefs			

☐ 530 Pete Mandley	.03	.01	.00
Kansas City Chiefs			
☐ 531 Chris Martin	.08	.04	.01
Kansas City Chiefs			
☐ 532 Christian Okoye	.10	.05	.01
Kansas City Chiefs			
☐ 533 Steve Pelluer	.06	.03	.00
Kansas City Chiefs			
☐ 534 Kevin Ross	.03	.01	.00
Kansas City Chiefs			
☐ 535 Dan Saleaumua	.06	.03	.00
Kansas City Chiefs			
☐ 536 Derrick Thomas	.25	.12	.02
Kansas City Chiefs			
☐ 537 Mike Webster	.06	.03	.00
Kansas City Chiefs			
☐ 538 Marcus Allen	.10	.05	.01
Los Angeles Raiders			
☐ 539 Greg Bell	.06	.03	.00
Los Angeles Raiders			
☐ 540 Thomas Benson	.08	.04	.01
Los Angeles Raiders			
☐ 541 Ron Brown	.06	.03	.00
Los Angeles Raiders			
☐ 542 Scott Davis	.08	.04	.01
Los Angeles Raiders			
☐ 543 Riki Ellison	.06	.03	.00
Los Angeles Raiders			
☐ 544 Jamie Holland	.03	.01	.00
Los Angeles Raiders			
☐ 545 Howie Long	.06	.03	.00
Los Angeles Raiders			
☐ 546 Terry McDaniel	.06	.03	.00
Los Angeles Raiders			
☐ 547 Max Montoya	.06	.03	.00
Los Angeles Raiders			
☐ 548 Jay Schroeder	.08	.04	.01
Los Angeles Raiders			
☐ 549 Lionel Washington	.03	.01	.00
Los Angeles Raiders			
☐ 550 Robert Delpino	.10	.05	.01
Los Angeles Rams			
☐ 551 Bobby Humphery	.03	.01	.00
Los Angeles Rams			
☐ 552 Mike Lansford	.03	.01	.00
Los Angeles Rams			
☐ 553 Michael Stewart	.08	.04	.01
Los Angeles Rams			
☐ 554 Doug Smith	.03	.01	.00
Los Angeles Rams			
☐ 555 Curt Warner	.08	.04	.01
Los Angeles Rams			
☐ 556 Alvin Wright	.08	.04	.01
Los Angeles Rams			
☐ 557 Jeff Cross	.06	.03	.00
Miami Dolphins			
☐ 558 Jeff Dellenbach	.08	.04	.01

Miami Dolphins			
☐ 559 Mark Duper	.06	.03	.00
Miami Dolphins			
☐ 560 Ferrell Edmunds	.06	.03	.00
Miami Dolphins			
☐ 561 Tim McKyer	.06	.03	.00
Miami Dolphins			
☐ 562 John Offerdahl	.06	.03	.00
Miami Dolphins			
☐ 563 Reggie Roby	.03	.01	.00
Miami Dolphins			
☐ 564 Pete Stoyanovich	.06	.03	.00
Miami Dolphins			
☐ 565 Alfred Anderson	.03	.01	.00
Minnesota Vikings			
☐ 566 Ray Berry	.06	.03	.00
Minnesota Vikings			
☐ 567 Rick Fenney	.06	.03	.00
Minnesota Vikings			
☐ 568 Rich Gannon	.25	.12	.02
Minnesota Vikings			
☐ 569 Tim Irwin	.08	.04	.01
Minnesota Vikings			
☐ 570 Hassan Jones	.06	.03	.00
Minnesota Vikings			
☐ 571 Cris Carter	.08	.04	.01
Minnesota Vikings			
☐ 572 Kirk Lowdermilk	.03	.01	.00
Minnesota Vikings			
☐ 573 Reggie Rutland	.08	.04	.01
Minnesota Vikings			
☐ 574 Ken Stills	.08	.04	.01
Minnesota Vikings			
☐ 575 Bruce Armstrong	.03	.01	.00
New England Patriots			
☐ 576 Irving Fryar	.06	.03	.00
New England Patriots			
☐ 577 Roland James	.03	.01	.00
New England Patriots			
☐ 578 Robert Perryman	.06	.03	.00
New England Patriots			
☐ 579 Cedric Jones	.10	.05	.01
New England Patriots			
☐ 580 Steve Grogan	.06	.03	.00
New England Patriots			
☐ 581 Johnny Rembert	.03	.01	.00
New England Patriots			
☐ 582 Ed Reynolds	.08	.04	.01
New England Patriots			
☐ 583 Brent Williams	.03	.01	.00
New England Patriots			
☐ 584 Marc Wilson	.06	.03	.00
New England Patriots			
☐ 585 Hoby Brenner	.03	.01	.00
New Orleans Saints			
☐ 586 Stan Brock	.03	.01	.00
New Orleans Saints			

☐ 587 Jim Dombrowski 10	.05	.01	
New Orleans Saints			
☐ 588 Joel Hilgenberg 12	.06	.01	
New Orleans Saints			
☐ 589 Robert Massey 06	.03	.00	
New Orleans Saints			
☐ 590 Floyd Turner 15	.07	.01	
New Orleans Saints			
☐ 591 Ottis Anderson 08	.04	.01	
New York Giants			
☐ 592 Mark Bavaro 06	.03	.00	
New York Giants			
☐ 593 Maurice Carthon 03	.01	.00	
New York Giants			
☐ 594 Eric Dorsey 15	.07	.01	
New York Giants			
☐ 595 Myron Guyton 06	.03	.00	
New York Giants			
☐ 596 Jeff Hostetler 50	.25	.05	
New York Giants			
☐ 597 Sean Landeta 03	.01	.00	
New York Giants			
☐ 598 Lionel Manual 06	.03	.00	
New York Giants			
☐ 599 Odessa Turner 20	.10	.02	
New York Giants			
☐ 600 Perry Williams 03	.01	.00	
New York Giants			
☐ 601 James Hasty 03	.01	.00	
New York Jets			
☐ 602 Erik McMillan 06	.03	.00	
New York Jets			
☐ 603 Alex Gordon UER 03	.01	.00	
New York Jets			
(reversed photo on back)			
☐ 604 Ron Stallworth 08	.04	.01	
New York Jets			
☐ 605 Byron Evans 08	.04	.01	
Philadelphia Eagles			
☐ 606 Ron Heller 08	.04	.01	
Philadelphia Eagles			
☐ 607 Wes Hopkins 03	.01	.00	
Philadelphia Eagles			
☐ 608 Mickey Shuler UER 03	.01	.00	
Philadelphia Eagles			
(reversed photo on back)			
☐ 609 Seth Joyner 06	.03	.00	
Philadelphia Eagles			
☐ 610 Jim McMahon 08	.04	.01	
Philadelphia Eagles			
☐ 611 Mike Pitts 03	.01	.00	
Philadelphia Eagles			
☐ 612 Izel Jenkins 10	.05	.01	
Philadelphia Eagles			
☐ 613 Anthony Bell 06	.03	.00	
Phoenix Cardinals			
☐ 614 David Galloway 03	.00		

Phoenix Cardinals			
☐ 615 Eric Hill 06	.03	.00	
Phoenix Cardinals			
☐ 616 Cedric Mack 03	.01	.00	
Phoenix Cardinals			
☐ 617 Freddie Joe Nunn 03	.01	.00	
Phoenix Cardinals			
☐ 618 Tootie Robbins 03	.01	.00	
Phoenix Cardinals			
☐ 619 Tom Tupa 15	.07	.01	
Phoenix Cardinals			
☐ 620 Joe Wolf 03	.01	.00	
Phoenix Cardinals			
☐ 621 Dermontti Dawson 03	.01	.00	
Pittsburgh Steelers			
☐ 622 Thomas Everett 03	.01	.00	
Pittsburgh Steelers			
☐ 623 Tunch Ilkin 03	.01	.00	
Pittsburgh Steelers			
☐ 624 Hardy Nickerson 03	.01	.00	
Pittsburgh Steelers			
☐ 625 Gerald Williams 10	.05	.01	
Pittsburgh Steelers			
☐ 626 Rod Woodson 08	.04	.01	
Pittsburgh Steelers			
☐ 627A Rod Bernstine TE ERR .50	.25	.05	
San Diego Chargers			
☐ 627B Rod Bernstine RB COR .10	.05	.01	
San Diego Chargers			
☐ 628 Courtney Hall 06	.03	.00	
San Diego Chargers			
☐ 629 Ronnie Harmon 06	.03	.00	
San Diego Chargers			
☐ 630A Anthony Miller ERR 30	.15	.03	
San Diego Chargers			
(Back says WR)			
☐ 630B Anthony Miller COR 10	.05	.01	
San Diego Chargers			
(Back says WR-KR)			
☐ 631 Joe Phillips 08	.04	.01	
San Diego Chargers			
☐ 632A Leslie O'Neal ERR 25	.12	.02	
San Diego Chargers			
(Listed as LB-DE on			
front and back)			
☐ 632B Leslie O'Neal ERR .. 2.00	1.00	.20	
San Diego Chargers			
(Listed as LB-DE on			
front and LB on back)			
☐ 632C Leslie O'Neal COR 08	.04	.01	
San Diego Chargers			
(Listed as LB on			
front and back)			
☐ 633A David Richards ERR 15	.07	.01	
San Diego Chargers			
(Back says G-T)			
☐ 633B David Richards COR 15	.07	.01	

San Diego Chargers
(Back says G)

☐ 634	Mark Vlasic	.15	.07	.01	
	San Diego Chargers				
☐ 635	Lee Williams	.06	.03	.00	
	San Diego Chargers				
☐ 636	Chet Brooks	.08	.04	.01	
	San Francisco 49ers				
☐ 637	Keena Turner	.03	.01	.00	
	San Francisco 49ers				
☐ 638	Kevin Fagan	.08	.04	.01	
	San Francisco 49ers				
☐ 639	Brent Jones	.15	.07	.01	
	San Francisco 49ers				
☐ 640	Matt Millen	.06	.03	.00	
	San Francisco 49ers				
☐ 641	Bubba Paris	.03	.01	.00	
	San Francisco 49ers				
☐ 642	Bill Romanowski	.06	.03	.00	
	San Francisco 49ers				
☐ 643	Fred Smerlas UER	.03	.01	.00	
	(Front 67, back 76)				
☐ 644	Dave Waymer	.03	.01	.00	
	San Francisco 49ers				
☐ 645	Steve Young	.12	.06	.01	
	San Francisco 49ers				
☐ 646	Brian Blades	.10	.05	.01	
	Seattle Seahawks				
☐ 647	Andy Heck	.03	.01	.00	
	Seattle Seahawks				
☐ 648	Dave Krieg	.08	.04	.01	
	Seattle Seahawks				
☐ 649	Rufus Porter	.06	.03	.00	
	Seattle Seahawks				
☐ 650	Kelly Stouffer	.08	.04	.01	
	Seattle Seahawks				
☐ 651	Tony Woods	.06	.03	.00	
	Seattle Seahawks				
☐ 652	Gary Anderson	.08	.04	.01	
	Tampa Bay Buccaneers				
☐ 653	Reuben Davis	.08	.04	.01	
	Tampa Bay Buccaneers				
☐ 654	Randy Grimes	.03	.01	.00	
	Tampa Bay Buccaneers				
☐ 655	Ron Hall	.06	.03	.00	
	Tampa Bay Buccaneers				
☐ 656	Eugene Marve	.03	.01	.00	
	Tampa Bay Buccaneers				
☐ 657A	Curt Jarvis ERR	.50	.25	.05	
	Tampa Bay Buccaneers				
	(No NFL logo on				
	front of card)				
☐ 657B	Curt Jarvis COR	.06	.03	.00	
	Tampa Bay Buccaneers				
☐ 658	Ricky Reynolds	.03	.01	.00	
	Tampa Bay Buccaneers				
☐ 659	Broderick Thomas	.08	.04	.01	
	Tampa Bay Buccaneers				
☐ 660	Jeff Bostic	.06	.03	.00	
	Washington Redskins				
☐ 661	Todd Bowles	.08	.04	.01	
	Washington Redskins				
☐ 662	Ravin Caldwell	.08	.04	.01	
	Washington Redskins				
☐ 663	Russ Grimm UER	.06	.03	.00	
	Washington Redskins				
	(Back photo is act-				
	ually Jeff Bostic)				
☐ 664	Joe Jacoby	.06	.03	.00	
	Washington Redskins				
☐ 665	Mark May	.03	.01	.00	
	Washington Redskins				
	(Front G, back G/T)				
☐ 666	Walter Stanley	.06	.03	.00	
	Washington Redskins				
☐ 667	Don Warren	.06	.03	.00	
	Washington Redskins				
☐ 668	Stan Humphries	.12	.06	.01	
	Washington Redskins				
☐ 669B	Jeff George	.75	.35	.07	
	Indianapolis Colts				
	(See 1st Series for				
	669A; pictured in				
	Colts uniform)				
☐ 670	Blair Thomas	.65	.30	.06	
	New York Jets				
	(No color stripe along				
	line with AFC symbol				
	and Jets logo)				
☐ 671	Cortez Kennedy UER	.30	.15	.03	
	Seattle Seahawks				
	(No scouting photo				
	line on back)				
☐ 672	Keith McCants	.20	.10	.02	
	Tampa Bay Buccaneers				
☐ 673	Junior Seau	.20	.10	.02	
	San Diego Chargers				
☐ 674	Mark Carrier	.35	.17	.03	
	Chicago Bears				
☐ 675	Andre Ware	.25	.12	.02	
	Detroit Lions				
☐ 676	Chris Singleton UER	.20	.10	.02	
	New England Patriots				
	(Parsippany High,				
	should be Parsippany				
	Hills High)				
☐ 677	Richmond Webb	.15	.07	.01	
	Miami Dolphins				
☐ 678	Ray Agnew	.10	.05	.01	
	New England Patriots				
☐ 679	Anthony Smith	.12	.06	.01	
	Los Angeles Raiders				
☐ 680	James Francis	.25	.12	.02	

Cincinnati Bengals
- ☐ 681 Percy Snow ....08 .04
Kansas City Chiefs
- ☐ 682 Renaldo Turnbull ....15 .07
New Orleans Saints
- ☐ 683 Lamar Lathon ....15 .07
Houston Oilers
- ☐ 684 James Williams ....08 .04
Buffalo Bills
- ☐ 685 Emmitt Smith ....2.50 1.25 .25
Dallas Cowboys
- ☐ 686 Tony Bennett ....20 .10 .02
Green Bay Packers
- ☐ 687 Darrell Thompson ....25 .12 .02
Green Bay Packers
- ☐ 688 Steve Broussard ....30 .15 .03
Atlanta Falcons
- ☐ 689 Eric Green ....45 .22 .04
Pittsburgh Steelers
- ☐ 690 Ben Smith ....10 .05 .01
Philadelphia Eagles
- ☐ 691 Bern Brostek UER ....08 .04 .01
Los Angeles Rams
(Listed as Center but
is playing Guard)
- ☐ 692 Rodney Hampton ....75 .35 .07
New York Giants
- ☐ 693 Dexter Carter ....25 .12 .02
San Francisco 49ers
- ☐ 694 Rob Moore ....65 .30 .06
New York Jets
- ☐ 695 Alexander Wright ....25 .12 .02
Dallas Cowboys
- ☐ 696 Darion Conner ....20 .10 .02
Atlanta Falcons
- ☐ 697 Reggie Rembert UER ....20 .10 .02
Cincinnati Bengals
(Missing Scouting Line
credit on the front)
- ☐ 698A Terry Wooden ERR ....25 .12 .02
Seattle Seahawks
(Number on back is 51)
- ☐ 698B Terry Wooden COR ......12 .06 .01
Seattle Seahawks
(Number on back is 90)
- ☐ 699 Reggie Cobb ....60 .30 .06
Tampa Bay Buccaneers
- ☐ 700 Anthony Thompson ....20 .10 .02
Phoenix Cardinals
- ☐ 701 Fred Washington ....03 .01 .00
Chicago Bears
(Final Update version
mentions his death;
this card does not)
- ☐ 702 Ron Cox ....08 .04 .01
Chicago Bears
- ☐ 703 Robert Blackmon ....08 .04 .01

Seattle Seahawks
- ☐ 704 Dan Owens ....12 .06 .01
Detroit Lions
- ☐ 705 Anthony Johnson ....15 .07 .01
Indianapolis Colts
- ☐ 706 Aaron Wallace ....15 .07 .01
Los Angeles Raiders
- ☐ 707 Harold Green ....45 .22 .04
Cincinnati Bengals
- ☐ 708 Keith Sims ....10 .05 .01
Miami Dolphins
- ☐ 709 Tim Grunhard ....08 .04 .01
Kansas City Chiefs
- ☐ 710 Jeff Alm ....08 .04 .01
Houston Oilers
- ☐ 711 Carwell Gardner ....20 .10 .02
Buffalo Bills
- ☐ 712 Kenny Davidson ....10 .05 .01
Pittsburgh Steelers
- ☐ 713 Vince Buck ....12 .06 .01
New Orleans Saints
- ☐ 714 Leroy Hoard ....40 .20 .04
Cleveland Browns
- ☐ 715 Andre Collins ....15 .07 .01
Washington Redskins
- ☐ 716 Dennis Brown ....08 .04 .01
San Francisco 49ers
- ☐ 717 LeRoy Butler ....08 .04 .01
Green Bay Packers
- ☐ 718A Pat Terrell 41 ERR ....30 .15 .03
Los Angeles Rams
- ☐ 718B Pat Terrell 37 COR ....15 .07 .01
Los Angeles Rams
- ☐ 719 Mike Bellamy ....12 .06 .01
Philadelphia Eagles
- ☐ 720 Mike Fox ....10 .05 .01
New York Giants
- ☐ 721 Alton Montgomery ....10 .05 .01
Denver Broncos
- ☐ 722 Eric Davis ....12 .06 .01
San Francisco 49ers
- ☐ 723A Oliver Barnett ERR ....50 .25 .05
Atlanta Falcons
(Front says DT)
- ☐ 723B Oliver Barnett COR ....15 .07 .01
Atlanta Falcons
(Front says NT)
- ☐ 724 Houston Hoover ....08 .04 .01
Atlanta Falcons
- ☐ 725 Howard Ballard ....08 .04 .01
Buffalo Bills
- ☐ 726 Keith McKeller ....30 .15 .03
Buffalo Bills
- ☐ 727 Wendell Davis ....30 .15 .03
Chicago Bears
(Pro Set Prospect in
white, not black)

☐ 728 Peter Tom Willis ....25 Chicago Bears	.12	.02	
☐ 729 Bernard Clark ....08 Cincinnati Bengals	.04	.01	
☐ 730 Doug Widell ....08 Denver Broncos	.04	.01	
☐ 731 Eric Andolsek ....08 Detroit Lions	.04	.01	
☐ 732 Jeff Campbell ....15 Detroit Lions	.07	.01	
☐ 733 Marc Spindler ....08 Detroit Lions	.04	.01	
☐ 734 Keith Woodside ....06 Green Bay Packers	.03	.00	
☐ 735 Willis Peguese ....08 Houston Oilers	.04	.01	
☐ 736 Frank Stams ....03 Los Angeles Rams	.01	.00	
☐ 737 Jeff Uhlenhake ....06 Miami Dolphins	.03	.00	
☐ 738 Todd Kalis ....08 Minnesota Vikings	.04	.01	
☐ 739 Tommy Hodson UER ....30 New England Patriots (Born Matthews, should be Mathews)	.15	.03	
☐ 740 Greg McMurtry ....30 New England Patriots	.15	.03	
☐ 741 Mike Buck ....08 New Orleans Saints	.04	.01	
☐ 742 Kevin Haverdink UER ..08 New Orleans Saints (Jersey says 70, back says 74)	.04	.01	
☐ 743A Johnny Bailey ....60 Chicago Bears (Back says 46)	.30	.06	
☐ 743B Johnny Bailey ....25 Chicago Bears (Back says 22)	.12	.02	
☐ 744A Eric Moore ....25 New York Giants (No Pro Set Prospect on front of card)	.12	.02	
☐ 744B Eric Moore ....08 New York Giants (Pro Set Prospect on front of card)	.04	.01	
☐ 745 Tony Stargell ....20 New York Jets	.10	.02	
☐ 746 Fred Barnett ....40 Philadelphia Eagles	.20	.04	
☐ 747 Walter Reeves ....08 Phoenix Cardinals	.04	.01	
☐ 748 Derek Hill ....08 Pittsburgh Steelers	.04	.01	
☐ 749 Quinn Early ....08 San Diego Chargers	.04	.01	
☐ 750 Ronald Lewis ....08 San Francisco 49ers	.04	.01	
☐ 751 Ken Clark ....08 Indianapolis Colts	.04	.01	
☐ 752 Garry Lewis ....08 Los Angeles Raiders	.04	.01	
☐ 781 American Bowl/London .03 Raiders vs. Saints	.01	.00	
☐ 782 American Bowl/Berlin ....03 Rams vs. Chiefs	.01	.00	
☐ 783 American Bowl/Tokyo ...03 Broncos vs. Seahawks	.01	.00	
☐ 784 American Bowl/Montreal .03 Steelers vs. Patriots	.01	.00	
☐ 785A Berlin Wall ....08 Paul Tagliabue ("Peered through the Berlin Wall")	.04	.01	
☐ 785B Berlin Wall ....08 Paul Tagliabue ("Posed at the Berlin Wall")	.04	.01	
☐ 786 Raiders Stay in LA ....08 (Al Davis)	.04	.01	
☐ 787 Falcons Back in Black ....06 (Jerry Glanville)	.03	.00	
☐ 788 NFL Goes International ..03 World League Spring Debut (Number on back is black, Newsreel cards are otherwise white; only Newsreel card with silver borders)	.01	.00	
☐ 789 Overseas Appeal ....08 (Cheerleaders)	.04	.01	
☐ 790 Photo Contest ....03 (Mike Mularkey awash)	.01	.00	
☐ 791 Photo Contest ....06 (Gary Reasons hitting Bobby Humphrey)	.03	.00	
☐ 792 Photo Contest ....03 (Maurice Hurst covering Drew Hill)	.01	.00	
☐ 793 Photo Contest ....06 (Ronnie Lott celebrating)	.03	.00	
☐ 794 Photo Contest ....20 (Felix Wright grabbing Barry Sanders' jersey)	.10	.02	
☐ 795 Photo Contest ....03 (George Seifert in Gatorade Shower)	.01	.00	
☐ 796 Photo Contest ....03 (Doug Smith praying)	.01	.00	
☐ 797 Photo Contest ....03 (Doug Widell keeping cool)	.01	.00	
☐ 798 Photo Contest ....03 (Todd Bowles covering Cris Carter)	.01	.00	

1990 Pro Set Final Update

*This 30-card standard size (2 1/2" by 3 1/2")
set was issued by Pro Set in a special mail-
away offer. This set consists of players either
not issued by Pro Set in their first two series or
players who were traded during the season.
The series also includes a special Ronnie Lott
stay in school card. And the 1990 Pro Set
Rookie of the Year card which introduced the
1991 Pro Set design. The key rookie cards in
this set are Johnny Johnson, Derrick Fenner
and Barry Word.*

	MINT	EXC	G-VG
COMPLETE SET (30)	4.00	2.00	.40
COMMON PLAYER	.05	.02	.00
☐ 753 James Lofton	.15	.07	.01
Buffalo Bills			
☐ 754 Steve Tasker UER	.10	.05	.01
Buffalo Bills			
(Back says photo is			
against Raiders, but			
front shows a Steeler)			
☐ 755 Jim Shofner CO	.05	.02	.00
Cleveland Browns			
☐ 756 Jimmie Jones	.08	.04	.01
Dallas Cowboys			
☐ 757 Jay Novacek	.30	.15	.03
Dallas Cowboys			
☐ 758 Jessie Hester	.20	.10	.02
Indianapolis Colts			
☐ 759 Barry Word	.65	.30	.06
Kansas City Chiefs			
☐ 760 Eddie Anderson	.10	.05	.01
Los Angeles Raiders			
☐ 761 Cleveland Gary	.10	.05	.01
Los Angeles Rams			

☐ 762 Marcus Dupree	.25	.12	.02
Los Angeles Rams			
☐ 763 David Griggs	.10	.05	.01
Miami Dolphins			
☐ 764 Rueben Mayes	.08	.04	.01
New Orleans Saints			
☐ 765 Stephen Baker	.10	.05	.01
New York Giants			
☐ 766 Reyna Thompson UER	.10	.05	.01
New York Giants			
(Front CB, back ST-CB)			
☐ 767 Everson Walls	.08	.04	.01
New York Giants			
☐ 768 Brad Baxter	.30	.15	.03
New York Jets			
☐ 769 Steve Walsh	.10	.05	.01
New Orleans Saints			
☐ 770 Heath Sherman	.25	.12	.02
Philadelphia Eagles			
☐ 771 Johnny Johnson	.75	.35	.07
Phoenix Cardinals			
☐ 772A Dexter Manley	25.00	10.00	2.00
Phoenix Cardinals			
(Back mentions sub-			
stance abuse violation)			
☐ 772B Dexter Manley	.08	.04	.01
Phoenix Cardinals			
(Bio on back changed;			
doesn't mention sub-			
stance abuse violation)			
☐ 773 Ricky Proehl	.35	.17	.03
Phoenix Cardinals			
☐ 774 Frank Cornish	.08	.04	.01
San Diego Chargers			
☐ 775 Tommy Kane	.30	.15	.03
Seattle Seahawks			
☐ 776 Derrick Fenner	.40	.20	.04
Seattle Seahawks			
☐ 777 Steve Christie	.08	.04	.01
Tampa Bay Buccaneers			
☐ 778 Wayne Haddix	.15	.07	.01
Tampa Bay Buccaneers			
☐ 779 Richard Williamson UER	.06	.03	.00
Tampa Bay Buccaneers			
(Experience is mis-			
spelled as experience)			
☐ 780 Brian Mitchell	.45	.22	.04
Washington Redskins			
☐ 799 Ronnie Lott School	.08	.04	.01
☐ 800D Mark Carrier D-ROY	.15	.07	.01
Chicago Bears			
☐ 800O Emmitt Smith O-ROY	1.25	.60	.12
Dallas Cowboys			
☐ SC4 Fred Washington UER	.08	.04	.01
Chicago Bears			
(Memorial to his death;			
word patches repeated			
in fourth line of text)			

1991 Pro Set I

This 405-card set marked the first series Pro Set produced in 1991. This set marked the third year Pro Set issued a major standard size (2 1/2" by 3 1/2") set. The set has 54 various special cards to start the set in subsets which include the Pro Set Rookies of the Year (both of whom are numbered 1, therefore there is no card 2 in the set). Cards numbered 3 through 19 are various NFL leaders, while cards 20-26 celebrate various milestones reached during the 1990 season. Cards numbered 27 through 31 feature the 1991 inductees into the Hall of Fame with original art drawings by Merv Corning, while cards number 32 through 36 feature various college award winners. Cards number 37 through 45 honor various past winners of the Heisman trophy, while cards number 46 through 54 relate to Super Bowl XXV. From card number 55 through 324 the cards are sequenced in alphabetical order by team, which are also in alphabetical order (except for the two participants in the Super Bowl). The only card for each team which is not in alphabetical order is the coach card, which is always the final card in a team's sequence. The team lists are as follows, New York Giants (55-72), Buffalo Bills (73-90), Atlanta Falcons (91-99), Cincinnati Bengals (109-117), Cleveland Browns (118-126), Dallas Cowboys (127-135), Denver Broncos (136-144), Detroit Lions (145-153), Green Bay Packers (154-162), Houston Oilers (163-171), Indianapolis Colts (172-180), Kansas City Chiefs (181-189), Los Angeles Raiders (190-198), Los Angeles Rams (199-207), Miami Dolphins (208-216), Minnesota VIkings (217-225), New England Patriots (226-234), New Orleans Saints (235-243), New York Jets (244-

252), Philadelphia Eagles (253-261), Phoenix Cardinals (262-270), Pittsburgh Steelers (271-279), San Diego Chargers (280-288), San Francisco 49ers (289-297), Seattle Seahawks (298-306), Tampa Bay Buccaneers (307-315), Washington Redskins (316-324). There are also 18 cards which highlight some of the special games of the 1990 season (325-342). In addition, like the 1990 second series there is a newsreel subset. Other special features include an 18 card subset about NFL officals (352-369), nine cards in the mode begun by 1990 Ronnie Lott's #799 Stay in School Card (370-378) and 27 All-NFC drawings again drawn by artist Merv Corning. The key rookies in this series are Ty Detmer, Rocket Ismail, and Russell Maryland.

	MINT	EXC	G-VG
COMPLETE SET (405)	10.00	5.00	1.00
COMMON PLAYER (1-405)	.03	.01	.00
☐ 1D Mark Carrier .... Defensive ROY	.08	.04	.01
☐ 1O Emmitt Smith .... Offensive ROY	.60	.30	.06
☐ 2 Does Not Exist	.00	.00	.00
☐ 3 Joe Montana .... NFL Player of the Year	.20	.10	.02
☐ 4 Art Shell .... NFL Coach of the Year	.06	.03	.00
☐ 5 Mike Singletary .... NFL Man of the Year	.06	.03	.00
☐ 6 Bruce Smith .... NFL Defensive Player of the Year	.06	.03	.00
☐ 7 Barry Word .... NFL Comeback Player of the Year	.12	.06	.01
☐ 8A Jim Kelly .... NFL Passing Leader (NFLPA logo on back)	.20	.10	.02
☐ 8B Jim Kelly .... NFL Passing Leader (No NFLPA logo on back)	.12	.06	.01
☐ 9 Warren Moon .... NFL Passing Yardage and TD Leader	.10	.05	.01
☐ 10 Barry Sanders .... NFL Rushing and TD Leader	.25	.12	.02
☐ 11 Jerry Rice .... NFL Receiving and Receiving Yardage Leader	.15	.07	.01
☐ 12 Jay Novacek .... Tight End Leader	.06	.03	.00

☐ 13 Thurman Thomas 15	.07	.01	
NFL Total Yardage Leader			
☐ 14 Nick Lowery 03	.01	:00	
NFL Scoring Leader, Kickers			
☐ 15 Mike Horan 03	.01	.00	
NFL Punting Leader			
☐ 16 Clarence Verdin 03	.01	.00	
NFL Punt Return Leader			
☐ 17 Kevin Clark 10	.05	.01	
NFL Kickoff Return Leader			
☐ 18 Mark Carrier 06	.03	.00	
NFL Interception Leader			
☐ 19A Derrick Thomas ERR 20.00	10.00	2.00	
NFL Sack Leader (Bills helmet on front)			
☐ 19B Derrick Thomas COR 12	.06	.01	
NFL Sack Leader (Chiefs helmet on front)			
☐ 20 Ottis Anderson ML 06	.03	.00	
10000 Career Rushing Yards			
☐ 21 Roger Craig ML 06	.03	.00	
Most Career Receptions by RB			
☐ 22 Art Monk ML 08	.04	.01	
700 Career Receptions			
☐ 23 Chuck Noll ML 03	.01	.00	
200 Victories			
☐ 24 Randall Cunningham ML ..08	.04	.01	
Leads team in rushing, fourth straight year UER (586 rushes, should be 486; average 5.9, should be 7.1)			
☐ 25 Dan Marino ML 15	.07	.01	
7th Straight 3000 yard season			
☐ 26 49ers Road Record 03	.01	.00	
18 victories in row, still alive			
☐ 27 Earl Campbell HOF 10	.05	.01	
☐ 28 John Hannah HOF 06	.03	.00	
☐ 29 Stan Jones HOF 06	.03	.00	
☐ 30 Tex Schramm HOF 06	.03	.00	
☐ 31 Jan Stenerud HOF 06	.03	.00	
☐ 32 Russell Maryland 45	.22	.04	
Outland Winner			
☐ 33 Chris Zorich 20	.10	.02	
Lombardi Winner			
☐ 34 Darryll Lewis UER 15	.07	.01	
Thorpe Winner (Name misspelled Darryl on card)			
☐ 35 Alfred Williams 15	.07	.01	
Butkus Winner			
☐ 36 Raghib(Rocket) Ismail .. 2.00	1.00	.20	
Walter Camp POY			
☐ 37 Ty Detmer HH 75	.35	.07	
☐ 38 Andre Ware HH 10	.05	.01	
☐ 39 Barry Sanders HH 25	.12	.02	
☐ 40 Tim Brown HH UER 06	.03	.00	
(No "Official Photo and Stat Card of the NFL" on card back)			
☐ 41 Vinny Testaverde HH 06	.03	.00	
☐ 42 Bo Jackson HH 15	.07	.01	
☐ 43 Mike Rozier HH 06	.03	.00	
☐ 44 Herschel Walker HH 08	.04	.01	
☐ 45 Marcus Allen HH 08	.04	.01	
☐ 46A James Lofton HH 10	.05	.01	
(NFLPA logo on back)			
☐ 46B James Lofton HH 06	.03	.00	
(No NFLPA logo on back)			
☐ 47A Bruce Smith SB 15	.07	.01	
(Official NFL Card in black letters)			
☐ 47B Bruce Smith SB 10	.05	.01	
(Official NFL Card in white letters)			
☐ 48 Myron Guyton SB 03	.01	.00	
☐ 49 Stephen Baker SB 06	.03	.00	
☐ 50 Mark Ingram SB UER 06	.03	.00	
(First repeated twice on back title)			
☐ 51 Ottis Anderson SB 06	.03	.00	
☐ 52 Thurman Thomas SB 15	.07	.01	
☐ 53 Matt Bahr SB 03	.01	.00	
☐ 54 Scott Norwood SB 03	.01	.00	
☐ 55 Stephen Baker SB 06	.03	.00	
☐ 56 Carl Banks 06	.03	.00	
☐ 57 Mark Collins 03	.01	.00	
☐ 58 Steve DeOssie 03	.01	.00	
☐ 59 Eric Dorsey 03	.01	.00	
☐ 60 John Elliott 03	.01	.00	
☐ 61 Myron Guyton 03	.01	.00	
☐ 62 Rodney Hampton 40	.20	.04	
☐ 63 Jeff Hostetler 20	.10	.02	
☐ 64 Erik Howard 03	.01	.00	
☐ 65 Mark Ingram 06	.03	.00	
☐ 66 Greg Jackson 08	.04	.01	
☐ 67 Leonard Marshall 06	.03	.00	
☐ 68 David Meggett 10	.05	.01	
☐ 69 Eric Moore 03	.01	.00	
☐ 70 Bart Oates 03	.01	.00	
☐ 71 Gary Reasons 03	.01	.00	
☐ 72 Bill Parcells CO 06	.03	.00	
☐ 73 Howard Ballard 03	.01	.00	
☐ 74A Cornelius Bennett 30	.15	.03	
(NFLPA logo on back)			
☐ 74B Cornelius Bennett 10	.05	.01	

(No NFLPA logo on back)

☐ 75 Shane Conlan	.06	.03	.00
☐ 76 Kent Hull	.03	.01	.00
☐ 77 Kirby Jackson	.08	.04	.01
☐ 78A Jim Kelly	.60	.30	.06

(NFLPA logo on back)

☐ 78B Jim Kelly	.25	.12	.02

(No NFLPA logo on back)

☐ 79 Mark Kelso	.03	.01	.00
☐ 80 Nate Odomes	.03	.01	.00
☐ 81 Andre Reed	.10	.05	.01
☐ 82 Jim Ritcher	.03	.01	.00
☐ 83 Bruce Smith	.08	.04	.01
☐ 84 Darryl Talley	.06	.03	.00
☐ 85 Steve Tasker	.03	.01	.00
☐ 86 Thurman Thomas	.45	.22	.04
☐ 87 James Williams	.03	.01	.00
☐ 88 Will Wolford	.03	.01	.00
☐ 89 Jeff Wright UER	.08	.04	.01

(Went to Central
Missouri State, not
Central Missouri)

☐ 90 Marv Levy CO	.03	.01	.00
☐ 91 Steve Broussard	.10	.05	.01
☐ 92A Darion Conner ERR	10.00	5.00	1.00

(Drafted 1st round, '99)

☐ 92B Darion Conner COR	.08	.04	.01

(Drafted 2nd round, '90)

☐ 93 Bill Fralic	.06	.03	.00
☐ 94 Tim Green	.03	.01	.00
☐ 95 Michael Haynes	.08	.04	.01
☐ 96 Chris Hinton	.06	.03	.00
☐ 97 Chris Miller UER	.15	.07	.01

(Two commas after city
in his birth info)

☐ 98 Deion Sanders UER	.20	.10	.02

(Career TD's 3, but
only 2 in yearly stats)

☐ 99 Jerry Glanville CO	.03	.01	.00
☐ 100 Kevin Butler	.03	.01	.00
☐ 101 Mark Carrier	.08	.04	.01
☐ 102 Jim Covert	.06	.03	.00
☐ 103 Richard Dent	.08	.04	.01
☐ 104 Jim Harbaugh	.10	.05	.01
☐ 105 Brad Muster	.06	.03	.00
☐ 106 Lemuel Stinson	.03	.01	.00
☐ 107 Keith Van Horne	.03	.01	.00
☐ 108 Mike Ditka CO UER	.06	.03	.00

(Winning percent in '87
was .733, not .753)

☐ 109 Lewis Billups	.03	.01	.00
☐ 110 James Brooks	.08	.04	.01
☐ 111 Boomer Esiason	.10	.05	.01
☐ 112 James Francis	.08	.04	.01
☐ 113 David Fulcher	.03	.01	.00
☐ 114 Rodney Holman	.03	.01	.00
☐ 115 Tim McGee	.06	.03	.00

☐ 116 Anthony Munoz	.08	.04	.01
☐ 117 Sam Wyche CO	.03	.01	.00
☐ 118 Paul Farren	.03	.01	.00
☐ 119 Thane Gash	.03	.01	.00
☐ 120 Mike Johnson	.03	.01	.00
☐ 121A Bernie Kosar	.15	.07	.01

(NFLPA logo on back)

☐ 121B Bernie Kosar	.10	.05	.01

(No NFLPA logo on back)

☐ 122 Clay Matthews	.03	.01	.00
☐ 123 Eric Metcalf	.06	.03	.00
☐ 124 Frank Minnifield	.03	.01	.00
☐ 125A Webster Slaughter	.10	.05	.01

(NFLPA logo on back)

☐ 125B Webster Slaughter	.06	.03	.00

(No NFLPA logo on back)

☐ 126 Bill Belichick CO	.03	.01	.00
☐ 127 Tommie Agee	.06	.03	.00
☐ 128 Troy Aikman	.35	.17	.03
☐ 129 Jack Del Rio	.03	.01	.00
☐ 130 John Gesek	.08	.04	.01
☐ 131 Issiac Holt	.03	.01	.00
☐ 132 Michael Irvin	.20	.10	.02
☐ 133 Ken Norton	.03	.01	.00
☐ 134 Daniel Stubbs	.03	.01	.00
☐ 135 Jimmy Johnson CO	.03	.01	.00
☐ 136 Steve Atwater	.06	.03	.00
☐ 137 Michael Brooks	.03	.01	.00
☐ 138 John Elway	.15	.07	.01
☐ 139 Wymon Henderson	.03	.01	.00
☐ 140 Bobby Humphrey	.10	.05	.01
☐ 141 Mark Jackson	.06	.03	.00
☐ 142 Karl Mecklenburg	.06	.03	.00
☐ 143 Doug Widell	.03	.01	.00
☐ 144 Dan Reeves CO	.03	.01	.00
☐ 145 Eric Andolsek	.03	.01	.00
☐ 146 Jerry Ball	.03	.01	.00
☐ 147 Bennie Blades	.06	.03	.00
☐ 148 Lomas Brown	.03	.01	.00
☐ 149 Robert Clark	.06	.03	.00
☐ 150 Michael Cofer	.03	.01	.00
☐ 151 Dan Owens	.03	.01	.00
☐ 152 Rodney Peete	.08	.04	.01
☐ 153 Wayne Fontes CO	.03	.01	.00
☐ 154 Tim Harris	.06	.03	.00
☐ 155 Johnny Holland	.03	.01	.00
☐ 156 Dan Majkowski	.08	.04	.01
☐ 157 Tony Mandarich	.06	.03	.00
☐ 158 Mark Murphy	.03	.01	.00
☐ 159 Brian Noble	.03	.01	.00
☐ 160 Jeff Query	.03	.01	.00
☐ 161 Sterling Sharpe	.10	.05	.01
☐ 162 Lindy Infante CO	.03	.01	.00
☐ 163 Ray Childress	.06	.03	.00
☐ 164 Ernest Givins	.08	.04	.01
☐ 165 Richard Johnson	.03	.01	.00
☐ 166 Bruce Matthews	.03	.01	.00

☐ 167 Warren Moon	.20	.10	.02
☐ 168 Mike Munchak	.06	.03	.00
☐ 169 Al Smith	.03	.01	.00
☐ 170 Lorenzo White	.06	.03	.00
☐ 171 Jack Pardee CO	.03	.01	.00
☐ 172 Albert Bentley	.06	.03	.00
☐ 173 Duane Bickett	.03	.01	.00
☐ 174 Bill Brooks	.03	.01	.00
☐ 175A Eric Dickerson	.75	.35	.07
(NFLPA logo on back)			
☐ 175B Eric Dickerson	1.50	.75	.15
(No NFLPA logo on back and 667 yards rushing for 1990 in text)			
☐ 175C Eric Dickerson	.35	.17	.03
(No NFLPA logo on back and 677 yards rushing for 1990 in text)			
☐ 176 Ray Donaldson	.03	.01	.00
☐ 177 Jeff George	.35	.17	.03
☐ 178 Jeff Herrod	.03	.01	.00
☐ 179 Clarence Verdin	.06	.03	.00
☐ 180 Ron Meyer CO	.03	.01	.00
☐ 181 John Alt	.03	.01	.00
☐ 182 Steve DeBerg	.08	.04	.01
☐ 183 Albert Lewis	.06	.03	.00
☐ 184 Nick Lowery UER	.06	.03	.00
(In his 13th year, not 12th)			
☐ 185 Christian Okoye	.08	.04	.01
☐ 186 Stephone Paige	.06	.03	.00
☐ 187 Kevin Porter	.03	.01	.00
☐ 188 Derrick Thomas	.15	.07	.01
☐ 189 Marty Schottenheimer CO	.03	.01	.00
☐ 190 Willie Gault	.06	.03	.00
☐ 191 Howie Long	.06	.03	.00
☐ 192 Terry McDaniel	.03	.01	.00
☐ 193 Jay Schroeder UER	.08	.04	.01
(Passing total yards 13863, should be 13683)			
☐ 194 Steve Smith	.03	.01	.00
☐ 195 Greg Townsend	.03	.01	.00
☐ 196 Lionel Washington	.03	.01	.00
☐ 197 Steve Wisniewski UER	.03	.01	.00
(Back says drafted, should say traded to)			
☐ 198 Art Shell CO	.06	.03	.00
☐ 199 Henry Ellard	.08	.04	.01
☐ 200 Jim Everett	.10	.05	.01
☐ 201 Jerry Gray	.03	.01	.00
☐ 202 Kevin Greene	.06	.03	.00
☐ 203 Buford McGee	.06	.03	.00
☐ 204 Tom Newberry	.03	.01	.00
☐ 205 Frank Stams	.03	.01	.00
☐ 206 Alvin Wright	.03	.01	.00
☐ 207 John Robinson CO	.03	.01	.00
☐ 208 Jeff Cross	.03	.01	.00
☐ 209 Mark Duper	.06	.03	.00
☐ 210 Dan Marino	.25	.12	.02
☐ 211A Tim McKyer	.35	.17	.03
(No Traded box on front)			
☐ 211B Tim McKyer	.08	.04	.01
(Traded box on front)			
☐ 212 John Offerdahl	.03	.01	.00
☐ 213 Sammie Smith	.08	.04	.01
☐ 214 Richmond Webb	.06	.03	.00
☐ 215 Jarvis Williams	.03	.01	.00
☐ 216 Don Shula CO	.06	.03	.00
☐ 217A Darrell Fullington ERR (No registered symbol on card back)	.15	.07	.01
☐ 217A Darrell Fullington COR (Registered symbol on card back)	.08	.04	.01
☐ 218 Tim Irwin	.03	.01	.00
☐ 219 Mike Merriweather	.03	.01	.00
☐ 220 Keith Millard	.06	.03	.00
☐ 221 Al Noga	.03	.01	.00
☐ 222 Henry Thomas	.03	.01	.00
☐ 223 Wade Wilson	.08	.04	.01
☐ 224 Gary Zimmerman	.03	.01	.00
☐ 225 Jerry Burns CO	.03	.01	.00
☐ 226 Bruce Armstrong	.03	.01	.00
☐ 227 Marv Cook	.10	.05	.01
☐ 228 Hart Lee Dykes	.03	.01	.00
☐ 229 Tommy Hodson	.15	.07	.01
☐ 230 Ronnie Lippett	.03	.01	.00
☐ 231 Ed Reynolds	.03	.01	.00
☐ 232 Chris Singleton	.06	.03	.00
☐ 233 John Stephens	.08	.04	.01
☐ 234 Dick MacPherson CO	.06	.03	.00
☐ 235 Stan Brock	.03	.01	.00
☐ 236 Craig Heyward	.08	.04	.01
☐ 237 Vaughan Johnson	.06	.03	.00
☐ 238 Robert Massey	.03	.01	.00
☐ 239 Brett Maxie	.08	.04	.01
☐ 240 Rueben Mayes	.06	.03	.00
☐ 241 Pat Swilling	.08	.04	.01
☐ 242 Renaldo Turnbull	.06	.03	.00
☐ 243 Jim Mora CO	.03	.01	.00
☐ 244 Kyle Clifton	.03	.01	.00
☐ 245 Jeff Criswell	.06	.03	.00
☐ 246 James Hasty	.03	.01	.00
☐ 247 Erik McMillan	.06	.03	.00
☐ 248 Scott Mersereau	.08	.04	.01
☐ 249 Ken O'Brien	.08	.04	.01
☐ 250A Blair Thomas	.65	.30	.06
(NFLPA logo on back)			
☐ 250B Blair Thomas	.50	.25	.05
(No NFLPA logo on back)			
☐ 251 Al Toon	.08	.04	.01
☐ 252 Bruce Coslet CO	.03	.01	.00
☐ 253 Eric Allen	.03	.01	.00

☐ 254 Fred Barnett	.15	.07	.01
☐ 255 Keith Byars	.06	.03	.00
☐ 256 Randall Cunningham	.15	.07	.01
☐ 257 Seth Joyner	.06	.03	.00
☐ 258 Clyde Simmons	.06	.03	.00
☐ 259 Jessie Small	.03	.01	.00
☐ 260 Andre Waters	.03	.01	.00
☐ 261 Rich Kotite CO	.06	.03	.00
☐ 262 Roy Green	.06	.03	.00
☐ 263 Ernie Jones	.06	.03	.00
☐ 264 Tim McDonald	.06	.03	.00
☐ 265 Timm Rosenbach	.10	.05	.01
☐ 266 Rod Saddler	.15	.07	.01
☐ 267 Luis Sharpe	.03	.01	.00
☐ 268 Anthony Thompson UER	.08	.04	.01
(Terra Haute should			
be Terre Haute)			
☐ 269 Marcus Turner	.10	.05	.01
☐ 270 Joe Bugel CO	.03	.01	.00
☐ 271 Gary Anderson	.03	.01	.00
☐ 272 Dermontti Dawson	.03	.01	.00
☐ 273 Eric Green	.15	.07	.01
☐ 274 Merril Hoge	.06	.03	.00
☐ 275 Tunch Ilkin	.03	.01	.00
☐ 276 David Johnson	.08	.04	.01
☐ 277 Louis Lipps	.06	.03	.00
☐ 278 Rod Woodson	.08	.04	.01
☐ 279 Chuck Noll CO	.03	.01	.00
☐ 280 Martin Bayless	.03	.01	.00
☐ 281 Marion Butts UER	.10	.05	.01
(2 years exp.,			
should be 3)			
☐ 282 Gill Byrd	.06	.03	.00
☐ 283 Burt Grossman	.06	.03	.00
☐ 284 Courtney Hall	.03	.01	.00
☐ 285 Anthony Miller	.08	.04	.01
☐ 286 Leslie O'Neal	.06	.03	.00
☐ 287 Billy Joe Tolliver	.08	.04	.01
☐ 288 Dan Henning CO	.03	.01	.00
☐ 289 Dexter Carter	.08	.04	.01
☐ 290 Michael Carter	.06	.03	.00
☐ 291 Kevin Fagan	.03	.01	.00
☐ 292 Pierce Holt	.03	.01	.00
☐ 293 Guy McIntyre	.03	.01	.00
☐ 294 Tom Rathman	.06	.03	.00
☐ 295 John Taylor	.12	.06	.01
☐ 296 Steve Young	.10	.05	.01
☐ 297 George Seifert CO	.03	.01	.00
☐ 298 Brian Blades	.06	.03	.00
☐ 299 Jeff Bryant	.03	.01	.00
☐ 300 Norm Johnson	.03	.01	.00
☐ 301 Tommy Kane	.12	.06	.01
☐ 302 Cortez Kennedy UER	.08	.04	.01
(Played for Seattle			
in '90, not Miami)			
☐ 303 Bryan Millard	.03	.01	.00
☐ 304 John L. Williams	.08	.04	.01

☐ 305 David Wyman	.03	.01	.00
☐ 306A Chuck Knox CO ERR	.08	.04	.01
(Has NFLPA logo,			
but should not)			
☐ 306B Chuck Knox CO COR	.12	.06	.01
(No NFLPA logo on back)			
☐ 307 Gary Anderson	.08	.04	.01
☐ 308 Reggie Cobb	.15	.07	.01
☐ 309 Randy Grimes	.03	.01	.00
☐ 310 Harry Hamilton	.03	.01	.00
☐ 311 Bruce Hill	.03	.01	.00
☐ 312 Eugene Marve	.03	.01	.00
☐ 313 Ervin Randle	.03	.01	.00
☐ 314 Vinny Testaverde	.08	.04	.01
☐ 315 Richard Williamson CO	.03	.01	.00
UER (Coach: 1st year,			
should be 2nd year)			
☐ 316 Earnest Byner	.08	.04	.01
☐ 317 Gary Clark	.12	.06	.01
☐ 318A Andre Collins	.10	.05	.01
(NFLPA logo on back)			
☐ 318B Andre Collins	.06	.03	.00
(No NFLPA logo on back)			
☐ 319 Darryl Grant	.03	.01	.00
☐ 320 Chip Lohmiller	.03	.01	.00
☐ 321 Martin Mayhew	.06	.03	.00
☐ 322 Mark Rypien	.20	.10	.02
☐ 323 Alvin Walton	.03	.01	.00
☐ 324 Joe Gibbs CO UER	.03	.01	.00
(Has registered			
symbol but should not)			
☐ 325 Jerry Glanville REP	.03	.01	.00
☐ 326A John Elway REP	.10	.05	.01
(NFLPA logo on back)			
☐ 326B John Elway REP	.06	.03	.00
(No NFLPA logo on back)			
☐ 327 Boomer Esiason REP	.06	.03	.00
☐ 328A Steve Tasker REP	.10	.05	.01
(NFLPA logo on back)			
☐ 328B Steve Tasker REP	.06	.03	.00
(No NFLPA logo on back)			
☐ 329 Jerry Rice REP	.15	.07	.01
☐ 330 Jeff Rutledge REP	.03	.01	.00
☐ 331 K.C. Defense REP	.03	.01	.00
☐ 332 49ers Streak REP	.03	.01	.00
(Cleveland Gary)			
☐ 333 Monday Meeting REP	.06	.03	.00
(John Taylor)			
☐ 334A Randall Cunningham	.15	.07	.01
REP			
(NFLPA logo on back)			
☐ 334B Randall Cunningham	.15	.07	.01
REP			
(No NFLPA logo on back)			
☐ 335A Bo Jackson and	.65	.30	.06
Barry Sanders REP			
(NFLPA logo on back)			

☐ 335B Bo Jackson and ....35 Barry Sanders REP (No NFLPA logo on back)	.17	.03
☐ 336 Lawrence Taylor REP 08	.04	.01
☐ 337 Warren Moon REP 10	.05	.01
☐ 338 Alan Grant REP 03	.01	.00
☐ 339 Todd McNair REP 03	.01	.00
☐ 340 Miami Dolphins REP ......06 (Mark Clayton)	.03	.00
☐ 341A Highest Scoring REP ...12 Jim Kelly Passing (NFLPA logo on back)	.06	.01
☐ 341B Highest Scoring REP ...08 Jim Kelly Passing (No NFLPA logo on back)	.04	.01
☐ 342 Matt Bahr REP 03	.01	.00
☐ 343 Robert Tisch NEW ....06 (With Wellington Mara)	.03	.00
☐ 344 Sam Jankovich NEW 03	.01	.00
☐ 345 In-the-Grasp NEW ....06 (John Elway)	.03	.00
☐ 346 Bo Jackson NEW ....15 (Career in Jeopardy)	.07	.01
☐ 347 NFL Teacher of the ....03 Year Jack Williams with Paul Tagliabue	.01	.00
☐ 348 Ronnie Lott NEW ....06 (Plan B Free Agent)	.03	.00
☐ 349 Super Bowl XXV ....06 Teleclinic NEW (Greg Gumbel with Warren Moon, Derrick Thomas, and Wade Wilson)	.03	.00
☐ 350 Whitney Houston NEW ...20	.10	.02
☐ 351 U.S. Troops in ....06 Saudia Arabia NEW (Troops watching TV with gas masks)	.03	.00
☐ 352 Art McNally OFF 06	.03	.00
☐ 353 Dick Jorgensen OFF 06	.03	.00
☐ 354 Jerry Seeman OFF 06	.03	.00
☐ 355 Jim Tunney OFF 06	.03	.00
☐ 356 Gerry Austin OFF 03	.01	.00
☐ 357 Gene Barth OFF 03	.01	.00
☐ 358 Red Cashion OFF 03	.01	.00
☐ 359 Tom Dooley OFF 03	.01	.00
☐ 360 Johnny Grier OFF 03	.01	.00
☐ 361 Pat Haggerty OFF 06	.03	.00
☐ 362 Dale Hamer OFF 03	.01	.00
☐ 363 Dick Hantak OFF 03	.01	.00
☐ 364 Jerry Markbreit OFF 06	.03	.00
☐ 365 Gordon McCarter OFF 03	.01	.00
☐ 366 Bob McElwee OFF 03	.01	.00
☐ 367 Howard Roe OFF ....03 (Illustrations on back smaller than other officials' cards)	.01	.00

☐ 368 Tom White OFF 03	.01	.00
☐ 369 Norm Schachter OFF 06	.03	.00
☐ 370A Warren Moon ....25 Crack Kills (Small type on back)	.12	.02
☐ 370B Warren Moon ....10 Crack Kills (Large type on back)	.05	.01
☐ 371A Boomer Esiason ....15 Don't Drink (Small type on back)	.07	.01
☐ 371B Boomer Esiason ....08 Don't Drink (Large type on back)	.04	.01
☐ 372A Troy Aikman ....30 Play It Straight (Small type on back)	.15	.03
☐ 372B Troy Aikman ....15 Play It Straight (Large type on back)	.07	.01
☐ 373A Carl Banks ....08 Read (Small type on back)	.04	.01
☐ 373B Carl Banks ....06 Read (Large type on back)	.03	.00
☐ 374A Jim Everett ....15 Study (Small type on back)	.07	.01
☐ 374B Jim Everett ....10 Study (Large type on back)	.05	.01
☐ 375A Anthony Munoz ....35 Quadante en la Escuela (Dificul)	.17	.03
☐ 375B Anthony Munoz ....35 Quadante en la Escuela (Dificil)	.17	.03
☐ 375C Anthony Munoz ....35 Quadante en la Escuela (Small type)	.17	.03
☐ 375D Anthony Munoz ....08 Quedate en la Escuela (Large type)	.04	.01
☐ 376A Ray Childress ....08 Don't Pollute (Small type on back)	.04	.01
☐ 376B Ray Childress ....06 Don't Pollute (Large type on back)	.03	.00
☐ 377A Charles Mann ....08 Steroids Destroy (Small type on back)	.04	.01
☐ 377B Charles Mann ....06 Steroids Destroy (Large type on back)	.03	.00
☐ 378A Jackie Slater 08	.04	.01

		MINT	EXC	G-VG

Keep the Peace
(Small type on back)
☐ 378B Jackie Slater .... .06 .03 .00

Keep the Peace
(Large type on back)
☐ 379 Jerry Rice NFC .... .15 .07 .01
☐ 380 Andre Rison NFC .... .10 .05 .01
☐ 381 Jim Lachey NFC .... .03 .01 .00
☐ 382 Jackie Slater NFC .... .03 .01 .00
☐ 383 Randall McDaniel NFC .. .03 .01 .00
☐ 384 Mark Bortz NFC .... .03 .01 .00
☐ 385 Jay Hilgenberg NFC ..... .03 .01 .00
☐ 386 Keith Jackson NFC .... .06 .03 .00
☐ 387 Joe Montana NFC .... .20 .10 .02
☐ 388 Barry Sanders NFC ...... .25 .12 .02
☐ 389 Neal Anderson NFC ...... .08 .04 .01
☐ 390 Reggie White NFC .... .06 .03 .00
☐ 391 Chris Doleman NFC ...... .06 .03 .00
☐ 392 Jerome Brown NFC ...... .03 .01 .00
☐ 393 Charles Haley NFC ...... .03 .01 .00
☐ 394 Lawrence Taylor NFC ... .08 .04 .01
☐ 395 Pepper Johnson NFC ... .03 .01 .00
☐ 396 Mike Singletary NFC .... .06 .03 .00
☐ 397 Darrell Green NFC .... .03 .01 .00
☐ 398 Carl Lee NFC .... .03 .01 .00
☐ 399 Joey Browner NFC .... .03 .01 .00
☐ 400 Ronnie Lott NFC .... .08 .04 .01
☐ 401 Sean Landeta NFC ...... .03 .01 .00
☐ 402 Morten Andersen NFC .. .03 .01 .00
☐ 403 Mel Gray NFC .... .03 .01 .00
☐ 404 Reyna Thompson NFC .. .03 .01 .00
☐ 405 Jimmy Johnson CO NFC .03 .01 .00

1991 Pro Set II

The second series of the 1991 Pro Set football set contains 407 cards measuring the standard

size (2 1/2" by 3 1/2"). The front design features full-bleed glossy color action photos, with player identification and team name at the bottom in two colored stripes reflecting the team's colors. The horizontally oriented backs have a color head shot on the right side, with player profile and/or statistics on the right. The cards are numbered on the back. The set begins with original artwork by Merv Corning of the All-AFC team (406-432). The player cards are then checklisted alphabetically within and according to teams as follows: Atlanta Falcons (433-441), Buffalo Bills (442-450), Chicago Bears (451-459), Cincinnati Bengals (460-468), Cleveland Browns (469-477), Dallas Cowboys (478-486), Denver Broncos (487-495), Detroit Lions (496-504), Green Bay Packers (505-513), Houston Oilers (514-522), Indianapolis Colts (523-531), Kansas City Chiefs (532-540), Los Angeles Raiders (541-549), Los Angeles Rams (550-558), Miami Dolphins (559-567), Minnesota Vikings (568-576), New England Patriots (577-585), New Orleans Saints (586-594), New York Giants (595-603), New York Jets (604-612), Philadelphia Eagles (613-621), Phoenix Cardinals (622-630), Pittsburgh Steelers (631-639), San Diego Chargers (640-648), San Francisco 49ers (649-657), Seattle Seahawks (658-666), Tampa Bay Buccaneers (667-675), and Washington Redskins (676-684). Additional subsets featured in this set are NFL Newsreel (685-693), Legends (694-702), World League Leaders (703-711), Hall of Fame Photo Contest (712-720), Think About It (721-729), First-Round Draft Choices (730-756), Second-Round Draft Choices (757-772), and Third-Round Draft Choices (785-812). The key rookie cards in this series are Ricky Ervins, Todd Marinovich, Dan McGwire, Leonard Russell, and Harvey Williams.

	MINT	EXC	G-VG
COMPLETE SET (407) 13.00	5.00	1.00
COMMON PLAYER (406-812) .... .03	.01	.00

☐ 406 Andre Reed AFC .... .06 .03 .00
Buffalo Bills
☐ 407 Anthony Miller AFC .... .06 .03 .00
San Diego Chargers
☐ 408 Anthony Munoz AFC ...... .06 .03 .00
Cincinnati Bengals
☐ 409 Bruce Armstrong AFC .... .03 .01 .00
New England Patriots
☐ 410 Bruce Matthews AFC .... .03 .01 .00
Houston Oilers
☐ 411 Mike Munchak AFC .... .03 .01 .00

	Houston Oilers		
☐ 412	Kent Hull AFC .... .03	.01	.00
	Buffalo Bills		
☐ 413	Rodney Holman AFC ...... .03	.01	.00
	Cincinnati Bengals		
☐ 414	Warren Moon AFC .... .10	.05	.01
	Houston Oilers		
☐ 415	Thurman Thomas AFC .... .15	.07	.01
	Buffalo Bills		
☐ 416	Marion Butts AFC .... .06	.03	.00
	San Diego Chargers		
☐ 417	Bruce Smith AFC .... .06	.03	.00
	Buffalo Bills		
☐ 418	Greg Townsend AFC ...... .03	.01	.00
	Los Angeles Raiders		
☐ 419	Ray Childress AFC .... .03	.01	.00
	Houston Oilers		
☐ 420	Derrick Thomas AFC ...... .08	.04	.01
	Kansas City Chiefs		
☐ 421	Leslie O'Neal AFC .... .03	.01	.00
	San Diego Chargers		
☐ 422	John Offerdahl AFC .... .03	.01	.00
	Miami Dolphins		
☐ 423	Shane Conlan AFC .... .03	.01	.00
	Buffalo Bills		
☐ 424	Rod Woodson AFC .... .06	.03	.00
	Pittsburgh Steelers		
☐ 425	Albert Lewis AFC .... .03	.01	.00
	Kansas City Chiefs		
☐ 426	Steve Atwater AFC .... .03	.01	.00
	Denver Broncos		
☐ 427	David Fulcher AFC .... .03	.01	.00
	Cincinnati Bengals		
☐ 428	Rohn Stark AFC .... .03	.01	.00
	Indianapolis Colts		
☐ 429	Nick Lowery AFC .... .03	.01	.00
	Kansas City Chiefs		
☐ 430	Clarence Verdin AFC ...... .03	.01	.00
	Indianapolis Colts		
☐ 431	Steve Tasker AFC .... .03	.01	.00
	Buffalo Bills		
☐ 432	Art Shell CO AFC .... .03	.01	.00
	Los Angeles Raiders		
☐ 433	Scott Case .... .03	.01	.00
☐ 434	Tory Epps UER .... .03	.01	.00
	(No TM next to Pro Set		
	on card back)		
☐ 435	Mike Gann UER .... .03	.01	.00
	(Text has 2 fumble		
	recoveries, stats		
	say 3)		
☐ 436	Brian Jordan UER .... .20	.10	.02
	(No TM next to Pro Set		
	on card back)		
☐ 437	Mike Kenn .... .03	.01	.00
☐ 438	John Rade .... .03	.01	.00
☐ 439	Andre Rison .... .15	.07	.01
☐ 440	Mike Rozier .... .06	.03	.00
☐ 441	Jessie Tuggle .... .03	.01	.00
☐ 442	Don Beebe .... .08	.04	.01
☐ 443	John Davis .... .12	.06	.01
☐ 444	James Lofton .... .12	.06	.01
☐ 445	Keith McKeller .... .08	.04	.01
☐ 446	Jamie Mueller .... .03	.01	.00
☐ 447	Scott Norwood .... .03	.01	.00
☐ 448	Frank Reich .... .06	.03	.00
☐ 449	Leon Seals .... .03	.01	.00
☐ 450	Leonard Smith .... .03	.01	.00
☐ 451	Neal Anderson .... .15	.07	.01
☐ 452	Trace Armstrong .... .03	.01	.00
☐ 453	Mark Bortz .... .03	.01	.00
☐ 454	Wendell Davis .... .12	.06	.01
☐ 455	Shaun Gayle .... .03	.01	.00
☐ 456	Jay Hilgenberg .... .06	.03	.00
☐ 457	Steve McMichael .... .06	.03	.00
☐ 458	Mike Singletary .... .08	.04	.01
☐ 459	Donnell Woolford .... .03	.01	.00
☐ 460	Jim Breech .... .03	.01	.00
☐ 461	Eddie Brown .... .06	.03	.00
☐ 462	Barney Bussey .... .08	.04	.01
☐ 463	Bruce Kozerski .... .03	.01	.00
☐ 464	Tim Krumrie .... .03	.01	.00
☐ 465	Bruce Reimers .... .15	.07	.01
☐ 466	Kevin Walker .... .03	.01	.00
☐ 467	Ickey Woods .... .06	.03	.00
☐ 468	Carl Zander UER .... .03	.01	.00
	(DOB: 4/12/63, should		
	be 3/23/63)		
☐ 469	Mike Baab .... .03	.01	.00
☐ 470	Brian Brennan .... .03	.01	.00
☐ 471	Rob Burnett .... .08	.04	.01
☐ 472	Raymond Clayborn .... .03	.01	.00
☐ 473	Reggie Langhorne .... .03	.01	.00
☐ 474	Kevin Mack .... .06	.03	.00
☐ 475	Anthony Pleasant .... .03	.01	.00
☐ 476	Joe Morris .... .06	.03	.00
☐ 477	Dan Fike .... .03	.01	.00
☐ 478	Ray Horton .... .03	.01	.00
☐ 479	Jim Jeffcoat .... .03	.01	.00
☐ 480	Jimmie Jones .... .03	.01	.00
☐ 481	Kelvin Martin .... .06	.03	.00
☐ 482	Nate Newton .... .03	.01	.00
☐ 483	Danny Noonan .... .03	.01	.00
☐ 484	Jay Novacek .... .10	.05	.01
☐ 485	Emmitt Smith 1.25	.60	.12
☐ 486	James Washington .... .08	.04	.01
☐ 487	Simon Fletcher .... .03	.01	.00
☐ 488	Ron Holmes .... .03	.01	.00
☐ 489	Mike Horan .... .03	.01	.00
☐ 490	Vance Johnson .... .06	.03	.00
☐ 491	Keith Kartz .... .08	.04	.01
☐ 492	Greg Kragen .... .03	.01	.00
☐ 493	Ken Lanier .... .03	.01	.00
☐ 494	Warren Powers .... .03	.01	.00

☐ 495	Dennis Smith	.03	.01	.00	☐ 545	Ethan Horton	.10	.05	.01
☐ 496	Jeff Campbell	.03	.01	.00	☐ 546	Ronnie Lott	.10	.05	.01
☐ 497	Ken Dallafior	.08	.04	.01	☐ 547	Don Mosebar	.03	.01	.00
☐ 498	Dennis Gibson	.03	.01	.00	☐ 548	Jerry Robinson	.03	.01	.00
☐ 499	Kevin Glover	.03	.01	.00	☐ 549	Aaron Wallace	.06	.03	.00
☐ 500	Mel Gray	.03	.01	.00	☐ 550	Flipper Anderson	.06	.03	.00
☐ 501	Eddie Murray	.03	.01	.00	☐ 551	Cleveland Gary	.06	.03	.00
☐ 502	Barry Sanders	.75	.35	.07	☐ 552	Damone Johnson	.08	.04	.01
☐ 503	Chris Spielman	.06	.03	.00	☐ 553	Duval Love	.08	.04	.01
☐ 504	William White	.03	.01	.00	☐ 554	Irv Pankey	.03	.01	.00
☐ 505	Matt Brock	.10	.05	.01	☐ 555	Mike Piel	.03	.01	.00
☐ 506	Robert Brown	.03	.01	.00	☐ 556	Jackie Slater	.06	.03	.00
☐ 507	LeRoy Butler	.03	.01	.00	☐ 557	Michael Stewart	.03	.01	.00
☐ 508	James Campen	.08	.04	.01	☐ 558	Pat Terrell	.03	.01	.00
☐ 509	Jerry Holmes	.03	.01	.00	☐ 559	J.B. Brown	.03	.01	.00
☐ 510	Perry Kemp	.03	.01	.00	☐ 560	Mark Clayton	.08	.04	.01
☐ 511	Ken Ruettgers	.03	.01	.00	☐ 561	Ferrell Edmunds	.03	.01	.00
☐ 512	Scott Stephen	.08	.04	.01	☐ 562	Harry Galbreath	.03	.01	.00
☐ 513	Ed West	.03	.01	.00	☐ 563	David Griggs	.03	.01	.00
☐ 514	Cris Dishman	.20	.10	.02	☐ 564	Jim C. Jensen	.03	.01	.00
☐ 515	Curtis Duncan	.06	.03	.00	☐ 565	Louis Oliver	.03	.01	.00
☐ 516	Drew Hill UER	.08	.04	.01	☐ 566	Tony Paige	.03	.01	.00
	(Text says 390 catches				☐ 567	Keith Sims	.03	.01	.00
	and 6368 yards, stats				☐ 568	Joey Browner	.06	.03	.00
	say 450 and 7715)				☐ 569	Anthony Carter	.08	.04	.01
☐ 517	Haywood Jeffires	.20	.10	.02	☐ 570	Chris Doleman	.06	.03	.00
☐ 518	Sean Jones	.03	.01	.00	☐ 571	Rich Gannon UER	.08	.04	.01
☐ 519	Lamar Lathon	.06	.03	.00		(Acquired in '87,			
☐ 520	Don Maggs	.03	.01	.00		not '88 as in text)			
☐ 521	Bubba McDowell	.03	.01	.00	☐ 572	Hassan Jones	.06	.03	.00
☐ 522	Johnny Meads	.03	.01	.00	☐ 573	Steve Jordan	.06	.03	.00
☐ 523A	Chip Banks ERR	.50	.25	.05	☐ 574	Carl Lee	.03	.01	.00
	(No text)				☐ 575	Randall McDaniel	.03	.01	.00
☐ 523B	Chip Banks COR	.06	.03	.00	☐ 576	Herschel Walker	.10	.05	.01
☐ 524	Pat Beach	.03	.01	.00	☐ 577	Ray Agnew	.03	.01	.00
☐ 525	Sam Clancy	.03	.01	.00	☐ 578	Vincent Brown	.06	.03	.00
☐ 526	Eugene Daniel	.03	.01	.00	☐ 579	Irving Fryar	.06	.03	.00
☐ 527	Jon Hand	.03	.01	.00	☐ 580	Tim Goad	.03	.01	.00
☐ 528	Jessie Hester	.06	.03	.00	☐ 581	Maurice Hurst	.03	.01	.00
☐ 529A	Mike Prior ERR	.50	.25	.05	☐ 582	Fred Marion	.03	.01	.00
	(No textual information)				☐ 583	Johnny Rembert	.03	.01	.00
☐ 529B	Mike Prior COR	.06	.03	.00	☐ 584	Andre Tippett	.06	.03	.00
☐ 530	Keith Taylor	.06	.03	.00	☐ 585	Brent Williams	.03	.01	.00
☐ 531	Donnell Thompson	.03	.01	.00	☐ 586	Morten Andersen	.06	.03	.00
☐ 532	Dino Hackett	.03	.01	.00	☐ 587	Toi Cook	.08	.04	.01
☐ 533	David Lutz	.08	.04	.01	☐ 588	Jim Dombrowski	.03	.01	.00
☐ 534	Chris Martin	.03	.01	.00	☐ 589	Dalton Hilliard	.06	.03	.00
☐ 535	Kevin Ross	.03	.01	.00	☐ 590	Rickey Jackson	.06	.03	.00
☐ 536	Dan Saleaumua	.03	.01	.00	☐ 591	Eric Martin	.06	.03	.00
☐ 537	Neil Smith	.06	.03	.00	☐ 592	Sam Mills	.06	.03	.00
☐ 538	Percy Snow	.06	.03	.00	☐ 593	Bobby Hebert	.08	.04	.01
☐ 539	Robb Thomas	.08	.04	.01	☐ 594	Steve Walsh	.06	.03	.00
☐ 540	Barry Word	.25	.12	.02	☐ 595	Ottis Anderson	.08	.04	.01
☐ 541	Marcus Allen	.10	.05	.01	☐ 596	Pepper Johnson	.06	.03	.00
☐ 542	Eddie Anderson	.03	.01	.00	☐ 597	Bob Kratch	.08	.04	.01
☐ 543	Scott Davis	.03	.01	.00	☐ 598	Sean Landeta	.03	.01	.00
☐ 544	Mervyn Fernandez	.06	.03	.00	☐ 599	Doug Riesenberg	.03	.01	.00

☐ 600 William Roberts	.03	.01	.00
☐ 601 Phil Simms	.08	.04	.01
☐ 602 Lawrence Taylor	.10	.05	.01
☐ 603 Everson Walls	.03	.01	.00
☐ 604 Brad Baxter	.10	.05	.01
☐ 605 Dennis Byrd	.03	.01	.00
☐ 606 Jeff Lageman	.06	.03	.00
☐ 607 Pat Leahy	.06	.03	.00
☐ 608 Rob Moore	.50	.25	.05
☐ 609 Joe Mott	.10	.05	.01
☐ 610 Tony Stargell	.06	.03	.00
☐ 611 Brian Washington	.03	.01	.00
☐ 612 Marvin Washington	.08	.04	.01
☐ 613 David Alexander	.03	.01	.00
☐ 614 Jerome Brown	.06	.03	.00
☐ 615 Byron Evans	.03	.01	.00
☐ 616 Ron Heller	.03	.01	.00
☐ 617 Wes Hopkins	.03	.01	.00
☐ 618 Keith Jackson	.08	.04	.01
☐ 619 Heath Sherman	.08	.04	.01
☐ 620 Reggie White	.08	.04	.01
☐ 621 Calvin Williams	.08	.04	.01
☐ 622 Ken Harvey	.03	.01	.00
☐ 623 Eric Hill	.03	.01	.00
☐ 624 Johnny Johnson	.25	.12	.02
☐ 625 Freddie Joe Nunn	.03	.01	.00
☐ 626 Ricky Proehl	.08	.04	.01
☐ 627 Tootie Robbins	.03	.01	.00
☐ 628 Jay Taylor	.08	.04	.01
☐ 629 Tom Tupa	.10	.05	.01
☐ 630 Jim Wahler	.08	.04	.01
☐ 631 Bubby Brister	.08	.04	.01
☐ 632 Thomas Everett	.03	.01	.00
☐ 633 Bryan Hinkle	.03	.01	.00
☐ 634 Carnell Lake	.03	.01	.00
☐ 635 David Little	.03	.01	.00
☐ 636 Hardy Nickerson	.03	.01	.00
☐ 637 Gerald Williams	.03	.01	.00
☐ 638 Keith Willis	.03	.01	.00
☐ 639 Tim Worley	.06	.03	.00
☐ 640 Rod Bernstine	.06	.03	.00
☐ 641 Frank Cornish	.03	.01	.00
☐ 642 Gary Plummer	.03	.01	.00
☐ 643 Henry Rolling	.08	.04	.01
☐ 644 Sam Seale	.08	.04	.01
☐ 645 Junior Seau	.08	.04	.01
☐ 646 Billy Ray Smith	.06	.03	.00
☐ 647 Broderick Thompson	.03	.01	.00
☐ 648 Derrick Walker	.10	.05	.01
☐ 649 Todd Bowles	.03	.01	.00
☐ 650 Don Griffin	.03	.01	.00
☐ 651 Charles Haley	.06	.03	.00
☐ 652 Brent Jones UER	.06	.03	.00
(Born in Santa Clara,			
not San Jose)			
☐ 653 Joe Montana	.45	.22	.04
☐ 654 Jerry Rice	.35	.17	.03

☐ 655 Bill Romanowski	.03	.01	.00
☐ 656 Michael Walter	.03	.01	.00
☐ 657 Dave Waymer	.03	.01	.00
☐ 658 Jeff Chadwick	.03	.01	.00
☐ 659 Derrick Fenner	.12	.06	.01
☐ 660 Nesby Glasgow	.03	.01	.00
☐ 661 Jacob Green	.06	.03	.00
☐ 662 Dwayne Harper	.15	.07	.01
☐ 663 Andy Heck	.03	.01	.00
☐ 664 Dave Krieg	.08	.04	.01
☐ 665 Rufus Porter	.03	.01	.00
☐ 666 Eugene Robinson	.03	.01	.00
☐ 667 Mark Carrier	.08	.04	.01
☐ 668 Steve Christie	.03	.01	.00
☐ 669 Reuben Davis	.03	.01	.00
☐ 670 Paul Gruber	.06	.03	.00
☐ 671 Wayne Haddix	.06	.03	.00
☐ 672 Ron Hall	.03	.01	.00
☐ 673 Keith McCants UER	.08	.04	.01
(Senior All-American,			
sic, left school			
after junior year)			
☐ 674 Ricky Reynolds	.03	.01	.00
☐ 675 Mark Robinson	.03	.01	.00
☐ 676 Jeff Bostic	.06	.03	.00
☐ 677 Darrell Green	.10	.05	.01
☐ 678 Markus Koch	.08	.04	.01
☐ 679 Jim Lachey	.06	.03	.00
☐ 680 Charles Mann	.06	.03	.00
☐ 681 Wilber Marshall	.06	.03	.00
☐ 682 Art Monk	.12	.06	.01
☐ 683 Gerald Riggs	.06	.03	.00
☐ 684 Ricky Sanders	.08	.04	.01
☐ 685 Ray Handley replaces	.03	.01	.00
Bill Parcells as			
Giants head coach			
☐ 686 NFL announces	.03	.01	.00
expansion			
☐ 687 Miami gets	.03	.01	.00
Super Bowl XXIX			
☐ 688 Giants' George Young	.03	.01	.00
is named NFL Executive			
of the Year by			
The Sporting News			
☐ 689 Five-millionth fan	.03	.01	.00
visits Pro Football			
Hall of Fame			
☐ 690 Sports Illustrated	.03	.01	.00
poll finds pro football			
is America's Number 1			
spectator sport			
☐ 691 American Bowl	.03	.01	.00
London Theme Art			
☐ 692 American Bowl	.03	.01	.00
Berlin Theme Art			
☐ 693 American Bowl	.03	.01	.00
Tokyo Theme Art			

□ 694 Joe Ferguson LEG .... .03	.01	.00
□ 695 Carl Hairston LEG .... .03	.01	.00
□ 696 Dan Hampton LEG .... .06	.03	.00
□ 697 Mike Haynes LEG .... .06	.03	.00
□ 698 Marty Lyons LEG .... .03	.01	.00
□ 699 Ozzie Newsome LEG .... .08	.04	.01
□ 700 Scott Studwell LEG .... .03	.01	.00
□ 701 Mike Webster LEG .... .06	.03	.00
□ 702 Dwayne Woodruff LEG .. .03	.01	.00
□ 703 Larry Kennan CO .... .03 London Monarchs	.01	.00
□ 704 Stan Gelbaugh .... .15 London Monarchs	.07	.01
□ 705 John Brantley .... .08 Birmingham Fire	.04	.01
□ 706 Danny Lockett .... .08 London Monarchs	.04	.01
□ 707 Anthony Parker .... .08 NY/NJ Knights	.04	.01
□ 708 Dan Crossman .... .08 London Monarchs	.04	.01
□ 709 Eric Wilkerson .... .08 NY/NJ Knights	.04	.01
□ 710 Judd Garrett .... .12 London Monarchs	.06	.01
□ 711 Tony Baker .... .12 Frankfurt Galaxy	.06	.01
□ 712 1st Place BW .... .08 Randall Cunningham	.04	.01
□ 713 2nd Place BW .... .03 Mark Ingram	.01	.00
□ 714 3rd Place BW .... .03 Pete Holohan Barney Bussey Carl Carter	.01	.00
□ 715 1st Place Color .... .06 Action Sterling Sharpe	.03	.00
□ 716 2nd Place Color .... .06 Action Jim Harbaugh	.03	.00
□ 717 3rd Place Color .... .06 Action Anthony Miller David Fulcher	.03	.00
□ 718 1st Place Color .... .06 Feature Bill Parcells CO Lawrence Taylor	.03	.00
□ 719 2nd Place Color .... .03 Feature Patriotic Crowd	.01	.00
□ 720 3rd Place Color .... .06 Feature Alfredo Roberts	.03	.00
□ 721 Ray Bentley .... .03 Read And Study	.01	.00

Buffalo Bills		
□ 722 Earnest Byner .... .08 Never Give Up Washington Redskins	.04	.01
□ 723 Bill Fralic .... .06 Steroids Destroy Atlanta Falcons	.03	.00
□ 724 Joe Jacoby .... .06 Don't Pollute Washington Redskins	.03	.00
□ 725 Howie Long .... .06 Aids Kills Los Angeles Raiders	.03	.00
□ 726 Dan Marino .... .15 School's The Ticket Miami Dolphins	.07	.01
□ 727 Ron Rivera .... .03 Leer Y Estudiar Chicago Bears	.01	.00
□ 728 Mike Singletary .... .06 Be The Best Chicago Bears	.03	.00
□ 729 Cornelius Bennett .... .06 Chill Buffalo Bills	.03	.00
□ 730 Russell Maryland .... .25 Dallas Cowboys	.12	.02
□ 731 Eric Turner .... .50 Cleveland Browns	.25	.05
□ 732 Bruce Pickens UER .... .20 Atlanta Falcons (Wearing 38, but card back lists 39)	.10	.02
□ 733 Mike Croel .... .75 Denver Broncos	.35	.07
□ 734 Todd Lyght .... .40 Los Angeles Rams	.20	.04
□ 735 Eric Swann .... .20 Phoenix Cardinals	.10	.02
□ 736 Charles McRae .... .15 Tampa Bay Buccaneers	.07	.01
□ 737 Antone Davis .... .12 Philadelphia Eagles	.06	.01
□ 738 Stanley Richard .... .25 San Diego Chargers	.12	.02
□ 739 Herman Moore .... .60 Detroit Lions	.30	.06
□ 740 Pat Harlow .... .15 New England Patriots	.07	.01
□ 741 Alvin Harper .... .50 Dallas Cowboys	.25	.05
□ 742 Mike Pritchard .... .60 Atlanta Falcons	.30	.06
□ 743 Leonard Russell .... 1.25 New England Patriots	.60	.12
□ 744 Huey Richardson .... .20 Pittsburgh Steelers	.10	.02

□ 745 Dan McGwire 1.25	.60	.12
Seattle Seahawks		
□ 746 Bobby Wilson .... .10	.05	.01
Washington Redskins		
□ 747 Alfred Williams .... .12	.06	.01
Cincinnati Bengals		
□ 748 Vinnie Clark .... .12	.06	.01
Green Bay Packers		
□ 749 Kelvin Pritchett .... .15	.07	.01
Detroit Lions		
□ 750 Harvey Williams .... .75	.35	.07
Kansas City Chiefs		
□ 751 Stan Thomas .... .10	.05	.01
Chicago Bears		
□ 752 Randal Hill .... .60	.30	.06
Phoenix Cardinals		
□ 753 Todd Marinovich 1.50	.75	.15
Los Angeles Raiders		
□ 754 Ted Washington .... .12	.06	.01
San Francisco 49ers		
□ 755 Henry Jones .... .15	.07	.01
Buffalo Bills		
□ 756 Jarrod Bunch .... .15	.07	.01
New York Giants		
□ 757 Mike Dumas .... .15	.07	.01
Houston Oilers		
□ 758 Ed King .... .15	.07	.01
Cleveland Browns		
□ 759 Reggie Johnson .... .25	.12	.02
Denver Broncos		
□ 760 Roman Phifer .... .15	.07	.01
Los Angeles Rams		
□ 761 Mike Jones .... .10	.05	.01
Phoenix Cardinals		
□ 762 Brett Favre .... .75	.35	.07
Atlanta Falcons		
□ 763 Browning Nagle .... .75	.35	.07
New York Jets		
□ 764 Esera Tuaolo .... .10	.05	.01
Green Bay Packers		
□ 765 George Thornton .... .15	.07	.01
San Diego Chargers		
□ 766 Dixon Edwards .... .10	.05	.01
Dallas Cowboys		
□ 767 Darryll Lewis .... .12	.06	.01
Houston Oilers		
□ 768 Eric Bieniemy .... .30	.15	.03
San Diego Chargers		
□ 769 Shane Curry .... .08	.04	.01
Indianapolis Colts		
□ 770 Jerome Henderson .... .15	.07	.01
New England Patriots		
□ 771 Wesley Carroll .... .40	.20	.04
New Orleans Saints		
□ 772 Nick Bell .... .75	.35	.07
Los Angeles Raiders		
□ 773 John Flannery .... .15	.07	.01

Houston Oilers		
□ 774 Ricky Watters .... .35	.17	.03
San Francisco 49ers		
□ 775 Jeff Graham .... .20	.10	.02
Pittsburgh Steelers		
□ 776 Eric Moten .... .15	.07	.01
San Diego Chargers		
□ 777 Jesse Campbell .... .12	.06	.01
Philadelphia Eagles		
□ 778 Chris Zorich .... .12	.06	.01
Chicago Bears		
□ 779 Joe Valerio .... .10	.05	.01
Kansas City Chiefs		
□ 780 Doug Thomas .... .15	.07	.01
Seattle Seahawks		
□ 781 Lamar Rogers UER .... .15	.07	.01
Cincinnati Bengals		
(No "Official Card of		
NFL" and TM on		
card front)		
□ 782 John Johnson .... .08	.04	.01
San Francisco 49ers		
□ 783 Phil Hansen .... .15	.07	.01
Buffalo Bills		
□ 784 Kanavis McGhee .... .25	.12	.02
New York Giants		
□ 785 Calvin Stephens UER ..... .15	.07	.01
New England Patriots		
(Card says New England,		
others say New England		
Patriots)		
□ 786 James Jones .... .10	.05	.01
Cleveland Browns		
□ 787 Reggie Barrett .... .20	.10	.02
Detroit Lions		
□ 788 Aeneas Williams .... .15	.07	.01
Phoenix Cardinals		
□ 789 Aaron Craver .... .20	.10	.02
Miami Dolphins		
□ 790 Keith Traylor .... .12	.06	.01
Denver Broncos		
□ 791 Godfrey Myles .... .08	.04	.01
Dallas Cowboys		
□ 792 Mo Lewis .... .20	.10	.02
New York Jets		
□ 793 James Richard .... .10	.05	.01
Dallas Cowboys		
□ 794 Carlos Jenkins .... .15	.07	.01
Minnesota Vikings		
□ 795 Lawrence Dawsey .... .40	.20	.04
Tampa Bay Buccaneers		
□ 796 Don Davey .... .20	.10	.02
Green Bay Packers		
□ 797 Jake Reed .... .15	.07	.01
Minnesota Vikings		
□ 798 Dave McCloughan .... .15	.07	.01
Indianapolis Colts		

☐ 799	Eric Williams ....12 Dallas Cowboys	.06	.01
☐ 800	Steve Jackson ....10 Houston Oilers	.05	.01
☐ 801	Bob Dahl ....12 Cincinnati Bengals	.06	.01
☐ 802	Ernie Mills ....20 Pittsburgh Steelers	.10	.02
☐ 803	David Daniels ....15 Seattle Seahawks	.07	.01
☐ 804	Rob Selby ....12 Philadelphia Eagles	.06	.01
☐ 805	Ricky Ervins .... 1.75 Washington Redskins	.85	.17
☐ 806	Tim Barnett ....30 Kansas City Chiefs	.15	.03
☐ 807	Chris Gardocki ....12 Chicago Bears	.06	.01
☐ 808	Kevin Donnalley ....10 Houston Oilers	.05	.01
☐ 809	Robert Wilson ....20 Tampa Bay Buccaneers	.10	.02
☐ 810	Chuck Webb ....20 Green Bay Packers	.10	.02
☐ 811	Darryl Wren ....10 Buffalo Bills	.05	.01
☐ 812	Ed McCaffrey ....30 New York Giants	.15	.03

1991 Pro Set Final Update

The 1991 Pro Set Final Update set features hot rookies, traded players, NFL Newsreel cards (813-815), and a Super Bowl XXV Theme

Art card. The cards measure the standard size (2 1/2" by 3 1/2"). The key rookie cards in this series are Erik Kramer, Hugh Millen, and Neil O'Donnell.

	MINT	EXC	G-VG
COMPLETE SET (39) 5.00		2.50	.50
COMMON PLAYER (813-850) ... .05		.02	.00
☐ 813 Shula's 300th Victory ..... .05 NEW		.02	.00
☐ 814 Raiders-49ers sell .... .05 out Coliseum NEW		.02	.00
☐ 815 NFL International NEW ... .05		.02	.00
☐ 816 Moe Gardner ....15 Atlanta Falcons		.07	.01
☐ 817 Tim McKyer ....05 Atlanta Falcons		.02	.00
☐ 818 Tom Waddle ....35 Chicago Bears		.17	.03
☐ 819 Michael Jackson ....35 Cleveland Browns		.17	.03
☐ 820 Tony Casillas .... .08 Dallas Cowboys		.04	.01
☐ 821 Gaston Green ....25 Denver Broncos		.12	.02
☐ 822 Kenny Walker ....45 Denver Broncos		.22	.04
☐ 823 Willie Green ....35 Detroit Lions		.17	.03
☐ 824 Erik Kramer .... 1.00 Detroit Lions		.50	.10
☐ 825 William Fuller .... .08 Houston Oilers		.04	.01
☐ 826 Allen Pinkett .... .08 Houston Oilers		.04	.01
☐ 827 Rick Venturi CO .... .08 Indianapolis Colts		.04	.01
☐ 828 Bill Maas .... .05 Kansas City Chiefs		.02	.00
☐ 829 Jeff Jaeger .... .05 Los Angeles Raiders		.02	.00
☐ 830 Robert Delpino .... .08 Los Angeles Rams		.04	.01
☐ 831 Mark Higgs ....60 Miami Dolphins		.30	.06
☐ 832 Reggie Roby .... .05 Miami Dolphins		.02	.00
☐ 833 Terry Allen ....40 Minnesota Vikings		.20	.04
☐ 834 Cris Carter ....10 Minnesota Vikings		.05	.01
☐ 835 John Randle ....12 Minnesota Vikings		.06	.01
☐ 836 Hugh Millen ....75 New England Patriots		.35	.07
☐ 837 Jon Vaughn 60		.30	.06

New England Patriots
- ☐ 838 Gill Fenerty ....10 .05 .01
  New Orleans Saints
- ☐ 839 Floyd Turner ....05 .02 .00
  New Orleans Saints
- ☐ 840 Irv Eatman ....05 .02 .00
  New York Jets
- ☐ 841 Lonnie Young ....05 .02 .00
  New York Jets
- ☐ 842 Jim McMahon ....08 .04 .01
  Philadelphia Eagles
- ☐ 843 Randal Hill ....25 .12 .02
  Phoenix Cardinals
- ☐ 844 Barry Foster ....15 .07 .01
  Pittsburgh Steelers
- ☐ 845 Neil O'Donnell ....1.00 .50 .10
  Pittsburgh Steelers
- ☐ 846 John Friesz ....30 .15 .03
  San Diego Chargers
- ☐ 847 Broderick Thomas ....10 .05 .01
  Tampa Bay Buccaneers
- ☐ 848 Brian Mitchell ....15 .07 .01
  Washington Redskins
- ☐ 849 Mike Utley ....35 .17 .03
  Detroit Lions
- ☐ 850 Mike Croel ROY ....35 .17 .03
  Denver Broncos
- ☐ xxx Super Bowl XXV ART .....15 .07 .01
  (Unnumbered)

1991 Pro Set Platinum I

The 1991 Pro Set Platinum I football set contains 150 cards measuring the standard size (2 1/2" by 3 1/2"). The front design has full-

bleed glossy color player photos capturing game action. The Pro Set Platinum icon appears in the lower left corner. The horizontally oriented backs feature other glossy color action photos. In the black rectangle below the picture, the player's name, team, and position are given, along with a "Platinum Performer" feature that highlights the player's outstanding performance. The cards are numbered on the back in the lower right corner and checklisted below alphabetically according to teams as follows: Atlanta Falcons (1-4), Buffalo Bills (5-9), Chicago Bears (10-14), Cincinnati Bengals (15-19), Cleveland Browns (20-23), Dallas Cowboys (24-27), Denver Broncos (28-31), Detroit Lions (32-35), Green Bay Packers (36-39), Houston Oilers (40-44), Indianapolis Colts (45-47), Kansas City Chiefs (48-51), Los Angeles Raiders (52-56), Los Angeles Rams (57-61), Miami Dolphins (62-67), Minnesota Vikings (68-71), New England Patriots (72-74), New Orleans Saints (75-78), New York Giants (79-82), New York Jets (83-87), Philadelphia Eagles (88-91), Phoenix Cardinals (92-95), Pittsburgh Steelers (96-100), San Diego Chargers (101-105), San Francisco 49ers (106-110), Seattle Seahawks (111-115), Tampa Bay Buccaneers (116-122), and Washington Redskins (123-127). Other subsets included in this set are Special Teams (128-135) and Platinum Performance (136-150).

	MINT	EXC	G-VG
COMPLETE SET (150) 11.00		5.50	1.10
COMMON PLAYER (1-150) 05		.02	.00

- ☐ 1 Chris Miller ....20 .10 .02
- ☐ 2 Andre Rison ....15 .07 .01
- ☐ 3 Tim Green ....05 .02 .00
- ☐ 4 Jessie Tuggle ....05 .02 .00
- ☐ 5 Thurman Thomas ....60 .30 .06
- ☐ 6 Darryl Talley ....08 .04 .01
- ☐ 7 Kent Hull ....05 .02 .00
- ☐ 8 Bruce Smith ....10 .05 .01
- ☐ 9 Shane Conlan ....08 .04 .01
- ☐ 10 Jim Harbaugh ....12 .06 .01
- ☐ 11 Neal Anderson ....15 .07 .01
- ☐ 12 Mark Bortz ....05 .02 .00
- ☐ 13 Richard Dent ....08 .04 .00
- ☐ 14 Steve McMichael ....08 .04 .01
- ☐ 15 James Brooks ....08 .04 .01
- ☐ 16 Boomer Esiason ....12 .06 .01
- ☐ 17 Tim Krumrie ....05 .02 .00
- ☐ 18 James Francis ....10 .05 .01
- ☐ 19 Lewis Billups ....05 .02 .00
- ☐ 20 Eric Metcalf ....08 .04 .01

☐ 21 Kevin Mack	.08	.04	.01
☐ 22 Clay Matthews	.05	.02	.00
☐ 23 Mike Johnson	.05	.02	.00
☐ 24 Troy Aikman	.40	.20	.04
☐ 25 Emmitt Smith	1.25	.60	.12
☐ 26 Daniel Stubbs	.05	.02	.00
☐ 27 Ken Norton	.05	.02	.00
☐ 28 John Elway	.15	.07	.01
☐ 29 Bobby Humphrey	.10	.05	.01
☐ 30 Simon Fletcher	.05	.02	.00
☐ 31 Karl Mecklenburg	.08	.04	.01
☐ 32 Rodney Peete	.10	.05	.01
☐ 33 Barry Sanders	.75	.35	.07
☐ 34 Michael Cofer	.05	.02	.00
☐ 35 Jerry Ball	.05	.02	.00
☐ 36 Sterling Sharpe	.12	.06	.01
☐ 37 Tony Mandarich	.08	.04	.01
☐ 38 Brian Noble	.05	.02	.00
☐ 39 Tim Harris	.08	.04	.01
☐ 40 Warren Moon	.20	.10	.02
☐ 41 Ernest Givins UER	.10	.05	.01
(Misspelled Givens on card back)			
☐ 42 Mike Munchak	.08	.04	.01
☐ 43 Sean Jones	.05	.02	.00
☐ 44 Ray Childress	.08	.04	.01
☐ 45 Jeff George	.35	.17	.03
☐ 46 Albert Bentley	.08	.04	.01
☐ 47 Duane Bickett	.05	.02	.00
☐ 48 Steve DeBerg	.08	.04	.01
☐ 49 Christian Okoye	.12	.06	.01
☐ 50 Neil Smith	.08	.04	.01
☐ 51 Derrick Thomas	.20	.10	.02
☐ 52 Willie Gault	.08	.04	.01
☐ 53 Don Mosebar	.05	.02	.00
☐ 54 Howie Long	.08	.04	.01
☐ 55 Greg Townsend	.05	.02	.00
☐ 56 Terry McDaniel	.05	.02	.00
☐ 57 Jackie Slater	.08	.04	.01
☐ 58 Jim Everett	.10	.05	.01
☐ 59 Cleveland Gary	.08	.04	.01
☐ 60 Mike Piel	.05	.02	.00
☐ 61 Jerry Gray	.05	.02	.00
☐ 62 Dan Marino	.25	.12	.02
☐ 63 Sammie Smith	.10	.05	.01
☐ 64 Richmond Webb	.08	.04	.01
☐ 65 Louis Oliver	.05	.02	.00
☐ 66 Ferrell Edmunds	.05	.02	.00
☐ 67 Jeff Cross	.05	.02	.00
☐ 68 Wade Wilson	.08	.04	.01
☐ 69 Chris Doleman	.08	.04	.01
☐ 70 Joey Browner	.08	.04	.01
☐ 71 Keith Millard	.08	.04	.01
☐ 72 John Stephens	.08	.04	.01
☐ 73 Andre Tippett	.08	.04	.01
☐ 74 Brent Williams	.05	.02	.00
☐ 75 Craig Heyward	.08	.04	.01

☐ 76 Eric Martin	.08	.04	.01
☐ 77 Pat Swilling	.10	.05	.01
☐ 78 Sam Mills	.08	.04	.01
☐ 79 Jeff Hostetler	.20	.10	.02
☐ 80 Ottis Anderson	.08	.04	.01
☐ 81 Lawrence Taylor	.12	.06	.01
☐ 82 Pepper Johnson	.08	.04	.01
☐ 83 Blair Thomas	.50	.25	.05
☐ 84 Al Toon	.08	.04	.01
☐ 85 Ken O'Brien	.08	.04	.01
☐ 86 Erik McMillan	.08	.04	.01
☐ 87 Dennis Byrd	.08	.04	.01
☐ 88 Randall Cunningham	.15	.07	.01
☐ 89 Fred Barnett	.15	.07	.01
☐ 90 Seth Joyner	.08	.04	.01
☐ 91 Reggie White	.08	.04	.01
☐ 92 Timm Rosenbach	.10	.05	.01
☐ 93 Johnny Johnson	.25	.12	.02
☐ 94 Tim McDonald	.08	.04	.01
☐ 95 Freddie Joe Nunn	.05	.02	.00
☐ 96 Bubby Brister	.08	.04	.01
☐ 97 Gary Anderson UER	.05	.02	.00
(Listed as RB)			
☐ 98 Merril Hoge	.08	.04	.01
☐ 99 Keith Willis	.05	.02	.00
☐ 100 Rod Woodson	.08	.04	.01
☐ 101 Billy Joe Tolliver	.08	.04	.01
☐ 102 Marion Butts	.10	.05	.01
☐ 103 Rod Bernstine	.08	.04	.01
☐ 104 Lee Williams	.08	.04	.01
☐ 105 Burt Grossman UER	.08	.04	.01
(Photo on back is reversed)			
☐ 106 Tom Rathman	.08	.04	.01
☐ 107 John Taylor	.12	.06	.01
☐ 108 Michael Carter	.08	.04	.01
☐ 109 Guy McIntyre	.05	.02	.00
☐ 110 Pierce Holt	.05	.02	.00
☐ 111 John L. Williams	.08	.04	.01
☐ 112 Dave Krieg	.08	.04	.01
☐ 113 Bryan Millard	.05	.02	.00
☐ 114 Cortez Kennedy	.10	.05	.01
☐ 115 Derrick Fenner	.12	.06	.01
☐ 116 Vinny Testaverde	.08	.04	.01
☐ 117 Reggie Cobb	.15	.07	.01
☐ 118 Gary Anderson	.08	.04	.01
☐ 119 Bruce Hill	.05	.02	.00
☐ 120 Wayne Haddix	.05	.02	.00
☐ 121 Broderick Thomas	.08	.04	.01
☐ 122 Keith McCants	.08	.04	.01
☐ 123 Andre Collins	.05	.02	.00
☐ 124 Earnest Byner	.08	.04	.01
☐ 125 Jim Lachey	.08	.04	.01
☐ 126 Mark Rypien	.20	.10	.02
☐ 127 Charles Mann	.08	.04	.01
☐ 128 Nick Lowery	.05	.02	.00
Kansas City Chiefs			

☐ 129	Chip Lohmiller ....05 Washington Redskins	.02	.00
☐ 130	Mike Horan ....05 Denver Broncos	.02	.00
☐ 131	Rohn Stark ....05 Indianapolis Colts	.02	.00
☐ 132	Sean Landeta ....05 New York Giants	.02	.00
☐ 133	Clarence Verdin ....05 Indianapolis Colts	.02	.00
☐ 134	Johnny Bailey ....08 Chicago Bears	.04	.01
☐ 135	Herschel Walker ....12 Minnesota Vikings	.06	.01
☐ 136	Bo Jackson PP ....40 Los Angeles Raiders	.20	.04
☐ 137	Dexter Carter PP ....10 San Francisco 49ers	.05	.01
☐ 138	Warren Moon PP ....20 Houston Oilers	.10	.02
☐ 139	Joe Montana PP ....60 San Francisco 49ers	.30	.06
☐ 140	Jerry Rice PP ....40 San Francisco 49ers	.20	.04
☐ 141	Deion Sanders PP ....20 Atlanta Falcons	.10	.02
☐ 142	Ronnie Lippett PP ....05 New England Patriots	.02	.00
☐ 143	Terance Mathis PP ....12 New York Jets	.06	.01
☐ 144	Gaston Green PP ....30 Los Angeles Rams	.15	.03
☐ 145	Dean Biasucci PP ....05 Indianapolis Colts	.02	.00
☐ 146	Charles Haley PP ....08 San Francisco 49ers	.04	.01
☐ 147	Derrick Thomas PP ....15 Kansas City Chiefs	.07	.01
☐ 148	Lawrence Taylor PP ....10 New York Giants	.05	.01
☐ 149	Art Shell CO PP ....08 Los Angeles Raiders	.04	.01
☐ 150	Bill Parcells CO PP ....08 New York Giants	.04	.01

1991 Pro Set Platinum II

The 1991 Pro Set Platinum II set contains 175 standard-size (2 1/2" by 3 1/2") cards. The

front design has a full-bleed glossy color player photo, with the silver Pro Set Platinum logo in one of the lower corners of the card face. In a horizontal format, the upper portion of the back features another color action photo, with player identification and career summary in a black stripe below the picture. The cards are numbered on the back and checklisted below alphabetically according to teams as follows: Atlanta Falcons (151-155), Buffalo Bills (156-160), Chicago Bears (161-165), Cincinnati Bengals (166-170), Cleveland Browns (171-174), Dallas Cowboys (175-179), Denver Broncos (180-184), Detroit Lions (185-189), Green Bay Packers (190-194), Houston Oilers (195-199), Indianapolis Colts (200-203), Kansas City Chiefs (204-208), Los Angeles Raiders (209-213), Los Angeles Rams (214-218), Miami Dolphins (219-222), Minnesota Vikings (223-227), New England Patriots (228-232), New Orleans Saints (233-237), New York Giants (238-242), New York Jets (243-246), Philadelphia Eagles (247-251), Phoenix Cardinals (252-256), Pittsburgh Steelers (257-261), San Diego Chargers (262-266), San Francisco 49ers (267-271), Seattle Seahawks (272-275), Tampa Bay Buccaneers (276-278), and Washington Redskins (279-284). A special subset features Platinum Prospects (286-315). Special Collectibles (PC1-PC10) cards are randomly distributed in 12-card foil packs. Also randomly inserted in the packs are bonus card certificates, which could be redeemed for a limited edition (1,500 made) platinum card of Paul Brown. The key rookie cards in this series are Nick Bell, Ricky Ervins, Todd Marinovich, Dan McGwire, Leonard Russell, and Harvey Williams.

	MINT	EXC	G-VG
COMPLETE SET (165)	14.00	7.00	1.40

COMMON PLAYER (151-315)	.05	.02	.00

☐ 151 Steve Broussard	.10	.05	.01
☐ 152 Darion Conner	.08	.04	.01
☐ 153 Bill Fralic	.08	.04	.01
☐ 154 Mike Gann	.05	.02	.00
☐ 155 Tim McKyer	.05	.02	.00
☐ 156 Don Beebe UER	.10	.05	.01
(4 TD's against Steelers, should be against Dolphins)			
☐ 157 Cornelius Bennett	.10	.05	.01
☐ 158 Andre Reed	.12	.06	.01
☐ 159 Leonard Smith	.05	.02	.00
☐ 160 Will Wolford	.05	.02	.00
☐ 161 Mark Carrier	.10	.05	.01
☐ 162 Wendell Davis	.15	.07	.01
☐ 163 Jay Hilgenberg	.08	.04	.01
☐ 164 Brad Muster	.08	.04	.01
☐ 165 Mike Singletary	.08	.04	.01
☐ 166 Eddie Brown	.08	.04	.01
☐ 167 David Fulcher	.05	.02	.00
☐ 168 Rodney Holman	.05	.02	.00
☐ 169 Anthony Munoz	.10	.05	.01
☐ 170 Craig Taylor	.15	.07	.01
☐ 171 Mike Baab	.05	.02	.00
☐ 172 David Grayson	.05	.02	.00
☐ 173 Reggie Langhorne	.05	.02	.00
☐ 174 Joe Morris	.08	.04	.01
☐ 175 Kevin Gogan	.12	.06	.01
☐ 176 Jack Del Rio	.05	.02	.00
☐ 177 Issiac Holt	.05	.02	.00
☐ 178 Michael Irvin	.20	.10	.02
☐ 179 Jay Novacek	.10	.05	.01
☐ 180 Steve Atwater	.08	.04	.01
☐ 181 Mark Jackson	.08	.04	.01
☐ 182 Ricky Nattiel	.08	.04	.01
☐ 183 Warren Powers	.05	.02	.00
☐ 184 Dennis Smith	.05	.02	.00
☐ 185 Bennie Blades	.08	.04	.01
☐ 186 Lomas Brown UER	.05	.02	.00
(Spent 6 seasons with Detroit, not 7)			
☐ 187 Robert Clark UER	.08	.04	.01
(Plan B acquisition in '89, not '90)			
☐ 188 Mel Gray	.05	.02	.00
☐ 189 Chris Spielman	.08	.04	.01
☐ 190 Johnny Holland	.05	.02	.00
☐ 191 Don Majkowski	.08	.04	.01
☐ 192 Bryce Paup	.20	.10	.02
☐ 193 Darrell Thompson	.12	.06	.01
☐ 194 Ed West UER	.05	.02	.00
(Photo on back is reversed)			
☐ 195 Cris Dishman	.20	.10	.02
☐ 196 Drew Hill	.08	.04	.01

☐ 197 Bruce Matthews	.05	.02	.00
☐ 198 Bubba McDowell	.05	.02	.00
☐ 199 Allen Pinkett	.08	.04	.01
☐ 200 Bill Brooks	.05	.02	.00
☐ 201 Jeff Herrod	.05	.02	.00
☐ 202 Anthony Johnson	.05	.02	.00
☐ 203 Mike Prior	.05	.02	.00
☐ 204 John Alt	.05	.02	.00
☐ 205 Stephone Paige	.08	.04	.01
☐ 206 Kevin Ross	.05	.02	.00
☐ 207 Dan Saleaumua	.05	.02	.00
☐ 208 Barry Word	.30	.15	.03
☐ 209 Marcus Allen	.10	.05	.01
☐ 210 Roger Craig	.10	.05	.01
☐ 211 Ronnie Lott	.10	.05	.01
☐ 212 Winston Moss	.05	.02	.00
☐ 213 Jay Schroeder	.08	.04	.01
☐ 214 Robert Delpino	.08	.04	.01
☐ 215 Henry Ellard	.08	.04	.01
☐ 216 Kevin Greene	.08	.04	.01
☐ 217 Tom Newberry	.05	.02	.00
☐ 218 Michael Stewart	.05	.02	.00
☐ 219 Mark Duper	.08	.04	.01
☐ 220 Mark Higgs	.60	.30	.06
☐ 221 John Offerdahl UER	.08	.04	.01
(2nd round pick in '86, not 6th)			
☐ 222 Keith Sims	.05	.02	.00
☐ 223 Anthony Carter	.08	.04	.01
☐ 224 Cris Carter	.08	.04	.01
☐ 225 Steve Jordan	.08	.04	.01
☐ 226 Randall McDaniel	.05	.02	.00
☐ 227 Al Noga	.05	.02	.00
☐ 228 Ray Agnew	.05	.02	.00
☐ 229 Bruce Armstrong	.05	.02	.00
☐ 230 Irving Fryar	.08	.04	.01
☐ 231 Greg McMurtry	.08	.04	.01
☐ 232 Chris Singleton	.08	.04	.01
☐ 233 Morten Andersen	.08	.04	.01
☐ 234 Vince Buck	.05	.02	.00
☐ 235 Gill Fenerty	.10	.05	.01
☐ 236 Rickey Jackson	.08	.04	.01
☐ 237 Vaughan Johnson	.08	.04	.01
☐ 238 Carl Banks	.08	.04	.01
☐ 239 Mark Collins	.05	.02	.00
☐ 240 Rodney Hampton	.40	.20	.04
☐ 241 David Meggett	.10	.05	.01
☐ 242 Bart Oates	.05	.02	.00
☐ 243 Kyle Clifton	.08	.04	.01
☐ 244 Jeff Lageman	.08	.04	.01
☐ 245 Freeman McNeil UER	.08	.04	.01
(Drafted in '81, not '80)			
☐ 246 Rob Moore	.50	.25	.05
☐ 247 Eric Allen	.05	.02	.00
☐ 248 Keith Byars	.08	.04	.01
☐ 249 Keith Jackson	.08	.04	.01

☐ 250	Jim McMahon 10	.05	.01
☐ 251	Andre Waters 05	.02	.00
☐ 252	Ken Harvey 05	.02	.00
☐ 253	Ernie Jones 08	.04	.01
☐ 254	Luis Sharpe 05	.02	.00
☐ 255	Anthony Thompson 10	.05	.01
☐ 256	Tom Tupa 10	.05	.01
☐ 257	Eric Green 15	.07	.01
☐ 258	Barry Foster 15	.07	.01
☐ 259	Bryan Hinkle 05	.02	.00
☐ 260	Tunch Ilkin 05	.02	.00
☐ 261	Louis Lipps 08	.04	.01
☐ 262	Gill Byrd 08	.04	.01
☐ 263	John Friesz 40	.20	.04
☐ 264	Anthony Miller 08	.04	.01
☐ 265	Junior Seau 10	.05	.01
☐ 266	Ronnie Harmon 08	.04	.01
☐ 267	Harris Barton 05	.02	.00
☐ 268	Todd Bowles 05	.02	.00
☐ 269	Don Griffin 05	.02	.00
☐ 270	Bill Romanowski 05	.02	.00
☐ 271	Steve Young 12	.06	.01
☐ 272	Brian Blades 08	.04	.01
☐ 273	Jacob Green 08	.04	.01
☐ 274	Rufus Porter 05	.02	.00
☐ 275	Eugene Robinson 05	.02	.00
☐ 276	Mark Carrier 08	.04	.01
☐ 277	Reuben Davis 05	.02	.00
☐ 278	Paul Gruber 08	.04	.01
☐ 279	Gary Clark 15	.07	.01
☐ 280	Darrell Green 10	.05	.01
☐ 281	Wilber Marshall 08	.04	.01
☐ 282	Matt Millen 05	.02	.00
☐ 283	Alvin Walton 05	.02	.00
☐ 284	Joe Gibbs CO UER 05	.02	.00
	(NFLPA logo on back)		
☐ 285	Don Shula CO UER 05	.02	.00
	Miami Dolphins		
	(NFLPA logo on back)		
☐ 286	Larry Brown 15	.07	.01
	Dallas Cowboys		
☐ 287	Mike Croel 75	.35	.07
	Denver Broncos		
☐ 288	Antone Davis 12	.06	.01
	Philadelphia Eagles		
☐ 289	Ricky Ervins UER 2.50	1.25	.25
	Washington Redskins		
	(2nd round choice,		
	should say 3rd)		
☐ 290	Brett Favre 75	.35	.07
	Atlanta Falcons		
☐ 291	Pat Harlow 15	.07	.01
	New England Patriots		
☐ 292	Michael Jackson 35	.17	.03
	Cleveland Browns		
☐ 293	Henry Jones 15	.07	.01
	Buffalo Bills		
☐ 294	Aaron Craver 20	.10	.02
	Miami Dolphins		
☐ 295	Nick Bell 75	.35	.07
	Los Angeles Raiders		
☐ 296	Todd Lyght 40	.20	.04
	Los Angeles Rams		
☐ 297	Todd Marinovich 1.50	.75	.15
	Los Angeles Raiders		
☐ 298	Russell Maryland 45	.22	.04
	Dallas Cowboys		
☐ 299	Kanavis McGhee 25	.12	.02
	New York Giants		
☐ 300	Dan McGwire 1.25	.60	.12
	Seattle Seahawks		
☐ 301	Charles McRae 20	.10	.02
	Tampa Bay Buccaneers		
☐ 302	Eric Moten 15	.07	.01
	San Diego Chargers		
☐ 303	Jerome Henderson 15	.07	.01
	New England Patriots		
☐ 304	Browning Nagle 75	.35	.07
	New York Jets		
☐ 305	Mike Pritchard 60	.30	.06
	Atlanta Falcons		
☐ 306	Stanley Richard 25	.12	.02
	San Diego Chargers		
☐ 307	Randal Hill 60	.30	.06
	Phoenix Cardinals		
☐ 308	Leonard Russell 1.25	.60	.12
	New England Patriots		
☐ 309	Eric Swann 25	.12	.02
	Phoenix Cardinals		
☐ 310	Phil Hansen 20	.10	.02
	Buffalo Bills		
☐ 311	Moe Gardner 20	.10	.02
	Atlanta Falcons		
☐ 312	Jon Vaughn 60	.30	.06
	New England Patriots		
☐ 313	Aeneas Williams UER 15	.07	.01
	Phoenix Cardinals		
	(Misspelled Aaneas		
	on card back)		
☐ 314	Alfred Williams 15	.07	.01
	Cincinnati Bengals		
☐ 315	Harvey Williams 1.00	.50	.10
	Kansas City Chiefs		

1991 Pro Set Platinum II PC

These ten Platinum Collectible cards were inserted in 1991 Pro Set Platinum II foil packs. The standard-size (2 1/2" by 3 1/2") cards feature full-bleed color player photos on the fronts, with a second color photo on the horizontally oriented backs. The set is subdivided as follows: Platinum Profile (1-3), Platinum Photo (4-5), and Platinum Game Breaker (6-10). The Platinum Game Breaker cards present in alphabetical order five standout NFL running backs. The cards are numbered on the back.

	MINT	EXC	G-VG
COMPLETE SET (10)	22.00	11.00	2.20
COMMON PLAYER (PC1-PC10)	1.00	.50	.10
☐ PC1 Bobby Hebert .... New Orleans Saints	1.00	.50	.10
☐ PC2 Art Monk .... Washington Redskins	1.50	.75	.15
☐ PC3 Kenny Walker .... Denver Broncos	1.75	.85	.17
☐ PC4 Low Fives .... Houston Oilers	1.00	.50	.10
☐ PC5 Touchdown .... Kevin Mack Cleveland Browns	1.00	.50	.10
☐ PC6 Neal Anderson .... Chicago Bears	1.25	.60	.12
☐ PC7 Gaston Green .... Denver Broncos	2.00	1.00	.20
☐ PC8 Barry Sanders .... Detroit Lions	4.50	2.25	.45
☐ PC9 Emmitt Smith .... Dallas Cowboys	7.50	3.75	.75
☐ PC10 Thurman Thomas ..... Buffalo Bills	3.50	1.75	.35

1992 Pro Set I

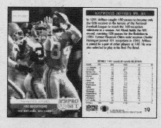

The 1992 Pro Set I football set contains 405 cards measuring the standard size (2 1/2" by 3 1/2"). The set features a four-card Emmitt Smith hologram subset, numbered ES1-ES4, which were randomly inserted into the foil packs. The ES1 card was the least difficult to find, while the ES4 card was the most difficult. Supposedly the numbered cases purchased directly from Pro Set by hobby dealers had a higher collation of the Smith holograms. The fronts feature full-bleed color player photos, with the player's name in a stripe at the card bottom and the NFL Pro Set logo in the lower right corner. In a horizontal format, the backs have a close-up color player photo, biography, career highlights, and complete statistical information. The cards are numbered on the back and checklisted below. The set opens with the following topical subsets: Statistical Leaders (1-18), Milestones (19-27), Draft Day (28-33), Innovators (34-36), 1991 Replays (37-63), and Super Bowl XXVI Replays (64-72). The Super Bowl teams are listed next (Washington Redskins (73-90), Buffalo Bills (91-108), and then the rest of the league alphabetically according to and within teams as follows: Atlanta Falcons (109-117), Chicago Bears (118-126), Cincinnati Bengals (127-135), Cleveland Browns (136-144), Dallas Cowboys (145-153), Denver Broncos (154-162), Detroit Lions (163-171), Green Bay Packers (172-180), Houston Oilers (181-189),

Indianapolis Colts (190-198), Kansas City Chiefs (199-207), Los Angeles Raiders (208-216), Los Angeles Rams (217-225), Miami Dolphins (226-234), Minnesota Vikings (235-243), New England Patriots (244-252), New Orleans Saints (253-261), New York Giants (262-270), New York Jets (271-279), Philadelphia Eagles (280-288), Phoenix Cardinals (289-297), Pittsburgh Steelers (298-306), San Diego Chargers (307-315), San Francisco 49ers (316-324), Seattle Seahawks (325-333), and Tampa Bay Buccaneers (334-342). The set closes with the following special subsets: Pro Set Newsreel (343-346), Magic Numbers (347-351), Play Smart (352-360), NFC Spirit of the Game (361-374), AFC Pro Bowl Stars (375-400), and Special Collectibles (SC1-SC5).

	MINT	EXC	G-VG
COMPLETE SET (400)	16.00	8.00	1.60
COMMON PLAYER (1-400)	.03	.01	.00
☐ 1 Mike Croel LL Rookie of the Year Denver Broncos	.12	.06	.01
☐ 2 Thurman Thomas LL Player of the Year Buffalo Bills	.17	.08	.01
☐ 3 Wayne Fontes CO LL Coach of the Year Detroit Lions	.03	.01	.00
☐ 4 Anthony Munoz LL Man of the Year Cincinnati Bengals	.06	.03	.01
☐ 5 Steve Young LL Passing Leader San Francisco 49ers	.08	.04	.01
☐ 6 Warren Moon LL Passing Yardage Leader Houston Oilers	.12	.06	.01
☐ 7 Emmitt Smith LL Rushing Leader Dallas Cowboys	.50	.25	.05
☐ 8 Haywood Jeffires LL Receiving Leader Houston Oilers	.10	.05	.01
☐ 9 Marv Cook LL Receiving Leader/TE New England Patriots	.06	.03	.00
☐ 10 Michael Irvin LL Receiving Yardage Leader Dallas Cowboys	.10	.05	.01
☐ 11 Thurman Thomas LL Total Yardage Leader Buffalo Bills	.17	.08	.01
☐ 12 Chip Lohmiller LL	.03	.01	.00

	MINT	EXC	G-VG
Scoring Leader Washington Redskins			
☐ 13 Barry Sanders LL Scoring Leader TD's Detroit Lions	.25	.12	.02
☐ 14 Reggie Roby LL Punting Leader Miami Dolphins	.03	.01	.00
☐ 15 Mel Gray LL Kickoff/Punt Return Leader Detroit Lions	.03	.01	.00
☐ 16 Ronnie Lott LL Interception Leader Los Angeles Raiders	.08	.04	.01
☐ 17 Pat Swilling LL Sack Leader New Orleans Saints	.06	.03	.00
☐ 18 Reggie White LL Defensive MVP Philadelphia Eagles	.08	.04	.01
☐ 19 Haywood Jeffires ML 100 Receptions Houston Oilers	.10	.05	.01
☐ 20 Pat Leahy LL 300 Field Goals New York Jets	.03	.01	.00
☐ 21 James Lofton ML 13,000 Yards Buffalo Bills	.08	.04	.01
☐ 22 Art Monk ML 800 Receptions Washington Redskins	.08	.04	.01
☐ 23 Don Shula ML 300 Wins Miami Dolphins	.06	.03	.00
☐ 24 Nick Lowery ML 9th 100-Point Season Kansas City Chiefs	.03	.01	.00
☐ 25 John Elway ML 2,000 Completed Passes Denver Broncos	.10	.05	.01
☐ 26 Chicago Bears ML 8 Straight Opening Wins	.03	.01	.00
☐ 27 Marcus Allen ML 2,000 Rushing Attempts Los Angeles Raiders	.06	.03	.00
☐ 28 Terrell Buckley Green Bay Packers	.75	.35	.07
☐ 29 Amp Lee San Francisco 49ers	.35	.17	.03
☐ 30 Chris Mims San Diego Chargers	.15	.07	.01
☐ 31 Leon Searcy Pittsburgh Steelers	.15	.07	.01
☐ 32 Jimmy Smith Dallas Cowboys	.20	.10	.02

☐ 33 Siran Stacy 35	.17	.03	
Philadelphia Eagles			
☐ 34 Pete Gogolak 03	.01	.00	
☐ 35 Cheerleaders 06	.03	.00	
Dallas Cowboys			
☐ 36 Houston Astrodome 03	.01	.00	
☐ 37 Week 1: 06	.03	.00	
Chiefs 14, Falcons 3			
(Christian Okoye)			
☐ 38 Week 2: 06	.03	.00	
Bills 52, Steelers 34			
(Don Beebe)			
☐ 39 Week 3: 06	.03	.00	
Bears 20, Giants 17			
(Wendell Davis)			
☐ 40 Week 4: 06	.03	.00	
Dolphins 16, Packers 13			
(Don Shula CO)			
☐ 41 Week 5: 06	.03	.00	
Raiders 12, 49ers 6			
(Ronnie Lott)			
☐ 42 Week 6: 06	.03	.00	
Redskins 20, Bears 7			
(Art Monk)			
☐ 43 Week 7: 17	.08	.01	
Bills 42, Colts 6			
(Thurman Thomas)			
☐ 44 Week 8: 06	.03	.00	
Patriots 26, Vikings 23			
(John Stephens)			
☐ 45 Week 9: UER 06	.03	.00	
Vikings 28, Cardinals 0			
(Herschel Walker;			
misspelled Hershel			
on card back)			
☐ 46 Week 10: 03	.01	.00	
Jets 19, Packers 16			
(Chris Burkett)			
☐ 47 Week 11: 03	.01	.00	
Colts 28, Jets 27			
(Line play)			
☐ 48 Week 12: 08	.04	.01	
Falcons 43, Buccaneers 7			
(Andre Rison)			
☐ 49 Week 13: 08	.04	.01	
Cowboys 24, Redskins 21			
(Steve Beuerlein			
and Michael Irvin)			
☐ 50 Week 14: 06	.03	.00	
Broncos 20, Patriots 3			
(Irving Fryar)			
☐ 51 Week 15: 03	.01	.00	
Bills 30, Raiders 27			
(Bills' Defense)			
☐ 52 Week 16: 03	.01	.00	
Cowboys 25, Eagles 13			
(Kelvin Martin)			

☐ 53 Week 17: 03	.01	.00	
Jets 23, Dolphins 20			
(Bruce Coslet CO)			
☐ 54 AFC Wild Card 03	.01	.00	
Chiefs 10, Raiders 6			
(Fred Jones)			
☐ 55 AFC Wild Card 06	.03	.00	
Oilers 17, Jets 10			
(Oilers' Run-and-Shoot)			
☐ 56 NFC Wild Card 03	.01	.00	
Cowboys 17, Bears 13			
(Bill Bates)			
☐ 57 NFC Wild Card 06	.03	.00	
Falcons 27, Saints 20			
(Michael Haynes)			
☐ 58 AFC Divisional Playoff ... 03	.01	.00	
Broncos 26, Oilers 24			
(Bronco interception)			
☐ 59 AFC Divisional Playoff ... 17	.08	.01	
Bills 37, Chiefs 14			
(Thurman Thomas)			
☐ 60 NFC Divisional Playoff ... 17	.08	.01	
Lions 38, Cowboys 6			
(Eric Kramer)			
☐ 61 NFC Divisional Playoff ... 06	.03	.00	
Redskins 24, Falcons 7			
(Darrell Green)			
☐ 62 AFC Championship 03	.01	.00	
Bills 10, Broncos 7			
(Carlton Bailey)			
☐ 63 NFC Championship 08	.04	.01	
Redskins 41, Lions 10			
(Mark Rypien)			
☐ 64 TD Reversed, ... 03	.01	.00	
FG Blocked			
☐ 65 (Brad) Edwards Picks 03	.01	.00	
Off First of Two			
☐ 66 Rypien to Byner, 10-0 ... 08	.04	.01	
☐ 67 Riggs Puts Redskins 06	.03	.00	
Up 17-10			
☐ 68 Gouveia Interception 03	.01	.00	
Buries Bills			
☐ 69 Thomas Scores Bills' 17	.08	.01	
First TD			
☐ 70 Clark Catches 08	.04	.01	
Rypien's Second TD			
☐ 71 Bills Convert Late 03	.01	.00	
Break			
☐ 72 Redskins Run Out 03	.01	.00	
the Clock			
☐ 73 Jeff Bostic 03	.01	.00	
☐ 74 Earnest Byner 08	.04	.01	
☐ 75 Gary Clark 12	.06	.01	
☐ 76 Andre Collins 03	.01	.00	
☐ 77 Darrell Green 10	.05	.01	
☐ 78 Joe Jacoby 03	.01	.00	
☐ 79 Jim Lachey 06	.03	.00	

☐ 80 Chip Lohmiller	.03	.01	.00
☐ 81 Charles Mann	.03	.01	.00
☐ 82 Martin Mayhew	.03	.01	.00
☐ 83 Matt Millen	.03	.01	.00
☐ 84 Brian Mitchell	.12	.06	.01
☐ 85 Art Monk	.12	.06	.01
☐ 86 Gerald Riggs	.06	.03	.00
☐ 87 Mark Rypien	.20	.10	.02
☐ 88 Fred Stokes	.03	.01	.00
☐ 89 Bobby Wilson	.03	.01	.00
☐ 90 Joe Gibbs CO	.03	.01	.00
☐ 91 Howard Ballard	.03	.01	.00
☐ 92 Cornelius Bennett	.10	.05	.01
☐ 93 Kenneth Davis	.06	.03	.00
☐ 94 Al Edwards	.03	.01	.00
☐ 95 Kent Hull	.03	.01	.00
☐ 96 Kirby Jackson	.03	.01	.00
☐ 97 Mark Kelso	.03	.01	.00
☐ 98 James Lofton	.15	.07	.01
☐ 99 Keith McKeller	.06	.03	.00
☐ 100 Nate Odomes	.03	.01	.00
☐ 101 Jim Ritcher	.03	.01	.00
☐ 102 Leon Seals	.03	.01	.00
☐ 103 Steve Tasker	.03	.01	.00
☐ 104 Darryl Talley	.06	.03	.00
☐ 105 Thurman Thomas	.40	.20	.04
☐ 106 Will Wolford	.03	.01	.00
☐ 107 Jeff Wright	.03	.01	.00
☐ 108 Marv Levy CO	.03	.01	.00
☐ 109 Darion Conner	.06	.03	.00
☐ 110 Bill Fralic	.06	.03	.00
☐ 111 Moe Gardner	.08	.04	.01
☐ 112 Michael Haynes	.20	.10	.02
☐ 113 Chris Miller	.15	.07	.01
☐ 114 Erric Pegram	.12	.06	.01
☐ 115 Bruce Pickens	.12	.06	.01
☐ 116 Andre Rison	.15	.07	.01
☐ 117 Jerry Glanville CO	.03	.01	.00
☐ 118 Neal Anderson	.12	.06	.01
☐ 119 Trace Armstrong	.03	.01	.00
☐ 120 Wendell Davis	.12	.06	.01
☐ 121 Richard Dent	.08	.04	.01
☐ 122 Jay Hilgenberg	.06	.03	.00
☐ 123 Lemuel Stinson	.03	.01	.00
☐ 124 Stan Thomas	.03	.01	.00
☐ 125 Tom Waddle	.15	.07	.01
☐ 126 Mike Ditka CO	.06	.03	.00
☐ 127 James Brooks	.08	.04	.01
☐ 128 Eddie Brown	.06	.03	.00
☐ 129 David Fulcher	.03	.01	.00
☐ 130 Harold Green	.15	.07	.01
☐ 131 Tim Krumrie	.03	.01	.00
☐ 132 Anthony Munoz	.10	.05	.01
☐ 133 Craig Taylor	.06	.03	.00
☐ 134 Eric Thomas	.03	.01	.00
☐ 135 David Shula CO	.10	.05	.01
☐ 136 Mike Baab	.03	.01	.00
☐ 137 Brian Brennan	.03	.01	.00
☐ 138 Michael Jackson	.15	.07	.01
☐ 139 James Jones	.03	.01	.00
☐ 140 Ed King	.03	.01	.00
☐ 141 Clay Matthews	.03	.01	.00
☐ 142 Eric Metcalf	.06	.03	.00
☐ 143 Joe Morris	.06	.03	.00
☐ 144 Bill Belichick CO	.03	.01	.00
☐ 145 Steve Beuerlein	.12	.06	.01
☐ 146 Larry Brown	.03	.01	.00
☐ 147 Ray Horton	.03	.01	.00
☐ 148 Ken Norton	.03	.01	.00
☐ 149 Mike Saxon	.03	.01	.00
☐ 150 Emmitt Smith	1.25	.60	.12
☐ 151 Mark Stepnoski	.03	.01	.00
☐ 152 Alexander Wright	.08	.04	.01
☐ 153 Jimmy Johnson CO	.03	.01	.00
☐ 154 Mike Croel	.25	.12	.02
☐ 155 John Elway	.15	.07	.01
☐ 156 Gaston Green	.20	.10	.02
☐ 157 Wymon Henderson	.03	.01	.00
☐ 158 Karl Mecklenburg	.06	.03	.00
☐ 159 Warren Powers	.03	.01	.00
☐ 160 Steve Sewell	.03	.01	.00
☐ 161 Doug Widell	.03	.01	.00
☐ 162 Dan Reeves CO	.03	.01	.00
☐ 163 Eric Andolsek	.03	.01	.00
☐ 164 Jerry Ball	.06	.03	.00
☐ 165 Bennie Blades	.06	.03	.00
☐ 166 Ray Crockett	.03	.01	.00
☐ 167 Willie Green	.15	.07	.01
☐ 168 Erik Kramer	.40	.20	.04
☐ 169 Barry Sanders	.75	.35	.07
☐ 170 Chris Spielman	.06	.03	.00
☐ 171 Wayne Fontes CO	.03	.01	.00
☐ 172 Vinnie Clark	.03	.01	.00
☐ 173 Tony Mandarich	.06	.03	.00
☐ 174 Brian Noble	.03	.01	.00
☐ 175 Bryce Paup	.03	.01	.00
☐ 176 Sterling Sharpe	.10	.05	.01
☐ 177 Darrell Thompson	.06	.03	.00
☐ 178 Esera Tuaolo	.03	.01	.00
☐ 179 Ed West	.03	.01	.00
☐ 180 Mike Holmgren CO	.06	.03	.00
☐ 181 Ray Childress	.06	.03	.00
☐ 182 Cris Dishman	.08	.04	.01
☐ 183 Curtis Duncan	.03	.01	.00
☐ 184 William Fuller	.03	.01	.00
☐ 185 Lamar Lathon	.06	.03	.00
☐ 186 Warren Moon	.20	.10	.02
☐ 187 Bo Orlando	.20	.10	.02
☐ 188 Lorenzo White	.06	.03	.00
☐ 189 Jack Pardee CO	.03	.01	.00
☐ 190 Chip Banks	.03	.01	.00
☐ 191 Dean Biasucci	.03	.01	.00
☐ 192 Bill Brooks	.03	.01	.00
☐ 193 Ray Donaldson	.03	.01	.00

☐ 194 Jeff Herrod	.03	.01	.00
☐ 195 Mike Prior	.03	.01	.00
☐ 196 Mark Vander Poel	.03	.01	.00
☐ 197 Clarence Verdin	.03	.01	.00
☐ 198 Ted Marchibroda CO	.03	.01	.00
☐ 199 John Alt	.03	.01	.00
☐ 200 Deron Cherry	.03	.01	.00
☐ 201 Steve DeBerg	.08	.04	.01
☐ 202 Nick Lowery	.06	.03	.00
☐ 203 Neil Smith	.03	.01	.00
☐ 204 Derrick Thomas	.17	.08	.01
☐ 205 Joe Valerio	.03	.01	.00
☐ 206 Barry Word	.17	.08	.01
☐ 207 M. Schottenheimer CO	.03	.01	.00
☐ 208 Marcus Allen	.10	.05	.01
☐ 209 Nick Bell	.35	.17	.03
☐ 210 Tim Brown	.08	.04	.01
☐ 211 Howie Long	.06	.03	.00
☐ 212 Ronnie Lott	.10	.05	.01
☐ 213 Todd Marinovich	.60	.30	.06
☐ 214 Greg Townsend	.03	.01	.00
☐ 215 Steve Wright	.03	.01	.00
☐ 216 Art Shell CO	.06	.03	.00
☐ 217 Flipper Anderson	.06	.03	.00
☐ 218 Robert Delpino	.06	.03	.00
☐ 219 Henry Ellard	.06	.03	.00
☐ 220 Kevin Greene	.06	.03	.00
☐ 221 Todd Lyght	.15	.07	.01
☐ 222 Tom Newberry	.03	.01	.00
☐ 223 Roman Phifer	.03	.01	.00
☐ 224 Michael Stewart	.03	.01	.00
☐ 225 Chuck Knox CO	.03	.01	.00
☐ 226 Aaron Craver	.06	.03	.00
☐ 227 Jeff Cross	.03	.01	.00
☐ 228 Mark Duper	.06	.03	.00
☐ 229 Ferrell Edmunds	.03	.01	.00
☐ 230 Jim C. Jensen	.03	.01	.00
☐ 231 Louis Oliver	.03	.01	.00
☐ 232 Reggie Roby	.03	.01	.00
☐ 233 Sammie Smith	.08	.04	.01
☐ 234 Don Shula CO	.06	.03	.00
☐ 235 Joey Browner	.06	.03	.00
☐ 236 Anthony Carter	.06	.03	.00
☐ 237 Chris Doleman	.06	.03	.00
☐ 238 Steve Jordan	.06	.03	.00
☐ 239 Kirk Lowdermilk	.03	.01	.00
☐ 240 Henry Thomas	.03	.01	.00
☐ 241 Herschel Walker	.10	.05	.01
☐ 242 Felix Wright	.03	.01	.00
☐ 243 Dennis Green CO	.08	.04	.01
☐ 244 Ray Agnew	.03	.01	.00
☐ 245 Marv Cook	.10	.05	.01
☐ 246 Irving Fryar	.06	.03	.00
☐ 247 Pat Harlow	.06	.03	.00
☐ 248 Hugh Millen	.40	.20	.04
☐ 249 Leonard Russell	.60	.30	.06
☐ 250 Andre Tippett	.06	.03	.00
☐ 251 Jon Vaughn	.30	.15	.03
☐ 252 Dick MacPherson CO	.03	.01	.00
☐ 253 Morten Andersen	.06	.03	.00
☐ 254 Bobby Hebert	.08	.04	.01
☐ 255 Joel Hilgenberg	.03	.01	.00
☐ 256 Vaughan Johnson	.03	.01	.00
☐ 257 Sam Mills	.03	.01	.00
☐ 258 Pat Swilling	.10	.05	.01
☐ 259 Floyd Turner	.03	.01	.00
☐ 260 Steve Walsh	.08	.04	.01
☐ 261 Jim Mora CO	.03	.01	.00
☐ 262 Stephen Baker	.06	.03	.00
☐ 263 Mark Collins	.03	.01	.00
☐ 264 Rodney Hampton	.20	.10	.02
☐ 265 Jeff Hostetler	.17	.08	.01
☐ 266 Erik Howard	.03	.01	.00
☐ 267 Sean Landeta	.03	.01	.00
☐ 268 Gary Reasons	.03	.01	.00
☐ 269 Everson Walls	.03	.01	.00
☐ 270 Ray Handley CO	.03	.01	.00
☐ 271 Louis Aguiar	.10	.05	.01
☐ 272 Brad Baxter	.06	.03	.00
☐ 273 Chris Burkett	.03	.01	.00
☐ 274 Irv Eatman	.03	.01	.00
☐ 275 Jeff Lageman	.06	.03	.00
☐ 276 Freeman McNeil	.08	.04	.01
☐ 277 Rob Moore	.25	.12	.02
☐ 278 Lonnie Young	.03	.01	.00
☐ 279 Bruce Coslet CO	.03	.01	.00
☐ 280 Jerome Brown	.03	.01	.00
☐ 281 Keith Byars	.06	.03	.00
☐ 282 Bruce Collie	.03	.01	.00
☐ 283 Keith Jackson	.06	.03	.00
☐ 284 James Joseph	.20	.10	.02
☐ 285 Seth Joyner	.06	.03	.00
☐ 286 Andre Waters	.03	.01	.00
☐ 287 Reggie White	.08	.04	.01
☐ 288 Rich Kotite CO	.03	.01	.00
☐ 289 Rich Camarillo	.03	.01	.00
☐ 290 Garth Jax	.03	.01	.00
☐ 291 Ernie Jones	.03	.01	.00
☐ 292 Tim McDonald	.03	.01	.00
☐ 293 Rod Saddler	.03	.01	.00
☐ 294 Anthony Thompson	.08	.04	.01
☐ 295 Tom Tupa	.06	.03	.00
☐ 296 Ron Wolfley	.03	.01	.00
☐ 297 Joe Bugel CO	.03	.01	.00
☐ 298 Gary Anderson	.03	.01	.00
☐ 299 Jeff Graham	.12	.06	.01
☐ 300 Eric Green	.12	.06	.01
☐ 301 Bryan Hinkle	.03	.01	.00
☐ 302 Tunch Ilkin	.03	.01	.00
☐ 303 Louis Lipps	.06	.03	.00
☐ 304 Neil O'Donnell	.40	.20	.04
☐ 305 Rod Woodson	.06	.03	.00
☐ 306 Bill Cowher CO	.06	.03	.00
☐ 307 Eric Bieniemy	.12	.06	.01

☐ 308 Marion Butts	10	.05	.01
☐ 309 John Friesz	15	.07	.01
☐ 310 Courtney Hall	03	.01	.00
☐ 311 Ronnie Harmon	03	.01	.00
☐ 312 Henry Rolling	03	.01	.00
☐ 313 Billy Ray Smith	03	.01	.00
☐ 314 George Thornton	03	.01	.00
☐ 315 Bobby Ross CO	06	.03	.00
☐ 316 Todd Bowles	03	.01	.00
☐ 317 Michael Carter	06	.03	.00
☐ 318 Don Griffin	03	.01	.00
☐ 319 Charles Haley	06	.03	.00
☐ 320 Brent Jones	06	.03	.00
☐ 321 John Taylor	10	.05	.01
☐ 322 Ted Washington	03	.01	.00
☐ 323 Steve Young	12	.06	.01
☐ 324 George Seifert CO	03	.01	.00
☐ 325 Brian Blades	06	.03	.00
☐ 326 Jacob Green	03	.01	.00
☐ 327 Patrick Hunter	03	.01	.00
☐ 328 Tommy Kane	12	.06	.01
☐ 329 Cortez Kennedy	06	.03	.00
☐ 330 Dave Krieg	06	.03	.00
☐ 331 Rufus Porter	03	.01	.00
☐ 332 John L. Williams	06	.03	.00
☐ 333 Tom Flores CO	03	.01	.00
☐ 334 Gary Anderson	06	.03	.00
☐ 335 Mark Carrier	06	.03	.00
☐ 336 Reuben Davis	03	.01	.00
☐ 337 Lawrence Dawsey	12	.06	.01
☐ 338 Keith McCants	06	.03	.00
☐ 339 Vinny Testaverde	08	.04	.01
☐ 340 Broderick Thomas	06	.03	.00
☐ 341 Robert Wilson	06	.03	.00
☐ 342 Sam Wyche CO	03	.01	.00
☐ 343 1991 Teacher of the Year	03	.01	.00
☐ 344 Owners Reject Instant Replay	03	.01	.00
☐ 345 NFL Experience Unveiled	03	.01	.00
☐ 346 Noll Retires Tosses Coin	03	.01	.00
☐ 347 Isaac Curtis Tim McGee Cincinnati Bengals	03	.01	.00
☐ 348 Drew Pearson Michael Irvin Dallas Cowboys	12	.06	.01
☐ 349 Billy Sims Barry Sanders Detroit Lions	30	.15	.03
☐ 350 Kenny Stabler Todd Marinovich Los Angeles Raiders	25	.12	.02
☐ 351 Craig James Leonard Russell New England Patriots	25	.12	.02
☐ 352 Bob Golic Graffiti It's a Sign of Ignorance	03	.01	.00
☐ 353 Pat Harlow Vote, Let Your Choice Be Heard	03	.01	.00
☐ 354 Esera Tuaolo Stand Tall, Be Proud of Your Heritage	03	.01	.00
☐ 355 Mark Schlereth Save The Environment Be a Team Player	10	.05	.01
☐ 356 Trace Armstrong Drug Abuse Stay in Control	03	.01	.00
☐ 357 Eric Bieniemy Save a Life Buckle Up	06	.03	.00
☐ 358 Bill Romanowski Education Stay In School	03	.01	.00
☐ 359 Irv Eatman Exercise Be Active	03	.01	.00
☐ 360 Jonathan Hayes Diabetes Be Your Best	03	.01	.00
☐ 361 Atlanta Falcons Spirit of the Game	03	.01	.00
☐ 362 Chicago Bears Spirit of the Game	03	.01	.00
☐ 363 Dallas Cowboys Spirit of the Game	03	.01	.00
☐ 364 Detroit Lions Spirit of the Game	03	.01	.00
☐ 365 Green Bay Packers Spirit of the Game	03	.01	.00
☐ 366 Los Angeles Rams Spirit of the Game	03	.01	.00
☐ 367 Minnesota Vikings Spirit of the Game	03	.01	.00
☐ 368 New Orleans Saints Spirit of the Game	03	.01	.00
☐ 369 New York Giants Spirit of the Game	03	.01	.00
☐ 370 Philadelphia Eagles Spirit of the Game	03	.01	.00
☐ 371 Phoenix Cardinals Spirit of the Game	03	.01	.00
☐ 372 San Francisco 49ers Spirit of the Game	03	.01	.00
☐ 373 Tampa Bay Buccaneers Spirit of the Game	03	.01	.00
☐ 374 Washington Redskins Spirit of the Game	03	.01	.00

☐ 375	Steve Atwater PB ....06 Denver Broncos	.03	.00
☐ 376	Cornelius Bennett PB .....06 Buffalo Bills	.03	.00
☐ 377	Tim Brown PB ....06 Los Angeles Raiders	.03	.00
☐ 378	Marion Butts PB ....06 San Diego Chargers	.03	.00
☐ 379	Ray Childress PB ....06 Houston Oilers	.03	.00
☐ 380	Mark Clayton PB ....06 Miami Dolphins	.03	.00
☐ 381	Marv Cook PB ....06 New England Patriots	.03	.00
☐ 382	Cris Dishman PB ....06 Houston Oilers	.03	.00
☐ 383	William Fuller PB ....03 Houston Oilers	.01	.00
☐ 384	Gaston Green PB ....10 Denver Broncos	.05	.01
☐ 385	Jeff Jaeger PB ....03 Los Angeles Raiders	.01	.00
☐ 386	Haywood Jeffires PB ....10 Houston Oilers	.05	.01
☐ 387	James Lofton PB ....08 Buffalo Bills	.04	.01
☐ 388	Ronnie Lott PB ....08 Los Angeles Raiders	.04	.01
☐ 389	Karl Mecklenburg PB ......06 Denver Broncos	.03	.00
☐ 390	Warren Moon PB ....12 Houston Oilers	.06	.01
☐ 391	Anthony Munoz PB ....08 Cincinnati Bengals	.04	.01
☐ 392	Dennis Smith PB ....03 Denver Broncos	.01	.00
☐ 393	Neil Smith PB ....03 Kansas City Chiefs	.01	.00
☐ 394	Darryl Talley PB ....06 Buffalo Bills	.03	.00
☐ 395	Derrick Thomas PB ....10 Kansas City Chiefs	.05	.01
☐ 396	Thurman Thomas PB ....17 Buffalo Bills	.08	.01
☐ 397	Greg Townsend PB ....03 Los Angeles Raiders	.01	.00
☐ 398	Richmond Webb PB ....03 Miami Dolphins	.01	.00
☐ 399	Rod Woodson PB ....06 Pittsburgh Steelers	.03	.00
☐ 400	Dan Reeves CO PB ....03 Denver Broncos	.01	.00
☐ SC1	Lem Barney HOF 50	.25	.05
☐ SC2	Al Davis HOF 60	.30	.06
☐ SC3	John Mackey HOF 50	.25	.05
☐ SC4	John Riggins HOF 50	.25	.05
☐ SC5	Super Bowl XXVI 50	.25	.05

1989 Score

This set of 330 football cards was Score's first
football set after two successful years of
baseball card issues. The cards are very similar
in design to the 1989 Score baseball cards.
The cards are standard size, 2 1/2" by 3 1/2",
and have full color on both sides. The front of
the card shows the player in an action photo
whereas the reverse photo of the player is a
portrait. The first 244 cards in the set are
regular player cards. Cards 245-272 are rookie
cards of players drafted in the spring '89 NFL
draft. Other creative subsets within this set are
post-season action (273-275), "combo" cards
showing related players like the Three Amigos
(277-284), all-pro selections (285-309),
"speedburners" (310-317), "predators" (318-
325), and record breakers (326-329). The last
card in the set is a tribute to Tom Landry. The
key rookie cards in this set are Troy Aikman,
Brian Blades, Bubby Brister, Gaston Green,
Michael Irvin, Keith Jackson, Don Majkowski,
Eric Metcalf, Anthony Miller, Chris Miller, Andre
Rison, Mark Rypien, Barry Sanders, Deion
Sanders, Sammie Smith, John Stephens, John
Taylor, Derrick Thomas, Thurman Thomas,
and Rod Woodson.

	MINT	EXC	G-VG
COMPLETE SET (330)	180.00	90.00	18.00
COMMON PLAYER (1-330)	.08	.04	.01
☐ 1 Joe Montana .... 2.00 San Francisco 49ers		1.00	.20
☐ 2 Bo Jackson .... 1.50 Los Angeles Raiders		.75	.15
☐ 3 Boomer Esiason .... .35 Cincinnati Bengals		.17	.03
☐ 4 Roger Craig .... .20		.10	.02

San Francisco 49ers			
☐ 5 Ed Too Tall Jones	.15	.07	.01
Dallas Cowboys			
☐ 6 Phil Simms	.30	.15	.03
New York Giants			
☐ 7 Dan Hampton	.15	.07	.01
Chicago Bears			
☐ 8 John Settle	.50	.25	.05
Atlanta Falcons			
☐ 9 Bernie Kosar	.35	.17	.03
Cleveland Browns			
☐ 10 Al Toon	.25	.12	.02
New York Jets			
☐ 11 Bubby Brister	1.00	.50	.10
Pittsburgh Steelers			
☐ 12 Mark Clayton	.20	.10	.02
Miami Dolphins			
☐ 13 Dan Marino	3.00	1.50	.30
Miami Dolphins			
☐ 14 Joe Morris	.12	.06	.01
New York Giants			
☐ 15 Warren Moon	1.75	.85	.17
Houston Oilers			
☐ 16 Chuck Long	.12	.06	.01
Detroit Lions			
☐ 17 Mark Jackson	.15	.07	.01
Denver Broncos			
☐ 18 Michael Irvin	16.00	8.00	1.60
Dallas Cowboys			
☐ 19 Bruce Smith	.30	.15	.03
Buffalo Bills			
☐ 20 Anthony Carter	.15	.07	.01
Minnesota Vikings			
☐ 21 Charles Haley	.12	.06	.01
San Francisco 49ers			
☐ 22 Dave Duerson	.08	.04	.01
Chicago Bears			
☐ 23 Troy Stradford	.12	.06	.01
Miami Dolphins			
☐ 24 Freeman McNeil	.15	.07	.01
New York Jets			
☐ 25 Jerry Gray	.08	.04	.01
Los Angeles Rams			
☐ 26 Bill Maas	.08	.04	.01
Kansas City Chiefs			
☐ 27 Chris Chandler	.30	.15	.03
Indianapolis Colts			
☐ 28 Tom Newberry	.25	.12	.02
Los Angeles Rams			
☐ 29 Albert Lewis	.20	.10	.02
Kansas City Chiefs			
☐ 30 Jay Schroeder	.25	.12	.02
Los Angeles Raiders			
☐ 31 Dalton Hilliard	.20	.10	.02
New Orleans Saints			
☐ 32 Tony Eason	.12	.06	.01
New England Patriots			

☐ 33 Rick Donnelly UER	.08	.04	.01
(229.11 yards per punt)			
Atlanta Falcons			
☐ 34 Herschel Walker	.75	.35	.07
Dallas Cowboys			
☐ 35 Wesley Walker	.15	.07	.01
New York Jets			
☐ 36 Chris Doleman	.15	.07	.01
Minnesota Vikings			
☐ 37 Pat Swilling	.50	.25	.05
New Orleans Saints			
☐ 38 Joey Browner	.20	.10	.02
Minnesota Vikings			
☐ 39 Shane Conlan	.25	.12	.02
Buffalo Bills			
☐ 40 Mike Tomczak	.15	.07	.01
Chicago Bears			
☐ 41 Webster Slaughter	.25	.12	.02
Cleveland Browns			
☐ 42 Ray Donaldson	.08	.04	.01
Indianapolis Colts			
☐ 43 Christian Okoye	1.25	.60	.12
Kansas City Chiefs			
☐ 44 John Bosa	.08	.04	.01
Miami Dolphins			
☐ 45 Aaron Cox	.40	.20	.04
Los Angeles Rams			
☐ 46 Bobby Hebert	.15	.07	.01
New Orleans Saints			
☐ 47 Carl Banks	.15	.07	.01
New York Giants			
☐ 48 Jeff Fuller	.12	.06	.01
San Francisco 49ers			
☐ 49 Gerald Willhite	.08	.04	.01
Denver Broncos			
☐ 50 Mike Singletary	.20	.10	.02
Chicago Bears			
☐ 51 Stanley Morgan	.15	.07	.01
New England Patriots			
☐ 52 Mark Bavaro	.12	.06	.01
New York Giants			
☐ 53 Mickey Shuler	.08	.04	.01
New York Jets			
☐ 54 Keith Millard	.12	.06	.01
Minnesota Vikings			
☐ 55 Andre Tippett	.12	.06	.01
New England Patriots			
☐ 56 Vance Johnson	.15	.07	.01
Denver Broncos			
☐ 57 Bennie Blades	.80	.40	.08
Detroit Lions			
☐ 58 Tim Harris	.15	.07	.01
Green Bay Packers			
☐ 59 Hanford Dixon	.08	.04	.01
Cleveland Browns			
☐ 60 Chris Miller	10.00	5.00	1.00
Atlanta Falcons			

☐ 61 Cornelius Bennett .... .75	.35	.07
Buffalo Bills		
☐ 62 Neal Anderson 2.00	1.00	.20
Chicago Bears		
☐ 63 Ickey Woods UER .... .50	.25	.05
(Jersey is 31 but		
listed as 30		
on card back)		
Cincinnati Bengals		
☐ 64 Gary Anderson .... .15	.07	.01
San Diego Chargers		
☐ 65 Vaughan Johnson .... .60	.30	.06
New Orleans Saints		
☐ 66 Ronnie Lippett .... .08	.04	.01
New England Patriots		
☐ 67 Mike Quick .... .12	.06	.01
Philadelphia Eagles		
☐ 68 Roy Green .... .15	.07	.01
Phoenix Cardinals		
☐ 69 Tim Krumrie .... .08	.04	.01
Cincinnati Bengals		
☐ 70 Mark Malone .... .12	.06	.01
San Diego Chargers		
☐ 71 James Jones .... .12	.06	.01
Detroit Lions		
☐ 72 Cris Carter 1.50	.75	.15
Philadelphia Eagles		
☐ 73 Ricky Nattiel .... .15	.07	.01
Denver Broncos		
☐ 74 Jim Arnold UER .... .08	.04	.01
(238.83 yards per punt)		
Detroit Lions		
☐ 75 Randall Cunningham 1.00	.50	.10
Philadelphia Eagles		
☐ 76 John L. Williams .... .35	.17	.03
Seattle Seahawks		
☐ 77 Paul Gruber .... .35	.17	.03
Tampa Bay Buccaneers		
☐ 78 Rod Woodson .... .90	.45	.09
Pittsburgh Steelers		
☐ 79 Ray Childress .... .12	.06	.01
Houston Oilers		
☐ 80 Doug Williams .... .15	.07	.01
Washington Redskins		
☐ 81 Deron Cherry .... .12	.06	.01
Kansas City Chiefs		
☐ 82 John Offerdahl .... .12	.06	.01
Miami Dolphins		
☐ 83 Louis Lipps .... .12	.06	.01
Pittsburgh Steelers		
☐ 84 Neil Lomax .... .12	.06	.01
Phoenix Cardinals		
☐ 85 Wade Wilson .... .15	.07	.01
Minnesota Vikings		
☐ 86 Tim Brown 1.75	.85	.17
Los Angeles Raiders		
☐ 87 Chris Hinton .... .12	.06	.01

Indianapolis Colts		
☐ 88 Stump Mitchell .... .12	.06	.01
Phoenix Cardinals		
☐ 89 Tunch Ilkin .... .15	.07	.01
Pittsburgh Steelers		
☐ 90 Steve Pelluer .... .12	.06	.01
Dallas Cowboys		
☐ 91 Brian Noble .... .08	.04	.01
Green Bay Packers		
☐ 92 Reggie White .... .45	.22	.04
Philadelphia Eagles		
☐ 93 Aundray Bruce .... .30	.15	.03
Atlanta Falcons		
☐ 94 Garry James .... .12	.06	.01
Detroit Lions		
☐ 95 Drew Hill .... .25	.12	.02
Houston Oilers		
☐ 96 Anthony Munoz .... .20	.10	.02
Cincinnati Bengals		
☐ 97 James Wilder .... .12	.06	.01
Tampa Bay Buccaneers		
☐ 98 Dexter Manley .... .12	.06	.01
Washington Redskins		
☐ 99 Lee Williams .... .12	.06	.01
San Diego Chargers		
☐ 100 Dave Krieg .... .15	.07	.01
Seattle Seahawks		
☐ 101A Keith Jackson ERR 3.00	1.50	.30
(Listed as 84		
on card back)		
Philadelphia Eagles		
☐ 101B Keith Jackson COR ... 4.00	2.00	.40
(Listed as 88		
on card back)		
Philadelphia Eagles		
☐ 102 Luis Sharpe .... .08	.04	.01
Phoenix Cardinals		
☐ 103 Kevin Greene .... .15	.07	.01
Los Angeles Rams		
☐ 104 Duane Bickett .... .12	.06	.01
Indianapolis Colts		
☐ 105 Mark Rypien 20.00	10.00	2.00
Washington Redskins		
☐ 106 Curt Warner .... .15	.07	.01
Seattle Seahawks		
☐ 107 Jacob Green .... .12	.06	.01
Seattle Seahawks		
☐ 108 Gary Clark .... .50	.25	.05
Washington Redskins		
☐ 109 Bruce Matthews .... .40	.20	.04
Houston Oilers		
☐ 110 Bill Fralic .... .12	.06	.01
Atlanta Falcons		
☐ 111 Bill Bates .... .12	.06	.01
Dallas Cowboys		
☐ 112 Jeff Bryant .... .08	.04	.01
Seattle Seahawks		

□ 113	Charles Mann	.12	.06	.01
	Washington Redskins			
□ 114	Richard Dent	.15	.07	.01
	Chicago Bears			
□ 115	Bruce Hill	.50	.25	.05
	Tampa Bay Buccaneers			
□ 116	Mark May	.20	.10	.02
	Washington Redskins			
□ 117	Mark Collins	.35	.17	.03
	New York Giants			
□ 118	Ron Holmes	.12	.06	.01
	Tampa Bay Buccaneers			
□ 119	Scott Case	.25	.12	.02
	Atlanta Falcons			
□ 120	Tom Rathman	.15	.07	.01
	San Francisco 49ers			
□ 121	Dennis McKinnon	.08	.04	.01
	Chicago Bears			
□ 122A	Ricky Sanders ERR	.40	.20	.04
	(Listed as 46			
	on card back)			
	Washington Redskins			
□ 122B	Ricky Sanders COR	1.25	.60	.12
	(Listed as 83			
	on card back)			
	Washington Redskins			
□ 123	Michael Carter	.12	.06	.01
	San Francisco 49ers			
□ 124	Ozzie Newsome	.20	.10	.02
	Cleveland Browns			
□ 125	Irving Fryar UER	.15	.07	.01
	New England Patriots			
	("wide reveiver")			
□ 126A	Ron Hall ERR	.25	.12	.02
	Tampa Bay Buccaneers			
	(Both photos actually			
	someone else, a black			
	player, whereas			
	Hall is white)			
□ 126B	Ron Hall COR	1.00	.50	.10
	Tampa Bay Buccaneers			
□ 127	Clay Matthews	.12	.06	.01
	Cleveland Browns			
□ 128	Leonard Marshall	.12	.06	.01
	New York Giants			
□ 129	Kevin Mack	.15	.07	.01
	Cleveland Browns			
□ 130	Art Monk	.50	.25	.05
	Washington Redskins			
□ 131	Garin Veris	.08	.04	.01
	New England Patriots			
□ 132	Steve Jordan	.12	.06	.01
	Minnesota Vikings			
□ 133	Frank Minnifield	.12	.06	.01
	Cleveland Browns			
□ 134	Eddie Brown	.15	.07	.01
	Cincinnati Bengals			
□ 135	Stacey Bailey	.08	.04	.01
	Atlanta Falcons			
□ 136	Rickey Jackson	.20	.10	.02
	New Orleans Saints			
□ 137	Henry Ellard	.15	.07	.01
	Los Angeles Rams			
□ 138	Jim Burt	.08	.04	.01
	New York Giants			
□ 139	Jerome Brown	.15	.07	.01
	Philadelphia Eagles			
□ 140	Rodney Holman	.50	.25	.05
	Cincinnati Bengals			
□ 141	Sammy Winder	.12	.06	.01
	Denver Broncos			
□ 142	Marcus Cotton	.25	.12	.02
	Atlanta Falcons			
□ 143	Jim Jeffcoat	.08	.04	.01
	Dallas Cowboys			
□ 144	Rueben Mayes	.12	.06	.01
	New Orleans Saints			
□ 145	Jim McMahon	.15	.07	.01
	Chicago Bears			
□ 146	Reggie Williams	.12	.06	.01
	Cincinnati Bengals			
□ 147	John Anderson	.08	.04	.01
	Green Bay Packers			
□ 148	Harris Barton	.15	.07	.01
	San Francisco 49ers			
□ 149	Phillip Epps	.12	.06	.01
	Green Bay Packers			
□ 150	Jay Hilgenberg	.12	.06	.01
	Chicago Bears			
□ 151	Earl Ferrell	.08	.04	.01
	Phoenix Cardinals			
□ 152	Andre Reed	.75	.35	.07
	Buffalo Bills			
□ 153	Dennis Gentry	.08	.04	.01
	Chicago Bears			
□ 154	Max Montoya	.12	.06	.01
	Cincinnati Bengals			
□ 155	Darrin Nelson	.12	.06	.01
	Minnesota Vikings			
□ 156	Jeff Chadwick	.08	.04	.01
	Detroit Lions			
□ 157	James Brooks	.15	.07	.01
	Cincinnati Bengals			
□ 158	Keith Bishop	.08	.04	.01
	Denver Broncos			
□ 159	Robert Awalt	.12	.06	.01
	Phoenix Cardinals			
□ 160	Marty Lyons	.12	.06	.01
	New York Jets			
□ 161	Johnny Hector	.12	.06	.01
	New York Jets			
□ 162	Tony Casillas	.25	.12	.02
	Atlanta Falcons			
□ 163	Kyle Clifton	.30	.15	.03

New York Jets			
☐ 164 Cody Risien	.08	.04	.01
Cleveland Browns			
☐ 165 Jamie Holland	.15	.07	.01
San Diego Chargers			
☐ 166 Merril Hoge	.50	.25	.05
Pittsburgh Steelers			
☐ 167 Chris Spielman	1.00	.50	.10
Detroit Lions			
☐ 168 Carlos Carson	.12	.06	.01
Kansas City Chiefs			
☐ 169 Jerry Ball	.35	.17	.03
Detroit Lions			
☐ 170 Don Majkowski	3.00	1.50	.30
Green Bay Packers			
☐ 171 Everson Walls	.12	.06	.01
Dallas Cowboys			
☐ 172 Mike Rozier	.15	.07	.01
Houston Oilers			
☐ 173 Matt Millen	.12	.06	.01
Los Angeles Raiders			
☐ 174 Karl Mecklenburg	.15	.07	.01
Denver Broncos			
☐ 175 Paul Palmer	.12	.06	.01
Kansas City Chiefs			
☐ 176 Brian Blades UER	4.00	2.00	.40
(Photo on back is			
reversed negative)			
Seattle Seahawks			
☐ 177 Brent Fullwood	.20	.10	.02
Green Bay Packers			
☐ 178 Anthony Miller	3.00	1.50	.30
San Diego Chargers			
☐ 179 Brian Sochia	.15	.07	.01
Miami Dolphins			
☐ 180 Stephen Baker	.80	.40	.08
New York Giants			
☐ 181 Jesse Solomon	.08	.04	.01
Minnesota Vikings			
☐ 182 John Grimsley	.08	.04	.01
Houston Oilers			
☐ 183 Timmy Newsome	.08	.04	.01
Dallas Cowboys			
☐ 184 Steve Sewell	.50	.25	.05
Denver Broncos			
☐ 185 Dean Biasucci	.08	.04	.01
Indianapolis Colts			
☐ 186 Alonzo Highsmith	.12	.06	.01
Houston Oilers			
☐ 187 Randy Grimes	.15	.07	.01
Tampa Bay Buccaneers			
☐ 188A Mark Carrier ERR	2.00	1.00	.20
(Photo on back is			
actually Bruce Hill)			
Tampa Bay Buccaneers			
☐ 188B Mark Carrier COR	2.50	1.25	.25
(Wearing helmet in			

photo on back)			
Tampa Bay Buccaneers			
☐ 189 Vann McElroy	.08	.04	.01
Los Angeles Raiders			
☐ 190 Greg Bell	.12	.06	.01
Los Angeles Rams			
☐ 191 Quinn Early	.30	.15	.03
San Diego Chargers			
☐ 192 Lawrence Taylor	.60	.30	.06
New York Giants			
☐ 193 Albert Bentley	.12	.06	.01
Indianapolis Colts			
☐ 194 Ernest Givins	.40	.20	.04
Houston Oilers			
☐ 195 Jackie Slater	.12	.06	.01
Los Angeles Rams			
☐ 196 Jim Sweeney	.15	.07	.01
New York Jets			
☐ 197 Freddie Joe Nunn	.08	.04	.01
Phoenix Cardinals			
☐ 198 Keith Byars	.15	.07	.01
Philadelphia Eagles			
☐ 199 Hardy Nickerson	.15	.07	.01
Pittsburgh Steelers			
☐ 200 Steve Beuerlein	1.75	.85	.17
Los Angeles Raiders			
☐ 201 Bruce Armstrong	.20	.10	.02
New England Patriots			
☐ 202 Lionel Manuel	.12	.06	.01
New York Giants			
☐ 203 J.T. Smith	.12	.06	.01
Phoenix Cardinals			
☐ 204 Mark Ingram	1.00	.50	.10
New York Giants			
☐ 205 Fred Smerlas	.12	.06	.01
Buffalo Bills			
☐ 206 Bryan Hinkle	.15	.07	.01
Pittsburgh Steelers			
☐ 207 Steve McMichael	.12	.06	.01
Chicago Bears			
☐ 208 Nick Lowery	.12	.06	.01
Kansas City Chiefs			
☐ 209 Jack Trudeau	.12	.06	.01
Indianapolis Colts			
☐ 210 Lorenzo Hampton	.12	.06	.01
Miami Dolphins			
☐ 211 Thurman Thomas	35.00	17.50	3.50
Buffalo Bills			
☐ 212 Steve Young	.50	.25	.05
San Francisco 49ers			
☐ 213 James Lofton	.45	.22	.04
Los Angeles Raiders			
☐ 214 Jim Covert	.12	.06	.01
Chicago Bears			
☐ 215 Ronnie Lott	.35	.17	.03
San Francisco 49ers			
☐ 216 Stephone Paige	.12	.06	.01

Kansas City Chiefs
- ☐ 217 Mark Duper .... .15 .07 .01
  Miami Dolphins
- ☐ 218A Willie Gault ERR .... .30 .15 .03
  (Front photo actually
  93 Greg Townsend)
  Los Angeles Raiders
- ☐ 218B Willie Gault COR .... .90 .45 .09
  (83 clearly visible)
  Los Angeles Raiders
- ☐ 219 Ken Ruettgers .... .30 .15 .03
  Green Bay Packers
- ☐ 220 Kevin Ross .... .35 .17 .03
  Kansas City Chiefs
- ☐ 221 Jerry Rice .... 2.50 1.25 .25
  San Francisco 49ers
- ☐ 222 Billy Ray Smith .... .12 .06 .01
  San Diego Chargers
- ☐ 223 Jim Kelly .... 2.50 1.25 .25
  Buffalo Bills
- ☐ 224 Vinny Testaverde .... .20 .10 .02
  Tampa Bay Buccaneers
- ☐ 225 Steve Largent .... .75 .35 .07
  Seattle Seahawks
- ☐ 226 Warren Williams .... .25 .12 .02
  Pittsburgh Steelers
- ☐ 227 Morten Andersen .... .12 .06 .01
  New Orleans Saints
- ☐ 228 Bill Brooks .... .12 .06 .01
  Indianapolis Colts
- ☐ 229 Reggie Langhorne .... .35 .17 .03
  Cleveland Browns
- ☐ 230 Pepper Johnson .... .12 .06 .01
  New York Giants
- ☐ 231 Pat Leahy .... .12 .06 .01
  New York Jets
- ☐ 232 Fred Marion .... .08 .04 .01
  New England Patriots
- ☐ 233 Gary Zimmerman .... .08 .04 .01
  Minnesota Vikings
- ☐ 234 Marcus Allen .... .25 .12 .02
  Los Angeles Raiders
- ☐ 235 Gaston Green .... 4.50 2.25 .45
  Los Angeles Rams
- ☐ 236 John Stephens .... 1.25 .60 .12
  New England Patriots
- ☐ 237 Terry Kinard .... .12 .06 .01
  New York Giants
- ☐ 238 John Taylor .... 5.00 2.50 .50
  San Francisco 49ers
- ☐ 239 Brian Bosworth .... .15 .07 .01
  Seattle Seahawks
- ☐ 240 Anthony Toney .... .08 .04 .01
  Philadelphia Eagles
- ☐ 241 Ken O'Brien .... .25 .12 .02
  New York Jets
- ☐ 242 Howie Long .... .15 .07 .01

Los Angeles Raiders
- ☐ 243 Doug Flutie .... .35 .17 .03
  New England Patriots
- ☐ 244 Jim Everett .... .40 .20 .04
  Los Angeles Rams
- ☐ 245 Broderick Thomas .... 1.50 .75 .15
  Tampa Bay Buccaneers
- ☐ 246 Deion Sanders .... 9.00 4.50 .90
  Atlanta Falcons
- ☐ 247 Donnell Woolford .... .45 .22 .04
  Chicago Bears
- ☐ 248 Wayne Martin .... .20 .10 .02
  New Orleans Saints
- ☐ 249 David Williams .... .20 .10 .02
  Houston Oilers
- ☐ 250 Bill Hawkins .... .15 .07 .01
  Los Angeles Rams
- ☐ 251 Eric Hill .... .25 .12 .02
  Phoenix Cardinals
- ☐ 252 Burt Grossman .... .35 .17 .03
  San Diego Chargers
- ☐ 253 Tracy Rocker .... .25 .12 .02
  Washington Redskins
- ☐ 254 Steve Wisniewski .... .50 .25 .05
  Los Angeles Raiders
- ☐ 255 Jessie Small .... .30 .15 .03
  Philadelphia Eagles
- ☐ 256 David Braxton .... .15 .07 .01
  Minnesota Vikings
- ☐ 257 Barry Sanders 50.00 25.00 5.00
  Detroit Lions
- ☐ 258 Derrick Thomas 10.00 5.00 1.00
  Kansas City Chiefs
- ☐ 259 Eric Metcalf .... 1.00 .50 .10
  Cleveland Browns
- ☐ 260 Keith DeLong .... .35 .17 .03
  San Francisco 49ers
- ☐ 261 Hart Lee Dykes .... .40 .20 .04
  New England Patriots
- ☐ 262 Sammie Smith .... 2.25 1.10 .22
  Miami Dolphins
- ☐ 263 Steve Atwater .... 2.00 1.00 .20
  Denver Broncos
- ☐ 264 Eric Ball .... .30 .15 .03
  Cincinnati Bengals
- ☐ 265 Don Beebe .... 2.50 1.25 .25
  Buffalo Bills
- ☐ 266 Brian Williams .... .15 .07 .01
  New York Giants
- ☐ 267 Jeff Lageman .... .60 .30 .06
  New York Jets
- ☐ 268 Tim Worley .... .20 .10 .02
  Pittsburgh Steelers
- ☐ 269 Tony Mandarich .... .40 .20 .04
  Green Bay Packers
- ☐ 270 Troy Aikman 28.00 14.00 2.80
  Dallas Cowboys

☐ 271 Andy Heck	.20	.10	.02
Seattle Seahawks			
☐ 272 Andre Rison	10.00	5.00	1.00
Indianapolis Colts			
☐ 273 AFC Championship	.20	.10	.02
Bengals over Bills			
(Ickey Woods and			
Boomer Esiason)			
☐ 274 NFC Championship	.50	.25	.05
49ers over Bears			
(Joe Montana)			
☐ 275 Super Bowl XXIII	.75	.35	.07
49ers over Bengals			
(Joe Montana and			
Jerry Rice)			
☐ 276 Rodney Carter	.15	.07	.01
Pittsburgh Steelers			
☐ 277 Mark Jackson,	.15	.07	.01
Vance Johnson,			
and Ricky Nattiel			
Denver Broncos			
☐ 278 John L. Williams	.12	.06	.01
and Curt Warner			
Seattle Seahawks			
☐ 279 Joe Montana and	1.00	.50	.10
Jerry Rice			
San Francisco 49ers			
☐ 280 Roy Green and	.12	.06	.01
Neil Lomax			
Phoenix Cardinals			
☐ 281 Randall Cunningham	.40	.20	.04
and Keith Jackson			
Philadelphia Eagles			
☐ 282 Chris Doleman and	.12	.06	.01
Keith Millard			
Minnesota Vikings			
☐ 283 Mark Duper and	.15	.07	.01
Mark Clayton			
Miami Dolphins			
☐ 284 Marcus Allen and	.75	.35	.07
Bo Jackson			
Los Angeles Raiders			
☐ 285 Frank Minnifield AP	.12	.06	.01
Cleveland Browns			
☐ 286 Bruce Matthews AP	.12	.06	.01
Houston Oilers			
☐ 287 Joey Browner AP	.12	.06	.01
Minnesota Vikings			
☐ 288 Jay Hilgenberg AP	.12	.06	.01
Chicago Bears			
☐ 289 Carl Lee AP	.20	.10	.02
Minnesota Vikings			
☐ 290 Scott Norwood AP	.25	.12	.02
Buffalo Bills			
☐ 291 John Taylor AP	.75	.35	.07
San Francisco 49ers			
☐ 292 Jerry Rice AP	.75	.35	.07

San Francisco 49ers			
☐ 293A Keith Jackson AP ERR	.90	.45	.09
(Listed as 84			
on card back)			
Philadelphia Eagles			
☐ 293B Keith Jackson AP COR	2.00	1.00	.20
(Listed as 88			
on card back)			
Philadelphia Eagles			
☐ 294 Gary Zimmerman AP	.12	.06	.01
Minnesota Vikings			
☐ 295 Lawrence Taylor AP	.20	.10	.02
New York Giants			
☐ 296 Reggie White AP	.15	.07	.01
Philadelphia Eagles			
☐ 297 Roger Craig AP	.15	.07	.01
San Francisco 49ers			
☐ 298 Boomer Esiason AP	.20	.10	.02
Cincinnati Bengals			
☐ 299 Cornelius Bennett AP	.25	.12	.02
Buffalo Bills			
☐ 300 Mike Horan AP	.08	.04	.01
Denver Broncos			
☐ 301 Deron Cherry AP	.12	.06	.01
Kansas City Chiefs			
☐ 302 Tom Newberry AP	.12	.06	.01
Los Angeles Rams			
☐ 303 Mike Singletary AP	.15	.07	.01
Chicago Bears			
☐ 304 Shane Conlan AP	.15	.07	.01
Buffalo Bills			
☐ 305A Tim Brown ERR AP	.65	.30	.06
(Photo on front act-			
ually 80 James Lofton)			
Los Angeles Raiders			
☐ 305B Tim Brown COR AP	1.00	.50	.10
(Dark jersey 81)			
Los Angeles Raiders			
☐ 306 Henry Ellard AP	.12	.06	.01
Los Angeles Rams			
☐ 307 Bruce Smith AP	.15	.07	.01
Buffalo Bills			
☐ 308 Tim Krumrie AP	.08	.04	.01
Cincinnati Bengals			
☐ 309 Anthony Munoz AP	.12	.06	.01
Cincinnati Bengals			
☐ 310 Darrell Green SPD	.25	.12	.02
Washington Redskins			
☐ 311 Anthony Miller SPD	.50	.25	.05
San Diego Chargers			
☐ 312 Wesley Walker SPD	.12	.06	.01
New York Jets			
☐ 313 Ron Brown SPD	.12	.06	.01
Los Angeles Rams			
☐ 314 Bo Jackson SPD	.65	.30	.06
Los Angeles Raiders			
☐ 315 Philip Epps SPD	.08	.04	.01

Green Bay Packers
- ☐ 316A Eric Thomas ERR SPD .35   .17   .03
  (Listed as 31
  on card back)
  Cincinnati Bengals
- ☐ 316B Eric Thomas COR SPD 1.00   .50   .10
  (Listed as 22
  on card back)
  Cincinnati Bengals
- ☐ 317 Herschel Walker SPD ..... .40   .20   .04
  Dallas Cowboys
- ☐ 318 Jacob Green PRED .... .12   .06   .01
  Seattle Seahawks
- ☐ 319 Andre Tippett PRED .... .12   .06   .01
  New England Patriots
- ☐ 320 Freddie Joe Nunn PRED .08   .04   .01
  Phoenix Cardinals
- ☐ 321 Reggie White PRED .... .15   .07   .01
  Philadelphia Eagles
- ☐ 322 Lawrence Taylor PRED ..20   .10   .02
  New York Giants
- ☐ 323 Greg Townsend PRED ...12   .06   .01
  Los Angeles Raiders
- ☐ 324 Tim Harris PRED .... .12   .06   .01
  Green Bay Packers
- ☐ 325 Bruce Smith PRED .... .15   .07   .01
  Buffalo Bills
- ☐ 326 Tony Dorsett RB .... .20   .10   .02
  Denver Broncos
- ☐ 327 Steve Largent RB .... .30   .15   .03
  Seattle Seahawks
- ☐ 328 Tim Brown RB .... .50   .25   .05
  Los Angeles Raiders
- ☐ 329 Joe Montana RB .... .60   .30   .06
  San Francisco 49ers
- ☐ 330 Tom Landry Tribute .... .75   .35   .07
  Dallas Cowboys

1989 Score Supplemental

The 1989 Score Football Supplemental set contains 110 standard-size (2 1/2" by 3 1/2") cards, numbered with the suffix "S". The fronts have purple borders; otherwise, the cards are identical to the regular issue 1989 Score football cards. This set is notable for the popular Bo Jackson football/baseball card (number 384S), similar to card number 697 in the 1990 Score baseball set. These cards were distributed

only as a complete boxed set. The key rookies in this set are Bobby Humphrey, Dave Meggett, Rodney Peete, Timm Rosenbach, Sterling Sharpe, and Steve Walsh.

	MINT	EXC	G-VG
COMPLETE SET (110)	18.00	9.00	1.80
COMMON PLAYER (331-440) ...	.05	.02	.00
☐ 331S Herschel Walker .... .40		.15	.03
Minnesota Vikings			
☐ 332S Allen Pinkett	.50	.25	.05
Houston Oilers			
☐ 333S Sterling Sharpe 3.00		1.50	.30
Green Bay Packers			
☐ 334S Alvin Walton	.15	.07	.01
Washington Redskins			
☐ 335S Frank Reich	.20	.10	.02
Buffalo Bills			
☐ 336S Jim Thornton	.20	.10	.02
Chicago Bears			
☐ 337S David Fulcher	.08	.04	.01
Cincinnati Bengals			
☐ 338S Raul Allegre	.05	.02	.00
New York Giants			
☐ 339S John Elway	.35	.17	.03
Denver Broncos			
☐ 340S Michael Cofer	.05	.02	.00
Detroit Lions			
☐ 341S Jim Skow	.10	.05	.01
Cincinnati Bengals			
☐ 342S Steve DeBerg	.12	.06	.01
Kansas City Chiefs			
☐ 343S Mervyn Fernandez	.35	.17	.03
Los Angeles Raiders			
☐ 344S Mike Lansford	.05	.02	.00
Los Angeles Rams			
☐ 345S Reggie Roby	.08	.04	.01
Miami Dolphins			
☐ 346S Raymond Clayborn	.05	.02	.00
New England Patriots			

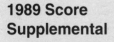

☐ 347S Lonzell Hill 12	.06	.01
New Orleans Saints		
☐ 348S Ottis Anderson 12	.06	.01
New York Giants		
☐ 349S Erik McMillan 35	.17	.03
New York Jets		
☐ 350S Al Harris 10	.05	.01
Philadelphia Eagles		
☐ 351S Jack Del Rio 10	.05	.01
Dallas Cowboys		
☐ 352S Gary Anderson 05	.02	.00
Pittsburgh Steelers		
☐ 353S Jim McMahon 12	.06	.01
San Diego Chargers		
☐ 354S Keena Turner 08	.04	.01
San Francisco 49ers		
☐ 355S Tony Woods 15	.07	.01
Seattle Seahawks		
☐ 356S Donald Igwebuike 05	.02	.00
Tampa Bay Buccaneers		
☐ 357S Gerald Riggs 10	.05	.01
Washington Redskins		
☐ 358S Eddie Murray 08	.04	.01
Detroit Lions		
☐ 359S Dino Hackett 05	.02	.00
Kansas City Chiefs		
☐ 360S Brad Muster 60	.30	.06
Chicago Bears		
☐ 361S Paul Palmer 08	.04	.01
Dallas Cowboys		
☐ 362S Jerry Robinson 08	.04	.01
Los Angeles Raiders		
☐ 363S Simon Fletcher 25	.12	.02
Denver Broncos		
☐ 364S Tommy Kramer 10	.05	.01
Minnesota Vikings		
☐ 365S Jim C. Jensen 12	.06	.01
Miami Dolphins		
☐ 366S Lorenzo White 30	.15	.03
Houston Oilers		
☐ 367S Fredd Young 08	.04	.01
Indianapolis Colts		
☐ 368S Ron Jaworski 08	.04	.01
Kansas City Chiefs		
☐ 369S Mel Owens 12	.06	.01
Los Angeles Rams		
☐ 370S Dave Waymer 05	.02	.00
New Orleans Saints		
☐ 371S Sean Landeta 05	.02	.00
New York Giants		
☐ 372S Sam Mills 15	.07	.01
New Orleans Saints		
☐ 373S Todd Blackledge 08	.04	.01
Pittsburgh Steelers		
☐ 374S Jo Jo Townsell 08	.04	.01
New York Jets		
☐ 375S Ron Wolfley 05	.02	.00

Phoenix Cardinals		
☐ 376S Ralf Mojsiejenko 05	.02	.00
Washington Redskins		
☐ 377S Eric Wright 05	.02	.00
San Francisco 49ers		
☐ 378S Nesby Glasgow 05	.02	.00
Seattle Seahawks		
☐ 379S Darryl Talley 12	.06	.01
Buffalo Bills		
☐ 380S Eric Allen 20	.10	.02
Philadelphia Eagles		
☐ 381S Dennis Smith 10	.05	.01
Denver Broncos		
☐ 382S John Tice 05	.02	.00
New Orleans Saints		
☐ 383S Jesse Solomon 05	.02	.00
Dallas Cowboys		
☐ 384S Bo Jackson 3.00	1.50	.30
(FB/BB Pose)		
Los Angeles Raiders		
☐ 385S Mike Merriweather 08	.04	.01
Minnesota Vikings		
☐ 386S Maurice Carthon 05	.02	.00
New York Giants		
☐ 387S Dave Grayson 15	.07	.01
Cleveland Browns		
☐ 388S Wilber Marshall 10	.05	.01
Washington Redskins		
☐ 389S David Wyman 10	.05	.01
Seattle Seahawks		
☐ 390S Thomas Everett 15	.07	.01
Pittsburgh Steelers		
☐ 391S Alex Gordon 05	.02	.00
New York Giants		
☐ 392S D.J. Dozier 25	.12	.02
Minnesota Vikings		
☐ 393S Scott Radecic 10	.05	.01
Buffalo Bills		
☐ 394S Eric Thomas 10	.05	.01
Cincinnati Bengals		
☐ 395S Mike Gann 08	.04	.01
Atlanta Falcons		
☐ 396S William Perry 10	.05	.01
Chicago Bears		
☐ 397S Carl Hairston 08	.04	.01
Cleveland Browns		
☐ 398S Billy Ard 15	.07	.01
Green Bay Packers		
☐ 399S Donnell Thompson 05	.02	.00
Indianapolis Colts		
☐ 400S Mike Webster 10	.05	.01
Kansas City Chiefs		
☐ 401S Scott Davis 20	.10	.02
Los Angeles Raiders		
☐ 402S Sean Farrell 05	.02	.00
New England Patriots		
☐ 403S Mike Golic 15	.07	.01

Philadelphia Eagles
☐ 404S Mike Kenn ....08 .04 .01
Atlanta Falcons
☐ 405S Keith Van Horne ....15 .07 .01
Chicago Bears
☐ 406S Bob Golic ....08 .04 .01
Los Angeles Raiders
☐ 407S Neil Smith ....30 .15 .03
Kansas City Chiefs
☐ 408S Dermontti Dawson ....12 .06 .01
Pittsburgh Steelers
☐ 409S Leslie O'Neal ....12 .06 .01
San Diego Chargers
☐ 410S Matt Bahr ....05 .02 .01
Cleveland Browns
☐ 411S Guy McIntyre ....15 .07 .01
San Francisco 49ers
☐ 412S Bryan Millard ....10 .05 .01
Seattle Seahawks
☐ 413S Joe Jacoby ....08 .04 .01
Washington Redskins
☐ 414S Rob Taylor ....15 .07 .01
Tampa Bay Buccaneers
☐ 415S Tony Zendejas ....05 .02 .00
Houston Oilers
☐ 416S Vai Sikahema ....08 .04 .01
Phoenix Cardinals
☐ 417S Gary Reasons ....20 .10 .02
New York Giants
☐ 418S Shawn Collins ....25 .12 .02
Atlanta Falcons
☐ 419S Mark Green ....15 .07 .01
Chicago Bears
☐ 420S Courtney Hall ....15 .07 .01
San Diego Chargers
☐ 421S Bobby Humphrey ...... 3.00 1.50 .30
Denver Broncos
☐ 422S Myron Guyton ....12 .06 .01
New York Giants
☐ 423S Darryl Ingram ....15 .07 .01
Minnesota Vikings
☐ 424S Chris Jacke ....10 .05 .01
Green Bay Packers
☐ 425S Keith Jones ....10 .05 .01
Atlanta Falcons
☐ 426S Robert Massey ....12 .06 .01
New Orleans Saints
☐ 427S Bubba McDowell ....20 .10 .02
Houston Oilers
☐ 428S Dave Meggett .... 2.00 1.00 .20
New York Giants
☐ 429S Louis Oliver ....20 .10 .02
Miami Dolphins
☐ 430S Danny Peebles ....08 .04 .01
Tampa Bay Buccaneers
☐ 431S Rodney Peete ....80 .40 .08
Detroit Lions

☐ 432S Jeff Query ....25 .12 .02
Green Bay Packers
☐ 433S Timm Rosenbach UER .75 .35 .07
Phoenix Cardinals
(Photo actually
Gary Hogeboom)
☐ 434S Frank Stams ....20 .10 .02
Los Angeles Rams
☐ 435S Lawyer Tillman ....20 .10 .02
Cleveland Browns
☐ 436S Billy Joe Tolliver ....40 .20 .04
San Diego Chargers
☐ 437S Floyd Turner ....30 .15 .03
New Orleans Saints
☐ 438S Steve Walsh ....80 .40 .08
Dallas Cowboys
☐ 439S Joe Wolf ....12 .06 .01
Phoenix Cardinals
☐ 440S Trace Armstrong ....20 .10 .02
Chicago Bears

1990 Score

The 1990 Score football set was issued in two separate series each featuring 330 standard-size (2 1/2" by 3 1/2") cards. The fronts have sharp color action photos and multicolored borders; the vertically oriented backs have large color mug shots and brief stats. Cards numbered 289-310 are draft picks, 311-320 are Hot Guns (HG), and 321-330 are Ground Force (GF). The Hot Gun and Ground Force cards indicate that there are 12 in each of these attractive subsets; however, only ten of each were included in this first series as the last two were saved for inclusion in Score's second series. The key rookie cards in the first

series are John Friesz, Rodney Hampton, Blair Thomas, and Andre Ware. The second series of 1990 Score football cards was very similar to the first series of 330. There are a number of special subsets, i.e., 551-555 are Crunch Crew (CC), 556-560 are Rocket Man (RM), 561-562 are Ground Force (GF), 563-564 are Hot Gun (HG), 565-590 are All-Pros, 591-594 are Record Breakers (RB), 595-601 are Hall of Famers (HOF), 606-617 are Class of '90, and 618-657 are Draft Picks. The key rookie cards in the second series are Mark Carrier, Jeff George and Eric Green.

	MINT	EXC	G-VG
COMPLETE SET (660)	13.50	6.00	1.00
COMMON PLAYER (1-330)	.03	.01	.00
COMMON PLAYER (331-660)	.03	.01	.00
☐ 1 Joe Montana	.50	.25	.05
San Francisco 49ers			
☐ 2 Christian Okoye	.10	.05	.01
Kansas City Chiefs			
☐ 3 Mike Singletary UER	.08	.04	.01
Chicago Bears			
(Text says 146 tackles			
in '89, should be 151)			
☐ 4 Jim Everett UER	.12	.06	.01
Los Angeles Rams			
(Text says 415 yards			
against Saints, should			
be 454)			
☐ 5 Phil Simms	.10	.05	.01
New York Giants			
☐ 6 Brent Fullwood	.06	.03	.00
Green Bay Packers			
☐ 7 Bill Fralic	.06	.03	.00
Atlanta Falcons			
☐ 8 Leslie O'Neal	.06	.03	.00
San Diego Chargers			
☐ 9 John Taylor	.15	.07	.01
San Francisco 49ers			
☐ 10 Bo Jackson	.35	.17	.03
Los Angeles Raiders			
☐ 11 John Stephens	.08	.04	.01
New England Patriots			
☐ 12 Art Monk	.15	.07	.01
Washington Redskins			
☐ 13 Dan Marino	.30	.15	.03
Miami Dolphins			
☐ 14 John Settle	.06	.03	.00
Atlanta Falcons			
☐ 15 Don Majkowski	.10	.05	.01
Green Bay Packers			
☐ 16 Bruce Smith	.08	.04	.01
Buffalo Bills			
☐ 17 Brad Muster	.08	.04	.01
Chicago Bears			
☐ 18 Jason Buck	.06	.03	.00
Cincinnati Bengals			
☐ 19 James Brooks	.08	.04	.01
Cincinnati Bengals			
☐ 20 Barry Sanders	.90	.45	.09
Detroit Lions			
☐ 21 Troy Aikman	.60	.30	.06
Dallas Cowboys			
☐ 22 Allen Pinkett	.08	.04	.01
Houston Oilers			
☐ 23 Duane Bickett	.03	.01	.00
Indianapolis Colts			
☐ 24 Kevin Ross	.03	.01	.00
Kansas City Chiefs			
☐ 25 John Elway	.20	.10	.02
Denver Broncos			
☐ 26 Jeff Query	.06	.03	.00
Green Bay Packers			
☐ 27 Eddie Murray	.06	.03	.00
Detroit Lions			
☐ 28 Richard Dent	.08	.04	.01
Chicago Bears			
☐ 29 Lorenzo White	.10	.05	.01
Houston Oilers			
☐ 30 Eric Metcalf	.08	.04	.01
Cleveland Browns			
☐ 31 Jeff Dellenbach	.08	.04	.01
Miami Dolphins			
☐ 32 Leon White	.06	.03	.00
Cincinnati Bengals			
☐ 33 Jim Jeffcoat	.03	.01	.00
Dallas Cowboys			
☐ 34 Herschel Walker	.15	.07	.01
Minnesota Vikings			
☐ 35 Mike Johnson UER	.06	.03	.00
Cleveland Browns			
(Front photo actually			
51 Eddie Johnson)			
☐ 36 Joe Phillips	.08	.04	.01
San Diego Chargers			
☐ 37 Willie Gault	.06	.03	.00
Los Angeles Raiders			
☐ 38 Keith Millard	.06	.03	.00
Minnesota Vikings			
☐ 39 Fred Marion	.03	.01	.00
New England Patriots			
☐ 40 Boomer Esiason	.10	.05	.01
Cincinnati Bengals			
☐ 41 Dermontti Dawson	.03	.01	.00
Pittsburgh Steelers			
☐ 42 Dino Hackett	.03	.01	.00
Kansas City Chiefs			
☐ 43 Reggie Roby	.03	.01	.00
Miami Dolphins			
☐ 44 Roger Vick	.03	.01	.00
New York Jets			

☐ 45	Bobby Hebert .... .08	.04	.01
	New Orleans Saints		
☐ 46	Don Beebe .... .12	.06	.01
	Buffalo Bills		
☐ 47	Neal Anderson .... .15	.07	.01
	Chicago Bears		
☐ 48	Johnny Holland .... .03	.01	.00
	Green Bay Packers		
☐ 49	Bobby Humphery .... .03	.01	.00
	New York Jets		
☐ 50	Lawrence Taylor .... .10	.05	.01
	New York Giants		
☐ 51	Billy Ray Smith .... .06	.03	.00
	San Diego Chargers		
☐ 52	Robert Perryman .... .06	.03	.00
	New England Patriots		
☐ 53	Gary Anderson .... .03	.01	.00
	Pittsburgh Steelers		
☐ 54	Raul Allegre .... .03	.01	.00
	New York Giants		
☐ 55	Pat Swilling .... .10	.05	.01
	New Orleans Saints		
☐ 56	Chris Doleman .... .06	.03	.00
	Minnesota Vikings		
☐ 57	Andre Reed .... .10	.05	.01
	Buffalo Bills		
☐ 58	Seth Joyner .... .06	.03	.00
	Philadelphia Eagles		
☐ 59	Bart Oates .... .03	.01	.00
	New York Giants		
☐ 60	Bernie Kosar .... .15	.07	.01
	Cleveland Browns		
☐ 61	Dave Krieg .... .08	.04	.01
	Seattle Seahawks		
☐ 62	Lars Tate .... .06	.03	.00
	Tampa Bay Buccaneers		
☐ 63	Scott Norwood .... .03	.01	.00
	Buffalo Bills		
☐ 64	Kyle Clifton .... .03	.01	.00
	New York Jets		
☐ 65	Alan Veingrad .... .08	.04	.01
	Green Bay Packers		
☐ 66	Gerald Riggs UER .... .06	.03	.00
	Washington Redskins		
	(Text begins Depite,		
	should be Despite)		
☐ 67	Tim Worley .... .06	.03	.00
	Pittsburgh Steelers		
☐ 68	Rodney Holman .... .06	.03	.00
	Cincinnati Bengals		
☐ 69	Tony Zendejas .... .03	.01	.00
	Houston Oilers		
☐ 70	Chris Miller .... .20	.10	.02
	Atlanta Falcons		
☐ 71	Wilber Marshall .... .06	.03	.00
	Washington Redskins		
☐ 72	Skip McClendon .... .10	.05	.01

	Cincinnati Bengals		
☐ 73	Jim Covert .... .06	.03	.00
	Chicago Bears		
☐ 74	Sam Mills .... .06	.03	.00
	New Orleans Saints		
☐ 75	Chris Hinton .... .06	.03	.00
	Indianapolis Colts		
☐ 76	Irv Eatman .... .03	.01	.00
	Kansas City Chiefs		
☐ 77	Bubba Paris UER .... .06	.03	.00
	San Francisco 49ers		
	(No team name on who		
	drafted him)		
☐ 78	John Elliott UER .... .06	.03	.00
	New York Giants		
	(No team name on who		
	drafted him; missing		
	Team/FA status)		
☐ 79	Thomas Everett .... .03	.01	.00
	Pittsburgh Steelers		
☐ 80	Steve Smith .... .06	.03	.00
	Los Angeles Raiders		
☐ 81	Jackie Slater .... .06	.03	.00
	Lost Angeles Rams		
☐ 82	Kelvin Martin .... .10	.05	.01
	Dallas Cowboys		
☐ 83	Jo Jo Townsell .... .06	.03	.00
	New York Jets		
☐ 84	Jim C. Jensen .... .03	.01	.00
	Miami Dolphins		
☐ 85	Bobby Humphrey .... .12	.06	.01
	Denver Broncos		
☐ 86	Mike Dyal .... .10	.05	.01
	Los Angeles Raiders		
☐ 87	Andre Rison UER .... .20	.10	.02
	Indianapolis Colts		
	(Front 87, back 85)		
☐ 88	Brian Sochia .... .03	.01	.00
	Miami Dolphins		
☐ 89	Greg Bell .... .06	.03	.00
	Los Angeles Rams		
☐ 90	Dalton Hilliard .... .06	.03	.00
	New Orleans Saints		
☐ 91	Carl Banks .... .06	.03	.00
	New York Giants		
☐ 92	Dennis Smith .... .03	.01	.00
	Denver Broncos		
☐ 93	Bruce Matthews .... .03	.01	.00
	Houston Oilers		
☐ 94	Charles Haley .... .06	.03	.00
	San Francisco 49ers		
☐ 95	Deion Sanders UER .... .30	.15	.03
	Atlanta Falcons		
	(Reversed photo on back)		
☐ 96	Stephone Paige .... .06	.03	.00
	Kansas City Chiefs		
☐ 97	Marion Butts .... .15	.07	.01

	San Diego Chargers			
☐ 98	Howie Long	.06	.03	.00
	Los Angeles Raiders			
☐ 99	Donald Igwebuike	.03	.01	.00
	Tampa Bay Buccaneers			
☐ 100	Roger Craig UER	.10	.05	.01
	San Francisco 49ers			
	(Text says 2 TD's in			
	SB XXIV, should be 1;			
	everything misspelled)			
☐ 101	Charles Mann	.06	.03	.00
	Washington Redskins			
☐ 102	Fredd Young	.03	.01	.00
	Indianapolis Colts			
☐ 103	Chris Jacke	.03	.01	.00
	Green Bay Packers			
☐ 104	Scott Case	.03	.01	.00
	Atlanta Falcons			
☐ 105	Warren Moon	.25	.12	.02
	Houston Oilers			
☐ 106	Clyde Simmons	.06	.03	.00
	Philadelphia Eagles			
☐ 107	Steve Atwater	.08	.04	.01
	Denver Broncos			
☐ 108	Morten Andersen	.06	.03	.00
	New Orleans Saints			
☐ 109	Eugene Marve	.03	.01	.00
	Tampa Bay Buccaneers			
☐ 110	Thurman Thomas	.60	.30	.06
	Buffalo Bills			
☐ 111	Carnell Lake	.06	.03	.00
	Pittsburgh Steelers			
☐ 112	Jim Kelly	.35	.17	.03
	Buffalo Bills			
☐ 113	Stanford Jennings	.03	.01	.00
	Cincinnati Bengals			
☐ 114	Jacob Green	.06	.03	.00
	Seattle Seahawks			
☐ 115	Karl Mecklenburg	.06	.03	.00
	Denver Broncos			
☐ 116	Ray Childress	.06	.03	.00
	Houston Oilers			
☐ 117	Erik McMillan	.06	.03	.00
	New York Jets			
☐ 118	Harry Newsome	.03	.01	.00
	Pittsburgh Steelers			
☐ 119	James Dixon	.08	.04	.01
	Dallas Cowboys			
☐ 120	Hassan Jones	.06	.03	.00
	Minnesoata Vikings			
☐ 121	Eric Allen	.06	.03	.00
	Philadelphia Eagles			
☐ 122	Felix Wright	.03	.01	.00
	Cleveland Browns			
☐ 123	Merril Hoge	.06	.03	.00
	Pittsburgh Steelers			
☐ 124	Eric Ball	.06	.03	.00

	Cincinnati Bengals			
☐ 125	Flipper Anderson	.10	.05	.01
	Los Angeles Rams			
☐ 126	James Jefferson	.06	.03	.00
	Seattle Seahawks			
☐ 127	Tim McDonald	.06	.03	.00
	Phoenix Cardinals			
☐ 128	Larry Kinnebrew	.03	.01	.00
	Buffalo Bills			
☐ 129	Mark Collins	.06	.03	.00
	New York Giants			
☐ 130	Ickey Woods	.06	.03	.00
	Cincinnati Bengals			
☐ 131	Jeff Donaldson UER	.03	.01	.00
	Houston Oilers			
	(Stats say 0 int. and			
	0 fumble rec., text			
	says 4 and 1)			
☐ 132	Rich Camarillo	.03	.01	.00
	Phoenix Cardinals			
☐ 133	Melvin Bratton	.12	.06	.01
	Denver Broncos			
☐ 134A	Kevin Butler	.60	.30	.06
	Chicago Bears			
	(Photo on back			
	has helmet on)			
☐ 134B	Kevin Butler	.06	.03	.00
	Chicago Bears			
	(Photo on back			
	has no helmet on)			
☐ 135	Albert Bentley	.06	.03	.00
	Indianapolis Colts			
☐ 136A	Vai Sikahema	.60	.30	.06
	Phoenix Cardinals			
	(Photo on back			
	has helmet on)			
☐ 136B	Vai Sikahema	.06	.03	.00
	Phoenix Cardinals			
	(Photo on back			
	has no helmet on)			
☐ 137	Todd McNair	.10	.05	.01
	Kansas City Chiefs			
☐ 138	Alonzo Highsmith	.06	.03	.00
	Houston Oilers			
☐ 139	Brian Blades	.12	.06	.01
	Seattle Seahawks			
☐ 140	Jeff Lageman	.06	.03	.00
	New York Jets			
☐ 141	Eric Thomas	.06	.03	.00
	Cincinnati Bengals			
☐ 142	Derek Hill	.08	.04	.01
	Pittsburgh Steelers			
☐ 143	Rick Fenney	.06	.03	.00
	Minnesota Vikings			
☐ 144	Herman Heard	.03	.01	.00
	Kansas City Chiefs			
☐ 145	Steve Young	.10	.05	.01

	San Francisco 49ers			
☐ 146	Kent Hull 03	.01	.00	
	Buffalo Bills			
☐ 147A	Joey Browner 50	.25	.05	
	Minnesota Vikings			
	(Photo on back			
	looking to side)			
☐ 147B	Joey Browner 06	.03	.00	
	Minnesota Vikings			
	(Photo on back			
	looking up)			
☐ 148	Frank Minnifield 03	.01	.00	
	Cleveland Browns			
☐ 149	Robert Massey 06	.03	.00	
	New Orleans Saints			
☐ 150	Dave Meggett 15	.07	.01	
	New York Giants			
☐ 151	Bubba McDowell 06	.03	.00	
	Houston Oilers			
☐ 152	Rickey Dixon 15	.07	.01	
	Cincinnati Bengals			
☐ 153	Ray Donaldson 03	.01	.00	
	Indianapolis Colts			
☐ 154	Alvin Walton 03	.01	.00	
	Washington Redskins			
☐ 155	Mike Cofer 03	.01	.00	
	San Francisco 49ers			
☐ 156	Darryl Talley 06	.03	.00	
	Buffalo Bills			
☐ 157	A.J. Johnson 06	.03	.00	
	Washington Redskins			
☐ 158	Jerry Gray 03	.01	.00	
	Los Angeles Rams			
☐ 159	Keith Byars 06	.03	.00	
	Philadelphia Eagles			
☐ 160	Andy Heck 03	.01	.00	
	Seattle Seahawks			
☐ 161	Mike Munchak 06	.03	.00	
	Houston Oilers			
☐ 162	Dennis Gentry 03	.01	.00	
	Chicago Bears			
☐ 163	Timm Rosenbach UER ...10	.05	.01	
	Phoenix Cardinals			
	(Born 1967 in Everett,			
	Wa., should be 1966			
	in Missoula, Mont.)			
☐ 164	Randall McDaniel 06	.03	.00	
	Minnesota Vikings			
☐ 165	Pat Leahy 06	.03	.00	
	New York Jets			
☐ 166	Bubby Brister 08	.04	.01	
	Pittsburgh Steelers			
☐ 167	Aundray Bruce 06	.03	.00	
	Atlanta Falcons			
☐ 168	Bill Brooks 03	.01	.00	
	Indianapolis Colts			
☐ 169	Eddie Anderson 10	.05	.01	

	Los Angeles Raiders			
☐ 170	Ronnie Lott 10	.05	.01	
	San Francisco 49ers			
☐ 171	Jay Hilgenberg 06	.03	.00	
	Chicago Bears			
☐ 172	Joe Nash 03	.01	.00	
	Seattle Seahawks			
☐ 173	Simon Fletcher 03	.01	.00	
	Denver Broncos			
☐ 174	Shane Conlan 06	.03	.00	
	Buffalo Bills			
☐ 175	Sean Landeta 03	.01	.00	
	New York Giants			
☐ 176	John Alt 10	.05	.01	
	Kansas City Chiefs			
☐ 177	Clay Matthews 03	.01	.00	
	Cleveland Browns			
☐ 178	Anthony Munoz 08	.04	.01	
	Cincinnati Bengals			
☐ 179	Pete Holohan 03	.01	.00	
	Los Angeles Rams			
☐ 180	Robert Awalt 03	.01	.00	
	Phoenix Cardinals			
☐ 181	Rohn Stark 03	.01	.00	
	Indianapolis Colts			
☐ 182	Vance Johnson 06	.03	.00	
	Denver Broncos			
☐ 183	David Fulcher 03	.01	.00	
	Cincinnati Bengals			
☐ 184	Robert Delpino 10	.05	.01	
	Los Angeles Rams			
☐ 185	Drew Hill 08	.04	.01	
	Houston Oilers			
☐ 186	Reggie Langhorne UER ..03	.01	.00	
	Cleveland Browns			
	(Stats read 1988,			
	not 1989)			
☐ 187	Lonzell Hill 06	.03	.00	
	New Orleans Saints			
☐ 188	Tom Rathman UER 06	.03	.00	
	San Francisco 49ers			
	(On back, blocker			
	misspelled)			
☐ 189	Greg Montgomery 08	.04	.01	
	Houston Oilers			
☐ 190	Leonard Smith 03	.01	.00	
	Buffalo Bills			
☐ 191	Chris Spielman 08	.04	.01	
	Detroit Lions			
☐ 192	Tom Newberry 03	.01	.00	
	Los Angeles Rams			
☐ 193	Cris Carter 06	.03	.00	
	Philadelphia Eagles			
☐ 194	Kevin Porter 10	.05	.01	
	Kansas City Chiefs			
☐ 195	Donnell Thompson 03	.01	.00	
	Indianapolis Colts			

☐ 196 Vaughan Johnson .... .06 .03 .00
New Orleans Saints
☐ 197 Steve McMichael .... .06 .03 .00
Chicago Bears
☐ 198 Jim Sweeney .... .06 .03 .00
New York Jets
☐ 199 Rich Karlis UER .... .03 .01 .00
Minnesota Vikings
(No comma between day
and year in birth data)
☐ 200 Jerry Rice .... .45 .22 .04
San Francisco 49ers
☐ 201 Dan Hampton UER .... .08 .04 .01
Chicago Bears
(Card says he's a DE,
should be DT)
☐ 202 Jim Lachey .... .06 .03 .00
Washington Redskins
☐ 203 Reggie White .... .08 .04 .01
Philadelphia Eagles
☐ 204 Jerry Ball .... .06 .03 .00
Detroit Lions
☐ 205 Russ Grimm .... .06 .03 .00
Washington Redskins
☐ 206 Tim Green .... .12 .06 .01
Atlanta Falcons
☐ 207 Shawn Collins .... .06 .03 .00
Atlanta Falcons
☐ 208A Ralf Mojsiejenko ERR 1.25 .60 .12
Washington Redskins
(Chargers stats)
☐ 208B Ralf Mojsiejenko COR .. .08 .04 .01
Washington Redskins
(Redskins stats)
☐ 209 Trace Armstrong .... .06 .03 .00
Chicago Bears
☐ 210 Keith Jackson .... .10 .05 .01
Philadelphia Eagles
☐ 211 Jamie Holland .... .03 .01 .00
San Diego Chargers
☐ 212 Mark Clayton .... .10 .05 .01
Miami Dolphins
☐ 213 Jeff Cross .... .06 .03 .00
Miami Dolphins
☐ 214 Bob Gagliano .... .08 .04 .01
Detroit Lions
☐ 215 Louis Oliver UER .... .06 .03 .00
Miami Dolphins
(Text says played at
Miami, should be
Florida as in bio)
☐ 216 Jim Arnold .... .03 .01 .00
Detroit Lions
☐ 217 Robert Clark .... .20 .10 .02
Detroit Lions
☐ 218 Gill Byrd .... .06 .03 .00
San Diego Chargers

☐ 219 Rodney Peete .... .12 .06 .01
Detroit Lions
☐ 220 Anthony Miller .... .10 .05 .01
San Diego Chargers
☐ 221 Steve Grogan .... .08 .04 .01
New England Patriots
☐ 222 Vince Newsome .... .10 .05 .01
Los Angeles Rams
☐ 223 Tom Benson .... .08 .04 .01
Los Angeles Raiders
☐ 224 Kevin Murphy .... .06 .03 .00
Tampa Bay Buccaneers
☐ 225 Henry Ellard .... .08 .04 .01
Los Angeles Rams
☐ 226 Richard Johnson .... .06 .03 .00
Detroit Lions
☐ 227 Jim Skow .... .03 .01 .00
Cincinnati Bengals
☐ 228 Keith Jones .... .06 .03 .00
Atlanta Falcons
☐ 229 Dave Brown .... .03 .01 .00
Green Bay Packers
☐ 230 Marcus Allen .... .10 .05 .01
Los Angeles Raiders
☐ 231 Steve Walsh .... .10 .05 .01
Dallas Cowboys
☐ 232 Jim Harbaugh .... .20 .10 .02
Chicago Bears
☐ 233 Mel Gray .... .06 .03 .00
Detroit Lions
☐ 234 David Treadwell .... .03 .01 .00
Denver Broncos
☐ 235 John Offerdahl .... .06 .03 .00
Miami Dolphins
☐ 236 Gary Reasons .... .03 .01 .00
New York Giants
☐ 237 Tim Krumrie .... .03 .01 .00
Cincinnati Bengals
☐ 238 Dave Duerson .... .03 .01 .00
Chicago Bears
☐ 239 Gary Clark UER .... .15 .07 .01
Washington Redskins
(Stats read 1988,
not 1989)
☐ 240 Mark Jackson .... .06 .03 .00
Denver Broncos
☐ 241 Mark Murphy .... .03 .01 .00
Green Bay Packers
☐ 242 Jerry Holmes .... .06 .03 .00
Detroit Lions
☐ 243 Tim McGee .... .08 .04 .01
Cincinnati Bengals
☐ 244 Mike Tomczak .... .08 .04 .01
Chicago Bears
☐ 245 Sterling Sharpe UER ...... .15 .07 .01
Green Bay Packers
(Broke 47-yard-old

☐ 246 Bennie Blades 06	.03	.00
Detroit Lions		
☐ 247 Ken Harvey UER 15	.07	.01
Phoenix Cardinals		
(Sacks and fumble		
recovery listings		
are switched; dis-		
appointing misspelled)		
☐ 248 Ron Heller 03	.01	.00
Philadelphia Eagles		
☐ 249 Louis Lipps 08	.04	.01
Pittsburgh Steelers		
☐ 250 Wade Wilson 08	.04	.01
Minnesota Vikings		
☐ 251 Freddie Joe Nunn 03	.01	.00
Phoenix Cardinals		
☐ 252 Jerome Brown UER 06	.03	.00
Philadelphia Eagles		
('89 stats show 2 fum-		
ble rec., should be 1)		
☐ 253 Myron Guyton 06	.03	.00
New York Giants		
☐ 254 Nate Odomes 10	.05	.01
Buffalo Bills		
☐ 255 Rod Woodson 08	.04	.01
Pittsburgh Steelers		
☐ 256 Cornelius Bennett 10	.05	.01
Buffalo Bills		
☐ 257 Keith Woodside 06	.03	.00
Green Bay Packers		
☐ 258 Jeff Uhlenhake UER 06	.03	.00
Miami Dolphins		
(Text calls him Ron)		
☐ 259 Harry Hamilton 03	.01	.00
Tampa Bay Buccaneers		
☐ 260 Mark Bavaro 06	.03	.00
New York Giants		
☐ 261 Vinny Testaverde 08	.04	.01
Tampa Bay Buccaneers		
☐ 262 Steve DeBerg 08	.04	.01
Kansas City Chiefs		
☐ 263 Steve Wisniewski UER .. .03	.01	.00
Los Angeles Raiders		
(Drafted by Dallas,		
not the Raiders)		
☐ 264 Pete Mandley 03	.01	.00
Kansas City Chiefs		
☐ 265 Tim Harris 06	.03	.00
Green Bay Packers		
☐ 266 Jack Trudeau 06	.03	.00
Indianapolis Colts		
☐ 267 Mark Kelso 03	.01	.00
Buffalo Bills		
☐ 268 Brian Noble 03	.01	.00
Green Bay Packers		
☐ 269 Jessie Tuggle 10	.05	.01
Atlanta Falcons		
☐ 270 Ken O'Brien 08	.04	.01
New York Jets		
☐ 271 David Little 03	.01	.00
Pittsburgh Steelers		
☐ 272 Pete Stoyanovich 06	.03	.00
Miami Dolphins		
☐ 273 Odessa Turner 20	.10	.02
New York Giants		
☐ 274 Anthony Toney 03	.01	.00
Philadelphia Eagles		
☐ 275 Tunch Ilkin 03	.01	.00
Pittsburgh Steelers		
☐ 276 Carl Lee 03	.01	.00
Minnesota Vikings		
☐ 277 Hart Lee Dykes 06	.03	.00
New England Patriots		
☐ 278 Al Noga 06	.03	.00
Minnesota Vikings		
☐ 279 Greg Lloyd 06	.03	.00
Pittsburgh Steelers		
☐ 280 Billy Joe Tolliver 08	.04	.01
San Diego Chargers		
☐ 281 Kirk Lowdermilk 06	.03	.00
Minnesota Vikings		
☐ 282 Earl Ferrell 03	.01	.00
Phoenix Cardinals		
☐ 283 Eric Sievers 10	.05	.01
New England Patriots		
☐ 284 Steve Jordan 06	.03	.00
Minnesota Vikings		
☐ 285 Burt Grossman 06	.03	.00
San Diego Chargers		
☐ 286 Johnny Rembert 06	.03	.00
New England Patriots		
☐ 287 Jeff Jaeger 08	.04	.01
Los Angeles Raiders		
☐ 288 James Hasty 06	.03	.00
New York Jets		
☐ 289 Tony Mandarich 06	.03	.00
Draft Pick		
☐ 290 Chris Singleton 20	.10	.02
Draft Pick		
☐ 291 Lynn James 12	.06	.01
Draft Pick		
☐ 292 Andre Ware 35	.17	.03
Draft Pick		
☐ 293 Ray Agnew 10	.05	.01
Draft Pick		
☐ 294 Joel Smeenge 08	.04	.01
Draft Pick		
☐ 295 Marc Spindler 08	.04	.01
Draft Pick		
☐ 296 Renaldo Turnbull 15	.07	.01
Draft Pick		
☐ 297 Reggie Rembert 20	.10	.02
Draft Pick		

☐ 298	Jeff Alm ....08 Draft Pick	.04	.01	
☐ 299	Cortez Kennedy ....30 Draft Pick	.15	.03	
☐ 300	Blair Thomas ....65 Draft Pick	.30	.06	
☐ 301	Pat Terrell ....15 Draft Pick	.07	.01	
☐ 302	Junior Seau ....20 Draft Pick	.10	.02	
☐ 303	Mohammed Elewonibi ...08 Draft Pick	.04	.01	
☐ 304	Tony Bennett ....20 Draft Pick	.10	.02	
☐ 305	Percy Snow ....15 Draft Pick	.07	.01	
☐ 306	Richmond Webb ....15 Draft Pick	.07	.01	
☐ 307	Rodney Hampton ....75 Draft Pick	.35	.07	
☐ 308	Barry Foster ....30 Draft Pick	.15	.03	
☐ 309	John Friesz ....1.00 Draft Pick	.50	.10	
☐ 310	Ben Smith ....10 Draft Pick	.05	.01	
☐ 311	Joe Montana HG ....20 San Francisco 49ers	.10	.02	
☐ 312	Jim Everett HG ....08 Los Angeles Rams	.04	.01	
☐ 313	Mark Rypien HG ....12 Washington Redskins	.06	.01	
☐ 314	Phil Simms HG UER ....08 New York Giants (Lists him as playing in the AFC)	.04	.01	
☐ 315	Don Majkowski HG ....06 Green Bay Packers	.03	.00	
☐ 316	Boomer Esiason HG ....08 Cincinnati Bengals	.04	.01	
☐ 317	Warren Moon HG ....25 Houston Oilers (Moon on card)	.12	.02	
☐ 318	Jim Kelly HG ....15 Buffalo Bills	.07	.01	
☐ 319	Bernie Kosar HG UER ...08 Cleveland Browns (Word just is mis- spelled as justs)	.04	.01	
☐ 320	Dan Marino HG UER ....15 Miami Dolphins (Text says 378 com- pletions in 1984, should be 1986)	.07	.01	
☐ 321	Christian Okoye GF ....08 Kansas City Chiefs	.04	.01	
☐ 322	Thurman Thomas GF ....20 Buffalo Bills	.10	.02	
☐ 323	James Brooks GF ....06 Cincinnati Bengals	.03	.00	
☐ 324	Bobby Humphrey GF ......08 Denver Broncos	.04	.01	
☐ 325	Barry Sanders GF ....35 Detroit Lions	.17	.03	
☐ 326	Neal Anderson GF ....08 Chicago Bears	.04	.01	
☐ 327	Dalton Hilliard GF ....03 New Orleans Saints	.01	.00	
☐ 328	Greg Bell GF ....03 Los Angeles Rams	.01	.00	
☐ 329	Roger Craig GF UER ......08 San Francisco 49ers (Text says 2 TD's in SB XXIV, should be 1)	.04	.01	
☐ 330	Bo Jackson GF ....15 Los Angeles Raiders	.07	.01	
☐ 331	Don Warren ....06 Washington Redskins	.03	.00	
☐ 332	Rufus Porter ....06 Seattle Seahawks	.03	.00	
☐ 333	Sammie Smith ....10 Miami Dolphins	.05	.01	
☐ 334	Lewis Tillman UER ....06 New York Giants (Born 4/16/67, should be 1966)	.03	.00	
☐ 335	Michael Walter ....03 San Francisco 49ers	.01	.00	
☐ 336	Marc Logan ....06 Miami Dolphins	.03	.00	
☐ 337	Ron Hallstrom ....10 Green Bay Packers	.05	.01	
☐ 338	Stanley Morgan ....08 New England Patriots	.04	.01	
☐ 339	Mark Robinson ....06 Tampa Bay Buccaneers	.03	.00	
☐ 340	Frank Reich ....08 Buffalo Bills	.04	.01	
☐ 341	Chip Lohmiller ....08 Washington Redskins	.04	.01	
☐ 342	Steve Beuerlein ....15 Los Angeles Raiders	.07	.01	
☐ 343	John L. Williams ....08 Seattle Seahawks	.04	.01	
☐ 344	Irving Fryar ....06 New England Patriots	.03	.00	
☐ 345	Anthony Carter ....08 Minnesota Vikings	.04	.01	
☐ 346	Al Toon ....08 New York Jets	.04	.01	
☐ 347	J.T. Smith ....06 Phoenix Cardinals	.03	.00	
☐ 348	Pierce Holt ....08 San Francisco 49ers	.04	.01	

☐ 349	Ferrell Edmunds 06	.03	.00	
	Miami Dolphins			
☐ 350	Mark Rypien 35	.17	.03	
	Washington Redskins			
☐ 351	Paul Gruber 06	.03	.00	
	Tampa Bay Buccaneers			
☐ 352	Ernest Givins 10	.05	.01	
	Houston Oilers			
☐ 353	Ervin Randle 03	.01	.00	
	Tampa Bay Buccaneers			
☐ 354	Guy McIntyre 03	.01	.00	
	San Francisco 49ers			
☐ 355	Webster Slaughter 06	.03	.00	
	Cleveland Browns			
☐ 356	Reuben Davis 08	.04	.01	
	Tampa Bay Buccaneers			
☐ 357	Rickey Jackson 06	.03	.00	
	New Orleans Saints			
☐ 358	Earnest Byner 08	.04	.01	
	Washington Redskins			
☐ 359	Eddie Brown 08	.04	.01	
	Cincinnati Bengals			
☐ 360	Troy Stradford 06	.03	.00	
	Miami Dolphins			
☐ 361	Pepper Johnson 06	.03	.00	
	New York Giants			
☐ 362	Ravin Caldwell 08	.04	.01	
	Washington Redskins			
☐ 363	Chris Mohr 08	.04	.01	
	Tampa Bay Buccaneers			
☐ 364	Jeff Bryant 03	.01	.00	
	Seattle Seahawks			
☐ 365	Bruce Collie 08	.04	.01	
	San Francisco 49ers			
☐ 366	Courtney Hall 03	.01	.00	
	San Diego Chargers			
☐ 367	Jerry Olsavsky 08	.04	.01	
	Pittsburgh Steelers			
☐ 368	David Galloway 03	.01	.00	
	Phoenix Cardinals			
☐ 369	Wes Hopkins 03	.01	.00	
	Philadelphia Eagles			
☐ 370	Johnny Hector 06	.03	.00	
	New York Jets			
☐ 371	Clarence Verdin 06	.03	.00	
	Indiananpolis Colts			
☐ 372	Nick Lowery 06	.03	.00	
	Kansas City Chiefs			
☐ 373	Tim Brown 10	.05	.01	
	Los Angeles Raiders			
☐ 374	Kevin Greene 06	.03	.00	
	Los Angeles Rams			
☐ 375	Leonard Marshall 06	.03	.00	
	New York Giants			
☐ 376	Roland James 03	.01	.00	
	New England Patriots			
☐ 377	Scott Studwell 03	.01	.00	
	Minnesota Vikins			
☐ 378	Jarvis Williams 06	.03	.00	
	Miami Dolphins			
☐ 379	Mike Saxon 03	.01	.00	
	Dallas Cowboys			
☐ 380	Kevin Mack 06	.03	.00	
	Cleveland Browns			
☐ 381	Joe Kelly 06	.03	.00	
	Cincinnati Bengals			
☐ 382	Tom Thayer 10	.05	.01	
	Chicago Bears			
☐ 383	Roy Green 08	.04	.01	
	Phoenix Cardinals			
☐ 384	Michael Brooks 10	.05	.01	
	Denver Broncos			
☐ 385	Michael Cofer 03	.01	.00	
	Detroit Lions			
☐ 386	Ken Ruettgers 06	.03	.00	
	Green Bay Packers			
☐ 387	Dean Steinkuhler 06	.03	.00	
	Houston Oilers			
☐ 388	Maurice Carthon 03	.01	.00	
	New York Giants			
☐ 389	Ricky Sanders 10	.05	.01	
	Washington Redskins			
☐ 390	Winston Moss 08	.04	.01	
	Tampa Bay Buccaneers			
☐ 391	Tony Woods 06	.03	.0C	
	Seattle Seahawks			
☐ 392	Keith DeLong 03	.01	.00	
	San Francisco 49ers			
☐ 393	David Wyman 03	.01	.00	
	Seattle Seahawks			
☐ 394	Vencie Glenn 03	.01	.00	
	San Diego Chargers			
☐ 395	Harris Barton 03	.01	.00	
	San Francisco 49ers			
☐ 396	Bryan Hinkle 03	.01	.00	
	Pittsburgh Steelers			
☐ 397	Derek Kennard 08	.04	.01	
	Phoenix Cardinals			
☐ 398	Heath Sherman 25	.12	.02	
	Philadelphia Eagles			
☐ 399	Troy Benson 03	.01	.00	
	New York Jets			
☐ 400	Gary Zimmerman 06	.03	.00	
	Minnesota Vikings			
☐ 401	Mark Duper 06	.03	.00	
	Miami Dolphins			
☐ 402	Eugene Lockhart 03	.01	.00	
	Dallas Cowboys			
☐ 403	Tim Manoa 08	.04	.01	
	Cleveland Browns			
☐ 404	Reggie Williams 06	.03	.00	
	Cincinnati Bengals			
☐ 405	Mark Bortz 08	.04	.01	
	Chicago Bears			

☐ 406 Mike Kenn 03	.01	.00	Miami Dolphins		
Atlanta Falcons			☐ 435 Henry Thomas 03	.01	.00
☐ 407 John Grimsley 03	.01	.00	Minnesota Vikings		
Houston Oilers			☐ 436 Chet Brooks 08	.04	.01
☐ 408 Bill Romanowski 08	.04	.01	San Francisco 49ers		
San Francisco 49ers			☐ 437 Mark Ingram 06	.03	.00
☐ 409 Perry Kemp 06	.03	.00	New York Giants		
Green Bay Packers			☐ 438 Jeff Gossett 03	.01	.00
☐ 410 Norm Johnson 03	.01	.00	Los Angles Raiders		
Seattle Seahawks			☐ 439 Mike Wilcher 03	.01	.00
☐ 411 Broderick Thomas 08	.04	.01	Los Angles Rams		
Tampa Bay Buccaneers			☐ 440 Deron Cherry UER 06	.03	.00
☐ 412 Joe Wolf 03	.01	.00	Kansas City Chiefs		
Phoenix Cardinals			(Text says 7 cons. Pro		
☐ 413 Andre Waters 03	.01	.00	Bowls, but he didn't		
Philadelphia Eagles			play in 1989 Pro Bowl)		
☐ 414 Jason Staurovsky 08	.04	.01	☐ 441 Mike Rozier 06	.03	.00
New England Patriots			Houston Oilers		
☐ 415 Eric Martin 06	.03	.00	☐ 442 Jon Hand 03	.01	.00
New Orleans Saints			Indianapolis Colts		
☐ 416 Joe Prokop 03	.01	.00	☐ 443 Ozzie Newsome 08	.04	.01
New York Jets			Cleveland Browns		
☐ 417 Steve Sewell 06	.03	.00	☐ 444 Sammy Martin 10	.05	.01
Denver Broncos			New England Patriots		
☐ 418 Cedric Jones 10	.05	.01	☐ 445 Luis Sharpe 03	.01	.00
New England Patriots			Phoenix Cardinals		
☐ 419 Alphonso Carreker 03	.01	.00	☐ 446 Lee Williams 06	.03	.00
Denver Broncos			San Diego Chargers		
☐ 420 Keith Willis 03	.01	.00	☐ 447 Chris Martin 08	.04	.01
Pittsburgh Steelers			Kansas City Chiefs		
☐ 421 Bobby Butler 03	.01	.00	☐ 448 Kevin Fagan 08	.04	.01
Atlanta Falcons			San Francisco 49ers		
☐ 422 John Roper 10	.05	.01	☐ 449 Gene Lang 03	.01	.00
Chicago Bears			Atlanta Falcons		
☐ 423 Tim Spencer 03	.01	.00	☐ 450 Greg Townsend 06	.03	.00
San Diego Chargers			Los Angeles Raiders		
☐ 424 Jesse Sapolu 08	.04	.01	☐ 451 Robert Lyles 06	.03	.00
San Francisco 49ers			Houston Oilers		
☐ 425 Ron Wolfley 03	.01	.00	☐ 452 Eric Hill 06	.03	.00
Phoenix Cardinals			Phoenix Cardinals		
☐ 426 Doug Smith 03	.01	.00	☐ 453 John Teltschik 03	.01	.00
Los Angeles Rams			Philadelphia Eagles		
☐ 427 William Howard 10	.05	.01	☐ 454 Vestee Jackson 06	.03	.00
Tampa Bay Buccaneers			Chicago Bears		
☐ 428 Keith Van Horne 03	.01	.00	☐ 455 Bruce Reimers 06	.03	.00
Chicago Bears			Cincinnati Bengals		
☐ 429 Tony Jordan 08	.04	.01	☐ 456 Butch Rolle 08	.04	.01
Phoenix Cardinals			Buffalo Bills		
☐ 430 Mervyn Fernandez 08	.04	.01	☐ 457 Lawyer Tillman 06	.03	.00
Los Angeles Raiders			Cleveland Browns		
☐ 431 Shaun Gayle 10	.05	.01	☐ 458 Andre Tippett 06	.03	.00
Chicago Bears			New England Patriots		
☐ 432 Ricky Nattiel 06	.03	.00	☐ 459 James Thornton 03	.01	.00
Denver Broncos			Chicago Bears		
☐ 433 Albert Lewis 08	.04	.01	☐ 460 Randy Grimes 03	.01	.00
Kansas City Chiefs			Tampa Bay Buccaneers		
☐ 434 Fred Banks 12	.06	.01	☐ 461 Larry Roberts 06	.03	.00

	San Francisco 49ers				New England Patriots			
☐ 462	Ron Holmes 03	.01	.00	☐ 490	Chris Chandler 06	.03	.00	
	Denver Broncos				Indianapolis Colts			
☐ 463	Mike Wise 06	.03	.00	☐ 491	Mark Lee 03	.01	.00	
	Los Angeles Rams				Green Bay Packers			
☐ 464	Danny Copeland 08	.04	.01	☐ 492	Johnny Meads 06	.03	.00	
	Kansas City Chiefs				Houston Oilers			
☐ 465	Bruce Wilkerson 10	.05	.01	☐ 493	Tim Irwin 08	.04	.01	
	Los Angeles Raiders				Minnesota Vikings			
☐ 466	Mike Quick 06	.03	.00	☐ 494	E.J. Junior 03	.01	.00	
	Philadelphia Eagles				Miami Dolphins			
☐ 467	Mickey Shuler 03	.01	.00	☐ 495	Hardy Nickerson 03	.01	.00	
	New York Jets				Pittsburgh Steelers			
☐ 468	Mike Prior 03	.01	.00	☐ 496	Rob McGovern 08	.04	.01	
	Indianapolis Colts				Kansas City Chiefs			
☐ 469	Ron Rivera 03	.01	.00	☐ 497	Fred Strickland 08	.04	.01	
	Chicago Bears				Los Angeles Rams			
☐ 470	Dean Biasucci 03	.01	.00	☐ 498	Reggie Rutland 08	.04	.01	
	Indianapolis Colts				Minnesota Vikings			
☐ 471	Perry Williams 06	.03	.00	☐ 499	Mel Owens 06			
	New York Giants						.03	.00
☐ 472	Darren Comeaux UER 08	.04	.01		Los Angeles Rams			
	Seattle Seahawks			☐ 500	Derrick Thomas 25	.12	.02	
	(Front 53, back 52)				Kansas City Chiefs			
☐ 473	Freeman McNeil 06	.03	.00	☐ 501	Jerrol Williams 06	.03	.00	
	New York Jets				Pittsburgh Steelers			
☐ 474	Tyrone Braxton 06	.03	.00	☐ 502	Maurice Hurst 12	.06	.01	
	Denver Broncos				New England Patriots			
☐ 475	Jay Schroeder 08	.04	.01	☐ 503	Larry Kelm 08	.04	.01	
	Los Angeles Raiders				Los Angeles Rams			
☐ 476	Naz Worthen 08	.04	.01	☐ 504	Herman Fontenot 03	.01	.00	
	Kansas City Chiefs				Green Bay Packers			
☐ 477	Lionel Washington 03	.01	.00	☐ 505	Pat Beach 03	.01	.00	
	Los Angeles Raiders				Indianapolis Colts			
☐ 478	Carl Zander 03	.01	.00	☐ 506	Haywood Jeffires 60	.30	.06	
	Cincinnati Bengals				Houston Oilers			
☐ 479	Al(Bubba) Baker 03	.01	.00	☐ 507	Neil Smith 06	.03	.00	
	Cleveland Browns				Kansas City Chiefs			
☐ 480	Mike Merriweather 03	.01	.00	☐ 508	Cleveland Gary 10	.05	.01	
	Minnesota Vikings				Los Angeles Rams			
☐ 481	Mike Gann 03	.01	.00	☐ 509	William Perry 08	.04	.01	
	Atlanta Falcons				Chicago Bears			
☐ 482	Brent Williams 06	.03	.00	☐ 510	Michael Carter 06	.03	.00	
	New England Patriots				San Francisco 49ers			
☐ 483	Eugene Robinson 06	.03	.00	☐ 511	Walker Lee Ashley 06	.03	.00	
	Seattle Seahawks				Kansas City Chiefs			
☐ 484	Ray Horton 03	.01	.00	☐ 512	Bob Golic 06	.03	.00	
	Dallas Cowboys				Los Angeles Raiders			
☐ 485	Bruce Armstrong 03	.01	.00	☐ 513	Danny Villa 08	.04	.01	
	New England Patriots				New England Patriots			
☐ 486	John Fourcade 06	.03	.00	☐ 514	Matt Millen 06	.03	.00	
	New Orleans Saints				San Francisco 49ers			
☐ 487	Lewis Billups 06	.03	.00	☐ 515	Don Griffin 03	.01	.00	
	Cincinnati Bengals				San Francisco 49ers			
☐ 488	Scott Davis 06	.03	.00	☐ 516	Jonathan Hayes 06	.03	.00	
	Los Angeles Raiders				Kansas City Chiefs			
☐ 489	Ken Sims 03	.01	.00	☐ 517	Gerald Williams 08	.04	.01	
					Pittsburgh Steelers			

☐ 518 Scott Fulhage 03	.01	.00	
Atlanta Falcons			
☐ 519 Irv Pankey 03	.01	.00	
Los Angeles Rams			
☐ 520 Randy Dixon 10	.05	.01	
Indianapolis Colts			
☐ 521 Terry McDaniel 06	.03	.00	
Los Angeles Raiders			
☐ 522 Dan Saleaumua 06	.03	.00	
Kansas City Chiefs			
☐ 523 Darrin Nelson 03	.01	.00	
San Diego Chargers			
☐ 524 Leonard Griffin 10	.05	.01	
Kansas City Chiefs			
☐ 525 Michael Ball 10	.05	.01	
Indianapolis Colts			
☐ 526 Ernie Jones 20	.10	.02	
Phoenix Cardinals			
☐ 527 Tony Eason UER 06	.03	.00	
New York Jets			
(Drafted in 1963,			
should be 1983)			
☐ 528 Ed Reynolds 08	.04	.01	
New England Patriots			
☐ 529 Gary Hogeboom 06	.03	.00	
Phoenix Cardinals			
☐ 530 Don Mosebar 06	.03	.00	
Los Angeles Raiders			
☐ 531 Ottis Anderson 08	.04	.01	
New York Giants			
☐ 532 Bucky Scribner 03	.01	.00	
Minnesota Vikins			
☐ 533 Aaron Cox 03	.01	.00	
Los Angeles Rams			
☐ 534 Sean Jones 03	.01	.00	
Houston Oilers			
☐ 535 Doug Flutie 15	.07	.01	
New England Patriots			
☐ 536 Leo Lewis 03	.01	.00	
Minnesota Vikings			
☐ 537 Art Still 06	.03	.00	
Buffalo Bills			
☐ 538 Matt Bahr 03	.01	.00	
Cleveland Browns			
☐ 539 Keena Turner 03	.01	.00	
San Francisco 49ers			
☐ 540 Sammy Winder 06	.03	.00	
Denver Broncos			
☐ 541 Mike Webster 06	.03	.00	
Kansas City Chiefs			
☐ 542 Doug Riesenberg 08	.04	.01	
New York Giants			
☐ 543 Dan Fike 08	.04	.01	
Cleveland Browns			
☐ 544 Clarence Kay 03	.01	.00	
Denver Broncos			
☐ 545 Jim Burt 03	.01	.00	

San Francisco 49ers			
☐ 546 Mike Horan 03	.01	.00	
Denver Broncos			
☐ 547 Al Harris 06	.03	.00	
Philadelphia Eagles			
☐ 548 Maury Buford 03	.01	.00	
Chicago Bears			
☐ 549 Jerry Robinson 03	.01	.00	
Los Angeles Raiders			
☐ 550 Tracy Rocker 03	.01	.00	
Washington Redskins			
☐ 551 Karl Mecklenburg CC 03	.01	.00	
Denver Broncos			
☐ 552 Lawrence Taylor CC 08	.04	.01	
New York Giants			
☐ 553 Derrick Thomas CC 10	.05	.01	
Kansas City Chiefs			
☐ 554 Mike Singletary CC 06	.03	.00	
Chicago Bears			
☐ 555 Tim Harris CC 06	.03	.00	
Green Bay Packers			
☐ 556 Jerry Rice RM 15	.07	.01	
San Francisco 49ers			
☐ 557 Art Monk RM 08	.04	.01	
Washington Redskins			
☐ 558 Mark Carrier RM 06	.03	.00	
Tampa Bay Buccaneers			
☐ 559 Andre Reed RM 08	.04	.01	
Buffalo Bills			
☐ 560 Sterling Sharpe RM 08	.04	.01	
Green Bay Packers			
☐ 561 Herschel Walker GF 10	.05	.01	
Minnesota Vikings			
☐ 562 Ottis Anderson GF 06	.03	.00	
New York Giants			
☐ 563 Randall Cunningham HG .10	.05	.01	
Philadelphia Eagles			
☐ 564 John Elway HG 10	.05	.01	
Denver Broncos			
☐ 565 David Fulcher AP 03	.01	.00	
Cincinnati Bengals			
☐ 566 Ronnie Lott AP 08	.04	.01	
San Francisco 49ers			
☐ 567 Jerry Gray AP 03	.01	.00	
Los Angeles Rams			
☐ 568 Albert Lewis AP 06	.03	.00	
Kansas City Chiefs			
☐ 569 Karl Mecklenburg AP 03	.01	.00	
Denver Broncos			
☐ 570 Mike Singletary AP 06	.03	.00	
Chicago Bears			
☐ 571 Lawrence Taylor AP 08	.04	.01	
New York Giants			
☐ 572 Tim Harris AP 06	.03	.00	
Green Bay Packers			
☐ 573 Keith Millard AP 06	.03	.00	
Minnesota Vikings			

☐ 574 Reggie White AP	.08	.04	.01
Philadelphia Eagles			
☐ 575 Chris Doleman AP	.06	.03	.00
Minnesota Vikings			
☐ 576 Dave Meggett AP	.08	.04	.01
New York Giants			
☐ 577 Rod Woodson AP	.06	.03	.00
Pittsburgh Steelers			
☐ 578 Sean Landeta AP	.03	.01	.00
New York Giants			
☐ 579 Eddie Murray AP	.03	.01	.00
Detroit Lions			
☐ 580 Barry Sanders AP	.35	.17	.03
Detroit Lions			
☐ 581 Christian Okoye AP	.08	.04	.01
Kansas City Chiefs			
☐ 582 Joe Montana AP	.20	.10	.02
San Francisco 49ers			
☐ 583 Jay Hilgenberg AP	.03	.01	.00
Chicago Bears			
☐ 584 Bruce Matthews AP	.03	.01	.00
Houston Oilers			
☐ 585 Tom Newberry AP	.03	.01	.00
Los Angeles Rams			
☐ 586 Gary Zimmerman AP	.03	.01	.00
Minnesota Vikings			
☐ 587 Anthony Munoz AP	.06	.03	.00
Cincinnati Bengals			
☐ 588 Keith Jackson AP	.08	.04	.01
Philadelphia Eagles			
☐ 589 Sterling Sharpe AP	.08	.04	.01
Green Bay Packers			
☐ 590 Jerry Rice AP	.15	.07	.01
San Francisco 49ers			
☐ 591 Bo Jackson RB	.15	.07	.01
Los Angeles Raiders			
☐ 592 Steve Largent RB	.15	.07	.01
Seattle Seahawks			
☐ 593 Flipper Anderson RB	.06	.03	.00
Los Angeles Rams			
☐ 594 Joe Montana RB	.15	.07	.01
San Francisco 49ers			
☐ 595 Franco Harris	.08	.04	.01
Hall of Famer			
☐ 596 Bob St. Clair	.06	.03	.00
Hall of Famer			
☐ 597 Tom Landry	.08	.04	.01
Hall of Famer			
☐ 598 Jack Lambert	.08	.04	.01
Hall of Famer			
☐ 599 Ted Hendricks UER	.06	.03	.00
Hall of Famer			
(Int. avg. says 12.8,			
should be 8.9)			
☐ 600A Buck Buchanan ERR	.08	.04	.01
Hall of Famer			
(Drafted in 1983)			

☐ 600B Buck Buchanan COR	.08	.04	.01
Hall of Famer			
(Drafted in 1963)			
☐ 601 Bob Griese	.08	.04	.01
Hall of Famer			
☐ 602 Super Bowl Wrap	.06	.03	.00
☐ 603A Vince Lombardi UER	.30	.15	.03
Lombardi Legend			
(Disciplinarian mis-			
spelled; no logo for			
Curtis Mgt. at bottom)			
☐ 603B Vince Lombardi UER	.30	.15	.03
Lombardi Legend			
(Disciplinarian mis-			
spelled; logo for			
Curtis Mgt. at bottom)			
☐ 604 Mark Carrier UER	.08	.04	.01
Tampa Bay Buccaneers			
(Front 88, back 89)			
☐ 605 Randall Cunningham	.15	.07	.01
Philadelphia Eagles			
☐ 606 Percy Snow	.08	.04	.01
Kansas City Chiefs			
(Class of '90)			
☐ 607 Andre Ware	.20	.10	.02
Detroit Lions			
(Class of '90)			
☐ 608 Blair Thomas	.40	.20	.04
New York Jets			
(Class of '90)			
☐ 609 Eric Green	.25	.12	.02
Pittsburgh Steelers			
(Class of '90)			
☐ 610 Reggie Rembert	.08	.04	.01
New York Jets			
(Class of '90)			
☐ 611 Richmond Webb	.08	.04	.01
Miami Dolphins			
(Class of '90)			
☐ 612 Bern Brostek	.06	.03	.00
Los Angeles Rams			
(Class of '90)			
☐ 613 James Williams	.06	.03	.00
Buffalo Bills			
(Class of '90)			
☐ 614 Mark Carrier	.15	.07	.01
Chicago Bears			
(Class of '90)			
☐ 615 Renaldo Turnbull	.08	.04	.01
New Orleans Saints			
(Class of '90)			
☐ 616 Cortez Kennedy	.15	.07	.01
Seattle Seahawks			
(Class of '90)			
☐ 617 Keith McCants	.12	.06	.01
Tampa Bay Buccaneers			
(Class of '90)			

☐ 618 Anthony Thompson ....30 Draft Pick	.15	.03
☐ 619 LeRoy Butler ....08 Draft Pick	.04	.01
☐ 620 Aaron Wallace ....15 Draft Pick	.07	.01
☐ 621 Alexander Wright ....25 Draft Pick	.12	.02
☐ 622 Keith McCants ....20 Draft Pick	.10	.02
☐ 623 Jimmie Jones UER ....08 Draft Pick (January misspelled)	.04	.01
☐ 624 Anthony Johnson ....15 Draft Pick	.07	.01
☐ 625 Fred Washington ....06 Draft Pick	.03	.00
☐ 626 Mike Bellamy ....12 Draft Pick	.06	.01
☐ 627 Mark Carrier ....35 Draft Pick	.17	.03
☐ 628 Harold Green ....45 Draft Pick	.22	.04
☐ 629 Eric Green ....45 Draft Pick	.22	.04
☐ 630 Andre Collins ....15 Draft Pick	.07	.01
☐ 631 Lamar Lathon ....15 Draft Pick	.07	.01
☐ 632 Terry Wooden ....12 Draft Pick	.06	.01
☐ 633 Jesse Anderson ....08 Draft Pick	.04	.01
☐ 634 Jeff George ....75 Draft Pick	.35	.07
☐ 635 Carwell Gardner ....25 Draft Pick	.12	.02
☐ 636 Darrell Thompson ....25 Draft Pick	.12	.02
☐ 637 Vince Buck ....12 Draft Pick	.06	.01
☐ 638 Mike Jones ....08 Draft Pick	.04	.01
☐ 639 Charles Arbuckle ....08 Draft Pick	.04	.01
☐ 640 Dennis Brown ....08 Draft Pick	.04	.01
☐ 641 James Williams ....08 Draft Pick	.04	.01
☐ 642 Bern Brostek ....08 Draft Pick	.04	.01
☐ 643 Darion Conner ....20 Draft Pick	.10	.02
☐ 644 Mike Fox ....10 Draft Pick	.05	.01
☐ 645 Cary Conklin ....20 Draft Pick	.10	.02
☐ 646 Tim Grunhard ....08 Draft Pick	.04	.01
☐ 647 Ron Cox ....08 Draft Pick	.04	.01
☐ 648 Keith Sims ....10 Draft Pick	.05	.01
☐ 649 Alton Montgomery ....10 Draft Pick	.05	.01
☐ 650 Greg McMurtry ....30 Draft Pick	.15	.03
☐ 651 Scott Mitchell ....25 Draft Pick	.12	.02
☐ 652 Tim Ryan ....10 Draft Pick	.05	.01
☐ 653 Jeff Mills ....10 Draft Pick	.05	.01
☐ 654 Ricky Proehl ....35 Draft Pick	.17	.03
☐ 655 Steve Broussard ....30 Draft Pick	.15	.03
☐ 656 Peter Tom Willis ....25 Draft Pick	.12	.02
☐ 657 Dexter Carter ....25 Draft Pick	.12	.02
☐ 658 Tony Casillas ....06 Atlanta Falcons	.03	.00
☐ 659 Joe Morris ....06 New York Giants	.03	.00
☐ 660 Greg Kragen ....06 Denver Broncos	.03	.00

1990 Score Final Five

This five-card set was a special insert in the 1990 Score Football Factory Sets. These cards,

which measure the standard 2 1/2" by 3 1/2",
honor the final five picks of the 1990 National
Football League Draft. These cards have a
"Final Five" logo on the front along with the
photo of the player, while the back has a brief
biographical description of the player.

	MINT	EXC	G-VG
COMPLETE SET (5)	.75	.35	.07
COMMON PLAYER (B1-B5)	.12	.06	.01
☐ B1 Judd Garrett Philadelphia Eagles	.25	.12	.02
☐ B2 Matt Stover New York Giants	.15	.07	.01
☐ B3 Ken McMichael Phoenix Cardinals	.12	.06	.01
☐ B4 Demetrius Davis Los Angeles Raiders	.15	.07	.01
☐ B5 Elliott Searcy San Diego Chargers	.15	.07	.01

1990 Score
Supplemental

This 110-card standard size set (2 1/2" by 3 1/
2") was issued in the same design as the
regular Score issue, but with blue and purple
borders. The set included cards of rookies and
cards of players who switched teams during
the off-season. The set was released through
Score's dealer outlets and was available only
in complete set form from the company. The
key rookies in the set are Reggie Cobb, Derrick

Fenner, Johnny Johnson, Rob Moore, Emmitt
Smith, and Barry Word.

	MINT	EXC	G-VG
COMPLETE SET (110)	65.00	32.50	6.50
COMMON PLAYER (1-110)	.08	.04	.01
☐ 1T Marcus Dupree Los Angeles Rams	.35	.17	.03
☐ 2T Jerry Kauric Cleveland Browns	.12	.06	.01
☐ 3T Everson Walls New York Giants	.08	.04	.01
☐ 4T Elliott Smith Denver Broncos	.15	.07	.01
☐ 5T Donald Evans UER Pittsburgh Steelers (Misspelled Pittsburg on card back)	.15	.07	.01
☐ 6T Jerry Holmes Green Bay Packers	.08	.04	.01
☐ 7T Dan Stryzinski Pittsburgh Steelers	.20	.10	.02
☐ 8T Gerald McNeil Houston Oilers	.08	.04	.01
☐ 9T Rick Tuten Buffalo Bills	.12	.06	.01
☐ 10T Mickey Shuler Philadelphia Eagles	.08	.04	.01
☐ 11T Jay Novacek Dallas Cowboys	1.50	.75	.15
☐ 12T Eric Williams Washington Redskins	.20	.10	.02
☐ 13T Stanley Morgan Indianapolis Colts	.12	.06	.01
☐ 14T Wayne Haddix Tampa Bay Buccaneers	.35	.17	.03
☐ 15T Gary Anderson Tampa Bay Buccaneers	.15	.07	.01
☐ 16T Stan Humphries Washington Redskins	.25	.12	.02
☐ 17T Raymond Clayborn Cleveland Browns	.08	.04	.01
☐ 18T Mark Boyer New York Jets	.15	.07	.01
☐ 19T Dave Waymer San Francisco 49ers	.08	.04	.01
☐ 20T Andre Rison Atlanta Falcons	1.25	.60	.12
☐ 21T Daniel Stubbs Dallas Cowboys	.12	.06	.01
☐ 22T Mike Rozier Atlanta Falcons	.12	.06	.01
☐ 23T Damian Johnson New England Patriots	.25	.12	.02
☐ 24T Don Smith Buffalo Bills	.15	.07	.01

☐ 25T Max Montoya 08	.04	.01
Los Angeles Raiders		
☐ 26T Terry Kinard 08	.04	.01
Houston Oilers		
☐ 27T Herb Welch 15	.07	.01
Detroit Lions		
☐ 28T Cliff Odom 08	.04	.01
Miami Dolphins		
☐ 29T John Kidd 12	.06	.01
San Diego Chargers		
☐ 30T Barry Word 2.00	1.00	.20
Kansas City Chiefs		
☐ 31T Rich Karlis 08	.04	.01
Detroit Lions		
☐ 32T Mike Baab 08	.04	.01
Cleveland Browns		
☐ 33T Ronnie Harmon 12	.06	.01
San Diego Chargers		
☐ 34T Jeff Donaldson 08	.04	.01
Kansas City Chiefs		
☐ 35T Riki Ellison 15	.07	.01
Los Angeles Raiders		
☐ 36T Steve Walsh 25	.12	.02
New Orleans Saints		
☐ 37T Bill Lewis 15	.07	.01
Phoenix Cardinals		
☐ 38T Tim McKyer 12	.06	.01
Miami Dolphins		
☐ 39T James Wilder 12	.06	.01
Detroit Lions		
☐ 40T Tony Paige 12	.06	.01
Miami Dolphins		
☐ 41T Derrick Fenner 1.25	.60	.12
Seattle Seahawks		
☐ 42T Thane Gash 25	.12	.02
Cleveland Browns		
☐ 43T Dave Duerson 08	.04	.01
New York Giants		
☐ 44T Clarence Weathers 15	.07	.01
Green Bay Packers		
☐ 45T Matt Bahr 08	.04	.01
New York Giants		
☐ 46T Alonzo Highsmith 12	.06	.01
Dallas Cowboys		
☐ 47T Joe Kelly 12	.06	.01
New York Jets		
☐ 48T Chris Hinton 15	.07	.01
Atlanta Falcons		
☐ 49T Bobby Humphery 08	.04	.01
Los Angeles Rams		
☐ 50T Greg Bell 15	.07	.01
Los Angeles Raiders		
☐ 51T Fred Smerlas 08	.04	.01
San Francisco 49ers		
☐ 52T Walter Stanley 12	.06	.01
Washington Redskins		
☐ 53T Jim Skow 08	.04	.01
Tampa Bay Buccaneers		

☐ 54T Renaldo Turnbull 15	.07	.01
New Orleans Saints		
☐ 55T Bern Brostek 12	.06	.01
Los Angeles Rams		
☐ 56T Charles Wilson 15	.07	.01
Green Bay Packers		
☐ 57T Keith McCants 50	.25	.05
Tampa Bay Buccaneers		
☐ 58T Alexander Wright 75	.35	.07
Dallas Cowboys		
☐ 59T Ian Beckles 20	.10	.02
Tampa Bay Buccaneers		
☐ 60T Eric Davis 40	.20	.04
San Francisco 49ers		
☐ 61T Chris Singleton 15	.07	.01
New England Patriots		
☐ 62T Rob Moore 6.00	3.00	.60
New York Jets		
☐ 63T Darion Conner 30	.15	.03
Atlanta Falcons		
☐ 64T Tim Grunhard 12	.06	.01
Kansas City Chiefs		
☐ 65T Junior Seau 60	.30	.06
San Diego Chargers		
☐ 66T Tony Stargell 50	.25	.05
New York Jets		
☐ 67T Anthony Thompson 1.00	.50	.10
Phoenix Cardinals		
☐ 68T Cortez Kennedy 1.00	.50	.10
Seattle Seahawks		
☐ 69T Darrell Thompson 1.25	.60	.12
Green Bay Packers		
☐ 70T Calvin Williams 1.00	.50	.10
Philadelphia Eagles		
☐ 71T Rodney Hampton 5.50	2.75	.55
New York Giants		
☐ 72T Terry Wooden 15	.07	.01
Seattle Seahawks		
☐ 73T Leo Goeas 15	.07	.01
San Diego Chargers		
☐ 74T Ken Willis 12	.06	.01
Dallas Cowboys		
☐ 75T Ricky Proehl 1.00	.50	.10
Phoenix Cardinals		
☐ 76T Steve Christie 15	.07	.01
Tampa Bay Buccaneers		
☐ 77T Andre Ware 60	.30	.06
Detroit Lions		
☐ 78T Jeff George 6.00	3.00	.60
Indianapolis Colts		
☐ 79T Walter Wilson 20	.10	.02
San Diego Chargers		
☐ 80T Johnny Bailey 1.00	.50	.10
Chicago Bears		
☐ 81T Harold Green 1.50	.75	.15
Cincinnati Bengals		
☐ 82T Mark Carrier 90	.45	.09

1991 Score

Chicago Bears
☐ 83T Frank Cornish ....12 .06 .01
San Diego Chargers
☐ 84T James Williams ....08 .04 .01
Buffalo Bills
☐ 85T James Francis ....80 .40 .08
Cincinnati Bengals
☐ 86T Percy Snow ....25 .12 .02
Kansas City Chiefs
☐ 87T Anthony Johnson ....25 .12 .02
Indianapolis Colts
☐ 88T Tim Ryan ....12 .06 .01
Chicago Bears
☐ 89T Dan Owens ....35 .17 .03
Detroit Lions
☐ 90T Aaron Wallace ....30 .15 .03
Los Angeles Raiders
☐ 91T Steve Broussard .... 1.00 .50 .10
Atlanta Falcons
☐ 92T Eric Green .... 2.75 1.35 .27
Pittsburgh Steelers
☐ 93T Blair Thomas .... 6.50 3.25 .65
New York Jets
☐ 94T Robert Blackmon ....30 .15 .03
Seattle Seahawks
☐ 95T Alan Grant ....25 .12 .02
Indianapolis Colts
☐ 96T Andre Collins ....25 .12 .02
Washington Redskins
☐ 97T Dexter Carter .... 1.25 .60 .12
San Francisco 49ers
☐ 98T Reggie Cobb .... 1.75 .85 .17
Tampa Bay Buccaneers
☐ 99T Dennis Brown ....08 .04 .01
San Francisco 49ers
☐ 100T Kenny Davidson ....25 .12 .02
Pittsburgh Steelers
☐ 101T Emmitt Smith 42.00 15.00 3.00
Dallas Cowboys
☐ 102T Jeff Alm ....12 .06 .01
Houston Oilers
☐ 103T Alton Montgomery ......15 .07 .01
Denver Broncos
☐ 104T Tony Bennett ....15 .07 .01
Green Bay Packers
☐ 105T Johnny Johnson ...... 3.00 1.50 .30
Phoenix Cardinals
☐ 106T Leroy Hoard .... 1.25 .60 .12
Cleveland Browns
☐ 107T Ray Agnew ....15 .07 .01
New England Patriots
☐ 108T Richmond Webb ....50 .25 .05
Miami Dolphins
☐ 109T Keith Sims ....15 .07 .01
Miami Dolphins
☐ 110T Barry Foster .... 1.25 .60 .12
Pittsburgh Steelers

The 1991 Score set consists of two series. The cards feature brilliant full-color photographs on the front and the backs have an horizontal format with the left half containing biographical and statistical information, while the right side of the card has a player portrait. The cards are standard size (2 1/2" by 3 1/2"). Notable subsets in the first series include a Draft Pick subset (311-319), the players who had plays which resulted in 90 or more yards (320-328), two Top Leaders (329-330), and a Dream Team subset (331-345). The key rookie cards in the first series are Nick Bell, Mike Croel, and Dan McGwire. The second series of the 1991 Score football set consists of 345 cards. As part of a promotion, the 11 offensive Dream Team members each signed 500 of their cards. Of this total, 5,478 were randomly inserted in Series II packs and 22 were given away in a mail-in sweepstakes. As with the first series, the fronts feature full-color photos with various color borders. The horizontally oriented backs have player information and the team helmet on the left half, while the right half has a color head shot. Topical subsets featured include 1991 Rookie Draft Picks (564-589, 591-596, 598-612, 614-616), Team MVP's (620-647), Crunch Crew (648-654), Sack Attack (655-661), The Leader (662-669), 1991 Hall of Fame (670-674), and Dream Team (676-686). The set closes with four bonus cards (B1-B4), which were available as part of each factory set. The key rookie cards in the second series are Ricky Ervins, Todd Marinovich, and Harvey Williams.

	MINT	EXC	G-VG
COMPLETE SET (690)	16.00	8.00	1.60

COMMON PLAYER (1-345)	.03	.01	.00
COMMON PLAYER (346-686)	.03	.01	.00
COMMON PLAYER (B1-B4)	.06	.03	.00

☐ 1 Joe Montana	.45	.22	.04
San Francisco 49ers			
☐ 2 Eric Allen	.03	.01	.00
Philadelphia Eagles			
☐ 3 Rohn Stark	.03	.01	.00
Indianapolis Colts			
☐ 4 Frank Reich	.08	.04	.01
Buffalo Bills			
☐ 5 Derrick Thomas	.15	.07	.01
Kansas City Chiefs			
☐ 6 Mike Singletary	.08	.04	.01
Chicago Bears			
☐ 7 Boomer Esiason	.10	.05	.01
Cincinnati Bengals			
☐ 8 Matt Millen	.03	.01	.00
San Francisco 49ers			
☐ 9 Chris Spielman	.06	.03	.00
Detroit Lions			
☐ 10 Gerald McNeil	.03	.01	.00
Houston Oilers			
☐ 11 Nick Lowery	.03	.01	.00
Kansas City Chiefs			
☐ 12 Randall Cunningham	.15	.07	.01
Philadelphia Eagles			
☐ 13 Marion Butts	.10	.05	.01
San Diego Chargers			
☐ 14 Tim Brown	.08	.04	.01
Los Angeles Raiders			
☐ 15 Emmitt Smith	1.25	.60	.12
Dallas Cowboys			
☐ 16 Rich Camarillo	.03	.01	.00
Phoenix Cardinals			
☐ 17 Mike Merriweather	.03	.01	.00
Minnesota Vikings			
☐ 18 Derrick Fenner	.12	.06	.01
Seattle Seahawks			
☐ 19 Clay Matthews	.03	.01	.00
Cleveland Browns			
☐ 20 Barry Sanders	.75	.35	.07
Detroit Lions			
☐ 21 James Brooks	.08	.04	.01
Cincinnati Bengals			
☐ 22 Alton Montgomery	.03	.01	.00
Denver Broncos			
☐ 23 Steve Atwater	.06	.03	.00
Denver Broncos			
☐ 24 Ron Morris	.03	.01	.00
Chicago Bears			
☐ 25 Brad Muster	.06	.03	.00
Chicago Bears			
☐ 26 Andre Rison	.15	.07	.01
Atlanta Falcons			
☐ 27 Brian Brennan	.03	.01	.00
Cleveland Browns			
☐ 28 Leonard Smith	.03	.01	.00
Buffalo Bills			
☐ 29 Kevin Butler	.03	.01	.00
Chicago Bears			
☐ 30 Tim Harris	.06	.03	.00
Green Bay Packers			
☐ 31 Jay Novacek	.10	.05	.01
Dallas Cowboys			
☐ 32 Eddie Murray	.03	.01	.00
Detroit Lions			
☐ 33 Keith Woodside	.06	.03	.00
Green Bay Packers			
☐ 34 Ray Crockett	.08	.04	.01
Detroit Lions			
☐ 35 Eugene Lockhart	.03	.01	.00
Dallas Cowboys			
☐ 36 Bill Romanowski	.03	.01	.00
San Francisco 49ers			
☐ 37 Eddie Brown	.08	.04	.01
Cincinnati Bengals			
☐ 38 Eugene Daniel	.03	.01	.00
Indianapolis Colts			
☐ 39 Scott Fulhage	.03	.01	.00
Atlanta Falcons			
☐ 40 Harold Green	.15	.07	.01
Cincinnati Bengals			
☐ 41 Mark Jackson	.06	.03	.00
Denver Broncos			
☐ 42 Sterling Sharpe	.10	.05	.01
Green Bay Packers			
☐ 43 Mel Gray	.03	.01	.00
Detroit Lions			
☐ 44 Jerry Holmes	.03	.01	.00
Green Bay Packers			
☐ 45 Allen Pinkett	.06	.03	.00
Houston Oilers			
☐ 46 Warren Powers	.06	.03	.00
Denver Broncos			
☐ 47 Rodney Peete	.08	.04	.01
Detroit Lions			
☐ 48 Lorenzo White	.06	.03	.00
Houston Oilers			
☐ 49 Dan Owens	.03	.01	.00
Detroit Lions			
☐ 50 James Francis	.08	.04	.01
Cincinnati Bengals			
☐ 51 Ken Norton	.06	.03	.00
Dallas Cowboys			
☐ 52 Ed West	.06	.03	.00
Green Bay Packers			
☐ 53 Andre Reed	.10	.05	.01
Buffalo Bills			
☐ 54 John Grimsley	.03	.01	.00
Houston Oilers			
☐ 55 Michael Cofer	.03	.01	.00
Detroit Lions			

☐ 56	Chris Doleman 06	.03	.00	
	Minnesota Vikings			
☐ 57	Pat Swilling 08	.04	.01	
	New Orleans Saints			
☐ 58	Jessie Tuggle 03	.01	.00	
	Atlanta Falcons			
☐ 59	Mike Johnson 03	.01	.00	
	Cleveland Browns			
☐ 60	Steve Walsh 08	.04	.01	
	New Orleans Saints			
☐ 61	Sam Mills 06	.03	.00	
	New Orleans Saints			
☐ 62	Don Mosebar 03	.01	.00	
	Los Angeles Raiders			
☐ 63	Jay Hilgenberg 06	.03	.00	
	Chicago Bears			
☐ 64	Cleveland Gary 06	.03	.00	
	Los Angeles Rams			
☐ 65	Andre Tippett 06	.03	.00	
	New England Patriots			
☐ 66	Tom Newberry 03	.01	.00	
	Los Angeles Rams			
☐ 67	Maurice Hurst 03	.01	.00	
	New England Patriots			
☐ 68	Louis Oliver 03	.01	.00	
	Miami Dolphins			
☐ 69	Fred Marion 03	.01	.00	
	New England Patriots			
☐ 70	Christian Okoye 08	.04	.01	
	Kansas City Chiefs			
☐ 71	Marv Cook 10	.05	.01	
	New England Patriots			
☐ 72	Darryl Talley 06	.03	.00	
	Buffalo Bills			
☐ 73	Rick Fenney 03	.01	.00	
	Minnesota Vikings			
☐ 74	Kelvin Martin 06	.03	.00	
	Dallas Cowboys			
☐ 75	Howie Long 06	.03	.00	
	Los Angeles Raiders			
☐ 76	Steve Wisniewski 03	.01	.00	
	Los Angeles Raiders			
☐ 77	Karl Mecklenburg 06	.03	.00	
	Denver Broncos			
☐ 78	Dan Saleaumua 03	.01	.00	
	Kansas City Chiefs			
☐ 79	Ray Childress 06	.03	.00	
	Houston Oilers			
☐ 80	Henry Ellard 08	.04	.01	
	Los Angeles Rams			
☐ 81	Ernest Givins UER 10	.05	.01	
	Houston Oilers			
	(3rd on Oilers in			
	receiving, not 4th)			
☐ 82	Ferrell Edmunds 03	.01	.00	
	Miami Dolphins			
☐ 83	Steve Jordan 06	.03	.00	

	Minnesota Vikings			
☐ 84	Tony Mandarich 06	.03	.00	
	Green Bay Packers			
☐ 85	Eric Martin 06	.03	.00	
	New Orleans Saints			
☐ 86	Rich Gannon 08	.04	.01	
	Minnesota Vikings			
☐ 87	Irving Fryar 06	.03	.00	
	New England Patriots			
☐ 88	Tom Rathman 06	.03	.00	
	San Francisco 49ers			
☐ 89	Dan Hampton 08	.04	.01	
	Chicago Bears			
☐ 90	Barry Word 25	.12	.02	
	Kansas City Chiefs			
☐ 91	Kevin Greene 06	.03	.00	
	Los Angeles Rams			
☐ 92	Sean Landeta 03	.01	.00	
	New York Giants			
☐ 93	Trace Armstrong 03	.01	.00	
	Chicago Bears			
☐ 94	Dennis Byrd 06	.03	.00	
	New York Jets			
☐ 95	Timm Rosenbach 10	.05	.01	
	Phoenix Cardinals			
☐ 96	Anthony Toney 03	.01	.00	
	Philadelphia Eagles			
☐ 97	Tim Krumrie 03	.01	.00	
	Cincinnati Bengals			
☐ 98	Jerry Ball 03	.01	.00	
	Detroit Lions			
☐ 99	Tim Green 03	.01	.00	
	Atlanta Falcons			
☐ 100	Bo Jackson 35	.17	.03	
	Los Angeles Raiders			
☐ 101	Myron Guyton 03	.01	.00	
	New York Giants			
☐ 102	Mike Mularkey 06	.03	.00	
	Pittsburgh Steelers			
☐ 103	Jerry Gray 06	.03	.00	
	Los Angeles Rams			
☐ 104	Scott Stephen 08	.04	.01	
	Green Bay Packers			
☐ 105	Anthony Bell 03	.01	.00	
	Phoenix Cardinals			
☐ 106	Lomas Brown 03	.01	.00	
	Detroit Lions			
☐ 107	David Little 03	.01	.00	
	Pittsburgh Steelers			
☐ 108	Brad Baxter 10	.05	.01	
	New York Jets			
☐ 109	Freddie Joe Nunn 03	.01	.00	
	Phoenix Cardinals			
☐ 110	Dave Meggett 10	.05	.01	
	New York Giants			
☐ 111	Mark Rypien 20	.10	.02	
	Washington Redskins			

☐ 112	Warren Williams .03 Pittsburgh Steelers	.01	.00
☐ 113	Ron Rivera .03 Chicago Bears	.01	.00
☐ 114	Terance Mathis .12 New York Jets	.06	.01
☐ 115	Anthony Munoz .08 Cincinnati Bengals	.04	.01
☐ 116	Jeff Bryant .03 Seattle Seahawks	.01	.00
☐ 117	Issiac Holt .03 Dallas Cowboys	.01	.00
☐ 118	Steve Sewell .06 Denver Broncos	.03	.00
☐ 119	Tim Newton .08 Tampa Bay Buccaneers	.04	.01
☐ 120	Emile Harry .06 Kansas City Chiefs	.03	.00
☐ 121	Gary Anderson .03 Pittsburgh Steelers	.01	.00
☐ 122	Mark Lee .03 Green Bay Packers	.01	.00
☐ 123	Alfred Anderson .03 Minnesota Vikings	.01	.00
☐ 124	Tony Blaylock .08 Cleveland Browns	.04	.01
☐ 125	Earnest Byner .08 Washington Redskins	.04	.01
☐ 126	Bill Maas .03 Kansas City Chiefs	.01	.00
☐ 127	Keith Taylor .06 Indianapolis Colts	.03	.00
☐ 128	Cliff Odom .03 Miami Dolphins	.01	.00
☐ 129	Bob Golic .06 Los Angeles Raiders	.03	.00
☐ 130	Bart Oates .03 New York Giants	.01	.00
☐ 131	Jim Arnold .03 Detroit Lions	.01	.00
☐ 132	Jeff Herrod .06 Indianapolis Colts	.03	.00
☐ 133	Bruce Armstrong .03 New England Patriots	.01	.00
☐ 134	Craig Heyward .08 New Orleans Saints	.04	.01
☐ 135	Joey Browner .06 Minnesota Vikings	.03	.00
☐ 136	Darren Comeaux .03 Seattle Seahawks	.01	.00
☐ 137	Pat Beach .03 Indianapolis Colts	.01	.00
☐ 138	Dalton Hilliard .06 New Orleans Saints	.03	.00
☐ 139	David Treadwell .03 Denver Broncos	.01	.00
☐ 140	Gary Anderson .06	.03	.00

	Tampa Bay Buccaneers		
☐ 141	Eugene Robinson .03 Seattle Seahawks	.01	.00
☐ 142	Scott Case .03 Atlanta Falcons	.01	.00
☐ 143	Paul Farren .06 Cleveland Browns	.03	.00
☐ 144	Gill Fenerty .08 New Orleans Saints	.04	.01
☐ 145	Tim Irwin .03 Minnesota Vikings	.01	.00
☐ 146	Norm Johnson .03 Seattle Seahawks	.01	.00
☐ 147	Willie Gault .06 Los Angeles Raiders	.03	.00
☐ 148	Clarence Verdin .03 Indianapolis Colts	.01	.00
☐ 149	Jeff Uhlenhake .03 Miami Dolphins	.01	.00
☐ 150	Erik McMillan .06 New York Jets	.03	.00
☐ 151	Kevin Ross .03 Kansas City Chiefs	.01	.00
☐ 152	Pepper Johnson .06 New York Giants	.03	.00
☐ 153	Bryan Hinkle .03 Pittsburgh Steelers	.01	.00
☐ 154	Gary Clark .10 Washington Redskins	.05	.01
☐ 155	Robert Delpino .06 Los Angeles Rams	.03	.00
☐ 156	Doug Smith .03 Los Angeles Rams	.01	.00
☐ 157	Chris Martin .03 Kansas City Chiefs	.01	.00
☐ 158	Ray Berry .03 Minnesota Vikings	.01	.00
☐ 159	Steve Christie .03 Tampa Bay Buccaneers	.01	.00
☐ 160	Don Smith .03 Buffalo Bills	.01	.00
☐ 161	Greg McMurtry .08 New England Patriots	.04	.01
☐ 162	Jack Del Rio .03 Dallas Cowboys	.01	.00
☐ 163	Floyd Dixon .03 Atlanta Falcons	.01	.00
☐ 164	Buford McGee .06 Los Angeles Rams	.03	.00
☐ 165	Brett Maxie .08 New Orleans Saints	.04	.01
☐ 166	Morten Andersen .06 New Orleans Saints	.03	.00
☐ 167	Kent Hull .03 Buffalo Bills	.01	.00
☐ 168	Skip McClendon .06 Cincinnati Bengals	.03	.00

☐ 169	Keith Sims .... .03 Miami Dolphins	.01	.00	
☐ 170	Leonard Marshall .... .06 New York Giants	.03	.00	
☐ 171	Tony Woods .... .06 Seattle Seahawks	.03	.00	
☐ 172	Byron Evans .... .03 Philadelphia Eagles	.01	.00	
☐ 173	Rob Burnett .... .08 Cleveland Browns	.04	.01	
☐ 174	Tory Epps .... .06 Atlanta Falcons	.03	.00	
☐ 175	Toi Cook .... .08 New Orleans Saints	.04	.01	
☐ 176	John Elliott .... .03 New York Giants	.01	.00	
☐ 177	Tommie Agee .... .06 Dallas Cowboys	.03	.00	
☐ 178	Keith Van Horne .... .03 Chicago Bears	.01	.00	
☐ 179	Dennis Smith .... .03 Denver Broncos	.01	.00	
☐ 180	James Lofton .... .12 Buffalo Bills	.06	.01	
☐ 181	Art Monk .... .12 Washington Redskins	.06	.01	
☐ 182	Anthony Carter .... .08 Minnesota Vikings	.04	.01	
☐ 183	Louis Lipps .... .06 Pittsburgh Steelers	.03	.00	
☐ 184	Bruce Hill .... .03 Tampa Bay Buccaneers	.01	.00	
☐ 185	Mike Young .... .06 Denver Broncos	.03	.00	
☐ 186	Eric Green .... .15 Pittsburgh Steelers	.07	.01	
☐ 187	Barney Bussey .... .08 Cincinnati Bengals	.04	.01	
☐ 188	Curtis Duncan .... .06 Houston Oilers	.03	.00	
☐ 189	Robert Awalt .... .03 Dallas Cowboys	.01	.00	
☐ 190	Johnny Johnson .... .25 Phoenix Cardinals	.12	.02	
☐ 191	Jeff Cross .... .03 Miami Dolphins	.01	.00	
☐ 192	Keith McKeller .... .08 Buffalo Bills	.04	.01	
☐ 193	Robert Brown .... .06 Green Bay Packers	.03	.00	
☐ 194	Vincent Brown .... .06 New England Patriots	.03	.00	
☐ 195	Calvin Williams .... .08 Philadelphia Eagles	.04	.01	
☐ 196	Sean Jones .... .03 Houston Oilers	.01	.00	
☐ 197	Willie Drewrey .... .03	.01	.00	
☐ 198	Tampa Bay Buccaneers Bubba McDowell .... .03 Houston Oilers	.01	.00	
☐ 199	Al Noga .... .03 Minnesota Vikings	.01	.00	
☐ 200	Ronnie Lott .... .10 San Francisco 49ers	.05	.01	
☐ 201	Warren Moon .... .20 Houston Oilers	.10	.02	
☐ 202	Chris Hinton .... .06 Atlanta Falcons	.03	.00	
☐ 203	Jim Sweeney .... .03 New York Jets	.01	.00	
☐ 204	Wayne Haddix .... .06 Tampa Bay Buccaneers	.03	.00	
☐ 205	Tim Jorden .... .08 Phoenix Cardinals	.04	.01	
☐ 206	Marvin Allen .... .03 New England Patriots	.01	.00	
☐ 207	Jim Morrissey .... .10 Chicago Bears	.05	.01	
☐ 208	Ben Smith .... .03 Philadelphia Eagles	.01	.00	
☐ 209	William White .... .06 Detroit Lions	.03	.00	
☐ 210	Jim Jensen .... .03 Miami Dolphins	.01	.00	
☐ 211	Doug Reed .... .08 Los Angeles Rams	.04	.01	
☐ 212	Ethan Horton .... .10 Los Angeles Raiders	.05	.01	
☐ 213	Chris Jacke .... .03 Green Bay Packers	.01	.00	
☐ 214	Johnny Hector .... .06 New York Jets	.03	.00	
☐ 215	Drew Hill UER .... .08 Houston Oilers (Tied for the NFC lead, should say AFC)	.04	.01	
☐ 216	Roy Green .... .06 Phoenix Cardinals	.03	.00	
☐ 217	Dean Steinkuhler .... .06 Houston Oilers	.03	.00	
☐ 218	Cedric Mack .... .03 Phoenix Cardinals	.01	.00	
☐ 219	Chris Miller .... .15 Atlanta Falcons	.07	.01	
☐ 220	Keith Byars .... .06 Philadelphia Eagles	.03	.00	
☐ 221	Lewis Billups .... .03 Cincinnati Bengals	.01	.00	
☐ 222	Roger Craig .... .10 San Francisco 49ers	.05	.01	
☐ 223	Shaun Gayle .... .03 Chicago Bears	.01	.00	
☐ 224	Mike Rozier .... .06 Atlanta Falcons	.03	.00	

☐ 225 Troy Aikman	.35	.17	.03
Dallas Cowboys			
☐ 226 Bobby Humphrey	.10	.05	.01
Denver Broncos			
☐ 227 Eugene Marve	.03	.01	.00
Tampa Bay Buccaneers			
☐ 228 Michael Carter	.06	.03	.00
San Francisco 49ers			
☐ 229 Richard Johnson	.08	.04	.01
Houston Oilers			
☐ 230 Billy Joe Tolliver	.08	.04	.01
San Diego Chargers			
☐ 231 Mark Murphy	.03	.01	.00
Green Bay Packers			
☐ 232 John L. Williams	.08	.04	.01
Seattle Seahawks			
☐ 233 Ronnie Harmon	.03	.01	.00
San Diego Chargers			
☐ 234 Thurman Thomas	.45	.22	.04
Buffalo Bills			
☐ 235 Martin Mayhew	.06	.03	.00
Washington Redskins			
☐ 236 Richmond Webb	.06	.03	.00
Miami Dolphins			
☐ 237 Gerald Riggs UER	.06	.03	.00
Washington Redskins			
(Earnest Byner mis-			
spelled as Ernest)			
☐ 238 Mike Prior	.03	.01	.00
Indianapolis Colts			
☐ 239 Mike Gann	.03	.01	.00
Atlanta Falcons			
☐ 240 Alvin Walton	.03	.01	.00
Washington Redskins			
☐ 241 Tim McGee	.06	.03	.00
Cincinnati Bengals			
☐ 242 Bruce Matthews	.03	.01	.00
Houston Oilers			
☐ 243 Johnny Holland	.03	.01	.00
Green Bay Packers			
☐ 244 Martin Bayless	.06	.03	.00
San Diego Chargers			
☐ 245 Eric Metcalf	.06	.03	.00
Cleveland Browns			
☐ 246 John Alt	.03	.01	.00
Kansas City Chiefs			
☐ 247 Max Montoya	.03	.01	.00
Los Angeles Raiders			
☐ 248 Rod Bernstine	.08	.04	.01
San Diego Chargers			
☐ 249 Paul Gruber	.06	.03	.00
Tampa Bay Buccaneers			
☐ 250 Charles Haley	.06	.03	.00
San Francisco 49ers			
☐ 251 Scott Norwood	.03	.01	.00
Buffalo Bills			
☐ 252 Michael Haddix	.06	.03	.00

Green Bay Packers			
☐ 253 Ricky Sanders	.08	.04	.01
Washington Redskins			
☐ 254 Ervin Randle	.03	.01	.00
Tampa Bay Buccaneers			
☐ 255 Duane Bickett	.03	.01	.00
Indianapolis Colts			
☐ 256 Mike Munchak	.06	.03	.00
Houston Oilers			
☐ 257 Keith Jones	.06	.03	.00
Atlanta Falcons			
☐ 258 Riki Ellison	.03	.01	.00
Los Angeles Raiders			
☐ 259 Vince Newsome	.03	.01	.00
Los Angeles Rams			
☐ 260 Lee Williams	.06	.03	.00
San Diego Chargers			
☐ 261 Steve Smith	.03	.01	.00
Los Angeles Raiders			
☐ 262 Sam Clancy	.03	.01	.00
Indianapolis Colts			
☐ 263 Pierce Holt	.03	.01	.00
San Francisco 49ers			
☐ 264 Jim Harbaugh	.10	.05	.01
Chicago Bears			
☐ 265 Dino Hackett	.03	.01	.00
Kansas City Chiefs			
☐ 266 Andy Heck	.03	.01	.00
Seattle Seahawks			
☐ 267 Leo Goeas	.03	.01	.00
San Diego Chargers			
☐ 268 Russ Grimm	.06	.03	.00
Washington Redskins			
☐ 269 Gill Byrd	.06	.03	.00
San Diego Chargers			
☐ 270 Neal Anderson	.15	.07	.01
Chicago Bears			
☐ 271 Jackie Slater	.06	.03	.00
Los Angeles Rams			
☐ 272 Joe Nash	.03	.01	.00
Seattle Seahawks			
☐ 273 Todd Bowles	.06	.03	.00
Washington Redskins			
☐ 274 D.J. Dozier	.08	.04	.01
Minnesota Vikings			
☐ 275 Kevin Fagan	.03	.01	.00
San Francisco 49ers			
☐ 276 Don Warren	.06	.03	.00
Washington Redskins			
☐ 277 Jim Jeffcoat	.03	.01	.00
Dallas Cowboys			
☐ 278 Bruce Smith	.08	.04	.01
Buffalo Bills			
☐ 279 Cortez Kennedy	.08	.04	.01
Seattle Seahawks			
☐ 280 Thane Gash	.03	.01	.00
Cleveland Browns			

☐ 281 Perry Kemp 03	.01	.00	
Green Bay Packers			
☐ 282 John Taylor 12	.06	.01	
San Francisco 49ers			
☐ 283 Stephone Paige 06	.03	.00	
Kansas City Chiefs			
☐ 284 Paul Skansi 06	.03	.00	
Seattle Seahawks			
☐ 285 Shawn Collins 06	.03	.00	
Atlanta Falcons			
☐ 286 Mervyn Fernandez 06	.03	.00	
Los Angeles Raiders			
☐ 287 Daniel Stubbs 03	.01	.00	
Dallas Cowboys			
☐ 288 Chip Lohmiller 03	.01	.00	
Washington Redskins			
☐ 289 Brian Blades 08	.04	.01	
Seattle Seahawks			
☐ 290 Mark Carrier 08	.04	.01	
Tampa Bay Buccaneers			
☐ 291 Carl Zander 03	.01	.00	
Cincinnati Bengals			
☐ 292 David Wyman 03	.01	.00	
Seattle Seahawks			
☐ 293 Jeff Bostic 06	.03	.00	
Washington Redskins			
☐ 294 Irv Pankey 03	.01	.00	
Los Angeles Rams			
☐ 295 Keith Millard 06	.03	.00	
Minnesota Vikings			
☐ 296 Jamie Mueller 06	.03	.00	
Buffalo Bills			
☐ 297 Bill Fralic 06	.03	.00	
Atlanta Falcons			
☐ 298 Wendell Davis 12	.06	.01	
Chicago Bears			
☐ 299 Ken Clarke 06	.03	.00	
Minnesota Vikings			
☐ 300 Wymon Henderson 03	.01	.00	
Denver Broncos			
☐ 301 Jeff Campbell 08	.04	.01	
Detroit Lions			
☐ 302 Cody Carlson 15	.07	.01	
Houston Oilers			
☐ 303 Matt Brock 10	.05	.01	
Green Bay Packers			
☐ 304 Maurice Carthon 03	.01	.00	
New York Giants			
☐ 305 Scott Mersereau 08	.04	.01	
New York Jets			
☐ 306 Steve Wright 08	.04	.01	
Los Angeles Raiders			
☐ 307 J.B. Brown 06	.03	.00	
Miami Dolphins			
☐ 308 Ricky Reynolds 03	.01	.00	
Tampa Bay Buccaneers			
☐ 309 Darryl Pollard 06	.03	.00	

San Francisco 49ers			
☐ 310 Donald Evans 03	.01	.00	
Pittsburgh Steelers			
☐ 311 Nick Bell 75	.35	.07	
Iowa			
☐ 312 Pat Harlow 15	.07	.01	
USC			
☐ 313 Dan McGwire 1.25	.60	.12	
San Diego State			
☐ 314 Mike Dumas 15	.07	.01	
Indiana			
☐ 315 Mike Croel 75	.35	.07	
Nebraska			
☐ 316 Chris Smith 10	.05	.01	
BYU			
☐ 317 Kenny Walker 45	.22	.04	
Nebraska			
☐ 318 Todd Lyght 40	.20	.04	
Notre Dame			
☐ 319 Mike Stonebreaker 10	.05	.01	
Notre Dame			
☐ 320 Randall Cunningham 90 .08	.04	.01	
Philadelphia Eagles			
☐ 321 Terance Mathis 90 08	.04	.01	
New York Jets			
☐ 322 Gaston Green 90 08	.04	.01	
Los Angeles Rams			
☐ 323 Johnny Bailey 90 08	.04	.01	
Chicago Bears			
☐ 324 Donnie Elder 90 03	.01	.00	
San Diego Chargers			
☐ 325 Dwight Stone 90 UER ...03	.01	.00	
Pittsburgh Steelers			
(No '91 copyright			
on card back)			
☐ 326 J.J. Birden 90 15	.07	.01	
Kansas City Chiefs			
☐ 327 Alexander Wright 90 10	.05	.01	
Dallas Cowboys			
☐ 328 Eric Metcalf 90 08	.04	.01	
Cleveland Browns			
☐ 329 Andre Rison TL 08	.04	.01	
Atlanta Falcons			
☐ 330 Warren Moon TL UER ...10	.05	.01	
Houston Oilers			
(Not Blanda's record,			
should be Van Brocklin)			
☐ 331 Steve Tasker DT 06	.03	.00	
Buffalo Bills			
☐ 332 Mel Gray DT 06	.03	.00	
Detroit Lions			
☐ 333 Nick Lowery DT 06	.03	.00	
Kansas City Chiefs			
☐ 334 Sean Landeta DT 06	.03	.00	
New York Giants			
☐ 335 David Fulcher DT 06	.03	.00	
Cincinnati Bengals			

☐ 336 Joey Browner DT	.06	.03	.00
Minnesota Vikings			
☐ 337 Albert Lewis DT	.06	.03	.00
Kansas City Chiefs			
☐ 338 Rod Woodson DT	.08	.04	.01
Pittsburgh Steelers			
☐ 339 Shane Conlan DT	.06	.03	.00
Buffalo Bills			
☐ 340 Pepper Johnson DT	.06	.03	.00
New York Giants			
☐ 341 Chris Spielman DT	.06	.03	.00
Detroit Lions			
☐ 342 Derrick Thomas DT	.10	.05	.01
Kansas City Chiefs			
☐ 343 Ray Childress DT	.06	.03	.00
Houston Oilers			
☐ 344 Reggie White DT	.08	.04	.01
Philadelphia Eagles			
☐ 345 Bruce Smith DT	.08	.04	.01
Buffalo Bills			
☐ 346 Darrell Green	.10	.05	.01
Washington Redskins			
☐ 347 Ray Bentley	.03	.01	.00
Buffalo Bills			
☐ 348 Herschel Walker	.12	.06	.01
Minnesota Vikings			
☐ 349 Rodney Holman	.03	.01	.00
Cincinnati Bengals			
☐ 350 Al Toon	.08	.04	.01
New York Jets			
☐ 351 Harry Hamilton	.03	.01	.00
Tampa Bay Buccaneers			
☐ 352 Albert Lewis	.06	.03	.00
Kansas City Chiefs			
☐ 353 Renaldo Turnbull	.06	.03	.00
New Orleans Saints			
☐ 354 Junior Seau	.08	.04	.01
San Diego Chargers			
☐ 355 Merril Hoge	.06	.03	.00
Pittsburgh Steelers			
☐ 356 Shane Conlan	.06	.03	.00
Buffalo Bills			
☐ 357 Jay Schroeder	.08	.04	.01
Los Angeles Raiders			
☐ 358 Steve Broussard	.10	.05	.01
Atlanta Falcons			
☐ 359 Mark Bavaro	.06	.03	.00
New York Giants			
☐ 360 Jim Lachey	.06	.03	.00
Washington Redskins			
☐ 361 Greg Townsend	.03	.01	.00
Los Angeles Raiders			
☐ 362 Dave Krieg	.08	.04	.01
Seattle Seahawks			
☐ 363 Jessie Hester	.06	.03	.00
Indianapolis Colts			
☐ 364 Steve Tasker	.03	.01	.00
Buffalo Bills			
☐ 365 Ron Hall	.03	.01	.00
Tampa Bay Buccaneers			
☐ 366 Pat Leahy	.06	.03	.00
New York Jets			
☐ 367 Jim Everett	.10	.05	.01
Los Angeles Rams			
☐ 368 Felix Wright	.03	.01	.00
Cleveland Browns			
☐ 369 Ricky Proehl	.10	.05	.01
Phoenix Cardinals			
☐ 370 Anthony Miller	.08	.04	.01
San Diego Chargers			
☐ 371 Keith Jackson	.08	.04	.01
Philadelphia Eagles			
☐ 372 Pete Stoyanovich	.03	.01	.00
Miami Dolphins			
☐ 373 Tommy Kane	.12	.06	.01
Seattle Seahawks			
☐ 374 Richard Johnson	.03	.01	.00
Detroit Lions			
☐ 375 Randall McDaniel	.03	.01	.00
Minnesota Vikings			
☐ 376 John Stephens	.08	.04	.01
New England Patriots			
☐ 377 Haywood Jeffires	.20	.10	.02
Houston Oilers			
☐ 378 Rodney Hampton	.40	.20	.04
New York Giants			
☐ 379 Tim Grunhard	.03	.01	.00
Kansas City Chiefs			
☐ 380 Jerry Rice	.35	.17	.03
San Francisco 49ers			
☐ 381 Ken Harvey	.03	.01	.00
Phoenix Cardinals			
☐ 382 Vaughan Johnson	.06	.03	.00
New Orleans Saints			
☐ 383 J.T. Smith	.06	.03	.00
Phoenix Cardinals			
☐ 384 Carnell Lake	.03	.01	.00
Pittsburgh Steelers			
☐ 385 Dan Marino	.25	.12	.02
Miami Dolphins			
☐ 386 Kyle Clifton	.03	.01	.00
New York Jets			
☐ 387 Wilber Marshall	.06	.03	.00
Washington Redskins			
☐ 388 Pete Holohan	.03	.01	.00
Los Angeles Rams			
☐ 389 Gary Plummer	.03	.01	.00
San Diego Chargers			
☐ 390 William Perry	.08	.04	.01
Chicago Bears			
☐ 391 Mark Robinson	.03	.01	.00
Buffalo Bills			
☐ 392 Nate Odomes	.03	.01	.00
Buffalo Bills			

☐ 393	Ickey Woods ....06 Cincinnati Bengals	.03	.00	
☐ 394	Reyna Thompson ....06 New York Giants	.03	.00	
☐ 395	Deion Sanders ....20 Atlanta Falcons	.10	.02	
☐ 396	Harris Barton ....03 San Francisco 49ers	.01	.00	
☐ 397	Sammie Smith ....08 Miami Dolphins	.04	.01	
☐ 398	Vinny Testaverde ....08 Tampa Bay Buccaneers	.04	.01	
☐ 399	Ray Donaldson ....03 Indianapolis Colts	.01	.00	
☐ 400	Tim McKyer ....03 Miami Dolphins	.01	.00	
☐ 401	Nesby Glasgow ....03 Seattle Seahawks	.01	.00	
☐ 402	Brent Williams ....03 New England Patriots	.01	.00	
☐ 403	Rob Moore ....50 New York Jets	.25	.05	
☐ 404	Bubby Brister ....08 Pittsburgh Steelers	.04	.01	
☐ 405	David Fulcher ....03 Cincinnati Bengals	.01	.00	
☐ 406	Reggie Cobb ....15 Tampa Bay Buccaneers	.07	.01	
☐ 407	Jerome Brown ....06 Philadelphia Eagles	.03	.00	
☐ 408	Erik Howard ....03 New York Giants	.01	.00	
☐ 409	Tony Paige ....03 Miami Dolphins	.01	.00	
☐ 410	John Elway ....15 Denver Broncos	.07	.01	
☐ 411	Charles Mann ....06 Washington Redskins	.03	.00	
☐ 412	Luis Sharpe ....03 Phoenix Cardinals	.01	.00	
☐ 413	Hassan Jones ....06 Minnesota Vikings	.03	.00	
☐ 414	Frank Minnifield ....03 Cleveland Browns	.01	.00	
☐ 415	Steve DeBerg ....08 Kansas City Chiefs	.04	.01	
☐ 416	Mark Carrier ....08 Chicago Bears	.04	.01	
☐ 417	Brian Jordan ....20 Atlanta Falcons	.10	.02	
☐ 418	Reggie Langhorne ....03 Cleveland Browns	.01	.00	
☐ 419	Don Majkowski ....08 Green Bay Packers	.04	.01	
☐ 420	Marcus Allen ....10 Los Angeles Raiders	.05	.01	
☐ 421	Michael Brooks 03	.01	.00	

	Denver Broncos			
☐ 422	Vai Sikahema ....03 Phoenix Cardinals	.01	.00	
☐ 423	Dermontti Dawson ....03 Pittsburgh Steelers	.01	.00	
☐ 424	Jacob Green ....06 Seattle Seahawks	.03	.00	
☐ 425	Flipper Anderson ....06 Los Angeles Rams	.03	.00	
☐ 426	Bill Brooks ....03 Indianapolis Colts	.01	.00	
☐ 427	Keith McCants ....08 Tampa Bay Buccaneers	.04	.01	
☐ 428	Ken O'Brien ....08 New York Jets	.04	.01	
☐ 429	Fred Barnett ....15 Philadelphia Eagles	.07	.01	
☐ 430	Mark Duper ....06 Miami Dolphins	.03	.00	
☐ 431	Mark Kelso ....03 Buffalo Bills	.01	.00	
☐ 432	Leslie O'Neal ....06 San Diego Chargers	.03	.00	
☐ 433	Ottis Anderson ....08 New York Giants	.04	.01	
☐ 434	Jesse Sapolu ....03 San Francisco 49ers	.01	.00	
☐ 435	Gary Zimmerman ....03 Minnesota Vikings	.01	.00	
☐ 436	Kevin Porter ....03 Kansas City Chiefs	.01	.00	
☐ 437	Anthony Thompson ....08 Phoenix Cardinals	.04	.01	
☐ 438	Robert Clark ....06 Detroit Lions	.03	.00	
☐ 439	Chris Warren ....06 Seattle Seahawks	.03	.00	
☐ 440	Gerald Williams ....03 Pittsburgh Steelers	.01	.00	
☐ 441	Jim Skow ....03 Tampa Bay Buccaneers	.01	.00	
☐ 442	Rick Donnelly ....03 Seattle Seahawks	.01	.00	
☐ 443	Guy McIntyre ....03 San Francisco 49ers	.01	.00	
☐ 444	Jeff Lageman ....06 New York Jets	.03	.00	
☐ 445	John Offerdahl ....03 Miami Dolphins	.01	.00	
☐ 446	Clyde Simmons ....06 Philadelphia Eagles	.03	.00	
☐ 447	John Kidd ....03 San Diego Chargers	.01	.00	
☐ 448	Chip Banks ....03 Indianapolis Colts	.01	.00	
☐ 449	Johnny Meads ....03 Houston Oilers	.01	.00	

☐ 450	Rickey Jackson 06	.03	.00	
	New Orleans Saints			
☐ 451	Lee Johnson 03	.01	.00	
	Cincinnati Bengals			
☐ 452	Michael Irvin 20	.10	.02	
	Dallas Cowboys			
☐ 453	Leon Seals 03	.01	.00	
	Buffalo Bills			
☐ 454	Darrell Thompson 12	.06	.01	
	Green Bay Packers			
☐ 455	Everson Walls 03	.01	.00	
	New York Giants			
☐ 456	LeRoy Butler 03	.01	.00	
	Green Bay Packers			
☐ 457	Marcus Dupree 06	.03	.00	
	Los Angeles Rams			
☐ 458	Kirk Lowdermilk 03	.01	.00	
	Minnesota Vikings			
☐ 459	Chris Singleton 06	.03	.00	
	New England Patriots			
☐ 460	Seth Joyner 06	.03	.00	
	Philadelphia Eagles			
☐ 461	Rueben Mayes UER 06	.03	.00	
	New Orleans Saints			
	(Hayes in bio should			
	be Heyward)			
☐ 462	Ernie Jones 06	.03	.00	
	Phoenix Cardinals			
☐ 463	Greg Kragen 03	.01	.00	
	Denver Broncos			
☐ 464	Bennie Blades 06	.03	.00	
	Detroit Lions			
☐ 465	Mark Bortz 03	.01	.00	
	Chicago Bears			
☐ 466	Tony Stargell 06	.03	.00	
	New York Jets			
☐ 467	Mike Cofer 03	.01	.00	
	San Francisco 49ers			
☐ 468	Randy Grimes 03	.01	.00	
	Tampa Bay Buccaneers			
☐ 469	Tim Worley 06	.03	.00	
	Pittsburgh Steelers			
☐ 470	Kevin Mack 06	.03	.00	
	Cleveland Browns			
☐ 471	Wes Hopkins 03	.01	.00	
	Philadelphia Eagles			
☐ 472	Will Wolford 03	.01	.00	
	Buffalo Bills			
☐ 473	Sam Seale 08	.04	.01	
	San Diego Chargers			
☐ 474	Jim Ritcher 03	.01	.00	
	Buffalo Bills			
☐ 475	Jeff Hostetler 20	.10	.02	
	New York Giants			
☐ 476	Mitchell Price 10	.05	.01	
	Cincinnati Bengals			
☐ 477	Ken Lanier 03	.01	.00	

	Denver Broncos			
☐ 478	Naz Worthen 03	.01	.00	
	Kansas City Chiefs			
☐ 479	Ed Reynolds 03	.01	.00	
	New England Patriots			
☐ 480	Mark Clayton 08	.04	.01	
	Miami Dolphins			
☐ 481	Matt Bahr 03	.01	.00	
	New York Giants			
☐ 482	Gary Reasons 03	.01	.00	
	New York Giants			
☐ 483	Dave Szott 08	.04	.01	
	Kansas City Chiefs			
☐ 484	Barry Foster 12	.06	.01	
	Pittsburgh Steelers			
☐ 485	Bruce Reimers 03	.01	.00	
	Cincinnati Bengals			
☐ 486	Dean Biasucci 03	.01	.00	
	Indianapolis Colts			
☐ 487	Cris Carter 06	.03	.00	
	Minnesota Vikings			
☐ 488	Albert Bentley 06	.03	.00	
	Indianapolis Colts			
☐ 489	Robert Massey 03	.01	.00	
	New Orleans Saints			
☐ 490	Al Smith 03	.01	.00	
	Houston Oilers			
☐ 491	Greg Lloyd 03	.01	.00	
	Pittsburgh Steelers			
☐ 492	Steve McMichael UER 06	.03	.00	
	Chicago Bears			
	(Photo on back act-			
	ually Dan Hampton)			
☐ 493	Jeff Wright 08	.04	.01	
	Buffalo Bills			
☐ 494	Scott Davis 06	.03	.00	
	Los Angeles Raiders			
☐ 495	Freeman McNeil 08	.04	.01	
	New York Jets			
☐ 496	Simon Fletcher 03	.01	.00	
	Denver Broncos			
☐ 497	Terry McDaniel 03	.01	.00	
	Los Angeles Raiders			
☐ 498	Heath Sherman 08	.04	.01	
	Philadelphia Eagles			
☐ 499	Jeff Jaeger 03	.01	.00	
	Los Angeles Raiders			
☐ 500	Mark Collins 06	.03	.00	
	New York Giants			
☐ 501	Tim Goad 03	.01	.00	
	New England Patriots			
☐ 502	Jeff George 35	.17	.03	
	Indianapolis Colts			
☐ 503	Jimmie Jones 03	.01	.00	
	Dallas Cowboys			
☐ 504	Henry Thomas 03	.01	.00	
	Minnesota Vikings			

☐ 505	Steve Young ....10 San Francisco 49ers	.05	.01
☐ 506	William Roberts ....03 New York Giants	.01	.00
☐ 507	Neil Smith ....06 Kansas City Chiefs	.03	.00
☐ 508	Mike Saxon ....03 Dallas Cowboys	.01	.00
☐ 509	Johnny Bailey ....08 Chicago Bears	.04	.01
☐ 510	Broderick Thomas ....06 Tampa Bay Buccaneers	.03	.00
☐ 511	Wade Wilson ....08 Minnesota Vikings	.04	.01
☐ 512	Hart Lee Dykes ....06 New England Patriots	.03	.00
☐ 513	Hardy Nickerson ....03 Pittsburgh Steelers	.01	.00
☐ 514	Tim McDonald ....06 Phoenix Cardinals	.03	.00
☐ 515	Frank Cornish ....03 San Diego Chargers	.01	.00
☐ 516	Jarvis Williams ....03 Miami Dolphins	.01	.00
☐ 517	Carl Lee ....03 Minnesota Vikings	.01	.00
☐ 518	Carl Banks ....06 New York Giants	.03	.00
☐ 519	Mike Golic ....03 Philadelphia Eagles	.01	.00
☐ 520	Brian Noble ....03 Green Bay Packers	.01	.00
☐ 521	James Hasty ....03 New York Jets	.01	.00
☐ 522	Bubba Paris ....03 San Francisco 49ers	.01	.00
☐ 523	Kevin Walker ....15 Cincinnati Bengals	.07	.01
☐ 524	William Fuller ....06 Houston Oilers	.03	.00
☐ 525	Eddie Anderson ....03 Los Angeles Raiders	.01	.00
☐ 526	Roger Ruzek ....03 Philadelphia Eagles	.01	.00
☐ 527	Robert Blackmon ....06 Seattle Seahawks	.03	.00
☐ 528	Vince Buck ....06 New Orleans Saints	.03	.00
☐ 529	Lawrence Taylor ....10 New York Giants	.05	.01
☐ 530	Reggie Roby ....03 Miami Dolphins	.01	.00
☐ 531	Doug Riesenberg ....03 New York Giants	.01	.00
☐ 532	Joe Jacoby ....06 Washington Redskins	.03	.00
☐ 533	Kirby Jackson 08	.04	.01

	Buffalo Bills		
☐ 534	Robb Thomas ....08 Kansas City Chiefs	.04	.01
☐ 535	Don Griffin ....03 San Francisco 49ers	.01	.00
☐ 536	Andre Waters ....03 Philadelphia Eagles	.01	.00
☐ 537	Marc Logan ....03 Miami Dolphins	.01	.00
☐ 538	James Thornton ....03 Chicago Bears	.01	.00
☐ 539	Ray Agnew ....03 New England Patriots	.01	.00
☐ 540	Frank Stams ....03 Los Angeles Rams	.01	.00
☐ 541	Brett Perriman ....06 New Orleans Saints	.03	.00
☐ 542	Andre Ware ....12 Detroit Lions	.06	.01
☐ 543	Kevin Haverdink ....03 New Orleans Saints	.01	.00
☐ 544	Greg Jackson ....08 New York Giants	.04	.01
☐ 545	Tunch Ilkin ....03 Pittsburgh Steelers	.01	.00
☐ 546	Dexter Carter ....08 San Francisco 49ers	.04	.01
☐ 547	Rod Woodson ....08 Pittsburgh Steelers	.04	.01
☐ 548	Donnell Woolford ....03 Chicago Bears	.01	.00
☐ 549	Mark Boyer ....03 New York Jets	.01	.00
☐ 550	Jeff Query ....03 Green Bay Packers	.01	.00
☐ 551	Burt Grossman ....06 San Diego Chargers	.03	.00
☐ 552	Mike Kenn ....03 Atlanta Falcons	.01	.00
☐ 553	Richard Dent ....08 Chicago Bears	.04	.01
☐ 554	Gaston Green ....25 Los Angeles Rams	.12	.02
☐ 555	Phil Simms ....08 New York Giants	.04	.01
☐ 556	Brent Jones ....06 San Francisco 49ers	.03	.00
☐ 557	Ronnie Lippett ....03 New England Patriots	.01	.00
☐ 558	Mike Horan ....03 Denver Broncos	.01	.00
☐ 559	Danny Noonan ....03 Dallas Cowboys	.01	.00
☐ 560	Reggie White ....08 Philadelphia Eagles	.04	.01
☐ 561	Rufus Porter ....03 Seattle Seahawks	.01	.00

☐ 562 Aaron Wallace 06	.03	.00	Pittsburgh Steelers	
Los Angeles Raiders			☐ 588 Harvey Williams 75	.35	.07
☐ 563 Vance Johnson 06	.03	.00	Kansas City Chiefs	
Denver Broncos			☐ 589 Alvin Harper 50	.25	.05
☐ 564 Aaron Craver UER 20	.10	.02	Dallas Cowboys	
Miami Dolphins			☐ 590 John Carney 06	.03	.00
(No copyright line			San Diego Chargers	
on back)			☐ 591 Mark Vander Poel 12	.06	.01
☐ 565A Russell Maryland ERR .45	.22	.04	Indianapolis Colts	
Dallas Cowboys			☐ 592 Mike Pritchard 60	.30	.06
(No copyright line			Atlanta Falcons	
on back)			☐ 593 Eric Moten 15	.07	.01
☐ 565B Russell Maryland COR .45	.22	.04	San Diego Chargers	
Dallas Cowboys			☐ 594 Moe Gardner 20	.10	.02
☐ 566 Paul Justin 08	.04	.01	Atlanta Falcons	
Chicago Bears			☐ 595 Wesley Carroll 40	.20	.04
☐ 567 Walter Dean 08	.04	.01	New Orleans Saints	
Green Bay Packers			☐ 596 Eric Swann 20	.10	.02
☐ 568 Herman Moore 60	.30	.06	Phoenix Cardinals	
Detroit Lions			☐ 597 Joe Kelly 03	.01	.00
☐ 569 Bill Musgrave 10	.05	.01	New York Jets	
Dallas Cowboys			☐ 598 Steve Jackson 10	.05	.01
☐ 570 Rob Carpenter 12	.06	.01	Houston Oilers	
Cincinnati Bengals			☐ 599 Kelvin Pritchett 15	.07	.01
☐ 571 Greg Lewis 35	.17	.03	Dallas Cowboys	
Denver Broncos			☐ 600 Jesse Campbell 12	.06	.01
☐ 572 Ed King 15	.07	.01	Philadelphia Eagles	
Cleveland Browns			☐ 601 Darryll Lewis UER 15	.07	.01
☐ 573 Ernie Mills 20	.10	.02	Houston Oilers	
Pittsburgh Steelers			(Misspelled Darryl	
☐ 574 Jake Reed 15	.07	.01	on card)	
Minnesota Vikings			☐ 602 Howard Griffith 08	.04	.01
☐ 575 Ricky Watters 35	.17	.03	Indianapolis Colts	
San Francisco 49ers			☐ 603 Blaise Bryant 10	.05	.01
☐ 576 Derek Russell 25	.12	.02	New York Jets	
Denver Broncos			☐ 604 Vinnie Clark 12	.06	.01
☐ 577 Shawn Moore 12	.06	.01	Green Bay Packers	
Denver Broncos			☐ 605 Mel Agee 08	.04	.01
☐ 578 Eric Bieniemy 30	.15	.03	Indianapolis Colts	
San Diego Chargers			☐ 606 Bobby Wilson 10	.05	.01
☐ 579 Chris Zorich 25	.12	.02	Washington Redskins	
Chicago Bears			☐ 607 Kevin Donnalley 08	.04	.01
☐ 580 Scott Miller 10	.05	.01	Houston Oilers	
Miami Dolphins			☐ 608 Randal Hill 60	.30	.06
☐ 581 Jarrod Bunch 15	.07	.01	Miami Dolphins	
New York Giants			☐ 609 Stan Thomas 10	.05	.01
☐ 582 Ricky Ervins 1.75	.85	.17	Chicago Bears	
Washington Redskins			☐ 610 Mike Heldt 08	.04	.01
☐ 583 Browning Nagle 75	.35	.07	San Diego Chargers	
New York Jets			☐ 611 Brett Favre 75	.35	.07
☐ 584 Eric Turner 50	.25	.05	Atlanta Falcons	
Cleveland Browns			☐ 612 Lawrence Dawsey UER ..40	.20	.04
☐ 585 William Thomas 10	.05	.01	Tampa Bay Buccaneers	
Philadelphia Eagles			(Went to Florida State,	
☐ 586 Stanley Richard 25	.12	.02	not Florida)	
San Diego Chargers			☐ 613 Dennis Gibson 03	.01	.00
☐ 587 Adrian Cooper 15	.07	.01	Detroit Lions	

□ 614	Dean Dingman	.08	.04	.01
	Pittsburgh Steelers			
□ 615	Bruce Pickens	.20	.10	.02
	Atlanta Falcons			
□ 616	Todd Marinovich	1.50	.75	.15
	Los Angeles Raiders			
□ 617	Gene Atkins	.03	.01	.00
	New Orleans Saints			
□ 618	Marcus Dupree	.06	.03	.00
	(Comeback Player)			
	Los Angeles Rams			
□ 619	Warren Moon	.10	.05	.01
	(Man of the Year)			
	Houston Oilers			
□ 620	Joe Montana	.20	.10	.02
	(Team MVP)			
	San Francisco 49ers			
□ 621	Neal Anderson	.08	.04	.01
	(Team MVP)			
	Chicago Bears			
□ 622	James Brooks	.06	.03	.00
	(Team MVP)			
	Cincinnati Bengals			
□ 623	Thurman Thomas	.15	.07	.01
	(Team MVP)			
	Buffalo Bills			
□ 624	Bobby Humphrey	.08	.04	.01
	(Team MVP)			
	Denver Broncos			
□ 625	Kevin Mack	.06	.03	.00
	(Team MVP)			
	Cleveland Browns			
□ 626	Mark Carrier	.06	.03	.00
	Tampa Bay Buccaneers			
□ 627	Johnny Johnson	.12	.06	.01
	(Team MVP)			
	Phoenix Cardinals			
□ 628	Marion Butts	.08	.04	.01
	(Team MVP)			
	San Diego Chargers			
□ 629	Steve DeBerg	.06	.03	.00
	(Team MVP)			
	Kansas City Chiefs			
□ 630	Jeff George	.15	.07	.01
	(Team MVP)			
	Indianapolis Colts			
□ 631	Troy Aikman	.15	.07	.01
	(Team MVP)			
	Dallas Cowboys			
□ 632	Dan Marino	.15	.07	.01
	(Team MVP)			
	Miami Dolphins			
□ 633	Randall Cunningham	.08	.04	.01
	(Team MVP)			
	Philadelphia Eagles			
□ 634	Andre Rison	.10	.05	.01
	(Team MVP)			
	Atlanta Falcons			
□ 635	Pepper Johnson	.06	.03	.00
	(Team MVP)			
	New York Giants			
□ 636	Pat Leahy	.03	.01	.00
	(Team MVP)			
	New York Jets			
□ 637	Barry Sanders	.25	.12	.02
	(Team MVP)			
	Detroit Lions			
□ 638	Warren Moon	.10	.05	.01
	(Team MVP)			
	Houston Oilers			
□ 639	Sterling Sharpe	.08	.04	.01
	(Team MVP)			
	Green Bay Packers			
□ 640	Bruce Armstrong	.03	.01	.00
	(Team MVP)			
	New England Patriots	*		
□ 641	Bo Jackson	.15	.07	.01
	(Team MVP)			
	Los Angeles Raiders			
□ 642	Henry Ellard	.06	.03	.00
	(Team MVP)			
	Los Angeles Rams			
□ 643	Earnest Byner	.06	.03	.00
	(Team MVP)			
	Washington Redskins			
□ 644	Pat Swilling	.06	.03	.00
	(Team MVP)			
	New Orleans Saints			
□ 645	John L. Williams	.06	.03	.00
	(Team MVP)			
	Seattle Seahawks			
□ 646	Rod Woodson	.06	.03	.00
	(Team MVP)			
	Pittsburgh Steelers			
□ 647	Chris Doleman	.06	.03	.00
	(Team MVP)			
	Minnesota Vikings			
□ 648	Joey Browner	.06	.03	.00
	(Crunch Crew)			
	Minnesota Vikings			
□ 649	Erik McMillan	.06	.03	.00
	(Crunch Crew)			
	New York Jets			
□ 650	David Fulcher	.03	.01	.00
	(Crunch Crew)			
	Cincinnati Bengals			
□ 651A	Ronnie Lott ERR	.08	.04	.01
	(Crunch Crew)			
	San Francisco 49ers			
	(Front 47, back 42)			
□ 651B	Ronnie Lott COR	.08	.04	.01
	(Crunch Crew)			
	San Francisco 49ers			

(Front 47, back 42
is now blacked out)

☐ 652 Louis Oliver .... .06 .03 .00
(Crunch Crew)
Miami Dolphins

☐ 653 Mark Robinson .... .03 .01 .00
(Crunch Crew)
Tampa Bay Buccaneers

☐ 654 Dennis Smith .... .03 .01 .00
(Crunch Crew)
Denver Broncos

☐ 655 Reggie White .... .06 .03 .00
(Sack Attack)
Philadelphia Eagles

☐ 656 Charles Haley .... .03 .01 .00
(Sack Attack)
San Francisco 49ers

☐ 657 Leslie O'Neal .... .03 .01 .00
(Sack Attack)
San Diego Chargers

☐ 658 Kevin Greene .... .03 .01 .00
(Sack Attack)
Los Angeles Rams

☐ 659 Dennis Byrd .... .03 .01 .00
(Sack Attack)
New York Jets

☐ 660 Bruce Smith .... .06 .03 .00
(Sack Attack)
Buffalo Bills

☐ 661 Derrick Thomas .... .08 .04 .01
(Sack Attack)
Kansas City Chiefs

☐ 662 Steve DeBerg .... .06 .03 .00
(Top Leader)
Kansas City Chiefs

☐ 663 Barry Sanders .... .25 .12 .02
(Top Leader)
Detroit Lions

☐ 664 Thurman Thomas ..... .15 .07 .01
(Top Leader)
Buffalo Bills

☐ 665 Jerry Rice .... .15 .07 .01
(Top Leader)
San Francisco 49ers

☐ 666 Derrick Thomas .... .08 .04 .01
(Top Leader)
Kansas City Chiefs

☐ 667 Bruce Smith .... .06 .03 .00
(Top Leader)
Buffalo Bills

☐ 668 Mark Carrier .... .06 .03 .00
(Top Leader)
Chicago Bears

☐ 669 Richard Johnson ...... .03 .01 .00
(Top Leader)
Houston Oilers

☐ 670 Jan Stenerud .... .06 .03 .00
(Hall of Fame)
Kansas City Chiefs
Green Bay Packers
Minnesota Vikings

☐ 671 Stan Jones .... .06 .03 .00
(Hall of Fame)
Chicago Bears
Washington Redskins

☐ 672 John Hannah .... .06 .03 .00
(Hall of Fame)
New England Patriots

☐ 673 Tex Schramm .... .06 .03 .00
(Hall of Fame)
Dallas Cowboys

☐ 674 Earl Campbell .... .10 .05 .01
(Hall of Fame)
Houston Oilers
New Orleans Saints

☐ 675 Mark Carrier and ..... .15 .07 .01
Emmitt Smith
(Rookies of the Year)

☐ 676 Warren Moon DT .... .10 .05 .01
Houston Oilers

☐ 677 Barry Sanders .... .30 .15 .03
Detroit Lions

☐ 678 Thurman Thomas DT ... .25 .12 .02
Buffalo Bills

☐ 679 Andre Reed DT .... .10 .05 .01
Buffalo Bills

☐ 680 Andre Rison DT .... .10 .05 .01
Atlanta Falcons

☐ 681 Keith Jackson DT ...... .08 .04 .01
Philadelphia Eagles

☐ 682 Bruce Armstrong DT ... .06 .03 .00
New England Patriots

☐ 683 Jim Lachey DT .... .06 .03 .00
Washington Redskins

☐ 684 Bruce Matthews DT .... .06 .03 .00
Houston Oilers

☐ 685 Mike Munchak DT ...... .06 .03 .00
Houston Oilers

☐ 686 Don Mosebar DT .... .06 .03 .00
Los Angeles Raiders

☐ B1 Jeff Hostetler .... .15 .07 .01
New York Giants
Super Bowl

☐ B2 Matt Bahr .... .06 .03 .00
New York Giants
Super Bowl

☐ B3 Ottis Anderson .... .08 .04 .01
New York Giants
Super Bowl

☐ B4 Ottis Anderson .... .08 .04 .01
New York Giants
Super Bowl

1991 Score Supplemental

*This 110-card standard size (2 1/2" by 3 1/2")
set features rookies and players who switched
teams during the off-season. The front design
is the same as the regular Score issue, but
with borders that shade from blue-green to
white. Within gold borders, the horizontally
oriented backs have player information and a
color head shot. The cards are numbered on
the back. The key rookie cards in this set are
Hugh Millen and Leonard Russell.*

	MINT	EXC	G-VG
COMPLETE SET (110)	12.00	6.00	1.20
COMMON PLAYER (1-110)	.05	.02	.00

☐ 1T Ronnie Lott	.10	.05	.01
Los Angeles Raiders			
☐ 2T Matt Millen	.05	.02	.00
Washington Redskins			
☐ 3T Tim McKyer	.05	.02	.00
Atlanta Falcons			
☐ 4T Vince Newsome	.05	.02	.00
Cleveland Browns			
☐ 5T Gaston Green	.30	.15	.03
Denver Broncos			
☐ 6T Brett Perriman	.08	.04	.01
Detroit Lions			
☐ 7T Roger Craig	.10	.05	.01
Los Angeles Raiders			
☐ 8T Pete Holohan	.05	.02	.00
Kansas City Chiefs			
☐ 9T Tony Zendejas	.05	.02	.00
Los Angeles Rams			
☐ 10T Lee Williams	.08	.04	.01
Houston Oilers			
☐ 11T Mike Stonebreaker	.08	.04	.01

Chicago Bears			
☐ 12T Felix Wright	.05	.02	.00
Minnesota Vikings			
☐ 13T Lonnie Young	.05	.02	.00
New York Jets			
☐ 14T Hugh Millen	.75	.35	.07
New England Patriots			
☐ 15T Roy Green	.08	.04	.01
Philadelphia Eagles			
☐ 16T Greg Davis	.10	.05	.01
Phoenix Cardinals			
☐ 17T Dexter Manley	.05	.02	.00
Tampa Bay Buccaneers			
☐ 18T Ted Washington	.15	.07	.01
San Francisco 49ers			
☐ 19T Norm Johnson	.05	.02	.00
Atlanta Falcons			
☐ 20T Joe Morris	.08	.04	.01
Cleveland Browns			
☐ 21T Robert Perryman	.08	.04	.01
Denver Broncos			
☐ 22T Mike Iaquaniello UER	.10	.05	.01
Miami Dolphins			
(Free agent in '91,			
not '87)			
☐ 23T Gerald Perry UER	.10	.05	.01
Los Angeles Rams			
(School should be			
Southern University)			
☐ 24T Zeke Mowatt	.05	.02	.00
New York Giants			
☐ 25T Rich Miano	.05	.02	.00
Philadelphia Eagles			
☐ 26T Nick Bell	.75	.35	.07
Los Angeles Raiders			
☐ 27T Terry Orr	.25	.12	.02
Washington Redskins			
☐ 28T Matt Stover	.10	.05	.01
Cleveland Browns			
☐ 29T Bubba Paris	.05	.02	.00
Indianapolis Colts			
☐ 30T Ron Brown	.08	.04	.01
Los Angeles Rams			
☐ 31T Don Davey	.15	.07	.01
Green Bay Packers			
☐ 32T Lee Rouson	.08	.04	.01
Cleveland Browns			
☐ 33T Terry Hoage UER	.05	.02	.00
Washington Redskins			
(Eaggles, sic)			
☐ 34T Tony Covington	.10	.05	.01
Tampa Bay Buccaneers			
☐ 35T John Rienstra	.05	.02	.00
Cleveland Browns			
☐ 36T Charles Dimry	.12	.06	.01
Denver Broncos			
☐ 37T Todd Marinovich	1.25	.60	.12

Los Angeles Raiders			
☐ 38T Winston Moss	.05	.02	.00
Los Angeles Raiders			
☐ 39T Vestee Jackson	.05	.02	.00
Miami Dolphins			
☐ 40T Brian Hansen	.05	.02	.00
Cleveland Browns			
☐ 41T Irv Eatman	.05	.02	.00
New York Jets			
☐ 42T Jarrod Bunch	.12	.06	.01
New York Giants			
☐ 43T Kanavis McGhee	.20	.10	.02
New York Giants			
☐ 44T Vai Sikahema	.05	.02	.00
Green Bay Packers			
☐ 45T Charles McRae	.15	.07	.01
Tampa Bay Buccaneers			
☐ 46T Quinn Early	.05	.02	.00
New Orleans Saints			
☐ 47T Jeff Faulkner	.15	.07	.01
Phoenix Cardinals			
☐ 48T William Frizzell	.15	.07	.01
Tampa Bay Buccaneers			
☐ 49T John Booty	.05	.02	.00
Philadelphia Eagles			
☐ 50T Tim Harris	.08	.04	.01
San Francisco 49ers			
☐ 51T Derek Russell	.15	.07	.01
Denver Broncos			
☐ 52T John Flannery	.15	.07	.01
Houston Oilers			
☐ 53T Tim Barnett	.25	.12	.02
Kansas City Chiefs			
☐ 54T Alfred Williams	.15	.07	.01
Cincinnati Bengals			
☐ 55T Dan McGwire	1.00	.50	.10
Seattle Seahawks			
☐ 56T Ernie Mills	.10	.05	.01
Pittsburgh Steelers			
☐ 57T Stanley Richard	.13	.06	.01
San Diego Chargers			
☐ 58T Huey Richardson	.20	.10	.02
Pittsburgh Steelers			
☐ 59T Jerome Henderson	.15	.07	.01
New England Patriots			
☐ 60T Bryan Cox	.15	.07	.01
Miami Dolphins			
☐ 61T Russell Maryland	.35	.17	.03
Dallas Cowboys			
☐ 62T Reggie Jones	.15	.07	.01
New Orleans Saints			
☐ 63T Mo Lewis	.15	.07	.01
New York Jets			
☐ 64T Moe Gardner	.12	.06	.01
Atlanta Falcons			
☐ 65T Wesley Carroll	.30	.15	.03
New Orleans Saints			
☐ 66T Michael Jackson	.35	.17	.03
Cleveland Browns			
☐ 67T Shawn Jefferson	.20	.10	.02
San Diego Chargers			
☐ 68T Chris Zorich	.12	.06	.01
Chicago Bears			
☐ 69T Kenny Walker	.35	.17	.03
Denver Broncos			
☐ 70T Erric Pegram	.25	.12	.02
Atlanta Falcons			
☐ 71T Alvin Harper	.35	.17	.03
Dallas Cowboys			
☐ 72T Harry Colon	.15	.07	.01
New England Patriots			
☐ 73T Scott Miller	.08	.04	.01
Miami Dolphins			
☐ 74T Lawrence Dawsey	.20	.10	.02
Tampa Bay Buccaneers			
☐ 75T Phil Hansen	.15	.07	.01
Buffalo Bills			
☐ 76T Roman Phifer	.15	.07	.01
Los Angeles Rams			
☐ 77T Greg Lewis	.25	.12	.02
Denver Broncos			
☐ 78T Merton Hanks	.08	.04	.01
San Francisco 49ers			
☐ 79T James Jones	.10	.05	.01
Cleveland Browns			
☐ 80T Vinnie Clark	.08	.04	.01
Green Bay Packers			
☐ 81T R.J. Kors	.10	.05	.01
New York Jets			
☐ 82T Mike Pritchard	.50	.25	.05
Atlanta Falcons			
☐ 83T Stan Thomas	.08	.04	.01
Chicago Bears			
☐ 84T Lamar Rogers	.12	.06	.01
Cincinnati Bengals			
☐ 85T Eric Williams	.12	.06	.01
Dallas Cowboys			
☐ 86T Keith Traylor	.10	.05	.01
Denver Broncos			
☐ 87T Mike Dumas	.12	.06	.01
Houston Oilers			
☐ 88T Mel Agee	.08	.04	.01
Indianapolis Colts			
☐ 89T Harvey Williams	1.00	.50	.10
Kansas City Chiefs			
☐ 90T Todd Lyght	.20	.10	.02
Los Angeles Rams			
☐ 91T Jake Reed	.15	.07	.01
Minnesota Vikings			
☐ 92T Pat Harlow	.12	.06	.01
New England Patriots			
☐ 93T Antone Davis	.12	.06	.01
Philadelphia Eagles			
☐ 94T Aeneas Williams	.15	.07	.01

Phoenix Cardinals
- [ ] 95T Eric Bieniemy ....25 .12 .02
San Diego Chargers
- [ ] 96T John Kasay ....12 .06 .01
Seattle Seahawks
- [ ] 97T Robert Wilson ....20 .10 .02
Tampa Bay Buccaneers
- [ ] 98T Ricky Ervins .... 2.50 1.25 .25
Washington Redskins
- [ ] 99T Mike Croel ....60 .30 .06
Denver Broncos
- [ ] 100T David Lang ....15 .07 .01
Los Angeles Rams
- [ ] 101T Esera Tuaolo ....10 .05 .01
Green Bay Packers
- [ ] 102T Randal Hill ....30 .15 .03
Phoenix Cardinals
- [ ] 103T Jon Vaughn ....60 .30 .06
New England Patriots
- [ ] 104T Dave McCloughan ....15 .07 .01
Indianapolis Colts
- [ ] 105T David Daniels ....20 .10 .02
Seattle Seahawks
- [ ] 106T Eric Moten ....08 .04 .01
San Diego Chargers
- [ ] 107T Anthony Morgan ....25 .12 .02
Chicago Bears
- [ ] 108T Ed King ....10 .05 .01
Cleveland Browns
- [ ] 109T Leonard Russell .... 1.25 .60 .12
New England Patriots
- [ ] 110T Aaron Craver ....15 .07 .01
Miami Dolphins

1991 Score Pinnacle

The premier edition of the 1991 Score Pinnacle set contains 415 cards measuring the standard size (2 1/2" by 3 1/2"). The front design of the veteran player cards features two color photos, an action photo and a head shot, on a black background with white borders. The card backs have a color action shot superimposed on a black background. The rookie cards have the same design, except with a green background on the front, and head shots rather than action shots on the back. The backs also include a biography, player profile, and statistics (where appropriate). The set includes 58 rookies (253,

281-336, 393) and four special cards. Special subsets featured are Head to Head (351-355), Technicians (356-362), Gamewinners (363-371), Idols (372-386), and Sideline (394-415). A patented anti-counterfeit device appears on the bottom border of each card back. The cards are numbered on the back. The key rookie cards in this set are Nick Bell, Ricky Ervins, Todd Marinovich, Dan McGwire, Mike Pritchard, Leonard Russell, and Harvey Williams.

	MINT	EXC	G-VG
COMPLETE SET (415)	50.00	25.00	5.00
COMMON PLAYER (1-415)	.07	.03	.01

- [ ] 1 Warren Moon ....50 .25 .05
Houston Oilers
- [ ] 2 Morten Andersen ....10 .05 .01
New Orleans Saints
- [ ] 3 Rohn Stark ....07 .03 .01
Indianapolis Colts
- [ ] 4 Mark Bortz ....07 .03 .01
Chicago Bears
- [ ] 5 Mark Higgs .... 1.25 .60 .12
Miami Dolphins
- [ ] 6 Troy Aikman .... 1.00 .50 .10
Dallas Cowboys
- [ ] 7 John Elway ....35 .17 .03
Denver Broncos
- [ ] 8 Neal Anderson ....25 .12 .02
Chicago Bears
- [ ] 9 Chris Doleman ....10 .05 .01
Minnesota Vikings
- [ ] 10 Jay Schroeder ....12 .06 .01
Los Angeles Raiders
- [ ] 11 Sterling Sharpe ....20 .10 .02
Green Bay Packers
- [ ] 12 Steve DeBerg ....12 .06 .01
Kansas City Chiefs
- [ ] 13 Ronnie Lott ....20 .10 .02

Los Angeles Raiders			
☐ 14 Sean Landeta	.07	.03	.01
New York Giants			
☐ 15 Jim Everett	.20	.10	.02
Los Angeles Rams			
☐ 16 Jim Breech	.07	.03	.01
Cincinnati Bengals			
☐ 17 Barry Foster	.30	.15	.03
Pittsburgh Steelers			
☐ 18 Mike Merriweather	.07	.03	.01
Minnesota Vikings			
☐ 19 Eric Metcalf	.10	.05	.01
Cleveland Browns			
☐ 20 Mark Carrier	.15	.07	.01
Chicago Bears			
☐ 21 James Brooks	.15	.07	.01
Cincinnati Bengals			
☐ 22 Nate Odomes	.07	.03	.01
Buffalo Bills			
☐ 23 Rodney Hampton	1.00	.50	.10
New York Giants			
☐ 24 Chris Miller	.35	.17	.03
Atlanta Falcons			
☐ 25 Roger Craig	.20	.10	.02
Los Angeles Raiders			
☐ 26 Louis Oliver	.07	.03	.01
Miami Dolphins			
☐ 27 Allen Pinkett	.10	.05	.01
Houston Oilers			
☐ 28 Bubby Brister	.15	.07	.01
Pittsburgh Steelers			
☐ 29 Reyna Thompson	.07	.03	.01
New York Giants			
☐ 30 Issiac Holt	.07	.03	.01
Dallas Cowboys			
☐ 31 Steve Broussard	.20	.10	.02
Atlanta Falcons			
☐ 32 Christian Okoye	.20	.10	.02
Kansas City Chiefs			
☐ 33 Dave Meggett	.20	.10	.02
New York Jets			
☐ 34 Andre Reed	.20	.10	.02
Buffalo Bills			
☐ 35 Shane Conlan	.10	.05	.01
Buffalo Bills			
☐ 36 Eric Ball	.07	.03	.01
Cincinnati Bengals			
☐ 37 Johnny Bailey	.12	.06	.01
Chicago Bears			
☐ 38 Don Majkowski	.15	.07	.01
Green Bay Packers			
☐ 39 Gerald Williams	.07	.03	.01
Pittsburgh Steelers			
☐ 40 Kevin Mack	.10	.05	.01
Cleveland Browns			
☐ 41 Jeff Herrod	.07	.03	.01
Indianapolis Colts			
☐ 42 Emmitt Smith	5.00	2.50	.50
Dallas Cowboys			
☐ 43 Wendell Davis	.30	.15	.03
Chicago Bears			
☐ 44 Lorenzo White	.12	.06	.01
Houston Oilers			
☐ 45 Andre Rison	.30	.15	.03
Atlanta Falcons			
☐ 46 Jerry Gray	.10	.05	.01
Los Angeles Rams			
☐ 47 Dennis Smith	.07	.03	.01
Denver Broncos			
☐ 48 Gaston Green	.50	.25	.05
Denver Broncos			
☐ 49 Dermontti Dawson	.07	.03	.01
Pittsburgh Steelers			
☐ 50 Jeff Hostetler	.40	.20	.04
New York Giants			
☐ 51 Nick Lowery	.10	.05	.01
Kansas City Chiefs			
☐ 52 Merril Hoge	.10	.05	.01
Pittsburgh Steelers			
☐ 53 Bobby Hebert	.15	.07	.01
New Orleans Saints			
☐ 54 Scott Case	.07	.03	.01
Atlanta Falcons			
☐ 55 Jack Del Rio	.07	.03	.01
Dallas Cowboys			
☐ 56 Cornelius Bennett	.20	.10	.02
Buffalo Bills			
☐ 57 Tony Mandarich	.10	.05	.01
Green Bay Packers			
☐ 58 Bill Brooks	.07	.03	.01
Indianapolis Colts			
☐ 59 Jessie Tuggle	.07	.03	.01
Atlanta Falcons			
☐ 60 Hugh Millen	1.50	.75	.15
New England Patriots			
☐ 61 Tony Bennett	.12	.06	.01
Green Bay Packers			
☐ 62 Cris Dishman	.40	.20	.04
Houston Oilers			
☐ 63 Darryl Henley	.30	.15	.03
Los Angeles Rams			
☐ 64 Duane Bickett	.07	.03	.01
Indianapolis Colts			
☐ 65 Jay Hilgenberg	.10	.05	.01
Chicago Bears			
☐ 66 Joe Montana	1.00	.50	.10
San Francisco 49ers			
☐ 67 Bill Fralic	.10	.05	.01
Atlanta Falcons			
☐ 68 Sam Mills	.10	.05	.01
New Orleans Saints			
☐ 69 Bruce Armstrong	.07	.03	.01
New England Patriots			
☐ 70 Dan Marino	.60	.30	.06

Miami Dolphins			
☐ 71 Jim Lachey	.10	.05	.01
Washington Redskins			
☐ 72 Rod Woodson	.15	.07	.01
Pittsburgh Steelers			
☐ 73 Simon Fletcher	.10	.05	.01
Denver Broncos			
☐ 74 Bruce Matthews	.07	.03	.01
Houston Oilers			
☐ 75 Howie Long	.10	.05	.01
Los Angeles Raiders			
☐ 76 John Friesz	.75	.35	.07
San Diego Chargers			
☐ 77 Karl Mecklenburg	.10	.05	.01
Denver Broncos			
☐ 78 John L. Williams UER	.15	.07	.01
Seattle Seahawks			
(Two photos show			
42 Chris Warren)			
☐ 79 Rob Burnett	.20	.10	.02
Cleveland Browns			
☐ 80 Anthony Carter	.15	.07	.01
Minnesota Vikings			
☐ 81 Henry Ellard	.15	.07	.01
Los Angeles Rams			
☐ 82 Don Beebe	.20	.10	.02
Buffalo Bills			
☐ 83 Louis Lipps	.12	.06	.01
Pittsburgh Steelers			
☐ 84 Greg McMurtry	.15	.07	.01
New England Patriots			
☐ 85 Will Wolford	.07	.03	.01
Buffalo Bills			
☐ 86 Eric Green	.30	.15	.03
Pittsburgh Steelers			
☐ 87 Irving Fryar	.12	.06	.01
New England Patriots			
☐ 88 John Offerdahl	.10	.05	.01
Miami Dolphins			
☐ 89 John Alt	.07	.03	.01
Kansas City Chiefs			
☐ 90 Tom Tupa	.15	.07	.01
Phoenix Cardinals			
☐ 91 Don Mosebar	.07	.03	.01
Los Angeles Raiders			
☐ 92 Jeff George	.75	.35	.07
Indianapolis Colts			
☐ 93 Vinny Testaverde	.15	.07	.01
Tampa Bay Buccaneers			
☐ 94 Greg Townsend	.07	.03	.01
Los Angeles Raiders			
☐ 95 Derrick Fenner	.30	.15	.03
Seattle Seahawks			
☐ 96 Brian Mitchell	.40	.20	.04
Washington Redskins			
☐ 97 Herschel Walker	.25	.12	.02
Minnesota Vikings			

☐ 98 Ricky Proehl	.20	.10	.02
Phoenix Cardinals			
☐ 99 Mark Clayton	.15	.07	.01
Miami Dolphins			
☐ 100 Derrick Thomas	.30	.15	.03
Kansas City Chiefs			
☐ 101 Jim Harbaugh	.20	.10	.02
Chicago Bears			
☐ 102 Barry Word	.50	.25	.05
Kansas City Chiefs			
☐ 103 Jerry Rice	.90	.45	.09
San Francisco 49ers			
☐ 104 Keith Byars	.10	.05	.01
Philadelphia Eagles			
☐ 105 Marion Butts	.15	.07	.01
San Diego Chargers			
☐ 106 Rich Moran	.07	.03	.01
Green Bay Packers			
☐ 107 Thurman Thomas	1.25	.60	.12
Buffalo Bills			
☐ 108 Stephone Paige	.10	.05	.01
Kansas City Chiefs			
☐ 109 David Johnson	.20	.10	.02
Pittsburgh Steelers			
☐ 110 William Perry	.12	.06	.01
Chicago Bears			
☐ 111 Haywood Jeffires	.40	.20	.04
Houston Oilers			
☐ 112 Rodney Peete	.15	.07	.01
Detroit Lions			
☐ 113 Andy Heck	.07	.03	.01
Seattle Seahawks			
☐ 114 Kevin Ross	.07	.03	.01
Kansas City Chiefs			
☐ 115 Michael Carter	.10	.05	.01
San Francisco 49ers			
☐ 116 Tim McKyer	.07	.03	.01
Atlanta Falcons			
☐ 117 Kenneth Davis	.10	.05	.01
Buffalo Bills			
☐ 118 Richmond Webb	.10	.05	.01
Miami Dolphins			
☐ 119 Rich Camarillo	.07	.03	.01
Phoenix Cardinals			
☐ 120 James Francis	.15	.07	.01
Cincinnati Bengals			
☐ 121 Craig Heyward	.12	.06	.01
New Orleans Saints			
☐ 122 Hardy Nickerson	.07	.03	.01
Pittsburgh Steelers			
☐ 123 Michael Brooks	.07	.03	.01
Denver Broncos			
☐ 124 Fred Barnett	.35	.17	.03
Philadelphia Eagles			
☐ 125 Cris Carter	.15	.07	.01
Minnesota Vikings			
☐ 126 Brian Jordan	.35	.17	.03

Atlanta Falcons			
☐ 127 Pat Leahy	.10	.05	.01
New York Jets			
☐ 128 Kevin Greene	.10	.05	.01
Los Angeles Rams			
☐ 129 Trace Armstrong	.07	.03	.01
Chicago Bears			
☐ 130 Eugene Lockhart	.07	.03	.01
New England Patriots			
☐ 131 Albert Lewis	.10	.05	.01
Kansas City Chiefs			
☐ 132 Ernie Jones	.10	.05	.01
Phoenix Cardinals			
☐ 133 Eric Martin	.10	.05	.01
New Orleans Saints			
☐ 134 Anthony Thompson	.20	.10	.02
Phoenix Cardinals			
☐ 135 Tim Krumrie	.07	.03	.01
Cincinnati Bengals			
☐ 136 James Lofton	.30	.15	.03
Buffalo Bills			
☐ 137 John Taylor	.30	.15	.03
San Francisco 49ers			
☐ 138 Jeff Cross	.10	.05	.01
Miami Dolphins			
☐ 139 Tommy Kane	.25	.12	.02
Seattle Seahawks			
☐ 140 Robb Thomas	.20	.10	.02
Kansas City Chiefs			
☐ 141 Gary Anderson	.07	.03	.01
Pittsburgh Steelers			
☐ 142 Mark Murphy	.07	.03	.01
Green Bay Packers			
☐ 143 Rickey Jackson	.10	.05	.01
New Orleans Saints			
☐ 144 Ken O'Brien	.12	.06	.01
New York Jets			
☐ 145 Ernest Givins	.20	.10	.02
Houston Oilers			
☐ 146 Jessie Hester	.15	.07	.01
Indianapolis Colts			
☐ 147 Deion Sanders	.50	.25	.05
Atlanta Falcons			
☐ 148 Keith Henderson	.40	.20	.04
San Francisco 49ers			
☐ 149 Chris Singleton	.12	.06	.01
New England Patriots			
☐ 150 Rod Bernstine	.12	.06	.01
San Diego Chargers			
☐ 151 Quinn Early	.07	.03	.01
New Orleans Saints			
☐ 152 Boomer Esiason	.15	.07	.01
Cincinnati Bengals			
☐ 153 Mike Gann	.07	.03	.01
Atlanta Falcons			
☐ 154 Dino Hackett	.07	.03	.01
Kansas City Chiefs			
☐ 155 Perry Kemp	.07	.03	.01
Green Bay Packers			
☐ 156 Mark Ingram	.07	.03	.01
New York Giants			
☐ 157 Daryl Johnston	.07	.03	.01
Dallas Cowboys			
☐ 158 Eugene Daniel	.07	.03	.01
Indianapolis Colts			
☐ 159 Dalton Hilliard	.10	.05	.01
New Orleans Saints			
☐ 160 Rufus Porter	.07	.03	.01
Seattle Seahawks			
☐ 161 Tunch Ilkin	.07	.03	.01
Pittsburgh Steelers			
☐ 162 James Hasty	.07	.03	.01
New York Jets			
☐ 163 Keith McKeller	.15	.07	.01
Buffalo Bills			
☐ 164 Heath Sherman	.15	.07	.01
Philadelphia Eagles			
☐ 165 Vai Sikahema	.07	.03	.01
Green Bay Packers			
☐ 166 Pat Terrell	.07	.03	.01
Los Angeles Rams			
☐ 167 Anthony Munoz	.15	.07	.01
Cincinnati Bengals			
☐ 168 Brad Edwards	.20	.10	.02
Washington Redskins			
☐ 169 Tom Rathman	.12	.06	.01
San Francisco 49ers			
☐ 170 Steve McMichael	.10	.05	.01
Chicago Bears			
☐ 171 Vaughan Johnson	.10	.05	.01
New Orleans Saints			
☐ 172 Nate Lewis	.30	.15	.03
San Diego Chargers			
☐ 173 Mark Rypien	.75	.35	.07
Washington Redskins			
☐ 174 Rob Moore	1.00	.50	.10
New York Jets			
☐ 175 Tim Green	.10	.05	.01
Atlanta Falcons			
☐ 176 Tony Casillas	.10	.05	.01
Dallas Cowboys			
☐ 177 Jon Hand	.10	.05	.01
Indianapolis Colts			
☐ 178 Todd McNair	.07	.03	.01
Kansas City Chiefs			
☐ 179 Toi Cook	.20	.10	.02
New Orleans Saints			
☐ 180 Eddie Brown	.12	.06	.01
Cincinnati Bengals			
☐ 181 Mark Jackson	.10	.05	.01
Denver Broncos			
☐ 182 Pete Stoyanovich	.07	.03	.01
Miami Dolphins			
☐ 183 Bryce Paup	.40	.20	.04

Green Bay Packers			
☐ 184 Anthony Miller 15	.07	.01	
San Diego Chargers			
☐ 185 Dan Saleaumua 07	.03	.01	
Kansas City Chiefs			
☐ 186 Guy McIntyre 07	.03	.01	
San Francisco			
☐ 187 Broderick Thomas 15	.07	.01	
Tampa Bay Buccaneers			
☐ 188 Frank Warren 07	.03	.01	
New Orleans Saints			
☐ 189 Drew Hill 15	.07	.01	
Houston Oilers			
☐ 190 Reggie White 15	.07	.01	
Philadelphia Eagles			
☐ 191 Chris Hinton 10	.05	.01	
Atlanta Falcons			
☐ 192 David Little 07	.03	.01	
Pittsburgh Steelers			
☐ 193 David Fulcher 07	.03	.01	
Cincinnati Bengals			
☐ 194 Clarence Verdin 10	.05	.01	
Indianapolis Colts			
☐ 195 Junior Seau 15	.07	.01	
San Diego Chargers			
☐ 196 Blair Thomas 1.25	.60	.12	
New York Jets			
☐ 197 Stan Brock 07	.03	.01	
New Orleans Saints			
☐ 198 Gary Clark 25	.12	.02	
Washington Redskins			
☐ 199 Michael Irvin 50	.25	.05	
Dallas Cowboys			
☐ 200 Ronnie Harmon 10	.05	.01	
San Diego Chargers			
☐ 201 Steve Young 25	.12	.02	
San Francisco 49ers			
☐ 202 Brian Noble 07	.03	.01	
Green Bay Packers			
☐ 203 Dan Stryzinski 07	.03	.01	
Pittsburgh Steelers			
☐ 204 Darryl Talley 10	.05	.01	
Buffalo Bills			
☐ 205 David Alexander 07	.03	.01	
Philadelphia Eagles			
☐ 206 Pat Swilling 15	.07	.01	
New Orleans Saints			
☐ 207 Gary Plummer 07	.03	.01	
San Diego Chargers			
☐ 208 Robert Delpino 10	.05	.01	
Los Angeles Rams			
☐ 209 Norm Johnson 07	.03	.01	
Atlanta Falcons			
☐ 210 Mike Singletary 15	.07	.01	
Chicago Bears			
☐ 211 Anthony Johnson 07	.03	.01	
Indianapolis Colts			
☐ 212 Eric Allen 07	.03	.01	
Philadelphia Eagles			
☐ 213 Gill Fenerty 15	.07	.01	
New Orleans Saints			
☐ 214 Neil Smith 10	.05	.01	
Kansas City Chiefs			
☐ 215 Joe Phillips 07	.03	.01	
San Diego Chargers			
☐ 216 Ottis Anderson 15	.07	.01	
New York Giants			
☐ 217 LeRoy Butler 07	.03	.01	
Green Bay Packers			
☐ 218 Ray Childress 10	.05	.01	
Houston Oilers			
☐ 219 Rodney Holman 07	.03	.01	
Cincinnati Bengals			
☐ 220 Kevin Fagan 07	.03	.01	
San Francisco 49ers			
☐ 221 Bruce Smith 15	.07	.01	
Buffalo Bills			
☐ 222 Brad Muster 12	.06	.01	
Chicago Bears			
☐ 223 Mike Horan 07	.03	.01	
Denver Broncos			
☐ 224 Steve Atwater 12	.06	.01	
Denver Broncos			
☐ 225 Rich Gannon 15	.07	.01	
Minnesota Vikings			
☐ 226 Anthony Pleasant 07	.03	.01	
Cleveland Browns			
☐ 227 Steve Jordan 10	.05	.01	
Minnesota Vikings			
☐ 228 Lomas Brown 07	.03	.01	
Detroit Lions			
☐ 229 Jackie Slater 10	.05	.01	
Los Angeles Rams			
☐ 230 Brad Baxter 20	.10	.02	
New York Jets			
☐ 231 Joe Morris 10	.05	.01	
Cleveland Browns			
☐ 232 Marcus Allen 20	.10	.02	
Los Angeles Raiders			
☐ 233 Chris Warren 12	.06	.01	
Seattle Seahawks			
☐ 234 Johnny Johnson 60	.30	.06	
Phoenix Cardinals			
☐ 235 Phil Simms 20	.10	.02	
New York Giants			
☐ 236 Dave Krieg 15	.07	.01	
Seattle Seahawks			
☐ 237 Jim McMahon 15	.07	.01	
Philadelphia Eagles			
☐ 238 Richard Dent 12	.06	.01	
Chicago Bears			
☐ 239 John Washington 20	.10	.02	
New York Giants			
☐ 240 Sammie Smith 15	.07	.01	

Miami Dolphins
☐ 241 Brian Brennan ....07 .03 .01
Cleveland Browns
☐ 242 Cortez Kennedy ....25 .12 .02
Seattle Seahawks
☐ 243 Tim McDonald ....10 .05 .01
Phoenix Cardinals
☐ 244 Charles Haley ....10 .05 .01
San Francisco 49ers
☐ 245 Joey Browner ....10 .05 .01
Minnesota Vikings
☐ 246 Eddie Murray ....07 .03 .01
Detroit Lions
☐ 247 Bob Golic ....07 .03 .01
Los Angeles Raiders
☐ 248 Myron Guyton ....07 .03 .01
New York Giants
☐ 249 Dennis Byrd ....07 .03 .01
New York Jets
☐ 250 Barry Sanders ....2.50 1.25 .25
Detroit Lions
☐ 251 Clay Matthews ....07 .03 .01
Cleveland Browns
☐ 252 Pepper Johnson ....10 .05 .01
New York Giants
☐ 253 Eric Swann ....60 .30 .06
Phoenix Cardinals
☐ 254 Lamar Lathon ....12 .06 .01
Houston Oilers
☐ 255 Andre Tippett ....10 .05 .01
New England Patriots
☐ 256 Tom Newberry ....07 .03 .01
Los Angeles Rams
☐ 257 Kyle Clifton ....07 .03 .01
New York Jets
☐ 258 Leslie O'Neal ....10 .05 .01
San Diego Chargers
☐ 259 Bubba McDowell ....07 .03 .01
Houston Oilers
☐ 260 Scott Davis ....10 .05 .01
Los Angeles Raiders
☐ 261 Wilber Marshall ....10 .05 .01
Washington Redskins
☐ 262 Marv Cook ....25 .12 .02
New England Patriots
☐ 263 Jeff Lageman ....12 .06 .01
New York Jets
☐ 264 Mike Young ....10 .05 .01
Denver Broncos
☐ 265 Gary Zimmerman ....07 .03 .01
Minnesota Vikings
☐ 266 Mike Munchak ....10 .05 .01
Houston Oilers
☐ 267 David Treadwell ....07 .03 .01
Denver Broncos
☐ 268 Steve Wisniewski ....07 .03 .01
Los Angeles Raiders

☐ 269 Mark Duper ....12 .06 .01
Miami Dolphins
☐ 270 Chris Spielman ....10 .05 .01
Detroit Lions
☐ 271 Brett Perriman ....10 .05 .01
Detroit Lions
☐ 272 Lionel Washington ....07 .03 .01
Los Angeles Raiders
☐ 273 Lawrence Taylor ....25 .12 .02
New York Giants
☐ 274 Mark Collins ....10 .05 .01
New York Giants
☐ 275 Mark Carrier ....15 .07 .01
Tampa Bay Buccaneers
☐ 276 Paul Gruber ....10 .05 .01
Tampa Bay Buccaneers
☐ 277 Earnest Byner ....15 .07 .01
Washington Redskins
☐ 278 Andre Collins ....10 .05 .01
Washington Redskins
☐ 279 Reggie Cobb ....35 .17 .03
Tampa Bay Buccaneers
☐ 280 Art Monk ....25 .12 .02
Washington Redskins
☐ 281 Henry Jones ....30 .15 .03
Buffalo Bills
☐ 282 Mike Pritchard ....1.50 .75 .15
Atlanta Falcons
☐ 283 Moe Gardner ....45 .22 .04
Atlanta Falcons
☐ 284 Chris Zorich ....45 .22 .04
Chicago Bears
☐ 285 Keith Traylor ....30 .15 .03
Denver Broncos
☐ 286 Mike Dumas ....30 .15 .03
Houston Oilers
☐ 287 Ed King ....30 .15 .03
Cleveland Browns
☐ 288 Russell Maryland ....90 .45 .09
Dallas Cowboys
☐ 289 Alfred Williams ....35 .17 .03
Cincinnati Bengals
☐ 290 Derek Russell ....60 .30 .06
Denver Broncos
☐ 291 Vinnie Clark ....30 .15 .03
Green Bay Packers
☐ 292 Mike Croel ....1.50 .75 .15
Denver Broncos
☐ 293 Todd Marinovich ....4.00 2.00 .40
Los Angeles Raiders
☐ 294 Phil Hansen ....35 .17 .03
Buffalo Bills
☐ 295 Aaron Craver ....60 .30 .06
Miami Dolphins
☐ 296 Nick Bell ....2.00 1.00 .20
Los Angeles Raiders
☐ 297 Kenny Walker ....1.25 .60 .12

	Denver Broncos			
☐ 298	Roman Phifer	.35	.17	.03
	Los Angeles Rams			
☐ 299	Kanavis McGhee	.50	.25	.05
	New York Giants			
☐ 300	Ricky Ervins	5.00	2.50	.50
	Washington Redskins			
☐ 301	Jim Price	.20	.10	.02
	Los Angeles Rams			
☐ 302	John Johnson	.30	.15	.03
	San Francisco 49ers			
☐ 303	George Thornton	.25	.12	.02
	San Diego Chargers			
☐ 304	Huey Richardson	.45	.22	.04
	Pittsburgh Steelers			
☐ 305	Harry Colon	.35	.17	.03
	New England Patriots			
☐ 306	Antone Davis	.25	.12	.02
	Philadelphia Eagles			
☐ 307	Todd Lyght	.90	.45	.09
	Los Angeles Rams			
☐ 308	Bryan Cox	.30	.15	.03
	Miami Dolphins			
☐ 309	Brad Goebel	.45	.22	.04
	Philadelphia Eagles			
☐ 310	Eric Moten	.30	.15	.03
	San Diego Chargers			
☐ 311	John Kasay	.30	.15	.03
	Atlanta Falcons			
☐ 312	Esera Tuaolo	.25	.12	.02
	Green Bay Packers			
☐ 313	Bobby Wilson	.20	.10	.02
	Washington Redskins			
☐ 314	Mo Lewis	.40	.20	.04
	New York Jets			
☐ 315	Harvey Williams	2.00	1.00	.20
	Kansas City Chiefs			
☐ 316	Mike Stonebreaker	.20	.10	.02
	Chicago Bears			
☐ 317	Charles McRae	.30	.15	.03
	Tampa Bay Buccaneers			
☐ 318	John Flannery	.30	.15	.03
	Houston Oilers			
☐ 319	Ted Washington	.30	.15	.03
	San Francisco 49ers			
☐ 320	Stanley Richard	.50	.25	.05
	San Diego Chargers			
☐ 321	Browning Nagle	1.50	.75	.15
	New York Jets			
☐ 322	Ed McCaffery	.60	.30	.06
	New York Giants			
☐ 323	Jeff Graham	.40	.20	.04
	Pittsburgh Steelers			
☐ 324	Stan Thomas	.20	.10	.02
	Chicago Bears			
☐ 325	Lawrence Dawsey	.75	.35	.07
	Tampa Bay Buccaneers			
☐ 326	Eric Bieniemy	.60	.30	.06
	San Diego Chargers			
☐ 327	Tim Barnett	.50	.25	.05
	Kansas City Chiefs			
☐ 328	Erric Pegram	.60	.30	.06
	Cincinnati Bengals			
☐ 329	Lamar Rogers	.30	.15	.03
	Cincinnati Bengals			
☐ 330	Ernie Mills	.40	.20	.04
	Pittsburgh Steelers			
☐ 331	Pat Harlow	.35	.17	.03
	New England Patriots			
☐ 332	Greg Lewis	.75	.35	.07
	Denver Broncos			
☐ 333	Jarrod Bunch	.50	.25	.05
	New York Giants			
☐ 334	Dan McGwire	3.00	1.50	.30
	Seattle Seahawks			
☐ 335	Randal Hill	1.50	.75	.15
	Phoenix Cardinals			
☐ 336	Leonard Russell	2.00	1.00	.20
	New England Patriots			
☐ 337	Carnell Lake	.07	.03	.01
	Pittsburgh Steelers			
☐ 338	Brian Blades	.15	.07	.01
	Seattle Seahawks			
☐ 339	Darrell Green	.20	.10	.02
	Washington Redskins			
☐ 340	Bobby Humphrey	.20	.10	.02
	Denver Broncos			
☐ 341	Mervyn Fernandez	.12	.06	.01
	Los Angeles Raiders			
☐ 342	Ricky Sanders	.15	.07	.01
	Washington Redskins			
☐ 343	Keith Jackson	.15	.07	.01
	Philadelphia Eagles			
☐ 344	Carl Banks	.12	.06	.01
	New York Giants			
☐ 345	Gill Byrd	.10	.05	.01
	San Diego Chargers			
☐ 346	Al Toon	.15	.07	.01
	New York Jets			
☐ 347	Stephen Baker	.10	.05	.01
	New York Giants			
☐ 348	Randall Cunningham	.30	.15	.03
	Philadelphia Eagles			
☐ 349	Flipper Anderson	.10	.05	.01
	Los Angeles Rams			
☐ 350	Jay Novacek	.20	.10	.02
	Dallas Cowboys			
☐ 351	Steve Young HH	.15	.07	.01
	vs. Bruce Smith			
☐ 352	Barry Sanders HH	.60	.30	.06
	vs. Joey Browner			
☐ 353	Joe Montana HH	.35	.17	.03
	vs. Mark Carrier			
☐ 354	Thurman Thomas HH	.50	.25	.05

	vs. Lawrence Taylor		
☐ 355	Jerry Rice HH 35	.17	.03
	vs. Darrell Green		
☐ 356	Warren Moon TECH 30	.15	.03
	Houston Oilers		
☐ 357	Anthony Munoz TECH 12	.06	.01
	Cincinnati Bengals		
☐ 358	Barry Sanders TECH ... 1.00	.50	.10
	Detroit Lions		
☐ 359	Jerry Rice TECH 50	.25	.05
	San Francisco 49ers		
☐ 360	Joey Browner TECH 10	.05	.01
	Minnesota Vikings		
☐ 361	Morten Andersen TECH ..10	.05	.01
	New Orleans Saints		
☐ 362	Sean Landeta TECH 07	.03	.01
	New York Giants		
☐ 363	Thurman Thomas GW 60	.30	.06
	·Buffalo Bills		
☐ 364	Emmitt Smith GW 2.50	1.25	.25
	Dallas Cowboys		
☐ 365	Gaston Green GW 30	.15	.03
	Denver Broncos		
☐ 366	Barry Sanders GW 1.00	.50	.10
	Detroit Lions		
☐ 367	Christian Okoye GW 15	.07	.01
	Kansas City Chiefs		
☐ 368	Earnest Byner GW 12	.06	.01
	Washington Redskins		
☐ 369	Neal Anderson GW 15	.07	.01
	Chicago Bears		
☐ 370	Herschel Walker GW 25	.12	.02
	Minnesota Vikings		
☐ 371	Rodney Hampton GW 45	.22	.04
	New York Giants		
☐ 372	Darryl Talley IDOL 10	.05	.01
	Ted Hendricks		
☐ 373	Mark Carrier IDOL 15	.07	.01
	Ronnie Lott		
☐ 374	Jim Breech IDOL 10	.05	.01
	Jan Stenerud		
☐ 375	Rodney Hampton IDOL ..35	.17	.03
	Ottis Anderson		
☐ 376	Kevin Mack IDOL 10	.05	.01
	Earnest Byner		
☐ 377	Steve Jordan IDOL 15	.07	.01
	Oscar Robertson		
☐ 378	Boomer Esiason IDOL ...15	.07	.01
	Bert Jones		
☐ 379	Steve DeBerg IDOL 15	.07	.01
	Roman Gabriel		
☐ 380	Al Toon IDOL 12	.06	.01
	Wesley Walker		
☐ 381	Ronnie Lott IDOL 15	.07	.01
	Charley Taylor		
☐ 382	Henry Ellard IDOL 12	.06	.01
	Bob Hayes		
☐ 383	Troy Aikman IDOL 50	.25	.05
	Roger Staubach		
☐ 384	Thurman Thomas IDOL ..50	.25	.05
	Earl Campbell		
☐ 385	Dan Marino IDOL 30	.15	.03
	Terry Bradshaw		
☐ 386	Howie Long IDOL 15	.07	.01
	Joe Green		
☐ 387	Franco Harris IDOL 15	.07	.01
	Pittsburgh Steelers		
	Immaculate Reception		
☐ 388	Esera Tuaolo 10	.05	.01
	Green Bay Packers		
☐ 389	Super Bowl XXVI 07	.03	.01
	(Super Bowl Records)		
☐ 390	Charles Mann 10	.05	.01
	Washington Redskins		
☐ 391	Kenny Walker 50	.25	.05
	Denver Broncos		
☐ 392	Reggie Roby 07	.03	.01
	Miami Dolphins		
☐ 393	Bruce Pickens 40	.20	.04
	Atlanta Falcons		
☐ 394	Ray Childress SL 10	.05	.01
	Houston Oilers		
☐ 395	Karl Mecklenburg SL 10	.05	.01
	Denver Broncos		
☐ 396	Dean Biasucci SL 07	.03	.01
	Indianapolis Colts		
☐ 397	John Alt SL 07	.03	.01
	Kansas City Chiefs		
☐ 398	Marcus Allen SL 12	.06	.01
	Los Angeles Raiders		
☐ 399	John Offerdahl SL 10	.05	.01
	Miami Dolphins		
☐ 400	Richard Tardits SL 15	.07	.01
	New England Patriots		
☐ 401	Al Toon SL 12	.06	.01
	New York Jets		
☐ 402	Joey Browner SL 10	.05	.01
	Minnesota Vikings		
☐ 403	Spencer Tillman SL 20	.10	.02
	New York Giants		
☐ 404	Jay Novacek SL 12	.06	.01
	Dallas Cowboys		
☐ 405	Stephen Braggs SL 07	.03	.01
	Cleveland Browns		
☐ 406	Mike Tice SL 20	.10	.02
	Seattle Seahawks		
☐ 407	Kevin Greene SL 10	.05	.01
	Los Angeles Rams		
☐ 408	Reggie White SL 15	.07	.01
	Philadelphia Eagles		
☐ 409	Brian Noble SL 07	.03	.01
	Green Bay Packers		
☐ 410	Bart Oates SL 07	.03	.01
	New York Giants		

☐ 411	Art Monk SL 20	.10	.02
	Washington Redskins		
☐ 412	Ron Wolfley SL 07	.03	.01
	Phoenix Cardinals		
☐ 413	Louis Lipps SL 10	.05	.01
	Pittsburgh Steelers		
☐ 414	Dante Jones SL 20	.10	.02
	Chicago Bears		
☐ 415	Kenneth Davis SL 10	.05	.01
	Buffalo Bills		

1992 Score

The 1992 Score football set contains 550 standard-size (2 1/2" by 3 1/2") cards. On a dark blue card face, the fronts display color action player photos enclosed by red borders. The player's name appears in a green stripe at the top, while his position is printed in the bottom dark blue border. The backs have a close-up photo (with goal posts serving as the borders) and player profile; biography and statistics (1991 and career) appear in a green box at the card bottom. Topical subsets featured include Draft Pick (476-514), Crunch Crew (515-519), Rookie of the Year (520-523), Little Big Men (524-528), Sack Attack (529-533), Hall of Fame (535-537), and 90 Plus Club (538-547). The cards are numbered on the back.

	MINT	EXC	G-VG
COMPLETE SET (550) 16.00		8.00	1.60
COMMON PLAYER (1-550) 03		.01	.00

☐ 1	Barry Sanders 75	.35	.07
	Detroit Lions		

☐ 2	Pat Swilling 08	.04	.01
	New Orleans Saints		
☐ 3	Moe Gardner 08	.04	.01
	Atlanta Falcons		
☐ 4	Steve Young 12	.06	.01
	San Francisco 49ers		
☐ 5	Chris Spielman 06	.03	.00
	Detroit Lions		
☐ 6	Richard Dent 08	.04	.01
	Chicago Bears		
☐ 7	Anthony Munoz 10	.05	.01
	Cincinnati Bengals		
☐ 8	Martin Mayhew 03	.01	.00
	Washington Redskins		
☐ 9	Terry McDaniel 03	.01	.00
	Los Angeles Raiders		
☐ 10	Thurman Thomas 40	.20	.04
	Buffalo Bills		
☐ 11	Ricky Sanders 06	.03	.00
	Washington Redskins		
☐ 12	Steve Atwater 06	.03	.00
	Denver Broncos		
☐ 13	Tony Tolbert 03	.01	.00
	Dallas Cowboys		
☐ 14	Vince Workman 10	.05	.01
	Green Bay Packers		
☐ 15	Haywood Jeffires 15	.07	.01
	Houston Oilers		
☐ 16	Duane Bickett 03	.01	.00
	Indianapolis Colts		
☐ 17	Jeff Uhlenhake 03	.01	.00
	Miami Dolphins		
☐ 18	Tim McDonald 03	.01	.00
	Phoenix Cardinals		
☐ 19	Cris Carter 06	.03	.00
	Minnesota Vikings		
☐ 20	Derrick Thomas 15	.07	.01
	Kansas City Chiefs		
☐ 21	Hugh Millen 40	.20	.04
	New England Patriots		
☐ 22	Bart Oates 03	.01	.00
	New York Giants		
☐ 23	Eugene Robinson 03	.01	.00
	Seattle Seahawks		
☐ 24	Jerrol Williams 03	.01	.00
	Pittsburgh Steelers		
☐ 25	Reggie White 08	.04	.01
	Philadelphia Eagles		
☐ 26	Marion Butts 08	.04	.01
	San Diego Chargers		
☐ 27	Jim Sweeney 03	.01	.00
	New York Jets		
☐ 28	Tom Newberry 03	.01	.00
	Los Angeles Rams		
☐ 29	Pete Stoyanovich 03	.01	.00
	Miami Dolphins		
☐ 30	Ronnie Lott 10	.05	.01

	Los Angeles Raiders			
☐ 31	Simon Fletcher 06	.03	.00
	Denver Broncos			
☐ 32	Dino Hackett 03	.01	.00
	Kansas City Chiefs			
☐ 33	Morten Andersen 06	.03	.00
	New Orleans Saints			
☐ 34	Clyde Simmons 06	.03	.00
	Philadelphia Eagles			
☐ 35	Mark Rypien 20	.10	.02
	Washington Redskins			
☐ 36	Greg Montgomery 03	.01	.00
	Houston Oilers			
☐ 37	Nate Lewis 03	.01	.00
	San Diego Chargers			
☐ 38	Henry Ellard 06	.03	.00
	Los Angeles Rams			
☐ 39	Luis Sharpe 03	.01	.00
	Phoenix Cardinals			
☐ 40	Michael Irvin 20	.10	.02
	Dallas Cowboys			
☐ 41	Louis Lipps 06	.03	.00
	Pittsburgh Steelers			
☐ 42	John L. Williams 06	.03	.00
	Seattle Seahawks			
☐ 43	Broderick Thomas 06	.03	.00
	Tampa Bay Buccaneers			
☐ 44	Michael Haynes 20	.10	.02
	Atlanta Falcons			
☐ 45	Don Majkowski 08	.04	.01
	Green Bay Packers			
☐ 46	William Perry 06	.03	.00
	Chicago Bears			
☐ 47	David Fulcher 03	.01	.00
	Cincinnati Bengals			
☐ 48	Tony Bennett 06	.03	.00
	Green Bay Packers			
☐ 49	Clay Matthews 03	.01	.00
	Cleveland Browns			
☐ 50	Warren Moon 20	.10	.02
	Houston Oilers			
☐ 51	Bruce Armstrong 03	.01	.00
	New England Patriots			
☐ 52	Harry Newsome 03	.01	.00
	Minnesota Vikings			
☐ 53	Bill Brooks 03	.01	.00
	Indianapolis Colts			
☐ 54	Greg Townsend 03	.01	.00
	Los Angeles Raiders			
☐ 55	Tom Rathman 06	.03	.00
	San Francisco 49ers			
☐ 56	Sean Landeta 03	.01	.00
	New York Giants			
☐ 57	Kyle Clifton 03	.01	.00
	New York Jets			
☐ 58	Steve Broussard 10	.05	.01
	Atlanta Falcons			
☐ 59	Mark Carrier 06	.03	.00
	Tampa Bay Buccaneers			
☐ 60	Mel Gray 03	.01	.00
	Detroit Lions			
☐ 61	Tim Krumrie 03	.01	.00
	Cincinnati Bengals			
☐ 62	Rufus Porter 03	.01	.00
	Seattle Seahawks			
☐ 63	Kevin Mack 06	.03	.00
	Cleveland Browns			
☐ 64	Todd Bowles 03	.01	.00
	San Francisco 49ers			
☐ 65	Emmitt Smith 1.25	.60	.12
	Dallas Cowboys			
☐ 66	Mike Croel 25	.12	.02
	Denver Broncos			
☐ 67	Brian Mitchell 12	.06	.01
	Washington Redskins			
☐ 68	Bennie Blades 06	.03	.00
	Detroit Lions			
☐ 69	Carnell Lake 03	.01	.00
	Pittsburgh Steelers			
☐ 70	Cornelius Bennett 10	.05	.01
	Buffalo Bills			
☐ 71	Darrell Thompson 08	.04	.01
	Green Bay Packers			
☐ 72	Wes Hopkins 03	.01	.00
	Philadelphia Eagles			
☐ 73	Jessie Hester 03	.01	.00
	Indianapolis Colts			
☐ 74	Irv Eatman 03	.01	.00
	New York Jets			
☐ 75	Marv Cook 10	.05	.01
	New England Patriots			
☐ 76	Tim Brown 06	.03	.00
	Los Angeles Raiders			
☐ 77	Pepper Johnson 03	.01	.00
	New York Giants			
☐ 78	Mark Duper 06	.03	.00
	Miami Dolphins			
☐ 79	Robert Delpino 06	.03	.00
	Los Angeles Rams			
☐ 80	Charles Mann 06	.03	.00
	Washington Redskins			
☐ 81	Brian Jordan 15	.07	.01
	Atlanta Falcons			
☐ 82	Wendell Davis 12	.06	.01
	Chicago Bears			
☐ 83	Lee Johnson 03	.01	.00
	Cincinnati Bengals			
☐ 84	Ricky Reynolds 03	.01	.00
	Tampa Bay Buccaneers			
☐ 85	Vaughan Johnson 03	.01	.00
	New Orleans Saints			
☐ 86	Brian Blades 06	.03	.00
	Seattle Seahawks			
☐ 87	Sam Seale 03	.01	.00

San Diego Chargers
| ☐ 88 Ed King | .03 | .01 | .00 |
Cleveland Browns
| ☐ 89 Gaston Green | .20 | .10 | .02 |
Denver Broncos
| ☐ 90 Christian Okoye | .10 | .05 | .01 |
Kansas City Chiefs
| ☐ 91 Chris Jacke | .03 | .01 | .00 |
Green Bay Packers
| ☐ 92 Rohn Stark | .03 | .01 | .00 |
Indianapolis Colts
| ☐ 93 Kevin Greene | .06 | .03 | .00 |
Los Angeles Rams
| ☐ 94 Jay Novacek | .10 | .05 | .01 |
Dallas Cowboys
| ☐ 95 Chip Lohmiller | .03 | .01 | .00 |
Washington Redskins
| ☐ 96 Cris Dishman | .08 | .04 | .01 |
Houston Oilers
| ☐ 97 Ethan Horton | .06 | .03 | .00 |
Los Angeles Raiders
| ☐ 98 Pat Harlow | .03 | .01 | .00 |
New England Patriots
| ☐ 99 Mark Ingram | .03 | .01 | .00 |
New York Giants
| ☐ 100 Mark Carrier | .06 | .03 | .00 |
Chicago Bears
| ☐ 101 Deron Cherry | .03 | .01 | .00 |
Kansas City Chiefs
| ☐ 102 Sam Mills | .03 | .01 | .00 |
New Orleans Saints
| ☐ 103 Mark Higgs | .25 | .12 | .02 |
Miami Dolphins
| ☐ 104 Keith Jackson | .08 | .04 | .01 |
Philadelphia Eagles
| ☐ 105 Steve Tasker | .03 | .01 | .00 |
Buffalo Bills
| ☐ 106 Ken Harvey | .03 | .01 | .00 |
Phoenix Cardinals
| ☐ 107 Bryan Hinkle | .03 | .01 | .00 |
Pittsburgh Steelers
| ☐ 108 Anthony Carter | .06 | .03 | .00 |
Minnesota Vikings
| ☐ 109 Johnny Hector | .03 | .01 | .00 |
New York Jets
| ☐ 110 Randall McDaniel | .03 | .01 | .00 |
Minnesota Vikings
| ☐ 111 Johnny Johnson | .15 | .07 | .01 |
Phoenix Cardinals
| ☐ 112 Shane Conlan | .06 | .03 | .00 |
Buffalo Bills
| ☐ 113 Ray Horton | .03 | .01 | .00 |
Dallas Cowboys
| ☐ 114 Sterling Sharpe | .10 | .05 | .01 |
Green Bay Packers
| ☐ 115 Guy McIntyre | .03 | .01 | .00 |
San Francisco 49ers

| ☐ 116 Tom Waddle | .15 | .07 | .01 |
Chicago Bears
| ☐ 117 Albert Lewis | .06 | .03 | .00 |
Kansas City Chiefs
| ☐ 118 Riki Ellison | .03 | .01 | .00 |
Los Angeles Raiders
| ☐ 119 Chris Doleman | .06 | .03 | .00 |
Minnesota Vikings
| ☐ 120 Andre Rison | .15 | .07 | .01 |
Atlanta Falcons
| ☐ 121 Bobby Hebert | .08 | .04 | .01 |
New Orleans Saints
| ☐ 122 Dan Owens | .03 | .01 | .00 |
Detroit Lions
| ☐ 123 Rodney Hampton | .20 | .10 | .02 |
New York Giants
| ☐ 124 Ron Holmes | .03 | .01 | .00 |
Denver Broncos
| ☐ 125 Ernie Jones | .03 | .01 | .00 |
Phoenix Cardinals
| ☐ 126 Michael Carter | .06 | .03 | .00 |
San Francisco 49ers
| ☐ 127 Reggie Cobb | .12 | .06 | .01 |
Tampa Bay Buccaneers
| ☐ 128 Esera Tuaolo | .03 | .01 | .00 |
Green Bay Packers
| ☐ 129 Wilber Marshall | .06 | .03 | .00 |
Washington Redskins
| ☐ 130 Mike Munchak | .06 | .03 | .00 |
Houston Oilers
| ☐ 131 Cortez Kennedy | .06 | .03 | .00 |
Seattle Seahawks
| ☐ 132 Lamar Lathon | .06 | .03 | .00 |
Houston Oilers
| ☐ 133 Todd Lyght | .15 | .07 | .01 |
Los Angeles Rams
| ☐ 134 Jeff Feagles | .03 | .01 | .00 |
Philadelphia Eagles
| ☐ 135 Burt Grossman | .06 | .03 | .00 |
San Diego Chargers
| ☐ 136 Mike Cofer | .03 | .01 | .00 |
San Francisco 49ers
| ☐ 137 Frank Warren | .03 | .01 | .00 |
New Orleans Saints
| ☐ 138 Jarvis Williams | .03 | .01 | .00 |
Miami Dolphins
| ☐ 139 Eddie Brown | .06 | .03 | .00 |
Cincinnati Bengals
| ☐ 140 John Elliott | .03 | .01 | .00 |
New York Giants
| ☐ 141 Jim Everett | .10 | .05 | .01 |
Los Angeles Rams
| ☐ 142 Hardy Nickerson | .03 | .01 | .00 |
Pittsburgh Steelers
| ☐ 143 Eddie Murray | .03 | .01 | .00 |
Detroit Lions
| ☐ 144 Andre Tippett | .06 | .03 | .00 |

New England Patriots
- [ ] 145 Heath Sherman .... .06 .03 .00
Philadelphia Eagles
- [ ] 146 Ronnie Harmon .... .03 .01 .00
San Diego Chargers
- [ ] 147 Eric Metcalf .... .06 .03 .00
Cleveland Browns
- [ ] 148 Tony Martin .... .03 .01 .00
Miami Dolphins
- [ ] 149 Chris Burkett .... .03 .01 .00
New York Jets
- [ ] 150 Andre Waters .... .03 .01 .00
Philadelphia Eagles
- [ ] 151 Ray Donaldson .... .03 .01 .00
Indianapolis Colts
- [ ] 152 Paul Gruber .... .03 .01 .00
Tampa Bay Buccaneers
- [ ] 153 Chris Singleton .... .06 .03 .00
New England Patriots
- [ ] 154 Clarence Kay .... .03 .01 .00
Denver Broncos
- [ ] 155 Ernest Givins .... .10 .05 .01
Houston Oilers
- [ ] 156 Eric Hill .... .03 .01 .00
Phoenix Cardinals
- [ ] 157 Jesse Sapolu .... .03 .01 .00
San Francisco 49ers
- [ ] 158 Jack Del Rio .... .03 .01 .00
Dallas Cowboys
- [ ] 159 Erric Pegram .... .10 .05 .01
Atlanta Falcons
- [ ] 160 Joey Browner .... .06 .03 .00
Minnesota Vikings
- [ ] 161 Marcus Allen .... .10 .05 .01
Los Angeles Raiders
- [ ] 162 Eric Moten .... .03 .01 .00
San Diego Chargers
- [ ] 163 Donnell Thompson .... .03 .01 .00
Indianapolis Colts
- [ ] 164 Chuck Cecil .... .03 .01 .00
Green Bay Packers
- [ ] 165 Matt Millen .... .03 .01 .00
Washington Redskins
- [ ] 166 Barry Foster .... .10 .05 .01
Pittsburgh Steelers
- [ ] 167 Kent Hull .... .03 .01 .00
Buffalo Bills
- [ ] 168 Tony Jones .... .06 .03 .00
Houston Oilers
- [ ] 169 Mike Prior .... .03 .01 .00
Indianapolis Colts
- [ ] 170 Neal Anderson .... .12 .06 .01
Chicago Bears
- [ ] 171 Roger Craig .... .10 .05 .01
Los Angeles Raiders
- [ ] 172 Felix Wright .... .03 .01 .00
Minnesota Vikings

- [ ] 173 James Francis .... .06 .03 .00
Cincinnati Bengals
- [ ] 174 Eugene Lockhart .... .03 .01 .00
New England Patriots
- [ ] 175 Dalton Hilliard .... .06 .03 .00
New Orleans Saints
- [ ] 176 Nick Lowery .... .06 .03 .00
Kansas City Chiefs
- [ ] 177 Tim McKyer .... .03 .01 .00
Atlanta Falcons
- [ ] 178 Lorenzo White .... .06 .03 .00
Houston Oilers
- [ ] 179 Jeff Hostetler .... .15 .07 .01
New York Giants
- [ ] 180 Jerome Brown .... .03 .01 .00
Philadelphia Eagles
- [ ] 181 Ken Norton .... .03 .01 .00
Dallas Cowboys
- [ ] 182 Flipper Anderson .... .06 .03 .00
Los Angeles Rams
- [ ] 183 Don Warren .... .03 .01 .00
Washington Redskins
- [ ] 184 Brad Baxter .... .06 .03 .00
New York Jets
- [ ] 185 John Taylor .... .10 .05 .01
San Francisco 49ers
- [ ] 186 Harold Green .... .15 .07 .01
Cincinnati Bengals
- [ ] 187 James Washington .... .03 .01 .00
Dallas Cowboys
- [ ] 188 Aaron Craver .... .06 .03 .00
Miami Dolphins
- [ ] 189 Mike Merriweather .... .03 .01 .00
Minnesota Vikings
- [ ] 190 Gary Clark .... .12 .06 .01
Washington Redskins
- [ ] 191 Vince Buck .... .03 .01 .00
New Orleans Saints
- [ ] 192 Cleveland Gary .... .06 .03 .00
Los Angeles Rams
- [ ] 193 Dan Saleaumua .... .03 .01 .00
Kansas City Chiefs
- [ ] 194 Gary Zimmerman .... .03 .01 .00
Minnesota Vikings
- [ ] 195 Richmond Webb .... .03 .01 .00
Miami Dolphins
- [ ] 196 Gary Plummer .... .03 .01 .00
San Diego Chargers
- [ ] 197 Willie Green .... .12 .06 .01
Detroit Lions
- [ ] 198 Chris Warren .... .06 .03 .00
Seattle Seahawks
- [ ] 199 Mike Pritchard .... .30 .15 .03
Atlanta Falcons
- [ ] 200 Art Monk .... .12 .06 .01
Washington Redskins
- [ ] 201 Matt Stover .... .03 .01 .00

Cleveland Browns			
☐ 202 Tim Grunhard 03	.01	.00
Kansas City Chiefs			
☐ 203 Mervyn Fernandez 06	.03	.00
Los Angeles Raiders			
☐ 204 Mark Jackson 06	.03	.00
Denver Broncos			
☐ 205 Freddie Joe Nunn 03	.01	.00
Phoenix Cardinals			
☐ 206 Stan Thomas 03	.01	.00
Chicago Bears			
☐ 207 Keith McKeller 06	.03	.00
Buffalo Bills			
☐ 208 Jeff Lageman 06	.03	.00
New York Jets			
☐ 209 Kenny Walker 20	.10	.02
Denver Broncos			
☐ 210 Dave Krieg 06	.03	.00
Seattle Seahawks			
☐ 211 Dean Biasucci 03	.01	.00
Indianapolis Colts			
☐ 212 Herman Moore 30	.15	.03
Detroit Lions			
☐ 213 Jon Vaughn 30	.15	.03
New England Patriots			
☐ 214 Howard Cross 03	.01	.00
New York Giants			
☐ 215 Greg Davis 03	.01	.00
Phoenix Cardinals			
☐ 216 Bubby Brister 08	.04	.01
Pittsburgh Steelers			
☐ 217 John Kasay 03	.01	.00
Seattle Seahawks			
☐ 218 Ron Hall 03	.01	.00
Tampa Bay Buccaneers			
☐ 219 Mo Lewis 08	.04	.01
New York Jets			
☐ 220 Eric Green 12	.06	.01
Pittsburgh Steelers			
☐ 221 Scott Case 03	.01	.00
Atlanta Falcons			
☐ 222 Sean Jones 03	.01	.00
Houston Oilers			
☐ 223 Winston Moss 03	.01	.00
Los Angeles Raiders			
☐ 224 Reggie Langhorne 03	.01	.00
Cleveland Browns			
☐ 225 Greg Lewis 12	.06	.01
Denver Broncos			
☐ 226 Todd McNair 03	.01	.00
Kansas City Chiefs			
☐ 227 Rod Bernstine 06	.03	.00
San Diego Chargers			
☐ 228 Joe Jacoby 03	.01	.00
Washington Redskins			
☐ 229 Brad Muster 06	.03	.00
Chicago Bears			

☐ 230 Nick Bell 35	.17	.03
Los Angeles Raiders			
☐ 231 Terry Allen 25	.12	.02
Minnesota Vikings			
☐ 232 Cliff Odom 03	.01	.00
Miami Dolphins			
☐ 233 Brian Hansen 03	.01	.00
Cleveland Browns			
☐ 234 William Fuller 03	.01	.00
Houston Oilers			
☐ 235 Issiac Holt 03	.01	.00
Dallas Cowboys			
☐ 236 Dexter Carter 06	.03	.00
San Francisco 49ers			
☐ 237 Gene Atkins 03	.01	.00
New Orleans Saints			
☐ 238 Pat Beach 03	.01	.00
Indianapolis Colts			
☐ 239 Tim McGee 03	.01	.00
Cincinnati Bengals			
☐ 240 Dermontti Dawson 03	.01	.00
Pittsburgh Steelers			
☐ 241 Dan Fike 03	.01	.00
Cleveland Browns			
☐ 242 Don Beebe 06	.03	.00
Buffalo Bills			
☐ 243 Jeff Bostic 03	.01	.00
Washington Redskins			
☐ 244 Mark Collins 03	.01	.00
New York Giants			
☐ 245 Steve Sewell 03	.01	.00
Denver Broncos			
☐ 246 Steve Walsh 08	.04	.01
New Orleans Saints			
☐ 247 Erik Kramer 40	.20	.04
Detroit Lions			
☐ 248 Scott Norwood 03	.01	.00
Buffalo Bills			
☐ 249 Jesse Solomon 03	.01	.00
Tampa Bay Buccaneers			
☐ 250 Jerry Ball 03	.01	.00
Detroit Lions			
☐ 251 Eugene Daniel 03	.01	.00
Indianapolis Colts			
☐ 252 Michael Stewart 03	.01	.00
Los Angeles Rams			
☐ 253 Fred Barnett 12	.06	.01
Philadelphia Eagles			
☐ 254 Rodney Holman 03	.01	.00
Cincinnati Bengals			
☐ 255 Stephen Baker 06	.03	.00
New York Giants			
☐ 256 Don Griffin 03	.01	.00
San Francisco 49ers			
☐ 257 Will Wolford 03	.01	.00
Buffalo Bills			
☐ 258 Perry Kemp 03	.01	.00

Green Bay Packers
| ☐ 259 Leonard Russell | .60 | .30 | .06 |

New England Patriots
| ☐ 260 Jeff Gossett | .03 | .01 | .00 |

Los Angeles Raiders
| ☐ 261 Dwayne Harper | .08 | .04 | .01 |

Seattle Seahawks
| ☐ 262 Vinny Testaverde | .08 | .04 | .01 |

Tampa Bay Buccaneers
| ☐ 263 Maurice Hurst | .03 | .01 | .00 |

New England Patriots
| ☐ 264 Tony Casillas | .03 | .01 | .00 |

Dallas Cowboys
| ☐ 265 Louis Oliver | .03 | .01 | .00 |

Miami Dolphins
| ☐ 266 Jim Morrissey | .03 | .01 | .00 |

Chicago Bears
| ☐ 267 Kenneth Davis | .06 | .03 | .00 |

Buffalo Bills
| ☐ 268 John Alt | .03 | .01 | .00 |

Kansas City Chiefs
| ☐ 269 Michael Zordich | .10 | .05 | .01 |

Phoenix Cardinals
| ☐ 270 Brian Brennan | .03 | .01 | .00 |

Cleveland Browns
| ☐ 271 Greg Kragen | .03 | .01 | .00 |

Denver Broncos
| ☐ 272 Andre Collins | .03 | .01 | .00 |

Washington Redskins
| ☐ 273 Dave Meggett | .08 | .04 | .01 |

New York Giants
| ☐ 274 Scott Fulhage | .03 | .01 | .00 |

Atlanta Falcons
| ☐ 275 Tony Zendejas | .03 | .01 | .00 |

Los Angeles Rams
| ☐ 276 Herschel Walker | .10 | .05 | .01 |

Minnesota Vikings
| ☐ 277 Keith Henderson | .10 | .05 | .01 |

San Francisco 49ers
| ☐ 278 Johnny Bailey | .06 | .03 | .00 |

Chicago Bears
| ☐ 279 Vince Newsome | .03 | .01 | .00 |

Cleveland Browns
| ☐ 280 Chris Hinton | .06 | .03 | .00 |

Atlanta Falcons
| ☐ 281 Robert Blackmon | .03 | .01 | .00 |

Seattle Seahawks
| ☐ 282 James Hasty | .03 | .01 | .00 |

New York Jets
| ☐ 283 John Offerdahl | .03 | .01 | .00 |

Miami Dolphins
| ☐ 284 Wesley Carroll | .20 | .10 | .02 |

New Orleans Saints
| ☐ 285 Lomas Brown | .03 | .01 | .00 |

Detroit Lions
| ☐ 286 Neil O'Donnell | .40 | .20 | .04 |

Pittsburgh Steelers

| ☐ 287 Kevin Porter | .03 | .01 | .00 |

Kansas City Chiefs
| ☐ 288 Lionel Washington | .03 | .01 | .00 |

Los Angeles Raiders
| ☐ 289 Carlton Bailey | .10 | .05 | .01 |

Buffalo Bills
| ☐ 290 Leonard Marshall | .06 | .03 | .00 |

New York Giants
| ☐ 291 John Carney | .03 | .01 | .00 |

San Diego Chargers
| ☐ 292 Bubba McDowell | .03 | .01 | .00 |

Houston Oilers
| ☐ 293 Nate Newton | .03 | .01 | .00 |

Dallas Cowboys
| ☐ 294 Dave Waymer | .03 | .01 | .00 |

San Francisco 49ers
| ☐ 295 Rob Moore | .25 | .12 | .02 |

New York Jets
| ☐ 296 Earnest Byner | .08 | .04 | .01 |

Washington Redskins
| ☐ 297 Jason Staurovsky | .03 | .01 | .00 |

New England Patriots
| ☐ 298 Keith McCants | .06 | .03 | .00 |

Tampa Bay Buccaneers
| ☐ 299 Floyd Turner | .03 | .01 | .00 |

New Orleans Saints
| ☐ 300 Steve Jordan | .06 | .03 | .00 |

Minnesota Vikings
| ☐ 301 Nate Odomes | .03 | .01 | .00 |

Buffalo Bills
| ☐ 302 Gerald Riggs | .06 | .03 | .00 |

Washington Redskins
| ☐ 303 Marvin Washington | .03 | .01 | .00 |

New York Jets
| ☐ 304 Anthony Thompson | .08 | .04 | .01 |

Phoenix Cardinals
| ☐ 305 Steve DeBerg | .08 | .04 | .01 |

Kansas City Chiefs
| ☐ 306 Jim Harbaugh | .08 | .04 | .01 |

Chicago Bears
| ☐ 307 Larry Brown | .03 | .01 | .00 |

Dallas Cowboys
| ☐ 308 Roger Ruzek | .03 | .01 | .00 |

Philadelphia Eagles
| ☐ 309 Jessie Tuggle | .03 | .01 | .00 |

Atlanta Falcons
| ☐ 310 Al Smith | .03 | .01 | .00 |

Houston Oilers
| ☐ 311 Mark Kelso | .03 | .01 | .00 |

Buffalo Bills
| ☐ 312 Lawrence Dawsey | .12 | .06 | .01 |

Tampa Bay Buccaneers
| ☐ 313 Steve Bono | .40 | .20 | .04 |

San Francisco 49ers
| ☐ 314 Greg Lloyd | .03 | .01 | .00 |

Pittsburgh Steelers
| ☐ 315 Steve Wisniewski | .03 | .01 | .00 |

	Los Angeles Raiders			
☐ 316	Gill Fenerty	.06	.03	.00
	New Orleans Saints			
☐ 317	Mark Stepnoski	.03	.01	.00
	Dallas Cowboys			
☐ 318	Derek Russell	.10	.05	.01
	Denver Broncos			
☐ 319	Chris Martin	.03	.01	.00
	Kansas City Chiefs			
☐ 320	Shaun Gayle	.03	.01	.00
	Chicago Bears			
☐ 321	Bob Golic	.03	.01	.00
	Los Angeles Raiders			
☐ 322	Larry Kelm	.03	.01	.00
	Los Angeles Rams			
☐ 323	Mike Brim	.10	.05	.01
	New York Jets			
☐ 324	Tommy Kane	.12	.06	.01
	Seattle Seahawks			
☐ 325	Mark Schlereth	.12	.06	.01
	Washington Redskins			
☐ 326	Ray Childress	.06	.03	.00
	Houston Oilers			
☐ 327	Richard Brown	.10	.05	.01
	Cleveland Browns			
☐ 328	Vincent Brown	.03	.01	.00
	New England Patriots			
☐ 329	Mike Farr	.03	.01	.00
	Detroit Lions			
☐ 330	Eric Swann	.08	.04	.01
	Phoenix Cardinals			
☐ 331	Bill Fralic	.06	.03	.00
	Atlanta Falcons			
☐ 332	Rodney Peete	.08	.04	.01
	Detroit Lions			
☐ 333	Jerry Gray	.03	.01	.00
	Los Angeles Rams			
☐ 334	Ray Berry	.03	.01	.00
	Minnesota Vikings			
☐ 335	Dennis Smith	.03	.01	.00
	Denver Broncos			
☐ 336	Jeff Herrod	.03	.01	.00
	Indianapolis Colts			
☐ 337	Tony Mandarich	.06	.03	.00
	Green Bay Packers			
☐ 338	Matt Bahr	.03	.01	.00
	New York Giants			
☐ 339	Mike Saxon	.03	.01	.00
	Dallas Cowboys			
☐ 340	Bruce Matthews	.03	.01	.00
	Houston Oilers			
☐ 341	Rickey Jackson	.06	.03	.00
	New Orleans Saints			
☐ 342	Eric Allen	.03	.01	.00
	Philadelphia Eagles			
☐ 343	Lonnie Young	.03	.01	.00
	New York Jets			
☐ 344	Steve McMichael	.06	.03	.00
	Chicago Bears			
☐ 345	Willie Gault	.06	.03	.00
	Los Angeles Raiders			
☐ 346	Barry Word	.15	.07	.01
	Kansas City Chiefs			
☐ 347	Rich Camarillo	.03	.01	.00
	Phoenix Cardinals			
☐ 348	Bill Romanowski	.03	.01	.00
	San Francisco 49ers			
☐ 349	Jim Lachey	.06	.03	.00
	Washington Redskins			
☐ 350	Jim Ritcher	.03	.01	.00
	Buffalo Bills			
☐ 351	Irving Fryar	.06	.03	.00
	New England Patriots			
☐ 352	Gary Anderson	.03	.01	.00
	Pittsburgh Steelers			
☐ 353	Henry Rolling	.03	.01	.00
	San Diego Chargers			
☐ 354	Mark Bortz	.03	.01	.00
	Chicago Bears			
☐ 355	Mark Clayton	.08	.04	.01
	Miami Dolphins			
☐ 356	Keith Woodside	.06	.03	.00
	Green Bay Packers			
☐ 357	Jonathan Hayes	.03	.01	.00
	Kansas City Chiefs			
☐ 358	Derrick Fenner	.08	.04	.01
	Seattle Seahawks			
☐ 359	Keith Byars	.06	.03	.00
	Philadelphia Eagles			
☐ 360	Drew Hill	.08	.04	.01
	Houston Oilers			
☐ 361	Harris Barton	.03	.01	.00
	San Francisco 49ers			
☐ 362	John Kidd	.03	.01	.00
	San Diego Chargers			
☐ 363	Aeneas Williams	.03	.01	.00
	Phoenix Cardinals			
☐ 364	Brian Washington	.03	.01	.00
	New York Jets			
☐ 365	John Stephens	.06	.03	.00
	New England Patriots			
☐ 366	Norm Johnson	.03	.01	.00
	Atlanta Falcons			
☐ 367	Darryl Henley	.03	.01	.00
	Los Angeles Rams			
☐ 368	William White	.03	.01	.00
	Detroit Lions			
☐ 369	Mark Murphy	.03	.01	.00
	Green Bay Packers			
☐ 370	Myron Guyton	.03	.01	.00
	New York Giants			
☐ 371	Leon Seals	.03	.01	.00
	Buffalo Bills			
☐ 372	Rich Gannon	.08	.04	.01

	Minnesota Vikings		
☐ 373	Toi Cook 03	.01	.00
	New Orleans Saints		
☐ 374	Anthony Johnson 03	.01	.00
	Indianapolis Colts		
☐ 375	Rod Woodson 06	.03	.00
	Pittsburgh Steelers		
☐ 376	Alexander Wright 08	.04	.01
	Dallas Cowboys		
☐ 377	Kevin Butler 03	.01	.00
	Chicago Bears		
☐ 378	Neil Smith 03	.01	.00
	Kansas City Chiefs		
☐ 379	Gary Anderson 06	.03	.00
	Tampa Bay Buccaneers		
☐ 380	Reggie Roby 03	.01	.00
	Miami Dolphins		
☐ 381	Jeff Bryant 03	.01	.00
	Seattle Seahawks		
☐ 382	Ray Crockett 03	.01	.00
	Detroit Lions		
☐ 383	Richard Johnson 03	.01	.00
	Houston Oilers		
☐ 384	Hassan Jones 03	.01	.00
	Minnesota Vikings		
☐ 385	Karl Mecklenburg 06	.03	.00
	Denver Broncos		
☐ 386	Jeff Jaeger 03	.01	.00
	Los Angeles Raiders		
☐ 387	Keith Willis 03	.01	.00
	Pittsburgh Steelers		
☐ 388	Phil Simms 10	.05	.01
	New York Giants		
☐ 389	Kevin Ross 03	.01	.00
	Kansas City Chiefs		
☐ 390	Chris Miller 15	.07	.01
	Atlanta Falcons		
☐ 391	Brian Noble 03	.01	.00
	Green Bay Packers		
☐ 392	Jamie Dukes 08	.04	.01
	Atlanta Falcons		
☐ 393	George Jamison 03	.01	.00
	Detroit Lions		
☐ 394	Rickey Dixon 03	.01	.00
	Cincinnati Bengals		
☐ 395	Carl Lee 03	.01	.00
	Minnesota Vikings		
☐ 396	Jon Hand 03	.01	.00
	Indianapolis Colts		
☐ 397	Kirby Jackson 03	.01	.00
	Buffalo Bills		
☐ 398	Pat Terrell 03	.01	.00
	Los Angeles Rams		
☐ 399	Howie Long 06	.03	.00
	Los Angeles Raiders		
☐ 400	Mike Young 03	.01	.00
	Denver Broncos		

☐ 401	Keith Sims 03	.01	.00
	Miami Dolphins		
☐ 402	Tommy Barnhardt 03	.01	.00
	New Orleans Saints		
☐ 403	Greg McMurtry 06	.03	.00
	New England Patriots		
☐ 404	Keith Van Horne 03	.01	.00
	Chicago Bears		
☐ 405	Seth Joyner 06	.03	.00
	Philadelphia Eagles		
☐ 406	Jim Jeffcoat 03	.01	.00
	Dallas Cowboys		
☐ 407	Courtney Hall 03	.01	.00
	San Diego Chargers		
☐ 408	Tony Covington 03	.01	.00
	Tampa Bay Buccaneers		
☐ 409	Jacob Green 03	.01	.00
	Seattle Seahawks		
☐ 410	Charles Haley 06	.03	.00
	San Francisco 49ers		
☐ 411	Darryl Talley 06	.03	.00
	Buffalo Bills		
☐ 412	Jeff Cross 03	.01	.00
	Miami Dolphins		
☐ 413	John Elway 15	.07	.01
	Denver Broncos		
☐ 414	Donald Evans 03	.01	.00
	Pittsburgh Steelers		
☐ 415	Jackie Slater 06	.03	.00
	Los Angeles Rams		
☐ 416	John Friesz 15	.07	.01
	San Diego Chargers		
☐ 417	Anthony Smith 03	.01	.00
	Los Angeles Raiders		
☐ 418	Gill Byrd 03	.01	.00
	San Diego Chargers		
☐ 419	Willie Drewrey 03	.01	.00
	Tampa Bay Buccaneers		
☐ 420	Jay Hilgenberg 06	.03	.00
	Chicago Bears		
☐ 421	David Treadwell 03	.01	.00
	Denver Broncos		
☐ 422	Curtis Duncan 06	.03	.00
	Houston Oilers		
☐ 423	Sammie Smith 08	.04	.01
	Miami Dolphins		
☐ 424	Henry Thomas 03	.01	.00
	Minnesota Vikings		
☐ 425	James Lofton 12	.06	.01
	Buffalo Bills		
☐ 426	Fred Marion 03	.01	.00
	New England Patriots		
☐ 427	Bryce Paup 03	.01	.00
	Green Bay Packers		
☐ 428	Eric Andolsek 03	.01	.00
	Detroit Lions		
☐ 429	Reyna Thompson 03	.01	.00

	New York Giants			
☐ 430	Mike Kenn 03	.01	.00	
	Atlanta Falcons			
☐ 431	Bill Maas 03	.01	.00	
	Kansas City Chiefs			
☐ 432	Quinn Early 03	.01	.00	
	New Orleans Saints			
☐ 433	Everson Walls 03	.01	.00	
	New York Giants			
☐ 434	Jimmie Jones 03	.01	.00	
	Dallas Cowboys			
☐ 435	Dwight Stone 03	.01	.00	
	Pittsburgh Steelers			
☐ 436	Harry Colon 03	.01	.00	
	New England Patriots			
☐ 437	Don Mosebar 03	.01	.00	
	Los Angeles Raiders			
☐ 438	Calvin Williams 06	.03	.00	
	Philadelphia Eagles			
☐ 439	Tom Tupa 06	.03	.00	
	Phoenix Cardinals			
☐ 440	Darrell Green 10	.05	.01	
	Washington Redskins			
☐ 441	Eric Thomas 03	.01	.00	
	Cincinnati Bengals			
☐ 442	Terry Wooden 03	.01	.00	
	Seattle Seahawks			
☐ 443	Brett Perriman 03	.01	.00	
	Detroit Lions			
☐ 444	Todd Marinovich 60	.30	.06	
	Los Angeles Raiders			
☐ 445	Jim Breech 03	.01	.00	
	Cincinnati Bengals			
☐ 446	Eddie Anderson 03	.01	.00	
	Los Angeles Raiders			
☐ 447	Jay Schroeder 08	.04	.01	
	Los Angeles Raiders			
☐ 448	William Roberts 03	.01	.00	
	New York Giants			
☐ 449	Brad Edwards 03	.01	.00	
	Washington Redskins			
☐ 450	Tunch Ilkin 03	.01	.00	
	Pittsburgh Steelers			
☐ 451	Joe Ivy 10	.05	.01	
	New England Patriots			
☐ 452	Robert Clark 06	.03	.00	
	Detroit Lions			
☐ 453	Tim Barnett 12	.06	.01	
	Kansas City Chiefs			
☐ 454	Jarrod Bunch 08	.04	.01	
	New York Giants			
☐ 455	Tim Harris 06	.03	.00	
	San Francisco 49ers			
☐ 456	James Brooks 08	.04	.01	
	Cincinnati Bengals			
☐ 457	Trace Armstrong 03	.01	.00	
	Chicago Bears			

☐ 458	Michael Brooks 03	.01	.00	
	Denver Broncos			
☐ 459	Andy Heck 03	.01	.00	
	Seattle Seahawks			
☐ 460	Greg Jackson 03	.01	.00	
	New York Giants			
☐ 461	Vance Johnson 06	.03	.00	
	Denver Broncos			
☐ 462	Kirk Lowdermilk 03	.01	.00	
	Minnesota Vikings			
☐ 463	Erik McMillan 03	.01	.00	
	New York Jets			
☐ 464	Scott Mersereau 03	.01	.00	
	New York Jets			
☐ 465	Jeff Wright 03	.01	.00	
	Buffalo Bills			
☐ 466	Mike Tomczak 08	.04	.01	
	Green Bay Packers			
☐ 467	David Alexander 03	.01	.00	
	Philadelphia Eagles			
☐ 468	Bryan Millard 03	.01	.00	
	Seattle Seahawks			
☐ 469	John Randle 03	.01	.00	
	Minnesota Vikings			
☐ 470	Joel Hilgenberg 03	.01	.00	
	New Orleans Saints			
☐ 471	Bennie Thompson 10	.05	.01	
	New Orleans Saints			
☐ 472	Freeman McNeil 08	.04	.01	
	New York Jets			
☐ 473	Terry Orr 10	.05	.01	
	Washington Redskins			
☐ 474	Mike Horan 03	.01	.00	
	Denver Broncos			
☐ 475	Leroy Hoard 08	.04	.01	
	Cleveland Browns			
☐ 476	Patrick Rowe DP 20	.10	.02	
	Cleveland Browns			
☐ 477	Siran Stacy DP 35	.17	.03	
	Philadelphia Eagles			
☐ 478	Amp Lee DP 35	.17	.03	
	San Francisco 49ers			
☐ 479	Eddie Blake DP 15	.07	.01	
	Miami Dolphins			
☐ 480	Joe Bowden DP 10	.05	.01	
	Houston Oilers			
☐ 481	Roderick Milstead DP 08	.04	.01	
	Dallas Cowboys			
☐ 482	Keith Hamilton DP 10	.05	.01	
	New York Giants			
☐ 483	Darryl Williams DP 20	.10	.02	
	Cincinnati Bengals			
☐ 484	Robert Porcher DP 20	.10	.02	
	Detroit Lions			
☐ 485	Ed Cunningham DP 08	.04	.01	
	Phoenix Cardinals			
☐ 486	Chris Mims DP 15	.07	.01	

San Diego Chargers				
☐ 487 Chris Hakel DP	.20	.10	.02	
Washington Redskins				
☐ 488 Jimmy Smith DP	.20	.10	.02	
Dallas Cowboys				
☐ 489 Todd Harrison DP	.12	.06	.01	
Chicago Bears				
☐ 490 Edgar Bennett DP	.25	.12	.02	
Green Bay Packers				
☐ 491 Dexter McNabb DP	.15	.07	.01	
Green Bay Packers				
☐ 492 Leon Searcy DP	.15	.07	.01	
Pittsburgh Steelers				
☐ 493 Tommy Vardell DP	.60	.30	.06	
Cleveland Browns				
☐ 494 Terrell Buckley DP	.75	.35	.07	
Green Bay Packers				
☐ 495 Kevin Turner DP	.15	.07	.01	
New England Patriots				
☐ 496 Russ Campbell DP	.10	.05	.01	
Pittsburgh Steelers				
☐ 497 Torrance Small DP	.12	.06	.01	
New Orleans Saints				
☐ 498 Nate Turner DP	.10	.05	.01	
Buffalo Bills				
☐ 499 Cornelius Benton DP	.15	.07	.01	
Pittsburgh Steelers				
☐ 500 Matt Elliott DP	.08	.04	.01	
Washington Redskins				
☐ 501 Robert Stewart DP	.10	.05	.01	
New Orleans Saints				
☐ 502 Muhammad Shamsid-Deen.12 DP		.06	.01	
Seattle Seahawks				
☐ 503 George Williams DP	.10	.05	.01	
Cleveland Browns				
☐ 504 Pumpy Tudors DP	.08	.04	.01	
Philadelphia Eagles				
☐ 505 Matt LaBounty DP	.08	.04	.01	
San Francisco 49ers				
☐ 506 Darryl Hardy DP	.10	.05	.01	
Atlanta Falcons				
☐ 507 Derrick Moore DP	.15	.07	.01	
Atlanta Falcons				
☐ 508 Willie Clay DP	.12	.06	.01	
Detroit Lions				
☐ 509 Bob Whitfield DP	.15	.07	.01	
Atlanta Falcons				
☐ 510 Ricardo McDonald DP	.10	.05	.01	
Cincinnati Bengals				
☐ 511 Carlos Huerta DP	.10	.05	.01	
San Diego Chargers				
☐ 512 Selwyn Jones DP	.10	.05	.01	
Cleveland Browns				
☐ 513 Steve Gordon DP	.08	.04	.01	
New England Patriots				
☐ 514 Bob Meeks DP	.08	.04	.01	

Denver Broncos				
☐ 515 Bennie Blades CC	.06	.03	.00	
Detroit Lions				
☐ 516 Andre Waters CC	.03	.01	.00	
Philadelphia Eagles				
☐ 517 Bubba McDowell CC	.03	.01	.00	
Houston Oilers				
☐ 518 Kevin Porter CC	.03	.01	.00	
Kansas City Chiefs				
☐ 519 Carnell Lake CC	.03	.01	.00	
Pittsburgh Steelers				
☐ 520 Leonard Russell ROY	.30	.15	.03	
New England Patriots				
☐ 521 Mike Croel ROY	.12	.06	.01	
Denver Broncos				
☐ 522 Lawrence Dawsey ROY	.06	.03	.00	
Tampa Bay Buccaneers				
☐ 523 Moe Gardner ROY	.06	.03	.00	
Atlanta Falcons				
☐ 524 Steve Broussard LBM	.06	.03	.00	
Atlanta Falcons				
☐ 525 Dave Meggett LBM	.06	.03	.00	
New York Giants				
☐ 526 Darrell Green LBM	.06	.03	.00	
Washington Redskins				
☐ 527 Tony Jones LBM	.03	.01	.00	
Houston Oilers				
☐ 528 Barry Sanders LBM	.25	.12	.02	
Detroit Lions				
☐ 529 Pat Swilling SA	.06	.03	.00	
New Orleans Saints				
☐ 530 Reggie White SA	.06	.03	.00	
Philadelphia Eagles				
☐ 531 William Fuller SA	.03	.01	.00	
Houston Oilers				
☐ 532 Simon Fletcher SA	.03	.01	.00	
Denver Broncos				
☐ 533 Derrick Thomas SA	.08	.04	.01	
Kansas City Chiefs				
☐ 534 Mark Rypien MOY	.10	.05	.01	
Washington Redskins				
☐ 535 John Mackey HOF	.06	.03	.00	
☐ 536 John Riggins HOF	.06	.03	.00	
☐ 537 Lem Barney HOF	.06	.03	.00	
☐ 538 Shawn McCarthy 90	.08	.04	.01	
New England Patriots				
☐ 539 Al Edwards 90	.03	.01	.00	
Buffalo Bills				
☐ 540 Alexander Wright 90	.06	.03	.00	
Dallas Cowboys				
☐ 541 Ray Crockett 90	.03	.01	.00	
Detroit Lions				
☐ 542 Steve Young 90	.08	.04	.01	
San Francisco 49ers				
☐ 543 Nate Lewis 90	.03	.01	.00	
San Diego Chargers				
☐ 544 Dexter Carter 90	.03	.01	.00	

	San Francisco 49ers		
☐ 545	Reggie Rutland 90	.03	.01	.00
☐ 546	Jon Vaughn 90	.15	.07	.01
	New England Patriots		
☐ 547	Chris Martin 90	.03	.01	.00
	Kansas City Chiefs		
☐ 548	Warren Moon HL	.12	.06	.01
	Houston Oilers		
☐ 549	Super Bowl Logo	.03	.01	.00
☐ 550	Robb Thomas	.06	.03	.00
	Kansas City Chiefs		

1992 SkyBox Impact

The 1992 SkyBox Impact football set consists of 350 standard-size (2 1/2" by 3 1/2") cards. The cards were sold in 12-card foil packs and 24-card jumbo packs. Twenty Major Impact player cards were randomly inserted in jumbo packs, while two hologram cards (featuring Jim Kelly and Lawrence Taylor) were inserted in foil packs. Five hundred Impact Playmakers cards featuring Magic Johnson and Jim Kelly bear autographs by both stars, and these cards were randomly inserted in the foil packs. Lastly, 2,500 gold foil-stamped Total Impact cards were autographed by Jim Kelly and randomly inserted in the foil packs. The full-bleed color action photos on the fronts have the player's last name printed in block lettering across the top of the picture. The team logo is superimposed at the lower left corner. The flipside shows another action photo, career highlights, biography, statistics, and the

player's position by a diagram of "X's" and "O's." In addition to 276 player cards, the set includes the following subsets: Team Checklists (277-304), High Impact League Leaders (305-314), Sudden Impact Hardest Hitters (315-320), and Instant Impact Rookies (321-350). The cards are numbered on the back.

	MINT	EXC	G-VG
COMPLETE SET (350)	18.00	9.00	1.80
COMMON PLAYER (1-350)	.03	.01	.00

☐ 1	Jim Kelly	.35	.17	.03
	Buffalo Bills		
☐ 2	Andre Rison	.15	.07	.01
	Atlanta Falcons		
☐ 3	Michael Dean Perry	.12	.06	.01
	Cleveland Browns		
☐ 4	Herman Moore	.30	.15	.03
	Detroit Lions		
☐ 5	Fred McAfee	.25	.12	.02
	New Orleans Saints		
☐ 6	Ricky Proehl	.06	.03	.00
	Phoenix Cardinals		
☐ 7	Jim Everett	.10	.05	.01
	Los Angeles Rams		
☐ 8	Mark Carrier	.06	.03	.00
	Chicago Bears		
☐ 9	Eric Martin	.03	.01	.00
	New Orleans Saints		
☐ 10	John Elway	.15	.07	.01
	Denver Broncos		
☐ 11	Michael Irvin	.20	.10	.02
	Dallas Cowboys		
☐ 12	Keith McCants	.06	.03	.00
	Tampa Bay Buccaneers		
☐ 13	Greg Lloyd	.03	.01	.00
	Pittsburgh Steelers		
☐ 14	Lawrence Taylor	.10	.05	.01
	New York Giants		
☐ 15	Mike Tomczak	.08	.04	.01
	Green Bay Packers		
☐ 16	Cortez Kennedy	.06	.03	.00
	Seattle Seahawks		
☐ 17	William Fuller	.03	.01	.00
	Houston Oilers		
☐ 18	James Lofton	.12	.06	.01
	Buffalo Bills		
☐ 19	Kevin Fagan	.03	.01	.00
	San Francisco 49ers		
☐ 20	Bill Brooks	.03	.01	.00
	Indianapolis Colts		
☐ 21	Roger Craig	.10	.05	.01
	Los Angeles Raiders		
☐ 22	Jay Novacek	.10	.05	.01
	Dallas Cowboys		

☐ 23 Steve Sewell	.03	.01	.00
Denver Broncos			
☐ 24 William Perry	.06	.03	.00
Chicago Bears			
☐ 25 Jerry Rice	.35	.17	.03
San Francisco 49ers			
☐ 26 James Joseph	.20	.10	.02
Philadelphia Eagles			
☐ 27 Timm Rosenbach	.08	.04	.01
Phoenix Cardinals			
☐ 28 Pat Terrell	.03	.01	.00
Los Angeles Rams			
☐ 29 Jon Vaughn	.30	.15	.03
New England Patriots			
☐ 30 Steve Walsh	.08	.04	.01
New Orleans Saints			
☐ 31 James Hasty	.03	.01	.00
New York Jets			
☐ 32 Dwight Stone	.03	.01	.00
Pittsburgh Steelers			
☐ 33 Derrick Fenner	.08	.04	.01
Seattle Seahawks			
☐ 34 Mark Bortz	.03	.01	.00
Chicago Bears			
☐ 35 Dan Saleaumua	.03	.01	.00
Kansas City Chiefs			
☐ 36 Sammie Smith	.08	.04	.01
Miami Dolphins			
☐ 37 Antone Davis	.03	.01	.00
Philadelphia Eagles			
☐ 38 Steve Young	.12	.06	.01
San Francisco 49ers			
☐ 39 Mike Baab	.03	.01	.00
Cleveland Browns			
☐ 40 Rick Fenney	.03	.01	.00
Minnesota Vikings			
☐ 41 Chris Hinton	.06	.03	.00
Atlanta Falcons			
☐ 42 Bart Oates	.03	.01	.00
New York Giants			
☐ 43 Bryan Hinkle	.03	.01	.00
Pittsburgh Steelers			
☐ 44 James Francis	.06	.03	.00
Cincinnati Bengals			
☐ 45 Ray Crockett	.03	.01	.00
Detroit Lions			
☐ 46 Eric Dickerson	.25	.12	.02
Indianapolis Colts			
☐ 47 Hart Lee Dykes	.03	.01	.00
New England Patriots			
☐ 48 Percy Snow	.06	.03	.00
Kansas City Chiefs			
☐ 49 Ron Hall	.03	.01	.00
Tampa Bay Buccaneers			
☐ 50 Warren Moon	.20	.10	.02
Houston Oilers			
☐ 51 Ed West	.03	.01	.00
Green Bay Packers			
☐ 52 Clarence Verdin	.03	.01	.00
Indianapolis Colts			
☐ 53 Eugene Lockhart	.03	.01	.00
New England Patriots			
☐ 54 Andre Reed	.10	.05	.01
Buffalo Bills			
☐ 55 Kevin Ross	.03	.01	.00
Kansas City Chiefs			
☐ 56 Al Noga	.03	.01	.00
Minnesota Vikings			
☐ 57 Wes Hopkins	.03	.01	.00
Philadelphia Eagles			
☐ 58 Rufus Porter	.03	.01	.00
Seattle Seahawks			
☐ 59 Brian Mitchell	.12	.06	.01
Washington Redskins			
☐ 60 Reggie Roby	.03	.01	.00
Miami Dolphins			
☐ 61 Rodney Peete	.08	.04	.01
Detroit Lions			
☐ 62 Jeff Herrod	.03	.01	.00
Indianapolis Colts			
☐ 63 Anthony Smith	.03	.01	.00
Los Angeles Raiders			
☐ 64 Brad Muster	.06	.03	.00
Chicago Bears			
☐ 65 Jessie Tuggle	.03	.01	.00
Atlanta Falcons			
☐ 66 Al Smith	.03	.01	.00
Houston Oilers			
☐ 67 Jeff Hostetler	.15	.07	.01
New York Giants			
☐ 68 John L. Williams	.08	.04	.01
Seattle Seahawks			
☐ 69 Paul Gruber	.03	.01	.00
Tampa Bay Buccaneers			
☐ 70 Cornelius Bennett	.08	.04	.01
Buffalo Bills			
☐ 71 William White	.03	.01	.00
Detroit Lions			
☐ 72 Tom Rathman	.06	.03	.00
San Francisco 49ers			
☐ 73 Boomer Esiason	.10	.05	.01
Cincinnati Bengals			
☐ 74 Neil Smith	.03	.01	.00
Kansas City Chiefs			
☐ 75 Sterling Sharpe	.10	.05	.01
Green Bay Packers			
☐ 76 James Jones	.03	.01	.00
Cleveland Browns			
☐ 77 David Treadwell	.03	.01	.00
Denver Broncos			
☐ 78 Flipper Anderson	.06	.03	.00
Los Angeles Rams			
☐ 79 Eric Allen	.03	.01	.00
Philadelphia Eagles			

☐ 80 Joe Jacoby .03 Washington Redskins	.01	.00
☐ 81 Keith Sims .03 Miami Dolphins	.01	.00
☐ 82 Bubba McDowell .03 Houston Oilers	.01	.00
☐ 83 Ronnie Lippett .03 New England Patriots	.01	.00
☐ 84 Cris Carter .06 Minnesota Vikings	.03	.00
☐ 85 Chris Burkett .03 New York Jets	.01	.00
☐ 86 Issiac Holt .03 Dallas Cowboys	.01	.00
☐ 87 Duane Bickett .03 Indianapolis Colts	.01	.00
☐ 88 Leslie O'Neal .06 San Diego Chargers	.03	.00
☐ 89 Gill Fenerty .06 New Orleans Saints	.03	.00
☐ 90 Pierce Holt .03 San Francisco 49ers	.01	.00
☐ 91 Willie Drewrey .03 Tampa Bay Buccaneers	.01	.00
☐ 92 Brian Blades .06 Seattle Seahawks	.03	.00
☐ 93 Tony Martin .03 Miami Dolphins	.01	.00
☐ 94 Jessie Hester .03 Indianapolis Colts	.01	.00
☐ 95 John Stephens .06 New England Patriots	.03	.00
☐ 96 Keith Willis .03 Pittsburgh Steelers	.01	.00
☐ 97 Vai Sikahema .03 Green Bay Packers	.01	.00
☐ 98 Mark Higgs .25 Miami Dolphins	.12	.02
☐ 99 Steve McMichael .06 Chicago Bears	.03	.00
☐ 100 Deion Sanders .20 Atlanta Falcons	.10	.02
☐ 101 Marvin Washington .03 New York Jets	.01	.00
☐ 102 Ken Norton .03 Dallas Cowboys	.01	.00
☐ 103 Barry Word .15 Kansas City Chiefs	.07	.01
☐ 104 Sean Jones .03 Houston Oilers	.01	.00
☐ 105 Ronnie Harmon .03 San Diego Chargers	.01	.00
☐ 106 Donnell Woolford .03 Chicago Bears	.01	.00
☐ 107 Ray Agnew .03 New England Patriots	.01	.00
☐ 108 Lemuel Stinson .03	.01	.00

Chicago Bears		
☐ 109 Dennis Smith .03 Denver Broncos	.01	.00
☐ 110 Lorenzo White .06 Houston Oilers	.03	.00
☐ 111 Craig Heyward .06 New Orleans Saints	.03	.00
☐ 112 Jeff Query .03 Green Bay Packers	.01	.00
☐ 113 Gary Plummer .03 San Diego Chargers	.01	.00
☐ 114 John Taylor .10 San Francisco 49ers	.05	.01
☐ 115 Rohn Stark .03 Indianapolis Colts	.01	.00
☐ 116 Tom Waddle .15 Chicago Bears	.07	.01
☐ 117 Jeff Cross .03 Miami Dolphins	.01	.00
☐ 118 Tim Green .03 Atlanta Falcons	.01	.00
☐ 119 Anthony Munoz .10 Cincinnati Bengals	.05	.01
☐ 120 Mel Gray .03 Detroit Lions	.01	.00
☐ 121 Ray Donaldson .03 Indianapolis Colts	.01	.00
☐ 122 Dennis Byrd .03 New York Jets	.01	.00
☐ 123 Carnell Lake .03 Pittsburgh Steelers	.01	.00
☐ 124 Broderick Thomas .06 Tampa Bay Buccaneers	.03	.00
☐ 125 Charles Mann .06 Washington Redskins	.03	.00
☐ 126 Darion Conner .06 Atlanta Falcons	.03	.00
☐ 127 John Roper .03 Chicago Bears	.01	.00
☐ 128 Jack Del Rio .03 Dallas Cowboys	.01	.00
☐ 129 Rickey Dixon .03 Cincinnati Bengals	.01	.00
☐ 130 Eddie Anderson .03 Los Angeles Raiders	.01	.00
☐ 131 Steve Broussard .10 Atlanta Falcons	.05	.01
☐ 132 Michael Young .03 Denver Broncos	.01	.00
☐ 133 Lamar Lathon .06 Houston Oilers	.03	.00
☐ 134 Rickey Jackson .06 New Orleans Saints	.03	.00
☐ 135 Billy Ray Smith .03 San Diego Chargers	.01	.00
☐ 136 Tony Casillas .03 Dallas Cowboys	.01	.00

☐ 137 Ickey Woods	.06	.03	.00
Cincinnati Bengals			
☐ 138 Ray Childress	.06	.03	.00
Houston Oilers			
☐ 139 Vance Johnson	.06	.03	.00
Denver Broncos			
☐ 140 Brett Perriman	.03	.01	.00
Detroit Lions			
☐ 141 Calvin Williams	.03	.01	.00
Philadelphia Eagles			
☐ 142 Dino Hackett	.03	.01	.00
Kansas City Chiefs			
☐ 143 Jacob Green	.03	.01	.00
Seattle Seahawks			
☐ 144 Robert Delpino	.06	.03	.00
Los Angeles Rams			
☐ 145 Marv Cook	.08	.04	.01
New England Patriots			
☐ 146 Dwayne Harper	.06	.03	.00
Seattle Seahawks			
☐ 147 Ricky Ervins	.75	.35	.07
Washington Redskins			
☐ 148 Kelvin Martin	.03	.01	.00
Dallas Cowboys			
☐ 149 Leroy Hoard	.08	.04	.01
Cleveland Browns			
☐ 150 Dan Marino	.25	.12	.02
Miami Dolphins			
☐ 151 Richard Johnson	.03	.01	.00
Houston Oilers			
☐ 152 Henry Ellard	.06	.03	.00
Los Angeles Rams			
☐ 153 Al Toon	.08	.04	.01
New York Jets			
☐ 154 Dermontti Dawson	.03	.01	.00
Pittsburgh Steelers			
☐ 155 Robert Blackmon	.03	.01	.00
Seattle Seahawks			
☐ 156 Howie Long	.06	.03	.00
Los Angeles Raiders			
☐ 157 David Fulcher	.03	.01	.00
Cincinnati Bengals			
☐ 158 Mike Merriweather	.03	.01	.00
Minnesota Vikings			
☐ 159 Gary Anderson	.03	.01	.00
Pittsburgh Steelers			
☐ 160 John Friesz	.15	.07	.01
San Diego Chargers			
☐ 161 Eugene Robinson	.03	.01	.00
Seattle Seahawks			
☐ 162 Brad Baxter	.06	.03	.00
New York Jets			
☐ 163 Bennie Blades	.06	.03	.00
Detroit Lions			
☐ 164 Harold Green	.15	.07	.01
Cincinnati Bengals			
☐ 165 Ernest Givins	.10	.05	.01

Houston Oilers			
☐ 166 Deron Cherry	.03	.01	.00
Kansas City Chiefs			
☐ 167 Carl Banks	.06	.03	.00
New York Giants			
☐ 168 Keith Jackson	.08	.04	.01
Philadelphia Eagles			
☐ 169 Pat Leahy	.03	.01	.00
New York Jets			
☐ 170 Alvin Harper	.20	.10	.02
Dallas Cowboys			
☐ 171 David Little	.06	.03	.00
Pittsburgh Steelers			
☐ 172 Anthony Carter	.08	.04	.01
Minnesota Vikings			
☐ 173 Willie Gault	.06	.03	.00
Los Angeles Raiders			
☐ 174 Bruce Armstrong	.03	.01	.00
New England Patriots			
☐ 175 Junior Seau	.08	.04	.01
San Diego Chargers			
☐ 176 Eric Metcalf	.06	.03	.00
Cleveland Browns			
☐ 177 Tony Mandarich	.06	.03	.00
Green Bay Packers			
☐ 178 Ernie Jones	.03	.01	.00
Phoenix Cardinals			
☐ 179 Albert Bentley	.06	.03	.00
Indianapolis Colts			
☐ 180 Mike Pritchard	.30	.15	.03
Atlanta Falcons			
☐ 181 Bubby Brister	.08	.04	.01
Pittsburgh Steelers			
☐ 182 Vaughan Johnson	.03	.01	.00
New Orleans Saints			
☐ 183 Robert Clark	.06	.03	.00
Detroit Lions			
☐ 184 Lawrence Dawsey	.12	.06	.01
Tampa Bay Buccaneers			
☐ 185 Eric Green	.12	.06	.01
Pittsburgh Steelers			
☐ 186 Jay Schroeder	.08	.04	.01
Los Angeles Raiders			
☐ 187 Andre Tippett	.06	.03	.00
New England Patriots			
☐ 188 Vinny Testaverde	.08	.04	.01
Tampa Bay Buccaneers			
☐ 189 Wendell Davis	.12	.06	.01
Chicago Bears			
☐ 190 Russell Maryland	.20	.10	.02
Dallas Cowboys			
☐ 191 Chris Singleton	.06	.03	.00
New England Patriots			
☐ 192 Ken O'Brien	.08	.04	.01
New York Jets			
☐ 193 Merril Hoge	.06	.03	.00
Pittsburgh Steelers			

☐ 194 Steve Bono .... .40 .20 .04
San Francisco 49ers
☐ 195 Earnest Byner .... .08 .04 .01
Washington Redskins
☐ 196 Mike Singletary .... .08 .04 .01
Chicago Bears
☐ 197 Gaston Green .... .20 .10 .02
Denver Broncos
☐ 198 Mark Carrier .... .06 .03 .00
Tampa Bay Buccaneers
☐ 199 Harvey Williams .... .45 .22 .04
Kansas City Chiefs
☐ 200 Randall Cunningham ...... .15 .07 .01
Philadelphia Eagles
☐ 201 Cris Dishman .... .08 .04 .01
Houston Oilers
☐ 202 Greg Townsend .... .03 .01 .00
Los Angeles Raiders
☐ 203 Christian Okoye .... .10 .05 .01
Kansas City Chiefs
☐ 204 Sam Mills .... .03 .01 .00
New Orleans Saints
☐ 205 Kyle Clifton .... .03 .01 .00
New York Jets
☐ 206 Jim Harbaugh .... .08 .04 .01
Chicago Bears
☐ 207 Anthony Thompson .... .08 .04 .01
Phoenix Cardinals
☐ 208 Rob Moore .... .25 .12 .02
New York Jets
☐ 209 Irving Fryar .... .06 .03 .00
New England Patriots
☐ 210 Derrick Thomas .... .15 .07 .01
Kansas City Chiefs
☐ 211 Chris Miller .... .15 .07 .01
Atlanta Falcons
☐ 212 Doug Smith .... .03 .01 .00
Houston Oilers
☐ 213 Michael Haynes .... .20 .10 .02
Atlanta Falcons
☐ 214 Phil Simms .... .10 .05 .01
New York Giants
☐ 215 Charles Haley .... .06 .03 .00
San Francisco 49ers
☐ 216 Burt Grossman .... .06 .03 .00
San Diego Chargers
☐ 217 Rod Bernstine .... .06 .03 .00
San Diego Chargers
☐ 218 Louis Lipps .... .06 .03 .00
Pittsburgh Steelers
☐ 219 Dan McGwire .... .60 .30 .06
Seattle Seahawks
☐ 220 Ethan Horton .... .06 .03 .00
Los Angeles Raiders
☐ 221 Michael Carter .... .06 .03 .00
San Francisco 49ers
☐ 222 Neil O'Donnell .... .40 .20 .04

Pittsburgh Steelers
☐ 223 Anthony Miller .... .06 .03 .00
San Diego Chargers
☐ 224 Eric Swann .... .08 .04 .01
Phoenix Cardinals
☐ 225 Thurman Thomas .... .40 .20 .04
Buffalo Bills
☐ 226 Jeff George .... .25 .12 .02
Indianapolis Colts
☐ 227 Joe Montana .... .45 .22 .04
San Francisco 49ers
☐ 228 Leonard Marshall .... .03 .01 .00
New York Giants
☐ 229 Haywood Jeffires .... .15 .07 .01
Houston Oilers
☐ 230 Mark Clayton .... .08 .04 .01
Miami Dolphins
☐ 231 Chris Doleman .... .06 .03 .00
Minnesota Vikings
☐ 232 Troy Aikman .... .35 .17 .03
Dallas Cowboys
☐ 233 Gary Anderson .... .06 .03 .00
Tampa Bay Buccaneers
☐ 234 Pat Swilling .... .08 .04 .01
New Orleans Saints
☐ 235 Ronnie Lott .... .10 .05 .01
Los Angeles Raiders
☐ 236 Brian Jordan .... .15 .07 .01
Atlanta Falcons
☐ 237 Bruce Smith .... .08 .04 .01
Buffalo Bills
☐ 238 Tony Jones .... .06 .03 .00
Houston Oilers
☐ 239 Tim McKyer .... .03 .01 .00
Atlanta Falcons
☐ 240 Gary Clark .... .12 .06 .01
Washington Redskins
☐ 241 Mitchell Price .... .03 .01 .00
Los Angeles Rams
☐ 242 John Kasay .... .03 .01 .00
Atlanta Falcons
☐ 243 Stephone Paige .... .06 .03 .00
Kansas City Chiefs
☐ 244 Jeff Wright .... .03 .01 .00
Buffalo Bills
☐ 245 Shannon Sharpe .... .03 .01 .00
Denver Broncos
☐ 246 Keith Byars .... .06 .03. .00
Philadelphia Eagles
☐ 247 Charles Dimry .... .03 .01 .00
Denver Broncos
☐ 248 Steve Smith .... .03 .01 .00
Los Angeles Raiders
☐ 249 Erric Pegram .... .12 .06 .01
Atlanta Falcons
☐ 250 Bernie Kosar .... .10 .05 .01
Cleveland Browns

☐ 251 Peter Tom Willis ....08 Chicago Bears	.04	.01	
☐ 252 Mark Ingram ....03 New York Giants	.01	.00	
☐ 253 Keith McKeller ....06 Buffalo Bills	.03	.00	
☐ 254 Lewis Billups ....03 Buffalo Bills	.01	.00	
☐ 255 Alton Montgomery ....03 Houston Oilers	.01	.00	
☐ 256 Jimmie Jones ....03 Dallas Cowboys	.01	.00	
☐ 257 Brent Williams ....03 New England Patriots	.01	.00	
☐ 258 Gene Atkins ....03 New Orleans Saints	.01	.00	
☐ 259 Reggie Rutland ....03 Minnesota Vikings	.01	.00	
☐ 260 Sam Seale ....03 San Diego Chargers	.01	.00	
☐ 261 Andre Ware ....10 Detroit Lions	.05	.01	
☐ 262 Fred Barnett ....12 Philadelphia Eagles	.06	.01	
☐ 263 Randal Hill ....30 Phoenix Cardinals	.15	.03	
☐ 264 Patrick Hunter ....03 Seattle Seahawks	.01	.00	
☐ 265 Johnny Rembert ....03 New England Patriots	.01	.00	
☐ 266 Monte Coleman ....03 Washington Redskins	.01	.00	
☐ 267 Aaron Wallace ....06 Los Angeles Raiders	.03	.00	
☐ 268 Ferrell Edmunds ....03 Miami Dolphins	.01	.00	
☐ 269 Stan Thomas ....03 Chicago Bears	.01	.00	
☐ 270 Robb Thomas ....06 Kansas City Chiefs	.03	.00	
☐ 271 Martin Bayless ....03 San Diego Chargers	.01	.00	
☐ 272 Dean Biasucci ....03 Indianapolis Colts	.01	.00	
☐ 273 Keith Henderson ....10 San Francisco 49ers	.05	.01	
☐ 274 Vinnie Clark ....03 Green Bay Packers	.01	.00	
☐ 275 Emmitt Smith ....1.25 Dallas Cowboys	.60	.12	
☐ 276 Mark Rypien ....20 Washington Redskins	.10	.02	
☐ 277 Atlanta Falcons ....08 Wing and a Prayer (Michael Haynes)	.04	.01	
☐ 278 Buffalo Bills ....15 Machine Gun	.07	.01	

(Jim Kelly)			
☐ 279 Chicago Bears ....08 Grizzly (Tom Waddle)	.04	.01	
☐ 280 Cincinnati Bengals ....03 Price is Right (Mitchell Price)	.01	.00	
☐ 281 Cleveland Browns ....06 Coasting (Bernie Kosar)	.03	.00	
☐ 282 Dallas Cowboys ....10 Gunned Down (Michael Irvin)	.05	.01	
☐ 283 Denver Broncos ....10 The Drive II (John Elway)	.05	.01	
☐ 284 Detroit Lions ....03 Lions Roar (Mel Gray)	.01	.00	
☐ 285 Green Bay Packers ....06 Razor Sharpe (Sterling Sharpe)	.03	.00	
☐ 286 Houston Oilers ....12 Oil's Well (Warren Moon)	.06	.01	
☐ 287 Indianapolis Colts ....12 Whew (Jeff George)	.06	.01	
☐ 288 Kansas City Chiefs ....08 Ambush (Derrick Thomas)	.04	.01	
☐ 289 Los Angeles Raiders ....06 Lott of Defense (Ronnie Lott)	.03	.00	
☐ 290 Los Angeles Rams ....06 Ram It (Robert Delpino)	.03	.00	
☐ 291 Miami Dolphins ....12 Miami Ice (Dan Marino)	.06	.01	
☐ 292 Minnesota Vikings ....06 Purple Blaze (Cris Carter)	.03	.00	
☐ 293 New England Patriots .....03 Surprise Attack (Irving Fryar)	.01	.00	
☐ 294 New Orleans Saints ....03 Marching In (Gene Atkins)	.01	.00	
☐ 295 New York Giants ....06 Almost Perfect (Phil Simms)	.03	.00	
☐ 296 New York Jets ....06 Playoff Bound (Ken O'Brien)	.03	.00	
☐ 297 Philadelphia Eagles ....06 Flying High (Keith Jackson)	.03	.00	

☐ 298 Phoenix Cardinals	.06	.03	.00
Airborne			
(Ricky Proehl)			
☐ 299 Pittsburgh Steelers	.03	.01	.00
Steel Curtain			
(Brian Hinkle)			
☐ 300 San Diego Chargers	.08	.04	.01
Lightning			
(John Friesz)			
☐ 301 San Francisco 49ers	.15	.07	.01
Instant Rice			
(Jerry Rice)			
☐ 302 Seattle Seahawks	.03	.01	.00
Defense Never Rests			
(Eugene Robinson)			
☐ 303 Tampa Bay Buccaneers	.03	.01	.00
Stunned			
(Broderick Thomas)			
☐ 304 Washington Redskins	.10	.05	.01
Super			
(Mark Rypien)			
☐ 305 Jim Kelly LL	.15	.07	.01
Buffalo Bills			
☐ 306 Steve Young LL	.08	.04	.01
San Francisco 49ers			
☐ 307 Thurman Thomas LL	.17	.08	.01
Buffalo Bills			
☐ 308 Emmitt Smith LL	.50	.25	.05
Dallas Cowboys			
☐ 309 Haywood Jeffires LL	.10	.05	.01
Houston Oilers			
☐ 310 Michael Irvin LL	.10	.05	.01
Dallas Cowboys			
☐ 311 William Fuller LL	.03	.01	.00
Houston Oilers			
☐ 312 Pat Swilling LL	.06	.03	.00
New Orleans Saints			
☐ 313 Ronnie Lott LL	.06	.03	.00
Los Angeles Raiders			
☐ 314 Deion Sanders LL	.10	.05	.01
Atlanta Falcons			
☐ 315 Cornelius Bennett HH	.06	.03	.00
Buffalo Bills			
☐ 316 David Fulcher HH	.03	.01	.00
Cincinnati Bengals			
☐ 317 Ronnie Lott HH	.06	.03	.00
Los Angeles Raiders			
☐ 318 Pat Swilling HH	.06	.03	.00
New Orleans Saints			
☐ 319 Lawrence Taylor HH	.08	.04	.01
New York Giants			
☐ 320 Derrick Thomas HH	.08	.04	.01
Kansas City Chiefs			
☐ 321 Steve Emtman	.90	.45	.09
Indianapolis Colts			
☐ 322 Carl Pickens	.75	.35	.07
Cincinnati Bengals			
☐ 323 David Klingler	1.25	.60	.12
Cincinnati Bengals			
☐ 324 Dale Carter	.15	.07	.01
Kansas City Chiefs			
☐ 325 Mike Gaddis	.20	.10	.02
Minnesota Vikings			
☐ 326 Quentin Coryatt	.90	.45	.09
Indianapolis Colts			
☐ 327 Darryl Williams	.15	.07	.01
Cincinnati Bengals			
☐ 328 Jeremy Lincoln	.10	.05	.01
Chicago Bears			
☐ 329 Robert Jones	.15	.07	.01
Dallas Cowboys			
☐ 330 Bucky Richardson	.15	.07	.01
Houston Oilers			
☐ 331 Tony Brooks	.15	.07	.01
Philadelphia Eagles			
☐ 332 Alonzo Spellman	.20	.10	.02
Chicago Bears			
☐ 333 Robert Brooks	.12	.06	.01
Green Bay Packers			
☐ 334 Marco Coleman	.20	.10	.02
Miami Dolphins			
☐ 335 Siran Stacy	.35	.17	.03
Philadelphia Eagles			
☐ 336 Tommy Maddox	.75	.35	.07
Denver Broncos			
☐ 337 Steve Israel	.15	.07	.01
Los Angeles Rams			
☐ 338 Vaughn Dunbar	.60	.30	.06
New Orleans Saints			
☐ 339 Shane Collins	.10	.05	.01
Washington Redskins			
☐ 340 Kevin Smith	.15	.07	.01
Dallas Cowboys			
☐ 341 Chris Mims	.15	.07	.01
San Diego Chargers			
☐ 342 Chester McGlockton	.12	.06	.01
Los Angeles Raiders			
☐ 343 Tracy Scroggins	.12	.06	.01
Detroit Lions			
☐ 344 Howard Dinkins	.10	.05	.01
Atlanta Falcons			
☐ 345 Levon Kirkland	.12	.06	.01
Pittsburgh Steelers			
☐ 346 Terrell Buckley	.75	.35	.07
Green Bay Packers			
☐ 347 Marquez Pope	.12	.06	.01
San Diego Chargers			
☐ 348 Phillippi Sparks	.12	.06	.01
New York Giants			
☐ 349 Joe Bowden	.12	.06	.01
Houston Oilers			
☐ 350 Edgar Bennett	.25	.12	.02
Green Bay Packers			

1991 Star Pics Pro Prospects

This 112-card set is numbered on the back and measures the standard size, 2 1/2" by 3 1/2". The front features an action color photo enclosed by a thin white border against a background of footballs. The player's name appears in white print on a maroon-colored box below the picture. The back has a full-color posed photo in the upper left hand corner and the card number (enclosed in a red star) in the upper right hand corner. The biographical information, including accomplishments, strengths, and weaknesses, is printed on a pale green diagram of a football field with a diagrammed play. The set also includes player agents and flashback cards of top young players.

	MINT	EXC	G-VG
COMPLETE SET (112)	10.00	5.00	1.00
COMMON PLAYER (1-112)	.05	.02	.00
☐ 1 1991 NFL Draft Overview	.05	.02	.00
☐ 2 Barry Sanders Flashback	.50	.25	.05
☐ 3 Nick Bell Iowa	.75	.35	.07
☐ 4 Kelvin Pritchett Mississippi	.20	.10	.02
☐ 5 Huey Richardson Florida	.20	.10	.02
☐ 6 Mike Croel Nebraska	.75	.35	.07
☐ 7 Paul Justin Arizona State	.15	.07	.01
☐ 8 Ivory Lee Brown Arkansas-Pine Bluff	.20	.10	.02
☐ 9 Herman Moore Virginia	.75	.35	.07
☐ 10 Derrick Thomas Flashback	.15	.07	.01
☐ 11 Keith Traylor Central State of Oklahoma	.20	.10	.02
☐ 12 Joe Johnson N.C. State	.05	.02	.00
☐ 13 Dan McGwire San Diego State	1.00	.50	.10
☐ 14 Harvey Williams LSU	1.00	.50	.10
☐ 15 Eric Moten Michigan State	.10	.05	.01
☐ 16 Steve Zucker Agent	.05	.02	.00
☐ 17 Randal Hill Miami (Florida)	.75	.35	.07
☐ 18 Browning Nagle Louisville	.75	.35	.07
☐ 19 Stan Thomas Texas	.10	.05	.01
☐ 20 Emmitt Smith Flashback	.50	.25	.05
☐ 21 Ted Washington Louisville	.20	.10	.02
☐ 22 Lamar Rogers Auburn	.10	.05	.01
☐ 23 Kenny Walker Nebraska	.60	.30	.06
☐ 24 Howard Griffith Illinois	.20	.10	.02
☐ 25 Reggie Johnson Florida State	.20	.10	.02
☐ 26 Lawrence Dawsey Florida State	.60	.30	.06
☐ 27 Joe Garten Colorado	.05	.02	.00
☐ 28 Moe Gardner Illinois	.25	.12	.02
☐ 29 Michael Stonebreaker Notre Dame	.15	.07	.01
☐ 30 Jeff George Flashback	.20	.10	.02
☐ 31 Leigh Steinberg Agent	.10	.05	.01
☐ 32 John Flannery Syracuse	.10	.05	.01
☐ 33 Pat Harlow USC	.20	.10	.02
☐ 34 Kanavis McGhee Colorado	.20	.10	.02
☐ 35 Mike Dumas Indiana	.20	.10	.02
☐ 36 Godfrey Myles	.15	.07	.01

☐ 37	Shawn Moore	.30	.15	.03
	Florida			
☐ 38	Jeff Graham	.20	.10	.02
	Virginia			
☐ 39	Ricky Watters	.25	.12	.02
	Ohio State			
☐ 40	Andre Ware	.10	.05	.01
	Notre Dame Flashback			
☐ 41	Henry Jones	.10	.05	.01
	Illinois			
☐ 42	Eric Turner	.50	.25	.05
	UCLA			
☐ 43	Bob Woolf	.05	.02	.00
	Agent			
☐ 44	Randy Baldwin	.15	.07	.01
	Mississippi			
☐ 45	Mo Lewis	.25	.12	.02
	Georgia			
☐ 46	Jerry Evans	.15	.07	.01
	Toledo University			
☐ 47	Derek Russell	.35	.17	.03
	Arkansas			
☐ 48	Merton Hanks	.10	.05	.01
	Iowa			
☐ 49	Kevin Donnalley	.10	.05	.01
	North Carolina			
☐ 50	Troy Aikman	.25	.12	.02
	Flashback			
☐ 51	William Thomas	.10	.05	.01
	Texas A and M			
☐ 52	Chris Thome	.05	.02	.00
	Minnesota			
☐ 53	Ricky Ervins	2.50	1.25	.25
	USC			
☐ 54	Jake Reed	.20	.10	.02
	Grambling			
☐ 55	Jerome Henderson	.10	.05	.01
	Clemson			
☐ 56	Mark Vander Poel	.10	.05	.01
	Colorado			
☐ 57	Bernard Ellison	.10	.05	.01
	Nevada (Reno)			
☐ 58	Jack Mills	.05	.02	.00
	Agent			
☐ 59	Jarrod Bunch	.20	.10	.02
	Michigan			
☐ 60	Mark Carrier	.10	.05	.01
	Flashback			
☐ 61	Rocen Keeton	.05	.02	.00
	UCLA			
☐ 62	Louis Riddick	.05	.02	.00
	Pittsburgh			
☐ 63	Bobby Wilson	.25	.12	.02
	Michigan State			
☐ 64	Steve Jackson	.10	.05	.01
	Purdue			
☐ 65	Brett Favre	.60	.30	.06
	Southern Miss			
☐ 66	Ernie Mills	.25	.12	.02
	Florida			
☐ 67	Joe Valerio	.10	.05	.01
	Pennsylvania			
☐ 68	Chris Smith	.10	.05	.01
	Brigham Young			
☐ 69	Ralph Cindrich	.05	.02	.00
	Agent			
☐ 70	Christian Okoye	.10	.05	.01
	Flashback			
☐ 71	Charles McRae	.15	.07	.01
	Tennessee			
☐ 72	Jon Vaughn	.40	.20	.04
	Michigan			
☐ 73	Eric Swann	.35	.17	.03
	No college			
☐ 74	Bill Musgrave	.20	.10	.02
	Oregon			
☐ 75	Eric Bieniemy	.35	.17	.03
	Colorado			
☐ 76	Pat Tyrance	.10	.05	.01
	Nebraska			
☐ 77	Vinnie Clark	.20	.10	.02
	Ohio State			
☐ 78	Eugene Williams	.05	.02	.00
	Iowa State			
☐ 79	Rob Carpenter	.20	.10	.02
	Syracuse			
☐ 80	Deion Sanders	.15	.07	.01
	Flashback			
☐ 81	Roman Phifer	.20	.10	.02
	UCLA			
☐ 82	Greg Lewis	.60	.30	.06
	Washington			
☐ 83	John Johnson	.10	.05	.01
	Clemson			
☐ 84	Richard Howell	.05	.02	.00
	Agent			
☐ 85	Jesse Campbell	.10	.05	.01
	N.C. State			
☐ 86	Stanley Richard	.30	.15	.03
	Texas			
☐ 87	Alfred Williams	.25	.12	.02
	Colorado			
☐ 88	Mike Pritchard	.75	.35	.07
	Colorado			
☐ 89	Mel Agee	.10	.05	.01
	Illinois			
☐ 90	Aaron Craver	.25	.12	.02
	Fresno State			
☐ 91	Tim Barnett	.45	.22	.04
	Jackson State			
☐ 92	Wesley Carroll	.40	.20	.04
	Miami (Florida)			
☐ 93	Kevin Scott	.10	.05	.01

	Stanford				
☐ 94	Darren Lewis	.40	.20	.04
	Texas A and M			
☐ 95	Tim Bruton	.15	.07	.01
	Missouri			
☐ 96	Tim James	.05	.02	.00
	Colorado			
☐ 97	Darryll Lewis	.30	.15	.03
	Arizona			
☐ 98	Shawn Jefferson	.10	.05	.01
	Central Florida			
☐ 99	Mitch Donahue·	.05	.02	.00
	Wyoming			
☐ 100	Marvin Demoff	.05	.02	.00
	Agent			
☐ 101	Adrian Cooper	.25	.12	.02
	Oklahoma			
☐ 102	Bruce Pickens	.20	.10	.02
	Nebraska			
☐ 103	Scott Zolak	.25	.12	.02
	Maryland			
☐ 104	Phil Hansen	.10	.05	.01
	No. Dakota State			
☐ 105	Ed King	.20	.10	.02
	Auburn			
☐ 106	Mike Jones	.10	.05	.01
	N.C. State			
☐ 107	Alvin Harper	.60	.30	.06
	Tennessee			
☐ 108	Robert Young	.05	.02	.00
	Mississippi State			
☐ 109	Offensive Prospects	.10	.05	.01
	Nick Bell			
	Brett Favre			
	Alvin Harper			
	Charles McRae			
☐ 110	Defensive Prospects	.10	.05	.01
	Mike Croel			
	Eric Swann			
	Eric Turner			
☐ 111	Checklist Card	.05	.02	.00
☐ 112	Checklist Card	.05	.02	.00
☐ xx	Salute/Advertisement	.05	.02	.00
	(American flag			
	background)			

1992 Star Pics Pro Prospects

This 100-card standard-size (2 1/2" by 3 1/2") set highlights over 80 of the top college prospects in the country. The set is available in ten-card foil StarPaks and factory sets, with randomly inserted autograph cards in both. It was reported that the production run did not exceed 195,000 factory sets and 12,000 ten-box foil cases. The fronts feature glossy color action photos bordered in white. A color stripe runs the length of the card on the right side, and the player's position and name are printed vertically. The Star Pics logo is superimposed at the lower right corner. The backs present an in-depth scouting report (accomplishments, strengths, and weaknesses), biographical information, and a color head shot in a circular format at the lower right corner. The five-card Flashback subset (10, 20, 30, 50, 70) displays illustrations by sports artist Scott Medlock. The StarStat subset, ten cards in all, compares the top pro prospects' stats to the collegiate stats of NFL greats; two of these were included in each set and eight others were randomly inserted in the foil packs. The cards are numbered on the back.

	MINT	EXC	G-VG
COMPLETE SET (100)	11.00	5.50	1.10
COMMON PLAYER (1-100)	.07	.03	.01

☐ 1	Steve Emtman SS	.50	.25	.05
	Washington			
☐ 2	Chris Hakel	.25	.12	.02
	William and Mary			
☐ 3	Phillipi Sparks	.15	.07	.01

Arizona State

☐ 4 Howard Dinkins	.12	.06	.01
Florida State			
☐ 5 Robert Brooks	.20	.10	.02
South Carolina			
☐ 6 Chris Pederson	.07	.03	.01
Iowa State			
☐ 7 Bucky Richardson	.15	.07	.01
Texas A and M			
☐ 8 Keith Goganious	.15	.07	.01
Penn State			
☐ 9 Robert Porcher	.20	.10	.02
South Carolina State			
☐ 10 Andre Rison	.15	.07	.01
(Flashback)			
☐ 11 Jason Hanson	.12	.06	.01
Washington State			
☐ 12 Tommy Vardell	.60	.30	.06
Stanford			
☐ 13 Kurt Barber	.15	.07	.01
Southern California			
☐ 14 Bernard Dafney	.10	.05	.01
Tennessee			
☐ 15 Levon Kirkland	.20	.10	.02
Clemson			
☐ 16 Corey Widmer	.10	.05	.01
Montana State			
☐ 17 Santana Dotson	.10	.05	.01
Baylor			
☐ 18 Chris Holder	.10	.05	.01
Tuskegee			
☐ 19 Elbert Turner	.10	.05	.01
Illinois			
☐ 20 Mike Croel	.20	.10	.02
(Flashback)			
☐ 21 Darren Perry	.10	.05	.01
Penn State			
☐ 22 Troy Vincent	.75	.35	.07
Wisconsin			
☐ 23 Quentin Coryatt	.75	.35	.07
Texas A and M			
☐ 24 John Brown III	.12	.06	.01
Houston			
☐ 25 John Ray	.07	.03	.01
West Virginia			
☐ 26 Vaughn Dunbar	.75	.35	.07
Indiana			
☐ 27 Stacey Dillard	.10	.05	.01
Oklahoma			
☐ 28 Alonzo Spellman	.25	.12	.02
Ohio State			
☐ 29 Darren Woodson	.15	.07	.01
Arizona State			
☐ 30 Pat Swilling	.07	.03	.01
(Flashback)			
☐ 31 Eddie Robinson	.15	.07	.01
Alabama State			
☐ 32 Tyji Armstrong	.15	.07	.01
Mississippi			
☐ 33 Bill Johnson	.15	.07	.01
Michigan State			
☐ 34 Eugene Chung	.15	.07	.01
Virginia Tech			
☐ 35 Ricardo McDonald	.15	.07	.01
Pittsburgh			
☐ 36 Sean Lumpkin	.10	.05	.01
Minnesota			
☐ 37 Greg Skrepenak	.20	.10	.02
Michigan			
☐ 38 Ashley Ambrose	.15	.07	.01
Mississippi Valley St.			
☐ 39 Kevin Smith	.20	.10	.02
Texas A and M			
☐ 40 Todd Collins	.12	.06	.01
Carson-Newman			
☐ 41 Shane Dronett	.15	.07	.01
Texas			
☐ 42 Ronnie West	.12	.06	.01
Pittsburg State			
☐ 43 Darryl Williams	.25	.12	.02
Miami			
☐ 44 Rodney Blackshear	.10	.05	.01
Texas Tech			
☐ 45 Dion Lambert	.10	.05	.01
UCLA			
☐ 46 Mike Saunders	.15	.07	.01
Iowa			
☐ 47 Keo Coleman	.12	.06	.01
Mississippi State			
☐ 48 Dana Hall	.20	.10	.02
Washington			
☐ 49 Arthur Marshall	.07	.03	.01
Georgia			
☐ 50 Leonard Russell	.35	.17	.03
(Flashback)			
☐ 51 Matt Rodgers	.25	.12	.02
Iowa			
☐ 52 Shane Collins	.15	.07	.01
Arizona State			
☐ 53 Courtney Hawkins	.35	.17	.03
Michigan State			
☐ 54 Chuck Smith	.15	.07	.01
Tennessee			
☐ 55 Joe Bowden	.10	.05	.01
Oklahoma			
☐ 56 Gene McGuire	.10	.05	.01
Notre Dame			
☐ 57 Tracy Scroggins	.15	.07	.01
Tulsa			
☐ 58 Mark D'Onofrio	.20	.10	.02
Penn State			
☐ 59 Jimmy Smith	.35	.17	.03
Jackson State			
☐ 60 Carl Pickens	.60	.30	.06

Tennessee
☐ 61 Robert Harris ....15 Southern	.07	.01
☐ 62 Erick Anderson ....25 Michigan	.12	.02
☐ 63 Doug Rigby ....10 Wyoming	.05	.01
☐ 64 Keith Hamilton ....12 Pittsburgh	.06	.01
☐ 65 Vaughn Dunbar SS ....50 Indiana	.25	.05
☐ 66 Willie Clay ....12 Georgia Tech	.06	.01
☐ 67 Robert Jones ....20 East Carolina	.10	.02
☐ 68 Leon Searcy Jr. ....20 Miami	.10	.02
☐ 69 Elliot Pilton ....07 Tennessee State	.03	.01
☐ 70 Thurman Thomas ....35 (Flashback)	.17	.03
☐ 71 Mark Wheeler ....12 Texas A and M	.06	.01
☐ 72 Jeremy Lincoln ....12 Tennessee	.06	.01
☐ 73 Tony McCoy ....10 Florida	.05	.01
☐ 74 Charles Davenport ....20 North Carolina State	.10	.02
☐ 75 Patrick Rowe ....25 San Diego State	.12	.02
☐ 76 Tommy Jeter ....12 Texas	.06	.01
☐ 77 Rod Smith ....15 Notre Dame	.07	.01
☐ 78 Johnny Mitchell ....35 Nebraska	.17	.03
☐ 79 Corey Barlow ....10 Auburn	.05	.01
☐ 80 Scottie Graham ....20 Ohio State	.10	.02
☐ 81 Mark Bounds ....07 Texas Tech	.03	.01
☐ 82 Chester McGlockton ....15 Clemson	.07	.01
☐ 83 Ray Roberts ....15 Virginia	.07	.01
☐ 84 Dale Carter ....25 Tennessee	.12	.02
☐ 85 James Patton ....12 Texas	.06	.01
☐ 86 Tyrone Legette ....15 Nebraska	.07	.01
☐ 87 Leodis Flowers ....10 Nebraska	.05	.01
☐ 88 Rico Smith ....15 Colorado	.07	.01

☐ 89 Kevin Turner ....20 Alabama	.10	.02
☐ 90 Steve Emtman ....1.25 Washington	.60	.12
☐ 91 Rodney Culver ....25 Notre Dame	.12	.02
☐ 92 Chris Mims ....15 Tennessee	.07	.01
☐ 93 Carlos Snow ....10 Ohio State	.05	.01
☐ 94 Corey Harris ....20 Vanderbilt	.10	.02
☐ 95 Nate Williams ....10 Mississippi State	.05	.01
☐ 96 Timothy Roberts ....10 Southern Mississippi	.05	.01
☐ 97 Steve Israel ....15 Pittsburgh	.07	.01
☐ 98 Tony Smith ....20 Notre Dame	.10	.02
☐ 99 Dwayne Sabb ....10 New Hampshire	.05	.01
☐ 100 Checklist 07	.03	.01

1950 Topps Felt Backs

The 1950 Topps felt-back set contains 100 small cards, each measuring approximately 7/ 8" by 1 7/16". Cards are sometimes found connected as a sheet of 25 cards all with the

same color background. The backs have a felt back depicting a college pennant. Cards with a yellow background are worth double the listed prices. The following players come with either brown or yellow backgrounds: Boldin, Botula, Burnett, Cecconi, Gitschier, Hart, Hester, Jensen, Lee, Malekoff, Martin, Mathews, McKissack, J. Miller, Nagel, Perini, Royal, Shaw, Sitko, Stalloni, Teninga, Towler, Turek, Walker, and Zinaich. The key rookie cards in this set are Joe Paterno, Darrell Royal, and Ernie Stautner.

	NRMT	VG-E	GOOD
COMPLETE SET (100)	2850.00	1350.00	350.00
COMMON PLAYER (1-100)	25.00	12.50	2.50
☐ 1 Lou Allen	25.00	12.50	2.50
Duke			
☐ 2 Morris Bailey	25.00	12.50	2.50
Texas Christian			
☐ 3 George Bell	25.00	12.50	2.50
Oregon			
☐ 4 Lindy Berry HOR	25.00	12.50	2.50
Texas Christian			
☐ 5 Mike Boldin	25.00	12.50	2.50
Pittsburgh			
☐ 6 Bernie Botula	25.00	12.50	2.50
Washington and Jefferson			
☐ 7 Bob Bowlby	25.00	12.50	2.50
North Carolina State			
☐ 8 Bob Bucher	25.00	12.50	2.50
Bucknell			
☐ 9 Al Burnett	25.00	12.50	2.50
Rutgers			
☐ 10 Don Burson	25.00	12.50	2.50
Northwestern			
☐ 11 Paul Campbell	25.00	12.50	2.50
Texas			
☐ 12 Herb Carey	25.00	12.50	2.50
Dartmouth			
☐ 13 Bimbo Cecconi	25.00	12.50	2.50
Pittsburgh			
☐ 14 Bill Chauncey	25.00	12.50	2.50
Iowa State			
☐ 15 Dick Clark	25.00	12.50	2.50
Cornell			
☐ 16 Tom Coleman	25.00	12.50	2.50
Georgia			
☐ 17 Billy Conn	25.00	12.50	2.50
Georgetown			
☐ 18 John Cox	25.00	12.50	2.50
Florida			
☐ 19 Lou Creekmur	35.00	17.50	3.50
William and Mary			
☐ 20 Glen Davis	33.00	16.50	3.30
Ohio University			
☐ 21 Warren Davis	25.00	12.50	2.50
Colgate			
☐ 22 Bob Deuber	25.00	12.50	2.50
Pennsylvania			
☐ 23 Ray Dooney	25.00	12.50	2.50
Pennsylvania			
☐ 24 Tom Dublinski	25.00	12.50	2.50
Utah			
☐ 25 Jeff Fleischman	25.00	12.50	2.50
Cornell			
☐ 26 Jack Friedland	25.00	12.50	2.50
Duke			
☐ 27 Bob Fuchs	25.00	12.50	2.50
Missouri			
☐ 28 Arnold Galiffa	35.00	17.50	3.50
Army			
☐ 29 Dick Gilman	25.00	12.50	2.50
Kansas			
☐ 30 Frank Gitschier	25.00	12.50	2.50
Louisville			
☐ 31 Gene Glick	25.00	12.50	2.50
Michigan State			
☐ 32 Bill Gregus	25.00	12.50	2.50
Wake Forest			
☐ 33 Harold Hagan	25.00	12.50	2.50
South Carolina			
☐ 34 Charles Hall	25.00	12.50	2.50
Arizona			
☐ 35 Leon Hart	40.00	20.00	4.00
Notre Dame			
☐ 36 Bob Hester	25.00	12.50	2.50
Marquette			
☐ 37 George Hughes	25.00	12.50	2.50
William and Mary			
☐ 38 Levi Jackson	30.00	15.00	3.00
Yale			
☐ 39 Jackie Jensen	120.00	60.00	12.00
California			
☐ 40 Charlie Justice	75.00	37.50	7.50
North Carolina			
☐ 41 Gary Kerkorian	25.00	12.50	2.50
Stanford			
☐ 42 Bernie Krueger	25.00	12.50	2.50
Illinois			
☐ 43 Bill Kuhn	25.00	12.50	2.50
North Carolina			
☐ 44 Dean Laun	25.00	12.50	2.50
Iowa State			
☐ 45 Chet Leach	25.00	12.50	2.50
Bucknell			
☐ 46 Bobby Lee	25.00	12.50	2.50
Pittsburgh			
☐ 47 Roger Lehew	25.00	12.50	2.50
Tulsa			
☐ 48 Glenn Lippman	25.00	12.50	2.50
Texas A and M			

☐ 49 Melvin Lyle	25.00	12.50	2.50
Louisiana State			
☐ 50 Len Makowski	25.00	12.50	2.50
Tulsa			
☐ 51 Al Malekoff	25.00	12.50	2.50
Rutgers			
☐ 52 Jim Martin	30.00	15.00	3.00
Notre Dame			
☐ 53 Frank Mataya	25.00	12.50	2.50
Washington State			
☐ 54 Ray Mathews	30.00	15.00	3.00
Clemson			
☐ 55 Dick McKissack	25.00	12.50	2.50
Southern Methodist			
☐ 56 Frank Miller	25.00	12.50	2.50
Cornell			
☐ 57 John Miller	25.00	12.50	2.50
Delaware			
☐ 58 Ed Modzelewski	35.00	17.50	3.50
Maryland			
☐ 59 Don Mouser	25.00	12.50	2.50
Baylor			
☐ 60 James Murphy	25.00	12.50	2.50
Holy Cross			
☐ 61 Ray Nagle	30.00	15.00	3.00
UCLA			
☐ 62 Leo Nomellini	90.00	45.00	9.00
Minnesota			
☐ 63 James O'Day	25.00	12.50	2.50
Duquesne			
☐ 64 Joe Paterno	350.00	175.00	35.00
Brown Univ.			
☐ 65 Andy Pavich	25.00	12.50	2.50
Denver			
☐ 66 Pete Perini	25.00	12.50	2.50
Ohio State			
☐ 67 Jim Powers	25.00	12.50	2.50
USC			
☐ 68 Dave Rakestraw	25.00	12.50	2.50
Tulsa			
☐ 69 Herb Rich	25.00	12.50	2.50
Vanderbilt			
☐ 70 Fran Rogel	30.00	15.00	3.00
Penn State			
☐ 71 Darrell Royal	70.00	35.00	7.00
Oklahoma			
☐ 72 Steve Sawle	25.00	12.50	2.50
Northwestern			
☐ 73 Nick Sebek	25.00	12.50	2.50
Indiana			
☐ 74 Herb Seidell	25.00	12.50	2.50
Fordham			
☐ 75 Charles Shaw	25.00	12.50	2.50
Oklahoma A and M			
☐ 76 Emil Sitko	30.00	15.00	3.00
Notre Dame			
☐ 77 Ed(Butch) Songin	33.00	16.50	3.30
Boston College			
☐ 78 Mariano Stalloni	25.00	12.50	2.50
Delaware			
☐ 79 Ernie Stautner	90.00	45.00	9.00
Boston College			
☐ 80 Don Stehley	25.00	12.50	2.50
Kansas State			
☐ 81 Gil Stevenson	30.00	15.00	3.00
Army			
☐ 82 Bishop Strickland	25.00	12.50	2.50
South Carolina			
☐ 83 Harry Szulborski	25.00	12.50	2.50
Purdue			
☐ 84 Wally Teninga	25.00	12.50	2.50
Michigan			
☐ 85 Clayton Tonnemaker	25.00	12.50	2.50
Minnesota			
☐ 86 Deacon Dan Towler	40.00	20.00	4.00
Washington and			
Jefferson			
☐ 87 Bert Turek	25.00	12.50	2.50
Marquette			
☐ 88 Harry Ulinski	25.00	12.50	2.50
Kentucky			
☐ 89 Leon Van Billingham	25.00	12.50	2.50
Columbia			
☐ 90 Langdon Viracola	25.00	12.50	2.50
Fordham			
☐ 91 Leo Wagner	25.00	12.50	2.50
CCNY			
☐ 92 Doak Walker	85.00	42.50	8.50
Southern Methodist			
☐ 93 Jim Ward	25.00	12.50	2.50
Columbia			
☐ 94 Art Weiner	25.00	12.50	2.50
North Carolina			
☐ 95 Dick Weiss	25.00	12.50	2.50
North Carolina			
☐ 96 Froggie Williams	25.00	12.50	2.50
Rice Institute			
☐ 97 Robert(Red) Wilson	30.00	15.00	3.00
Wisconsin			
☐ 98 Roger(Red) Wilson	25.00	12.50	2.50
South Carolina			
☐ 99 Carl Wren	25.00	12.50	2.50
Rochester			
☐ 100 Pete Zinaich	25.00	12.50	2.50
West Virginia			

1951 Topps Magic

The 1951 Topps Magic football set was Topps first major football "card" issue. The set features 75 cards of the country's best collegiate players. The cards measure approximately 2 1/16" by 2 15/16". The backs contain a scratch-off section which gives the answer to a football quiz. Cards with the scratch-off back intact are valued at 50 percent more than the prices listed below. The key rookie cards in this set are Marion Campbell, Vic Janowicz, Babe Parilli, and Bill Wade. The player's college nicknames are provided as they are listed physically on the card fronts.

	NRMT	VG-E	GOOD
COMPLETE SET (75)	900.00	450.00	90.00
COMMON PLAYER (1-75)	12.50	6.25	1.25
☐ 1 Jimmy Monahan	25.00	7.50	1.50
Queensmen			
☐ 2 Bill Wade	27.00	13.50	2.70
Commodores			
☐ 3 Bill Reichardt	12.50	6.25	1.25
Hawkeyes			
☐ 4 Babe Parilli	27.00	13.50	2.70
Wildcats			
☐ 5 Billie Burkhalter	12.50	6.25	1.25
Owls			
☐ 6 Ed Weber	12.50	6.25	1.25
Indians			
☐ 7 Tom Scott	12.50	6.25	1.25
Cavaliers			
☐ 8 Frank Guthridge	12.50	6.25	1.25
Blue Hens			
☐ 9 John Karras	12.50	6.25	1.25
Fighting Illini			
☐ 10 Vic Janowicz	27.00	13.50	2.70
Buckeyes			
☐ 11 Lloyd Hill	12.00	6.00	1.20
Bruins			
☐ 12 Jim Weatherall	16.00	8.00	1.60
Sooners			
☐ 13 Howard Hansen	12.50	6.25	1.25
Lions			
☐ 14 Lou D'Achille	12.50	6.25	1.25
Hoosiers			
☐ 15 Johnny Turco	12.50	6.25	1.25
Crusaders			
☐ 16 Jerrell Price	12.50	6.25	1.25
Red Raiders			
☐ 17 John Coatta	12.50	6.25	1.25
Badgers			
☐ 18 Bruce Patton	12.50	6.25	1.25
Hilltoppers			
☐ 19 Marion Campbell	22.00	11.00	2.20
Bulldogs			
☐ 20 Blaine Earon	12.50	6.25	1.25
Blue Devils			
☐ 21 Dewey McConnell	12.50	6.25	1.25
Cowboys			
☐ 22 Ray Beck	12.50	6.25	1.25
Yellow Jackets			
☐ 23 Jim Prewett	12.50	6.25	1.25
Golden Hurricane			
☐ 24 Bob Steele	12.50	6.25	1.25
Aggies			
☐ 25 Art Betts	12.50	6.25	1.25
Nittany Lions			
☐ 26 Walt Trillhaase	12.50	6.25	1.25
Engineers			
☐ 27 Gil Bartosh	12.50	6.25	1.25
Horned Frogs			
☐ 28 Bob Bestwick	12.50	6.25	1.25
Panthers			
☐ 29 Tom Rushing	12.50	6.25	1.25
Maroons			
☐ 30 Bert Rechichar	20.00	10.00	2.00
Volunteers			
☐ 31 Bill Owens	12.50	6.25	1.25
Raiders			
☐ 32 Mike Goggins	12.50	6.25	1.25
Titans			
☐ 33 John Petitbon	12.50	6.25	1.25
Fighting Irish			
☐ 34 Byron Townsend	12.50	6.25	1.25
Longhorns			
☐ 35 Ed Rotticci	12.50	6.25	1.25
Broncos			
☐ 36 Steve Wadiak	12.50	6.25	1.25
Gamecocks			
☐ 37 Bobby Marlow	16.00	8.00	1.60
Crimson Tide			
☐ 38 Bill Fuchs	12.50	6.25	1.25
Tigers			

☐ 39 Ralph Staub 12.50		6.25	1.25
Bearcats			
☐ 40 Bill Vesprini 12.50		6.25	1.25
Indians			
☐ 41 Zack Jordan 12.50		6.25	1.25
Tigers			
☐ 42 Bob Smith 12.50		6.25	1.25
Aggies			
☐ 43 Charles Hanson 12.50		6.25	1.25
Terriers			
☐ 44 Glenn Smith 12.50		6.25	1.25
Tigers			
☐ 45 Armand Kitto 12.50		6.25	1.25
Tigers			
☐ 46 Vinnie Drake 12.50		6.25	1.25
Rams			
☐ 47 Bill Putich 12.50		6.25	1.25
Wolverines			
☐ 48 George Young 18.00		9.00	1.80
Bisons			
☐ 49 Don McRae 12.50		6.25	1.25
Wildcats			
☐ 50 Frank Smith 12.50		6.25	1.25
Hurricanes			
☐ 51 Dick Hightower 12.50		6.25	1.25
Mustangs			
☐ 52 Clyde Pickard 12.50		6.25	1.25
Deacons			
☐ 53 Bob Reynolds 12.50		6.25	1.25
Cornhuskers			
☐ 54 Dick Gregory 12.50		6.25	1.25
Gophers			
☐ 55 Dale Samuels 12.50		6.25	1.25
Boilermakers			
☐ 56 Gale Galloway 12.50		6.25	1.25
Bears			
☐ 57 Vic Pujo 12.50		6.25	1.25
Big Red			
☐ 58 Dave Waters 12.50		6.25	1.25
Generals			
☐ 59 Joe Ernest 12.50		6.25	1.25
Green Wave			
☐ 60 Elmer Costa 12.50		6.25	1.25
Wolfpack			
☐ 61 Nick Liotta 12.50		6.25	1.25
Wildcats			
☐ 62 John Dottley 12.50		6.25	1.25
Rebels			
☐ 63 Hi Faubion 12.50		6.25	1.25
Wildcats			
☐ 64 David Harr 12.50		6.25	1.25
Diplomats			
☐ 65 Bill Matthews 12.50		.25	1.25
Violets			
☐ 66 Carroll McDonald 12.50		6.25	1.25
Gators			
☐ 67 Dick Dewing 12.50		6.25	1.25

Wildcats			
☐ 68 Joe Johnson 12.50		6.25	1.25
Eagles			
☐ 69 Arnold Burwitz 12.50		6.25	1.25
Wildcats			
☐ 70 Ed Dobrowolski 12.50		6.25	1.25
Orangemen			
☐ 71 Joe Dudeck 12.50		6.25	1.25
Tar Heels			
☐ 72 John Bright 16.00		8.00	1.60
Bulldogs			
☐ 73 Harold Loehlein 12.50		6.25	1.25
Cadets			
☐ 74 Lawrence Hairston 12.50		6.25	1.25
Wolfpack			
☐ 75 Bob Carey 20.00		7.50	1.50
Spartans			

1955 Topps All-American

The 1955 Topps All-American set features 100 cards of college football greats. The cards measure approximately 2 5/8" by 3 5/8". There are many numbers which were printed in lesser supply; these short-printed cards are denoted in the checklist below by SP. The key rookies in this set are Doc Blanchard, The Four Horseman (Notre Dame backfield in 1924), Tommy Harmon, Don Hutson, Ernie Nevers, and Amos Alonzo Stagg.

	NRMT	VG-E	GOOD
COMPLETE SET (100) 2900.00	1350.00	350.00	
COMMON PLAYER (1-92) 12.50	6.25	1.25	
COMMON PLAYER SP 18.00	9.00	1.80	

COMMON PLAYER (93-100) . 22.00   11.00   2.20

☐ 1 Herman Hickman 85.00 42.50 8.50		
Tennessee		
☐ 2 John Kimbrough 12.50 6.25 1.25		
Texas A and M		
☐ 3 Ed Weir 12.50 6.25 1.25		
Nebraska		
☐ 4 Ernie Pinckert 12.50 6.25 1.25		
USC		
☐ 5 Bobby Grayson 12.50 6.25 1.25		
Stanford		
☐ 6 Nile Kinnick UER 21.00 10.50 2.10		
Iowa		
(Misspelled Niles		
on card)		
☐ 7 Andy Bershak 12.50 6.25 1.25		
North Carolina		
☐ 8 George Cafego 12.50 6.25 1.25		
Tennessee		
☐ 9 Tom Hamilton SP 18.00 9.00 1.80		
Navy		
☐ 10 Bill Dudley 22.00 11.00 2.20		
Virginia		
☐ 11 Bobby Dodd SP 18.00 9.00 1.80		
Tennessee		
☐ 12 Otto Graham 150.00 75.00 15.00		
Northwestern		
☐ 13 Aaron Rosenberg 12.50 6.25 1.25		
USC		
☐ 14A Gaynell Tinsley ERR . 21.00 10.50 2.10		
(Wrong back 21 with		
Whizzer White bio)		
Louisiana State		
☐ 14B Gaynell Tinsley COR . 17.00 8.50 1.70		
Louisiana State		
☐ 15 Ed Kaw SP 18.00 9.00 1.80		
Cornell		
☐ 16 Knute Rockne 225.00 110.00 22.00		
Notre Dame		
☐ 17 Bob Reynolds 12.50 6.25 1.25		
Nebraska		
☐ 18 Pudge Heffelfinger SP . 22.00 11.00 2.20		
Yale		
☐ 19 Bruce Smith 15.00 7.50 1.50		
Minnesota		
☐ 20 Sammy Baugh 140.00 70.00 14.00		
Texas Christian		
☐ 21A Whizzer White ERR SP 33.00 16.50 3.30		
(Wrong back 14 with		
Gaynell Tinsley bio)		
Colorado		
☐ 21B Whizzer White COR SP 42.00 20.00 4.00		
Colorado		
☐ 22 Brick Muller 12.50 6.25 1.25		
California		
☐ 23 Dick Kazmaier 18.00 9.00 1.80		

Princeton
☐ 24 Ken Strong 20.00   10.00   2.00
NYU
☐ 25 Casimir Myslinski SP . 18.00   9.00   1.80
Army
☐ 26 Larry Kelley SP 18.00   9.00   1.80
Yale
☐ 27 Red Grange UER 240.00   100.00   20.00
(Card says he was QB,
should say halfback)
Illinois
☐ 28 Mel Hein SP 25.00   12.50   2.50
Washington State
☐ 29 Leo Nomellini SP 28.00   14.00   2.80
Minnesota
☐ 30 Wes E. Fesler 12.50   6.25   1.25
Ohio State
☐ 31 George Sauer Sr. 15.00   7.50   1.50
Nebraska
☐ 32 Hank Foldberg 12.50   6.25   1.25
Army
☐ 33 Bob Higgins 12.50   6.25   1.25
Penn State
☐ 34 Davey O'Brien 21.00   10.50   2.10
Texas Christian
☐ 35 Tom Harmon SP 25.00   12.50   2.50
Michigan
☐ 36 Turk Edwards SP 21.00   10.50   2.10
Washington State
☐ 37 Jim Thorpe 275.00   135.00   27.00
Carlisle
☐ 38A Amos Alonzo Stagg . 45.00   22.50   4.50
(wrong back 19) ERR
Yale
☐ 38B Amos Alonzo Stagg . 33.00   16.50   3.30
COR Yale
☐ 39 Jerome Holland 15.00   7.50   1.50
Cornell
☐ 40 Donn Moomaw 12.50   6.25   1.25
UCLA
☐ 41 Joseph Alexander SP . 18.00   9.00   1.80
Syracuse
☐ 42 J. Edward Tryon SP 18.00   9.00   1.80
Colgate
☐ 43 George Savitsky 12.50   6.25   1.25
Pennsylvania
☐ 44 Ed Garbisch 12.50   6.25   1.25
Army
☐ 45 Elmer Oliphant 12.50   6.25   1.25
Army
☐ 46 Arnold Lassman 12.50   6.25   1.25
NYU
☐ 47 Bo McMillan 12.50   6.25   1.25
Centre
☐ 48 Ed Widseth 12.50   6.25   1.25
Minnesota
☐ 49 Don Zimmerman 12.50   6.25   1.25

	Tulane		
☐ 50	Ken Kavanaugh 17.00	8.50	1.70
	Louisiana State		
☐ 51	Duane Purvis SP 18.00	9.00	1.80
	Purdue		
☐ 52	John Lujack 25.00	12.50	2.50
	Notre Dame		
☐ 53	John F. Green 12.50	6.25	1.25
	Army		
☐ 54	Edwin Dooley SP 18.00	9.00	1.80
	Dartmouth		
☐ 55	Frank Merritt SP 18.00	9.00	1.80
	Army		
☐ 56	Ernie Nevers 42.00	20.00	4.00
	Stanford		
☐ 57	Vic Hanson SP 18.00	9.00	1.80
	Syracuse		
☐ 58	Ed Franco 12.50	6.25	1.25
	Fordham		
☐ 59	Doc Blanchard 40.00	20.00	4.00
	Army		
☐ 60	Dan Hill 12.50	25	1.25
	Duke		
☐ 61	Charles Brickley SP 18.00	9.00	1.80
	Harvard		
☐ 62	Harry Newman 12.50	6.25	1.25
	Michigan		
☐ 63	Charlie Justice 17.00	8.50	1.70
	North Carolina		
☐ 64	Benny Friedman 15.00	7.50	1.50
	Michigan		
☐ 65	Joe Donchess SP 18.00	9.00	1.80
	Pittsburgh		
☐ 66	Bruiser Kinard 18.00	9.00	1.80
	Ole Miss		
☐ 67	Frankie Albert 18.00	9.00	1.80
	Stanford		
☐ 68	Four Horsemen SP 375.00	175.00	37.00
	Jim Crowley		
	Elmer Layden		
	Creighton Miller		
	Harry Stuhldreher		
	Notre Dame		
☐ 69	Frank Sinkwich 16.00	8.00	1.60
	Georgia		
☐ 70	Bill Daddio 12.50	6.25	1.25
	Pittsburgh		
☐ 71	Bob Wilson 12.50	6.25	1.25
	Southern Methodist		
☐ 72	Chub Peabody 12.50	6.25	1.25
	Harvard		
☐ 73	Paul Governali 12.50	6.25	1.25
	Columbia		
☐ 74	Gene McEver 12.50	6.25	1.25
	Tennessee		
☐ 75	Hugh Gallarneau 12.50	6.25	1.25
	Stanford		

☐ 76	Angelo Bertelli 18.00	9.00	1.80
	Notre Dame		
☐ 77	Bowden Wyatt SP 18.00	9.00	1.80
	Tennessee		
☐ 78	Jay Berwanger 17.00	8.50	1.70
	Chicago		
☐ 79	Pug Lund 12.50	6.25	1.25
	Minnesota		
☐ 80	Bennie Oosterbaan 12.50	6.25	1.25
	Michigan		
☐ 81	Cotton Warburton 12.50	6.25	1.25
	USC		
☐ 82	Alex Wojciechowicz 18.00	9.00	1.80
	Fordham		
☐ 83	Ted Coy SP 18.00	9.00	1.80
	Yale		
☐ 84	Ace Parker SP 33.00	16.50	3.30
	Duke		
☐ 85	Sid Luckman 65.00	32.50	6.50
	Columbia		
☐ 86	Albie Booth SP 18.00	9.00	1.80
	Yale		
☐ 87	Adolph Schultz SP 18.00	9.00	1.80
	Michigan		
☐ 88	Ralph G. Kercheval 12.50	6.25	1.25
	Kentucky		
☐ 89	Marshall Goldberg 12.50	6.25	1.25
	Pittsburgh		
☐ 90	Charlie O'Rourke 12.50	6.25	1.25
	Boston College		
☐ 91	Bob Odell 12.50	6.25	1.25
	Pennsylvania		
☐ 92	Biggie Munn 12.50	6.25	1.25
	Minnesota		
☐ 93	Willie Heston SP 22.00	11.00	2.20
	Michigan		
☐ 94	Joe Bernard SP 22.00	11.00	2.20
	Michigan		
☐ 95	Red Cagle SP 25.00	12.50	2.50
	Army		
☐ 96	Bill Hollenback SP 22.00	11.00	2.20
	Pennsylvania		
☐ 97	Don Hutson SP 125.00	60.00	12.50
	Alabama		
☐ 98	Beattie Feathers SP 28.00	14.00	2.80
	Tennessee		
☐ 99	Don Whitmire SP 22.00	11.00	2.20
	Alabama/Navy		
☐ 100	Fats Henry SP 135.00	35.00	7.00
	Washington and		
	Jefferson		

1956 Topps

The 1956 Topps football set of 120 (numbered) cards contains NFL players. The cards measure 2 5/8" by 3 5/8". The first football team cards (produced by Topps) were included in this set. Players from the Washington Redskins and the Chicago Cardinals were apparently produced in lesser quantities, as they are more difficult to find compared to the other teams. The card backs were printed in red and black on gray card stock. Statistical information from the immediate past season and career totals are given at the bottom of the reverse. A checklist card and six contest cards were also issued along with this set, although in much lesser quantities. The complete price below refers to the 120 numbered cards plus the unnumbered checklist card. There also exists a three-card advertising panel consisting of the obverses of Lou Groza, Don Colo, and Darrell Brewster with ad copy on the reverse. The key rookie cards in this set are Roosevelt Brown, Bill George, Rosey Grier, Stan Jones, Lenny Moore, and Joe Schmidt.

	NRMT	VG-E	GOOD
COMPLETE SET (121)	1650.00	750.00	185.00
COMMON PLAYER (1-120)	5.00	2.50	.50
COMMON CARDINALS	16.00	8.00	1.60
COMMON REDSKINS	12.00	6.00	1.20

☐ 1 Jack Carson SP	50.00	7.50	1.50
Washington Redskins			
☐ 2 Gordon Soltau	5.00	2.50	.50
San Francisco 49ers			
☐ 3 Frank Varrichione	5.00	2.50	.50
Pittsburgh Steelers			
☐ 4 Eddie Bell	5.00	2.50	.50
Philadelphia Eagles			
☐ 5 Alex Webster	12.50	6.25	1.25
New York Giants			
☐ 6 Norm Van Brocklin	24.00	12.00	2.40
Los Angeles Rams			
☐ 7 Green Bay Packers	15.00	7.50	1.50
Team Card			
☐ 8 Lou Creekmur	6.00	3.00	.60
Detroit Lions			
☐ 9 Lou Groza	24.00	12.00	2.40
Cleveland Browns			
☐ 10 Tom Bienemann SP	16.00	8.00	1.60
Chicago Cardinals			
☐ 11 George Blanda	50.00	25.00	5.00
Chicago Bears			
☐ 12 Alan Ameche	9.00	4.50	.90
Baltimore Colts			
☐ 13 Vic Janowicz SP	16.00	8.00	1.60
Washington Redskins			
☐ 14 Dick Moegle	6.00	3.00	.60
San Francisco 49ers			
☐ 15 Fran Rogel	5.00	2.50	.50
Pittsburgh Steelers			
☐ 16 Harold Giancanelli	5.00	2.50	.50
Philadelphia Eagles			
☐ 17 Emlen Tunnell	12.50	6.25	1.25
New York Giants			
☐ 18 Paul(Tank) Younger	6.00	3.00	.60
Los Angeles Rams			
☐ 19 Bill Howton	8.00	4.00	.80
Green Bay Packers			
☐ 20 Jack Christiansen	12.50	6.25	1.25
Detroit Lions			
☐ 21 Darrell Brewster	5.00	2.50	.50
Cleveland Browns			
☐ 22 Chicago Cardinals SP	60.00	30.00	6.00
Team Card			
☐ 23 Ed Brown	7.00	3.50	.70
Chicago Bears			
☐ 24 Joe Campanella	5.00	2.50	.50
Baltimore Colts			
☐ 25 Leon Heath SP	12.00	6.00	1.20
Washington Redskins			
☐ 26 San Francisco 49ers	15.00	7.50	1.50
Team Card			
☐ 27 Dick Flanagan	5.00	2.50	.50
Pittsburgh Steelers			
☐ 28 Chuck Bednarik	17.00	8.50	1.70
Philadelphia Eagles			
☐ 29 Kyle Rote	11.00	5.50	1.10
New York Giants			
☐ 30 Les Richter	6.00	3.00	.60
Los Angeles Rams			
☐ 31 Howard Ferguson	5.00	2.50	.50
Green Bay Packers			
☐ 32 Dorne Dibble	5.00	2.50	.50
Detroit Lions			

☐ 33 Kenny Konz .... 5.00   2.50   .50
     Cleveland Browns
☐ 34 Dave Mann SP 16.00   8.00   1.60
     Chicago Cardinals
☐ 35 Rick Casares .... 7.00   3.50   .70
     Chicago Bears
☐ 36 Art Donovan 14.00   7.00   1.40
     Baltimore Colts
☐ 37 Chuck Drazenovich SP 12.00   6.00   1.20
     Washington Redskins
☐ 38 Joe Arenas .... 5.00   2.50   .50
     San Francisco 49ers
☐ 39 Lynn Chandnois .... 5.00   2.50   .50
     Pittsburgh Steelers
☐ 40 Philadelphia Eagles 15.00   7.50   1.50
     Team Card
☐ 41 Roosevelt Brown 33.00   16.50   3.30
     New York Giants
☐ 42 Tom Fears 12.50   6.25   1.25
     Los Angeles Rams
☐ 43 Gary Knafelc .... 5.00   2.50   .50
     Green Bay Packers
☐ 44 Joe Schmidt 45.00   22.50   4.50
     Detroit Lions
☐ 45 Cleveland Browns 15.00   7.50   1.50
     Team Card UER
     (Card back does not
     credit the Browns with
     being Champs in 1955)
☐ 46 Len Teeuws SP 18.00   9.00   1.80
     Chicago Cardinals
☐ 47 Bill George 32.00   16.00   3.20
     Chicago Bears
☐ 48 Baltimore Colts 15.00   7.50   1.50
     Team Card
☐ 49 Eddie LeBaron SP 21.00   10.50   2.10
     Washington Redskins
☐ 50 Hugh McElhenny 16.00   8.00   1.60
     San Francisco 49ers
☐ 51 Ted Marchibroda .... 7.00   3.50   .70
     Pittsburgh Steelers
☐ 52 Adrian Burk .... 5.00   2.50   .50
     Philadelphia Eagles
☐ 53 Frank Gifford 150.00   75.00   15.00
     New York Giants
☐ 54 Charley Toogood .... 5.00   2.50   .50
     Los Angeles Rams
☐ 55 Tobin Rote .... 7.00   3.50   .70
     Green Bay Packers
☐ 56 Bill Stits .... 5.00   2.50   .50
     Detroit Lions
☐ 57 Don Colo .... 5.00   2.50   .50
     Cleveland Browns
☐ 58 Ollie Matson SP .... 32.00   16.00   .3.20
     Chicago Cardinals
☐ 59 Harlon Hill .... 7.00   3.50   .70
     Chicago Bears

☐ 60 Lenny Moore 80.00   40.00   8.00
     Baltimore Colts
☐ 61 Washington Redskins . 50.00   25.00   5.00
     Team Card SP
☐ 62 Billy Wilson .... 7.00   3.50   .70
     San Francisco 49ers
☐ 63 Pittsburgh Steelers 15.00   7.50   1.50
     Team Card
☐ 64 Bob Pellegrini .... 5.00   2.50   .50
     Philadelphia Eagles
☐ 65 Ken MacAfee .... 7.00   3.50   .70
     New York Giants
☐ 66 Willard Sherman .... 5.00   2.50   .50
     Los Angeles Rams
☐ 67 Roger Zatkoff .... 5.00   2.50   .50
     Green Bay Packers
☐ 68 Dave Middleton .... 5.00   2.50   .50
     Detroit Lions
☐ 69 Ray Renfro .... 7.00   3.50   .70
     Cleveland Browns
☐ 70 Don Stonesifer SP 16.00   8.00   1.60
     Chicago Cardinals
☐ 71 Stan Jones 27.00   13.50   2.70
     Chicago Bears
☐ 72 Jim Mutscheller .... 5.00   2.50   .50
     Baltimore Colts
☐ 73 Volney Peters SP 12.00   6.00   1.20
     Washington Redskins
☐ 74 Leo Nomellini 13.50   6.50   1.25
     San Francisco 49ers
☐ 75 Ray Mathews .... 5.00   2.50   .50
     Pittsburgh Steelers
☐ 76 Dick Bielski .... 5.00   2.50   .50
     Philadelphia Eagles
☐ 77 Charley Conerly 22.00   11.00   2.20
     New York Giants
☐ 78 Elroy Hirsch 16.00   8.00   1.60
     Los Angeles Rams
☐ 79 Bill Forester .... 8.00   4.00   .80
     Green Bay Packers
☐ 80 Jim Doran .... 5.00   2.50   .50
     Detroit Lions
☐ 81 Fred Morrison .... 5.00   2.50   .50
     Cleveland Browns
☐ 82 Jack Simmons SP 16.00   8.00   1.60
     Chicago Cardinals
☐ 83 Bill McColl .... 5.00   2.50   .50
     Chicago Bears
☐ 84 Bert Rechichar .... 5.00   2.50   .50
     Baltimore Colts
☐ 85 Joe Scudero SP 12.00   6.00   1.20
     Washington Redskins
☐ 86 Y.A. Tittle 36.00   18.00   3.60
     San Francisco 49ers
☐ 87 Ernie Stautner 13.50   6.50   1.25
     Pittsburgh Steelers
☐ 88 Norm Willey .... 5.00   2.50   .50

Philadelphia Eagles
☐ 89	Bob Schnelker 7.00	3.50	.70

New York Giants
☐ 90	Dan Towler 7.00	3.50	.70

Los Angeles Rams
☐ 91	John Martinkovic 5.00	2.50	.50

Green Bay Packers
☐ 92	Detroit Lions 15.00	7.50	1.50

Team Card
☐ 93	George Ratterman 6.00	3.00	.60

Cleveland Browns
☐ 94	Chuck Ulrich SP 18.00	9.00	1.80

Chicago Cardinals
☐ 95	Bobby Watkins 5.00	2.50	.50

Chicago Bears
☐ 96	Buddy Young 7.00	3.50	.70

Baltimore Colts
☐ 97	Billy Wells SP 12.00	6.00	1.20

Washington Redskins
☐ 98	Bob Toneff 5.00	2.50	.50

San Francisco 49ers
☐ 99	Bill McPeak 5.00	2.50	.50

Pittsburgh Steelers
☐ 100	Bobby Thomason 6.00	3.00	.60

Philadelphia Eagles
☐ 101	Roosevelt Grier 25.00	12.50	2.50

New York Giants
☐ 102	Ron Waller 5.00	2.50	.50

Los Angeles Rams
☐ 103	Bobby Dillon 5.00	2.50	.50

Green Bay Packers
☐ 104	Leon Hart 8.00	4.00	.80

Detroit Lions
☐ 105	Mike McCormack 12.00	6.00	1.20

Cleveland Browns
☐ 106	John Olszewski SP 16.00	8.00	1.60

Chicago Cardinals
☐ 107	Bill Wightkin 5.00	2.50	.50

Chicago Bears
☐ 108	George Shaw 7.00	3.50	.70

Baltimore Colts
☐ 109	Dale Atkeson SP 12.00	6.00	1.20

Washington Redskins
☐ 110	Joe Perry 17.00	8.50	1.70

San Francisco 49ers
☐ 111	Dale Dodrill 5.00	2.50	.50

Pittsburgh Steelers
☐ 112	Tom Scott 5.00	2.50	.50

Philadelphia Eagles
☐ 113	New York Giants 15.00	7.50	1.50

Team Card
☐ 114	Los Angeles Rams 15.00	7.50	1.50

Team Card UER
(back incorrect, Rams
were not 1955 champs)
☐ 115	Al Carmichael 5.00	2.50	.50

Green Bay Packers

☐ 116	Bobby Layne 33.00	16.50	3.30

Detroit Lions
☐ 117	Ed Modzelewski 6.00	3.00	.60

Cleveland Browns
☐ 118	Lamar McHan SP 18.00	9.00	1.80

Chicago Cardinals
☐ 119	Chicago Bears 15.00	7.50	1.50

Team Card
☐ 120	Billy Vessels 28.00	7.50	1.50

Baltimore Colts
☐ NNO	Checklist Card 275.00	50.00	10.00

(unnumbered)

1957 Topps

The 1957 Topps football set contains 154 cards of NFL players, each card measuring 2 1/2" by 3 1/2". The second series (89-154) is more difficult to obtain than the first series. The fronts include both a bust and an action picture. The card backs were printed in red and black on gray card stock. Statistical information from the immediate past season and career totals are given at the bottom of the reverse. The rookie cards of Johnny Unitas, Bart Starr, and Paul Hornung are included in this set. Other notable rookie cards in this set are Raymond Berry, Dick "Night Train" Lane, Tommy McDonald, and Earl Morrall. A checklist card was also issued along with this set. The complete set price below refers to the 154 numbered cards plus the unnumbered checklist card.

	NRMT	VG-E	GOOD
COMPLETE SET (155)	2800.00	1300.00	325.00

COMMON PLAYER (1-88) .... 3.75   1.85   .37
COMMON PLAYER (89-154) ... 6.50   3.25   .65

☐ 1 Eddie LeBaron 36.00   5.00   1.00
   Washington Redskins
☐ 2 Pete Retzlaff .... 6.50   3.25   .65
   Philadelphia Eagles
☐ 3 Mike McCormack ....9.00   4.50   .90
   Cleveland Browns
☐ 4 Lou Baldacci .... 3.75   1.85   .37
   Pittsburgh Steelers
☐ 5 Gino Marchetti 13.50   6.50   1.35
   Baltimore Colts
☐ 6 Leo Nomellini 11.00   5.50   1.10
   San Francisco 49ers
☐ 7 Bobby Watkins .... 3.75   1.85   .37
   Chicago Bears
☐ 8 Dave Middleton .... 3.75   1.85   .37
   Detroit Lions
☐ 9 Bobby Dillon .... 3.75   1.85   .37
   Green Bay Packers
☐ 10 Les Richter .... 4.50   2.25   .45
   Los Angeles Rams
☐ 11 Roosevelt Brown 11.00   5.50   1.10
   New York Giants
☐ 12 Lavern Torgeson .... 4.50   2.25   .45
   Washington Redskins
☐ 13 Dick Bielski .... 3.75   1.85   .37
   Philadelphia Eagles
☐ 14 Pat Summerall 11.00   5.50   1.10
   Chicago Cardinals
☐ 15 Jack Butler .... 4.50   2.25   .45
   Pittsburgh Steelers
☐ 16 John Henry Johnson ... 11.00   5.50   1.10
   Cleveland Browns
☐ 17 Art Spinney .... 3.75   1.85   .37
   Baltimore Colts
☐ 18 Bob St. Clair ....9.00   4.50   .90
   San Francisco 49ers
☐ 19 Perry Jeter .... 3.75   1.85   .37
   Chicago Bears
☐ 20 Lou Creekmur .... 4.50   2.25   .45
   Detroit Lions
☐ 21 Dave Hanner .... 4.50   2.25   .45
   Green Bay Packers
☐ 22 Norm Van Brocklin 20.00   10.00   2.00
   Los Angeles Rams
☐ 23 Don Chandler .... 7.50   3.75   .75
   New York Giants
☐ 24 Al Dorow .... 3.75   1.85   .37
   Washington Redskins
☐ 25 Tom Scott .... 3.75   1.85   .37
   Philadelphia Eagles
☐ 26 Ollie Matson 12.00   6.00   1.20
   Chicago Cardinals
☐ 27 Fran Rogel .... 3.75   1.85   .37
   Pittsburgh Steelers

☐ 28 Lou Groza 20.00   10.00   2.00
   Cleveland Browns
☐ 29 Billy Vessels .... 5.00   2.50   .50
   Baltimore Colts
☐ 30 Y.A. Tittle 35.00   17.50   3.50
   San Francisco 49ers
☐ 31 George Blanda 42.00   20.00   4.00
   Chicago Bears
☐ 32 Bobby Layne 32.00   16.00   3.20
   Detroit Lions
☐ 33 Bill Howton .... 5.00   2.50   .50
   Green Bay Packers
☐ 34 Bill Wade .... 4.50   2.25   .45
   Los Angeles Rams
☐ 35 Emlen Tunnell 11.00   5.50   1.10
   New York Giants
☐ 36 Leo Elter .... 3.75   1.85   .37
   Washington Redskins
☐ 37 Clarence Peaks .... 5.50   2.75   .55
   Philadelphia Eagles
☐ 38 Don Stonesifer .... 3.75   1.85   .37
   Chicago Cardinals
☐ 39 George Tarasovic .... 3.75   1.85   .37
   Pittsburgh Steelers
☐ 40 Darrell Brewster .... 3.75   1.85   .37
   Cleveland Browns
☐ 41 Bert Rechichar .... 3.75   1.85   .37
   Baltimore Colts
☐ 42 Billy Wilson .... 4.50   2.25   .45
   San Francisco 49ers
☐ 43 Ed Brown .... 4.50   2.25   .45
   Chicago Bears
☐ 44 Gene Gedman .... 3.75   1.85   .37
   Detroit Lions
☐ 45 Gary Knafelc .... 3.75   1.85   .37
   Green Bay Packers
☐ 46 Elroy Hirsch 13.50   6.50   1.25
   Los Angeles Rams
☐ 47 Don Heinrich .... 4.50   2.25   .45
   New York Giants
☐ 48 Gene Brito .... 4.50   2.25   .45
   Washington Redskins
☐ 49 Chuck Bednarik 13.50   6.50   1.25
   Philadelphia Eagles
☐ 50 Dave Mann .... 3.75   1.85   .37
   Chicago Cardinals
☐ 51 Bill McPeak .... 3.75   1.85   .37
   Pittsburgh Steelers
☐ 52 Kenny Konz .... 3.75   1.85   .37
   Cleveland Browns
☐ 53 Alan Ameche .... 7.50   3.75   .75
   Baltimore Colts
☐ 54 Gordon Soltau .... 3.75   1.85   .37
   San Francisco 49ers
☐ 55 Rick Casares .... 5.00   2.50   .50
   Chicago Bears
☐ 56 Charlie Ane .... 3.75   1.85   .37

Detroit Lions
- [ ] 57 Al Carmichael .... 3.75   1.85   .37
  Green Bay Packers
- [ ] 58A Willard Sherman ERR 16.00   8.00   1.60
  (no team on front)
  Los Angeles Rams
- [ ] 58B Willard Sherman COR . 3.75   1.85   .37
  Los Angeles Rams
- [ ] 59 Kyle Rote .... 7.50   3.75   .75
  New York Giants
- [ ] 60 Chuck Drazenovich .... 3.75   1.85   .37
  Washington Redskins
- [ ] 61 Bobby Walston .... 3.75   1.85   .37
  Philadelphia Eagles
- [ ] 62 John Olszewski .... 3.75   1.85   .37
  Chicago Cardinals
- [ ] 63 Ray Mathews .... 3.75   1.85   .37
  Pittsburgh Steelers
- [ ] 64 Maurice Bassett .... 3.75   1.85   .37
  Cleveland Browns
- [ ] 65 Art Donovan 12.00   6.00   1.20
  Baltimore Colts
- [ ] 66 Joe Arenas .... 3.75   1.85   .37
  San Francisco 49ers
- [ ] 67 Harlon Hill .... 4.50   2.25   .45
  Chicago Bears
- [ ] 68 Yale Lary .... 9.00   4.50   .90
  Detroit Lions
- [ ] 69 Bill Forester .... 5.00   2.50   .50
  Green Bay Packers
- [ ] 70 Bob Boyd .... 3.75   1.85   .37
  Los Angeles Rams
- [ ] 71 Andy Robustelli 12.50   6.25   1.25
  New York Giants
- [ ] 72 Sam Baker .... 5.50   2.75   .55
  Washington Redskins
- [ ] 73 Bob Pellegrini .... 3.75   1.85   .37
  Philadelphia Eagles
- [ ] 74 Leo Sanford .... 3.75   1.85   .37
  Chicago Cardinals
- [ ] 75 Sid Watson .... 3.75   1.85   .37
  Pittsburgh Steelers
- [ ] 76 Ray Renfro .... 4.50   2.25   .45
  Cleveland Browns
- [ ] 77 Carl Taseff .... 3.75   1.85   .37
  Baltimore Colts
- [ ] 78 Clyde Conner .... 3.75   1.85   .37
  San Francisco 49ers
- [ ] 79 J.C. Caroline .... 3.75   1.85   .37
  Chicago Bears
- [ ] 80 Howard Cassady .... 8.50   4.25   .85
  ("Hopalong")
  Detroit Lions
- [ ] 81 Tobin Rote .... 5.00   2.50   .50
  Green Bay Packers
- [ ] 82 Ron Waller .... 3.75   1.85   .37
  Los Angeles Rams
- [ ] 83 Jim Patton .... 5.50   2.75   .55
  New York Giants
- [ ] 84 Volney Peters .... 3.75   1.85   .37
  Washington Redskins
- [ ] 85 Dick Lane 35.00   17.50   3.50
  ("Night Train")
  Chicago Cardinals
- [ ] 86 Royce Womble .... 3.75   1.85   .37
  Baltimore Colts
- [ ] 87 Duane Putnam .... 5.00   2.50   .50
  Los Angeles Rams
- [ ] 88 Frank Gifford 110.00   55.00   11.00
  New York Giants
- [ ] 89 Steve Meilinger .... 6.50   3.25   .65
  Washington Redskins
- [ ] 90 Buck Lansford .... 6.50   3.25   .65
  Philadelphia Eagles
- [ ] 91 Lindon Crow .... 6.50   3.25   .65
  Chicago Cardinals
- [ ] 92 Ernie Stautner 12.50   6.25   1.25
  Pittsburgh Steelers
- [ ] 93 Preston Carpenter ..... 8.00   4.00   .80
  Cleveland Browns
- [ ] 94 Raymond Berry 85.00   42.50   8.50
  Baltimore Colts
- [ ] 95 Hugh McElhenny 15.00   7.50   1.50
  San Francisco 49ers
- [ ] 96 Stan Jones 12.50   6.25   1.25
  Chicago Bears
- [ ] 97 Dorne Dibble .... 6.50   3.25   .65
  Detroit Lions
- [ ] 98 Joe Scudero .... 6.50   3.25   .65
  Washington Redskins
- [ ] 99 Eddie Bell .... 6.50   3.25   .65
  Philadelphia Eagles
- [ ] 100 Joe Childress .... 6.50   3.25   .65
  Chicago Cardinals
- [ ] 101 Elbert Nickel .... 6.50   3.25   .65
  Pittsburgh Steelers
- [ ] 102 Walt Michaels .... 8.00   4.00   .80
  Cleveland Browns
- [ ] 103 Jim Mutscheller ...... 6.50   3.25   .65
  Baltimore Colts
- [ ] 104 Earl Morrall 25.00   12.50   2.50
  San Francisco 49ers
- [ ] 105 Larry Strickland ..... 6.50   3.25   .65
  Chicago Bears
- [ ] 106 Jack Christiansen ... 12.50   6.25   1.25
  Detroit Lions
- [ ] 107 Fred Cone .... 6.50   3.25   .65
  Green Bay Packers
- [ ] 108 Bud McFadin .... 7.50   3.75   .75
  Los Angeles Rams
- [ ] 109 Charley Conerly 22.00   11.00   2.20
  New York Giants
- [ ] 110 Tom Runnels .... 6.50   3.25   .65
  Washington Redskins

☐ 111	Ken Keller 6.50	3.25	.65
	Philadelphia Eagles		
☐ 112	James Root 6.50	3.25	.65
	Chicago Cardinals		
☐ 113	Ted Marchibroda 8.00	4.00	.80
	Pittsburgh Steelers		
☐ 114	Don Paul 6.50	3.25	.65
	Cleveland Browns		
☐ 115	George Shaw 7.50	3.75	.75
	Baltimore Colts		
☐ 116	Dick Moegle 7.50	3.75	.75
	San Francisco 49ers		
☐ 117	Don Bingham 6.50	3.25	.65
	Chicago Bears		
☐ 118	Leon Hart 8.50	4.25	.85
	Detroit Lions		
☐ 119	Bart Starr 425.00	200.00	42.00
	Green Bay Packers		
☐ 120	Paul Miller 6.50	3.25	.65
	Los Angeles Rams		
☐ 121	Alex Webster 8.50	4.25	.85
	New York Giants		
☐ 122	Ray Wietecha 6.50	3.25	.65
	New York Giants		
☐ 123	Johnny Carson 6.50	3.25	.65
	Washington Redskins		
☐ 124	Tommy McDonald 12.50	6.25	1.25
	Philadelphia Eagles		
☐ 125	Jerry Tubbs 8.50	4.25	.85
	Chicago Cardinals		
☐ 126	Jack Scarbath 6.50	3.25	.65
	Pittsburgh Steelers		
☐ 127	Ed Modzelewski 7.50	3.75	.75
	Cleveland Browns		
☐ 128	Lenny Moore 28.00	14.00	2.80
	Baltimore Colts		
☐ 129	Joe Perry 22.00	11.00	2.20
	San Francisco 49ers		
☐ 130	Bill Wightkin 6.50	3.25	.65
	Chicago Bears		
☐ 131	Jim Doran 6.50	3.25	.65
	Detroit Lions		
☐ 132	Howard Ferguson 6.50	3.25	.65
	Green Bay Packers		
☐ 133	Tom Wilson 7.50	3.75	.75
	Los Angeles Rams		
☐ 134	Dick James 6.50	3.25	.65
	Washington Redskins		
☐ 135	Jimmy Harris 6.50	3.25	.65
	Philadelphia Eagles		
☐ 136	Chuck Ulrich 6.50	3.25	.65
	Chicago Cardinals		
☐ 137	Lynn Chandnois 6.50	3.25	.65
	Pittsburgh Steelers		
☐ 138	John Unitas 575.00	250.00	50.00
	Baltimore Colts		
☐ 139	Jim Ridlon 6.50	3.25	.65

	San Francisco 49ers		
☐ 140	Zeke Bratkowski 9.00	4.50	.90
	Chicago Bears		
☐ 141	Ray Krouse 6.50	3.25	.65
	Detroit Lions		
☐ 142	John Martinkovic 6.50	3.25	.65
	Green Bay Packers		
☐ 143	Jim Cason 6.50	3.25	.65
	Los Angeles Rams		
☐ 144	Ken MacAfee 7.50	3.75	.75
	New York Giants		
☐ 145	Sid Youngelman 6.50	3.25	.65
	Philadelphia Eagles		
☐ 146	Paul Larson 6.50	3.25	.65
	Chicago Cardinals		
☐ 147	Len Ford 12.50	6.25	1.25
	Cleveland Browns		
☐ 148	Bob Toneff 6.50	3.25	.65
	San Francisco 49ers		
☐ 149	Ronnie Knox 7.50	3.75	.75
	Chicago Bears		
☐ 150	Jim David 8.00	4.00	.80
	Detroit Lions		
☐ 151	Paul Hornung 425.00	200.00	42.00
	Green Bay Packers		
☐ 152	Paul(Tank) Younger 7.50	3.75	.75
	Los Angeles Rams		
☐ 153	Bill Svoboda 6.50	3.25	.65
	New York Giants		
☐ 154	Fred Morrison 35.00	5.00	1.00
	Cleveland Browns		
☐ NNO	Unnumbered Checklist 375.00	75.00	15.00
	(Red, white, and blue)		
☐ NNO	Unnumbered Checklist 375.00	75.00	15.00
	(Red, yellow, and blue)		

1958 Topps

The 1958 Topps football set of 132 cards contains NFL players. After a one-year interruption, team cards are back in the Topps football cards. The cards measure 2 1/2" by 3 1/2". The backs are easily distinguished from other years, as they are printed in bright red ink on white stock. The right-hand side of the reverse gives a trivia question; the answer could be obtained by rubbing with a coin over the blank space. The key rookie cards in this set are Jim Brown and Sonny Jurgensen.

JOHN H. JOHNSON
HALFBACK DETROIT LIONS

	NRMT	VG-E	GOOD
COMPLETE SET (132)	1250.00	600.00	150.00
COMMON PLAYER (1-132)	2.50	1.25	.25
☐ 1 Gene Filipski	16.00	2.50	.50
New York Giants			
☐ 2 Bobby Layne	25.00	12.50	2.50
Detroit Lions			
☐ 3 Joe Schmidt	8.50	4.25	.85
Detroit Lions			
☐ 4 Bill Barnes	2.50	1.25	.25
Philadelphia Eagles			
☐ 5 Milt Plum	5.50	2.75	.55
Cleveland Browns			
☐ 6 Bill Howton	3.50	1.75	.35
Green Bay Packers			
☐ 7 Howard Cassady	3.75	1.85	.37
Detroit Lions			
☐ 8 Jim Dooley	3.00	1.50	.30
Chicago Bears			
☐ 9 Cleveland Browns	6.50	3.25	.65
Team Card			
☐ 10 Lenny Moore	13.50	6.00	1.20
Baltimore Colts			
☐ 11 Darrell Brewster	2.50	1.25	.25
Cleveland Browns			
☐ 12 Alan Ameche	4.25	2.10	.42
Baltimore Colts			
☐ 13 Jim David	2.50	1.25	.25
Detroit Lions			
☐ 14 Jim Mutscheller	2.50	1.25	.25
Baltimore Colts			
☐ 15 Andy Robustelli	8.00	4.00	.80
New York Giants			
☐ 16 Gino Marchetti	8.00	4.00	.80
Baltimore Colts			
☐ 17 Ray Renfro	3.00	1.50	.30
Cleveland Browns			
☐ 18 Yale Lary	7.00	3.50	.70
Detroit Lions			
☐ 19 Gary Glick	2.50	1.25	.25
Pittsburgh Steelers			
☐ 20 Jon Arnett	7.00	3.50	.70
Los Angeles Rams			
☐ 21 Bob Boyd	2.50	1.25	.25
Los Angeles Rams			
☐ 22 John Unitas UER	160.00	80.00	16.00
(College: Pittsburgh should be Louisville) Baltimore Colts			
☐ 23 Zeke Bratkowski	4.00	2.00	.40
Chicago Bears			
☐ 24 Sid Youngelman UER	2.50	1.25	.25
(Misspelled Youngleman on card back) Philadelphia Eagles			
☐ 25 Leo Elter	2.50	1.25	.25
Washington Redskins			
☐ 26 Kenny Konz	2.50	1.25	.25
Cleveland Browns			
☐ 27 Washington Redskins	6.50	3.25	.65
Team Card			
☐ 28 Carl Brettschneider	2.50	1.25	.25
UER (Misspelled on back as Brettschneider) Chicago Cardinals			
☐ 29 Chicago Bears	6.50	3.25	.65
Team Card			
☐ 30 Alex Webster	3.50	1.75	.35
New York Giants			
☐ 31 Al Carmichael	2.50	1.25	.25
Green Bay Packers			
☐ 32 Bobby Dillon	2.50	1.25	.25
Green Bay Packers			
☐ 33 Steve Meilinger	2.50	1.25	.25
Washington Redskins			
☐ 34 Sam Baker	3.00	1.50	.30
Washington Redskins			
☐ 35 Chuck Bednarik UER	9.00	4.50	.90
(Misspelled Bednarick on card back) Philadelphia Eagles			
☐ 36 Bert Vic Zucco	2.50	1.25	.25
Chicago Bears			
☐ 37 George Tarasovic	2.50	1.25	.25
Pittsburgh Steelers			
☐ 38 Bill Wade	3.50	1.75	.35
Los Angeles Rams			
☐ 39 Dick Stanfel	3.00	1.50	.30
Washington Redskins			
☐ 40 Jerry Norton	2.50	1.25	.25
Philadelphia Eagles			
☐ 41 San Francisco 49ers	6.50	3.25	.65
Team Card			
☐ 42 Emlen Tunnell	8.00	4.00	.80
New York Giants			
☐ 43 Jim Doran	2.50	1.25	.25
Detroit Lions			

☐ 44 Ted Marchibroda .... 3.50 Chicago Cardinals	1.75	.35
☐ 45 Chet Hanulak .... 2.50 Cleveland Browns	1.25	.25
☐ 46 Dale Dodrill .... 2.50 Pittsburgh Steelers	1.25	.25
☐ 47 Johnny Carson .... 2.50 Washington Redskins	1.25	.25
☐ 48 Dick Deschaine .... 2.50 Green Bay Packers	1.25	.25
☐ 49 Billy Wells .... 2.50 Philadelphia Eagles	1.25	.25
☐ 50 Larry Morris .... 2.50 Los Angeles Rams	1.25	.25
☐ 51 Jack McClairen .... 2.50 Pittsburgh Steelers	1.25	.25
☐ 52 Lou Groza .... 18.00 Cleveland Browns	9.00	1.80
☐ 53 Rick Casares .... 3.75 Chicago Bears	1.85	.37
☐ 54 Don Chandler .... 3.50 New York Giants	1.75	.35
☐ 55 Duane Putnam .... 2.50 Los Angeles Rams	1.25	.25
☐ 56 Gary Knafelc .... 2.50 Green Bay Packers	1.25	.25
☐ 57 Earl Morrall .... 6.00 Pittsburgh Steelers	3.00	.60
☐ 58 Ron Kramer .... 4.00 Green Bay Packers	2.00	.40
☐ 59 Mike McCormack .... 6.50 Cleveland Browns	3.25	.65
☐ 60 Gern Nagler .... 2.50 Chicago Bears	1.25	.25
☐ 61 New York Giants .... 6.50 Team Card	3.25	.65
☐ 62 Jim Brown .... 400.00 Cleveland Browns	200.00	40.00
☐ 63 Joe Marconi .... 3.50 Los Angeles Rams	1.75	.35
☐ 64 R.C. Owens UER .... 4.00 San Francisco 49ers (Photo actually Don Owens)	2.00	.40
☐ 65 Jimmy Carr .... 3.50 Chicago Cardinals	1.75	.35
☐ 66 Bart Starr UER .... 100.00 Green Bay Packers (Life and year stats reversed)	50.00	10.00
☐ 67 Tom Wilson .... 3.00 Los Angeles Rams	1.50	.30
☐ 68 Lamar McHan .... 3.00 Chicago Cardinals	1.50	.30
☐ 69 Chicago Cardinals .... 6.50 Team Card	3.25	.65
☐ 70 Jack Christiansen .... 7.00 Detroit Lions	3.50	.70
☐ 71 Don McIlhenny .... 3.50 Green Bay Packers	1.75	.35
☐ 72 Ron Waller .... 2.50 Los Angeles Rams	1.25	.25
☐ 73 Frank Gifford .... 75.00 New York Giants	37.50	7.50
☐ 74 Bert Rechichar .... 2.50 Baltimore Colts	1.25	.25
☐ 75 John Henry Johnson ..... 7.50 Detroit Lions	3.75	.75
☐ 76 Jack Butler .... 2.50 Pittsburgh Steelers	1.25	.25
☐ 77 Frank Varrichione .... 2.50 Pittsburgh Steelers	1.25	.25
☐ 78 Ray Mathews .... 2.50 Pittsburgh Steelers	1.25	.25
☐ 79 Marv Matuszak UER ..... 2.50 (Misspelled Matuzsak on card front) San Francisco 49ers	1.25	.25
☐ 80 Harlon Hill .... 3.00 Chicago Bears	1.50	.30
☐ 81 Lou Creekmur .... 3.00 Detroit Lions	1.50	.30
☐ 82 Woodley Lewis UER ...... 2.50 Chicago Cardinals (misspelled Woodly on front; end on front and halfback on back)	1.25	.25
☐ 83 Don Heinrich .... 3.50 New York Giants	1.75	.35
☐ 84 Charley Conerly .... 13.50 New York Giants	6.50	1.25
☐ 85 Los Angeles Rams .... 6.50 Team Card	3.25	.65
☐ 86 Y.A. Tittle .... 28.00 San Francisco 49ers	14.00	2.80
☐ 87 Bobby Walston .... 2.50 Philadelphia Eagles	1.25	.25
☐ 88 Earl Putman .... 2.50 Chicago Cardinals	1.25	.25
☐ 89 Leo Nomellini .... 7.50 San Francisco 49ers	3.75	.75
☐ 90 Sonny Jurgensen ...... 100.00 Philadelphia Eagles	50.00	10.00
☐ 91 Don Paul .... 2.50 Cleveland Browns	1.25	.25
☐ 92 Paige Cothren .... 2.50 Los Angeles Rams	1.25	.25
☐ 93 Joe Perry .... 12.00 San Francisco 49ers	6.00	1.20
☐ 94 Tobin Rote .... 3.75 Detroit Lions	1.85	.37
☐ 95 Billy Wilson .... 3.00 San Francisco 49ers	1.50	.30
☐ 96 Green Bay Packers .... 6.50 Team Card	3.25	.65

Team Card
- [ ] 97 Lavern Torgeson .... 2.50   1.25   .25
Washington Redskins
- [ ] 98 Milt Davis .... 2.50   1.25   .25
Baltimore Colts
- [ ] 99 Larry Strickland .... 2.50   1.25   .25
Chicago Bears
- [ ] 100 Matt Hazeltine .... 3.50   1.75   .35
San Francisco 49ers
- [ ] 101 Walt Yowarski .... 2.50   1.25   .25
San Francisco 49ers
- [ ] 102 Roosevelt Brown .... 7.50   3.75   .75
New York Giants
- [ ] 103 Jim Ringo .... 7.00   3.50   .70
Green Bay Packers
- [ ] 104 Joe Krupa .... 2.50   1.25   .25
Pittsburgh Steelers
- [ ] 105 Les Richter .... 3.00   1.50   .30
Los Angeles Rams
- [ ] 106 Art Donovan .... 7.50   3.75   .75
Baltimore Colts
- [ ] 107 John Olszewski .... 2.50   1.25   .25
Pittsburgh Steelers
- [ ] 108 Ken Keller .... 2.50   1.25   .25
Philadelphia Eagles
- [ ] 109 Philadelphia Eagles ..... 6.50   3.25   .65
Team Card
- [ ] 110 Baltimore Colts .... 6.50   3.25   .65
Team Card
- [ ] 111 Dick Bielski .... 2.50   1.25   .25
Philadelphia Eagles
- [ ] 112 Eddie LeBaron .... 3.75   1.85   .37
Washington Redskins
- [ ] 113 Gene Brito .... 3.00   1.50   .30
Washington Redskins
- [ ] 114 Willie Galimore .... 8.00   4.00   .80
Chicago Bears
- [ ] 115 Detroit Lions .... 6.50   3.25   .65
Team Card
- [ ] 116 Pittsburgh Steelers ..... 6.50   3.25   .65
Team Card
- [ ] 117 L.G. Dupre .... 3.00   1.50   .30
Baltimore Colts
- [ ] 118 Babe Parilli .... 3.50   1.75   .35
Green Bay Packers
- [ ] 119 Bill George .... 7.00   3.50   .70
Chicago Bears
- [ ] 120 Raymond Berry 20.00   10.00   2.00
Baltimore Colts
- [ ] 121 Jim Podoley UER .... 2.50   1.25   .25
Washington Redskins
(photo actually
Volney Peters)
- [ ] 122 Hugh McElhenny 10.00   5.00   1.00
San Francisco 49ers
- [ ] 123 Ed Brown .... 3.00   1.50   .30
Chicago Bears

- [ ] 124 Dick Moegle .... 2.50   1.25   .25
San Francisco 49ers
- [ ] 125 Tom Scott .... 2.50   1.25   .25
Philadelphia Eagles
- [ ] 126 Tommy McDonald .... 4.00   2.00   .40
Philadelphia Eagles
- [ ] 127 Ollie Matson 10.00   5.00   1.00
Chicago Cardinals
- [ ] 128 Preston Carpenter .... 2.50   1.25   .25
Cleveland Browns
- [ ] 129 George Blanda 35.00   17.50   3.50
Chicago Bears
- [ ] 130 Gordon Soltau .... 2.50   1.25   .25
San Francisco 49ers
- [ ] 131 Dick Nolan .... 3.50   1.75   .35
Chicago Cardinals5
- [ ] 132 Don Bosseler .... 16.00   2.50   .50
Washington Redskins

1959 Topps

ALEX KARRAS
DEF. TACKLE   DETROIT LIONS

PUB EDGE OF COIN OVER THIS
SPACE FOR **MAGIC ANSWER**

*The 1959 Topps football set contains 176
cards which were issued in two series. The
cards measure 2 1/2" by 3 1/2". Card backs
include a scratch-off quiz. Team cards (with
checklist backs) as well as team pennant
cards are included in the set. The card backs
were printed in gray on white card stock.
Statistical information from the immediate past
season and career totals are given on the
reverse. The key rookie cards in this set are
Sam Huff, Alex Karras, Jerry Kramer, Bobby
Mitchell, Jim Parker, and Jim Taylor (although
his card does not picture him).*

	NRMT	VG-E	GOOD
COMPLETE SET (176)	950.00	475.00	95.00

COMMON PLAYER (1-88) .... 1.75   .85   .17
COMMON PLAYER (89-176) ... 1.25   .60   .12

☐ 1 Johnny Unitas 115.00   40.00   8.00
    Baltimore Colts
☐ 2 Gene Brito .... 1.75   .85   .17
    Los Angeles Rams
☐ 3 Detroit Lions .... 5.00   1.50   .30
    Team Card
    (checklist back)
☐ 4 Max McGee .... 7.00   3.50   .70
    Green Bay Packers
☐ 5 Hugh McElhenny .... 7.50   3.75   .75
    San Francisco 49ers
☐ 6 Joe Schmidt .... 6.00   3.00   .60
    Detroit Lions
☐ 7 Kyle Rote .... 4.00   2.00   .40
    New York Giants
☐ 8 Clarence Peaks .... 1.75   .85   .17
    Philadelphia Eagles
☐ 9 Pittsburgh Steelers .... 2.25   1.10   .22
    Pennant Card
☐ 10 Jim Brown 165.00   80.00   16.00
    Cleveland Browns
☐ 11 Ray Mathews .... 1.75   .85   .17
    Pittsburgh Steelers
☐ 12 Bobby Dillon .... 1.75   .85   .17
    Green Bay Packers
☐ 13 Joe Childress .... 1.75   .85   .17
    Chicago Cardinals
☐ 14 Terry Barr .... 3.00   1.50   .30
    Detroit Lions
☐ 15 Del Shofner .... 4.00   2.00   .40
    Los Angeles Rams
☐ 16 Bob Pellegrini .... 1.75   .85   .17
    Philadelphia Eagles
☐ 17 Baltimore Colts .... 5.00   1.50   .30
    Team Card
    (checklist back)
☐ 18 Preston Carpenter .... 1.75   .85   .17
    Cleveland Browns
☐ 19 Leo Nomellini .... 6.00   3.00   .60
    San Francisco 49ers
☐ 20 Frank Gifford 55.00   27.50   5.50
    New York Giants
☐ 21 Charlie Ane .... 1.75   .85   .17
    Detroit Lions
☐ 22 Jack Butler .... 1.75   .85   .17
    Pittsburgh Steelers
☐ 23 Bart Starr 55.00   27.50   5.50
    Green Bay Packers
☐ 24 Chicago Cardinals .... 2.25   1.10   .22
    Pennant Card
☐ 25 Bill Barnes .... 1.75   .85   .17
    Philadelphia Eagles
☐ 26 Walt Michaels .... 2.25   1.10   .22
    Cleveland Browns

☐ 27 Clyde Conner .... 1.75   .85   .17
    San Francisco 49ers
☐ 28 Paige Cothren .... 1.75   .85   .17
    Philadelphia Eagles
☐ 29 Roosevelt Grier .... 4.00   2.00   .40
    New York Giants
☐ 30 Alan Ameche .... 3.75   1.85   .37
    Baltimore Colts
☐ 31 Philadelphia Eagles .... 5.00   1.50   .30
    Team Card
    (checklist back)
☐ 32 Dick Nolan .... 2.25   1.10   .22
    New York Giants
☐ 33 R.C. Owens .... 2.25   1.10   .22
    San Francisco 49ers
☐ 34 Dale Dodrill .... 1.75   .85   .17
    Pittsburgh Steelers
☐ 35 Gene Gedman .... 1.75   .85   .17
    Detroit Lions
☐ 36 Gene Lipscomb .... 7.00   3.50   .70
    Baltimore Colts
☐ 37 Ray Renfro .... 2.25   1.10   .22
    Cleveland Browns
☐ 38 Cleveland Browns .... 2.25   1.10   .22
    Pennant Card
☐ 39 Bill Forester .... 2.25   1.10   .22
    Green Bay Packers
☐ 40 Bobby Layne 22.00   11.00   2.20
    Pittsburgh Steelers
☐ 41 Pat Summerall .... 5.50   2.75   .55
    New York Giants
☐ 42 Jerry Mertens .... 1.75   .85   .17
    San Francisco 49ers
☐ 43 Steve Myhra .... 1.75   .85   .17
    Baltimore Colts
☐ 44 John Henry Johnson ...... 6.00   3.00   .60
    Detroit Lions
☐ 45 Woodley Lewis UER ...... 1.75   .85   .17
    Chicago Cardinals
    (misspelled Woody)
☐ 46 Green Bay Packers .... 5.00   1.50   .30
    Team Card
    (checklist back)
☐ 47 Don Owens UER .... 1.75   .85   .17
    (Def.Tackle on front,
    Linebacker on back)
    Philadelphia Eagles
☐ 48 Ed Beatty .... 1.75   .85   .17
    Pittsburgh Steelers
☐ 49 Don Chandler .... 2.25   1.10   .22
    New York Giants
☐ 50 Ollie Matson .... 8.00   4.00   .80
    Los Angeles Rams
☐ 51 Sam Huff 55.00   27.50   5.50
    New York Giants
☐ 52 Tom Miner .... 1.75   .85   .17
    Pittsburgh Steelers

☐ 53 New York Giants 2.25	1.10	.22
Pennant Card		
☐ 54 Kenny Konz 1.75	.85	.17
Cleveland Browns		
☐ 55 Raymond Berry 9.00	4.50	.90
Baltimore Colts		
☐ 56 Howard Ferguson 1.75	.85	.17
Green Bay Packers		
☐ 57 Chuck Ulrich 1.75	.85	.17
Chicago Cardinals		
☐ 58 Bob St. Clair 5.25	2.60	.50
San Francisco 49ers		
☐ 59 Don Burroughs 3.00	1.50	.30
Los Angeles Rams		
☐ 60 Lou Groza 10.00	5.00	1.00
Cleveland Browns		
☐ 61 San Francisco 49ers 5.00	1.50	.30
Team Card		
(checklist back)		
☐ 62 Andy Nelson 1.75	.85	.17
Baltimore Colts		
☐ 63 Hal Bradley 1.75	.85	.17
Philadelphia Eagles		
☐ 64 Dave Hanner 2.25	1.10	.22
Green Bay Packers		
☐ 65 Charley Conerly 11.00	5.50	1.10
New York Giants		
☐ 66 Gene Cronin 1.75	.85	.17
Detroit Lions		
☐ 67 Duane Putnam 1.75	.85	.17
Los Angeles Rams		
☐ 68 Baltimore Colts 2.25	1.10	.22
Pennant Card		
☐ 69 Ernie Stautner 6.00	3.00	.60
Pittsburgh Steelers		
☐ 70 Jon Arnett 2.75	1.35	.27
Los Angeles Rams		
☐ 71 Ken Panfil 1.75	.85	.17
Chicago Cardinals		
☐ 72 Matt Hazeltine 1.75	.85	.17
San Francisco 49ers		
☐ 73 Harley Sewell 1.75	.85	.17
Detroit Lions		
☐ 74 Mike McCormack 5.25	2.60	.50
Cleveland Browns		
☐ 75 Jim Ringo 5.25	2.60	.50
Green Bay Packers		
☐ 76 Los Angeles Rams 5.00	1.50	.30
Team Card		
(checklist back)		
☐ 77 Bob Gain 1.75	.85	.17
Cleveland Browns		
☐ 78 Buzz Nutter 1.75	.85	.17
Baltimore Colts		
☐ 79 Jerry Norton 1.75	.85	.17
Philadelphia Eagles		
☐ 80 Joe Perry 8.00	4.00	.80

San Francisco 49ers		
☐ 81 Carl Brettschneider 1.75	.85	.17
Chicago Cardinals		
☐ 82 Paul Hornung 55.00	27.50	5.50
Green Bay Packers		
☐ 83 Philadelphia Eagles 2.25	1.10	.22
Pennant Card		
☐ 84 Les Richter 2.25	1.10	.22
Los Angeles Rams		
☐ 85 Howard Cassady 2.75	1.35	.27
("Hopalong")		
Detroit Lions		
☐ 86 Art Donovan 6.00	3.00	.60
Baltimore Colts		
☐ 87 Jim Patton 2.25	1.10	.22
New York Giants		
☐ 88 Pete Retzlaff 2.75	1.35	.27
Philadelphia Eagles		
☐ 89 Jim Mutscheller 1.25	.60	.12
Baltimore Colts		
☐ 90 Zeke Bratkowski 2.75	1.35	.27
Chicago Bears		
☐ 91 Washington Redskins .. 3.75	1.25	.25
Team Card		
(Checklist back)		
☐ 92 Art Hunter 1.25	.60	.12
Cleveland Browns		
☐ 93 Gern Nagler 1.25	.60	.12
Chicago Cardinals		
☐ 94 Chuck Weber 1.25	.60	.12
Philadelphia Eagles		
☐ 95 Lew Carpenter 2.00	1.00	.20
Green Bay Packers		
☐ 96 Stan Jones 5.00	2.50	.50
Chicago Bears		
☐ 97 Ralph Guglielmi UER 1.75	.85	.17
Washington Redskins		
(Misspelled Gugliemi		
on card front)		
☐ 98 Green Bay Packers 1.75	.85	.17
Pennant Card		
☐ 99 Ray Wietecha 1.25	.60	.12
New York Giants		
☐ 100 Lenny Moore 8.00	4.00	.80
Baltimore Colts		
☐ 101 Jim Ray Smith UER 3.00	1.50	.30
Cleveland Browns		
(Lions logo on front)		
☐ 102 Abe Woodson 3.50	1.75	.35
San Francisco 49ers		
☐ 103 Alex Karras 65.00	32.50	6.50
Detroit Lions		
☐ 104 Chicago Bears 3.75	1.25	.25
Team Card		
(checklist back)		
☐ 105 John David Crow 8.50	4.25	.85
Chicago Cardinals		

☐ 106	Joe Fortunato	3.75	1.85	.37
	Chicago Bears			
☐ 107	Babe Parilli	2.75	1.35	.27
	Green Bay Packers			
☐ 108	Proverb Jacobs	1.25	.60	.12
	Philadelphia Eagles			
☐ 109	Gino Marchetti	6.00	3.00	.60
	Baltimore Colts			
☐ 110	Bill Wade	1.75	.85	.17
	Los Angeles Rams			
☐ 111	San Francisco 49ers	1.75	.85	.17
	Pennant Card			
☐ 112	Karl Rubke	1.25	.60	.12
	San Francisco 49ers			
☐ 113	Dave Middleton UER	1.75	.85	.17
	Detroit Lions			
	(Browns logo in			
	upper left corner)			
☐ 114	Roosevelt Brown	5.50	2.75	.55
	New York Giants			
☐ 115	John Olszewski	1.25	.60	.12
	Washington Redskins			
☐ 116	Jerry Kramer	22.00	11.00	2.20
	Green Bay Packers			
☐ 117	King Hill	3.50	1.75	.35
	Chicago Cardinals			
☐ 118	Chicago Cardinals	3.75	1.25	.25
	Team Card			
	(Checklist back)			
☐ 119	Frank Varrichione	1.25	.60	.12
	Pittsburgh Steelers			
☐ 120	Rick Casares	1.75	.85	.17
	Chicago Bears			
☐ 121	George Strugar	1.25	.60	.12
	Los Angeles Rams			
☐ 122	Bill Glass UER	2.50	1.25	.25
	(Center on front,			
	tackle on back)			
	Detroit Lions			
☐ 123	Don Bosseler	1.25	.60	.12
	Washington Redskins			
☐ 124	John Reger	1.25	.60	.12
	Pittsburgh Steelers			
☐ 125	Jim Ninowski	2.50	1.25	.25
	Cleveland Browns			
☐ 126	Los Angeles Rams	1.75	.85	.17
	Pennant Card			
☐ 127	Willard Sherman	1.25	.60	.12
	Los Angeles Rams			
☐ 128	Bob Schnelker	1.75	.85	.17
	New York Giants			
☐ 129	Ollie Spencer	1.25	.60	.12
	Green Bay Packers			
☐ 130	Y.A. Tittle	24.00	12.00	2.40
	San Francisco 49ers			
☐ 131	Yale Lary	5.50	2.75	.55
	Detroit Lions			
☐ 132	Jim Parker	25.00	12.50	2.50
	Baltimore Colts			
☐ 133	New York Giants	3.75	1.25	.25
	Team Card			
	(Checklist back)			
☐ 134	Jim Schrader	1.25	.60	.12
	Washington Redskins			
☐ 135	M.C. Reynolds	1.25	.60	.12
	Chicago Cardinals			
☐ 136	Mike Sandusky	1.25	.60	.12
	Pittsburgh Steelers			
☐ 137	Ed Brown	1.75	.85	.17
	Chicago Bears			
☐ 138	Al Barry	1.25	.60	.12
	New York Giants			
☐ 139	Detroit Lions	1.75	.85	.17
	Pennant Card			
☐ 140	Bobby Mitchell	33.00	16.50	3.30
	Cleveland Browns			
☐ 141	Larry Morris	1.25	.60	.12
	Washington Redskins			
☐ 142	Jim Phillips	2.50	1.25	.25
	Los Angeles Rams			
☐ 143	Jim David	1.25	.60	.12
	Detroit Lions			
☐ 144	Joe Krupa	1.25	.60	.12
	Pittsburgh Steelers			
☐ 145	Willie Galimore	2.50	1.25	.25
	Chicago Bears			
☐ 146	Pittsburgh Steelers	3.75	1.25	.25
	Team Card			
	(Checklist back)			
☐ 147	Andy Robustelli	6.00	3.00	.60
	New York Giants			
☐ 148	Billy Wilson	1.75	.85	.17
	San Francisco 49ers			
☐ 149	Leo Sanford	1.25	.60	.12
	Baltimore Colts			
☐ 150	Eddie LeBaron	3.00	1.50	.30
	Washington Redskins			
☐ 151	Bill McColl	1.25	.60	.12
	Chicago Bears			
☐ 152	Buck Lansford UER	1.25	.60	.12
	(Tackle on front,			
	guard on back)			
	Los Angeles Rams			
☐ 153	Chicago Bears	1.75	.85	.17
	Pennant Card			
☐ 154	Leo Sugar	1.25	.60	.12
	Chicago Cardinals			
☐ 155	Jim Taylor UER	18.00	9.00	1.80
	Green Bay Packers			
	(Photo actually			
	Jim Taylor,			
	Cardinal LB)			
☐ 156	Lindon Crow	1.25	.60	.12
	New York Giants			

☐ 157	Jack McClairen 1.25	.60	.12
	Pittsburgh Steelers		
☐ 158	Vince Costello UER 2.25	1.10	.22
	(Linebacker on front,		
	Guard on back)		
	Cleveland Browns		
☐ 159	Stan Wallace 1.25	.60	.12
	Chicago Bears		
☐ 160	Mel Triplett 2.50	1.25	.25
	New York Giants		
☐ 161	Cleveland Browns 3.75	1.25	.25
	Team Card		
	(Checklist back)		
☐ 162	Dan Currie 1.25	.60	.12
	Green Bay Packers		
☐ 163	L.G. Dupre UER 1.25	.60	.12
	(Misspelled DuPre		
	on back)		
	Baltimore Colts		
☐ 164	John Morrow UER 1.25	.60	.12
	(Center on front,		
	Linebacker on back)		
	Los Angeles Rams		
☐ 165	Jim Podoley 1.25	.60	.12
	Washington Redskins		
☐ 166	Bruce Bosley 2.50	1.25	.25
	San Francisco 49ers		
☐ 167	Harlon Hill 1.75	.85	.17
	Chicago Bears		
☐ 168	Washington Redskins . 1.75	.85	.17
	Pennant Card		
☐ 169	Junior Wren 1.25	.60	.12
	Cleveland Browns		
☐ 170	Tobin Rote 2.25	1.10	.22
	Detroit Lions		
☐ 171	Art Spinney 1.25	.60	.12
	Baltimore Colts		
☐ 172	Chuck Drazenovich UER 1.25	.60	.12
	(Linebacker on front,		
	Defensive Back on back)		
	Washington Redskins		
☐ 173	Bobby Joe Conrad 4.00	2.00	.40
	Chicage Cardinals		
☐ 174	Jesse Richardson 1.25	.60	.12
	Philadelphia Eagles		
☐ 175	Sam Baker 1.75	.85	.17
	Washington Redskins		
☐ 176	Tom Tracy 7.50	1.75	.35
	Pittsburgh Steelers		

1960 Topps

The 1960 Topps football set contains 132 cards, each measuring 2 1/2" by 3 1/2". The card backs are printed in green on white card stock. Statistical information from the immediate past season and career totals are given on the reverse. The set marks the debut of the Dallas Cowboys into the National Football League. The backs feature a "Football Funnies" scratch-off quiz; answer was revealed by rubbing with an edge of a coin. The team cards feature numerical checklist backs. The cards are numbered in team order, for example: Baltimore Colts (1-11), Chicago Bears (12-21), Cleveland Browns (22-31), Dallas Cowboys (32-40), Detroit Lions (41-50), Green Bay Packers (51-60), Los Angeles Rams (61-71), New York Giants (72-82), Philadelphia Eagles (83-92), Pittsburgh Steelers (93-102), St. Louis Cardinals (103-112), San Francisco 49ers (113-122), and Washington Redskins (123-132). The key rookie card in this set is Forrest Gregg.

	MINT	VG-E	GOOD
COMPLETE SET (132)	650.00	325.00	65.00
COMMON PLAYER (1-132)	1.65	.80	.15
☐ 1 John Unitas	100.00	30.00	6.00
☐ 2 Alan Ameche	3.25	1.60	.32
☐ 3 Lenny Moore	6.50	3.25	.65
☐ 4 Raymond Berry	6.50	3.25	.65
☐ 5 Jim Parker	5.00	2.50	.50
☐ 6 George Preas	1.65	.80	.15
☐ 7 Art Spinney	1.65	.80	.15
☐ 8 Bill Pellington	2.25	1.10	.22
☐ 9 John Sample	2.50	1.25	.25
☐ 10 Gene Lipscomb	3.00	1.50	.30
☐ 11 Baltimore Colts	5.00	1.50	.30

Team Card
(Checklist 67-132)

☐ 12	Ed Brown	2.25	1.10	.22
☐ 13	Rick Casares	2.50	1.25	.25
☐ 14	Willie Galimore	2.50	1.25	.25
☐ 15	Jim Dooley	2.25	1.10	.22
☐ 16	Harlon Hill	2.25	1.10	.22
☐ 17	Stan Jones	4.50	2.25	.45
☐ 18	Bill George	4.50	2.25	.45
☐ 19	Erich Barnes	3.00	1.50	.30
☐ 20	Doug Atkins UER	5.00	2.50	.50

(reversed negative)

☐ 21	Chicago Bears	5.00	1.50	.30

Team Card
(Checklist 1-66)

☐ 22	Milt Plum	3.00	1.50	.30
☐ 23	Jim Brown	95.00	45.00	9.00
☐ 24	Sam Baker	2.25	1.10	.22
☐ 25	Bobby Mitchell	9.00	4.50	.90
☐ 26	Ray Renfro	2.25	1.10	.22
☐ 27	Bill Howton	2.50	1.25	.25
☐ 28	Jim Ray Smith	2.25	1.10	.22
☐ 29	Jim Shofner	3.00	1.50	.30
☐ 30	Bob Gain	1.65	.80	.15
☐ 31	Cleveland Browns	5.00	1.50	.30

Team Card
(Checklist 1-66)

☐ 32	Don Heinrich	2.50	1.25	.25
☐ 33	Ed Modzelewski	2.50	1.25	.25
☐ 34	Fred Cone	2.25	1.10	.22
☐ 35	L.G. Dupre	2.50	1.25	.25
☐ 36	Dick Bielski	2.25	1.10	.22
☐ 37	Charlie Ane	2.25	1.10	.22
☐ 38	Jerry Tubbs	2.50	1.25	.25
☐ 39	Doyle Nix	2.25	1.10	.22
☐ 40	Ray Krouse	2.25	1.10	.22
☐ 41	Earl Morrall	3.75	1.85	.37
☐ 42	Howard Cassady	2.50	1.25	.25
☐ 43	Dave Middleton	1.65	.80	.15
☐ 44	Jim Gibbons	2.50	1.25	.25
☐ 45	Darris McCord	1.65	.80	.15
☐ 46	Joe Schmidt	5.00	2.50	.50
☐ 47	Terry Barr	1.65	.80	.15
☐ 48	Yale Lary UER	4.50	2.25	.45

(Def.back on front,
halfback on back)

☐ 49	Gil Mains	1.65	.80	.15
☐ 50	Detroit Lions	5.00	1.50	.30

Team Card
(Checklist 1-66)

☐ 51	Bart Starr	36.00	18.00	3.60
☐ 52	Jim Taylor UER	6.50	3.25	.65

(photo actually
Jim Taylor,
Cardinal LB)

☐ 53	Lew Carpenter	1.65	.80	.15
☐ 54	Paul Hornung UER	30.00	15.00	3.00

(Halfback on front,
fullback on back)

☐ 55	Max McGee	2.75	1.35	.27
☐ 56	Forrest Gregg	27.00	13.50	2.70
☐ 57	Jim Ringo	4.50	2.25	.45
☐ 58	Bill Forester	2.25	1.10	.22
☐ 59	Dave Hanner	2.25	1.10	.22
☐ 60	Green Bay Packers	5.00	1.50	.30

Team Card
(Checklist 67-132)

☐ 61	Bill Wade	2.50	1.25	.25
☐ 62	Frank Ryan	6.00	3.00	.60
☐ 63	Ollie Matson	6.50	3.25	.65
☐ 64	Jon Arnett	2.50	1.25	.25
☐ 65	Del Shofner	2.50	1.25	.25
☐ 66	Jim Phillips	2.00	1.00	.20
☐ 67	Art Hunter	1.65	.80	.15
☐ 68	Les Richter	2.25	1.10	.22
☐ 69	Lou Michaels	3.00	1.50	.30
☐ 70	John Baker	1.65	.80	.15
☐ 71	Los Angeles Rams	5.00	1.50	.30

Team Card
(Checklist 1-66)

☐ 72	Charley Conerly	10.00	5.00	1.00
☐ 73	Mel Triplett	1.65	.80	.15
☐ 74	Frank Gifford	50.00	25.00	5.00
☐ 75	Alex Webster	2.50	1.25	.25
☐ 76	Bob Schnelker	2.25	1.10	.22
☐ 77	Pat Summerall	4.00	2.00	.40
☐ 78	Roosevelt Brown	4.50	2.25	.45
☐ 79	Jim Patton	2.25	1.10	.22
☐ 80	Sam Huff UER	12.00	6.00	1.20

(Def.tackle on front,
linebacker on back)

☐ 81	Andy Robustelli	5.00	2.50	.50
☐ 82	New York Giants	5.00		
			1.50	
				.30

Team Card
(Checklist 1-66)

☐ 83	Clarence Peaks	1.65	.80	.15
☐ 84	Bill Barnes	1.65	.80	.15
☐ 85	Pete Retzlaff	2.25	1.10	.22
☐ 86	Bobby Walston	1.65	.80	.15
☐ 87	Chuck Bednarik UER	5.00	2.50	.50

(Misspelled Bednarik
on both sides of card)

☐ 88	Bob Pellegrini	1.65	.80	.15
☐ 89	Tom Brookshier	4.50	2.25	.45
☐ 90	Marion Campbell	2.25	1.10	.22
☐ 91	Jesse Richardson	1.65	.80	.15
☐ 92	Philadelphia Eagles	5.00	1.50	.30

Team Card
(Checklist 1-66)

☐ 93	Bobby Layne	20.00	10.00	2.00
☐ 94	John Henry Johnson	5.00	2.50	.50
☐ 95	Tom Tracy UER	2.25	1.10	.22

(Halfback on front,

☐ 96 Preston Carpenter	1.65	.80	.15
☐ 97 Frank Varrichione UER	1.65	.80	.15
(Reversed negative)			
☐ 98 John Nisby	1.65	.80	.15
☐ 99 Dean Derby	1.65	.80	.15
☐ 100 George Tarasovic	1.65	.80	.15
☐ 101 Ernie Stautner	5.00	2.50	.50
☐ 102 Pittsburgh Steelers	5.00	1.50	.30
Team Card			
(Checklist 67-132)			
☐ 103 King Hill	2.50	1.25	.25
☐ 104 Mal Hammack	1.65	.80	.15
☐ 105 John David Crow	3.50	1.75	.35
☐ 106 Bobby Joe Conrad	2.50	1.25	.25
☐ 107 Woodley Lewis	1.65	.80	.15
☐ 108 Don Gillis	1.65	.80	.15
☐ 109 Carl Brettschneider	1.65	.80	.15
☐ 110 Leo Sugar	1.65	.80	.15
☐ 111 Frank Fuller	1.65	.80	.15
☐ 112 St. Louis Cardinals	5.00	1.50	.30
Team Card			
(Checklist 67-132)			
☐ 113 Y.A. Tittle	25.00	12.50	2.50
☐ 114 Joe Perry	6.50	3.25	.65
☐ 115 J.D. Smith	2.50	1.25	.25
☐ 116 Hugh McElhenny	5.50	2.75	.55
☐ 117 Billy Wilson	2.25	1.10	.22
☐ 118 Bob St. Clair	4.50	2.25	.45
☐ 119 Matt Hazeltine	1.65	.80	.15
☐ 120 Abe Woodson	2.50	1.25	.25
☐ 121 Leo Nomellini	5.00	2.50	.50
☐ 122 San Francisco 49ers	5.00	1.50	.30
Team Card			
(Checklist 67-132)			
☐ 123 Ralph Guglielmi UER	2.25	1.10	.22
(Misspelled Gugliemi			
on card front)			
☐ 124 Don Bosseler	1.65	.80	.15
☐ 125 John Olszewski	1.65	.80	.15
☐ 126 Bill Anderson UER	1.65	.80	.15
(Walt on back)			
☐ 127 Joe Walton	3.75	1.85	.37
☐ 128 Jim Schrader	1.65	.80	.15
☐ 129 Ralph Felton	1.65	.80	.15
☐ 130 Gary Glick	1.65	.80	.15
☐ 131 Bob Toneff	1.65	.80	.15
☐ 132 Washington Redskins	22.00	2.50	.50
Team Card			
(Checklist 67-132)			

1961 Topps

The 1961 Topps football set of 198 cards contains NFL players (1-132) and AFL players (133-197). The cards measure 2 1/2" by 3 1/2". The fronts are very similar to the Topps 1961 baseball issue. The card backs are printed in light blue on white card stock. Statistical information from the immediate past season and career totals are given on the reverse. A "coin-rub" picture was featured on the right of the reverse. Cards are essentially numbered in team order, i.e., Baltimore Colts (1-9), Chicago Bears (10-18), Dallas Cowboys (19-28), Detroit Lions (29-37), Green Bay Packers (38-47), Los Angeles Rams (48-56), San Francisco 49ers (58-66), Cleveland Browns (67-77), Minnesota Vikings (78-84), New York Giants (85-94), Philadelphia Eagles (95-103), Pittsburgh Steelers (104-113), St. Louis Cardinals (114-121), and Washington Redskins (123-131) in the NFL; and Dallas Texans (133-140), Houston Oilers (141-148), New York Titans (149-156), Buffalo Bills (157-165), Los Angeles Chargers (166-173), Boston Patriots (174-181), Oakland Raiders (182-189), and Denver Broncos (190-197) in the AFL. There are three checklist cards in the set, numbers 67, 122, and 198. The key rookie cards in this set are John Brodie, Tom Flores, Don Maynard, and Jim Otto.

	NRMT	VG-E	GOOD
COMPLETE SET (198)	1050.00	475.00	135.00
COMMON PLAYER (1-132)	1.50	.75	.15
COMMON PLAYER (133-198)	1.75	.85	.17
☐ 1 Johnny Unitas	100.00	30.00	6.00
☐ 2 Lenny Moore	6.00	3.00	.60
☐ 3 Alan Ameche	3.00	1.50	.30

☐ 4 Raymond Berry	6.00	3.00	.60
☐ 5 Jim Mutscheller	1.50	.75	.15
☐ 6 Jim Parker	4.25	2.10	.42
☐ 7 Gino Marchetti	5.25	2.60	.50
☐ 8 Gene Lipscomb	3.00	1.50	.30
☐ 9 Baltimore Colts	3.75	1.85	.37
Team Card			
☐ 10 Bill Wade	2.00	1.00	.20
☐ 11 Johnny Morris	6.00	3.00	.60
☐ 12 Rick Casares	2.50	1.25	.25
☐ 13 Harlon Hill	2.00	1.00	.20
☐ 14 Stan Jones	4.00	2.00	.40
☐ 15 Doug Atkins	4.50	2.25	.45
☐ 16 Bill George	4.25	2.10	.42
☐ 17 J.C. Caroline	1.50	.75	.15
☐ 18 Chicago Bears	3.75	1.85	.37
Team Card			
☐ 19 Big Time Football	3.25	1.60	.32
Comes to Texas			
(Eddie LeBaron)			
☐ 20 Eddie LeBaron	3.00	1.50	.30
☐ 21 Don McIlhenny	2.00	1.00	.20
☐ 22 L.G. Dupre	2.00	1.00	.20
☐ 23 Jim Doran	2.00	1.00	.20
☐ 24 Bill Howton	2.50	1.25	.25
☐ 25 Buzz Guy	2.00	1.00	.20
☐ 26 Jack Patera	2.50	1.25	.25
☐ 27 Tom Frankhauser	2.00	1.00	.20
☐ 28 Dallas Cowboys	5.50	2.75	.55
Team Card			
☐ 29 Jim Ninowski	2.00	1.00	.20
☐ 30 Dan Lewis	2.25	1.10	.22
☐ 31 Nick Pietrosante	3.25	1.60	.32
☐ 32 Gail Cogdill	2.25	1.10	.22
☐ 33 Jim Gibbons	2.00	1.00	.20
☐ 34 Jim Martin	1.50	.75	.15
☐ 35 Alex Karras	27.00	13.50	2.70
☐ 36 Joe Schmidt	5.00	2.50	.50
☐ 37 Detroit Lions	3.75	1.85	.37
Team Card			
☐ 38 Packers' Hornung	8.50	4.25	.85
Sets NFL Scoring			
Record			
☐ 39 Bart Starr	30.00	15.00	3.00
☐ 40 Paul Hornung	25.00	12.50	2.50
☐ 41 Jim Taylor	21.00	10.50	2.10
☐ 42 Max McGee	2.50	1.25	.25
☐ 43 Boyd Dowler	4.50	2.25	.45
☐ 44 Jim Ringo	4.25	2.10	.42
☐ 45 Henry Jordan	4.25	2.10	.42
☐ 46 Bill Forester	2.00	1.00	.20
☐ 47 Green Bay Packers	3.75	1.85	.37
Team Card			
☐ 48 Frank Ryan	2.75	1.35	.27
☐ 49 Jon Arnett	2.00	1.00	.20
☐ 50 Ollie Matson	6.00	3.00	.60
☐ 51 Jim Phillips	2.00	1.00	.20
☐ 52 Del Shofner	2.50	1.25	.25
☐ 53 Art Hunter	1.50	.75	.15
☐ 54 Gene Brito	1.50	.75	.15
☐ 55 Lindon Crow	1.50	.75	.15
☐ 56 Los Angeles Rams	3.75	1.85	.37
Team Card			
☐ 57 Colts' Unitas	12.50	6.25	1.25
25 TD Passes			
☐ 58 Y.A. Tittle	20.00	10.00	2.00
☐ 59 John Brodie	45.00	22.50	4.50
☐ 60 J.D. Smith	2.00	1.00	.20
☐ 61 R.C. Owens	2.00	1.00	.20
☐ 62 Clyde Conner	1.50	.75	.15
☐ 63 Bob St. Clair	4.00	2.00	.40
☐ 64 Leo Nomellini	4.25	2.10	.42
☐ 65 Abe Woodson	2.00	1.00	.20
☐ 66 San Francisco 49ers	3.75	1.85	.37
Team Card			
☐ 67 Checklist Card	35.00	3.50	.75
☐ 68 Milt Plum	2.50	1.25	.25
☐ 69 Ray Renfro	2.00	1.00	.20
☐ 70 Bobby Mitchell	6.00	3.00	.60
☐ 71 Jim Brown	85.00	42.50	8.50
☐ 72 Mike McCormack	3.75	1.85	.37
☐ 73 Jim Ray Smith	1.50	.75	.15
☐ 74 Sam Baker	2.00	1.00	.20
☐ 75 Walt Michaels	2.00	1.00	.20
☐ 76 Cleveland Browns	3.75	1.85	.37
Team Card			
☐ 77 Jimmy Brown Gains	25.00	12.50	2.50
1257 Yards			
☐ 78 George Shaw	2.00	1.00	.20
☐ 79 Hugh McElhenny	5.50	2.75	.55
☐ 80 Clancy Osborne	1.50	.75	.15
☐ 81 Dave Middleton	1.50	.75	.15
☐ 82 Frank Youso	1.50	.75	.15
☐ 83 Don Joyce	1.50	.75	.15
☐ 84 Ed Culpepper	1.50	.75	.15
☐ 85 Charley Conerly	8.50	4.25	.85
☐ 86 Mel Triplett	1.50	.75	.15
☐ 87 Kyle Rote	3.50	1.75	.35
☐ 88 Roosevelt Brown	4.25	2.10	.42
☐ 89 Ray Wietecha	1.50	.75	.15
☐ 90 Andy Robustelli	4.50	2.25	.45
☐ 91 Sam Huff	7.00	3.50	.70
☐ 92 Jim Patton	2.00	1.00	.20
☐ 93 New York Giants	3.75	1.85	.37
Team Card			
☐ 94 Charley Conerly	4.25	2.10	.42
Leads Giants for			
13th Year			
☐ 95 Sonny Jurgensen	20.00	10.00	2.00
☐ 96 Tommy McDonald	2.25	1.10	.22
☐ 97 Bill Barnes	1.50	.75	.15
☐ 98 Bobby Walston	1.50	.75	.15
☐ 99 Pete Retzlaff	2.00	1.00	.20
☐ 100 Jim McCusker	1.50	.75	.15

☐ 101 Chuck Bednarik	4.50	2.25	.45
☐ 102 Tom Brookshier	3.00	1.50	.30
☐ 103 Philadelphia Eagles	3.75	1.85	.37
Team Card			
☐ 104 Bobby Layne	18.00	9.00	1.80
☐ 105 John Henry Johnson	4.50	2.25	.45
☐ 106 Tom Tracy	2.00	1.00	.20
☐ 107 Buddy Dial	3.00	1.50	.30
☐ 108 Jimmy Orr	3.00	1.50	.30
☐ 109 Mike Sandusky	1.50	.75	.15
☐ 110 John Reger	1.50	.75	.15
☐ 111 Junior Wren	1.50	.75	.15
☐ 112 Pittsburgh Steelers	3.75	1.85	.37
Team Card			
☐ 113 Bobby Layne Sets	5.00	2.50	.50
New Passing Record			
☐ 114 Ron Roach	1.50	.75	.15
☐ 115 Sam Etcheverry	2.50	1.25	.25
☐ 116 John David Crow	2.75	1.35	.27
☐ 117 Mal Hammack	1.50	.75	.15
☐ 118 Sonny Randle	2.50	1.25	.25
☐ 119 Leo Sugar	1.50	.75	.15
☐ 120 Jerry Norton	1.50	.75	.15
☐ 121 St. Louis Cardinals	3.75	1.85	.37
Team Card			
☐ 122 Checklist Card	35.00	3.50	.75
☐ 123 Ralph Guglielmi	2.00	1.00	.20
☐ 124 Dick James	1.50	.75	.15
☐ 125 Don Bosseler	1.50	.75	.15
☐ 126 Joe Walton	2.50	1.25	.25
☐ 127 Bill Anderson	1.50	.75	.15
☐ 128 Vince Promuto	2.75	1.35	.27
☐ 129 Bob Toneff	1.50	.75	.15
☐ 130 John Paluck	1.50	.75	.15
☐ 131 Washington Redskins	3.75	1.85	.37
Team Card			
☐ 132 Browns' Plum Wins	2.50	1.25	.25
NFL Passing Title			
☐ 133 Abner Haynes	4.00	2.00	.40
☐ 134 Mel Branch	2.50	1.25	.25
☐ 135 Jerry Cornelison	1.75	.85	.17
☐ 136 Bill Krisher	1.75	.85	.17
☐ 137 Paul Miller	1.75	.85	.17
☐ 138 Jack Spikes	2.50	1.25	.25
☐ 139 Johnny Robinson	6.00	3.00	.60
☐ 140 Cotton Davidson	3.75	1.85	.37
☐ 141 Dave Smith	1.75	.85	.17
☐ 142 Bill Groman	2.50	1.25	.25
☐ 143 Rich Michael	1.75	.85	.17
☐ 144 Mike Dukes	1.75	.85	.17
☐ 145 George Blanda	25.00	12.50	2.50
☐ 146 Billy Cannon	4.00	2.00	.40
☐ 147 Dennit Morris	1.75	.85	.17
☐ 148 Jacky Lee	2.50	1.25	.25
☐ 149 Al Dorow	1.75	.85	.17
☐ 150 Don Maynard	50.00	25.00	5.00
☐ 151 Art Powell	4.50	2.25	.45
☐ 152 Sid Youngelman	1.75	.85	.17
☐ 153 Bob Mischak	1.75	.85	.17
☐ 154 Larry Grantham	2.50	1.25	.25
☐ 155 Tom Saidock	1.75	.85	.17
☐ 156 Roger Donnahoo	1.75	.85	.17
☐ 157 Laverne Torczon	1.75	.85	.17
☐ 158 Archie Matsos	2.50	1.25	.25
☐ 159 Elbert Dubenion	3.00	1.50	.30
☐ 160 Wray Carlton	3.00	1.50	.30
☐ 161 Rich McCabe	2.50	1.25	.25
☐ 162 Ken Rice	1.75	.85	.17
☐ 163 Art Baker	1.75	.85	.17
☐ 164 Tom Rychlec	1.75	.85	.17
☐ 165 Mack Yoho	1.75	.85	.17
☐ 166 Jack Kemp	110.00	55.00	11.00
☐ 167 Paul Lowe	4.00	2.00	.40
☐ 168 Ron Mix	8.50	4.25	.85
☐ 169 Paul Maguire	3.50	1.75	.35
☐ 170 Volney Peters	1.75	.85	.17
☐ 171 Ernie Wright	1.75	.85	.17
☐ 172 Ron Nery	1.75	.85	.17
☐ 173 Dave Kocourek	2.75	1.35	.27
☐ 174 Jim Colclough	1.75	.85	.17
☐ 175 Babe Parilli	3.50	1.75	.35
☐ 176 Billy Lott	2.75	1.35	.27
☐ 177 Fred Bruney	1.75	.85	.17
☐ 178 Ross O'Hanley	1.75	.85	.17
☐ 179 Walt Cudzik	1.75	.85	.17
☐ 180 Charley Leo	1.75	.85	.17
☐ 181 Bob Dee	1.75	.85	.17
☐ 182 Jim Otto	34.00	16.50	3.00
☐ 183 Eddie Macon	1.75	.85	.17
☐ 184 Dick Christy	1.75	.85	.17
☐ 185 Alan Miller	1.75	.85	.17
☐ 186 Tom Flores	12.50	6.25	1.25
☐ 187 Joe Cannavino	1.75	.85	.17
☐ 188 Don Manoukian	1.75	.85	.17
☐ 189 Bob Coolbaugh	1.75	.85	.17
☐ 190 Lionel Taylor	6.50	3.25	.65
☐ 191 Bud McFadin	1.75	.85	.17
☐ 192 Goose Gonsoulin	3.75	1.85	.37
☐ 193 Frank Tripucka	3.00	1.50	.30
☐ 194 Gene Mingo	3.00	1.50	.30
☐ 195 Eldon Danenhauer	2.50	1.25	.25
☐ 196 Bob McNamara	1.75	.85	.17
☐ 197 Dave Rolle	1.75	.85	.17
☐ 198 Checklist Card	90.00	9.00	1.75

1962 Topps

The 1962 Topps football set contains 176 black-bordered cards. The cards measure 2 1/2" by 3 1/2". In designing the 1962 set, Topps chose a horizontally oriented card front for the first time since 1957. The black borders make it quite difficult to put together a set in Mint condition. The single-printed (SP) cards are in shorter supply than the others. The shortage is probably attributable to the fact that the set size is not the standard 132-card, single-sheet size; hence all cards were not printed in equal amounts. Cards are again organized numerically in team order, for example: Baltimore Colts (1-12), Chicago Bears (13-25), Cleveland Browns (26-37), Dallas Cowboys (38-49), Detroit Lions (50-62), Green Bay Packers (63-75), Los Angeles Rams (77-89), Minnesota Vikings (90-101), New York Giants (102-114), Philadelphia Eagles (115-126), Pittsburgh Steelers (127-138), St. Louis Cardinals (139-150), San Francisco 49ers (151-163), and Washington Redskins (164-175). The last card within each team grouping was a "rookie prospect" for that team. Many of the black and white inset photos on the card fronts are not the player pictured and described on the card. The key rookie cards in this set are Ernie Davis, Mike Ditka, Roman Gabriel, Bill Kilmer, and Fran Tarkenton.

	NRMT	VG-E	GOOD
COMPLETE SET (176)	1600.00	700.00	200.00
COMMON PLAYER (1-176)	2.00	1.00	.20
COMMON PLAYER SP	5.00	2.50	.50
☐ 1 John Unitas	120.00	30.00	6.00
☐ 2 Lenny Moore	6.50	3.25	.65
☐ 3 Alex Hawkins SP	6.50	3.25	.65
☐ 4 Joe Perry	6.50	3.25	.65
☐ 5 Raymond Berry SP	15.00	7.50	1.50
☐ 6 Steve Myhra	2.00	1.00	.20
☐ 7 Tom Gilburg SP	5.00	2.50	.50
☐ 8 Gino Marchetti	5.25	2.60	.50
☐ 9 Bill Pellington	2.00	1.00	.20
☐ 10 Andy Nelson	2.00	1.00	.20
☐ 11 Wendell Harris SP	5.00	2.50	.50
☐ 12 Baltimore Colts Team Card	5.00	2.50	.50
☐ 13 Bill Wade SP	5.50	2.75	.55
☐ 14 Willie Galimore	2.50	1.25	.25
☐ 15 Johnny Morris SP	6.00	3.00	.60
☐ 16 Rick Casares	2.50	1.25	.25
☐ 17 Mike Ditka	110.00	55.00	11.00
☐ 18 Stan Jones	4.00	2.00	.40
☐ 19 Roger LeClerc	2.00	1.00	.20
☐ 20 Angelo Coia	2.00	1.00	.20
☐ 21 Doug Atkins	5.00	2.50	.50
☐ 22 Bill George	4.25	2.10	.42
☐ 23 Richie Petitbon	6.00	3.00	.60
☐ 24 Ron Bull SP	6.50	3.25	.65
☐ 25 Chicago Bears Team Card	5.00	2.50	.50
☐ 26 Howard Cassady	2.50	1.25	.25
☐ 27 Ray Renfro SP	5.50	2.75	.55
☐ 28 Jim Brown	100.00	50.00	10.00
☐ 29 Rich Kreitling	2.00	1.00	.20
☐ 30 Jim Ray Smith	2.00	1.00	.20
☐ 31 John Morrow	2.00	1.00	.20
☐ 32 Lou Groza	8.00	4.00	.80
☐ 33 Bob Gain	2.00	1.00	.20
☐ 34 Bernie Parrish	2.50	1.25	.25
☐ 35 Jim Shofner	2.50	1.25	.25
☐ 36 Ernie Davis SP	45.00	22.50	4.50
☐ 37 Cleveland Browns Team Card	5.00	2.50	.50
☐ 38 Eddie LeBaron	3.00	1.50	.30
☐ 39 Don Meredith SP	75.00	37.50	7.50
☐ 40 J.W. Lockett SP	5.00	2.50	.50
☐ 41 Don Perkins	4.50	2.25	.45
☐ 42 Bill Howton	2.50	1.25	.25
☐ 43 Dick Bielski	2.00	1.00	.20
☐ 44 Mike Connelly	3.00	1.50	.30
☐ 45 Jerry Tubbs SP	5.50	2.75	.55
☐ 46 Don Bishop SP	5.00	2.50	.50
☐ 47 Dick Moegle	2.00	1.00	.20
☐ 48 Bobby Plummer SP	5.00	2.50	.50
☐ 49 Dallas Cowboys Team Card	6.50	3.25	.65
☐ 50 Milt Plum	3.00	1.50	.30
☐ 51 Dan Lewis	2.00	1.00	.20
☐ 52 Nick Pietrosante SP	5.50	2.75	.55
☐ 53 Gail Cogdill	2.00	1.00	.20
☐ 54 Jim Gibbons	2.00	1.00	.20
☐ 55 Jim Martin	2.00	1.00	.20
☐ 56 Yale Lary	4.50	2.25	.45

☐ 57	Darris McCord	2.00	1.00	.20
☐ 58	Alex Karras	13.50	6.00	1.20
☐ 59	Joe Schmidt	5.00	2.50	.50
☐ 60	Dick Lane	4.50	2.25	.45
☐ 61	John Lomakoski SP	5.00	2.50	.50
☐ 62	Detroit Lions SP	11.00	5.50	1.10
	Team Card			
☐ 63	Bart Starr SP	40.00	20.00	4.00
☐ 64	Paul Hornung SP	36.00	18.00	3.60
☐ 65	Tom Moore SP	6.00	3.00	.60
☐ 66	Jim Taylor SP	25.00	12.50	2.50
☐ 67	Max McGee SP	6.00	3.00	.60
☐ 68	Jim Ringo SP	11.00	5.50	1.10
☐ 69	Fuzzy Thurston SP	11.00	5.50	1.10
☐ 70	Forrest Gregg	5.00	2.50	.50
☐ 71	Boyd Dowler	2.50	1.25	.25
☐ 72	Henry Jordan SP	5.50	2.75	.55
☐ 73	Bill Forester SP	5.50	2.75	.55
☐ 74	Earl Gros SP	5.50	2.75	.55
☐ 75	Green Bay Packers SP	17.00	8.50	1.70
	Team Card			
☐ 76	Checklist SP	70.00	7.00	1.50
☐ 77	Zeke Bratkowski SP	6.50	3.25	.65
	(Inset photo is			
	Johnny Unitas)			
☐ 78	Jon Arnett SP	6.00	3.00	.60
☐ 79	Ollie Matson SP	15.00	7.50	1.50
☐ 80	Dick Bass SP	6.00	3.00	.60
☐ 81	Jim Phillips	2.00	1.00	.20
☐ 82	Carroll Dale	3.50	1.75	.35
☐ 83	Frank Varrichione	2.00	1.00	.20
☐ 84	Art Hunter	2.00	1.00	.20
☐ 85	Danny Villanueva	2.50	1.25	.25
☐ 86	Les Richter SP	5.50	2.75	.55
☐ 87	Lindon Crow	2.00	1.00	.20
☐ 88	Roman Gabriel SP	33.00	15.00	3.00
	(Inset photo is			
	Y.A. Tittle)			
☐ 89	Los Angeles Rams SP	11.00	5.50	1.10
	Team Card			
☐ 90	Fran Tarkenton SP UER	325.00	160.00	32.00
	(Small photo actually			
	Jurgensen with air-			
	brushed jersey)			
☐ 91	Jerry Reichow SP	5.00	2.50	.50
☐ 92	Hugh McElhenny SP	12.00	6.00	1.20
☐ 93	Mel Triplett SP	5.00	2.50	.50
☐ 94	Tommy Mason SP	6.50	3.25	.65
☐ 95	Dave Middleton SP	5.00	2.50	.50
☐ 96	Frank Youso SP	5.00	2.50	.50
☐ 97	Mike Mercer SP	5.00	2.50	.50
☐ 98	Rip Hawkins SP	5.00	2.50	.50
☐ 99	Cliff Livingston SP	5.00	2.50	.50
☐ 100	Roy Winston SP	6.50	3.25	.65
☐ 101	Minnesota Vikings SP	13.00	6.50	1.30
	Team Card			
☐ 102	Y.A. Tittle	20.00	10.00	2.00
☐ 103	Joe Walton	2.50	1.25	.25
☐ 104	Frank Gifford	50.00	25.00	5.00
☐ 105	Alex Webster	2.50	1.25	.25
☐ 106	Del Shofner	2.50	1.25	.25
☐ 107	Don Chandler	2.50	1.25	.25
☐ 108	Andy Robustelli	4.50	2.25	.45
☐ 109	Jim Katcavage	3.00	1.50	.30
☐ 110	Sam Huff SP	13.50	6.50	1.30
☐ 111	Erich Barnes	2.50	1.25	.25
☐ 112	Jim Patton	2.50	1.25	.25
☐ 113	Jerry Hillebrand SP	5.00	2.50	.50
☐ 114	New York Giants	5.00	2.50	.50
	Team Card			
☐ 115	Sonny Jurgensen	20.00	10.00	2.00
☐ 116	Tommy McDonald	2.50	1.25	.25
☐ 117	Ted Dean SP	5.00	2.50	.50
☐ 118	Clarence Peaks	2.00	1.00	.20
☐ 119	Bobby Walston	2.00	1.00	.20
☐ 120	Pete Retzlaff SP	5.50	2.75	.55
☐ 121	Jim Schrader SP	5.00	2.50	.50
☐ 122	J.D. Smith	2.00	1.00	.20
	(tackle)			
☐ 123	King Hill	2.50	1.25	.25
☐ 124	Maxie Baughan	3.75	1.85	.37
☐ 125	Pete Case SP	5.00	2.50	.50
☐ 126	Philadelphia Eagles	5.00	2.50	.50
	Team Card			
☐ 127	Bobby Layne UER	18.00	9.00	1.80
	(Bears until 1958,			
	should be Lions)			
☐ 128	Tom Tracy	2.50	1.25	.25
☐ 129	John Henry Johnson	4.50	2.25	.45
☐ 130	Buddy Dial SP	5.50	2.75	.55
☐ 131	Preston Carpenter	2.00	1.00	.20
☐ 132	Lou Michaels SP	5.50	2.75	.55
☐ 133	Gene Lipscomb SP	6.00	3.00	.60
☐ 134	Ernie Stautner SP	10.00	5.00	1.00
☐ 135	John Reger SP	5.00	2.50	.50
☐ 136	Myron Pottios	2.50	1.25	.25
☐ 137	Bob Ferguson SP	5.50	2.75	.55
☐ 138	Pittsburgh Steelers	11.00	5.50	1.10
	Team Card SP			
☐ 139	Sam Etcheverry	2.50	1.25	.25
☐ 140	John David Crow SP	6.00	3.00	.60
☐ 141	Bobby Joe Conrad SP	5.50	2.75	.55
☐ 142	Prentice Gautt SP	6.00	3.00	.60
☐ 143	Frank Mestnick	2.00	1.00	.20
☐ 144	Sonny Randle	2.50	1.25	.25
☐ 145	Gerry Perry	2.00	1.00	.20
☐ 146	Jerry Norton	2.00	1.00	.20
☐ 147	Jimmy Hill	2.00	1.00	.20
☐ 148	Bill Stacy	2.00	1.00	.20
☐ 149	Fate Echols SP	5.00	2.50	.50
☐ 150	St. Louis Cardinals	5.00	2.50	.50
	Team Card			
☐ 151	Bill Kilmer	15.00	7.50	1.50
☐ 152	John Brodie	15.00	7.50	1.50

☐ 153 J.D. Smith 2.50	1.25	.25
(halfback)			
☐ 154 C.R. Roberts SP 5.00	2.50	.50
☐ 155 Monty Stickles 2.00	1.00	.20
☐ 156 Clyde Conner 2.00	1.00	.20
☐ 157 Bob St. Clair 4.25	2.10	.42
☐ 158 Tommy Davis 2.75	1.35	.27
☐ 159 Leo Nomellini 4.50	2.25	.45
☐ 160 Matt Hazeltine 2.00	1.00	.20
☐ 161 Abe Woodson 2.50	1.25	.25
☐ 162 Dave Baker 2.00	1.00	.20
☐ 163 San Francisco 49ers .. 5.00	2.50	.50
Team Card			
☐ 164 Norm Snead SP 14.00	7.00	1.40
☐ 165 Dick James 2.00	1.00	.20
(Inset photo is			
Don Bosseler)			
☐ 166 Bobby Mitchell 5.50	2.75	.55
☐ 167 Sam Horner 2.00	1.00	.20
☐ 168 Bill Barnes 2.00	1.00	.20
☐ 169 Bill Anderson 2.00	1.00	.20
☐ 170 Fred Dugan 2.00	1.00	.20
☐ 171 John Aveni SP 5.00	2.50	.50
☐ 172 Bob Toneff 2.00	1.00	.20
☐ 173 Jim Kerr 2.00	1.00	.20
☐ 174 Leroy Jackson SP 5.00	2.50	.50
☐ 175 Washington Redskins .. 5.00	2.50	.50
Team Card			
☐ 176 Checklist 100.00	10.00	2.00

1963 Topps

The 1963 Topps set contains 170 cards of NFL players grouped together by teams. The teams are ordered as follows: Baltimore Colts (1-12), Cleveland Browns (13-24), Detroit Lions (25-36), Los Angeles Rams (37-48), New York

Giants (49-60), Chicago Bears (61-72), Dallas Cowboys (73-84), Green Bay Packers (86-97), Minnesota Vikings (98-109), Philadelphia Eagles (110-121), Pittsburgh Steelers (122-133), San Francisco 49ers (134-145), St. Louis Cardinals (146-157), and Washington Redskins (158-169). The cards measure 2 1/2" by 3 1/2". The card backs are printed in light orange ink on white card stock. Statistical information from the immediate past season and career totals are given on the reverse. The illustrated trivia question on the reverse (of each card) could be answered by placing red cellophane paper (which was inserted into wax packs) over the card. The 76 cards indicated by SP below are in shorter supply than the others because the set size is not the standard 132-card, single-sheet size; hence, all cards were not printed in equal amounts. The key rookie cards in this set are defensive stalwarts Deacon Jones, Bob Lilly, Jim Marshall, Ray Nitschke, Larry Wilson, and Willie Wood.

	MINT	VG-E	GOOD
COMPLETE SET (170)	1100.00	500.00	135.00
COMMON PLAYER (1-170)	1.75	.85	.17
COMMON PLAYER SP	4.50	2.25	.45

☐ 1 John Unitas 100.00	30.00	6.00
☐ 2 Lenny Moore 6.00	3.00	.60
☐ 3 Jimmy Orr 2.25	1.10	.22
☐ 4 Raymond Berry 6.00	3.00	.60
☐ 5 Jim Parker 4.50	2.25	.45
☐ 6 Alex Sandusky 1.75	.85	.17
☐ 7 Dick Szymanski 1.75	.85	.17
☐ 8 Gino Marchetti 4.75	2.35	.45
☐ 9 Billy Ray Smith 2.75	1.35	.27
☐ 10 Bill Pellington 1.75	.85	.17
☐ 11 Bob Boyd 2.50	1.25	.25
☐ 12 Baltimore Colts SP 10.00	5.00	1.00
Team Card			
☐ 13 Frank Ryan SP 5.25	2.60	.50
☐ 14 Jim Brown SP 135.00	65.00	13.50
☐ 15 Ray Renfro SP 5.25	2.60	.50
☐ 16 Rich Kreitling SP 4.50	2.25	.45
☐ 17 Mike McCormack SP 8.00	4.00	.80
☐ 18 Jim Ray Smith SP 4.50	2.25	.45
☐ 19 Lou Groza SP 13.50	6.50	1.25
☐ 20 Bill Glass SP 5.25	2.60	.50
☐ 21 Galen Fiss SP 4.50	2.25	.45
☐ 22 Don Fleming SP 5.25	2.60	.50
☐ 23 Bob Gain SP 4.50	2.25	.45
☐ 24 Cleveland Browns SP .. 10.00	5.00	1.00
Team Card			
☐ 25 Milt Plum 2.25	1.10	.22
☐ 26 Dan Lewis 1.75	.85	.17

☐ 27	Nick Pietrosante	2.25	1.10	.22
☐ 28	Gail Cogdill	1.75	.85	.17
☐ 29	Harley Sewell	1.75	.85	.17
☐ 30	Jim Gibbons	1.75	.85	.17
☐ 31	Carl Brettschneider	1.75	.85	.17
☐ 32	Dick Lane	4.50	2.25	.45
☐ 33	Yale Lary	4.50	2.25	.45
☐ 34	Roger Brown	3.00	1.50	.30
☐ 35	Joe Schmidt	5.00	2.50	.50
☐ 36	Detroit Lions SP Team Card	10.00	5.00	1.00
☐ 37	Roman Gabriel	5.50	2.75	.55
☐ 38	Zeke Bratkowski	2.50	1.25	.25
☐ 39	Dick Bass	2.25	1.10	.22
☐ 40	Jon Arnett	2.25	1.10	.22
☐ 41	Jim Phillips	1.75	.85	.17
☐ 42	Frank Varrichione	1.75	.85	.17
☐ 43	Danny Villanueva	2.25	1.10	.22
☐ 44	Deacon Jones	50.00	25.00	5.00
☐ 45	Lindon Crow	1.75	.85	.17
☐ 46	Marlin McKeever	2.25	1.10	.22
☐ 47	Ed Meador	2.50	1.25	.25
☐ 48	Los Angeles Rams Team Card	4.00	2.00	.40
☐ 49	Y.A. Tittle SP	25.00	12.50	2.50
☐ 50	Del Shofner SP	5.25	2.60	.50
☐ 51	Alex Webster SP	5.25	2.60	.50
☐ 52	Phil King SP	4.50	2.25	.45
☐ 53	Jack Stroud SP	4.50	2.25	.45
☐ 54	Darrell Dess SP	4.50	2.25	.45
☐ 55	Jim Katcavage SP	5.25	2.60	.50
☐ 56	Roosevelt Grier SP	7.00	3.50	.70
☐ 57	Erich Barnes SP	5.25	2.60	.50
☐ 58	Jim Patton SP	5.25	2.60	.50
☐ 59	Sam Huff SP	12.00	6.00	1.20
☐ 60	New York Giants Team Card	4.00	2.00	.40
☐ 61	Bill Wade	2.25	1.10	.22
☐ 62	Mike Ditka	34.00	16.00	3.00
☐ 63	Johnny Morris	2.50	1.25	.25
☐ 64	Roger LeClerc	1.75	.85	.17
☐ 65	Roger Davis	1.75	.85	.17
☐ 66	Joe Marconi	1.75	.85	.17
☐ 67	Herman Lee	1.75	.85	.17
☐ 68	Doug Atkins	4.50	2.25	.45
☐ 69	Joe Fortunato	2.25	1.10	.22
☐ 70	Bill George	4.50	2.25	.45
☐ 71	Richie Petitbon	2.50	1.25	.25
☐ 72	Chicago Bears SP Team Card	10.00	5.00	1.00
☐ 73	Eddie LeBaron SP	5.25	2.60	.50
☐ 74	Don Meredith SP	45.00	22.50	4.50
☐ 75	Don Perkins SP	5.25	2.60	.50
☐ 76	Amos Marsh SP	4.50	2.25	.45
☐ 77	Bill Howton SP	5.25	2.60	.50
☐ 78	Andy Cvercko SP	4.50	2.25	.45
☐ 79	Sam Baker SP	5.25	2.60	.50
☐ 80	Jerry Tubbs SP	5.25	2.60	.50
☐ 81	Don Bishop SP	4.50	2.25	.45
☐ 82	Bob Lilly SP	90.00	45.00	9.00
☐ 83	Jerry Norton SP	4.50	2.25	.45
☐ 84	Dallas Cowboys SP Team Card	12.50	6.25	1.25
☐ 85	Checklist Card	25.00	2.50	.50
☐ 86	Bart Starr	28.00	14.00	2.80
☐ 87	Jim Taylor	13.50	6.50	1.25
☐ 88	Boyd Dowler	2.50	1.25	.25
☐ 89	Forrest Gregg	4.50	2.25	.45
☐ 90	Fuzzy Thurston	2.75	1.35	.27
☐ 91	Jim Ringo	4.50	2.25	.45
☐ 92	Ron Kramer	2.25	1.10	.22
☐ 93	Henry Jordan	2.25	1.10	.22
☐ 94	Bill Forester	2.25	1.10	.22
☐ 95	Willie Wood	25.00	12.50	2.50
☐ 96	Ray Nitschke	60.00	30.00	6.00
☐ 97	Green Bay Packers Team Card	4.00	2.00	.40
☐ 98	Fran Tarkenton	75.00	37.50	7.50
☐ 99	Tommy Mason	2.25	1.10	.22
☐ 100	Mel Triplett	1.75	.85	.17
☐ 101	Jerry Reichow	1.75	.85	.17
☐ 102	Frank Youso	1.75	.85	.17
☐ 103	Hugh McElhenny	5.00	2.50	.50
☐ 104	Gerry Huth	1.75	.85	.17
☐ 105	Ed Sharockman	1.75	.85	.17
☐ 106	Rip Hawkins	1.75	.85	.17
☐ 107	Jim Marshall	20.00	10.00	2.00
☐ 108	Jim Prestel	1.75	.85	.17
☐ 109	Minnesota Vikings Team Card	4.00	2.00	.40
☐ 110	Sonny Jurgensen SP	20.00	10.00	2.00
☐ 111	Tim Brown SP	7.50	3.75	.75
☐ 112	Tommy McDonald SP	5.25	2.60	.50
☐ 113	Clarence Peaks SP	4.50	2.25	.45
☐ 114	Pete Retzlaff SP	4.50	2.25	.45
☐ 115	Jim Schrader SP	4.50	2.25	.45
☐ 116	Jim McCusker SP	4.50	2.25	.45
☐ 117	Don Burroughs SP	4.50	2.25	.45
☐ 118	Maxie Baughan SP	5.25	2.60	.50
☐ 119	Riley Gunnels SP	4.50	2.25	.45
☐ 120	Jimmy Carr SP	4.50	2.25	.45
☐ 121	Philadelphia Eagles Team Card SP	10.00	5.00	1.00
☐ 122	Ed Brown SP	5.25	2.60	.50
☐ 123	John Henry Johnson SP	8.50	4.25	.85
☐ 124	Buddy Dial SP	5.25	2.60	.50
☐ 125	Red Mack SP	4.50	2.25	.45
☐ 126	Preston Carpenter SP	4.50	2.25	.45
☐ 127	Ray Lemek SP	4.50	2.25	.45
☐ 128	Buzz Nutter SP	4.50	2.25	.45
☐ 129	Ernie Stautner SP	10.00	5.00	1.00
☐ 130	Lou Michaels SP	4.50	2.25	.45
☐ 131	Clendon Thomas SP	6.00	3.00	.60
☐ 132	Tom Bettis SP	4.50	2.25	.45

			NRMT	VG-E	GOOD
☐ 133	Pittsburgh Steelers .... Team Card SP	10.00	5.00	1.00
☐ 134	John Brodie 8.50	4.25	.85
☐ 135	J.D. Smith 2.25	1.10	.22
☐ 136	Bill Kilmer 4.50	2.25	.45
☐ 137	Bernie Casey 3.50	1.75	.35
☐ 138	Tommy Davis 1.75	.85	.17
☐ 139	Ted Connolly 1.75	.85	.17
☐ 140	Bob St. Clair 4.25	2.10	.42
☐ 141	Abe Woodson 2.25	1.10	.22
☐ 142	Matt Hazeltine 1.75	.85	.17
☐ 143	Leo Nomellini 4.50	2.25	.45
☐ 144	Dan Colchico 1.75	.85	.17
☐ 145	San Francisco 49ers . 10.00 Team Card SP	5.00	1.00

			NRMT	VG-E	GOOD
☐ 146	Charlie Johnson 6.50	3.25	.65
☐ 147	John David Crow 2.50	1.25	.25
☐ 148	Bobby Joe Conrad 2.25	1.10	.22
☐ 149	Sonny Randle 2.25	1.10	.22
☐ 150	Prentice Gautt 2.25	1.10	.22
☐ 151	Taz Anderson 1.75	.85	.17
☐ 152	Ernie McMillan 2.50	1.25	.25
☐ 153	Jimmy Hill 1.75	.85	.17
☐ 154	Bill Koman 1.75	.85	.17
☐ 155	Larry Wilson 28.00	14.00	2.80
☐ 156	Don Owens 1.75	.85	.17
☐ 157	St. Louis Cardinals .... 10.00 Team Card SP	5.00	1.00
☐ 158	Norm Snead SP 6.00	3.00	.60
☐ 159	Bobby Mitchell SP 9.00	4.50	.90
☐ 160	Bill Barnes SP 4.50	2.25	.45
☐ 161	Fred Dugan SP 4.50	2.25	.45
☐ 162	Don Bosseler SP 4.50	2.25	.45
☐ 163	John Nisby SP 4.50	2.25	.45
☐ 164	Riley Mattson SP 4.50	2.25	.45
☐ 165	Bob Toneff SP 4.50	2.25	.45
☐ 166	Rod Breedlove SP 4.50	2.25	.45
☐ 167	Dick James SP 4.50	2.25	.45
☐ 168	Claud Crabb SP 4.50	2.25	.45
☐ 169	Washington Redskins . 10.00 Team Card SP	5.00	1.00
☐ 170	Checklist Card 56.00	5.00	1.00

1964 Topps

The 1964 Topps football set contains 176 American Football League (AFL) player cards. The cards measure the standard 2 1/2" by 3 1/2" and are grouped by teams. Because the cards were not printed on a standard 132-card sheet, some cards are printed in lesser

quantities than others. These cards are marked in the checklist with SP for short print. The backs of the cards contain the card number, vital statistics, a short biography, the player's record for the past year and his career, and a cartoon-illustrated question and answer section. The cards are organized alphabetically within teams, for example: Boston Patriots (1-21), Buffalo Bills (22-43), Denver Broncos (44-65), Houston Oilers (66-88), Kansas City Chiefs (89-110), New York Jets (111-131), Oakland Raiders (132-153), and San Diego Chargers (154-175). The key rookie cards in this set are Bobby Bell, Buck Buchanan, John Hadl, and Daryle Lamonica.

	NRMT	VG-E	GOOD
COMPLETE SET (176) 1275.00	600.00	165.00
COMMON PLAYER (1-176) 2.50	1.25	.25
COMMON PLAYER SP 6.00	3.00	.60

			NRMT	VG-E	GOOD
☐ 1	Tommy Addison SP 30.00	5.00	1.00
☐ 2	Houston Antwine 3.75	1.85	.37
☐ 3	Nick Buoniconti 8.50	4.25	.85
☐ 4	Ron Burton SP 7.00	3.50	.70
☐ 5	Gino Cappelletti 4.00	2.00	.40
☐ 6	Jim Colclough SP 6.00	3.00	.60
☐ 7	Bob Dee SP 6.00	3.00	.60
☐ 8	Larry Eisenhauer 3.75	1.85	.37
☐ 9	Dick Felt SP 6.00	3.00	.60
☐ 10	Larry Garron 2.50	1.25	.25
☐ 11	Art Graham 2.50	1.25	.25
☐ 12	Ron Hall 2.50	1.25	.25
☐ 13	Charles Long 2.50	1.25	.25
☐ 14	Don McKinnon 2.50	1.25	.25
☐ 15	Don Oakes SP 6.00	3.00	.60
☐ 16	Ross O'Hanley SP 6.00	3.00	.60
☐ 17	Babe Parilli SP 7.50	3.75	.75
☐ 18	Jesse Richardson SP ... 6.00	3.00	.60
☐ 19	Jack Rudolph SP 6.00	3.00	.60
☐ 20	Don Webb 3.75	1.85	.37

☐ 21 Boston Patriots 6.50	3.25	.65
Team Card		
☐ 22 Ray Abbruzzese 2.50	1.25	.25
☐ 23 Stew Barber 3.75	1.85	.37
☐ 24 Dave Behrman 2.50	1.25	.25
☐ 25 Al Bemiller 2.50	1.25	.25
☐ 26 Elbert Dubenion SP 7.50	3.75	.75
☐ 27 Jim Dunaway SP 8.50	4.25	.85
☐ 28 Booker Edgerson SP 6.00	3.00	.60
☐ 29 Cookie Gilchrist SP 8.50	4.25	.85
☐ 30 Jack Kemp SP 125.00	60.00	12.50
☐ 31 Daryle Lamonica 50.00	25.00	5.00
☐ 32 Bill Miller 2.50	1.25	.25
☐ 33 Herb Paterra 3.75	1.85	.37
☐ 34 Ken Rice SP 6.00	3.00	.60
☐ 35 Ed Rutkowski 2.50	1.25	.25
☐ 36 George Saimes 4.50	2.25	.45
☐ 37 Tom Sestak 3.75	1.85	.37
☐ 38 Billy Shaw SP 6.00	3.00	.60
☐ 39 Mike Stratton 3.00	1.50	.30
☐ 40 Gene Sykes 2.50	1.25	.25
☐ 41 John Tracey SP 6.00	3.00	.60
☐ 42 Sid Youngelman SP 6.00	3.00	.60
☐ 43 Buffalo Bills 6.50	3.25	.65
Team Card		
☐ 44 Eldon Danenhauer SP 7.00	3.50	.70
☐ 45 Jim Fraser SP 6.00	3.00	.60
☐ 46 Chuck Gavin SP 6.00	3.00	.60
☐ 47 Goose Gonsoulin SP 7.00	3.50	.70
☐ 48 Ernie Barnes 4.00	2.00	.40
☐ 49 Tom Janik 2.50	1.25	.25
☐ 50 Billy Joe 4.00	2.00	.40
☐ 51 Ike Lassiter 4.00	2.00	.40
☐ 52 John McCormick SP 6.00	3.00	.60
☐ 53 Bud McFadin SP 6.00	3.00	.60
☐ 54 Gene Mingo SP 6.00	3.00	.60
☐ 55 Charlie Mitchell 2.50	1.25	.25
☐ 56 John Nocera SP 6.00	3.00	.60
☐ 57 Tom Nomina SP 2.50	1.25	.25
☐ 58 Harold Olson SP 6.00	3.00	.60
☐ 59 Bob Scarpitto 2.50	1.25	.25
☐ 60 John Sklopan 2.50	1.25	.25
☐ 61 Mickey Slaughter 3.50	1.75	.35
☐ 62 Don Stone 2.50	1.25	.25
☐ 63 Jerry Sturm 2.50	1.25	.25
☐ 64 Lionel Taylor SP 8.50	4.25	.85
☐ 65 Denver Broncos SP 12.50	6.25	1.25
Team Card		
☐ 66 Scott Appleton 4.50	2.25	.45
☐ 67 Tony Banfield SP 6.00	3.00	.60
☐ 68 George Blanda SP 60.00	30.00	6.00
☐ 69 Billy Cannon 4.50	2.25	.45
☐ 70 Doug Cline SP 6.00	3.00	.60
☐ 71 Gary Cutsinger SP 6.00	3.00	.60
☐ 72 Willard Dewveall SP 6.00	3.00	.60
☐ 73 Don Floyd SP 6.00	3.00	.60
☐ 74 Freddy Glick SP 6.00	3.00	.60
☐ 75 Charlie Hennigan SP 7.50	3.75	.75
☐ 76 Ed Husmann SP 6.00	3.00	.60
☐ 77 Bobby Jancik SP 7.50	3.75	.75
☐ 78 Jacky Lee SP 7.00	3.50	.70
☐ 79 Bob McLeod SP 5.00	2.50	.50
☐ 80 Rich Michael SP 5.00	2.50	.50
☐ 81 Larry Onesti 2.50	1.25	.25
☐ 82 Checklist Card 30.00	3.00	.60
☐ 83 Bob Schmidt SP 6.00	3.00	.60
☐ 84 Walt Suggs SP 6.00	3.00	.60
☐ 85 Bob Talamini SP 6.00	3.00	.60
☐ 86 Charley Tolar SP 7.00	3.50	.70
☐ 87 Don Trull 4.00	2.00	.40
☐ 88 Houston Oilers 6.50	3.25	.65
Team Card		
☐ 89 Fred Arbanas 3.75	1.85	.37
☐ 90 Bobby Bell 27.00	13.50	2.70
☐ 91 Mel Branch SP 7.00	3.50	.70
☐ 92 Buck Buchanan 27.00	13.50	2.70
☐ 93 Ed Budde 7.00	3.50	.70
☐ 94 Chris Burford SP 7.00	3.50	.70
☐ 95 Walt Corey 2.50	1.25	.25
☐ 96 Len Dawson SP 65.00	32.50	6.50
☐ 97 Dave Grayson 4.00	2.00	.40
☐ 98 Abner Haynes 4.50	2.25	.45
☐ 99 Sherrill Headrick SP 7.00	3.50	.70
☐ 100 E.J. Holub 4.00	2.00	.40
☐ 101 Bobby Hunt 3.00	1.50	.30
☐ 102 Frank Jackson SP 6.00	3.00	.60
☐ 103 Curtis McClinton 4.00	2.00	.40
☐ 104 Jerry Mays SP 7.00	3.50	.70
☐ 105 Johnny Robinson SP 7.50	3.75	.75
☐ 106 Jack Spikes SP 7.00	3.50	.70
☐ 107 Smokey Stover SP 6.00	3.00	.60
☐ 108 Jim Tyrer SP 7.00	3.50	.70
☐ 109 Duane Wood SP 7.00	3.50	.70
☐ 110 Kansas City Chiefs 6.50	3.25	.65
Team Card		
☐ 111 Dick Christy SP 6.00	3.00	.60
☐ 112 Dan Ficca SP 6.00	3.00	.60
☐ 113 Larry Grantham 3.75	1.85	.37
☐ 114 Curley Johnson SP 6.00	3.00	.60
☐ 115 Gene Heeter 2.50	1.25	.25
☐ 116 Jack Klotz 2.50	1.25	.25
☐ 117 Pete Liske 4.00	2.00	.40
☐ 118 Bob McAdam 2.50	1.25	.25
☐ 119 Dee Mackey SP 6.00	3.00	.60
☐ 120 Bill Mathis SP 6.00	3.00	.60
☐ 121 Don Maynard 21.00	10.50	2.10
☐ 122 Dainard Paulson SP 6.00	3.00	.60
☐ 123 Gerry Philbin 4.00	2.00	.40
☐ 124 Mark Smolinski SP 6.00	3.00	.60
☐ 125 Matt Snell 10.00	5.00	1.00
☐ 126 Mike Taliaferro 3.00	1.50	.30
☐ 127 Bake Turner SP 8.00	4.00	.80
☐ 128 Jeff Ware 2.50	1.25	.25
☐ 129 Clyde Washington 2.50	1.25	.25

☐ 130	Dick Wood	3.50	1.75	.35
☐ 131	New York Jets Team Card	6.50	3.25	.65
☐ 132	Dalva Allen SP	6.00	3.00	.60
☐ 133	Dan Birdwell	2.50	1.25	.25
☐ 134	Dave Costa	3.50	1.75	.35
☐ 135	Dobie Craig	2.50	1.25	.25
☐ 136	Clem Daniels	3.75	1.85	.37
☐ 137	Cotton Davidson SP	7.00	3.50	.70
☐ 138	Claude Gibson	2.50	1.25	.25
☐ 139	Tom Flores SP	10.00	5.00	1.00
☐ 140	Wayne Hawkins SP	6.00	3.00	.60
☐ 141	Ken Herock	2.50	1.25	.25
☐ 142	Jon Jelacic SP	6.00	3.00	.60
☐ 143	Joe Krakoski	2.50	1.25	.25
☐ 144	Archie Matsos SP	6.00	3.00	.60
☐ 145	Mike Mercer	2.50	1.25	.25
☐ 146	Alan Miller SP	6.00	3.00	.60
☐ 147	Bob Mischak SP	6.00	3.00	.60
☐ 148	Jim Otto SP	17.00	8.50	1.70
☐ 149	Clancy Osborne SP	6.00	3.00	.60
☐ 150	Art Powell SP	8.00	4.00	.80
☐ 151	Bo Roberson (Raider helmet placed over his foot)	2.50	1.25	.25
☐ 152	Fred Williamson SP	8.00	4.00	.80
☐ 153	Oakland Raiders Team Card	6.50	3.25	.65
☐ 154	Chuck Allen SP	6.00	3.00	.60
☐ 155	Lance Alworth	32.00	16.00	3.20
☐ 156	George Blair	2.50	1.25	.25
☐ 157	Earl Faison	3.00	1.50	.30
☐ 158	Sam Gruniesen	2.50	1.25	.25
☐ 159	John Hadl	20.00	10.00	2.00
☐ 160	Dick Harris SP	6.00	3.00	.60
☐ 161	Emil Karas SP	6.00	3.00	.60
☐ 162	Dave Kocourek SP	7.00	3.50	.70
☐ 163	Ernie Ladd	5.00	2.50	.50
☐ 164	Keith Lincoln	4.50	2.25	.45
☐ 165	Paul Lowe SP	8.00	4.00	.80
☐ 166	Charles McNeil	3.75	1.85	.37
☐ 167	Jacque MacKinnon SP	6.00	3.00	.60
☐ 168	Ron Mix SP	13.50	6.50	1.25
☐ 169	Don Norton SP	6.00	3.00	.60
☐ 170	Don Rogers SP	6.00	3.00	.60
☐ 171	Tobin Rote SP	7.50	3.75	.75
☐ 172	Henry Schmidt SP	6.00	3.00	.60
☐ 173	Bud Whitehead	2.50	1.25	.25
☐ 174	Ernie Wright SP	6.00	3.00	.60
☐ 175	San Diego Chargers Team Card	6.50	3.25	.65
☐ 176	Checklist SP	125.00	12.50	2.50

1965 Topps

JACK KEMP quarterback

The 1965 Topps football card set contains 176 oversized (2 1/2" by 4 11/16") cards of American Football League players. The cards are grouped together and numbered in basic alphabetical order by teams: for example, Boston Patriots (1-22), Buffalo Bills (23-44), Denver Broncos (45-65), Houston Oilers (66-88), Kansas City Chiefs (89-110), New York Jets (111-131), Oakland Raiders (132-153), and San Diego Chargers (154-175). Since this set was not printed in the standard fashion, many of the cards were printed in lesser quantities than others. These cards are marked in the checklist with SP for short print. This set is somewhat significant in that it contains the rookie card of Joe Namath. Other notable rookie cards in this set are Fred Biletnikoff, Willie Brown, and Ben Davidson.

	NRMT	VG-E	GOOD
COMPLETE SET (176)	3650.00	1650.00	425.00
COMMON PLAYER (1-176)	6.00	3.00	.60
COMMON PLAYER	12.00	6.00	1.20

☐ 1	Tommy Addison SP	42.00	7.50	1.50
☐ 2	Houston Antwine SP	12.00	6.00	1.20
☐ 3	Nick Buoniconti SP	18.00	9.00	1.80
☐ 4	Ron Burton SP	13.50	6.50	1.35
☐ 5	Gino Cappelletti SP	16.50	8.00	1.65
☐ 6	Jim Colclough	6.00	3.00	.60
☐ 7	Bob Dee SP	12.00	6.00	1.20
☐ 8	Larry Eisenhauer	7.00	3.50	.70
☐ 9	J.D. Garrett	6.00	3.00	.60

☐ 10 Larry Garron	6.00	3.00	.60
☐ 11 Art Graham SP	12.00	6.00	1.20
☐ 12 Ron Hall	6.00	3.00	.60
☐ 13 Charles Long	6.00	3.00	.60
☐ 14 Jon Morris	8.00	4.00	.80
☐ 15 Bill Neighbors SP	12.00	6.00	1.20
☐ 16 Ross O'Hanley	6.00	3.00	.60
☐ 17 Babe Parilli SP	13.50	6.50	1.35
☐ 18 Tony Romeo SP	12.00	6.00	1.20
☐ 19 Jack Rudolph SP	12.00	6.00	1.20
☐ 20 Bob Schmidt	6.00	3.00	.60
☐ 21 Don Webb SP	12.00	6.00	1.20
☐ 22 Jim Whalen SP	12.00	6.00	1.20
☐ 23 Stew Barber	6.00	3.00	.60
☐ 24 Glenn Bass SP	12.00	6.00	1.20
☐ 25 Al Bemiller SP	12.00	6.00	1.20
☐ 26 Wray Carlton SP	13.50	6.50	1.35
☐ 27 Tom Day	6.00	3.00	.60
☐ 28 Elbert Dubenion SP	13.50	6.50	1.35
☐ 29 Jim Dunaway	6.00	3.00	.60
☐ 30 Pete Gogolak SP	15.00	7.50	1.50
☐ 31 Dick Hudson SP	12.00	6.00	1.20
☐ 32 Harry Jacobs SP	12.00	6.00	1.20
☐ 33 Billy Joe SP	13.50	6.50	1.35
☐ 34 Tom Keating SP	15.00	7.50	1.50
☐ 35 Jack Kemp SP	210.00	90.00	18.00
☐ 36 Daryle Lamonica SP	24.00	12.00	2.40
☐ 37 Paul Maguire SP	16.00	8.00	1.60
☐ 38 Ron McDole SP	15.00	7.50	1.50
☐ 39 George Saimes SP	13.50	6.50	1.35
☐ 40 Tom Sestak SP	13.50	6.50	1.35
☐ 41 Billy Shaw SP	12.00	6.00	1.20
☐ 42 Mike Stratton SP	13.50	6.50	1.35
☐ 43 John Tracey SP	12.00	6.00	1.20
☐ 44 Ernie Warlick	6.00	3.00	.60
☐ 45 Odell Barry	6.00	3.00	.60
☐ 46 Willie Brown SP	50.00	25.00	5.00
☐ 47 Gerry Bussell SP	12.00	6.00	1.20
☐ 48 Eldon Danenhauer SP	13.50	6.50	1.35
☐ 49 Al Denson SP	12.00	6.00	1.20
☐ 50 Hewritt Dixon SP	15.00	7.50	1.50
☐ 51 Cookie Gilchrist SP	16.00	8.00	1.60
☐ 52 Goose Gonsoulin SP	13.50	6.50	1.35
☐ 53 Abner Haynes SP	16.00	8.00	1.60
☐ 54 Jerry Hopkins	6.00	3.00	.60
☐ 55 Ray Jacobs SP	12.00	6.00	1.20
☐ 56 Jacky Lee SP	13.50	6.50	1.35
☐ 57 John McCormick	6.00	3.00	.60
☐ 58 Bob McCullough SP	12.00	6.00	1.20
☐ 59 John McGeever	6.00	3.00	.60
☐ 60 Charlie Mitchell SP	12.00	6.00	1.20
☐ 61 Jim Perkins SP	12.00	6.00	1.20
☐ 62 Bob Scarpitto SP	12.00	6.00	1.20
☐ 63 Mickey Slaughter SP	12.00	6.00	1.20
☐ 64 Jerry Sturm SP	12.00	6.00	1.20
☐ 65 Lionel Taylor SP	16.00	8.00	1.60
☐ 66 Scott Appleton SP	13.50	6.50	1.35
☐ 67 Johnny Baker SP	12.00	6.00	1.20
☐ 68 Sonny Bishop SP	12.00	6.00	1.20
☐ 69 George Blanda SP	80.00	40.00	8.00
☐ 70 Sid Blanks SP	12.00	6.00	1.20
☐ 71 Ode Burrell SP	12.00	6.00	1.20
☐ 72 Doug Cline SP	12.00	6.00	1.20
☐ 73 Willard Dewveall	6.00	3.00	.60
☐ 74 Larry Elkins	9.00	4.50	.90
☐ 75 Don Floyd SP	12.00	6.00	1.20
☐ 76 Freddy Glick	6.00	3.00	.60
☐ 77 Tom Goode SP	12.00	6.00	1.20
☐ 78 Charlie Hennigan SP	16.00	8.00	1.60
☐ 79 Ed Husmann	6.00	3.00	.60
☐ 80 Bobby Jancik SP	12.00	6.00	1.20
☐ 81 Bud McFadin SP	12.00	6.00	1.20
☐ 82 Bob McLeod SP	12.00	6.00	1.20
☐ 83 Jim Norton SP	12.00	6.00	1.20
☐ 84 Walt Suggs	6.00	3.00	.60
☐ 85 Bob Talamini	6.00	3.00	.60
☐ 86 Charley Tolar SP	13.50	6.50	1.35
☐ 87 Checklist 1-88 SP	120.00	12.50	2.50
☐ 88 Don Trull SP	13.50	6.50	1.35
☐ 89 Fred Arbanas SP	13.50	6.50	1.35
☐ 90 Pete Beathard SP	22.00	11.00	2.20
☐ 91 Bobby Bell SP	22.00	11.00	2.20
☐ 92 Mel Branch SP	12.00	6.00	1.20
☐ 93 Tommy Brooker SP	12.00	6.00	1.20
☐ 94 Buck Buchanan SP	22.00	11.00	2.20
☐ 95 Ed Budde SP	15.00	7.50	1.50
☐ 96 Chris Burford SP	13.50	6.50	1.35
☐ 97 Walt Corey	6.00	3.00	.60
☐ 98 Jerry Cornelison	6.00	3.00	.60
☐ 99 Len Dawson SP	65.00	32.50	6.50
☐ 100 Jon Gilliam SP	12.00	6.00	1.20
☐ 101 Sherrill Headrick SP	13.50	6.50	1.35
☐ 102 Dave Hill SP	12.00	6.00	1.20
☐ 103 E.J. Holub SP	13.50	6.50	1.35
☐ 104 Bobby Hunt SP	12.00	6.00	1.20
☐ 105 Frank Jackson SP	12.00	6.00	1.20
☐ 106 Jerry Mays	7.00	3.50	.70
☐ 107 Curtis McClinton SP	13.50	6.50	1.35
☐ 108 Bobby Ply SP	12.00	6.00	1.20
☐ 109 Johnny Robinson SP	15.00	7.50	1.50
☐ 110 Jim Tyrer SP	13.50	6.50	1.35
☐ 111 Bill Baird SP	12.00	6.00	1.20
☐ 112 Ralph Baker SP	13.50	6.50	1.35
☐ 113 Sam DeLuca SP	12.00	6.00	1.20
☐ 114 Larry Grantham SP	13.50	6.50	1.35
☐ 115 Gene Heeter SP	12.00	6.00	1.20
☐ 116 Winston Hill SP	16.00	8.00	1.60
☐ 117 John Huarte SP	22.00	11.00	2.20
☐ 118 Cosmo Iacavazzi SP	12.00	6.00	1.20
☐ 119 Curley Johnson SP	12.00	6.00	1.20
☐ 120 Dee Mackey UER	6.00	3.00	.60
(College WVU, should			
be East Texas State)			
☐ 121 Don Maynard	35.00	17.50	3.50

☐ 122 Joe Namath SP	1250.00	450.00	90.00
☐ 123 Dainard Paulson	6.00	3.00	.60
☐ 124 Gerry Philbin SP	12.00	6.00	1.20
☐ 125 Sherman Plunkett SP	15.00	7.50	1.50
☐ 126 Mark Smolinski	6.00	3.00	.60
☐ 127 Matt Snell SP	16.00	8.00	1.60
☐ 128 Mike Taliaferro SP	12.00	6.00	1.20
☐ 129 Bake Turner SP	13.50	6.50	1.35
☐ 130 Clyde Washington SP	12.00	6.00	1.20
☐ 131 Verlon Biggs SP	15.00	7.50	1.50
☐ 132 Dalva Allen	6.00	3.00	.60
☐ 133 Fred Biletnikoff SP	150.00	75.00	15.00
☐ 134 Billy Cannon SP	16.00	8.00	1.60
☐ 135 Dave Costa SP	12.00	6.00	1.20
☐ 136 Clem Daniels SP	13.50	6.50	1.35
☐ 137 Ben Davidson SP	35.00	17.50	3.50
☐ 138 Cotton Davidson SP	13.50	6.50	1.35
☐ 139 Tom Flores SP	16.00	8.00	1.60
☐ 140 Claude Gibson	6.00	3.00	.60
☐ 141 Wayne Hawkins	6.00	3.00	.60
☐ 142 Archie Matsos SP	12.00	6.00	1.20
☐ 143 Mike Mercer SP	12.00	6.00	1.20
☐ 144 Bob Mischak SP	12.00	6.00	1.20
☐ 145 Jim Otto	22.00	11.00	2.20
☐ 146 Art Powell SP	16.00	8.00	1.60
☐ 147 Warren Powers SP	13.50	6.50	1.35
☐ 148 Ken Rice SP	12.00	6.00	1.20
☐ 149 Bo Roberson SP	12.00	6.00	1.20
☐ 150 Harry Schuh	9.00	4.50	.90
☐ 151 Larry Todd SP	12.00	6.00	1.20
☐ 152 Fred Williamson SP	16.00	8.00	1.60
☐ 153 J.R. Williamson	6.00	3.00	.60
☐ 154 Chuck Allen	6.00	3.00	.60
☐ 155 Lance Alworth	50.00	25.00	5.00
☐ 156 Frank Buncom	6.00	3.00	.60
☐ 157 Steve DeLong SP	15.00	7.50	1.50
☐ 158 Earl Faison SP	12.00	6.00	1.20
☐ 159 Kenny Graham SP	12.00	6.00	1.20
☐ 160 George Gross SP	12.00	6.00	1.20
☐ 161 John Hadl SP	20.00	10.00	2.00
☐ 162 Emil Karas SP	12.00	6.00	1.20
☐ 163 Dave Kocourek SP	13.50	6.50	1.35
☐ 164 Ernie Ladd SP	17.00	8.50	1.70
☐ 165 Keith Lincoln SP	17.00	8.50	1.70
☐ 166 Paul Lowe SP	16.00	8.00	1.60
☐ 167 Jacque MacKinnon	6.00	3.00	.60
☐ 168 Ron Mix	16.00	8.00	1.60
☐ 169 Don Norton SP	12.00	6.00	1.20
☐ 170 Bob Petrich	6.00	3.00	.60
☐ 171 Rick Redman SP	12.00	6.00	1.20
☐ 172 Pat Shea	6.00	3.00	.60
☐ 173 Walt Sweeney SP	16.00	8.00	1.60
☐ 174 Dick Westmoreland SP	8.00	4.00	.80
☐ 175 Ernie Wright SP	12.00	6.00	1.20
☐ 176 Checklist 89-176 SP	180.00	17.50	3.50

1966 Topps

The 1966 Topps set of 132 cards contains AFL players grouped together and numbered alphabetically within teams, for example: Boston Patriots (1-14), Buffalo Bills (16-30), Denver Broncos (31-45), Houston Oilers (46-60), Kansas City Chiefs (62-75), Miami Dolphins (76-89), New York Jets (90-103), Oakland Raiders (104-117), and San Diego Chargers (118-131). The cards measure 2 1/2" by 3 1/2". The card backs are printed in black and pink on white card stock. In actuality, card number 15 is not a football card at all but a "Funny Ring" checklist card; nevertheless, it is considered part of the set and is now regarded as the toughest card in the set to find in mint condition. The only notable rookie cards in this set are George Sauer Jr., Otis Taylor, and Jim Turner.

	NRMT	VG-E	GOOD
COMPLETE SET (132)	1250.00	125.00	25.00
COMMON PLAYER (1-132)	3.25	1.60	.32

☐ 1 Tommy Addison	21.00	2.50	.50
☐ 2 Houston Antwine	3.25	1.60	.32
☐ 3 Nick Buoniconti	6.50	3.25	.65
☐ 4 Gino Cappelletti	4.50	2.25	.45
☐ 5 Bob Dee	3.25	1.60	.32
☐ 6 Larry Garron	3.25	1.60	.32
☐ 7 Art Graham	3.25	1.60	.32
☐ 8 Ron Hall	3.25	1.60	.32
☐ 9 Charles Long	3.25	1.60	.32
☐ 10 Jon Morris	3.25	1.60	.32
☐ 11 Don Oakes	3.25	1.60	.32
☐ 12 Babe Parilli	4.50	2.25	.45
☐ 13 Don Webb	3.25	1.60	.32
☐ 14 Jim Whalen	3.25	1.60	.32
☐ 15 Funny Ring Checklist	325.00	50.00	10.00

☐ 16 Stew Barber	3.25	1.60	.32
☐ 17 Glenn Bass	3.25	1.60	.32
☐ 18 Dave Behrman	3.25	1.60	.32
☐ 19 Al Bemiller	3.25	1.60	.32
☐ 20 George(Butch) Byrd	4.50	2.25	.45
☐ 21 Wray Carlton	3.75	1.85	.37
☐ 22 Tom Day	3.25	1.60	.32
☐ 23 Elbert Dubenion	4.00	2.00	.40
☐ 24 Jim Dunaway	3.25	1.60	.32
☐ 25 Dick Hudson	3.25	1.60	.32
☐ 26 Jack Kemp	120.00	60.00	12.00
☐ 27 Daryle Lamonica	6.50	3.25	.65
☐ 28 Tom Sestak	4.00	2.00	.40
☐ 29 Billy Shaw	3.25	1.60	.32
☐ 30 Mike Stratton	3.75	1.85	.37
☐ 31 Eldon Danenhauer	3.75	1.85	.37
☐ 32 Cookie Gilchrist	4.50	2.25	.45
☐ 33 Goose Gonsoulin	3.75	1.85	.37
☐ 34 Wendell Hayes	5.50	2.75	.55
☐ 35 Abner Haynes	4.50	2.25	.45
☐ 36 Jerry Hopkins	3.25	1.60	.32
☐ 37 Ray Jacobs	3.25	1.60	.32
☐ 38 Charlie Janerette	3.25	1.60	.32
☐ 39 Ray Kubala	3.25	1.60	.32
☐ 40 John McCormick	3.25	1.60	.32
☐ 41 Leroy Moore	3.25	1.60	.32
☐ 42 Bob Scarpitto	3.25	1.60	.32
☐ 43 Mickey Slaughter	3.25	1.60	.32
☐ 44 Jerry Sturm	3.25	1.60	.32
☐ 45 Lionel Taylor	4.50	2.25	.45
☐ 46 Scott Appleton	3.75	1.85	.37
☐ 47 Johnny Baker	3.25	1.60	.32
☐ 48 George Blanda	38.00	17.00	3.50
☐ 49 Sid Blanks	3.25	1.60	.32
☐ 50 Danny Brabham	3.25	1.60	.32
☐ 51 Ode Burrell	3.25	1.60	.32
☐ 52 Gary Cutsinger	3.25	1.60	.32
☐ 53 Larry Elkins	3.75	1.85	.37
☐ 54 Don Floyd	3.25	1.60	.32
☐ 55 Willie Frazier	5.00	2.50	.50
☐ 56 Freddy Glick	3.25	1.60	.32
☐ 57 Charlie Hennigan	4.50	2.25	.45
☐ 58 Bobby Jancik	3.25	1.60	.32
☐ 59 Rich Michael	3.25	1.60	.32
☐ 60 Don Trull	4.00	2.00	.40
☐ 61 Checklist Card	35.00	3.50	.75
☐ 62 Fred Arbanas	4.00	2.00	.40
☐ 63 Pete Beathard	4.50	2.25	.45
☐ 64 Bobby Bell	7.50	3.75	.75
☐ 65 Ed Budde	4.00	2.00	.40
☐ 66 Chris Burford	3.75	1.85	.37
☐ 67 Len Dawson	21.00	10.50	2.10
☐ 68 Jon Gilliam	3.25	1.60	.32
☐ 69 Sherrill Headrick	3.75	1.85	.37
☐ 70 E.J. Holub UER	4.00	2.00	.40
(College: TCU, should be Texas Tech)			

☐ 71 Bobby Hunt	3.25	1.60	.32
☐ 72 Curtis McClinton	4.00	2.00	.40
☐ 73 Jerry Mays	4.00	2.00	.40
☐ 74 Johnny Robinson	4.50	2.25	.45
☐ 75 Otis Taylor	12.50	6.25	1.25
☐ 76 Tom Erlandson	3.25	1.60	.32
☐ 77 Norm Evans UER	4.50	2.25	.45
(Flanker on front, tackle on back)			
☐ 78 Tom Goode	3.25	1.60	.32
☐ 79 Mike Hudock	3.25	1.60	.32
☐ 80 Frank Jackson	3.25	1.60	.32
☐ 81 Billy Joe	3.25	1.60	.32
☐ 82 Dave Kocourek	3.25	1.60	.32
☐ 83 Bo Roberson	3.25	1.60	.32
☐ 84 Jack Spikes	4.00	2.00	.40
☐ 85 Jim Warren	4.50	2.25	.45
☐ 86 Willie West	4.50	2.25	.45
☐ 87 Dick Westmoreland	3.25	1.60	.32
☐ 88 Eddie Wilson	3.25	1.60	.32
☐ 89 Dick Wood	3.25	1.60	.32
☐ 90 Verlon Biggs	4.00	2.00	.40
☐ 91 Sam DeLuca	3.25	1.60	.32
☐ 92 Winston Hill	3.25	1.60	.32
☐ 93 Dee Mackey	3.25	1.60	.32
☐ 94 Bill Mathis	3.25	1.60	.32
☐ 95 Don Maynard	18.00	9.00	1.80
☐ 96 Joe Namath	250.00	125.00	25.00
☐ 97 Dainard Paulson	3.25	1.60	.32
☐ 98 Gerry Philbin	3.25	1.60	.32
☐ 99 Sherman Plunkett	3.25	1.60	.32
☐ 100 Paul Rochester	3.25	1.60	.32
☐ 101 George Sauer Jr.	7.50	3.75	.75
☐ 102 Matt Snell	4.50	2.25	.45
☐ 103 Jim Turner	5.50	2.75	.55
☐ 104 Fred Biletnikoff UER	50.00	25.00	5.00
(Misspelled on back as Bilentnikoff)			
☐ 105 Bill Budness	3.25	1.60	.32
☐ 106 Billy Cannon	4.50	2.25	.45
☐ 107 Clem Daniels	4.00	2.00	.40
☐ 108 Ben Davidson	4.50	2.25	.45
☐ 109 Cotton Davidson	4.00	2.00	.40
☐ 110 Claude Gibson	3.25	1.60	.32
☐ 111 Wayne Hawkins	3.25	1.60	.32
☐ 112 Ken Herock	3.25	1.60	.32
☐ 113 Bob Mischak	3.25	1.60	.32
☐ 114 Gus Otto	3.25	1.60	.32
☐ 115 Jim Otto	12.50	6.25	1.25
☐ 116 Art Powell	4.50	2.25	.45
☐ 117 Harry Schuh	3.25	1.60	.32
☐ 118 Chuck Allen	3.25	1.60	.32
☐ 119 Lance Alworth	25.00	12.50	2.50
☐ 120 Frank Buncom	3.25	1.60	.32
☐ 121 Steve DeLong	3.25	1.60	.32
☐ 122 John Farris	3.25	1.60	.32
☐ 123 Kenny Graham	3.25	1.60	.32

☐ 124 Sam Gruniesen	3.25	1.60	.32
☐ 125 John Hadl	7.00	3.50	.70
☐ 126 Walt Sweeney	3.75	1.85	.37
☐ 127 Keith Lincoln	4.50	2.25	.45
☐ 128 Ron Mix	7.00	3.50	.70
☐ 129 Don Norton	3.25	1.60	.32
☐ 130 Pat Shea	3.25	1.60	.32
☐ 131 Ernie Wright	3.25	1.60	.32
☐ 132 Checklist Card	80.00	7.50	1.50

1967 Topps

The 1967 Topps set of 132 cards contains AFL players only, with players grouped together and numbered by teams, for example: Boston Patriots (1-14), Buffalo Bills (15-29), Denver Broncos (30-43), Houston Oilers (44-58), Kansas City Chiefs (60-73), Miami Dolphins (74-88), New York Jets (89-102), Oakland Raiders (103-116), and San Diego Chargers (117-131). The cards measure 2 1/2" by 3 1/2". The card backs are printed in gold and black on white card stock. A question (with upside-down answer) is given on the bottom of the reverse. The only notable rookie card in this set is Wahoo McDaniel, who gained greater fame as a professional wrestler.

	MINT	VG-E	GOOD
COMPLETE SET (132)	525.00	250.00	50.00
COMMON PLAYER (1-132)	2.00	1.00	.20
☐ 1 John Huarte	10.00	2.00	.40
☐ 2 Babe Parilli	2.50	1.25	.25
☐ 3 Gino Cappelletti	3.00	1.50	.30
☐ 4 Larry Garron	2.00	1.00	.20
☐ 5 Tommy Addison	2.00	1.00	.20

☐ 6 Jon Morris	2.00	1.00	.20
☐ 7 Houston Antwine	2.00	1.00	.20
☐ 8 Don Oakes	2.00	1.00	.20
☐ 9 Larry Eisenhauer	2.50	1.25	.25
☐ 10 Jim Hunt	2.00	1.00	.20
☐ 11 Jim Whalen	2.00	1.00	.20
☐ 12 Art Graham	2.00	1.00	.20
☐ 13 Nick Buoniconti	3.50	1.75	.35
☐ 14 Bob Dee	2.00	1.00	.20
☐ 15 Keith Lincoln	3.25	1.60	.32
☐ 16 Tom Flores	3.50	1.75	.35
☐ 17 Art Powell	3.00	1.50	.30
☐ 18 Stew Barber	2.00	1.00	.20
☐ 19 Wray Carlton	2.50	1.25	.25
☐ 20 Elbert Dubenion	2.50	1.25	.25
☐ 21 Jim Dunaway	2.00	1.00	.20
☐ 22 Dick Hudson	2.00	1.00	.20
☐ 23 Harry Jacobs	2.00	1.00	.20
☐ 24 Jack Kemp	70.00	35.00	7.00
☐ 25 Ron McDole	2.50	1.25	.25
☐ 26 George Saimes	2.50	1.25	.25
☐ 27 Tom Sestak	2.50	1.25	.25
☐ 28 Billy Shaw	2.00	1.00	.20
☐ 29 Mike Stratton	2.50	1.25	.25
☐ 30 Nemiah Wilson	3.00	1.50	.30
☐ 31 John McCormick	2.00	1.00	.20
☐ 32 Rex Mirich	2.00	1.00	.20
☐ 33 Dave Costa	2.00	1.00	.20
☐ 34 Goose Gonsoulin	2.50	1.25	.25
☐ 35 Abner Haynes	3.25	1.60	.32
☐ 36 Wendell Hayes	2.50	1.25	.25
☐ 37 Archie Matsos	2.00	1.00	.20
☐ 38 John Bramlett	2.00	1.00	.20
☐ 39 Jerry Sturm	2.00	1.00	.20
☐ 40 Max Leetzow	2.00	1.00	.20
☐ 41 Bob Scarpitto	2.00	1.00	.20
☐ 42 Lionel Taylor	3.25	1.60	.32
☐ 43 Al Denson	2.00	1.00	.20
☐ 44 Miller Farr	3.00	1.50	.30
☐ 45 Don Trull	2.50	1.25	.25
☐ 46 Jacky Lee	2.50	1.25	.25
☐ 47 Bobby Jancik	2.00	1.00	.20
☐ 48 Ode Burrell	2.00	1.00	.20
☐ 49 Larry Elkins	2.50	1.25	.25
☐ 50 W.K. Hicks	2.00	1.00	.20
☐ 51 Sid Blanks	2.00	1.00	.20
☐ 52 Jim Norton	2.00	1.00	.20
☐ 53 Bobby Maples	3.00	1.50	.30
☐ 54 Bob Talamini	2.00	1.00	.20
☐ 55 Walt Suggs	2.00	1.00	.20
☐ 56 Gary Cutsinger	2.00	1.00	.20
☐ 57 Danny Brabham	2.00	1.00	.20
☐ 58 Ernie Ladd	4.00	2.00	.40
☐ 59 Checklist Card	27.00	2.50	.50
☐ 60 Pete Beathard	3.00	1.50	.30
☐ 61 Len Dawson	18.00	9.00	1.80
☐ 62 Bobby Hunt	2.00	1.00	.20

☐ 63	Bert Coan	2.00	1.00	.20
☐ 64	Curtis McClinton	2.50	1.25	.25
☐ 65	Johnny Robinson	2.75	1.35	.27
☐ 66	E.J. Holub	2.50	1.25	.25
☐ 67	Jerry Mays	2.50	1.25	.25
☐ 68	Jim Tyrer	2.50	1.25	.25
☐ 69	Bobby Bell	5.25	2.60	.50
☐ 70	Fred Arbanas	2.50	1.25	.25
☐ 71	Buck Buchanan	5.25	2.60	.50
☐ 72	Chris Burford	2.50	1.25	.25
☐ 73	Otis Taylor	4.00	2.00	.40
☐ 74	Cookie Gilchrist	3.25	1.60	.32
☐ 75	Earl Faison	2.00	1.00	.20
☐ 76	George Wilson	2.00	1.00	.20
☐ 77	Rick Norton	2.00	1.00	.20
☐ 78	Frank Jackson	2.00	1.00	.20
☐ 79	Joe Auer	2.00	1.00	.20
☐ 80	Willie West	2.50	1.25	.25
☐ 81	Jim Warren	2.50	1.25	.25
☐ 82	Wahoo McDaniel	13.50	6.50	1.35
☐ 83	Ernie Park	2.00	1.00	.20
☐ 84	Bill Neighbors	2.00	1.00	.20
☐ 85	Norm Evans	2.50	1.25	.25
☐ 86	Tom Nomina	2.00	1.00	.20
☐ 87	Rich Zecher	2.00	1.00	.20
☐ 88	Dave Kocourek	2.00	1.00	.20
☐ 89	Bill Baird	2.00	1.00	.20
☐ 90	Ralph Baker	2.00	1.00	.20
☐ 91	Verlon Biggs	2.00	1.00	.20
☐ 92	Sam DeLuca	2.00	1.00	.20
☐ 93	Larry Grantham	2.50	1.25	.25
☐ 94	Jim Harris	2.00	1.00	.20
☐ 95	Winston Hill	2.00	1.00	.20
☐ 96	Bill Mathis	2.00	1.00	.20
☐ 97	Don Maynard	15.00	7.50	1.50
☐ 98	Joe Namath	135.00	65.00	13.50
☐ 99	Gerry Philbin	2.00	1.00	.20
☐ 100	Paul Rochester	2.00	1.00	.20
☐ 101	George Sauer Jr.	3.25	1.60	.32
☐ 102	Matt Snell	3.25	1.60	.32
☐ 103	Daryle Lamonica	4.50	2.25	.45
☐ 104	Glenn Bass	2.00	1.00	.20
☐ 105	Jim Otto	5.50	2.75	.55
☐ 106	Fred Biletnikoff	20.00	10.00	2.00
☐ 107	Cotton Davidson	2.50	1.25	.25
☐ 108	Larry Todd	2.00	1.00	.20
☐ 109	Billy Cannon	3.25	1.60	.32
☐ 110	Clem Daniels	2.50	1.25	.25
☐ 111	Dave Grayson	2.00	1.00	.20
☐ 112	Kent McCloughan	2.50	1.25	.25
☐ 113	Bob Svihus	2.00	1.00	.20
☐ 114	Ike Lassiter	2.00	1.00	.20
☐ 115	Harry Schuh	2.00	1.00	.20
☐ 116	Ben Davidson	3.50	1.75	.35
☐ 117	Tom Day	2.00	1.00	.20
☐ 118	Scott Appleton	2.50	1.25	.25
☐ 119	Steve Tensi	3.00	1.50	.30

☐ 120	John Hadl	4.25	2.10	.42
☐ 121	Paul Lowe	3.25	1.60	.32
☐ 122	Jim Allison	2.00	1.00	.20
☐ 123	Lance Alworth	18.00	9.00	1.80
☐ 124	Jacque MacKinnon	2.00	1.00	.20
☐ 125	Ron Mix	5.00	2.50	.50
☐ 126	Bob Petrich	2.00	1.00	.20
☐ 127	Howard Kindig	2.00	1.00	.20
☐ 128	Steve DeLong	2.00	1.00	.20
☐ 129	Chuck Allen	2.00	1.00	.20
☐ 130	Frank Buncom	2.00	1.00	.20
☐ 131	Speedy Duncan	3.25	1.60	.32
☐ 132	Checklist Card	50.00	5.00	1.00

1968 Topps

The 1968 Topps football set of 219 cards is Topps' first set in five years (since 1963) to contain NFL players. In fact, the set also includes AFL players even though the two rival leagues didn't formally merge until 1970. The second series (132-219) is slightly more difficult to obtain than the first series. The cards in the second series have blue printing on the back whereas the cards in the first series had green printing on the back. Cards for players from the previous year's Super Bowl teams, the Green Bay Packers and the Oakland Raiders, are oriented horizontally; the rest of the cards are oriented vertically. The cards measure 2 1/2" by 3 1/2". Card backs of some of the cards in the second series can be used to form a ten-card puzzle of Bart Starr (141, 148, 153, 155, 168, 172, 196, 197, 201, and 213) or Len Dawson (145, 146, 151, 152, 163, 166, 170, 195, 199, and 200). The set features the

rookie cards of quarterbacks Bob Griese, Jim Hart, and Craig Morton, and (ex-Syracuse) running backs Floyd Little and Jim Nance.

	NRMT	VG-E	GOOD
COMPLETE SET (219)	600.00	300.00	60.00
COMMON PLAYER (1-131)	.75	.35	.07
COMMON PLAYER (132-219)	1.00	.50	.10

☐ 1	Bart Starr .... 35.00 Green Bay Packers	35.00	10.00	2.00
☐ 2	Dick Bass .... 1.00 Los Angeles Rams	1.00	.50	.10
☐ 3	Grady Alderman .... .75 Minnesota Vikings	.75	.35	.07
☐ 4	Obert Logan .... .75 New Orleans Saints	.75	.35	.07
☐ 5	Ernie Koy .... 1.25 New York Giants	1.25	.60	.12
☐ 6	Don Hultz .... .75 Philadelphia Eagles	.75	.35	.07
☐ 7	Earl Gros .... .75 Pittsburgh Steelers	.75	.35	.07
☐ 8	Jim Bakken .... 1.00 St. Louis Cardinals	1.00	.50	.10
☐ 9	George Mira .... 1.00 San Francisco 49ers	1.00	.50	.10
☐ 10	Carl Kammerer .... .75 Washington Redskins	.75	.35	.07
☐ 11	Willie Frazier .... 1.00 San Diego Chargers	1.00	.50	.10
☐ 12	Kent McCloughan UER ..... .75 Oakland Raiders (McCloughlan on card back)	.75	.35	.07
☐ 13	George Sauer Jr. .... 1.25 New York Jets	1.25	.60	.12
☐ 14	Jack Clancy .... 1.00 Miami Dolphins	1.00	.50	.10
☐ 15	Jim Tyrer .... 1.00 Kansas City Chiefs	1.00	.50	.10
☐ 16	Bobby Maples .... .75 Houston Oilers	.75	.35	.07
☐ 17	Bo Hickey .... .75 Denver Broncos	.75	.35	.07
☐ 18	Frank Buncom .... .75 Cincinnati Bengals	.75	.35	.07
☐ 19	Keith Lincoln .... 1.50 Buffalo Bills	1.50	.75	.15
☐ 20	Jim Whalen .... .75 Boston Patriots	.75	.35	.07
☐ 21	Junior Coffey .... .75 Atlanta Falcons	.75	.35	.07
☐ 22	Billy Ray Smith .... .75 Baltimore Colts	.75	.35	.07
☐ 23	Johnny Morris .... 1.00 Chicago Bears	1.00	.50	.10
☐ 24	Ernie Green .... 1.00 Cleveland Browns	1.00	.50	.10
☐ 25	Don Meredith .... 18.00 Dallas Cowboys	18.00	9.00	1.80
☐ 26	Wayne Walker .... 1.00 Detroit Lions	1.00	.50	.10
☐ 27	Carroll Dale .... 1.00 Green Bay Packers	1.00	.50	.10
☐ 28	Bernie Casey .... 1.00 Los Angeles Rams	1.00	.50	.10
☐ 29	Dave Osborn .... 2.00 Minnesota Vikings	2.00	1.00	.20
☐ 30	Ray Poage .... .75 New Orleans Saints	.75	.35	.07
☐ 31	Homer Jones .... 1.00 New York Jets	1.00	.50	.10
☐ 32	Sam Baker .... 1.00 Philadelphia Eagles	1.00	.50	.10
☐ 33	Bill Saul .... .75 Pittsburgh Steelers	.75	.35	.07
☐ 34	Ken Willard .... 1.25 San Francisco 49ers	1.25	.60	.12
☐ 35	Bobby Mitchell .... 4.00 Washington Redskins	4.00	2.00	.40
☐ 36	Gary Garrison .... 1.50 San Diego Chargers	1.50	.75	.15
☐ 37	Billy Cannon .... 2.00 Oakland Raiders	2.00	1.00	.20
☐ 38	Ralph Baker .... .75 New York Jets	.75	.35	.07
☐ 39	Howard Twilley .... 2.50 Miami Dophins	2.50	1.25	.25
☐ 40	Wendell Hayes .... 1.00 Kansas City Chiefs	1.00	.50	.10
☐ 41	Jim Norton .... .75 Houston Oilers	.75	.35	.07
☐ 42	Tom Beer .... .75 Denver Broncos	.75	.35	.07
☐ 43	Chris Burford .... 1.00 Cincinnati Bengals	1.00	.50	.10
☐ 44	Stew Barber .... .75 Buffalo Bills	.75	.35	.07
☐ 45	Leroy Mitchell .... .75 Boston Patriots	.75	.35	.07
☐ 46	Dan Grimm .... .75 Atlanta Falcons	.75	.35	.07
☐ 47	Jerry Logan .... .75 Baltimore Colts	.75	.35	.07
☐ 48	Andy Livingston .... .75 Chicago Bears	.75	.35	.07
☐ 49	Paul Warfield .... 7.00 Cleveland Browns	7.00	3.50	.70
☐ 50	Don Perkins .... 1.50 Dallas Cowboys	1.50	.75	.15
☐ 51	Ron Kramer .... 1.00 Detroit Lions	1.00	.50	.10
☐ 52	Bob Jeter 1.75	1.75	.85	.17

Green Bay Packers			
☐ 53 Les Josephson 1.75	.85	.17	
Los Angeles Rams			
☐ 54 Bobby Walden .... .75	.35	.07	
Minnesota Vikings			
☐ 55 Checklist Card 9.00	.75	.15	
☐ 56 Walter Roberts .... .75	.35	.07	
New Orleans Saints			
☐ 57 Henry Carr 1.00	.50	.10	
New York Giants			
☐ 58 Gary Ballman 1.00	.50	.10	
Philadelphia Eagles			
☐ 59 J.R. Wilburn .... .75	.35	.07	
Pittsburgh Steelers			
☐ 60 Jim Hart 7.50	3.75	.75	
St. Louis Cardinals			
☐ 61 Jim Johnson 1.00	.50	.10	
San Francisco 49ers			
☐ 62 Chris Hanburger 1.25	.60	.12	
Washington Redskins			
☐ 63 John Hadl 3.00	1.50	.30	
San Diego Chargers			
☐ 64 Hewritt Dixon 1.00	.50	.10	
Oakland Raiders			
☐ 65 Joe Namath 80.00	40.00	8.00	
New York Jets			
☐ 66 Jim Warren .... .75	.35	.07	
Miami Dolphins			
☐ 67 Curtis McClinton 1.00	.50	.10	
Kansas City Chiefs			
☐ 68 Bob Talamini .... .75	.35	.07	
Houston Oilers			
☐ 69 Steve Tensi 1.25	.60	.12	
Denver Broncos			
☐ 70 Dick Van Raaphorst UER .75	.35	.07	
Cincinnati Bengals			
(Van Raap Horst			
on card back)			
☐ 71 Art Powell 1.50	.75	.15	
Buffalo Bills			
☐ 72 Jim Nance 3.75	1.85	.37	
Boston Patriots			
☐ 73 Bob Riggle .... .75	.35	.07	
Atlanta Falcons			
☐ 74 John Mackey 2.50	1.25	.25	
Baltimore Colts			
☐ 75 Gale Sayers 75.00	37.50	7.50	
Chicago Bears			
☐ 76 Gene Hickerson .... .75	.35	.07	
Cleveland Browns			
☐ 77 Dan Reeves 4.25	2.10	.42	
Dallas Cowboys			
☐ 78 Tom Nowatzke .... .75	.35	.07	
Detroit Lions			
☐ 79 Elijah Pitts 1.00	.50	.10	
Green Bay Packers			
☐ 80 Lamar Lundy 1.00	.50	.10	

Los Angeles Rams			
☐ 81 Paul Flatley 1.00	.50	.10	
Minnesota Vikings			
☐ 82 Dave Whitsell .... .75	.35	.07	
New Orleans Saints			
☐ 83 Spider Lockhart 1.00	.50	.10	
New York Giants			
☐ 84 Dave Lloyd .... .75	.35	.07	
Philadelphia Eagles			
☐ 85 Roy Jefferson 1.00	.50	.10	
Pittsburgh Steelers			
☐ 86 Jackie Smith 1.50	.75	.15	
St. Louis Cardinals			
☐ 87 John David Crow 1.50	.75	.15	
San Francisco 49ers			
☐ 88 Sonny Jurgensen 7.00	3.50	.70	
Washington Redskins			
☐ 89 Ron Mix 3.25	1.60	.32	
San Diego Chargers			
☐ 90 Clem Daniels 1.00	.50	.10	
Oakland Raiders			
☐ 91 Cornell Gordon .... .75	.35	.07	
New York Jets			
☐ 92 Tom Goode .... .75	.35	.07	
Miami Dolphins			
☐ 93 Bobby Bell 3.75	1.85	.37	
Kansas City Chiefs			
☐ 94 Walt Suggs .... .75	.35	.07	
Houston Oilers			
☐ 95 Eric Crabtree .... .75	.35	.07	
Denver Broncos			
☐ 96 Sherrill Headrick 1.00	.50	.10	
Cincinnati Bengals			
☐ 97 Wray Carlton 1.00	.50	.10	
Buffalo Bills			
☐ 98 Gino Cappelletti 1.25	.60	.12	
Boston Patriots			
☐ 99 Tommy McDonald 1.25	.60	.12	
Atlanta Falcons			
☐ 100 John Unitas 27.00	13.50	2.70	
Baltimore Colts			
☐ 101 Richie Petitbon 1.00	.50	.10	
Chicago Bears			
☐ 102 Erich Barnes 1.00	.50	.10	
Cleveland Browns			
☐ 103 Bob Hayes 2.00	1.00	.20	
Dallas Cowboys			
☐ 104 Milt Plum 1.25	.60	.12	
Detroit Lions			
☐ 105 Boyd Dowler 1.25	.60	.12	
Green Bay Packers			
☐ 106 Ed Meador 1.00	.50	.10	
Los Angeles Rams			
☐ 107 Fred Cox 1.00	.50	.10	
Minnesota Vikings			
☐ 108 Steve Stonebreaker 1.25	.60	.12	
New Orleans Saints			

☐ 109	Aaron Thomas .... .75 New York Giants	.35	.07
☐ 110	Norm Snead .... 1.75 Philadelphia Eagles	.85	.17
☐ 111	Paul Martha .... 1.50 Pittsburgh Steelers	.75	.15
☐ 112	Jerry Stovall .... 1.00 St. Louis Cardinals	.50	.10
☐ 113	Kay McFarland .... .75 San Francisco 49ers	.35	.07
☐ 114	Pat Richter .... .75 Washington Redskins	.35	.07
☐ 115	Rick Redman .... .75 San Diego Chargers	.35	.07
☐ 116	Tom Keating .... .75 Oakland Raiders	.35	.07
☐ 117	Matt Snell .... 2.25 New York Jets	1.10	.22
☐ 118	Dick Westmoreland .... .75 Miami Dolphins	.35	.07
☐ 119	Jerry Mays .... 1.00 Kansas City Chiefs	.50	.10
☐ 120	Sid Blanks .... .75 Houston Oilers	.35	.07
☐ 121	Al Denson .... .75 Denver Broncos	.35	.07
☐ 122	Bobby Hunt .... .75 Cincinnati Bengals	.35	.07
☐ 123	Mike Mercer .... .75 Buffalo Bills	.35	.07
☐ 124	Nick Buoniconti .... 2.50 Boston Patriots	1.25	.25
☐ 125	Ron Vanderkelen .... 1.50 Minnesota Vikings	.75	.15
☐ 126	Ordell Braase .... .75 Baltimore Colts	.35	.07
☐ 127	Dick Butkus .... 33.00 Chicago Bears	16.00	3.00
☐ 128	Gary Collins .... 1.00 Cleveland Browns	.50	.10
☐ 129	Mel Renfro .... 2.00 Dallas Cowboys	1.00	.20
☐ 130	Alex Karras .... 5.00 Detroit Lions	2.50	.50
☐ 131	Herb Adderley .... 3.25 Green Bay Packers	1.60	.32
☐ 132	Roman Gabriel .... 3.25 Los Angeles Rams	1.60	.32
☐ 133	Bill Brown .... 1.25 Minnesota Vikings	.60	.12
☐ 134	Kent Kramer .... 1.00 New Orleans Saints	.50	.10
☐ 135	Tucker Frederickson ...... 1.50 New York Giants	.75	.15
☐ 136	Nate Ramsey .... 1.00 Philadelphia Eagles	.50	.10
☐ 137	Marv Woodson 1.25	.60	.12
	Pittsburgh Steelers		
☐ 138	Ken Gray .... 1.00 St. Louis Cardinals	.50	.10
☐ 139	John Brodie .... 5.50 San Francisco 49ers	2.75	.55
☐ 140	Jerry Smith .... 1.25 Washington Redskins	.60	.12
☐ 141	Brad Hubbert .... 1.00 San Diego Chargers	.50	.10
☐ 142	George Blanda .... 21.00 Oakland Raiders	10.50	2.10
☐ 143	Pete Lammons .... 1.75 New York Jets	.85	.17
☐ 144	Doug Moreau .... 1.25 Miami Dolphins	.60	.12
☐ 145	E.J. Holub .... 1.25 Kansas City Chiefs	.60	.12
☐ 146	Ode Burrell .... 1.00 Houston Oilers	.50	.10
☐ 147	Bob Scarpitto .... 1.00 Denver Broncos	.50	.10
☐ 148	Andre White .... 1.00 Cincinnati Bengals	.50	.10
☐ 149	Jack Kemp .... 38.00 Buffalo Bills	17.00	3.50
☐ 150	Art Graham .... 1.00 Boston Patriots	.50	.10
☐ 151	Tommy Nobis .... 3.50 Atlanta Falcons	1.75	.35
☐ 152	Willie Richardson .... 2.00 Baltimore Colts	1.00	.20
☐ 153	Jack Concannon .... 1.50 Chicago Bears	.75	.15
☐ 154	Bill Glass .... 1.25 Cleveland Browns	.60	.12
☐ 155	Craig Morton .... 9.00 Dallas Cowboys	4.50	.90
☐ 156	Pat Studstill .... 1.25 Detroit Lions	.60	.12
☐ 157	Ray Nitschke .... 4.50 Green Bay Packers	2.25	.45
☐ 158	Roger Brown .... 1.25 Los Angeles Rams	.60	.12
☐ 159	Joe Kapp .... 5.00 Minnesota Vikings	2.50	.50
☐ 160	Jim Taylor .... 7.00 (Shown in uniform of Green Bay Packers) New Orleans Saints	3.50	.70
☐ 161	Fran Tarkenton .... 25.00 New York Giants	12.50	2.50
☐ 162	Mike Ditka .... 6.50 Philadelphia Eagles	3.25	.65
☐ 163	Andy Russell .... 4.00 Pittsburgh Steelers	2.00	.40
☐ 164	Larry Wilson .... 3.50 St. Louis Cardinals	1.75	.35

☐ 165	Tommy Davis 1.00	.50	.10
	San Francisco 49ers		
☐ 166	Paul Krause 2.50	1.25	.25
	Washington Redskins		
☐ 167	Speedy Duncan 1.25	.60	.12
	San Diego Chargers		
☐ 168	Fred Biletnikoff 8.00	4.00	.80
	Oakland Raiders		
☐ 169	Don Maynard 7.00	3.50	.70
	New York Jets		
☐ 170	Frank Emanuel 1.00	.50	.10
	Miami Dolphins		
☐ 171	Len Dawson 8.00	4.00	.80
	Kansas City Chiefs		
☐ 172	Miller Farr 1.00	.50	.10
	Houston Oilers		
☐ 173	Floyd Little 14.00	7.00	1.40
	Denver Broncos		
☐ 174	Lonnie Wright 1.00	.50	.10
	Cincinnati Bengals		
☐ 175	Paul Costa 1.00	.50	.10
	Buffalo Bills		
☐ 176	Don Trull 1.25	.60	.12
	Houston Oilers		
☐ 177	Jerry Simmons 1.00	.50	.10
	Atlanta Falcons		
☐ 178	Tom Matte 1.50	.75	.15
	Baltimore Colts		
☐ 179	Bennie McRae 1.00	.50	.10
	Chicago Bears		
☐ 180	Jim Kanicki 1.00	.50	.10
	Cleveland Browns		
☐ 181	Bob Lilly 5.50	2.75	.55
	Dallas Cowboys		
☐ 182	Tom Watkins 1.00	.50	.10
	Detroit Lions		
☐ 183	Jim Grabowski 3.25	1.60	.32
	Green Bay Packers		
☐ 184	Jack Snow 3.25	1.60	.32
	Los Angeles Rams		
☐ 185	Gary Cuozzo 1.50	.75	.15
	Minnesota Vikings		
☐ 186	Bill Kilmer 3.00	1.50	.30
	New Orleans Saints		
☐ 187	Jim Katcavage 1.25	.60	.12
	New York Giants		
☐ 188	Floyd Peters 1.25	.60	.12
	Philadelphia Eagles		
☐ 189	Bill Nelsen 1.50	.75	.15
	Cleveland Browns		
☐ 190	Bobby Joe Conrad 1.25	.60	.12
	St. Louis Cardinals		
☐ 191	Kermit Alexander 1.25	.60	.12
	San Francisco 49ers		
☐ 192	Charley Taylor UER 5.00	2.50	.50
	(Called Charley		
	and Charlie on back)		

	Washington Redskins		
☐ 193	Lance Alworth 8.00	4.00	.80
	San Diego Chargers		
☐ 194	Daryle Lamonica 3.50	1.75	.35
	Oakland Raiders		
☐ 195	Al Atkinson 1.00	.50	.10
	New York Jets		
☐ 196	Bob Griese 90.00	45.00	9.00
	Miami Dolphins		
☐ 197	Buck Buchanan 3.75	1.85	.37
	Kansas City Chiefs		
☐ 198	Pete Beathard 1.50	.75	.15
	Kansas City Chiefs		
☐ 199	Nemiah Wilson 1.25	.60	.12
	Denver Broncos		
☐ 200	Ernie Wright 1.00	.50	.10
	Cincinnati Bengals		
☐ 201	George Saimes 1.25	.60	.12
	Buffalo Bills		
☐ 202	John Charles 1.00	.50	.10
	Boston Patriots		
☐ 203	Randy Johnson 1.25	.60	.12
	Atlanta Falcons		
☐ 204	Tony Lorick 1.00	.50	.10
	Baltimore Colts		
☐ 205	Dick Evey 1.00	.50	.10
	Chicago Bears		
☐ 206	Leroy Kelly 4.50	2.25	.45
	Cleveland Browns		
☐ 207	Lee Roy Jordan 3.50	1.75	.35
	Dallas Cowboys		
☐ 208	Jim Gibbons 1.00	.50	.10
	Detroit Lions		
☐ 209	Donny Anderson 3.50	1.75	.35
	Green Bay Packers		
☐ 210	Maxie Baughan 1.25	.60	.12
	Los Angeles Rams		
☐ 211	Joe Morrison 1.25	.60	.12
	New York Giants		
☐ 212	Jim Snowden 1.00	.50	.10
	Washington Redskins		
☐ 213	Lenny Lyles 1.00	.50	.10
	Baltimore Colts		
☐ 214	Bobby Joe Green 1.00	.50	.10
	Chicago Bears		
☐ 215	Frank Ryan 1.75	.85	.17
	Cleveland Browns		
☐ 216	Cornell Green 1.50	.75	.15
	Dallas Cowboys		
☐ 217	Karl Sweetan 1.25	.60	.12
	Detroit Lions		
☐ 218	Dave Williams 1.25	.60	.12
	St. Louis Cardinals		
☐ 219A	Checklist 132-218 ... 16.00	1.50	.30
	(green print on back)		
☐ 219B	Checklist 132-218 ... 20.00	2.00	.40
	(blue print on back)		

1969 Topps

The 1969 Topps football set of 263 cards contains 132 borderless cards (1-132), whereas the remaining 131 cards do have white borders. The lack of borders makes the first series especially difficult to find in mint condition. The checklist card 132 was obviously printed with each series as it is found in both styles (with and without borders). The cards in the set measure the standard 2 1/2" by 3 1/2". The backs of the cards are predominantly black, but with a green and white accent. This set is distinctive in that it contains the late Brian Piccolo's only card. Another notable rookie card in this set is Larry Csonka.

	NRMT	VG-E	GOOD
COMPLETE SET (263)	500.00	250.00	50.00
COMMON PLAYER (1-132)	.75	.35	.07
COMMON PLAYER (133-263)	1.00	.50	.10

☐ 1	Leroy Kelly	7.50	1.50	.30
	Cleveland Browns			
☐ 2	Paul Flatley	.75	.35	.07
	Atlanta Falcons			
☐ 3	Jim Cadile	.75	.35	.07
	Chicago Bears			
☐ 4	Erich Barnes	1.00	.50	.10
	Cleveland Browns			
☐ 5	Willie Richardson	1.00	.50	.10
	Baltimore Colts			
☐ 6	Bob Hayes	2.00	1.00	.20
	Dallas Cowboys			
☐ 7	Bob Jeter	1.00	.50	.10
	Green Bay Packers			
☐ 8	Jim Colclough	.75	.35	.07
	Boston Patriots			
☐ 9	Sherrill Headrick	1.00	.50	.10
	Cincinnati Bengals			

☐ 10	Jim Dunaway	.75	.35	.07
	Buffalo Bills			
☐ 11	Bill Munson	1.00	.50	.10
	Detroit Lions			
☐ 12	Jack Pardee	2.00	1.00	.20
	Los Angeles Rams			
☐ 13	Jim Lindsey	.75	.35	.07
	Minnesota Vikings			
☐ 14	Dave Whitsell	.75	.35	.07
	New Orleans Saints			
☐ 15	Tucker Frederickson	1.00	.50	.10
	New York Giants			
☐ 16	Alvin Haymond	.75	.35	.07
	Philadelphia Eagles			
☐ 17	Andy Russell	1.25	.60	.12
	Pittsburgh Steelers			
☐ 18	Tom Beer	.75	.35	.07
	Denver Broncos			
☐ 19	Bobby Maples	.75	.35	.07
	Houston Oilers			
☐ 20	Len Dawson	5.50	2.75	.55
	Kansas City Chiefs			
☐ 21	Willis Crenshaw	.75	.35	.07
	St. Louis Cardinals			
☐ 22	Tommy Davis	.75	.35	.07
	San Francisco 49ers			
☐ 23	Rickie Harris	.75	.35	.07
	Washington Redskins			
☐ 24	Jerry Simmons	.75	.35	.07
	Atlanta Falcons			
☐ 25	John Unitas	27.00	13.50	2.70
	Baltimore Colts			
☐ 26	Brian Piccolo UER	60.00	30.00	6.00
	Chicago Bears			
	(Misspelled Bryon			
	on back and Bryan			
	on card front)			
☐ 27	Bob Matheson	1.00	.50	.10
	Cleveland Browns			
☐ 28	Howard Twilley	1.25	.60	.12
	Miami Dolphins			
☐ 29	Jim Turner	1.00	.50	.10
	New York Jets			
☐ 30	Pete Banaszak	1.50	.75	.15
	Oakland Raiders			
☐ 31	Lance Rentzel	1.50	.75	.15
	Dallas Cowboys			
☐ 32	Bill Triplett	.75	.35	.07
	Detroit Lions			
☐ 33	Boyd Dowler	1.00	.50	.10
	Green Bay Packers			
☐ 34	Merlin Olsen	5.50	2.75	.55
	Los Angeles Rams			
☐ 35	Joe Kapp	1.50	.75	.15
	Minnesota Vikings			
☐ 36	Dan Abramowicz	2.50	1.25	.25
	New Orleans Saints			

☐ 37	Spider Lockhart .... .75	.35	.07	
	New York Giants			
☐ 38	Tom Day .... .75	.35	.07	
	Buffalo Bills			
☐ 39	Art Graham .... .75	.35	.07	
	Boston Patriots			
☐ 40	Bob Cappadona .... .75	.35	.07	
	Buffalo Bills			
☐ 41	Gary Ballman 1.00	.50	.10	
	Philadelphia Eagles			
☐ 42	Clendon Thomas .... .75	.35	.07	
	Pittsburgh Steelers			
☐ 43	Jackie Smith 1.25	.60	.12	
	St. Louis Cardinals			
☐ 44	Dave Wilcox 1.25	.60	.12	
	San Francisco 49ers			
☐ 45	Jerry Smith 1.00	.50	.10	
	Washington Redskins			
☐ 46	Dan Grimm .... .75	.35	.07	
	Baltimore Colts			
☐ 47	Tom Matte 1.25	.60	.12	
	Baltimore Colts			
☐ 48	John Stofa .... .75	.35	.07	
	Cincinnati Bengals			
☐ 49	Rex Mirich .... .75	.35	.07	
	Denver Broncos			
☐ 50	Miller Farr .... .75	.35	.07	
	Houston Oilers			
☐ 51	Gale Sayers 55.00	27.50	5.50	
	Chicago Bears			
☐ 52	Bill Nelsen 1.25	.60	.12	
	Cleveland Browns			
☐ 53	Bob Lilly 5.00	2.50	.50	
	Dallas Cowboys			
☐ 54	Wayne Walker 1.00	.50	.10	
	Detroit Lions			
☐ 55	Ray Nitschke 3.50	1.75	.35	
	Green Bay Packers			
☐ 56	Ed Meador 1.00	.50	.10	
	Los Angeles Rams			
☐ 57	Lonnie Warwick .... .75	.35	.07	
	Minnesota Vikings			
☐ 58	Wendell Hayes 1.00	.50	.10	
	Kansas City Chiefs			
☐ 59	Dick Anderson 3.00	1.50	.30	
	Miami Dolphins			
☐ 60	Don Maynard 5.50	2.75	.55	
	New York Jets			
☐ 61	Tony Lorick .... .75	.35	.07	
	New Orleans Saints			
☐ 62	Pete Gogolak 1.00	.50	.10	
	New York Giants			
☐ 63	Nate Ramsey .... .75	.35	.07	
	Philadelphia Eagles			
☐ 64	Dick Shiner 1.00	.50	.10	
	Pittsburgh Steelers			
☐ 65	Larry Wilson 3.00	1.50	.30	

	St. Louis Cardinals			
☐ 66	Ken Willard 1.25	.60	.12	
	San Francisco 49ers			
☐ 67	Charley Taylor UER 5.00	2.50	.50	
	Washington Redskins			
	(Led Redskins in			
	pass interceptions)			
☐ 68	Billy Cannon 2.00	1.00	.20	
	Oakland Raiders			
☐ 69	Lance Alworth 6.00	3.00	.60	
	San Diego Chargers			
☐ 70	Jim Nance 1.25	.60	.12	
	Boston Patriots			
☐ 71	Nick Rassas .... .75	.35	.07	
	Atlanta Falcons			
☐ 72	Lenny Lyles .... .75	.35	.07	
	Baltimore Colts			
☐ 73	Bennie McRae .... .75	.35	.07	
	Chicago Bears			
☐ 74	Bill Glass .... .75	.35	.07	
	Cleveland Browns			
☐ 75	Don Meredith 17.00	8.50	1.70	
	Dallas Cowboys			
☐ 76	Dick LeBeau 1.00	.50	.10	
	Detroit Lions			
☐ 77	Carroll Dale .... .75	.35	.07	
	Green Bay Packers			
☐ 78	Ron McDole .... .75	.35	.07	
	Buffalo Bills			
☐ 79	Charley King .... .75	.35	.07	
	Cincinnati Bengals			
☐ 80	Checklist 1-132 .... 8.50	.75	.15	
☐ 81	Dick Bass 1.00	.50	.10	
	Los Angeles Rams			
☐ 82	Roy Winston 1.00	.50	.10	
	Minnesota Vikings			
☐ 83	Don McCall .... .75	.35	.07	
	New Orleans Saints			
☐ 84	Jim Katcavage 1.00	.50	.10	
	New York Giants			
☐ 85	Norm Snead 1.75	.85	.17	
	Philadelphia Eagles			
☐ 86	Earl Gros .... .75	.35	.07	
	Pittsburgh Steelers			
☐ 87	Don Brumm .... .75	.35	.07	
	St. Louis Cardinals			
☐ 88	Sonny Bishop .... .75	.35	.07	
	Houston Oilers			
☐ 89	Fred Arbanas 1.00	.50	.10	
	Kansas City Chiefs			
☐ 90	Karl Noonan .... .75	.35	.07	
	Miami Dolphins			
☐ 91	Dick Witcher .... .75	.35	.07	
	San Francisco 49ers			
☐ 92	Vince Promuto .... .75	.35	.07	
	Washington Redskins			
☐ 93	Tommy Nobis 2.50	1.25	.25	

Atlanta Falcons			
☐ 94 Jerry Hill	.75	.35	.07
Baltimore Colts			
☐ 95 Ed O'Bradovich	1.00	.50	.10
Chicago Bears			
☐ 96 Ernie Kellerman	.75	.35	.07
Cleveland Browns			
☐ 97 Chuck Howley	1.25	.60	.12
Dallas Cowboys			
☐ 98 Hewritt Dixon	1.00	.50	.10
Oakland Raiders			
☐ 99 Ron Mix	3.25	1.60	.32
San Diego Chargers			
☐ 100 Joe Namath	65.00	32.50	6.50
New York Jets			
☐ 101 Billy Gambrell	.75	.35	.07
Detroit Lions			
☐ 102 Elijah Pitts	1.00	.50	.10
Green Bay Packers			
☐ 103 Billy Truax	1.00	.50	.10
Los Angeles Rams			
☐ 104 Ed Sharockman	.75	.35	.07
Minnesota Vikings			
☐ 105 Doug Atkins	3.25	1.60	.32
New Orleans Saints			
☐ 106 Greg Larson	.75	.35	.07
New York Giants			
☐ 107 Israel Lang	.75	.35	.07
Philadelphia Eagles			
☐ 108 Houston Antwine	.75	.35	.07
Boston Patriots			
☐ 109 Paul Guidry	.75	.35	.07
Buffalo Bills			
☐ 110 Al Denson	.75	.35	.07
Denver Broncos			
☐ 111 Roy Jefferson	1.00	.50	.10
Pittsburgh Steelers			
☐ 112 Chuck Latourette	.75	.35	.07
St. Louis Cardinals			
☐ 113 Jim Johnson	1.00	.50	.10
San Francisco 49ers			
☐ 114 Bobby Mitchell	4.00	2.00	.40
Washington Redskins			
☐ 115 Randy Johnson	1.00	.50	.10
Atlanta Falcons			
☐ 116 Lou Michaels	.75	.35	.07
Baltimore Colts			
☐ 117 Rudy Kuechenberg	.75	.35	.07
Chicago Bears			
☐ 118 Walt Suggs	.75	.35	.07
Houston Oilers			
☐ 119 Goldie Sellers	.75	.35	.07
Kansas City Chiefs			
☐ 120 Larry Csonka	70.00	35.00	7.00
Miami Dolphins			
☐ 121 Jim Houston	1.00	.50	.10
Cleveland Browns			
☐ 122 Craig Baynham	1.00	.50	.10
Dallas Cowboys			
☐ 123 Alex Karras	5.50	2.75	.55
Detroit Lions			
☐ 124 Jim Grabowski	1.00	.50	.10
Green Bay Packers			
☐ 125 Roman Gabriel	3.00	1.50	.30
Los Angeles Rams			
☐ 126 Larry Bowie	.75	.35	.07
Minnesota Vikings			
☐ 127 Dave Parks	1.00	.50	.10
New Orleans Saints			
☐ 128 Ben Davidson	2.50	1.25	.25
Oakland Raiders			
☐ 129 Steve DeLong	.75	.35	.07
San Diego Chargers			
☐ 130 Fred Hill	.75	.35	.07
Philadelphia Eagles			
☐ 131 Ernie Koy	1.00	.50	.10
New York Giants			
☐ 132A Checklist 133-263	9.50	.75	.15
(no border)			
☐ 132B Checklist 133-263	14.00	1.00	.20
(thin white border like second series)			
☐ 133 Dick Hoak	1.00	.50	.10
Pittsburgh Steelers			
☐ 134 Larry Stallings	1.50	.75	.15
St. Louis Cardinals			
☐ 135 Clifton McNeil	1.75	.85	.17
San Francisco 49ers			
☐ 136 Walter Rock	1.00	.50	.10
Washington Redskins			
☐ 137 Billy Lothridge	1.00	.50	.10
Atlanta Falcons			
☐ 138 Bob Vogel	1.00	.50	.10
Baltimore Colts			
☐ 139 Dick Butkus	17.00	8.50	1.70
Chicago Bears			
☐ 140 Frank Ryan	1.50	.75	.15
Cleveland Browns			
☐ 141 Larry Garron	1.00	.50	.10
Boston Patriots			
☐ 142 George Saimes	1.25	.60	.12
Buffalo Bills			
☐ 143 Frank Buncom	1.00	.50	.10
Cincinnati Bengals			
☐ 144 Don Perkins	1.50	.75	.15
Dallas Cowboys			
☐ 145 Johnny Robinson	1.50	.75	.15
Kansas City Chiefs			
☐ 146 Lee Roy Caffey	1.25	.60	.12
Green Bay Packers			
☐ 147 Bernie Casey	1.25	.60	.12
Los Angeles Rams			
☐ 148 Billy Martin	1.00	.50	.10
Minnesota Vikings			

☐ 149	Gene Howard .... 1.00 New Orleans Saints	.50	.10
☐ 150	Fran Tarkenton .... 22.00 New York Giants	11.00	2.20
☐ 151	Eric Crabtree .... 1.00 Denver Broncos	.50	.10
☐ 152	W.K. Hicks .... 1.00 Houston Oilers	.50	.10
☐ 153	Bobby Bell .... 3.75 Kansas City Chiefs	1.85	.37
☐ 154	Sam Baker .... 1.25 Philadelphia Eagles	.60	.12
☐ 155	Marv Woodson .... 1.25 Pittsburgh Steelers	.60	.12
☐ 156	Dave Williams .... 1.00 St. Louis Cardinals	.50	.10
☐ 157	Bruce Bosley .... 1.00 San Francisco 49ers	.50	.10
☐ 158	Carl Kammerer .... 1.00 Washington Redskins	.50	.10
☐ 159	Jim Burson .... 1.00 Atlanta Falcons	.50	.10
☐ 160	Roy Hilton .... 1.00 Baltimore Colts	.50	.10
☐ 161	Bob Griese .... 22.00 Miami Dolphins	11.00	2.20
☐ 162	Bob Talamini .... 1.00 New York Jets	.50	.10
☐ 163	Jim Otto .... 3.50 Oakland Raiders	1.75	.35
☐ 164	Ron Bull .... 1.25 Chicago Bears	.60	.12
☐ 165	Walter Johnson .... 1.50 Cleveland Browns	.75	.15
☐ 166	Lee Roy Jordan .... 3.25 Dallas Cowboys	1.60	.32
☐ 167	Mike Lucci .... 1.25 Detroit Lions	.60	.12
☐ 168	Willie Wood .... 3.50 Green Bay Packers	1.75	.35
☐ 169	Maxie Baughan .... 1.25 Los Angeles Rams	.60	.12
☐ 170	Bill Brown .... 1.25 Minnesota Vikings	.60	.12
☐ 171	John Hadl .... 2.25 San Diego Chargers	1.10	.22
☐ 172	Gino Cappelletti .... 1.50 Boston Patriots	.75	.15
☐ 173	George Byrd .... 1.25 Buffalo Bills	.60	.12
☐ 174	Steve Stonebreaker ..... 1.00 New Orleans Saints	.50	.10
☐ 175	Joe Morrison .... 1.25 New York Giants	.60	.12
☐ 176	Joe Scarpati .... 1.00 Philadelphia Eagles	.50	.10
☐ 177	Bobby Walden 1.00	.50	.10
☐ 178	Pittsburgh Steelers Roy Shivers .... 1.00 St. Louis Cardinals	.50	.10
☐ 179	Kermit Alexander .... 1.25 San Francisco 49ers	.60	.12
☐ 180	Pat Richter .... 1.00 Washington Redskins	.50	.10
☐ 181	Pete Perreault .... 1.00 Cincinnati Bengals	.50	.10
☐ 182	Pete Duranko .... 1.00 Denver Broncos	.50	.10
☐ 183	Leroy Mitchell .... 1.00 Boston Patriots	.50	.10
☐ 184	Jim Simon .... 1.00 Atlanta Falcons	.50	.10
☐ 185	Billy Ray Smith .... 1.00 Baltimore Colts	.50	.10
☐ 186	Jack Concannon .... 1.25 Chicago Bears	.60	.12
☐ 187	Ben Davis .... 1.00 Cleveland Browns	.50	.10
☐ 188	Mike Clark .... 1.00 Dallas Cowboys	.50	.10
☐ 189	Jim Gibbons .... 1.00 Detroit Lions	.50	.10
☐ 190	Dave Robinson .... 1.25 Green Bay Packers	.60	.12
☐ 191	Otis Taylor .... 1.75 Kansas City Chiefs	.85	.17
☐ 192	Nick Buoniconti .... 2.50 Miami Dolphins	1.25	.25
☐ 193	Matt Snell .... 2.00 New York Jets	1.00	.20
☐ 194	Bruce Gossett .... 1.00 Los Angeles Rams	.50	.10
☐ 195	Mick Tingelhoff .... 1.50 Minnesota Vikings	.75	.15
☐ 196	Earl Leggett .... 1.00 New Orleans Saints	.50	.10
☐ 197	Pete Case .... 1.00 New York Giants	.50	.10
☐ 198	Tom Woodeshick .... 1.50 Philadelphia Eagles	.75	.15
☐ 199	Ken Kortas .... 1.00 Pittsburgh Steelers	.50	.10
☐ 200	Jim Hart .... 2.50 St. Louis Cardinals	1.25	.25
☐ 201	Fred Biletnikoff .... 6.50 Oakland Raiders	3.25	.65
☐ 202	Jacque MacKinnon ...... 1.00 San Diego Chargers	.50	.10
☐ 203	Jim Whalen .... 1.00 Boston Patriots	.50	.10
☐ 204	Matt Hazeltine .... 1.00 San Francisco 49ers	.50	.10
☐ 205	Charlie Gogolak .... 1.25 Washington Redskins	.60	.12

☐ 206	Ray Ogden	1.00	.50	.10
	Atlanta Falcons			
☐ 207	John Mackey	2.50	1.25	.25
	Baltimore Colts			
☐ 208	Roosevelt Taylor	1.25	.60	.12
	Chicago Bears			
☐ 209	Gene Hickerson	1.00	.50	.10
	Cleveland Browns			
☐ 210	Dave Edwards	1.50	.75	.15
	Dallas Cowboys			
☐ 211	Tom Sestak	1.00	.50	.10
	Buffalo Bills			
☐ 212	Ernie Wright	1.00	.50	.10
	Cincinnati Bengals			
☐ 213	Dave Costa	1.00	.50	.10
	Denver Broncos			
☐ 214	Tom Vaughn	1.00	.50	.10
	Detroit Lions			
☐ 215	Bart Starr	22.00	11.00	2.20
	Green Bay Packers			
☐ 216	Les Josephson	1.25	.60	.12
	Los Angeles Rams			
☐ 217	Fred Cox	1.25	.60	.12
	Minnesota Vikings			
☐ 218	Mike Tilleman	1.00	.50	.10
	New Orleans Saints			
☐ 219	Darrell Dess	1.00	.50	.10
	New York Giants			
☐ 220	Dave Lloyd	1.00	.50	.10
	Philadelphia Eagles			
☐ 221	Pete Beathard	1.25	.60	.12
	Houston Oilers			
☐ 222	Buck Buchanan	3.75	1.85	.37
	Kansas City Chiefs			
☐ 223	Frank Emanuel	1.00	.50	.10
	Miami Dolphins			
☐ 224	Paul Martha	1.25	.60	.12
	Pittsburgh Steelers			
☐ 225	Johnny Roland	1.25	.60	.12
	St. Louis Cardinals			
☐ 226	Gary Lewis	1.00	.50	.10
	San Francisco 49ers			
☐ 227	Sonny Jurgensen UER	6.50	3.25	.65
	Washington Redskins			
	(Chiefs logo)			
☐ 228	Jim Butler	1.00	.50	.10
	Atlanta Falcons			
☐ 229	Mike Curtis	3.00	1.50	.30
	Baltimore Colts			
☐ 230	Richie Petitbon	1.25	.60	.12
	Chicago Bears			
☐ 231	George Sauer Jr.	1.25	.60	.12
	New York Jets			
☐ 232	George Blanda	18.00	9.00	1.80
	Oakland Raiders			
☐ 233	Gary Garrison	1.25	.60	.12
	San Diego Chargers			
☐ 234	Gary Collins	1.25	.60	.12
	Cleveland Browns			
☐ 235	Craig Morton	3.50	1.75	.35
	Dallas Cowboys			
☐ 236	Tom Nowatzke	1.00	.50	.10
	Detroit Lions			
☐ 237	Donny Anderson	1.50	.75	.15
	Green Bay Packers			
☐ 238	Deacon Jones	3.50	1.75	.35
	Los Angeles Rams			
☐ 239	Grady Alderman	1.00	.50	.10
	Minnesota Vikings			
☐ 240	Bill Kilmer	2.50	1.25	.25
	New Orleans Saints			
☐ 241	Mike Taliaferro	1.00	.50	.10
	Boston Patriots			
☐ 242	Stew Barber	1.00	.50	.10
	Buffalo Bills			
☐ 243	Bobby Hunt	1.00	.50	.10
	Kansas City Chiefs			
☐ 244	Homer Jones	1.25	.60	.12
	New York Giants			
☐ 245	Bob Brown	1.25	.60	.12
	Los Angeles Rams			
☐ 246	Bill Asbury	1.00	.50	.10
	Pittsburgh Steelers			
☐ 247	Charlie Johnson	1.75	.85	.17
	St. Louis Cardinals			
☐ 248	Chris Hanburger	1.25	.60	.12
	Washington Redskins			
☐ 249	John Brodie	5.50	2.75	.55
	San Francisco 49ers			
☐ 250	Earl Morrall	2.50	1.25	.25
	Baltimore Colts			
☐ 251	Floyd Little	2.50	1.25	.25
	Denver Broncos			
☐ 252	Jerrel Wilson	1.50	.75	.15
	Kansas City Chiefs			
☐ 253	Jim Keyes	1.00	.50	.10
	Miami Dolphins			
☐ 254	Mel Renfro	2.00	1.00	.20
	Dallas Cowboys			
☐ 255	Herb Adderley	3.50	1.75	.35
	Green Bay Packers			
☐ 256	Jack Snow	1.25	.60	.12
	Los Angeles Rams			
☐ 257	Charlie Durkee	1.00	.50	.10
	New Orleans Saints			
☐ 258	Charlie Harper	1.00	.50	.10
	New York Giants			
☐ 259	J.R. Wilburn	1.00	.50	.10
	Pittsburgh Steelers			
☐ 260	Charlie Krueger	1.25	.60	.12
	San Francisco 49ers			
☐ 261	Pete Jacques	1.00	.50	.10
	Denver Broncos			
☐ 262	Gerry Philbin	1.00	.50	.10

New York Jets
☐ 263 Daryle Lamonica .... 9.00 2.50 .50
Oakland Raiders

1970 Topps

The 1970 Topps football set contains 263 cards. The cards measure 2 1/2" by 3 1/2". The second series was printed in slightly lesser quantities than the first series. There are no scarcities, although O.J. Simpson's rookie card appears in this set. Other notable rookie cards in this set are Lem Barney, Bill Bergey, Larry Brown, Fred Dryer, Calvin Hill, Harold Jackson, Tom Mack, Alan Page, Bubba Smith, Jan Stenerud, Bob Trumpy, and both Gene Washingtons. The card backs are done in orange, purple, and white. In the second series, the offensive and defensive linemen are styled on the card back with no statistics and a coin rub-off cartoon rather than a printed cartoon as seen on all the other cards in the set.

	NRMT	VG-E	GOOD
COMPLETE SET (263)	475.00	225.00	47.00
COMMON PLAYER (1-132)	.50	.25	.05
COMMON PLAYER (133-263)	.75	.35	.07

☐ 1 Len Dawson UER .... 12.00 3.50 .75
Kansas City Chiefs
(Cartoon caption
says, "AFL AN NFL")
☐ 2 Doug Hart .... .50 .25 .05
Green Bay Packers
☐ 3 Verlon Biggs .... .50 .25 .05
New York Jets
☐ 4 Ralph Neely .... 1.00 .50 .10

Dallas Cowboys
☐ 5 Harmon Wages .... .50 .25 .05
Atlanta Falcons
☐ 6 Dan Conners .... .50 .25 .05
Oakland Raiders
☐ 7 Gino Cappelletti .... 1.00 .50 .10
Boston Patriots
☐ 8 Erich Barnes .... .75 .35 .07
Cleveland Browns
☐ 9 Checklist 1-132 .... 8.00 .75 .15
☐ 10 Bob Griese 10.00 5.00 1.00
Miami Dolphins
☐ 11 Ed Flanagan .... .50 .25 .05
Detroit Lions
☐ 12 George Seals .... .50 .25 .05
Chicago Bears
☐ 13 Harry Jacobs .... .50 .25 .05
Buffalo Bills
☐ 14 Mike Haffner .... .50 .25 .05
Denver Broncos
☐ 15 Bob Vogel .... .50 .25 .05
Baltimore Colts
☐ 16 Bill Peterson .... .50 .25 .05
Cincinnati Bengals
☐ 17 Spider Lockhart .... .50 .25 .05
New York Giants
☐ 18 Billy Truax .... .50 .25 .05
Los Angeles Rams
☐ 19 Jim Beirne .... .50 .25 .05
Houston Oilers
☐ 20 Leroy Kelly .... 3.50 1.75 .35
Cleveland Browns
☐ 21 Dave Lloyd .... .50 .25 .05
Philadelphia Eagles
☐ 22 Mike Tilleman .... .50 .25 .05
New Orleans Saints
☐ 23 Gary Garrison .... .75 .35 .07
San Diego Chargers
☐ 24 Larry Brown .... 5.00 2.50 .50
Washington Redskins
☐ 25 Jan Stenerud 10.00 5.00 1.00
Kansas City Chiefs
☐ 26 Rolf Krueger .... .50 .25 .05
St. Louis Cardinals
☐ 27 Roland Lakes .... .50 .25 .05
San Francisco 49ers
☐ 28 Dick Hoak .... .50 .25 .05
Pittsburgh Steelers
☐ 29 Gene Washington .... 1.00 .50 .10
Minnesota Vikings
☐ 30 Bart Starr 18.00 9.00 1.80
Green Bay Packers
☐ 31 Dave Grayson .... .50 .25 .05
Oakland Raiders
☐ 32 Jerry Rush .... .50 .25 .05
Detroit Lions
☐ 33 Len St. Jean .... .50 .25 .05

Boston Patriots
| ☐ 34 | Randy Edmunds | .50 | .25 | .05 |

Miami Dolphins
| ☐ 35 | Matt Snell | 1.00 | .50 | .10 |

New York Jets
| ☐ 36 | Paul Costa | .50 | .25 | .05 |

Buffalo Bills
| ☐ 37 | Mike Pyle | .50 | .25 | .05 |

Chicago Bears
| ☐ 38 | Roy Hilton | .50 | .25 | .05 |

Baltimore Colts
| ☐ 39 | Steve Tensi | .75 | .35 | .07 |

Denver Broncos
| ☐ 40 | Tommy Nobis | 1.75 | .85 | .17 |

Atlanta Falcons
| ☐ 41 | Pete Case | .50 | .25 | .05 |

New York Giants
| ☐ 42 | Andy Rice | .50 | .25 | .05 |

Cincinnati Bengals
| ☐ 43 | Elvin Bethea | 2.50 | 1.25 | .25 |

Houston Oilers
| ☐ 44 | Jack Snow | .75 | .35 | .07 |

Los Angeles Rams
| ☐ 45 | Mel Renfro | 1.50 | .75 | .15 |

Dallas Cowboys
| ☐ 46 | Andy Livingston | .50 | .25 | .05 |

New Orleans Saints
| ☐ 47 | Gary Ballman | .75 | .35 | .07 |

Philadelphia Eagles
| ☐ 48 | Bob DeMarco | .50 | .25 | .05 |

St. Louis Cardinals
| ☐ 49 | Steve DeLong | .50 | .25 | .05 |

San Diego Chargers
| ☐ 50 | Daryle Lamonica | 3.00 | 1.50 | .30 |

Oakland Raiders
| ☐ 51 | Jim Lynch | 1.25 | .60 | .12 |

Kansas City Chiefs
| ☐ 52 | Mel Farr | 1.25 | .60 | .12 |

Detroit Lions
| ☐ 53 | Bob Long | .50 | .25 | .05 |

Washington Redskins
| ☐ 54 | John Elliott | .50 | .25 | .05 |

New York Jets
| ☐ 55 | Ray Nitschke | 3.50 | 1.75 | .35 |

Green Bay Packers
| ☐ 56 | Jim Shorter | .50 | .25 | .05 |

Pittsburgh Steelers
| ☐ 57 | Dave Wilcox | 1.00 | .50 | .10 |

San Francisco 49ers
| ☐ 58 | Eric Crabtree | .50 | .25 | .05 |

Cincinnati Bengals
| ☐ 59 | Alan Page | 22.00 | 11.00 | 2.20 |

Minnesota Vikings
| ☐ 60 | Jim Nance | 1.00 | .50 | .10 |

Boston Patriots
| ☐ 61 | Glen Ray Hines | .50 | .25 | .05 |

Houston Oilers

| ☐ 62 | John Mackey | 2.50 | 1.25 | .25 |

Baltimore Colts
| ☐ 63 | Ron McDole | .50 | .25 | .05 |

Buffalo Bills
| ☐ 64 | Tom Beier | .50 | .25 | .05 |

San Francisco 49ers
| ☐ 65 | Bill Nelsen | .75 | .35 | .07 |

Cleveland Browns
| ☐ 66 | Paul Flatley | .50 | .25 | .05 |

Atlanta Falcons
| ☐ 67 | Sam Brunelli | .50 | .25 | .05 |

Denver Broncos
| ☐ 68 | Jack Pardee | 1.75 | .85 | .17 |

Los Angeles Rams
| ☐ 69 | Brig Owens | .50 | .25 | .05 |

Washington Redskins
| ☐ 70 | Gale Sayers | 45.00 | 22.50 | 4.50 |

Chicago Bears
| ☐ 71 | Lee Roy Jordan | 1.75 | .85 | .17 |

Dallas Cowboys
| ☐ 72 | Harold Jackson | 6.00 | 3.00 | .60 |

Philadelphia Eagles
| ☐ 73 | John Hadl | 2.00 | 1.00 | .20 |

San Diego Chargers
| ☐ 74 | Dave Parks | .75 | .35 | .07 |

New Orleans Saints
| ☐ 75 | Lem Barney | 9.00 | 4.50 | .90 |

Detroit Lions
| ☐ 76 | Johnny Roland | .75 | .35 | .07 |

St. Louis Cardinals
| ☐ 77 | Ed Budde | .75 | .35 | .07 |

Kansas City Chiefs
| ☐ 78 | Ben McGee | .50 | .25 | .05 |

Pittsburgh Steelers
| ☐ 79 | Ken Bowman | .50 | .25 | .05 |

Green Bay Packers
| ☐ 80 | Fran Tarkenton | 20.00 | 10.00 | 2.00 |

New York Giants
| ☐ 81 | Gene Washington | 4.00 | 2.00 | .40 |

San Francisco 49ers
| ☐ 82 | Larry Grantham | .75 | .35 | .07 |

New York Jets
| ☐ 83 | Bill Brown | .75 | .35 | .07 |

Minnesota Vikings
| ☐ 84 | John Charles | .50 | .25 | .05 |

New England Patriots
| ☐ 85 | Fred Biletnikoff | 4.50 | 2.25 | .45 |

Oakland Raiders
| ☐ 86 | Royce Berry | .50 | .25 | .05 |

Cincinnati Bengals
| ☐ 87 | Bob Lilly | 4.00 | 2.00 | .40 |

Dallas Cowboys
| ☐ 88 | Earl Morrall | 2.00 | 1.00 | .20 |

Baltimore Colts
| ☐ 89 | Jerry LeVias | 1.00 | .50 | .10 |

Houston Oilers
| ☐ 90 | O.J. Simpson | 150.00 | 75.00 | 15.00 |

	Buffalo Bills			
□ 91	Mike Howell	.50	.25	.05
	Cleveland Browns			
□ 92	Ken Gray	.50	.25	.05
	St. Louis Cardinals			
□ 93	Chris Hanburger	1.00	.50	.10
	Washington Redskins			
□ 94	Larry Seiple	1.00	.50	.10
	Miami Dolphins			
□ 95	Rich Jackson	.75	.35	.07
	Denver Broncos			
□ 96	Rockne Freitas	.50	.25	.05
	Detroit Lions			
□ 97	Dick Post	1.00	.50	.10
	San Diego Chargers			
□ 98	Ben Hawkins	.50	.25	.05
	Philadelphia Eagles			
□ 99	Ken Reaves	.50	.25	.05
	Atlanta Falcons			
□ 100	Roman Gabriel	2.50	1.25	.25
	Los Angeles Rams			
□ 101	Dave Rowe	.50	.25	.05
	New Orleans Saints			
□ 102	Dave Robinson	.75	.35	.07
	Green Bay Packers			
□ 103	Otis Taylor	1.50	.75	.15
	Kansas City Chiefs			
□ 104	Jim Turner	.75	.35	.07
	New York Jets			
□ 105	Joe Morrison	.75	.35	.07
	New York Giants			
□ 106	Dick Evey	.50	.25	.05
	Chicago Bears			
□ 107	Ray Mansfield	.50	.25	.05
	Pittsburgh Steelers			
□ 108	Grady Alderman	.50	.25	.05
	Minnesota Vikings			
□ 109	Bruce Gossett	.50	.25	.05
	San Francisco 49ers			
□ 110	Bob Trumpy	9.00	4.50	.90
	Cincinnati Bengals			
□ 111	Jim Hunt	.50	.25	.05
	Boston Patriots			
□ 112	Larry Stallings	.75	.35	.07
	St. Louis Cardinals			
□ 113A	Lance Rentzel	1.00	.50	.10
	Dallas Cowboys			
	(name in red)			
□ 113B	Lance Rentzel	1.00	.50	.10
	Dallas Cowboys			
	(name in black)			
□ 114	Bubba Smith	25.00	12.50	2.50
	Baltimore Colts			
□ 115	Norm Snead	1.50	.75	.15
	Philadelphia Eagles			
□ 116	Jim Otto	3.50	1.75	.35
	Oakland Raiders			
□ 117	Bo Scott	1.00	.50	.10
	Cleveland Browns			
□ 118	Rick Redman	.50	.25	.05
	San Diego Chargers			
□ 119	George Byrd	.75	.35	.07
	Buffalo Bills			
□ 120	George Webster	2.00	1.00	.20
	Houston Oilers			
□ 121	Chuck Walton	.50	.25	.05
	Detroit Lions			
□ 122	Dave Costa	.50	.25	.05
	Denver Broncos			
□ 123	Al Dodd	.50	.25	.05
	New Orleans Saints			
□ 124	Len Hauss	.75	.35	.07
	Washington Redskins			
□ 125	Deacon Jones	3.25	1.60	.32
	Los Angeles Rams			
□ 126	Randy Johnson	.75	.35	.07
	Atlanta Falcons			
□ 127	Ralph Heck	.50	.25	.05
	New York Giants			
□ 128	Emerson Boozer	2.25	1.10	.22
	New York Jets			
□ 129	Johnny Robinson	.75	.35	.07
	Kansas City Chiefs			
□ 130	John Brodie	5.50	2.75	.55
	San Francisco 49ers			
□ 131	Gale Gillingham	1.50	.75	.15
	Green Bay Packers			
□ 132	Checklist 133-263 DP	6.00	.60	.12
□ 133	Chuck Walker	.75	.35	.07
	St. Louis Cardinals			
□ 134	Bennie McRae	.75	.35	.07
	Chicago Bears			
□ 135	Paul Warfield	5.00	2.50	.50
	Miami Dolphins			
□ 136	Dan Darragh	.75	.35	.07
	Buffalo Bills			
□ 137	Paul Robinson	1.25	.60	.12
	Cincinnati Bengals			
□ 138	Ed Philpott	.75	.35	.07
	Boston Patriots			
□ 139	Craig Morton	2.00	1.00	.20
	Dallas Cowboys			
□ 140	Tom Dempsey	3.50	1.75	.35
	New Orleans Saints			
□ 141	Al Nelson	.75	.35	.07
	Philadelphia Eagles			
□ 142	Tom Matte	1.25	.60	.12
	Baltimore Colts			
□ 143	Dick Schafrath	.75	.35	.07
	Cleveland Browns			
□ 144	Willie Brown	4.00	2.00	.40
	Oakland Raiders			
□ 145	Charley Taylor UER	5.00	2.50	.50
	(Charlie on front)			

Washington Redskins
- 146 John Huard .... .75 .35 .07
Denver Broncos
- 147 Dave Osborn .... 1.00 .50 .10
Minnesota Vikings
- 148 Gene Mingo .... .75 .35 .07
Pittsburgh Steelers
- 149 Larry Hand .... .75 .35 .07
Detroit Lions
- 150 Joe Namath 55.00 27.50 5.50
New York Jets
- 151 Tom Mack .... 6.00 3.00 .60
Los Angeles Rams
- 152 Kenny Graham .... .75 .35 .07
San Diego Chargers
- 153 Don Herrmann .... .75 .35 .07
New York Giants
- 154 Bobby Bell .... 3.50 1.75 .35
Kansas City Chiefs
- 155 Hoyle Granger .... .75 .35 .07
Houston Oilers
- 156 Claude Humphrey .... 1.75 .85 .17
Atlanta Falcons
- 157 Clifton McNeil .... 1.00 .50 .10
New York Giants
- 158 Mick Tingelhoff .... 1.25 .60 .12
Minnesota Vikings
- 159 Don Horn .... 1.25 .60 .12
Green Bay Packers
- 160 Larry Wilson .... 3.25 1.60 .32
St. Louis Cardinals
- 161 Tom Neville .... .75 .35 .07
Boston Patriots
- 162 Larry Csonka 18.00 9.00 1.80
Miami Dolphins
- 163 Doug Buffone .... 1.50 .75 .15
Chicago Bears
- 164 Cornell Green .... 1.25 .60 .12
Dallas Cowboys
- 165 Haven Moses .... 2.25 1.10 .22
Buffalo Bills
- 166 Bill Kilmer .... 2.50 1.25 .25
New Orleans Saints
- 167 Tim Rossovich .... 1.50 .75 .15
Philadelphia Eagles
- 168 Bill Bergey .... 4.25 2.10 .42
Cincinnati Bengals
- 169 Gary Collins .... 1.25 .60 .12
Cleveland Browns
- 170 Floyd Little .... 2.50 1.25 .25
Denver Broncos
- 171 Tom Keating .... .75 .35 .07
Oakland Raiders
- 172 Pat Fischer .... 1.00 .50 .10
Washington Redskins
- 173 Walt Sweeney .... .75 .35 .07
San Diego Chargers

- 174 Greg Larson .... .75 .35 .07
New York Giants
- 175 Carl Eller .... 3.00 1.50 .30
Minnesota Vikings
- 176 George Sauer Jr. .... 1.25 .60 .12
New York Jets
- 177 Jim Hart .... 2.50 1.25 .25
St. Louis Cardinals
- 178 Bob Brown .... 1.25 .60 .12
Los Angeles Rams
- 179 Mike Garrett .... 3.00 1.50 .30
Kansas City Chiefs
- 180 John Unitas 25.00 12.50 2.50
Baltimore Colts
- 181 Tom Regner .... .75 .35 .07
Houston Oilers
- 182 Bob Jeter .... 1.00 .50 .10
Green Bay Packers
- 183 Gail Cogdill .... .75 .35 .07
Atlanta Falcons
- 184 Earl Gros .... .75 .35 .07
Pittsburgh Steelers
- 185 Dennis Partee .... .75 .35 .07
San Diego Chargers
- 186 Charlie Krueger .... .75 .35 .07
San Francisco 49ers
- 187 Martin Baccaglio .... .75 .35 .07
Cincinnati Bengals
- 188 Charles Long .... .75 .35 .07
Boston Patriots
- 189 Bob Hayes .... 2.00 1.00 .20
Dallas Cowboys
- 190 Dick Butkus 14.00 7.00 1.40
Chicago Bears
- 191 Al Bemiller .... .75 .35 .07
Buffalo Bills
- 192 Dick Westmoreland ...... .75 .35 .07
Minnesota Vikings
- 193 Joe Scarpati .... .75 .35 .07
New Orleans Saints
- 194 Ron Snidow .... .75 .35 .07
Cleveland Browns
- 195 Earl McCullouch .... 1.25 .60 .12
Detroit Lions
- 196 Jake Kupp .... .75 .35 .07
New Orleans Saints
- 197 Bob Lurtsema .... .75 .35 .07
New York Giants
- 198 Mike Current .... .75 .35 .07
Denver Broncos
- 199 Charlie Smith .... .75 .35 .07
Oakland Raiders
- 200 Sonny Jurgensen .... 6.00 3.00 .60
Washington Redskins
- 201 Mike Curtis .... 1.25 .60 .12
Baltimore Colts
- 202 Aaron Brown .... .75 .35 .07

	Kansas City Chiefs			
☐ 203	Richie Petitbon 1.00	.50	.10	
	Los Angeles Rams			
☐ 204	Walt Suggs .... .75	.35	.07	
	Houston Oilers			
☐ 205	Roy Jefferson 1.00	.50	.10	
	Pittsburgh Steelers			
☐ 206	Russ Washington 1.50	.75	.15	
	San Diego Chargers			
☐ 207	Woody Peoples 1.25	.60	.12	
	San Francisco 49ers			
☐ 208	Dave Williams .... .75	.35	.07	
	St. Louis Cardinals			
☐ 209	John Zook 1.50	.75	.15	
	Atlanta Falcons			
☐ 210	Tom Woodeshick .... .75	.35	.07	
	Philadelphia Eagles			
☐ 211	Howard Fest .... .75	.35	.07	
	Cincinnati Bengals			
☐ 212	Jack Concannon 1.00	.50	.10	
	Chicago Bears			
☐ 213	Jim Marshall 3.00	1.50	.30	
	Minnesota Vikings			
☐ 214	Jon Morris .... .75	.35	.07	
	Boston Patriots			
☐ 215	Dan Abramowicz 1.25	.60	.12	
	New Orleans Saints			
☐ 216	Paul Martha 1.00	.50	.10	
	Denver Broncos			
☐ 217	Ken Willard 1.25	.60	.12	
	San Francisco 49ers			
☐ 218	Walter Rock .... .75	.35	.07	
	Washington Redskins			
☐ 219	Garland Boyette .... .75	.35	.07	
	Houston Oilers			
☐ 220	Buck Buchanan 3.50	1.75	.35	
	Kansas City Chiefs			
☐ 221	Bill Munson 1.25	.60	.12	
	Detroit Lions			
☐ 222	David Lee 1.00	.50	.10	
	Baltimore Colts			
☐ 223	Karl Noonan .... .75	.35	.07	
	Miami Dolphins			
☐ 224	Harry Schuh .... .75	.35	.07	
	Oakland Raiders			
☐ 225	Jackie Smith 1.25	.60	.12	
	St. Louis Cardinals			
☐ 226	Gerry Philbin .... .75	.35	.07	
	New York Jets			
☐ 227	Ernie Koy .... .75	.35	.07	
	New York Giants			
☐ 228	Chuck Howley 1.25	.60	.12	
	Dallas Cowboys			
☐ 229	Billy Shaw .... .75	.35	.07	
	Buffalo Bills			
☐ 230	Jerry Hillebrand .... .75	.35	.07	
	Pittsburgh Steelers			
☐ 231	Bill Thompson 1.75	.85	.17	
	Denver Broncos			
☐ 232	Carroll Dale .... .75	.35	.07	
	Green Bay Packers			
☐ 233	Gene Hickerson .... .75	.35	.07	
	Cleveland Browns			
☐ 234	Jim Butler .... .75	.35	.07	
	Atlanta Falcons			
☐ 235	Greg Cook 1.50	.75	.15	
	Cincinnati Bengals			
☐ 236	Lee Roy Caffey .... .75	.35	.07	
	Chicago Bears			
☐ 237	Merlin Olsen 5.50	2.75	.55	
	Los Angeles Rams			
☐ 238	Fred Cox 1.00	.50	.10	
	Minnesota Vikings			
☐ 239	Nate Ramsey .... .75	.35	.07	
	Philadelphia Eagles			
☐ 240	Lance Alworth 5.00	2.50	.50	
	San Diego Chargers			
☐ 241	Chuck Hinton .... .75	.35	.07	
	Pittsburgh Steelers			
☐ 242	Jerry Smith 1.00	.50	.10	
	Washington Redskins			
☐ 243	Tony Baker .... .75	.35	.07	
	New Orleans Saints			
☐ 244	Nick Buoniconti 2.25	1.10	.22	
	Miami Dolphins			
☐ 245	Jim Johnson 1.00	.50	.10	
	San Francisco 49ers			
☐ 246	Willie Richardson 1.00	.50	.10	
	Baltimore Colts			
☐ 247	Fred Dryer 16.00	8.00	1.60	
	New York Giants			
☐ 248	Bobby Maples .... .75	.35	.07	
	Houston Oilers			
☐ 249	Alex Karras 5.50	2.75	.55	
	Detroit Lions			
☐ 250	Joe Kapp 1.25	.60	.12	
	Minnesota Vikings			
☐ 251	Ben Davidson 2.50	1.25	.25	
	Oakland Raiders			
☐ 252	Mike Stratton .... .75	.35	.07	
	Buffalo Bills			
☐ 253	Les Josephson 1.00	.50	.10	
	Los Angeles Rams			
☐ 254	Don Maynard 5.00	2.50	.50	
	New York Jets			
☐ 255	Houston Antwine .... .75	.35	.07	
	Boston Patriots			
☐ 256	Mac Percival .... .75	.35	.07	
	Chicago Bears			
☐ 257	George Goeddeke .... .75	.35	.07	
	Denver Broncos			
☐ 258	Homer Jones 1.00	.50	.10	
	Cleveland Browns			
☐ 259	Bob Berry 1.00	.50	.10	

Atlanta Falcons
☐ 260A Calvin Hill .... 4.50   2.25   .45
    Dallas Cowboys
    (Name in red)
☐ 260B Calvin Hill .... 4.50   2.25   .45
    Dallas Cowboys
    (Name in black)
☐ 261 Willie Wood .... 3.00   1.50   .30
    Green Bay Packers
☐ 262 Ed Weisacosky .... .75   .35   .07
    Miami Dolphins
☐ 263 Jim Tyrer .... 3.00   .75   .15
    Kansas City Chiefs

1971 Topps

The 1971 Topps set contains 263 cards. The cards measure 2 1/2" by 3 1/2". The second series was printed in slightly lesser quantities than the first series. There are no known scarcities, although the first cards of two Steeler greats, Terry Bradshaw and Mean Joe Greene, occur in this set. Other notable rookie cards in this set are Hall of Famers Ken Houston and Willie Lanier. The card backs are printed in black ink with a gold accent on gray card stock. The card fronts have red borders for AFC players, blue borders for NFC players, and blue over red borders for the respective conference All-Pros.

	NRMT	VG-E	GOOD
COMPLETE SET (263)	450.00	225.00	45.00
COMMON PLAYER (1-132)	.50	.25	.05
COMMON PLAYER (133-263)	.75	.35	*07

☐ 1 John Unitas 32.00   10.00   2.00
    Baltimore Colts
☐ 2 Jim Butler .... .50   .25   .05
    Atlanta Falcons
☐ 3 Marty Schottenheimer ..... 8.00   4.00   .80
    New England Patriots
☐ 4 Joe O'Donnell .... .50   .25   .05
    Buffalo Bills
☐ 5 Tom Dempsey .... 1.00   .50   .10
    New Orleans Saints
☐ 6 Chuck Allen .... .50   .25   .05
    Pittsburgh Steelers
☐ 7 Ernie Kellerman .... .50   .25   .05
    Cleveland Browns
☐ 8 Walt Garrison .... 1.50   .75   15
    Dallas Cowboys
☐ 9 Bill Van Heusen .... .50   .25   .05
    Denver Broncos
☐ 10 Lance Alworth .... 4.50   2.25   .45
    San Diego Chargers
☐ 11 Greg Landry .... 2.75   1.35   .27
    Detroit Lions
☐ 12 Larry Krause .... .50   .25   .05
    Green Bay Packers
☐ 13 Buck Buchanan .... 2.50   1.25   .25
    Kansas City Chiefs
☐ 14 Roy Gerela .... 1.00   .50   .10
    Houston Oilers
☐ 15 Clifton McNeil .... .75   .35   .07
    New York Giants
☐ 16 Bob Brown .... .75   .35   .07
    Los Angeles Rams
☐ 17 Lloyd Mumphord .... .50   .25   .05
    Miami Dolphins
☐ 18 Gary Cuozzo .... .75   .35   .07
    Minnesota Vikings
☐ 19 Don Maynard .... 4.00   2.00   .40
    New York Jets
☐ 20 Larry Wilson .... 2.50   1.25   .25
    St. Louis Cardinals
☐ 21 Charlie Smith .... .50   .25   .05
    Oakland Raiders
☐ 22 Ken Avery .... .50   .25   .05
    Cincinnati Bengals
☐ 23 Billy Walik .... .50   .25   .05
    Philadelphia Eagles
☐ 24 Jim Johnson .... .75   .35   .07
    San Francisco 49ers
☐ 25 Dick Butkus .... 9.00   4.50   .90
    Chicago Bears
☐ 26 Charley Taylor UER .... 3.50   1.75   .35
    (Charlie on front)
    Washington Redskins
☐ 27 Checklist 1-132 .... 8.00   .75   .15
☐ 28 Lionel Aldridge .... 1.00   .50   .10
    Green Bay Packers
☐ 29 Billy Lothridge .... .50   .25   .05

	Atlanta Falcons		
☐ 30	Terry Hanratty 1.25	.60	.12
	Pittsburgh Steelers		
☐ 31	Lee Roy Jordan 1.75	.85	.17
	Dallas Cowboys		
☐ 32	Rick Volk .... .75	.35	.07
	Baltimore Colts		
☐ 33	Howard Kindig .... .50	.25	.05
	Buffalo Bills		
☐ 34	Carl Garrett 1.00	.50	.10
	New England Patriots		
☐ 35	Bobby Bell 2.50	1.25	.25
	Kansas City Chiefs		
☐ 36	Gene Hickerson .... .50	.25	.05
	Cleveland Browns		
☐ 37	Dave Parks .... .75	.35	.07
	New Orleans Saints		
☐ 38	Paul Martha .... .75	.35	.07
	Denver Broncos		
☐ 39	George Blanda 12.00	6.00	1.20
	Oakland Raiders		
☐ 40	Tom Woodeshick .... .50	.25	.05
	Philadelphia Eagles		
☐ 41	Alex Karras 4.00	2.00	.40
	Detroit Lions		
☐ 42	Rick Redman .... .50	.25	.05
	San Diego Chargers		
☐ 43	Zeke Moore .... .50	.25	.05
	Houston Oilers		
☐ 44	Jack Snow .... .75	.35	.07
	Los Angeles Rams		
☐ 45	Larry Csonka 6.00	3.00	.60
	Miami Dolphins		
☐ 46	Karl Kassulke .... .50	.25	.05
	Minnesota Vikings		
☐ 47	Jim Hart 1.75	.85	.17
	St. Louis Cardinals		
☐ 48	Al Atkinson .... .50	.25	.05
	New York Jets		
☐ 49	Horst Muhlmann .... .75	.35	.07
	Cincinnati Bengals		
☐ 50	Sonny Jurgensen 5.50	2.75	.55
	Washington Redskins		
☐ 51	Ron Johnson 2.50	1.25	.25
	New York Giants		
☐ 52	Cas Banaszek .... .50	.25	.05
	San Francisco 49ers		
☐ 53	Bubba Smith 6.00	3.00	.60
	Baltimore Colts		
☐ 54	Bobby Douglass 1.25	.60	.12
	Chicago Bears		
☐ 55	Willie Wood 2.25	1.10	.22
	Green Bay Packers		
☐ 56	Bake Turner .... .75	.35	.07
	New England Patriots		
☐ 57	Mike Morgan .... .50	.25	.05
	New Orleans Saints		
☐ 58	George Byrd .... .75	.35	.07
	Buffalo Bills		
☐ 59	Don Horn .... .75	.35	.07
	Denver Broncos		
☐ 60	Tommy Nobis 1.50	.75	.15
	Atlanta Falcons		
☐ 61	Jan Stenerud 3.00	1.50	.30
	Kansas City Chiefs		
☐ 62	Altie Taylor 1.00	.50	.10
	Detroit Lions		
☐ 63	Gary Pettigrew .... .50	.25	.05
	Philadelphia Eagles		
☐ 64	Spike Jones .... .50	.25	.05
	Buffalo Bills		
☐ 65	Duane Thomas 2.50	1.25	.25
	Dallas Cowboys		
☐ 66	Marty Domres .... .75	.35	.07
	San Diego Chargers		
☐ 67	Dick Anderson .... .75	.35	.07
	Miami Dolphins		
☐ 68	Ken Iman .... .50	.25	.05
	Los Angeles Rams		
☐ 69	Miller Farr .... .50	.25	.05
	St. Louis Cardinals		
☐ 70	Daryle Lamonica 2.25	1.10	.22
	Oakland Raiders		
☐ 71	Alan Page 6.50	3.25	.65
	Minnesota Vikings		
☐ 72	Pat Matson .... .50	.25	.05
	Cincinnati Bengals		
☐ 73	Emerson Boozer .... .75	.35	.07
	New York Jets		
☐ 74	Pat Fischer .... .75	.35	.07
	Washington Redskins		
☐ 75	Gary Collins .... .75	.35	.07
	Cleveland Browns		
☐ 76	John Fuqua 1.00	.50	.10
	Pittsburgh Steelers		
☐ 77	Bruce Gossett .... .50	.25	.05
	San Francisco 49ers		
☐ 78	Ed O'Bradovich .... .50	.25	.05
	Chicago Bears		
☐ 79	Bob Tucker 1.25	.60	.12
	New York Giants		
☐ 80	Mike Curtis .... .75	.35	.07
	Baltimore Colts		
☐ 81	Rich Jackson .... .50	.25	.05
	Denver Broncos		
☐ 82	Tom Janik .... .50	.25	.05
	New England Patriots		
☐ 83	Gale Gillingham .... .50	.25	.05
	Green Bay Packers		
☐ 84	Jim Mitchell .... .50	.25	.05
	Atlanta Falcons		
☐ 85	Charlie Johnson 1.50	.75	.15
	Houston Oilers		
☐ 86	Edgar Chandler .... .50	.25	.05

Buffalo Bills			
☐ 87 Cyril Pinder .... .50	.25	.05	
Philadelphia Eagles			
☐ 88 Johnny Robinson .... .75	.35	.07	
Kansas City Chiefs			
☐ 89 Ralph Neely .... .75	.35	.07	
Dallas Cowboys			
☐ 90 Dan Abramowicz .... .75	.35	.07	
New Orleans Saints			
☐ 91 Mercury Morris 2.75	1.35	.27	
Miami Dolphins			
☐ 92 Steve DeLong .... .50	.25	.05	
San Diego Chargers			
☐ 93 Larry Stallings .... .50	.25	.05	
St. Louis Cardinals			
☐ 94 Tom Mack 1.50	.75	.15	
Los Angeles Rams			
☐ 95 Hewritt Dixon .... .75	.35	.07	
Oakland Raiders			
☐ 96 Fred Cox .... .75	.35	.07	
Minnesota Vikings			
☐ 97 Chris Hanburger .... .75	.35	.07	
Washington Redskins			
☐ 98 Gerry Philbin .... .50	.25	.05	
New York Jets			
☐ 99 Ernie Wright .... .50	.25	.05	
Cincinnati Bengals			
☐ 100 John Brodie 5.00	2.50	.50	
San Francisco 49ers			
☐ 101 Tucker Frederickson .75	.35	.07	
New York Giants			
☐ 102 Bobby Walden .... .50	.25	.05	
Pittsburgh Steelers			
☐ 103 Dick Gordon .... .75	.35	.07	
Chicago Bears			
☐ 104 Walter Johnson .... .50	.25	.05	
Cleveland Browns			
☐ 105 Mike Lucci .... .75	.35	.07	
Detroit Lions			
☐ 106 Checklist 133-263 DP .5.50	.50	.10	
☐ 107 Ron Berger .... .50	.25	.05	
New England Patriots			
☐ 108 Dan Sullivan .... .50	.25	.05	
Baltimore Colts			
☐ 109 George Kunz 2.00	1.00	.20	
Atlanta Falcons			
☐ 110 Floyd Little 2.25	1.10	.22	
Denver Broncos			
☐ 111 Zeke Bratkowski 1.00	.50	.10	
Green Bay Packers			
☐ 112 Haven Moses .... .75	.35	.07	
Buffalo Bills			
☐ 113 Ken Houston 16.00	8.00	1.60	
Houston Oilers			
☐ 114 Willie Lanier 16.00	8.00	1.60	
Kansas City Chiefs			
☐ 115 Larry Brown 1.50	.75	.15	
Washington Redskins			
☐ 116 Tim Rossovich .... .75	.35	.07	
Philadelphia Eagles			
☐ 117 Errol Linden .... .50	.25	.05	
New Orleans Saints			
☐ 118 Mel Renfro 1.25	.60	.12	
Dallas Cowboys			
☐ 119 Mike Garrett 1.00	.50	.10	
San Diego Chargers			
☐ 120 Fran Tarkenton 20.00	10.00	2.00	
New York Giants			
☐ 121 Garo Yepremian 2.25	1.10	.22	
Miami Dolphins			
☐ 122 Glen Condren .... .50	.25	.05	
Atlanta Falcons			
☐ 123 Johnny Roland .... .75	.35	.07	
St. Louis Cardinals			
☐ 124 Dave Herman .... .50	.25	.05	
New York Jets			
☐ 125 Merlin Olsen 3.50	1.75	.35	
Los Angeles Rams			
☐ 126 Doug Buffone .... .50	.25	.05	
Chicago Bears			
☐ 127 Earl McCullouch ...... .75	.35	.07	
Detroit Lions			
☐ 128 Spider Lockhart ...... .50	.25	.05	
New York Giants			
☐ 129 Ken Willard .... .75	.35	.07	
San Francisco 49ers			
☐ 130 Gene Washington ..... .75	.35	.07	
Minnesota Vikings			
☐ 131 Mike Phipps 1.50	.75	.15	
Cleveland Browns			
☐ 132 Andy Russell .... .75	.35	.07	
Pittsburgh Steelers			
☐ 133 Ray Nitschke 3.75	1.85	.37	
Green Bay Packers			
☐ 134 Jerry Logan .... .75	.35	.07	
Baltimore Colts			
☐ 135 MacArthur Lane 1.75	.85	.17	
St. Louis Cardinals			
☐ 136 Jim Turner 1.00	.50	.10	
Denver Broncos			
☐ 137 Kent McCloughan .... .75	.35	.07	
Oakland Raiders			
☐ 138 Paul Guidry .... .75	.35	.07	
Buffalo Bills			
☐ 139 Otis Taylor 1.50	.75	.15	
Kansas City Chiefs			
☐ 140 Virgil Carter 1.00	.50	.10	
Cincinnati Bengals			
☐ 141 Joe Dawkins .... .75	.35	.07	
Houston Oilers			
☐ 142 Steve Preece .... .75	.35	.07	
Philadelphia Eagles			
☐ 143 Mike Bragg 1.00	.50	.10	
Washington Redskins			

□ 144 Bob Lilly .... 4.25   2.10   .42
     Dallas Cowboys
□ 145 Joe Kapp .... 1.25   .60   .12
     New England Patriots
□ 146 Al Dodd .... .75   .35   .07
     New Orleans Saints
□ 147 Nick Buoniconti ... 2.00   1.00   .20
     Miami Dolphins
□ 148 Speedy Duncan ... 1.00   .50   .10
     (Back mentions his
     trade to Redskins)
     San Diego Chargers
□ 149 Cedric Hardman ... 1.00   .50   .10
     San Francisco 49ers
□ 150 Gale Sayers 35.00   17.50   3.50
     Chicago Bears
□ 151 Jim Otto .... 3.50   1.75   .35
     Oakland Raiders
□ 152 Billy Truax .... .75   .35   .07
     Dallas Cowboys
□ 153 John Elliott .... .75   .35   .07
     New York Jets
□ 154 Dick LeBeau .... 1.00   .50   .10
     Detroit Lions
□ 155 Bill Bergey .... 1.50   .75   .15
     Cincinnati Bengals
□ 156 Terry Bradshaw 125.00   60.00   12.50
     Pittsburgh Steelers
□ 157 Leroy Kelly .... 2.50   1.25   .25
     Cleveland Browns
□ 158 Paul Krause .... 1.75   .85   .17
     Minnesota Vikings
□ 159 Ted Vactor .... .75   .35   .07
     Washington Redskins
□ 160 Bob Griese 10.00   5.00   1.00
     Miami Dolphins
□ 161 Ernie McMillan .... .75   .35   .07
     St. Louis Cardinals
□ 162 Donny Anderson ... 1.25   .60   .12
     Green Bay Packers
□ 163 John Pitts .... .75   .35   .07
     Buffalo Bills
□ 164 Dave Costa .... .75   .35   .07
     Denver Broncos
□ 165 Gene Washington ... 1.25   .60   .12
     San Francisco 49ers
□ 166 John Zook .... 1.00   .50   .10
     Atlanta Falcons
□ 167 Pete Gogolak .... 1.00   .50   .10
     New York Giants
□ 168 Erich Barnes .... .75   .35   .07
     Cleveland Browns
□ 169 Alvin Reed .... .75   .35   .07
     Houston Oilers
□ 170 Jim Nance .... 1.00   .50   .10
     New England Patriots
□ 171 Craig Morton .... 1.75   .85   .17

     Dallas Cowboys
□ 172 Gary Garrison .... 1.00   .50   .10
     San Diego Chargers
□ 173 Joe Scarpati .... .75   .35   .07
     New Orleans Saints
□ 174 Adrian Young .... .75   .35   .07
     Philadelphia Eagles
□ 175 John Mackey .... 2.25   1.10   .22
     Baltimore Colts
□ 176 Mac Percival .... .75   .35   .07
     Chicago Bears
□ 177 Preston Pearson ... 2.25   1.10   .22
     Pittsburgh Steelers
□ 178 Fred Biletnikoff ...... 4.50   2.25   .45
     Oakland Raiders
□ 179 Mike Battle .... 1.00   .50   .10
     New York Jets
□ 180 Len Dawson .... 5.50   2.75   .55
     Kansas City Chiefs
□ 181 Les Josephson ...... 1.00   .50   .10
     Los Angeles Rams
□ 182 Royce Berry .... .75   .35   .07
     Cincinnati Bengals
□ 183 Herman Weaver ...... .75   .35   .07
     Detroit Lions
□ 184 Norm Snead .... 1.50   .75   .15
     Minnesota Vikings
□ 185 Sam Brunelli .... .75   .35   .07
     Denver Broncos
□ 186 Jim Kiick .... 3.00   1.50   .30
     Miami Dolphins
□ 187 Austin Denney .... .75   .35   .07
     Buffalo Bills
□ 188 Roger Wehrli .... 3.00   1.50   .30
     St. Louis Cardinals
□ 189 Dave Wilcox .... 1.00   .50   .10
     San Francisco 49ers
□ 190 Bob Hayes .... 1.75   .85   .17
     Dallas Cowboys
□ 191 Joe Morrison .... 1.00   .50   .10
     New York Giants
□ 192 Manny Sistrunk .... .75   .35   .07
     Washington Redskins
□ 193 Don Cockroft .... 1.00   .50   .10
     Cleveland Browns
□ 194 Lee Bouggess .... .75   .35   .07
     Philadelphia Eagles
□ 195 Bob Berry .... 1.00   .50   .10
     Atlanta Falcons
□ 196 Ron Sellers .... 1.00   .50   .10
     New England Patriots
□ 197 George Webster ..... 1.00   .50   .10
     Houston Oilers
□ 198 Hoyle Granger .... .75   .35   .07
     New Orleans Saints
□ 199 Bob Vogel .... .75   .35   .07
     Baltimore Colts

☐ 200	Batt Starr 20.00	10.00	2.00
	Green Bay Packers		
☐ 201	Mike Mercer .... .75	.35	.07
	San Diego Chargers		
☐ 202	Dave Smith .... .75	.35	.07
	Pittsburgh Steelers		
☐ 203	Lee Roy Caffey .... .75	.35	.07
	Chicago Bears		
☐ 204	Mick Tingelhoff 1.00	.50	.10
	Minnesota Vikings		
☐ 205	Matt Snell 1.25	.60	.12
	New York Jets		
☐ 206	Jim Tyrer 1.00	.50	.10
	Kansas City Chiefs		
☐ 207	Willie Brown 3.50	1.75	.35
	Oakland Raiders		
☐ 208	Bob Johnson 1.50	.75	.15
	Cincinnati Bengals		
☐ 209	Deacon Jones 3.50	1.75	.35
	Los Angeles Rams		
☐ 210	Charlie Sanders 4.50	2.25	.45
	Detroit Lions		
☐ 211	Jake Scott 2.75	1.35	.27
	Miami Dolphins		
☐ 212	Bob Anderson 1.75	.85	.17
	Denver Broncos		
☐ 213	Charlie Krueger .... .75	.35	.07
	San Francisco 49ers		
☐ 214	Jim Bakken 1.00	.50	.10
	St. Louis Cardinals		
☐ 215	Harold Jackson 2.25	1.10	.22
	Philadelphia Eagles		
☐ 216	Bill Brundige .... .75	.35	.07
	Washington Redskins		
☐ 217	Calvin Hill 2.00	1.00	.20
	Dallas Cowboys		
☐ 218	Claude Humphrey 1.00	.50	.10
	Atlanta Falcons		
☐ 219	Glen Ray Hines .... .75	.35	.07
	Houston Oilers		
☐ 220	Bill Nelsen 1.00	.50	.10
	Cleveland Browns		
☐ 221	Roy Hilton .... .75	.35	.07
	Baltimore Colts		
☐ 222	Don Herrmann .... .75	.35	.07
	New York Giants		
☐ 223	John Bramlett .... .75	.35	.07
	Atlanta Falcons		
☐ 224	Ken Ellis .... .75	.35	.07
	Green Bay Packers		
☐ 225	Dave Osborn 1.00	.50	.10
	Minnesota Vikings		
☐ 226	Edd Hargett 1.25	.60	.12
	New Orleans Saints		
☐ 227	Gene Mingo .... .75	.35	.07
	Pittsburgh Steelers		
☐ 228	Larry Grantham 1.00	.50	.10

	New York Jets		
☐ 229	Dick Post .... .75	.35	.07
	San Diego Chargers		
☐ 230	Roman Gabriel 2.50	1.25	.25
	Los Angeles Rams		
☐ 231	Mike Eischeid .... .75	.35	.07
	Oakland Raiders		
☐ 232	Jim Lynch 1.00	.50	.10
	Kansas City Chiefs		
☐ 233	Lemar Parrish 3.00	1.50	.30
	Cincinnati Bengals		
☐ 234	Cecil Turner .... .75	.35	.07
	Chicago Bears		
☐ 235	Dennis Shaw 1.00	.50	.10
	Buffalo Bills		
☐ 236	Mel Farr 1.00	.50	.10
	Detroit Lions		
☐ 237	Curt Knight .... .75	.35	.07
	Washington Redskins		
☐ 238	Chuck Howley 1.00	.50	.10
	Dallas Cowboys		
☐ 239	Bruce Taylor 1.25	.60	.12
	San Francisco 49ers		
☐ 240	Jerry LeVias 1.00	.50	.10
	Houston Oilers		
☐ 241	Bob Lurtsema .... .75	.35	.07
	New York Giants		
☐ 242	Earl Morrall 2.00	1.00	.20
	Baltimore Colts		
☐ 243	Kermit Alexander 1.00	.50	.10
	Los Angeles Rams		
☐ 244	Jackie Smith 1.00	.50	.10
	St. Louis Cardinals		
☐ 245	Joe Greene 45.00	22.50	4.50
	Pittsburgh Steelers		
☐ 246	Harmon Wages .... .75	.35	.07
	Atlanta Falcons		
☐ 247	Errol Mann .... .75	.35	.07
	Detroit Lions		
☐ 248	Mike McCoy 1.00	.50	.10
	Green Bay Packers		
☐ 249	Milt Morin 1.00	.50	.10
	Cleveland Browns		
☐ 250	Joe Namath 50.00	25.00	5.00
	New York Jets		
☐ 251	Jackie Burkett 1.00	.50	.10
	New Orleans Saints		
☐ 252	Steve Chomyszak .... .75	.35	.07
	Cincinnati Bengals		
☐ 253	Ed Sharockman .... .75	.35	.07
	Minnesota Vikings		
☐ 254	Robert Holmes 1.00	.50	.10
	Kansas City Chiefs		
☐ 255	John Hadl 2.00	1.00	.20
	San Diego Chargers		
☐ 256	Cornell Gordon .... .75	.35	.07
	Denver Broncos		

□ 257	Mark Moseley	5.50	2.75	.55
	Philadelphia Eagles			
□ 258	Gus Otto	.75	.35	.07
	Oakland Raiders			
□ 259	Mike Taliaferro	.75	.35	.07
	New England Patriots			
□ 260	O.J. Simpson	50.00	25.00	5.00
	Buffalo Bills			
□ 261	Paul Warfield	4.50	2.25	.45
	Miami Dolphins			
□ 262	Jack Concannon	1.00	.50	.10
	Chicago Bears			
□ 263	Tom Matte	2.50	.60	.12
	Baltimore Colts			

1972 Topps

The 1972 Topps football set contains 351 cards. The cards measure 2 1/2" by 3 1/2". The second series was printed in slightly lesser quantities than the first series. The third series (264-351) is considerably more difficult to obtain than cards in the first two series. In-Action cards (IA in the checklist below) are included as numbers 119-132, 250-263, and 338-351, as are All-Pro selections (AP below) numbered 264-287. The first eight (1-8) cards in the set feature statistical league leaders for the AFC and NFC. Cards 133-139 show the results of the previous season's playoff action. The card backs are printed in blue and green on gray card stock. The key rookie cards in this set are Lyle Alzado, Ted Hendricks, Charlie Joiner, Archie Manning, Jim Plunkett, John Riggins, Steve Spurrier, Roger Staubach, and Gene Upshaw.

		NRMT	VG-E	GOOD
COMPLETE SET (351)		1800.00	800.00	225.00
COMMON PLAYER (1-132)		.45	.22	.04
COMMON PLAYER (133-263)		.65	.30	.06
COMMON PLAYER (264-351)		15.00	7.50	1.50
□ 1	AFC Rushing Leaders	3.25	.75	.15
	Floyd Little			
	Larry Csonka			
	Marv Hubbard			
□ 2	NFC Rushing Leaders	.80	.40	.08
	John Brockington			
	Steve Owens			
	Willie Ellison			
□ 3	AFC Passing Leaders	1.50	.75	.15
	Bob Griese			
	Len Dawson			
	Virgil Carter			
□ 4	NFC Passing Leaders	3.25	1.60	.32
	Roger Staubach			
	Greg Landry			
	Bill Kilmer			
□ 5	AFC Receiving Leaders	.80	.40	.08
	Fred Biletnikoff			
	Otis Taylor			
	Randy Vataha			
□ 6	NFC Receiving Leaders	.80	.40	.08
	Bob Tucker			
	Ted Kwalick			
	Harold Jackson			
	Roy Jefferson			
□ 7	AFC Scoring Leaders	.65	.30	.06
	Garo Yepremian			
	Jan Stenerud			
	Jim O'Brien			
□ 8	NFC Scoring Leaders	.65	.30	.06
	Curt Knight			
	Errol Mann			
	Bruce Gossett			
□ 9	Jim Kiick	.65	.30	.06
	Miami Dolphins			
□ 10	Otis Taylor	1.00	.50	.10
	Kansas City Chiefs			
□ 11	Bobby Joe Green	.45	.22	.04
	Chicago Bears			
□ 12	Ken Ellis	.45	.22	.04
	Green Bay Packers			
□ 13	John Riggins	25.00	12.50	2.50
	New York Jets			
□ 14	Dave Parks	.65	.30	.06
	New Orleans Saints			
□ 15	John Hadl	1.50	.75	.15
	San Diego Chargers			
□ 16	Ron Hornsby	.45	.22	.04
	New York Giants			
□ 17	Chip Myers	.65	.30	.06
	Cincinnati Bengals			

☐ 18 Bill Kilmer 1.50	.75	.15	
Washington Redskins			
☐ 19 Fred Hoaglin .... .45	.22	.04	
Cleveland Browns			
☐ 20 Carl Eller 1.50	.75	.15	
Minnesota Vikings			
☐ 21 Steve Zabel .... .45	.22	.04	
Philadelphia Eagles			
☐ 22 Vic Washington 1.00	.50	.10	
San Francisco 49ers			
☐ 23 Len St. Jean .... .45	.22	.04	
New England Patriots			
☐ 24 Bill Thompson .... .65	.30	.06	
Denver Broncos			
☐ 25 Steve Owens 1.75	.85	.17	
Detroit Lions			
☐ 26 Ken Burrough 1.25	.60	.12	
Houston Oilers			
☐ 27 Mike Clark .... .45	.22	.04	
Dallas Cowboys			
☐ 28 Willie Brown 3.25	1.60	.32	
Oakland Raiders			
☐ 29 Checklist 1-132 .... 5.50	.50	.10	
☐ 30 Marlin Briscoe 1.00	.50	.10	
Buffalo Bills			
☐ 31 Jerry Logan .... .45	.22	.04	
Baltimore Colts			
☐ 32 Donny Anderson .... .65	.30	.06	
St. Louis Cardinals			
☐ 33 Rich McGeorge .... .45	.22	.04	
Green Bay Packers			
☐ 34 Charlie Durkee .... .45	.22	.04	
New Orleans Saints			
☐ 35 Willie Lanier 3.50	1.75	.35	
Kansas City Chiefs			
☐ 36 Chris Farasopoulos .... .65	.30	.06	
New York Jets			
☐ 37 Ron Shanklin .... .65	.30	.06	
Pittsburgh Steelers			
☐ 38 Forrest Blue 1.00	.50	.10	
San Francisco 49ers			
☐ 39 Ken Reaves .... .45	.22	.04	
Atlanta Falcons			
☐ 40 Roman Gabriel 2.00	1.00	.20	
Los Angeles Rams			
☐ 41 Mac Percival .... .45	.22	.04	
Chicago Bears			
☐ 42 Lem Barney 2.25	1.10	.22	
Detroit Lions			
☐ 43 Nick Buoniconti 1.75	.85	.17	
Miami Dolphins			
☐ 44 Charlie Gogolak .... .65	.30	.06	
New England Patriots			
☐ 45 Bill Bradley 1.75	.85	.17	
Philadelphia Eagles			
☐ 46 Joe Jones .... .45	.22	.04	
Cleveland Browns			
☐ 47 Dave Williams .... .45	.22	.04	
St. Louis Cardinals			
☐ 48 Pete Athas .... .45	.22	.04	
New York Giants			
☐ 49 Virgil Carter .... .65	.30	.06	
Cincinnati Bengals			
☐ 50 Floyd Little 2.00	1.00	.20	
Denver Broncos			
☐ 51 Curt Knight .... .45	.22	.04	
Washington Redskins			
☐ 52 Bobby Maples .... .45	.22	.04	
Houston Oilers			
☐ 53 Charlie West .... .65	.30	.06	
Minnesota Vikings			
☐ 54 Marv Hubbard 1.25	.60	.12	
Oakland Raiders			
☐ 55 Archie Manning 13.50	6.50	1.35	
New Orleans Saints			
☐ 56 Jim O'Brien 1.00	.50	.10	
Baltimore Colts			
☐ 57 Wayne Patrick .... .45	.22	.04	
Buffalo Bills			
☐ 58 Ken Bowman .... .45	.22	.04	
Green Bay Packers			
☐ 59 Roger Wehrli .... .65	.30	.06	
St. Louis Cardinals			
☐ 60 Charlie Sanders UER 1.00	.50	.10	
Detroit Lions			
(Front WR, back TE)			
☐ 61 Jan Stenerud 2.00	1.00	.20	
Kansas City Chiefs			
☐ 62 Willie Ellison .... .65	.30	.06	
Los Angeles Rams			
☐ 63 Walt Sweeney .... .45	.22	.04	
San Diego Chargers			
☐ 64 Ron Smith .... .45	.22	.04	
Chicago Bears			
☐ 65 Jim Plunkett 22.00	11.00	2.20	
New England Patriots			
☐ 66 Herb Adderley UER 2.50	1.25	.25	
Dallas Cowboys			
(misspelled Adderly)			
☐ 67 Mike Reid 3.00	1.50	.30	
Cincinnati Bengals			
☐ 68 Richard Caster 1.50	.75	.15	
New York Jets			
☐ 69 Dave Wilcox .... .65	.30	.06	
San Francisco 49ers			
☐ 70 Leroy Kelly 1.75	.85	.17	
Cleveland Browns			
☐ 71 Bob Lee 1.00	.50	.10	
Minnesota Vikings			
☐ 72 Verlon Biggs .... .45	.22	.04	
Washington Redskins			
☐ 73 Henry Allison .... .45	.22	.04	
Philadelphia Eagles			
☐ 74 Steve Ramsey .... .65	.30	.06	

	Denver Broncos			
☐ 75	Claude Humphrey 65	.30	.06	
	Atlanta Falcons			
☐ 76	Bob Grim 1.00	.50	.10	
	New York Giants			
☐ 77	John Fuqua 65	.30	.06	
	Pittsburgh Steelers			
☐ 78	Ken Houston 3.25	1.60	.32	
	Houston Oilers			
☐ 79	Checklist 133-263 DP ... 4.50	.50	.10	
☐ 80	Bob Griese 6.50	3.25	.65	
	Miami Dolphins			
☐ 81	Lance Rentzel 65	.30	.06	
	Los Angeles Rams			
☐ 82	Ed Podolak 1.50	.75	.15	
	Kansas City Chiefs			
☐ 83	Ike Hill 45	.22	.04	
	Buffalo Bills			
☐ 84	George Farmer 45	.22	.04	
	Chicago Bears			
☐ 85	John Brockington 3.00	1.50	.30	
	Green Bay Packers			
☐ 86	Jim Otto 2.50	1.25	.25	
	Oakland Raiders			
☐ 87	Richard Neal 45	.22	.04	
	New Orleans Saints			
☐ 88	Jim Hart 1.50	.75	.15	
	St. Louis Cardinals			
☐ 89	Bob Babich 45	.22	.04	
	San Diego Chargers			
☐ 90	Gene Washington 1.00	.50	.10	
	San Francisco 49ers			
☐ 91	John Zook 65	.30	.06	
	Atlanta Falcons			
☐ 92	Bobby Duhon 45	.22	.04	
	New York Giants			
☐ 93	Ted Hendricks 16.00	8.00	1.60	
	Baltimore Colts			
☐ 94	Rockne Freitas 45	.22	.04	
	Detroit Lions			
☐ 95	Larry Brown 1.50	.75	.15	
	Washington Redskins			
☐ 96	Mike Phipps 1.00	.50	.10	
	Cleveland Browns			
☐ 97	Julius Adams 80	.40	.08	
	New England Patriots			
☐ 98	Dick Anderson 65	.30	.06	
	Miami Dolphins			
☐ 99	Fred Willis 45	.22	.04	
	Cincinnati Bengals			
☐ 100	Joe Namath 36.00	18.00	3.60	
	New York Jets			
☐ 101	L.C. Greenwood 12.00	6.00	1.20	
	Pittsburgh Steelers			
☐ 102	Mark Nordquist 45	.22	.04	
	Philadelphia Eagles			
☐ 103	Robert Holmes 65	.30	.06	
	Kansas City Chiefs			
☐ 104	Ron Yary 3.25	1.60	.32	
	Minnesota Vikings			
☐ 105	Bob Hayes 1.50	.75	.15	
	Dallas Cowboys			
☐ 106	Lyle Alzado 14.00	7.00	1.40	
	Denver Broncos			
☐ 107	Bob Berry 65	.30	.06	
	Atlanta Falcons			
☐ 108	Phil Villapiano 1.50	.75	.15	
	Oakland Raiders			
☐ 109	Dave Elmendorf 65	.30	.06	
	Los Angeles Rams			
☐ 110	Gale Sayers 25.00	12.50	2.50	
	Chicago Bears			
☐ 111	Jim Tyrer 65	.30	.06	
	Kansas City Chiefs			
☐ 112	Mel Gray 2.50	1.25	.25	
	St. Louis Cardinals			
☐ 113	Gerry Philbin 45	.22	.04	
	New York Jets			
☐ 114	Bob James 45	.22	.04	
	Buffalo Bills			
☐ 115	Garo Yepremian 80	.40	.08	
	Miami Dolphins			
☐ 116	Dave Robinson 65	.30	.06	
	Green Bay Packers			
☐ 117	Jeff Queen 45	.22	.04	
	San Diego Chargers			
☐ 118	Norm Snead 1.00	.50	.10	
	New York Giants			
☐ 119	Jim Nance IA 65	.30	.06	
	New England Patriots			
☐ 120	Terry Bradshaw IA ... 11.00	5.50	1.10	
	Pittsburgh Steelers			
☐ 121	Jim Kiick IA 65	.30	.06	
	Miami Dolphins			
☐ 122	Roger Staubach IA 17.00	8.50	1.70	
	Dallas Cowboys			
☐ 123	Bo Scott IA 45	.22	.04	
	Cleveland Browns			
☐ 124	John Brodie IA 2.00	1.00	.20	
	San Francisco 49ers			
☐ 125	Rick Volk IA 45	.22	.04	
	Baltimore Colts			
☐ 126	John Riggins IA 6.00	3.00	.60	
	New York Jets			
☐ 127	Bubba Smith IA 1.50	.75	.15	
	Baltimore Colts			
☐ 128	Roman Gabriel IA 1.00	.50	.10	
	Los Angeles Rams			
☐ 129	Calvin Hill IA 65	.30	.06	
	Dallas Cowboys			
☐ 130	Bill Nelsen IA 65	.30	.06	
	Cleveland Browns			
☐ 131	Tom Matte IA 65	.30	.06	
	Baltimore Colts			

☐ 132 Bob Griese IA .... 3.00 ... 1.50 ... .30
Miami Dolphins

☐ 133 AFC Semi-Final .... 1.00 ... .50 ... .10
Dolphins 27,
Chiefs 24

☐ 134 NFC Semi-Final .... 1.00 ... .50 ... .10
Cowboys 20,
Vikings 12
(Duane Thomas
getting tackled)

☐ 135 AFC Semi-Final .... 1.00 ... .50 ... .10
Colts 20,
Browns 3
(Don Nottingham)

☐ 136 NFC Semi-Final .... 1.00 ... .50 ... .10
49ers 24,
Redskins 20

☐ 137 AFC Title Game .... 2.00 ... 1.00 ... .20
Dolphins 21,
Colts 0
(Johnny Unitas
getting tackled)

☐ 138 NFC Title Game .... 2.00 ... 1.00 ... .20
Cowboys 14,
49ers 3
(Bob Lilly
making tackle)

☐ 139 Super Bowl .... 5.00 ... 2.50 ... .50
Cowboys 24,
Dolphins 3
(Roger Staubach
rolling out)

☐ 140 Larry Csonka .... 5.00 ... 2.50 ... .50
Miami Dolphins

☐ 141 Rick Volk ....65 ... .30 ... .06
Baltimore Colts

☐ 142 Roy Jefferson ....80 ... .40 ... .08
Washington Redskins

☐ 143 Raymond Chester .... 1.50 ... .75 ... .15
Oakland Raiders

☐ 144 Bobby Douglass ....80 ... .40 ... .08
Chicago Bears

☐ 145 Bob Lilly .... 4.00 ... 2.00 ... .40
Dallas Cowboys

☐ 146 Harold Jackson .... 2.00 ... 1.00 ... .20
Philadelphia Eagles

☐ 147 Pete Gogolak ....80 ... .40 ... .08
New York Giants

☐ 148 Art Malone ....65 ... .30 ... .06
Atlanta Falcons

☐ 149 Ed Flanagan ....65 ... .30 ... .06
Detroit Lions

☐ 150 Terry Bradshaw .... 35.00 ... 17.50 ... 3.50
Pittsburgh Steelers

☐ 151 MacArthur Lane .... 1.00 ... .50 ... .10
Green Bay Packers

☐ 152 Jack Snow ....80 ... .40 ... .08

Los Angeles Rams

☐ 153 Al Beauchamp ....65 ... .30 ... .06
Cincinnati Bengals

☐ 154 Bob Anderson ....80 ... .40 ... .08
Denver Broncos

☐ 155 Ted Kwalick .... 1.50 ... .75 ... .15
San Francisco 49ers

☐ 156 Dan Pastorini .... 1.75 ... .85 ... .17
Houston Oilers

☐ 157 Emmitt Thomas .... 1.25 ... .60 ... .12
Kansas City Chiefs

☐ 158 Randy Vataha .... 1.25 ... .60 ... .12
New England Patriots

☐ 159 Al Atkinson ....65 ... .30 ... .06
New York Jets

☐ 160 O.J. Simpson .... 35.00 ... 17.50 ... 3.50
Buffalo Bills

☐ 161 Jackie Smith ....80 ... .40 ... .08
St. Louis Cardinals

☐ 162 Ernie Kellerman ....65 ... .30 ... .06
Cleveland Browns

☐ 163 Dennis Partee ....65 ... .30 ... .06
San Diego Chargers

☐ 164 Jake Kupp ....65 ... .30 ... .06
New Orleans Saints

☐ 165 John Unitas .... 21.00 ... 10.50 ... 2.10
Baltimore Colts

☐ 166 Clint Jones .... 1.00 ... .50 ... .10
Minnesota Vikings

☐ 167 Paul Warfield .... 4.00 ... 2.00 ... .40
Miami Dolphins

☐ 168 Roland McDole ....65 ... .30 ... .06
Washington Redskins

☐ 169 Daryle Lamonica .... 2.00 ... 1.00 ... .20
Oakland Raiders

☐ 170 Dick Butkus .... 7.50 ... 3.75 ... .75
Chicago Bears

☐ 171 Jim Butler ....65 ... .30 ... .06
Atlanta Falcons

☐ 172 Mike McCoy ....65 ... .30 ... .06
Green Bay Packers

☐ 173 Dave Smith ....65 ... .30 ... .06
Pittsburgh Steelers

☐ 174 Greg Landry .... 1.00 ... .50 ... .10
Detroit Lions

☐ 175 Tom Dempsey ....80 ... .40 ... .08
Philadelphia Eagles

☐ 176 John Charles ....65 ... .30 ... .06
Houston Oilers

☐ 177 Bobby Bell .... 2.25 ... 1.10 ... .22
Kansas City Chiefs

☐ 178 Don Horn ....80 ... .40 ... .08
Denver Broncos

☐ 179 Bob Trumpy .... 1.75 ... .85 ... .17
Cincinnati Bengals

☐ 180 Duane Thomas .... 1.25 ... .60 ... .12
Dallas Cowboys

☐ 181	Merlin Olsen 3.50	1.75	.35
	Los Angeles Rams		
☐ 182	Dave Herman .... .65	.30	.06
	New York Jets		
☐ 183	Jim Nance .... .80	.40	.08
	New England Patriots		
☐ 184	Pete Beathard 1.00	.50	.10
	St. Louis Cardinals		
☐ 185	Bob Tucker .... .80	.40	.08
	New York Giants		
☐ 186	Gene Upshaw 17.00	8.50	1.70
	Oakland Raiders		
☐ 187	Bo Scott .... .65	.30	.06
	Cleveland Browns		
☐ 188	J.D. Hill 1.00	.50	.10
	Buffalo Bills		
☐ 189	Bruce Gossett .... .65	.30	.06
	San Francisco 49ers		
☐ 190	Bubba Smith 3.25	1.60	.32
	Baltimore Colts		
☐ 191	Edd Hargett .... .80	.40	.08
	New Orleans Saints		
☐ 192	Gary Garrison .... .80	.40	.08
	San Diego Chargers		
☐ 193	Jake Scott 1.00	.50	.10
	Miami Dolphins		
☐ 194	Fred Cox .... .80	.40	.08
	Minnesota Vikings		
☐ 195	Sonny Jurgensen 3.75	1.85	.37
	Washington Redskins		
☐ 196	Greg Brezina 1.00	.50	.10
	Atlanta Falcons		
☐ 197	Ed O'Bradovich .... .65	.30	.06
	Chicago Bears		
☐ 198	John Rowser .... .65	.30	.06
	Pittsburgh Steelers		
☐ 199	Altie Taylor UER .... .80	.40	.08
	Detroit Lions		
	(Taylor misspelled as		
	Tayor on front)		
☐ 200	Roger Staubach 110.00	55.00	11.00
	Dallas Cowboys		
☐ 201	Leroy Keyes 1.75	.85	.17
	Philadelphia Eagles		
☐ 202	Garland Boyette .... .65	.30	.06
	Houston Oilers		
☐ 203	Tom Beer .... .65	.30	.06
	New England Patriots		
☐ 204	Buck Buchanan 2.25	1.10	.22
	Kansas City Chiefs		
☐ 205	Larry Wilson 2.25	1.10	.22
	St. Louis Cardinals		
☐ 206	Scott Hunter 1.00	.50	.10
	Green Bay Packers		
☐ 207	Ron Johnson 1.00	.50	.10
	New York Giants		
☐ 208	Sam Brunelli .... .65	.30	.06
☐ 209	Deacon Jones 3.50	1.75	.35
	Los Angeles Rams		
☐ 210	Fred Biletnikoff 4.50	2.25	.45
	Oakland Raiders		
☐ 211	Bill Nelsen .... .80	.40	.08
	Cleveland Browns		
☐ 212	George Nock .... .65	.30	.06
	New York Jets		
☐ 213	Dan Abramowicz .... .80	.40	.08
	New Orleans Saints		
☐ 214	Irv Goode .... .65	.30	.06
	Buffalo Bills		
☐ 215	Isiah Robertson 1.50	.75	.15
	Los Angeles Rams		
☐ 216	Tom Matte 1.00	.50	.10
	Baltimore Colts		
☐ 217	Pat Fischer .... .80	.40	.08
	Washington Redskins		
☐ 218	Gene Washington 1.00	.50	.10
	San Francisco 49ers		
☐ 219	Paul Robinson .... .80	.40	.08
	Cincinnati Bengals		
☐ 220	John Brodie 3.75	1.85	.37
	San Francisco 49ers		
☐ 221	Manny Fernandez 1.50	.75	.15
	Miami Dolphins		
☐ 222	Errol Mann .... .65	.30	.06
	Detroit Lions		
☐ 223	Dick Gordon .... .65	.30	.06
	Chicago Bears		
☐ 224	Calvin Hill 1.50	.75	.15
	Dallas Cowboys		
☐ 225	Fran Tarkenton 20.00	10.00	2.00
	New York Giants		
☐ 226	Jim Turner .... .80	.40	.08
	Denver Broncos		
☐ 227	Jim Mitchell .... .80	.40	.08
	Atlanta Falcons		
☐ 228	Pete Liske .... .65	.30	.06
	Philadelphia Eagles		
☐ 229	Carl Garrett .... .65	.30	.06
	New England Patriots		
☐ 230	Joe Greene 11.00	5.50	1.10
	Pittsburgh Steelers		
☐ 231	Gale Gillingham .... .65	.30	.06
	Green Bay Packers		
☐ 232	Norm Bulaich 1.25	.60	.12
	Baltimore Colts		
☐ 233	Spider Lockhart .... .65	.30	.06
	New York Giants		
☐ 234	Ken Willard .... .80	.40	.08
	San Francisco 49ers		
☐ 235	George Blanda 8.50	4.25	.85
	Oakland Raiders		
☐ 236	Wayne Mulligan .... .65	.30	.06
	St. Louis Cardinals		

☐ 237	Dave Lewis 65	.30	.06
	Cincinnati Bengals		
☐ 238	Dennis Shaw 80	.40	.08
	Buffalo Bills		
☐ 239	Fair Hooker 80	.40	.08
	Cleveland Browns		
☐ 240	Larry Little 4.00	2.00	.40
	Miami Dolphins		
☐ 241	Mike Garrett 80	.40	.08
	San Diego Chargers		
☐ 242	Glen Ray Hines 65	.30	.06
	New Orleans Saints		
☐ 243	Myron Pottios 65	.30	.06
	Washington Redskins		
☐ 244	Charlie Joiner 22.00	11.00	2.20
	Houston Oilers		
☐ 245	Len Dawson 3.75	1.85	.37
	Kansas City Chiefs		
☐ 246	W.K. Hicks 65	.30	.06
	New York Jets		
☐ 247	Les Josephson 80	.40	.08
	Los Angeles Rams		
☐ 248	Lance Alworth UER 3.75	1.85	.37
	Dallas Cowboys		
	(Front TE, back WR)		
☐ 249	Frank Nunley 65	.30	.06
	San Francisco 49ers		
☐ 250	Mel Farr IA 65	.30	.06
	Detroit Lions		
☐ 251	Johnny Unitas IA 7.50	3.75	.75
	Baltimore Colts		
☐ 252	George Farmer IA 65	.30	.06
	Chicago Bears		
☐ 253	Duane Thomas IA 80	.40	.08
	Dallas Cowboys		
☐ 254	John Hadl IA 1.00	.50	.10
	San Diego Chargers		
☐ 255	Vic Washington IA 65	.30	.06
	San Francisco 49ers		
☐ 256	Don Horn IA 65	.30	.06
	Denver Broncos		
☐ 257	L.C. Greenwood IA 2.50	1.25	.25
	Pittsburgh Steelers		
☐ 258	Bob Lee IA 65	.30	.06
	Minnesota Vikings		
☐ 259	Larry Csonka IA 3.00	1.50	.30
	Miami Dolphins		
☐ 260	Mike McCoy IA 65	.30	.06
	Green Bay Packers		
☐ 261	Greg Landry IA 80	.40	.08
	Detroit Lions		
☐ 262	Ray May IA 65	.30	.06
	Baltimore Colts		
☐ 263	Bobby Douglass IA 65	.30	.06
	Chicago Bears		
☐ 264	Charlie Sanders AP ...16.00	8.00	1.60
	Detroit Lions		
☐ 265	Ron Yary AP 20.00	10.00	2.00
	Minnesota Vikings		
☐ 266	Rayfield Wright AP 16.00	8.00	1.60
	Dallas Cowboys		
☐ 267	Larry Little AP 16.00	8.00	1.60
	Miami Dolphins		
☐ 268	John Niland AP 16.00	8.00	1.60
	Dallas Cowboys		
☐ 269	Forrest Blue AP 16.00	8.00	1.60
	San Francisco 49ers		
☐ 270	Otis Taylor AP 16.00	8.00	1.60
	Kansas City Chiefs		
☐ 271	Paul Warfield AP 30.00	15.00	3.00
	Miami Dolphins		
☐ 272	Bob Griese AP 35.00	17.50	3.50
	Miami Dolphins		
☐ 273	John Brockington AP 16.00	8.00	1.60
	Green Bay Packers		
☐ 274	Floyd Little AP 22.00	11.00	2.20
	Denver Broncos		
☐ 275	Garo Yepremian AP ...16.00	8.00	1.60
	Miami Dolphins		
☐ 276	Jerrel Wilson AP 16.00	8.00	1.60
	Kansas City Chiefs		
☐ 277	Carl Eller AP 22.00	11.00	2.20
	Minnesota Vikings		
☐ 278	Bubba Smith AP 25.00	12.50	2.50
	Baltimore Colts		
☐ 279	Alan Page AP 24.00	12.00	2.40
	Minnesota Vikings		
☐ 280	Bob Lilly AP 34.00	16.00	3.00
	Dallas Cowboys		
☐ 281	Ted Hendricks AP 36.00	18.00	3.60
	Baltimore Colts		
☐ 282	Dave Wilcox AP 16.00	8.00	1.60
	San Francisco 49ers		
☐ 283	Willie Lanier AP 22.00	11.00	2.20
	Kansas City Chiefs		
☐ 284	Jim Johnson AP 16.00	8.00	1.60
	San Francisco 49ers		
☐ 285	Willie Brown AP 22.00	11.00	2.20
	Oakland Raiders		
☐ 286	Bill Bradley AP 16.00	8.00	1.60
	Philadelphia Eagles		
☐ 287	Ken Houston AP 22.00	11.00	2.20
	Houston Oilers		
☐ 288	Mel Farr 16.00	8.00	1.60
	Detroit Lions		
☐ 289	Kermit Alexander 16.00	8.00	1.60
	Los Angeles Rams		
☐ 290	John Gilliam 18.00	9.00	1.80
	St. Louis Cardinals		
☐ 291	Steve Spurrier 35.00	17.50	3.50
	San Francisco 49ers		
☐ 292	Walter Johnson 15.00	7.50	1.50
	Cleveland Browns		
☐ 293	Jack Pardee 18.00	9.00	1.80

	Washington Redskins			
☐ 294	Checklist 264-351 ..... 50.00	9.00	1.75	
☐ 295	Winston Hill 15.00	7.50	1.50	
	New York Jets			
☐ 296	Hugo Hollas 15.00	7.50	1.50	
	New Orleans Saints			
☐ 297	Ray May 18.00	9.00	1.80	
	Baltimore Colts			
☐ 298	Jim Bakken 16.00	8.00	1.60	
	St. Louis Cardinals			
☐ 299	Larry Carwell 15.00	7.50	1.50	
	New England Patriots			
☐ 300	Alan Page 25.00	12.50	2.50	
	Minnesota Vikings			
☐ 301	Walt Garrison 18.00	9.00	1.80	
	Dallas Cowboys			
☐ 302	Mike Lucci 16.00	8.00	1.60	
	Detroit Lions			
☐ 303	Nemiah Wilson 15.00	7.50	1.50	
	Oakland Raiders			
☐ 304	Carroll Dale 16.00	8.00	1.60	
	Green Bay Packers			
☐ 305	Jim Kanicki 15.00	7.50	1.50	
	New York Giants			
☐ 306	Preston Pearson 18.00	9.00	1.80	
	Pittsburgh Steelers			
☐ 307	Lemar Parrish 16.00	8.00	1.60	
	Cincinnati Bengals			
☐ 308	Earl Morrall 18.00	9.00	1.80	
	Miami Dolphins			
☐ 309	Tommy Nobis 24.00	12.00	2.40	
*	Atlanta Falcons			
☐ 310	Rich Jackson 15.00	7.50	1.50	
	Denver Broncos			
☐ 311	Doug Cunningham 15.00	7.50	1.50	
	San Francisco 49ers			
☐ 312	Jim Marsalis 16.00	8.00	1.60	
	Kansas City Chiefs			
☐ 313	Jim Beirne 15.00	7.50	1.50	
	Houston Oilers			
☐ 314	Tom McNeill 15.00	7.50	1.50	
	Philadelphia Eagles			
☐ 315	Milt Morin 15.00	7.50	1.50	
	Cleveland Browns			
☐ 316	Rayfield Wright 20.00	10.00	2.00	
	Dallas Cowboys			
☐ 317	Jerry LeVias 16.00	8.00	1.60	
	San Diego Chargers			
☐ 318	Travis Williams 24.00	12.00	2.40	
	Los Angeles Rams			
☐ 319	Edgar Chandler 15.00	7.50	1.50	
	Buffalo Bills			
☐ 320	Bob Wallace 15.00	7.50	1.50	
	Chicago Bears			
☐ 321	Delles Howell 15.00	7.50	1.50	
	New Orleans Saints			
☐ 322	Emerson Boozer 16.00	8.00	1.60	
	New York Jets			

☐ 323	George Atkinson 16.00	8.00	1.60	
	Oakland Raiders			
☐ 324	Mike Montler 15.00	7.50	1.50	
	New England Patriots			
☐ 325	Randy Johnson 15.00	7.50	1.50	
	New York Jets			
☐ 326	Mike Curtis 16.00	8.00	1.60	
	Baltimore Colts			
☐ 327	Miller Farr 15.00	7.50	1.50	
	St. Louis Cardinals			
☐ 328	Horst Muhlmann 15.00	7.50	1.50	
	Cincinnati Bengals			
☐ 329	John Niland 18.00	9.00	1.80	
	Dallas Cowboys			
☐ 330	Andy Russell 16.00	8.00	1.60	
	Pittsburgh Steelers			
☐ 331	Mercury Morris 22.00	11.00	2.20	
	Miami Dolphins			
☐ 332	Jim Johnson 16.00	8.00	1.60	
	San Francisco 49ers			
☐ 333	Jerrel Wilson 16.00	8.00	1.60	
	Kansas City Chiefs			
☐ 334	Charley Taylor 27.00	13.50	2.70	
	Washington Redskins			
☐ 335	Dick LeBeau 16.00	8.00	1.60	
	Detroit Lions			
☐ 336	Jim Marshall 22.00	11.00	2.20	
	Minnesota Vikings			
☐ 337	Tom Mack 18.00	9.00	1.80	
	Los Angeles Rams			
☐ 338	Steve Spurrier IA 22.00	11.00	2.20	
	San Francisco 49ers			
☐ 339	Floyd Little IA 22.00	11.00	2.20	
	Denver Broncos			
☐ 340	Len Dawson IA 32.00	16.00	3.20	
	Kansas City Chiefs			
☐ 341	Dick Butkus IA 40.00	20.00	4.00	
	Chicago Bears			
☐ 342	Larry Brown IA 22.00	11.00	2.20	
	Washington Redskins			
☐ 343	Joe Namath IA 225.00	110.00	22.00	
	New York Jets			
☐ 344	Jim Turner IA 16.00	8.00	1.60	
	Denver Broncos			
☐ 345	Doug Cunningham IA 15.00	7.50	1.50	
	San Francisco 49ers			
☐ 346	Edd Hargett IA 16.00	8.00	1.60	
	New Orleans Saints			
☐ 347	Steve Owens IA 16.00	8.00	1.60	
	Detroit Lions			
☐ 348	George Blanda IA 42.00	20.00	4.00	
	Oakland Raiders			
☐ 349	Ed Podolak IA 16.00	8.00	1.60	
	Kansas City Chiefs			
☐ 350	Rich Jackson IA 15.00	7.50	1.50	
	Denver Broncos			
☐ 351	Ken Willard IA 36.00	10.00	2.00	
	San Francisco 49ers			

1973 Topps

The 1973 Topps football set marks the first of ten years in a row that Topps settled on a 528-card football set. This is Topps' first large football set which was not issued in series. The cards measure 2 1/2" by 3 1/2". The first six cards in the set are statistical league leader cards. Cards 133-139 show the results of the previous season's playoff games. Cards 265-267 are Kid Pictures (KP) showing the player in a boyhood photo. No known scarcities exist. The card backs are printed in blue ink with a red background on gray card stock. The bottom portion of each card back gives a cartoon and trivia question; the question's answer is given upside down. The key rookie cards in this set are Ken Anderson, Dan Dierdorf, Jack Ham, Franco Harris, Jim Langer, Art Shell, Ken Stabler, and Jack Youngblood.

	NRMT	VG-E	GOOD
COMPLETE SET (528)	435.00	200.00	50.00
COMMON PLAYER (1-528)	.40	.20	.04

☐ 1	Rushing Leaders Larry Brown O.J. Simpson	5.00	2.50	.50
☐ 2	Passing Leaders Norm Snead Earl Morrall	.80	.40	.08
☐ 3	Receiving Leaders Harold Jackson Fred Biletnikoff	1.00	.50	.10
☐ 4	Scoring Leaders Chester Marcol Bobby Howfield	.60	.30	.06
☐ 5	Interception Leaders Bill Bradley	.60	.30	.06
☐ 6	Punting Leaders Dave Chapple Jerrel Wilson	.60	.30	.06
☐ 7	Bob Trumpy Cincinnati Bengals	1.25	.60	.12
☐ 8	Mel Tom Philadelphia Eagles	.40	.20	.04
☐ 9	Clarence Ellis Atlanta Falcons	.40	.20	.04
☐ 10	John Niland Dallas Cowboys	.40	.20	.04
☐ 11	Randy Jackson San Francisco 49ers	.40	.20	.04
☐ 12	Greg Landry Detroit Lions	1.00	.50	.10
☐ 13	Cid Edwards San Diego Chargers	.40	.20	.04
☐ 14	Phil Olsen Los Angeles Rams	.40	.20	.04
☐ 15	Terry Bradshaw Pittsburgh Steelers	15.00	7.50	1.50
☐ 16	Al Cowlings Houston Oilers	.40	.20	.04
☐ 17	Walker Gillette St. Louis Cardinals	.60	.30	.06
☐ 18	Bob Atkins Houston Oilers	.40	.20	.04
☐ 19	Diron Talbert Washington Redskins	.80	.40	.08
☐ 20	Jim Johnson San Francisco 49ers	.60	.30	.06
☐ 21	Howard Twilley Miami Dolphins	.60	.30	.06
☐ 22	Dick Enderle New York Giants	.40	.20	.04
☐ 23	Wayne Colman New Orleans Saints	.40	.20	.04
☐ 24	John Schmitt New York Jets	.40	.20	.04
☐ 25	George Blanda Oakland Raiders	7.00	3.50	.70
☐ 26	Milt Morin Cleveland Browns	.40	.20	.04
☐ 27	Mike Current Denver Broncos	.40	.20	.04
☐ 28	Rex Kern Baltimore Colts	.60	.30	.06
☐ 29	MacArthur Lane Green Bay Packers	.60	.30	.06
☐ 30	Alan Page Minnesota Vikings	2.50	1.25	.25
☐ 31	Randy Vataha New England Patriots	.60	.30	.06
☐ 32	Jim Kearney Kansas City Chiefs	.40	.20	.04
☐ 33	Steve Smith	.40	.20	.04

	Philadelphia Eagles			
☐ 34	Ken Anderson	25.00	12.50	2.50
	Cincinnati Bengals			
☐ 35	Calvin Hill	1.00	.50	.10
	Dallas Cowboys			
☐ 36	Andy Maurer	.40	.20	.04
	Atlanta Falcons			
☐ 37	Joe Taylor	.40	.20	.04
	Chicago Bears			
☐ 38	Deacon Jones	2.50	1.25	.25
	San Diego Chargers			
☐ 39	Mike Weger	.40	.20	.04
	Detroit Lions			
☐ 40	Roy Gerela	.40	.20	.04
	Pittsburgh Steelers			
☐ 41	Les Josephson	.60	.30	.06
	Los Angeles Rams			
☐ 42	Dave Washington	.40	.20	.04
	Buffalo Bills			
☐ 43	Bill Curry	1.25	.60	.12
	Houston Oilers			
☐ 44	Fred Heron	.40	.20	.04
	St. Louis Cardinals			
☐ 45	John Brodie	3.25	1.60	.32
	San Francisco 49ers			
☐ 46	Roy Winston	.40	.20	.04
	Minnesota Vikings			
☐ 47	Mike Bragg	.40	.20	.04
	Washington Redskins			
☐ 48	Mercury Morris	1.00	.50	.10
	Miami Dolphins			
☐ 49	Jim Files	.40	.20	.04
	New York Giants			
☐ 50	Gene Upshaw	3.00	1.50	.30
	Oakland Raiders			
☐ 51	Hugo Hollas	.40	.20	.04
	New Orleans Saints			
☐ 52	Rod Sherman	.40	.20	.04
	Denver Broncos			
☐ 53	Ron Snidow	.40	.20	.04
	Cleveland Browns			
☐ 54	Steve Tannen	.80	.40	.08
	New York Jets			
☐ 55	Jim Carter	.40	.20	.04
	Green Bay Packers			
☐ 56	Lydell Mitchell	3.00	1.50	.30
	Baltimore Colts			
☐ 57	Jack Rudnay	.80	.40	.08
	Kansas City Chiefs			
☐ 58	Halvor Hagen	.40	.20	.04
	Buffalo Bills			
☐ 59	Tom Dempsey	.60	.30	.06
	Philadelphia Eagles			
☐ 60	Fran Tarkenton	14.00	7.00	1.40
	Minnesota Vikings			
☐ 61	Lance Alworth	3.00	1.50	.30
	Dallas Cowboys			
☐ 62	Vern Holland	.40	.20	.04
	Cincinnati Bengals			
☐ 63	Steve DeLong	.40	.20	.04
	Chicago Bears			
☐ 64	Art Malone	.40	.20	.04
	Atlanta Falcons			
☐ 65	Isiah Robertson	.60	.30	.06
	Los Angeles Rams			
☐ 66	Jerry Rush	.40	.20	.04
	Detroit Lions			
☐ 67	Bryant Salter	.40	.20	.04
	San Diego Chargers			
☐ 68	Checklist 1-132	3.50	.35	.07
☐ 69	J.D. Hill	.60	.30	.06
	Buffalo Bills			
☐ 70	Forrest Blue	.60	.30	.06
	San Francisco 49ers			
☐ 71	Myron Pottios	.40	.20	.04
	Washington Redskins			
☐ 72	Norm Thompson	.80	.40	.08
	St. Louis Cardinals			
☐ 73	Paul Robinson	.40	.20	.04
	Houston Oilers			
☐ 74	Larry Grantham	.60	.30	.06
	New York Jets			
☐ 75	Manny Fernandez	.60	.30	.06
	Miami Dolphins			
☐ 76	Kent Nix	.40	.20	.04
	New Orleans Saints			
☐ 77	Art Shell	25.00	12.50	2.50
	Oakland Raiders			
☐ 78	George Saimes	.60	.30	.06
	Denver Broncos			
☐ 79	Don Cockroft	.60	.30	.06
	Cleveland Browns			
☐ 80	Bob Tucker	.60	.30	.06
	New York Giants			
☐ 81	Don McCauley	.80	.40	.08
	Baltimore Colts			
☐ 82	Bob Brown	.40	.20	.04
	Green Bay Packers			
☐ 83	Larry Carwell	.40	.20	.04
	New England Patriots			
☐ 84	Mo Moorman	.40	.20	.04
	Kansas City Chiefs			
☐ 85	John Gilliam	.60	.30	.06
	Minnesota Vikings			
☐ 86	Wade Key	.40	.20	.04
	Philadelphia Eagles			
☐ 87	Ross Brupbacher	.40	.20	.04
	Chicago Bears			
☐ 88	Dave Lewis	.40	.20	.04
	Cincinnati Bengals			
☐ 89	Franco Harris	65.00	32.50	6.50
	Pittsburgh Steelers			
☐ 90	Tom Mack	1.00	.50	.10
	Los Angeles Rams			

☐ 91	Mike Tilleman 40	.20	.04	
	Atlanta Falcons			
☐ 92	Carl Mauck 40	.20	.04	
	San Diego Chargers			
☐ 93	Larry Hand 40	.20	.04	
	Detroit Lions			
☐ 94	Dave Foley 40	.20	.04	
	Buffalo Bills			
☐ 95	Frank Nunley 40	.20	.04	
	San Francisco 49ers			
☐ 96	John Charles 40	.20	.04	
	Houston Oilers			
☐ 97	Jim Bakken 60	.30	.06	
	St. Louis Cardinals			
☐ 98	Pat Fischer 60	.30	.06	
	Washington Redskins			
☐ 99	Randy Rasmussen 40	.20	.04	
	New York Jets			
☐ 100	Larry Csonka 3.50	1.75	.35	
	Miami Dolphins			
☐ 101	Mike Siani 80	.40	.08	
	Oakland Raiders			
☐ 102	Tom Roussel 40	.20	.04	
	New Orleans Saints			
☐ 103	Clarence Scott 80	.40	.08	
	Cleveland Browns			
☐ 104	Charlie Johnson 80	.40	.08	
	Denver Broncos			
☐ 105	Rick Volk 40	.20	.04	
	Baltimore Colts			
☐ 106	Willie Young 40	.20	.04	
	New York Giants			
☐ 107	Emmitt Thomas 60	.30	.06	
	Kansas City Chiefs			
☐ 108	Jon Morris 40	.20	.04	
	New England Patriots			
☐ 109	Clarence Williams 40	.20	.04	
	Green Bay Packers			
☐ 110	Rayfield Wright 40	.20	.04	
	Dallas Cowboys			
☐ 111	Norm Bulaich 60	.30	.06	
	Philadelphia Eagles			
☐ 112	Mike Eischeid 40	.20	.04	
	Minnesota Vikings			
☐ 113	Speedy Thomas 40	.20	.04	
	Cincinnati Bengals			
☐ 114	Glen Holloway 40	.20	.04	
	Chicago Bears			
☐ 115	Jack Ham 21.00	10.50	2.10	
	Pittsburgh Steelers			
☐ 116	Jim Nettles 40	.20	.04	
	Los Angeles Rams			
☐ 117	Errol Mann 40	.20	.04	
	Detroit Lions			
☐ 118	John Mackey 1.75	.85	.17	
	San Diego Chargers			
☐ 119	George Kunz 60	.30	.06	

	Atlanta Falcons			
☐ 120	Bob James 40	.20	.04	
	Buffalo Bills			
☐ 121	Garland Boyette 40	.20	.04	
	Houston Oilers			
☐ 122	Mel Phillips 60	.30	.06	
	San Francisco 49ers			
☐ 123	Johnny Roland 60	.30	.06	
	New York Giants			
☐ 124	Doug Swift 40	.20	.04	
	Miami Dolphins			
☐ 125	Archie Manning 2.75	1.35	.27	
	New Orleans Saints			
☐ 126	Dave Herman 40	.20	.04	
	New York Jets			
☐ 127	Carleton Oats 40	.20	.04	
	Oakland Raiders			
☐ 128	Bill Van Heusen 40	.20	.04	
	Denver Broncos			
☐ 129	Rich Jackson 40	.20	.04	
	Cleveland Browns			
☐ 130	Len Hauss 60	.30	.06	
	Washington Redskins			
☐ 131	Billy Parks 80	.40	.08	
	Dallas Cowboys			
☐ 132	Ray May 40	.20	.04	
	Baltimore Colts			
☐ 133	NFC Semi-Final 2.75	1.35	.27	
	Cowboys 30,			
	49ers 28			
	(Roger Staubach			
	dropping back)			
☐ 134	AFC Semi-Final 80	.40	.08	
	Steelers 13,			
	Raiders 7			
	(line play)			
☐ 135	NFC Semi-Final 80	.40	.08	
	Redskins 16,			
	Packers 3			
	(Redskins defense)			
☐ 136	AFC Semi-Final 1.75	.85	.17	
	Dolphins 20,			
	Browns 14			
	(Bob Griese			
	handing off to			
	Larry Csonka)			
☐ 137	NFC Title Game 1.25	.60	.12	
	Redskins 26,			
	Cowboys 3			
	(Bill Kilmer			
	handing off to			
	Larry Brown)			
☐ 138	AFC Title Game 80	.40	.08	
	Dolphins 21,			
	Steelers 17			
	(Miami defense			
	stops Fuqua)			

☐ 139	Super Bowl .... 1.50 Dolphins 14, Redskins 7 (Miami defense)	.75	.15
☐ 140	Dwight White UER ...... 1.50 Pittsburgh Steelers (College North Texas State, should be East Texas State)	.75	.15
☐ 141	Jim Marsalis .... .40 Kansas City Chiefs	.20	.04
☐ 142	Doug Van Horn .... .40 New York Giants	.20	.04
☐ 143	Al Matthews .... .40 Green Bay Packers	.20	.04
☐ 144	Bob Windsor .... .40 New England Patriots	.20	.04
☐ 145	Dave Hampton .... 1.00 Atlanta Falcons	.50	.10
☐ 146	Horst Muhlmann .... .40 Cincinnati Bengals	.20	.04
☐ 147	Wally Hilgenberg .... 1.25 Minnesota Vikings	.60	.12
☐ 148	Ron Smith .... .40 Chicago Bears	.20	.04
☐ 149	Coy Bacon .... 1.25 San Diego Chargers	.60	.12
☐ 150	Winston Hill .... .40 New York Jets	.20	.04
☐ 151	Ron Jessie .... 1.25 Detroit Lions	.60	.12
☐ 152	Ken Iman .... .40 Los Angeles Rams	.20	.04
☐ 153	Ron Saul .... .40 Houston Oilers	.20	.04
☐ 154	Jim Braxton .... .80 Buffalo Bills	.40	.08
☐ 155	Bubba Smith .... 2.75 Baltimore Colts	1.35	.27
☐ 156	Gary Cuozzo .... .60 St. Louis Cardinals	.30	.06
☐ 157	Charlie Krueger .... .40 San Francisco 49ers	.20	.04
☐ 158	Tim Foley .... .80 Miami Dolphins	.40	.08
☐ 159	Lee Roy Jordan .... 1.75 Dallas Cowboys	.85	.17
☐ 160	Bob Brown .... .60 Oakland Raiders	.30	.06
☐ 161	Margene Adkins .... .40 New Orleans Saints	.20	.04
☐ 162	Ron Widby .... .60 Green Bay Packers	.30	.06
☐ 163	Jim Houston .... .60 Cleveland Browns	.30	.06
☐ 164	Joe Dawkins .... .40 Denver Broncos	.20	.04
☐ 165	L.C. Greenwood .... 2.50 Pittsburgh Steelers	1.25	.25
☐ 166	Richmond Flowers .... .60 New York Giants	.30	.06
☐ 167	Curley Culp .... 1.50 Kansas City Chiefs	.75	.15
☐ 168	Len St. Jean .... .40 New England Patriots	.20	.04
☐ 169	Walter Rock .... .40 Washington Redskins	.20	.04
☐ 170	Bill Bradley .... .60 Philadelphia Eagles	.30	.06
☐ 171	Ken Riley .... 1.75 Cincinnati Bengals	.85	.17
☐ 172	Rich Coady .... .40 Chicago Bears	.20	.04
☐ 173	Don Hansen .... .40 Atlanta Falcons	.20	.04
☐ 174	Lionel Aldridge .... .40 San Diego Chargers	.20	.04
☐ 175	Don Maynard .... 2.50 St. Louis Cardinals	1.25	.25
☐ 176	Dave Osborn .... .60 Minnesota Vikings	.30	.06
☐ 177	Jim Bailey .... .40 Baltimore Colts	.20	.04
☐ 178	John Pitts .... .40 Buffalo Bills	.20	.04
☐ 179	Dave Parks .... .60 Houston Oilers	.30	.06
☐ 180	Chester Marcol .... .80 Green Bay Packers	.40	.08
☐ 181	Len Rohde .... .40 San Francisco 49ers	.20	.04
☐ 182	Jeff Staggs .... .40 St. Louis Cardinals	.20	.04
☐ 183	Gene Hickerson .... .40 Cleveland Browns	.20	.04
☐ 184	Charlie Evans .... .40 New York Giants	.20	.04
☐ 185	Mel Renfro .... 1.00 Dallas Cowboys	.50	.10
☐ 186	Marvin Upshaw .... .40 Kansas City Chiefs	.20	.04
☐ 187	George Atkinson .... .60 Oakland Raiders	.30	.06
☐ 188	Norm Evans .... .60 Miami Dolphins	.30	.06
☐ 189	Steve Ramsey .... .60 Denver Broncos	.30	.06
☐ 190	Dave Chapple .... .40 Los Angeles Rams	.20	.04
☐ 191	Gerry Mullins .... .40 Pittsburgh Steelers	.20	.04
☐ 192	John Didion .... .40 New Orleans Saints	.20	.04
☐ 193	Bob Gladieux .... .40	.20	.04

		New England Patriots			
☐ 194	Don Hultz	.40	.20	.04
	Philadelphia Eagles			
☐ 195	Mike Lucci	.60	.30	.06
	Detroit Lions			
☐ 196	John Wilbur	.40	.20	.04
	Washington Redskins			
☐ 197	George Farmer	.40	.20	.04
	Chicago Bears			
☐ 198	Tommy Casanova	1.25	.60	.12
	Cincinnati Bengals			
☐ 199	Russ Washington	.40	.20	.04
	San Diego Chargers			
☐ 200	Claude Humphrey	.60	.30	.06
	Atlanta Falcons			
☐ 201	Pat Hughes	.40	.20	.04
	New York Jets			
☐ 202	Zeke Moore	.40	.20	.04
	Houston Oilers			
☐ 203	Chip Glass	.40	.20	.04
	Cleveland Browns			
☐ 204	Glenn Ressler	.40	.20	.04
	Baltimore Colts			
☐ 205	Willie Ellison	.40	.20	.04
	Kansas City Chiefs			
☐ 206	John Leypoldt	.40	.20	.04
	Buffalo Bills			
☐ 207	Johnny Fuller	.40	.20	.04
	San Francisco 49ers			
☐ 208	Bill Hayhoe	.40	.20	.04
	Green Bay Packers			
☐ 209	Ed Bell	.40	.20	.04
	New York Jets			
☐ 210	Willie Brown	2.00	1.00	.20
	Oakland Raiders			
☐ 211	Carl Eller	1.50	.75	.15
	Minnesota Vikings			
☐ 212	Mark Nordquist	.40	.20	.04
	Philadelphia Eagles			
☐ 213	Larry Willingham	.40	.20	.04
	St. Louis Cardinals			
☐ 214	Nick Buoniconti	1.50	.75	.15
	Miami Dolphins			
☐ 215	John Hadl	1.50	.75	.15
	Los Angeles Rams			
☐ 216	Jethro Pugh	1.00	.50	.10
	Dallas Cowboys			
☐ 217	Leroy Mitchell	.40	.20	.04
	Denver Broncos			
☐ 218	Billy Newsome	.40	.20	.04
	New Orleans Saints			
☐ 219	John McMakin	.40	.20	.04
	Pittsburgh Steelers			
☐ 220	Larry Brown	1.25	.60	.12
	Washington Redskins			
☐ 221	Clarence Scott	.40	.20	.04
	New England Patriots			

☐ 222	Paul Naumoff	.40	.20	.04
	Detroit Lions			
☐ 223	Ted Fritsch Jr.	.40	.20	.04
	Atlanta Falcons			
☐ 224	Checklist 133-264	3.50	.35	.07
☐ 225	Dan Pastorini	.80	.40	.08
	Houston Oilers			
☐ 226	Joe Beauchamp	.40	.20	.04
	San Diego Chargers			
☐ 227	Pat Matson	.40	.20	.04
	Cincinnati Bengals			
☐ 228	Tony McGee	.40	.20	.04
	Chicago Bears			
☐ 229	Mike Phipps	.60	.30	.06
	Cleveland Browns			
☐ 230	Harold Jackson	1.25	.60	.12
	Los Angeles Rams			
☐ 231	Willie Williams	.40	.20	.04
	New York Giants			
☐ 232	Spike Jones	.40	.20	.04
	Buffalo Bills			
☐ 233	Jim Tyrer	.60	.30	.06
	Kansas City Chiefs			
☐ 234	Roy Hilton	.40	.20	.04
	Baltimore Colts			
☐ 235	Phil Villapiano	.60	.30	.06
	Oakland Raiders			
☐ 236	Charley Taylor UER	3.00	1.50	.30
	(Charlie on front)			
	Washington Redskins			
☐ 237	Malcolm Snider	.40	.20	.04
	Green Bay Packers			
☐ 238	Vic Washington	.60	.30	.06
	San Francisco 49ers			
☐ 239	Grady Alderman	.40	.20	.04
	Minnesota Vikings			
☐ 240	Dick Anderson	.60	.30	.06
	Miami Dolphins			
☐ 241	Ron Yankowski	.40	.20	.04
	St. Louis Cardinals			
☐ 242	Billy Masters	.40	.20	.04
	Denver Broncos			
☐ 243	Herb Adderley	2.25	1.10	.22
	Dallas Cowboys			
☐ 244	David Ray	.40	.20	.04
	Los Angeles Rams			
☐ 245	John Riggins	6.50	3.25	.65
	New York Jets			
☐ 246	Mike Wagner	1.25	.60	.12
	Pittsburgh Steelers			
☐ 247	Don Morrison	.40	.20	.04
	New Orleans Saints			
☐ 248	Earl McCullouch	.60	.30	.06
	Detroit Lions			
☐ 249	Dennis Wirgowski	.40	.20	.04
	Philadelphia Eagles			
☐ 250	Chris Hanburger	.60	.30	.06

Washington Redskins
| ☐ 251 Pat Sullivan | 1.50 | .75 | .15 |

Atlanta Falcons
| ☐ 252 Walt Sweeney | .40 | .20 | .04 |

San Diego Chargers
| ☐ 253 Willie Alexander | .40 | .20 | .04 |

Houston Oilers
| ☐ 254 Doug Dressler | .40 | .20 | .04 |

Cincinnati Bengals
| ☐ 255 Walter Johnson | .40 | .20 | .04 |

Cleveland Browns
| ☐ 256 Ron Hornsby | .40 | .20 | .04 |

New York Giants
| ☐ 257 Ben Hawkins | .40 | .20 | .04 |

Philadelphia Eagles
| ☐ 258 Donnie Green | .40 | .20 | .04 |

Buffalo Bills
| ☐ 259 Fred Hoaglin | .40 | .20 | .04 |

Baltimore Colts
| ☐ 260 Jerrel Wilson | .60 | .30 | .06 |

Kansas City Chiefs
| ☐ 261 Horace Jones | .40 | .20 | .04 |

Oakland Raiders
| ☐ 262 Woody Peoples | .40 | .20 | .04 |

San Francisco 49ers
| ☐ 263 Jim Hill | .40 | .20 | .04 |

Green Bay Packers
| ☐ 264 John Fuqua | .60 | .30 | .06 |

Pittsburgh Steelers
| ☐ 265 Donny Anderson KP | .60 | .30 | .06 |

St. Louis Cardinals
| ☐ 266 Roman Gabriel KP | .80 | .40 | .08 |

Philadelphia Eagles
| ☐ 267 Mike Garrett KP | .60 | .30 | .06 |

San Diego Chargers
| ☐ 268 Rufus Mayes | .60 | .30 | .06 |

Cincinnati Bengals
| ☐ 269 Chip Myrtle | .40 | .20 | .04 |

Denver Broncos
| ☐ 270 Bill Stanfill | .80 | .40 | .08 |

Miami Dolphins
| ☐ 271 Clint Jones | .60 | .30 | .06 |

San Diego Chargers
| ☐ 272 Miller Farr | .40 | .20 | .04 |

Detroit Lions
| ☐ 273 Harry Schuh | .40 | .20 | .04 |

Los Angeles Rams
| ☐ 274 Bob Hayes | 1.25 | .60 | .12 |

Dallas Cowboys
| ☐ 275 Bobby Douglass | .60 | .30 | .06 |

Chicago Bears
| ☐ 276 Gus Hollomon | .40 | .20 | .04 |

New York Jets
| ☐ 277 Del Williams | .40 | .20 | .04 |

New Orleans Saints
| ☐ 278 Julius Adams | .40 | .20 | .04 |

New England Patriots
| ☐ 279 Herman Weaver | .40 | .20 | .04 |

Detroit Lions
| ☐ 280 Joe Greene | 4.50 | 2.25 | .45 |

Pittsburgh Steelers
| ☐ 281 Wes Chesson | .40 | .20 | .04 |

Atlanta Falcons
| ☐ 282 Charlie Harraway | .40 | .20 | .04 |

Washington Redskins
| ☐ 283 Paul Guidry | .40 | .20 | .04 |

Houston Oilers
| ☐ 284 Terry Owens | .60 | .30 | .06 |

San Diego Chargers
| ☐ 285 Jan Stenerud | 1.50 | .75 | .15 |

Kansas City Chiefs
| ☐ 286 Pete Athas | .40 | .20 | .04 |

New York Giants
| ☐ 287 Dale Lindsey | .40 | .20 | .04 |

Cleveland Browns
| ☐ 288 Jack Tatum | 4.00 | 2.00 | .40 |

Oakland Raiders
| ☐ 289 Floyd Little | 1.50 | .75 | .15 |

Denver Broncos
| ☐ 290 Bob Johnson | .40 | .20 | .04 |

Cincinnati Bengals
| ☐ 291 Tommy Hart | .60 | .30 | .06 |

San Francisco 49ers
| ☐ 292 Tom Mitchell | .40 | .20 | .04 |

Baltimore Colts
| ☐ 293 Walt Patulski | .60 | .30 | .06 |

Buffalo Bills
| ☐ 294 Jim Skaggs | .40 | .20 | .04 |

Philadelphia Eagles
| ☐ 295 Bob Griese | 6.00 | 3.00 | .60 |

Miami Dolphins
| ☐ 296 Mike McCoy | .40 | .20 | .04 |

Green Bay Packers
| ☐ 297 Mel Gray | .60 | .30 | .06 |

St. Louis Cardinals
| ☐ 298 Bobby Bryant | .40 | .20 | .04 |

Minnesota Vikings
| ☐ 299 Blaine Nye | .60 | .30 | .06 |

Dallas Cowboys
| ☐ 300 Dick Butkus | 6.00 | 3.00 | .60 |

Chicago Bears
| ☐ 301 Charlie Cowan | .60 | .30 | .06 |

Los Angeles Rams
| ☐ 302 Mark Lomas | .40 | .20 | .04 |

New York Jets
| ☐ 303 Josh Ashton | .40 | .20 | .04 |

New England Patriots
| ☐ 304 Happy Feller | .40 | .20 | .04 |

New Orleans Saints
| ☐ 305 Ron Shanklin | .40 | .20 | .04 |

Pittsburgh Steelers
| ☐ 306 Wayne Rasmussen | .40 | .20 | .04 |

Detroit Lions
| ☐ 307 Jerry Smith | .60 | .30 | .06 |

Washington Redskins			
☐ 308 Ken Reaves	.40	.20	.04
Atlanta Falcons			
☐ 309 Ron East	.40	.20	.04
San Diego Chargers			
☐ 310 Otis Taylor	1.00	.50	.10
Kansas City Chiefs			
☐ 311 John Garlington	.40	.20	.04
Cleveland Browns			
☐ 312 Lyle Alzado	3.50	1.75	.35
Denver Broncos			
☐ 313 Remi Prudhomme	.40	.20	.04
Buffalo Bills			
☐ 314 Cornelius Johnson	.40	.20	.04
Baltimore Colts			
☐ 315 Lemar Parrish	.60	.30	.06
Cincinnati Bengals			
☐ 316 Jim Kiick	.60	.30	.06
Miami Dolphins			
☐ 317 Steve Zabel	.40	.20	.04
Philadelphia Eagles			
☐ 318 Alden Roche	.40	.20	.04
Green Bay Packers			
☐ 319 Tom Blanchard	.40	.20	.04
New York Giants			
☐ 320 Fred Biletnikoff	3.25	1.60	.32
Oakland Raiders			
☐ 321 Ralph Neely	.60	.30	.06
Dallas Cowboys			
☐ 322 Dan Dierdorf	12.00	6.00	1.20
St. Louis Cardinals			
☐ 323 Richard Caster	.60	.30	.06
New York Jets			
☐ 324 Gene Howard	.40	.20	.04
Los Angeles Rams			
☐ 325 Elvin Bethea	.60	.30	.06
Houston Oilers			
☐ 326 Carl Garrett	.40	.20	.04
Chicago Bears			
☐ 327 Ron Billingsley	.40	.20	.04
New Orleans Saints			
☐ 328 Charlie West	.40	.20	.04
Minnesota Vikings			
☐ 329 Tom Neville	.40	.20	.04
New England Patriots			
☐ 330 Ted Kwalick	.60	.30	.06
San Francisco 49ers			
☐ 331 Rudy Redmond	.40	.20	.04
Detroit Lions			
☐ 332 Henry Davis	.40	.20	.04
Pittsburgh Steelers			
☐ 333 John Zook	.60	.30	.06
Atlanta Falcons			
☐ 334 Jim Turner	.60	.30	.06
Denver Broncos			
☐ 335 Len Dawson	3.50	1.75	.35
Kansas City Chiefs			

☐ 336 Bob Chandler	.80	.40	.08
Buffalo Bills			
☐ 337 Al Beauchamp	.40	.20	.04
Cincinnati Bengals			
☐ 338 Tom Matte	.60	.30	.06
San Diego Chargers			
☐ 339 Paul Laaveg	.40	.20	.04
Washington Redskins			
☐ 340 Ken Ellis	.40	.20	.04
Green Bay Packers			
☐ 341 Jim Langer	12.50	6.25	1.25
Miami Dolphins			
☐ 342 Ron Porter	.40	.20	.04
Philadelphia Eagles			
☐ 343 Jack Youngblood	10.00	5.00	1.00
Los Angeles Rams			
☐ 344 Cornell Green	.60	.30	.06
Dallas Cowboys			
☐ 345 Marv Hubbard	.60	.30	.06
Oakland Raiders			
☐ 346 Bruce Taylor	.60	.30	.06
San Francisco 49ers			
☐ 347 Sam Havrilak	.40	.20	.04
Baltimore Colts			
☐ 348 Walt Sumner	.40	.20	.04
Cleveland Browns			
☐ 349 Steve O'Neal	.40	.20	.04
New York Jets			
☐ 350 Ron Johnson	.60	.30	.06
New York Giants			
☐ 351 Rockne Freitas	.40	.20	.04
Detroit Lions			
☐ 352 Larry Stallings	.40	.20	.04
St. Louis Cardinals			
☐ 353 Jim Cadile	.40	.20	.04
Chicago Bears			
☐ 354 Ken Burrough	.60	.30	.06
Houston Oilers			
☐ 355 Jim Plunkett	4.00	2.00	.40
New England Patriots			
☐ 356 Dave Long	.40	.20	.04
New Orleans Saints			
☐ 357 Ralph Anderson	.40	.20	.04
Pittsburgh Steelers			
☐ 358 Checklist 265-396	3.50	.35	.07
☐ 359 Gene Washington	.60	.30	.06
Minnesota Vikings			
☐ 360 Dave Wilcox	.60	.30	.06
San Francisco 49ers			
☐ 361 Paul Smith	.60	.30	.06
Denver Broncos			
☐ 362 Alvin Wyatt	.40	.20	.04
Buffalo Bills			
☐ 363 Charlie Smith	.40	.20	.04
Oakland Raiders			
☐ 364 Royce Berry	.40	.20	.04
Cincinnati Bengals			

☐ 365	Dave Elmendorf 40	.20	.04
	Los Angeles Rams		
☐ 366	Scott Hunter 60	.30	.06
	Green Bay Packers		
☐ 367	Bob Kuechenberg 2.25	1.10	.22
	Miami Dolphins		
☐ 368	Pete Gogolak 60	.30	.06
	New York Giants		
☐ 369	Dave Edwards 60	.30	.06
	Dallas Cowboys		
☐ 370	Lem Barney 1.75	.85	.17
	Detroit Lions		
☐ 371	Verlon Biggs 40	.20	.04
	Washington Redskins		
☐ 372	John Reaves 60	.30	.06
	Philadelphia Eagles		
☐ 373	Ed Podolak 60	.30	.06
	Kansas City Chiefs		
☐ 374	Chris Farasopoulos 40	.20	.04
	New York Jets		
☐ 375	Gary Garrison 60	.30	.06
	San Diego Chargers		
☐ 376	Tom Funchess 40	.20	.04
	Houston Oilers		
☐ 377	Bobby Joe Green 40	.20	.04
	Chicago Bears		
☐ 378	Don Brumm 40	.20	.04
	St. Louis Cardinals		
☐ 379	Jim O'Brien 40	.20	.04
	Baltimore Colts		
☐ 380	Paul Krause 1.00	.50	.10
	Minnesota Vikings		
☐ 381	Leroy Kelly 1.25	.60	.12
	Cleveland Browns		
☐ 382	Ray Mansfield 40	.20	.04
	Pittsburgh Steelers		
☐ 383	Dan Abramowicz 60	.30	.06
	New Orleans Saints		
☐ 384	John Outlaw 40	.20	.04
	New England Patriots		
☐ 385	Tommy Nobis 1.50	.75	.15
	Atlanta Falcons		
☐ 386	Tom Domres 40	.20	.04
	Denver Broncos		
☐ 387	Ken Willard 60	.30	.06
	San Francisco 49ers		
☐ 388	Mike Stratton 40	.20	.04
	San Diego Chargers		
☐ 389	Fred Dryer 3.00	1.50	.30
	Los Angeles Rams		
☐ 390	Jake Scott 60	.30	.06
	Miami Dolphins		
☐ 391	Rich Houston 40	.20	.04
	New York Giants		
☐ 392	Virgil Carter 60	.30	.06
	Cincinnati Bengals		
☐ 393	Tody Smith 40	.20	.04
	Dallas Cowboys		
☐ 394	Ernie Calloway 40	.20	.04
	Philadelphia Eagles		
☐ 395	Charlie Sanders 60	.30	.06
	Detroit Lions		
☐ 396	Fred Willis 40	.20	.04
	Houston Oilers		
☐ 397	Curt Knight 40	.20	.04
	Washington Redskins		
☐ 398	Nemiah Wilson 40	.20	.04
	Oakland Raiders		
☐ 399	Carroll Dale 40	.20	.04
	Green Bay Packers		
☐ 400	Joe Namath 28.00	14.00	2.80
	New York Jets		
☐ 401	Wayne Mulligan 40	.20	.04
	St. Louis Cardinals		
☐ 402	Jim Harrison 40	.20	.04
	Chicago Bears		
☐ 403	Tim Rossovich 60	.30	.06
	San Diego Chargers		
☐ 404	David Lee 40	.20	.04
	Baltimore Colts		
☐ 405	Frank Pitts 40	.20	.04
	Cleveland Browns		
☐ 406	Jim Marshall 1.50	.75	.15
	Minnesota Vikings		
☐ 407	Bob Brown 40	.20	.04
	New Orleans Saints		
☐ 408	John Rowser 40	.20	.04
	Pittsburgh Steelers		
☐ 409	Mike Montler 40	.20	.04
	New England Patriots		
☐ 410	Willie Lanier 2.50	1.25	.25
	Kansas City Chiefs		
☐ 411	Bill Bell 40	.20	.04
	Atlanta Falcons		
☐ 412	Cedric Hardman 60	.30	.06
	San Francisco 49ers		
☐ 413	Bob Anderson 60	.30	.06
	Denver Broncos		
☐ 414	Earl Morrall 1.25	.60	.12
	Miami Dolphins		
☐ 415	Ken Houston 2.25	1.10	.22
	Houston Oilers		
☐ 416	Jack Snow 60	.30	.06
	Los Angeles Rams		
☐ 417	Dick Cunningham 40	.20	.04
	Buffalo Bills		
☐ 418	Greg Larson 40	.20	.04
	New York Giants		
☐ 419	Mike Bass 40	.20	.04
	Washington Redskins		
☐ 420	Mike Reid 1.25	.60	.12
	Cincinnati Bengals		
☐ 421	Walt Garrison 80	.40	.08
	Dallas Cowboys		

☐ 422	Pete Liske	40	.20	.04
	Philadelphia Eagles			
☐ 423	Jim Yarbrough	.40	.20	.04
	Detroit Lions			
☐ 424	Rich McGeorge	.40	.20	.04
	Green Bay Packers			
☐ 425	Bobby Howfield	.40	.20	.04
	New York Jets			
☐ 426	Pete Banaszak	.40	.20	.04
	Oakland Raiders			
☐ 427	Willie Holman	.40	.20	.04
	Chicago Bears			
☐ 428	Dale Hackbart	.40	.20	.04
	St. Louis Cardinals			
☐ 429	Fair Hooker	.40	.20	.04
	Cleveland Browns			
☐ 430	Ted Hendricks	4.00	2.00	.40
	Baltimore Colts			
☐ 431	Mike Garrett	.60	.30	.06
	San Diego Chargers			
☐ 432	Glen Ray Hines	.40	.20	.04
	New Orleans Saints			
☐ 433	Fred Cox	.60	.30	.06
	Minnesota Vikings			
☐ 434	Bobby Walden	.40	.20	.04
	Pittsburgh Steelers			
☐ 435	Bobby Bell	2.00	1.00	.20
	Kansas City Chiefs			
☐ 436	Dave Rowe	.40	.20	.04
	New England Patriots			
☐ 437	Bob Berry	.60	.30	.06
	Atlanta Falcons			
☐ 438	Bill Thompson	.60	.30	.06
	Denver Broncos			
☐ 439	Jim Beirne	.40	.20	.04
	Houston Oilers			
☐ 440	Larry Little	1.00	.50	.10
	Miami Dolphins			
☐ 441	Rocky Thompson	.40	.20	.04
	New York Giants			
☐ 442	Brig Owens	.40	.20	.04
	Washington Redskins			
☐ 443	Richard Neal	.40	.20	.04
	New York Jets			
☐ 444	Al Nelson	.40	.20	.04
	Philadelphia Eagles			
☐ 445	Chip Myers	.40	.20	.04
	Cincinnati Bengals			
☐ 446	Ken Bowman	.40	.20	.04
	Green Bay Packers			
☐ 447	Jim Purnell	.40	.20	.04
	Los Angeles Rams			
☐ 448	Altie Taylor	.40	.20	.04
	Detroit Lions			
☐ 449	Linzy Cole	.40	.20	.04
	Buffalo Bills			
☐ 450	Bob Lilly	4.00	2.00	.40
	Dallas Cowboys			
☐ 451	Charlie Ford	.40	.20	.04
	Chicago Bears			
☐ 452	Milt Sunde	.40	.20	.04
	Minnesota Vikings			
☐ 453	Doug Wyatt	.40	.20	.04
	New Orleans Saints			
☐ 454	Don Nottingham	.80	.40	.08
	Baltimore Colts			
☐ 455	John Unitas	18.00	9.00	1.80
	San Diego Chargers			
☐ 456	Frank Lewis	1.50	.75	.15
	Pittsburgh Steelers			
☐ 457	Roger Wehrli	.60	.30	.06
	St. Louis Cardinals			
☐ 458	Jim Cheyunski	.40	.20	.04
	New England Patriots			
☐ 459	Jerry Sherk	1.00	.50	.10
	Cleveland Browns			
☐ 460	Gene Washington	.80	.40	.08
	San Francisco 49ers			
☐ 461	Jim Otto	2.25	1.10	.22
	Oakland Raiders			
☐ 462	Ed Budde	.60	.30	.06
	Kansas City Chiefs			
☐ 463	Jim Mitchell	.40	.20	.04
	Atlanta Falcons			
☐ 464	Emerson Boozer	.60	.30	.06
	New York Jets			
☐ 465	Garo Yepremian	.60	.30	.06
	Miami Dolphins			
☐ 466	Pete Duranko	.40	.20	.04
	Denver Broncos			
☐ 467	Charlie Joiner	4.50	2.25	.45
	Cincinnati Bengals			
☐ 468	Spider Lockhart	.60	.30	.06
	New York Giants			
☐ 469	Marty Domres	.60	.30	.06
	Baltimore Colts			
☐ 470	John Brockington	1.00	.50	.10
	Green Bay Packers			
☐ 471	Ed Flanagan	.40	.20	.04
	Detroit Lions			
☐ 472	Roy Jefferson	.60	.30	.06
	Washington Redskins			
☐ 473	Julian Fagan	.40	.20	.04
	New Orleans Saints			
☐ 474	Bill Brown	.60	.30	.06
	Minnesota Vikings			
☐ 475	Roger Staubach	30.00	15.00	3.00
	Dallas Cowboys			
☐ 476	Jan White	.40	.20	.04
	Buffalo Bills			
☐ 477	Pat Holmes	.40	.20	.04
	Houston Oilers			
☐ 478	Bob DeMarco	.40	.20	.04
	Cleveland Browns			

☐ 479	Merlin Olsen 3.25	1.60	.32
	Los Angeles Rams		
☐ 480	Andy Russell .... .60	.30	.06
	Pittsburgh Steelers		
☐ 481	Steve Spurrier 1.75	.85	.17
	San Francisco 49ers		
☐ 482	Nate Ramsey .... .40	.20	.04
	Philadelphia Eagles		
☐ 483	Dennis Partee .... .40	.20	.04
	San Diego Chargers		
☐ 484	Jerry Simmons .... .40	.20	.04
	Denver Broncos		
☐ 485	Donny Anderson .... .60	.30	.06
	St. Louis Cardinals		
☐ 486	Ralph Baker .... .40	.20	.04
	New York Jets		
☐ 487	Ken Stabler 25.00	12.50	2.50
	Oakland Raiders		
☐ 488	Ernie McMillan .... .40	.20	.04
	St. Louis Cardinals		
☐ 489	Ken Burrow .... .40	.20	.04
	Atlanta Falcons		
☐ 490	Jack Gregory .... .60	.30	.06
	New York Giants		
☐ 491	Larry Seiple .... .40	.20	.04
	Miami Dolphins		
☐ 492	Mick Tingelhoff .... .80	.40	.08
	Minnesota Vikings		
☐ 493	Craig Morton 1.50	.75	.15
	Dallas Cowboys		
☐ 494	Cecil Turner .... .40	.20	.04
	Chicago Bears		
☐ 495	Steve Owens .... .80	.40	.08
	Detroit Lions		
☐ 496	Rickie Harris .... .40	.20	.04
	New England Patriots		
☐ 497	Buck Buchanan 1.50	.75	.15
	Kansas City Chiefs		
☐ 498	Checklist 397-528 ...... 3.50	.35	.07
☐ 499	Bill Kilmer 1.25	.60	.12
	Washington Redskins		
☐ 500	O.J. Simpson 22.00	11.00	2.20
	Buffalo Bills		
☐ 501	Bruce Gossett .... .40	.20	.04
	San Francisco 49ers		
☐ 502	Art Thoms .... .40	.20	.04
	Oakland Raiders		
☐ 503	Larry Kaminski .... .40	.20	.04
	Denver Broncos		
☐ 504	Larry Smith .... .40	.20	.04
	Los Angeles Rams		
☐ 505	Bruce Van Dyke .... .40	.20	.04
	Pittsburgh Steelers		
☐ 506	Alvin Reed .... .40	.20	.04
	Houston Oilers		
☐ 507	Delles Howell .... .40	.20	.04
	New York Jets		
☐ 508	Leroy Keyes .... .80	.40	.08
	Philadelphia Eagles		
☐ 509	Bo Scott .... .60	.30	.06
	Cleveland Browns		
☐ 510	Ron Yary .... .80	.40	.08
	Minnesota Vikings		
☐ 511	Paul Warfield 3.00	1.50	.30
	Miami Dolphins		
☐ 512	Mac Percival .... .40	.20	.04
	Chicago Bears		
☐ 513	Essex Johnson .... .40	.20	.04
	Cincinnati Bengals		
☐ 514	Jackie Smith .... .60	.30	.06
	St. Louis Cardinals		
☐ 515	Norm Snead .... .80	.40	.08
	New York Giants		
☐ 516	Charlie Stukes .... .40	.20	.04
	Los Angeles Rams		
☐ 517	Reggie Rucker 1.25	.60	.12
	New England Patriots		
☐ 518	Bill Sandeman .... .40	.20	.04
	Atlanta Falcons		
☐ 519	Mel Farr .... .60	.30	.06
	Detroit Lions		
☐ 520	Raymond Chester .... .60	.30	.06
	Baltimore Colts		
☐ 521	Fred Carr 1.00	.50	.10
	Green Bay Packers		
☐ 522	Jerry LeVias .... .60	.30	.06
	San Diego Chargers		
☐ 523	Jim Strong .... .40	.20	.04
	New Orleans Saints		
☐ 524	Roland McDole .... .40	.20	.04
	Washington Redskins		
☐ 525	Dennis Shaw .... .60	.30	.06
	Buffalo Bills		
☐ 526	Dave Manders .... .60	.30	.06
	Dallas Cowboys		
☐ 527	Skip Vanderbundt .... .40	.20	.04
	San Francisco 49ers		
☐ 528	Mike Sensibaugh 1.25	.30	.06
	Kansas City Chiefs		

1974 Topps

The 1974 Topps set contains 528 cards. The cards measure 2 1/2" by 3 1/2". Cards 328-333 present the statistical league leaders from each league. This set contains the rookie cards of Harold Carmichael, Chuck Foreman, Ray Guy, John Hannah, Bert Jones, Ed

Marinaro, and Ahmad Rashad. No known
scarcities exist. The card backs are printed in
blue and yellow on gray card stock. The bottom
of the reverse provided part of a simulated
football game which could be played by drawing
cards. All-Pro selections (AP) are provided as
card numbers 121-144. Statistical league
leaders are featured on cards 328-333. Post-
season action is summarized on cards 460-
463. The cards have either one or two asterisks
on the back before the TCG notation. Cards
with two asterisks include 26, 129, 130, 156,
162, 219, 265-364, 367-422, and 424-528; the
rest have only one asterisk. Topps also printed
a very similar (and very confusing) 50-card set
for Parker Brothers in early 1974 as part of a
football board game. The only players in this
set (game) were offensive players (with an
emphasis on the skill positions) and all come
from the first 132 cards in the 1974 Topps
football card set. There are several notable
differences between these Parker Brothers
Pro Draft cards and the 1974 Topps regular
issue. Those cards with 1972 statistics on the
back (unlike the 1974 Topps regular issue) are
obviously Parker Brothers cards. Parker
Brothers game cards can also be distinguished
by the presence of two asterisks rather than
one on the copyright line. However, as noted
above, there are cards in the regular 1974
Topps set that do have two asterisks but are
not Parker Brothers Pro Draft cards. In fact,
variations 23A, 49A, 116A, 124A, 126A, and
127A listed in this 1974 Topps checklist below
are probably Parker Brothers cards, but they
are impossible to identify as such, since they
are exceptions to all the identification criteria
with respect to Parker Brothers cards.

	NRMT	VG-E	GOOD
COMPLETE SET (528)	325.00	160.00	32.00

COMMON PLAYER (1-528)	.35	.17	.03
☐ 1 O.J. Simpson RB UER	18.00	5.00	1.00
Buffalo Bills			
(Text on back says			
100 years, should say			
100 yards)			
☐ 2 Blaine Nye	.35	.17	.03
Dallas Cowboys			
☐ 3 Don Hansen	.35	.17	.03
Atlanta Falcons			
☐ 4 Ken Bowman	.35	.17	.03
Green Bay Packers			
☐ 5 Carl Eller	1.25	.60	.12
Minnesota Vikings			
☐ 6 Jerry Smith	.50	.25	.05
Washington Redskins			
☐ 7 Ed Podolak	.50	.25	.05
Kansas City Chiefs			
☐ 8 Mel Gray	.50	.25	.05
St. Louis Cardinals			
☐ 9 Pat Matson	.35	.17	.03
Cincinnati Bengals			
☐ 10 Floyd Little	1.25	.60	.12
Denver Broncos			
☐ 11 Frank Pitts	.35	.17	.03
Cleveland Browns			
☐ 12 Vern Den Herder	.50	.25	.05
Miami Dolphins			
☐ 13 John Fuqua	.50	.25	.05
Pittsburgh Steelers			
☐ 14 Jack Tatum	.90	.45	.09
Oakland Raiders			
☐ 15 Winston Hill	.35	.17	.03
New York Jets			
☐ 16 John Beasley	.35	.17	.03
New Orleans Saints			
☐ 17 David Lee	.35	.17	.03
Baltimore Colts			
☐ 18 Rich Coady	.35	.17	.03
Chicago Bears			
☐ 19 Ken Willard	.50	.25	.05
San Francisco 49ers			
☐ 20 Coy Bacon	.35	.17	.03
San Diego Chargers			
☐ 21 Ben Hawkins	.35	.17	.03
Philadelphia Eagles			
☐ 22 Paul Guidry	.35	.17	.03
Houston Oilers			
☐ 23A Norm Snead	5.00	2.50	.50
New York Giants			
(Vertical pose; 1973			
stats; one asterisk			
before TCG on back)			
☐ 23B Norm Snead HOR	.70	.35	.07
New York Giants			
☐ 24 Jim Yarbrough	.35	.17	.03

Detroit Lions

☐ 25 Jack Reynolds	2.00	1.00	.20

Los Angeles Rams

☐ 26 Josh Ashton	.35	.17	.03

New England Patriots

☐ 27 Donnie Green	.35	.17	.03

Buffalo Bills

☐ 28 Bob Hayes	.90	.45	.09

Dallas Cowboys

☐ 29 John Zook	.50	.25	.05

Atlanta Falcons

☐ 30 Bobby Bryant	.35	.17	.03

Minnesota Vikings

☐ 31 Scott Hunter	.50	.25	.05

Green Bay Packers

☐ 32 Dan Dierdorf	2.75	1.35	.27

St. Louis Cardinals

☐ 33 Curt Knight	.35	.17	.03

Washington Redskins

☐ 34 Elmo Wright	.90	.45	.09

Kansas City Chiefs

☐ 35 Essex Johnson	.35	.17	.03

Cincinnati Bengals

☐ 36 Walt Sumner	.35	.17	.03

Cleveland Browns

☐ 37 Marv Montgomery	.35	.17	.03

Denver Broncos

☐ 38 Tim Foley	.50	.25	.05

Miami Dolphins

☐ 39 Mike Siani	.35	.17	.03

Oakland Raiders

☐ 40 Joe Greene	4.00	2.00	.40

Pittsburgh Steelers

☐ 41 Bobby Howfield	.35	.17	.03

New York Jets

☐ 42 Del Williams	.35	.17	.03

New Orleans Saints

☐ 43 Don McCauley	.35	.17	.03

Baltimore Colts

☐ 44 Randy Jackson	.35	.17	.03

Chicago Bears

☐ 45 Ron Smith	.35	.17	.03

San Diego Chargers

☐ 46 Gene Washington	.70	.35	.07

San Francisco 49ers

☐ 47 Po James	.45	.22	.04

Philadelphia Eagles

☐ 48 Solomon Freelon	.45	.22	.04

Houston Oilers

☐ 49A Bob Windsor	3.00	1.50	.30

New England Patriots
(Vertical pose; 1973
stats; one asterisk
before TCG on back)

☐ 49B Bob Windsor HOR	.45	.22	.04

New England Patriots

☐ 50 John Hadl	1.25	.60	.12

☐ 51 Greg Larson	.35	.17	.03

New York Giants

☐ 52 Steve Owens	.50	.25	.05

Detroit Lions

☐ 53 Jim Cheyunski	.35	.17	.03

Buffalo Bills

☐ 54 Rayfield Wright	.35	.17	.03

Dallas Cowboys

☐ 55 Dave Hampton	.35	.17	.03

Atlanta Falcons

☐ 56 Ron Widby	.35	.17	.03

Green Bay Packers

☐ 57 Milt Sunde	.35	.17	.03

Minnesota Viking

☐ 58 Bill Kilmer	1.25	.60	.12

Washington Redskins

☐ 59 Bobby Bell	2.00	1.00	.20

Kansas City Chiefs

☐ 60 Jim Bakken	.50	.25	.05

St. Louis Cardinals

☐ 61 Rufus Mayes	.35	.17	.03

Cincinnati Bengals

☐ 62 Vic Washington	.35	.17	.03

San Francisco 49ers

☐ 63 Gene Washington	.50	.25	.05

Denver Broncos

☐ 64 Clarence Scott	.35	.17	.03

Cleveland Browns

☐ 65 Gene Upshaw	1.75	.85	.17

Oakland Raiders

☐ 66 Larry Seiple	.35	.17	.03

Miami Dolphins

☐ 67 John McMakin	.35	.17	.03

Pittsburgh Steelers

☐ 68 Ralph Baker	.35	.17	.03

New York Jets

☐ 69 Lydell Mitchell	.90	.45	.09

Baltimore Colts

☐ 70 Archie Manning	1.50	.75	.15

New Orleans Saints

☐ 71 George Farmer	.35	.17	.03

Chicago Bears

☐ 72 Ron East	.35	.17	.03

San Diego Chargers

☐ 73 Al Nelson	.35	.17	.03

Philadelphia Eagles

☐ 74 Pat Hughes	.35	.17	.03

New York Giants

☐ 75 Fred Willis	.35	.17	.03

Houston Oilers

☐ 76 Larry Walton	.35	.17	.03

Detroit Lions

☐ 77 Tom Neville	.35	.17	.03

New England Patriots

☐ 78 Ted Kwalick	.50	.25	.05

San Francisco 49ers

☐ 79	Walt Patulski 35	.17	.03
	Buffalo Bills		
☐ 80	John Niland 35	.17	.03
	Dallas Cowboys		
☐ 81	Ted Fritsch Jr. 35	.17	.03
	Atlanta Falcons		
☐ 82	Paul Krause 90	.45	.09
	Minnesota Vikings		
☐ 83	Jack Snow 50	.25	.05
	Los Angeles Rams		
☐ 84	Mike Bass 35	.17	.03
	Washington Redskins		
☐ 85	Jim Tyrer 50	.25	.05
	Kansas City Chiefs		
☐ 86	Ron Yankowski 35	.17	.03
	St. Louis Cardinals		
☐ 87	Mike Phipps 50	.25	.05
	Cleveland Browns		
☐ 88	Al Beauchamp 35	.17	.03
	Cincinnati Bengals		
☐ 89	Riley Odoms 2.00	1.00	.20
	Denver Broncos		
☐ 90	MacArthur Lane 50	.25	.05
	Green Bay Packers		
☐ 91	Art Thoms 35	.17	.03
	Oakland Raiders		
☐ 92	Marlin Briscoe 50	.25	.05
	Miami Dolphins		
☐ 93	Bruce Van Dyke 35	.17	.03
	Pittsburgh Steelers		
☐ 94	Tom Myers 50	.25	.05
	New Orleans Saints		
☐ 95	Calvin Hill 70	.35	.07
	Dallas Cowboys		
☐ 96	Bruce Laird 35	.17	.03
	Baltimore Colts		
☐ 97	Tony McGee 35	.17	.03
	Chicago Bears		
☐ 98	Len Rohde 35	.17	.03
	San Francisco 49ers		
☐ 99	Tom McNeill 35	.17	.03
	Philadelphia Eagles		
☐ 100	Delles Howell 35	.17	.03
	New York Jets		
☐ 101	Gary Garrison 50	.25	.05
	San Diego Chargers		
☐ 102	Dan Goich 35	.17	.03
	New York Giants		
☐ 103	Len St. Jean 35	.17	.03
	New England Patriots		
☐ 104	Zeke Moore 35	.17	.03
	Houston Oilers		
☐ 105	Ahmad Rashad 15.00	7.50	1.50
	Buffalo Bills		
☐ 106	Mel Renfro 90	.45	.09
	Dallas Cowboys		
☐ 107	Jim Mitchell 35	.17	.03
	Detroit Lions		
☐ 108	Ed Budde 50	.25	.05
	Kansas City Chiefs		
☐ 109	Harry Schuh 35	.17	.03
	Los Angeles Rams		
☐ 110	Greg Pruitt 3.00	1.50	.30
	Cleveland Browns		
☐ 111	Ed Flanagan 35	.17	.03
	Detroit Lions		
☐ 112	Larry Stallings 35	.17	.03
	St. Louis Cardinals		
☐ 113	Chuck Foreman 3.25	1.60	.32
	Minnesota Vikings		
☐ 114	Royce Berry 35	.17	.03
	Cincinnati Bengals		
☐ 115	Gale Gillingham 35	.17	.03
	Green Bay Packers		
☐ 116A	Charlie Johnson 5.00	2.50	.50
	Denver Broncos		
	(Vertical pose; 1973		
	stats; one asterisk		
	before TCG on back)		
☐ 116B	Charlie Johnson HOR ..70	.35	.07
	Denver Broncos		
☐ 117	Checklist 1-132 ....3.00	.30	.06
☐ 118	Bill Butler 35	.17	.03
	New Orleans Saints		
☐ 119	Roy Jefferson 50	.25	.05
	Washington Redskins		
☐ 120	Bobby Douglass 50	.25	.05
	Chicago Bears		
☐ 121	Harold Carmichael AP 12.50	6.25	1.25
	Philadelphia Eagles		
☐ 122	George Kunz AP 50	.25	.05
	Atlanta Falcons		
☐ 123	Larry Little AP 70	.35	.07
	Miami Dolphins		
☐ 124A	Forrest Blue AP 3.00	1.50	.30
	San Francisco 49ers		
	(Not All-Pro style; 1973		
	stats; one asterisk		
	before TCG on back)		
☐ 124B	Forrest Blue AP 50	.25	.05
	San Francisco 49ers		
☐ 125	Ron Yary AP 70	.35	.07
	Minnesota Vikings		
☐ 126A	Tom Mack 4.00	2.00	.40
	Los Angeles Rams		
	(Not All-Pro style; 1973		
	stats; one asterisk		
	before TCG on back)		
☐ 126B	Tom Mack AP 70	.35	.07
	Los Angeles Rams		
☐ 127A	Bob Tucker 4.00	2.00	.40
	New York Giants		
	(Not All-Pro style; 1973		
	stats; one asterisk		

before TCG on back)

☐ 127B Bob Tucker AP 50	.25	.05
New York Giants		
☐ 128 Paul Warfield AP 2.75	1.35	.27
Miami Dolphins		
☐ 129 Fran Tarkenton AP ... 9.00	4.50	.90
Minnesota Vikings		
☐ 130 O.J. Simpson AP 18.00	9.00	1.80
Buffalo Bills		
☐ 131 Larry Csonka AP 3.00	1.50	.30
Miami Dolphins		
☐ 132 Bruce Gossett AP 35	.17	.03
San Francisco 49ers		
☐ 133 Bill Stanfill AP 50	.25	.05
Miami Dolphins		
☐ 134 Alan Page AP 2.25	1.10	.22
Minnesota Vikings		
☐ 135 Paul Smith AP 35	.17	.03
Denver Broncos		
☐ 136 Claude Humphrey AP 50	.25	.05
Atlanta Falcons		
☐ 137 Jack Ham AP 4.50	2.25	.45
Pittsburgh Steelers		
☐ 138 Lee Roy Jordan AP 1.00	.50	.10
Dallas Cowboys		
☐ 139 Phil Villapiano AP 50	.25	.05
Oakland Raiders		
☐ 140 Ken Ellis AP 35	.17	.03
Green Bay Packers		
☐ 141 Willie Brown AP 1.75	.85	.17
Oakland Raiders		
☐ 142 Dick Anderson AP 50	.25	.05
Miami Dolphins		
☐ 143 Bill Bradley AP 50	.25	.05
Philadelphia Eagles		
☐ 144 Jerrel Wilson AP 35	.17	.03
Kansas City Chiefs		
☐ 145 Reggie Rucker 50	.25	.05
New England Patriots		
☐ 146 Marty Domres 50	.25	.05
Baltimore Colts		
☐ 147 Bob Kowalkowski 35	.17	.03
Detroit Lions		
☐ 148 John Matuszak 3.50	1.75	.35
Houston Oilers		
☐ 149 Mike Adamle 70	.35	.07
New York Jets		
☐ 150 John Unitas 15.00	7.50	1.50
San Diego Chargers		
☐ 151 Charlie Ford 35	.17	.03
Chicago Bears		
☐ 152 Bob Klein 50	.25	.05
Los Angeles Rams		
☐ 153 Jim Merlo 35	.17	.03
New Orleans Saints		
☐ 154 Willie Young 35	.17	.03
New York Giants		

☐ 155 Donny Anderson 50	.25	.05
St. Louis Cardinals		
☐ 156 Brig Owens 35	.17	.03
Washington Redskins		
☐ 157 Bruce Jarvis 35	.17	.03
Buffalo Bills		
☐ 158 Ron Carpenter 35	.17	.03
Cincinnati Bengals		
☐ 159 Don Cockroft 50	.25	.05
Cleveland Browns		
☐ 160 Tommy Nobis 1.00	.50	.10
Atlanta Falcons		
☐ 161 Craig Morton 1.25	.60	.12
Dallas Cowboys		
☐ 162 Jon Staggers 35	.17	.03
Green Bay Packers		
☐ 163 Mike Eischeid 35	.17	.03
Minnesota Vikings		
☐ 164 Jerry Sisemore 70	.35	.07
Philadelphia Eagles		
☐ 165 Cedric Hardman 50	.25	.05
San Francisco 49ers		
☐ 166 Bill Thompson 50	.25	.05
Denver Broncos		
☐ 167 Jim Lynch 35	.17	.03
Kansas City Chiefs		
☐ 168 Bob Moore 50	.25	.05
Oakland Raiders		
☐ 169 Glen Edwards 35	.17	.03
Pittsburgh Steelers		
☐ 170 Mercury Morris 70	.35	.07
Miami Dolphins		
☐ 171 Julius Adams 35	.17	.03
New England Patriots		
☐ 172 Cotton Speyrer 50	.25	.05
Baltimore Colts		
☐ 173 Bill Munson 50	.25	.05
Detroit Lions		
☐ 174 Benny Johnson 35	.17	.03
Houston Oilers		
☐ 175 Burgess Owens 70	.35	.07
New York Jets		
☐ 176 Cid Edwards 35	.17	.03
San Diego Chargers		
☐ 177 Doug Buffone 35	.17	.03
Chicago Bears		
☐ 178 Charlie Cowan 35	.17	.03
Los Angeles Rams		
☐ 179 Bob Newland 35	.17	.03
New Orleans Saints		
☐ 180 Ron Johnson 50	.25	.05
New York Giants		
☐ 181 Bob Rowe 35	.17	.03
St. Louis Cardinals		
☐ 182 Len Hauss 50	.25	.05
Washington Redskins		
☐ 183 Joe DeLamielleure 1.25	.60	.12

Buffalo Bills
| ☐ 184 | Sherman White | .50 | .25 | .05 |

Cincinnati Bengals
| ☐ 185 | Fair Hooker | .35 | .17 | .03 |

Cleveland Browns
| ☐ 186 | Nick Mike-Mayer | .35 | .17 | .03 |

Atlanta Falcons
| ☐ 187 | Ralph Neely | .50 | .25 | .05 |

Dallas Cowboys
| ☐ 188 | Rich McGeorge | .35 | .17 | .03 |

Green Bay Packers
| ☐ 189 | Ed Marinaro | 4.00 | 2.00 | .40 |

Minnesota Vikings
| ☐ 190 | Dave Wilcox | .50 | .25 | .05 |

San Francisco 49ers
| ☐ 191 | Joe Owens | .35 | .17 | .03 |

New Orleans Saints
| ☐ 192 | Bill Van Heusen | .35 | .17 | .03 |

Denver Broncos
| ☐ 193 | Jim Kearney | .35 | .17 | .03 |

Kansas City Chiefs
| ☐ 194 | Otis Sistrunk | 1.50 | .75 | .15 |

Oakland Raiders
| ☐ 195 | Ron Shanklin | .35 | .17 | .03 |

Pittsburgh Steelers
| ☐ 196 | Bill Lenkaitis | .35 | .17 | .03 |

New England Patriots
| ☐ 197 | Tom Drougas | .35 | .17 | .03 |

Baltimore Colts
| ☐ 198 | Larry Hand | .35 | .17 | .03 |

Detroit Lions
| ☐ 199 | Mack Alston | .35 | .17 | .03 |

Houston Oilers
| ☐ 200 | Bob Griese | 5.00 | 2.50 | .50 |

Miami Dolphins
| ☐ 201 | Earlie Thomas | .35 | .17 | .03 |

New York Jets
| ☐ 202 | Carl Gerbach | .35 | .17 | .03 |

San Diego Chargers
| ☐ 203 | Jim Harrison | .35 | .17 | .03 |

Chicago Bears
| ☐ 204 | Jake Kupp | .35 | .17 | .03 |

New Orleans Saints
| ☐ 205 | Merlin Olsen | 3.00 | 1.50 | .30 |

Los Angeles Rams
| ☐ 206 | Spider Lockhart | .50 | .25 | .05 |

New York Giants
| ☐ 207 | Walker Gillette | .35 | .17 | .03 |

St. Louis Cardinals
| ☐ 208 | Verlon Biggs | .35 | .17 | .03 |

Washington Redskins
| ☐ 209 | Bob James | .35 | .17 | .03 |

Buffalo Bills
| ☐ 210 | Bob Trumpy | 1.00 | .50 | .10 |

Cincinnati Bengals
| ☐ 211 | Jerry Sherk HOR | .50 | .25 | .05 |

Cleveland Browns

| ☐ 212 | Andy Maurer | .35 | .17 | .03 |

Atlanta Falcons
| ☐ 213 | Fred Carr | .50 | .25 | .05 |

Green Bay Packers
| ☐ 214 | Mick Tingelhoff | .70 | .35 | .07 |

Minnesota Vikings
| ☐ 215 | Steve Spurrier | 1.00 | .50 | .10 |

San Francisco 49ers
| ☐ 216 | Richard Harris | .35 | .17 | .03 |

Philadelphia Eagles
| ☐ 217 | Charlie Greer | .35 | .17 | .03 |

Denver Broncos
| ☐ 218 | Buck Buchanan | 1.75 | .85 | .17 |

Kansas City Chiefs
| ☐ 219 | Ray Guy | 7.00 | 3.50 | .70 |

Oakland Raiders
| ☐ 220 | Franco Harris | 20.00 | 10.00 | 2.00 |

Pittsburgh Steelers
| ☐ 221 | Darryl Stingley | 2.50 | 1.25 | .25 |

New England Patriots
| ☐ 222 | Rex Kern | .50 | .25 | .05 |

Baltimore Colts
| ☐ 223 | Toni Fritsch | .50 | .25 | .05 |

Dallas Cowboys
| ☐ 224 | Levi Johnson | .35 | .17 | .03 |

Detroit Lions
| ☐ 225 | Bob Kuechenberg | .70 | .35 | .07 |

Miami Dolphins
| ☐ 226 | Elvin Bethea | .50 | .25 | .05 |

Houston Oilers
| ☐ 227 | Al Woodall | .50 | .25 | .05 |

New York Jets
| ☐ 228 | Terry Owens | .50 | .25 | .05 |

San Diego Chargers
| ☐ 229 | Bivian Lee | .35 | .17 | .03 |

New Orleans Saints
| ☐ 230 | Dick Butkus | 5.00 | 2.50 | .50 |

Chicago Bears
| ☐ 231 | Jim Bertelsen | .70 | .35 | .07 |

Los Angeles Rams
| ☐ 232 | John Mendenhall | .50 | .25 | .05 |

New York Giants
| ☐ 233 | Conrad Dobler | 2.50 | 1.25 | .25 |

St. Louis Cardinals
| ☐ 234 | J.D. Hill | .50 | .25 | .05 |

Buffalo Bills
| ☐ 235 | Ken Houston | 1.25 | .60 | .12 |

Washington Redskins
| ☐ 236 | Dave Lewis | .35 | .17 | .03 |

Cincinnati Bengals
| ☐ 237 | John Garlington | .35 | .17 | .03 |

Cleveland Browns
| ☐ 238 | Bill Sandeman | .35 | .17 | .03 |

Atlanta Falcons
| ☐ 239 | Alden Roche | .35 | .17 | .03 |

Green Bay Packers
| ☐ 240 | John Gilliam | .50 | .25 | .05 |

	Minnesota Vikings			
☐ 241	Bruce Taylor	.50	.25	.05
	San Francisco 49ers			
☐ 242	Vern Winfield	.35	.17	.03
	Philadelphia Eagles			
☐ 243	Bobby Maples	.35	.17	.03
	Denver Broncos			
☐ 244	Wendell Hayes	.50	.25	.05
	Kansas City Chiefs			
☐ 245	George Blanda	6.00	3.00	.60
	Oakland Raiders			
☐ 246	Dwight White	.50	.25	.05
	Pittsburgh Steelers			
☐ 247	Sandy Durko	.35	.17	.03
	New England Patriots			
☐ 248	Tom Mitchell	.35	.17	.03
	Baltimore Colts			
☐ 249	Chuck Walton	.35	.17	.03
	Detroit Lions			
☐ 250	Bob Lilly	3.75	1.85	.37
	Dallas Cowboys			
☐ 251	Doug Swift	.35	.17	.03
	Miami Dolphins			
☐ 252	Lynn Dickey	3.50	1.75	.35
	Houston Oilers			
☐ 253	Jerome Barkum	1.50	.75	.15
	New York Jets			
☐ 254	Clint Jones	.50	.25	.05
	San Diego Chargers			
☐ 255	Billy Newsome	.35	.17	.03
	New Orleans Saints			
☐ 256	Bob Asher	.35	.17	.03
	Chicago Bears			
☐ 257	Joe Scibelli	.50	.25	.05
	Los Angeles Rams			
☐ 258	Tom Blanchard	.35	.17	.03
	New York Giants			
☐ 259	Norm Thompson	.35	.17	.03
	St. Louis Cardinals			
☐ 260	Larry Brown	.70	.35	.07
	Washington Redskins			
☐ 261	Paul Seymour	.35	.17	.03
	Buffalo Bills			
☐ 262	Checklist 133-264	3.00	.30	.06
☐ 263	Doug Dieken	.70	.35	.07
	Cleveland Browns			
☐ 264	Lemar Parrish	.50	.25	.05
	Cincinnati Bengals			
☐ 265	Bob Lee UER	.50	.25	.05
	Atlanta Falcons			
	(listed as Atlanta			
	Hawks on card back)			
☐ 266	Bob Brown	.35	.17	.03
	Green Bay Packers			
☐ 267	Roy Winston	.35	.17	.03
	Minnesota Vikings			
☐ 268	Randy Beisler	.35	.17	.03
	San Francisco 49ers			
☐ 269	Joe Dawkins	.35	.17	.03
	Denver Broncos			
☐ 270	Tom Dempsey	.50	.25	.05
	Philadelphia Eagles			
☐ 271	Jack Rudnay	.35	.17	.03
	Kansas City Chiefs			
☐ 272	Art Shell	6.00	3.00	.60
	Oakland Raiders			
☐ 273	Mike Wagner	.50	.25	.05
	Pittsburgh Steelers			
☐ 274	Rick Cash	.35	.17	.03
	New England Patriots			
☐ 275	Greg Landry	.90	.45	.09
	Detroit Lions			
☐ 276	Glenn Ressler	.35	.17	.03
	Baltimore Colts			
☐ 277	Billy Joe DuPree	3.25	1.60	.32
	Dallas Cowboys			
☐ 278	Norm Evans	.50	.25	.05
	Miami Dolphins			
☐ 279	Billy Parks	.50	.25	.05
	Houston Oilers			
☐ 280	John Riggins	5.00	2.50	.50
	New York Jets			
☐ 281	Lionel Aldridge	.35	.17	.03
	San Diego Chargers			
☐ 282	Steve O'Neal	.35	.17	.03
	New Orleans Saints			
☐ 283	Craig Clemons	.35	.17	.03
	Chicago Bears			
☐ 284	Willie Williams	.35	.17	.03
	New York Giants			
☐ 285	Isiah Robertson	.50	.25	.05
	Los Angeles Rams			
☐ 286	Dennis Shaw	.50	.25	.05
	Buffalo Bills			
☐ 287	Bill Brundige	.35	.17	.03
	Washington Redskins			
☐ 288	John Leypoldt	.35	.17	.03
	Buffalo Bills			
☐ 289	John DeMarie	.35	.17	.03
	Cleveland Browns			
☐ 290	Mike Reid	1.00	.50	.10
	Cincinnati Bengals			
☐ 291	Greg Brezina	.50	.25	.05
	Atlanta Falcons			
☐ 292	Willie Buchanon	1.75	.85	.17
	Green Bay Packers			
☐ 293	Dave Osborn	.50	.25	.05
	Minnesota Vikings			
☐ 294	Mel Phillips	.35	.17	.03
	San Francisco 49ers			
☐ 295	Haven Moses	.50	.25	.05
	Denver Broncos			
☐ 296	Wade Key	.35	.17	.03
	Philadelphia Eagles			

☐ 297	Marvin Upshaw .... .35 Kansas City Chiefs	.17	.03
☐ 298	Ray Mansfield .... .35 Pittsburgh Steelers	.17	.03
☐ 299	Edgar Chandler .... .35 New England Patriots	.17	.03
☐ 300	Marv Hubbard .... .50 Oakland Raiders	.25	.05
☐ 301	Herman Weaver .... .35 Detroit Lions	.17	.03
☐ 302	Jim Bailey .... .35 Baltimore Colts	.17	.03
☐ 303	D.D. Lewis .... 1.50 Dallas Cowboys	.75	.15
☐ 304	Ken Burrough .... .50 Houston Oilers	.25	.05
☐ 305	Jake Scott .... .50 Miami Dolphins	.25	.05
☐ 306	Randy Rasmussen .... .35 New York Jets	.17	.03
☐ 307	Pettis Norman .... .35 San Diego Chargers	.17	.03
☐ 308	Carl Johnson .... .35 New Orleans Saints	.17	.03
☐ 309	Joe Taylor .... .35 Chicago Bears	.17	.03
☐ 310	Pete Gogolak .... .50 New York Giants	.25	.05
☐ 311	Tony Baker .... .35 Los Angeles Rams	.17	.03
☐ 312	John Richardson .... .35 St. Louis Cardinals	.17	.03
☐ 313	Dave Robinson .... .50 Washington Redskins	.25	.05
☐ 314	Reggie McKenzie .... 2.25 Buffalo Bills	1.10	.22
☐ 315	Isaac Curtis .... 2.50 Cincinnati Bengals	1.25	.25
☐ 316	Thom Darden .... .50 Cleveland Browns	.25	.05
☐ 317	Ken Reaves .... .35 Atlanta Falcons	.17	.03
☐ 318	Malcolm Snider .... .35 Green Bay Packers	.17	.03
☐ 319	Jeff Siemon .... 1.50 Minnesota Vikings	.75	.15
☐ 320	Dan Abramowicz .... .50 San Francisco 49ers	.25	.05
☐ 321	Lyle Alzado .... 2.50 Denver Broncos	1.25	.25
☐ 322	John Reaves .... .50 Philadelphia Eagles	.25	.05
☐ 323	Morris Stroud .... .35 Kansas City Chiefs	.17	.03
☐ 324	Bobby Walden .... .35 Pittsburgh Steelers	.17	.03
☐ 325	Randy Vataha .... .50 	.25	.05

	New England Patriots		
☐ 326	Nemiah Wilson .... .35 Oakland Raiders	.17	.03
☐ 327	Paul Naumoff .... .35 Detroit Lions	.17	.03
☐ 328	Rushing Leaders .... 2.50 O.J. Simpson John Brockington	1.25	.25
☐ 329	Passing Leaders .... 2.50 Ken Stabler Roger Staubach	1.25	.25
☐ 330	Receiving Leaders .... .90 Fred Willis Harold Carmichael	.45	.09
☐ 331	Scoring Leaders .... .50 Roy Gerela David Ray	.25	.05
☐ 332	Interception Leaders ...... .50 Dick Anderson Mike Wagner Bobby Bryant	.25	.05
☐ 333	Punting Leaders .... .50 Jerrel Wilson Tom Wittum	.25	.05
☐ 334	Dennis Nelson .... .35 Baltimore Colts	.17	.03
☐ 335	Walt Garrison .... .70 Dallas Cowboys	.35	.07
☐ 336	Tody Smith .... .35 Houston Oilers	.17	.03
☐ 337	Ed Bell .... .35 New York Jets	.17	.03
☐ 338	Bryant Salter .... .35 San Diego Chargers	.17	.03
☐ 339	Wayne Colman .... .35 New Orleans Saints	.17	.03
☐ 340	Garo Yepremian .... .50 Miami Dolphins	.25	.05
☐ 341	Bob Newton .... .35 Chicago Bears	.17	.03
☐ 342	Vince Clements .... .70 New York Giants	.35	.07
☐ 343	Ken Iman .... .35 Los Angeles Rams	.17	.03
☐ 344	Jim Tolbert .... .35 St. Louis Cardinals	.17	.03
☐ 345	Chris Hanburger .... .50 Washington Redskins	.25	.05
☐ 346	Dave Foley .... .35 Buffalo Bills	.17	.03
☐ 347	Tommy Casanova .... .70 Cincinnati Bengals	.35	.07
☐ 348	John James .... .35 Atlanta Falcons	.17	.03
☐ 349	Clarence Williams .... .35 Green Bay Packers	.17	.03
☐ 350	Leroy Kelly 1.00	.50	.10

	Cleveland Browns		
☐ 351	Stu Voigt 1.00	.50	.10
	Minnesota Vikings		
☐ 352	Skip Vanderbundt .... .35	.17	.03
	San Francisco 49ers		
☐ 353	Pete Duranko .... .35	.17	.03
	Denver Broncos		
☐ 354	John Outlaw .... .35	.17	.03
	Philadelphia Eagles		
☐ 355	Jan Stenerud 1.25	.60	.12
	Kansas City Chiefs		
☐ 356	Barry Pearson .... .35	.17	.03
	Pittsburgh Steelers		
☐ 357	Brian Dowling .... .70	.35	.07
	New England Patriots		
☐ 358	Dan Conners .... .35	.17	.03
	Oakland Raiders		
☐ 359	Bob Bell .... .35	.17	.03
	Detroit Lions		
☐ 360	Rick Volk .... .35	.17	.03
	Baltimore Colts		
☐ 361	Pat Toomay .... .35	.17	.03
	Dallas Cowboys		
☐ 362	Bob Gresham .... .35	.17	.03
	Houston Oilers		
☐ 363	John Schmitt .... .35	.17	.03
	New York Jets		
☐ 364	Mel Rogers .... .35	.17	.03
	San Diego Chargers		
☐ 365	Manny Fernandez .... .35	.17	.03
	Miami Dolphins		
☐ 366	Ernie Jackson .... .35	.17	.03
	New Orleans Saints		
☐ 367	Gary Huff 1.00	.50	.10
	Chicago Bears		
☐ 368	Bob Grim .... .50	.25	.05
	New York Giants		
☐ 369	Ernie McMillan .... .35	.17	.03
	St. Louis Cardinals		
☐ 370	Dave Elmendorf .... .35	.17	.03
	Los Angeles Rams		
☐ 371	Mike Bragg .... .35	.17	.03
	Washington Redskins		
☐ 372	John Skorupan .... .35	.17	.03
	Buffalo Bills		
☐ 373	Howard Fest .... .35	.17	.03
	Cincinnati Bengals		
☐ 374	Jerry Tagge 1.00	.50	.10
	Green Bay Packers		
☐ 375	Art Malone .... .35	.17	.03
	Atlanta Falcons		
☐ 376	Bob Babich .... .35	.17	.03
	Cleveland Browns		
☐ 377	Jim Marshall 1.25	.60	.12
	Minnesota Vikings		
☐ 378	Bob Hoskins .... .35	.17	.03
	San Francisco 49ers		
☐ 379	Don Zimmerman .... .35	.17	.03
	Philadelphia Eagles		
☐ 380	Ray May .... .35	.17	.03
	Baltimore Colts		
☐ 381	Emmitt Thomas .... .35	.17	.03
	Kansas City Chiefs		
☐ 382	Terry Hanratty .... .50	.25	.05
	Pittsburgh Steelers		
☐ 383	John Hannah 14.00	7.00	1.40
	New England Patriots		
☐ 384	George Atkinson .... .50	.25	.05
	Oakland Raiders		
☐ 385	Ted Hendricks 2.00	1.00	.20
	Baltimore Colts		
☐ 386	Jim O'Brien .... .35	.17	.03
	Detroit Lions		
☐ 387	Jethro Pugh .... .50	.25	.05
	Dallas Cowboys		
☐ 388	Elbert Drungo .... .35	.17	.03
	Houston Oilers		
☐ 389	Richard Caster .... .50	.25	.05
	New York Jets		
☐ 390	Deacon Jones 2.00	1.00	.20
	San Diego Chargers		
☐ 391	Checklist 265-396 .... 3.00	.30	.06
☐ 392	Jess Phillips .... .35	.17	.03
	New Orleans Saints		
☐ 393	Garry Lyle .... .35	.17	.03
	Chicago Bears		
☐ 394	Jim Files .... .35	.17	.03
	New York Giants		
☐ 395	Jim Hart 1.25	.60	.12
	St. Louis Cardinals		
☐ 396	Dave Chapple .... .35	.17	.03
	Los Angeles Rams		
☐ 397	Jim Langer 2.50	1.25	.25
	Miami Dolphins		
☐ 398	John Wilbur .... .35	.17	.03
	Washington Redskins		
☐ 399	Dwight Harrison .... .35	.17	.03
	Buffalo Bills		
☐ 400	John Brockington .... .70	.35	.07
	Green Bay Packers		
☐ 401	Ken Anderson 6.00	3.00	.60
	Cincinnati Bengals		
☐ 402	Mike Tilleman .... .35	.17	.03
	Atlanta Falcons		
☐ 403	Charlie Hall .... .35	.17	.03
	Cleveland Browns		
☐ 404	Tommy Hart .... .35	.17	.03
	San Francisco 49ers		
☐ 405	Norm Bulaich .... .50	.25	.05
	Philadelphia Eagles		
☐ 406	Jim Turner .... .50	.25	.05
	Denver Broncos		
☐ 407	Mo Moorman .... .35	.17	.03
	Kansas City Chiefs		

☐ 408	Ralph Anderson ....35 New England Patriots	.17	.03	
☐ 409	Jim Otto .... 2.00 Oakland Raiders	1.00	.20	
☐ 410	Andy Russell ....50 Pittsburgh Steelers	.25	.05	
☐ 411	Glenn Doughty ....35 Baltimore Colts	.17	.03	
☐ 412	Altie Taylor ....35 Detroit Lions	.17	.03	
☐ 413	Marv Bateman ....35 Dallas Cowboys	.17	.03	
☐ 414	Willie Alexander ....35 Houston Oilers	.17	.03	
☐ 415	Bill Zapalac ....35 New York Jets	.17	.03	
☐ 416	Russ Washington ....35 San Diego Chargers	.17	.03	
☐ 417	Joe Federspiel ....35 New Orleans Saints	.17	.03	
☐ 418	Craig Cotton ....35 Chicago Bears	.17	.03	
☐ 419	Randy Johnson ....35 New York Giants	.17	.03	
☐ 420	Harold Jackson .... 1.00 Los Angeles Rams	.50	.10	
☐ 421	Roger Wehrli ....50 St. Louis Cardinals	.25	.05	
☐ 422	Charlie Harraway ....35 Washington Redskins	.17	.03	
☐ 423	Spike Jones ....35 Buffalo Bills	.17	.03	
☐ 424	Bob Johnson ....35 Cincinnati Bengals	.17	.03	
☐ 425	Mike McCoy ....35 Green Bay Packers	.17	.03	
☐ 426	Dennis Havig HOR ....35 Atlanta Falcons	.17	.03	
☐ 427	Bob McKay ....35 Cleveland Browns	.17	.03	
☐ 428	Steve Zabel ....35 Philadelphia Eagles	.17	.03	
☐ 429	Horace Jones ....35 Oakland Raiders	.17	.03	
☐ 430	Jim Johnson ....50 San Francisco 49ers	.25	.05	
☐ 431	Roy Gerela ....35 Pittsburgh Steelers	.17	.03	
☐ 432	Tom Graham ....35 Denver Broncos	.17	.03	
☐ 433	Curley Culp ....70 Kansas City Chiefs	.35	.07	
☐ 434	Ken Mendenhall ....35 Baltimore Colts	.17	.03	
☐ 435	Jim Plunkett .... 2.50 New England Patriots	1.25	.25	
☐ 436	Julian Fagan 35	.17	.03	
	New York Jets			
☐ 437	Mike Garrett ....50 San Diego Chargers	.25	.05	
☐ 438	Bobby Joe Green ....35 Chicago Bears	.17	.03	
☐ 439	Jack Gregory HOR ....50 New York Giants	.25	.05	
☐ 440	Charlie Sanders ....50 Detroit Lions	.25	.05	
☐ 441	Bill Curry ....70 Houston Oilers	.35	.07	
☐ 442	Bob Pollard ....35 New Orleans Saints	.17	.03	
☐ 443	David Ray ....35 Los Angeles Rams	.17	.03	
☐ 444	Terry Metcalf .... 2.50 St. Louis Cardinals	1.25	.25	
☐ 445	Pat Fischer ....50 Washington Redskins	.25	.05	
☐ 446	Bob Chandler ....50 Buffalo Bills	.25	.05	
☐ 447	Bill Bergey ....90 Cincinnati Bengals	.45	.09	
☐ 448	Walter Johnson ....35 Cleveland Browns	.17	.03	
☐ 449	Charley Young .... 1.25 Philadelphia Eagles	.60	.12	
☐ 450	Chester Marcol ....50 Green Bay Packers	.25	.05	
☐ 451	Ken Stabler .... 6.00 Oakland Raiders	3.00	.60	
☐ 452	Preston Pearson ....70 Pittsburgh Steelers	.35	.07	
☐ 453	Mike Current ....35 Denver Broncos	.17	.03	
☐ 454	Ron Bolton ....35 New England Patriots	.17	.03	
☐ 455	Mark Lomas ....35 New York Jets	.17	.03	
☐ 456	Raymond Chester ....50 Baltimore Colts	.25	.05	
☐ 457	Jerry LeVias ....50 San Diego Chargers	.25	.05	
☐ 458	Skip Butler ....35 Houston Oilers	.17	.03	
☐ 459	Mike Livingston ....70 Kansas City Chiefs	.35	.07	
☐ 460	AFC Semi-Finals ....70 Raiders 33, Steelers 14 and Dolphins 34, Bengals 16	.35	.07	
☐ 461	NFC Semi-Finals .... 2.25 Vikings 27, Redskins 20 and Cowboys 27, Rams 16	1.10	.22	

(Staubach)

☐ 462 Playoff Championship . 2.00   1.00   .20
Dolphins 27,
Raiders 10 and
Vikings 27,
Cowboys 10
(Stabler/Tarkenton)

☐ 463 Super Bowl .... 2.00   1.00   .20
Dolphins 24,
Vikings 7

☐ 464 Wayne Mulligan .... .35   .17   .03
St. Louis Cardinals

☐ 465 Horst Muhlmann .... .35   .17   .03
Cincinnati Bengals

☐ 466 Milt Morin .... .35   .17   .03
Cleveland Browns

☐ 467 Don Parish .... .35   .17   .03
Kansas City Chiefs

☐ 468 Richard Neal .... .35   .17   .03
New York Jets

☐ 469 Ron Jessie .... .50   .25   .05
Detroit Lions

☐ 470 Terry Bradshaw 12.00   6.00   1.20
Pittsburgh Steelers

☐ 471 Fred Dryer .... 2.25   1.10   .22
Los Angeles Rams

☐ 472 Jim Carter .... .35   .17   .03
Green Bay Packers

☐ 473 Ken Burrow .... .35   .17   .03
Atlanta Falcons

☐ 474 Wally Chambers .... 1.00   .50   .10
Chicago Bears

☐ 475 Dan Pastorini .... .70   .35   .07
Houston Oilers

☐ 476 Don Morrison .... .35   .17   .03
New Orleans Saints

☐ 477 Carl Mauck .... .35   .17   .03
San Diego Chargers

☐ 478 Larry Cole .... .70   .35   .07
Dallas Cowboys

☐ 479 Jim Kiick .... .50   .25   .05
Miami Dolphins

☐ 480 Willie Lanier .... 2.00   1.00   .20
Kansas City Chiefs

☐ 481 Don Herrmann .... .35   .17   .03
New York Giants

☐ 482 George Hunt .... .35   .17   .03
Baltimore Colts

☐ 483 Bob Howard .... .35   .17   .03
San Diego Chargers

☐ 484 Myron Pottios .... .35   .17   .03
Washington Redskins

☐ 485 Jackie Smith .... .50   .25   .05
St. Louis Cardinals

☐ 486 Vern Holland .... .35   .17   .03
Cincinnati Bengals

☐ 487 Jim Braxton .... .35   .17   .03
Buffalo Bills

☐ 488 Joe Reed .... .50   .25   .05
San Francisco 49ers

☐ 489 Wally Hilgenberg .... .35   .17   .03
Minnesota Vikings

☐ 490 Fred Biletnikoff .... 2.50   1.25   .25
Oakland Raiders

☐ 491 Bob DeMarco HOR .... .35   .17   .03
Cleveland Browns

☐ 492 Mark Nordquist .... .35   .17   .03
Philadelphia Eagles

☐ 493 Larry Brooks .... .35   .17   .03
Los Angeles Rams

☐ 494 Pete Athas .... .35   .17   .03
New York Giants

☐ 495 Emerson Boozer .... .50   .25   .05
New York Jets

☐ 496 L.C. Greenwood .... 1.25   .60   .12
Pittsburgh Steelers

☐ 497 Rockne Freitas .... .35   .17   .03
Detroit Lions

☐ 498 Checklist 397-528 .... 3.00   .30   .06

☐ 499 Joe Schmiesing .... .35   .17   .03
Baltimore Colts

☐ 500 Roger Staubach 22.00   11.00   2.20
Dallas Cowboys

☐ 501 Al Cowlings .... .35   .17   .03
Houston Oilers

☐ 502 Sam Cunningham .... 1.50   .75   .15
New England Patriots

☐ 503 Dennis Partee .... .35   .17   .03
San Diego Chargers

☐ 504 John Didion .... .35   .17   .03
New Orleans Saints

☐ 505 Nick Buoniconti .... 1.50   .75   .15
Miami Dolphins

☐ 506 Carl Garrett .... .35   .17   .03
Chicago Bears

☐ 507 Doug Van Horn .... .35   .17   .03
New York Giants

☐ 508 Jamie Rivers .... .35   .17   .03
St. Louis Cardinals

☐ 509 Jack Youngblood .... 2.50   1.25   .25
Los Angeles Rams

☐ 510 Charley Taylor UER ...... 2.50   1.25   .25
(Charlie on front)
Washington Redskins

☐ 511 Ken Riley .... .70   .35   .07
Cincinnati Bengals

☐ 512 Joe Ferguson .... 2.00   1.00   .20
Buffalo Bills

☐ 513 Bill Lueck .... .35   .17   .03
Green Bay Packers

☐ 514 Ray Brown .... .35   .17   .03
Atlanta Falcons

☐ 515 Fred Cox .... .50   .25   .05
Minnesota Vikings

		NRMT	VG-E	GOOD
☐ 516	Joe Jones .... .35		.17	.03
	Cleveland Browns			
☐ 517	Larry Schreiber .... .35		.17	.03
	San Francisco 49ers			
☐ 518	Dennis Wirgowski .... .35		.17	.03
	Philadelphia Eagles			
☐ 519	Leroy Mitchell .... .35		.17	.03
	Denver Broncos			
☐ 520	Otis Taylor .... .70		.35	.07
	Kansas City Chiefs			
☐ 521	Henry Davis .... .35		.17	.03
	Pittsburgh Steelers			
☐ 522	Bruce Barnes .... .35		.17	.03
	New England Patriots			
☐ 523	Charlie Smith .... .35		.17	.03
	Oakland Raiders			
☐ 524	Bert Jones 3.00		1.50	.30
	Baltimore Colts			
☐ 525	Lem Barney 1.25		.60	.12
	Detroit Lions			
☐ 526	John Fitzgerald .... .50		.25	.05
	Dallas Cowboys			
☐ 527	Tom Funchess .... .35		.17	.03
	Houston Oilers			
☐ 528	Steve Tannen .... .70		.25	.05
	New York Jets			

1975 Topps

MERLIN OLSEN

The 1975 Topps football set contains 528 cards. The cards measure 2 1/2" by 3 1/2". The first six cards in the set depict the statistical league leaders from each league. Cards 7 and 8 both show George Blanda in a very similar pose but with a different color jersey. Cards 201-225 are the All-Pro (AP) selections at each position. Record Breakers (351-356) and Highlights (452-460) are also featured in this

set. Post-season action is summarized on cards 526-528. No known scarcities exist. The card backs are printed in black ink with a green background on gray card stock. The key rookie cards in this set are Otis Armstrong, Rocky Bleier, Mel Blount, Cliff Branch, Dan Fouts, Drew Pearson and Lynn Swann. The set also includes Joe Theismann's first American football card marking his return from the CFL.

		NRMT	VG-E	GOOD
	COMPLETE SET (528)	315.00	145.00	35.00
	COMMON PLAYER (1-528) ...	.30	.15	.03
☐ 1	Rushing Leaders 1.50		.50	.10
	Lawrence McCutcheon			
	Otis Armstrong			
☐ 2	Passing Leaders 1.25		.60	.12
	Sonny Jurgensen			
	Ken Anderson			
☐ 3	Receiving Leaders .... .50		.25	.05
	Charley Young			
	Lydell Mitchell			
☐ 4	Scoring Leaders .... .50		.25	.05
	Chester Marcol			
	Roy Gerela			
☐ 5	Interception Leaders .... .50		.25	.05
	Ray Brown			
	Emmitt Thomas			
☐ 6	Punting Leaders .... .50		.25	.05
	Tom Blanchard			
	Ray Guy			
☐ 7	George Blanda 5.00		2.50	.50
	Oakland Raiders			
	(black jersey;			
	highlights on back)			
☐ 8	George Blanda 5.00		2.50	.50
	Oakland Raiders			
	(white jersey;			
	career record on back)			
☐ 9	Ralph Baker .... .30		.15	.03
	New York Jets			
☐ 10	Don Woods .... .30		.15	.03
	San Diego Chargers			
☐ 11	Bob Asher .... .30		.15	.03
	Chicago Bears			
☐ 12	Mel Blount 16.00		8.00	1.60
	Pittsburgh Steelers			
☐ 13	Sam Cunningham .... .70		.35	.07
	New England Patriots			
☐ 14	Jackie Smith .... .50		.25	.05
	St. Louis Cardinals			
☐ 15	Greg Landry .... .70		.35	.07
	Detroit Lions			
☐ 16	Buck Buchanan 1.50		.75	.15
	Kansas City Chiefs			
☐ 17	Haven Moses .... .50		.25	.05

Denver Broncos				
☐ 18 Clarence Ellis	.30	.15	.03
Atlanta Falcons			
☐ 19 Jim Carter	.30	.15	.03
Green Bay Packers			
☐ 20 Charley Taylor UER	2.00	1.00	.20
Washington Redskins			
(misspelled Charlie			
on card front)			
☐ 21 Jess Phillips	.30	.15	.03
New Orleans Saints			
☐ 22 Larry Seiple	.30	.15	.03
Miami Dolphins			
☐ 23 Doug Dieken	.30	.15	.03
Cleveland Browns			
☐ 24 Ron Saul	.30	.15	.03
Houston Oilers			
☐ 25 Isaac Curtis	.70	.35	.07
Cincinnati Bengals			
☐ 26 Gary Larsen	.70	.35	.07
Minnesota Vikings			
☐ 27 Bruce Jarvis	.30	.15	.03
Buffalo Bills			
☐ 28 Steve Zabel	.30	.15	.03
Philadelphia Eagles			
☐ 29 John Mendenhall	.30	.15	.03
New York Giants			
☐ 30 Rick Volk	.30	.15	.03
Baltimore Colts			
☐ 31 Checklist 1-132	2.50	.25	.05
☐ 32 Dan Abramowicz	.50	.25	.05
San Francisco 49ers			
☐ 33 Bubba Smith	1.75	.85	.17
Oakland Raiders			
☐ 34 David Ray	.30	.15	.03
Los Angeles Rams			
☐ 35 Dan Dierdorf	1.75	.85	.17
St. Louis Cardinals			
☐ 36 Randy Rasmussen	.30	.15	.03
New York Jets			
☐ 37 Bob Howard	.30	.15	.03
New England Patriots			
☐ 38 Gary Huff	.50	.25	.05
Chicago Bears			
☐ 39 Rocky Bleier	6.00	3.00	.60
Pittsburgh Steelers			
☐ 40 Mel Gray	.50	.25	.05
St. Louis Cardinals			
☐ 41 Tony McGee	.30	.15	.03
New England Patriots			
☐ 42 Larry Hand	.30	.15	.03
Detroit Lions			
☐ 43 Wendell Hayes	.50	.25	.05
Kansas City Chiefs			
☐ 44 Doug Wilkerson	.70	.35	.07
San Diego Chargers			
☐ 45 Paul Smith	.50	.25	.05
Denver Broncos			
☐ 46 Dave Robinson	.50	.25	.05
Washington Redskins			
☐ 47 Bivian Lee	.30	.15	.03
New York Jets			
☐ 48 Jim Mandich	.70	.35	.07
Miami Dolphins			
☐ 49 Greg Pruitt	.90	.45	.09
Cleveland Browns			
☐ 50 Dan Pastorini	.70	.35	.07
Houston Oilers			
☐ 51 Ron Pritchard	.30	.15	.03
Cincinnati Bengals			
☐ 52 Dan Conners	.30	.15	.03
Oakland Raiders			
☐ 53 Fred Cox	.50	.25	.05
Minnesota Vikings			
☐ 54 Tony Greene	.30	.15	.03
Buffalo Bills			
☐ 55 Craig Morton	1.00	.50	.10
New York Giants			
☐ 56 Jerry Sisemore	.50	.25	.05
Philadelphia Eagles			
☐ 57 Glenn Doughty	.30	.15	.03
Baltimore Colts			
☐ 58 Larry Schreiber	.30	.15	.03
San Francisco 49ers			
☐ 59 Charlie Waters	2.50	1.25	.25
Dallas Cowboys			
☐ 60 Jack Youngblood	1.25	.60	.12
Los Angeles Rams			
☐ 61 Bill Lenkaitis	.30	.15	.03
New England Patriots			
☐ 62 Greg Brezina	.50	.25	.05
Atlanta Falcons			
☐ 63 Bob Pollard	.30	.15	.03
New Orleans Saints			
☐ 64 Mack Alston	.30	.15	.03
Houston Oilers			
☐ 65 Drew Pearson	5.50	2.75	.55
Dallas Cowboys			
☐ 66 Charlie Stukes	.30	.15	.03
Los Angeles Rams			
☐ 67 Emerson Boozer	.50	.25	.05
New York Jets			
☐ 68 Dennis Partee	.30	.15	.03
San Diego Chargers			
☐ 69 Bob Newton	.30	.15	.03
Chicago Bears			
☐ 70 Jack Tatum	.70	.35	.07
Oakland Raiders			
☐ 71 Frank Lewis	.50	.25	.05
Pittsburgh Steelers			
☐ 72 Bob Young	.30	.15	.03
St. Louis Cardinals			
☐ 73 Julius Adams	.30	.15	.03
New England Patriots			

☐ 74 Paul Naumoff .... .30		.15	.03
Detroit Lions			
☐ 75 Otis Taylor .... .70		.35	.07
Kansas City Chiefs			
☐ 76 Dave Hampton .... .50		.25	.05
Atlanta Falcons			
☐ 77 Mike Current .... .30		.15	.03
Denver Broncos			
☐ 78 Brig Owens .... .30		.15	.03
Washington Redskins			
☐ 79 Bobby Scott .... .50		.25	.05
New Orleans Saints			
☐ 80 Harold Carmichael 2.50		1.25	.25
Philadelphia Eagles			
☐ 81 Bill Stanfill .... .50		.25	.05
Miami Dolphins			
☐ 82 Bob Babich .... .30		.15	.03
Cleveland Browns			
☐ 83 Vic Washington .... .30		.15	.03
Houston Oilers			
☐ 84 Mick Tingelhoff .... .50		.25	.05
Minnesota Vikings			
☐ 85 Bob Trumpy 1.00		.50	.10
Cincinnati Bengals			
☐ 86 Earl Edwards .... .30		.15	.03
Buffalo Bills			
☐ 87 Ron Hornsby .... .30		.15	.03
New York Giants			
☐ 88 Don McCauley .... .30		.15	.03
Baltimore Colts			
☐ 89 Jim Johnson .... .50		.25	.05
San Francisco 49ers			
☐ 90 Andy Russell .... .50		.25	.05
Pittsburgh Steelers			
☐ 91 Cornell Green .... .50		.25	.05
Dallas Cowboys			
☐ 92 Charlie Cowan .... .30		.15	.03
Los Angeles Rams			
☐ 93 Jon Staggers .... .30		.15	.03
Green Bay Packers			
☐ 94 Billy Newsome .... .30		.15	.03
New York Jets			
☐ 95 Willie Brown 1.50		.75	.15
Oakland Raiders			
☐ 96 Carl Mauck .... .30		.15	.03
San Diego Chargers			
☐ 97 Doug Buffone .... .30		.15	.03
Chicago Bears			
☐ 98 Preston Pearson .... .70		.35	.07
Pittsburgh Steelers			
☐ 99 Jim Bakken .... .50		.25	.05
St. Louis Cardinals			
☐ 100 Bob Griese 4.50		2.25	.45
Miami Dolphins			
☐ 101 Bob Windsor .... .30		.15	.03
New England Patriots			
☐ 102 Rockne Freitas .... .30		.15	.03

Detroit Lions			
☐ 103 Jim Marsalis .... .30		.15	.03
Kansas City Chiefs			
☐ 104 Bill Thompson .... .50		.25	.05
Denver Broncos			
☐ 105 Ken Burrow .... .30		.15	.03
Atlanta Falcons			
☐ 106 Diron Talbert .... .50		.25	.05
Washington Redskins			
☐ 107 Joe Federspiel .... .30		.15	.03
New Orleans Saints			
☐ 108 Norm Bulaich .... .50		.25	.05
Philadelphia Eagles			
☐ 109 Bob DeMarco .... .30		.15	.03
Cleveland Browns			
☐ 110 Tom Wittum .... .30		.15	.03
San Francisco 49ers			
☐ 111 Larry Hefner .... .30		.15	.03
Green Bay Packers			
☐ 112 Tody Smith .... .30		.15	.03
Houston Oilers			
☐ 113 Stu Voigt .... .50		.25	.05
Minnesota Vikings			
☐ 114 Horst Muhlmann .... .30		.15	.03
Cincinnati Bengals			
☐ 115 Ahmad Rashad 4.00		2.00	.40
Buffalo Bills			
☐ 116 Joe Dawkins .... .30		.15	.03
New York Giants			
☐ 117 George Kunz .... .50		.25	.05
Atlanta Falcons			
☐ 118 D.D. Lewis .... .50		.25	.05
Dallas Cowboys			
☐ 119 Levi Johnson .... .30		.15	.03
Detroit Lions			
☐ 120 Len Dawson 3.00		1.50	.30
Kansas City Chiefs			
☐ 121 Jim Bertelsen .... .50		.25	.05
Los Angeles Rams			
☐ 122 Ed Bell .... .30		.15	.03
New York Jets			
☐ 123 Art Thoms .... .30		.15	.03
Oakland Raiders			
☐ 124 Joe Beauchamp .... .30		.15	.03
San Diego Chargers			
☐ 125 Jack Ham 2.50		1.25	.25
Pittsburgh Steelers			
☐ 126 Carl Garrett .... .30		.15	.03
Chicago Bears			
☐ 127 Roger Finnie .... .30		.15	.03
St. Louis Cardinals			
☐ 128 Howard Twilley .... .50		.25	.05
Miami Dolphins			
☐ 129 Bruce Barnes .... .30		.15	.03
New England Patriots			
☐ 130 Nate Wright .... .50		.25	.05
Minnesota Vikings			

☐ 131	Jerry Tagge .... .50	.25	.05
	Green Bay Packers		
☐ 132	Floyd Little 1.00	.50	.10
	Denver Broncos		
☐ 133	John Zook .... .50	.25	.05
	Atlanta Falcons		
☐ 134	Len Hauss .... .50	.25	.05
	Washington Redskins		
☐ 135	Archie Manning 1.25	.60	.12
	New Orleans Saints		
☐ 136	Po James .... .30	.15	.03
	Philadelphia Eagles		
☐ 137	Walt Sumner .... .30	.15	.03
	Cleveland Browns		
☐ 138	Randy Beisler .... .30	.15	.03
	San Francisco 49ers		
☐ 139	Willie Alexander .... .30	.15	.03
	Houston Oilers		
☐ 140	Garo Yepremian .... .50	.25	.05
	Miami Dolphins		
☐ 141	Chip Myers .... .30	.15	.03
	Cincinnati Bengals		
☐ 142	Jim Braxton .... .30	.15	.03
	Buffalo Bills		
☐ 143	Doug Van Horn .... .30	.15	.03
	New York Giants		
☐ 144	Stan White .... .30	.15	.03
	Baltimore Colts		
☐ 145	Roger Staubach 17.00	8.50	1.70
	Dallas Cowboys		
☐ 146	Herman Weaver .... .30	.15	.03
	Detroit Lions		
☐ 147	Marvin Upshaw .... .30	.15	.03
	Kansas City Chiefs		
☐ 148	Bob Klein .... .30	.15	.03
	Los Angeles Rams		
☐ 149	Earlie Thomas .... .30	.15	.03
	New York Jets		
☐ 150	John Brockington .... .70	.35	.07
	Green Bay Packers		
☐ 151	Mike Siani .... .30	.15	.03
	Oakland Raiders		
☐ 152	Sam Davis .... .30	.15	.03
	Pittsburgh Steelers		
☐ 153	Mike Wagner .... .50	.25	.05
	Pittsburgh Steelers		
☐ 154	Larry Stallings .... .30	.15	.03
	St. Louis Cardinals		
☐ 155	Wally Chambers .... .50	.25	.05
	Chicago Bears		
☐ 156	Randy Vataha .... .50	.25	.05
	New England Patriots		
☐ 157	Jim Marshall 1.25	.60	.12
	Minnesota Vikings		
☐ 158	Jim Turner .... .50	.25	.05
	Denver Broncos		
☐ 159	Walt Sweeney .... .30	.15	.03
	Washington Redskins		
☐ 160	Ken Anderson 3.50	1.75	.35
	Cincinnati Bengals		
☐ 161	Ray Brown .... .30	.15	.03
	Atlanta Falcons		
☐ 162	John Didion .... .30	.15	.03
	New Orleans Saints		
☐ 163	Tom Dempsey .... .50	.25	.05
	Philadelphia Eagles		
☐ 164	Clarence Scott .... .30	.15	.03
	Cleveland Browns		
☐ 165	Gene Washington .... .70	.35	.07
	San Francisco 49ers		
☐ 166	Willie Rogers .... .30	.15	.03
	Houston Oilers		
☐ 167	Doug Swift .... .30	.15	.03
	Miami Dolphins		
☐ 168	Rufus Mayes .... .30	.15	.03
	Cincinnati Bengals		
☐ 169	Marv Bateman .... .30	.15	.03
	Buffalo Bills		
☐ 170	Lydell Mitchell .... .70	.35	.07
	Baltimore Colts		
☐ 171	Ron Smith .... .30	.15	.03
	San Diego Chargers		
☐ 172	Bill Munson .... .50	.25	.05
	Detroit Lions		
☐ 173	Bob Grim .... .50	.25	.05
	New York Giants		
☐ 174	Ed Budde .... .50	.25	.05
	Kansas City Chiefs		
☐ 175	Bob Lilly UER 3.00	1.50	.30
	(Was first draft,		
	not first player)		
	Dallas Cowboys		
☐ 176	Jim Youngblood .... .90	.45	.09
	Los Angeles Rams		
☐ 177	Steve Tannen .... .30	.15	.03
	New York Jets		
☐ 178	Rich McGeorge .... .30	.15	.03
	Green Bay Packers		
☐ 179	Jim Tyrer .... .50	.25	.05
	Washington Redskins		
☐ 180	Forrest Blue .... .50	.25	.05
	San Francisco 49ers		
☐ 181	Jerry LeVias .... .50	.25	.05
	San Diego Chargers		
☐ 182	Joe Gilliam .... .70	.35	.07
	Pittsburgh Steelers		
☐ 183	Jim Otis .... .90	.45	.09
	St. Louis Cardinals		
☐ 184	Mel Tom .... .30	.15	.03
	Chicago Bears		
☐ 185	Paul Seymour .... .30	.15	.03
	Buffalo Bills		
☐ 186	George Webster .... .50	.25	.05
	New England Patriots		

□			
187	Pete Duranko 30	.15	.03
	Denver Broncos		
188	Essex Johnson 30	.15	.03
	Cincinnati Bengals		
189	Bob Lee 50	.25	.05
	Atlanta Falcons		
190	Gene Upshaw 1.50	.75	.15
	Oakland Raiders		
191	Tom Myers 30	.15	.03
	New Orleans Saints		
192	Don Zimmerman 30	.15	.03
	Philadelphia Eagles		
193	John Garlington 30	.15	.03
	Cleveland Browns		
194	Skip Butler 30	.15	.03
	Houston Oilers		
195	Tom Mitchell 30	.15	.03
	San Francisco 49ers		
196	Jim Langer 1.50	.75	.15
	Miami Dolphins		
197	Ron Carpenter 30	.15	.03
	Cincinnati Bengals		
198	Dave Foley 30	.15	.03
	Buffalo Bills		
199	Bert Jones 1.00	.50	.10
	Baltimore Colts		
200	Larry Brown 70	.35	.07
	Washington Redskins		
201	All Pro Receivers 1.75	.85	.17
	Charley Taylor		
	Fred Biletnikoff		
202	All Pro Tackles 50	.25	.05
	Rayfield Wright		
	Russ Washington		
203	All Pro Guards 70	.35	.07
	Tom Mack		
	Larry Little		
204	All Pro Centers 50	.25	.05
	Jeff Van Note		
	Jack Rudnay		
205	All Pro Guards 1.00	.50	.10
	Gale Gillingham		
	John Hannah		
206	All Pro Tackles 70	.35	.07
	Dan Dierdorf		
	Winston Hill		
207	All Pro Tight Ends 50	.25	.05
	Charley Young		
	Riley Odoms		
208	All Pro Quarterbacks ...2.25	1.10	.22
	Fran Tarkenton		
	Ken Stabler		
209	All Pro Backs 2.25	1.10	.22
	Lawrence McCutcheon		
	O.J. Simpson		
210	All Pro Backs 70	.35	.07
	Terry Metcalf		

□			
	Otis Armstrong		
211	All Pro Receivers 50	.25	.05
	Mel Gray		
	Isaac Curtis		
212	All Pro Kickers 50	.25	.05
	Chester Marcol		
	Roy Gerela		
213	All Pro Ends 70	.35	.07
	Jack Youngblood		
	Elvin Bethea		
214	All Pro Tackles 50	.25	.05
	Alan Page		
	Otis Sistrunk		
215	All Pro Tackles 1.00	.50	.10
	Merlin Olsen		
	Mike Reid		
216	All Pro Ends 90	.45	.09
	Carl Eller		
	Lyle Alzado		
217	All Pro Linebackers 70	.35	.07
	Ted Hendricks		
	Phil Villapiano		
218	All Pro Linebackers 90	.45	.09
	Lee Roy Jordan		
	Willie Lanier		
219	All Pro Linebackers 50	.25	.05
	Isiah Robertson		
	Andy Russell		
220	All Pro Cornerbacks 50	.25	.05
	Nate Wright		
	Emmitt Thomas		
221	All Pro Cornerbacks 50	.25	.05
	Willie Buchanon		
	Lemar Parrish		
222	All Pro Safeties 70	.35	.07
	Ken Houston		
	Dick Anderson		
223	All Pro Safeties 70	.35	.07
	Cliff Harris		
	Jack Tatum		
224	All Pro Punters 50	.25	.05
	Tom Wittum		
	Ray Guy		
225	All Pro Returners 50	.25	.05
	Terry Metcalf		
	Greg Pruitt		
226	Ted Kwalick 50	.25	.05
	San Francisco 49ers		
227	Spider Lockhart 50	.25	.05
	New York Giants		
228	Mike Livingston 50	.25	.05
	Kansas City Chiefs		
229	Larry Cole 30	.15	.03
	Dallas Cowboys		
230	Gary Garrison 50	.25	.05
	San Diego Chargers		
231	Larry Brooks 30	.15	.03

	Los Angeles Rams					Cleveland Browns		
☐ 232	Bobby Howfield	.30	.15	.03	☐ 261	Al Matthews	.30	.15	.03
	New York Jets					Green Bay Packers		
☐ 233	Fred Carr	.50	.25	.05	☐ 262	Bob Kuechenberg	.50	.25	.05
	Green Bay Packers					Miami Dolphins		
☐ 234	Norm Evans	.30	.15	.03	☐ 263	Ron Yankowski	.30	.15	.03
	Miami Dolphins					St. Louis Cardinals		
☐ 235	Dwight White	.50	.25	.05	☐ 264	Ron Shanklin	.30	.15	.03
	Pittsburgh Steelers					Pittsburgh Steelers		
☐ 236	Conrad Dobler	.70	.35	.07	☐ 265	Bobby Douglass	.50	.25	.05
	St. Louis Cardinals					Chicago Bears		
☐ 237	Garry Lyle	.30	.15	.03	☐ 266	Josh Ashton	.30	.15	.03
	Chicago Bears					New England Patriots		
☐ 238	Darryl Stingley	.70	.35	.07	☐ 267	Bill Van Heusen	.30	.15	.03
	New England Patriots					Denver Broncos		
☐ 239	Tom Graham	.30	.15	.03	☐ 268	Jeff Siemon	.50	.25	.05
	Denver Broncos					Minnesota Vikings		
☐ 240	Chuck Foreman	1.00	.50	.10	☐ 269	Bob Newland	.30	.15	.03
	Minnesota Vikings					New Orleans Saints		
☐ 241	Ken Riley	.50	.25	.05	☐ 270	Gale Gillingham	.30	.15	.03
	Cincinnati Bengals					Green Bay Packers		
☐ 242	Don Morrison	.30	.15	.03	☐ 271	Zeke Moore	.30	.15	.03
	New Orleans Saints					Houston Oilers		
☐ 243	Lynn Dickey	.70	.35	.07	☐ 272	Mike Tilleman	.30	.15	.03
	Houston Oilers					Atlanta Falcons		
☐ 244	Don Cockroft	.30	.15	.03	☐ 273	John Leypoldt	.30	.15	.03
	Cleveland Browns					Buffalo Bills		
☐ 245	Claude Humphrey	.50	.25	.05	☐ 274	Ken Mendenhall	.30	.15	.03
	Atlanta Falcons					Baltimore Colts		
☐ 246	John Skorupan	.30	.15	.03	☐ 275	Norm Snead	.70	.35	.07
	Buffalo Bills					San Francisco 49ers		
☐ 247	Raymond Chester	.50	.25	.05	☐ 276	Bill Bradley	.50	.25	.05
	Oakland Raiders					Philadelphia Eagles		
☐ 248	Cas Banaszek	.30	.15	.03	☐ 277	Jerry Smith	.50	.25	.05
	San Francisco 49ers					Washington Redskins		
☐ 249	Art Malone	.30	.15	.03	☐ 278	Clarence Davis	.30	.15	.03
	Atlanta Falcons					Oakland Raiders		
☐ 250	Ed Flanagan	.30	.15	.03	☐ 279	Jim Yarbrough	.30	.15	.03
	Detroit Lions					Detroit Lions		
☐ 251	Checklist 133-264	2.50	.25	.05	☐ 280	Lemar Parrish	.50	.25	.05
☐ 252	Nemiah Wilson	.30	.15	.03		Cincinnati Bengals		
	Oakland Raiders				☐ 281	Bobby Bell	1.50	.75	.15
☐ 253	Ron Jessie	.50	.25	.05		Kansas City Chiefs		
	Detroit Lions				☐ 282	Lynn Swann UER	28.00	14.00	2.80
☐ 254	Jim Lynch	.30	.15	.03		Pittsburgh Steelers		
	Kansas City Chiefs					(Wide Reciever on front)		
☐ 255	Bob Tucker	.50	.25	.05	☐ 283	John Hicks	.50	.25	.05
	New York Giants					New York Giants		
☐ 256	Terry Owens	.50	.25	.05	☐ 284	Coy Bacon	.30	.15	.03
	San Diego Chargers					San Diego Chargers		
☐ 257	John Fitzgerald	.50	.25	.05	☐ 285	Lee Roy Jordan	1.00	.50	.10
	Dallas Cowboys					Dallas Cowboys		
☐ 258	Jack Snow	.50	.25	.05	☐ 286	Willie Buchanon	.50	.25	.05
	Los Angeles Rams					Green Bay Packers		
☐ 259	Garry Puetz	.30	.15	.03	☐ 287	Al Woodall	.50	.25	.05
	New York Jets					New York Jets		
☐ 260	Mike Phipps	.50	.25	.05	☐ 288	Reggie Rucker	.50	.25	.05

Cleveland Browns			
☐ 289 John Schmitt 30	.15	.03
Green Bay Packers			
☐ 290 Carl Eller 1.00	.50	.10
Minnesota Vikings			
☐ 291 Jake Scott 50	.25	.05
Miami Dolphins			
☐ 292 Donny Anderson 50	.25	.05
St. Louis Cardinals			
☐ 293 Charley Wade 30	.15	.03
Chicago Bears			
☐ 294 John Tanner 30	.15	.03
New England Patriots			
☐ 295 Charlie Johnson 50	.25	.05
Denver Broncos			
☐ 296 Tom Blanchard 30	.15	.03
New Orleans Saints			
☐ 297 Curley Culp 50	.25	.05
Houston Oilers			
☐ 298 Jeff Van Note 1.50	.75	.15
Atlanta Falcons			
☐ 299 Bob James 30	.15	.03
Buffalo Bills			
☐ 300 Franco Harris 11.00	5.50	1.10
Pittsburgh Steelers			
☐ 301 Tim Berra 50	.25	.05
Baltimore Colts			
☐ 302 Bruce Gossett 30	.15	.03
San Francisco 49ers			
☐ 303 Verlon Biggs 30	.15	.03
Washington Redskins			
☐ 304 Bob Kowalkowski 30	.15	.03
Detroit Lions			
☐ 305 Marv Hubbard 50	.25	.05
Oakland Raiders			
☐ 306 Ken Avery 30	.15	.03
Kansas City Chiefs			
☐ 307 Mike Adamle 50	.25	.05
New York Jets			
☐ 308 Don Herrmann 30	.15	.03
New York Giants			
☐ 309 Chris Fletcher 30	.15	.03
San Diego Chargers			
☐ 310 Roman Gabriel 1.25	.60	.12
Philadelphia Eagles			
☐ 311 Billy Joe DuPree 90	.45	.09
Dallas Cowboys			
☐ 312 Fred Dryer 2.00	1.00	.20
Los Angeles Rams			
☐ 313 John Riggins 4.00	2.00	.40
New York Jets			
☐ 314 Bob McKay 30	.15	.03
Cleveland Browns			
☐ 315 Ted Hendricks 1.50	.75	.15
Green Bay Packers			
☐ 316 Bobby Bryant 30	.15	.03
Minnesota Vikings			

☐ 317 Don Nottingham 30	.15	.03
Miami Dolphins			
☐ 318 John Hannah 3.00	1.50	.30
New England Patriots			
☐ 319 Rich Coady 30	.15	.03
Chicago Bears			
☐ 320 Phil Villapiano 50	.25	.05
Oakland Raiders			
☐ 321 Jim Plunkett 1.75	.85	.17
New England Patriots			
☐ 322 Lyle Alzado 1.25	.60	.12
Denver Broncos			
☐ 323 Ernie Jackson 30	.15	.03
New Orleans Saints			
☐ 324 Billy Parks 30	.15	.03
Houston Oilers			
☐ 325 Willie Lanier 1.50	.75	.15
Kansas City Chiefs			
☐ 326 John James 30	.15	.03
Atlanta Falcons			
☐ 327 Joe Ferguson 90	.45	.09
Buffalo Bills			
☐ 328 Ernie Holmes 90	.45	.09
Pittsburgh Steelers			
☐ 329 Bruce Laird 30	.15	.03
Baltimore Colts			
☐ 330 Chester Marcol 30	.15	.03
Green Bay Packers			
☐ 331 Dave Wilcox 50	.25	.05
San Francisco 49ers			
☐ 332 Pat Fischer 50	.25	.05
Washington Redskins			
☐ 333 Steve Owens 70	.35	.07
Detroit Lions			
☐ 334 Royce Berry 30	.15	.03
Cincinnati Bengals			
☐ 335 Russ Washington 30	.15	.03
San Diego Chargers			
☐ 336 Walker Gillette 30	.15	.03
New York Giants			
☐ 337 Mark Nordquist 30	.15	.03
Philadelphia Eagles			
☐ 338 James Harris 1.00	.50	.10
Los Angeles Rams			
☐ 339 Warren Koegel 30	.15	.03
New York Jets			
☐ 340 Emmitt Thomas 50	.25	.05
Kansas City Chiefs			
☐ 341 Walt Garrison 70	.35	.07
Dallas Cowboys			
☐ 342 Thom Darden 30	.15	.03
Cleveland Browns			
☐ 343 Mike Eischeid 30	.15	.03
Minnesota Vikings			
☐ 344 Ernie McMillan 30	.15	.03
St. Louis Cardinals			
☐ 345 Nick Buoniconti 1.25	.60	.12

	Miami Dolphins			
☐ 346	George Farmer .... .30	.15	.03	
	Chicago Bears			
☐ 347	Sam Adams .... .30	.15	.03	
	New England Patriots			
☐ 348	Larry Cipa .... .30	.15	.03	
	New Orleans Saints			
☐ 349	Bob Moore .... .30	.15	.03	
	Oakland Raiders			
☐ 350	Otis Armstrong 3.75	1.85	.37	
	Denver Broncos			
☐ 351	George Blanda RB 1.75	.85	.17	
	All Time Scoring Leader			
☐ 352	Fred Cox RB .... .50	.25	.05	
	151 Straight PAT's			
☐ 353	Tom Dempsey RB .... .50	.25	.05	
	63 Yard FG			
☐ 354	Ken Houston RB .... .70	.35	.07	
	9th Int. for TD (Shown as Oiler, should be Redskin)			
☐ 355	O.J. Simpson RB 4.25	2.10	.42	
	2003 Yard Season			
☐ 356	Ron Smith RB .... .50	.25	.05	
	All Time Return Yardage Mark			
☐ 357	Bob Atkins .... .30	.15	.03	
	Houston Oilers			
☐ 358	Pat Sullivan .... .50	.25	.05	
	Atlanta Falcons			
☐ 359	Joe DeLamielleure .... .50	.25	.05	
	Buffalo Bills			
☐ 360	Lawrence McCutcheon 2.50	1.25	.25	
	Los Angeles Rams			
☐ 361	David Lee .... .30	.15	.03	
	Baltimore Colts			
☐ 362	Mike McCoy .... .30	.15	.03	
	Green Bay Packers			
☐ 363	Skip Vanderbundt .... .30	.15	.03	
	San Francisco 49ers			
☐ 364	Mark Moseley .... .50	.25	.05	
	Washington Redskins			
☐ 365	Lem Barney 1.00	.50	.10	
	Detroit Lions			
☐ 366	Doug Dressler .... .30	.15	.03	
	Cincinnati Bengals			
☐ 367	Dan Fouts 55.00	27.50	5.50	
	San Diego Chargers			
☐ 368	Bob Hyland .... .30	.15	.03	
	New York Giants			
☐ 369	John Outlaw .... .30	.15	.03	
	Philadelphia Eagles			
☐ 370	Roy Gerela .... .30	.15	.03	
	Pittsburgh Steelers			
☐ 371	Isiah Robertson .... .50	.25	.05	
	Los Angeles Rams			
☐ 372	Jerome Barkum .... .50	.25	.05	
	New York Jets			
☐ 373	Ed Podolak .... .50	.25	.05	
	Kansas City Chiefs			
☐ 374	Milt Morin .... .30	.15	.03	
	Cleveland Browns			
☐ 375	John Niland .... .30	.15	.03	
	Dallas Cowboys			
☐ 376	Checklist 265-396 .... 2.50	.25	.05	
☐ 377	Ken Iman .... .30	.15	.03	
	St. Louis Cardinals			
☐ 378	Manny Fernandez .... .30	.15	.03	
	Miami Dolphins			
☐ 379	Dave Gallagher .... .30	.15	.03	
	Chicago Bears			
☐ 380	Ken Stabler 3.50	1.75	.35	
	Oakland Raiders			
☐ 381	Mack Herron .... .50	.25	.05	
	New England Patriots			
☐ 382	Bill McClard .... .30	.15	.03	
	New Orleans Saints			
☐ 383	Ray May .... .30	.15	.03	
	Denver Broncos			
☐ 384	Don Hansen .... .30	.15	.03	
	Atlanta Falcons			
☐ 385	Elvin Bethea .... .50	.25	.05	
	Houston Oilers			
☐ 386	Joe Scibelli .... .30	.15	.03	
	Los Angeles Rams			
☐ 387	Neal Craig .... .30	.15	.03	
	Buffalo Bills			
☐ 388	Marty Domres .... .50	.25	.05	
	Baltimore Colts			
☐ 389	Ken Ellis .... .30	.15	.03	
	Green Bay Packers			
☐ 390	Charley Young .... .50	.25	.05	
	Philadelphia Eagles			
☐ 391	Tommy Hart .... .30	.15	.03	
	San Francisco 49ers			
☐ 392	Moses Denson .... .30	.15	.03	
	Washington Redskins			
☐ 393	Larry Walton .... .30	.15	.03	
	Detroit Lions			
☐ 394	Dave Green .... .30	.15	.03	
	Cincinnati Bengals			
☐ 395	Ron Johnson .... .50	.25	.05	
	New York Giants			
☐ 396	Ed Bradley .... .30	.15	.03	
	Pittsburgh Steelers			
☐ 397	J.T. Thomas .... .30	.15	.03	
	Pittsburgh Steelers			
☐ 398	Jim Bailey .... .30	.15	.03	
	Baltimore Colts			
☐ 399	Barry Pearson .... .30	.15	.03	
	Kansas City Chiefs			
☐ 400	Fran Tarkenton 8.50	4.25	.85	
	Minnesota Vikings			

☐ 401	Jack Rudnay 30	.15	.03
	Kansas City Chiefs		
☐ 402	Rayfield Wright 30	.15	.03
	Dallas Cowboys		
☐ 403	Roger Wehrli 50	.25	.05
	St. Louis Cardinals		
☐ 404	Vern Den Herder 30	.15	.03
	Miami Dolphins		
☐ 405	Fred Biletnikoff 2.50	1.25	.25
	Oakland Raiders		
☐ 406	Ken Grandberry 30	.15	.03
	Chicago Bears		
☐ 407	Bob Adams 30	.15	.03
	New England Patriots		
☐ 408	Jim Merlo 30	.15	.03
	New Orleans Saints		
☐ 409	John Pitts 30	.15	.03
	Denver Broncos		
☐ 410	Dave Osborn 50	.25	.05
	Minnesota Vikings		
☐ 411	Dennis Havig 30	.15	.03
	Atlanta Falcons		
☐ 412	Bob Johnson 30	.15	.03
	Cincinnati Bengals		
☐ 413	Ken Burrough 50	.25	.05
	Houston Oilers		
☐ 414	Jim Cheyunski 30	.15	.03
	Buffalo Bills		
☐ 415	MacArthur Lane 50	.25	.05
	Green Bay Packers		
☐ 416	Joe Theismann 18.00	9.00	1.80
	Washington Redskins		
☐ 417	Mike Boryla 50	.25	.05
	Philadelphia Eagles		
☐ 418	Bruce Taylor 50	.25	.05
	San Francisco 49ers		
☐ 419	Chris Hanburger 50	.25	.05
	Washington Redskins		
☐ 420	Tom Mack 70	.35	.07
	Los Angeles Rams		
☐ 421	Errol Mann 30	.15	.03
	Detroit Lions		
☐ 422	Jack Gregory 50	.25	.05
	New York Giants		
☐ 423	Harrison Davis 30	.15	.03
	San Diego Chargers		
☐ 424	Burgess Owens 30	.15	.03
	New York Jets		
☐ 425	Joe Greene 3.00	1.50	.30
	Pittsburgh Steelers		
☐ 426	Morris Stroud 30	.15	.03
	Kansas City Chiefs		
☐ 427	John DeMarie 30	.15	.03
	Cleveland Browns		
☐ 428	Mel Renfro 70	.35	.07
	Dallas Cowboys		
☐ 429	Cid Edwards 30	.15	.03

	Chicago Bears		
☐ 430	Mike Reid 70	.35	.07
	Cincinnati Bengals		
☐ 431	Jack Mildren 70	.35	.07
	New England Patriots		
☐ 432	Jerry Simmons 30	.15	.03
	Denver Broncos		
☐ 433	Ron Yary 50	.25	.05
	Minnesota Vikings		
☐ 434	Howard Stevens 50	.25	.05
	New Orleans Saints		
☐ 435	Ray Guy 1.75	.85	.17
	Oakland Raiders		
☐ 436	Tommy Nobis 1.00	.50	.10
	Atlanta Falcons		
☐ 437	Solomon Freelon 30	.15	.03
	Houston Oilers		
☐ 438	J.D. Hill 50	.25	.05
	Buffalo Bills		
☐ 439	Toni Linhart 30	.15	.03
	Baltimore Colts		
☐ 440	Dick Anderson 50	.25	.05
	Miami Dolphins		
☐ 441	Guy Morriss 30	.15	.03
	Philadelphia Eagles		
☐ 442	Bob Hoskins 30	.15	.03
	San Francisco 49ers		
☐ 443	John Hadl 1.00	.50	.10
	Los Angeles Rams		
☐ 444	Roy Jefferson 50	.25	.05
	Washington Redskins		
☐ 445	Charlie Sanders 50	.25	.05
	Detroit Lions		
☐ 446	Pat Curran 30	.15	.03
	Los Angeles Rams		
☐ 447	David Knight 30	.15	.03
	New York Jets		
☐ 448	Bob Brown 50	.25	.05
	San Diego Chargers		
☐ 449	Pete Gogolak 50	.25	.05
	New York Giants		
☐ 450	Terry Metcalf 70	.35	.07
	St. Louis Cardinals		
☐ 451	Bill Bergey 70	.35	.07
	Philadelphia Eagles		
☐ 452	Dan Abramowicz 50	.25	.05
	105 Straight Games		
☐ 453	Otis Armstrong HL 90	.45	.09
	183 Yard Game		
☐ 454	Cliff Branch HL 1.25	.60	.12
	13 TD Passes		
☐ 455	John James HL 50	.25	.05
	Record 96 Punts		
☐ 456	Lydell Mitchell HL 50	.25	.05
	13 Passes in Game		
☐ 457	Lemar Parrish HL 50	.25	.05
	3 TD Punt Returns		

☐ 458 Ken Stabler HL 1.25	.60	.12	
26 TD Passes			
in One Season			
☐ 459 Lynn Swann HL 4.50	2.25	.45	
577 Yards in			
Punt Returns			
☐ 460 Emmitt Thomas HL 50	.25	.05	
73 Yd. Interception			
☐ 461 Terry Bradshaw 9.00	4.50	.90	
Pittsburgh Steelers			
☐ 462 Jerrel Wilson 50	.25	.05	
Kansas City Chiefs			
☐ 463 Walter Johnson 30	.15	.03	
Cleveland Browns			
☐ 464 Golden Richards 50	.25	.05	
Dallas Cowboys			
☐ 465 Tommy Casanova 50	.25	.05	
Cincinnati Bengals			
☐ 466 Randy Jackson 30	.15	.03	
Chicago Bears			
☐ 467 Ron Bolton 30	.15	.03	
New England Patriots			
☐ 468 Joe Owens 30	.15	.03	
New Orleans Saints			
☐ 469 Wally Hilgenberg 30	.15	.03	
Minnesota Vikings			
☐ 470 Riley Odoms 50	.25	.05	
Denver Broncos			
☐ 471 Otis Sistrunk 50	.25	.05	
Oakland Raiders			
☐ 472 Eddie Ray 30	.15	.03	
Atlanta Falcons			
☐ 473 Reggie McKenzie 70	.35	.07	
Buffalo Bills			
☐ 474 Elbert Drungo 30	.15	.03	
Houston Oilers			
☐ 475 Mercury Morris 70	.35	.07	
Miami Dolphins			
☐ 476 Dan Dickel 30	.15	.03	
Baltimore Colts			
☐ 477 Merritt Kersey 30	.15	.03	
Philadelphia Eagles			
☐ 478 Mike Holmes 30	.15	.03	
San Francisco 49ers			
☐ 479 Clarence Williams 30	.15	.03	
Green Bay Packers			
☐ 480 Bill Kilmer 1.00	.50	.10	
Washington Redskins			
☐ 481 Altie Taylor 30	.15	.03	
Detroit Lions			
☐ 482 Dave Elmendorf 30	.15	.03	
Los Angeles Rams			
☐ 483 Bob Rowe 30	.15	.03	
St. Louis Cardinals			
☐ 484 Pete Athas 30	.15	.03	
New York Giants			
☐ 485 Winston Hill 30	.15	.03	

New York Jets			
☐ 486 Bo Matthews 30	.15	.03	
San Diego Chargers			
☐ 487 Earl Thomas 30	.15	.03	
St. Louis Cardinals			
☐ 488 Jan Stenerud 1.00	.50	.10	
Kansas City Chiefs			
☐ 489 Steve Holden 30	.15	.03	
Cleveland Browns			
☐ 490 Cliff Harris 2.50	1.25	.25	
Dallas Cowboys			
☐ 491 Boobie Clark 50	.25	.05	
Cincinnati Bengals			
☐ 492 Joe Taylor 30	.15	.03	
Chicago Bears			
☐ 493 Tom Neville 30	.15	.03	
New England Patriots			
☐ 494 Wayne Colman 30	.15	.03	
New Orleans Saints			
☐ 495 Jim Mitchell 30	.15	.03	
Atlanta Falcons			
☐ 496 Paul Krause 70	.35	.07	
Minnesota Vikings			
☐ 497 Jim Otto 1.50	.75	.15	
Oakland Raiders			
☐ 498 John Rowser 30	.15	.03	
Denver Broncos			
☐ 499 Larry Little 50	.25	.05	
Miami Dolphins			
☐ 500 O.J. Simpson 12.00	6.00	1.20	
Buffalo Bills			
☐ 501 John Dutton 1.25	.60	.12	
Baltimore Colts			
☐ 502 Pat Hughes 30	.15	.03	
New York Giants			
☐ 503 Malcolm Snider 30	.15	.03	
Green Bay Packers			
☐ 504 Fred Willis 30	.15	.03	
Houston Oilers			
☐ 505 Harold Jackson 1.00	.50	.10	
Los Angeles Rams			
☐ 506 Mike Bragg 30	.15	.03	
Washington Redskins			
☐ 507 Jerry Sherk 50	.25	.05	
Cleveland Browns			
☐ 508 Mirro Roder 30	.15	.03	
Chicago Bears			
☐ 509 Tom Sullivan 30	.15	.03	
Philadelphia Eagles			
☐ 510 Jim Hart 1.00	.50	.10	
St. Louis Cardinals			
☐ 511 Cedric Hardman 50	.25	.05	
San Francisco 49ers			
☐ 512 Blaine Nye 30	.15	.03	
Dallas Cowboys			
☐ 513 Elmo Wright 50	.25	.05	
Kansas City Chiefs			

☐ 514	Herb Orvis .... .30 Detroit Lions	.15	.03
☐ 515	Richard Caster .... .50 New York Jets	.25	.05
☐ 516	Doug Kotar .... .50 New York Giants	.25	.05
☐ 517	Checklist 397-528 .. 2.50	.25	.05
☐ 518	Jesse Freitas .... .30 San Diego Chargers	.15	.03
☐ 519	Ken Houston .... 1.25 Washington Redskins	.60	.12
☐ 520	Alan Page .... 1.50 Minnesota Vikings	.75	.15
☐ 521	Tim Foley .... .50 Miami Dolphins	.25	.05
☐ 522	Bill Olds .... .30 Baltimore Colts	.15	.03
☐ 523	Bobby Maples .... .30 Denver Broncos	.15	.03
☐ 524	Cliff Branch .... 5.50 Oakland Raiders	2.75	.55
☐ 525	Merlin Olsen .... 2.75 Los Angeles Rams	1.35	.27
☐ 526	AFC Champs .... 2.50 Pittsburgh 24, Oakland 13 (Bradshaw and Franco Harris)	1.25	.25
☐ 527	NFC Champs .... 1.00 Minnesota 14, Los Angeles 10 (C.Foreman tackled)	.50	.10
☐ 528	Super Bowl IX .... 3.75 Steelers 16, Vikings 6 (Bradshaw watching pass)	1.00	.20

1976 Topps

The 1976 Topps football set contains 528 cards. The cards measure 2 1/2" by 3 1/2". No known scarcities exist, although Walter Payton's first card is in great demand. Other notable rookie cards in this set are defensive stalwarts Randy Gradishar, Ed Too Tall Jones, Jack Lambert, Harvey Martin, and Randy White. The first eight cards are dedicated to Record-Breaking (RB) performances for the previous season. Statistical league leaders are depicted on cards 201-206. Post-season playoff action is summarized on cards 331-333. Cards 451-478 are team checklist cards. All-Pro (AP) selections are designated on the player's regular card, not a special card. The card backs are printed in orange and blue on gray card stock.

	NRMT	VG-E	GOOD
COMPLETE SET (528)	365.00	175.00	42.00
COMMON PLAYER (1-528) ...	.20	.10	.02
☐ 1 George Blanda RB .... 5.00 First to Score 2000 Points		2.00	.40
☐ 2 Neal Colzie RB .... .30 Punt Returns		.15	.03
☐ 3 Chuck Foreman RB .... .40 Catches 73 Passes		.20	.04
☐ 4 Jim Marshall RB .... .50 26th Fumble Recovery		.25	.05
☐ 5 Terry Metcalf RB .... .40		.20	.04
☐ 6 O.J. Simpson RB .... 3.75 23 Touchdowns		1.85	.37
☐ 7 Fran Tarkenton RB 2.50		1.25	.25
☐ 8 Charley Taylor RB .... .75 Career Receptions		.35	.07
☐ 9 Ernie Holmes .... .30 Pittsburgh Steelers		.15	.03
☐ 10 Ken Anderson AP .... 2.25 Cincinnati Bengals		1.10	.22
☐ 11 Bobby Bryant .... .20 Minnesota Vikings		.10	.02
☐ 12 Jerry Smith .... .30 Washington Redskins		.15	.03
☐ 13 David Lee .... .20 Baltimore Colts		.10	.02
☐ 14 Robert Newhouse .... 1.25 Dallas Cowboys		.60	.12
☐ 15 Vern Den Herder .... .20 Miami Dolphins		.10	.02

☐ 16 John Hannah	1.75	.85	.17
New England Patriots			
☐ 17 J.D. Hill	.30	.15	.03
Buffalo Bills			
☐ 18 James Harris	.40	.20	.04
Los Angeles Rams			
☐ 19 Willie Buchanon	.40	.20	.04
Green Bay Packers			
☐ 20 Charley Young AP	.30	.15	.03
Philadelphia Eagles			
☐ 21 Jim Yarbrough	.20	.10	.02
Detroit Lions			
☐ 22 Ronnie Coleman	.20	.10	.02
Houston Oilers			
☐ 23 Don Cockroft	.20	.10	.02
Cleveland Browns			
☐ 24 Willie Lanier	1.25	.60	.12
Kansas City Chiefs			
☐ 25 Fred Biletnikoff	2.00	1.00	.20
Oakland Raiders			
☐ 26 Ron Yankowski	.20	.10	.02
St. Louis Cardinals			
☐ 27 Spider Lockhart	.30	.15	.03
New York Giants			
☐ 28 Bob Johnson	.20	.10	.02
Cincinnati Bengals			
☐ 29 J.T. Thomas	.20	.10	.02
Pittsburgh Steelers			
☐ 30 Ron Yary AP	.40	.20	.04
Minnesota Vikings			
☐ 31 Brad Dusek	.50	.25	.05
Washington Redskins			
☐ 32 Raymond Chester	.30	.15	.03
Baltimore Colts			
☐ 33 Larry Little	.30	.15	.03
Miami Dolphins			
☐ 34 Pat Leahy	2.25	1.10	.22
New York Jets			
☐ 35 Steve Bartkowski	2.50	1.25	.25
Atlanta Falcons			
☐ 36 Tom Myers	.20	.10	.02
New Orleans Saints			
☐ 37 Bill Van Heusen	.20	.10	.02
Denver Broncos			
☐ 38 Russ Washington	.20	.10	.02
San Diego Chargers			
☐ 39 Tom Sullivan	.20	.10	.02
Philadelphia Eagles			
☐ 40 Curly Culp AP	.40	.20	.04
Houston Oilers			
☐ 41 Johnnie Gray	.20	.10	.02
Green Bay Packers			
☐ 42 Bob Klein	.20	.10	.02
Los Angeles Rams			
☐ 43 Lem Barney	.75	.35	.07
Detroit Lions			
☐ 44 Harvey Martin	3.00	1.50	.30

Dallas Cowboys			
☐ 45 Reggie Rucker	.30	.15	.03
Cleveland Browns			
☐ 46 Neil Clabo	.20	.10	.02
Minnesota Vikings			
☐ 47 Ray Hamilton	.40	.20	.04
New England Patriots			
☐ 48 Joe Ferguson	.75	.35	.07
Buffalo Bills			
☐ 49 Ed Podolak	.30	.15	.03
Kansas City Chiefs			
☐ 50 Ray Guy AP	1.00	.50	.10
Oakland Raiders			
☐ 51 Glen Edwards	.20	.10	.02
Pittsburgh Steelers			
☐ 52 Jim LeClair	.40	.20	.04
Cincinnati Bengals			
☐ 53 Mike Barnes	.20	.10	.02
Baltimore Colts			
☐ 54 Nat Moore	2.25	1.10	.22
Miami Dolphins			
☐ 55 Bill Kilmer	1.00	.50	.10
Washington Redskins			
☐ 56 Larry Stallings	.20	.10	.02
St. Louis Cardinals			
☐ 57 Jack Gregory	.30	.15	.03
New York Giants			
☐ 58 Steve Mike-Mayer	.20	.10	.02
San Francisco 49ers			
☐ 59 Virgil Livers	.20	.10	.02
Chicago Bears			
☐ 60 Jerry Sherk AP	.30	.15	.03
Cleveland Browns			
☐ 61 Guy Morriss	.20	.10	.02
Philadelphia Eagles			
☐ 62 Barty Smith	.20	.10	.02
Green Bay Packers			
☐ 63 Jerome Barkum	.30	.15	.03
New York Jets			
☐ 64 Ira Gordon	.20	.10	.02
Tampa Bay Buccaneers			
☐ 65 Paul Krause	.60	.30	.06
Minnesota Vikings			
☐ 66 John McMakin	.20	.10	.02
Seattle Seahawks			
☐ 67 Checklist 1-132	2.00	.20	.04
☐ 68 Charlie Johnson	.40	.20	.04
Denver Broncos			
☐ 69 Tommy Nobis	.75	.35	.07
Atlanta Falcons			
☐ 70 Lydell Mitchell	.40	.20	.04
Baltimore Colts			
☐ 71 Vern Holland	.20	.10	.02
Cincinnati Bengals			
☐ 72 Tim Foley	.30	.15	.03
Miami Dolphins			
☐ 73 Golden Richards	.30	.15	.03

Dallas Cowboys
| □ 74 Bryant Salter | .20 | .10 | .02 |

Washington Redskins
| □ 75 Terry Bradshaw | 6.50 | 3.25 | .65 |

Pittsburgh Steelers
| □ 76 Ted Hendricks | 1.00 | .50 | .10 |

Oakland Raiders
| □ 77 Rich Saul | .30 | .15 | .03 |

Los Angeles Rams
| □ 78 John Smith | .20 | .10 | .02 |

New England Patriots
| □ 79 Altie Taylor | .20 | .10 | .02 |

Detroit Lions
| □ 80 Cedric Hardman AP | .30 | .15 | .03 |

San Francisco 49ers
| □ 81 Ken Payne | .20 | .10 | .02 |

Green Bay Packers
| □ 82 Zeke Moore | .20 | .10 | .02 |

Houston Oilers
| □ 83 Alvin Maxson | .30 | .15 | .03 |

New Orleans Saints
| □ 84 Wally Hilgenberg | .20 | .10 | .02 |

Minnesota Vikings
| □ 85 John Niland | .20 | .10 | .02 |

Philadelphia Eagles
| □ 86 Mike Sensibaugh | .20 | .10 | .02 |

Kansas City Chiefs
| □ 87 Ron Johnson | .30 | .15 | .03 |

New York Giants
| □ 88 Winston Hill | .20 | .10 | .02 |

New York Jets
| □ 89 Charlie Joiner | 1.75 | .85 | .17 |

Cincinnati Bengals
| □ 90 Roger Wehrli AP | .30 | .15 | .03 |

St. Louis Cardinals
| □ 91 Mike Bragg | .20 | .10 | .02 |

Washington Redskins
| □ 92 Dan Dickel | .20 | .10 | .02 |

Baltimore Colts
| □ 93 Earl Morrall | .90 | .45 | .09 |

Miami Dolphins
| □ 94 Pat Toomay | .20 | .10 | .02 |

Buffalo Bills
| □ 95 Gary Garrison | .30 | .15 | .03 |

San Diego Chargers
| □ 96 Ken Geddes | .20 | .10 | .02 |

Seattle Seahawks
| □ 97 Mike Current | .20 | .10 | .02 |

Tampa Bay Buccaneers
| □ 98 Bob Avellini | .30 | .15 | .03 |

Chicago Bears
| □ 99 Dave Pureifory | .30 | .15 | .03 |

Green Bay Packers
| □ 100 Franco Harris AP | 6.50 | 3.25 | .65 |

Pittsburgh Steelers
| □ 101 Randy Logan | .20 | .10 | .02 |

Philadelphia Eagles

| □ 102 John Fitzgerald | .30 | .15 | .03 |

Dallas Cowboys
| □ 103 Gregg Bingham | .50 | .25 | .05 |

Houston Oilers
| □ 104 Jim Plunkett | 1.50 | .75 | .15 |

New England Patriots
| □ 105 Carl Eller | 1.00 | .50 | .10 |

Minnesota Vikings
| □ 106 Larry Walton | .20 | .10 | .02 |

Detroit Lions
| □ 107 Clarence Scott | .20 | .10 | .02 |

Cleveland Browns
| □ 108 Skip Vanderbundt | .20 | .10 | .02 |

San Francisco 49ers
| □ 109 Boobie Clark | .30 | .15 | .03 |

Cincinnati Bengals
| □ 110 Tom Mack AP | .50 | .25 | .05 |

Los Angeles Rams
| □ 111 Bruce Laird | .20 | .10 | .02 |

Baltimore Colts
| □ 112 Dave Dalby | .75 | .35 | .07 |

Oakland Raiders
| □ 113 John Leypoldt | .20 | .10 | .02 |

Buffalo Bills
| □ 114 Barry Pearson | .20 | .10 | .02 |

Kansas City Chiefs
| □ 115 Larry Brown | .50 | .25 | .05 |

Washington Redskins
| □ 116 Jackie Smith | .40 | .20 | .04 |

St. Louis Cardinals
| □ 117 Pat Hughes | .20 | .10 | .02 |

New York Giants
| □ 118 Al Woodall | .30 | .15 | .03 |

New York Jets
| □ 119 John Zook | .30 | .15 | .03 |

Atlanta Falcons
| □ 120 Jake Scott AP | .30 | .15 | .03 |

Miami Dolphins
| □ 121 Rich Glover | .20 | .10 | .02 |

Philadelphia Eagles
| □ 122 Ernie Jackson | .20 | .10 | .02 |

New Orleans Saints
| □ 123 Otis Armstrong | .75 | .35 | .07 |

Denver Broncos
| □ 124 Bob Grim | .30 | .15 | .03 |

Chicago Bears
| □ 125 Jeff Siemon | .30 | .15 | .03 |

Minnesota Vikings
| □ 126 Harold Hart | .20 | .10 | .02 |

Tampa Bay Buccaneers
| □ 127 John DeMarie | .20 | .10 | .02 |

Seattle Seahawks
| □ 128 Dan Fouts | 18.00 | 9.00 | 1.80 |

San Diego Chargers
| □ 129 Jim Kearney | .20 | .10 | .02 |

Kansas City Chiefs
| □ 130 John Dutton AP | .50 | .25 | .05 |

Baltimore Colts
| ☐ 131 | Calvin Hill | .50 | .25 | .05 |

Washington Redskins
| ☐ 132 | Toni Fritsch | .20 | .10 | .02 |

Dallas Cowboys
| ☐ 133 | Ron Jessie | .30 | .15 | .03 |

Los Angeles Rams
| ☐ 134 | Don Nottingham | .20 | .10 | .02 |

Miami Dolphins
| ☐ 135 | Lemar Parrish | .30 | .15 | .03 |

Cincinnati Bengals
| ☐ 136 | Russ Francis | 2.50 | 1.25 | .25 |

New England Patriots
| ☐ 137 | Joe Reed | .30 | .15 | .03 |

Detroit Lions
| ☐ 138 | C.L. Whittington | .20 | .10 | .02 |

Houston Oilers
| ☐ 139 | Otis Sistrunk | .30 | .15 | .03 |

Oakland Raiders
| ☐ 140 | Lynn Swann AP | 6.50 | 3.25 | .65 |

Pittsburgh Steelers
| ☐ 141 | Jim Carter | .20 | .10 | .02 |

Green Bay Packers
| ☐ 142 | Mike Montler | .20 | .10 | .02 |

Buffalo Bills
| ☐ 143 | Walter Johnson | .20 | .10 | .02 |

Cleveland Browns
| ☐ 144 | Doug Kotar | .20 | .10 | .02 |

New York Giants
| ☐ 145 | Roman Gabriel | 1.00 | .50 | .10 |

Philadelphia Eagles
| ☐ 146 | Billy Newsome | .20 | .10 | .02 |

New York Jets
| ☐ 147 | Ed Bradley | .20 | .10 | .02 |

Seattle Seahawks
| ☐ 148 | Walter Payton | 150.00 | 75.00 | 15.00 |

Chicago Bears
| ☐ 149 | Johnny Fuller | .20 | .10 | .02 |

New Orleans Saints
| ☐ 150 | Alan Page AP | 1.25 | .60 | .12 |

Minnesota Vikings
| ☐ 151 | Frank Grant | .20 | .10 | .02 |

Washington Redskins
| ☐ 152 | Dave Green | .20 | .10 | .02 |

Cincinnati Bengals
| ☐ 153 | Nelson Munsey | .20 | .10 | .02 |

Baltimore Colts
| ☐ 154 | Jim Mandich | .30 | .15 | .03 |

Miami Dolphins
| ☐ 155 | Lawrence McCutcheon | .60 | .30 | .06 |

Los Angeles Rams
| ☐ 156 | Steve Ramsey | .30 | .15 | .03 |

Denver Broncos
| ☐ 157 | Ed Flanagan | .20 | .10 | .02 |

San Diego Chargers
| ☐ 158 | Randy White | 22.00 | 11.00 | 2.20 |

Dallas Cowboys
| ☐ 159 | Gerry Mullins | .20 | .10 | .02 |

Pittsburgh Steelers
| ☐ 160 | Jan Stenerud AP | 1.00 | .50 | .10 |

Kansas City Chiefs
| ☐ 161 | Steve Odom | .40 | .20 | .04 |

Green Bay Packers
| ☐ 162 | Roger Finnie | .20 | .10 | .02 |

St. Louis Cardinals
| ☐ 163 | Norm Snead | .50 | .25 | .05 |

San Francisco 49ers
| ☐ 164 | Jeff Van Note | .40 | .20 | .04 |

Atlanta Falcons
| ☐ 165 | Bill Bergey | .60 | .30 | .06 |

Philadelphia Eagles
| ☐ 166 | Allen Carter | .20 | .10 | .02 |

New England Patriots
| ☐ 167 | Steve Holden | .20 | .10 | .02 |

Cleveland Browns
| ☐ 168 | Sherman White | .20 | .10 | .02 |

Cincinnati Bengals
| ☐ 169 | Bob Berry | .30 | .15 | .03 |

Minnesota Vikings
| ☐ 170 | Ken Houston AP | 1.00 | .50 | .10 |

Washington Redskins
| ☐ 171 | Bill Olds | .20 | .10 | .02 |

Baltimore Colts
| ☐ 172 | Larry Seiple | .20 | .10 | .02 |

Miami Dolphins
| ☐ 173 | Cliff Branch | 1.50 | .75 | .15 |

Oakland Raiders
| ☐ 174 | Reggie McKenzie | .30 | .15 | .03 |

Buffalo Bills
| ☐ 175 | Dan Pastorini | .40 | .20 | .04 |

Houston Oilers
| ☐ 176 | Paul Naumoff | .20 | .10 | .02 |

Detroit Lions
| ☐ 177 | Checklist 133-264 | 2.00 | .20 | .04 |
| ☐ 178 | Durwood Keeton | .20 | .10 | .02 |

Tampa Bay Buccaneers
| ☐ 179 | Earl Thomas | .20 | .10 | .02 |

St. Louis Cardinals
| ☐ 180 | L.C. Greenwood AP | .75 | .35 | .07 |

Pittsburgh Steelers
| ☐ 181 | John Outlaw | .20 | .10 | .02 |

Philadelphia Eagles
| ☐ 182 | Frank Nunley | .20 | .10 | .02 |

San Francisco 49ers
| ☐ 183 | Dave Jennings | .75 | .35 | .07 |

New York Giants
| ☐ 184 | MacArthur Lane | .30 | .15 | .03 |

Kansas City Chiefs
| ☐ 185 | Chester Marcol | .30 | .15 | .03 |

Green Bay Packers
| ☐ 186 | J.J. Jones | .20 | .10 | .02 |

New York Jets
| ☐ 187 | Tom DeLeone | .20 | .10 | .02 |

Cleveland Browns

☐ 188	Steve Zabel ....20 New England Patriots	.10	.02
☐ 189	Ken Johnson ....20 Cincinnati Bengals	.10	.02
☐ 190	Rayfield Wright AP .....20 Dallas Cowboys	.10	.02
☐ 191	Brent McClanahan ....20 Minnesota Vikings	.10	.02
☐ 192	Pat Fischer ....30 Washington Redskins	.15	.03
☐ 193	Roger Carr ....75 Baltimore Colts	.35	.07
☐ 194	Manny Fernandez ....30 Miami Dolphins	.15	.03
☐ 195	Roy Gerela ....20 Pittsburgh Steelers	.10	.02
☐ 196	Dave Elmendorf ....20 Los Angeles Rams	.10	.02
☐ 197	Bob Kowalkowski ....20 Detroit Lions	.10	.02
☐ 198	Phil Villapiano ....30 Oakland Raiders	.15	.03
☐ 199	Will Wynn ....20 Philadelphia Eagles	.10	.02
☐ 200	Terry Metcalf ....50 St. Louis Cardinals	.25	.05
☐ 201	Passing Leaders ....1.75 Ken Anderson Fran Tarkenton	.85	.17
☐ 202	Receiving Leaders ....50 Reggie Rucker Lydell Mitchell Chuck Foreman	.25	.05
☐ 203	Rushing Leaders ....1.75 O.J. Simpson Jim Otis	.85	.17
☐ 204	Scoring Leaders ....1.75 O.J. Simpson Chuck Foreman	.85	.17
☐ 205	Interception Leaders ......60 Mel Blount Paul Krause	.30	.06
☐ 206	Punting Leaders ....40 Ray Guy Herman Weaver	.20	.04
☐ 207	Ken Ellis ....20 Green Bay Packers	.10	.02
☐ 208	Ron Saul ....20 Houston Oilers	.10	.02
☐ 209	Toni Linhart ....20 Baltimore Colts	.10	.02
☐ 210	Jim Langer AP ....1.00 Miami Dolphins	.50	.10
☐ 211	Jeff Wright ....20 Minnesota Vikings	.10	.02
☐ 212	Moses Denson ....20 Washington Redskins	.10	.02
☐ 213	Earl Edwards ....20 Buffalo Bills	.10	.02
☐ 214	Walker Gillette ....20 New York Giants	.10	.02
☐ 215	Bob Trumpy ....75 Cincinnati Bengals	.35	.07
☐ 216	Emmitt Thomas ....30 Kansas City Chiefs	.15	.03
☐ 217	Lyle Alzado 1.00	.50	.10
	Denver Broncos		
☐ 218	Carl Garrett ....20 New York Jets	.10	.02
☐ 219	Van Green ....20 Cleveland Browns	.10	.02
☐ 220	Jack Lambert AP ....22.00 Pittsburgh Steelers	11.00	2.20
☐ 221	Spike Jones ....20 Philadelphia Eagles	.10	.02
☐ 222	John Hadl ....75 Green Bay Packers	.35	.07
☐ 223	Billy Johnson ....2.25 Houston Oilers	1.10	.22
☐ 224	Tony McGee ....20 New England Patriots	.10	.02
☐ 225	Preston Pearson ....50 Dallas Cowboys	.25	.05
☐ 226	Isiah Robertson ....30 Los Angeles Rams	.15	.03
☐ 227	Errol Mann ....20 Detroit Lions	.10	.02
☐ 228	Paul Seal ....20 New Orleans Saints	.10	.02
☐ 229	Roland Harper ....75 Chicago Bears	.35	.07
☐ 230	Ed White AP ....75 Minnesota Vikings	.35	.07
☐ 231	Joe Theismann ....6.00 Washington Redskins	3.00	.60
☐ 232	Jim Cheyunski ....20 Baltimore Colts	.10	.02
☐ 233	Bill Stanfill ....30 Miami Dolphins	.15	.03
☐ 234	Marv Hubbard ....30 Oakland Raiders	.15	.03
☐ 235	Tommy Casanova ....30 Cincinnati Bengals	.15	.03
☐ 236	Bob Hyland ....20 New York Giants	.10	.02
☐ 237	Jesse Freitas ....20 San Diego Chargers	.10	.02
☐ 238	Norm Thompson ....20 St. Louis Cardinals	.10	.02
☐ 239	Charlie Smith ....20 Philadelphia Eagles	.10	.02
☐ 240	John James AP ....20 Atlanta Falcons	.10	.02
☐ 241	Alden Roche 20	.10	.02

Green Bay Packers			☐ 270	Jack Tatum AP 40	.20	.04

Green Bay Packers
☐ 242 Gordon Jolley ....20 .10 .02
Seattle Seahawks
☐ 243 Larry Ely ....20 .10 .02
Tampa Bay Buccaneers
☐ 244 Richard Caster ....30 .15 .03
New York Jets
☐ 245 Joe Greene .... 3.00 1.50 .30
Pittsburgh Steelers
☐ 246 Larry Schreiber ....20 .10 .02
San Francisco 49ers
☐ 247 Terry Schmidt ....20 .10 .02
New Orleans Saints
☐ 248 Jerrel Wilson ....20 .10 .02
Kansas City Chiefs
☐ 249 Marty Domres ....30 .15 .03
Baltimore Colts
☐ 250 Isaac Curtis AP ....40 .20 .04
Cincinnati Bengals
☐ 251 Harold McLinton ....20 .10 .02
Washington Redskins
☐ 252 Fred Dryer .... 2.00 1.00 .20
Los Angeles Rams
☐ 253 Bill Lenkaitis ....20 .10 .02
New England Patriots
☐ 254 Don Hardeman ....20 .10 .02
Houston Oilers
☐ 255 Bob Griese .... 3.00 1.50 .30
Miami Dolphins
☐ 256 Oscar Roan ....40 .20 .04
Cleveland Browns
☐ 257 Randy Gradishar ..... 4.50 2.25 .45
Denver Broncos
☐ 258 Bob Thomas ....40 .20 .04
Chicago Bears
☐ 259 Joe Owens ....20 .10 .02
Seattle Seahawks
☐ 260 Cliff Harris AP ....75 .35 .07
Dallas Cowboys
☐ 261 Frank Lewis ....40 .20 .04
Pittsburgh Steelers
☐ 262 Mike McCoy ....20 .10 .02
Green Bay Packers
☐ 263 Rickey Young ....75 .35 .07
San Diego Chargers
☐ 264 Brian Kelley ....50 .25 .05
New York Giants
☐ 265 Charlie Sanders ....30 .15 .03
Detroit Lions
☐ 266 Jim Hart ....75 .35 .07
St. Louis Cardinals
☐ 267 Greg Gantt ....20 .10 .02
New York Jets
☐ 268 John Ward ....20 .10 .02
Tampa Bay Buccaneers
☐ 269 Al Beauchamp ....20 .10 .02
Cincinnati Bengals

☐ 270 Jack Tatum AP ....40 .20 .04
Oakland Raiders
☐ 271 Jim Lash ....20 .10 .02
Minnesota Vikings
☐ 272 Diron Talbert ....30 .15 .03
Washington Redskins
☐ 273 Checklist 265-396 .... 2.00 .20 .04
☐ 274 Steve Spurrier .... 1.00 .50 .10
San Francisco 49ers
☐ 275 Greg Pruitt ....60 .30 .06
Cleveland Browns
☐ 276 Jim Mitchell ....20 .10 .02
Detroit Lions
☐ 277 Jack Rudnay ....20 .10 .02
Kansas City Chiefs
☐ 278 Freddie Solomon ....1.00 .50 .10
Miami Dolphins
☐ 279 Frank LeMaster ....20 .10 .02
Philadelphia Eagles
☐ 280 Wally Chambers AP ...30 .15 .03
Chicago Bears
☐ 281 Mike Collier ....20 .10 .02
Pittsburgh Steelers
☐ 282 Clarence Williams ....20 .10 .02
Green Bay Packers
☐ 283 Mitch Hoopes ....20 .10 .02
Dallas Cowboys
☐ 284 Ron Bolton ....20 .10 .02
New England Patriots
☐ 285 Harold Jackson ....90 .45 .09
Los Angeles Rams
☐ 286 Greg Landry ....60 .30 .06
Detroit Lions
☐ 287 Tony Greene ....20 .10 .02
Buffalo Bills
☐ 288 Howard Stevens ....30 .15 .03
Baltimore Colts
☐ 289 Roy Jefferson ....30 .15 .03
Washington Redskins
☐ 290 Jim Bakken AP ....30 .15 .03
St. Louis Cardinals
☐ 291 Doug Sutherland ....40 .20 .04
Minnesota Vikings
☐ 292 Marvin Cobb ....20 .10 .02
Cincinnati Bengals
☐ 293 Mack Alston ....20 .10 .02
Houston Oilers
☐ 294 Rod McNeil ....20 .10 .02
New Orleans Saints
☐ 295 Gene Upshaw ....1.00 .50 .10
Oakland Raiders
☐ 296 Dave Gallagher ....20 .10 .02
New York Giants
☐ 297 Larry Ball ....20 .10 .02
Tampa Bay Buccaneers
☐ 298 Ron Howard ....20 .10 .02
Seattle Seahawks

☐ 299	Don Strock 1.50	.75	.15
	Miami Dolphins		
☐ 300	O.J. Simpson AP 8.50	4.25	.85
	Buffalo Bills		
☐ 301	Ray Mansfield .... .20	.10	.02
	Pittsburgh Steelers		
☐ 302	Larry Marshall .... .20	.10	.02
	Philadelphia Eagles		
☐ 303	Dick Himes .... .20	.10	.02
	Green Bay Packers		
☐ 304	Ray Wersching .... .40	.20	.04
	San Diego Chargers		
☐ 305	John Riggins 3.50	1.75	.35
	New York Jets		
☐ 306	Bob Parsons .... .20	.10	.02
	Chicago Bears		
☐ 307	Ray Brown .... .20	.10	.02
	Atlanta Falcons		
☐ 308	Len Dawson 2.50	1.25	.25
	Kansas City Chiefs		
☐ 309	Andy Maurer .... .20	.10	.02
	Minnesota Vikings		
☐ 310	Jack Youngblood AP ... 1.00	.50	.10
	Los Angeles Rams		
☐ 311	Essex Johnson .... .20	.10	.02
	Cincinnati Bengals		
☐ 312	Stan White .... .20	.10	.02
	Baltimore Colts		
☐ 313	Drew Pearson 1.50	.75	.15
	Dallas Cowboys		
☐ 314	Rockne Freitas .... .20	.10	.02
	Detroit Lions		
☐ 315	Mercury Morris .... .60	.30	.06
	Miami Dolphins		
☐ 316	Willie Alexander .... .20	.10	.02
	Houston Oilers		
☐ 317	Paul Warfield 2.25	1.10	.22
	Cleveland Browns		
☐ 318	Bob Chandler .... .30	.15	.03
	Buffalo Bills		
☐ 319	Bobby Walden .... .20	.10	.02
	Pittsburgh Steelers		
☐ 320	Riley Odoms AP .... .40	.20	.04
	Denver Broncos		
☐ 321	Mike Boryla .... .30	.15	.03
	Philadelphia Eagles		
☐ 322	Bruce Van Dyke .... .20	.10	.02
	Green Bay Packers		
☐ 323	Pete Banaszak .... .20	.10	.02
	Oakland Raiders		
☐ 324	Darryl Stingley .... .40	.20	.04
	New England Patriots		
☐ 325	John Mendenhall .... .20	.10	.02
	New York Giants		
☐ 326	Dan Dierdorf 1.50	.75	.15
	St. Louis Cardinals		
☐ 327	Bruce Taylor .... .30	.15	.03
	San Francisco 49ers		
☐ 328	Don McCauley .... .20	.10	.02
	Baltimore Colts		
☐ 329	John Reaves .... .30	.15	.03
	Cincinnati Bengals		
☐ 330	Chris Hanburger AP ...... .40	.20	.04
	Washington Redskins		
☐ 331	NFC Champions 2.75	1.35	.27
	Cowboys 37,		
	Rams 7		
	(Roger Staubach)		
☐ 332	AFC Champions 1.75	.85	.17
	Steelers 16,		
	Raiders 10		
	(Franco Harris)		
☐ 333	Super Bowl X 2.00	1.00	.20
	Steelers 21,		
	Cowboys 17		
	(Terry Bradshaw)		
☐ 334	Godwin Turk .... .20	.10	.02
	New York Jets		
☐ 335	Dick Anderson .... .30	.15	.03
	Miami Dolphins		
☐ 336	Woody Green .... .20	.10	.02
	Kansas City Chiefs		
☐ 337	Pat Curran .... .20	.10	.02
	San Diego Chargers		
☐ 338	Council Rudolph .... .20	.10	.02
	Tampa Bay Buccaneers		
☐ 339	Joe Lavender .... .20	.10	.02
	Philadelphia Eagles		
☐ 340	John Gilliam AP .... .30	.15	.03
	Minnesota Vikings		
☐ 341	Steve Furness .... .50	.25	.05
	Pittsburgh Steelers		
☐ 342	D.D. Lewis .... .40	.20	.04
	Dallas Cowboys		
☐ 343	Duane Carrell .... .20	.10	.02
	Los Angeles Rams		
☐ 344	Jon Morris .... .20	.10	.02
	Detroit Lions		
☐ 345	John Brockington .... .40	.20	.04
	Green Bay Packers		
☐ 346	Mike Phipps .... .40	.20	.04
	Cleveland Browns		
☐ 347	Lyle Blackwood .... .60	.30	.06
	Seattle Seahawks		
☐ 348	Julius Adams .... .20	.10	.02
	New England Patriots		
☐ 349	Terry Hermeling .... .20	.10	.02
	Washington Redskins		
☐ 350	Rolland Lawrence AP .... .60	.30	.06
	Atlanta Falcons		
☐ 351	Glenn Doughty .... .20	.10	.02
	Baltimore Colts		
☐ 352	Doug Swift .... .20	.10	.02
	Miami Dolphins		

☐ 353 Mike Strachan	.20	.10	.02
New Orleans Saints			
☐ 354 Craig Morton	.90	.45	.09
New York Giants			
☐ 355 George Blanda	5.50	2.75	.55
Oakland Raiders			
☐ 356 Garry Puetz	.20	.10	.02
New York Jets			
☐ 357 Carl Mauck	.20	.10	.02
Houston Oilers			
☐ 358 Walt Patulski	.20	.10	.02
Buffalo Bills			
☐ 359 Stu Voigt	.30	.15	.03
Minnesota Vikings			
☐ 360 Fred Carr AP	.30	.15	.03
Green Bay Packers			
☐ 361 Po James	.20	.10	.02
Philadelphia Eagles			
☐ 362 Otis Taylor	.50	.25	.05
Kansas City Chiefs			
☐ 363 Jeff West	.20	.10	.02
St. Louis Cardinals			
☐ 364 Gary Huff	.30	.15	.03
Chicago Bears			
☐ 365 Dwight White	.30	.15	.03
Pittsburgh Steelers			
☐ 366 Dan Ryczek	.20	.10	.02
Tampa Bay Buccaneers			
☐ 367 Jon Keyworth	.50	.25	.05
Denver Broncos			
☐ 368 Mel Renfro	.60	.30	.06
Dallas Cowboys			
☐ 369 Bruce Coslet	2.50	1.25	.25
Cincinnati Bengals			
☐ 370 Len Hauss AP	.30	.15	.03
Washington Redskins			
☐ 371 Rick Volk	.20	.10	.02
Baltimore Colts			
☐ 372 Howard Twilley	.30	.15	.03
Miami Dolphins			
☐ 373 Cullen Bryant	.30	.15	.03
Los Angeles Rams			
☐ 374 Bob Babich	.20	.10	.02
Cleveland Browns			
☐ 375 Herman Weaver	.20	.10	.02
Detroit Lions			
☐ 376 Steve Grogan	6.50	3.25	.65
New England Patriots			
☐ 377 Bubba Smith	1.50	.75	.15
Houston Oilers			
☐ 378 Burgess Owens	.20	.10	.02
New York Jets			
☐ 379 Alvin Matthews	.20	.10	.02
Green Bay Packers			
☐ 380 Art Shell	1.75	.85	.17
Oakland Raiders			
☐ 381 Larry Brown	.20	.10	.02

Pittsburgh Steelers			
☐ 382 Horst Muhlmann	.20	.10	.02
Philadelphia Eagles			
☐ 383 Ahmad Rashad	2.50	1.25	.25
Buffalo Bills			
☐ 384 Bobby Maples	.20	.10	.02
Denver Broncos			
☐ 385 Jim Marshall	1.00	.50	.10
Minnesota Vikings			
☐ 386 Joe Dawkins	.20	.10	.02
New York Giants			
☐ 387 Dennis Partee	.20	.10	.02
San Diego Chargers			
☐ 388 Eddie McMillan	.20	.10	.02
Seattle Seahawks			
☐ 389 Randy Johnson	.30	.15	.03
Washington Redskins			
☐ 390 Bob Kuechenberg AP	.40	.20	.04
Miami Dolphins			
☐ 391 Rufus Mayes	.20	.10	.02
Cincinnati Bengals			
☐ 392 Lloyd Mumphord	.20	.10	.02
Baltimore Colts			
☐ 393 Ike Harris	.20	.10	.02
St. Louis Cardinals			
☐ 394 Dave Hampton	.30	.15	.03
Atlanta Falcons			
☐ 395 Roger Staubach	12.50	6.25	1.25
Dallas Cowboys			
☐ 396 Doug Buffone	.20	.10	.02
Chicago Bears			
☐ 397 Howard Fest	.20	.10	.02
Tampa Bay Buccaneers			
☐ 398 Wayne Mulligan	.20	.10	.02
New York Jets			
☐ 399 Bill Bradley	.40	.20	.04
Philadelphia Eagles			
☐ 400 Chuck Foreman AP	.60	.30	.06
Minnesota Vikings			
☐ 401 Jack Snow	.30	.15	.03
Los Angeles Rams			
☐ 402 Bob Howard	.20	.10	.02
New England Patriots			
☐ 403 John Matuszak	.90	.45	.09
Kansas City Chiefs			
☐ 404 Bill Munson	.30	.15	.03
Detroit Lions			
☐ 405 Andy Russell	.30	.15	.03
Pittsburgh Steelers			
☐ 406 Skip Butler	.20	.10	.02
Houston Oilers			
☐ 407 Hugh McKinnis	.20	.10	.02
Cleveland Browns			
☐ 408 Bob Penchion	.20	.10	.02
Seattle Seahawks			
☐ 409 Mike Bass	.20	.10	.02
Washington Redskins			

☐ 410	George Kunz AP 40	.20	.04
	Baltimore Colts		
☐ 411	Ron Pritchard 20	.10	.02
	Cincinnati Bengals		
☐ 412	Barry Smith 20	.10	.02
	Green Bay Packers		
☐ 413	Norm Bulaich 30	.15	.03
	Miami Dolphins		
☐ 414	Marv Bateman 20	.10	.02
	Buffalo Bills		
☐ 415	Ken Stabler 2.25	1.10	.22
	Oakland Raiders		
☐ 416	Conrad Dobler 40	.20	.04
	St. Louis Cardinals		
☐ 417	Bob Tucker 30	.15	.03
	New York Giants		
☐ 418	Gene Washington 40	.20	.04
	San Francisco 49ers		
☐ 419	Ed Marinaro 90	.45	.09
	Minnesota Vikings		
☐ 420	Jack Ham AP 3.00	1.50	.30
	Pittsburgh Steelers		
☐ 421	Jim Turner 30	.15	.03
	Denver Broncos		
☐ 422	Chris Fletcher 20	.10	.02
	San Diego Chargers		
☐ 423	Carl Barzilauskas 20	.10	.02
	New York Jets		
☐ 424	Robert Brazile 2.25	1.10	.22
	Houston Oilers		
☐ 425	Harold Carmichael ... 1.25	.60	.12
	Philadelphia Eagles		
☐ 426	Ron Jaworski 3.25	1.60	.32
	Los Angeles Rams		
☐ 427	Ed Too Tall Jones ... 14.00	7.00	1.40
	Dallas Cowboys		
☐ 428	Larry McCarren 20	.10	.02
	Green Bay Packers		
☐ 429	Mike Thomas 50	.25	.05
	Washington Redskins		
☐ 430	Joe DeLamielleure AP 30	.15	.03
	Buffalo Bills		
☐ 431	Tom Blanchard 20	.10	.02
	New Orleans Saints		
☐ 432	Ron Carpenter 20	.10	.02
	Cincinnati Bengals		
☐ 433	Levi Johnson 20	.10	.02
	Detroit Lions		
☐ 434	Sam Cunningham 40	.20	.04
	New England Patriots		
☐ 435	Garo Yepremian 30	.15	.03
	Miami Dolphins		
☐ 436	Mike Livingston 30	.15	.03
	Kansas City Chiefs		
☐ 437	Larry Csonka 2.25	1.10	.22
	New York Giants		
☐ 438	Doug Dieken 20	.10	.02
	Cleveland Browns		
☐ 439	Bill Lueck 20	.10	.02
	Philadelphia Eagles		
☐ 440	Tom MacLeod AP 20	.10	.02
	Baltimore Colts		
☐ 441	Mick Tingelhoff 40	.20	.04
	Minnesota Vikings		
☐ 442	Terry Hanratty 40	.20	.04
	Pittsburgh Steelers		
☐ 443	Mike Siani 20	.10	.02
	Oakland Raiders		
☐ 444	Dwight Harrison 20	.10	.02
	Buffalo Bills		
☐ 445	Jim Otis 40	.20	.04
	St. Louis Cardinals		
☐ 446	Jack Reynolds 40	.20	.04
	Los Angeles Rams		
☐ 447	Jean Fugett 30	.15	.03
	Dallas Cowboys		
☐ 448	Dave Beverly 20	.10	.02
	Green Bay Packers		
☐ 449	Bernard Jackson 1.00	.50	.10
	Cincinnati Bengals		
☐ 450	Charley Taylor 1.75	.85	.17
	Washington Redskins		
☐ 451	Atlanta Falcons 1.50	.30	.06
	Team Checklist		
☐ 452	Baltimore Colts 1.50	.30	.06
	Team Checklist		
☐ 453	Buffalo Bills 1.50	.30	.06
	Team Checklist		
☐ 454	Chicago Bears 1.50	.30	.06
	Team Checklist		
☐ 455	Cincinnati Bengals 1.50	.30	.06
	Team Checklist		
☐ 456	Cleveland Browns 1.50	.30	.06
	Team Checklist		
☐ 457	Dallas Cowboys 1.50	.30	.06
	Team Checklist		
☐ 458	Denver Broncos 1.50	.30	.06
	Team Checklist		
☐ 459	Detroit Lions 1.50	.30	.06
	Team Checklist		
☐ 460	Green Bay Packers 1.50	.30	.06
	Team Checklist		
☐ 461	Houston Oilers 1.50	.30	.06
	Team Checklist		
☐ 462	Kansas City Chiefs 1.50	.30	.06
	Team Checklist		
☐ 463	Los Angeles Rams 1.50	.30	.06
	Team Checklist		
☐ 464	Miami Dolphins 1.50	.30	.06
	Team Checklist		
☐ 465	Minnesota Vikings 1.50	.30	.06
	Team Checklist		
☐ 466	New England Patriots . 1.50	.30	.06
	Team Checklist		

☐ 467	New Orleans Saints 1.50	.30	.06
	Team Checklist		
☐ 468	New York Giants 1.50	.30	.06
	Team Checklist		
☐ 469	New York Jets 1.50	.30	.06
	Team Checklist		
☐ 470	Oakland Raiders 1.50	.30	.06
	Team Checklist		
☐ 471	Philadelphia Eagles 1.50	.30	.06
	Team Checklist		
☐ 472	Pittsburgh Steelers 1.50	.30	.06
	Team Checklist		
☐ 473	St. Louis Cardinals 1.50	.30	.06
	Team Checklist		
☐ 474	San Diego Chargers 1.50	.30	.06
	Team Checklist		
☐ 475	San Francisco 49ers ... 1.50	.30	.06
	Team Checklist		
☐ 476	Seattle Seahawks 1.50	.30	.06
	Team Checklist		
☐ 477	Tampa Bay Buccaneers 1.50	.30	.06
	Team Checklist		
☐ 478	Washington Redskins . 1.50	.30	.06
	Team Checklist		
☐ 479	Fred Cox .... .30	.15	.03
	Minnesota Vikings		
☐ 480	Mel Blount AP 4.00	2.00	.40
	Pittsburgh Steelers		
☐ 481	John Bunting .... .20	.10	.02
	Philadelphia Eagles		
☐ 482	Ken Mendenhall .... .20	.10	.02
	Baltimore Colts		
☐ 483	Will Harrell .... .40	.20	.04
	Green Bay Packers		
☐ 484	Marlin Briscoe .... .40	.20	.04
	San Diego Chargers		
☐ 485	Archie Manning 1.00	.50	.10
	New Orleans Saints		
☐ 486	Tody Smith .... .20	.10	.02
	Houston Oilers		
☐ 487	George Hunt .... .20	.10	.02
	New York Giants		
☐ 488	Roscoe Word .... .20	.10	.02
	New York Jets		
☐ 489	Paul Seymour .... .20	.10	.02
	Buffalo Bills		
☐ 490	Lee Roy Jordan AP .... .90	.45	.09
	Dallas Cowboys		
☐ 491	Chip Myers .... .20	.10	.02
	Cincinnati Bengals		
☐ 492	Norm Evans .... .30	.15	.03
	Miami Dolphins		
☐ 493	Jim Bertelsen .... .30	.15	.03
	Los Angeles Rams		
☐ 494	Mark Moseley .... .50	.25	.05
	Washington Redskins		
☐ 495	George Buehler .... .20	.10	.02
	Oakland Raiders		
☐ 496	Charlie Hall .... .20	.10	.02
	Cleveland Browns		
☐ 497	Marvin Upshaw .... .20	.10	.02
	Kansas City Chiefs		
☐ 498	Tom Banks .... .50	.25	.05
	St. Louis Cardinals		
☐ 499	Randy Vataha .... .30	.15	.03
	New England Patriots		
☐ 500	Fran Tarkenton AP 7.50	3.75	.75
	Minnesota Vikings		
☐ 501	Mike Wagner .... .30	.15	.03
	Pittsburgh Steelers		
☐ 502	Art Malone .... .20	.10	.02
	Philadelphia Eagles		
☐ 503	Fred Cook .... .40	.20	.04
	Baltimore Colts		
☐ 504	Rich McGeorge .... .20	.10	.02
	Green Bay Packers		
☐ 505	Ken Burrough .... .30	.15	.03
	Houston Oilers		
☐ 506	Nick Mike-Mayer .... .20	.10	.02
	Atlanta Falcons		
☐ 507	Checklist 397-528 .... 2.00	.20	.04
☐ 508	Steve Owens .... .40	.20	.04
	Detroit Lions		
☐ 509	Brad Van Pelt 1.00	.50	.10
	New York Giants		
☐ 510	Ken Riley AP .... .40	.20	.04
	Cincinnati Bengals		
☐ 511	Art Thoms .... .20	.10	.02
	Oakland Raiders		
☐ 512	Ed Bell .... .20	.10	.02
	New York Jets		
☐ 513	Tom Wittum .... .20	.10	.02
	San Francisco 49ers		
☐ 514	Jim Braxton .... .20	.10	.02
	Buffalo Bills		
☐ 515	Nick Buoniconti .... .90	.45	.09
	Miami Dolphins		
☐ 516	Brian Sipe 1.75	.85	.17
	Cleveland Browns		
☐ 517	Jim Lynch .... .30	.15	.03
	Kansas City Chiefs		
☐ 518	Prentice McCray .... .20	.10	.02
	New England Patriots		
☐ 519	Tom Dempsey .... .30	.15	.03
	Los Angeles Rams		
☐ 520	Mel Gray AP .... .40	.20	.04
	St. Louis Cardinals		
☐ 521	Nate Wright .... .20	.10	.02
	Minnesota Vikings		
☐ 522	Rocky Bleier 1.25	.60	.12
	Pittsburgh Steelers		
☐ 523	Dennis Johnson .... .20	.10	.02
	Washington Redskins		
☐ 524	Jerry Sisemore .... .30	.15	.03

Philadelphia Eagles
- ☐ 525 Bert Jones .... 1.00 .50 .10
  Baltimore Colts
- ☐ 526 Perry Smith .... .20 .10 .02
  Green Bay Packers
- ☐ 527 Blaine Nye .... .20 .10 .02
  Dallas Cowboys
- ☐ 528 Bob Moore .... .50 .15 .03
  Oakland Raiders

1977 Topps

The 1977 Topps football set contains 528 cards. The cards measure 2 1/2" by 3 1/2". The first six cards in the set are the statistical league leaders from each conference. Cards 451 to 455 are Record Breaker (RB) cards featuring players breaking individual records during the previous season. Cards 201-228 are team checklist cards. The Falcons checklist erroneously does not list 79 Jim Mitchell. Cards 526-528 feature post-season action from the previous season. All-Pro (AP) selections are designated on the player's regular card, not a special card. No known scarcities exist. The card backs are printed in purple and black on gray card stock. The key rookie card in this set is Steve Largent. Other notable rookie cards include Harry Carson, Dave Casper, Archie Griffin, Lee Roy Selmon, Mike Webster, Danny White, and Jim Zorn. There also exists a Mexican version of the Topps 1977 set. The Mexican set contains the same 528 players but is done completely in Spanish (front and back) and is obviously quite a bit rarer than the 1977 regular football issue and valued at five to ten times the values listed below.

	NRMT	VG-E	GOOD
COMPLETE SET (528)	260.00	120.00	30.00
COMMON PLAYER (1-528)	.15	.07	.01
☐ 1 Passing Leaders	1.75	.85	.17
James Harris			
Ken Stabler			
☐ 2 Receiving Leaders	.35	.17	.03
Drew Pearson			
MacArthur Lane			
☐ 3 Rushing Leaders	6.00	3.00	.60
Walter Payton			
O.J. Simpson			
☐ 4 Scoring Leaders	.25	.12	.02
Mark Moseley			
Toni Linhart			
☐ 5 Interception Leaders	.25	.12	.02
Monte Jackson			
Ken Riley			
☐ 6 Punting Leaders	.25	.12	.02
John James			
Marv Bateman			
☐ 7 Mike Phipps	.30	.15	.03
Cleveland Browns			
☐ 8 Rick Volk	.15	.07	.01
New York Giants			
☐ 9 Steve Furness	.15	.07	.01
Pittsburgh Steelers			
☐ 10 Isaac Curtis	.35	.17	.03
Cincinnati Bengals			
☐ 11 Nate Wright	.15	.07	.01
Minnesota Vikings			
☐ 12 Jean Fugett	.15	.07	.01
Washington Redskins			
☐ 13 Ken Mendenhall	.15	.07	.01
Baltimore Colts			
☐ 14 Sam Adams	.15	.07	.01
New England Patriots			
☐ 15 Charlie Waters	.60	.30	.06
Dallas Cowboys			
☐ 16 Bill Stanfill	.25	.12	.02
Miami Dolphins			
☐ 17 John Holland	.15	.07	.01
Buffalo Bills			
☐ 18 Pat Haden	2.25	1.10	.22
Los Angeles Rams			
☐ 19 Bob Young	.15	.07	.01
St. Louis Cardinals			
☐ 20 Wally Chambers AP	.25	.12	.02
Chicago Bears			
☐ 21 Lawrence Gaines	.15	.07	.01
Detroit Lions			
☐ 22 Larry McCarren	.15	.07	.01
Green Bay Packers			
☐ 23 Horst Muhlmann	.15	.07	.01
Philadelphia Eagles			
☐ 24 Phil Villapiano	.25	.12	.02

Oakland Raiders			
☐ 25 Greg Pruitt 40	.20	.04	
Cleveland Browns			
☐ 26 Ron Howard 15	.07	.01	
Seattle Seahawks			
☐ 27 Craig Morton 75	.35	.07	
New York Giants			
☐ 28 Rufus Mayes 15	.07	.01	
Cincinnati Bengals			
☐ 29 Lee Roy Selmon UER 2.75	1.35	.27	
Tampa Bay Buccaneers			
(Misspelled Leroy)			
☐ 30 Ed White AP 25	.12	.02	
Minnesota Vikings			
☐ 31 Harold McLinton 15	.07	.01	
Washington Redskins			
☐ 32 Glenn Doughty 15	.07	.01	
Baltimore Colts			
☐ 33 Bob Kuechenberg 25	.12	.02	
Miami Dolphins			
☐ 34 Duane Carrell 15	.07	.01	
New York Jets			
☐ 35 Riley Odoms 30	.15	.03	
Denver Broncos			
☐ 36 Bobby Scott 25	.12	.02	
New Orleans Saints			
☐ 37 Nick Mike-Mayer 15	.07	.01	
Atlanta Falcons			
☐ 38 Bill Lenkaitis 15	.07	.01	
New England Patriots			
☐ 39 Roland Harper 25	.12	.02	
Chicago Bears			
☐ 40 Tommy Hart AP 15	.07	.01	
San Francisco 49ers			
☐ 41 Mike Sensibaugh 15	.07	.01	
St. Louis Cardinals			
☐ 42 Rusty Jackson 15	.07	.01	
Los Angeles Rams			
☐ 43 Levi Johnson 15	.07	.01	
Detroit Lions			
☐ 44 Mike McCoy 15	.07	.01	
Green Bay Packers			
☐ 45 Roger Staubach 9.00	4.50	.90	
Dallas Cowboys			
☐ 46 Fred Cox 25	.12	.02	
Minnesota Vikings			
☐ 47 Bob Babich 15	.07	.01	
Cleveland Browns			
☐ 48 Reggie McKenzie 25	.12	.02	
Buffalo Bills			
☐ 49 Dave Jennings 25	.12	.02	
New York Giants			
☐ 50 Mike Haynes AP 5.00	2.50	.50	
New England Patriots			
☐ 51 Larry Brown 15	.07	.01	
Pittsburgh Steelers			
☐ 52 Marvin Cobb 15	.07	.01	
Cincinnati Bengals			
☐ 53 Fred Cook 15	.07	.01	
Baltimore Colts			
☐ 54 Freddie Solomon 35	.17	.03	
Miami Dolphins			
☐ 55 John Riggins 2.00	1.00	.20	
Washington Redskins			
☐ 56 John Bunting 15	.07	.01	
Philadelphia Eagles			
☐ 57 Ray Wersching 15	.07	.01	
San Diego Chargers			
☐ 58 Mike Livingston 25	.12	.02	
Kansas City Chiefs			
☐ 59 Billy Johnson 50	.25	.05	
Houston Oilers			
☐ 60 Mike Wagner AP 25	.12	.02	
Pittsburgh Steelers			
☐ 61 Waymond Bryant 25	.12	.02	
Chicago Bears			
☐ 62 Jim Otis 25	.12	.02	
St. Louis Cardinals			
☐ 63 Ed Galigher 15	.07	.01	
New York Jets			
☐ 64 Randy Vataha 25	.12	.02	
New England Patriots			
☐ 65 Jim Zorn 3.00	1.50	.30	
Seattle Seahawks			
☐ 66 Jon Keyworth 25	.12	.02	
Denver Broncos			
☐ 67 Checklist 1-132 .... 1.50	.15	.03	
☐ 68 Henry Childs 15	.07	.01	
New Orleans Saints			
☐ 69 Thom Darden 15	.07	.01	
Cleveland Browns			
☐ 70 George Kunz AP 25	.12	.02	
Baltimore Colts			
☐ 71 Lenvil Elliott 15	.07	.01	
Cincinnati Bengals			
☐ 72 Curtis Johnson 15	.07	.01	
Miami Dolphins			
☐ 73 Doug Van Horn 15	.07	.01	
New York Giants			
☐ 74 Joe Theismann 3.25	1.60	.32	
Washington Redskins			
☐ 75 Dwight White 25	.12	.02	
Pittsburgh Steelers			
☐ 76 Scott Laidlaw 15	.07	.01	
Dallas Cowboys			
☐ 77 Monte Johnson 25	.12	.02	
Oakland Raiders			
☐ 78 Dave Beverly 15	.07	.01	
Green Bay Packers			
☐ 79 Jim Mitchell 15	.07	.01	
Atlanta Falcons			
☐ 80 Jack Youngblood AP 75	.35	.07	
Los Angeles Rams			
☐ 81 Mel Gray 25	.12	.02	

St. Louis Cardinals			
☐ 82 Dwight Harrison 15	.07	.01	
Buffalo Bills			
☐ 83 John Hadl 60	.30	.06	
Houston Oilers			
☐ 84 Matt Blair 1.75	.85	.17	
Minnesota Vikings			
☐ 85 Charlie Sanders 25	.12	.02	
Detroit Lions			
☐ 86 Noah Jackson 15	.07	.01	
Chicago Bears			
☐ 87 Ed Marinaro 50	.25	.05	
New York Jets			
☐ 88 Bob Howard 15	.07	.01	
New England Patriots			
☐ 89 John McDaniel 15	.07	.01	
Cincinnati Bengals			
☐ 90 Dan Dierdorf AP 1.25	.60	.12	
St. Louis Cardinals			
☐ 91 Mark Moseley 35	.17	.03	
Washington Redskins			
☐ 92 Cleo Miller 15	.07	.01	
Cleveland Browns			
☐ 93 Andre Tillman 15	.07	.01	
Miami Dolphins			
☐ 94 Bruce Taylor 25	.12	.02	
San Francisco 49ers			
☐ 95 Bert Jones 75	.35	.07	
Baltimore Colts			
☐ 96 Anthony Davis 1.00	.50	.10	
Tampa Bay Buccaneers			
☐ 97 Don Goode 15	.07	.01	
San Diego Chargers			
☐ 98 Ray Rhodes 30	.15	.03	
New York Giants			
☐ 99 Mike Webster 8.00	4.00	.80	
Pittsburgh Steelers			
☐ 100 O.J. Simpson AP 7.50	3.75	.75	
Buffalo Bills			
☐ 101 Doug Plank 60	.30	.06	
Chicago Bears			
☐ 102 Efren Herrera 15	.07	.01	
Dallas Cowboys			
☐ 103 Charlie Smith 15	.07	.01	
Philadelphia Eagles			
☐ 104 Carlos Brown 35	.17	.03	
Green Bay Packers			
☐ 105 Jim Marshall 90	.45	.09	
Minnesota Vikings			
☐ 106 Paul Naumoff 15	.07	.01	
Detroit Lions			
☐ 107 Walter White 15	.07	.01	
Kansas City Chiefs			
☐ 108 John Cappelletti 1.75	.85	.17	
Los Angeles Rams			
☐ 109 Chip Myers 15	.07	.01	
San Diego Chargers			

☐ 110 Ken Stabler AP 1.50	.75	.15	
Oakland Raiders			
☐ 111 Joe Ehrmann 15	.07	.01	
Baltimore Colts			
☐ 112 Rick Engles 15	.07	.01	
Seattle Seahawks			
☐ 113 Jack Dolbin 30	.15	.03	
Denver Broncos			
☐ 114 Ron Bolton 15	.07	.01	
Cleveland Browns			
☐ 115 Mike Thomas 25	.12	.02	
Washington Redskins			
☐ 116 Mike Fuller 15	.07	.01	
San Diego Chargers			
☐ 117 John Hill 15	.07	.01	
New Orleans Saints			
☐ 118 Richard Todd 75	.35	.07	
New York Jets			
☐ 119 Duriel Harris 40	.20	.04	
Miami Dolphins			
☐ 120 John James AP 15	.07	.01	
Atlanta Falcons			
☐ 121 Lionel Antoine 15	.07	.01	
Chicago Bears			
☐ 122 John Skorupan 15	.07	.01	
Buffalo Bills			
☐ 123 Skip Butler 15	.07	.01	
Houston Oilers			
☐ 124 Bob Tucker 25	.12	.02	
New York Giants			
☐ 125 Paul Krause 50	.25	.05	
Minnesota Vikings			
☐ 126 Dave Hampton 15	.07	.01	
Philadelphia Eagles			
☐ 127 Tom Wittum 15	.07	.01	
San Francisco 49ers			
☐ 128 Gary Huff 25	.12	.02	
Tampa Bay Buccaneers			
☐ 129 Emmitt Thomas 25	.12	.02	
Kansas City Chiefs			
☐ 130 Drew Pearson AP 1.25	.60	.12	
Dallas Cowboys			
☐ 131 Ron Saul 15	.07	.01	
Washington Redskins			
☐ 132 Steve Niehaus 15	.07	.01	
Seattle Seahawks			
☐ 133 Fred Carr 25	.12	.02	
Green Bay Packers			
☐ 134 Norm Bulaich 25	.12	.02	
Miami Dolphins			
☐ 135 Bob Trumpy 60	.30	.06	
Cincinnati Bengals			
☐ 136 Greg Landry 50	.25	.05	
Detroit Lions			
☐ 137 George Buehler 15	.07	.01	
Oakland Raiders			
☐ 138 Reggie Rucker 25	.12	.02	

Cleveland Browns			
☐ 139 Julius Adams	.15	.07	.01
New England Patriots			
☐ 140 Jack Ham AP	2.00	1.00	.20
Pittsburgh Steelers			
☐ 141 Wayne Morris	.30	.15	.03
St. Louis Cardinals			
☐ 142 Marv Bateman	.15	.07	.01
Buffalo Bills			
☐ 143 Bobby Maples	.15	.07	.01
Denver Broncos			
☐ 144 Harold Carmichael	1.00	.50	.10
Philadelphia Eagles			
☐ 145 Bob Avellini	.25	.12	.02
Chicago Bears			
☐ 146 Harry Carson	7.00	3.50	.70
New York Giants			
☐ 147 Lawrence Pillers	.15	.07	.01
New York Jets			
☐ 148 Ed Williams	.15	.07	.01
Tampa Bay Buccaneers			
☐ 149 Dan Pastorini	.35	.17	.03
Houston Oilers			
☐ 150 Ron Yary AP	.25	.12	.02
Minnesota Vikings			
☐ 151 Joe Lavender	.15	.07	.01
Washington Redskins			
☐ 152 Pat McInally	.75	.35	.07
Cincinnati Bengals			
☐ 153 Lloyd Mumphord	.15	.07	.01
Baltimore Colts			
☐ 154 Cullen Bryant	.25	.12	.02
Los Angeles Rams			
☐ 155 Willie Lanier	1.00	.50	.10
Kansas City Chiefs			
☐ 156 Gene Washington	.35	.17	.03
San Francisco 49ers			
☐ 157 Scott Hunter	.25	.12	.02
Atlanta Falcons			
☐ 158 Jim Merlo	.15	.07	.01
New Orleans Saints			
☐ 159 Randy Grossman	.15	.07	.01
Pittsburgh Steelers			
☐ 160 Blaine Nye AP	.15	.07	.01
Dallas Cowboys			
☐ 161 Ike Harris	.15	.07	.01
St. Louis Cardinals			
☐ 162 Doug Dieken	.15	.07	.01
Cleveland Browns			
☐ 163 Guy Morriss	.15	.07	.01
Philadelphia Eagles			
☐ 164 Bob Parsons	.15	.07	.01
Chicago Bears			
☐ 165 Steve Grogan	1.50	.75	.15
New England Patriots			
☐ 166 John Brockington	.30	.15	.03
Green Bay Packers			
☐ 167 Charlie Joiner	1.25	.60	.12
San Diego Chargers			
☐ 168 Ron Carpenter	.15	.07	.01
Cincinnati Bengals			
☐ 169 Jeff Wright	.15	.07	.01
Minnesota Vikings			
☐ 170 Chris Hanburger AP	.25	.12	.02
Washington Redskins			
☐ 171 Roosevelt Leaks	.50	.25	.05
Baltimore Colts			
☐ 172 Larry Little	.25	.12	.02
Miami Dolphins			
☐ 173 John Matuszak	.30	.15	.03
Oakland Raiders			
☐ 174 Joe Ferguson	.50	.25	.05
Buffalo Bills			
☐ 175 Brad Van Pelt	.40	.20	.04
New York Giants			
☐ 176 Dexter Bussey	.40	.20	.04
Detroit Lions			
☐ 177 Steve Largent	60.00	30.00	6.00
Seattle Seahawks			
☐ 178 Dewey Selmon	.25	.12	.02
Tampa Bay Buccaneers			
☐ 179 Randy Gradishar	.75	.35	.07
Denver Broncos			
☐ 180 Mel Blount AP	2.00	1.00	.20
Pittsburgh Steelers			
☐ 181 Dan Neal	.15	.07	.01
Chicago Bears			
☐ 182 Rich Szaro	.15	.07	.01
New Orleans Saints			
☐ 183 Mike Boryla	.25	.12	.02
Philadelphia Eagles			
☐ 184 Steve Jones	.15	.07	.01
St. Louis Cardinals			
☐ 185 Paul Warfield	1.75	.85	.17
Cleveland Browns			
☐ 186 Greg Buttle	.50	.25	.05
New York Jets			
☐ 187 Rich McGeorge	.15	.07	.01
Green Bay Packers			
☐ 188 Leon Gray	.50	.25	.05
New England Patriots			
☐ 189 John Shinners	.15	.07	.01
Cincinnati Bengals			
☐ 190 Toni Linhart AP	.15	.07	.01
Baltimore Colts			
☐ 191 Robert Miller	.15	.07	.01
Minnesota Vikings			
☐ 192 Jake Scott	.25	.12	.02
Washington Redskins			
☐ 193 Jon Morris	.15	.07	.01
Detroit Lions			
☐ 194 Randy Crowder	.15	.07	.01
Miami Dolphins			
☐ 195 Lynn Swann UER	5.00	2.50	.50

Pittsburgh Steelers
(Interception Record
on card back)

☐ 196	Marsh White 15	.07	.01	
	New York Giants			
☐ 197	Rod Perry 35	.17	.03	
	Los Angeles Rams			
☐ 198	Willie Hall 15	.07	.01	
	Oakland Raiders			
☐ 199	Mike Hartenstine 15	.07	.01	
	Chicago Bears			
☐ 200	Jim Bakken AP 25	.12	.02	
	St. Louis Cardinals			
☐ 201	Atlanta Falcons UER 90	.15	.03	
	(79 Jim Mitchell			
	is not listed)			
	Team Checklist			
☐ 202	Baltimore Colts 90	.15	.03	
	Team Checklist			
☐ 203	Buffalo Bills 90	.15	.03	
	Team Checklist			
☐ 204	Chicago Bears 90	.15	.03	
	Team Checklist			
☐ 205	Cincinnati Bengals 90	.15	.03	
	Team Checklist			
☐ 206	Cleveland Browns 90	.15	.03	
	Team Checklist			
☐ 207	Dallas Cowboys 90	.15	.03	
	Team Checklist			
☐ 208	Denver Broncos 90	.15	.03	
	Team Checklist			
☐ 209	Detroit Lions 90	.15	.03	
	Team Checklist			
☐ 210	Green Bay Packers 90	.15	.03	
	Team Checklist			
☐ 211	Houston Oilers 90	.15	.03	
	Team Checklist			
☐ 212	Kansas City Chiefs 90	.15	.03	
	Team Checklist			
☐ 213	Los Angeles Rams 90	.15	.03	
	Team Checklist			
☐ 214	Miami Dolphins 90	.15	.03	
	Team Checklist			
☐ 215	Minnesota Vikings 90	.15	.03	
	Team Checklist			
☐ 216	New England Patriots 90	.15	.03	
	Team Checklist			
☐ 217	New Orleans Saints 90	.15	.03	
	Team Checklist			
☐ 218	New York Giants 90	.15	.03	
	Team Checklist			
☐ 219	New York Jets 90	.15	.03	
	Team Checklist			
☐ 220	Oakland Raiders 90	.15	.03	
	Team Checklist			
☐ 221	Philadelphia Eagles 90	.15	.03	
	Team Checklist			
☐ 222	Pittsburgh Steelers 90	.15	.03	
	Team Checklist			
☐ 223	St. Louis Cardinals 90	.15	.03	
	Team Checklist			
☐ 224	San Diego Chargers 90	.15	.03	
	Team Checklist			
☐ 225	San Francisco 49ers 90	.15	.03	
	Team Checklist			
☐ 226	Seattle Seahawks 90	.15	.03	
	Team Checklist			
☐ 227	Tampa Bay Buccaneers ...90	.15	.03	
	Team Checklist UER			
	(Lee Roy Selmon mis-			
	spelled as Leroy)			
☐ 228	Washington Redskins 90	.15	.03	
	Team Checklist			
☐ 229	Sam Cunningham 30	.15	.03	
	New England Patriots			
☐ 230	Alan Page AP 1.25	.60	.12	
	Minnesota Vikings			
☐ 231	Eddie Brown 15	.07	.01	
	Washington Redskins			
☐ 232	Stan White 15	.07	.01	
	Baltimore Colts			
☐ 233	Vern Den Herder 15	.07	.01	
	Miami Dolphins			
☐ 234	Clarence Davis 15	.07	.01	
	Oakland Raiders			
☐ 235	Ken Anderson 1.50	.75	.15	
	Cincinnati Bengals			
☐ 236	Karl Chandler 15	.07	.01	
	New York Giants			
☐ 237	Will Harrell 15	.07	.01	
	Green Bay Packers			
☐ 238	Clarence Scott 15	.07	.01	
	Cleveland Browns			
☐ 239	Bo Rather 35	.17	.03	
	Chicago Bears			
☐ 240	Robert Brazile AP 35	.17	.03	
	Houston Oilers			
☐ 241	Bob Bell 15	.07	.01	
	St. Louis Cardinals			
☐ 242	Rolland Lawrence 25	.12	.02	
	Atlanta Falcons			
☐ 243	Tom Sullivan 15	.07	.01	
	Philadelphia Eagles			
☐ 244	Larry Brunson 15	.07	.01	
	Kansas City Chiefs			
☐ 245	Terry Bradshaw 4.50	2.25	.45	
	Pittsburgh Steelers			
☐ 246	Rich Saul 15	.07	.01	
	Los Angeles Rams			
☐ 247	Cleveland Elam 15	.07	.01	
	San Francisco 49ers			
☐ 248	Don Woods 15	.07	.01	
	San Diego Chargers			
☐ 249	Bruce Laird 15	.07	.01	

Baltimore Colts
- ☐ 250 Coy Bacon AP ....15 .07 .01
  Cincinnati Bengals
- ☐ 251 Russ Francis ....50 .25 .05
  New England Patriots
- ☐ 252 Jim Braxton ....15 .07 .01
  Buffalo Bills
- ☐ 253 Perry Smith ....15 .07 .01
  Green Bay Packers
- ☐ 254 Jerome Barkum ....25 .12 .02
  New York Jets
- ☐ 255 Garo Yepremian ....25 .12 .02
  Miami Dolphins
- ☐ 256 Checklist 133-264 .. 1.50 .15 .03
- ☐ 257 Tony Galbreath ....35 .17 .03
  New Orleans Saints
- ☐ 258 Troy Archer ....25 .12 .02
  New York Giants
- ☐ 259 Brian Sipe ....75 .35 .07
  Cleveland Browns
- ☐ 260 Billy Joe DuPree AP ....50 .25 .05
  Dallas Cowboys
- ☐ 261 Bobby Walden ....15 .07 .01
  Pittsburgh Steelers
- ☐ 262 Larry Marshall ....15 .07 .01
  Philadelphia Eagles
- ☐ 263 Ted Fritsch Jr. ....15 .07 .01
  Washington Redskins
- ☐ 264 Larry Hand ....15 .07 .01
  Detroit Lions
- ☐ 265 Tom Mack ....35 .17 .03
  Los Angeles Rams
- ☐ 266 Ed Bradley ....15 .07 .01
  Seattle Seahawks
- ☐ 267 Pat Leahy ....75 .35 .07
  New York Jets
- ☐ 268 Louis Carter ....15 .07 .01
  Tampa Bay Buccaneers
- ☐ 269 Archie Griffin .... 3.50 1.75 .35
  Cincinnati Bengals
- ☐ 270 Art Shell AP .... 1.25 .60 .12
  Oakland Raiders
- ☐ 271 Stu Voigt ....25 .12 .02
  Minnesota Vikings
- ☐ 272 Prentice McCray ....15 .07 .01
  New England Patriots
- ☐ 273 MacArthur Lane ....25 .12 .02
  Kansas City Chiefs
- ☐ 274 Dan Fouts .... 7.50 3.75 .75
  San Diego Chargers
- ☐ 275 Charley Young ....25 .12 .02
  Los Angeles Rams
- ☐ 276 Wilbur Jackson ....50 .25 .05
  San Francisco 49ers
- ☐ 277 John Hicks ....15 .07 .01
  New York Giants
- ☐ 278 Nat Moore ....60 .30 .06

Miami Dolphins
- ☐ 279 Virgil Livers ....15 .07 .01
  Chicago Bears
- ☐ 280 Curley Culp AP ....25 .12 .02
  Houston Oilers
- ☐ 281 Rocky Bleier ....75 .35 :07
  Pittsburgh Steelers
- ☐ 282 John Zook ....25 .12 .02
  St. Louis Cardinals
- ☐ 283 Tom DeLeone ....15 .07 .01
  Cleveland Browns
- ☐ 284 Danny White .... 3.25 1.60 .32
  Dallas Cowboys
- ☐ 285 Otis Armstrong ....50 .25 .05
  Denver Broncos
- ☐ 286 Larry Walton ....15 .07 .01
  Detroit Lions
- ☐ 287 Jim Carter ....15 .07 .01
  Green Bay Packers
- ☐ 288 Don McCauley ....15 .07 .01
  Baltimore Colts
- ☐ 289 Frank Grant ....15 .07 .01
  Washington Redskins
- ☐ 290 Roger Wehrli AP ....25 .12 .02
  St. Louis Cardinals
- ☐ 291 Mick Tingelhoff ....30 .15 .03
  Minnesota Vikings
- ☐ 292 Bernard Jackson ....25 .12 .02
  Denver Broncos
- ☐ 293 Tom Owen ....40 .20 .04
  New England Patriots
- ☐ 294 Mike Esposito ....15 .07 .01
  Atlanta Falcons
- ☐ 295 Fred Biletnikoff .... 1.75 .85 .17
  Oakland Raiders
- ☐ 296 Revie Sorey ....35 .17 .03
  Chicago Bears
- ☐ 297 John McMakin ....15 .07 .01
  Seattle Seahawks
- ☐ 298 Dan Ryczek ....15 .07 .01
  Tampa Bay Buccaneers
- ☐ 299 Wayne Moore ....15 .07 .01
  Miami Dolphins
- ☐ 300 Franco Harris AP .... 3.75 1.85 .37
  Pittsburgh Steelers
- ☐ 301 Rick Upchurch .... 1.50 .75 .15
  Denver Broncos
- ☐ 302 Jim Stienke ....15 .07 .01
  New York Giants
- ☐ 303 Charlie Davis ....15 .07 .01
  St. Louis Cardinals
- ☐ 304 Don Cockroft ....15 .07 .01
  Cleveland Browns
- ☐ 305 Ken Burrough ....25 .12 .02
  Houston Oilers
- ☐ 306 Clark Gaines ....15 .07 .01
  New York Jets

☐ 307	Bobby Douglass ....25 New Orleans Saints	.12	.02
☐ 308	Ralph Perretta ....15 San Diego Chargers	.07	.01
☐ 309	Wally Hilgenberg ....15 Minnesota Vikings	.07	.01
☐ 310	Monte Jackson AP ....50 Los Angeles Rams	.25	.05
☐ 311	Chris Bahr ....60 Cincinnati Bengals	.30	.06
☐ 312	Jim Cheyunski ....15 Baltimore Colts	.07	.01
☐ 313	Mike Patrick ....15 New England Patriots	.07	.01
☐ 314	Ed Too Tall Jones ....3.50 Dallas Cowboys	1.75	.35
☐ 315	Bill Bradley ....25 Philadelphia Eagles	.12	.02
☐ 316	Benny Malone ....15 Miami Dolphins	.07	.01
☐ 317	Paul Seymour ....15 Buffalo Bills	.07	.01
☐ 318	Jim Laslavic ....15 Detroit Lions	.07	.01
☐ 319	Frank Lewis ....25 Pittsburgh Steelers	.12	.02
☐ 320	Ray Guy AP ....60 Oakland Raiders	.30	.06
☐ 321	Allan Ellis ....15 Chicago Bears	.07	.01
☐ 322	Conrad Dobler ....30 St. Louis Cardinals	.15	.03
☐ 323	Chester Marcol ....15 Green Bay Packers	.07	.01
☐ 324	Doug Kotar ....15 New York Giants	.07	.01
☐ 325	Lemar Parrish ....25 Cincinnati Bengals	.12	.02
☐ 326	Steve Holden ....15 Cleveland Browns	.07	.01
☐ 327	Jeff Van Note ....25 Atlanta Falcons	.12	.02
☐ 328	Howard Stevens ....15 Baltimore Colts	.07	.01
☐ 329	Brad Dusek ....15 Washington Redskins	.07	.01
☐ 330	Joe DeLamielleure AP ....25 Buffalo Bills	.12	.02
☐ 331	Jim Plunkett ....1.00 San Francisco 49ers	.50	.10
☐ 332	Checklist 265-396 ....1.50	.15	.03
☐ 333	Lou Piccone ....15 New York Jets	.07	.01
☐ 334	Ray Hamilton ....25 New England Patriots	.12	.02
☐ 335	Jan Stenerud ....75 Kansas City Chiefs	.35	.07
☐ 336	Jeris White ....15 Miami Dolphins	.07	.01
☐ 337	Sherman Smith ....35 Seattle Seahawks	.17	.03
☐ 338	Dave Green ....15 Tampa Bay Buccaneers	.07	.01
☐ 339	Terry Schmidt ....15 Chicago Bears	.07	.01
☐ 340	Sammie White AP ....1.00 Minnesota Vikings	.50	.10
☐ 341	Jon Kolb ....30 Pittsburgh Steelers	.15	.03
☐ 342	Randy White ....4.50 Dallas Cowboys	2.25	.45
☐ 343	Bob Klein ....15 Los Angeles Rams	.07	.01
☐ 344	Bob Kowalkowski ....15 Detroit Lions	.07	.01
☐ 345	Terry Metcalf ....35 St. Louis Cardinals	.17	.03
☐ 346	Joe Danelo ....15 New York Giants	.07	.01
☐ 347	Ken Payne ....15 Green Bay Packers	.07	.01
☐ 348	Neal Craig ....15 Cleveland Browns	.07	.01
☐ 349	Dennis Johnson ....15 Washington Redskins	.07	.01
☐ 350	Bill Bergey AP ....40 Philadelphia Eagles	.20	.04
☐ 351	Raymond Chester ....25 Baltimore Colts	.12	.02
☐ 352	Bob Matheson ....25 Miami Dolphins	.12	.02
☐ 353	Mike Kadish ....15 Buffalo Bills	.07	.01
☐ 354	Mark Van Eeghen ....75 Oakland Raiders	.35	.07
☐ 355	L.C. Greenwood ....60 Pittsburgh Steelers	.30	.06
☐ 356	Sam Hunt ....15 New England Patriots	.07	.01
☐ 357	Darrell Austin ....15 New York Jets	.07	.01
☐ 358	Jim Turner ....25 Denver Broncos	.12	.02
☐ 359	Ahmad Rashad ....1.75 Minnesota Vikings	.85	.17
☐ 360	Walter Payton AP ....35.00 Chicago Bears	17.50	3.50
☐ 361	Mark Arneson ....15 St. Louis Cardinals	.07	.01
☐ 362	Jerrel Wilson ....15 Kansas City Chiefs	.07	.01
☐ 363	Steve Bartkowski ....75 Atlanta Falcons	.35	.07
☐ 364	John Watson 15	.07	.01

	San Francisco 49ers			
□ 365	Ken Riley	.25	.12	.02
	Cincinnati Bengals			
□ 366	Gregg Bingham	.15	.07	.01
	Houston Oilers			
□ 367	Golden Richards	.25	.12	.02
	Dallas Cowboys			
□ 368	Clyde Powers	.15	.07	.01
	New York Giants			
□ 369	Diron Talbert	.25	.12	.02
	Washington Redskins			
□ 370	Lydell Mitchell	.30	.15	.03
	Baltimore Colts			
□ 371	Bob Jackson	.15	.07	.01
	Cleveland Browns			
□ 372	Jim Mandich	.25	.12	.02
	Miami Dolphins			
□ 373	Frank LeMaster	.15	.07	.01
	Philadelphia Eagles			
□ 374	Benny Ricardo	.15	.07	.01
	Buffalo Bills			
□ 375	Lawrence McCutcheon	.35	.17	.03
	Los Angeles Rams			
□ 376	Lynn Dickey	.50	.25	.05
	Green Bay Packers			
□ 377	Phil Wise	.15	.07	.01
	New York Jets			
□ 378	Tony McGee	.15	.07	.01
	New England Patriots			
□ 379	Norm Thompson	.25	.12	.02
	Baltimore Colts			
□ 380	Dave Casper AP	3.50	1.75	.35
	Oakland Raiders			
□ 381	Glen Edwards	.15	.07	.01
	Pittsburgh Steelers			
□ 382	Bob Thomas	.15	.07	.01
	Chicago Bears			
□ 383	Bob Chandler	.25	.12	.02
	Buffalo Bills			
□ 384	Rickey Young	.25	.12	.02
	San Diego Chargers			
□ 385	Carl Eller	.75	.35	.07
	Minnesota Vikings			
□ 386	Lyle Alzado	1.00	.50	.10
	Denver Broncos			
□ 387	John Leypoldt	.15	.07	.01
	Seattle Seahawks			
□ 388	Gordon Bell	.15	.07	.01
	New York Giants			
□ 389	Mike Bragg	.15	.07	.01
	Washington Redskins			
□ 390	Jim Langer AP	.90	.45	.09
	Miami Dolphins			
□ 391	Vern Holland	.15	.07	.01
	Cincinnati Bengals			
□ 392	Nelson Munsey	.15	.07	.01
	Baltimore Colts			

□ 393	Mack Mitchell	.15	.07	.01
	Cleveland Browns			
□ 394	Tony Adams	.25	.12	.02
	Kansas City Chiefs			
□ 395	Preston Pearson	.35	.17	.03
	Dallas Cowboys			
□ 396	Emanuel Zanders	.15	.07	.01
	New Orleans Saints			
□ 397	Vince Papale	.15	.07	.01
	Philadelphia Eagles			
□ 398	Joe Fields	.50	.25	.05
	New York Jets			
□ 399	Craig Clemons	.15	.07	.01
	Chicago Bears			
□ 400	Fran Tarkenton AP	5.50	2.75	.55
	Minnesota Vikings			
□ 401	Andy Johnson	.25	.12	.02
	New England Patriots			
□ 402	Willie Buchanon	.25	.12	.02
	Green Bay Packers			
□ 403	Pat Curran	.15	.07	.01
	San Diego Chargers			
□ 404	Ray Jarvis	.15	.07	.01
	Detroit Lions			
□ 405	Joe Greene	2.25	1.10	.22
	Pittsburgh Steelers			
□ 406	Bill Simpson	.15	.07	.01
	Los Angeles Rams			
□ 407	Ronnie Coleman	.15	.07	.01
	Houston Oilers			
□ 408	J.K. McKay	.30	.15	.03
	Tampa Bay Buccaneers			
□ 409	Pat Fischer	.25	.12	.02
	Washington Redskins			
□ 410	John Dutton AP	.25	.12	.02
	Baltimore Colts			
□ 411	Boobie Clark	.25	.12	.02
	Cincinnati Bengals			
□ 412	Pat Tilley	1.00	.50	.10
	St. Louis Cardinals			
□ 413	Don Strock	.30	.15	.03
	Miami Dolphins			
□ 414	Brian Kelley	.25	.12	.02
	New York Giants			
□ 415	Gene Upshaw	.90	.45	.09
	Oakland Raiders			
□ 416	Mike Montler	.15	.07	.01
	Buffalo Bills			
□ 417	Checklist 397-528	1.50	.15	.03
□ 418	John Gilliam	.25	.12	.02
	Atlanta Falcons			
□ 419	Brent McClanahan	.15	.07	.01
	Minnesota Vikings			
□ 420	Jerry Sherk AP	.25	.12	.02
	Cleveland Browns			
□ 421	Roy Gerela	.15	.07	.01
	Pittsburgh Steelers			

☐ 422 Tim Fox ....15 .07 .01		
New England Patriots		
☐ 423 John Ebersole ....15 .07 .01		
New York Jets		
☐ 424 James Scott ....25 .12 .02		
Chicago Bears		
☐ 425 Delvin Williams ....75 .35 .07		
San Francisco 49ers		
☐ 426 Spike Jones ....15 .07 .01		
Philadelphia Eagles		
☐ 427 Harvey Martin ....75 .35 .07		
Dallas Cowboys		
☐ 428 Don Herrmann ....15 .07 .01		
New Orleans Saints		
☐ 429 Calvin Hill ....50 .25 .05		
Washington Redskins		
☐ 430 Isiah Robertson AP ....25 .12 .02		
Los Angeles Rams		
☐ 431 Tony Greene ....15 .07 .01		
Buffalo Bills		
☐ 432 Bob Johnson ....15 .07 .01		
Cincinnati Bengals		
☐ 433 Lem Barney ....60 .30 .06		
Detroit Lions		
☐ 434 Eric Torkelson ....15 .07 .01		
Green Bay Packers		
☐ 435 John Mendenhall ....15 .07 .01		
New York Giants		
☐ 436 Larry Seiple ....15 .07 .01		
Miami Dolphins		
☐ 437 Art Kuehn ....15 .07 .01		
Seattle Seahawks		
☐ 438 John Vella ....15 .07 .01		
Oakland Raiders		
☐ 439 Greg Latta ....15 .07 .01		
Chicago Bears		
☐ 440 Roger Carr AP ....25 .12 .02		
Baltimore Colts		
☐ 441 Doug Sutherland ....15 .07 .01		
Minnesota Vikings		
☐ 442 Mike Kruczek ....25 .12 .02		
Pittsburgh Steelers		
☐ 443 Steve Zabel ....15 .07 .01		
New England Patriots		
☐ 444 Mike Pruitt ....1.25 .60 .12		
Cleveland Browns		
☐ 445 Harold Jackson ....60 .30 .06		
Los Angeles Rams		
☐ 446 George Jakowenko ....15 .07 .01		
Buffalo Bills		
☐ 447 John Fitzgerald ....25 .12 .02		
Dallas Cowboys		
☐ 448 Carey Joyce ....15 .07 .01		
St. Louis Cardinals		
☐ 449 Jim LeClair ....15 .07 .01		
Cincinnati Bengals		
☐ 450 Ken Houston AP ....1.00 .50 .10		

Washington Redskins		
☐ 451 Steve Grogan RB ....50 .25 .05		
Most Touchdowns Rush-		
ing by QB, Season		
☐ 452 Jim Marshall RB ....40 .20 .04		
Most Games		
Played, Lifetime		
☐ 453 O.J. Simpson RB ....3.50 1.75 .35		
Most Yardage,		
Rushing, Game		
☐ 454 Fran Tarkenton RB ....2.75 1.35 .27		
Most Yardage,		
Passing, Lifetime		
☐ 455 Jim Zorn RB ....40 .20 .04		
Most Passing Yards		
Season, Rookie		
☐ 456 Robert Pratt ....15 .07 .01		
Baltimore Colts		
☐ 457 Walker Gillette ....15 .07 .01		
New York Giants		
☐ 458 Charlie Hall ....15 .07 .01		
Cleveland Browns		
☐ 459 Robert Newhouse ....35 .17 .03		
Dallas Cowboys		
☐ 460 John Hannah AP ....1.25 .60 .12		
New England Patriots		
☐ 461 Ken Reaves ....15 .07 .01		
St. Louis Cardinals		
☐ 462 Herman Weaver ....15 .07 .01		
Detroit Lions		
☐ 463 James Harris ....35 .17 .03		
Los Angeles Rams		
☐ 464 Howard Twilley ....25 .12 .02		
Miami Dolphins		
☐ 465 Jeff Siemon ....25 .12 .02		
Minnesota Vikings		
☐ 466 John Outlaw ....15 .07 .01		
Philadelphia Eagles		
☐ 467 Chuck Muncie ....1.25 .60 .12		
New Orleans Saints		
☐ 468 Bob Moore ....15 .07 .01		
Tampa Bay Buccaneers		
☐ 469 Robert Woods ....15 .07 .01		
New York Jets		
☐ 470 Cliff Branch AP ....1.25 .60 .12		
Oakland Raiders		
☐ 471 Johnnie Gray ....15 .07 .01		
Green Bay Packers		
☐ 472 Don Hardeman ....15 .07 .01		
Houston Oilers		
☐ 473 Steve Ramsey ....25 .12 .02		
Denver Broncos		
☐ 474 Steve Mike-Mayer ....15 .07 .01		
San Francisco 49ers		
☐ 475 Gary Garrison ....25 .12 .02		
San Diego Chargers		
☐ 476 Walter Johnson ....15 .07 .01		

	Cleveland Browns			
☐ 477	Neil Clabo	.15	.07	.01
	Minnesota Vikings			
☐ 478	Len Hauss	.25	.12	.02
	Washington Redskins			
☐ 479	Darryl Stingley	.30	.15	.03
	New England Patriots			
☐ 480	Jack Lambert AP	4.50	2.25	.45
	Pittsburgh Steelers			
☐ 481	Mike Adamle	.25	.12	.02
	Chicago Bears			
☐ 482	David Lee	.15	.07	.01
	Baltimore Colts			
☐ 483	Tom Mullen	.15	.07	.01
	New York Giants			
☐ 484	Claude Humphrey	.25	.12	.02
	Atlanta Falcons			
☐ 485	Jim Hart	.60	.30	.06
	St. Louis Cardinals			
☐ 486	Bobby Thompson	.15	.07	.01
	Detroit Lions			
☐ 487	Jack Rudnay	.15	.07	.01
	Kansas City Chiefs			
☐ 488	Rich Sowells	.15	.07	.01
	New York Jets			
☐ 489	Reuben Gant	.15	.07	.01
	Buffalo Bills			
☐ 490	Cliff Harris AP	.50	.25	.05
	Dallas Cowboys			
☐ 491	Bob Brown	.15	.07	.01
	Cincinnati Bengals			
☐ 492	Don Nottingham	.15	.07	.01
	Miami Dolphins			
☐ 493	Ron Jessie	.25	.12	.02
	Los Angeles Rams			
☐ 494	Otis Sistrunk	.25	.12	.02
	Oakland Raiders			
☐ 495	Bill Kilmer	.75	.35	.07
	Washington Redskins			
☐ 496	Oscar Roan	.25	.12	.02
	Cleveland Browns			
☐ 497	Bill Van Heusen	.15	.07	.01
	Denver Broncos			
☐ 498	Randy Logan	.15	.07	.01
	Philadelphia Eagles			
☐ 499	John Smith	.15	.07	.01
	New England Patriots			
☐ 500	Chuck Foreman AP	.50	.25	.05
	Minnesota Vikings			
☐ 501	J.T. Thomas	.15	.07	.01
	Pittsburgh Steelers			
☐ 502	Steve Schubert	.15	.07	.01
	Chicago Bears			
☐ 503	Mike Barnes	.15	.07	.01
	Baltimore Colts			
☐ 504	J.V. Cain	.15	.07	.01
	St. Louis Cardinals			
☐ 505	Larry Csonka	1.75	.85	.17
	New York Giants			
☐ 506	Elvin Bethea	.25	.12	.02
	Houston Oilers			
☐ 507	Ray Easterling	.15	.07	.01
	Atlanta Falcons			
☐ 508	Joe Reed	.25	.12	.02
	Detroit Lions			
☐ 509	Steve Odom	.25	.12	.02
	Green Bay Packers			
☐ 510	Tommy Casanova AP	.25	.12	.02
	Cincinnati Bengals			
☐ 511	Dave Dalby	.25	.12	.02
	Oakland Raiders			
☐ 512	Richard Caster	.25	.12	.02
	New York Jets			
☐ 513	Fred Dryer	1.25	.60	.12
	Los Angeles Rams			
☐ 514	Jeff Kinney	.25	.12	.02
	Kansas City Chiefs			
☐ 515	Bob Griese	3.00	1.50	.30
	Miami Dolphins			
☐ 516	Butch Johnson	.75	.35	.07
	Dallas Cowboys			
☐ 517	Gerald Irons	.15	.07	.01
	Cleveland Browns			
☐ 518	Don Calhoun	.15	.07	.01
	New England Patriots			
☐ 519	Jack Gregory	.25	.12	.02
	New York Giants			
☐ 520	Tom Banks AP	.25	.12	.02
	St. Louis Cardinals			
☐ 521	Bobby Bryant	.15	.07	.01
	Minnesota Vikings			
☐ 522	Reggie Harrison	.15	.07	.01
	Pittsburgh Steelers			
☐ 523	Terry Hermeling	.15	.07	.01
	Washington Redskins			
☐ 524	David Taylor	.15	.07	.01
	Baltimore Colts			
☐ 525	Brian Baschnagel	.50	.25	.05
	Chicago Bears			
☐ 526	AFC Championship	.50	.25	.05
	Raiders 24,			
	Steelers 7			
	(Stabler)			
☐ 527	NFC Championship	.40	.20	.04
	Vikings 24,			
	Rams 13			
☐ 528	Super Bowl XI	1.50	.50	.10
	Raiders 32,			
	Vikings 14			
	(line play)			

1978 Topps

The 1978 Topps football set contains 528 cards. The cards measure 2 1/2" by 3 1/2". No known scarcities exist. The first six cards in the set feature Highlights (HL) of the previous season. Cards 501 through 528 are Team Leader (TL) cards depicting typically four individual team (statistical) leaders on the front and a team checklist on the back. Post-season playoff action is featured on cards 166-168. Statistical league leaders are depicted on cards 331-336. All-Pro (AP) selections are designated on the player's regular card, not a special card. The card backs are printed in black and green on gray card stock. The key rookie card in this set is Tony Dorsett. Other notable rookie cards in the set include Tom Jackson, Joe Klecko, Stanley Morgan, John Stallworth, Wesley Walker, and Reggie Williams.

	NRMT	VG-E	GOOD
COMPLETE SET (528)	130.00	55.00	17.00
COMMON PLAYER (1-528)	.10	.05	.01

☐ 1 Gary Huff HL Huff Leads Bucs to First Win	.60	.10	.02
☐ 2 Craig Morton HL Morton Passes Broncos to Super Bowl	.25	.12	.02
☐ 3 Walter Payton HL Rushes for 275 Yards	3.50	1.75	.35
☐ 4 O.J. Simpson HL Reaches 10,000 Yards	2.75	1.35	.27
☐ 5 Fran Tarkenton HL Completes 17 of 18	1.50	.75	.15
☐ 6 Bob Thomas HL Thomas' FG Sends	.20	.10	.02

Bears to Playoffs			
☐ 7 Joe Pisarcik New York Giants	.20	.10	.02
☐ 8 Skip Thomas Oakland Raiders	.10	.05	.01
☐ 9 Roosevelt Leaks Baltimore Colts	.20	.10	.02
☐ 10 Ken Houston AP Washington Redskins	.75	.35	.07
☐ 11 Tom Blanchard New Orleans Saints	.10	.05	.01
☐ 12 Jim Turner Denver Broncos	.15	.07	.01
☐ 13 Tom DeLeone Cleveland Browns	.10	.05	.01
☐ 14 Jim LeClair Cincinnati Bengals	.10	.05	.01
☐ 15 Bob Avellini Chicago Bears	.15	.07	.01
☐ 16 Tony McGee New England Patriots	.10	.05	.01
☐ 17 James Harris San Diego Chargers	.20	.10	.02
☐ 18 Terry Nelson Los Angeles Rams	.10	.05	.01
☐ 19 Rocky Bleier Pittsburgh Steelers	.60	.30	.06
☐ 20 Joe DeLamielleure AP Buffalo Bills	.15	.07	.01
☐ 21 Richard Caster New York Jets	.15	.07	.01
☐ 22 A.J. Duhe Miami Dolphins	.60	.30	.06
☐ 23 John Outlaw Philadelphia Eagles	.10	.05	.01
☐ 24 Danny White Dallas Cowboys	1.00	.50	.10
☐ 25 Larry Csonka New York Giants	1.50	.75	.15
☐ 26 David Hill Detroit Lions	.10	.05	.01
☐ 27 Mark Arneson St. Louis Cardinals	.10	.05	.01
☐ 28 Jack Tatum Oakland Raiders	.20	.10	.02
☐ 29 Norm Thompson Baltimore Colts	.10	.05	.01
☐ 30 Sammie White Minnesota Vikings	.30	.15	.03
☐ 31 Dennis Johnson Washington Redskins	.10	.05	.01
☐ 32 Robin Earl Chicago Bears	.10	.05	.01
☐ 33 Don Cockroft Cleveland Browns	.10	.05	.01
☐ 34 Bob Johnson Cincinnati Bengals	.10	.05	.01

☐ 35 John Hannah 75	.35	.07	
New England Patriots			
☐ 36 Scott Hunter 15	.07	.01	
Atlanta Falcons			
☐ 37 Ken Burrough 15	.07	.01	
Houston Oilers			
☐ 38 Wilbur Jackson 15	.07	.01	
San Francisco 49ers			
☐ 39 Rich McGeorge 10	.05	.01	
Green Bay Packers			
☐ 40 Lyle Alzado AP 75	.35	.07	
Denver Broncos			
☐ 41 John Ebersole 10	.05	.01	
New York Jets			
☐ 42 Gary Green 25	.12	.02	
Kansas City Chiefs			
☐ 43 Art Kuehn 10	.05	.01	
Seattle Seahawks			
☐ 44 Glen Edwards 10	.05	.01	
Pittsburgh Steelers			
☐ 45 Lawrence McCutcheon 20	.10	.02	
Los Angeles Rams			
☐ 46 Duriel Harris 15	.07	.01	
Miami Dolphins			
☐ 47 Rich Szaro 10	.05	.01	
New Orleans Saints			
☐ 48 Mike Washington 10	.05	.01	
Tampa Bay Buccaneers			
☐ 49 Stan White 10	.05	.01	
Baltimore Colts			
☐ 50 Dave Casper AP 1.00	.50	.10	
Oakland Raiders			
☐ 51 Len Hauss 15	.07	.01	
Washington Redskins			
☐ 52 James Scott 10	.05	.01	
Chicago Bears			
☐ 53 Brian Sipe 50	.25	.05	
Cleveland Browns			
☐ 54 Gary Shirk 10	.05	.01	
New York Giants			
☐ 55 Archie Griffin 60	.30	.06	
Cincinnati Bengals			
☐ 56 Mike Patrick 10	.05	.01	
New England Patriots			
☐ 57 Mario Clark 10	.05	.01	
Buffalo Bills			
☐ 58 Jeff Siemon 15	.07	.01	
Minnesota Vikings			
☐ 59 Steve Mike-Mayer 10	.05	.01	
Detroit Lions			
☐ 60 Randy White AP 2.00	1.00	.20	
Dallas Cowboys			
☐ 61 Darrell Austin 10	.05	.01	
New York Jets			
☐ 62 Tom Sullivan 10	.05	.01	
Philadelphia Eagles			
☐ 63 Johnny Rodgers 1.50	.75	.15	

San Diego Chargers			
☐ 64 Ken Reaves 10	.05	.01	
St. Louis Cardinals			
☐ 65 Terry Bradshaw 3.50	1.75	.35	
Pittsburgh Steelers			
☐ 66 Fred Steinfort 10	.05	.01	
Atlanta Falcons			
☐ 67 Curley Culp 15	.07	.01	
Houston Oilers			
☐ 68 Ted Hendricks 75	.35	.07	
Oakland Raiders			
☐ 69 Raymond Chester 15	.07	.01	
Oakland Raiders			
☐ 70 Jim Langer AP 75	.35	.07	
Miami Dolphins			
☐ 71 Calvin Hill 30	.15	.03	
Washington Redskins			
☐ 72 Mike Hartenstine 10	.05	.01	
Chicago Bears			
☐ 73 Gerald Irons 10	.05	.01	
Cleveland Browns			
☐ 74 Billy Brooks 20	.10	.02	
Cincinnati Bengals			
☐ 75 John Mendenhall 10	.05	.01	
New York Giants			
☐ 76 Andy Johnson 10	.05	.01	
New England Patriots			
☐ 77 Tom Wittum 10	.05	.01	
San Francisco 49ers			
☐ 78 Lynn Dickey 30	.15	.03	
Green Bay Packers			
☐ 79 Carl Eller 60	.30	.06	
Minnesota Vikings			
☐ 80 Tom Mack 30	.15	.03	
Los Angeles Rams			
☐ 81 Clark Gaines 10	.05	.01	
New York Jets			
☐ 82 Lem Barney 60	.30	.06	
Detroit Lions			
☐ 83 Mike Montler 10	.05	.01	
Detroit Lions			
☐ 84 Jon Kolb 10	.05	.01	
Pittsburgh Steelers			
☐ 85 Bob Chandler 15	.07	.01	
Buffalo Bills			
☐ 86 Robert Newhouse 20	.10	.02	
Dallas Cowboys			
☐ 87 Frank LeMaster 10	.05	.01	
Philadelphia Eagles			
☐ 88 Jeff West 10	.05	.01	
San Diego Chargers			
☐ 89 Lyle Blackwood 15	.07	.01	
Baltimore Colts			
☐ 90 Gene Upshaw AP 75	.35	.07	
Oakland Raiders			
☐ 91 Frank Grant 10	.05	.01	
Washington Redskins			

☐ 92 Tom Hicks 10	.05	.01
Chicago Bears		
☐ 93 Mike Pruitt 30	.15	.03
Cleveland Browns		
☐ 94 Chris Bahr 15	.07	.01
Cincinnati Bengals		
☐ 95 Russ Francis 35	.17	.03
New England Patriots		
☐ 96 Norris Thomas 10	.05	.01
Miami Dolphins		
☐ 97 Gary Barbaro 50	.25	.05
Kansas City Chiefs		
☐ 98 Jim Merlo 10	.05	.01
New Orleans Saints		
☐ 99 Karl Chandler 10	.05	.01
New York Giants		
☐ 100 Fran Tarkenton 4.50	2.25	.45
Minnesota Vikings		
☐ 101 Abdul Salaam 10	.05	.01
New York Jets		
☐ 102 Marv Kellum 10	.05	.01
St. Louis Cardinals		
☐ 103 Herman Weaver 10	.05	.01
Seattle Seahawks		
☐ 104 Roy Gerela 10	.05	.01
Pittsburgh Steelers		
☐ 105 Harold Jackson 50	.25	.05
New England Patriots		
☐ 106 Dewey Selmon 15	.07	.01
Tampa Bay Buccaneers		
☐ 107 Checklist 1-132 ....1.00	.10	.02
☐ 108 Clarence Davis 10	.05	.01
Oakland Raiders		
☐ 109 Robert Pratt 10	.05	.01
Baltimore Colts		
☐ 110 Harvey Martin AP 50	.25	.05
Dallas Cowboys		
☐ 111 Brad Dusek 10	.05	.01
Washington Redskins		
☐ 112 Greg Latta 10	.05	.01
Chicago Bears		
☐ 113 Tony Peters 10	.05	.01
Cleveland Browns		
☐ 114 Jim Braxton 10	.05	.01
Buffalo Bills		
☐ 115 Ken Riley 15	.07	.01
Cincinnati Bengals		
☐ 116 Steve Nelson 10	.05	.01
New England Patriots		
☐ 117 Rick Upchurch 35	.17	.03
Denver Broncos		
☐ 118 Spike Jones 10	.05	.01
Philadelphia Eagles		
☐ 119 Doug Kotar 10	.05	.01
New York Giants		
☐ 120 Bob Griese AP 2.25	1.10	.22
Miami Dolphins		
☐ 121 Burgess Owens 10	.05	.01
New York Jets		
☐ 122 Rolf Benirschke 50	.25	.05
San Diego Chargers		
☐ 123 Haskel Stanback 35	.17	.03
Atlanta Falcons		
☐ 124 J.T. Thomas 10	.05	.01
Pittsburgh Steelers		
☐ 125 Ahmad Rashad 1.00	.50	.10
Minnesota Vikings		
☐ 126 Rick Kane 10	.05	.01
Detroit Lions		
☐ 127 Elvin Bethea 15	.07	.01
Houston Oilers		
☐ 128 Dave Dalby 15	.07	.01
Oakland Raiders		
☐ 129 Mike Barnes 10	.05	.01
Baltimore Colts		
☐ 130 Isiah Robertson 15	.07	.01
Los Angeles Rams		
☐ 131 Jim Plunkett 75	.35	.07
San Francisco 49ers		
☐ 132 Allan Ellis 10	.05	.01
Chicago Bears		
☐ 133 Mike Bragg 10	.05	.01
Washington Redskins		
☐ 134 Bob Jackson 15	.07	.01
Cleveland Browns		
☐ 135 Coy Bacon 10	.05	.01
Cincinnati Bengals		
☐ 136 John Smith 10	.05	.01
New England Patriots		
☐ 137 Chuck Muncie 30	.15	.03
New Orleans Saints		
☐ 138 Johnnie Gray 10	.05	.01
Green Bay Packers		
☐ 139 Jimmy Robinson 10	.05	.01
New York Giants		
☐ 140 Tom Banks 15	.07	.01
St. Louis Cardinals		
☐ 141 Marvin Powell 50	.25	.05
New York Jets		
☐ 142 Jerrel Wilson 10	.05	.01
Kansas City Chiefs		
☐ 143 Ron Howard 10	.05	.01
Seattle Seahawks		
☐ 144 Rob Lytle 30	.15	.03
Denver Broncos		
☐ 145 L.C. Greenwood 50	.25	.05
Pittsburgh Steelers		
☐ 146 Morris Owens 10	.05	.01
Tampa Bay Buccaneers		
☐ 147 Joe Reed 15	.07	.01
Detroit Lions		
☐ 148 Mike Kadish 10	.05	.01
Buffalo Bills		
☐ 149 Phil Villapiano 15	.07	.01

	Oakland Raiders			
☐ 150	Lydell Mitchell	.25	.12	.02
	Baltimore Colts			
☐ 151	Randy Logan	.10	.05	.01
	Philadelphia Eagles			
☐ 152	Mike Williams	.10	.05	.01
	San Diego Chargers			
☐ 153	Jeff Van Note	.20	.10	.02
	Atlanta Falcons			
☐ 154	Steve Schubert	.10	.05	.01
	Chicago Bears			
☐ 155	Bill Kilmer	.60	.30	.06
	Washington Redskins			
☐ 156	Boobie Clark	.15	.07	.01
	Cincinnati Bengals			
☐ 157	Charlie Hall	.10	.05	.01
	Cleveland Browns			
☐ 158	Raymond Clayborn	.75	.35	.07
	New England Patriots			
☐ 159	Jack Gregory	.15	.07	.01
	New York Giants			
☐ 160	Cliff Harris AP	.50	.25	.05
	Dallas Cowboys			
☐ 161	Joe Fields	.15	.07	.01
	New York Jets			
☐ 162	Don Nottingham	.10	.05	.01
	Miami Dolphins			
☐ 163	Ed White	.15	.07	.01
	Minnesota Vikings			
☐ 164	Toni Fritsch	.10	.05	.01
	Houston Oilers			
☐ 165	Jack Lambert	2.00	1.00	.20
	Pittsburgh Steelers			
☐ 166	NFC Champions	1.50	.75	.15
	Cowboys 23,			
	Vikings 6			
	(Roger Staubach)			
☐ 167	AFC Champions	.30	.15	.03
	Broncos 20,			
	Raiders 17			
	(Lytle running)			
☐ 168	Super Bowl XII	2.50	1.25	.25
	Cowboys 27,			
	Broncos 10			
	(Tony Dorsett)			
☐ 169	Neal Colzie	.35	.17	.03
	Oakland Raiders			
☐ 170	Cleveland Elam AP	.10	.05	.01
	San Francisco 49ers			
☐ 171	David Lee	.10	.05	.01
	Baltimore Colts			
☐ 172	Jim Otis	.15	.07	.01
	St. Louis Cardinals			
☐ 173	Archie Manning	.60	.30	.06
	New Orleans Saints			
☐ 174	Jim Carter	.10	.05	.01
	Green Bay Packers			
☐ 175	Jean Fugett	.10	.05	.01
	Washington Redskins			
☐ 176	Willie Parker	.10	.05	.01
	Buffalo Bills			
☐ 177	Haven Moses	.15	.07	.01
	Denver Broncos			
☐ 178	Horace King	.10	.05	.01
	Detroit Lions			
☐ 179	Bob Thomas	.10	.05	.01
	Chicago Bears			
☐ 180	Monte Jackson	.15	.07	.01
	Los Angeles Rams			
☐ 181	Steve Zabel	.10	.05	.01
	New England Patriots			
☐ 182	John Fitzgerald	.15	.07	.01
	Dallas Cowboys			
☐ 183	Mike Livingston	.15	.07	.01
	Kansas City Chiefs			
☐ 184	Larry Poole	.10	.05	.01
	Cleveland Browns			
☐ 185	Isaac Curtis	.20	.10	.02
	Cincinnati Bengals			
☐ 186	Chuck Ramsey	.10	.05	.01
	New York Jets			
☐ 187	Bob Klein	.10	.05	.01
	San Diego Chargers			
☐ 188	Ray Rhodes	.10	.05	.01
	New York Giants			
☐ 189	Otis Sistrunk	.15	.07	.01
	Oakland Raiders			
☐ 190	Bill Bergey	.30	.15	.03
	Philadelphia Eagles			
☐ 191	Sherman Smith	.15	.07	.01
	Seattle Seahawks			
☐ 192	Dave Green	.10	.05	.01
	Tampa Bay Buccaneers			
☐ 193	Carl Mauck	.10	.05	.01
	Houston Oilers			
☐ 194	Reggie Harrison	.10	.05	.01
	Pittsburgh Steelers			
☐ 195	Roger Carr	.15	.07	.01
	Baltimore Colts			
☐ 196	Steve Bartkowski	.60	.30	.06
	Atlanta Falcons			
☐ 197	Ray Wersching	.10	.05	.01
	San Francisco 49ers			
☐ 198	Willie Buchanon	.15	.07	.01
	Green Bay Packers			
☐ 199	Neil Clabo	.10	.05	.01
	Minnesota Vikings			
☐ 200	Walter Payton AP	15.00	7.50	1.50
	Chicago Bears			
	UER (Born 7/5/54,			
	should be 7/25/54)			
☐ 201	Sam Adams	.10	.05	.01
	New England Patriots			
☐ 202	Larry Gordon	.10	.05	.01

Miami Dolphins			
☐ 203 Pat Tilley	.20	.10	.02
St. Louis Cardinals			
☐ 204 Mack Mitchell	.10	.05	.01
Cleveland Browns			
☐ 205 Ken Anderson	1.25	.60	.12
Cincinnati Bengals			
☐ 206 Scott Dierking	.10	.05	.01
New York Jets			
☐ 207 Jack Rudnay	.10	.05	.01
Kansas City Chiefs			
☐ 208 Jim Stienke	.10	.05	.01
Atlanta Falcons			
☐ 209 Bill Simpson	.10	.05	.01
Los Angeles Rams			
☐ 210 Errol Mann	.10	.05	.01
Oakland Raiders			
☐ 211 Bucky Dilts	.10	.05	.01
Denver Broncos			
☐ 212 Reuben Gant	.10	.05	.01
Buffalo Bills			
☐ 213 Thomas Henderson	.50	.25	.05
Dallas Cowboys			
☐ 214 Steve Furness	.10	.05	.01
Pittsburgh Steelers			
☐ 215 John Riggins	1.25	.60	.12
Washington Redskins			
☐ 216 Keith Krepfle	.35	.17	.03
Philadelphia Eagles			
☐ 217 Fred Dean	1.00	.50	.10
San Diego Chargers			
☐ 218 Emanuel Zanders	.10	.05	.01
New Orleans Saints			
☐ 219 Don Testerman	.10	.05	.01
Seattle Seahawks			
☐ 220 George Kunz	.15	.07	.01
Baltimore Colts			
☐ 221 Darryl Stingley	.25	.12	.02
New England Patriots			
☐ 222 Ken Sanders	.10	.05	.01
Detroit Lions			
☐ 223 Gary Huff	.20	.10	.02
Tampa Bay Buccaneers			
☐ 224 Gregg Bingham	.15	.07	.01
Houston Oilers			
☐ 225 Jerry Sherk	.15	.07	.01
Cleveland Browns			
☐ 226 Doug Plank	.15	.07	.01
Chicago Bears			
☐ 227 Ed Taylor	.10	.05	.01
New York Jets			
☐ 228 Emery Moorehead	.10	.05	.01
New York Giants			
☐ 229 Reggie Williams	2.00	1.00	.20
Cincinnati Bengals			
☐ 230 Claude Humphrey	.15	.07	.01
Atlanta Falcons			
☐ 231 Randy Cross	1.00	.50	.10
San Francisco 49ers			
☐ 232 Jim Hart	.40	.20	.04
St. Louis Cardinals			
☐ 233 Bobby Bryant	.10	.05	.01
Minnesota Vikings			
☐ 234 Larry Brown	.10	.05	.01
Pittsburgh Steelers			
☐ 235 Mark Van Eeghen	.15	.07	.01
Oakland Raiders			
☐ 236 Terry Hermeling	.10	.05	.01
Washington Redskins			
☐ 237 Steve Odom	.15	.07	.01
Green Bay Packers			
☐ 238 Jan Stenerud	.60	.30	.06
Kansas City Chiefs			
☐ 239 Andre Tillman	.10	.05	.01
Miami Dolphins			
☐ 240 Tom Jackson AP	2.50	1.25	.25
Denver Broncos			
☐ 241 Ken Mendenhall	.10	.05	.01
Baltimore Colts			
☐ 242 Tim Fox	.10	.05	.01
New England Patriots			
☐ 243 Don Herrmann	.10	.05	.01
New Orleans Saints			
☐ 244 Eddie McMillan	.10	.05	.01
Seattle Seahawks			
☐ 245 Greg Pruitt	.35	.17	.03
Cleveland Browns			
☐ 246 J.K. McKay	.15	.07	.01
Tampa Bay Buccaneers			
☐ 247 Larry Keller	.10	.05	.01
New York Jets			
☐ 248 Dave Jennings	.15	.07	.01
New York Giants			
☐ 249 Bo Harris	.10	.05	.01
Cincinnati Bengals			
☐ 250 Revie Sorey	.10	.05	.01
Chicago Bears			
☐ 251 Tony Greene	.10	.05	.01
Buffalo Bills			
☐ 252 Butch Johnson	.30	.15	.03
Dallas Cowboys			
☐ 253 Paul Naumoff	.10	.05	.01
Detroit Lions			
☐ 254 Rickey Young	.15	.07	.01
Minnesota Vikings			
☐ 255 Dwight White	.15	.07	.01
Pittsburgh Steelers			
☐ 256 Joe Lavender	.10	.05	.01
Washington Redskins			
☐ 257 Checklist 133-264	1.00	.10	.02
☐ 258 Ronnie Coleman	.10	.05	.01
Houston Oilers			
☐ 259 Charlie Smith	.10	.05	.01
Philadelphia Eagles			

☐ 260	Ray Guy AP 50	.25	.05
	Oakland Raiders		
☐ 261	David Taylor 10	.05	.01
	Baltimore Colts		
☐ 262	Bill Lenkaitis 10	.05	.01
	New England Patriots		
☐ 263	Jim Mitchell 10	.05	.01
	Atlanta Falcons		
☐ 264	Delvin Williams 15	.07	.01
	San Francisco 49ers		
☐ 265	Jack Youngblood 75	.35	.07
	Los Angeles Rams		
☐ 266	Chuck Crist 10	.05	.01
	New Orleans Saints		
☐ 267	Richard Todd 30	.15	.03
	New York Jets		
☐ 268	Dave Logan 30	.15	.03
	Cleveland Browns		
☐ 269	Rufus Mayes 10	.05	.01
	Cincinnati Bengals		
☐ 270	Brad Van Pelt 20	.10	.02
	New York Giants		
☐ 271	Chester Marcol 10	.05	.01
	Green Bay Packers		
☐ 272	J.V. Cain 10	.05	.01
	St. Louis Cardinals		
☐ 273	Larry Seiple 10	.05	.01
	Miami Dolphins		
☐ 274	Brent McClanahan 10	.05	.01
	Minnesota Vikings		
☐ 275	Mike Wagner 15	.07	.01
	Pittsburgh Steelers		
☐ 276	Diron Talbert 15	.07	.01
	Washington Redskins		
☐ 277	Brian Baschnagel 15	.07	.01
	Chicago Bears		
☐ 278	Ed Podolak 15	.07	.01
	Kansas City Chiefs		
☐ 279	Don Goode 10	.05	.01
	San Diego Chargers		
☐ 280	John Dutton 15	.07	.01
	Baltimore Colts		
☐ 281	Don Calhoun 10	.05	.01
	New England Patriots		
☐ 282	Monte Johnson 15	.07	.01
	Oakland Raiders		
☐ 283	Ron Jessie 15	.07	.01
	Los Angeles Rams		
☐ 284	Jon Morris 10	.05	.01
	Detroit Lions		
☐ 285	Riley Odoms 15	.07	.01
	Denver Broncos		
☐ 286	Marv Bateman 10	.05	.01
	Buffalo Bills		
☐ 287	Joe Klecko 3.50	1.75	.35
	New York Jets		
☐ 288	Oliver Davis 10	.05	.01

	Cleveland Browns		
☐ 289	John McDaniel 10	.05	.01
	Cincinnati Bengals		
☐ 290	Roger Staubach 6.00	3.00	.60
	Dallas Cowboys		
☐ 291	Brian Kelley 15	.07	.01
	New York Giants		
☐ 292	Mike Hogan 10	.05	.01
	Philadelphia Eagles		
☐ 293	John Leypoldt 10	.05	.01
	Seattle Seahawks		
☐ 294	Jack Novak 10	.05	.01
	Tampa Bay Buccaneers		
☐ 295	Joe Greene 1.25	.60	.12
	Pittsburgh Steelers		
☐ 296	John Hill 10	.05	.01
	New Orleans Saints		
☐ 297	Danny Buggs 10	.05	.01
	Washington Redskins		
☐ 298	Ted Albrecht 10	.05	.01
	Chicago Bears		
☐ 299	Nelson Munsey 10	.05	.01
	Baltimore Colts		
☐ 300	Chuck Foreman 50	.25	.05
	Minnesota Vikings		
☐ 301	Dan Pastorini 25	.12	.02
	Houston Oilers		
☐ 302	Tommy Hart 10	.05	.01
	Chicago Bears		
☐ 303	Dave Beverly 10	.05	.01
	Green Bay Packers		
☐ 304	Tony Reed 35	.17	.03
	Kansas City Chiefs		
☐ 305	Cliff Branch 60	.30	.06
	Oakland Raiders		
☐ 306	Clarence Duren 10	.05	.01
	San Diego Chargers		
☐ 307	Randy Rasmussen 10	.05	.01
	New York Jets		
☐ 308	Oscar Roan 10	.05	.01
	Cleveland Browns		
☐ 309	Lenvil Elliott 10	.05	.01
	Cincinnati Bengals		
☐ 310	Dan Dierdorf AP 75	.35	.07
	St. Louis Cardinals		
☐ 311	Johnny Perkins 10	.05	.01
	New York Giants		
☐ 312	Rafael Septien 30	.15	.03
	Los Angeles Rams		
☐ 313	Terry Beeson 10	.05	.01
	Seattle Seahawks		
☐ 314	Lee Roy Selmon 60	.30	.06
	Tampa Bay Buccaneers		
☐ 315	Tony Dorsett 32.00	16.00	3.20
	Dallas Cowboys		
☐ 316	Greg Landry 30	.15	.03
	Detroit Lions		

☐ 317	Jake Scott	.15	.07	.01
	Washington Redskins			
☐ 318	Dan Peiffer	.10	.05	.01
	Chicago Bears			
☐ 319	John Bunting	.10	.05	.01
	Philadelphia Eagles			
☐ 320	John Stallworth	12.00	6.00	1.20
	Pittsburgh Steelers			
☐ 321	Bob Howard	.10	.05	.01
	New England Patriots			
☐ 322	Larry Little	.15	.07	.01
	Miami Dolphins			
☐ 323	Reggie McKenzie	.15	.07	.01
	Buffalo Bills			
☐ 324	Duane Carrell	.10	.05	.01
	St. Louis Cardinals			
☐ 325	Ed Simonini	.10	.05	.01
	Baltimore Colts			
☐ 326	John Vella	.10	.05	.01
	Oakland Raiders			
☐ 327	Wesley Walker	3.00	1.50	.30
	New York Jets			
☐ 328	Jon Keyworth	.15	.07	.01
	Denver Broncos			
☐ 329	Ron Bolton	.10	.05	.01
	Cleveland Browns			
☐ 330	Tommy Casanova	.15	.07	.01
	Cincinnati Bengals			
☐ 331	Passing Leaders	2.50	1.25	.25
	Bob Griese			
	Roger Staubach			
☐ 332	Receiving Leaders	.35	.17	.03
	Lydell Mitchell			
	Ahmad Rashad			
☐ 333	Rushing Leaders	2.00	1.00	.20
	Mark Van Eeghen			
	Walter Payton			
☐ 334	Scoring Leaders	2.00	1.00	.20
	Errol Mann			
	Walter Payton			
☐ 335	Interception Leaders	.20	.10	.02
	Lyle Blackwood			
	Rolland Lawrence			
☐ 336	Punting Leaders	.20	.10	.02
	Ray Guy			
	Tom Blanchard			
☐ 337	Robert Brazile	.15	.07	.01
	Houston Oilers			
☐ 338	Charlie Joiner	.75	.35	.07
	San Diego Chargers			
☐ 339	Joe Ferguson	.30	.15	.03
	Buffalo Bills			
☐ 340	Bill Thompson	.15	.07	.01
	Denver Broncos			
☐ 341	Sam Cunningham	.20	.10	.02
	New England Patriots			
☐ 342	Curtis Johnson	.10	.05	.01
	Miami Dolphins			
☐ 343	Jim Marshall	.60	.30	.06
	Minnesota Vikings			
☐ 344	Charlie Sanders	.15	.07	.01
	Detroit Lions			
☐ 345	Willie Hall	.10	.05	.01
	Oakland Raiders			
☐ 346	Pat Haden	.60	.30	.06
	Los Angeles Rams			
☐ 347	Jim Bakken	.15	.07	.01
	St. Louis Cardinals			
☐ 348	Bruce Taylor	.15	.07	.01
	San Francisco 49ers			
☐ 349	Barty Smith	.10	.05	.01
	Green Bay Packers			
☐ 350	Drew Pearson AP	.75	.35	.07
	Dallas Cowboys			
☐ 351	Mike Webster	1.50	.75	.15
	Pittsburgh Steelers			
☐ 352	Bobby Hammond	.10	.05	.01
	New York Giants			
☐ 353	Dave Mays	.10	.05	.01
	Cleveland Browns			
☐ 354	Pat McInally	.20	.10	.02
	Cincinnati Bengals			
☐ 355	Toni Linhart	.10	.05	.01
	Baltimore Colts			
☐ 356	Larry Hand	.10	.05	.01
	Detroit Lions			
☐ 357	Ted Fritsch Jr.	.10	.05	.01
	Washington Redskins			
☐ 358	Larry Marshall	.10	.05	.01
	Philadelphia Eagles			
☐ 359	Waymond Bryant	.10	.05	.01
	Chicago Bears			
☐ 360	Louie Kelcher	.30	.15	.03
	San Diego Chargers			
☐ 361	Stanley Morgan	6.50	3.25	.65
	New England Patriots			
☐ 362	Bruce Harper	.15	.07	.01
	New York Jets			
☐ 363	Bernard Jackson	.15	.07	.01
	Denver Broncos			
☐ 364	Walter White	.10	.05	.01
	Kansas City Chiefs			
☐ 365	Ken Stabler	1.25	.60	.12
	Oakland Raiders			
☐ 366	Fred Dryer	.90	.45	.09
	Los Angeles Rams			
☐ 367	Ike Harris	.10	.05	.01
	New Orleans Saints			
☐ 368	Norm Bulaich	.15	.07	.01
	Miami Dolphins			
☐ 369	Merv Krakau	.10	.05	.01
	Buffalo Bills			
☐ 370	John James	.10	.05	.01
	Atlanta Falcons			

☐ 371	Bennie Cunningham	.30	.15	.03	☐ 400	O.J. Simpson	5.00	2.50	.50
	Pittsburgh Steelers					San Francisco 49ers		
☐ 372	Doug Van Horn	.10	.05	.01	☐ 401	Julius Adams	.10	.05	.01
	New York Giants					New England Patriots		
☐ 373	Thom Darden	.10	.05	.01	☐ 402	Artimus Parker	.10	.05	.01
	Cleveland Browns					New York Jets		
☐ 374	Eddie Edwards	.30	.15	.03	☐ 403	Gene Washington	.25	.12	.02
	Cincinnati Bengals					San Francisco 49ers		
☐ 375	Mike Thomas	.15	.07	.01	☐ 404	Herman Edwards	.10	.05	.01
	Washington Redskins					Philadelphia Eagles		
☐ 376	Fred Cook	.15	.07	.01	☐ 405	Craig Morton	.50	.25	.05
	Baltimore Colts					Denver Broncos		
☐ 377	Mike Phipps	.20	.10	.02	☐ 406	Alan Page	1.00	.50	.10
	Chicago Bears					Minnesota Vikings		
☐ 378	Paul Krause	.25	.12	.02	☐ 407	Larry McCarren	.10	.05	.01
	Minnesota Vikings					Green Bay Packers		
☐ 379	Harold Carmichael	.75	.35	.07	☐ 408	Tony Galbreath	.15	.07	.01
	Philadelphia Eagles					New Orleans Saints		
☐ 380	Mike Haynes AP	.90	.45	.09	☐ 409	Roman Gabriel	.50	.25	.05
	New England Patriots					Los Angeles Rams		
☐ 381	Wayne Morris	.10	.05	.01	☐ 410	Efren Herrera AP	.10	.05	.01
	St. Louis Cardinals					Dallas Cowboys		
☐ 382	Greg Buttle	.15	.07	.01	☐ 411	Jim Smith	.50	.25	.05
	New York Jets					Pittsburgh Steelers		
☐ 383	Jim Zorn	.75	.35	.07	☐ 412	Bill Bryant	.10	.05	.01
	Seattle Seahawks					New York Giants		
☐ 384	Jack Dolbin	.15	.07	.01	☐ 413	Doug Dieken	.10	.05	.01
	Denver Broncos					Cleveland Browns		
☐ 385	Charlie Waters	.45	.22	.04	☐ 414	Marvin Cobb	.10	.05	.01
	Dallas Cowboys					Cincinnati Bengals		
☐ 386	Dan Ryczek	.10	.05	.01	☐ 415	Fred Biletnikoff	1.50	.75	.15
	Los Angeles Rams					Oakland Raiders		
☐ 387	Joe Washington	1.00	.50	.10	☐ 416	Joe Theismann	2.00	1.00	.20
	San Diego Chargers					Washington Redskins		
☐ 388	Checklist 265-396	1.00	.10	.02	☐ 417	Roland Harper	.15	.07	.01
☐ 389	James Hunter	.10	.05	.01		Chicago Bears		
	Detroit Lions				☐ 418	Derrel Luce	.10	.05	.01
☐ 390	Billy Johnson	.25	.12	.02		Baltimore Colts		
	Houston Oilers				☐ 419	Ralph Perretta	.10	.05	.01
☐ 391	Jim Allen	.10	.05	.01		San Diego Chargers		
	Pittsburgh Steelers				☐ 420	Louis Wright	1.00	.50	.10
☐ 392	George Buehler	.10	.05	.01		Denver Broncos		
	Oakland Raiders				☐ 421	Prentice McCray	.10	.05	.01
☐ 393	Harry Carson	1.25	.60	.12		New England Patriots		
	New York Giants				☐ 422	Garry Puetz	.10	.05	.01
☐ 394	Cleo Miller	.10	.05	.01		New York Jets		
	Cleveland Browns				☐ 423	Alfred Jenkins	.50	.25	.05
☐ 395	Gary Burley	.10	.05	.01		Atlanta Falcons		
	Cincinnati Bengals				☐ 424	Paul Seymour	.10	.05	.01
☐ 396	Mark Moseley	.30	.15	.03		Buffalo Bills		
	Washington Redskins				☐ 425	Garo Yepremian	.15	.07	.01
☐ 397	Virgil Livers	.10	.05	.01		Miami Dolphins		
	Chicago Bears				☐ 426	Emmitt Thomas	.15	.07	.01
☐ 398	Joe Ehrmann	.10	.05	.01		Kansas City Chiefs		
	Baltimore Colts				☐ 427	Dexter Bussey	.10	.05	.01
☐ 399	Freddie Solomon	.15	.07	.01		Detroit Lions		
	Miami Dolphins				☐ 428	John Sanders	.10	.05	.01

	Philadelphia Eagles				
☐ 429	Ed Too Tall Jones 1.75	.85	.17		
	Dallas Cowboys				
☐ 430	Ron Yary 15	.07	.01		
	Minnesota Vikings				
☐ 431	Frank Lewis 15	.07	.01		
	Buffalo Bills				
☐ 432	Jerry Golsteyn 10	.05	.01		
	New York Giants				
☐ 433	Clarence Scott 10	.05	.01		
	Cleveland Browns				
☐ 434	Pete Johnson 50	.25	.05		
	Cincinnati Bengals				
☐ 435	Charley Young 15	.07	.01		
	Los Angeles Rams				
☐ 436	Harold McLinton 10	.05	.01		
	Washington Redskins				
☐ 437	Noah Jackson 10	.05	.01		
	Chicago Bears				
☐ 438	Bruce Laird 10	.05	.01		
	Baltimore Colts				
☐ 439	John Matuszak 20	.10	.02		
	Oakland Raiders				
☐ 440	Nat Moore AP 35	.17	.03		
	Miami Dolphins				
☐ 441	Leon Gray 15	.07	.01		
	New England Patriots				
☐ 442	Jerome Barkum 15	.07	.01		
	New York Jets				
☐ 443	Steve Largent 16.00	8.00	1.60		
	Seattle Seahawks				
☐ 444	John Zook 15	.07	.01		
	St. Louis Cardinals				
☐ 445	Preston Pearson 35	.17	.03		
	Dallas Cowboys				
☐ 446	Conrad Dobler 15	.07	.01		
	New Orleans Saints				
☐ 447	Wilbur Summers 10	.05	.01		
	Detroit Lions				
☐ 448	Lou Piccone 10	.05	.01		
	Buffalo Bills				
☐ 449	Ron Jaworski 60	.30	.06		
	Philadelphia Eagles				
☐ 450	Jack Ham AP 1.25	.60	.12		
	Pittsburgh Steelers				
☐ 451	Mick Tingelhoff 20	.10	.02		
	Minnesota Vikings				
☐ 452	Clyde Powers 10	.05	.01		
	New York Giants				
☐ 453	John Cappelletti 35	.17	.03		
	Los Angeles Rams				
☐ 454	Dick Ambrose 10	.05	.01		
	Cleveland Browns				
☐ 455	Lemar Parrish 15	.07	.01		
	Cincinnati Bengals				
☐ 456	Ron Saul 10	.05	.01		
	Washington Redskins				

☐ 457	Bob Parsons 10	.05	.01		
	Chicago Bears				
☐ 458	Glenn Doughty 10	.05	.01		
	Baltimore Colts				
☐ 459	Don Woods 10	.05	.01		
	San Diego Chargers				
☐ 460	Art Shell AP 1.00	.50	.10		
	Oakland Raiders				
☐ 461	Sam Hunt 10	.05	.01		
	New England Patriots				
☐ 462	Lawrence Pillers 10	.05	.01		
	New York Jets				
☐ 463	Henry Childs 10	.05	.01		
	New Orleans Saints				
☐ 464	Roger Wehrli 15	.07	.01		
	St. Louis Cardinals				
☐ 465	Otis Armstrong 30	.15	.03		
	Denver Broncos				
☐ 466	Bob Baumhower 60	.30	.06		
	Miami Dolphins				
☐ 467	Ray Jarvis 10	.05	.01		
	Detroit Lions				
☐ 468	Guy Morriss 10	.05	.01		
	Philadelphia Eagles				
☐ 469	Matt Blair 25	.12	.02		
	Minnesota Vikings				
☐ 470	Billy Joe DuPree 35	.17	.03		
	Dallas Cowboys				
☐ 471	Roland Hooks 10	.05	.01		
	Buffalo Bills				
☐ 472	Joe Danelo 10	.05	.01		
	New York Giants				
☐ 473	Reggie Rucker 15	.07	.01		
	Cleveland Browns				
☐ 474	Vern Holland 10	.05	.01		
	Cincinnati Bengals				
☐ 475	Mel Blount 1.00	.50	.10		
	Pittsburgh Steelers				
☐ 476	Eddie Brown 10	.05	.01		
	Washington Redskins				
☐ 477	Bo Rather 10	.05	.01		
	Chicago Bears				
☐ 478	Don McCauley 10	.05	.01		
	Baltimore Colts				
☐ 479	Glen Walker 10	.05	.01		
	Los Angeles Rams				
☐ 480	Randy Gradishar AP 60	.30	.06		
	Denver Broncos				
☐ 481	Dave Rowe 10	.05	.01		
	Oakland Raiders				
☐ 482	Pat Leahy 50	.25	.05		
	New York Jets				
☐ 483	Mike Fuller 10	.05	.01		
	San Diego Chargers				
☐ 484	David Lewis 10	.05	.01		
	Tampa Bay Buccaneers				
☐ 485	Steve Grogan 75	.35	.07		

New England Patriots
| □ 486 | Mel Gray | .15 | .07 | .01 |

St. Louis Cardinals
| □ 487 | Eddie Payton | .35 | .17 | .03 |

Detroit Lions
| □ 488 | Checklist 397-528 | 1.00 | .10 | .02 |
| □ 489 | Stu Voigt | .15 | .07 | .01 |

Minnesota Vikings
| □ 490 | Rolland Lawrence AP | .15 | .07 | .01 |

Atlanta Falcons
| □ 491 | Nick Mike-Mayer | .10 | .05 | .01 |

Philadelphia Eagles
| □ 492 | Troy Archer | .15 | .07 | .01 |

New York Giants
| □ 493 | Benny Malone | .10 | .05 | .01 |

Miami Dolphins
| □ 494 | Golden Richards | .15 | 07 | .01 |

Dallas Cowboys
| □ 495 | Chris Hanburger | .15 | .07 | .01 |

Washington Redskins
| □ 496 | Dwight Harrison | .10 | .05 | .01 |

Buffalo Bills
| □ 497 | Gary Fencik | 1.00 | .50 | .10 |

Chicago Bears
| □ 498 | Rich Saul | .10 | .05 | .01 |

Los Angeles Rams
| □ 499 | Dan Fouts | 4.50 | 2.25 | .45 |

San Diego Chargers
| □ 500 | Franco Harris AP | 2.25 | 1.10 | .22 |

Pittsburgh Steelers
| □ 501 | Atlanta Falcons TL | .40 | .20 | .04 |

Haskel Stanback
Alfred Jenkins
Claude Humphrey
Jeff Merrow
Rolland Lawrence
| □ 502 | Baltimore Colts TL | .40 | .20 | .04 |

Lydell Mitchell
Lydell Mitchell
Lyle Blackwood
Fred Cook
| □ 503 | Buffalo Bills TL | 1.00 | .50 | .10 |

O.J. Simpson
Bob Chandler
Tony Greene
Sherman White
| □ 504 | Chicago Bears TL | 1.50 | .75 | .15 |

Walter Payton
James Scott
Allan Ellis
Ron Rydalch
| □ 505 | Cincinnati Bengals TL | .75 | .35 | .07 |

Pete Johnson
Billy Brooks
Lemar Parrish
Reggie Williams
Gary Burley

| □ 506 | Cleveland Browns TL | .40 | .20 | .04 |

Greg Pruitt
Reggie Rucker
Thom Darden
Mack Mitchell
| □ 507 | Dallas Cowboys TL | 1.50 | .75 | .15 |

Tony Dorsett
Drew Pearson
Cliff Harris
Harvey Martin
| □ 508 | Denver Broncos TL | .50 | .25 | .05 |

Otis Armstrong
Haven Moses
Bill Thompson
Rick Upchurch
| □ 509 | Detroit Lions TL | .40 | .20 | .04 |

Horace King
David Hill
James Hunter
Ken Sanders
| □ 510 | Green Bay Packers TL | .40 | .20 | .04 |

Barty Smith
Steve Odom
Steve Luke
Mike C. McCoy
Dave Pureifory
Dave Roller
| □ 511 | Houston Oilers TL | .40 | .20 | .04 |

Ronnie Coleman
Ken Burrough
Mike Reinfeldt
James Young
| □ 512 | Kansas City Chiefs TL | .40 | .20 | .04 |

Ed Podolak
Walter White
Gary Barbaro
Wilbur Young
| □ 513 | Los Angeles Rams TL | .50 | .25 | .05 |

Lawrence McCutcheon
Harold Jackson
Bill Simpson
Jack Youngblood
| □ 514 | Miami Dolphins TL | .40 | .20 | .04 |

Benny Malone
Nat Moore
Curtis Johnson
A.J. Duhe
| □ 515 | Minnesota Vikings TL | .40 | .20 | .04 |

Chuck Foreman
Sammie White
Bobby Bryant
Carl Eller
| □ 516 | New England Pats TL | .50 | .25 | .05 |

Sam Cunningham
Darryl Stingley
Mike Haynes
Tony McGee

☐ 517	New Orleans Saints TL ..40	.20	.04
	Chuck Muncie		
	Don Herrmann		
	Chuck Crist		
	Elois Grooms		
☐ 518	New York Giants TL .... .40	.20	.04
	Bobby Hammond		
	Jimmy Robinson		
	Bill Bryant		
	John Mendenhall		
☐ 519	New York Jets TL .... .75	.35	.07
	Clark Gaines		
	Wesley Walker		
	Burgess Owens		
	Joe Klecko		
☐ 520	Oakland Raiders TL .... .50	.25	.05
	Mark Van Eeghen		
	Dave Casper		
	Jack Tatum		
	Neal Colzie		
☐ 521	Philadelphia Eagles TL ..40	.20	.04
	Mike Hogan		
	Harold Carmichael		
	Herman Edwards		
	John Sanders		
	Lem Burnham		
☐ 522	Pittsburgh Steelers TL 1.00	.50	.10
	Franco Harris		
	Jim Smith		
	Mel Blount		
	Steve Furness		
☐ 523	St.Louis Cardinals TL ..... .40	.20	.04
	Terry Metcalf		
	Mel Gray		
	Roger Wehrli		
	Mike Dawson		
☐ 524	San Diego Chargers TL ..40	.20	.04
	Rickey Young		
	Charlie Joiner		
	Mike Fuller		
	Gary Johnson		
☐ 525	San Francisco 49ers TL .40	.20	.04
	Delvin Williams		
	Gene Washington		
	Mel Phillips		
	Dave Washington		
	Cleveland Elam		
☐ 526	Seattle Seahawks TL ... 1.25	.60	.12
	Sherman Smith		
	Steve Largent		
	Autry Beamon		
	Walter Packer		
☐ 527	Tampa Bay Bucs TL .... .40	.20	.04
	Morris Owens		
	Isaac Hagins		
	Mike Washington		
	Lee Roy Selmon		

☐ 528	Wash. Redskins TL .... .75	.25	.05
	Mike Thomas		
	Jean Fugett		
	Ken Houston		
	Dennis Johnson		

1979 Topps

The 1979 Topps football set contains 528 cards. The cards measure 2 1/2" by 3 1/2". No known scarcities exist. The first six cards feature the AFC and NFC statistical leaders from the previous season. Post-season playoff action is summarized on cards 166-168. Record Breakers (RB) of the past season are featured on cards 331-336. Distributed throughout the set are Team Leader (TL) cards depicting, typically, four individual team (statistical) leaders on the front and a team checklist on the back. All-Pro (AP) selections are designated on the player's regular card, not a special card. The set features the first and only Topps cards of Earl Campbell. Other notable rookie cards in this set are Steve DeBerg, James Lofton, Ozzie Newsome, and Doug Williams. The card backs are printed in yellow and blue.

	NRMT	VG-E	GOOD
COMPLETE SET (528)	120.00	60.00	12.00
COMMON PLAYER (1-528)	.08	.04	.01
☐ 1 Passing Leaders 4.50		1.25	.25
Roger Staubach			
Terry Bradshaw			
☐ 2 Receiving Leaders .... .75		.35	.07
Rickey Young			

Steve Largent
- [ ] 3 Rushing Leaders .... 5.50   2.75   .55
  Walter Payton
  Earl Campbell
- [ ] 4 Scoring Leaders .... .20   .10   .02
  Frank Corral
  Pat Leahy
- [ ] 5 Interception Leaders .... .15   .07   .01
  Willie Buchanon
  Ken Stone
  Thom Darden
- [ ] 6 Punting Leaders .... .15   .07   .01
  Tom Skladany
  Pat McInally
- [ ] 7 Johnny Perkins .... .08   .04   .01
  New York Giants
- [ ] 8 Charles Phillips .... .08   .04   .01
  Oakland Raiders
- [ ] 9 Derrel Luce .... .08   .04   .01
  Baltimore Colts
- [ ] 10 John Riggins .... 1.25   .60   .12
  Washington Redskins
- [ ] 11 Chester Marcol .... .08   .04   .01
  Green Bay Packers
- [ ] 12 Bernard Jackson .... .12   .06   .01
  Denver Broncos
- [ ] 13 Dave Logan .... .12   .06   .01
  Cleveland Browns
- [ ] 14 Bo Harris .... .08   .04   .01
  Cincinnati Bengals
- [ ] 15 Alan Page .... .75   .35   .07
  Minnesota Vikings
- [ ] 16 John Smith .... .08   .04   .01
  New England Patriots
- [ ] 17 Dwight McDonald .... .08   .04   .01
  San Diego Chargers
- [ ] 18 John Cappelletti .... .25   .12   .02
  Los Angeles Rams
- [ ] 19 Pittsburgh Steelers TL ...... .75   .35   .07
  Franco Harris
  Larry Anderson
  Tony Dungy
  L.C. Greenwood
- [ ] 20 Bill Bergey AP .... .30   .15   .03
  Philadelphia Eagles
- [ ] 21 Jerome Barkum .... .12   .06   .01
  New York Jets
- [ ] 22 Larry Csonka .... 1.25   .60   .12
  Miami Dolphins
- [ ] 23 Joe Ferguson .... .20   .10   .02
  Buffalo Bills
- [ ] 24 Ed Too Tall Jones .... 1.00   .50   .10
  Dallas Cowboys
- [ ] 25 Dave Jennings .... .12   .06   .01
  New York Giants
- [ ] 26 Horace King .... .08   .04   .01
  Detroit Lions
- [ ] 27 Steve Little .... .08   .04   .01
  St. Louis Cardinals
- [ ] 28 Morris Bradshaw .... .08   .04   .01
  Oakland Raiders
- [ ] 29 Joe Ehrmann .... .08   .04   .01
  Baltimore Colts
- [ ] 30 Ahmad Rashad AP .... .75   .35   .07
  Minnesota Vikings
- [ ] 31 Joe Lavender .... .08   .04   .01
  Washington Redskins
- [ ] 32 Dan Neal .... .08   .04   .01
  Chicago Bears
- [ ] 33 Johnny Evans .... .08   .04   .01
  Cleveland Browns
- [ ] 34 Pete Johnson .... .12   .06   .01
  Cincinnati Bengals
- [ ] 35 Mike Haynes AP .... .50   .25   .05
  New England Patriots
- [ ] 36 Tim Mazzetti .... .08   .04   .01
  Atlanta Falcons
- [ ] 37 Mike Barber .... .20   .10   .02
  Houston Oilers
- [ ] 38 San Francisco 49ers TL ...... .90   .45   .09
  O.J. Simpson
  Freddie Solomon
  Chuck Crist
  Cedrick Hardman
- [ ] 39 Bill Gregory .... .08   .04   .01
  Seattle Seahawks
- [ ] 40 Randy Gradishar AP .... .45   .22   .04
  Denver Broncos
- [ ] 41 Richard Todd .... .25   .12   .02
  New York Jets
- [ ] 42 Henry Marshall .... .08   .04   .01
  Kansas City Chiefs
- [ ] 43 John Hill .... .08   .04   .01
  New Orleans Saints
- [ ] 44 Sidney Thornton .... .08   .04   .01
  Pittsburgh Steelers
- [ ] 45 Ron Jessie .... .12   .06   .01
  Los Angeles Rams
- [ ] 46 Bob Baumhower .... .15   .07   .01
  Miami Dolphins
- [ ] 47 Johnnie Gray .... .08   .04   .01
  Green Bay Packers
- [ ] 48 Doug Williams .... 1.75   .85   .17
  Tampa Bay Buccaneers
- [ ] 49 Don McCauley .... .08   .04   .01
  Baltimore Colts
- [ ] 50 Ray Guy AP .... .35   .17   .03
  Oakland Raiders
- [ ] 51 Bob Klein .... .08   .04   .01
  San Diego Chargers
- [ ] 52 Golden Richards .... .12   .06   .01
  Chicago Bears
- [ ] 53 Mark Miller .... .12   .06   .01
  Cleveland Browns

☐ 54 John Sanders	.08	.04	.01
Philadelphia Eagles			
☐ 55 Gary Burley	.08	.04	.01
Cincinnati Bengals			
☐ 56 Steve Nelson	.08	.04	.01
New England Patriots			
☐ 57 Buffalo Bills TL	.30	.15	.03
Terry Miller			
Frank Lewis			
Mario Clark			
Lucius Sanford			
☐ 58 Bobby Bryant	.08	.04	.01
Minnesota Vikings			
☐ 59 Rick Kane	.08	.04	.01
Detroit Lions			
☐ 60 Larry Little	.15	.07	.01
Miami Dolphins			
☐ 61 Ted Fritsch Jr.	.08	.04	.01
Washington Redskins			
☐ 62 Larry Mallory	.08	.04	.01
New York Giants			
☐ 63 Marvin Powell	.12	.06	.01
New York Jets			
☐ 64 Jim Hart	.35	.17	.03
St. Louis Cardinals			
☐ 65 Joe Greene AP	1.25	.60	.12
Pittsburgh Steelers			
☐ 66 Walter White	.08	.04	.01
Kansas City Chiefs			
☐ 67 Gregg Bingham	.12	.06	.01
Houston Oilers			
☐ 68 Errol Mann	.08	.04	.01
Oakland Raiders			
☐ 69 Bruce Laird	.08	.04	.01
Baltimore Colts			
☐ 70 Drew Pearson	.60	.30	.06
Dallas Cowboys			
☐ 71 Steve Bartkowski	.60	.30	.06
Atlanta Falcons			
☐ 72 Ted Albrecht	.08	.04	.01
Chicago Bears			
☐ 73 Charlie Hall	.08	.04	.01
Cleveland Browns			
☐ 74 Pat McInally	.15	.07	.01
Cincinnati Bengals			
☐ 75 Al(Bubba) Baker AP	.60	.30	.06
Detroit Lions			
☐ 76 New England Pats TL	.40	.20	.04
Sam Cunningham			
Stanley Morgan			
Mike Haynes			
Tony McGee			
☐ 77 Steve DeBerg	7.00	3.50	.70
San Francisco 49ers			
☐ 78 John Yarno	.08	.04	.01
Seattle Seahawks			
☐ 79 Stu Voigt	.12	.06	.01
Minnesota Vikings			
☐ 80 Frank Corral AP	.08	.04	.01
Los Angeles Rams			
☐ 81 Troy Archer	.08	.04	.01
New York Giants			
☐ 82 Bruce Harper	.08	.04	.01
New York Jets			
☐ 83 Tom Jackson	.75	.35	.07
Denver Broncos			
☐ 84 Larry Brown	.08	.04	.01
Pittsburgh Steelers			
☐ 85 Wilbert Montgomery AP	1.00	.50	.10
Philadelphia Eagles			
☐ 86 Butch Johnson	.20	.10	.02
Dallas Cowboys			
☐ 87 Mike Kadish	.08	.04	.01
Buffalo Bills			
☐ 88 Ralph Perretta	.08	.04	.01
San Diego Chargers			
☐ 89 David Lee	.08	.04	.01
Baltimore Colts			
☐ 90 Mark Van Eeghen	.12	.06	.01
Oakland Raiders			
☐ 91 John McDaniel	.08	.04	.01
Washington Redskins			
☐ 92 Gary Fencik	.15	.07	.01
Chicago Bears			
☐ 93 Mack Mitchell	.08	.04	.01
Cleveland Browns			
☐ 94 Cincinnati Bengals TL	.35	.17	.03
Pete Johnson			
Isaac Curtis			
Dick Jauron			
Ross Browner			
☐ 95 Steve Grogan	.50	.25	.05
New England Patriots			
☐ 96 Garo Yepremian	.15	.07	.01
Miami Dolphins			
☐ 97 Barty Smith	.08	.04	.01
Green Bay Packers			
☐ 98 Frank Reed	.08	.04	.01
Atlanta Falcons			
☐ 99 Jim Clark	.08	.04	.01
New York Giants			
☐ 100 Chuck Foreman	.40	.20	.04
Minnesota Vikings			
☐ 101 Joe Klecko	.75	.35	.07
New York Jets			
☐ 102 Pat Tilley	.15	.07	.01
St. Louis Cardinals			
☐ 103 Conrad Dobler	.15	.07	.01
New Orleans Saints			
☐ 104 Craig Colquitt	.15	.07	.01
Pittsburgh Steelers			
☐ 105 Dan Pastorini	.20	.10	.02
Houston Oilers			
☐ 106 Rod Perry AP	.12	.06	.01

Los Angeles Rams			
☐ 107 Nick Mike-Mayer 08	.04	.01	
Philadelphia Eagles			
☐ 108 John Matuszak 15	.07	.01	
Oakland Raiders			
☐ 109 David Taylor 08	.04	.01	
Baltimore Colts			
☐ 110 Billy Joe DuPree AP 25	.12	.02	
Dallas Cowboys			
☐ 111 Harold McLinton 08	.04	.01	
Washington Redskins			
☐ 112 Virgil Livers 08	.04	.01	
Chicago Bears			
☐ 113 Cleveland Browns TL 35	.17	.03	
Greg Pruitt			
Reggie Rucker			
Thom Darden			
Mack Mitchell			
☐ 114 Checklist 1-132 80	.08	.01	
☐ 115 Ken Anderson 1.00	.50	.10	
Cincinnati Bengals			
☐ 116 Bill Lenkaitis 08	.04	.01	
New England Patriots			
☐ 117 Bucky Dilts 08	.04	.01	
Denver Broncos			
☐ 118 Tony Greene 08	.04	.01	
Buffalo Bills			
☐ 119 Bobby Hammond 08	.04	.01	
New York Giants			
☐ 120 Nat Moore 15	.07	.01	
Miami Dolphins			
☐ 121 Pat Leahy AP 35	.17	.03	
New York Jets			
☐ 122 James Harris 15	.07	.01	
San Diego Chargers			
☐ 123 Lee Roy Selmon 35	.17	.03	
Tampa Bay Buccaneers			
☐ 124 Bennie Cunningham 12	.06	.01	
Pittsburgh Steelers			
☐ 125 Matt Blair AP 15	.07	.01	
Minnesota Vikings			
☐ 126 Jim Allen 08	.04	.01	
Detroit Lions			
☐ 127 Alfred Jenkins 12	.06	.01	
Atlanta Falcons			
☐ 128 Arthur Whittington 15	.07	.01	
Oakland Raiders			
☐ 129 Norm Thompson 08	.04	.01	
Baltimore Colts			
☐ 130 Pat Haden 40	.20	.04	
Los Angeles Rams			
☐ 131 Freddie Solomon 12	.06	.01	
San Francisco 49ers			
☐ 132 Chicago Bears TL 1.00	.50	.10	
Walter Payton			
James Scott			
Gary Fencik			

Alan Page			
☐ 133 Mark Moseley 20	.10	.02	
Washington Redskins			
☐ 134 Cleo Miller 08	.04	.01	
Cleveland Browns			
☐ 135 Ross Browner 30	.15	.03	
Cincinnati Bengals			
☐ 136 Don Calhoun 08	.04	.01	
New England Patriots			
☐ 137 David Whitehurst 15	.07	.01	
Green Bay Packers			
☐ 138 Terry Beeson 08	.04	.01	
Seattle Seahawks			
☐ 139 Ken Stone 08	.04	.01	
St. Louis Cardinals			
☐ 140 Brad Van Pelt AP 15	.07	.01	
New York Giants			
☐ 141 Wesley Walker AP 75	.35	.07	
New York Jets			
☐ 142 Jan Stenerud 50	.25	.05	
Kansas City Chiefs			
☐ 143 Henry Childs 08	.04	.01	
New Orleans Saints			
☐ 144 Otis Armstrong 25	.12	.02	
Denver Broncos			
☐ 145 Dwight White 12	.06	.01	
Pittsburgh Steelers			
☐ 146 Steve Wilson 08	.04	.01	
Tampa Bay Buccaneers			
☐ 147 Tom Skladany AP 20	.10	.02	
Detroit Lions			
☐ 148 Lou Piccone 08	.04	.01	
Buffalo Bills			
☐ 149 Monte Johnson 12	.06	.01	
Oakland Raiders			
☐ 150 Joe Washington 20	.10	.02	
Baltimore Colts			
☐ 151 Philadelphia Eagles TL ..35	.17	.03	
Wilbert Montgomery			
Harold Carmichael			
Herman Edwards			
Dennis Harrison			
☐ 152 Fred Dean 20	.10	.02	
San Diego Chargers			
☐ 153 Rolland Lawrence 12	.06	.01	
Atlanta Falcons			
☐ 154 Brian Baschnagel 12	.06	.01	
Chicago Bears			
☐ 155 Joe Theismann 1.50	.75	.15	
Washington Redskins			
☐ 156 Marvin Cobb 08	.04	.01	
Cincinnati Bengals			
☐ 157 Dick Ambrose 08	.04	.01	
Cleveland Browns			
☐ 158 Mike Patrick 08	.04	.01	
New England Patriots			
☐ 159 Gary Shirk 08	.04	.01	

New York Giants
☐ 160 Tony Dorsett .... 6.50 | 3.25 | .65

Dallas Cowboys
☐ 161 Greg Buttle .... .12 | .06 | .01

New York Jets
☐ 162 A.J. Duhe .... .12 | .06 | .01

Miami Dolphins
☐ 163 Mick Tingelhoff .... .15 | .07 | .01

Minnesota Vikings
☐ 164 Ken Burrough .... .12 | .06 | .01

Houston Oilers
☐ 165 Mike Wagner .... .12 | .06 | .01

Pittsburgh Steelers
☐ 166 AFC Championship ...... 1.00 | .50 | .10
Steelers 34,
Oilers 5
(Franco Harris)

☐ 167 NFC Championship .... .30 | .15 | .03
Cowboys 28,
Rams 0
(line of scrimmage)

☐ 168 Super Bowl XIII .... 1.25 | .60 | .12
Steelers 35,
Cowboys 31
(Franco Harris)

☐ 169 Oakland Raiders TL .... .50 | .25 | .05
Mark Van Eeghen
Dave Casper
Charles Phillips
Ted Hendricks

☐ 170 O.J. Simpson .... 4.50 | 2.25 | .45
San Francisco 49ers

☐ 171 Doug Nettles .... .08 | .04 | .01
Baltimore Colts

☐ 172 Dan Dierdorf AP .... .60 | .30 | .06
St. Louis Cardinals

☐ 173 Dave Beverly .... .08 | .04 | .01
Green Bay Packers

☐ 174 Jim Zorn .... .35 | .17 | .03
Seattle Seahawks

☐ 175 Mike Thomas .... .12 | .06 | .01
Washington Redskins

☐ 176 John Outlaw .... .08 | .04 | .01
Philadelphia Eagles

☐ 177 Jim Turner .... .12 | .06 | .01
Denver Broncos

☐ 178 Freddie Scott .... .08 | .04 | .01
Detroit Lions

☐ 179 Mike Phipps .... .15 | .07 | .01
Chicago Bears

☐ 180 Jack Youngblood AP ...... .75 | .35 | .07
Los Angeles Rams

☐ 181 Sam Hunt .... .08 | .04 | .01
New England Patriots

☐ 182 Tony Hill .... 1.25 | .60 | .12
Dallas Cowboys

☐ 183 Gary Barbaro .... .15 | .07 | .01

Kansas City Chiefs
☐ 184 Archie Griffin .... .30 | .15 | .03

Cincinnati Bengals
☐ 185 Jerry Sherk .... .12 | .06 | .01

Cleveland Browns
☐ 186 Bobby Jackson .... .08 | .04 | .01

New York Jets
☐ 187 Don Woods .... .08 | .04 | .01

San Diego Chargers
☐ 188 New York Giants TL .... .30 | .15 | .03
Doug Kotar
Jimmy Robinson
Terry Jackson
George Martin

☐ 189 Raymond Chester .... .12 | .06 | .01
Oakland Raiders

☐ 190 Joe DeLamielleure AP .... .12 | .06 | .01
Buffalo Bills

☐ 191 Tony Galbreath .... .12 | .06 | .01
New Orleans Saints

☐ 192 Robert Brazile AP .... .12 | .06 | .01
Houston Oilers

☐ 193 Neil O'Donoghue .... .08 | .04 | .01
Tampa Bay Buccaneers

☐ 194 Mike Webster AP .... .75 | .35 | .07
Pittsburgh Steelers

☐ 195 Ed Simonini .... .08 | .04 | .01
Baltimore Colts

☐ 196 Benny Malone .... .08 | .04 | .01
Washington Redskins

☐ 197 Tom Wittum .... .08 | .04 | .01
San Francisco 49ers

☐ 198 Steve Largent AP .... 7.50 | 3.75 | .75
Seattle Seahawks

☐ 199 Tommy Hart .... .08 | .04 | .01
Chicago Bears

☐ 200 Fran Tarkenton .... 4.00 | 2.00 | .40
Minnesota Vikings

☐ 201 Leon Gray AP .... .12 | .06 | .01
New England Patriots

☐ 202 Leroy Harris .... .08 | .04 | .01
Miami Dolphins

☐ 203 Eric Williams .... .08 | .04 | .01
St. Louis Cardinals

☐ 204 Thom Darden AP .... .12 | .06 | .01
Cleveland Browns

☐ 205 Ken Riley .... .15 | .07 | .01
Cincinnati Bengals

☐ 206 Clark Gaines .... .08 | .04 | .01
New York Jets

☐ 207 Kansas City Chiefs TL .... .35 | .17 | .03
Tony Reed
Tony Reed
Tim Gray
Art Still

☐ 208 Joe Danelo .... .08 | .04 | .01
New York Giants

☐ 209	Glen Walker 08	.04	.01	
	Los Angeles Rams			
☐ 210	Art Shell 75	.35	.07	
	Oakland Raiders			
☐ 211	Jon Keyworth 12	.06	.01	
	Denver Broncos			
☐ 212	Herman Edwards 08	.04	.01	
	Philadelphia Eagles			
☐ 213	John Fitzgerald 12	.06	.01	
	Dallas Cowboys			
☐ 214	Jim Smith 15	.07	.01	
	Pittsburgh Steelers			
☐ 215	Coy Bacon 08	.04	.01	
	Washington Redskins			
☐ 216	Dennis Johnson 08	.04	.01	
	Buffalo Bills			
☐ 217	John Jefferson 2.50	1.25	.25	
	San Diego Chargers			
☐ 218	Gary Weaver 08	.04	.01	
	Green Bay Packers			
☐ 219	Tom Blanchard 08	.04	.01	
	New Orleans Saints			
☐ 220	Bert Jones 50	.25	.05	
	Baltimore Colts			
☐ 221	Stanley Morgan 1.50	.75	.15	
	New England Patriots			
☐ 222	James Hunter 08	.04	.01	
	Detroit Lions			
☐ 223	Jim O'Bradovich 08	.04	.01	
	Tampa Bay Buccaneers			
☐ 224	Carl Mauck 08	.04	.01	
	Houston Oilers			
☐ 225	Chris Bahr 12	.06	.01	
	Cincinnati Bengals			
☐ 226	New York Jets TL 50	.25	.05	
	Kevin Long			
	Wesley Walker			
	Bobby Jackson			
	Burgess Owens			
	Joe Klecko			
☐ 227	Roland Harper 12	.06	.01	
	Chicago Bears			
☐ 228	Randy Dean 08	.04	.01	
	New York Giants			
☐ 229	Bob Jackson 08	.04	.01	
	Cleveland Browns			
☐ 230	Sammie White 20	.10	.02	
	Minnesota Vikings			
☐ 231	Mike Dawson 12	.06	.01	
	St. Louis Cardinals			
☐ 232	Checklist 133-264 80	.08	.01	
☐ 233	Ken MacAfee 15	.07	.01	
	San Francisco 49ers			
☐ 234	Jon Kolb AP 12	.06	.01	
	Pittsburgh Steelers			
☐ 235	Willie Hall 08	.04	.01	
	Oakland Raiders			

☐ 236	Ron Saul AP 08	.04	.01	
	Washington Redskins			
☐ 237	Haskel Stanback 20	.10	.02	
	Atlanta Falcons			
☐ 238	Zenon Andrusyshyn 08	.04	.01	
	Kansas City Chiefs			
☐ 239	Norris Thomas 08	.04	.01	
	Miami Dolphins			
☐ 240	Rick Upchurch 25	.12	.02	
	Denver Broncos			
☐ 241	Robert Pratt 08	.04	.01	
	Baltimore Colts			
☐ 242	Julius Adams 08	.04	.01	
	New England Patriots			
☐ 243	Rich McGeorge 08	.04	.01	
	Green Bay Packers			
☐ 244	Seattle Seahawks TL 75	.35	.07	
	Sherman Smith			
	Steve Largent			
	Cornell Webster			
	Bill Gregory			
☐ 245	Blair Bush 30	.15	.03	
	Cincinnati Bengals			
☐ 246	Billy Johnson 20	.10	.02	
	Houston Oilers			
☐ 247	Randy Rasmussen 08	.04	.01	
	New York Jets			
☐ 248	Brian Kelley 12	.06	.01	
	New York Giants			
☐ 249	Mike Pruitt 20	.10	.02	
	Cleveland Browns			
☐ 250	Harold Carmichael AP ...60	.30	.06	
	Philadelphia Eagles			
☐ 251	Mike Hartenstine 08	.04	.01	
	Chicago Bears			
☐ 252	Robert Newhouse 20	.10	.02	
	Dallas Cowboys			
☐ 253	Gary Danielson 30	.15	.03	
	Detroit Lions			
☐ 254	Mike Fuller 08	.04	.01	
	San Diego Chargers			
☐ 255	L.C. Greenwood AP 35	.17	.03	
	Pittsburgh Steelers			
☐ 256	Lemar Parrish 12	.06	.01	
	Washington Redskins			
☐ 257	Ike Harris 08	.04	.01	
	New Orleans Saints			
☐ 258	Ricky Bell 1.25	.60	.12	
	Tampa Bay Buccaneers			
☐ 259	Willie Parker 08	.04	.01	
	Buffalo Bills			
☐ 260	Gene Upshaw 60	.30	.06	
	Oakland Raiders			
☐ 261	Glenn Doughty 08	.04	.01	
	Baltimore Colts			
☐ 262	Steve Zabel 08	.04	.01	
	New England Patriots			

☐ 263	Atlanta Falcons TL .... .30	.15	.03
	Bubba Bean		
	Wallace Francis		
	Rolland Lawrence		
	Greg Brezina		
☐ 264	Ray Wersching .... .08	.04	.01
	San Francisco 49ers		
☐ 265	Lawrence McCutcheon .. .20	.10	.02
	Los Angeles Rams		
☐ 266	Willie Buchanon AP .... .15	.07	.01
	Green Bay Packers		
☐ 267	Matt Robinson .... .15	.07	.01
	New York Jets		
☐ 268	Reggie Rucker .... .12	.06	.01
	Cleveland Browns		
☐ 269	Doug Van Horn .... .08	.04	.01
	New York Giants		
☐ 270	Lydell Mitchell .... .15	.07	.01
	San Diego Chargers		
☐ 271	Vern Holland .... .08	.04	.01
	Cincinnati Bengals		
☐ 272	Eason Ramson .... .08	.04	.01
	St. Louis Cardinals		
☐ 273	Steve Towle .... .08	.04	.01
	Miami Dolphins		
☐ 274	Jim Marshall .... .50	.25	.05
	Minnesota Vikings		
☐ 275	Mel Blount .... .75	.35	.07
	Pittsburgh Steelers		
☐ 276	Bob Kuziel .... .08	.04	.01
	Washington Redskins		
☐ 277	James Scott .... .08	.04	.01
	Chicago Bears		
☐ 278	Tony Reed .... .12	.06	.01
	Kansas City Chiefs		
☐ 279	Dave Green .... .08	.04	.01
	Tampa Bay Buccaneers		
☐ 280	Toni Linhart .... .08	.04	.01
	Baltimore Colts		
☐ 281	Andy Johnson .... .08	.04	.01
	New England Patriots		
☐ 282	Los Angeles Rams TL .... .30	.15	.03
	Cullen Bryant		
	Willie Miller		
	Rod Perry		
	Pat Thomas		
	Larry Brooks		
☐ 283	Phil Villapiano .... .12	.06	.01
	Oakland Raiders		
☐ 284	Dexter Bussey .... .08	.04	.01
	Detroit Lions		
☐ 285	Craig Morton .... .50	.25	.05
	Denver Broncos		
☐ 286	Guy Morriss .... .08	.04	.01
	Philadelphia Eagles		
☐ 287	Lawrence Pillers .... .08	.04	.01
	New York Jets		
☐ 288	Gerald Irons .... .08	.04	.01
	Cleveland Browns		
☐ 289	Scott Perry .... .08	.04	.01
	Cincinnati Bengals		
☐ 290	Randy White AP 1.25	.60	.12
	Dallas Cowboys		
☐ 291	Jack Gregory .... .12	.06	.01
	New York Giants		
☐ 292	Bob Chandler .... .12	.06	.01
	Buffalo Bills		
☐ 293	Rich Szaro .... .08	.04	.01
	New Orleans Saints		
☐ 294	Sherman Smith .... .12	.06	.01
	Seattle Seahawks		
☐ 295	Tom Banks AP .... .12	.06	.01
	St. Louis Cardinals		
☐ 296	Revie Sorey AP .... .12	.06	.01
	Chicago Bears		
☐ 297	Ricky Thompson .... .08	.04	.01
	Washington Redskins		
☐ 298	Ron Yary .... .15	.07	.01
	Minnesota Vikings		
☐ 299	Lyle Blackwood .... .12	.06	.01
	Baltimore Colts		
☐ 300	Franco Harris 2.00	1.00	.20
	Pittsburgh Steelers		
☐ 301	Houston Oilers TL 2.75	1.35	.27
	Earl Campbell		
	Ken Burrough		
	Willie Alexander		
	Elvin Bethea		
☐ 302	Scott Bull .... .15	.07	.01
	San Francisco 49ers		
☐ 303	Dewey Selmon .... .12	.06	.01
	Tampa Bay Buccaneers		
☐ 304	Jack Rudnay .... .08	.04	.01
	Kansas City Chiefs		
☐ 305	Fred Biletnikoff 1.25	.60	.12
	Oakland Raiders		
☐ 306	Jeff West .... .08	.04	.01
	San Diego Chargers		
☐ 307	Shafer Suggs .... .08	.04	.01
	New York Jets		
☐ 308	Ozzie Newsome 24.00	12.00	2.40
	Cleveland Browns		
☐ 309	Boobie Clark .... .12	.06	.01
	Cincinnati Bengals		
☐ 310	James Lofton 40.00	20.00	4.00
	Green Bay Packers		
☐ 311	Joe Pisarcik .... .12	.06	.01
	New York Giants		
☐ 312	Bill Simpson AP .... .08	.04	.01
	Los Angeles Rams		
☐ 313	Haven Moses .... .12	.06	.01
	Denver Broncos		
☐ 314	Jim Merlo .... .08	.04	.01
	New Orleans Saints		

☐ 315	Preston Pearson 15	.07	.01
	Dallas Cowboys		
☐ 316	Larry Tearry 08	.04	.01
	Detroit Lions		
☐ 317	Tom Dempsey 12	.06	.01
	Buffalo Bills		
☐ 318	Greg Latta 08	.04	.01
	Chicago Bears		
☐ 319	Wash. Redskins TL 50	.25	.05
	John Riggins		
	John McDaniel		
	Jake Scott		
	Coy Bacon		
☐ 320	Jack Ham AP 1.00	.50	.10
	Pittsburgh Steelers		
☐ 321	Harold Jackson 40	.20	.04
	New England Patriots		
☐ 322	George Roberts 08	.04	.01
	Miami Dolphins		
☐ 323	Ron Jaworski 40	.20	.04
	Philadelphia Eagles		
☐ 324	Jim Otis 15	.07	.01
	St. Louis Cardinals		
☐ 325	Roger Carr 12	.06	.01
	Baltimore Colts		
☐ 326	Jack Tatum 15	.07	.01
	Oakland Raiders		
☐ 327	Derrick Gaffney 08	.04	.01
	New York Jets		
☐ 328	Reggie Williams 50	.25	.05
	Cincinnati Bengals		
☐ 329	Doug Dieken 08	.04	.01
	Cleveland Browns		
☐ 330	Efren Herrera 08	.04	.01
	Seattle Seahawks		
☐ 331	Earl Campbell RB 5.00	2.50	.50
	Most Yards		
	Rushing, Rookie		
☐ 332	Tony Galbreath RB 15	.07	.01
	Most Receptions,		
	Running Back, Game		
☐ 333	Bruce Harper RB 15	.07	.01
	Most Combined Kick		
	Return Yards, Season		
☐ 334	John James RB 12	.06	.01
	Most Punts, Season		
☐ 335	Walter Payton RB 2.25	1.10	.22
	Most Combined		
	Attempts, Season		
☐ 336	Rickey Young RB 15	.07	.01
	Most Receptions,		
	Running Back, Season		
☐ 337	Jeff Van Note 15	.07	.01
	Atlanta Falcons		
☐ 338	San Diego Chargers TL ..50	.25	.05
	Lydell Mitchell		
	John Jefferson		

	Mike Fuller		
	Fred Dean		
☐ 339	Stan Walters AP 25	.12	.02
	Philadelphia Eagles		
☐ 340	Louis Wright AP 20	.10	.02
	Denver Broncos		
☐ 341	Horace Ivory 08	.04	.01
	New England Patriots		
☐ 342	Andre Tillman 08	.04	.01
	Miami Dolphins		
☐ 343	Greg Coleman 15	.07	.01
	Minnesota Vikings		
☐ 344	Doug English AP 75	.35	.07
	Detroit Lions		
☐ 345	Ted Hendricks 60	.30	.06
	Oakland Raiders		
☐ 346	Rich Saul 08	.04	.01
	Los Angeles Rams		
☐ 347	Mel Gray 15	.07	.01
	St. Louis Cardinals		
☐ 348	Toni Fritsch 08	.04	.01
	Houston Oilers		
☐ 349	Cornell Webster 08	.04	.01
	Seattle Seahawks		
☐ 350	Ken Houston 75	.35	.07
	Washington Redskins		
☐ 351	Ron Johnson 08	.04	.01
	Pittsburgh Steelers		
☐ 352	Doug Kotar 08	.04	.01
	New York Giants		
☐ 353	Brian Sipe 40	.20	.04
	Cleveland Browns		
☐ 354	Billy Brooks 12	.06	.01
	Cincinnati Bengals		
☐ 355	John Dutton 15	.07	.01
	Baltimore Colts		
☐ 356	Don Goode 08	.04	.01
	San Diego Chargers		
☐ 357	Detroit Lions TL 30	.15	.03
	Dexter Bussey		
	David Hill		
	Jim Allen		
	Al(Bubba) Baker		
☐ 358	Reuben Gant 08	.04	.01
	Buffalo Bills		
☐ 359	Bob Parsons 08	.04	.01
	Chicago Bears		
☐ 360	Cliff Harris AP 30	.15	.03
	Dallas Cowboys		
☐ 361	Raymond Clayborn 20	.10	.02
	New England Patriots		
☐ 362	Scott Dierking 08	.04	.01
	New York Jets		
☐ 363	Bill Bryan 08	.04	.01
	Denver Broncos		
☐ 364	Mike Livingston 12	.06	.01
	Kansas City Chiefs		

☐ 365	Otis Sistrunk 12	.06	.01	
	Oakland Raiders			
☐ 366	Charley Young 12	.06	.01	
	Los Angeles Rams			
☐ 367	Keith Wortman 08	.04	.01	
	St. Louis Cardinals			
☐ 368	Checklist 265-396 80	.08	.01	
☐ 369	Mike Michel 08	.04	.01	
	Philadelphia Eagles			
☐ 370	Delvin Williams AP 15	.07	.01	
	Miami Dolphins			
☐ 371	Steve Furness 08	.04	.01	
	Pittsburgh Steelers			
☐ 372	Emery Moorehead 08	.04	.01	
	New York Giants			
☐ 373	Clarence Scott 08	.04	.01	
	Cleveland Browns			
☐ 374	Rufus Mayes 08	.04	.01	
	Cincinnati Bengals			
☐ 375	Chris Hanburger 12	.06	.01	
	Washington Redskins			
☐ 376	Baltimore Colts TL 30	.15	.03	
	Joe Washington			
	Roger Carr			
	Norm Thompson			
	John Dutton			
☐ 377	Bob Avellini 12	.06	.01	
	Chicago Bears			
☐ 378	Jeff Siemon 12	.06	.01	
	Minnesota Vikings			
☐ 379	Roland Hooks 08	.04	.01	
	Buffalo Bills			
☐ 380	Russ Francis 15	.07	.01	
	New England Patriots			
☐ 381	Roger Wehrli 12	.06	.01	
	St. Louis Cardinals			
☐ 382	Joe Fields 12	.06	.01	
	New York Jets			
☐ 383	Archie Manning 45	.22	.04	
	New Orleans Saints			
☐ 384	Rob Lytle 12	.06	.01	
	Denver Broncos			
☐ 385	Thomas Henderson 15	.07	.01	
	Dallas Cowboys			
☐ 386	Morris Owens 08	.04	.01	
	Tampa Bay Buccaneers			
☐ 387	Dan Fouts 3.00	1.50	.30	
	San Diego Chargers			
☐ 388	Chuck Crist 08	.04	.01	
	San Francisco 49ers			
☐ 389	Ed O'Neil 08	.04	.01	
	Detroit Lions			
☐ 390	Earl Campbell AP 35.00	17.50	3.50	
	Houston Oilers			
☐ 391	Randy Grossman 08	.04	.01	
	Pittsburgh Steelers			
☐ 392	Monte Jackson 12	.06	.01	

	Oakland Raiders			
☐ 393	John Mendenhall 08	.04	.01	
	New York Giants			
☐ 394	Miami Dolphins TL 35	.17	.03	
	Delvin Williams			
	Duriel Harris			
	Tim Foley			
	Vern Den Herder			
☐ 395	Isaac Curtis 15	.07	.01	
	Cincinnati Bengals			
☐ 396	Mike Bragg 08	.04	.01	
	Washington Redskins			
☐ 397	Doug Plank 12	.06	.01	
	Chicago Bears			
☐ 398	Mike Barnes 08	.04	.01	
	Baltimore Colts			
☐ 399	Calvin Hill 20	.10	.02	
	Cleveland Browns			
☐ 400	Roger Staubach AP 4.50	2.25	.45	
	Dallas Cowboys			
☐ 401	Doug Beaudoin 08	.04	.01	
	New England Patriots			
☐ 402	Chuck Ramsey 08	.04	.01	
	New York Jets			
☐ 403	Mike Hogan 08	.04	.01	
	Philadelphia Eagles			
☐ 404	Mario Clark 08	.04	.01	
	Buffalo Bills			
☐ 405	Riley Odoms 15	.07	.01	
	Denver Broncos			
☐ 406	Carl Eller 50	.25	.05	
	Minnesota Vikings			
☐ 407	Green Bay Packers TL ..2.50	1.25	.25	
	Terdell Middleton			
	James Lofton			
	Willie Buchanon			
	Ezra Johnson			
☐ 408	Mark Arneson 08	.04	.01	
	St. Louis Cardinals			
☐ 409	Vince Ferragamo 75	.35	.07	
	Los Angeles Rams			
☐ 410	Cleveland Elam 08	.04	.01	
	San Francisco 49ers			
☐ 411	Donnie Shell 1.50	.75	.15	
	Pittsburgh Steelers			
☐ 412	Ray Rhodes 08	.04	.01	
	New York Giants			
☐ 413	Don Cockroft 08	.04	.01	
	Cleveland Browns			
☐ 414	Don Bass 15	.07	.01	
	Cincinnati Bengals			
☐ 415	Cliff Branch 50	.25	.05	
	Oakland Raiders			
☐ 416	Diron Talbert 12	.06	.01	
	Washington Redskins			
☐ 417	Tom Hicks 08	.04	.01	
	Chicago Bears			

☐ 418	Roosevelt Leaks 12	.06	.01	
	Baltimore Colts			
☐ 419	Charlie Joiner 75	.35	.07	
	San Diego Chargers			
☐ 420	Lyle Alzado AP 60	.30	.06	
	Denver Broncos			
☐ 421	Sam Cunningham 15	.07	.01	
	New England Patriots			
☐ 422	Larry Keller 08	.04	.01	
	New York Jets			
☐ 423	Jim Mitchell 08	.04	.01	
	Atlanta Falcons			
☐ 424	Randy Logan 08	.04	.01	
	Philadelphia Eagles			
☐ 425	Jim Langer 50	.25	.05	
	Miami Dolphins			
☐ 426	Gary Green 12	.06	.01	
	Kansas City Chiefs			
☐ 427	Luther Blue 08	.04	.01	
	Detroit Lions			
☐ 428	Dennis Johnson 08	.04	.01	
	Buffalo Bills			
☐ 429	Danny White 60	.30	.06	
	Dallas Cowboys			
☐ 430	Roy Gerela 08	.04	.01	
	Pittsburgh Steelers			
☐ 431	Jimmy Robinson 08	.04	.01	
	New York Giants			
☐ 432	Minnesota Vikings TL 35	.17	.03	
	Chuck Foreman			
	Ahmad Rashad			
	Bobby Bryant			
	Mark Mullaney			
☐ 433	Oliver Davis 08	.04	.01	
	Cleveland Browns			
☐ 434	Lenvil Elliott 08	.04	.01	
	Cincinnati Bengals			
☐ 435	Willie Miller 15	.07	.01	
	Los Angeles Rams			
☐ 436	Brad Dusek 08	.04	.01	
	Washington Redskins			
☐ 437	Bob Thomas 08	.04	.01	
	Chicago Bears			
☐ 438	Ken Mendenhall 08	.04	.01	
	Baltimore Colts			
☐ 439	Clarence Davis 08	.04	.01	
	Oakland Raiders			
☐ 440	Bob Griese 1.75	.85	.17	
	Miami Dolphins			
☐ 441	Tony McGee 08	.04	.01	
	New England Patriots			
☐ 442	Ed Taylor 08	.04	.01	
	New York Jets			
☐ 443	Ron Howard 08	.04	.01	
	Seattle Seahawks			
☐ 444	Wayne Morris 08	.04	.01	
	St. Louis Cardinals			

☐ 445	Charlie Waters 35	.17	.03	
	Dallas Cowboys			
☐ 446	Rick Danmeier 08	.04	.01	
	Minnesota Vikings			
☐ 447	Paul Naumoff 08	.04	.01	
	Detroit Lions			
☐ 448	Keith Krepfle 08	.04	.01	
	Philadelphia Eagles			
☐ 449	Rusty Jackson 08	.04	.01	
	Buffalo Bills			
☐ 450	John Stallworth 2.50	1.25	.25	
	Pittsburgh Steelers			
☐ 451	New Orleans Saints TL ...30	.15	.03	
	Tony Galbreath			
	Henry Childs			
	Tom Myers			
	Elex Price			
☐ 452	Ron Mikolajczyk 08	.04	.01	
	New York Giants			
☐ 453	Fred Dryer 75	.35	.07	
	Los Angeles Rams			
☐ 454	Jim LeClair 08	.04	.01	
	Cincinnati Bengals			
☐ 455	Greg Pruitt 30	.15	.03	
	Cleveland Browns			
☐ 456	Jake Scott 12	.06	.01	
	Washington Redskins			
☐ 457	Steve Schubert 08	.04	.01	
	Chicago Bears			
☐ 458	George Kunz 15	.07	.01	
	Baltimore Colts			
☐ 459	Mike Williams 08	.04	.01	
	San Diego Chargers			
☐ 460	Dave Casper AP 15	.07	.01	
	Oakland Raiders			
☐ 461	Sam Adams 08	.04	.01	
	New England Patriots			
☐ 462	Abdul Salaam 08	.04	.01	
	New York Jets			
☐ 463	Terdell Middleton 15	.07	.01	
	Green Bay Packers			
☐ 464	Mike Wood 08	.04	.01	
	St. Louis Cardinals			
☐ 465	Bill Thompson AP 12	.06	.01	
	Denver Broncos			
☐ 466	Larry Gordon 08	.04	.01	
	Miami Dolphins			
☐ 467	Benny Ricardo 08	.04	.01	
	Detroit Lions			
☐ 468	Reggie McKenzie 12	.06	.01	
	Buffalo Bills			
☐ 469	Dallas Cowboys TL 75	.35	.07	
	Tony Dorsett			
	Tony Hill			
	Benny Barnes			
	Harvey Martin			
	Randy White			

	Chicago Bears			
☐ 470	Rickey Young 12	.06	.01	
	Minnesota Vikings			
☐ 498	Billy Waddy 15	.07	.01
	Los Angeles Rams			
☐ 471	Charlie Smith 08	.04	.01	
	Philadelphia Eagles			
☐ 499	Hank Bauer 15	.07	.01
	San Diego Chargers			
☐ 472	Al Dixon 08	.04	.01	
	New York Giants			
☐ 500	Terry Bradshaw AP UER3.25	1.60	.32
	(Stat headers on back			
☐ 473	Tom DeLeone 08	.04	.01	
	Cleveland Browns			
	are for a runner)			
	Pittsburgh Steelers			
☐ 474	Louis Breeden 08	.04	.01	
	Cincinnati Bengals			
☐ 501	Larry McCarren 08	.04	.01
	Green Bay Packers			
☐ 475	Jack Lambert 1.25	.60	.12	
	Pittsburgh Steelers			
☐ 502	Fred Cook 12	.06	.01
	Baltimore Colts			
☐ 476	Terry Hermeling 08	.04	.01	
	Los Angeles Rams			
☐ 503	Chuck Muncie 20	.10	.02
	New Orleans Saints			
☐ 477	J.K. McKay 12	.06	.01	
	Tampa Bay Buccaneers			
☐ 504	Herman Weaver 08	.04	.01
	Seattle Seahawks			
☐ 478	Stan White 08	.04	.01	
	Baltimore Colts			
☐ 505	Eddie Edwards 08	.04	.01
	Cincinnati Bengals			
☐ 479	Terry Nelson 08	.04	.01	
	Los Angeles Rams			
☐ 506	Tony Peters 08	.04	.01
	Cleveland Browns			
☐ 480	Walter Payton AP 8.50	4.25	.85	
	Chicago Bears			
☐ 507	Denver Broncos TL 35	.17	.03
	Lonnie Perrin			
☐ 481	Dave Dalby 12	.06	.01	
	Oakland Raiders			
	Riley Odoms			
	Steve Foley			
☐ 482	Burgess Owens 08	.04	.01	
	New York Jets			
	Bernard Jackson			
	Lyle Alzado			
☐ 483	Rolf Benirschke 20	.10	.02	
	San Diego Chargers			
☐ 508	Jimbo Elrod 08	.04	.01
	Kansas City Chiefs			
☐ 484	Jack Dolbin 12	.06	.01	
	Denver Broncos			
☐ 509	David Hill 08	.04	.01
	Detroit Lions			
☐ 485	John Hannah AP 75	.35	.07	
	New England Patriots			
☐ 510	Harvey Martin 35	.17	.03
	Dallas Cowboys			
☐ 486	Checklist 397-528 80	.08	.01	
☐ 487	Greg Landry 25	.12	.02	
	Detroit Lions			
☐ 511	Terry Miller 20	.10	.02
	Buffalo Bills			
☐ 488	St. Louis Cardinals TL .... .30	.15	.03	
	Jim Otis			
☐ 512	June Jones 15	.07	.01
	Atlanta Falcons			
	Pat Tilley			
	Ken Stone			
☐ 513	Randy Cross 30	.15	.03
	San Francisco 49ers			
	Mike Dawson			
☐ 514	Duriel Harris 12	.06	.01
	Miami Dolphins			
☐ 489	Paul Krause 20	.10	.02	
	Minnesota Vikings			
☐ 515	Harry Carson 60	.30	.06
	New York Giants			
☐ 490	John James 08	.04	.01	
	Atlanta Falcons			
☐ 516	Tim Fox 08	.04	.01
	New England Patriots			
☐ 491	Merv Krakau 08	.04	.01	
	Buffalo Bills			
☐ 517	John Zook 12	.06	.01
	St. Louis Cardinals			
☐ 492	Dan Doornink 08	.04	.01	
	New York Giants			
☐ 518	Bob Tucker 12	.06	.01
	Minnesota Vikings			
☐ 493	Curtis Johnson 08	.04	.01	
	Miami Dolphins			
☐ 519	Kevin Long 08	.04	.01
	New York Jets			
☐ 494	Rafael Septien 15	.07	.01	
	Dallas Cowboys			
☐ 520	Ken Stabler 1.00	.50	.10
	Oakland Raiders			
☐ 495	Jean Fugett 08	.04	.01	
	Washington Redskins			
☐ 521	John Bunting 08	.04	.01
	Philadelphia Eagles			
☐ 496	Frank LeMaster 08	.04	.01	
	Philadelphia Eagles			
☐ 522	Rocky Bleier 50	.25	.05
	Pittsburgh Steelers			
☐ 497	Allan Ellis 08	.04	.01	

	MINT	EXC	G-VG
COMPLETE SET (528)	80.00	40.00	8.00
COMMON PLAYER (1-528)	.07	.03	.01

☐ 523 Noah Jackson .... .08 .04 .01
  Chicago Bears
☐ 524 Cliff Parsley .... .08 .04 .01
  Houston Oilers
☐ 525 Louie Kelcher AP .... .12 .06 .01
  San Diego Chargers
☐ 526 Tampa Bay Bucs TL .... .60 .30 .06
  Ricky Bell
  Morris Owens
  Cedric Brown
  Lee Roy Selmon
☐ 527 Bob Brudzinski .... .12 .06 .01
  Los Angeles Rams
☐ 528 Danny Buggs .... .15 .05 .01
  Washington Redskins

1980 Topps

The 1980 Topps football card set contains 528 cards of NFL players. The cards measure 2 1/ 2" by 3 1/2". The backs of the cards contain vital statistics, year-by-year career records, and a cartoon-illustrated fact section within a simulated football. No scarcities are known. The first six cards in the set recognize Record-Breaking (RB) performances from the previous season. Statistical league leaders are depicted on cards 331-336. Post-season playoff action is summarized on cards 492-494. All-Pro selections are designated on the player's regular card and are indicated by AP in the checklist below. Distributed throughout the set are Team Leader (TL) cards depicting, typically, four individual team (statistical) leaders on the front and a team checklist on the back. The key rookie cards in this set are Ottis Anderson and Phil Simms.

☐ 1 Ottis Anderson RB .... 1.50 .40 .08
  Most Yardage,
  Rushing, Rookie
☐ 2 Harold Carmichael RB ...... .15 .07 .01
  Most Consec. Games,
  One or More Receptions
☐ 3 Dan Fouts RB .... .60 .30 .06
  Most Yardage,
  Passing, Season
☐ 4 Paul Krause RB .... .15 .07 .01
  Most Interceptions,
  Lifetime
☐ 5 Rick Upchurch RB .... .12 .06 .01
  Most Punt Return
  Yards, Lifetime
☐ 6 Garo Yepremian RB .... .12 .06 .01
  Most Consecutive
  Field Goals
☐ 7 Harold Jackson .... .30 .15 .03
  New England Patriots
☐ 8 Mike Williams .... .07 .03 .01
  Kansas City Chiefs
☐ 9 Calvin Hill .... .15 .07 .01
  Cleveland Browns
☐ 10 Jack Ham AP .... .75 .35 .07
  Pittsburgh Steelers
☐ 11 Dan Melville .... .07 .03 .01
  San Francisco 49ers
☐ 12 Matt Robinson .... .12 .06 .01
  Denver Broncos
☐ 13 Billy Campfield .... .07 .03 .01
  Philadelphia Eagles
☐ 14 Phil Tabor .... .07 .03 .01
  New York Giants
☐ 15 Randy Hughes UER .... .12 .06 .01
  Dallas Cowboys
  (Cowboys didn't play
  in SB VII)
☐ 16 Andre Tillman .... .07 .03 .01
  Miami Dolphins
☐ 17 Isaac Curtis .... .12 .06 .01
  Cincinnati Bengals
☐ 18 Charley Hannah .... .07 .03 .01
  Tampa Bay Buccaneers
☐ 19 Wash. Redskins TL .... .35 .17 .03
  John Riggins
  Danny Buggs
  Joe Lavender
  Coy Bacon
☐ 20 Jim Zorn .... .30 .15 .03
  Seattle Seahawks
☐ 21 Brian Baschnagel .... .12 .06 .01
  Chicago Bears

☐ 22 Jon Keyworth 12	.06	.01	☐ 49 Oliver Davis 07	.03	.01

☐ 22 Jon Keyworth ....12 .06 .01
Denver Broncos

☐ 23 Phil Villapiano ....12 .06 .01
Oakland Raiders

☐ 24 Richard Osborne ....07 .03 .01
St. Louis Cardinals

☐ 25 Rich Saul AP ....07 .03 .01
Los Angeles Rams

☐ 26 Doug Beaudoin ....07 .03 .01
New England Patriots

☐ 27 Cleveland Elam ....07 .03 .01
Detroit Lions

☐ 28 Charlie Joiner ....75 .35 .07
San Diego Chargers

☐ 29 Dick Ambrose ....07 .03 .01
Cleveland Browns

☐ 30 Mike Reinfeldt AP ....15 .07 .01
Houston Oilers

☐ 31 Matt Bahr ....1.00 .50 .10
Pittsburgh Steelers

☐ 32 Keith Krepfle ....07 .03 .01
Philadelphia Eagles

☐ 33 Herbert Scott ....12 .06 .01
Dallas Cowboys

☐ 34 Doug Kotar ....07 .03 .01
New York Giants

☐ 35 Bob Griese ....1.75 .85 .17
Miami Dolphins

☐ 36 Jerry Butler ....60 .30 .06
Buffalo Bills

☐ 37 Rolland Lawrence ....12 .06 .01
Atlanta Falcons

☐ 38 Gary Weaver ....07 .03 .01
Green Bay Packers

☐ 39 Kansas City Chiefs TL ......40 .20 .04
Ted McKnight
J.T. Smith
Gary Barbaro
Art Still

☐ 40 Chuck Muncie ....15 .07 .01
New Orleans Saints

☐ 41 Mike Hartenstine ....07 .03 .01
Chicago Bears

☐ 42 Sammie White ....15 .07 .01
Minnesota Vikings

☐ 43 Ken Clark ....07 .03 .01
Los Angeles Rams

☐ 44 Clarence Harmon ....07 .03 .01
Washington Redskins

☐ 45 Bert Jones ....30 .15 .03
Baltimore Colts

☐ 46 Mike Washington ....07 .03 .01
Tampa Bay Buccaneers

☐ 47 Joe Fields ....12 .06 .01
New York Jets

☐ 48 Mike Wood ....07 .03 .01
San Diego Chargers

☐ 49 Oliver Davis ....07 .03 .01
Cleveland Browns

☐ 50 Stan Walters AP ....07 .03 .01
Philadelphia Eagles

☐ 51 Riley Odoms ....12 .06 .01
Denver Broncos

☐ 52 Steve Pisarkiewicz ....12 .06 .01
St. Louis Cardinals

☐ 53 Tony Hill ....30 .15 .03
Dallas Cowboys

☐ 54 Scott Perry ....07 .03 .01
San Francisco 49ers

☐ 55 George Martin ....50 .25 .05
New York Giants

☐ 56 George Roberts ....07 .03 .01
Miami Dolphins

☐ 57 Seattle Seahawks TL ......60 .30 .06
Sherman Smith
Steve Largent
Dave Brown
Manu Tuiasosopo

☐ 58 Billy Johnson ....15 .07 .01
Houston Oilers

☐ 59 Reuben Gant ....07 .03 .01
Buffalo Bills

☐ 60 Dennis Harrah AP ....15 .07 .01
Los Angeles Rams

☐ 61 Rocky Bleier ....35 .17 .03
Pittsburgh Steelers

☐ 62 Sam Hunt ....07 .03 .01
New England Patriots

☐ 63 Allan Ellis ....07 .03 .01
Chicago Bears

☐ 64 Ricky Thompson ....07 .03 .01
Washington Redskins

☐ 65 Ken Stabler ....75 .35 .07
Houston Oilers

☐ 66 Dexter Bussey ....07 .03 .01
Detroit Lions

☐ 67 Ken Mendenhall ....07 .03 .01
Baltimore Colts

☐ 68 Woodrow Lowe ....07 .03 .01
San Diego Chargers

☐ 69 Thom Darden ....07 .03 .01
Cleveland Browns

☐ 70 Randy White AP ....1.00 .50 .10
Dallas Cowboys

☐ 71 Ken MacAfee ....12 .06 .01
San Francisco 49ers

☐ 72 Ron Jaworski ....30 .15 .03
Philadelphia Eagles

☐ 73 William Andrews ....60 .30 .06
Atlanta Falcons

☐ 74 Jimmy Robinson ....07 .03 .01
New York Giants

☐ 75 Roger Wehrli AP ....12 .06 .01
St. Louis Cardinals

☐ 76 Miami Dolphins TL .... .35	.17	.03	
Larry Csonka			
Nat Moore			
Neal Colzie			
Gerald Small			
Vern Den Herder			
☐ 77 Jack Rudnay .... .07	.03	.01	
Kansas City Chiefs			
☐ 78 James Lofton 9.00	4.50	.90	
Green Bay Packers			
☐ 79 Robert Brazile .... .12	.06	.01	
Houston Oilers			
☐ 80 Russ Francis .... .15	.07	.01	
New England Patriots			
☐ 81 Ricky Bell .... .30	.15	.03	
Tampa Bay Buccaneers			
☐ 82 Bob Avellini .... .12	.06	.01	
Chicago Bears			
☐ 83 Bobby Jackson .... .07	.03	.01	
New York Jets			
☐ 84 Mike Bragg .... .07	.03	.01	
Washington Redskins			
☐ 85 Cliff Branch .... .40	.20	.04	
Oakland Raiders			
☐ 86 Blair Bush .... .07	.03	.01	
Cincinnati Bengals			
☐ 87 Sherman Smith .... .07	.03	.01	
Seattle Seahawks			
☐ 88 Glen Edwards .... .07	.03	.01	
San Diego Chargers			
☐ 89 Don Cockroft .... .07	.03	.01	
Cleveland Browns			
☐ 90 Louis Wright AP .... .15	.07	.01	
Denver Broncos			
☐ 91 Randy Grossman .... .07	.03	.01	
Pittsburgh Steelers			
☐ 92 Carl Hairston .... .75	.35	.07	
Philadelphia Eagles			
☐ 93 Archie Manning .... .35	.17	.03	
New Orleans Saints			
☐ 94 New York Giants TL .... .20	.10	.02	
Billy Taylor			
Earnest Gray			
George Martin			
☐ 95 Preston Pearson .... .15	.07	.01	
Dallas Cowboys			
☐ 96 Rusty Chambers .... .07	.03	.01	
Miami Dolphins			
☐ 97 Greg Coleman .... .07	.03	.01	
Minnesota Vikings			
☐ 98 Charley Young .... .12	.06	.01	
Los Angeles Rams			
☐ 99 Matt Cavanaugh .... .35	.17	.03	
New England Patriots			
☐ 100 Jesse Baker .... .12	.06	.01	
Houston Oilers			
☐ 101 Doug Plank .... .12	.06	.01	

Chicago Bears			
☐ 102 Checklist 1-132 .... .65	.06	.01	
☐ 103 Luther Bradley .... .15	.07	.01	
Detroit Lions			
☐ 104 Bob Kuziel .... .07	.03	.01	
Washington Redskins			
☐ 105 Craig Morton .... .40	.20	.04	
Denver Broncos			
☐ 106 Sherman White .... .07	.03	.01	
Buffalo Bills			
☐ 107 Jim Breech .... .60	.30	.06	
Oakland Raiders			
☐ 108 Hank Bauer .... .07	.03	.01	
San Diego Chargers			
☐ 109 Tom Blanchard .... .07	.03	.01	
Tampa Bay Buccaneers			
☐ 110 Ozzie Newsome AP 6.00	3.00	.60	
Cleveland Browns			
☐ 111 Steve Furness .... .07	.03	.01	
Pittsburgh Steelers			
☐ 112 Frank LeMaster .... .07	.03	.01	
Philadelphia Eagles			
☐ 113 Dallas Cowboys TL .... .75	.35	.07	
Tony Dorsett			
Tony Hill			
Harvey Martin			
☐ 114 Doug Van Horn .... .07	.03	.01	
New York Giants			
☐ 115 Delvin Williams .... .12	.06	.01	
Miami Dolphins			
☐ 116 Lyle Blackwood .... .07	.03	.01	
Baltimore Colts			
☐ 117 Derrick Gaffney .... .07	.03	.01	
New York Jets			
☐ 118 Cornell Webster .... .07	.03	.01	
Seattle Seahawks			
☐ 119 Sam Cunningham .... .12	.06	.01	
New England Patriots			
☐ 120 Jim Youngblood AP ...... .12	.06	.01	
Los Angeles Rams			
☐ 121 Bob Thomas .... .07	.03	.01	
Chicago Bears			
☐ 122 Jack Thompson .... .15	.07	.01	
Cincinnati Bengals			
☐ 123 Randy Cross .... .12	.06	.01	
San Francisco 49ers			
☐ 124 Karl Lorch .... .07	.03	.01	
Washington Redskins			
☐ 125 Mel Gray .... .12	.06	.01	
St. Louis Cardinals			
☐ 126 John James .... .07	.03	.01	
Atlanta Falcons			
☐ 127 Terdell Middleton .... .07	.03	.01	
Green Bay Packers			
☐ 128 Leroy Jones .... .07	.03	.01	
San Diego Chargers			
☐ 129 Tom DeLeone .... .07	.03	.01	

	Cleveland Browns		
☐ 130	John Stallworth AP 1.00	.50	.10
	Pittsburgh Steelers		
☐ 131	Jimmie Giles .... .50	.25	.05
	Tampa Bay Buccaneers		
☐ 132	Philadelphia Eagles TL ...25	.12	.02
	Wilbert Montgomery		
	Harold Carmichael		
	Brenard Wilson		
	Carl Hairston		
☐ 133	Gary Green 12	.06	.01
	Kansas City Chiefs		
☐ 134	John Dutton 15	.07	.01
	Dallas Cowboys		
☐ 135	Harry Carson AP 50	.25	.05
	New York Giants		
☐ 136	Bob Kuechenberg 12	.06	.01
	Miami Dolphins		
☐ 137	Ike Harris 07	.03	.01
	New Orleans Saints		
☐ 138	Tommy Kramer 1.00	.50	.10
	Minnesota Vikings		
☐ 139	Sam Adams 07	.03	.01
	New England Patriots		
☐ 140	Doug English AP 20	.10	.02
	Detroit Lions		
☐ 141	Steve Schubert 07	.03	.01
	Chicago Bears		
☐ 142	Rusty Jackson 07	.03	.01
	Buffalo Bills		
☐ 143	Reese McCall 07	.03	.01
	Baltimore Colts		
☐ 144	Scott Dierking 07	.03	.01
	New York Jets		
☐ 145	Ken Houston AP 75	.35	.07
	Washington Redskins		
☐ 146	Bob Martin 07	.03	.01
	New York Jets		
☐ 147	Sam McCullum 12	.06	.01
	Seattle Seahawks		
☐ 148	Tom Banks 12	.06	.01
	St. Louis Cardinals		
☐ 149	Willie Buchanon 12	.06	.01
	San Diego Chargers		
☐ 150	Greg Pruitt 20	.10	.02
	Cleveland Browns		
☐ 151	Denver Broncos TL 25	.12	.02
	Otis Armstrong		
	Rick Upchurch		
	Steve Foley		
	Brison Manor		
☐ 152	Don Smith 07	.03	.01
	Atlanta Falcons		
☐ 153	Pete Johnson 12	.06	.01
	Cincinnati Bengals		
☐ 154	Charlie Smith 07	.03	.01
	Philadelphia Eagles		
☐ 155	Mel Blount 75	.35	.07
	Pittsburgh Steelers		
☐ 156	John Mendenhall 07	.03	.01
	New York Giants		
☐ 157	Danny White 50	.25	.05
	Dallas Cowboys		
☐ 158	Jimmy Cefalo 50	.25	.05
	Miami Dolphins		
☐ 159	Richard Bishop AP 07	.03	.01
	New England Patriots		
☐ 160	Walter Payton AP 7.50	3.75	.75
	Chicago Bears		
☐ 161	Dave Dalby 12	.06	.01
	Oakland Raiders		
☐ 162	Preston Dennard 07	.03	.01
	Los Angeles Rams		
☐ 163	Johnnie Gray 07	.03	.01
	Green Bay Packers		
☐ 164	Russell Erxleben 07	.03	.01
	New Orleans Saints		
☐ 165	Toni Fritsch AP 07	.03	.01
	Houston Oilers		
☐ 166	Terry Hermeling 07	.03	.01
	Washington Redskins		
☐ 167	Roland Hooks 07	.03	.01
	Buffalo Bills		
☐ 168	Roger Carr 12	.06	.01
	Baltimore Colts		
☐ 169	San Diego Chargers TL ...20	.10	.02
	Clarence Williams		
	John Jefferson		
	Woodrow Lowe		
	Ray Preston		
	Wilbur Young		
☐ 170	Ottis Anderson AP 10.00	5.00	1.00
	St. Louis Cardinals		
☐ 171	Brian Sipe 30	.15	.03
	Cleveland Browns		
☐ 172	Leonard Thompson 12	.06	.01
	Detroit Lions		
☐ 173	Tony Reed 12	.06	.01
	Kansas City Chiefs		
☐ 174	Bob Tucker 12	.06	.01
	Minnesota Vikings		
☐ 175	Joe Greene 1.00	.50	.10
	Pittsburgh Steelers		
☐ 176	Jack Dolbin 07	.03	.01
	Denver Broncos		
☐ 177	Chuck Ramsey 07	.03	.01
	New York Jets		
☐ 178	Paul Hofer 12	.06	.01
	San Francisco 49ers		
☐ 179	Randy Logan 07	.03	.01
	Philadelphia Eagles		
☐ 180	David Lewis AP 07	.03	.01
	Tampa Bay Buccaneers		
☐ 181	Duriel Harris 07	.03	.01

	Miami Dolphins			
☐ 182	June Jones 07	.03	.01	
	Atlanta Falcons			
☐ 183	Larry McCarren 07	.03	.01	
	Green Bay Packers			
☐ 184	Ken Johnson 07	.03	.01	
	New York Jets			
☐ 185	Charlie Waters 25	.12	.02	
	Dallas Cowboys			
☐ 186	Noah Jackson 07	.03	.01	
	Chicago Bears			
☐ 187	Reggie Williams 30	.15	.03	
	Cincinnati Bengals			
☐ 188	New England Pats TL 25	.12	.02	
	Sam Cunningham			
	Harold Jackson			
	Raymond Clayborn			
	Tony McGee			
☐ 189	Carl Eller 40	.20	.04	
	Seattle Seahawks			
☐ 190	Ed White AP 12	.06	.01	
	San Diego Chargers			
☐ 191	Mario Clark 07	.03	.01	
	Buffalo Bills			
☐ 192	Roosevelt Leaks 12	.06	.01	
	Baltimore Colts			
☐ 193	Ted McKnight 07	.03	.01	
	Kansas City Chiefs			
☐ 194	Danny Buggs 07	.03	.01	
	Washington Redskins			
☐ 195	Lester Hayes 1.75	.85	.17	
	Oakland Raiders			
☐ 196	Clarence Scott 07	.03	.01	
	Cleveland Browns			
☐ 197	New Orleans Saints TL .. .35	.17	.03	
	Chuck Muncie			
	Wes Chandler			
	Tom Myers			
	Elois Grooms			
	Don Reese			
☐ 198	Richard Caster 12	.06	.01	
	Houston Oilers			
☐ 199	Louie Giammona 07	.03	.01	
	Philadelphia Eagles			
☐ 200	Terry Bradshaw 2.50	1.25	.25	
	Pittsburgh Steelers			
☐ 201	Ed Newman 07	.03	.01	
	Miami Dolphins			
☐ 202	Fred Dryer 60	.30	.06	
	Los Angeles Rams			
☐ 203	Dennis Franks 07	.03	.01	
	Detroit Lions			
☐ 204	Bob Breunig 50	.25	.05	
	Dallas Cowboys			
☐ 205	Alan Page 60	.30	.06	
	Chicago Bears			
☐ 206	Earnest Gray 15	.07	.01	

	New York Giants			
☐ 207	Minnesota Vikings TL 25	.12	.02	
	Rickey Young			
	Ahmad Rashad			
	Tom Hannon			
	Nate Wright			
	Mark Mullaney			
☐ 208	Horace Ivory 07	.03	.01	
	New England Patriots			
☐ 209	Isaac Hagins 07	.03	.01	
	Tampa Bay Buccaneers			
☐ 210	Gary Johnson AP 12	.06	.01	
	San Diego Chargers			
☐ 211	Kevin Long 07	.03	.01	
	New York Jets			
☐ 212	Bill Thompson 12	.06	.01	
	Denver Broncos			
☐ 213	Don Bass 12	.06	.01	
	Cincinnati Bengals			
☐ 214	George Starke 20	.10	.02	
	Washington Redskins			
☐ 215	Efren Herrera 07	.03	.01	
	Seattle Seahawks			
☐ 216	Theo Bell 07	.03	.01	
	Pittsburgh Steelers			
☐ 217	Monte Jackson 12	.06	.01	
	Oakland Raiders			
☐ 218	Reggie McKenzie 12	.06	.01	
	Buffalo Bills			
☐ 219	Bucky Dilts 07	.03	.01	
	Baltimore Colts			
☐ 220	Lyle Alzado 50	.25	.05	
	Cleveland Browns			
☐ 221	Tim Foley 12	.06	.01	
	Miami Dolphins			
☐ 222	Mark Arneson 07	.03	.01	
	St. Louis Cardinals			
☐ 223	Fred Quillan 07	.03	.01	
	San Francisco 49ers			
☐ 224	Benny Ricardo 07	.03	.01	
	Detroit Lions			
☐ 225	Phil Simms 16.00	8.00	1.60	
	New York Giants			
☐ 226	Chicago Bears TL 1.00	.50	.10	
	Walter Payton			
	Brian Baschnagel			
	Gary Fencik			
	Terry Schmidt			
	Jim Osborne			
☐ 227	Max Runager 07	.03	.01	
	Philadelphia Eagles			
☐ 228	Barty Smith 07	.03	.01	
	Green Bay Packers			
☐ 229	Jay Saldi 07	.03	.01	
	Dallas Cowboys			
☐ 230	John Hannah AP 50	.25	.05	
	New England Patriots			

☐ 231 Tim Wilson	.07	.03	.01
Houston Oilers			
☐ 232 Jeff Van Note	.12	.06	.01
Atlanta Falcons			
☐ 233 Henry Marshall	.07	.03	.01
Kansas City Chiefs			
☐ 234 Diron Talbert	.12	.06	.01
Washington Redskins			
☐ 235 Garo Yepremian	.12	.06	.01
New Orleans Saints			
☐ 236 Larry Brown	.07	.03	.01
Pittsburgh Steelers			
☐ 237 Clarence Williams	.07	.03	.01
San Diego Chargers			
☐ 238 Burgess Owens	.07	.03	.01
New York Jets			
☐ 239 Vince Ferragamo	.25	.12	.02
Los Angeles Rams			
☐ 240 Rickey Young	.12	.06	.01
Minnesota Vikings			
☐ 241 Dave Logan	.07	.03	.01
Cleveland Browns			
☐ 242 Larry Gordon	.07	.03	.01
Miami Dolphins			
☐ 243 Terry Miller	.12	.06	.01
Buffalo Bills			
☐ 244 Baltimore Colts TL	.20	.10	.02
Joe Washington			
Joe Washington			
Fred Cook			
☐ 245 Steve DeBerg	2.00	1.00	.20
San Francisco 49ers			
☐ 246 Checklist 133-264	.65	.06	.01
☐ 247 Greg Latta	.07	.03	.01
Chicago Bears			
☐ 248 Raymond Clayborn	.12	.06	.01
New England Patriots			
☐ 249 Jim Clark	.07	.03	.01
New York Giants			
☐ 250 Drew Pearson	.45	.22	.04
Dallas Cowboys			
☐ 251 John Bunting	.07	.03	.01
Philadelphia Eagles			
☐ 252 Rob Lytle	.12	.06	.01
Denver Broncos			
☐ 253 Jim Hart	.30	.15	.03
St. Louis Cardinals			
☐ 254 John McDaniel	.07	.03	.01
Washington Redskins			
☐ 255 Dave Pear AP	.07	.03	.01
Oakland Raiders			
☐ 256 Donnie Shell	.35	.17	.03
Pittsburgh Steelers			
☐ 257 Dan Doornink	.07	.03	.01
Seattle Seahawks			
☐ 258 Wallace Francis	.35	.17	.03
Atlanta Falcons			

☐ 259 Dave Beverly	.07	.03	.01
Green Bay Packers			
☐ 260 Lee Roy Selmon AP	.25	.12	.02
Tampa Bay Buccaneers			
☐ 261 Doug Dieken	.07	.03	.01
Cleveland Browns			
☐ 262 Gary Davis	.07	.03	.01
Miami Dolphins			
☐ 263 Bob Rush	.07	.03	.01
San Diego Chargers			
☐ 264 Buffalo Bills TL	.20	.10	.02
Curtis Brown			
Frank Lewis			
Keith Moody			
Sherman White			
☐ 265 Greg Landry	.20	.10	.02
Baltimore Colts			
☐ 266 Jan Stenerud	.50	.25	.05
Kansas City Chiefs			
☐ 267 Tom Hicks	.07	.03	.01
Chicago Bears			
☐ 268 Pat McInally	.15	.07	.01
Cincinnati Bengals			
☐ 269 Tim Fox	.07	.03	.01
New England Patriots			
☐ 270 Harvey Martin	.25	.12	.02
Dallas Cowboys			
☐ 271 Dan Lloyd	.07	.03	.01
St. Louis Cardinals			
☐ 272 Mike Barber	.12	.06	.01
Houston Oilers			
☐ 273 Wendell Tyler	.60	.30	.06
Los Angeles Rams			
☐ 274 Jeff Komlo	.12	.06	.01
Detroit Lions			
☐ 275 Wes Chandler	2.50	1.25	.25
New Orleans Saints			
☐ 276 Brad Dusek	.07	.03	.01
Washington Redskins			
☐ 277 Charlie Johnson	.07	.03	.01
Philadelphia Eagles			
☐ 278 Dennis Swilley	.15	.07	.01
Minnesota Vikings			
☐ 279 Johnny Evans	.07	.03	.01
Cleveland Browns			
☐ 280 Jack Lambert AP	1.00	.50	.10
Pittsburgh Steelers			
☐ 281 Vern Den Herder	.07	.03	.01
Miami Dolphins			
☐ 282 Tampa Bay Bucs TL	.25	.12	.02
Ricky Bell			
Isaac Hagins			
Lee Roy Selmon			
☐ 283 Bob Klein	.07	.03	.01
San Diego Chargers			
☐ 284 Jim Turner	.12	.06	.01
Denver Broncos			

☐ 285 Marvin Powell AP .... .12   .06   .01
    New York Jets
☐ 286 Aaron Kyle .... .12   .06   .01
    Dallas Cowboys
☐ 287 Dan Neal .... .07   .03   .01
    Chicago Bears
☐ 288 Wayne Morris .... .07   .03   .01
    St. Louis Cardinals
☐ 289 Steve Bartkowski .... .35   .17   .03
    Atlanta Falcons
☐ 290 Dave Jennings AP .... .12   .06   .01
    New York Giants
☐ 291 John Smith .... .07   .03   .01
    New England Patriots
☐ 292 Bill Gregory .... .07   .03   .01
    Seattle Seahawks
☐ 293 Frank Lewis .... .12   .06   .01
    Buffalo Bills
☐ 294 Fred Cook .... .12   .06   .01
    Baltimore Colts
☐ 295 David Hill AP .... .07   .03   .01
    Detroit Lions
☐ 296 Wade Key .... .07   .03   .01
    Philadelphia Eagles
☐ 297 Sidney Thornton .... .07   .03   .01
    Pittsburgh Steelers
☐ 298 Charlie Hall .... .07   .03   .01
    Cleveland Browns
☐ 299 Joe Lavender .... .07   .03   .01
    Washington Redskins
☐ 300 Tom Rafferty .... .15   .07   .01
    Dallas Cowboys
☐ 301 Mike Renfro .... .20   .10   .02
    Houston Oilers
☐ 302 Wilbur Jackson .... .12   .06   .01
    San Francisco 49ers
☐ 303 Green Bay Packers TL . 1.25   .60   .12
    Terdell Middleton
    James Lofton
    Johnnie Gray
    Robert Barber
    Ezra Johnson
☐ 304 Henry Childs .... .07   .03   .01
    New Orleans Saints
☐ 305 Russ Washington AP ..... .07   .03   .01
    San Diego Chargers
☐ 306 Jim LeClair .... .07   .03   .01
    Cincinnati Bengals
☐ 307 Tommy Hart .... .07   .03   .01
    Chicago Bears
☐ 308 Gary Barbaro .... .12   .06   .01
    Kansas City Chiefs
☐ 309 Billy Taylor .... .12   .06   .01
    New York Giants
☐ 310 Ray Guy .... .25   .12   .02
    Oakland Raiders
☐ 311 Don Hasselbeck .... .12   .06   .01

    New England Patriots
☐ 312 Doug Williams .... .60   .30   .06
    Tampa Bay Buccaneers
☐ 313 Nick Mike-Mayer .... .07   .03   .01
    Buffalo Bills
☐ 314 Don McCauley .... .07   .03   .01
    Baltimore Colts
☐ 315 Wesley Walker .... .50   .25   .05
    New York Jets
☐ 316 Dan Dierdorf .... .50   .25   .05
    St. Louis Cardinals
☐ 317 Dave Brown .... .50   .25   .05
    Seattle Seahawks
☐ 318 Leroy Harris .... .07   .03   .01
    Philadelphia Eagles
☐ 319 Pittsburgh Steelers TL ... .75   .35   .07
    Franco Harris
    John Stallworth
    Jack Lambert
    Steve Furness
    L.C. Greenwood
☐ 320 Mark Moseley AP .... .15   .07   .01
    Washington Redskins
☐ 321 Mark Dennard .... .07   .03   .01
    Miami Dolphins
☐ 322 Terry Nelson .... .07   .03   .01
    Los Angeles Rams
☐ 323 Tom Jackson .... .45   .22   .04
    Denver Broncos
☐ 324 Rick Kane .... .07   .03   .01
    Detroit Lions
☐ 325 Jerry Sherk .... .12   .06   .01
    Cleveland Browns
☐ 326 Ray Preston .... .07   .03   .01
    San Diego Chargers
☐ 327 Golden Richards .... .12   .06   .01
    Chicago Bears
☐ 328 Randy Dean .... .07   .03   .01
    New York Giants
☐ 329 Rick Danmeier .... .07   .03   .01
    Minnesota Vikings
☐ 330 Tony Dorsett .... 4.00   2.00   .40
    Dallas Cowboys
☐ 331 Passing Leaders .... 2.00   1.00   .20
    Dan Fouts
    Roger Staubach
☐ 332 Receiving Leaders .... .25   .12   .02
    Joe Washington
    Ahmad Rashad
☐ 333 Sacks Leaders .... .15   .07   .01
    Jesse Baker
    Al(Bubba) Baker
    Jack Youngblood
☐ 334 Scoring Leaders .... .15   .07   .01
    John Smith
    Mark Moseley
☐ 335 Interception Leaders ...... .15   .07   .01

Mike Reinfeldt
Lemar Parrish

☐ 336	Punting Leaders 12	.06	.01	
	Bob Grupp			
	Dave Jennings			
☐ 337	Freddie Solomon 12	.06	.01	
	San Francisco 49ers			
☐ 338	Cincinnati Bengals TL 20	.10	.02	
	Pete Johnson			
	Don Bass			
	Dick Jauron			
	Gary Burley			
☐ 339	Ken Stone 07	.03	.01	
	St. Louis Cardinals			
☐ 340	Greg Buttle AP 12	.06	.01	
	New York Jets			
☐ 341	Bob Baumhower 12	.06	.01	
	Miami Dolphins			
☐ 342	Billy Waddy 07	.03	.01	
	Los Angeles Rams			
☐ 343	Cliff Parsley 07	.03	.01	
	Houston Oilers			
☐ 344	Walter White 07	.03	.01	
	Kansas City Chiefs			
☐ 345	Mike Thomas 07	.03	.01	
	San Diego Chargers			
☐ 346	Neil O'Donoghue 07	.03	.01	
	Tampa Bay Buccaneers			
☐ 347	Freddie Scott 07	.03	.01	
	Detroit Lions			
☐ 348	Joe Ferguson 20	.10	.02	
	Buffalo Bills			
☐ 349	Doug Nettles 07	.03	.01	
	Baltimore Colts			
☐ 350	Mike Webster AP 45	.22	.04	
	Pittsburgh Steelers			
☐ 351	Ron Saul 07	.03	.01	
	Washington Redskins			
☐ 352	Julius Adams 07	.03	.01	
	New England Patriots			
☐ 353	Rafael Septien 15	.07	.01	
	Dallas Cowboys			
☐ 354	Cleo Miller 07	.03	.01	
	Cleveland Browns			
☐ 355	Keith Simpson AP 07	.03	.01	
	Seattle Seahawks			
☐ 356	Johnny Perkins 07	.03	.01	
	New York Jets			
☐ 357	Jerry Sisemore 07	.03	.01	
	Philadelphia Eagles			
☐ 358	Arthur Whittington 07	.03	.01	
	Oakland Raiders			
☐ 359	St. Louis Cardinals TL 45	.22	.04	
	Ottis Anderson			
	Pat Tilley			
	Ken Stone			
	Bob Pollard			
☐ 360	Rick Upchurch 15	.07	.01	
	Denver Broncos			
☐ 361	Kim Bokamper 15	.07	.01	
	Miami Dolphins			
☐ 362	Roland Harper 12	.06	.01	
	Chicago Bears			
☐ 363	Pat Leahy 20	.10	.02	
	New York Jets			
☐ 364	Louis Breeden 07	.03	.01	
	Cincinnati Bengals			
☐ 365	John Jefferson 60	.30	.06	
	San Diego Chargers			
☐ 366	Jerry Eckwood 15	.07	.01	
	Tampa Bay Buccaneers			
☐ 367	David Whitehurst 12	.06	.01	
	Green Bay Packers			
☐ 368	Willie Parker 07	.03	.01	
	Buffalo Bills			
☐ 369	Ed Simonini 07	.03	.01	
	Baltimore Colts			
☐ 370	Jack Youngblood AP 50	.25	.05	
	Los Angeles Rams			
☐ 371	Don Warren 1.25	.60	.12	
	Washington Redskins			
☐ 372	Andy Johnson 07	.03	.01	
	New England Patriots			
☐ 373	D.D. Lewis 15	.07	.01	
	Dallas Cowboys			
☐ 374	Beasley Reece 07	.03	.01	
	Tampa Bay Buccaneers			
☐ 375	L.C. Greenwood 35	.17	.03	
	Pittsburgh Steelers			
☐ 376	Cleveland Browns TL 20	.10	.02	
	Mike Pruitt			
	Dave Logan			
	Thom Darden			
	Jerry Sherk			
☐ 377	Herman Edwards 07	.03	.01	
	Philadelphia Eagles			
☐ 378	Rob Carpenter 30	.15	.03	
	Houston Oilers			
☐ 379	Herman Weaver 07	.03	.01	
	Seattle Seahawks			
☐ 380	Gary Fencik AP 15	.07	.01	
	Chicago Bears			
☐ 381	Don Strock 15	.07	.01	
	Miami Dolphins			
☐ 382	Art Shell 60	.30	.06	
	Oakland Raiders			
☐ 383	Tim Mazzetti 07	.03	.01	
	Atlanta Falcons			
☐ 384	Bruce Harper 07	.03	.01	
	New York Jets			
☐ 385	Al(Bubba) Baker 15	.07	.01	
	Detroit Lions			
☐ 386	Conrad Dobler 15	.07	.01	
	New Orleans Saints			

☐ 387 Stu Voigt 12	.06	.01	
Minnesota Vikings			
☐ 388 Ken Anderson 75	.35	.07	
Cincinnati Bengals			
☐ 389 Pat Tilley 12	.06	.01	
St. Louis Cardinals			
☐ 390 John Riggins 1.00	.50	.10	
Washington Redskins			
☐ 391 Checklist 265-396 ...65	.06	.01	
☐ 392 Fred Dean AP 15	.07	.01	
San Diego Chargers			
☐ 393 Benny Barnes 15	.07	.01	
Dallas Cowboys			
☐ 394 Los Angeles Rams TL ...25	.12	.02	
Wendell Tyler			
Preston Dennard			
Nolan Cromwell			
Jim Youngblood			
Jack Youngblood			
☐ 395 Brad Van Pelt 12	.06	.01	
New York Giants			
☐ 396 Eddie Hare 07	.03	.01	
New England Patriots			
☐ 397 John Sciarra 20	.10	.02	
Philadelphia Eagles			
☐ 398 Bob Jackson 07	.03	.01	
Cleveland Browns			
☐ 399 John Yarno 07	.03	.01	
Seattle Seahawks			
☐ 400 Franco Harris AP 1.75	.85	.17	
Pittsburgh Steelers			
☐ 401 Ray Wersching 07	.03	.01	
San Francisco 49ers			
☐ 402 Virgil Livers 07	.03	.01	
Chicago Bears			
☐ 403 Raymond Chester 12	.06	.01	
Oakland Raiders			
☐ 404 Leon Gray 12	.06	.01	
Houston Oilers			
☐ 405 Richard Todd 20	.10	.02	
New York Jets			
☐ 406 Larry Little 15	.07	.01	
Miami Dolphins			
☐ 407 Ted Fritsch Jr. 07	.03	.01	
Washington Redskins			
☐ 408 Larry Mucker 07	.03	.01	
Tampa Bay Buccaneers			
☐ 409 Jim Allen 07	.03	.01	
Detroit Lions			
☐ 410 Randy Gradishar 30	.15	.03	
Denver Broncos			
☐ 411 Atlanta Falcons TL 20	.10	.02	
William Andrews			
Wallace Francis			
Rolland Lawrence			
Don Smith			
☐ 412 Louie Kelcher 12	.06	.01	

San Diego Chargers			
☐ 413 Robert Newhouse 15	.07	.01	
Dallas Cowboys			
☐ 414 Gary Shirk 07	.03	.01	
New York Giants			
☐ 415 Mike Haynes AP 25	.12	.02	
New England Patriots			
☐ 416 Craig Colquitt 07	.03	.01	
Pittsburgh Steelers			
☐ 417 Lou Piccone 07	.03	.01	
Buffalo Bills			
☐ 418 Clay Matthews 1.00	.50	.10	
Cleveland Browns			
☐ 419 Marvin Cobb 07	.03	.01	
Cincinnati Bengals			
☐ 420 Harold Carmichael AP ...50	.25	.05	
Philadelphia Eagles			
☐ 421 Uwe Von Schamann 15	.07	.01	
Miami Dolphins			
☐ 422 Mike Phipps 15	.07	.01	
Chicago Bears			
☐ 423 Nolan Cromwell 1.50	.75	.15	
Los Angeles Rams			
☐ 424 Glenn Doughty 07	.03	.01	
Baltimore Colts			
☐ 425 Bob Young AP 07	.03	.01	
St. Louis Cardinals			
☐ 426 Tony Galbreath...........12	.06	.01	
New Orleans Saints			
☐ 427 Luke Prestridge 07	.03	.01	
Denver Broncos			
☐ 428 Terry Beeson 07	.03	.01	
Seattle Seahawks			
☐ 429 Jack Tatum 15	.07	.01	
Oakland Raiders			
☐ 430 Lemar Parrish AP 12	.06	.01	
Washington Redskins			
☐ 431 Chester Marcol 07	.03	.01	
Green Bay Packers			
☐ 432 Houston Oilers TL 25	.12	.02	
Dan Pastorini			
Ken Burrough			
Mike Reinfeldt			
Jesse Baker			
☐ 433 John Fitzgerald 12	.06	.01	
Dallas Cowboys			
☐ 434 Gary Jeter 50	.25	.05	
New York Giants			
☐ 435 Steve Grogan 40	.20	.04	
New England Patriots			
☐ 436 Jon Kolb 07	.03	.01	
Pittsburgh Steelers			
☐ 437 Jim O'Bradovich 07	.03	.01	
Tampa Bay Buccaneers			
☐ 438 Gerald Irons 07	.03	.01	
Cleveland Browns			
☐ 439 Jeff West 07	.03	.01	

San Diego Chargers
☐ 440 Wilbert Montgomery	.30	.15	.03

Philadelphia Eagles
☐ 441 Norris Thomas	.07	.03	.01

Miami Dolphins
☐ 442 James Scott	.07	.03	.01

Chicago Bears
☐ 443 Curtis Brown	.07	.03	.01

Buffalo Bills
☐ 444 Ken Fantetti	.07	.03	.01

Detroit Lions
☐ 445 Pat Haden	.30	.15	.03

Los Angeles Rams
☐ 446 Carl Mauck	.07	.03	.01

Houston Oilers
☐ 447 Bruce Laird	.07	.03	.01

Baltimore Colts
☐ 448 Otis Armstrong	.20	.10	.02

Denver Broncos
☐ 449 Gene Upshaw	.50	.25	.05

Oakland Raiders
☐ 450 Steve Largent AP	4.00	2.00	.40

Seattle Seahawks
☐ 451 Benny Malone	.07	.03	.01

Washington Redskins
☐ 452 Steve Nelson	.07	.03	.01

New England Patriots
☐ 453 Mark Cotney	.07	.03	.01

Tampa Bay Buccaneers
☐ 454 Joe Danelo	.07	.03	.01

New York Giants
☐ 455 Billy Joe DuPree	.20	.10	.02

Dallas Cowboys
☐ 456 Ron Johnson	.07	.03	.01

Pittsburgh Steelers
☐ 457 Archie Griffin	.20	.10	.02

Cincinnati Bengals
☐ 458 Reggie Rucker	.12	.06	.01

Cleveland Browns
☐ 459 Claude Humphrey	.12	.06	.01

Philadelphia Eagles
☐ 460 Lydell Mitchell	.15	.07	.01

San Diego Chargers
☐ 461 Steve Towle	.07	.03	.01

Miami Dolphins
☐ 462 Revie Sorey	.07	.03	.01

Chicago Bears
☐ 463 Tom Skladany	.12	.06	.01

Detroit Lions
☐ 464 Clark Gaines	.07	.03	.01

New York Jets
☐ 465 Frank Corral	.07	.03	.01

Los Angeles Rams
☐ 466 Steve Fuller	.30	.15	.03

Kansas City Chiefs
☐ 467 Ahmad Rashad AP	.75	.35	.07

Minnesota Vikings

☐ 468 Oakland Raiders TL	.30	.15	.03

Mark Van Eeghen
Cliff Branch
Lester Hayes
Willie Jones
☐ 469 Brian Peets	.07	.03	.01

Seattle Seahawks
☐ 470 Pat Donovan AP	.20	.10	.02

Dallas Cowboys
☐ 471 Ken Burrough	.12	.06	.01

Houston Oilers
☐ 472 Don Calhoun	.07	.03	.01

New England Patriots
☐ 473 Bill Bryan	.07	.03	.01

Denver Broncos
☐ 474 Terry Jackson	.07	.03	.01

New York Giants
☐ 475 Joe Theismann	1.50	.75	.15

Washington Redskins
☐ 476 Jim Smith	.12	.06	.01

Pittsburgh Steelers
☐ 477 Joe DeLamielleure	.12	.06	.01

Buffalo Bills
☐ 478 Mike Pruitt AP	.15	.07	.01

Cleveland Browns
☐ 479 Steve Mike-Mayer	.07	.03	.01

Baltimore Colts
☐ 480 Bill Bergey	.20	.10	.02

Philadelphia Eagles
☐ 481 Mike Fuller	.07	.03	.01

San Diego Chargers
☐ 482 Bob Parsons	.07	.03	.01

Chicago Bears
☐ 483 Billy Brooks	.12	.06	.01

Cincinnati Bengals
☐ 484 Jerome Barkum	.12	.06	.01

New York Jets
☐ 485 Larry Csonka	.90	.45	.09

Miami Dolphins
☐ 486 John Hill	.07	.03	.01

New Orleans Saints
☐ 487 Mike Dawson	.07	.03	.01

St. Louis Cardinals
☐ 488 Detroit Lions TL	.20	.10	.02

Dexter Bussey
Freddie Scott
Jim Allen
Luther Bradley
Al(Bubba) Baker
☐ 489 Ted Hendricks	.50	.25	.05

Oakland Raiders
☐ 490 Dan Pastorini	.15	.07	.01

Oakland Raiders
☐ 491 Stanley Morgan	.75	.35	.07

New England Patriots
☐ 492 AFC Championship	.20	.10	.02

Steelers 27,

Oilers 13
(Rocky Bleier running)

☐ 493	NFC Championship	.20	.10	.02

Rams 9,
Buccaneers 0
(Vince Ferragamo)

☐ 494	Super Bowl XIV	.45	.22	.04

Steelers 31,
Rams 19
(line play)

☐ 495	Dwight White	.12	.06	.01

Pittsburgh Steelers

☐ 496	Haven Moses	.12	.06	.01

Denver Broncos

☐ 497	Guy Morriss	.07	.03	.01

Philadelphia Eagles

☐ 498	Dewey Selmon	.12	.06	.01

Tampa Bay Buccaneers

☐ 499	Dave Butz	1.50	.75	.15

Washington Redskins

☐ 500	Chuck Foreman	.25	.12	.02

Minnesota Vikings

☐ 501	Chris Bahr	.12	.06	.01

Cincinnati Bengals

☐ 502	Mark Miller	.07	.03	.01

Cleveland Browns

☐ 503	Tony Greene	.07	.03	.01

Buffalo Bills

☐ 504	Brian Kelley	.12	.06	.01

New York Giants

☐ 505	Joe Washington	.15	.07	.01

Baltimore Colts

☐ 506	Butch Johnson	.15	.07	.01

Dallas Cowboys

☐ 507	New York Jets TL	.25	.12	.02

Clark Gaines
Wesley Walker
Burgess Owens
Joe Klecko

☐ 508	Steve Little	.07	.03	.01

St. Louis Cardinals

☐ 509	Checklist 397-528	.65	.06	.01
☐ 510	Mark Van Eeghen	.12	.06	.01

Oakland Raiders

☐ 511	Gary Danielson	.15	.07	.01

Detroit Lions

☐ 512	Manu Tuiasosopo	.12	.06	.01

Seattle Seahawks

☐ 513	Paul Coffman	.40	.20	.04

Green Bay Packers

☐ 514	Cullen Bryant	.07	.03	.01

Los Angeles Rams

☐ 515	Nat Moore	.15	.07	.01

Miami Dolphins

☐ 516	Bill Lenkaitis	.07	.03	.01

Atlanta Falcons

☐ 517	Lynn Cain	.25	.12	.02

Atlanta Falcons

☐ 518	Gregg Bingham	.07	.03	.01

Houston Oilers

☐ 519	Ted Albrecht	.07	.03	.01

Chicago Bears

☐ 520	Dan Fouts AP	2.00	1.00	.20

San Diego Chargers

☐ 521	Bernard Jackson	.12	.06	.01

Denver Broncos

☐ 522	Coy Bacon	.07	.03	.01

Washington Redskins

☐ 523	Tony Franklin	.30	.15	.03

Philadelphia Eagles

☐ 524	Bo Harris	.07	.03	.01

Cincinnati Bengals

☐ 525	Bob Grupp JP	.07	.03	.01

Kansas City Chiefs

☐ 526	San Francisco 49ers TL	.20	.10	.02

Paul Hofer
Freddie Solomon
James Owens
Dwaine Board

☐ 527	Steve Wilson	.07	.03	.01

Tampa Bay Buccaneers

☐ 528	Bennie Cunningham	.12	.06	.01

Pittsburgh Steelers

1981 Topps

*The 1981 Topps football card set contains 528
cards of NFL players. The cards measure the
standard 2 1/2" by 3 1/2". The backs of the
cards contain player vital statistics, year-by-
year records, and a short biography of the
player. The fronts of the cards contain the
name "Topps" in the frame line. The term SA
refers to a Super Action card as stated on the
obverse; the SA card is a special card issued*

in addition to the player's regular card. The first six cards in the set feature statistical league leaders from the previous season. Record-Breaking (RB) performances from the previous season are commemorated on cards 331-336. Post-season playoff action is summarized on cards 492-494. All-Pro (AP) selections are designated on the player's regular card, not a special card. Distributed throughout the set are Team Leader (TL) cards, typically, featuring four individual team statistical leaders on the front, as well as a team checklist on the back. The key rookie cards in this set are Art Monk and Joe Montana.

	MINT	EXC	G-VG
COMPLETE SET (528)	225.00	110.00	22.00
COMMON PLAYER (1-528)	.07	.03	.01

☐ 1 Passing Leaders Ron Jaworski Brian Sipe	.35	.10	.02
☐ 2 Receiving Leaders Earl Cooper Kellen Winslow	.45	.22	.04
☐ 3 Sack Leaders Al(Bubba) Baker Gary Johnson	.12	.06	.01
☐ 4 Scoring Leaders Ed Murray John Smith	.10	.05	.01
☐ 5 Interception Leaders Nolan Cromwell Lester Hayes	.15	.07	.01
☐ 6 Punting Leaders Dave Jennings Luke Prestridge	.10	.05	.01
☐ 7 Don Calhoun New England Patriots	.07	.03	.01
☐ 8 Jack Tatum Houston Oilers	.12	.06	.01
☐ 9 Reggie Rucker Cleveland Browns	.10	.05	.01
☐ 10 Mike Webster AP Pittsburgh Steelers	.35	.17	.03
☐ 11 Vince Evans Chicago Bears	.50	.25	.05
☐ 12 Ottis Anderson SA St. Louis Cardinals	.60	.30	.06
☐ 13 Leroy Harris Philadelphia Eagles	.07	.03	.01
☐ 14 Gordon King New York Giants	.07	.03	.01
☐ 15 Harvey Martin Dallas Cowboys	.20	.10	.02
☐ 16 Johnny "Lam" Jones New York Jets	.20	.10	.02
☐ 17 Ken Greene St. Louis Cardinals	.07	.03	.01
☐ 18 Frank Lewis Buffalo Bills	.10	.05	.01
☐ 19 Seattle Seahawks TL Jim Jodat Dave Brown John Harris Steve Largent Jacob Green	.50	.25	.05
☐ 20 Lester Hayes AP Oakland Raiders	.30	.15	.03
☐ 21 Uwe Von Schamann Miami Dolphins	.07	.03	.01
☐ 22 Joe Washington Baltimore Colts	.12	.06	.01
☐ 23 Louie Kelcher San Diego Chargers	.10	.05	.01
☐ 24 Willie Miller Los Angeles Rams	.07	.03	.01
☐ 25 Steve Grogan New England Patriots	.35	.17	.03
☐ 26 John Hill New Orleans Saints	.07	.03	.01
☐ 27 Stan White Detroit Lions	.07	.03	.01
☐ 28 William Andrews SA Atlanta Falcons	.12	.06	.01
☐ 29 Clarence Scott Cleveland Browns	.07	.03	.01
☐ 30 Leon Gray AP Houston Oilers	.10	.05	.01
☐ 31 Craig Colquitt Pittsburgh Steelers	.07	.03	.01
☐ 32 Doug Williams Tampa Bay Buccaneers	.35	.17	.03
☐ 33 Bob Breunig Dallas Cowboys	.15	.07	.01
☐ 34 Billy Taylor New York Giants	.10	.05	.01
☐ 35 Harold Carmichael Philadelphia Eagles	.35	.17	.03
☐ 36 Ray Wersching San Francisco 49ers	.07	.03	.01
☐ 37 Dennis Johnson Minnesota Vikings	.07	.03	.01
☐ 38 Archie Griffin Cincinnati Bengals	.15	.07	.01
☐ 39 Los Angeles Rams TL Cullen Bryant Billy Waddy Nolan Cromwell Jack Youngblood	.20	.10	.02
☐ 40 Gary Fencik AP Chicago Bears	.12	.06	.01
☐ 41 Lynn Dickey Green Bay Packers	.15	.07	.01

☐ 42 Steve Bartkowski SA	.15	.07	.01
Atlanta Falcons			
☐ 43 Art Shell	.60	.30	.06
Oakland Raiders			
☐ 44 Wilbur Jackson	.10	.05	.01
Washington Redskins			
☐ 45 Frank Corral	.07	.03	.01
Los Angeles Rams			
☐ 46 Ted McKnight	.07	.03	.01
Kansas City Chiefs			
☐ 47 Joe Klecko	.30	.15	.03
New York Jets			
☐ 48 Dan Doornink	.07	.03	.01
Seattle Seahawks			
☐ 49 Doug Dieken	.07	.03	.01
Cleveland Browns			
☐ 50 Jerry Robinson AP	1.00	.50	.10
Philadelphia Eagles			
☐ 51 Wallace Francis	.10	.05	.01
Atlanta Falcons			
☐ 52 Dave Preston	.15	.07	.01
Denver Broncos			
☐ 53 Jay Saldi	.07	.03	.01
Dallas Cowboys			
☐ 54 Rush Brown	.07	.03	.01
St. Louis Cardinals			
☐ 55 Phil Simms	3.25	1.60	.32
New York Giants			
☐ 56 Nick Mike-Mayer	.07	.03	.01
Buffalo Bills			
☐ 57 Wash. Redskins TL	1.25	.60	.12
Wilbur Jackson			
Art Monk			
Lemar Parrish			
Coy Bacon			
☐ 58 Mike Renfro	.10	.05	.01
Houston Oilers			
☐ 59 Ted Brown SA	.07	.03	.01
Minnesota Vikings			
☐ 60 Steve Nelson AP	.10	.05	.01
New England Patriots			
☐ 61 Sidney Thornton	.07	.03	.01
Pittsburgh Steelers			
☐ 62 Kent Hill	.12	.06	.01
Los Angeles Rams			
☐ 63 Don Bessillieu	.07	.03	.01
Miami Dolphins			
☐ 64 Fred Cook	.07	.03	.01
Baltimore Colts			
☐ 65 Raymond Chester	.12	.06	.01
Oakland Raiders			
☐ 66 Rick Kane	.07	.03	.01
Detroit Lions			
☐ 67 Mike Fuller	.07	.03	.01
San Diego Chargers			
☐ 68 Dewey Selmon	.10	.05	.01
Tampa Bay Buccaneers			
☐ 69 Charles White	1.25	.60	.12
Cleveland Browns			
☐ 70 Jeff Van Note AP	.12	.06	.01
Atlanta Falcons			
☐ 71 Robert Newhouse	.12	.06	.01
Dallas Cowboys			
☐ 72 Roynell Young	.35	.17	.03
Philadelphia Eagles			
☐ 73 Lynn Cain SA	.07	.03	.01
Atlanta Falcons			
☐ 74 Mike Friede	.07	.03	.01
New York Giants			
☐ 75 Earl Cooper	.15	.07	.01
San Francisco 49ers			
☐ 76 New Orleans Saints TL	.15	.07	.01
Jimmy Rogers			
Wes Chandler			
Tom Myers			
Elois Grooms			
Derland Moore			
☐ 77 Rick Danmeier	.07	.03	.01
Minnesota Vikings			
☐ 78 Darrol Ray	.12	.06	.01
New York Jets			
☐ 79 Gregg Bingham	.10	.05	.01
Houston Oilers			
☐ 80 John Hannah AP	.50	.25	.05
New England Patriots			
☐ 81 Jack Thompson	.10	.05	.01
Cincinnati Bengals			
☐ 82 Rick Upchurch	.15	.07	.01
Denver Broncos			
☐ 83 Mike Butler	.07	.03	.01
Green Bay Packers			
☐ 84 Don Warren	.25	.12	.02
Washington Redskins			
☐ 85 Mark Van Eeghen	.10	.05	.01
Oakland Raiders			
☐ 86 J.T. Smith	2.00	1.00	.20
Kansas City Chiefs			
☐ 87 Herman Weaver	.07	.03	.01
Seattle Seahawks			
☐ 88 Terry Bradshaw SA	1.00	.50	.10
Pittsburgh Steelers			
☐ 89 Charlie Hall	.07	.03	.01
Cleveland Browns			
☐ 90 Donnie Shell	.20	.10	.02
Pittsburgh Steelers			
☐ 91 Ike Harris	.07	.03	.01
New Orleans Saints			
☐ 92 Charlie Johnson	.07	.03	.01
Philadelphia Eagles			
☐ 93 Rickey Watts	.07	.03	.01
Chicago Bears			
☐ 94 New England Pats TL	.20	.10	.02
Vagas Ferguson			
Stanley Morgan			

Raymond Clayborn
Julius Adams

☐ 95	Drew Pearson 35	.17	.03
	Dallas Cowboys		
☐ 96	Neil O'Donoghue 07	.03	.01
	St. Louis Cardinals		
☐ 97	Conrad Dobler 12	.06	.01
	Buffalo Bills		
☐ 98	Jewerl Thomas 15	.07	.01
	Los Angeles Rams		
☐ 99	Mike Barber 10	.05	.01
	Houston Oilers		
☐ 100	Billy Sims AP 1.50	.75	.15
	Detroit Lions		
☐ 101	Vern Den Herder 07	.03	.01
	Miami Dolphins		
☐ 102	Greg Landry 15	.07	.01
	Baltimore Colts		
☐ 103	Joe Cribbs SA 12	.06	.01
	Buffalo Bills		
☐ 104	Mark Murphy 40	.20	.04
	Washington Redskins		
☐ 105	Chuck Muncie 15	.07	.01
	San Diego Chargers		
☐ 106	Alfred Jackson 10	.05	.01
	Atlanta Falcons		
☐ 107	Chris Bahr 10	.05	.01
	Oakland Raiders		
☐ 108	Gordon Jones 12	.06	.01
	Tampa Bay Buccaneers		
☐ 109	Willie Harper 25	.12	.02
	San Francisco 49ers		
☐ 110	Dave Jennings AP 12	.06	.01
	New York Giants		
☐ 111	Bennie Cunningham 10	.05	.01
	Pittsburgh Steelers		
☐ 112	Jerry Sisemore 07	.03	.01
	Philadelphia Eagles		
☐ 113	Cleveland Browns TL 20	.10	.02
	Mike Pruitt		
	Dave Logan		
	Ron Bolton		
	Lyle Alzado		
☐ 114	Rickey Young 12	.06	.01
	Minnesota Vikings		
☐ 115	Ken Anderson 60	.30	.06
	Cincinnati Bengals		
☐ 116	Randy Gradishar 30	.15	.03
	Denver Broncos		
☐ 117	Eddie Lee Ivery 35	.17	.03
	Green Bay Packers		
☐ 118	Wesley Walker 35	.17	.03
	New York Jets		
☐ 119	Chuck Foreman 20	.10	.02
	New England Patriots		
☐ 120	Nolan Cromwell AP 30	.15	.03
	Los Angeles Rams		

UER (Rushing TD's
added wrong)

☐ 121	Curtis Dickey SA 12	.06	.01
	Baltimore Colts		
☐ 122	Wayne Morris 07	.03	.01
	St. Louis Cardinals		
☐ 123	Greg Stemrick 07	.03	.01
	Houston Oilers		
☐ 124	Coy Bacon 07	.03	.01
	Washington Redskins		
☐ 125	Jim Zorn 20	.10	.02
	Seattle Seahawks		
☐ 126	Henry Childs 07	.03	.01
	New Orleans Saints		
☐ 127	Checklist 1-132 45	.05	.01
☐ 128	Len Walterscheid 07	.03	.01
	Chicago Bears		
☐ 129	Johnny Evans 07	.03	.01
	Cleveland Browns		
☐ 130	Gary Barbaro AP 12	.06	.01
	Kansas City Chiefs		
☐ 131	Jim Smith 10	.05	.01
	Pittsburgh Steelers		
☐ 132	New York Jets TL 20	.10	.02
	Scott Dierking		
	Bruce Harper		
	Ken Schroy		
	Mark Gastineau		
☐ 133	Curtis Brown 07	.03	.01
	Buffalo Bills		
☐ 134	D.D. Lewis 12	.06	.01
	Dallas Cowboys		
☐ 135	Jim Plunkett 50	.25	.05
	Oakland Raiders		
☐ 136	Nat Moore 12	.06	.01
	Miami Dolphins		
☐ 137	Don McCauley 07	.03	.01
	Baltimore Colts		
☐ 138	Tony Dorsett SA 1.00	.50	.10
	Dallas Cowboys		
☐ 139	Julius Adams 07	.03	.01
	New England Patriots		
☐ 140	Ahmad Rashad AP 50	.25	.05
	Minnesota Vikings		
☐ 141	Rich Saul 07	.03	.01
	Los Angeles Rams		
☐ 142	Ken Fantetti 07	.03	.01
	Detroit Lions		
☐ 143	Kenny Johnson 07	.03	.01
	Buffalo Bills		
☐ 144	Clark Gaines 07	.03	.01
	New York Jets		
☐ 145	Mark Moseley 12	.06	.01
	Washington Redskins		
☐ 146	Vernon Perry 15	.07	.01
	Houston Oilers		
☐ 147	Jerry Eckwood 10	.05	.01

Tampa Bay Buccaneers			
☐ 148 Freddie Solomon 12	.06	.01	
San Francisco 49ers			
☐ 149 Jerry Sherk 10	.05	.01	
Cleveland Browns			
☐ 150 Kellen Winslow AP 8.00	4.00	.80	
San Diego Chargers			
☐ 151 Green Bay Packers TL 75	.35	.07	
Eddie Lee Ivery			
James Lofton			
Johnnie Gray			
Mike Butler			
☐ 152 Ross Browner 10	.05	.01	
Cincinnati Bengals			
☐ 153 Dan Fouts SA 65	.30	.06	
San Diego Chargers			
☐ 154 Woody Peoples 07	.03	.01	
Philadelphia Eagles			
☐ 155 Jack Lambert 75	.35	.07	
Pittsburgh Steelers			
☐ 156 Mike Dennis 07	.03	.01	
New York Giants			
☐ 157 Rafael Septien 10	.05	.01	
Dallas Cowboys			
☐ 158 Archie Manning 35	.17	.03	
New Orleans Saints			
☐ 159 Don Hasselbeck 07	.03	.01	
New England Patriots			
☐ 160 Alan Page AP 50	.25	.05	
Chicago Bears			
☐ 161 Arthur Whittington 07	.03	.01	
Oakland Raiders			
☐ 162 Billy Waddy 07	.03	.01	
Los Angeles Rams			
☐ 163 Horace Belton 07	.03	.01	
Kansas City Chiefs			
☐ 164 Luke Prestridge 07	.03	.01	
Denver Broncos			
☐ 165 Joe Theismann 1.25	.60	.12	
Washington Redskins			
☐ 166 Morris Towns 07	.03	.01	
Houston Oilers			
☐ 167 Dave Brown 15	.07	.01	
Seattle Seahawks			
☐ 168 Ezra Johnson 07	.03	.01	
Green Bay Packers			
☐ 169 Tampa Bay Bucs TL 25	.12	.02	
Ricky Bell			
Gordon Jones			
Mike Washington			
Lee Roy Selmon			
☐ 170 Joe DeLamielleure AP 10	.05	.01	
Cleveland Browns			
☐ 171 Earnest Gray SA 10	.05	.01	
New York Giants			
☐ 172 Mike Thomas 07	.03	.01	
San Diego Chargers			
☐ 173 Jim Haslett 07	.03	.01	
Buffalo Bills			
☐ 174 David Woodley 35	.17	.03	
Miami Dolphins			
☐ 175 Al(Bubba) Baker 15	.07	.01	
Detroit Lions			
☐ 176 Nesby Glasgow 20	.10	.02	
Baltimore Colts			
☐ 177 Pat Leahy 15	.07	.01	
New York Jets			
☐ 178 Tom Brahaney 07	.03	.01	
St. Louis Cardinals			
☐ 179 Herman Edwards 07	.03	.01	
Philadelphia Eagles			
☐ 180 Junior Miller AP 30	.15	.03	
Atlanta Falcons			
☐ 181 Richard Wood 30	.15	.03	
Tampa Bay Buccaneers			
☐ 182 Lenvil Elliott 07	.03	.01	
San Francisco 49ers			
☐ 183 Sammie White 15	.07	.01	
Minnesota Vikings			
☐ 184 Russell Erxleben 07	.03	.01	
New Orleans Saints			
☐ 185 Ed Too Tall Jones 60	.30	.06	
Dallas Cowboys			
☐ 186 Ray Guy SA 15	.07	.01	
Oakland Raiders			
☐ 187 Haven Moses 10	.05	.01	
Denver Broncos			
☐ 188 New York Giants TL 15	.07	.01	
Billy Taylor			
Earnest Gray			
Mike Dennis			
Gary Jeter			
☐ 189 David Whitehurst 10	.05	.01	
Green Bay Packers			
☐ 190 John Jefferson AP 20	.10	.02	
San Diego Chargers			
☐ 191 Terry Beeson 07	.03	.01	
Seattle Seahawks			
☐ 192 Dan Ross 50	.25	.05	
Cincinnati Bengals			
☐ 193 Dave Williams 07	.03	.01	
Chicago Bears			
☐ 194 Art Monk 45.00	22.50	4.50	
Washington Redskins			
☐ 195 Roger Wehrli 10	.05	.01	
St. Louis Cardinals			
☐ 196 Ricky Feacher 07	.03	.01	
Cleveland Browns			
☐ 197 Miami Dolphins TL 20	.10	.02	
Delvin Williams			
Tony Nathan			
Gerald Small			
Kim Bokamper			
A.J. Duhe			

☐ 198	Carl Roaches 15	.07	.01	
	Houston Oilers			
☐ 199	Billy Campfield 07	.03	.01	
	Philadelphia Eagles			
☐ 200	Ted Hendricks AP 45	.22	.04	
	Oakland Raiders			
☐ 201	Fred Smerlas 1.25	.60	.12	
	Buffalo Bills			
☐ 202	Walter Payton SA 1.50	.75	.15	
	Chicago Bears			
☐ 203	Luther Bradley 10	.05	.01	
	Detroit Lions			
☐ 204	Herbert Scott 10	.05	.01	
	Dallas Cowboys			
☐ 205	Jack Youngblood 35	.17	.03	
	Los Angeles Rams			
☐ 206	Danny Pittman 07	.03	.01	
	New York Giants			
☐ 207	Houston Oilers TL 20	.10	.02	
	Carl Roaches			
	Mike Barber			
	Jack Tatum			
	Jesse Baker			
	Robert Brazile			
☐ 208	Vagas Ferguson 25	.12	.02	
	Buffalo Bills			
☐ 209	Mark Dennard 07	.03	.01	
	Miami Dolphins			
☐ 210	Lemar Parrish AP 07	.03	.01	
	Washington Redskins			
☐ 211	Bruce Harper 07	.03	.01	
	New York Jets			
☐ 212	Ed Simonini 07	.03	.01	
	Baltimore Colts			
☐ 213	Nick Lowery 2.50	1.25	.25	
	Kansas City Chiefs			
☐ 214	Kevin House 35	.17	.03	
	Tampa Bay Buccaneers			
☐ 215	Mike Kenn 75	.35	.07	
	Atlanta Falcons			
☐ 216	Joe Montana 150.00	75.00	15.00	
	San Francisco 49ers			
☐ 217	Joe Senser 15	.07	.01	
	Minnesota Vikings			
☐ 218	Lester Hayes SA 12	.06	.01	
	Oakland Raiders			
☐ 219	Gene Upshaw 45	.22	.04	
	Oakland Raiders			
☐ 220	Franco Harris 1.25	.60	.12	
	Pittsburgh Steelers			
☐ 221	Ron Bolton 07	.03	.01	
	Cleveland Browns			
☐ 222	Charles Alexander 15	.07	.01	
	Cincinnati Bengals			
☐ 223	Matt Robinson 10	.05	.01	
	Denver Broncos			
☐ 224	Ray Oldham 07	.03	.01	

	Detroit Lions			
☐ 225	George Martin 12	.06	.01	
	New York Giants			
☐ 226	Buffalo Bills TL 15	.07	.01	
	Joe Cribbs			
	Jerry Butler			
	Steve Freeman			
	Ben Williams			
☐ 227	Tony Franklin 10	.05	.01	
	Philadelphia Eagles			
☐ 228	George Cumby 07	.03	.01	
	Green Bay Packers			
☐ 229	Butch Johnson 15	.07	.01	
	Dallas Cowboys			
☐ 230	Mike Haynes AP 20	.10	.02	
	New England Patriots			
☐ 231	Rob Carpenter 10	.05	.01	
	Houston Oilers			
☐ 232	Steve Fuller 15	.07	.01	
	Kansas City Chiefs			
☐ 233	John Sawyer 07	.03	.01	
	Seattle Seahawks			
☐ 234	Kenny King SA 12	.06	.01	
	Oakland Raiders			
☐ 235	Jack Ham 60	.30	.06	
	Pittsburgh Steelers			
☐ 236	Jimmy Rogers 07	.03	.01	
	New Orleans Saints			
☐ 237	Bob Parsons 07	.03	.01	
	Chicago Bears			
☐ 238	Marty Lyons 60	.30	.06	
	New York Jets			
☐ 239	Pat Tilley 12	.06	.01	
	St. Louis Cardinals			
☐ 240	Dennis Harrah AP 10	.05	.01	
	Los Angeles Rams			
☐ 241	Thom Darden 07	.03	.01	
	Cleveland Browns			
☐ 242	Rolf Benirschke 15	.07	.01	
	San Diego Chargers			
☐ 243	Gerald Small 07	.03	.01	
	Miami Dolphins			
☐ 244	Atlanta Falcons TL 15	.07	.01	
	William Andrews			
	Alfred Jenkins			
	Al Richardson			
	Joel Williams			
☐ 245	Roger Carr 10	.05	.01	
	Baltimore Colts			
☐ 246	Sherman White 07	.03	.01	
	Buffalo Bills			
☐ 247	Ted Brown 10	.05	.01	
	Minnesota Vikings			
☐ 248	Matt Cavanaugh 15	.07	.01	
	New England Patriots			
☐ 249	John Dutton 12	.06	.01	
	Dallas Cowboys			

☐	250	Bill Bergey AP	.15	.07	.01
		Philadelphia Eagles			
☐	251	Jim Allen	.07	.03	.01
		Detroit Lions			
☐	252	Mike Nelms SA	.10	.05	.01
		Washington Redskins			
☐	253	Tom Blanchard	.07	.03	.01
		Tampa Bay Buccaneers			
☐	254	Ricky Thompson	.07	.03	.01
		Washington Redskins			
☐	255	John Matuszak	.12	.06	.01
		Oakland Raiders			
☐	256	Randy Grossman	.07	.03	.01
		Pittsburgh Steelers			
☐	257	Ray Griffin	.07	.03	.01
		Cincinnati Bengals			
☐	258	Lynn Cain	.10	.05	.01
		Atlanta Falcons			
☐	259	Checklist 133-264	.45	.05	.01
☐	260	Mike Pruitt AP	.12	.06	.01
		Cleveland Browns			
☐	261	Chris Ward	.07	.03	.01
		New York Jets			
☐	262	Fred Steinfort	.07	.03	.01
		Denver Broncos			
☐	263	James Owens	.12	.06	.01
		San Francisco 49ers			
☐	264	Chicago Bears TL	1.25	.60	.12
		Walter Payton			
		James Scott			
		Len Walterscheid			
		Dan Hampton			
☐	265	Dan Fouts	1.50	.75	.15
		San Diego Chargers			
☐	266	Arnold Morgado	.07	.03	.01
		Kansas City Chiefs			
☐	267	John Jefferson SA	.12	.06	.01
		San Diego Chargers			
☐	268	Bill Lenkaitis	.07	.03	.01
		New England Patriots			
☐	269	James Jones	.12	.06	.01
		Dallas Cowboys			
☐	270	Brad Van Pelt	.10	.05	.01
		New York Giants			
☐	271	Steve Largent	3.00	1.50	.30
		Seattle Seahawks			
☐	272	Elvin Bethea	.12	.06	.01
		Houston Oilers			
☐	273	Cullen Bryant	.10	.05	.01
		Los Angeles Rams			
☐	274	Gary Danielson	.15	.07	.01
		Detroit Lions			
☐	275	Tony Galbreath	.10	.05	.01
		New Orleans Saints			
☐	276	Dave Butz	.30	.15	.03
		Washington Redskins			
☐	277	Steve Mike-Mayer	.07	.03	.01
☐	278	Ron Johnson	.07	.03	.01
		Pittsburgh Steelers			
☐	279	Tom DeLeone	.07	.03	.01
		Cleveland Browns			
☐	280	Ron Jaworski	.20	.10	.02
		Philadelphia Eagles			
☐	281	Mel Gray	.12	.06	.01
		St. Louis Cardinals			
☐	282	San Diego Chargers TL	.20	.10	.02
		Chuck Muncie			
		John Jefferson			
		Glen Edwards			
		Gary Johnson			
☐	283	Mark Brammer	.07	.03	.01
		Buffalo Bills			
☐	284	Alfred Jenkins SA	.07	.03	.01
		Atlanta Falcons			
☐	285	Greg Buttle	.10	.05	.01
		New York Jets			
☐	286	Randy Hughes	.10	.05	.01
		Dallas Cowboys			
☐	287	Delvin Williams	.10	.05	.01
		Miami Dolphins			
☐	288	Brian Baschnagel	.10	.05	.01
		Chicago Bears			
☐	289	Gary Jeter	.10	.05	.01
		New York Giants			
☐	290	Stanley Morgan AP	.50	.25	.05
		New England Patriots			
☐	291	Gerry Ellis	.07	.03	.01
		Green Bay Packers			
☐	292	Al Richardson	.07	.03	.01
		Atlanta Falcons			
☐	293	Jimmie Giles	.10	.05	.01
		Tampa Bay Buccaneers			
☐	294	Dave Jennings SA	.07	.03	.01
		New York Giants			
☐	295	Wilbert Montgomery	.20	.10	.02
		Philadelphia Eagles			
☐	296	Dave Pureifory	.07	.03	.01
		Detroit Lions			
☐	297	Greg Hawthorne	.10	.05	.01
		Pittsburgh Steelers			
☐	298	Dick Ambrose	.07	.03	.01
		Cleveland Browns			
☐	299	Terry Hermeling	.07	.03	.01
		Washington Redskins			
☐	300	Danny White	.50	.25	.05
		Dallas Cowboys			
☐	301	Ken Burrough	.12	.06	.01
		Houston Oilers			
☐	302	Paul Hofer	.07	.03	.01
		San Francisco 49ers			
☐	303	Denver Broncos TL	.15	.07	.01
		Jim Jensen			
		Haven Moses			

Steve Foley
Rulon Jones

☐ 304 Eddie Payton ....12 .06 .01
Minnesota Vikings
☐ 305 Isaac Curtis ....12 .06 .01
Cincinnati Bengals
☐ 306 Benny Ricardo ....07 .03 .01
New Orleans Saints
☐ 307 Riley Odoms ....12 .06 .01
Denver Broncos
☐ 308 Bob Chandler ....10 .05 .01
Oakland Raiders
☐ 309 Larry Heater ....07 .03 .01
New York Giants
☐ 310 Art Still AP ....75 .35 .07
Kansas City Chiefs
☐ 311 Harold Jackson ....25 .12 .02
New England Patriots
☐ 312 Charlie Joiner SA ....25 .12 .02
San Diego Chargers
☐ 313 Jeff Nixon ....07 .03 .01
Buffalo Bills
☐ 314 Aundra Thompson ....12 .06 .01
Green Bay Packers
☐ 315 Richard Todd ....15 .07 .01
New York Jets
☐ 316 Dan Hampton 11.00 5.50 1.10
Chicago Bears
☐ 317 Doug Marsh ....07 .03 .01
St. Louis Cardinals
☐ 318 Louie Giammona ....07 .03 .01
Philadelphia Eagles
☐ 319 San Francisco 49ers TL .45 .22 .04
Earl Cooper
Dwight Clark
Ricky Churchman
Dwight Hicks
Jim Stuckey
☐ 320 Manu Tuiasosopo ....07 .03 .01
Seattle Seahawks
☐ 321 Rich Milot ....07 .03 .01
Washington Redskins
☐ 322 Mike Guman ....07 .03 .01
Los Angeles Rams
☐ 323 Bob Kuechenberg ....10 .05 .01
Miami Dolphins
☐ 324 Tom Skladany ....07 .03 .01
Detroit Lions
☐ 325 Dave Logan ....07 .03 .01
Cleveland Browns
☐ 326 Bruce Laird ....07 .03 .01
Baltimore Colts
☐ 327 James Jones SA ....10 .05 .01
Dallas Cowboys
☐ 328 Joe Danelo ....07 .03 .01
New York Giants
☐ 329 Kenny King ....35 .17 .03

Oakland Raiders
☐ 330 Pat Donovan AP ....12 .06 .01
Dallas Cowboys
☐ 331 Earl Cooper RB ....12 .06 .01
Most Receptions,
Running Back,
Season, Rookie
☐ 332 John Jefferson RB ....12 .06 .01
Most Cons. Seasons,
1000 Yards Receiving,
Start of Career
☐ 333 Kenny King RB ....12 .06 .01
Longest Pass Caught,
Super Bowl History
☐ 334 Rod Martin RB ....12 .06 .01
Most Interceptions
Super Bowl Game
☐ 335 Jim Plunkett RB ....15 .07 .01
Longest Pass,
Super Bowl History
☐ 336 Bill Thompson RB ....12 .06 .01
Most Touchdowns,
Fumble Recoveries,
Lifetime
☐ 337 John Cappelletti ....15 .07 .01
San Diego Chargers
☐ 338 Detroit Lions TL ....30 .15 .03
Billy Sims
Freddie Scott
Jim Allen
James Hunter
Al(Bubba) Baker
☐ 339 Don Smith ....07 .03 .01
Atlanta Falcons
☐ 340 Rod Perry AP ....12 .06 .01
Los Angeles Rams
☐ 341 David Lewis ....07 .03 .01
Tampa Bay Buccaneers
☐ 342 Mark Gastineau ....1.25 .60 .12
New York Jets
☐ 343 Steve Largent SA ....1.50 .75 .15
Seattle Seahawks
☐ 344 Charley Young ....12 .06 .01
San Francisco 49ers
☐ 345 Toni Fritsch ....07 .03 .01
Houston Oilers
☐ 346 Matt Blair ....12 .06 .01
Minnesota Vikings
☐ 347 Don Bass ....07 .03 .01
Cincinnati Bengals
☐ 348 Jim Jensen ....40 .20 .04
Denver Broncos
☐ 349 Karl Lorch ....07 .03 .01
Washington Redskins
☐ 350 Brian Sipe AP ....20 .10 .02
Cleveland Browns
☐ 351 Theo Bell ....07 .03 .01

	Pittsburgh Steelers		
☐ 352	Sam Adams 07	.03	.01
	New Orleans Saints		
☐ 353	Paul Coffman 10	.05	.01
	Green Bay Packers		
☐ 354	Eric Harris 07	.03	.01
	Kansas City Chiefs		
☐ 355	Tony Hill 15	.07	.01
	Dallas Cowboys		
☐ 356	J.T. Turner 07	.03	.01
	New York Giants		
☐ 357	Frank LeMaster 07	.03	.01
	Philadelphia Eagles		
☐ 358	Jim Jodat 07	.03	.01
	Seattle Seahawks		
☐ 359	Oakland Raiders TL 30	.15	.03
	Mark Van Eeghen		
	Cliff Branch		
	Lester Hayes		
	Cedric Hardman		
	Ted Hendricks		
☐ 360	Joe Cribbs AP 1.00	.50	.10
	Buffalo Bills		
☐ 361	James Lofton SA 1.75	.85	.17
	Green Bay Packers		
☐ 362	Dexter Bussey 07	.03	.01
	Detroit Lions		
☐ 363	Bobby Jackson 07	.03	.01
	New York Jets		
☐ 364	Steve DeBerg 1.25	.60	.12
	San Francisco 49ers		
☐ 365	Ottis Anderson 2.50	1.25	.25
	St. Louis Cardinals		
☐ 366	Tom Myers 07	.03	.01
	New Orleans Saints		
☐ 367	John James 07	.03	.01
	Atlanta Falcons		
☐ 368	Reese McCall 07	.03	.01
	Baltimore Colts		
☐ 369	Jack Reynolds 12	.06	.01
	Los Angeles Rams		
☐ 370	Gary Johnson AP 12	.06	.01
	San Diego Chargers		
☐ 371	Jimmy Cefalo 12	.06	.01
	Miami Dolphins		
☐ 372	Horace Ivory 07	.03	.01
	New England Patriots		
☐ 373	Garo Yepremian 10	.05	.01
	Tampa Bay Buccaneers		
☐ 374	Brian Kelley 10	.05	.01
	New York Giants		
☐ 375	Terry Bradshaw 2.25	1.10	.22
	Pittsburgh Steelers		
☐ 376	Dallas Cowboys TL 65	.30	.06
	Tony Dorsett		
	Tony Hill		
	Dennis Thurman		
	Charlie Waters		
	Harvey Martin		
☐ 377	Randy Logan 07	.03	.01
	Philadelphia Eagles		
☐ 378	Tim Wilson 07	.03	.01
	Houston Oilers		
☐ 379	Archie Manning SA 15	.07	.01
	New Orleans Saints		
☐ 380	Revie Sorey AP 07	.03	.01
	Chicago Bears		
☐ 381	Randy Holloway 07	.03	.01
	Minnesota Vikings		
☐ 382	Henry Lawrence 07	.03	.01
	Oakland Raiders		
☐ 383	Pat McInally 10	.05	.01
	Cincinnati Bengals		
☐ 384	Kevin Long 07	.03	.01
	New York Jets		
☐ 385	Louis Wright 15	.07	.01
	Denver Broncos		
☐ 386	Leonard Thompson 07	.03	.01
	Detroit Lions		
☐ 387	Jan Stenerud 35	.17	.03
	Green Bay Packers		
☐ 388	Raymond Butler 35	.17	.03
	Baltimore Colts		
☐ 389	Checklist 265-396 45	.05	.01
☐ 390	Steve Bartkowski AP 25	.12	.02
	Atlanta Falcons		
☐ 391	Clarence Harmon 07	.03	.01
	Washington Redskins		
☐ 392	Wilbert Montgomery SA .10	.05	.01
	Philadelphia Eagles		
☐ 393	Billy Joe DuPree 20	.10	.02
	Dallas Cowboys		
☐ 394	Kansas City Chiefs TL 15	.07	.01
	Ted McKnight		
	Henry Marshall		
	Gary Barbaro		
	Art Still		
☐ 395	Earnest Gray 10	.05	.01
	New York Giants		
☐ 396	Ray Hamilton 10	.05	.01
	New England Patriots		
☐ 397	Brenard Wilson 07	.03	.01
	Philadelphia Eagles		
☐ 398	Calvin Hill 12	.06	.01
	Cleveland Browns		
☐ 399	Robin Cole 07	.03	.01
	Pittsburgh Steelers		
☐ 400	Walter Payton AP 4.00	2.00	.40
	Chicago Bears		
☐ 401	Jim Hart 25	.12	.02
	St. Louis Cardinals		
☐ 402	Ron Yary 12	.06	.01
	Minnesota Vikings		
☐ 403	Cliff Branch 35	.17	.03

	Oakland Raiders			Green Bay Packers	
☐ 404	Roland Hooks .... .07	.03	.01	☐ 431 Tony Reed .... .10	.05	.01
	Buffalo Bills			Kansas City Chiefs	
☐ 405	Ken Stabler .... .60	.30	.06	☐ 432 Minnesota Vikings TL .. .25	.12	.02
	Houston Oilers			Ted Brown	
☐ 406	Chuck Ramsey .... .07	.03	.01	Ahmad Rashad	
	New York Jets			John Turner	
☐ 407	Mike Nelms .... .20	.10	.02	Doug Sutherland	
	Washington Redskins			☐ 433 Ron Springs .... .15	.07	.01
☐ 408	Ron Jaworski SA .... .10	.05	.01	Dallas Cowboys	
	Philadelphia Eagles			☐ 434 Tim Fox .... .07	.03	.01
☐ 409	James Hunter .... .07	.03	.01	New England Patriots	
	Detroit Lions			☐ 435 Ozzie Newsome 2.50	1.25	.25
☐ 410	Lee Roy Selmon AP ...... .15	.07	.01	Cleveland Browns	
	Tampa Bay Buccaneers			☐ 436 Steve Furness .... .07	.03	.01
☐ 411	Baltimore Colts TL .... .15	.07	.01	Pittsburgh Steelers	
	Curtis Dickey			☐ 437 Will Lewis .... .07	.03	.01
	Roger Carr			Seattle Seahawks	
	Bruce Laird			☐ 438 Mike Hartenstine .... .07	.03	.01
	Mike Barnes			Chicago Bears	
☐ 412	Henry Marshall .... .07	.03	.01	☐ 439 John Bunting .... .07	.03	.01
	Kansas City Chiefs			Philadelphia Eagles	
☐ 413	Preston Pearson .... .15	.07	.01	☐ 440 Ed Murray 1.00	.50	.10
	Dallas Cowboys			Detroit Lions	
☐ 414	Richard Bishop .... .07	.03	.01	☐ 441 Mike Pruitt SA .... .12	.06	.01
	New England Patriots			Cleveland Browns	
☐ 415	Greg Pruitt .... .15	.07	.01	☐ 442 Larry Swider .... .07	.03	.01
	Cleveland Browns			St. Louis Cardinals	
☐ 416	Matt Bahr .... .25	.12	.02	☐ 443 Steve Freeman .... .07	.03	.01
	Pittsburgh Steelers			Buffalo Bills	
☐ 417	Tom Mullady .... .07	.03	.01	☐ 444 Bruce Hardy .... .12	.06	.01
	New York Giants			Miami Dolphins	
☐ 418	Glen Edwards .... .07	.03	.01	☐ 445 Pat Haden .... .25	.12	.02
	San Diego Chargers			Los Angeles Rams	
☐ 419	Sam McCullum .... .12	.06	.01	☐ 446 Curtis Dickey .... .35	.17	.03
	Seattle Seahawks			Baltimore Colts	
☐ 420	Stan Walters AP .... .07	.03	.01	☐ 447 Doug Wilkerson .... .07	.03	.01
	Philadelphia Eagles			San Diego Chargers	
☐ 421	George Roberts .... .07	.03	.01	☐ 448 Alfred Jenkins .... .10	.05	.01
	Miami Dolphins			Atlanta Falcons	
☐ 422	Dwight Clark 4.00	2.00	.40	☐ 449 Dave Dalby .... .10	.05	.01
	San Francisco 49ers			Oakland Raiders	
☐ 423	Pat Thomas .... .15	.07	.01	☐ 450 Robert Brazile AP .... .12	.06	.01
	Los Angeles Rams			Houston Oilers	
☐ 424	Bruce Harper SA .... .07	.03	.01	☐ 451 Bobby Hammond .... .07	.03	.01
	New York Jets			Washington Redskins	
☐ 425	Craig Morton .... .30	.15	.03	☐ 452 Raymond Clayborn .... .10	.05	.01
	Denver Broncos			New England Patriots	
☐ 426	Derrick Gaffney .... .07	.03	.01	☐ 453 Jim Miller .... .07	.03	.01
	New York Jets			San Francisco 49ers	
☐ 427	Pete Johnson .... .10	.05	.01	☐ 454 Roy Simmons .... .07	.03	.01
	Cincinnati Bengals			New York Giants	
☐ 428	Wes Chandler .... .45	.22	.04	☐ 455 Charlie Waters .... .15	.07	.01
	New Orleans Saints			Dallas Cowboys	
☐ 429	Burgess Owens .... .07	.03	.01	☐ 456 Ricky Bell .... .15	.07	.01
	Oakland Raiders			Tampa Bay Buccaneers	
☐ 430	James Lofton AP 4.25	2.10	.42	☐ 457 Ahmad Rashad SA .... .25	.12	.02

	Minnesota Vikings		
☐ 458	Don Cockroft 07	.03	.01
	Cleveland Browns		
☐ 459	Keith Krepfle 07	.03	.01
	Philadelphia Eagles.		
☐ 460	Marvin Powell AP 12	.06	.01
	New York Jets		
☐ 461	Tommy Kramer 30	.15	.03
	Minnesota Vikings		
☐ 462	Jim LeClair 07	.03	.01
	Cincinnati Bengals		
☐ 463	Freddie Scott 07	.03	.01
	Detroit Lions		
☐ 464	Rob Lytle 10	.05	.01
	Denver Broncos		
☐ 465	Johnnie Gray 07	.03	.01
	Green Bay Packers		
☐ 466	Doug France 20	.10	.02
	Los Angeles Rams		
☐ 467	Carlos Carson 50	.25	.05
	Kansas City Chiefs		
☐ 468	St. Louis Cardinals TL 35	.17	.03
	Ottis Anderson		
	Pat Tilley		
	Ken Stone		
	Curtis Greer		
	Steve Neils		
☐ 469	Efren Herrera 07	.03	.01
	Seattle Seahawks		
☐ 470	Randy White AP 75	.35	.07
	Dallas Cowboys		
☐ 471	Richard Caster 12	.06	.01
	Houston Oilers		
☐ 472	Andy Johnson 07	.03	.01
	New England Patriots		
☐ 473	Billy Sims SA 30	.15	.03
	Detroit Lions		
☐ 474	Joe Lavender 07	.03	.01
	Washington Redskins		
☐ 475	Harry Carson 45	.22	.04
	New York Giants		
☐ 476	John Stallworth 50	.25	.05
	Pittsburgh Steelers		
☐ 477	Bob Thomas 07	.03	.01
	Chicago Bears		
☐ 478	Keith Wright 07	.03	.01
	Cleveland Browns		
☐ 479	Ken Stone 07	.03	.01
	St. Louis Cardinals		
☐ 480	Carl Hairston AP 12	.06	.01
	Philadelphia Eagles		
☐ 481	Reggie McKenzie 12	.06	.01
	Buffalo Bills		
☐ 482	Bob Griese 1.50	.75	.15
	Miami Dolphins		
☐ 483	Mike Bragg 07	.03	.01
	Baltimore Colts		

☐ 484	Scott Dierking 07	.03	.01
	New York Jets		
☐ 485	David Hill 07	.03	.01
	Detroit Lions		
☐ 486	Brian Sipe SA 12	.06	.01
	Cleveland Browns		
☐ 487	Rod Martin 35	.17	.03
	Oakland Raiders		
☐ 488	Cincinnati Bengals TL ...15	.07	.01
	Pete Johnson		
	Dan Ross		
	Louis Breeden		
	Eddie Edwards		
☐ 489	Preston Dennard 07	.03	.01
	Los Angeles Rams		
☐ 490	John Smith AP 07	.03	.01
	New England Patriots		
☐ 491	Mike Reinfeldt 07	.03	.01
	Houston Oilers		
☐ 492	1980 NFC Champions 15	.07	.01
	Eagles 20,		
	Cowboys 7		
	(Ron Jaworski)		
☐ 493	1980 AFC Champions 20	.10	.02
	Raiders 34,		
	Chargers 27		
	(Jim Plunkett)		
☐ 494	Super Bowl XV 50	.25	.05
	Raiders 27,		
	Eagles 10		
	(Plunkett hand-		
	ing off to King)		
☐ 495	Joe Greene 90	.45	.09
	Pittsburgh Steelers		
☐ 496	Charlie Joiner 60	.30	.06
	San Diego Chargers		
☐ 497	Rolland Lawrence 10	.05	.01
	Atlanta Falcons		
☐ 498	Al(Bubba) Baker SA 10	.05	.01
	Detroit Lions		
☐ 499	Brad Dusek 07	.03	.01
	Washington Redskins		
☐ 500	Tony Dorsett 2.00	1.00	.20
	Dallas Cowboys		
☐ 501	Robin Earl 07	.03	.01
	Chicago Bears		
☐ 502	Theotis Brown 15	.07	.01
	St. Louis Cardinals		
☐ 503	Joe Ferguson 15	.07	.01
	Buffalo Bills		
☐ 504	Beasley Reece 07	.03	.01
	New York Giants		
☐ 505	Lyle Alzado 35	.17	.03
	Cleveland Browns		
☐ 506	Tony Nathan 50	.25	.05
	Miami Dolphins		
☐ 507	Philadelphia Eagles TL ...15	.07	.01

Wilbert Montgomery
Charlie Smith
Brenard Wilson
Claude Humphrey

☐ 508	Herb Orvis 07	.03	.01
	Baltimore Colts		
☐ 509	Clarence Williams 07	.03	.01
	San Diego Chargers		
☐ 510	Ray Guy AP 25	.12	.02
	Oakland Raiders		
☐ 511	Jeff Komlo 10	.05	.01
	Detroit Lions		
☐ 512	Freddie Solomon SA 10	.05	.01
	San Francisco 49ers		
☐ 513	Tim Mazzetti 07	.03	.01
	Atlanta Falcons		
☐ 514	Elvis Peacock 15	.07	.01
	Los Angeles Rams		
☐ 515	Russ Francis 12	.06	.01
	New England Patriots		
☐ 516	Roland Harper 10	.05	.01
	Chicago Bears		
☐ 517	Checklist 397-528 45	.05	.01
☐ 518	Billy Johnson 15	.07	.01
	Houston Oilers		
☐ 519	Dan Dierdorf 35	.17	.03
	St. Louis Cardinals		
☐ 520	Fred Dean AP 12	.06	.01
	San Diego Chargers		
☐ 521	Jerry Butler 15	.07	.01
	Buffalo Bills		
☐ 522	Ron Saul 07	.03	.01
	Washington Redskins		
☐ 523	Charlie Smith 07	.03	.01
	Philadelphia Eagles		
☐ 524	Kellen Winslow SA 1.75	.85	.17
	San Diego Chargers		
☐ 525	Bert Jones 25	.12	.02
	Baltimore Colts		
☐ 526	Pittsburgh Steelers TL ...75	.35	.07
	Franco Harris		
	Theo Bell		
	Donnie Shell		
	L.C. Greenwood		
☐ 527	Duriel Harris 07	.03	.01
	Miami Dolphins		
☐ 528	William Andrews 20	.07	.01
	Atlanta Falcons		

1982 Topps

The 1982 Topps football set features 528 cards. The cards measure 2 1/2" by 3 1/2". The team helmets appear on the fronts for the first time, as Topps apparently received permission from the teams for the use of their insignias. Again, the fronts contain the stylized Topps logo within the frame line. The backs contain blue and yellow-green ink on a gray card stock. Many special cards, e.g., Playoffs and Super Bowl (7-9), Record Breakers (RB, cards 1-6), and statistical leaders (257-262) are included in the set. Cards 263-270 feature brothers playing in the NFL. All-Pro (AP) selections are denoted on each player's regular card. Some players also have an additional special card with an In-Action (IA) pose. Distributed throughout the set are Team Leader (TL) cards typically featuring four individual team statistical leaders on the front, as well as a team checklist on the back. The set is organized in team order alphabetically by team within conference (and with players within teams in alphabetical order), for example, Baltimore Colts (10-20), Buffalo Bills (21-35), Cincinnati Bengals (36-54), Cleveland Browns (55-75), Denver Broncos (76-91), Houston Oilers (92-108), Kansas City Chiefs (109-124), Miami Dolphins (125-140), New England Patriots (141-159), New York Jets (160-184), Oakland Raiders (185-201), Pittsburgh Steelers (202-222), San Diego Chargers (223-242), Seattle Seahawks (243-256), Atlanta Falcons (271-291), Chicago Bears (292-306), Dallas Cowboys (307-332), Detroit Lions (333-353), Green Bay Packers (354-368), Los Angeles Rams (369-388), Minnesota Vikings (389-403), New Orleans Saints (404-414), New

*York Giants (415-436), Philadelphia Eagles
(437-461), St. Louis Cardinals (462-476), San
Francisco 49ers (477-494), Tampa Bay
Buccaneers (495-508), and Washington
Redskins (509-524). The last four cards in the
set (525-528) are checklist cards. The key
rookie cards in this set are James Brooks,
Ronnie Lott, Anthony Munoz, and Lawrence
Taylor.*

	MINT	EXC	G-VG
COMPLETE SET (528)	100.00	50.00	10.00
COMMON PLAYER (1-528)	.06	.03	.00
☐ 1 Ken Anderson RB	.50	.25	.05
Cincinnati Bengals			
Most Completions,			
Super Bowl Game			
☐ 2 Dan Fouts RB	.40	.20	.04
San Diego Chargers			
Most Passing Yards,			
Playoff Game			
☐ 3 LeRoy Irvin RB	.12	.06	.01
Los Angeles Rams			
Most Punt Return			
Yardage, Game			
☐ 4 Stump Mitchell RB	.12	.06	.01
St. Louis Cardinals			
Most Return			
Yardage, Season			
☐ 5 George Rogers RB	.15	.07	.01
New Orleans Saints			
Most Rushing Yards,			
Rookie Season			
☐ 6 Dan Ross RB	.12	.06	.01
Cincinnati Bengals			
Most Receptions,			
Super Bowl Game			
☐ 7 AFC Championship	.12	.06	.01
Bengals 27,			
Chargers 7			
(Ken Anderson			
handing off to			
Pete Johnson)			
☐ 8 NFC Championship	.12	.06	.01
49ers 28,			
Cowboys 27			
(Earl Cooper)			
☐ 9 Super Bowl XVI	.60	.30	.06
49ers 26,			
Bengals 7			
(Anthony Munoz			
blocking)			
☐ 10 Baltimore Colts TL	.15	.07	.01
Curtis Dickey			
Raymond Butler			
Larry Braziel			

Bruce Laird			
☐ 11 Raymond Butler	.10	.05	.01
☐ 12 Roger Carr	.10	.05	.01
☐ 13 Curtis Dickey	.12	.06	.01
☐ 14 Zachary Dixon	.06	.03	.00
☐ 15 Nesby Glasgow	.06	.03	.00
☐ 16 Bert Jones	.20	.10	.02
☐ 17 Bruce Laird	.06	.03	.00
☐ 18 Reese McCall	.06	.03	.00
☐ 19 Randy McMillan	.10	.05	.01
☐ 20 Ed Simonini	.06	.03	.00
☐ 21 Buffalo Bills TL	.15	.07	.01
Joe Cribbs			
Frank Lewis			
Mario Clark			
Fred Smerlas			
☐ 22 Mark Brammer	.06	.03	.00
☐ 23 Curtis Brown	.06	.03	.00
☐ 24 Jerry Butler	.10	.05	.01
☐ 25 Mario Clark	.06	.03	.00
☐ 26 Joe Cribbs	.20	.10	.02
☐ 27 Joe Cribbs IA	.10	.05	.01
☐ 28 Joe Ferguson	.15	.07	.01
☐ 29 Jim Haslett	.06	.03	.00
☐ 30 Frank Lewis AP	.10	.05	.01
☐ 31 Frank Lewis IA	.06	.03	.00
☐ 32 Shane Nelson	.06	.03	.00
☐ 33 Charles Romes	.06	.03	.00
☐ 34 Bill Simpson	.06	.03	.00
☐ 35 Fred Smerlas	.20	.10	.02
☐ 36 Cincinnati Bengals TL	.25	.12	.02
Pete Johnson			
Cris Collinsworth			
Ken Riley			
Reggie Williams			
☐ 37 Charles Alexander	.06	.03	.00
☐ 38 Ken Anderson AP	.50	.25	.05
☐ 39 Ken Anderson IA	.25	.12	.02
☐ 40 Jim Breech	.06	.03	.00
☐ 41 Jim Breech IA	.06	.03	.00
☐ 42 Louis Breeden	.06	.03	.00
☐ 43 Ross Browner	.10	.05	.01
☐ 44 Cris Collinsworth	2.00	1.00	.20
☐ 45 Cris Collinsworth IA	.75	.35	.07
☐ 46 Isaac Curtis	.12	.06	.01
☐ 47 Pete Johnson	.10	.05	.01
☐ 48 Pete Johnson IA	.06	.03	.00
☐ 49 Steve Kreider	.06	.03	.00
☐ 50 Pat McInally AP	.12	.06	.01
☐ 51 Anthony Munoz AP	10.00	5.00	1.00
☐ 52 Dan Ross	.10	.05	.01
☐ 53 David Verser	.06	.03	.00
☐ 54 Reggie Williams	.12	.06	.01
☐ 55 Cleveland Browns TL	.30	.15	.03
Mike Pruitt			
Ozzie Newsome			
Clarence Scott			

Lyle Alzado

☐ 56 Lyle Alzado	.30	.15	.03
☐ 57 Dick Ambrose	.06	.03	.00
☐ 58 Ron Bolton	.06	.03	.00
☐ 59 Steve Cox	.06	.03	.00
☐ 60 Joe DeLamielleure	.10	.05	.01
☐ 61 Tom DeLeone	.06	.03	.00
☐ 62 Doug Dieken	.06	.03	.00
☐ 63 Ricky Feacher	.06	.03	.00
☐ 64 Don Goode	.06	.03	.00
☐ 65 Robert L. Jackson	.20	.10	.02
☐ 66 Dave Logan	.06	.03	.00
☐ 67 Ozzie Newsome	1.25	.60	.12
☐ 68 Ozzie Newsome IA	.50	.25	.05
☐ 69 Greg Pruitt	.15	.07	.01
☐ 70 Mike Pruitt	.12	.06	.01
☐ 71 Mike Pruitt IA	.10	.05	.01
☐ 72 Reggie Rucker	.10	.05	.01
☐ 73 Clarence Scott	.06	.03	.00
☐ 74 Brian Sipe	.15	.07	.01
☐ 75 Charles White	.20	.10	.02
☐ 76 Denver Broncos TL	.12	.06	.01

Rick Parros
Steve Watson
Steve Foley
Rulon Jones

☐ 77 Rubin Carter	.06	.03	.00
☐ 78 Steve Foley	.06	.03	.00
☐ 79 Randy Gradishar	.20	.10	.02
☐ 80 Tom Jackson	.20	.10	.02
☐ 81 Craig Morton	.20	.10	.02
☐ 82 Craig Morton IA	.12	.06	.01
☐ 83 Riley Odoms	.12	.06	.01
☐ 84 Rick Parros	.06	.03	.00
☐ 85 Dave Preston	.10	.05	.01
☐ 86 Tony Reed	.10	.05	.01
☐ 87 Bob Swenson	.20	.10	.02
☐ 88 Bill Thompson	.10	.05	.01
☐ 89 Rick Upchurch	.12	.06	.01
☐ 90 Steve Watson AP	.50	.25	.05
☐ 91 Steve Watson IA	.20	.10	.02
☐ 92 Houston Oilers TL	.12	.06	.01

Carl Roaches
Ken Burrough
Carter Hartwig
Greg Stemrick
Jesse Baker

☐ 93 Mike Barber	.10	.05	.01
☐ 94 Elvin Bethea	.12	.06	.01
☐ 95 Gregg Bingham	.06	.03	.00
☐ 96 Robert Brazile AP	.12	.06	.01
☐ 97 Ken Burrough	.10	.05	.01
☐ 98 Toni Fritsch	.06	.03	.00
☐ 99 Leon Gray	.10	.05	.01
☐ 100 Gifford Nielsen	.30	.15	.03
☐ 101 Vernon Perry	.06	.03	.00
☐ 102 Mike Reinfeldt	.06	.03	.00

☐ 103 Mike Renfro	.10	.05	.01
☐ 104 Carl Roaches AP	.10	.05	.01
☐ 105 Ken Stabler	.50	.25	.05
☐ 106 Greg Stemrick	.06	.03	.00
☐ 107 J.C. Wilson	.06	.03	.00
☐ 108 Tim Wilson	.06	.03	.00
☐ 109 Kansas City Chiefs TL	.15	.07	.01

Joe Delaney
J.T. Smith
Eric Harris
Ken Kremer

☐ 110 Gary Barbaro AP	.12	.06	.01
☐ 111 Brad Budde	.06	.03	.00
☐ 112 Joe Delaney AP	.40	.20	.04
☐ 113 Joe Delaney IA	.15	.07	.01
☐ 114 Steve Fuller	.10	.05	.01
☐ 115 Gary Green	.06	.03	.00
☐ 116 James Hadnot	.10	.05	.01
☐ 117 Eric Harris	.06	.03	.00
☐ 118 Billy Jackson	.06	.03	.00
☐ 119 Bill Kenney	.20	.10	.02
☐ 120 Nick Lowery AP	.50	.25	.05
☐ 121 Nick Lowery IA	.20	.10	.02
☐ 122 Henry Marshall	.06	.03	.00
☐ 123 J.T. Smith	.35	.17	.03
☐ 124 Art Still	.20	.10	.02
☐ 125 Miami Dolphins TL	.15	.07	.01

Tony Nathan
Duriel Harris
Glenn Blackwood
Bob Baumhower

☐ 126 Bob Baumhower AP	.10	.05	.01
☐ 127 Glenn Blackwood	.10	.05	.01
☐ 128 Jimmy Cefalo	.10	.05	.01
☐ 129 A.J. Duhe	.10	.05	.01
☐ 130 Andra Franklin	.20	.10	.02
☐ 131 Duriel Harris	.06	.03	.00
☐ 132 Nat Moore	.12	.06	.01
☐ 133 Tony Nathan	.12	.06	.01
☐ 134 Ed Newman	.06	.03	.00
☐ 135 Earnie Rhone	.06	.03	.00
☐ 136 Don Strock	.12	.06	.01
☐ 137 Tommy Vigorito	.06	.03	.00
☐ 138 Uwe Von Schamann	.06	.03	.00
☐ 139 Uwe Von Schamann IA	.06	.03	.00
☐ 140 David Woodley	.10	.05	.01
☐ 141 New England Pats TL	.12	.06	.01

Tony Collins
Stanley Morgan
Tim Fox
Rick Sanford
Tony McGee

☐ 142 Julius Adams	.06	.03	.00
☐ 143 Richard Bishop	.06	.03	.00
☐ 144 Matt Cavanaugh	.10	.05	.01
☐ 145 Raymond Clayborn	.10	.05	.01
☐ 146 Tony Collins	.30	.15	.03

☐ 147	Vagas Ferguson	.12	.06	.01
☐ 148	Tim Fox	.06	.03	.00
☐ 149	Steve Grogan	.25	.12	.02
☐ 150	John Hannah AP	.45	.22	.04
☐ 151	John Hannah IA	.20	.10	.02
☐ 152	Don Hasselbeck	.06	.03	.00
☐ 153	Mike Haynes	.15	.07	.01
☐ 154	Harold Jackson	.20	.10	.02
☐ 155	Andy Johnson	.06	.03	.00
☐ 156	Stanley Morgan	.35	.17	.03
☐ 157	Stanley Morgan IA	.15	.07	.01
☐ 158	Steve Nelson	.06	.03	.00
☐ 159	Rod Shoate	.06	.03	.00
☐ 160	New York Jets TL	.45	.22	.04
	Freeman McNeil			
	Wesley Walker			
	Darrol Ray			
	Joe Klecko			
☐ 161	Dan Alexander	.06	.03	.00
☐ 162	Mike Augustyniak	.06	.03	.00
☐ 163	Jerome Barkum	.10	.05	.01
☐ 164	Greg Buttle	.10	.05	.01
☐ 165	Scott Dierking	.06	.03	.00
☐ 166	Joe Fields	.10	.05	.01
☐ 167	Mark Gastineau AP	.25	.12	.02
☐ 168	Mark Gastineau IA	.10	.05	.01
☐ 169	Bruce Harper	.06	.03	.00
☐ 170	Johnny "Lam" Jones	.10	.05	.01
☐ 171	Joe Klecko AP	.20	.10	.02
☐ 172	Joe Klecko IA	.10	.05	.01
☐ 173	Pat Leahy	.15	.07	.01
☐ 174	Pat Leahy IA	.10	.05	.01
☐ 175	Marty Lyons	.12	.06	.01
☐ 176	Freeman McNeil	3.25	1.60	.32
☐ 177	Marvin Powell AP	.10	.05	.01
☐ 178	Chuck Ramsey	.06	.03	.00
☐ 179	Darrol Ray	.10	.05	.01
☐ 180	Abdul Salaam	.06	.03	.00
☐ 181	Richard Todd	.15	.07	.01
☐ 182	Richard Todd IA	.10	.05	.01
☐ 183	Wesley Walker	.30	.15	.03
☐ 184	Chris Ward	.06	.03	.00
☐ 185	Oakland Raiders TL	.15	.07	.01
	Kenny King			
	Derrick Ramsey			
	Lester Hayes			
	Odis McKinney			
	Rod Martin			
☐ 186	Cliff Branch	.30	.15	.03
☐ 187	Bob Chandler	.10	.05	.01
☐ 188	Ray Guy	.20	.10	.02
☐ 189	Lester Hayes AP	.12	.06	.01
☐ 190	Ted Hendricks AP	.35	.17	.03
☐ 191	Monte Jackson	.10	.05	.01
☐ 192	Derrick Jensen	.06	.03	.00
☐ 193	Kenny King	.12	.06	.01
☐ 194	Rod Martin	.12	.06	.01

☐ 195	John Matuszak	.12	.06	.01
☐ 196	Matt Millen	1.50	.75	.15
☐ 197	Derrick Ramsey	.06	.03	.00
☐ 198	Art Shell	.50	.25	.05
☐ 199	Mark Van Eeghen	.10	.05	.01
☐ 200	Arthur Whittington	.06	.03	.00
☐ 201	Marc Wilson	.35	.17	.03
☐ 202	Pittsburgh Steelers TL	.60	.30	.06
	Franco Harris			
	John Stallworth			
	Mel Blount			
	Jack Lambert			
	Gary Dunn			
☐ 203	Mel Blount AP	.50	.25	.05
☐ 204	Terry Bradshaw	1.50	.75	.15
☐ 205	Terry Bradshaw IA	.75	.35	.07
☐ 206	Craig Colquitt	.06	.03	.00
☐ 207	Bennie Cunningham	.06	.03	.00
☐ 208	Russell Davis	.06	.03	.00
☐ 209	Gary Dunn	.06	.03	.00
☐ 210	Jack Ham	.50	.25	.05
☐ 211	Franco Harris	1.00	.50	.10
☐ 212	Franco Harris IA	.45	.22	.04
☐ 213	Jack Lambert AP	.60	.30	.06
☐ 214	Jack Lambert IA	.30	.15	.03
☐ 215	Mark Malone	.30	.15	.03
☐ 216	Frank Pollard	.30	.15	.03
☐ 217	Donnie Shell AP	.15	.07	.01
☐ 218	Jim Smith	.10	.05	.01
☐ 219	John Stallworth	.35	.17	.03
☐ 220	John Stallworth IA	.15	.07	.01
☐ 221	David Trout	.06	.03	.00
☐ 222	Mike Webster AP	.35	.17	.03
☐ 223	San Diego Chargers TL	.15	.07	.01
	Chuck Muncie			
	Charlie Joiner			
	Willie Buchanon			
	Gary Johnson			
☐ 224	Rolf Benirschke	.10	.05	.01
☐ 225	Rolf Benirschke IA	.06	.03	.00
☐ 226	James Brooks	6.50	3.25	.65
☐ 227	Willie Buchanon	.05	.05	.01
☐ 228	Wes Chandler	.15	.07	.01
☐ 229	Wes Chandler IA	.10	.05	.01
☐ 230	Dan Fouts	1.25	.60	.12
☐ 231	Dan Fouts IA	.60	.30	.06
☐ 232	Gary Johnson AP	.10	.05	.01
☐ 233	Charlie Joiner	.40	.20	.04
☐ 234	Charlie Joiner IA	.20	.10	.02
☐ 235	Louie Kelcher	.10	.05	.01
☐ 236	Chuck Muncie AP	.15	.07	.01
☐ 237	Chuck Muncie IA	.10	.05	.01
☐ 238	George Roberts	.06	.03	.00
☐ 239	Ed White	.10	.05	.01
☐ 240	Doug Wilkerson AP	.06	.03	.00
☐ 241	Kellen Winslow AP	1.50	.75	.15
☐ 242	Kellen Winslow IA	.60	.30	.06

☐ 243	Seattle Seahawks TL	.35	.17	.03
	Theotis Brown			
	Steve Largent			
	John Harris			
	Jacob Green			
☐ 244	Theotis Brown	.10	.05	.01
☐ 245	Dan Doornink	.06	.03	.00
☐ 246	John Harris	.06	.03	.00
☐ 247	Efren Herrera	.06	.03	.00
☐ 248	David Hughes	.06	.03	.00
☐ 249	Steve Largent	1.75	.85	.17
☐ 250	Steve Largent IA	.80	.40	.08
☐ 251	Sam McCullum	.06	.03	.00
☐ 252	Sherman Smith	.06	.03	.00
☐ 253	Manu Tuiasosopo	.06	.03	.00
☐ 254	John Yarno	.06	.03	.00
☐ 255	Jim Zorn	.15	.07	.01
☐ 256	Jim Zorn IA	.10	.05	.01
☐ 257	Passing Leaders	1.50	.75	.15
	Ken Anderson			
	Joe Montana			
☐ 258	Receiving Leaders	.35	.17	.03
	Kellen Winslow			
	Dwight Clark			
☐ 259	QB Sack Leaders	.15	.07	.01
	Joe Klecko			
	Curtis Greer			
☐ 260	Scoring Leaders	.12	.06	.01
	Jim Breech			
	Nick Lowery			
	Ed Murray			
	Rafael Septien			
☐ 261	Interception Leaders	.20	.10	.02
	John Harris			
	Everson Walls			
☐ 262	Punting Leaders	.12	.06	.01
	Pat McInally			
	Tom Skladany			
☐ 263	Brothers: Bahr	.12	.06	.01
	Chris and Matt			
☐ 264	Brothers: Blackwood	.12	.06	.01
	Lyle and Glenn			
☐ 265	Brothers: Brock	.12	.06	.01
	Pete and Stan			
☐ 266	Brothers: Griffin	.12	.06	.01
	Archie and Ray			
☐ 267	Brothers: Hannah	.20	.10	.02
	John and Charlie			
☐ 268	Brothers: Jackson	.12	.06	.01
	Monte and Terry			
☐ 269	Brothers: Payton	.75	.35	.07
	Eddie and Walter			
☐ 270	Brothers: Selmon	.12	.06	.01
	Dewey and Lee Roy			
☐ 271	Atlanta Falcons TL	.12	.06	.01
	William Andrews			
	Alfred Jenkins			
	Tom Pridemore			
	Al Richardson			
☐ 272	William Andrews	.15	.07	.01
☐ 273	William Andrews IA	.10	.05	.01
☐ 274	Steve Bartkowski	.25	.12	.02
☐ 275	Steve Bartkowski IA	.12	.06	.01
☐ 276	Bobby Butler	.06	.03	.00
☐ 277	Lynn Cain	.10	.05	.01
☐ 278	Wallace Francis	.10	.05	.01
☐ 279	Alfred Jackson	.10	.05	.01
☐ 280	John James	.06	.03	.00
☐ 281	Alfred Jenkins AP	.10	.05	.01
☐ 282	Alfred Jenkins IA	.06	.03	.00
☐ 283	Kenny Johnson	.06	.03	.00
☐ 284	Mike Kenn AP	.15	.07	.01
☐ 285	Fulton Kuykendall	.06	.03	.00
☐ 286	Mick Luckhurst	.15	.07	.01
☐ 287	Mick Luckhurst IA	.10	.05	.01
☐ 288	Junior Miller	.10	.05	.01
☐ 289	Al Richardson	.06	.03	.00
☐ 290	R.C. Thielemann	.15	.07	.01
☐ 291	Jeff Van Note	.12	.06	.01
☐ 292	Chicago Bears TL	.75	.35	.07
	Walter Payton			
	Ken Margerum			
	Gary Fencik			
	Dan Hampton			
	Alan Page			
☐ 293	Brian Baschnagel	.06	.03	.00
☐ 294	Robin Earl	.06	.03	.00
☐ 295	Vince Evans	.10	.05	.01
☐ 296	Gary Fencik AP	.12	.06	.01
☐ 297	Dan Hampton	2.75	1.35	.27
☐ 298	Noah Jackson	.06	.03	.00
☐ 299	Ken Margerum	.10	.05	.01
☐ 300	Jim Osborne	.06	.03	.00
☐ 301	Bob Parsons	.06	.03	.00
☐ 302	Walter Payton	2.50	1.25	.25
☐ 303	Walter Payton IA	1.00	.50	.10
☐ 304	Revie Sorey	.06	.03	.00
☐ 305	Matt Suhey	.35	.17	.03
☐ 306	Rickey Watts	.06	.03	.00
☐ 307	Dallas Cowboys TL	.50	.25	.05
	Tony Dorsett			
	Tony Hill			
	Everson Walls			
	Harvey Martin			
☐ 308	Bob Breunig	.12	.06	.01
☐ 309	Doug Cosbie	.35	.17	.03
☐ 310	Pat Donovan AP	.10	.05	.01
☐ 311	Tony Dorsett AP	1.25	.60	.12
☐ 312	Tony Dorsett IA	.50	.25	.05
☐ 313	Michael Downs	.15	.07	.01
☐ 314	Billy Joe DuPree	.15	.07	.01
☐ 315	John Dutton	.12	.06	.01
☐ 316	Tony Hill	.15	.07	.01
☐ 317	Butch Johnson	.10	.05	.01

☐ 318 Ed Too Tall Jones AP	.40	.20	.04
☐ 319 James Jones	.06	.03	.00
☐ 320 Harvey Martin	.20	.10	.02
☐ 321 Drew Pearson	.30	.15	.03
☐ 322 Herbert Scott AP	.06	.03	.00
☐ 323 Rafael Septien AP	.10	.05	.01
☐ 324 Rafael Septien IA	.06	.03	.00
☐ 325 Ron Springs	.06	.03	.00
☐ 326 Dennis Thurman	.15	.07	.01
☐ 327 Everson Walls	2.50	1.25	.25
☐ 328 Everson Walls IA	.75	.35	.07
☐ 329 Danny White	.30	.15	.03
☐ 330 Danny White IA	.15	.07	.01
☐ 331 Randy White AP	.60	.30	.06
☐ 332 Randy White IA	.30	.15	.03
☐ 333 Detroit Lions TL	.12	.06	.01
Billy Sims			
Freddie Scott			
Jim Allen			
Dave Pureifory			
☐ 334 Jim Allen	.06	.03	.00
☐ 335 Al(Bubba) Baker	.10	.05	.01
☐ 336 Dexter Bussey	.06	.03	.00
☐ 337 Doug English AP	.12	.06	.01
☐ 338 Ken Fantetti	.06	.03	.00
☐ 339 William Gay	.06	.03	.00
☐ 340 David Hill	.06	.03	.00
☐ 341 Eric Hipple	.30	.15	.03
☐ 342 Rick Kane	.06	.03	.00
☐ 343 Ed Murray	.25	.12	.02
☐ 344 Ed Murray IA	.12	.06	.01
☐ 345 Ray Oldham	.06	.03	.00
☐ 346 Dave Pureifory	.06	.03	.00
☐ 347 Freddie Scott	.06	.03	.00
☐ 348 Freddie Scott IA	.06	.03	.00
☐ 349 Billy Sims AP	.35	.17	.03
☐ 350 Billy Sims IA	.15	.07	.01
☐ 351 Tom Skladany AP	.06	.03	.00
☐ 352 Leonard Thompson	.06	.03	.00
☐ 353 Stan White	.06	.03	.00
☐ 354 Green Bay Packers TL	.40	.20	.04
Gerry Ellis			
James Lofton			
Maurice Harvey			
Mark Lee			
Mike Butler			
☐ 355 Paul Coffman	.10	.05	.01
☐ 356 George Cumby	.06	.03	.00
☐ 357 Lynn Dickey	.15	.07	.01
☐ 358 Lynn Dickey IA	.10	.05	.01
☐ 359 Gerry Ellis	.06	.03	.00
☐ 360 Maurice Harvey	.06	.03	.00
☐ 361 Harlan Huckleby	.15	.07	.01
☐ 362 John Jefferson	.15	.07	.01
☐ 363 Mark Lee	.35	.17	.03
☐ 364 James Lofton AP	2.25	1.10	.22
☐ 365 James Lofton IA	.90	.45	.09
☐ 366 Jan Stenerud	.25	.12	.02
☐ 367 Jan Stenerud IA	.12	.06	.01
☐ 368 Rich Wingo	.06	.03	.00
☐ 369 Los Angeles Rams TL	.15	.07	.01
Wendell Tyler			
Preston Dennard			
Nolan Cromwell			
Jack Youngblood			
☐ 370 Frank Corral	.06	.03	.00
☐ 371 Nolan Cromwell AP	.15	.07	.01
☐ 372 Nolan Cromwell IA	.10	.05	.01
☐ 373 Preston Dennard	.06	.03	.00
☐ 374 Mike Fanning	.06	.03	.00
☐ 375 Doug France	.10	.05	.01
☐ 376 Mike Guman	.06	.03	.00
☐ 377 Pat Haden	.20	.10	.02
☐ 378 Dennis Harrah	.10	.05	.01
☐ 379 Drew Hill	4.00	2.00	.40
☐ 380 LeRoy Irvin	.50	.25	.05
☐ 381 Cody Jones	.06	.03	.00
☐ 382 Rod Perry	.10	.05	.01
☐ 383 Rich Saul AP	.06	.03	.00
☐ 384 Pat Thomas	.06	.03	.00
☐ 385 Wendell Tyler	.15	.07	.01
☐ 386 Wendell Tyler IA	.10	.05	.01
☐ 387 Billy Waddy	.06	.03	.00
☐ 388 Jack Youngblood	.30	.15	.03
☐ 389 Minnesota Vikings TL	.12	.06	.01
Ted Brown			
Joe Senser			
Tom Hannon			
Willie Teal			
Matt Blair			
☐ 390 Matt Blair AP	.12	.06	.01
☐ 391 Ted Brown	.10	.05	.01
☐ 392 Ted Brown IA	.06	.03	.00
☐ 393 Rick Danmeier	.06	.03	.00
☐ 394 Tommy Kramer	.25	.12	.02
☐ 395 Mark Mullaney	.10	.05	.01
☐ 396 Eddie Payton	.10	.05	.01
☐ 397 Ahmad Rashad	.35	.17	.03
☐ 398 Joe Senser	.06	.03	.00
☐ 399 Joe Senser IA	.06	.03	.00
☐ 400 Sammie White	.10	.05	.01
☐ 401 Sammie White IA	.06	.03	.00
☐ 402 Ron Yary	.12	.06	.01
☐ 403 Rickey Young	.10	.05	.01
☐ 404 New Orleans Saints TL	.35	.17	.03
George Rogers			
Guido Merkens			
Dave Waymer			
Rickey Jackson			
☐ 405 Russell Erxleben	.06	.03	.00
☐ 406 Elois Grooms	.06	.03	.00
☐ 407 Jack Holmes	.06	.03	.00
☐ 408 Archie Manning	.30	.15	.03
☐ 409 Derland Moore	.06	.03	.00

☐ 410 George Rogers	1.00	.50	.10
☐ 411 George Rogers IA	.30	.15	.03
☐ 412 Toussaint Tyler	.06	.03	.00
☐ 413 Dave Waymer	.20	.10	.02
☐ 414 Wayne Wilson	.10	.05	.01
☐ 415 New York Giants TL	.12	.06	.01
Rob Carpenter			
Johnny Perkins			
Beasley Reece			
George Martin			
☐ 416 Scott Brunner	.25	.12	.02
☐ 417 Rob Carpenter	.10	.05	.01
☐ 418 Harry Carson AP	.30	.15	.03
☐ 419 Bill Currier	.06	.03	.00
☐ 420 Joe Danelo	.06	.03	.00
☐ 421 Joe Danelo IA	.06	.03	.00
☐ 422 Mark Haynes	.50	.25	.05
☐ 423 Terry Jackson	.06	.03	.00
☐ 424 Dave Jennings	.10	.05	.01
☐ 425 Gary Jeter	.10	.05	.01
☐ 426 Brian Kelley	.10	.05	.01
☐ 427 George Martin	.10	.05	.01
☐ 428 Curtis McGriff	.06	.03	.00
☐ 429 Bill Neill	.06	.03	.00
☐ 430 Johnny Perkins	.06	.03	.00
☐ 431 Beasley Reece	.06	.03	.00
☐ 432 Gary Shirk	.06	.03	.00
☐ 433 Phil Simms	1.50	.75	.15
☐ 434 Lawrence Taylor AP	27.00	13.50	2.70
☐ 435 Lawrence Taylor IA	7.50	3.75	.75
☐ 436 Brad Van Pelt	.10	.05	.01
☐ 437 Philadelphia Eagles TL	.15	.07	.01
Wilbert Montgomery			
Harold Carmichael			
Brenard Wilson			
Carl Hairston			
☐ 438 John Bunting	.06	.03	.00
☐ 439 Billy Campfield	.06	.03	.00
☐ 440 Harold Carmichael	.30	.15	.03
☐ 441 Harold Carmichael IA	.15	.07	.01
☐ 442 Herman Edwards	.06	.03	.00
☐ 443 Tony Franklin	.06	.03	.00
☐ 444 Tony Franklin IA	.06	.03	.00
☐ 445 Carl Hairston	.10	.05	.01
☐ 446 Dennis Harrison	.06	.03	.00
☐ 447 Ron Jaworski	.15	.07	.01
☐ 448 Charlie Johnson	.06	.03	.00
☐ 449 Keith Krepfle	.06	.03	.00
☐ 450 Frank LeMaster	.06	.03	.00
☐ 451 Randy Logan	.06	.03	.00
☐ 452 Wilbert Montgomery	.15	.07	.01
☐ 453 Wilbert Montgomery IA	.10	.05	.01
☐ 454 Hubert Oliver	.10	.05	.01
☐ 455 Jerry Robinson	.25	.12	.02
☐ 456 Jerry Robinson IA	.12	.06	.01
☐ 457 Jerry Sisemore	.10	.05	.01
☐ 458 Charlie Smith	.06	.03	.00
☐ 459 Stan Walters	.06	.03	.00
☐ 460 Brenard Wilson	.06	.03	.00
☐ 461 Roynell Young AP	.12	.06	.01
☐ 462 St. Louis Cardinals TL	.20	.10	.02
Ottis Anderson			
Pat Tilley			
Ken Greene			
Curtis Greer			
☐ 463 Ottis Anderson	1.00	.50	.10
☐ 464 Ottis Anderson IA	.40	.20	.04
☐ 465 Carl Birdsong	.06	.03	.00
☐ 466 Rush Brown	.06	.03	.00
☐ 467 Mel Gray	.10	.05	.01
☐ 468 Ken Greene	.06	.03	.00
☐ 469 Jim Hart	.15	.07	.01
☐ 470 E.J. Junior	.60	.30	.06
☐ 471 Neil Lomax	1.00	.50	.10
☐ 472 Stump Mitchell	.50	.25	.05
☐ 473 Wayne Morris	.06	.03	.00
☐ 474 Neil O'Donoghue	.06	.03	.00
☐ 475 Pat Tilley	.10	.05	.01
☐ 476 Pat Tilley IA	.06	.03	.00
☐ 477 San Francisco 49ers TL	.25	.12	.02
Ricky Patton			
Dwight Clark			
Dwight Hicks			
Fred Dean			
☐ 478 Dwight Clark	1.00	.50	.10
☐ 479 Dwight Clark IA	.40	.20	.04
☐ 480 Earl Cooper	.06	.03	.00
☐ 481 Randy Cross AP	.10	.05	.01
☐ 482 Johnny Davis	.06	.03	.00
☐ 483 Fred Dean	.10	.05	.01
☐ 484 Fred Dean IA	.06	.03	.00
☐ 485 Dwight Hicks	.60	.30	.06
☐ 486 Ronnie Lott AP	30.00	15.00	3.00
☐ 487 Ronnie Lott IA	7.50	3.75	.75
☐ 488 Joe Montana AP	25.00	12.50	2.50
☐ 489 Joe Montana IA	6.00	3.00	.60
☐ 490 Ricky Patton	.06	.03	.00
☐ 491 Jack Reynolds	.12	.06	.01
☐ 492 Freddie Solomon	.12	.06	.01
☐ 493 Ray Wersching	.06	.03	.00
☐ 494 Charley Young	.10	.05	.01
☐ 495 Tampa Bay Bucs TL	.12	.06	.01
Jerry Eckwood			
Kevin House			
Cedric Brown			
Lee Roy Selmon			
☐ 496 Cedric Brown	.06	.03	.00
☐ 497 Neal Colzie	.06	.03	.00
☐ 498 Jerry Eckwood	.10	.05	.01
☐ 499 Jimmie Giles AP	.10	.05	.01
☐ 500 Hugh Green	.75	.35	.07
☐ 501 Kevin House	.10	.05	.01
☐ 502 Kevin House IA	.10	.05	.01
☐ 503 Cecil Johnson	.06	.03	.00

		MINT	EXC	G-VG
☐ 504	James Owens	.10	.05	.01
☐ 505	Lee Roy Selmon AP	.15	.07	.01
☐ 506	Mike Washington	.06	.03	.00
☐ 507	James Wilder	1.00	.50	.10
☐ 508	Doug Williams	.20	.10	.02
☐ 509	Wash. Redskins TL	.75	.35	.07
	Joe Washington			
	Art Monk			
	Mark Murphy			
	Perry Brooks			
☐ 510	Perry Brooks	.06	.03	.00
☐ 511	Dave Butz	.20	.10	.02
☐ 512	Wilbur Jackson	.10	.05	.01
☐ 513	Joe Lavender	.06	.03	.00
☐ 514	Terry Metcalf	.15	.07	.01
☐ 515	Art Monk	12.00	6.00	1.20
☐ 516	Mark Moseley	.12	.06	.01
☐ 517	Mark Murphy	.06	.03	.00
☐ 518	Mike Nelms AP	.10	.05	.01
☐ 519	Lemar Parrish	.10	.05	.01
☐ 520	John Riggins	.75	.35	.07
☐ 521	Joe Theismann	.90	.45	.09
☐ 522	Ricky Thompson	.06	.03	.00
☐ 523	Don Warren UER	.12	.06	.01
	(photo actually			
	Ricky Thompson)			
☐ 524	Joe Washington	.12	.06	.01
☐ 525	Checklist 1-132	.25	.03	.00
☐ 526	Checklist 133-264	.25	.03	.00
☐ 527	Checklist 265-396	.25	.03	.00
☐ 528	Checklist 397-528	.30	.03	.00

1983 Topps

The 1983 Topps football set decreased in number from previous years, as only 396

cards are contained in this year's set. The cards measure 2 1/2" by 3 1/2". Although there are only 396 cards, the set was printed on four sheets; therefore, there are 132 double-printed cards, which are denoted in the checklist below by DP. The cards themselves contain the player's name at the bottom in a rectangular area, while the team names are in block letters at the top of the cards. The first nine cards in the set recognize Record-Breaking (RB) achievements occurring during the previous season. Cards 10-12 summarize the playoff action of the previous year. Statistical league leaders are recognized on cards 202-207. Players who appeared in the Pro Bowl game (designated PB in the checklist below) are identified as such in a rectangular area on the obverse of the player's regular card. The backs of the cards are printed in black ink with red borders and a faintly identifiable helmet of the player's team covering the center of the back in a screened red color. The Team Leader (TL) cards are distributed throughout the set as the first card of the team sequence; this year only one leader (usually the team's rushing leader) is pictured and the backs contain team scoring information from the previous year. The team numbering is arranged alphabetically within each conference (with players ordered alphabetically within team) as follows: Atlanta Falcons (13-27), Chicago Bears (28-41), Dallas Cowboys (42-57), Detroit Lions (58-73), Green Bay Packers (74-85), Los Angeles Rams (86-96), Minnesota Vikings (97-108), New Orleans Saints (109-119), New York Giants (120-135), Philadelphia Eagles (136-151), St. Louis Cardinals (152-162), San Francisco 49ers (163-173), Tampa Bay Buccaneers (174-185), Washington Redskins (186-201), Baltimore Colts (208-218), Buffalo Bills (219-229), Cincinnati Bengals (230-243), Cleveland Browns (244-259), Denver Broncos (260-270), Houston Oilers (271-281), Kansas City Chiefs (282-292), Los Angeles Raiders (293-307), Miami Dolphins (308-323), New England Patriots (324-337), New York Jets (338-354), Pittsburgh Steelers (355-369), San Diego Chargers (370-382), and Seattle Seahawks (383-393). The last three cards in the set (394-396) are checklist cards. The key rookies in this set are Marcus Allen, Roy Green, Jim McMahon, and Mike Singletary.

	MINT	EXC	G-VG
COMPLETE SET (396)	60.00	30.00	6.00
COMMON PLAYER (1-396)	.06	.03	.00
COMMON PLAYER DP	.04	.02	.00

☐ 1	Ken Anderson RB ....35 20 Consecutive Pass Completions	.10	.02
☐ 2	Tony Dorsett RB ....35 99 Yard Run	.17	.03
☐ 3	Dan Fouts RB ....30 30 Games Over 300 Yards Passing	.15	.03
☐ 4	Joe Montana RB ....1.25 Five Straight 300 Yard Games	.60	.12
☐ 5	Mark Moseley RB ....10 21 Straight Field Goals	.05	.01
☐ 6	Mike Nelms RB ....10 Most Yards, Punt Returns, Super Bowl Game	.05	.01
☐ 7	Darrol Ray RB ....10 Longest Interception Return, Playoff Game	.05	.01
☐ 8	John Riggins RB ....20 Most Yards Rushing, Super Bowl Game	.10	.02
☐ 9	Fulton Walker RB ....10 Most Yards, Kickoff Returns, Super Bowl Game	.05	.01
☐ 10	NFC Championship ....20 Redskins 31, Cowboys 17 (John Riggins tackled)	.10	.02
☐ 11	AFC Championship ....10 Dolphins 14, Jets 0	.05	.01
☐ 12	Super Bowl XVII ....35 Redskins 27, Dolphins 17 (John Riggins running)	.17	.03
☐ 13	Atlanta Falcons TL ....10 William Andrews	.05	.01
☐ 14	William Andrews DP PB ..10	.05	.01
☐ 15	Steve Bartkowski 20	.10	.02
☐ 16	Bobby Butler 06	.03	.00
☐ 17	Buddy Curry 06	.03	.00
☐ 18	Alfred Jackson DP 06	.03	.00
☐ 19	Alfred Jenkins 10	.05	.01
☐ 20	Kenny Johnson 06	.03	.00
☐ 21	Mike Kenn PB 10	.05	.01
☐ 22	Mick Luckhurst 06	.03	.00
☐ 23	Junior Miller 10	.05	.01
☐ 24	Al Richardson 06	.03	.00
☐ 25	Gerald Riggs DP 2.00	1.00	.20
☐ 26	R.C. Thielemann PB 10	.05	.01
☐ 27	Jeff Van Note PB 10	.05	.01
☐ 28	Chicago Bears TL ....50 Walter Payton	.25	.05
☐ 29	Brian Baschnagel 06	.03	.00
☐ 30	Dan Hampton PB 1.25	.60	.12
☐ 31	Mike Hartenstine 06	.03	.00
☐ 32	Noah Jackson 06	.03	.00
☐ 33	Jim McMahon 3.25	1.60	.32
☐ 34	Emery Moorehead DP 04	.02	.00
☐ 35	Bob Parsons 06	.03	.00
☐ 36	Walter Payton 2.00	1.00	.20
☐ 37	Terry Schmidt 06	.03	.00
☐ 38	Mike Singletary 10.00	5.00	1.00
☐ 39	Matt Suhey DP 04	.02	.00
☐ 40	Rickey Watts DP 04	.02	.00
☐ 41	Otis Wilson DP 25	.12	.02
☐ 42	Dallas Cowboys TL ....30 Tony Dorsett	.15	.03
☐ 43	Bob Breunig PB 10	.05	.01
☐ 44	Doug Cosbie 12	.06	.01
☐ 45	Pat Donovan PB 10	.05	.01
☐ 46	Tony Dorsett DP PB 75	.35	.07
☐ 47	Tony Hill 12	.06	.01
☐ 48	Butch Johnson DP 06	.03	.00
☐ 49	Ed Jones DP PB 15	.07	.01
☐ 50	Harvey Martin DP 10	.05	.01
☐ 51	Drew Pearson 20	.10	.02
☐ 52	Rafael Septien 06	.03	.00
☐ 53	Ron Springs DP 04	.02	.00
☐ 54	Dennis Thurman 06	.03	.00
☐ 55	Everson Walls PB 60	.30	.06
☐ 56	Danny White DP PB 15	.07	.01
☐ 57	Randy White PB 50	.25	.05
☐ 58	Detroit Lions TL ....15 Billy Sims	.07	.01
☐ 59	Al(Bubba) Baker DP 06	.03	.00
☐ 60	Dexter Bussey DP 04	.02	.00
☐ 61	Gary Danielson DP 06	.03	.00
☐ 62	Keith Dorney DP PB 04	.02	.00
☐ 63	Doug English PB 10	.05	.01
☐ 64	Ken Fantetti DP 04	.02	.00
☐ 65	Alvin Hall 04	.02	.00
☐ 66	David Hill DP 04	.02	.00
☐ 67	Eric Hipple 10	.05	.01
☐ 68	Ed Murray DP 10	.05	.01
☐ 69	Freddie Scott 06	.03	.00
☐ 70	Billy Sims DP PB 12	.06	.01
☐ 71	Tom Skladany DP 04	.02	.00
☐ 72	Leonard Thompson DP 04	.02	.00
☐ 73	Bobby Watkins 06	.03	.00
☐ 74	Green Bay Packers TL ....10 Eddie Lee Ivery	.05	.01
☐ 75	John Anderson 10	.05	.01
☐ 76	Paul Coffman PB 10	.05	.01
☐ 77	Lynn Dickey 12	.06	.01
☐ 78	Mike Douglass DP 04	.02	.00
☐ 79	Eddie Lee Ivery 10	.05	.01
☐ 80	John Jefferson DP 12	.06	.01
☐ 81	Ezra Johnson 06	.03	.00
☐ 82	Mark Lee 10	.05	.01

☐ 83 James Lofton PB 1.25	.60	.12	
☐ 84 Larry McCarren PB .... .06	.03	.00	
☐ 85 Jan Stenerud DP .... .15	.07	.01	
☐ 86 Los Angeles Rams TL .... .10	.05	.01	
Wendell Tyler			
☐ 87 Bill Bain DP .... .04	.02	.00	
☐ 88 Nolan Cromwell PB .... .10	.05	.01	
☐ 89 Preston Dennard .... .06	.03	.00	
☐ 90 Vince Ferragamo DP .... .10	.05	.01	
☐ 91 Mike Guman .... .06	.03	.00	
☐ 92 Kent Hill PB .... .06	.03	.00	
☐ 93 Mike Lansford DP .... .12	.06	.01	
☐ 94 Rod Perry .... .06	.03	.00	
☐ 95 Pat Thomas DP .... .04	.02	.00	
☐ 96 Jack Youngblood .... .20	.10	.02	
☐ 97 Minnesota Vikings TL ... .10	.05	.01	
Ted Brown			
☐ 98 Matt Blair PB .... .10	.05	.01	
☐ 99 Ted Brown .... .10	.05	.01	
☐ 100 Greg Coleman .... .06	.03	.00	
☐ 101 Randy Holloway .... .06	.03	.00	
☐ 102 Tommy Kramer .... .20	.10	.02	
☐ 103 Doug Martin DP .... .04	.02	.00	
☐ 104 Mark Mullaney .... .06	.03	.00	
☐ 105 Joe Senser .... .06	.03	.00	
☐ 106 Willie Teal DP .... .04	.02	.00	
☐ 107 Sammie White .... .10	.05	.01	
☐ 108 Rickey Young .... .10	.05	.01	
☐ 109 New Orleans Saints TL .. .10	.05	.01	
George Rogers			
☐ 110 Stan Brock .... .20	.10	.02	
☐ 111 Bruce Clark .... .12	.06	.01	
☐ 112 Russell Erxleben DP ...... .04	.02	.00	
☐ 113 Russell Gary .... .06	.03	.00	
☐ 114 Jeff Groth DP .... .06	.03	.00	
☐ 115 John Hill DP .... .04	.02	.00	
☐ 116 Derland Moore .... .06	.03	.00	
☐ 117 George Rogers PB .... .20	.10	.02	
☐ 118 Ken Stabler .... .35	.17	.03	
☐ 119 Wayne Wilson .... .10	.05	.01	
☐ 120 New York Giants TL .... .10	.05	.01	
Butch Woolfolk			
☐ 121 Scott Brunner .... .10	.05	.01	
☐ 122 Rob Carpenter .... .06	.03	.00	
☐ 123 Harry Carson PB .... .20	.10	.02	
☐ 124 Joe Danelo DP .... .04	.02	.00	
☐ 125 Earnest Gray .... .06	.03	.00	
☐ 126 Mark Haynes DP PB ...... .10	.05	.01	
☐ 127 Terry Jackson .... .06	.03	.00	
☐ 128 Dave Jennings PB .... .10	.05	.01	
☐ 129 Brian Kelley .... .10	.05	.01	
☐ 130 George Martin .... .10	.05	.01	
☐ 131 Tom Mullady .... .06	.03	.00	
☐ 132 Johnny Perkins .... .06	.03	.00	
☐ 133 Lawrence Taylor PB 6.50	3.25	.65	
☐ 134 Brad Van Pelt .... .10	.05	.01	
☐ 135 Butch Woolfolk DP .... .06	.03	.00	

☐ 136 Philadelphia Eagles TL .. .10	.05	.01	
Wilbert Montgomery			
☐ 137 Harold Carmichael .... .20	.10	.02	
☐ 138 Herman Edwards .... .06	.03	.00	
☐ 139 Tony Franklin DP .... .06	.03	.00	
☐ 140 Carl Hairston DP .... .06	.03	.00	
☐ 141 Dennis Harrison DP PB .. .04	.02	.00	
☐ 142 Ron Jaworski DP .... .10	.05	.01	
☐ 143 Frank LeMaster .... .06	.03	.00	
☐ 144 Wilbert Montgomery DP .10	.05	.01	
☐ 145 Guy Morriss .... .06	.03	.00	
☐ 146 Jerry Robinson .... .10	.05	.01	
☐ 147 Max Runager .... .06	.03	.00	
☐ 148 Ron Smith DP .... .04	.02	.00	
☐ 149 John Spagnola .... .06	.03	.00	
☐ 150 Stan Walters DP .... .06	.03	.00	
☐ 151 Roynell Young DP .... .06	.03	.00	
☐ 152 St. Louis Cardinals TL .. .20	.10	.02	
Ottis Anderson			
☐ 153 Ottis Anderson .... .50	.25	.05	
☐ 154 Carl Birdsong .... .06	.03	.00	
☐ 155 Dan Dierdorf DP .... .15	.07	.01	
☐ 156 Roy Green 2.00	1.00	.20	
☐ 157 Elois Grooms .... .06	.03	.00	
☐ 158 Neil Lomax DP .... .15	.07	.01	
☐ 159 Wayne Morris .... .06	.03	.00	
☐ 160 Tootie Robbins .... .15	.07	.01	
☐ 161 Luis Sharpe .... .35	.17	.03	
☐ 162 Pat Tilley .... .10	.05	.01	
☐ 163 San Francisco 49ers TL .10	.05	.01	
Jeff Moore			
☐ 164 Dwight Clark PB .... .35	.17	.03	
☐ 165 Randy Cross PB .... .10	.05	.01	
☐ 166 Russ Francis .... .10	.05	.01	
☐ 167 Dwight Hicks PB .... .12	.06	.01	
☐ 168 Ronnie Lott PB 7.00	3.50	.70	
☐ 169 Joe Montana DP 6.50	3.25	.65	
☐ 170 Jeff Moore .... .10	.05	.01	
☐ 171 Renaldo Nehemiah DP .. .30	.15	.03	
☐ 172 Freddie Solomon .... .10	.05	.01	
☐ 173 Ray Wersching DP .... .04	.02	.00	
☐ 174 Tampa Bay Bucs TL .... .10	.05	.01	
James Wilder			
☐ 175 Cedric Brown .... .06	.03	.00	
☐ 176 Bill Capece .... .06	.03	.00	
☐ 177 Neal Colzie .... .06	.03	.00	
☐ 178 Jimmie Giles PB .... .10	.05	.01	
☐ 179 Hugh Green PB .... .15	.07	.01	
☐ 180 Kevin House DP .... .06	.03	.00	
☐ 181 James Owens .... .10	.05	.01	
☐ 182 Lee Roy Selmon PB ...... .12	.06	.01	
☐ 183 Mike Washington .... .06	.03	.00	
☐ 184 James Wilder .... .20	.10	.02	
☐ 185 Doug Williams DP .... .10	.05	.01	
☐ 186 Wash. Redskins TL .... .15	.07	.01	
John Riggins			
☐ 187 Jeff Bostic DP .... .30	.15	.03	

☐ 188	Charlie Brown PB	.20	.10	.02
☐ 189	Vernon Dean DP	.06	.03	.00
☐ 190	Joe Jacoby	.75	.35	.07
☐ 191	Dexter Manley	.35	.17	.03
☐ 192	Rich Milot	.06	.03	.00
☐ 193	Art Monk DP	3.00	1.50	.30
☐ 194	Mark Moseley DP PB	.10	.05	.01
☐ 195	Mike Nelms PB	.10	.05	.01
☐ 196	Neal Olkewicz DP	.06	.03	.00
☐ 197	Tony Peters PB	.10	.05	.01
☐ 198	John Riggins DP	.35	.17	.03
☐ 199	Joe Theismann PB	.75	.35	.07
☐ 200	Don Warren	.12	.06	.01
☐ 201	Jeris White DP	.04	.02	.00
☐ 202	Passing Leaders	.20	.10	.02
	Joe Theismann			
	Ken Anderson			
☐ 203	Receiving Leaders	.15	.07	.01
	Dwight Clark			
	Kellen Winslow			
☐ 204	Rushing Leaders	.40	.20	.04
	Tony Dorsett			
	Freeman McNeil			
☐ 205	Scoring Leaders	.50	.25	.05
	Wendell Tyler			
	Marcus Allen			
☐ 206	Interception Leaders	.10	.05	.01
	Everson Walls			
	AFC Tie (Four)			
☐ 207	Punting Leaders	.10	.05	.01
	Carl Birdsong			
	Luke Prestridge			
☐ 208	Baltimore Colts TL	.10	.05	.01
	Randy McMillan			
☐ 209	Matt Bouza	.06	.03	.00
☐ 210	Johnie Cooks DP	.12	.06	.01
☐ 211	Curtis Dickey	.10	.05	.01
☐ 212	Nesby Glasgow DP	.04	.02	.00
☐ 213	Derrick Hatchett	.06	.03	.00
☐ 214	Randy McMillan	.10	.05	.01
☐ 215	Mike Pagel	.15	.07	.01
☐ 216	Rohn Stark DP	.20	.10	.02
☐ 217	Donnell Thompson DP	.20	.10	.02
☐ 218	Leo Wisniewski DP	.04	.02	.00
☐ 219	Buffalo Bills TL	.10	.05	.01
	Joe Cribbs			
☐ 220	Curtis Brown	.06	.03	.00
☐ 221	Jerry Butler	.10	.05	.01
☐ 222	Greg Cater DP	.04	.02	.00
☐ 223	Joe Cribbs	.15	.07	.01
☐ 224	Joe Ferguson	.12	.06	.01
☐ 225	Roosevelt Leaks	.10	.05	.01
☐ 226	Frank Lewis	.10	.05	.01
☐ 227	Eugene Marve	.15	.07	.01
☐ 228	Fred Smerlas DP PB	.10	.05	.01
☐ 229	Ben Williams DP PB	.06	.03	.00
☐ 230	Cincinnati Bengals TL	.10	.05	.01
	Pete Johnson			
☐ 231	Charles Alexander	.10	.05	.01
☐ 232	Ken Anderson DP PB	.20	.10	.02
☐ 233	Jim Breech DP	.04	.02	.00
☐ 234	Ross Browner	.10	.05	.01
☐ 235	Cris Collinsworth	.35	.17	.03
	DP PB			
☐ 236	Isaac Curtis	.12	.06	.01
☐ 237	Pete Johnson	.10	.05	.01
☐ 238	Steve Kreider DP	.04	.02	.00
☐ 239	Max Montoya DP	.25	.12	.02
☐ 240	Anthony Munoz PB	2.50	1.25	.25
☐ 241	Ken Riley	.10	.05	.01
☐ 242	Dan Ross PB	.10	.05	.01
☐ 243	Reggie Williams	.12	.06	.01
☐ 244	Cleveland Browns TL	.10	.05	.01
	Mike Pruitt			
☐ 245	Chip Banks DP PB	.30	.15	.03
☐ 246	Tom Cousineau DP	.12	.06	.01
☐ 247	Joe DeLamielleure DP	.06	.03	.00
☐ 248	Doug Dieken DP	.04	.02	.00
☐ 249	Hanford Dixon	.50	.25	.05
☐ 250	Ricky Feacher DP	.04	.02	.00
☐ 251	Lawrence Johnson DP	.04	.02	.00
☐ 252	Dave Logan DP	.04	.02	.00
☐ 253	Paul McDonald DP	.10	.05	.01
☐ 254	Ozzie Newsome DP	.40	.20	.04
☐ 255	Mike Pruitt	.10	.05	.01
☐ 256	Clarence Scott DP	.04	.02	.00
☐ 257	Brian Sipe DP	.12	.06	.01
☐ 258	Dwight Walker DP	.04	.02	.00
☐ 259	Charles White	.12	.06	.01
☐ 260	Denver Broncos TL	.10	.05	.01
	Gerald Willhite			
☐ 261	Steve DeBerg DP	.60	.30	.06
☐ 262	Randy Gradishar DP PB	.15	.07	.01
☐ 263	Rulon Jones DP	.15	.07	.01
☐ 264	Rick Karlis DP	.04	.02	.00
☐ 265	Don Latimer	.06	.03	.00
☐ 266	Rick Parros DP	.04	.02	.00
☐ 267	Luke Prestridge PB	.06	.03	.00
☐ 268	Rick Upchurch PB	.12	.06	.01
☐ 269	Steve Watson DP	.10	.05	.01
☐ 270	Gerald Willhite DP	.10	.05	.01
☐ 271	Houston Oilers TL	.10	.05	.01
	Gifford Nielsen			
☐ 272	Harold Bailey	.06	.03	.00
☐ 273	Jesse Baker DP	.06	.03	.00
☐ 274	Gregg Bingham DP	.04	.02	.00
☐ 275	Robert Brazile DP PB	.06	.03	.00
☐ 276	Donnie Craft	.06	.03	.00
☐ 277	Daryl Hunt	.06	.03	.00
☐ 278	Archie Manning DP	.15	.07	.01
☐ 279	Gifford Nielsen	.10	.05	.01
☐ 280	Mike Renfro	.10	.05	.01
☐ 281	Carl Roaches DP	.06	.03	.00
☐ 282	Kansas City Chiefs TL	.10	.05	.01

Joe Delaney

☐ 283 Gary Barbaro PB	.10	.05	.01
☐ 284 Joe Delaney	.12	.06	.01
☐ 285 Jeff Gossett	.30	.15	.03
☐ 286 Gary Green DP PB	.06	.03	.00
☐ 287 Eric Harris DP	.04	.02	.00
☐ 288 Billy Jackson DP	.04	.02	.00
☐ 289 Bill Kenney DP	.10	.05	.01
☐ 290 Nick Lowery	.30	.15	.03
☐ 291 Henry Marshall	.06	.03	.00
☐ 292 Art Still DP PB	.10	.05	.01
☐ 293 Los Angeles Raiders TL	.75	.35	.07

Marcus Allen

☐ 294 Marcus Allen DP PB	9.00	4.50	.90
☐ 295 Lyle Alzado	.20	.10	.02
☐ 296 Chris Bahr DP	.06	.03	.00
☐ 297 Cliff Branch	.20	.10	.02
☐ 298 Todd Christensen	1.50	.75	.15
☐ 299 Ray Guy	.20	.10	.02
☐ 300 Frank Hawkins DP	.04	.02	.00
☐ 301 Lester Hayes DP PB	.10	.05	.01
☐ 302 Ted Hendricks DP PB	.15	.07	.01
☐ 303 Kenny King DP	.06	.03	.00
☐ 304 Rod Martin	.10	.05	.01
☐ 305 Matt Millen DP	.25	.12	.02
☐ 306 Burgess Owens	.06	.03	.00
☐ 307 Jim Plunkett	.30	.15	.03
☐ 308 Miami Dolphins TL	.10	.05	.01

Andra Franklin

☐ 309 Bob Baumhower PB	.10	.05	.01
☐ 310 Glenn Blackwood	.06	.03	.00
☐ 311 Lyle Blackwood DP	.04	.02	.00
☐ 312 A.J. Duhe	.10	.05	.01
☐ 313 Andra Franklin PB	.10	.05	.01
☐ 314 Duriel Harris	.06	.03	.00
☐ 315 Bob Kuechenberg DP PB	.06	.03	.00
☐ 316 Don McNeal	.10	.05	.01
☐ 317 Tony Nathan	.10	.05	.01
☐ 318 Ed Newman PB	.10	.05	.01
☐ 319 Earnie Rhone DP	.04	.02	.00
☐ 320 Joe Rose DP	.06	.03	.00
☐ 321 Don Strock DP	.06	.03	.00
☐ 322 Uwe Von Schamann	.06	.03	.00
☐ 323 David Woodley DP	.06	.03	.00
☐ 324 New England Pats TL	.10	.05	.01

Tony Collins

☐ 325 Julius Adams	.06	.03	.00
☐ 326 Pete Brock	.06	.03	.00
☐ 327 Rich Camarillo DP	.12	.06	.01
☐ 328 Tony Collins DP	.10	.05	.01
☐ 329 Steve Grogan	.15	.07	.01
☐ 330 John Hannah PB	.30	.15	.03
☐ 331 Don Hasselbeck	.06	.03	.00
☐ 332 Mike Haynes DP	.12	.06	.01
☐ 333 Roland James	.06	.03	.00
☐ 334A Stanley Morgan ERR	.75	.35	.07

("Inside Linebacker"

printed upside down
on card back)

☐ 334B Stanley Morgan COR	.25	.12	.02
☐ 335 Steve Nelson	.06	.03	.00
☐ 336 Kenneth Sims DP	.10	.05	.01
☐ 337 Mark Van Eeghen	.10	.05	.01
☐ 338 New York Jets TL	.10	.05	.01

Freeman McNeil

☐ 339 Greg Buttle	.10	.05	.01
☐ 340 Joe Fields PB	.10	.05	.01
☐ 341 Mark Gastineau DP PB	.10	.05	.01
☐ 342 Bruce Harper	.06	.03	.00
☐ 343 Bobby Jackson	.06	.03	.00
☐ 344 Bobby Jones	.06	.03	.00
☐ 345 Johnny"Lam" Jones DP	.06	.03	.00
☐ 346 Joe Klecko	.12	.06	.01
☐ 347 Marty Lyons	.10	.05	.01
☐ 348 Freeman McNeil PB	.60	.30	.06
☐ 349 Lance Mehl	.25	.12	.02
☐ 350 Marvin Powell DP PB	.06	.03	.00
☐ 351 Darrol Ray DP	.06	.03	.00
☐ 352 Abdul Salaam	.06	.03	.00
☐ 353 Richard Todd	.12	.06	.01
☐ 354 Wesley Walker PB	.20	.10	.02
☐ 355 Pittsburgh Steelers TL	.30	.15	.03

Franco Harris

☐ 356 Gary Anderson DP	.20	.10	.02
☐ 357 Mel Blount DP	.15	.07	.01
☐ 358 Terry Bradshaw DP	.75	.35	.07
☐ 359 Larry Brown PB	.06	.03	.00
☐ 360 Bennie Cunningham	.06	.03	.00
☐ 361 Gary Dunn	.06	.03	.00
☐ 362 Franco Harris	.75	.35	.07
☐ 363 Jack Lambert PB	.50	.25	.05
☐ 364 Frank Pollard	.10	.05	.01
☐ 365 Donnie Shell DP	.12	.06	.01
☐ 366 John Stallworth PB	.20	.10	.02
☐ 367 Loren Toews	.12	.06	.01
☐ 368 Mike Webster DP PB	.15	.07	.01
☐ 369 Dwayne Woodruff	.20	.10	.02
☐ 370 San Diego Chargers TL	.10	.05	.01

Chuck Muncie

☐ 371 Rolf Benirschke DP PB	.06	.03	.00
☐ 372 James Brooks	1.50	.75	.15
☐ 373 Wes Chandler PB	.12	.06	.01
☐ 374 Dan Fouts DP PB	.60	.30	.06
☐ 375 Tim Fox	.06	.03	.00
☐ 376 Gary Johnson PB	.10	.05	.01
☐ 377 Charlie Joiner DP	.20	.10	.02
☐ 378 Louie Kelcher	.10	.05	.01
☐ 379 Chuck Muncie PB	.10	.05	.01
☐ 380 Cliff Thrift	.06	.03	.00
☐ 381 Doug Wilkerson DP	.06	.03	.00
☐ 382 Kellen Winslow PB	.50	.25	.05
☐ 383 Seattle Seahawks TL	.10	.05	.01

Sherman Smith

☐ 384 Kenny Easley PB	.75	.35	.07

	MINT	EXC	G-VG
☐ 385 Jacob Green	1.00	.50	.10
☐ 386 John Harris	.06	.03	.00
☐ 387 Michael Jackson	.06	.03	.00
☐ 388 Norm Johnson	.35	.17	.03
☐ 389 Steve Largent	1.00	.50	.10
☐ 390 Keith Simpson	.06	.03	.00
☐ 391 Sherman Smith	.06	.03	.00
☐ 392 Jeff West DP	.04	.02	.00
☐ 393 Jim Zorn DP	.10	.05	.01
☐ 394 Checklist 1-132	.15	.02	.00
☐ 395 Checklist 133-264	.15	.02	.00
☐ 396 Checklist 265-396	.20	.02	.00

1984 Topps

The 1984 Topps football card set contains 396 cards featuring players of the NFL. Cards are standard size, 2 1/2" by 3 1/2". The first six cards in the set recognize Record-Breaking (RB) achievements during the previous season. Post-season playoff games are featured on cards 7-9. Statistical league leaders are depicted on cards 202-207. The Team Leader (TL) cards are distributed throughout the set as the first card of the team sequence; this year only one leader (usually the team's rushing leader) is pictured and the backs contain team scoring information from the previous year. Instant Replay (IR) cards were issued as a special card for certain players in addition to (and immediately following) their regular card. Players who appeared in the Pro Bowl game (designated PB in the checklist below) are identified as such on the obverse of the player's regular card. Cards are numbered and alphabetically arranged within teams in the following order: Indianapolis Colts (10-20),

Buffalo Bills (21-31), Cincinnati Bengals (32-46), Cleveland Browns (47-60), Denver Broncos (61-72), Houston Oilers (73-83), Kansas City Chiefs (84-96), Los Angeles Raiders (97-115), Miami Dolphins (116-130), New England Patriots (131-143), New York Jets (144-158), Pittsburgh Steelers (159-173), San Diego Chargers (174-187), Seattle Seahawks (188-201), Atlanta Falcons (208-220), Chicago Bears (221-234), Dallas Cowboys (235-249), Detroit Lions (250-262), Green Bay Packers (263-275), Los Angeles Rams (276-287), Minnesota Vikings (288-298), New Orleans Saints (299-309), New York Giants (310-324), Philadelphia Eagles (325-336), St. Louis Cardinals (337-348), San Francisco 49ers (349-363), Tampa Bay Buccaneers (364-374), and Washington Redskins (375-393). The teams themselves were ordered alphabetically by team name with the exception of Indianapolis, who had very recently moved from Baltimore. The last three cards in the set (394-396) are checklist cards. The set features the rookie cards of Roger Craig, Eric Dickerson, John Elway, Darrell Green, Dan Marino, and Curt Warner.

	MINT	EXC	G-VG
COMPLETE SET (396)	100.00	50.00	10.00
COMMON PLAYER (1-396)	.05	.02	.00
☐ 1 Eric Dickerson RB Sets Rookie Mark With 1808 Yards	.60	.15	.03
☐ 2 Ali Haji-Sheikh RB Sets Field Goal Mark as a Rookie	.08	.04	.01
☐ 3 Franco Harris RB Records Eighth 1000 Yard Year	.20	.10	.02
☐ 4 Mark Moseley RB 161 Points Sets Mark for Kickers	.08	.04	.01
☐ 5 John Riggins RB 24 Rushing TD's	.15	.07	.01
☐ 6 Jan Stenerud RB 338th Career FG	.12	.06	.01
☐ 7 AFC Championship Raiders 30, Seahawks 14 (Marcus Allen running)	.15	.07	.01
☐ 8 NFC Championship Redskins 24, 49ers 21 (John Riggins running)	.15	.07	.01
☐ 9 Super Bowl XVIII UER Raiders 38,	.35	.17	.03

Redskins 9
(hand-off to Marcus
Allen; score wrong,
28-9 on card front)

☐ 10	Indianapolis Colts TL 10	.05	.01
	Curtis Dickey		
☐ 11	Raul Allegre 10	.05	.01
☐ 12	Curtis Dickey 10	.05	.01
☐ 13	Ray Donaldson 20	.10	.02
☐ 14	Nesby Glasgow 05	.02	.00
☐ 15	Chris Hinton PB 1.50	.75	.15
☐ 16	Vernon Maxwell 25	.12	.02
☐ 17	Randy McMillan 08	.04	.01
☐ 18	Mike Pagel 08	.04	.01
☐ 19	Rohn Stark 08	.04	.01
☐ 20	Leo Wisniewski 05	.02	.00
☐ 21	Buffalo Bills TL 10	.05	.01
	Joe Cribbs		
☐ 22	Jerry Butler 10	.05	.01
☐ 23	Joe Danelo 05	.02	.00
☐ 24	Joe Ferguson 10	.05	.01
☐ 25	Steve Freeman 05	.02	.00
☐ 26	Roosevelt Leaks 08	.04	.01
☐ 27	Frank Lewis 08	.04	.01
☐ 28	Eugene Marve 08	.04	.01
☐ 29	Booker Moore 05	.02	.00
☐ 30	Fred Smerlas PB 08	.04	.01
☐ 31	Ben Williams 05	.02	.00
☐ 32	Cincinnati Bengals TL 10	.05	.01
	Cris Collinsworth		
☐ 33	Charles Alexander 05	.02	.00
☐ 34	Ken Anderson 25	.12	.02
☐ 35	Ken Anderson IR 12	.06	.01
☐ 36	Jim Breech 05	.02	.00
☐ 37	Cris Collinsworth PB 15	.07	.01
☐ 38	Cris Collinsworth 08	.04	.01
☐ 39	Isaac Curtis 10	.05	.01
☐ 40	Eddie Edwards 05	.02	.00
☐ 41	Ray Horton 35	.17	.03
☐ 42	Pete Johnson 08	.04	.01
☐ 43	Steve Kreider 05	.02	.00
☐ 44	Max Montoya 10	.05	.01
☐ 45	Anthony Munoz PB 1.00	.50	.10
☐ 46	Reggie Williams 10	.05	.01
☐ 47	Cleveland Browns TL 10	.05	.01
	Mike Pruitt		
☐ 48	Matt Bahr 08	.04	.01
☐ 49	Chip Banks PB 10	.05	.01
☐ 50	Tom Cousineau 08	.04	.01
☐ 51	Joe DeLamielleure 08	.04	.01
☐ 52	Doug Dieken 05	.02	.00
☐ 53	Bob Golic 75	.35	.07
☐ 54	Bobby Jones 05	.02	.00
☐ 55	Dave Logan 05	.02	.00
☐ 56	Clay Matthews 25	.12	.02
☐ 57	Paul McDonald 08	.04	.01
☐ 58	Ozzie Newsome 50	.25	.05
☐ 59	Ozzie Newsome IR 25	.12	.02
☐ 60	Mike Pruitt 08	.04	.01
☐ 61	Denver Broncos TL 10	.05	.01
	Steve Watson		
☐ 62	Barney Chavous 20	.10	.02
☐ 63	John Elway 18.00	9.00	1.80
☐ 64	Steve Foley 05	.02	.00
☐ 65	Tom Jackson 15	.07	.01
☐ 66	Rich Karlis 05	.02	.00
☐ 67	Luke Prestridge 05	.02	.00
☐ 68	Zack Thomas 05	.02	.00
☐ 69	Rick Upchurch 10	.05	.01
☐ 70	Steve Watson 08	.04	.01
☐ 71	Sammy Winder 35	.17	.03
☐ 72	Louis Wright PB 10	.05	.01
☐ 73	Houston Oilers TL 10	.05	.01
	Tim Smith		
☐ 74	Jesse Baker 05	.02	.00
☐ 75	Gregg Bingham 05	.02	.00
☐ 76	Robert Brazile 08	.04	.01
☐ 77	Steve Brown 05	.02	.00
☐ 78	Chris Dressel 05	.02	.00
☐ 79	Doug France 05	.02	.00
☐ 80	Florian Kempf 05	.02	.00
☐ 81	Carl Roaches 08	.04	.01
☐ 82	Tim Smith 15	.07	.01
☐ 83	Willie Tullis 05	.02	.00
☐ 84	Kansas City Chiefs TL 10	.05	.01
	Carlos Carson		
☐ 85	Mike Bell 08	.04	.01
☐ 86	Theotis Brown 08	.04	.01
☐ 87	Carlos Carson PB 15	.07	.01
☐ 88	Carlos Carson IR 08	.04	.01
☐ 89	Deron Cherry PB 1.75	.85	.17
☐ 90	Gary Green PB 08	.04	.01
☐ 91	Billy Jackson 05	.02	.00
☐ 92	Bill Kenney 10	.05	.01
☐ 93	Bill Kenney IR 08	.04	.01
☐ 94	Nick Lowery 25	.12	.02
☐ 95	Henry Marshall 05	.02	.00
☐ 96	Art Still 08	.04	.01
☐ 97	Los Angeles Raiders TL 12	.06	.01
	Todd Christensen		
☐ 98	Marcus Allen 2.00	1.00	.20
☐ 99	Marcus Allen IR 1.00	.50	.10
☐ 100	Lyle Alzado 15	.07	.01
☐ 101	Lyle Alzado IR 10	.05	.01
☐ 102	Chris Bahr 08	.04	.01
☐ 103	Malcolm Barnwell 12	.06	.01
☐ 104	Cliff Branch 20	.10	.02
☐ 105	Todd Christensen PB 35	.17	.03
☐ 106	Todd Christensen IR ...15	.07	.01
☐ 107	Ray Guy 20	.10	.02
☐ 108	Frank Hawkins 05	.02	.00
☐ 109	Lester Hayes PB 10	.05	.01
☐ 110	Ted Hendricks PB 15	.07	.01
☐ 111	Howie Long PB 2.25	1.10	.22

☐ 112	Rod Martin PB 08	.04	.01
☐ 113	Vann McElroy PB 20	.10	.02
☐ 114	Jim Plunkett 20	.10	.02
☐ 115	Greg Pruitt PB 10	.05	.01
☐ 116	Miami Dolphins TL 45	.22	.04
	Mark Duper		
☐ 117	Bob Baumhower PB 08	.04	.01
☐ 118	Doug Betters PB 15	.07	.01
☐ 119	A.J. Duhe 08	.04	.01
☐ 120	Mark Duper PB 3.00	1.50	.30
☐ 121	Andra Franklin 08	.04	.01
☐ 122	William Judson 05	.02	.00
☐ 123	Dan Marino PB 48.00	20.00	4.00
☐ 124	Dan Marino IR 6.50	3.25	.65
☐ 125	Nat Moore 08	.04	.01
☐ 126	Ed Newman PB 05	.02	.00
☐ 127	Reggie Roby 75	.35	.07
☐ 128	Gerald Small 05	.02	.00
☐ 129	Dwight Stephenson PB .50	.25	.05
☐ 130	Uwe Von Schamann 05	.02	.00
☐ 131	New England Pats TL ..10	.05	.01
	Tony Collins		
☐ 132	Rich Camarillo PB 05	.02	.00
☐ 133	Tony Collins PB 08	.04	.01
☐ 134	Tony Collins IR 05	.02	.00
☐ 135	Bob Cryder 05	.02	.00
☐ 136	Steve Grogan 15	.07	.01
☐ 137	John Hannah PB 20	.10	.02
☐ 138	Brian Holloway PB 15	.07	.01
☐ 139	Roland James 05	.02	.00
☐ 140	Stanley Morgan 20	.10	.02
☐ 141	Rick Sanford 05	.02	.00
☐ 142	Mosi Tatupu 15	.07	.01
☐ 143	Andre Tippett 2.00	1.00	.20
☐ 144	New York Jets TL 12	.06	.01
	Wesley Walker		
☐ 145	Jerome Barkum 08	.04	.01
☐ 146	Mark Gastineau PB 12	.06	.01
☐ 147	Mark Gastineau IR 08	.04	.01
☐ 148	Bruce Harper 05	.02	.00
☐ 149	Johnny "Lam" Jones 08	.04	.01
☐ 150	Joe Klecko PB 12	.06	.01
☐ 151	Pat Leahy 10	.05	.01
☐ 152	Freeman McNeil 25	.12	.02
☐ 153	Lance Mehl 08	.04	.01
☐ 154	Marvin Powell PB 08	.04	.01
☐ 155	Darrol Ray 05	.02	.00
☐ 156	Pat Ryan 15	.07	.01
☐ 157	Kirk Springs 05	.02	.00
☐ 158	Wesley Walker 20	.10	.02
☐ 159	Pittsburgh Steelers TL ..20	.10	.02
	Franco Harris		
☐ 160	Walter Abercrombie 15	.07	.01
☐ 161	Gary Anderson PB 08	.04	.01
☐ 162	Terry Bradshaw 75	.35	.07
☐ 163	Craig Colquitt 05	.02	.00
☐ 164	Bennie Cunningham 05	.02	.00

☐ 165	Franco Harris 60	.30	.06
☐ 166	Franco Harris IR 25	.12	.02
☐ 167	Jack Lambert PB 40	.20	.04
☐ 168	Jack Lambert IR 15	.07	.01
☐ 169	Frank Pollard 08	.04	.01
☐ 170	Donnie Shell 10	.05	.01
☐ 171	Mike Webster PB 20	.10	.02
☐ 172	Keith Willis 15	.07	.01
☐ 173	Rick Woods 05	.02	.00
☐ 174	San Diego Chargers TL ..10	.05	.01
	Kellen Winslow		
☐ 175	Rolf Benirschke 08	.04	.01
☐ 176	James Brooks 60	.30	.06
☐ 177	Maury Buford 05	.02	.00
☐ 178	Wes Chandler PB 10	.05	.01
☐ 179	Dan Fouts PB 60	.30	.06
☐ 180	Dan Fouts IR 25	.12	.02
☐ 181	Charlie Joiner 20	.10	.02
☐ 182	Linden King 05	.02	.00
☐ 183	Chuck Muncie 10	.05	.01
☐ 184	Billy Ray Smith 35	.17	.03
☐ 185	Danny Walters 15	.07	.01
☐ 186	Kellen Winslow PB 30	.15	.03
☐ 187	Kellen Winslow IR 15	.07	.01
☐ 188	Seattle Seahawks TL 15	.07	.01
	Curt Warner		
☐ 189	Steve August 05	.02	.00
☐ 190	Dave Brown 08	.04	.01
☐ 191	Zachary Dixon 05	.02	.00
☐ 192	Kenny Easley 15	.07	.01
☐ 193	Jacob Green 25	.12	.02
☐ 194	Norm Johnson 10	.05	.01
☐ 195	Dave Krieg 3.00	1.50	.30
☐ 196	Steve Largent 1.00	.50	.10
☐ 197	Steve Largent IR 50	.25	.05
☐ 198	Curt Warner PB 75	.35	.07
☐ 199	Curt Warner IR 25	.12	.02
☐ 200	Jeff West 05	.02	.00
☐ 201	Charley Young 08	.04	.01
☐ 202	Passing Leaders 2.00	1.00	.20
	Dan Marino		
	Steve Bartkowski		
☐ 203	Receiving Leaders 10	.05	.01
	Todd Christensen		
	Charlie Brown		
	Earnest Gray		
	Roy Green		
☐ 204	Rushing Leaders 70	.35	.07
	Curt Warner		
	Eric Dickerson		
☐ 205	Scoring Leaders 08	.04	.01
	Gary Anderson		
	Mark Moseley		
☐ 206	Interception Leaders 08	.04	.01
	Vann McElroy		
	Ken Riley		
	Mark Murphy		

☐ 207	Punting Leaders 08	.04	.01
	Rich Camarillo		
	Greg Coleman		
☐ 208	Atlanta Falcons TL 10	.05	.01
	William Andrews		
☐ 209	William Andrews PB 10	.05	.01
☐ 210	William Andrews IR 08	.04	.01
☐ 211	Stacey Bailey 25	.12	.02
☐ 212	Steve Bartkowski 15	.07	.01
☐ 213	Steve Bartkowski IR 10	.05	.01
☐ 214	Ralph Giacomarro 05	.02	.00
☐ 215	Billy Johnson PB 10	.05	.01
☐ 216	Mike Kenn PB 08	.04	.01
☐ 217	Mick Luckhurst 05	.02	.00
☐ 218	Gerald Riggs 50	.25	.05
☐ 219	R.C. Thielemann PB 08	.04	.01
☐ 220	Jeff Van Note 08	.04	.01
☐ 221	Chicago Bears TL 50	.25	.05
	Walter Payton		
☐ 222	Jim Covert 1.00	.50	.10
☐ 223	Leslie Frazier 05	.02	.00
☐ 224	Willie Gault 1.50	.75	.15
☐ 225	Mike Hartenstine 05	.02	.00
☐ 226	Noah Jackson UER 08	.04	.01
	(photo actually		
	Jim Osborne)		
☐ 227	Jim McMahon 1.00	.50	.10
☐ 228	Walter Payton PB 1.50	.75	.15
☐ 229	Walter Payton IR 75	.35	.07
☐ 230	Mike Richardson 30	.15	.03
☐ 231	Terry Schmidt 05	.02	.00
☐ 232	Mike Singletary PB ... 2.00	1.00	.20
☐ 233	Matt Suhey 05	.02	.00
☐ 234	Bob Thomas 05	.02	.00
☐ 235	Dallas Cowboys TL 25	.12	.02
	Tony Dorsett		
☐ 236	Bob Breunig 08	.04	.01
☐ 237	Doug Cosbie PB 08	.04	.01
☐ 238	Tony Dorsett PB 75	.35	.07
☐ 239	Tony Dorsett IR 35	.17	.03
☐ 240	John Dutton 08	.04	.01
☐ 241	Tony Hill 10	.05	.01
☐ 242	Ed Jones PB 20	.10	.02
☐ 243	Drew Pearson 20	.10	.02
☐ 244	Rafael Septien 05	.02	.00
☐ 245	Ron Springs 05	.02	.00
☐ 246	Dennis Thurman 05	.02	.00
☐ 247	Everson Walls PB 35	.17	.03
☐ 248	Danny White 20	.10	.02
☐ 249	Randy White PB 40	.20	.04
☐ 250	Detroit Lions TL 12	.06	.01
	Billy Sims		
☐ 251	Jeff Chadwick 35	.17	.03
☐ 252	Garry Cobb 10	.05	.01
☐ 253	Doug English PB 10	.05	.01
☐ 254	William Gay 05	.02	.00
☐ 255	Eric Hipple 08	.04	.01
☐ 256	James Jones 25	.12	.02
☐ 257	Bruce McNorton 10	.05	.01
☐ 258	Ed Murray 10	.05	.01
☐ 259	Ulysses Norris 05	.02	.00
☐ 260	Billy Sims 15	.07	.01
☐ 261	Billy Sims IR 10	.05	.01
☐ 262	Leonard Thompson 05	.02	.00
☐ 263	Green Bay Packers TL ...25	.12	.02
	James Lofton		
☐ 264	John Anderson 05	.02	.00
☐ 265	Paul Coffman PB 08	.04	.01
☐ 266	Lynn Dickey 10	.05	.01
☐ 267	Gerry Ellis 05	.02	.00
☐ 268	John Jefferson 15	.07	.01
☐ 269	John Jefferson IR 08	.04	.01
☐ 270	Ezra Johnson 05	.02	.00
☐ 271	Tim Lewis 08	.04	.01
☐ 272	James Lofton PB 1.25	.60	.12
☐ 273	James Lofton IR 50	.25	.05
☐ 274	Larry McCarren PB 05	.02	.00
☐ 275	Jan Stenerud 20	.10	.02
☐ 276	Los Angeles Rams TL ...75	.35	.07
	Eric Dickerson		
☐ 277	Mike Barber 05	.02	.00
☐ 278	Jim Collins 05	.02	.00
☐ 279	Nolan Cromwell PB 10	.05	.01
☐ 280	Eric Dickerson PB 16.00	8.00	1.60
☐ 281	Eric Dickerson IR 3.00	1.50	.30
☐ 282	George Farmer 05	.02	.00
☐ 283	Vince Ferragamo 10	.05	.01
☐ 284	Kent Hill PB 08	.04	.01
☐ 285	John Misko 05	.02	.00
☐ 286	Jackie Slater PB 1.50	.75	.15
☐ 287	Jack Youngblood 20	.10	.02
☐ 288	Minnesota Vikings TL 10	.05	.01
	Darrin Nelson		
☐ 289	Ted Brown 08	.04	.01
☐ 290	Greg Coleman 05	.02	.00
☐ 291	Steve Dils 08	.04	.01
☐ 292	Tony Galbreath 08	.04	.01
☐ 293	Tommy Kramer 15	.07	.01
☐ 294	Doug Martin 05	.02	.00
☐ 295	Darrin Nelson 35	.17	.03
☐ 296	Benny Ricardo 05	.02	.00
☐ 297	John Swain 05	.02	.00
☐ 298	John Turner 05	.02	.00
☐ 299	New Orleans Saints TL ...10	.05	.01
	George Rogers		
☐ 300	Morten Andersen 1.75	.85	.17
☐ 301	Russell Erxleben 05	.02	.00
☐ 302	Jeff Groth 05	.02	.00
☐ 303	Rickey Jackson PB 1.50	.75	.15
☐ 304	Johnnie Poe 05	.02	.00
☐ 305	George Rogers 15	.07	.01
☐ 306	Richard Todd 10	.05	.01
☐ 307	Jim Wilks 05	.02	.00
☐ 308	Dave Wilson 10	.05	.01

☐ 309	Wayne Wilson	.08	.04	.01
☐ 310	New York Giants TL Earnest Gray	.10	.05	.01
☐ 311	Leon Bright	.05	.02	.00
☐ 312	Scott Brunner	.08	.04	.01
☐ 313	Rob Carpenter	.08	.04	.01
☐ 314	Harry Carson PB	.20	.10	.02
☐ 315	Earnest Gray	.08	.04	.01
☐ 316	Ali Haji-Sheikh PB	.10	.05	.01
☐ 317	Mark Haynes PB	.08	.04	.01
☐ 318	Dave Jennings	.08	.04	.01
☐ 319	Brian Kelley	.08	.04	.01
☐ 320	Phil Simms	.60	.30	.06
☐ 321	Lawrence Taylor PB	1.50	.75	.15
☐ 322	Lawrence Taylor IR	.75	.35	.07
☐ 323	Brad Van Pelt	.08	.04	.01
☐ 324	Butch Woolfolk	.08	.04	.01
☐ 325	Philadelphia Eagles TL Mike Quick	.12	.06	.01
☐ 326	Harold Carmichael	.15	.07	.01
☐ 327	Herman Edwards	.05	.02	.00
☐ 328	Michael Haddix	.15	.07	.01
☐ 329	Dennis Harrison	.05	.02	.00
☐ 330	Ron Jaworski	.12	.06	.01
☐ 331	Wilbert Montgomery	.10	.05	.01
☐ 332	Hubert Oliver	.05	.02	.00
☐ 333	Mike Quick PB	.75	.35	.07
☐ 334	Jerry Robinson	.08	.04	.01
☐ 335	Max Runager	.05	.02	.00
☐ 336	Michael Williams	.05	.02	.00
☐ 337	St. Louis Cardinals TL Ottis Anderson	.15	.07	.01
☐ 338	Ottis Anderson	.40	.20	.04
☐ 339	Al(Bubba) Baker	.08	.04	.01
☐ 340	Carl Birdsong PB	.05	.02	.00
☐ 341	David Galloway	.05	.02	.00
☐ 342	Roy Green PB	.40	.20	.04
☐ 343	Roy Green IR	.15	.07	.01
☐ 344	Curtis Greer	.25	.12	.02
☐ 345	Neil Lomax	.15	.07	.01
☐ 346	Doug Marsh	.05	.02	.00
☐ 347	Stump Mitchell	.12	.06	.01
☐ 348	Lionel Washington	.45	.22	.04
☐ 349	San Francisco 49ers TL Dwight Clark	.12	.06	.01
☐ 350	Dwaine Board	.05	.02	.00
☐ 351	Dwight Clark	.20	.10	.02
☐ 352	Dwight Clark IR	.10	.05	.01
☐ 353	Roger Craig	6.50	3.25	.65
☐ 354	Fred Dean	.10	.05	.01
☐ 355	Fred Dean IR	.08	.04	.01
☐ 356	Dwight Hicks PB	.08	.04	.01
☐ 357	Ronnie Lott PB	2.00	1.00	.20
☐ 358	Joe Montana PB	4.50	2.25	.45
☐ 359	Joe Montana IR	2.25	1.10	.22
☐ 360	Freddie Solomon	.08	.04	.01
☐ 361	Wendell Tyler	.08	.04	.01

☐ 362	Ray Wersching	.05	.02	.00
☐ 363	Eric Wright	.25	.12	.02
☐ 364	Tampa Bay Bucs TL Kevin House	.10	.05	.01
☐ 365	Gerald Carter	.05	.02	.00
☐ 366	Hugh Green PB	.10	.05	.01
☐ 367	Kevin House	.08	.04	.01
☐ 368	Michael Morton	.05	.02	.00
☐ 369	James Owens	.08	.04	.01
☐ 370	Booker Reese	.05	.02	.00
☐ 371	Lee Roy Selmon PB	.12	.06	.01
☐ 372	Jack Thompson	.08	.04	.01
☐ 373	James Wilder	.15	.07	.01
☐ 374	Steve Wilson	.05	.02	.00
☐ 375	Wash. Redskins TL John Riggins	.15	.07	.01
☐ 376	Jeff Bostic PB	.12	.06	.01
☐ 377	Charlie Brown PB	.10	.05	.01
☐ 378	Charlie Brown IR	.08	.04	.01
☐ 379	Dave Butz PB	.12	.06	.01
☐ 380	Darrell Green	7.00	3.50	.70
☐ 381	Russ Grimm PB	.50	.25	.05
☐ 382	Joe Jacoby PB	.12	.06	.01
☐ 383	Dexter Manley	.12	.06	.01
☐ 384	Art Monk	1.50	.75	.15
☐ 385	Mark Moseley	.08	.04	.01
☐ 386	Mark Murphy PB	.05	.02	.00
☐ 387	Mike Nelms	.08	.04	.01
☐ 388	John Riggins	.55	.27	.05
☐ 389	John Riggins IR	.20	.10	.02
☐ 390	Joe Theismann PB	.50	.25	.05
☐ 391	Joe Theismann IR	.20	.10	.02
☐ 392	Don Warren	.08	.04	.01
☐ 393	Joe Washington	.08	.04	.01
☐ 394	Checklist 1-132	.12	.02	.00
☐ 395	Checklist 133-264	.12	.02	.00
☐ 396	Checklist 265-396	.15	.02	.00

1984 Topps USFL

The 1984 Topps USFL set contains 132 cards, which were available as a pre-packaged set from Topps housed in its own specially made box. The cards are in full color and measure the standard 2 1/2" by 3 1/2". The cards in the set are numbered in alphabetical team order (with players arranged alphabetically within teams), for example, Arizona Wranglers (1-8), Birmingham Stallions (9-16), Chicago Blitz (17-24), Denver Gold (25-32), Houston Gamblers (33-38), Jacksonville Bulls (39-44),

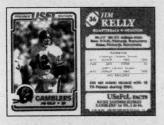

Los Angeles Express (45-52), Memphis Showboats (53-58), Michigan Panthers (59-66), New Jersey Generals (67-74), New Orleans Breakers (75-82), Oakland Invaders (83-90), Oklahoma Outlaws (91-96), Philadelphia Stars (97-104), Pittsburgh Maulers (105-110), San Antonio Gunslingers (111-116), Tampa Bay Bandits (117-124), and Washington Federals (125-131). The last card in the set is a checklist card. The key rookie cards in this set are Anthony Carter, Jim Kelly, Ricky Sanders, Herschel Walker, Reggie White, and Steve Young.

	MINT	EXC	G-VG
COMPLETE SET (132)	400.00	200.00	40.00
COMMON PLAYER (1-132)	.75	.35	.07

		MINT	EXC	G-VG
☐ 1	Luther Bradley	1.00	.50	.10
☐ 2	Frank Corral	1.00	.50	.10
☐ 3	Trumaine Johnson	1.25	.60	.12
☐ 4	Greg Landry	1.00	.50	.10
☐ 5	Kit Lathrop	.75	.35	.07
☐ 6	Kevin Long	.75	.35	.07
☐ 7	Tim Spencer	1.50	.75	.15
☐ 8	Stan White	.75	.35	.07
☐ 9	Buddy Aydelette	.75	.35	.07
☐ 10	Tom Banks	.75	.35	.07
☐ 11	Fred Bohannon	.75	.35	.07
☐ 12	Joe Cribbs	1.00	.50	.10
☐ 13	Joey Jones	1.00	.50	.10
☐ 14	Scott Norwood	4.00	2.00	.40
☐ 15	Jim Smith	1.00	.50	.10
☐ 16	Cliff Stoudt	1.00	.50	.10
☐ 17	Vince Evans	1.00	.50	.10
☐ 18	Vagas Ferguson	1.00	.50	.10
☐ 19	John Gillen	.75	.35	.07
☐ 20	Kris Haines	.75	.35	.07
☐ 21	Glenn Hyde	.75	.35	.07
☐ 22	Mark Keel	.75	.35	.07
☐ 23	Gary Lewis	.75	.35	.07
☐ 24	Doug Plank	1.00	.50	.10
☐ 25	Neil Balholm	.75	.35	.07
☐ 26	David Dumars	.75	.35	.07
☐ 27	David Martin	.75	.35	.07
☐ 28	Craig Penrose	.75	.35	.07
☐ 29	Dave Stalls	.75	.35	.07
☐ 30	Harry Sydney	2.00	1.00	.20
☐ 31	Vincent White	.75	.35	.07
☐ 32	George Yarno	.75	.35	.07
☐ 33	Kiki DeAyala	.75	.35	.07
☐ 34	Sam Harrell	.75	.35	.07
☐ 35	Mike Hawkins	.75	.35	.07
☐ 36	Jim Kelly	185.00	75.00	15.00
☐ 37	Mark Rush	.75	.35	.07
☐ 38	Ricky Sanders	18.00	9.00	1.80
☐ 39	Paul Bergmann	.75	.35	.07
☐ 40	Tom Dinkel	.75	.35	.07
☐ 41	Wyatt Henderson	.75	.35	.07
☐ 42	Vaughan Johnson	10.00	5.00	1.00
☐ 43	Willie McClendon	1.00	.50	.10
☐ 44	Matt Robinson	1.00	.50	.10
☐ 45	George Achica	1.00	.50	.10
☐ 46	Mark Adickes	1.00	.50	.10
☐ 47	Howard Carson	.75	.35	.07
☐ 48	Kevin Nelson	.75	.35	.07
☐ 49	Jeff Partridge	.75	.35	.07
☐ 50	Jo Jo Townsell	1.50	.75	.15
☐ 51	Eddie Weaver	.75	.35	.07
☐ 52	Steve Young	40.00	20.00	4.00
☐ 53	Derrick Crawford	.75	.35	.07
☐ 54	Walter Lewis	.75	.35	.07
☐ 55	Phil McKinnely	.75	.35	.07
☐ 56	Vic Minore	.75	.35	.07
☐ 57	Gary Shirk	.75	.35	.07
☐ 58	Reggie White	45.00	22.50	4.50
☐ 59	Anthony Carter	18.00	9.00	1.80
☐ 60	John Corker	1.00	.50	.10
☐ 61	David Greenwood	1.00	.50	.10
☐ 62	Bobby Hebert	12.50	6.25	1.25
☐ 63	Derek Holloway	.75	.35	.07
☐ 64	Ken Lacy	.75	.35	.07
☐ 65	Tyrone McGriff	.75	.35	.07
☐ 66	Ray Pinney	.75	.35	.07
☐ 67	Gary Barbaro	.75	.50	.10
☐ 68	Sam Bowers	.75	.35	.07
☐ 69	Clarence Collins	.75	.35	.07
☐ 70	Willie Harper	.75	.35	.07
☐ 71	Jim LeClair	.75	.35	.07
☐ 72	Bob Leopold	.75	.35	.07
☐ 73	Brian Sipe	1.00	.50	.10
☐ 74	Herschel Walker	65.00	32.50	6.50
☐ 75	Junior Ah You	.75	.35	.07
☐ 76	Marcus Dupree	3.50	1.75	.35
☐ 77	Marcus Marek	1.00	.50	.10
☐ 78	Tim Mazzetti	1.00	.50	.10
☐ 79	Mike Robinson	1.00	.50	.10
☐ 80	Dan Ross	1.00	.50	.10

☐ 81	Mark Schellen	1.00	.50	.10
☐ 82	Johnnie Walton	.75	.35	.07
☐ 83	Gordon Banks	1.00	.50	.10
☐ 84	Fred Besana	.75	.35	.07
☐ 85	Dave Browning	.75	.35	.07
☐ 86	Eric Jordan	.75	.35	.07
☐ 87	Frank Manumaleuga	.75		
			.35	.07
☐ 88	Gary Plummer	2.00	1.00	.20
☐ 89	Stan Talley	.75	.35	.07
☐ 90	Arthur Whittington	.75	.35	.07
☐ 91	Terry Beeson	.75	.35	.07
☐ 92	Mel Gray	1.00	.50	.10
☐ 93	Mike Katolin	.75	.35	.07
☐ 94	Dewey McClain	.75	.35	.07
☐ 95	Sidney Thornton	1.00	.50	.10
☐ 96	Doug Williams	1.50	.75	.15
☐ 97	Kelvin Bryant	4.00	2.00	.40
☐ 98	John Bunting	.75	.35	.07
☐ 99	Irv Eatman	1.50	.75	.15
☐ 100	Scott Fitzkee	1.00	.50	.10
☐ 101	Chuck Fusina	1.00	.50	.10
☐ 102	Sean Landeta	3.00	1.50	.30
☐ 103	David Trout	.75	.35	.07
☐ 104	Scott Woerner	.75	.35	.07
☐ 105	Glenn Carano	.75	.35	.07
☐ 106	Ron Crosby	.75	.35	.07
☐ 107	Jerry Holmes	1.50	.75	.15
☐ 108	Bruce Huther	.75	.35	.07
☐ 109	Mike Rozier	10.00	5.00	1.00
☐ 110	Larry Swider	.75	.35	.07
☐ 111	Danny Buggs	.75	.35	.07
☐ 112	Putt Choate	.75	.35	.07
☐ 113	Rich Garza	.75	.35	.07
☐ 114	Joey Hackett	.75	.35	.07
☐ 115	Rick Neuheisel	1.00	.50	.10
☐ 116	Mike St. Clair	.75	.35	.07
☐ 117	Gary Anderson	12.00	6.00	1.20
☐ 118	Zenon Andrusyshyn	.75	.35	.07
☐ 119	Doug Beaudoin	.75	.35	.07
☐ 120	Mike Butler	.75	.35	.07
☐ 121	Willie Gillespie	.75	.35	.07
☐ 122	Fred Nordgren	.75	.35	.07
☐ 123	John Reaves	1.00	.50	.10
☐ 124	Eric Truvillion	.75	.35	.07
☐ 125	Reggie Collier	1.00	.50	.10
☐ 126	Mike Guess	.75	.35	.07
☐ 127	Mike Hohensee	.75	.35	.07
☐ 128	Craig James	2.00	1.00	.20
☐ 129	Eric Robinson	.75	.35	.07
☐ 130	Billy Taylor	1.00	.50	.10
☐ 131	Joey Walters	.75	.35	.07
☐ 132	Checklist 1-132	1.25	.40	.08

1985 Topps

The 1985 Topps football card set contains 396 cards featuring players of the NFL. Cards are standard size 2 1/2" by 3 1/2". The set is distinguished by the black border on the fronts of the cards, as well as the horizontal orientation of the card fronts. The first six cards in the set recognize Record-Breaking (RB) achievements during the previous season. Cards 7-9 provide a summary of the post-season playoff action. Statistical league leaders are featured on cards 192-197. The Team Leader (TL) cards are distributed throughout the set as the first card of the team sequence; this year an action scene is pictured and captioned, and the backs contain team scoring information from the previous year. All-Pro (AP) selections are denoted on the player's regular card in small yellow print in the upper left black border of the obverse. The order of teams (alphabetically arranged by conference with players themselves alphabetically ordered within each team) is as follows: Atlanta Falcons (10-21), Chicago Bears (22-36), Dallas Cowboys (37-52), Detroit Lions (53-65), Green Bay Packers (66-76), Los Angeles Rams (77-88), Minnesota Vikings (89-99), New Orleans Saints (100-109), New York Giants (110-124), Philadelphia Eagles (125-136), St. Louis Cardinals (137-147), San Francisco 49ers (148-165), Tampa Bay Buccaneers (166-176), Washington Redskins (177-191), Buffalo Bills (198-208), Cincinnati Bengals (209-220), Cleveland Browns (221-234), Denver Broncos (235-247), Houston Oilers (258-257), Indianapolis Colts (258-268), Kansas City Chiefs (269-280), Los Angeles Raiders (281-299), Miami Dolphins (300-319), New England Patriots (320-334), New York Jets (335-350),

Pittsburgh Steelers (351-366), San Diego Chargers (367-379), and Seattle Seahawks (380-393) are checklist cards. The last three cards in the set (394-396) are checklist cards. Although they are not considered part of the complete set price, Topps also printed cards on the bottoms of the wax pack boxes. There were four different boxes. There were four different players. These box bottom cards are distinguished by their red border (instead of black) and the fact that they are "lettered" rather than "numbered". The key rookie card in this set is Warren Moon (although he had already appeared in several JOGO CFL card issues). Other notable rookie cards in this set are Carl Banks, Mark Clayton, Richard Dent, Henry Ellard, Louis Lipps, and Darryl Talley.

	MINT	EXC	G-VG
COMPLETE SET (396)	80.00	40.00	8.00
COMMON PLAYER (1-396)	.05	.02	.00

☐ 1 Mark Clayton RB Most Touchdown Receptions, Season	.60	.10	.02
☐ 2 Eric Dickerson RB Most Yards Rushing, Season	.50	.25	.05
☐ 3 Charlie Joiner RB Most Receptions, Career	.10	.05	.01
☐ 4 Dan Marino RB UER Most Touchdown Passes, Season (Dolphins misspelled as Dophins)	2.00	1.00	.20
☐ 5 Art Monk RB Most Receptions, Season	.15	.07	.01
☐ 6 Walter Payton RB Most Yards Rushing, Career	.50	.25	.05
☐ 7 NFC Championship 49ers 23, Bears 0 (Matt Suhey tackled)	.10	.05	.01
☐ 8 AFC Championship Dolphins 45, Steelers 28 (Woody Bennett over)	.10	.05	.01
☐ 9 Super Bowl XIX 49ers 38, Dolphins 16 (Wendell Tyler)	.15	.07	.01
☐ 10 Atlanta Falcons TL Stretching For The First Down (Gerald Riggs)	.10	.05	.01
☐ 11 William Andrews	.08	.04	.01
☐ 12 Stacey Bailey	.08	.04	.01
☐ 13 Steve Bartkowski	.15	.07	.01
☐ 14 Rick Bryan	.50	.25	.05
☐ 15 Alfred Jackson	.08	.04	.01
☐ 16 Kenny Johnson	.05	.02	.00
☐ 17 Mike Kenn AP	.08	.04	.01
☐ 18 Mike Pitts	.25	.12	.02
☐ 19 Gerald Riggs	.25	.12	.02
☐ 20 Sylvester Stamps	.05	.02	.00
☐ 21 R.C. Thielemann	.05	.02	.00
☐ 22 Chicago Bears TL Sweetness Sets Record Straight (Walter Payton)	.45	.22	.04
☐ 23 Todd Bell AP	.25	.12	.02
☐ 24 Richard Dent AP	5.00	2.50	.50
☐ 25 Gary Fencik	.08	.04	.01
☐ 26 Dave Finzer	.05	.02	.00
☐ 27 Leslie Frazier	.05	.02	.00
☐ 28 Steve Fuller	.08	.04	.01
☐ 29 Willie Gault	.35	.17	.03
☐ 30 Dan Hampton AP	.60	.30	.06
☐ 31 Jim McMahon	.50	.25	.05
☐ 32 Steve McMichael	2.00	1.00	.20
☐ 33 Walter Payton AP	1.50	.75	.15
☐ 34 Mike Singletary	.75	.35	.07
☐ 35 Matt Suhey	.05	.02	.00
☐ 36 Bob Thomas	.05	.02	.00
☐ 37 Dallas Cowboys TL Busting Through The Defense (Tony Dorsett)	.25	.12	.02
☐ 38 Bill Bates	.50	.25	.05
☐ 39 Doug Cosbie	.08	.04	.01
☐ 40 Tony Dorsett	.50	.25	.05
☐ 41 Michael Downs	.05	.02	.00
☐ 42 Mike Hegman UER (reference to SB VIII, should be SB XIII)	.10	.05	.01
☐ 43 Tony Hill	.08	.04	.01
☐ 44 Gary Hogeboom	.15	.07	.01
☐ 45 Jim Jeffcoat	.35	.17	.03
☐ 46 Ed Too Tall Jones	.20	.10	.02
☐ 47 Matt Renfro	.05	.02	.00
☐ 48 Rafael Septien	.05	.02	.00
☐ 49 Dennis Thurman	.05	.02	.00
☐ 50 Everson Walls	.10	.05	.01
☐ 51 Danny White	.15	.07	.01
☐ 52 Randy White	.35	.17	.03
☐ 53 Detroit Lions TL Popping One Loose (Lions' Defense)	.08	.04	.01
☐ 54 Jeff Chadwick	.08	.04	.01
☐ 55 Mike Cofer	.50	.25	.05
☐ 56 Gary Danielson	.08	.04	.01
☐ 57 Keith Dorney	.05	.02	.00

☐ 58 Doug English	.08	.04	.01
☐ 59 William Gay	.05	.02	.00
☐ 60 Ken Jenkins	.05	.02	.00
☐ 61 James Jones	.08	.04	.01
☐ 62 Ed Murray	.08	.04	.01
☐ 63 Billy Sims	.12	.06	.01
☐ 64 Leonard Thompson	.05	.02	.00
☐ 65 Bobby Watkins	.05	.02	.00
☐ 66 Green Bay Packers TL	.08	.04	.01
Spotting His			
Deep Receiver			
(Lynn Dickey)			
☐ 67 Paul Coffman	.08	.04	.01
☐ 68 Lynn Dickey	.10	.05	.01
☐ 69 Mike Douglass	.05	.02	.00
☐ 70 Tom Flynn	.10	.05	.01
☐ 71 Eddie Lee Ivery	.08	.04	.01
☐ 72 Ezra Johnson	.05	.02	.00
☐ 73 Mark Lee	.08	.04	.01
☐ 74 Tim Lewis	.08	.04	.01
☐ 75 James Lofton	.75	.35	.07
☐ 76 Bucky Scribner	.05	.02	.00
☐ 77 Los Angeles Rams TL	.30	.15	.03
Record-Setting			
Ground Attack			
(Eric Dickerson)			
☐ 78 Nolan Cromwell	.08	.04	.01
☐ 79 Eric Dickerson AP	3.50	1.75	.35
☐ 80 Henry Ellard	3.75	1.85	.37
☐ 81 Kent Hill	.05	.02	.00
☐ 82 LeRoy Irvin	.08	.04	.01
☐ 83 Jeff Kemp	.45	.22	.04
☐ 84 Mike Lansford	.05	.02	.00
☐ 85 Barry Redden	.05	.02	.00
☐ 86 Jackie Slater	.35	.17	.03
☐ 87 Doug Smith	.25	.12	.02
☐ 88 Jack Youngblood	.12	.06	.01
☐ 89 Minnesota Vikings TL	.08	.04	.01
Smothering The			
Opposition			
(Vikings' Defense)			
☐ 90 Alfred Anderson	.25	.12	.02
☐ 91 Ted Brown	.08	.04	.01
☐ 92 Greg Coleman	.05	.02	.00
☐ 93 Tommy Hannon	.05	.02	.00
☐ 94 Tommy Kramer	.12	.06	.01
☐ 95 Leo Lewis	.25	.12	.02
☐ 96 Doug Martin	.05	.02	.00
☐ 97 Darrin Nelson	.08	.04	.01
☐ 98 Jan Stenerud AP	.20	.10	.02
☐ 99 Sammie White	.08	.04	.01
☐ 100 New Orleans Saints TL	.08	.04	.01
Hurdling Over			
Front Line			
☐ 101 Morten Andersen	.45	.22	.04
☐ 102 Hoby Brenner	.15	.07	.01
☐ 103 Bruce Clark	.08	.04	.01
☐ 104 Hokie Gajan	.12	.06	.01
☐ 105 Brian Hansen	.12	.06	.01
☐ 106 Rickey Jackson	.45	.22	.04
☐ 107 George Rogers	.15	.07	.01
☐ 108 Dave Wilson	.08	.04	.01
☐ 109 Tyrone Young	.15	.07	.01
☐ 110 New York Giants TL	.08	.04	.01
Engulfing The			
Quarterback			
(Giants' Defense)			
☐ 111 Carl Banks	4.50	2.25	.45
☐ 112 Jim Burt	.45	.22	.04
☐ 113 Rob Carpenter	.05	.02	.00
☐ 114 Harry Carson	.20	.10	.02
☐ 115 Earnest Gray	.05	.02	.00
☐ 116 Ali Haji-Sheikh	.05	.02	.00
☐ 117 Mark Haynes AP	.08	.04	.01
☐ 118 Bobby Johnson	.05	.02	.00
☐ 119 Lionel Manuel	.20	.10	.02
☐ 120 Joe Morris	1.00	.50	.10
☐ 121 Zeke Mowatt	.30	.15	.03
☐ 122 Jeff Rutledge	.25	.12	.02
☐ 123 Phil Simms	.40	.20	.04
☐ 124 Lawrence Taylor AP	1.25	.60	.12
☐ 125 Philadelphia Eagles TL	.08	.04	.01
Finding The Wide			
Open Spaces			
(Wilbert Montgomery)			
☐ 126 Greg Brown	.05	.02	.00
☐ 127 Ray Ellis	.05	.02	.00
☐ 128 Dennis Harrison	.05	.02	.00
☐ 129 Wes Hopkins	.25	.12	.02
☐ 130 Mike Horan	.05	.02	.00
☐ 131 Kenny Jackson	.20	.10	.02
☐ 132 Ron Jaworski	.12	.06	.01
☐ 133 Paul McFadden	.05	.02	.00
☐ 134 Wilbert Montgomery	.10	.05	.01
☐ 135 Mike Quick	.15	.07	.01
☐ 136 John Spagnola	.05	.02	.00
☐ 137 St.Louis Cardinals TL	.10	.05	.01
Exploiting The			
Air Route			
(Neil Lomax)			
☐ 138 Ottis Anderson	.30	.15	.03
☐ 139 Al(Bubba) Baker	.08	.04	.01
☐ 140 Roy Green	.20	.10	.02
☐ 141 Curtis Greer	.08	.04	.01
☐ 142 E.J. Junior AP	.12	.06	.01
☐ 143 Neil Lomax	.12	.06	.01
☐ 144 Stump Mitchell	.10	.05	.01
☐ 145 Neil O'Donoghue	.05	.02	.00
☐ 146 Pat Tilley	.08	.04	.01
☐ 147 Lionel Washington	.10	.05	.01
☐ 148 San Francisco 49ers TL	.50	.25	.05
The Road To			
Super Bowl XIX			
(Joe Montana)			

☐ 149	Dwaine Board .05	.02	.00
☐ 150	Dwight Clark .20	.10	.02
☐ 151	Roger Craig 1.50	.75	.15
☐ 152	Randy Cross AP .08	.04	.01
☐ 153	Fred Dean .08	.04	.01
☐ 154	Keith Fahnhorst .12	.06	.01
☐ 155	Dwight Hicks .08	.04	.01
☐ 156	Ronnie Lott 1.25	.60	.12
☐ 157	Joe Montana 3.75	1.85	.37
☐ 158	Renaldo Nehemiah .10	.05	.01
☐ 159	Fred Quillan .05	.02	.00
☐ 160	Jack Reynolds .08	.04	.01
☐ 161	Freddie Solomon .08	.04	.01
☐ 162	Keena Turner .60	.30	.06
☐ 163	Wendell Tyler .08	.04	.01
☐ 164	Ray Wersching .05	.02	.00
☐ 165	Carlton Williamson .05	.02	.00
☐ 166	Tampa Bay Bucs TL .12	.06	.01
	Protecting The		
	Quarterback		
	(Steve DeBerg)		
☐ 167	Gerald Carter .05	.02	.00
☐ 168	Mark Cotney .05	.02	.00
☐ 169	Steve DeBerg .50	.25	.05
☐ 170	Sean Farrell .12	.06	.01
☐ 171	Hugh Green .10	.05	.01
☐ 172	Kevin House .08	.04	.01
☐ 173	David Logan .05	.02	.00
☐ 174	Michael Morton .05	.02	.00
☐ 175	Lee Roy Selmon .12	.06	.01
☐ 176	James Wilder .12	.06	.01
☐ 177	Wash. Redskins TL .15	.07	.01
	Diesel Named Desire		
	(John Riggins)		
☐ 178	Charlie Brown .08	.04	.01
☐ 179	Monte Coleman .50	.25	.05
☐ 180	Vernon Dean .05	.02	.00
☐ 181	Darrell Green 2.00	1.00	.20
☐ 182	Russ Grimm .15	.07	.01
☐ 183	Joe Jacoby .12	.06	.01
☐ 184	Dexter Manley .10	.05	.01
☐ 185	Art Monk AP 1.25	.60	.12
☐ 186	Mark Moseley .08	.04	.01
☐ 187	Calvin Muhammad .08	.04	.01
☐ 188	Mike Nelms .05	.02	.00
☐ 189	John Riggins .45	.22	.04
☐ 190	Joe Theismann .45	.22	.04
☐ 191	Joe Washington .08	.04	.01
☐ 192	Passing Leaders 3.00	1.50	.30
	Dan Marino		
	Joe Montana		
☐ 193	Receiving Leaders .35	.17	.03
	Ozzie Newsome		
	Art Monk		
☐ 194	Rushing Leaders .35	.17	.03
	Earnest Jackson		
	Eric Dickerson		
☐ 195	Scoring Leaders .08	.04	.01
	Gary Anderson		
	Ray Wersching		
☐ 196	Interception Leaders .08	.04	.01
	Kenny Easley		
	Tom Flynn		
☐ 197	Punting Leaders .08	.04	.01
	Jim Arnold		
	Brian Hansen		
☐ 198	Buffalo Bills TL .15	.07	.01
	Rushing Toward		
	Rookie Stardom		
	(Greg Bell)		
☐ 199	Greg Bell 1.00	.50	.10
☐ 200	Preston Dennard .05	.02	.00
☐ 201	Joe Ferguson .10	.05	.01
☐ 202	Byron Franklin .05	.02	.00
☐ 203	Steve Freeman .05	.02	.00
☐ 204	Jim Haslett .05	.02	.00
☐ 205	Charles Romes .05	.02	.00
☐ 206	Fred Smerlas .08	.04	.01
☐ 207	Darryl Talley 3.00	1.50	.30
☐ 208	Van Williams .05	.02	.00
☐ 209	Cincinnati Bengals TL .10	.05	.01
	Advancing The		
	Ball Downfield		
	(Ken Anderson and		
	Larry Kinnebrew)		
☐ 210	Ken Anderson .20	.10	.02
☐ 211	Jim Breech .05	.02	.00
☐ 212	Louis Breeden .05	.02	.00
☐ 213	James Brooks .30	.15	.03
☐ 214	Ross Browner .08	.04	.01
☐ 215	Eddie Edwards .05	.02	.00
☐ 216	M.L. Harris .05	.02	.00
☐ 217	Bobby Kemp .05	.02	.00
☐ 218	Larry Kinnebrew .20	.10	.02
☐ 219	Anthony Munoz AP .50	.25	.05
☐ 220	Reggie Williams .10	.05	.01
☐ 221	Cleveland Browns TL .08	.04	.01
	Evading The		
	Defensive Pursuit		
	(Boyce Green)		
☐ 222	Matt Bahr .08	.04	.01
☐ 223	Chip Banks .08	.04	.01
☐ 224	Reggie Camp .05	.02	.00
☐ 225	Tom Cousineau .08	.04	.01
☐ 226	Joe DeLamielleure .08	.04	.01
☐ 227	Ricky Feacher .05	.02	.00
☐ 228	Boyce Green .10	.05	.01
☐ 229	Al Gross .05	.02	.00
☐ 230	Clay Matthews .10	.05	.01
☐ 231	Paul McDonald .08	.04	.01
☐ 232	Ozzie Newsome AP .35	.17	.03
☐ 233	Mike Pruitt .08	.04	.01
☐ 234	Don Rogers .08	.04	.01
☐ 235	Denver Broncos TL .30	.15	.03

Thousand Yarder
Gets The Ball
(Sammy Winder and
John Elway)

☐ 236	Rubin Carter	.05	.02	.00
☐ 237	Barney Chavous	.05	.02	.00
☐ 238	John Elway	3.50	1.75	.35
☐ 239	Steve Foley	.05	.02	.00
☐ 240	Mike Harden	.25	.12	.02
☐ 241	Tom Jackson	.15	.07	.01
☐ 242	Butch Johnson	.08	.04	.01
☐ 243	Rulon Jones	.08	.04	.01
☐ 244	Rich Karlis	.05	.02	.00
☐ 245	Steve Watson	.08	.04	.01
☐ 246	Gerald Willhite	.08	.04	.01
☐ 247	Sammy Winder	.08	.04	.01
☐ 248	Houston Oilers TL	.08	.04	.01

Eluding A
Traffic Jam
(Larry Moriarty)

☐ 249	Jesse Baker	.05	.02	.00
☐ 250	Carter Hartwig	.05	.02	.00
☐ 251	Warren Moon	27.00	13.50	2.70
☐ 252	Larry Moriarty	.10	.05	.01
☐ 253	Mike Munchak	1.50	.75	.15
☐ 254	Carl Roaches	.08	.04	.01
☐ 255	Tim Smith	.05	.02	.00
☐ 256	Willie Tullis	.05	.02	.00
☐ 257	Jamie Williams	.05	.02	.00
☐ 258	Indianapolis Colts TL	.08	.04	.01

Start Of A
Long Gainer
(Art Schlichter)

☐ 259	Raymond Butler	.08	.04	.01
☐ 260	Johnie Cooks	.08	.04	.01
☐ 261	Eugene Daniel	.05	.02	.00
☐ 262	Curtis Dickey	.08	.04	.01
☐ 263	Chris Hinton	.25	.12	.02
☐ 264	Vernon Maxwell	.08	.04	.01
☐ 265	Randy McMillan	.08	.04	.01
☐ 266	Art Schlichter	.15	.07	.01
☐ 267	Rohn Stark	.08	.04	.01
☐ 268	Leo Wisniewski	.05	.02	.00
☐ 269	Kansas City Chiefs TL	.08	.04	.01

Pigskin About To
Soar Upward
(Bill Kenney)

☐ 270	Jim Arnold	.08	.04	.01
☐ 271	Mike Bell	.05	.02	.00
☐ 272	Todd Blackledge	.15	.07	.01
☐ 273	Carlos Carson	.08	.04	.01
☐ 274	Deron Cherry	.35	.17	.03
☐ 275	Herman Heard	.12	.06	.01
☐ 276	Bill Kenney	.10	.05	.01
☐ 277	Nick Lowery	.20	.10	.02
☐ 278	Bill Maas	.35	.17	.03
☐ 279	Henry Marshall	.05	.02	.00

☐ 280	Art Still	.08	.04	.01
☐ 281	Los Angeles Raiders TL	.25	.12	.02

Diving For The
Goal Line
(Marcus Allen)

☐ 282	Marcus Allen	1.00	.50	.10
☐ 283	Lyle Alzado	.15	.07	.01
☐ 284	Chris Bahr	.08	.04	.01
☐ 285	Malcolm Barnwell	.05	.02	.00
☐ 286	Cliff Branch	.15	.07	.01
☐ 287	Todd Christensen	.10	.05	.01
☐ 288	Ray Guy	.15	.07	.01
☐ 289	Lester Hayes	.08	.04	.01
☐ 290	Mike Haynes AP	.12	.06	.01
☐ 291	Henry Lawrence	.05	.02	.00
☐ 292	Howie Long	.75	.35	.07
☐ 293	Rod Martin AP	.08	.04	.01
☐ 294	Vann McElroy	.05	.02	.00
☐ 295	Matt Millen	.12	.06	.01
☐ 296	Bill Pickel	.15	.07	.01
☐ 297	Jim Plunkett	.15	.07	.01
☐ 298	Dokie Williams	.20	.10	.02
☐ 299	Marc Wilson	.10	.05	.01
☐ 300	Miami Dolphins TL	.15	.07	.01

Super Duper
Performance
(Mark Duper)

☐ 301	Bob Baumhower	.08	.04	.01
☐ 302	Doug Betters	.08	.04	.01
☐ 303	Glenn Blackwood	.05	.02	.00
☐ 304	Lyle Blackwood	.05	.02	.00
☐ 305	Kim Bokamper	.05	.02	.00
☐ 306	Charles Bowser	.05	.02	.00
☐ 307	Jimmy Cefalo	.08	.04	.01
☐ 308	Mark Clayton AP	7.00	3.50	.70
☐ 309	A.J. Duhe	.08	.04	.01
☐ 310	Mark Duper	1.00	.50	.10
☐ 311	Andra Franklin	.08	.04	.01
☐ 312	Bruce Hardy	.05	.02	.00
☐ 313	Pete Johnson	.08	.04	.01
☐ 314	Dan Marino AP	15.00	7.50	1.50
☐ 315	Tony Nathan	.08	.04	.01
☐ 316	Ed Newman	.05	.02	.00
☐ 317	Reggie Roby AP	.15	.07	.01
☐ 318	Dwight Stephenson AP	.12	.06	.01
☐ 319	Uwe Von Schamann	.05	.02	.00
☐ 320	New England Pats TL	.08	.04	.01

Refusing To
Be Denied
(Tony Collins)

☐ 321	Raymond Clayborn	.05	.02	.00
☐ 322	Tony Collins	.08	.04	.01
☐ 323	Tony Eason	.35	.17	.03
☐ 324	Tony Franklin	.05	.02	.00
☐ 325	Irving Fryar	1.50	.75	.15
☐ 326	John Hannah AP	.15	.07	.01
☐ 327	Brian Holloway	.08	.04	.01

☐ 328	Craig James	.20	.10	.02
☐ 329	Stanley Morgan	.15	.07	.01
☐ 330	Steve Nelson AP	.05	.02	.00
☐ 331	Derrick Ramsey	.05	.02	.00
☐ 332	Stephen Starring	.05	.02	.00
☐ 333	Mosi Tatupu	.05	.02	.00
☐ 334	Andre Tippett	.45	.22	.04
☐ 335	New York Jets TL	.10	.05	.01
	Thwarting The			
	Passing Game			
	(Mark Gastineau			
	and Joe Ferguson)			
☐ 336	Russell Carter	.15	.07	.01
☐ 337	Mark Gastineau AP	.12	.06	.01
☐ 338	Bruce Harper	.05	.02	.00
☐ 339	Bobby Humphery	.15	.07	.01
☐ 340	Johnny "Lam" Jones	.08	.04	.01
☐ 341	Joe Klecko	.12	.06	.01
☐ 342	Pat Leahy	.12	.06	.01
☐ 343	Marty Lyons	.08	.04	.01
☐ 344	Freeman McNeil	.20	.10	.02
☐ 345	Lance Mehl	.08	.04	.01
☐ 346	Ken O'Brien	2.00	1.00	.20
☐ 347	Marvin Powell	.08	.04	.01
☐ 348	Pat Ryan	.12	.06	.01
☐ 349	Mickey Shuler	.50	.25	.05
☐ 350	Wesley Walker	.15	.07	.01
☐ 351	Pittsburgh Steelers TL	.08	.04	.01
	Testing Defensive			
	Pass Coverage			
	(Mark Malone)			
☐ 352	Walter Abercrombie	.08	.04	.01
☐ 353	Gary Anderson	.05	.02	.00
☐ 354	Robin Cole	.05	.02	.00
☐ 355	Bennie Cunningham	.05	.02	.00
☐ 356	Rich Erenberg	.08	.04	.01
☐ 357	Jack Lambert	.35	.17	.03
☐ 358	Louis Lipps	2.50	1.25	.25
☐ 359	Mark Malone	.12	.06	.01
☐ 360	Mike Merriweather	.75	.35	.07
☐ 361	Frank Pollard	.08	.04	.01
☐ 362	Donnie Shell	.10	.05	.01
☐ 363	John Stallworth	.15	.07	.01
☐ 364	Sam Washington	.05	.02	.00
☐ 365	Mike Webster	.15	.07	.01
☐ 366	Dwayne Woodruff	.05	.02	.00
☐ 367	San Diego Chargers TL	.08	.04	.01
	Jarring The			
	Ball Loose			
	(Chargers' Defense)			
☐ 368	Rolf Benirschke	.08	.04	.01
☐ 369	Gill Byrd	1.25	.60	.12
☐ 370	Wes Chandler	.12	.06	.01
☐ 371	Bobby Duckworth	.05	.02	.00
☐ 372	Dan Fouts	.50	.25	.05
☐ 373	Mike Green	.05	.02	.00
☐ 374	Pete Holohan	.60	.30	.06

☐ 375	Earnest Jackson	.30	.15	.03
☐ 376	Lionel James	.30	.15	.03
☐ 377	Charlie Joiner	.20	.10	.02
☐ 378	Billy Ray Smith	.08	.04	.01
☐ 379	Kellen Winslow	.20	.10	.02
☐ 380	Seattle Seahawks TL	.10	.05	.01
	Setting Up For			
	The Air Attack			
	(Dave Krieg)			
☐ 381	Dave Brown	.08	.04	.01
☐ 382	Jeff Bryant	.05	.02	.00
☐ 383	Dan Doornink	.05	.02	.00
☐ 384	Kenny Easley AP	.10	.05	.01
☐ 385	Jacob Green	.12	.06	.01
☐ 386	David Hughes	.05	.02	.00
☐ 387	Norm Johnson	.08	.04	.01
☐ 388	Dave Krieg	.60	.30	.06
☐ 389	Steve Largent	.75	.35	.07
☐ 390	Joe Nash	.20	.10	.02
☐ 391	Daryl Turner	.15	.07	.01
☐ 392	Curt Warner	.15	.07	.01
☐ 393	Fredd Young	.25	.12	.02
☐ 394	Checklist 1-132	.12	.02	.00
☐ 395	Checklist 133-264	.12	.02	.00
☐ 396	Checklist 265-396	.15	.02	.00

1985 Topps USFL

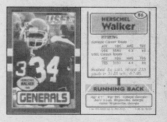

The 1985 Topps USFL set contains 132 football cards, which were available as a pre-packaged set from Topps housed in its own specially made box. The cards are in full color and measure the standard 2 1/2" by 3 1/2". The card backs are printed in red and blue on white card stock. The card fronts have a heavy red border with a blue and white stripe in the middle. Card backs describe each player's

highlights of the previous USFL season. The cards in the set are ordered numerically by team location with players within teams also ordered alphabetically, i.e., Arizona Outlaws (1-9), Baltimore Stars (10-19), Birmingham Stallions (20-29), Denver Gold (30-38), Houston Gamblers (39-48), Jacksonville Bulls (49-57), Los Angeles Express (58-66), Memphis Showboats (67-76), New Jersey Generals (77-86), Oakland Invaders (87-96), Orlando Renegades (97-104), Portland Breakers (105-113), San Antonio Gunslingers (114-121), and Tampa Bay Bandits (122-131). The last card in the set is a checklist card. The key rookie cards in this set are Gary Clark and Doug Flutie. Other key cards in the set include the second USFL cards of Jim Kelly, Herschel Walker, Reggie White, and Steve Young.

	MINT	EXC	G-VG
COMPLETE SET (132)	135.00	65.00	13.50
COMMON PLAYER (1-132)	.20	.10	.02

☐ 1	Case DeBruijn	.40	.12	.02
☐ 2	Mike Katolin	.20	.10	.02
☐ 3	Bruce Laird	.20	.10	.02
☐ 4	Kit Lathrop	.20	.10	.02
☐ 5	Kevin Long	.20	.10	.02
☐ 6	Karl Lorch	.20	.10	.02
☐ 7	Dave Tipton	.20	.10	.02
☐ 8	Doug Williams	.50	.25	.05
☐ 9	Luis Zendejas	.35	.17	.03
☐ 10	Kelvin Bryant	.75	.35	.07
☐ 11	Willie Collier	.20	.10	.02
☐ 12	Irv Eatman	.45	.22	.04
☐ 13	Scott Fitzkee	.30	.15	.03
☐ 14	William Fuller	1.50	.75	.15
☐ 15	Chuck Fusina	.30	.15	.03
☐ 16	Pete Kugler	.35	.17	.03
☐ 17	Garcia Lane	.30	.15	.03
☐ 18	Mike Lush	.20	.10	.02
☐ 19	Sam Mills	8.00	4.00	.80
☐ 20	Buddy Aydelette	.30	.15	.03
☐ 21	Joe Cribbs	.50	.25	.05
☐ 22	David Dumars	.20	.10	.02
☐ 23	Robin Earl	.20	.10	.02
☐ 24	Joey Jones	.30	.15	.03
☐ 25	Leon Perry	.20	.10	.02
☐ 26	Dave Pureifory	.30	.15	.03
☐ 27	Bill Roe	.20	.10	.02
☐ 28	Doug Smith	1.50	.75	.15
☐ 29	Cliff Stoudt	.30	.15	.03
☐ 30	Jeff Delaney	.20	.10	.02
☐ 31	Vince Evans	.40	.20	.04
☐ 32	Leonard Harris	.20	.10	.02
☐ 33	Bill Johnson	.20	.10	.02
☐ 34	Marc Lewis	.20	.10	.02
☐ 35	David Martin	.20	.10	.02
☐ 36	Bruce Thornton	.20	.10	.02
☐ 37	Craig Walls	.20	.10	.02
☐ 38	Vincent White	.20	.10	.02
☐ 39	Luther Bradley	.30	.15	.03
☐ 40	Pete Catan	.20	.10	.02
☐ 41	Kiki DeAyala	.30	.15	.03
☐ 42	Toni Fritsch	.30	.15	.03
☐ 43	Sam Harrell	.30	.15	.03
☐ 44	Richard Johnson	2.00	1.00	.20
☐ 45	Jim Kelly	65.00	32.50	6.50
☐ 46	Gerald McNeil	1.50	.75	.15
☐ 47	Clarence Verdin	1.50	.75	.15
☐ 48	Dale Walters	.20	.10	.02
☐ 49	Gary Clark	50.00	25.00	5.00
☐ 50	Tom Dinkel	.20	.10	.02
☐ 51	Mike Edwards	.20	.10	.02
☐ 52	Brian Franco	.20	.10	.02
☐ 53	Bob Gruber	.20	.10	.02
☐ 54	Robbie Mahfouz	.20	.10	.02
☐ 55	Mike Rozier	2.00	1.00	.20
☐ 56	Brian Sipe	.50	.25	.05
☐ 57	J.T. Turner	.20	.10	.02
☐ 58	Howard Carson	.30	.15	.03
☐ 59	Wymon Henderson	.45	.22	.04
☐ 60	Kevin Nelson	.20	.10	.02
☐ 61	Jeff Partridge	.20	.10	.02
☐ 62	Ben Rudolph	.20	.10	.02
☐ 63	Jo Jo Townsell	.35	.17	.03
☐ 64	Eddie Weaver	.20	.10	.02
☐ 65	Steve Young	14.00	7.00	1.40
☐ 66	Tony Zendejas	.50	.25	.05
☐ 67	Mossy Cade	.20	.10	.02
☐ 68	Leonard Coleman	.50	.25	.05
☐ 69	John Corker	.30	.15	.03
☐ 70	Derrick Crawford	.20	.10	.02
☐ 71	Art Kuehn	.20	.10	.02
☐ 72	Walter Lewis	.20	.10	.02
☐ 73	Tyrone McGriff	.20	.10	.02
☐ 74	Tim Spencer	.35	.17	.03
☐ 75	Reggie White	16.00	8.00	1.60
☐ 76	Gizmo Williams	.75	.35	.07
☐ 77	Sam Bowers	.20	.10	.02
☐ 78	Maurice Carthon	1.25	.60	.12
☐ 79	Clarence Collins	.30	.15	.03
☐ 80	Doug Flutie	12.00	6.00	1.20
☐ 81	Freddie Gilbert	.20	.10	.02
☐ 82	Kerry Justin	.20	.10	.02
☐ 83	Dave Lapham	.20	.10	.02
☐ 84	Rick Partridge	.20	.10	.02
☐ 85	Roger Ruzek	.75	.35	.07
☐ 86	Herschel Walker	18.00	9.00	1.80
☐ 87	Gordon Banks	.30	.15	.03
☐ 88	Monte Bennett	.20	.10	.02
☐ 89	Albert Bentley	3.50	1.75	.35
☐ 90	Novo Bojovic	.20	.10	.02
☐ 91	Dave Browning	.20	.10	.02

☐ 92	Anthony Carter	4.00	2.00	.40
☐ 93	Bobby Hebert	4.00	2.00	.40
☐ 94	Ray Pinney	.20	.10	.02
☐ 95	Stan Talley	.20	.10	.02
☐ 96	Ruben Vaughan	.20	.10	.02
☐ 97	Curtis Bledsoe	.20	.10	.02
☐ 98	Reggie Collier	.30	.15	.03
☐ 99	Jerry Doerger	.20	.10	.02
☐ 100	Jerry Golsteyn	.30	.15	.03
☐ 101	Bob Niziolek	.20	.10	.02
☐ 102	Joel Patten	.20	.10	.02
☐ 103	Ricky Simmons	.20	.10	.02
☐ 104	Joey Walters	.20	.10	.02
☐ 105	Marcus Dupree	1.00	.50	.10
☐ 106	Jeff Gossett	.30	.15	.03
☐ 107	Frank Lockett	.20	.10	.02
☐ 108	Marcus Marek	.30	.15	.03
☐ 109	Kenny Neil	.30	.15	.03
☐ 110	Robert Pennywell	.20	.10	.02
☐ 111	Matt Robinson	.30	.15	.03
☐ 112	Dan Ross	.30	.15	.03
☐ 113	Doug Woodward	.20	.10	.02
☐ 114	Danny Buggs	.20	.10	.02
☐ 115	Putt Choate	.20	.10	.02
☐ 116	Greg Fields	.20	.10	.02
☐ 117	Ken Hartley	.20	.10	.02
☐ 118	Nick Mike-Mayer	.20	.10	.02
☐ 119	Rick Neuheisel	.30	.15	.03
☐ 120	Peter Raeford	.20	.10	.02
☐ 121	Gary Worthy	.20	.10	.02
☐ 122	Gary Anderson	3.00	1.50	.30
☐ 123	Zenon Andrusyshyn	.20	.10	.02
☐ 124	Greg Boone	.20	.10	.02
☐ 125	Mike Butler	.20	.10	.02
☐ 126	Mike Clark	.20	.10	.02
☐ 127	Willie Gillespie	.30	.15	.03
☐ 128	James Harrell	.20	.10	.02
☐ 129	Marvin Harvey	.20	.10	.02
☐ 130	John Reaves	.30	.15	.03
☐ 131	Eric Truvillion	.20	.10	.02
☐ 132	Checklist 1-132	.40	.10	.02

1986 Topps

The 1986 Topps football card set contains 396 cards featuring players of the NFL. Cards are standard size, 2 1/2" by 3 1/2". The set is distinguished by the green border on the fronts of the cards. The first seven cards in the set recognize Record-Breaking (RB) achievements during the previous season.

Statistical league leaders are featured on cards 225-229. Team cards feature a distinctive yellow border on the front with the team's results and leaders (from the previous season) listed on the back. All-Pro (AP) selections are designated on the player's regular card, not a special card. The set numbering is again ordered by teams, i.e., Chicago Bears (9-28), New England Patriots (29-43), Miami Dolphins (44-59), Los Angeles Raiders (60-75), Los Angeles Rams (76-93), New York Jets (94-110), Denver Broncos (111-123), Dallas Cowboys (124-136), New York Giants (137-154), San Francisco 49ers (155-169), Washington Redskins (170-184), Cleveland Browns (185-199), Seattle Seahawks (200-212), Green Bay Packers (213-224), San Diego Chargers (230-241), Detroit Lions (242-253), Cincinnati Bengals (254-267), Philadelphia Eagles (268-279), Pittsburgh Steelers (280-291), Minnesota Vikings (292-302), Kansas City Chiefs (303-313), Indianapolis Colts (314-325), St. Louis Cardinals (326-337), New Orleans Saints (338-348), Houston Oilers (349-359), Atlanta Falcons (360-371), Tampa Bay Buccaneers (372-382), and Buffalo Bills (383-393). The last three cards in the set (394-396) are checklist cards. Although they are not considered part of the complete set price, Topps also printed cards on the sides of the wax pack boxes. There were four different boxes each with a different playoff team pictured. These box cards are "lettered" rather than numbered and are listed at the end of the checklist below. The key rookie cards in this set are Mark Bavaro, Eddie Brown, Earnest Byner, Boomer Esiason, Bernie Kosar, Wilbur Marshall, Karl Mecklenburg, William Perry, Andre Reed, Jerry Rice, Jay Schroeder, Bruce Smith, and Al Toon. In addition, Anthony Carter, Gary Clark, and Steve Young are rookie cards, although they had each appeared in a previous Topps USFL set.

	MINT	EXC	G-VG
COMPLETE SET (396)	90.00	45.00	9.00
COMMON PLAYER (1-396)	.05	.02	.00

☐ 1	Marcus Allen RB Los Angeles Raiders Most Yards From Scrimmage, Season	.35	.08	.01
☐ 2	Eric Dickerson RB Los Angeles Rams Most Yards Rushing, Playoff Game	.25	.12	.02
☐ 3	Lionel James RB San Diego Chargers Most All-Purpose Yards, Season	.08	.04	.01
☐ 4	Steve Largent RB Seattle Seahawks Most Seasons, 50 or More Receptions	.30	.15	.03
☐ 5	George Martin RB New York Giants Most Touchdowns, Def. Lineman, Career	.08	.04	.01
☐ 6	Stephone Paige RB Kansas City Chiefs Most Yards Receiving, Game	.12	.06	.01
☐ 7	Walter Payton RB Chicago Bears Most Consecutive Games, 100 or More Yards Rushing	.35	.17	.03
☐ 8	Super Bowl XX Bears 46, Patriots 10 (Jim McMahon handing off)	.15	.07	.01
☐ 9	Chicago Bears Team Card (Walter Payton in Motion)	.35	.17	.03
☐ 10	Jim McMahon	.35	.17	.03
☐ 11	Walter Payton AP	1.25	.60	.12
☐ 12	Matt Suhey	.05	.02	.00
☐ 13	Willie Gault	.25	.12	.02
☐ 14	Dennis McKinnon	.30	.15	.03
☐ 15	Emery Moorehead	.05	.02	.00
☐ 16	Jim Covert AP	.15	.07	.01
☐ 17	Jay Hilgenberg AP	1.75	.85	.17
☐ 18	Kevin Butler	.60	.30	.06
☐ 19	Richard Dent AP	.75	.35	.07
☐ 20	William Perry	.60	.30	.06
☐ 21	Steve McMichael	.50	.25	.05
☐ 22	Dan Hampton	.35	.17	.03
☐ 23	Otis Wilson	.08	.04	.01
☐ 24	Mike Singletary	.60	.30	.06
☐ 25	Wilber Marshall	2.00	1.00	.20
☐ 26	Leslie Frazier	.05	.02	.00
☐ 27	Dave Duerson	.75	.35	.07
☐ 28	Gary Fencik	.08	.04	.01
☐ 29	New England Patriots Team Card (Craig James on the Run)	.08	.04	.01
☐ 30	Tony Eason	.15	.07	.01
☐ 31	Steve Grogan	.12	.06	.01
☐ 32	Craig James	.12	.06	.01
☐ 33	Tony Collins	.08	.04	.01
☐ 34	Irving Fryar	.30	.15	.03
☐ 35	Brian Holloway AP	.08	.04	.01
☐ 36	John Hannah AP	.15	.07	.01
☐ 37	Tony Franklin	.05	.02	.00
☐ 38	Garin Veris	.15	.07	.01
☐ 39	Andre Tippett AP	.12	.06	.01
☐ 40	Steve Nelson	.05	.02	.00
☐ 41	Raymond Clayborn	.08	.04	.01
☐ 42	Fred Marion	.25	.12	.02
☐ 43	Rich Camarillo	.05	.02	.00
☐ 44	Miami Dolphins Team Card (Dan Marino Sets Up)	.50	.25	.05
☐ 45	Dan Marino AP	5.00	2.50	.50
☐ 46	Tony Nathan	.08	.04	.01
☐ 47	Ron Davenport	.10	.05	.01
☐ 48	Mark Duper	.35	.17	.03
☐ 49	Mark Clayton	1.50	.75	.15
☐ 50	Nat Moore	.08	.04	.01
☐ 51	Bruce Hardy	.05	.02	.00
☐ 52	Roy Foster	.05	.02	.00
☐ 53	Dwight Stephenson	.08	.04	.01
☐ 54	Fuad Reveiz	.05	.02	.00
☐ 55	Bob Baumhower	.08	.04	.01
☐ 56	Mike Charles	.05	.02	.00
☐ 57	Hugh Green	.08	.04	.01
☐ 58	Glenn Blackwood	.05	.02	.00
☐ 59	Reggie Roby	.08	.04	.01
☐ 60	Los Angeles Raiders Team Card (Marcus Allen Cuts Upfield)	.25	.12	.02
☐ 61	Marc Wilson	.10	.05	.01
☐ 62	Marcus Allen AP	.75	.35	.07
☐ 63	Dokie Williams	.08	.04	.01
☐ 64	Todd Christensen	.12	.06	.01
☐ 65	Chris Bahr	.05	.02	.00
☐ 66	Fulton Walker	.05	.02	.00
☐ 67	Howie Long	.25	.12	.02
☐ 68	Bill Pickel	.08	.04	.01
☐ 69	Ray Guy	.15	.07	.01
☐ 70	Greg Townsend	1.25	.60	.12
☐ 71	Rod Martin	.08	.04	.01

☐ 72 Matt Millen	.12	.06	.01
☐ 73 Mike Haynes AP	.12	.06	.01
☐ 74 Lester Hayes	.08	.04	.01
☐ 75 Vann McElroy	.05	.02	.00
☐ 76 Los Angeles Rams	.30	.15	.03
Team Card			
(Eric Dickerson			
Stiff-Arm)			
☐ 77 Dieter Brock	.15	.07	.01
☐ 78 Eric Dickerson	1.25	.60	.12
☐ 79 Henry Ellard	.75	.35	.07
☐ 80 Ron Brown	.50	.25	.05
☐ 81 Tony Hunter	.10	.05	.01
☐ 82 Kent Hill AP	.05	.02	.00
☐ 83 Doug Smith	.08	.04	.01
☐ 84 Dennis Harrah	.05	.02	.00
☐ 85 Jackie Slater	.20	.10	.02
☐ 86 Mike Lansford	.05	.02	.00
☐ 87 Gary Jeter	.08	.04	.01
☐ 88 Mike Wilcher	.05	.02	.00
☐ 89 Jim Collins	.05	.02	.00
☐ 90 LeRoy Irvin	.08	.04	.01
☐ 91 Gary Green	.05	.02	.00
☐ 92 Nolan Cromwell	.08	.04	.01
☐ 93 Dale Hatcher	.15	.07	.01
☐ 94 New York Jets	.10	.05	.01
Team Card			
(Freeman McNeil			
Powers)			
☐ 95 Ken O'Brien	.50	.25	.05
☐ 96 Freeman McNeil	.15	.07	.01
☐ 97 Tony Paige	.40	.20	.04
☐ 98 Johnny "Lam" Jones	.05	.02	.00
☐ 99 Wesley Walker	.15	.07	.01
☐ 100 Kurt Sohn	.05	.02	.00
☐ 101 Al Toon	6.00	3.00	.60
☐ 102 Mickey Shuler	.08	.04	.01
☐ 103 Marvin Powell	.08	.04	.01
☐ 104 Pat Leahy	.10	.05	.01
☐ 105 Mark Gastineau	.10	.05	.01
☐ 106 Joe Klecko AP	.10	.05	.01
☐ 107 Marty Lyons	.08	.04	.01
☐ 108 Lance Mehl	.08	.04	.01
☐ 109 Bobby Jackson	.05	.02	.00
☐ 110 Dave Jennings	.08	.04	.01
☐ 111 Denver Broncos	.08	.04	.01
Team Card			
(Sammy Winder			
Up Middle)			
☐ 112 John Elway	1.50	.75	.15
☐ 113 Sammy Winder	.08	.04	.01
☐ 114 Gerald Willhite	.08	.04	.01
☐ 115 Steve Watson	.08	.04	.01
☐ 116 Vance Johnson	1.50	.75	.15
☐ 117 Rich Karlis	.05	.02	.00
☐ 118 Rulon Jones	.08	.04	.01
☐ 119 Karl Mecklenburg AP	3.00	1.50	.30
☐ 120 Louis Wright	.10	.05	.01
☐ 121 Mike Harden	.05	.02	.00
☐ 122 Dennis Smith	1.25	.60	.12
☐ 123 Steve Foley	.05	.02	.00
☐ 124 Dallas Cowboys	.08	.04	.01
Team Card			
(Tony Hill Evades			
Defender)			
☐ 125 Danny White	.15	.07	.01
☐ 126 Tony Dorsett	.40	.20	.04
☐ 127 Timmy Newsome	.05	.02	.00
☐ 128 Mike Renfro	.05	.02	.00
☐ 129 Tony Hill	.08	.04	.01
☐ 130 Doug Cosbie AP	.08	.04	.01
☐ 131 Rafael Septien	.05	.02	.00
☐ 132 Ed Too Tall Jones	.20	.10	.02
☐ 133 Randy White	.25	.12	.02
☐ 134 Jim Jeffcoat	.05	.02	.00
☐ 135 Everson Walls AP	.10	.05	.01
☐ 136 Dennis Thurman	.05	.02	.00
☐ 137 New York Giants	.08	.04	.01
Team Card			
(Joe Morris Opening)			
☐ 138 Phil Simms	.35	.17	.03
☐ 139 Joe Morris	.25	.12	.02
☐ 140 George Adams	.15	.07	.01
☐ 141 Lionel Manuel	.08	.04	.01
☐ 142 Bobby Johnson	.05	.02	.00
☐ 143 Phil McConkey	.15	.07	.01
☐ 144 Mark Bavaro	1.00	.50	.10
☐ 145 Zeke Mowatt	.05	.02	.00
☐ 146 Brad Benson	.10	.05	.01
☐ 147 Bart Oates	.50	.25	.05
☐ 148 Leonard Marshall AP	1.50	.75	.15
☐ 149 Jim Burt	.10	.05	.01
☐ 150 George Martin	.08	.04	.01
☐ 151 Lawrence Taylor AP	.75	.35	.07
☐ 152 Harry Carson AP	.20	.10	.02
☐ 153 Elvis Patterson	.15	.07	.01
☐ 154 Sean Landeta	.35	.17	.03
☐ 155 San Francisco 49ers	.20	.10	.02
Team Card			
(Roger Craig			
Scampers)			
☐ 156 Joe Montana	2.00	1.00	.20
☐ 157 Roger Craig	.65	.30	.06
☐ 158 Wendell Tyler	.08	.04	.01
☐ 159 Carl Monroe	.05	.02	.00
☐ 160 Dwight Clark	.15	.07	.01
☐ 161 Jerry Rice	45.00	22.50	4.50
☐ 162 Randy Cross	.08	.04	.01
☐ 163 Keith Fahnhorst	.05	.02	.00
☐ 164 Jeff Stover	.05	.02	.00
☐ 165 Michael Carter	1.25	.60	.12
☐ 166 Dwaine Board	.05	.02	.00
☐ 167 Eric Wright	.08	.04	.01
☐ 168 Ronnie Lott	.75	.35	.07

☐ 169	Carlton Williamson 05	.02	.00
☐ 170	Washington Redskins 08	.04	.01
	Team Card		
	(Dave Butz Gets		
	His Man)		
☐ 171	Joe Theismann 35	.17	.03
☐ 172	Jay Schroeder 1.75	.85	.17
☐ 173	George Rogers 12	.06	.01
☐ 174	Ken Jenkins 05	.02	.00
☐ 175	Art Monk AP 75	.35	.07
☐ 176	Gary Clark 7.50	3.75	.75
☐ 177	Joe Jacoby 10	.05	.01
☐ 178	Russ Grimm 10	.05	.01
☐ 179	Mark Moseley 08	.04	.01
☐ 180	Dexter Manley 10	.05	.01
☐ 181	Charles Mann 1.00	.50	.10
☐ 182	Vernon Dean 05	.02	.00
☐ 183	Raphel Cherry 25	.12	.02
☐ 184	Curtis Jordan 05	.02	.00
☐ 185	Cleveland Browns 25	.12	.02
	Team Card		
	(Bernie Kosar Fakes		
	Handoff)		
☐ 186	Gary Danielson 08	.04	.01
☐ 187	Bernie Kosar 5.00	2.50	.50
☐ 188	Kevin Mack 65	.30	.06
☐ 189	Earnest Byner 3.50	1.75	.35
☐ 190	Glen Young 05	.02	.00
☐ 191	Ozzie Newsome 25	.12	.02
☐ 192	Mike Baab 05	.02	.00
☐ 193	Cody Risien 08	.04	.01
☐ 194	Bob Golic 15	.07	.01
☐ 195	Reggie Camp 05	.02	.00
☐ 196	Chip Banks 08	.04	.01
☐ 197	Tom Cousineau 08	.04	.01
☐ 198	Frank Minnifield 40	.20	.04
☐ 199	Al Gross 05	.02	.00
☐ 200	Seattle Seahawks 10	.05	.01
	Team Card		
	(Curt Warner Breaks		
	Free)		
☐ 201	Dave Krieg 30	.15	.03
☐ 202	Curt Warner 10	.05	.01
☐ 203	Steve Largent AP 60	.30	.06
☐ 204	Norm Johnson 08	.04	.01
☐ 205	Daryl Turner 08	.04	.01
☐ 206	Jacob Green 10	.05	.01
☐ 207	Joe Nash 08	.04	.01
☐ 208	Jeff Bryant 05	.02	.00
☐ 209	Randy Edwards 05	.02	.00
☐ 210	Fredd Young 10	.05	.01
☐ 211	Kenny Easley 08	.04	.01
☐ 212	John Harris 05	.02	.00
☐ 213	Green Bay Packers 08	.04	.00
	Team Card		
	(Paul Coffman		
	Conquers)		
☐ 214	Lynn Dickey 08	.04	.01
☐ 215	Gerry Ellis 05	.02	.00
☐ 216	Eddie Lee Ivery 08	.04	.01
☐ 217	Jessie Clark 05	.02	.00
☐ 218	James Lofton 50	.25	.05
☐ 219	Paul Coffman 08	.04	.01
☐ 220	Alphonso Carreker 05	.02	.00
☐ 221	Ezra Johnson 05	.02	.00
☐ 222	Mike Douglass 05	.02	.00
☐ 223	Tim Lewis 08	.04	.01
☐ 224	Mark Murphy 40	.20	.04
☐ 225	Passing Leaders: 75	.35	.07
	Ken O'Brien AFC,		
	New York Jets		
	Joe Montana NFC,		
	San Francisco 49ers		
☐ 226	Receiving Leaders: 12	.06	.01
	Lionel James AFC,		
	San Diego Chargers		
	Roger Craig NFC,		
	San Francisco 49ers		
☐ 227	Rushing Leaders: 25	.12	.02
	Marcus Allen AFC,		
	Los Angeles Raiders		
	Gerald Riggs NFC,		
	Atlanta Falcons		
☐ 228	Scoring Leaders: 08	.04	.01
	Gary Anderson AFC,		
	Pittsburgh Steelers		
	Kevin Butler NFC,		
	Chicago Bears		
☐ 229	Interception Leaders: 10	.05	.01
	Eugene Daniel AFC,		
	Indianapolis Colts		
	Albert Lewis AFC,		
	Kansas City Chiefs		
	Everson Walls NFC,		
	Dallas Cowboys		
☐ 230	San Diego Chargers 12	.06	.01
	Team Card		
	(Dan Fouts Over Top)		
☐ 231	Dan Fouts 35	.17	.03
☐ 232	Lionel James 10	.05	.01
☐ 233	Gary Anderson 1.25	.60	.12
☐ 234	Tim Spencer 15	.07	.01
☐ 235	Wes Chandler 10	.05	.01
☐ 236	Charlie Joiner 20	.10	.02
☐ 237	Kellen Winslow 20	.10	.02
☐ 238	Jim Lachey 1.50	.75	.15
☐ 239	Bob Thomas 05	.02	.00
☐ 240	Jeffery Dale 05	.02	.00
☐ 241	Ralf Mojsiejenko 05	.02	.00
☐ 242	Detroit Lions 08	.04	.01
	Team Card		
	(Eric Hipple Spots		
	Receiver)		
☐ 243	Eric Hipple 08	.04	.01

☐ 244	Billy Sims	.10	.05	.01
☐ 245	James Jones	.08	.04	.01
☐ 246	Pete Mandley	.12	.06	.01
☐ 247	Leonard Thompson	.08	.04	.01
☐ 248	Lomas Brown	.35	.17	.03
☐ 249	Ed Murray	.10	.05	.01
☐ 250	Curtis Green	.05	.02	.00
☐ 251	William Gay	.05	.02	.00
☐ 252	Jimmy Williams	.05	.02	.00
☐ 253	Bobby Watkins	.05	.02	.00
☐ 254	Cincinnati Bengals	.45	.22	.04
	Team Card			
	(Boomer Esiason			
	Zeroes In)			
☐ 255	Boomer Esiason	6.50	3.25	.65
☐ 256	James Brooks	.20	.10	.02
☐ 257	Larry Kinnebrew	.08	.04	.01
☐ 258	Cris Collinsworth	.10	.05	.01
☐ 259	Mike Martin	.05	.02	.00
☐ 260	Eddie Brown	1.75	.85	.17
☐ 261	Anthony Munoz	.25	.12	.02
☐ 262	Jim Breech	.05	.02	.00
☐ 263	Ross Browner	.08	.04	.01
☐ 264	Carl Zander	.05	.02	.00
☐ 265	James Griffin	.05	.02	.00
☐ 266	Robert Jackson	.05	.02	.00
☐ 267	Pat McInally	.08	.04	.01
☐ 268	Philadelphia Eagles	.08	.04	.01
	Team Card			
	(Ron Jaworski Surveys)			
☐ 269	Ron Jaworski	.10	.05	.01
☐ 270	Earnest Jackson	.08	.04	.01
☐ 271	Mike Quick	.10	.05	.01
☐ 272	John Spagnola	.05	.02	.00
☐ 273	Mark Dennard	.05	.02	.00
☐ 274	Paul McFadden	.05	.02	.00
☐ 275	Reggie White	6.00	3.00	.60
☐ 276	Greg Brown	.05	.02	.00
☐ 277	Herman Edwards	.05	.02	.00
☐ 278	Roynell Young	.08	.04	.01
☐ 279	Wes Hopkins AP	.08	.04	.01
☐ 280	Pittsburgh Steelers	.08	.04	.01
	Team Card			
	(Walter Abercrombie			
	Inches)			
☐ 281	Mark Malone	.08	.04	.01
☐ 282	Frank Pollard	.05	.02	.00
☐ 283	Walter Abercrombie	.08	.04	.01
☐ 284	Louis Lipps	.60	.30	.06
☐ 285	John Stallworth	.12	.06	.01
☐ 286	Mike Webster	.12	.06	.01
☐ 287	Gary Anderson AP	.05	.02	.00
☐ 288	Keith Willis	.05	.02	.00
☐ 289	Mike Merriweather	.20	.10	.02
☐ 290	Dwayne Woodruff	.05	.02	.00
☐ 291	Donnie Shell	.08	.04	.01
☐ 292	Minnesota Vikings	.08	.04	.01
	Team Card			
	(Tommy Kramer Audible)			
☐ 293	Tommy Kramer	.10	.05	.01
☐ 294	Darrin Nelson	.08	.04	.01
☐ 295	Ted Brown	.08	.04	.01
☐ 296	Buster Rhymes	.15	.07	.01
☐ 297	Anthony Carter	1.75	.85	.17
☐ 298	Steve Jordan	1.50	.75	.15
☐ 299	Keith Millard	1.00	.50	.10
☐ 300	Joey Browner	1.50	.75	.15
☐ 301	John Turner	.05	.02	.00
☐ 302	Greg Coleman	.05	.02	.00
☐ 303	Kansas City Chiefs	.08	.04	.01
	Team Card			
	(Todd Blackledge)			
☐ 304	Bill Kenney	.08	.04	.01
☐ 305	Herman Heard	.05	.02	.00
☐ 306	Stephone Paige	1.50	.75	.15
☐ 307	Carlos Carson	.08	.04	.01
☐ 308	Nick Lowery	.12	.06	.01
☐ 309	Mike Bell	.05	.02	.00
☐ 310	Bill Maas	.10	.05	.01
☐ 311	Art Still	.08	.04	.01
☐ 312	Albert Lewis	1.50	.75	.15
☐ 313	Deron Cherry AP	.20	.10	.02
☐ 314	Indianapolis Colts	.08	.04	.01
	Team Card			
	(Rohn Stark Booms It)			
☐ 315	Mike Pagel	.08	.04	.01
☐ 316	Randy McMillan	.08	.04	.01
☐ 317	Albert Bentley	.40	.20	.04
☐ 318	George Wonsley	.10	.05	.01
☐ 319	Robbie Martin	.05	.02	.00
☐ 320	Pat Beach	.08	.04	.01
☐ 321	Chris Hinton	.15	.07	.01
☐ 322	Duane Bickett	.50	.25	.05
☐ 323	Eugene Daniel	.05	.02	.00
☐ 324	Cliff Odom	.20	.10	.02
☐ 325	Rohn Stark AP	.05	.02	.00
☐ 326	St. Louis Cardinals	.08	.04	.01
	Team Card			
	(Stump Mitchell			
	Outside)			
☐ 327	Neil Lomax	.10	.05	.01
☐ 328	Stump Mitchell	.10	.05	.01
☐ 329	Ottis Anderson	.25	.12	.02
☐ 330	J.T. Smith	.12	.06	.01
☐ 331	Pat Tilley	.08	.04	.01
☐ 332	Roy Green	.15	.07	.01
☐ 333	Lance Smith	.05	.02	.00
☐ 334	Curtis Greer	.08	.04	.01
☐ 335	Freddie Joe Nunn	.30	.15	.03
☐ 336	E.J. Junior	.10	.05	.01
☐ 337	Lonnie Young	.15	.07	.01
☐ 338	New Orleans Saints	.08	.04	.01
	Team Card			
	(Wayne Wilson running)			

□ 339	Bobby Hebert	1.00	.50	.10
□ 340	Dave Wilson	.08	.04	.01
□ 341	Wayne Wilson	.05	.02	.00
□ 342	Hoby Brenner	.05	.02	.00
□ 343	Stan Brock	.05	.02	.00
□ 344	Morten Andersen	.20	.10	.02
□ 345	Bruce Clark	.08	.04	.01
□ 346	Rickey Jackson	.20	.10	.02
□ 347	Dave Waymer	.05	.02	.00
□ 348	Brian Hansen	.05	.02	.00
□ 349	Houston Oilers Team Card (Warren Moon Throws Bomb)	.60	.30	.06
□ 350	Warren Moon	7.50	3.75	.75
□ 351	Mike Rozier	.60	.30	.06
□ 352	Butch Woolfolk	.08	.04	.01
□ 353	Drew Hill	.45	.22	.04
□ 354	Willie Drewrey	.08	.04	.01
□ 355	Tim Smith	.05	.02	.00
□ 356	Mike Munchak	.20	.10	.02
□ 357	Ray Childress	1.50	.75	.15
□ 358	Frank Bush	.05	.02	.00
□ 359	Steve Brown	.05	.02	.00
□ 360	Atlanta Falcons Team Card (Gerald Riggs Around End)	.08	.04	.01
□ 361	Dave Archer	.35	.17	.03
□ 362	Gerald Riggs	.20	.10	.02
□ 363	William Andrews	.08	.04	.01
□ 364	Billy Johnson	.08	.04	.01
□ 365	Arthur Cox	.05	.02	.00
□ 366	Mike Kenn	.08	.04	.01
□ 367	Bill Fralic	.75	.35	.07
□ 368	Mick Luckhurst	.08	.04	.01
□ 369	Rick Bryan	.10	.05	.01
□ 370	Bobby Butler	.05	.02	.00
□ 371	Rick Donnelly	.15	.07	.01
□ 372	Tampa Bay Buccaneers	.08	.04	.01
	Team Card (James Wilder Sweeps Left)			
□ 373	Steve DeBerg	.30	.15	.03
□ 374	Steve Young	5.00	2.50	.50
□ 375	James Wilder	.10	.05	.01
□ 376	Kevin House	.08	.04	.01
□ 377	Gerald Carter	.05	.02	.00
□ 378	Jimmie Giles	.08	.04	.01
□ 379	Sean Farrell	.08	.04	.01
□ 380	Donald Igwebuike	.10	.05	.01
□ 381	David Logan	.05	.02	.00
□ 382	Jeremiah Castille	.10	.05	.01
□ 383	Buffalo Bills Team Card (Greg Bell Sees Daylight)	.08	.04	.01

□ 384	Bruce Mathison	.15	.07	.01
□ 385	Joe Cribbs	.10	.05	.01
□ 386	Greg Bell	.20	.10	.02
□ 387	Jerry Butler	.08	.04	.01
□ 388	Andre Reed	10.00	5.00	1.00
□ 389	Bruce Smith	6.50	3.25	.65
□ 390	Fred Smerlas	.08	.04	.01
□ 391	Darryl Talley	.75	.35	.07
□ 392	Jim Haslett	.05	.02	.00
□ 393	Charles Romes	.05	.02	.00
□ 394	Checklist 1-132	.10	.01	.00
□ 395	Checklist 133-264	.10	.01	.00
□ 396	Checklist 265-396	.12	.01	.00

1987 Topps

The 1987 Topps football set is standard size, 2 1/2" by 3 1/2", and consists of 396 cards featuring players of the NFL. The first eight cards in the set recognize the Super Bowl winning Giants and seven Record-Breaking (RB) achievements during the previous season. All-Pro (AP) selections are designated on the player's regular card, not a special card. Statistical league leaders are featured on cards 227-231. The set numbering is again ordered by teams, i.e., New York Giants (9-29), Denver Broncos (30-42), Chicago Bears (43-62), Washington Redskins (63-78), Cleveland Browns (79-95), New England Patriots (96-110), San Francisco 49ers (111-125), New York Jets (126-143), Los Angeles Rams (144-159), Kansas City Chiefs (160-171), Seattle Seahawks (172-183), Cincinnati Bengals (184-197), Minnesota Vikings (198-212), Los Angeles Raiders (213-226), Miami Dolphins (232-247), Atlanta Falcons (248-259), Dallas

Cowboys (260-271), New Orleans Saints (272-282), Pittsburgh Steelers (283-293), Philadelphia Eagles (294-305), Houston Oilers (306-316), Detroit Lions (317-327), St. Louis Cardinals (328-338), San Diego Chargers (339-349), Green Bay Packers (350-360), Buffalo Bills (361-371), Indianapolis Colts (372-382), and Tampa Bay Buccaneers (383-393). The last three cards in the set (394-396) are checklist cards. Team cards feature an action photo on the front with the team's statistical leaders and week-by-week game results from the previous season. Although they are not considered part of the complete set price, Topps also printed cards on the bottoms of the wax pack boxes. There were four different boxes each with four different players. These box bottom cards are distinguished by their yellow border (instead of white) and the fact that they are "lettered" rather than numbered. The key rookies in this set are Randall Cunningham, Jim Everett, and Jim Kelly.

	MINT	EXC	G-VG
COMPLETE SET (396)	50.00	25.00	5.00
COMMON PLAYER (1-396)	.05	.02	.00
☐ 1 Super Bowl XXI	.15	.04	.01
Giants 39,			
Broncos 20			
(Line play shown)			
☐ 2 Todd Christensen RB	.08	.04	.01
Most Seasons,			
80 or More Receptions			
☐ 3 Dave Jennings RB	.08	.04	.01
Most Punts, Career			
☐ 4 Charlie Joiner RB	.10	.05	.01
Most Receiving			
Yards, Career			
☐ 5 Steve Largent RB	.25	.12	.02
Most Cons. Games			
With a Reception			
☐ 6 Dan Marino RB	.50	.25	.05
Most Cons. Seasons,			
30 or More TD Passes			
☐ 7 Donnie Shell RB	.08	.04	.01
Most Interceptions,			
Strong Safety, Career			
☐ 8 Phil Simms RB	.15	.07	.01
Highest Completion			
Percentage, Super Bowl			
☐ 9 New York Giants	.08	.04	.01
Team Card			
(Mark Bavaro Pulls Free)			
☐ 10 Phil Simms	.30	.15	.03
☐ 11 Joe Morris AP	.15	.07	.01
☐ 12 Maurice Carthon	.20	.10	.02
☐ 13 Lee Rouson	.05	.02	.00
☐ 14 Bobby Johnson	.05	.02	.00
☐ 15 Lionel Manuel	.08	.04	.01
☐ 16 Phil McConkey	.08	.04	.01
☐ 17 Mark Bavaro AP	.25	.12	.02
☐ 18 Zeke Mowatt	.05	.02	.00
☐ 19 Raul Allegre	.05	.02	.00
☐ 20 Sean Landeta	.08	.04	.01
☐ 21 Brad Benson	.05	.02	.00
☐ 22 Jim Burt	.05	.02	.00
☐ 23 Leonard Marshall	.35	.17	.03
☐ 24 Carl Banks	.60	.30	.06
☐ 25 Harry Carson	.15	.07	.01
☐ 26 Lawrence Taylor AP	.65	.30	.06
☐ 27 Terry Kinard	.20	.10	.02
☐ 28 Pepper Johnson	1.00	.50	.10
☐ 29 Erik Howard	.15	.07	.01
☐ 30 Denver Broncos	.08	.04	.01
Team Card			
(Gerald Willhite Dives)			
☐ 31 John Elway	1.00	.50	.10
☐ 32 Gerald Willhite	.08	.04	.01
☐ 33 Sammy Winder	.08	.04	.01
☐ 34 Ken Bell	.05	.02	.00
☐ 35 Steve Watson	.08	.04	.01
☐ 36 Rich Karlis	.05	.02	.00
☐ 37 Keith Bishop	.05	.02	.00
☐ 38 Rulon Jones	.08	.04	.01
☐ 39 Karl Mecklenburg AP	.60	.30	.06
☐ 40 Louis Wright	.10	.05	.01
☐ 41 Mike Harden	.05	.02	.00
☐ 42 Dennis Smith	.25	.12	.02
☐ 43 Chicago Bears	.30	.15	.03
Team Card			
(Walter Payton Barrels)			
☐ 44 Jim McMahon	.15	.07	.01
☐ 45 Doug Flutie	1.75	.85	.17
☐ 46 Walter Payton	1.00	.50	.10
☐ 47 Matt Suhey	.05	.02	.00
☐ 48 Willie Gault	.15	.07	.01
☐ 49 Dennis Gentry	.40	.20	.04
☐ 50 Kevin Butler	.15	.07	.01
☐ 51 Jim Covert AP	.08	.04	.01
☐ 52 Jay Hilgenberg	.25	.12	.02
☐ 53 Dan Hampton	.20	.10	.02
☐ 54 Steve McMichael	.15	.07	.01
☐ 55 William Perry	.15	.07	.01
☐ 56 Richard Dent	.35	.17	.03
☐ 57 Otis Wilson	.08	.04	.01
☐ 58 Mike Singletary AP	.50	.25	.05
☐ 59 Wilber Marshall	.50	.25	.05
☐ 60 Mike Richardson	.05	.02	.00
☐ 61 Dave Duerson	.15	.07	.01
☐ 62 Gary Fencik	.08	.04	.01
☐ 63 Washington Redskins	.08	.04	.01
Team Card			
(George Rogers Plunges)			

☐ 64 Jay Schroeder	.50	.25	.05
☐ 65 George Rogers	.10	.05	.01
☐ 66 Kelvin Bryant	.25	.12	.02
☐ 67 Ken Jenkins	.05	.02	.00
☐ 68 Gary Clark	1.50	.75	.15
☐ 69 Art Monk	.60	.30	.06
☐ 70 Clint Didier	.20	.10	.02
☐ 71 Steve Cox	.05	.02	.00
☐ 72 Joe Jacoby	.08	.04	.01
☐ 73 Russ Grimm	.08	.04	.01
☐ 74 Charles Mann	.30	.15	.03
☐ 75 Dave Butz	.08	.04	.01
☐ 76 Dexter Manley AP	.10	.05	.01
☐ 77 Darrell Green AP	.50	.25	.05
☐ 78 Curtis Jordan	.05	.02	.00
☐ 79 Cleveland Browns	.08	.04	.01
Team Card			
(Harry Holt Sees			
Daylight)			
☐ 80 Bernie Kosar	1.00	.50	.10
☐ 81 Curtis Dickey	.08	.04	.01
☐ 82 Kevin Mack	.20	.10	.02
☐ 83 Herman Fontenot	.05	.02	.00
☐ 84 Brian Brennan	.25	.12	.02
☐ 85 Ozzie Newsome	.20	.10	.02
☐ 86 Jeff Gossett	.05	.02	.00
☐ 87 Cody Risien AP	.05	.02	.00
☐ 88 Reggie Camp	.05	.02	.00
☐ 89 Bob Golic	.08	.04	.01
☐ 90 Carl Hairston	.08	.04	.01
☐ 91 Chip Banks	.08	.04	.01
☐ 92 Frank Minnifield	.08	.04	.01
☐ 93 Hanford Dixon AP	.08	.04	.01
☐ 94 Gerald McNeil	.20	.10	.02
☐ 95 Dave Puzzuoli	.08	.04	.01
☐ 96 New England Patriots	.08	.04	.01
Team Card			
(Andre Tippett Gets			
His Man)			
☐ 97 Tony Eason	.10	.05	.01
☐ 98 Craig James	.10	.05	.01
☐ 99 Tony Collins	.08	.04	.01
☐ 100 Mosi Tatupu	.08	.04	.01
☐ 101 Stanley Morgan	.15	.07	.01
☐ 102 Irving Fryar	.20	.10	.02
☐ 103 Stephen Starring	.05	.02	.00
☐ 104 Tony Franklin AP	.05	.02	.00
☐ 105 Rich Camarillo	.05	.02	.00
☐ 106 Garin Veris	.05	.02	.00
☐ 107 Andre Tippett AP	.10	.05	.01
☐ 108 Don Blackmon	.05	.02	.00
☐ 109 Ronnie Lippett	.30	.15	.03
☐ 110 Raymond Clayborn	.08	.04	.01
☐ 111 San Francisco 49ers	.12	.06	.01
Team Card			
(Roger Craig Up			
the Middle)			

☐ 112 Joe Montana	1.50	.75	.15
☐ 113 Roger Craig	.35	.17	.03
☐ 114 Joe Cribbs	.08	.04	.01
☐ 115 Jerry Rice AP	8.00	4.00	.80
☐ 116 Dwight Clark	.12	.06	.01
☐ 117 Ray Wersching	.05	.02	.00
☐ 118 Max Runager	.05	.02	.00
☐ 119 Jeff Stover	.05	.02	.00
☐ 120 Dwaine Board	.05	.02	.00
☐ 121 Tim McKyer	.75	.35	.07
☐ 122 Don Griffin	.40	.20	.04
☐ 123 Ronnie Lott AP	.50	.25	.05
☐ 124 Tom Holmoe	.05	.02	.00
☐ 125 Charles Haley	1.50	.75	.15
☐ 126 New York Jets	.08	.04	.01
Team Card			
(Mark Gastineau Seeks)			
☐ 127 Ken O'Brien	.30	.15	.03
☐ 128 Pat Ryan	.08	.04	.01
☐ 129 Freeman McNeil	.15	.07	.01
☐ 130 Johnny Hector	.50	.25	.05
☐ 131 Al Toon AP	1.25	.60	.12
☐ 132 Wesley Walker	.12	.06	.01
☐ 133 Mickey Shuler	.05	.02	.00
☐ 134 Pat Leahy	.10	.05	.01
☐ 135 Mark Gastineau	.10	.05	.01
☐ 136 Joe Klecko	.10	.05	.01
☐ 137 Marty Lyons	.08	.04	.01
☐ 138 Bob Crable	.05	.02	.00
☐ 139 Lance Mehl	.05	.02	.00
☐ 140 Dave Jennings	.05	.02	.00
☐ 141 Harry Hamilton	.25	.12	.02
☐ 142 Lester Lyles	.05	.02	.00
☐ 143 Bobby Humphery UER	.05	.02	.00
(Misspelled Humphrey			
on card front)			
☐ 144 Los Angeles Rams	.15	.07	.01
Team Card			
(Eric Dickerson			
Through the Line)			
☐ 145 Jim Everett	6.50	3.25	.65
☐ 146 Eric Dickerson AP	.75	.35	.07
☐ 147 Barry Redden	.08	.04	.01
☐ 148 Ron Brown	.15	.07	.01
☐ 149 Kevin House	.05	.02	.00
☐ 150 Henry Ellard	.35	.17	.03
☐ 151 Doug Smith	.05	.02	.00
☐ 152 Dennis Harrah AP	.05	.02	.00
☐ 153 Jackie Slater	.15	.07	.01
☐ 154 Gary Jeter	.05	.02	.00
☐ 155 Carl Ekern	.05	.02	.00
☐ 156 Mike Wilcher	.05	.02	.00
☐ 157 Jerry Gray	.50	.25	.05
☐ 158 LeRoy Irvin	.08	.04	.01
☐ 159 Nolan Cromwell	.08	.04	.01
☐ 160 Kansas City Chiefs	.08	.04	.01
Team Card			

(Todd Blackledge
Hands Off)

☐ 161	Bill Kenney 08	.04	.01
☐ 162	Stephone Paige 30	.15	.03
☐ 163	Henry Marshall 05	.02	.00
☐ 164	Carlos Carson 08	.04	.01
☐ 165	Nick Lowery 12	.06	.01
☐ 166	Irv Eatman 12	.06	.01
☐ 167	Brad Budde 05	.02	.00
☐ 168	Art Still 08	.04	.01
☐ 169	Bill Maas AP 08	.04	.01
☐ 170	Lloyd Burruss 20	.10	.02
☐ 171	Deron Cherry AP 15	.07	.01
☐ 172	Seattle Seahawks 10	.05	.01

Team Card
(Curt Warner Finds
Opening)

☐ 173	Dave Krieg 20	.10	.02
☐ 174	Curt Warner 12	.06	.01
☐ 175	John L. Williams 2.00	1.00	.20
☐ 176	Bobby Joe Edmonds 25	.12	.02
☐ 177	Steve Largent 50	.25	.05
☐ 178	Bruce Scholtz 05	.02	.00
☐ 179	Norm Johnson 08	.04	.01
☐ 180	Jacob Green 10	.05	.01
☐ 181	Fredd Young 08	.04	.01
☐ 182	Dave Brown 08	.04	.01
☐ 183	Kenny Easley 08	.04	.01
☐ 184	Cincinnati Bengals 10	.05	.01

Team Card
(James Brooks
Stiff-Arm)

☐ 185	Boomer Esiason 1.25	.60	.12
☐ 186	James Brooks 15	.07	.01
☐ 187	Larry Kinnebrew 05	.02	.00
☐ 188	Cris Collinsworth 08	.04	.01
☐ 189	Eddie Brown 40	.20	.04
☐ 190	Tim McGee 1.00	.50	.10
☐ 191	Jim Breech 05	.02	.00
☐ 192	Anthony Munoz 20	.10	.02
☐ 193	Max Montoya 08	.04	.01
☐ 194	Eddie Edwards 05	.02	.00
☐ 195	Ross Browner 05	.02	.00
☐ 196	Emanuel King 05	.02	.00
☐ 197	Louis Breeden 05	.02	.00
☐ 198	Minnesota Vikings 08	.04	.01

Team Card
(Darrin Nelson In
Motion)

☐ 199	Tommy Kramer 10	.05	.01
☐ 200	Darrin Nelson 08	.04	.01
☐ 201	Allen Rice 05	.02	.00
☐ 202	Anthony Carter 35	.17	.03
☐ 203	Leo Lewis 08	.04	.01
☐ 204	Steve Jordan 30	.15	.03
☐ 205	Chuck Nelson 10	.05	.01
☐ 206	Greg Coleman 05	.02	.00

☐ 207	Gary Zimmerman 30	.15	.03
☐ 208	Doug Martin 05	.02	.00
☐ 209	Keith Millard 25	.12	.02
☐ 210	Issiac Holt 35	.17	.03
☐ 211	Joey Browner 35	.17	.03
☐ 212	Rufus Bess 10	.05	.01
☐ 213	Los Angeles Raiders 15	.07	.01

Team Card
(Marcus Allen
Quick Feet)

☐ 214	Jim Plunkett 15	.07	.01
☐ 215	Marcus Allen 40	.20	.04
☐ 216	Napoleon McCallum 15	.07	.01
☐ 217	Dokie Williams 08	.04	.01
☐ 218	Todd Christensen 10	.05	.01
☐ 219	Chris Bahr 05	.02	.00
☐ 220	Howie Long 15	.07	.01
☐ 221	Bill Pickel 08	.04	.01
☐ 222	Sean Jones 35	.17	.03
☐ 223	Lester Hayes 08	.04	.01
☐ 224	Mike Haynes 12	.06	.01
☐ 225	Vann McElroy 05	.02	.00
☐ 226	Fulton Walker 05	.02	.00
☐ 227	Passing Leaders 45	.22	.04

Tommy Kramer,
Minnesota Vikings
Dan Marino,
Miami Dolphins

☐ 228	Receiving Leaders 45	.22	.04

Jerry Rice,
San Francisco 49ers
Todd Christensen,
Los Angeles Raiders

☐ 229	Rushing Leaders 25	.12	.02

Eric Dickerson,
Los Angeles Rams
Curt Warner,
Seattle Seahawks

☐ 230	Scoring Leaders 08	.04	.01

Kevin Butler,
Chicago Bears
Tony Franklin,
New England Patriots

☐ 231	Interception Leaders 15	.07	.01

Ronnie Lott,
San Francisco 49ers
Deron Cherry,
Kansas City Chiefs

☐ 232	Miami Dolphins 08	.04	.01

Team Card
(Reggie Roby Booms It)

☐ 233	Dan Marino AP 3.50	1.75	.35
☐ 234	Lorenzo Hampton 15	.07	.01
☐ 235	Tony Nathan 08	.04	.01
☐ 236	Mark Duper 20	.10	.02
☐ 237	Mark Clayton 60	.30	.06
☐ 238	Nat Moore 08	.04	.01

☐ 239 Bruce Hardy	.05	.02	.00
☐ 240 Reggie Roby	.08	.04	.01
☐ 241 Roy Foster	.05	.02	.00
☐ 242 Dwight Stephenson AP	.08	.04	.01
☐ 243 Hugh Green	.08	.04	.01
☐ 244 John Offerdahl	.75	.35	.07
☐ 245 Mark Brown	.05	.02	.00
☐ 246 Doug Betters	.05	.02	.00
☐ 247 Bob Baumhower	.08	.04	.01
☐ 248 Atlanta Falcons	.08	.04	.01
Team Card			
(Gerald Riggs Uses			
Blockers)			
☐ 249 Dave Archer	.15	.07	.01
☐ 250 Gerald Riggs	.12	.06	.01
☐ 251 William Andrews	.08	.04	.01
☐ 252 Charlie Brown	.08	.04	.01
☐ 253 Arthur Cox	.05	.02	.00
☐ 254 Rick Donnelly	.05	.02	.00
☐ 255 Bill Fralic AP	.12	.06	.01
☐ 256 Mike Gann	.12	.06	.01
☐ 257 Rick Bryan	.10	.05	.01
☐ 258 Bret Clark	.05	.02	.00
☐ 259 Mike Pitts	.05	.02	.00
☐ 260 Dallas Cowboys	.15	.07	.01
Team Card			
(Tony Dorsett Cuts)			
☐ 261 Danny White	.12	.06	.01
☐ 262 Steve Pelluer	.15	.07	.01
☐ 263 Tony Dorsett	.35	.17	.03
☐ 264 Herschel Walker UER	2.25	1.10	.22
(Stats show 12 TD's			
in '86, text says 14)			
☐ 265 Timmy Newsome	.05	.02	.00
☐ 266 Tony Hill	.08	.04	.01
☐ 267 Mike Sherrard	1.00	.50	.10
☐ 268 Jim Jeffcoat	.08	.04	.01
☐ 269 Ron Fellows	.05	.02	.00
☐ 270 Bill Bates	.08	.04	.01
☐ 271 Michael Downs	.05	.02	.00
☐ 272 New Orleans Saints	.08	.04	.01
Team Card			
(Bobby Hebert Fakes)			
☐ 273 Dave Wilson	.08	.04	.01
☐ 274 Rueben Mayes UER	.30	.15	.03
(Stats show 1353 comple-			
tions, should be yards)			
☐ 275 Hoby Brenner	.05	.02	.00
☐ 276 Eric Martin	.90	.45	.09
☐ 277 Morten Andersen	.20	.10	.02
☐ 278 Brian Hansen	.05	.02	.00
☐ 279 Rickey Jackson	.20	.10	.02
☐ 280 Dave Waymer	.05	.02	.00
☐ 281 Bruce Clark	.08	.04	.01
☐ 282 James Geathers	.12	.06	.01
☐ 283 Pittsburgh Steelers	.08	.04	.01
Team Card			

(Walter Abercrombie			
Resists)			
☐ 284 Mark Malone	.08	.04	.01
☐ 285 Earnest Jackson	.08	.04	.01
☐ 286 Walter Abercrombie	.08	.04	.01
☐ 287 Louis Lipps	.20	.10	.02
☐ 288 John Stallworth UER	.12	.06	.01
(Stats only go up			
through 1981)			
☐ 289 Gary Anderson	.05	.02	.00
☐ 290 Keith Willis	.05	.02	.00
☐ 291 Mike Merriweather	.10	.05	.01
☐ 292 Lupe Sanchez	.05	.02	.00
☐ 293 Donnie Shell	.08	.04	.01
☐ 294 Philadelphia Eagles	.08	.04	.01
Team Card			
(Keith Byars			
Inches Ahead)			
☐ 295 Mike Reichenbach	.05	.02	.00
☐ 296 Randall Cunningham	15.00	7.50	1.50
☐ 297 Keith Byars	1.00	.50	.10
☐ 298 Mike Quick	.10	.05	.01
☐ 299 Kenny Jackson	.08	.04	.01
☐ 300 John Teltschik	.15	.07	.01
☐ 301 Reggie White AP	1.00	.50	.10
☐ 302 Ken Clarke	.05	.02	.00
☐ 303 Greg Brown	.05	.02	.00
☐ 304 Roynell Young	.08	.04	.01
☐ 305 Andre Waters	.50	.25	.05
☐ 306 Houston Oilers	.35	.17	.03
Team Card			
(Warren Moon			
Plots Play)			
☐ 307 Warren Moon	3.50	1.75	.35
☐ 308 Mike Rozier	.15	.07	.01
☐ 309 Drew Hill	.25	.12	.02
☐ 310 Ernest Givins	3.25	1.60	.32
☐ 311 Lee Johnson	.05	.02	.00
☐ 312 Kent Hill	.05	.02	.00
☐ 313 Dean Steinkuhler	.40	.20	.04
☐ 314 Ray Childress	.30	.15	.03
☐ 315 John Grimsley	.15	.07	.01
☐ 316 Jesse Baker	.05	.02	.00
☐ 317 Detroit Lions	.08	.04	.01
Team Card			
(Eric Hipple Surveys)			
☐ 318 Chuck Long	.15	.07	.01
☐ 319 James Jones	.08	.04	.01
☐ 320 Garry James	.12	.06	.01
☐ 321 Jeff Chadwick	.08	.04	.01
☐ 322 Leonard Thompson	.08	.04	.01
☐ 323 Pete Mandley	.05	.02	.00
☐ 324 Jimmie Giles	.08	.04	.01
☐ 325 Herman Hunter	.05	.02	.00
☐ 326 Keith Ferguson	.10	.05	.01
☐ 327 Devon Mitchell	.05	.02	.00
☐ 328 St. Louis Cardinals	.08	.04	.01

Team Card
(Neil Lomax Audible)

☐ 329 Neil Lomax	.10	.05	.01
☐ 330 Stump Mitchell	.08	.04	.01
☐ 331 Earl Ferrell	.10	.05	.01
☐ 332 Vai Sikahema	.25	.12	.02
☐ 333 Ron Wolfley	.15	.07	.01
☐ 334 J.T. Smith	.10	.05	.01
☐ 335 Roy Green	.12	.06	.01
☐ 336 Al(Bubba) Baker	.08	.04	.01
☐ 337 Freddie Joe Nunn	.08	.04	.01
☐ 338 Cedric Mack	.08	.04	.01
☐ 339 San Diego Chargers	.08	.04	.01

Team Card
(Gary Anderson Evades)

☐ 340 Dan Fouts	.30	.15	.03
☐ 341 Gary Anderson UER	.25	.12	.02

(Two Topps logos
on card front)

☐ 342 Wes Chandler	.10	.05	.01
☐ 343 Kellen Winslow	.15	.07	.01
☐ 344 Ralf Mojsiejenko	.05	.02	.00
☐ 345 Rolf Benirschke	.08	.04	.01
☐ 346 Lee Williams	.50	.25	.05
☐ 347 Leslie O'Neal	.75	.35	.07
☐ 348 Billy Ray Smith	.08	.04	.01
☐ 349 Gill Byrd	.25	.12	.02
☐ 350 Green Bay Packers	.08	.04	.01

Team Card
(Paul Ott Carruth
Around End)

☐ 351 Randy Wright	.10	.05	.01
☐ 352 Kenneth Davis	.75	.35	.07
☐ 353 Gerry Ellis	.05	.02	.00
☐ 354 James Lofton	.40	.20	.04
☐ 355 Phillip Epps	.12	.06	.01
☐ 356 Walter Stanley	.35	.17	.03
☐ 357 Eddie Lee Ivery	.08	.04	.01
☐ 358 Tim Harris	1.50	.75	.15
☐ 359 Mark Lee UER	.08	.04	.01

(Red flag, rest of
Packers have yellow)

☐ 360 Mossy Cade	.05	.02	.00
☐ 361 Buffalo Bills	1.50	.75	.15

Team Card
(Jim Kelly Works
Ground)

☐ 362 Jim Kelly	18.00	9.00	1.80
☐ 363 Robb Riddick	.15	.07	.01
☐ 364 Greg Bell	.12	.06	.01
☐ 365 Andre Reed	2.50	1.25	.25
☐ 366 Pete Metzelaars	.05	.02	.00
☐ 367 Sean McNanie	.05	.02	.00
☐ 368 Fred Smerlas	.08	.04	.01
☐ 369 Bruce Smith	1.75	.85	.17
☐ 370 Darryl Talley	.30	.15	.03
☐ 371 Charles Romes	.05	.02	.00

☐ 372 Indianapolis Colts	.08	.04	.01

Team Card
(Rohn Stark High
and Far)

☐ 373 Jack Trudeau	.25	.12	.02
☐ 374 Gary Hogeboom	.10	.05	.01
☐ 375 Randy McMillan	.08	.04	.01
☐ 376 Albert Bentley	.15	.07	.01
☐ 377 Matt Bouza	.05	.02	.00
☐ 378 Bill Brooks	.50	.25	.05
☐ 379 Rohn Stark AP	.05	.02	.00
☐ 380 Chris Hinton	.15	.07	.01
☐ 381 Ray Donaldson	.05	.02	.00
☐ 382 Jon Hand	.30	.15	.03
☐ 383 Tampa Bay Buccaneers	.08	.04	.01

Team Card
(James Wilder Braces)

☐ 384 Steve Young	1.00	.50	.10
☐ 385 James Wilder	.08	.04	.01
☐ 386 Frank Garcia	.05	.02	.00
☐ 387 Gerald Carter	.05	.02	.00
☐ 388 Phil Freeman	.05	.02	.00
☐ 389 Calvin Magee	.08	.04	.01
☐ 390 Donald Igwebuike	.05	.02	.00
☐ 391 David Logan	.05	.02	.00
☐ 392 Jeff Davis	.05	.02	.00
☐ 393 Chris Washington	.05	.02	.00
☐ 394 Checklist 1-132	.08	.02	.00
☐ 395 Checklist 133-264	.08	.02	.00
☐ 396 Checklist 265-396	.10	.02	.00

1988 Topps

This 396-card set is essentially in team order as follows: Washington Redskins (7-21), Denver Broncos (22-36), San Francisco 49ers (37-53), New Orleans Saints (54-67), Chicago

Bears (68-84), Cleveland Browns (85-101), Houston Oilers (102-115), Indianapolis Colts (116-129), Seattle Seahawks (130-145), Minnesota Vikings (146-161), Pittsburgh Steelers (162-174), New England Patriots (175-188), Miami Dolphins (189-202), San Diego Chargers (203-214), Buffalo Bills (220-232), Philadelphia Eagles (233-247), Phoenix Cardinals (248-258), Dallas Cowboys (259-270), New York Giants (271-286), Los Angeles Rams (287-300), New York Jets (301-313), Green Bay Packers (314-324), Los Angeles Raiders (325-338), Cincinnati Bengals (339-349), Kansas City Chiefs (361-371), Detroit Lions (372-382), and Atlanta Falcons (383-393). The cards are standard size 2 1/2" by 3 1/2". The Team Leader (TL) cards show an action scene for each team; the caption and featured players are identified in the checklist below. All-Pro selections are identified on the player's regular card. Some of the younger players are also designated by Topps as "Super Rookies" (SR). The wax box cards carry the theme of current pro players who were past college trophy winners, e.g., Heisman, Outland, or Lombardi. They are not included in the complete set price below. The key rookie cards in this set are Neal Anderson, Cornelius Bennett, Chris Doleman, Dalton Hilliard, Bo Jackson, Christian Okoye, Tom Rathman, Pat Swilling, and Vinny Testaverde.

	MINT	EXC	G-VG
COMPLETE SET (396)	20.00	10.00	2.00
COMMON PLAYER (1-396)	.03	.01	.00

☐ 1 Super Bowl XXII	.12	.03	.01
Redskins 42,			
Broncos 10			
(Redskins celebrating)			
☐ 2 Vencie Glenn RB	.06	.03	.00
Longest Interception			
Return			
☐ 3 Steve Largent RB	.15	.07	.01
Most Receptions,			
Career			
☐ 4 Joe Montana RB	.30	.15	.03
Most Consecutive			
Pass Completions			
☐ 5 Walter Payton RB	.25	.12	.02
Most Rushing			
Touchdowns, Career			
☐ 6 Jerry Rice RB	.30	.15	.03
Most Touchdown			
Receptions, Season			
☐ 7 Redskins TL	.06	.03	.00

Kelvin Bryant Sees			
Daylight			
☐ 8 Doug Williams	.10	.05	.01
☐ 9 George Rogers	.08	.04	.01
☐ 10 Kelvin Bryant	.08	.04	.01
☐ 11 Timmy Smith SR	.10	.05	.01
☐ 12 Art Monk	.35	.17	.03
☐ 13 Gary Clark	.50	.25	.05
☐ 14 Ricky Sanders	.75	.35	.07
☐ 15 Steve Cox	.03	.01	.00
☐ 16 Joe Jacoby	.06	.03	.00
☐ 17 Charles Mann	.12	.06	.01
☐ 18 Dave Butz	.06	.03	.00
☐ 19 Darrell Green AP	.30	.15	.03
☐ 20 Dexter Manley	.08	.04	.01
☐ 21 Barry Wilburn	.10	.05	.01
☐ 22 Broncos TL	.06	.03	.00
Sammy Winder Winds			
Through			
☐ 23 John Elway AP	.45	.22	.04
☐ 24 Sammy Winder	.06	.03	.00
☐ 25 Vance Johnson	.15	.07	.01
☐ 26 Mark Jackson	.30	.15	.03
☐ 27 Ricky Nattiel SR	.30	.15	.03
☐ 28 Clarence Kay	.03	.01	.00
☐ 29 Rich Karlis	.03	.01	.00
☐ 30 Keith Bishop	.03	.01	.00
☐ 31 Mike Horan	.03	.01	.00
☐ 32 Rulon Jones	.06	.03	.00
☐ 33 Karl Mecklenburg	.15	.07	.01
☐ 34 Jim Ryan	.03	.01	.00
☐ 35 Mark Haynes	.06	.03	.00
☐ 36 Mike Harden	.03	.01	.00
☐ 37 49ers TL	.10	.05	.01
Roger Craig Gallops			
For Yardage			
☐ 38 Joe Montana	.90	.45	.09
☐ 39 Steve Young	.35	.17	.03
☐ 40 Roger Craig	.25	.12	.02
☐ 41 Tom Rathman	.50	.25	.05
☐ 42 Joe Cribbs	.08	.04	.01
☐ 43 Jerry Rice AP	1.25	.60	.12
☐ 44 Mike Wilson	.12	.06	.01
☐ 45 Ron Heller	.15	.07	.01
☐ 46 Ray Wersching	.03	.01	.00
☐ 47 Michael Carter	.12	.06	.01
☐ 48 Dwaine Board	.03	.01	.00
☐ 49 Michael Walter	.03	.01	.00
☐ 50 Don Griffin	.08	.04	.01
☐ 51 Ronnie Lott	.30	.15	.03
☐ 52 Charles Haley	.25	.12	.02
☐ 53 Dana McLemore	.03	.01	.00
☐ 54 Saints TL	.08	.04	.01
Bobby Hebert Hands Off			
☐ 55 Bobby Hebert	.20	.10	.02
☐ 56 Rueben Mayes	.12	.06	.01
☐ 57 Dalton Hilliard	.60	.30	.06

☐ 58 Eric Martin	.20	.10	.02
☐ 59 John Tice	.15	.07	.01
☐ 60 Brad Edelman	.03	.01	.00
☐ 61 Morten Andersen AP	.10	.05	.01
☐ 62 Brian Hansen	.03	.01	.00
☐ 63 Mel Gray	.20	.10	.02
☐ 64 Rickey Jackson	.12	.06	.01
☐ 65 Sam Mills	.50	.25	.05
☐ 66 Pat Swilling	1.25	.60	.12
☐ 67 Dave Waymer	.03	.01	.00
☐ 68 Bears TL	.08	.04	.01
Willie Gault Powers			
Forward			
☐ 69 Jim McMahon	.10	.05	.01
☐ 70 Mike Tomczak	.35	.17	.03
☐ 71 Neal Anderson	2.75	1.35	.27
☐ 72 Willie Gault	.12	.06	.01
☐ 73 Dennis Gentry	.06	.03	.00
☐ 74 Dennis McKinnon	.03	.01	.00
☐ 75 Kevin Butler	.03	.01	.00
☐ 76 Jim Covert	.06	.03	.00
☐ 77 Jay Hilgenberg	.08	.04	.01
☐ 78 Steve McMichael	.08	.04	.01
☐ 79 William Perry	.12	.06	.01
☐ 80 Richard Dent	.15	.07	.01
☐ 81 Ron Rivera	.10	.05	.01
☐ 82 Mike Singletary AP	.20	.10	.02
☐ 83 Dan Hampton	.12	.06	.01
☐ 84 Dave Duerson	.06	.03	.00
☐ 85 Browns TL	.10	.05	.01
Bernie Kosar Lets			
It Go			
☐ 86 Bernie Kosar	.35	.17	.03
☐ 87 Earnest Byner	.35	.17	.03
☐ 88 Kevin Mack	.12	.06	.01
☐ 89 Webster Slaughter	.50	.25	.05
☐ 90 Gerald McNeil	.06	.03	.00
☐ 91 Brian Brennan	.03	.01	.00
☐ 92 Ozzie Newsome	.15	.07	.01
☐ 93 Cody Risien	.03	.01	.00
☐ 94 Bob Golic	.06	.03	.00
☐ 95 Carl Hairston	.06	.03	.00
☐ 96 Mike Johnson	.20	.10	.02
☐ 97 Clay Matthews	.06	.03	.00
☐ 98 Frank Minnifield	.06	.03	.00
☐ 99 Hanford Dixon AP	.06	.03	.00
☐ 100 Dave Puzzuoli	.03	.01	.00
☐ 101 Felix Wright	.15	.07	.01
☐ 102 Oilers TL	.25	.12	.02
Warren Moon Over			
The Top			
☐ 103 Warren Moon	1.25	.60	.12
☐ 104 Mike Rozier	.08	.04	.01
☐ 105 Alonzo Highsmith SR	.15	.07	.01
☐ 106 Drew Hill	.20	.10	.02
☐ 107 Ernest Givins	.75	.35	.07
☐ 108 Curtis Duncan	.35	.17	.03

☐ 109 Tony Zendejas	.10	.05	.01
☐ 110 Mike Munchak AP	.12	.06	.01
☐ 111 Kent Hill	.03	.01	.00
☐ 112 Ray Childress	.08	.04	.01
☐ 113 Al Smith	.25	.12	.02
☐ 114 Keith Bostic	.10	.05	.01
☐ 115 Jeff Donaldson	.03	.01	.00
☐ 116 Colts TL	.15	.07	.01
Eric Dickerson Finds			
Opening			
☐ 117 Jack Trudeau	.10	.05	.01
☐ 118 Eric Dickerson AP	.50	.25	.05
☐ 119 Albert Bentley	.08	.04	.01
☐ 120 Matt Bouza	.03	.01	.00
☐ 121 Bill Brooks	.12	.06	.01
☐ 122 Dean Biasucci	.15	.07	.01
☐ 123 Chris Hinton	.08	.04	.01
☐ 124 Ray Donaldson	.03	.01	.00
☐ 125 Ron Solt	.15	.07	.01
☐ 126 Donnell Thompson	.03	.01	.00
☐ 127 Barry Krauss	.10	.05	.01
☐ 128 Duane Bickett	.08	.04	.01
☐ 129 Mike Prior	.15	.07	.01
☐ 130 Seahawks TL	.06	.03	.00
Curt Warner Follows			
Blocking			
☐ 131 Dave Krieg	.12	.06	.01
☐ 132 Curt Warner	.10	.05	.01
☐ 133 John L. Williams	.35	.17	.03
☐ 134 Bobby Joe Edmonds	.06	.03	.00
☐ 135 Steve Largent	.40	.20	.04
☐ 136 Raymond Butler	.06	.03	.00
☐ 137 Norm Johnson	.06	.03	.00
☐ 138 Ruben Rodriguez	.10	.05	.01
☐ 139 Blair Bush	.03	.01	.00
☐ 140 Jacob Green	.06	.03	.00
☐ 141 Joe Nash	.06	.03	.00
☐ 142 Jeff Bryant	.03	.01	.00
☐ 143 Fredd Young AP	.06	.03	.00
☐ 144 Brian Bosworth SR	.25	.12	.02
☐ 145 Kenny Easley AP	.06	.03	.00
☐ 146 Vikings TL	.08	.04	.01
Tommy Kramer Spots			
His Man			
☐ 147 Wade Wilson	.35	.17	.03
☐ 148 Tommy Kramer	.10	.05	.01
☐ 149 Darrin Nelson	.06	.03	.00
☐ 150 D.J. Dozier SR	.50	.25	.05
☐ 151 Anthony Carter	.15	.07	.01
☐ 152 Leo Lewis	.06	.03	.00
☐ 153 Steve Jordan	.15	.07	.01
☐ 154 Gary Zimmerman	.06	.03	.00
☐ 155 Chuck Nelson	.03	.01	.00
☐ 156 Henry Thomas SR	.25	.12	.02
☐ 157 Chris Doleman	.60	.30	.06
☐ 158 Scott Studwell	.15	.07	.01
☐ 159 Jesse Solomon	.10	.05	.01

☐ 160 Joey Browner AP	.15	.07	.01
☐ 161 Neal Guggemos	.03	.01	.00
☐ 162 Steelers TL	.08	.04	.01
Louis Lipps In a Crowd			
☐ 163 Mark Malone	.08	.04	.01
☐ 164 Walter Abercrombie	.06	.03	.00
☐ 165 Earnest Jackson	.06	.03	.00
☐ 166 Frank Pollard	.03	.01	.00
☐ 167 Dwight Stone	.12	.06	.01
☐ 168 Gary Anderson	.03	.01	.00
☐ 169 Harry Newsome	.10	.05	.01
☐ 170 Keith Willis	.03	.01	.00
☐ 171 Keith Gary	.03	.01	.00
☐ 172 David Little	.12	.06	.01
☐ 173 Mike Merriweather	.06	.03	.00
☐ 174 Dwayne Woodruff	.03	.01	.00
☐ 175 Patriots TL	.08	.04	.01
Irving Fryar One on One			
☐ 176 Steve Grogan	.10	.05	.01
☐ 177 Tony Eason	.08	.04	.01
☐ 178 Tony Collins	.06	.03	.00
☐ 179 Mosi Tatupu	.06	.03	.00
☐ 180 Stanley Morgan	.10	.05	.01
☐ 181 Irving Fryar	.08	.04	.01
☐ 182 Stephen Starring	.03	.01	.00
☐ 183 Tony Franklin	.03	.01	.00
☐ 184 Rich Camarillo	.03	.01	.00
☐ 185 Garin Veris	.03	.01	.00
☐ 186 Andre Tippett AP	.08	.04	.01
☐ 187 Ronnie Lippett	.06	.03	.00
☐ 188 Fred Marion	.03	.01	.00
☐ 189 Dolphins TL	.35	.17	.03
Dan Marino Play-Action Pass			
☐ 190 Dan Marino	1.25	.60	.12
☐ 191 Troy Stradford SR	.15	.07	.01
☐ 192 Lorenzo Hampton	.06	.03	.00
☐ 193 Mark Duper	.12	.06	.01
☐ 194 Mark Clayton	.25	.12	.02
☐ 195 Reggie Roby	.06	.03	.00
☐ 196 Dwight Stephenson AP	.06	.03	.00
☐ 197 T.J. Turner	.06	.03	.00
☐ 198 John Bosa SR	.10	.05	.01
☐ 199 Jackie Shipp	.06	.03	.00
☐ 200 John Offerdahl	.10	.05	.01
☐ 201 Mark Brown	.03	.01	.00
☐ 202 Paul Lankford	.03	.01	.00
☐ 203 Chargers TL	.06	.03	.00
Kellen Winslow Sure Hands			
☐ 204 Tim Spencer	.03	.01	.00
☐ 205 Gary Anderson	.10	.05	.01
☐ 206 Curtis Adams	.03	.01	.00
☐ 207 Lionel James	.06	.03	.00
☐ 208 Chip Banks	.06	.03	.00
☐ 209 Kellen Winslow	.12	.06	.01
☐ 210 Ralf Mojsiejenko	.03	.01	.00
☐ 211 Jim Lachey	.20	.10	.02
☐ 212 Lee Williams	.10	.05	.01
☐ 213 Billy Ray Smith	.06	.03	.00
☐ 214 Vencie Glenn	.15	.07	.01
☐ 215 Passing Leaders	.40	.20	.04
Bernie Kosar			
Joe Montana			
☐ 216 Receiving Leaders	.08	.04	.01
Al Toon			
J.T. Smith			
☐ 217 Rushing Leaders	.15	.07	.01
Charles White			
Eric Dickerson			
☐ 218 Scoring Leaders	.20	.10	.02
Jim Breech			
Jerry Rice			
☐ 219 Interception Leaders	.06	.03	.00
Keith Bostic			
Mark Kelso			
Mike Prior			
Barry Wilburn			
☐ 220 Bills TL	.35	.17	.03
Jim Kelly Plots His Course			
☐ 221 Jim Kelly	2.50	1.25	.25
☐ 222 Ronnie Harmon	.30	.15	.03
☐ 223 Robb Riddick	.06	.03	.00
☐ 224 Andre Reed	.60	.30	.06
☐ 225 Chris Burkett	.30	.15	.03
☐ 226 Pete Metzelaars	.03	.01	.00
☐ 227 Bruce Smith AP	.40	.20	.04
☐ 228 Darryl Talley	.12	.06	.01
☐ 229 Eugene Marve	.03	.01	.00
☐ 230 Cornelius Bennett SR	1.75	.85	.17
☐ 231 Mark Kelso	.30	.15	.03
☐ 232 Shane Conlan SR	.90	.45	.09
☐ 233 Eagles TL	.20	.10	.02
Randall Cunningham QB Keeper			
☐ 234 Randall Cunningham	1.25	.60	.12
☐ 235 Keith Byars	.15	.07	.01
☐ 236 Anthony Toney	.15	.07	.01
☐ 237 Mike Quick	.08	.04	.01
☐ 238 Kenny Jackson	.06	.03	.00
☐ 239 John Spagnola	.03	.01	.00
☐ 240 Paul McFadden	.03	.01	.00
☐ 241 Reggie White AP	.35	.17	.03
☐ 242 Ken Clarke	.03	.01	.00
☐ 243 Mike Pitts	.03	.01	.00
☐ 244 Clyde Simmons	.50	.25	.05
☐ 245 Seth Joyner	.50	.25	.05
☐ 246 Andre Waters	.06	.03	.00
☐ 247 Jerome Brown SR	.50	.25	.05
☐ 248 Cardinals TL	.06	.03	.00
Stump Mitchell On the Run			
☐ 249 Neil Lomax	.08	.04	.01

☐ 250 Stump Mitchell	.08	.04	.01
☐ 251 Earl Ferrell	.03	.01	.00
☐ 252 Vai Sikahema	.06	.03	.00
☐ 253 J.T. Smith AP	.08	.04	.01
☐ 254 Roy Green	.10	.05	.01
☐ 255 Robert Awalt SR	.15	.07	.01
☐ 256 Freddie Joe Nunn	.06	.03	.00
☐ 257 Leonard Smith	.10	.05	.01
☐ 258 Travis Curtis	.03	.01	.00
☐ 259 Cowboys TL	.15	.07	.01
Herschel Walker			
Around End			
☐ 260 Danny White	.10	.05	.01
☐ 261 Herschel Walker	.50	.25	.05
☐ 262 Tony Dorsett	.25	.12	.02
☐ 263 Doug Cosbie	.06	.03	.00
☐ 264 Roger Ruzek	.08	.04	.01
☐ 265 Darryl Clack	.08	.04	.01
☐ 266 Ed Too Tall Jones	.12	.06	.01
☐ 267 Jim Jeffcoat	.03	.01	.00
☐ 268 Everson Walls	.08	.04	.01
☐ 269 Bill Bates	.06	.03	.00
☐ 270 Michael Downs	.03	.01	.00
☐ 271 Giants TL	.06	.03	.00
Mark Bavaro Drives			
Ahead			
☐ 272 Phil Simms	.15	.07	.01
☐ 273 Joe Morris	.08	.04	.01
☐ 274 Lee Rouson	.03	.01	.00
☐ 275 George Adams	.03	.01	.00
☐ 276 Lionel Manuel	.06	.03	.00
☐ 277 Mark Bavaro AP	.10	.05	.01
☐ 278 Raul Allegre	.03	.01	.00
☐ 279 Sean Landeta	.03	.01	.00
☐ 280 Erik Howard	.03	.01	.00
☐ 281 Leonard Marshall	.12	.06	.01
☐ 282 Carl Banks AP	.20	.10	.02
☐ 283 Pepper Johnson	.15	.07	.01
☐ 284 Harry Carson	.10	.05	.01
☐ 285 Lawrence Taylor	.35	.17	.03
☐ 286 Terry Kinard	.06	.03	.00
☐ 287 Rams TL	.12	.06	.01
Jim Everett Races			
Downfield			
☐ 288 Jim Everett	.65	.30	.06
☐ 289 Charles White AP	.08	.04	.01
☐ 290 Ron Brown	.08	.04	.01
☐ 291 Henry Ellard	.12	.06	.01
☐ 292 Mike Lansford	.03	.01	.00
☐ 293 Dale Hatcher	.03	.01	.00
☐ 294 Doug Smith	.03	.01	.00
☐ 295 Jackie Slater AP	.08	.04	.01
☐ 296 Jim Collins	.03	.01	.00
☐ 297 Jerry Gray	.08	.04	.01
☐ 298 LeRoy Irvin	.06	.03	.00
☐ 299 Nolan Cromwell	.06	.03	.00
☐ 300 Kevin Greene	.35	.17	.03

☐ 301 Jets TL	.06	.03	.00
Ken O'Brien Reads			
Defense			
☐ 302 Ken O'Brien	.15	.07	.01
☐ 303 Freeman McNeil	.10	.05	.01
☐ 304 Johnny Hector	.06	.03	.00
☐ 305 Al Toon	.35	.17	.03
☐ 306 Jo Jo Townsell	.10	.05	.01
☐ 307 Mickey Shuler	.06	.03	.00
☐ 308 Pat Leahy	.08	.04	.01
☐ 309 Roger Vick	.12	.06	.01
☐ 310 Alex Gordon	.15	.07	.01
☐ 311 Troy Benson	.03	.01	.00
☐ 312 Bob Crable	.06	.03	.00
☐ 313 Harry Hamilton	.06	.03	.00
☐ 314 Packers TL	.06	.03	.00
Phillip Epps Ready			
for Contact			
☐ 315 Randy Wright	.06	.03	.00
☐ 316 Kenneth Davis	.15	.07	.01
☐ 317 Phillip Epps	.06	.03	.00
☐ 318 Walter Stanley	.06	.03	.00
☐ 319 Frankie Neal	.03	.01	.00
☐ 320 Don Bracken	.03	.01	.00
☐ 321 Brian Noble	.15	.07	.01
☐ 322 Johnny Holland SR	.30	.15	.03
☐ 323 Tim Harris	.25	.12	.02
☐ 324 Mark Murphy	.06	.03	.00
☐ 325 Raiders TL	.40	.20	.04
Bo Jackson All Alone			
☐ 326 Marc Wilson	.06	.03	.00
☐ 327 Bo Jackson SR	4.00	2.00	.40
☐ 328 Marcus Allen	.25	.12	.02
☐ 329 James Lofton	.20	.10	.02
☐ 330 Todd Christensen	.08	.04	.01
☐ 331 Chris Bahr	.03	.01	.00
☐ 332 Stan Talley	.03	.01	.00
☐ 333 Howie Long	.10	.05	.01
☐ 334 Sean Jones	.03	.01	.00
☐ 335 Matt Millen	.08	.04	.01
☐ 336 Stacey Toran	.06	.03	.00
☐ 337 Vann McElroy	.03	.01	.00
☐ 338 Greg Townsend	.15	.07	.01
☐ 339 Bengals TL	.10	.05	.01
Boomer Esiason			
Calls Signals			
☐ 340 Boomer Esiason	.30	.15	.03
☐ 341 Larry Kinnebrew	.03	.01	.00
☐ 342 Stanford Jennings	.15	.07	.01
☐ 343 Eddie Brown	.15	.07	.01
☐ 344 Jim Breech	.03	.01	.00
☐ 345 Anthony Munoz AP	.15	.07	.01
☐ 346 Scott Fulhage	.10	.05	.01
☐ 347 Tim Krumrie	.25	.12	.02
☐ 348 Reggie Williams	.06	.03	.00
☐ 349 David Fulcher	.25	.12	.02
☐ 350 Buccaneers TL	.06	.03	.00

James Wilder Free
and Clear

☐ 351 Frank Garcia	.03	.01	.00
☐ 352 Vinny Testaverde SR	.75	.35	.07
☐ 353 James Wilder	.06	.03	.00
☐ 354 Jeff Smith	.03	.01	.00
☐ 355 Gerald Carter	.03	.01	.00
☐ 356 Calvin Magee	.03	.01	.00
☐ 357 Donald Igwebuike	.03	.01	.00
☐ 358 Ron Holmes	.15	.07	.01
☐ 359 Chris Washington	.03	.01	.00
☐ 360 Ervin Randle	.03	.01	.00
☐ 361 Chiefs TL	.06	.03	.00

Bill Kenney Ground
Attack

☐ 362 Bill Kenney	.06	.03	.00
☐ 363 Christian Okoye SR	1.75	.85	.17
☐ 364 Paul Palmer	.10	.05	.01
☐ 365 Stephone Paige	.12	.06	.01
☐ 366 Carlos Carson	.06	.03	.00
☐ 367 Kelly Goodburn	.03	.01	.00
☐ 368 Bill Maas AP	.06	.03	.00
☐ 369 Mike Bell	.03	.01	.00
☐ 370 Dino Hackett	.25	.12	.02
☐ 371 Deron Cherry	.08	.04	.01
☐ 372 Lions TL	.08	.04	.01

James Jones Stretches
For More

☐ 373 Chuck Long	.08	.04	.01
☐ 374 Garry James	.06	.03	.00
☐ 375 James Jones	.06	.03	.00
☐ 376 Pete Mandley	.03	.01	.00
☐ 377 Gary Lee SR	.10	.05	.01
☐ 378 Ed Murray	.06	.03	.00
☐ 379 Jim Arnold	.03	.01	.00
☐ 380 Dennis Gibson SR	.15	.07	.01
☐ 381 Mike Cofer	.08	.04	.01
☐ 382 James Griffin	.03	.01	.00
☐ 383 Falcons TL	.06	.03	.00

Gerald Riggs Carries
Heavy Load

☐ 384 Scott Campbell	.06	.03	.00
☐ 385 Gerald Riggs	.12	.06	.01
☐ 386 Floyd Dixon	.15	.07	.01
☐ 387 Rick Donnelly AP	.03	.01	.00
☐ 388 Bill Fralic AP	.08	.04	.01
☐ 389 Major Everett	.03	.01	.00
☐ 390 Mike Gann	.03	.01	.00
☐ 391 Tony Casillas	.45	.22	.04
☐ 392 Rick Bryan	.06	.03	.00
☐ 393 John Rade	.10	.05	.01
☐ 394 Checklist 1-132	.06	.01	.00
☐ 395 Checklist 133-264	.06	.01	.00
☐ 396 Checklist 265-396	.08	.01	.00

1989 Topps

This 396-card set is similar to the Topps football efforts of the past few years. The cards are standard size, 2 1/2" by 3 1/2". The cards are ordered in team order and the teams themselves are ordered according to their finish in the 1988 standings, e.g., San Francisco 49ers (6-22), Cincinnati Bengals (23-39), Buffalo Bills (40-56), Chicago Bears (57-73), Minnesota Vikings (74-89), Houston Oilers (90-105), Philadelphia Eagles (106-121), Los Angeles Rams (122-137), Cleveland Browns (138-151), New Orleans Saints (152-164), New York Giants (165-180), Seattle Seahawks (181-192), New England Patriots (193-204), Indianapolis Colts (205-216), New York Jets (222-237), Denver Broncos (238-249), Washington Redskins (250-263), Los Angeles Raiders (264-275), Phoenix Cardinals (276-289), Miami Dolphins (290-302), San Diego Chargers (303-313), Pittsburgh Steelers (314-324), Tampa Bay Buccaneers (325-335), Atlanta Falcons (336-347), Kansas City Chiefs (348-359), Detroit Lions (360-370), Green Bay Packers (371-381), and Dallas Cowboys (382-393). The card backs are printed in green and yellow on gray card stock. The team cards are actually Team Leader cards showing an action scene on the front and giving the recap of the team's success in the previous season on the back. The key rookie cards in this set are Brian Blades, Michael Irvin, Don Majkowski, Chris Miller, Michael Dean Perry, Mark Rypien, Sterling Sharpe, John Taylor, and Thurman Thomas.

	MINT	EXC	G-VG
COMPLETE SET (396)	13.50	6.00	1.50
COMMON PLAYER (1-396)	.03	.01	.00

☐ 1 Super Bowl XXIII 15	.05	.01	
(Joe Montana back			
to pass)			
☐ 2 Tim Brown RB 10	.05	.01	
Most Combined Net			
Yards Gained,			
Rookie Season			
☐ 3 Eric Dickerson RB 12	.06	.01	
Most Consecutive			
Seasons, Start of			
Career, 1000 or More			
Yards Rushing			
☐ 4 Steve Largent RB 12	.06	.01	
Most Yards Receiving,			
Career			
☐ 5 Dan Marino RB 15	.07	.01	
Most Seasons 4000 or			
More Yards Passing			
☐ 6 49ers Team 15	.07	.01	
Joe Montana On The Run			
☐ 7 Jerry Rice 75	.35	.07	
☐ 8 Roger Craig 12	.06	.01	
☐ 9 Ronnie Lott 15	.07	.01	
☐ 10 Michael Carter 06	.03	.00	
☐ 11 Charles Haley 06	.03	.00	
☐ 12 Joe Montana 75	.35	.07	
☐ 13 John Taylor 90	.45	.09	
☐ 14 Michael Walter 03	.01	.00	
☐ 15 Mike Cofer K 10	.05	.01	
☐ 16 Tom Rathman 08	.04	.01	
☐ 17 Danny Stubbs 08	.04	.01	
☐ 18 Keena Turner 06	.03	.00	
☐ 19 Tim McKyer 08	.04	.01	
☐ 20 Larry Roberts 12	.06	.01	
☐ 21 Jeff Fuller 06	.03	.00	
☐ 22 Bubba Paris 08	.04	.01	
☐ 23 Bengals Team UER 08	.04	.01	
Boomer Esiason Measures			
Up (Should be versus			
Steelers in week three)			
☐ 24 Eddie Brown 08	.04	.01	
☐ 25 Boomer Esiason 20	.10	.02	
☐ 26 Tim Krumrie 03	.01	.00	
☐ 27 Ickey Woods 25	.12	.02	
☐ 28 Anthony Munoz 10	.05	.01	
☐ 29 Tim McGee 10	.05	.01	
☐ 30 Max Montoya 06	.03	.00	
☐ 31 David Grant 08	.04	.01	
☐ 32 Rodney Holman 25	.12	.02	
(Cincinnati Bengals on			
card front is subject to			
various printing errors)			
☐ 33 David Fulcher 06	.03	.00	
☐ 34 Jim Skow 08	.04	.01	
☐ 35 James Brooks 10	.05	.01	
☐ 36 Reggie Williams 06	.03	.00	
☐ 37 Eric Thomas 15	.07	.01	

☐ 38 Stanford Jennings 03	.01	.00	
☐ 39 Jim Breech 03	.01	.00	
☐ 40 Bills Team 15	.07	.01	
Jim Kelly Reads Defense			
☐ 41 Shane Conlan 10	.05	.01	
☐ 42 Scott Norwood 08	.04	.01	
☐ 43 Cornelius Bennett 25	.12	.02	
☐ 44 Bruce Smith 12	.06	.01	
☐ 45 Thurman Thomas 3.50	1.75	.35	
☐ 46 Jim Kelly 60	.30	.06	
☐ 47 John Kidd 08	.04	.01	
☐ 48 Kent Hull 10	.05	.01	
☐ 49 Art Still 06	.03	.00	
☐ 50 Fred Smerlas 06	.03	.00	
☐ 51A Derrick Burroughs 06	.03	.00	
(White name plate)			
☐ 51B Derrick Burroughs 06	.03	.00	
(Yellow name plate)			
☐ 52 Andre Reed 15	.07	.01	
☐ 53 Robb Riddick 03	.01	.00	
☐ 54 Chris Burkett 03	.01	.00	
☐ 55 Ronnie Harmon 06	.03	.00	
☐ 56 Mark Kelso UER 06	.03	.00	
(team shown as			
"Buffalo Bill")			
☐ 57 Bears Team 06	.03	.00	
Thomas Sanders			
Changes Pace			
☐ 58 Mike Singletary 12	.06	.01	
☐ 59 Jay Hilgenberg UER 08	.04	.01	
(letter "g" is miss-			
ing from Chicago)			
☐ 60 Richard Dent 10	.05	.01	
☐ 61 Ron Rivera 03	.01	.00	
☐ 62 Jim McMahon 08	.04	.01	
☐ 63 Mike Tomczak 08	.04	.01	
☐ 64 Neal Anderson 40	.20	.04	
☐ 65 Dennis Gentry 03	.01	.00	
☐ 66 Dan Hampton 08	.04	.01	
☐ 67 David Tate 08	.04	.01	
☐ 68 Thomas Sanders 12	.06	.01	
☐ 69 Steve McMichael 06	.03	.00	
☐ 70 Dennis McKinnon 03	.01	.00	
☐ 71 Brad Muster 25	.12	.02	
☐ 72 Vestee Jackson 10	.05	.01	
☐ 73 Dave Duerson 06	.03	.00	
☐ 74 Vikings Team 06	.03	.00	
Millard Gets His Man			
☐ 75 Joey Browner 08	.04	.01	
☐ 76 Carl Lee 10	.05	.01	
☐ 77 Gary Zimmerman 06	.03	.00	
☐ 78 Hassan Jones 15	.07	.01	
☐ 79 Anthony Carter 08	.04	.01	
☐ 80 Ray Berry 10	.05	.01	
☐ 81 Steve Jordan 08	.04	.01	
☐ 82 Issiac Holt 06	.03	.00	
☐ 83 Wade Wilson 10	.05	.01	

☐ 84 Chris Doleman	.10	.05	.01
☐ 85 Alfred Anderson	.03	.01	.00
☐ 86 Keith Millard	.08	.04	.01
☐ 87 Darrin Nelson	.06	.03	.00
☐ 88 D.J. Dozier	.10	.05	.01
☐ 89 Scott Studwell	.03	.01	.00
☐ 90 Oilers Team	.06	.03	.00
Tony Zendejas Big Boot			
☐ 91 Bruce Matthews	.15	.07	.01
☐ 92 Curtis Duncan	.06	.03	.00
☐ 93 Warren Moon	.45	.22	.04
☐ 94 Johnny Meads	.15	.07	.01
☐ 95 Drew Hill	.12	.06	.01
☐ 96 Alonzo Highsmith	.08	.04	.01
☐ 97 Mike Munchak	.06	.03	.00
☐ 98 Mike Rozier	.08	.04	.01
☐ 99 Tony Zendejas	.03	.01	.00
☐ 100 Jeff Donaldson	.03	.01	.00
☐ 101 Ray Childress	.06	.03	.00
☐ 102 Sean Jones	.03	.01	.00
☐ 103 Ernest Givins	.12	.06	.01
☐ 104 William Fuller	.12	.06	.01
☐ 105 Allen Pinkett	.20	.10	.02
☐ 106 Eagles Team	.10	.05	.01
Randall Cunningham			
Fakes Field			
☐ 107 Keith Jackson	.50	.25	.05
☐ 108 Reggie White	.12	.06	.01
☐ 109 Clyde Simmons	.08	.04	.01
☐ 110 John Teltschik	.03	.01	.00
☐ 111 Wes Hopkins	.03	.01	.00
☐ 112 Keith Byars	.08	.04	.01
☐ 113 Jerome Brown	.08	.04	.01
☐ 114 Mike Quick	.06	.03	.00
☐ 115 Randall Cunningham	.30	.15	.03
☐ 116 Anthony Toney	.03	.01	.00
☐ 117 Ron Johnson	.10	.05	.01
☐ 118 Terry Hoage	.03	.01	.00
☐ 119 Seth Joyner	.10	.05	.01
☐ 120 Eric Allen	.15	.07	.01
☐ 121 Cris Carter	.45	.22	.04
☐ 122 Rams Team	.06	.03	.00
Greg Bell Runs To Glory			
☐ 123 Tom Newberry	.12	.06	.01
☐ 124 Pete Holohan	.03	.01	.00
☐ 125 Robert Delpino UER	.35	.17	.03
(Listed as Raider			
on card back)			
☐ 126 Carl Ekern	.03	.01	.00
☐ 127 Greg Bell	.08	.04	.01
☐ 128 Mike Lansford	.03	.01	.00
☐ 129 Jim Everett	.15	.07	.01
☐ 130 Mike Wilcher	.03	.01	.00
☐ 131 Jerry Gray	.06	.03	.00
☐ 132 Dale Hatcher	.03	.01	.00
☐ 133 Doug Smith	.03	.01	.00
☐ 134 Kevin Greene	.06	.03	.00

☐ 135 Jackie Slater	.06	.03	.00
☐ 136 Aaron Cox	.15	.07	.01
☐ 137 Henry Ellard	.08	.04	.01
☐ 138 Browns Team	.08	.04	.01
Bernie Kosar Quick			
Release			
☐ 139 Frank Minnifield	.06	.03	.00
☐ 140 Webster Slaughter	.12	.06	.01
☐ 141 Bernie Kosar	.15	.07	.01
☐ 142 Charles Buchanan	.08	.04	.01
☐ 143 Clay Matthews	.06	.03	.00
☐ 144 Reggie Langhorne	.20	.10	.02
☐ 145 Hanford Dixon	.03	.01	.00
☐ 146 Brian Brennan	.03	.01	.00
☐ 147 Earnest Byner	.12	.06	.01
☐ 148 Michael Dean Perry	2.00	1.00	.20
☐ 149 Kevin Mack	.06	.03	.00
☐ 150 Matt Bahr	.03	.01	.00
☐ 151 Ozzie Newsome	.10	.05	.01
☐ 152 Saints Team	.06	.03	.00
Craig Heyward Motors			
Forward			
☐ 153 Morten Andersen	.06	.03	.00
☐ 154 Pat Swilling	.15	.07	.01
☐ 155 Sam Mills	.08	.04	.01
☐ 156 Lonzell Hill	.12	.06	.01
☐ 157 Dalton Hilliard	.10	.05	.01
☐ 158 Craig Heyward	.15	.07	.01
☐ 159 Vaughan Johnson	.25	.12	.02
☐ 160 Rueben Mayes	.08	.04	.01
☐ 161 Gene Atkins	.10	.05	.01
☐ 162 Bobby Hebert	.10	.05	.01
☐ 163 Rickey Jackson	.08	.04	.01
☐ 164 Eric Martin	.08	.04	.01
☐ 165 Giants Team	.06	.03	.00
Joe Morris Up			
The Middle			
☐ 166 Lawrence Taylor	.15	.07	.01
☐ 167 Bart Oates	.03	.01	.00
☐ 168 Carl Banks	.08	.04	.01
☐ 169 Eric Moore	.10	.05	.01
☐ 170 Sheldon White	.08	.04	.01
☐ 171 Mark Collins	.15	.07	.01
☐ 172 Phil Simms	.15	.07	.01
☐ 173 Jim Burt	.03	.01	.00
☐ 174 Stephen Baker	.25	.12	.02
☐ 175 Mark Bavaro	.06	.03	.00
☐ 176 Pepper Johnson	.06	.03	.00
☐ 177 Lionel Manuel	.06	.03	.00
☐ 178 Joe Morris	.08	.04	.01
☐ 179 John Elliott	.12	.06	.01
☐ 180 Gary Reasons	.12	.06	.01
☐ 181 Seahawks Team	.06	.03	.00
Dave Krieg Winds Up			
☐ 182 Brian Blades	.90	.45	.09
☐ 183 Steve Largent	.25	.12	.02
☐ 184 Rufus Porter	.12	.06	.01

□	185	Ruben Rodriguez	.03	.01	.00
□	186	Curt Warner	.08	.04	.01
□	187	Paul Moyer	.08	.04	.01
□	188	Dave Krieg	.10	.05	.01
□	189	Jacob Green	.06	.03	.00
□	190	John L. Williams	.10	.05	.01
□	191	Eugene Robinson	.08	.04	.01
□	192	Brian Bosworth	.08	.04	.01
□	193	Patriots Team	.06	.03	.00
		Tony Eason Behind			
		Blocking			
□	194	John Stephens	.50	.25	.05
□	195	Robert Perryman	.10	.05	.01
□	196	Andre Tippett	.06	.03	.00
□	197	Fred Marion	.03	.01	.00
□	198	Doug Flutie	.20	.10	.02
□	199	Stanley Morgan	.08	.04	.01
□	200	Johnny Rembert	.12	.06	.01
□	201	Tony Eason	.08	.04	.01
□	202	Marvin Allen	.08	.04	.01
□	203	Raymond Clayborn	.03	.01	.00
□	204	Irving Fryar	.06	.03	.00
□	205	Colts Team	.06	.03	.00
		Chris Chandler			
		All Alone			
□	206	Eric Dickerson	.30	.15	.03
□	207	Chris Hinton	.06	.03	.00
□	208	Duane Bickett	.06	.03	.00
□	209	Chris Chandler	.15	.07	.01
□	210	Jon Hand	.06	.03	.00
□	211	Ray Donaldson	.03	.01	.00
□	212	Dean Biasucci	.03	.01	.00
□	213	Bill Brooks	.06	.03	.00
□	214	Chris Goode	.08	.04	.01
□	215	Clarence Verdin	.08	.04	.01
□	216	Albert Bentley	.06	.03	.00
□	217	Passing Leaders	.08	.04	.01
		Wade Wilson			
		Boomer Esiason			
□	218	Receiving Leaders	.08	.04	.01
		Henry Ellard			
		Al Toon			
□	219	Rushing Leaders	.15	.07	.01
		Herschel Walker			
		Eric Dickerson			
□	220	Scoring Leaders	.06	.03	.00
		Mike Cofer			
		Scott Norwood			
□	221	Intercept Leaders	.06	.03	.00
		Scott Case			
		Erik McMillan			
□	222	Jets Team	.06	.03	.00
		Ken O'Brien Surveys			
		Scene			
□	223	Erik McMillan	.25	.12	.02
□	224	James Hasty	.12	.06	.01
□	225	Al Toon	.12	.06	.01

□	226	John Booty	.10	.05	.01
□	227	Johnny Hector	.06	.03	.00
□	228	Ken O'Brien	.10	.05	.01
□	229	Marty Lyons	.06	.03	.00
□	230	Mickey Shuler	.03	.01	.00
□	231	Robin Cole	.03	.01	.00
□	232	Freeman McNeil	.08	.04	.01
□	233	Marion Barber	.08	.04	.01
□	234	Jo Jo Townsell	.06	.03	.00
□	235	Wesley Walker	.08	.04	.01
□	236	Roger Vick	.06	.03	.00
□	237	Pat Leahy	.03	.01	.00
□	238	Broncos Team UER	.08	.04	.01
		John Elway Ground Attack			
		(Score of week 15 says			
		42-21, should be 42-14)			
□	239	Mike Horan	.03	.01	.00
□	240	Tony Dorsett	.15	.07	.01
□	241	John Elway	.30	.15	.03
□	242	Mark Jackson	.08	.04	.01
□	243	Sammy Winder	.06	.03	.00
□	244	Rich Karlis	.03	.01	.00
□	245	Vance Johnson	.08	.04	.01
□	246	Steve Sewell	.20	.10	.02
□	247	Karl Mecklenburg UER	.08	.04	.01
		(Drafted 2, should be 12)			
□	248	Rulon Jones	.06	.03	.00
□	249	Simon Fletcher	.20	.10	.02
□	250	Redskins Team	.06	.03	.00
		Doug Williams Sets Up			
□	251	Chip Lohmiller	.15	.07	.01
□	252	Jamie Morris	.08	.04	.01
□	253	Mark Rypien UER	2.00	1.00	.20
		(14 1988 completions,			
		should be 114)			
□	254	Barry Wilburn	.03	.01	.00
□	255	Mark May	.10	.05	.01
□	256	Wilber Marshall	.06	.03	.00
□	257	Charles Mann	.06	.03	.00
□	258	Gary Clark	.20	.10	.02
□	259	Doug Williams	.06	.03	.00
□	260	Art Monk	.20	.10	.02
□	261	Kelvin Bryant	.06	.03	.00
□	262	Dexter Manley	.06	.03	.00
□	263	Ricky Sanders	.12	.06	.01
□	264	Raiders Team	.08	.04	.01
		Marcus Allen Through			
		the Line			
□	265	Tim Brown	.50	.25	.05
□	266	Jay Schroeder	.12	.06	.01
□	267	Marcus Allen	.10	.05	.01
□	268	Mike Haynes	.06	.03	.00
□	269	Bo Jackson	.70	.35	.07
□	270	Steve Beuerlein	.45	.22	.04
□	271	Vann McElroy	.03	.01	.00
□	272	Willie Gault	.08	.04	.01
□	273	Howie Long	.08	.04	.01

☐ 274 Greg Townsend	.06	.03	.00
☐ 275 Mike Wise	.08	.04	.01
☐ 276 Cardinals Team	.06	.03	.00
Neil Lomax Looks Long			
☐ 277 Luis Sharpe	.03	.01	.00
☐ 278 Scott Dill	.08	.04	.01
☐ 279 Vai Sikahema	.06	.03	.00
☐ 280 Ron Wolfley	.03	.01	.00
☐ 281 David Galloway	.03	.01	.00
☐ 282 Jay Novacek	.50	.25	.05
☐ 283 Neil Lomax	.08	.04	.01
☐ 284 Robert Awalt	.06	.03	.00
☐ 285 Cedric Mack	.03	.01	.00
☐ 286 Freddie Joe Nunn	.03	.01	.00
☐ 287 J.T. Smith	.06	.03	.00
☐ 288 Stump Mitchell	.06	.03	.00
☐ 289 Roy Green	.08	.04	.01
☐ 290 Dolphins Team	.15	.07	.01
Dan Marino High and Far			
☐ 291 Jarvis Williams	.12	.06	.01
☐ 292 Troy Stradford	.06	.03	.00
☐ 293 Dan Marino	.50	.25	.05
☐ 294 T.J. Turner	.06	.03	.00
☐ 295 John Offerdahl	.06	.03	.00
☐ 296 Ferrell Edmunds	.15	.07	.01
☐ 297 Scott Schwedes	.10	.05	.01
☐ 298 Lorenzo Hampton	.03	.01	.00
☐ 299 Jim Jensen	.10	.05	.01
☐ 300 Brian Sochia	.08	.04	.01
☐ 301 Reggie Roby	.03	.01	.00
☐ 302 Mark Clayton	.12	.06	.01
☐ 303 Chargers Team	.06	.03	.00
Tim Spencer Leads			
the Way			
☐ 304 Lee Williams	.06	.03	.00
☐ 305 Gary Plummer	.08	.04	.01
☐ 306 Gary Anderson	.08	.04	.01
☐ 307 Gill Byrd	.06	.03	.00
☐ 308 Jamie Holland	.08	.04	.01
☐ 309 Billy Ray Smith	.06	.03	.00
☐ 310 Lionel James	.06	.03	.00
☐ 311 Mark Vlasic	.30	.15	.03
☐ 312 Curtis Adams	.03	.01	.00
☐ 313 Anthony Miller	.60	.30	.06
☐ 314 Steelers Team	.06	.03	.00
Frank Pollard Set			
for Action			
☐ 315 Bubby Brister	.35	.17	.03
☐ 316 David Little	.03	.01	.00
☐ 317 Tunch Ilkin	.08	.04	.01
☐ 318 Louis Lipps	.08	.04	.01
☐ 319 Warren Williams	.12	.06	.01
☐ 320 Dwight Stone	.03	.01	.00
☐ 321 Merril Hoge	.20	.10	.02
☐ 322 Thomas Everett	.12	.06	.01
☐ 323 Rod Woodson	.25	.12	.02
☐ 324 Gary Anderson	.03	.01	.00

☐ 325 Buccaneers Team	.06	.03	.00
Ron Hall in Pursuit			
☐ 326 Donnie Elder	.08	.04	.01
☐ 327 Vinny Testaverde	.10	.05	.01
☐ 328 Harry Hamilton	.03	.01	.00
☐ 329 James Wilder	.06	.03	.00
☐ 330 Lars Tate	.12	.06	.01
☐ 331 Mark Carrier	.35	.17	.03
☐ 332 Bruce Hill	.25	.12	.02
☐ 333 Paul Gruber	.15	.07	.01
☐ 334 Ricky Reynolds	.10	.05	.01
☐ 335 Eugene Marve	.03	.01	.00
☐ 336 Falcons Team	.06	.03	.00
Joel Williams Holds On			
☐ 337 Aundray Bruce	.10	.05	.01
☐ 338 John Rade	.03	.01	.00
☐ 339 Scott Case	.12	.06	.01
☐ 340 Robert Moore	.08	.04	.01
☐ 341 Chris Miller	1.25	.60	.12
☐ 342 Gerald Riggs	.10	.05	.01
☐ 343 Gene Lang	.08	.04	.01
☐ 344 Marcus Cotton	.10	.05	.01
☐ 345 Rick Donnelly	.03	.01	.00
☐ 346 John Settle	.20	.10	.02
☐ 347 Bill Fralic	.06	.03	.00
☐ 348 Chiefs Team	.06	.03	.00
Dino Hackett Zeros In			
☐ 349 Steve DeBerg	.10	.05	.01
☐ 350 Mike Stensrud	.10	.05	.01
☐ 351 Dino Hackett	.06	.03	.00
☐ 352 Deron Cherry	.06	.03	.00
☐ 353 Christian Okoye	.25	.12	.02
☐ 354 Bill Maas	.06	.03	.00
☐ 355 Carlos Carson	.06	.03	.00
☐ 356 Albert Lewis	.08	.04	.01
☐ 357 Paul Palmer	.06	.03	.00
☐ 358 Nick Lowery	.06	.03	.00
☐ 359 Stephone Paige	.06	.03	.00
☐ 360 Lions Team	.06	.03	.00
Chuck Long Gets			
the Snap			
☐ 361 Chris Spielman	.30	.15	.03
☐ 362 Jim Arnold	.03	.01	.00
☐ 363 Devon Mitchell	.03	.01	.00
☐ 364 Mike Cofer	.06	.03	.00
☐ 365 Bennie Blades	.30	.15	.03
☐ 366 James Jones	.06	.03	.00
☐ 367 Garry James	.06	.03	.00
☐ 368 Pete Mandley	.03	.01	.00
☐ 369 Keith Ferguson	.06	.03	.00
☐ 370 Dennis Gibson	.06	.03	.00
☐ 371 Packers Team UER	.06	.03	.00
Johnny Holland Over			
the Top (Week 16 has			
vs. Vikings, but			
they played Bears)			
☐ 372 Brent Fullwood	.10	.05	.01

☐ 373	Don Majkowski	.60	.30	.06
☐ 374	Tim Harris	.08	.04	.01
☐ 375	Keith Woodside	.15	.07	.01
☐ 376	Mark Murphy	.06	.03	.00
☐ 377	Dave Brown	.06	.03	.00
☐ 378	Perry Kemp	.10	.05	.01
☐ 379	Sterling Sharpe	1.50	.75	.15
☐ 380	Chuck Cecil	.10	.05	.01
☐ 381	Walter Stanley	.06	.03	.00
☐ 382	Cowboys Team	.06	.03	.00
	Steve Pelluer Lets			
	It Go			
☐ 383	Michael Irvin	2.00	1.00	.20
☐ 384	Bill Bates	.06	.03	.00
☐ 385	Herschel Walker	.35	.17	.03
☐ 386	Darryl Clack	.03	.01	.00
☐ 387	Danny Noonan	.08	.04	.01
☐ 388	Eugene Lockhart	.08	.04	.01
☐ 389	Ed Too Tall Jones	.08	.04	.01
☐ 390	Steve Pelluer	.06	.03	.00
☐ 391	Ray Alexander	.08	.04	.01
☐ 392	Nate Newton	.08	.04	.01
☐ 393	Garry Cobb	.03	.01	.00
☐ 394	Checklist 1-132	.06	.01	.00
☐ 395	Checklist 133-264	.06	.01	.00
☐ 396	Checklist 265-396	.08	.01	.00

1989 Topps Traded

The 1989 Topps Traded set contains 132 standard-size (2 1/2" by 3 1/2") cards, numbered with the suffix "T". The cards are nearly identical to the 1989 Topps regular issue football set, except this traded series was printed on white stock and was distributed

only as a boxed set. The key rookie cards in this set are Troy Aikman, Marion Butts, Bobby Humphrey, Dave Meggett, Eric Metcalf, Rodney Peete, Andre Rison, Barry Sanders, Deion Sanders, Sammie Smith, Derrick Thomas, and Steve Walsh.

	MINT	EXC	G-VG
COMPLETE SET (132)	8.00	4.00	.80
COMMON PLAYER (1T-132T)	.03	.01	.00

☐ 1T	Eric Ball	.10	.05	.01
	Cincinnati Bengals			
☐ 2T	Tony Mandarich	.15	.07	.01
	Green Bay Packers			
☐ 3T	Shawn Collins	.15	.07	.01
	Atlanta Falcons			
☐ 4T	Ray Bentley	.10	.05	.01
	Buffalo Bills			
☐ 5T	Tony Casillas	.08	.04	.01
	Atlanta Falcons			
☐ 6T	Al Del Greco	.08	.04	.01
	Phoenix Cardinals			
☐ 7T	Dan Saleaumua	.08	.04	.01
	Kansas City Chiefs			
☐ 8T	Keith Bishop	.03	.01	.00
	Denver Broncos			
☐ 9T	Rodney Peete	.25	.12	.02
	Detroit Lions			
☐ 10T	Lorenzo White	.15	.07	.01
	Houston Oilers			
☐ 11T	Steve Smith	.10	.05	.01
	Los Angeles Raiders			
☐ 12T	Pete Mandley	.03	.01	.00
	Kansas City Chiefs			
☐ 13T	Mervyn Fernandez	.20	.10	.02
	Los Angeles Raiders			
☐ 14T	Flipper Anderson	.20	.10	.02
	Los Angeles Rams			
☐ 15T	Louis Oliver	.10	.05	.01
	Miami Dolphins			
☐ 16T	Rick Fenney	.10	.05	.01
	Minnesota Vikings			
☐ 17T	Gary Jeter	.06	.03	.00
	New England Patriots			
☐ 18T	Greg Cox	.08	.04	.01
	New York Giants			
☐ 19T	Bubba McDowell	.15	.07	.01
	Houston Oilers			
☐ 20T	Ron Heller	.06	.03	.00
	Philadelphia Eagles			
☐ 21T	Tim McDonald	.12	.06	.01
	Phoenix Cardinals			
☐ 22T	Jerrol Williams	.10	.05	.01
	Pittsburgh Steelers			
☐ 23T	Marion Butts	.50	.25	.05
	San Diego Chargers			

☐ 24T	Steve Young 15	.07	.01
	San Francisco 49ers		
☐ 25T	Mike Merriweather 06	.03	.00
	Minnesota Vikings		
☐ 26T	Richard Johnson 08	.04	.01
	Detroit Lions		
☐ 27T	Gerald Riggs 08	.04	.01
	Washington Redskins		
☐ 28T	Dave Waymer 03	.01	.00
	New Orleans Saints		
☐ 29T	Issiac Holt 03	.01	.00
	Dallas Cowboys		
☐ 30T	Deion Sanders 1.00	.50	.10
	Atlanta Falcons		
☐ 31T	Todd Blackledge 06	.03	.00
	Pittsburgh Steelers		
☐ 32T	Jeff Cross 10	.05	.01
	Miami Dolphins		
☐ 33T	Steve Wisniewski 15	.07	.01
	Los Angeles Raiders		
☐ 34T	Ron Brown 06	.03	.00
	Los Angeles Rams		
☐ 35T	Rod Bernstine 20	.10	.02
	San Diego Chargers		
☐ 36T	Jeff Uhlenhake 08	.04	.01
	Miami Dolphins		
☐ 37T	Donnell Woolford 12	.06	.01
	Chicago Bears		
☐ 38T	Bob Gagliano 10	.05	.01
	Detroit Lions		
☐ 39T	Ezra Johnson 03	.01	.00
	Indianapolis Colts		
☐ 40T	Ron Jaworski 06	.03	.00
	Kansas City Chiefs		
☐ 41T	Lawyer Tillman 12	.06	.01
	Clevelands Browns		
☐ 42T	Lorenzo Lynch 08	.04	.01
	Chicago Bears		
☐ 43T	Mike Alexander 08	.04	.01
	Los Angeles Raiders		
☐ 44T	Tim Worley 08	.04	.01
	Pittsburgh Steelers		
☐ 45T	Guy Bingham 08	.04	.01
	Atlanta Falcons		
☐ 46T	Cleveland Gary 15	.07	.01
	Los Angeles Rams		
☐ 47T	Danny Peebles 03	.01	.00
	Tampa Bay Buccaneers		
☐ 48T	Clarence Weathers 08	.04	.01
	Kansas City Chiefs		
☐ 49T	Jeff Lageman 15	.07	.01
	New York Jets		
☐ 50T	Eric Metcalf 20	.10	.02
	Cleveland Browns		
☐ 51T	Myron Guyton 10	.05	.01
	New York Giants		
☐ 52T	Steve Atwater 25	.12	.02

	Denver Broncos		
☐ 53T	John Fourcade 08	.04	.01
	New Orleans Saints		
☐ 54T	Randall McDaniel 10	.05	.01
	Minnesota Vikings		
☐ 55T	Al Noga 08	.04	.01
	Minnesota Vikings		
☐ 56T	Sammie Smith 35	.17	.03
	Miami Dolphins		
☐ 57T	Jesse Solomon 03	.01	.00
	Dallas Cowboys		
☐ 58T	Greg Kragen 08	.04	.01
	Denver Broncos		
☐ 59T	Don Beebe 30	.15	.03
	Buffalo Bills		
☐ 60T	Hart Lee Dykes 15	.07	.01
	New England Patriots		
☐ 61T	Trace Armstrong 12	.06	.01
	Chicago Bears		
☐ 62T	Steve Pelluer 06	.03	.00
	Kansas City Chiefs		
☐ 63T	Barry Krauss 03	.01	.00
	Miami Dolphins		
☐ 64T	Kevin Murphy 08	.04	.01
	Tampa Bay Buccaneers		
☐ 65T	Steve Tasker 15	.07	.01
	Buffalo Bills		
☐ 66T	Jessie Small 15	.07	.01
	Philadelphia Eagles		
☐ 67T	Dave Meggett 40	.20	.04
	New York Giants		
☐ 68T	Dean Hamel 08	.04	.01
	Dallas Cowboys		
☐ 69T	Jim Covert 06	.03	.00
	Chicago Bears		
☐ 70T	Troy Aikman 2.25	1.10	.22
	Dallas Cowboys		
☐ 71T	Raul Allegre 03	.01	.00
	New York Giants		
☐ 72T	Chris Jacke 08	.04	.01
	Green Bay Packers		
☐ 73T	Leslie O'Neal 06	.03	.00
	San Diego Chargers		
☐ 74T	Keith Taylor 10	.05	.01
	Indianapolis Colts		
☐ 75T	Steve Walsh 30	.15	.03
	Dallas Cowboys		
☐ 76T	Tracy Rocker 12	.06	.01
	Washington Redskins		
☐ 77T	Robert Massey 10	.05	.01
	New Orleans Saints		
☐ 78T	Bryan Wagner 08	.04	.01
	Cleveland Browns		
☐ 79T	Steve DeOssie 08	.04	.01
	New York Giants		
☐ 80T	Carnell Lake 10	.05	.01
	Pittsburgh Steelers		

☐ 81T Frank Reich	.15	.07	.01
Buffalo Bills			
☐ 82T Tyrone Braxton	.12	.06	.01
Denver Broncos			
☐ 83T Barry Sanders	4.00	2.00	.40
Detroit Lions			
☐ 84T Pete Stoyanovich	.08	.04	.01
Miami Dolphins			
☐ 85T Paul Palmer	.06	.03	.00
Dallas Cowboys			
☐ 86T Billy Joe Tolliver	.20	.10	.02
San Diego Chargers			
☐ 87T Eric Hill	.10	.05	.01
Phoenix Cardinals			
☐ 88T Gerald McNeil	.06	.03	.00
Cleveland Browns			
☐ 89T Bill Hawkins	.08	.04	.01
Los Angeles Rams			
☐ 90T Derrick Thomas	.75	.35	.07
Kansas City Chiefs			
☐ 91T Jim Harbaugh	.35	.17	.03
Chicago Bears			
☐ 92T Brian Williams	.08	.04	.01
New York Giants			
☐ 93T Jack Trudeau	.06	.03	.00
Indianapolis Colts			
☐ 94T Leonard Smith	.03	.01	.00
Buffalo Bills			
☐ 95T Gary Hogeboom	.06	.03	.00
Phoenix Cardinals			
☐ 96T A.J. Johnson	.08	.04	.01
Washington Redskins			
☐ 97T Jim McMahon	.08	.04	.01
San Diego Chargers			
☐ 98T David Williams	.08	.04	.01
Houston Oilers			
☐ 99T Rohn Stark	.03	.01	.00
Indianapolis Colts			
☐ 100T Sean Landeta	.03	.01	.00
New York Giants			
☐ 101T Tim Johnson	.08	.04	.01
Pittsburgh Steelers			
☐ 102T Andre Rison	.75	.35	.07
Indianapolis Colts			
☐ 103T Earnest Byner	.08	.04	.01
Washington Redskins			
☐ 104T Don McPherson	.08	.04	.01
Philadelphia Eagles			
☐ 105T Zefross Moss	.08	.04	.01
Indianapolis Colts			
☐ 106T Frank Stams	.10	.05	.01
Los Angeles Rams			
☐ 107T Courtney Hall	.10	.05	.01
San Diego Chargers			
☐ 108T Marc Logan	.08	.04	.01
Miami Dolphins			
☐ 109T James Lofton	.12	.06	.01
Buffalo Bills			
☐ 110T Lewis Tillman	.10	.05	.01
New York Giants			
☐ 111T Irv Pankey	.08	.04	.01
Los Angeles Rams			
☐ 112T Ralf Mojsiejenko	.03	.01	.00
Washington Redskins			
☐ 113T Bobby Humphrey	.50	.25	.05
Denver Broncos			
☐ 114T Chris Burkett	.06	.03	.00
New York Jets			
☐ 115T Greg Lloyd	.10	.05	.01
Pittsburgh Steelers			
☐ 116T Matt Millen	.06	.03	.00
San Francisco 49ers			
☐ 117T Carl Zander	.03	.01	.00
Cincinnati Bengals			
☐ 118T Wayne Martin	.08	.04	.01
New Orleans Saints			
☐ 119T Mike Saxon	.08	.04	.01
Dallas Cowboys			
☐ 120T Herschel Walker	.15	.07	.01
Minnesota Vikings			
☐ 121T Andy Heck	.08	.04	.01
Seattle Seahawks			
☐ 122T Mark Robinson	.08	.04	.01
Tampa Bay Buccaneers			
☐ 123T Keith Van Horne	.10	.05	.01
Chicago Bears			
☐ 124T Ricky Hunley	.08	.04	.01
Los Angeles Raiders			
☐ 125T Timm Rosenbach	.20	.10	.02
Phoenix Cardinals			
☐ 126T Steve Grogan	.08	.04	.01
New England Patriots			
☐ 127T Stephen Braggs	.08	.04	.01
Cleveland Browns			
☐ 128T Terry Long	.08	.04	.01
Pittsburgh Steelers			
☐ 129T Evan Cooper	.08	.04	.01
Atlanta Falcons			
☐ 130T Robert Lyles	.08	.04	.01
Houston Oilers			
☐ 131T Mike Webster	.08	.04	.01
Kansas City Chiefs			
☐ 132T Checklist 1-132	.06	.01	.00

1990 Topps

This 528-card set is similar to the Topps football efforts of the past few years. The cards are standard size, 2 1/2" by 3 1/2". The cards are arranged in team order and the teams themselves are ordered according to their finish in the 1989 standings, e.g., San Francisco 49ers (6-27), Denver Broncos (29-47), New York Giants (48-66), Los Angeles Rams (67-83), Philadelphia Eagles (84-101), Minnesota Vikings (102-119), Washington Redskins (120-138), Green Bay Packers (139-155), Cleveland Browns (156-174), Pittsburgh Steelers (175-192), Buffalo Bills (194-211), Houston Oilers (212-228), New Orleans Saints (230-246), Kansas City Chiefs (247-264), Cincinnati Bengals (265-280), Los Angeles Raiders (281-297), Indianapolis Colts (298-316), Miami Dolphins (317-334), Seattle Seahawks (335-348), Detroit Lions (349-364), Chicago Bears (365-381), San Diego Chargers (382-398), Tampa Bay Buccaneers (399-415), New England Patriots (416-430), Phoenix Cardinals (432-447), New York Jets (448-465), Atlanta Falcons (466-480), Dallas Cowboys (481-496), Checklists (497-500), and Team Cards (501-528). Topps also produced a Tiffany edition of the set; this upscale version features exactly the same cards, but with a glossy coating on white card stock. Individual card Tiffany values are approximately five times the values listed below. The key rookies in this set are Jeff George, Rodney Hampton, Michael Haynes, Haywood Jeffires, Blair Thomas, and Andre Ware.

	MINT	EXC	G-VG
COMPLETE SET (528)	12.50	6.25	1.25
COMMON PLAYER (1-528)	.03	.01	.00

☐ 1 Joe Montana RB Most TD Passes, Super Bowl	.20	.07	.01
☐ 2 Flipper Anderson RB Most Receiving Yards, Game	.06	.03	.00
☐ 3 Troy Aikman RB Most Passing Yards, Game, Rookie	.15	.07	.01
☐ 4 Kevin Butler RB Most Consecutive Field Goals	.06	.03	.00
☐ 5 Super Bowl XXIV 49ers 55 Broncos 10 (line of scrimmage)	.06	.03	.00
☐ 6 Dexter Carter	.25	.12	.02
☐ 7 Matt Millen	.06	.03	.00
☐ 8 Jerry Rice	.40	.20	.04
☐ 9 Ronnie Lott	.10	.05	.01
☐ 10 John Taylor	.15	.07	.01
☐ 11 Guy McIntyre	.06	.03	.00
☐ 12 Roger Craig	.10	.05	.01
☐ 13 Joe Montana	.50	.25	.05
☐ 14 Brent Jones	.15	.07	.01
☐ 15 Tom Rathman	.06	.03	.00
☐ 16 Harris Barton	.06	.03	.00
☐ 17 Charles Haley	.06	.03	.00
☐ 18 Pierce Holt	.08	.04	.01
☐ 19 Michael Carter	.06	.03	.00
☐ 20 Chet Brooks	.08	.04	.01
☐ 21 Eric Wright	.03	.01	.00
☐ 22 Mike Cofer	.03	.01	.00
☐ 23 Jim Fahnhorst	.06	.03	.00
☐ 24 Keena Turner	.03	.01	.00
☐ 25 Don Griffin	.03	.01	.00
☐ 26 Kevin Fagan	.08	.04	.01
☐ 27 Bubba Paris	.03	.01	.00
☐ 28 Rushing Leaders Barry Sanders Christian Okoye	.15	.07	.01
☐ 29 Steve Atwater	.06	.03	.00
☐ 30 Tyrone Braxton	.03	.01	.00
☐ 31 Ron Holmes	.03	.01	.00
☐ 32 Bobby Humphrey	.12	.06	.01
☐ 33 Greg Kragen	.03	.01	.00
☐ 34 David Treadwell	.06	.03	.00
☐ 35 Karl Mecklenburg	.06	.03	.00
☐ 36 Dennis Smith	.03	.01	.00
☐ 37 John Elway	.20	.10	.02
☐ 38 Vance Johnson	.06	.03	.00
☐ 39 Simon Fletcher UER (Front DL, back LB)	.03	.01	.00
☐ 40 Jim Juriga	.08	.04	.01
☐ 41 Mark Jackson	.06	.03	.00
☐ 42 Melvin Bratton	.12	.06	.01
☐ 43 Wymon Henderson	.06	.03	.00

☐ 44 Ken Bell	.06	.03	.00	☐ 101 Wes Hopkins	.03	.01	.00
☐ 45 Sammy Winder	.06	.03	.00	☐ 102 Kirk Lowdermilk	.06	.03	.00
☐ 46 Alphonso Carreker	.03	.01	.00	☐ 103 Rick Fenney	.06	.03	.00
☐ 47 Orson Mobley	.10	.05	.01	☐ 104 Randall McDaniel	.06	.03	.00
☐ 48 Rodney Hampton	.75	.35	.07	☐ 105 Herschel Walker	.15	.07	.01
☐ 49 Dave Meggett	.15	.07	.01	☐ 106 Al Noga	.03	.01	.00
☐ 50 Myron Guyton	.06	.03	.00	☐ 107 Gary Zimmerman	.03	.01	.00
☐ 51 Phil Simms	.10	.05	.01	☐ 108 Chris Doleman	.06	.03	.00
☐ 52 Lawrence Taylor	.10	.05	.01	☐ 109 Keith Millard	.06	.03	.00
☐ 53 Carl Banks	.06	.03	.00	☐ 110 Carl Lee	.03	.01	.00
☐ 54 Pepper Johnson	.06	.03	.00	☐ 111 Joey Browner	.06	.03	.00
☐ 55 Leonard Marshall	.06	.03	.00	☐ 112 Steve Jordan	.06	.03	.00
☐ 56 Mark Collins	.06	.03	.00	☐ 113 Reggie Rutland	.08	.04	.01
☐ 57 Erik Howard	.03	.01	.00	☐ 114 Wade Wilson	.08	.04	.01
☐ 58 Eric Dorsey	.15	.07	.01	☐ 115 Anthony Carter	.08	.04	.01
☐ 59 Ottis Anderson	.08	.04	.01	☐ 116 Rick Karlis	.03	.01	.00
☐ 60 Mark Bavaro	.06	.03	.00	☐ 117 Hassan Jones	.06		
☐ 61 Odessa Turner	.20	.10	.02			.03	.00
☐ 62 Gary Reasons	.03	.01	.00	☐ 118 Henry Thomas	.03	.01	.00
☐ 63 Maurice Carthon	.03	.01	.00	☐ 119 Scott Studwell	.03	.01	.00
☐ 64 Lionel Manuel	.03	.01	.00	☐ 120 Ralf Mojsiejenko	.03	.01	.00
☐ 65 Sean Landeta	.03	.01	.00	☐ 121 Earnest Byner	.08	.04	.01
☐ 66 Perry Williams	.06	.03	.00	☐ 122 Gerald Riggs	.06	.03	.00
☐ 67 Pat Terrell	.15	.07	.01	☐ 123 Tracy Rocker	.06	.03	.00
☐ 68 Flipper Anderson	.10	.05	.01	☐ 124 A.J. Johnson	.06	.03	.00
☐ 69 Jackie Slater	.06	.03	.00	☐ 125 Charles Mann	.06	.03	.00
☐ 70 Tom Newberry	.06	.03	.00	☐ 126 Art Monk	.15	.07	.01
☐ 71 Jerry Gray	.03	.01	.00	☐ 127 Ricky Sanders	.08	.04	.01
☐ 72 Henry Ellard	.08	.04	.01	☐ 128 Gary Clark	.15	.07	.01
☐ 73 Doug Smith	.03	.01	.00	☐ 129 Jim Lachey	.06	.03	.00
☐ 74 Kevin Greene	.06	.03	.00	☐ 130 Martin Mayhew	.08	.04	.01
☐ 75 Jim Everett	.12	.06	.01	☐ 131 Ravin Caldwell	.08	.04	.01
☐ 76 Mike Lansford	.03	.01	.00	☐ 132 Don Warren	.06	.03	.00
☐ 77 Greg Bell	.06	.03	.00	☐ 133 Mark Rypien	.35	.17	.03
☐ 78 Pete Holohan	.03	.01	.00	☐ 134 Ed Simmons	.08	.04	.01
☐ 79 Robert Delpino	.06	.03	.00	☐ 135 Darryl Grant	.06	.03	.00
☐ 80 Mike Wilcher	.03	.01	.00	☐ 136 Darrell Green	.15	.07	.01
☐ 81 Mike Piel	.10	.05	.01	☐ 137 Chip Lohmiller	.03	.01	.00
☐ 82 Mel Owens	.06	.03	.00	☐ 138 Tony Bennett	.20	.10	.02
☐ 83 Michael Stewart	.08	.04	.01	☐ 139 Tony Mandarich	.06	.03	.00
☐ 84 Ben Smith	.08	.04	.01	☐ 140 Sterling Sharpe	.15	.07	.01
☐ 85 Keith Jackson	.10	.05	.01	☐ 141 Tim Harris	.06	.03	.00
☐ 86 Reggie White	.08	.04	.01	☐ 142 Don Majkowski	.10	.05	.01
☐ 87 Eric Allen	.06	.03	.00	☐ 143 Rich Moran	.10	.05	.01
☐ 88 Jerome Brown	.06	.03	.00	☐ 144 Jeff Query	.06	.03	.00
☐ 89 Robert Drummond	.06	.03	.00	☐ 145 Brent Fullwood	.06	.03	.00
☐ 90 Anthony Toney	.03	.01	.00	☐ 146 Chris Jacke	.03	.01	.00
☐ 91 Keith Byars	.06	.03	.00	☐ 147 Keith Woodside	.06	.03	.00
☐ 92 Cris Carter	.08	.04	.01	☐ 148 Perry Kemp	.06	.03	.00
☐ 93 Randall Cunningham	.15	.07	.01	☐ 149 Herman Fontenot	.03	.01	.00
☐ 94 Ron Johnson	.06	.03	.00	☐ 150 Dave Brown	.03	.01	.00
☐ 95 Mike Quick	.06	.03	.00	☐ 151 Brian Noble	.03	.01	.00
☐ 96 Clyde Simmons	.06	.03	.00	☐ 152 Johnny Holland	.03	.01	.00
☐ 97 Mike Pitts	.03	.01	.00	☐ 153 Mark Murphy	.03	.01	.00
☐ 98 Izel Jenkins	.10	.05	.01	☐ 154 Bob Nelson	.10	.05	.01
☐ 99 Seth Joyner	.06	.03	.00	☐ 155 Darrell Thompson	.25	.12	.02
☐ 100 Mike Schad	.08	.04	.01	☐ 156 Lawyer Tillman	.06	.03	.00
				☐ 157 Eric Metcalf	.08	.04	.01

☐ 158 Webster Slaughter	.06	.03	.00
☐ 159 Frank Minnifield	.03	.01	.00
☐ 160 Brian Brennan	.03	.01	.00
☐ 161 Thane Gash	.08	.04	.01
☐ 162 Robert Banks	.10	.05	.01
☐ 163 Bernie Kosar	.15	.07	.01
☐ 164 David Grayson	.06	.03	.00
☐ 165 Kevin Mack	.06	.03	.00
☐ 166 Mike Johnson	.03	.01	.00
☐ 167 Tim Manoa	.08	.04	.01
☐ 168 Ozzie Newsome	.08	.04	.01
☐ 169 Felix Wright	.03	.01	.00
☐ 170 Al(Bubba) Baker	.03	.01	.00
☐ 171 Reggie Langhorne	.03	.01	.00
☐ 172 Clay Matthews	.03	.01	.00
☐ 173 Andrew Stewart	.08	.04	.01
☐ 174 Barry Foster	.30	.15	.03
☐ 175 Tim Worley	.06	.03	.00
☐ 176 Tim Johnson	.03	.01	.00
☐ 177 Carnell Lake	.03	.01	.00
☐ 178 Greg Lloyd	.03	.01	.00
☐ 179 Rod Woodson	.08	.04	.01
☐ 180 Tunch Ilkin	.03	.01	.00
☐ 181 Dermontti Dawson	.06	.03	.00
☐ 182 Gary Anderson	.03	.01	.00
☐ 183 Bubby Brister	.10	.05	.01
☐ 184 Louis Lipps	.08	.04	.01
☐ 185 Merril Hoge	.06	.03	.00
☐ 186 Mike Mularkey	.10	.05	.01
☐ 187 Derek Hill	.08	.04	.01
☐ 188 Rodney Carter	.06	.03	.00
☐ 189 Dwayne Woodruff	.03	.01	.00
☐ 190 Keith Willis	.03	.01	.00
☐ 191 Jerry Olsavsky	.08	.04	.01
☐ 192 Mark Stock	.08	.04	.01
☐ 193 Sacks Leaders	.06	.03	.00
Chris Doleman			
Lee Williams			
☐ 194 Leonard Smith	.03	.01	.00
☐ 195 Darryl Talley	.06	.03	.00
☐ 196 Mark Kelso	.03	.01	.00
☐ 197 Kent Hull	.03	.01	.00
☐ 198 Nate Odomes	.10	.05	.01
☐ 199 Pete Metzelaars	.03	.01	.00
☐ 200 Don Beebe	.10	.05	.01
☐ 201 Ray Bentley	.06	.03	.00
☐ 202 Steve Tasker	.06	.03	.00
☐ 203 Scott Norwood	.03	.01	.00
☐ 204 Andre Reed	.10	.05	.01
☐ 205 Bruce Smith	.08	.04	.01
☐ 206 Thurman Thomas	.60	.30	.06
☐ 207 Jim Kelly	.35	.17	.03
☐ 208 Cornelius Bennett	.12	.06	.01
☐ 209 Shane Conlan	.06	.03	.00
☐ 210 Larry Kinnebrew	.03	.01	.00
☐ 211 Jeff Alm	.08	.04	.01
☐ 212 Robert Lyles	.03	.01	.00
☐ 213 Bubba McDowell	.06	.03	.00
☐ 214 Mike Munchak	.06	.03	.00
☐ 215 Bruce Matthews	.03	.01	.00
☐ 216 Warren Moon	.25	.12	.02
☐ 217 Drew Hill	.08	.04	.01
☐ 218 Ray Childress	.06	.03	.00
☐ 219 Steve Brown	.03	.01	.00
☐ 220 Alonzo Highsmith	.06	.03	.00
☐ 221 Allen Pinkett	.06	.03	.00
☐ 222 Sean Jones	.03	.01	.00
☐ 223 Johnny Meads	.06	.03	.00
☐ 224 John Grimsley	.03	.01	.00
☐ 225 Haywood Jeffires	.60	.30	.06
☐ 226 Curtis Duncan	.03	.01	.00
☐ 227 Greg Montgomery	.08	.04	.01
☐ 228 Ernest Givins	.08	.04	.01
☐ 229 Passing Leaders	.15	.07	.01
Joe Montana			
Boomer Esiason			
☐ 230 Robert Massey	.03	.01	.00
☐ 231 John Fourcade	.08	.04	.01
☐ 232 Dalton Hilliard	.06	.03	.00
☐ 233 Vaughan Johnson	.06	.03	.00
☐ 234 Hoby Brenner	.03	.01	.00
☐ 235 Pat Swilling	.10	.05	.01
☐ 236 Kevin Haverdink	.08	.04	.01
☐ 237 Bobby Hebert	.08	.04	.01
☐ 238 Sam Mills	.08	.04	.01
☐ 239 Eric Martin	.06	.03	.00
☐ 240 Lonzell Hill	.06	.03	.00
☐ 241 Steve Trapilo	.08	.04	.01
☐ 242 Rickey Jackson	.06	.03	.00
☐ 243 Craig Heyward	.08	.04	.01
☐ 244 Rueben Mayes	.06	.03	.00
☐ 245 Morten Andersen	.06	.03	.00
☐ 246 Percy Snow	.15	.07	.01
☐ 247 Pete Mandley	.03	.01	.00
☐ 248 Derrick Thomas	.25	.12	.02
☐ 249 Dan Saleaumua	.06	.03	.00
☐ 250 Todd McNair	.08	.04	.01
☐ 251 Leonard Griffin	.08	.04	.01
☐ 252 Jonathan Hayes	.06	.03	.00
☐ 253 Christian Okoye	.10	.05	.01
☐ 254 Albert Lewis	.08	.04	.01
☐ 255 Nick Lowery	.06	.03	.00
☐ 256 Kevin Ross	.06	.03	.00
☐ 257 Steve DeBerg UER	.08	.04	.01
(Total 45,046,			
should be 25,046)			
☐ 258 Stephone Paige	.06	.03	.00
☐ 259 James Saxon	.10	.05	.01
☐ 260 Herman Heard	.03	.01	.00
☐ 261 Deron Cherry	.06	.03	.00
☐ 262 Dino Hackett	.03	.01	.00
☐ 263 Neil Smith	.06	.03	.00
☐ 264 Steve Pelluer	.06	.03	.00
☐ 265 Eric Thomas	.06	.03	.00

☐ 266 Eric Ball	.06	.03	.00
☐ 267 Leon White	.06	.03	.00
☐ 268 Tim Krumrie	.03	.01	.00
☐ 269 Jason Buck	.06	.03	.00
☐ 270 Boomer Esiason	.10	.05	.01
☐ 271 Carl Zander	.03	.01	.00
☐ 272 Eddie Brown	.08	.04	.01
☐ 273 David Fulcher	.06	.03	.00
☐ 274 Tim McGee	.08	.04	.01
☐ 275 James Brooks	.08	.04	.01
☐ 276 Rickey Dixon	.15	.07	.01
☐ 277 Ickey Woods	.08	.04	.01
☐ 278 Anthony Munoz	.08	.04	.01
☐ 279 Rodney Holman	.06	.03	.00
☐ 280 Mike Alexander	.06	.03	.00
☐ 281 Mervyn Fernandez	.10	.05	.01
☐ 282 Steve Wisniewski	.03	.01	.00
☐ 283 Steve Smith	.03	.01	.00
☐ 284 Howie Long	.06	.03	.00
☐ 285 Bo Jackson	.40	.20	.04
☐ 286 Mike Dyal	.10	.05	.01
☐ 287 Thomas Benson	.08	.04	.01
☐ 288 Willie Gault	.06	.03	.00
☐ 289 Marcus Allen	.10	.05	.01
☐ 290 Greg Townsend	.06	.03	.00
☐ 291 Steve Beuerlein	.15	.07	.01
☐ 292 Scott Davis	.08	.04	.01
☐ 293 Eddie Anderson	.10	.05	.01
☐ 294 Terry McDaniel	.06	.03	.00
☐ 295 Tim Brown	.10	.05	.01
☐ 296 Bob Golic	.06	.03	.00
☐ 297 Jeff Jaeger	.08	.04	.01
☐ 298 Jeff George	.75	.35	.07
☐ 299 Chip Banks	.06	.03	.00
☐ 300 Andre Rison UER	.20	.10	.02
(Photo actually			
Clarence Weathers)			
☐ 301 Rohn Stark	.03	.01	.00
☐ 302 Keith Taylor	.06	.03	.00
☐ 303 Jack Trudeau	.06	.03	.00
☐ 304 Chris Hinton	.06	.03	.00
☐ 305 Ray Donaldson	.03	.01	.00
☐ 306 Jeff Herrod	.10	.05	.01
☐ 307 Clarence Verdin	.06	.03	.00
☐ 308 Jon Hand	.06	.03	.00
☐ 309 Bill Brooks	.03	.01	.00
☐ 310 Albert Bentley	.06	.03	.00
☐ 311 Mike Prior	.03	.01	.00
☐ 312 Pat Beach	.03	.01	.00
☐ 313 Eugene Daniel	.03	.01	.00
☐ 314 Duane Bickett	.03	.01	.00
☐ 315 Dean Biasucci	.03	.01	.00
☐ 316 Richmond Webb	.15	.07	.01
☐ 317 Jeff Cross	.06	.03	.00
☐ 318 Louis Oliver	.06	.03	.00
☐ 319 Sammie Smith	.10	.05	.01
☐ 320 Pete Stoyanovich	.03	.01	.00

☐ 321 John Offerdahl	.06	.03	.00
☐ 322 Ferrell Edmunds	.03	.01	.00
☐ 323 Dan Marino	.30	.15	.03
☐ 324 Andre Brown	.10	.05	.01
☐ 325 Reggie Roby	.03	.01	.00
☐ 326 Jarvis Williams	.03	.01	.00
☐ 327 Roy Foster	.03	.01	.00
☐ 328 Mark Clayton	.10	.05	.01
☐ 329 Brian Sochia	.03	.01	.00
☐ 330 Mark Duper	.06	.03	.00
☐ 331 T.J. Turner	.03	.01	.00
☐ 332 Jeff Uhlenhake	.03	.01	.00
☐ 333 Jim Jensen	.03	.01	.00
☐ 334 Cortez Kennedy	.30	.15	.03
☐ 335 Andy Heck	.03	.01	.00
☐ 336 Rufus Porter	.03	.01	.00
☐ 337 Brian Blades	.10	.05	.01
☐ 338 Dave Krieg	.08	.04	.01
☐ 339 John L. Williams	.08	.04	.01
☐ 340 David Wyman	.06	.03	.00
☐ 341 Paul Skansi	.08	.04	.01
☐ 342 Eugene Robinson	.03	.01	.00
☐ 343 Joe Nash	.03	.01	.00
☐ 344 Jacob Green	.06	.03	.00
☐ 345 Jeff Bryant	.03	.01	.00
☐ 346 Ruben Rodriguez	.03	.01	.00
☐ 347 Norm Johnson	.03	.01	.00
☐ 348 Darren Comeaux	.08	.04	.01
☐ 349 Andre Ware	.35	.17	.03
☐ 350 Richard Johnson	.06	.03	.00
☐ 351 Rodney Peete	.12	.06	.01
☐ 352 Barry Sanders	.90	.45	.09
☐ 353 Chris Spielman	.06	.03	.00
☐ 354 Eddie Murray	.06	.03	.00
☐ 355 Jerry Ball	.08	.04	.01
☐ 356 Mel Gray	.06	.03	.00
☐ 357 Eric Williams	.08	.04	.01
☐ 358 Robert Clark	.20	.10	.02
☐ 359 Jason Phillips	.10	.05	.01
☐ 360 Terry Taylor	.10	.05	.01
☐ 361 Bennie Blades	.06	.03	.00
☐ 362 Michael Cofer	.03		
		.01	.00
☐ 363 Jim Arnold	.03	.01	.00
☐ 364 Marc Spindler	.08	.04	.01
☐ 365 Jim Covert	.06	.03	.00
☐ 366 Jim Harbaugh	.20	.10	.02
☐ 367 Neal Anderson	.15	.07	.01
☐ 368 Mike Singletary	.08	.04	.01
☐ 369 John Roper	.10	.05	.01
☐ 370 Steve McMichael	.06	.03	.00
☐ 371 Dennis Gentry	.03	.01	.00
☐ 372 Brad Muster	.08	.04	.01
☐ 373 Ron Morris	.06	.03	.00
☐ 374 James Thornton	.06	.03	.00
☐ 375 Kevin Butler	.03	.01	.00
☐ 376 Richard Dent	.08	.04	.01
☐ 377 Dan Hampton	.08	.04	.01

☐ 378 Jay Hilgenberg	.06	.03	.00	☐ 433 Gary Hogeboom	.06	.03	.00
☐ 379 Donnell Woolford	.03	.01	.00	☐ 434 Timm Rosenbach UER	.10	.05	.01
☐ 380 Trace Armstrong	.03	.01	.00	(Born 1967 in Everett,
☐ 381 Junior Seau	.20	.10	.02	Wa., should be 1966
☐ 382 Rod Bernstine	.10	.05	.01	in Missoula, Mont.)
☐ 383 Marion Butts	.15	.07	.01	☐ 435 Tim McDonald	.06	.03	.00
☐ 384 Burt Grossman	.08	.04	.01	☐ 436 Rich Camarillo	.03	.01	.00
☐ 385 Darrin Nelson	.03	.01	.00	☐ 437 Luis Sharpe	.03	.01	.00
☐ 386 Leslie O'Neal	.06	.03	.01	☐ 438 J.T. Smith	.06	.03	.00
☐ 387 Billy Joe Tolliver	.08	.04	.01	☐ 439 Roy Green	.08	.04	.01
☐ 388 Courtney Hall	.03	.01	.00	☐ 440 Ernie Jones	.25	.12	.02
☐ 389 Lee Williams	.06	.03	.00	☐ 441 Robert Awalt	.03	.01	.00
☐ 390 Anthony Miller	.10	.05	.01	☐ 442 Vai Sikahema	.03	.01	.00
☐ 391 Gill Byrd	.06	.03	.00	☐ 443 Joe Wolf	.06	.03	.00
☐ 392 Wayne Walker	.10	.05	.01	☐ 444 Stump Mitchell	.03	.01	.00
☐ 393 Billy Ray Smith	.06	.03	.01	☐ 445 David Galloway	.03	.01	.00
☐ 394 Vencie Glenn	.03	.01	.00	☐ 446 Ron Wolfley	.03	.01	.00
☐ 395 Tim Spencer	.03	.01	.00	☐ 447 Freddie Joe Nunn	.03	.01	.00
☐ 396 Gary Plummer	.03	.01	.00	☐ 448 Blair Thomas	.65	.30	.06
☐ 397 Arthur Cox	.06	.03	.00	☐ 449 Jeff Lageman	.06	.03	.00
☐ 398 Jamie Holland	.03	.01	.00	☐ 450 Tony Eason	.06	.03	.00
☐ 399 Keith McCants	.20	.10	.02	☐ 451 Erik McMillan	.06	.03	.00
☐ 400 Kevin Murphy	.06	.03	.00	☐ 452 Jim Sweeney	.06	.03	.00
☐ 401 Danny Peebles	.03	.01	.00	☐ 453 Ken O'Brien	.08	.04	.01
☐ 402 Mark Robinson	.03	.01	.00	☐ 454 Johnny Hector	.06	.03	.00
☐ 403 Broderick Thomas	.08	.04	.01	☐ 455 Jo Jo Townsell	.06	.03	.00
☐ 404 Ron Hall	.06	.03	.00	☐ 456 Roger Vick	.03	.01	.00
☐ 405 Mark Carrier	.08	.04	.01	☐ 457 James Hasty	.03	.01	.00
☐ 406 Paul Gruber	.06	.03	.00	☐ 458 Dennis Byrd	.10	.05	.01
☐ 407 Vinny Testaverde	.08	.04	.01	☐ 459 Ron Stallworth	.08	.04	.01
☐ 408 Bruce Hill	.03	.01	.00	☐ 460 Mickey Shuler	.03	.01	.00
☐ 409 Lars Tate	.06	.03	.00	☐ 461 Bobby Humphery	.03	.01	.00
☐ 410 Harry Hamilton	.03	.01	.00	☐ 462 Kyle Clifton	.06	.03	.00
☐ 411 Ricky Reynolds	.03	.01	.00	☐ 463 Al Toon	.08	.04	.01
☐ 412 Donald Igwebuike	.03	.01	.00	☐ 464 Freeman McNeil	.08	.04	.01
☐ 413 Reuben Davis	.08	.04	.01	☐ 465 Pat Leahy	.06	.03	.00
☐ 414 William Howard	.10	.05	.01	☐ 466 Scott Case	.03	.01	.00
☐ 415 Winston Moss	.10	.05	.01	☐ 467 Shawn Collins	.06	.03	.00
☐ 416 Chris Singleton	.20	.10	.02	☐ 468 Floyd Dixon	.03	.01	.00
☐ 417 Hart Lee Dykes	.06	.03	.00	☐ 469 Deion Sanders	.30	.15	.03
☐ 418 Steve Grogan	.08	.04	.01	☐ 470 Tony Casillas	.06	.03	.00
☐ 419 Bruce Armstrong	.06	.03	.00	☐ 471 Michael Haynes	.50	.25	.05
☐ 420 Robert Perryman	.06	.03	.00	☐ 472 Chris Miller	.20	.10	.02
☐ 421 Andre Tippett	.06	.03	.00	☐ 473 John Settle	.06	.03	.00
☐ 422 Sammy Martin	.10	.05	.01	☐ 474 Aundray Bruce	.06	.03	.00
☐ 423 Stanley Morgan	.08	.04	.01	☐ 475 Gene Lang	.03	.01	.00
☐ 424 Cedric Jones	.10	.05	.01	☐ 476 Tim Gordon	.10	.05	.01
☐ 425 Sean Farrell	.03	.01	.00	☐ 477 Scott Fulhage	.03	.01	.00
☐ 426 Marc Wilson	.06	.03	.00	☐ 478 Bill Fralic	.06	.03	.00
☐ 427 John Stephens	.08	.04	.01	☐ 479 Jessie Tuggle	.10	.05	.01
☐ 428 Eric Sievers	.10	.05	.01	☐ 480 Marcus Cotton	.03	.01	.00
☐ 429 Maurice Hurst	.12	.06	.01	☐ 481 Steve Walsh	.10	.05	.01
☐ 430 Johnny Rembert	.06	.03	.00	☐ 482 Troy Aikman	.60	.30	.06
☐ 431 Receiving Leaders	.15	.07	.01	☐ 483 Ray Horton	.03	.01	.00
Jerry Rice				☐ 484 Tony Tolbert	.08	.04	.01
Andre Reed				☐ 485 Steve Folsom	.06	.03	.00
☐ 432 Eric Hill	.06	.03	.00	☐ 486 Ken Norton	.15	.07	.01

☐ 487 Kelvin Martin	.10	.05	.01
☐ 488 Jack Del Rio	.06	.03	.00
☐ 489 Daryl Johnston	.08	.04	.01
☐ 490 Bill Bates	.06	.03	.00
☐ 491 Jim Jeffcoat	.03	.01	.00
☐ 492 Vince Albritton	.08	.04	.01
☐ 493 Eugene Lockhart	.03	.01	.00
☐ 494 Mike Saxon	.03	.01	.00
☐ 495 James Dixon	.08	.04	.01
☐ 496 Willie Broughton	.08	.04	.01
☐ 497 Checklist 1-132	.06	.01	.00
☐ 498 Checklist 133-264	.06	.01	.00
☐ 499 Checklist 265-396	.06	.01	.00
☐ 500 Checklist 397-528	.06	.01	.00
☐ 501 Bears Team	.06	.03	.00
Harbaugh Eludes			
The Pursuit			
☐ 502 Bengals Team	.08	.04	.01
Boomer Studies			
The Defense			
☐ 503 Bills Team	.06	.03	.00
Conlan Calls			
Defensive Scheme			
☐ 504 Broncos Team	.06	.03	.00
Bratton Breaks Away			
☐ 505 Browns Team	.08	.04	.01
Kosar Calls The Play			
☐ 506 Buccaneers Team	.06	.03	.00
Moss Assists In			
Squeeze Play			
☐ 507 Cardinals Team	.06	.03	.00
Zordich Saves The Day			
☐ 508 Chargers Team	.06	.03	.00
Williams Plugs			
The Hole			
☐ 509 Chiefs Team	.06	.03	.00
Cherry Applies The "D"			
☐ 510 Colts Team	.06	.03	.00
Trudeau Begins			
A Reverse			
☐ 511 Cowboys Team	.10	.05	.01
Aikman Directs			
Ground Attack			
☐ 512 Dolphins Team	.06	.03	.00
Double-Decker By			
Oliver and Williams			
☐ 513 Eagles Team	.06	.03	.00
Toney Bangs Into			
The Line			
☐ 514 Falcons Team	.06	.03	.00
Tuggle Falls On Fumble			
☐ 515 49ers Team	.15	.07	.01
Montana To Craig,			
A Winning Duo			
☐ 516 Giants Team	.08	.04	.01
Simms Likes His O.J.			
☐ 517 Jets Team	.06	.03	.00

A Hasty Return			
☐ 518 Lions Team	.06	.03	.00
Gagliano Orchestrates			
The Offense			
☐ 519 Oilers Team	.10	.05	.01
Moon Scrambles			
To Daylight			
☐ 520 Packers Team	.08	.04	.01
A Bit Of Packer "Majik"			
☐ 521 Patriots Team	.06	.03	.00
Stephens Steams Ahead			
☐ 522 Raiders Team	.10	.05	.01
Bo Knows Yardage			
☐ 523 Rams Team	.08	.04	.01
Everett Rolls Right			
☐ 524 Redskins Team	.06	.03	.00
Riggs Rumbles			
Downfield			
☐ 525 Saints Team	.06	.03	.00
Mills Takes A Stand			
☐ 526 Seahawks Team	.06	.03	.00
Feasel Sets To Snap			
☐ 527 Steelers Team	.06	.03	.00
Brister Has A			
Clear Lane			
☐ 528 Vikings Team	.06	.03	.00
Fenney Spots Opening			

1990 Topps Traded

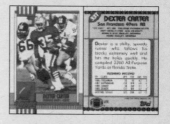

*This 132-card set measures 2 1/2" by 3 1/2"
and was released by Topps as an update to
their regular issue set. The set features players
who were traded after Topps printed their
regular set and rookies who were not in the
1990 Topps football set. The set was issued in
its own custom box and was distributed through*

the Topps hobby distribution system. The cards were printed on white card stock. The key rookies in the set are Reggie Cobb, Johnny Johnson, Rob Moore, and Emmitt Smith.

	MINT	EXC	G-VG
COMPLETE SET (132)	15.00	7.50	1.50
COMMON PLAYER (1T-132T)	.05	.02	.00
☐ 1T Gerald McNeil Houston Oilers	.08	.04	.01
☐ 2T Andre Rison Atlanta Falcons	.20	.10	.02
☐ 3T Steve Walsh New Orleans Saints	.12	.06	.01
☐ 4T Lorenzo White Houston Oilers	.12	.06	.01
☐ 5T Max Montoya Los Angeles Raiders	.05	.02	.00
☐ 6T William Roberts New York Giants	.10	.05	.01
☐ 7T Alonzo Highsmith Dallas Cowboys	.08	.04	.01
☐ 8T Chris Hinton Atlanta Falcons	.08	.04	.01
☐ 9T Stanley Morgan Indianapolis Colts	.10	.05	.01
☐ 10T Mickey Shuler Philadelphia Eagles	.05	.02	.00
☐ 11T Bobby Humphery Los Angeles Rams	.05	.02	.00
☐ 12T Gary Anderson Tampa Bay Buccaneers	.10	.05	.01
☐ 13T Mike Tomczak Chicago Bears	.08	.04	.01
☐ 14T Anthony Pleasant Cleveland Browns	.10	.05	.01
☐ 15T Walter Stanley Washington Redskins	.05	.02	.00
☐ 16T Greg Bell Los Angeles Raiders	.08	.04	.01
☐ 17T Tony Martin Miami Dolphins	.10	.05	.01
☐ 18T Terry Kinard Houston Oilers	.05	.02	.00
☐ 19T Cris Carter Minnesota Vikings	.10	.05	.01
☐ 20T James Wilder Detroit Lions	.08	.04	.01
☐ 21T Jerry Kauric Cleveland Browns	.10	.05	.01
☐ 22T Irving Fryar New England Patriots	.10	.05	.01
☐ 23T Ken Harvey Phoenix Cardinals	.15	.07	.01
☐ 24T James Williams Buffalo Bills	.12	.06	.01
☐ 25T Ron Cox Chicago Bears	.12	.06	.01
☐ 26T Andre Ware Detroit Lions	.30	.15	.03
☐ 27T Emmitt Smith Dallas Cowboys	7.50	3.75	.75
☐ 28T Junior Seau San Diego Chargers	.20	.10	.02
☐ 29T Mark Carrier Chicago Bears	.40	.20	.04
☐ 30T Rodney Hampton New York Giants	1.00	.50	.10
☐ 31T Rob Moore New York Jets	1.00	.50	.10
☐ 32T Bern Brostek Los Angeles Rams	.10	.05	.01
☐ 33T Dexter Carter San Francisco 49ers	.20	.10	.02
☐ 34T Blair Thomas New York Jets	.75	.35	.07
☐ 35T Harold Green Cincinnati Bengals	.50	.25	.05
☐ 36T Darrell Thompson Green Bay Packers	.45	.22	.04
☐ 37T Eric Green Pittsburgh Steelers	.75	.35	.07
☐ 38T Renaldo Turnbull New Orleans Saints	.20	.10	.02
☐ 39T Leroy Hoard Cleveland Browns	.40	.20	.04
☐ 40T Anthony Thompson Phoenix Cardinals	.35	.17	.03
☐ 41T Jeff George Indianapolis Colts	1.00	.50	.10
☐ 42T Alexander Wright Dallas Cowboys	.30	.15	.03
☐ 43T Richmond Webb Miami Dolphins	.15	.07	.01
☐ 44T Cortez Kennedy Seattle Seahawks	.20	.10	.02
☐ 45T Ray Agnew New England Patriots	.12	.06	.01
☐ 46T Percy Snow Kansas City Chiefs	.12	.06	.01
☐ 47T Chris Singleton New England Patriots	.10	.05	.01
☐ 48T James Francis Cincinnati Bengals	.40	.20	.04
☐ 49T Tony Bennett Green Bay Packers	.10	.05	.01
☐ 50T Reggie Cobb Tampa Bay Buccaneers	.75	.35	.07
☐ 51T Barry Foster Pittsburgh Steelers	.30	.15	.03
☐ 52T Ben Smith Philadelphia Eagles	.10	.05	.01
☐ 53T Anthony Smith	.15	.07	.01

Los Angeles Raiders
- ☐ 54T Steve Christie ....08 .04 .01
Tampa Bay Buccaneers
- ☐ 55T Johnny Bailey ....25 .12 .02
Chicago Bears
- ☐ 56T Alan Grant ....15 .07 .01
Indianapolis Colts
- ☐ 57T Eric Floyd ....08 .04 .01
San Diego Chargers
- ☐ 58T Robert Blackmon ....10 .05 .01
Seattle Seahawks
- ☐ 59T Brent Williams ....08 .04 .01
New England Patriots
- ☐ 60T Raymond Clayborn ....05 .02 .00
Cleveland Browns
- ☐ 61T Dave Duerson ....05 .02 .00
New York Giants
- ☐ 62T Derrick Fenner ....40 .20 .04
Seattle Seahawks
- ☐ 63T Ken Willis ....08 .04 .01
Dallas Cowboys
- ☐ 64T Brad Baxter ....35 .17 .03
New York Jets
- ☐ 65T Tony Paige ....08 .04 .01
Miami Dolphins
- ☐ 66T Jay Schroeder ....10 .05 .01
Los Angeles Raiders
- ☐ 67T Jim Breech ....05 .02 .00
Cincinnati Bengals
- ☐ 68T Barry Word ....80 .40 .08
Kansas City Chiefs
- ☐ 69T Anthony Dilweg ....10 .05 .01
Green Bay Packers
- ☐ 70T Rich Gannon ....30 .15 .03
Minnesota Vikings
- ☐ 71T Stan Humphries ....12 .06 .01
Washington Redskins
- ☐ 72T Jay Novacek ....30 .15 .03
Dallas Cowboys
- ☐ 73T Tommy Kane ....35 .17 .03
Seattle Seahawks
- ☐ 74T Everson Walls ....05 .02 .00
New York Giants
- ☐ 75T Mike Rozier ....08 .04 .01
Atlanta Falcons
- ☐ 76T Robb Thomas ....20 .10 .02
Kansas City Chiefs
- ☐ 77T Terance Mathis ....40 .20 .04
New York Jets
- ☐ 78T LeRoy Irvin ....05 .02 .00
Detroit Lions
- ☐ 79T Jeff Donaldson ....05 .02 .00
Kansas City Chiefs
- ☐ 80T Ethan Horton ....25 .12 .02
Los Angeles Raiders
- ☐ 81T J.B. Brown ....12 .06 .01
Miami Dolphins

- ☐ 82T Joe Kelly ....08 .04 .01
New York Jets
- ☐ 83T John Carney ....10 .05 .01
San Diego Chargers
- ☐ 84T Dan Stryzinski ....10 .05 .01
Pittsburgh Steelers
- ☐ 85T John Kidd ....05 .02 .00
San Diego Chargers
- ☐ 86T Al Smith ....08 .04 .01
Houston Oilers
- ☐ 87T Travis McNeal ....10 .05 .01
Seattle Seahawks
- ☐ 88T Reyna Thompson ....12 .06 .01
New York Giants
- ☐ 89T Rick Donnelly ....05 .02 .00
Seattle Seahawks
- ☐ 90T Marv Cook ....10 .05 .01
New England Patriots
- ☐ 91T Mike Farr ....12 .06 .01
Detroit Lions
- ☐ 92T Daniel Stubbs ....05 .02 .00
Dallas Cowboys
- ☐ 93T Jeff Campbell ....20 .10 .02
Detroit Lions
- ☐ 94T Tim McKyer ....08 .04 .01
Miami Dolphins
- ☐ 95T Ian Beckles ....12 .06 .01
Tampa Bay Buccaneers
- ☐ 96T Lemuel Stinson ....08 .04 .01
Chicago Bears
- ☐ 97T Frank Cornish ....10 .05 .01
San Diego Chargers
- ☐ 98T Riki Ellison ....08 .04 .01
Los Angeles Raiders
- ☐ 99T Jamie Mueller ....10 .05 .01
Buffalo Bills
- ☐ 100T Brian Hansen ....05 .02 .00
New England Patriots
- ☐ 101T Warren Powers ....10 .05 .01
Denver Broncos
- ☐ 102T Howard Cross ....12 .06 .01
New York Giants
- ☐ 103T Tim Grunhard ....10 .05 .01
Kansas City Chiefs
- ☐ 104T Johnny Johnson ....90 .45 .09
Phoenix Cardinals
- ☐ 105T Calvin Williams ....30 .15 .03
Philadelphia Eagles
- ☐ 106T Keith McCants ....15 .07 .01
Tampa Bay Buccaneers
- ☐ 107T Lamar Lathon ....20 .10 .02
Houston Oilers
- ☐ 108T Steve Broussard ....40 .20 .04
Atlanta Falcons
- ☐ 109T Glenn Parker ....08 .04 .01
Buffalo Bills
- ☐ 110T Alton Montgomery ....10 .05 .01

Denver Broncos
☐ 111T Jim McMahon .... .10   .05   .01
Philadelphia Eagles
☐ 112T Aaron Wallace .... .15   .07   .01
Los Angeles Raiders
☐ 113T Keith Sims .... .12   .06   .01
Miami Dolphins
☐ 114T Ervin Randle .... .05   .02   .00
Tampa Bay Buccaneers
☐ 115T Walter Wilson .... .10   .05   .01
San Diego Chargers
☐ 116T Terry Wooden .... .12   .06   .01
Seattle Seahawks
☐ 117T Bernard Clark .... .10   .05   .01
Buffalo Bills
☐ 118T Tony Stargell .... .20   .10   .02
New York Jets
☐ 119T Jimmie Jones .... .08   .04   .01
Dallas Cowboys
☐ 120T Andre Collins .... .20   .10   .02
Washington Redskins
☐ 121T Ricky Proehl .... .35   .17   .03
Phoenix Cardinals
☐ 122T Darion Conner .... .20   .10   .02
Atlanta Falcons
☐ 123T Jeff Rutledge .... .10   .05   .01
Washington Redskins
☐ 124T Heath Sherman .... .25   .12   .02
Philadelphia Eagles
☐ 125T Tommie Agee .... .10   .05   .01
Dallas Cowboys
☐ 126T Tory Epps .... .10   .05   .01
Atlanta Falcons
☐ 127T Tommy Hodson .... .35   .17   .03
New England Patriots
☐ 128T Jessie Hester .... .20   .10   .02
Indianapolis Colts
☐ 129T Alfred Oglesby .... .10   .05   .01
Miami Dolphins
☐ 130T Chris Chandler .... .10   .05   .01
Tampa Bay Buccaneers
☐ 131T Fred Barnett .... .40   .20   .04
Philadelphia Eagles
☐ 132T Checklist Card .... .05   .01   .00

1991 Topps

This 660-card standard size (2 1/2" by 3 1/2")
set was issued by Topps. This set marked the
largest football card set Topps had ever issued.
The set numbering is according to teams as

follows, Highlights (2-7), League Leaders (8-
12), New York Giants (13-36), Buffalo Bills
(37-59), San Francisco 49ers (60-82), Los
Angeles Raiders (83-107), Miami Dolphins
(108-129), Kansas City Chiefs (130-153),
Chicago Bears (154-177), Washington
Redskins (178-200), Philadelphia Eagles (201-
221), Houston Oilers (222-243), Cincinnati
Bengals (244-265), Seattle Seahawks (266-
287), Pittsburgh Steelers (288-309), New
Orleans Saints (310-331), Indianapolis Colts
(332-352), Dallas Cowboys (353-375),
Minnesota Vikings (376-396), Detroit Lions
(397-417), San Diego Chargers (418-438),
Green Bay Packers (439-460), New York Jets
(461-481), Tampa Bay Buccaneers (482-501),
Phoenix Cardinals (502-522), Los Angeles
Rams (523-544), Denver Broncos (545-566),
Atlanta Falcons (567-588), Cleveland Browns
(589-607), New England Patriots (608-627),
Team Cards (628-655), and Checklist Cards
(656-660). The key rookies in the set are Nick
Bell, Ricky Ervins, Todd Marinovich, Dan
McGwire, Browning Nagle, and Harvey
Williams.

	MINT	EXC	G-VG
COMPLETE SET (660) 15.00		7.50	1.50
COMMON PLAYER (1-660) .... .03		.01	.00
☐ 1 Super Bowl XXV .... .08		.04	.01
☐ 2 Roger Craig HL .... .06		.03	.00
☐ 3 Derrick Thomas HL .... .08		.04	.01
☐ 4 Pete Stoyanovich HL .... .03		.01	.00
☐ 5 Ottis Anderson HL .... .06		.03	.01
☐ 6 Jerry Rice HL .... .15		.07	.01
☐ 7 Warren Moon HL .... .10		.05	.01
☐ 8 Leaders Passing Yards .... .10		.05	.01
Warren Moon			
Jim Everett			
☐ 9 Leaders Rushing .... .25		.12	.02

Barry Sanders
Thurman Thomas
- [ ] 10 Leaders Receiving ....15 .07 .01
  Jerry Rice
  Haywood Jeffires
- [ ] 11 Leaders Interceptions ......06 .03 .00
  Mark Carrier
  Richard Johnson
- [ ] 12 Leaders Sacks ....08 .04 .01
  Derrick Thomas
  Charles Haley
- [ ] 13 Jumbo Elliott ....03 .01 .00
- [ ] 14 Leonard Marshall ....06 .03 .00
- [ ] 15 William Roberts ....03 .01 .00
- [ ] 16 Lawrence Taylor ....10 .05 .01
- [ ] 17 Mark Ingram ....06 .03 .00
- [ ] 18 Rodney Hampton ....40 .20 .04
- [ ] 19 Carl Banks ....06 .03 .00
- [ ] 20 Ottis Anderson ....08 .04 .01
- [ ] 21 Mark Collins ....03 .01 .00
- [ ] 22 Pepper Johnson ....06 .03 .00
- [ ] 23 Dave Meggett ....10 .05 .01
- [ ] 24 Reyna Thompson ....06 .03 .00
- [ ] 25 Stephen Baker ....06 .03 .00
- [ ] 26 Mike Fox ....06 .03 .00
- [ ] 27 Maurice Carthon UER ......03 .01 .00
  (Herschel Walker mis-
  spelled as Herschell)
- [ ] 28 Jeff Hostetler ....20 .10 .02
- [ ] 29 Greg Jackson ....08 .04 .01
- [ ] 30 Sean Landeta ....03 .01 .00
- [ ] 31 Bart Oates ....03 .01 .00
- [ ] 32 Phil Simms ....08 .04 .01
- [ ] 33 Erik Howard ....03 .01 .00
- [ ] 34 Myron Guyton ....03 .01 .00
- [ ] 35 Mark Bavaro ....06 .03 .00
- [ ] 36 Jarrod Bunch ....15 .07 .01
- [ ] 37 Will Wolford ....03 .01 .00
- [ ] 38 Ray Bentley ....03 .01 .00
- [ ] 39 Nate Odomes ....03 .01 .00
- [ ] 40 Scott Norwood ....03 .01 .00
- [ ] 41 Darryl Talley ....06 .03 .00
- [ ] 42 Carwell Gardner ....08 .04 .01
- [ ] 43 James Lofton ....12 .06 .01
- [ ] 44 Shane Conlan ....06 .03 .01
- [ ] 45 Steve Tasker ....03 .01 .00
- [ ] 46 James Williams ....03 .01 .00
- [ ] 47 Kent Hull ....03 .01 .00
- [ ] 48 Al Edwards ....08 .04 .01
- [ ] 49 Frank Reich ....08 .04 .01
- [ ] 50 Leon Seals ....06 .03 .00
- [ ] 51 Keith McKeller ....08 .04 .01
- [ ] 52 Thurman Thomas ....45 .22 .04
- [ ] 53 Leonard Smith ....03 .01 .00
- [ ] 54 Andre Reed ....10 .05 .01
- [ ] 55 Kenneth Davis ....06 .03 .00
- [ ] 56 Jeff Wright ....08 .04 .01
- [ ] 57 Jamie Mueller ....03 .01 .00
- [ ] 58 Jim Ritcher ....03 .01 .00
- [ ] 59 Bruce Smith ....08 .04 .01
- [ ] 60 Ted Washington ....12 .06 .01
- [ ] 61 Guy McIntyre ....03 .01 .00
- [ ] 62 Michael Carter ....06 .03 .00
- [ ] 63 Pierce Holt ....03 .01 .00
- [ ] 64 Darryl Pollard ....06 .03 .00
- [ ] 65 Mike Sherrard ....08 .04 .01
- [ ] 66 Dexter Carter ....08 .04 .01
- [ ] 67 Bubba Paris ....03 .01 .00
- [ ] 68 Harry Sydney ....08 .04 .01
- [ ] 69 Tom Rathman ....06 .03 .00
- [ ] 70 Jesse Sapolu ....06 .03 .00
- [ ] 71 Mike Cofer ....03 .01 .00
- [ ] 72 Keith DeLong ....06 .03 .00
- [ ] 73 Joe Montana ....40 .20 .04
- [ ] 74 Bill Romanowski ....06 .03 .00
- [ ] 75 John Taylor ....12 .06 .01
- [ ] 76 Brent Jones ....06 .03 .00
- [ ] 77 Harris Barton ....03 .01 .00
- [ ] 78 Charles Haley ....06 .03 .00
- [ ] 79 Eric Davis ....06 .03 .00
- [ ] 80 Kevin Fagan ....03 .01 .00
- [ ] 81 Jerry Rice ....35 .17 .03
- [ ] 82 Dave Waymer ....03 .01 .00
- [ ] 83 Todd Marinovich ....1.50 .75 .15
- [ ] 84 Steve Smith ....03 .01 .00
- [ ] 85 Tim Brown ....08 .04 .01
- [ ] 86 Ethan Horton ....10 .05 .01
- [ ] 87 Marcus Allen ....10 .05 .01
- [ ] 88 Terry McDaniel ....03 .01 .00
- [ ] 89 Thomas Benson ....03 .01 .00
- [ ] 90 Roger Craig ....10 .05 .01
- [ ] 91 Don Mosebar ....03 .01 .00
- [ ] 92 Aaron Wallace ....06 .03 .00
- [ ] 93 Eddie Anderson ....03 .01 .00
- [ ] 94 Willie Gault ....06 .03 .00
- [ ] 95 Howie Long ....06 .03 .00
- [ ] 96 Jay Schroeder ....08 .04 .01
- [ ] 97 Ronnie Lott ....10 .05 .01
- [ ] 98 Bob Golic ....03 .01 .00
- [ ] 99 Bo Jackson ....35 .17 .03
- [ ] 100 Max Montoya ....03 .01 .00
- [ ] 101 Scott Davis ....03 .01 .00
- [ ] 102 Greg Townsend ....03 .01 .00
- [ ] 103 Garry Lewis ....06 .03 .00
- [ ] 104 Mervyn Fernandez ....06 .03 .00
- [ ] 105 Steve Wisniewski UER .....03 .01 .00
  (Back has drafted,
  should be traded to)
- [ ] 106 Jeff Jaeger ....03 .01 .00
- [ ] 107 Nick Bell ....75 .35 .07
- [ ] 108 Mark Dennis ....08 .04 .01
- [ ] 109 Jarvis Williams ....03 .01 .00
- [ ] 110 Mark Clayton ....08 .04 .01
- [ ] 111 Harry Galbreath ....06 .03 .00

☐ 112 Dan Marino	.25	.12	.02
☐ 113 Louis Oliver	.03	.01	.00
☐ 114 Pete Stoyanovich	.03	.01	.00
☐ 115 Ferrell Edmunds	.03	.01	.00
☐ 116 Jeff Cross	.03	.01	.00
☐ 117 Richmond Webb	.06	.03	.00
☐ 118 Jim C. Jensen	.03	.01	.00
☐ 119 Keith Sims	.03	.01	.00
☐ 120 Mark Duper	.06	.03	.00
☐ 121 Shawn Lee	.08	.04	.01
☐ 122 Reggie Roby	.03	.01	.00
☐ 123 Jeff Uhlenhake	.03	.01	.00
☐ 124 Sammie Smith	.08	.04	.01
☐ 125 John Offerdahl	.06	.03	.00
☐ 126 Hugh Green	.06	.03	.00
☐ 127 Tony Paige	.03	.01	.00
☐ 128 David Griggs	.06	.03	.00
☐ 129 J.B. Brown	.03	.01	.00
☐ 130 Harvey Williams	.75	.35	.07
☐ 131 John Alt	.06	.03	.00
☐ 132 Albert Lewis	.06	.03	.00
☐ 133 Robb Thomas	.08	.04	.01
☐ 134 Neil Smith	.06	.03	.00
☐ 135 Stephone Paige	.06	.03	.00
☐ 136 Nick Lowery	.06	.03	.00
☐ 137 Steve DeBerg	.08	.04	.01
☐ 138 Rich Baldinger	.08	.04	.00
☐ 139 Percy Snow	.08	.04	.01
☐ 140 Kevin Porter	.06	.03	.00
☐ 141 Chris Martin	.03	.01	.00
☐ 142 Deron Cherry	.06	.03	.00
☐ 143 Derrick Thomas	.15	.07	.01
☐ 144 Tim Grunhard	.03	.01	.00
☐ 145 Todd McNair	.03	.01	.00
☐ 146 David Szott	.08	.04	.01
☐ 147 Dan Saleaumua	.03	.01	.00
☐ 148 Jonathan Hayes	.03	.01	.00
☐ 149 Christian Okoye	.08	.04	.01
☐ 150 Dino Hackett	.03	.01	.00
☐ 151 Bryan Barker	.10	.05	.01
☐ 152 Kevin Ross	.03	.01	.00
☐ 153 Barry Word	.25	.12	.02
☐ 154 Stan Thomas	.10	.05	.01
☐ 155 Brad Muster	.06	.03	.00
☐ 156 Donnell Woolford	.03	.01	.00
☐ 157 Neal Anderson	.15	.07	.01
☐ 158 Jim Covert	.06	.03	.00
☐ 159 Jim Harbaugh	.10	.05	.01
☐ 160 Shaun Gayle	.06	.03	.00
☐ 161 William Perry	.08	.04	.01
☐ 162 Ron Morris	.04	.02	.00
☐ 163 Mark Bortz	.03	.01	.00
☐ 164 James Thornton	.03	.01	.00
☐ 165 Ron Rivera	.03	.01	.00
☐ 166 Kevin Butler	.03	.01	.00
☐ 167 Jay Hilgenberg	.06	.03	.00
☐ 168 Peter Tom Willis	.10	.05	.01

☐ 169 Johnny Bailey	.08	.04	.01
☐ 170 Ron Cox	.03	.01	.00
☐ 171 Keith Van Horne	.03	.01	.00
☐ 172 Mark Carrier	.08	.04	.01
☐ 173 Richard Dent	.08	.04	.01
☐ 174 Wendell Davis	.12	.06	.01
☐ 175 Trace Armstrong	.03	.01	.00
☐ 176 Mike Singletary	.08	.04	.01
☐ 177 Chris Zorich	.25	.12	.02
☐ 178 Gerald Riggs	.06	.03	.00
☐ 179 Jeff Bostic	.06	.03	.00
☐ 180 Kurt Gouveia	.08	.04	.01
☐ 181 Stan Humphries	.08	.04	.01
☐ 182 Chip Lohmiller	.03	.01	.00
☐ 183 Raleigh McKenzie	.10	.05	.01
☐ 184 Alvin Walton	.06	.03	.00
☐ 185 Earnest Byner	.08	.04	.01
☐ 186 Markus Koch	.08	.04	.01
☐ 187 Art Monk	.10	.05	.01
☐ 188 Ed Simmons	.03	.01	.00
☐ 189 Bobby Wilson	.08	.04	.01
☐ 190 Charles Mann	.06	.03	.00
☐ 191 Darrell Green	.10	.05	.01
☐ 192 Mark Rypien	.20	.10	.02
☐ 193 Ricky Sanders	.08	.04	.01
☐ 194 Jim Lachey	.06	.03	.00
☐ 195 Martin Mayhew	.03	.01	.00
☐ 196 Gary Clark	.12	.06	.01
☐ 197 Wilber Marshall	.06	.03	.00
☐ 198 Darryl Grant	.03	.01	.00
☐ 199 Don Warren	.06	.03	.00
☐ 200 Ricky Ervins UER	1.75	.85	.17
(Front has Chiefs, back has Redskins)			
☐ 201 Eric Allen	.03	.01	.00
☐ 202 Anthony Toney	.03	.01	.00
☐ 203 Ben Smith UER	.03	.01	.00
(Front CB, back S)			
☐ 204 David Alexander	.06	.03	.00
☐ 205 Jerome Brown	.06	.03	.00
☐ 206 Mike Golic	.06	.03	.00
☐ 207 Roger Ruzek	.03	.01	.00
☐ 208 Andre Waters	.03	.01	.00
☐ 209 Fred Barnett	.15	.07	.01
☐ 210 Randall Cunningham	.15	.07	.01
☐ 211 Mike Schad	.03	.01	.00
☐ 212 Reggie White	.08	.04	.01
☐ 213 Mike Bellamy	.08	.04	.01
☐ 214 Jeff Feagles	.08	.04	.01
☐ 215 Wes Hopkins	.03	.01	.00
☐ 216 Clyde Simmons	.06	.03	.00
☐ 217 Keith Byars	.06	.03	.00
☐ 218 Seth Joyner	.06	.03	.00
☐ 219 Byron Evans	.06	.03	.00
☐ 220 Keith Jackson	.08	.04	.01
☐ 221 Calvin Williams	.08	.04	.01
☐ 222 Mike Dumas	.15	.07	.01

☐ 223 Ray Childress	.06	.03	.00
☐ 224 Ernest Givins	.10	.05	.01
☐ 225 Lamar Lathon	.06	.03	.00
☐ 226 Greg Montgomery	.03	.01	.00
☐ 227 Mike Munchak	.06	.03	.00
☐ 228 Al Smith	.03	.01	.00
☐ 229 Bubba McDowell	.03	.01	.00
☐ 230 Haywood Jeffires	.20	.10	.02
☐ 231 Drew Hill	.08	.04	.01
☐ 232 William Fuller	.06	.03	.00
☐ 233 Warren Moon	.20	.10	.02
☐ 234 Doug Smith	.08	.04	.01
☐ 235 Cris Dishman	.20	.10	.02
☐ 236 Teddy Garcia	.08	.04	.01
☐ 237 Richard Johnson	.08	.04	.01
☐ 238 Bruce Matthews	.03	.01	.00
☐ 239 Gerald McNeil	.03	.01	.00
☐ 240 Johnny Meads	.03	.01	.00
☐ 241 Curtis Duncan	.06	.03	.00
☐ 242 Sean Jones	.03	.01	.00
☐ 243 Lorenzo White	.06	.03	.00
☐ 244 Rob Carpenter	.12	.06	.01
☐ 245 Bruce Reimers	.06	.03	.00
☐ 246 Ickey Woods	.06	.03	.00
☐ 247 Lewis Billups	.03	.01	.00
☐ 248 Boomer Esiason	.10	.05	.01
☐ 249 Tim Krumrie	.03	.01	.00
☐ 250 David Fulcher	.03	.01	.00
☐ 251 Jim Breech	.03	.01	.00
☐ 252 Mitchell Price	.08	.04	.01
☐ 253 Carl Zander	.03	.01	.00
☐ 254 Barney Bussey	.08	.04	.01
☐ 255 Leon White	.03	.01	.00
☐ 256 Eddie Brown	.08	.04	.01
☐ 257 James Francis	.08	.04	.01
☐ 258 Harold Green	.15	.07	.01
☐ 259 Anthony Munoz	.08	.04	.01
☐ 260 James Brooks	.08	.04	.01
☐ 261 Kevin Walker UER	.15	.07	.01
(Hometown should be			
West Milford Township)			
☐ 262 Bruce Kozerski	.03	.01	.00
☐ 263 David Grant	.03	.01	.00
☐ 264 Tim McGee	.06	.03	.00
☐ 265 Rodney Holman	.03	.01	.00
☐ 266 Dan McGwire	1.25	.60	.12
☐ 267 Andy Heck	.03	.01	.00
☐ 268 Dave Krieg	.08	.04	.01
☐ 269 David Wyman	.03	.01	.00
☐ 270 Robert Blackmon	.06	.03	.00
☐ 271 Grant Feasel	.06	.03	.00
☐ 272 Patrick Hunter	.12	.06	.01
☐ 273 Travis McNeal	.06	.03	.00
☐ 274 John L. Williams	.08	.04	.01
☐ 275 Tony Woods	.06	.03	.00
☐ 276 Derrick Fenner	.12	.06	.01
☐ 277 Jacob Green	.06	.03	.00

☐ 278 Brian Blades	.08	.04	.01
☐ 279 Eugene Robinson	.03	.01	.00
☐ 280 Terry Wooden	.06	.03	.00
☐ 281 Jeff Bryant	.03	.01	.00
☐ 282 Norm Johnson	.03	.01	.00
☐ 283 Joe Nash UER	.03	.01	.00
Front DT, Back NT)			
☐ 284 Rick Donnelly	.03	.01	.00
☐ 285 Chris Warren	.06	.03	.00
☐ 286 Tommy Kane	.12	.06	.01
☐ 287 Cortez Kennedy	.08	.04	.01
☐ 288 Ernie Mills	.20	.10	.02
☐ 289 Dermontti Dawson	.03	.01	.00
☐ 290 Tunch Ilkin	.03	.01	.00
☐ 291 Tim Worley	.06	.03	.00
☐ 292 David Little	.03	.01	.00
☐ 293 Gary Anderson	.03	.01	.00
☐ 294 Chris Calloway	.06	.03	.00
☐ 295 Carnell Lake	.03	.01	.00
☐ 296 Dan Stryzinski	.03	.01	.00
☐ 297 Rod Woodson	.08	.04	.01
☐ 298 Johnny Jackson	.10	.05	.01
☐ 299 Bubby Brister	.08	.04	.01
☐ 300 Thomas Everett	.03	.01	.00
☐ 301 Merril Hoge	.06	.03	.00
☐ 302 Eric Green	.15	.07	.01
☐ 303 Greg Lloyd	.03	.01	.00
☐ 304 Gerald Williams	.06	.03	.00
☐ 305 Bryan Hinkle	.03	.01	.00
☐ 306 Keith Willis	.03	.01	.00
☐ 307 Louis Lipps	.06	.03	.00
☐ 308 Donald Evans	.06	.03	.00
☐ 309 David Johnson	.08	.04	.01
☐ 310 Wesley Carroll	.45	.22	.04
☐ 311 Eric Martin	.06	.03	.00
☐ 312 Brett Maxie	.08	.04	.01
☐ 313 Rickey Jackson	.06	.03	.00
☐ 314 Robert Massey	.03	.01	.00
☐ 315 Pat Swilling	.08	.04	.01
☐ 316 Morten Andersen	.03	.01	.00
☐ 317 Toi Cook	.08	.04	.01
☐ 318 Sam Mills	.06	.03	.00
☐ 319 Steve Walsh	.08	.04	.01
☐ 320 Tommy Barnhardt	.08	.04	.01
☐ 321 Vince Buck	.08	.04	.01
☐ 322 Joel Hilgenberg	.06	.03	.00
☐ 323 Rueben Mayes	.06	.03	.00
☐ 324 Renaldo Turnbull	.06	.03	.00
☐ 325 Brett Perriman	.06	.03	.00
☐ 326 Vaughan Johnson	.06	.03	.00
☐ 327 Gill Fenerty	.08	.04	.01
☐ 328 Stan Brock	.03	.01	.00
☐ 329 Dalton Hilliard	.06	.03	.00
☐ 330 Hoby Brenner	.03	.01	.00
☐ 331 Craig Heyward	.08	.04	.01
☐ 332 Jon Hand	.03	.01	.00
☐ 333 Duane Bickett	.03	.01	.00

☐ 334 Jessie Hester	.08	.04	.01
☐ 335 Rohn Stark	.03	.01	.00
☐ 336 Zefross Moss	.03	.01	.00
☐ 337 Bill Brooks	.03	.01	.00
☐ 338 Clarence Verdin	.06	.03	.00
☐ 339 Mike Prior	.03	.01	.00
☐ 340 Chip Banks	.06	.03	.00
☐ 341 Dean Biasucci	.03	.01	.00
☐ 342 Ray Donaldson	.03	.01	.00
☐ 343 Jeff Herrod	.03	.01	.00
☐ 344 Donnell Thompson	.03	.01	.00
☐ 345 Chris Goode	.03	.01	.00
☐ 346 Eugene Daniel	.03	.01	.00
☐ 347 Pat Beach	.03	.01	.00
☐ 348 Keith Taylor	.06	.03	.00
☐ 349 Jeff George	.35	.17	.03
☐ 350 Tony Siragusa	.08	.04	.01
☐ 351 Randy Dixon	.10	.05	.01
☐ 352 Albert Bentley	.06	.03	.00
☐ 353 Russell Maryland	.45	.22	.04
☐ 354 Mike Saxon	.03	.01	.00
☐ 355 Godfrey Myles UER	.08	.04	.01
(Misspelled Miles			
on card front)			
☐ 356 Mark Stepnoski	.08	.04	.01
☐ 357 James Washington	.08	.04	.01
☐ 358 Jay Novacek	.12	.06	.01
☐ 359 Kelvin Martin	.06	.03	.00
☐ 360 Emmitt Smith UER	1.25	.60	.12
(Played for Florida,			
not Florida State)			
☐ 361 Jim Jeffcoat	.03	.01	.00
☐ 362 Alexander Wright	.15	.07	.01
☐ 363 James Dixon UER	.03	.01	.00
(Photo is not Dixon			
on card front)			
☐ 364 Alonzo Highsmith	.06	.03	.00
☐ 365 Daniel Stubbs	.03	.01	.00
☐ 366 Jack Del Rio	.03	.01	.00
☐ 367 Mark Tuinei	.08	.04	.01
☐ 368 Michael Irvin	.20	.10	.02
☐ 369 John Gesek	.08	.04	.01
☐ 370 Ken Willis	.03	.01	.00
☐ 371 Troy Aikman	.35	.17	.03
☐ 372 Jimmie Jones	.06	.03	.00
☐ 373 Nate Newton	.03	.01	.00
☐ 374 Issiac Holt	.03	.01	.00
☐ 375 Alvin Harper	.45	.22	.04
☐ 376 Todd Kalis	.06	.03	.00
☐ 377 Wade Wilson	.08	.04	.01
☐ 378 Joey Browner	.06	.03	.00
☐ 379 Chris Doleman	.06	.03	.00
☐ 380 Hassan Jones	.06	.03	.00
☐ 381 Henry Thomas	.03	.01	.00
☐ 382 Darrell Fullington	.06	.03	.00
☐ 383 Steve Jordan	.06	.03	.00
☐ 384 Gary Zimmerman	.03	.01	.00
☐ 385 Ray Berry	.03	.01	.00
☐ 386 Cris Carter	.06	.03	.00
☐ 387 Mike Merriweather	.03	.01	.00
☐ 388 Carl Lee	.03	.01	.00
☐ 389 Keith Millard	.06	.03	.00
☐ 390 Reggie Rutland	.03	.01	.00
☐ 391 Anthony Carter	.08	.04	.01
☐ 392 Mark Dusbabek	.08	.04	.01
☐ 393 Kirk Lowdermilk	.03	.01	.00
☐ 394 Al Noga UER	.03	.01	.00
(Card says DT,			
should be DE)			
☐ 395 Herschel Walker	.10	.05	.01
☐ 396 Randall McDaniel	.03	.01	.00
☐ 397 Herman Moore	.60	.30	.06
☐ 398 Eddie Murray	.03	.01	.00
☐ 399 Lomas Brown	.03	.01	.00
☐ 400 Marc Spindler	.03	.01	.00
☐ 401 Bennie Blades	.06	.03	.00
☐ 402 Kevin Glover	.06	.03	.00
☐ 403 Aubrey Matthews	.08	.04	.01
☐ 404 Michael Cofer	.03	.01	.00
☐ 405 Robert Clark	.06	.03	.00
☐ 406 Eric Andolsek	.06	.03	.00
☐ 407 William White	.06	.03	.00
☐ 408 Rodney Peete	.08	.04	.01
☐ 409 Mel Gray	.03	.01	.00
☐ 410 Jim Arnold	.03	.01	.00
☐ 411 Jeff Campbell	.08	.04	.01
☐ 412 Chris Spielman	.06	.03	.00
☐ 413 Jerry Ball	.03	.01	.00
☐ 414 Dan Owens	.06	.03	.00
☐ 415 Barry Sanders	.75	.35	.07
☐ 416 Andre Ware	.12	.06	.01
☐ 417 Stanley Richard	.25	.12	.02
☐ 418 Gill Byrd	.06	.03	.00
☐ 419 John Kidd	.03	.01	.00
☐ 420 Sam Seale	.10	.05	.01
☐ 421 Gary Plummer	.03	.01	.00
☐ 422 Anthony Miller	.08	.04	.01
☐ 423 Ronnie Harmon	.03	.01	.00
☐ 424 Frank Cornish	.03	.01	.00
☐ 425 Marion Butts	.10	.05	.01
☐ 426 Leo Goeas	.06	.03	.00
☐ 427 Junior Seau	.08	.04	.01
☐ 428 Courtney Hall	.03	.01	.00
☐ 429 Leslie O'Neal	.06	.03	.00
☐ 430 Martin Bayless	.06	.03	.00
☐ 431 John Carney	.03	.01	.00
☐ 432 Lee Williams	.06	.03	.00
☐ 433 Arthur Cox	.03	.01	.00
☐ 434 Burt Grossman	.06	.03	.00
☐ 435 Nate Lewis	.12	.06	.01
☐ 436 Rod Bernstine	.06	.03	.00
☐ 437 Henry Rolling	.08	.04	.01
☐ 438 Billy Joe Tolliver	.08	.04	.01
☐ 439 Vinnie Clark	.12	.06	.01

☐ 440	Brian Noble	.03	.01	.00	☐ 486	Steve Christie	.03	.01	.00
☐ 441	Charles Wilson	.06	.03	.00	☐ 487	Paul Gruber	.06	.03	.00
☐ 442	Don Majkowski	.08	.04	.01	☐ 488	Jesse Anderson	.06	.03	.00
☐ 443	Tim Harris	.06	.03	.00	☐ 489	Reggie Cobb	.15	.07	.01
☐ 444	Scott Stephen	.08	.04	.01	☐ 490	Harry Hamilton	.03	.01	.00
☐ 445	Perry Kemp	.03	.01	.00	☐ 491	Vinny Testaverde	.08	.04	.01
☐ 446	Darrell Thompson	.12	.06	.01	☐ 492	Mark Royals	.08	.04	.01
☐ 447	Chris Jacke	.03	.01	.00	☐ 493	Keith McCants	.08	.04	.01
☐ 448	Mark Murphy	.03	.01	.00	☐ 494	Ron Hall	.03	.01	.00
☐ 449	Ed West	.03	.01	.00	☐ 495	Ian Beckles	.03	.01	.00
☐ 450	LeRoy Butler	.06	.03	.00	☐ 496	Mark Robinson	.03	.01	.00
☐ 451	Keith Woodside	.06	.03	.01	☐ 497	Reuben Davis	.03	.01	.00
☐ 452	Tony Bennett	.06	.03	.00	☐ 498	Wayne Haddix	.06	.03	.00
☐ 453	Mark Lee	.03	.01	.00	☐ 499	Kevin Murphy	.03	.01	.00
☐ 454	James Campen	.08	.04	.01	☐ 500	Eugene Marve	.03	.01	.00
☐ 455	Robert Brown	.03	.01	.00	☐ 501	Broderick Thomas	.06	.03	.00
☐ 456	Sterling Sharpe	.10	.05	.01	☐ 502	Eric Swann UER	.20	.10	.02
☐ 457A	Tony Mandarich ERR	2.25	1.10	.22		(Draft pick logo miss-			
	Denver Broncos					ing from card front)			
☐ 457B	Tony Mandarich COR	.12	.06	.01	☐ 503	Ernie Jones	.08	.04	.01
	Green Bay Packers				☐ 504	Rich Camarillo	.03	.01	.00
☐ 458	Johnny Holland	.03	.01	.00	☐ 505	Tim McDonald	.06	.03	.00
☐ 459	Matt Brock	.12	.06	.01	☐ 506	Freddie Joe Nunn	.03	.01	.00
☐ 460A	Esera Tuaolo ERR	.20	.10	.02	☐ 507	Tim Jorden	.08	.04	.01
	(See also 462; no 1991				☐ 508	Johnny Johnson	.25	.12	.02
	NFL Draft Pick logo)				☐ 509	Eric Hill	.03	.01	.00
☐ 460B	Esera Tuaolo COR	.10	.05	.01	☐ 510	Derek Kennard	.06	.03	.00
	(See also 462; 1991 NFL				☐ 511	Ricky Proehl	.10	.05	.01
	Draft Pick logo on front)				☐ 512	Bill Lewis	.06	.03	.00
☐ 461	Freeman McNeil	.08	.04	.01	☐ 513	Roy Green	.06	.03	.00
☐ 462	Terance Mathis UER	.15	.07	.01	☐ 514	Anthony Bell	.03	.01	.00
	(Card numbered in-				☐ 515	Timm Rosenbach	.10	.05	.01
	correctly as 460)				☐ 516	Jim Wahler	.08	.04	.01
☐ 463	Rob Moore	.45	.22	.04	☐ 517	Anthony Thompson	.08	.04	.01
☐ 464	Darrell Davis	.15	.07	.01	☐ 518	Ken Harvey	.03	.01	.00
☐ 465	Chris Burkett	.03	.01	.00	☐ 519	Luis Sharpe	.03	.01	.00
☐ 466	Jeff Criswell	.06	.03	.00	☐ 520	Walter Reeves	.03	.01	.00
☐ 467	Tony Stargell	.03	.01	.00	☐ 521	Lonnie Young	.03	.01	.00
☐ 468	Ken O'Brien	.08	.04	.01	☐ 522	Rod Saddler	.15	.07	.01
☐ 469	Erik McMillan	.06	.03	.00	☐ 523	Todd Lyght	.40	.20	.04
☐ 470	Jeff Lageman UER	.06	.03	.00	☐ 524	Alvin Wright	.06	.03	.00
	(Front DE, back LB)				☐ 525	Flipper Anderson	.06	.03	.00
☐ 471	Pat Leahy	.06	.03	.00	☐ 526	Jackie Slater	.06	.03	.00
☐ 472	Dennis Byrd	.03	.01	.00	☐ 527	Damone Johnson	.08	.04	.01
☐ 473	Jim Sweeney	.03	.01	.00	☐ 528	Cleveland Gary	.06	.03	.00
☐ 474	Brad Baxter	.10	.05	.01	☐ 529	Mike Piel	.03	.01	.00
☐ 475	Joe Kelly	.03	.01	.00	☐ 530	Buford McGee	.06	.03	.00
☐ 476	Al Toon	.08	.04	.01	☐ 531	Michael Stewart	.03	.01	.00
☐ 477	Joe Prokop	.08	.04	.01	☐ 532	Jim Everett	.10	.05	.01
☐ 478	Mark Boyer	.06	.03	.00	☐ 533	Mike Wilcher	.03	.01	.00
☐ 479	Kyle Clifton	.03	.01	.00	☐ 534	Irv Pankey	.03	.01	.00
☐ 480	James Hasty	.03	.01	.00	☐ 535	Bern Brostek	.03	.01	.00
☐ 481	Browning Nagle	.75	.35	.07	☐ 536	Henry Ellard	.08	.04	.01
☐ 482	Gary Anderson	.08	.04	.01	☐ 537	Doug Smith	.03	.01	.00
☐ 483	Mark Carrier	.08	.04	.01	☐ 538	Larry Kelm	.06	.03	.00
☐ 484	Ricky Reynolds	.03	.01	.00	☐ 539	Pat Terrell	.03	.01	.00
☐ 485	Bruce Hill	.03	.01	.00	☐ 540	Tom Newberry	.03	.01	.00

☐ 541 Jerry Gray	.06	.03	.00
☐ 542 Kevin Greene	.06	.03	.00
☐ 543 Duval Love	.08	.04	.01
☐ 544 Frank Stams	.03	.01	.00
☐ 545 Mike Croel	.75	.35	.07
☐ 546 Mark Jackson	.06	.03	.00
☐ 547 Greg Kragen	.03	.01	.00
☐ 548 Karl Mecklenburg	.06	.03	.00
☐ 549 Simon Fletcher	.03	.01	.00
☐ 550 Bobby Humphrey	.10	.05	.01
☐ 551 Ken Lanier	.03	.01	.00
☐ 552 Vance Johnson	.06	.03	.00
☐ 553 Ron Holmes	.03	.01	.00
☐ 554 John Elway	.15	.07	.01
☐ 555 Melvin Bratton	.06	.03	.00
☐ 556 Dennis Smith	.03	.01	.00
☐ 557 Ricky Nattiel	.06	.03	.00
☐ 558 Clarence Kay	.03	.01	.00
☐ 559 Michael Brooks	.06	.03	.00
☐ 560 Mike Horan	.03	.01	.00
☐ 561 Warren Powers	.03	.01	.00
☐ 562 Keith Kartz	.08	.04	.01
☐ 563 Shannon Sharpe	.10	.05	.01
☐ 564 Wymon Henderson	.03	.01	.00
☐ 565 Steve Atwater	.06	.03	.00
☐ 566 David Treadwell	.03	.01	.00
☐ 567 Bruce Pickens	.20	.10	.02
☐ 568 Jessie Tuggle	.03	.01	.00
☐ 569 Chris Hinton	.06	.03	.00
☐ 570 Keith Jones	.06	.03	.00
☐ 571 Bill Fralic	.06	.03	.00
☐ 572 Mike Rozier	.06	.03	.00
☐ 573 Scott Fulhage	.03	.01	.00
☐ 574 Floyd Dixon	.03	.01	.00
☐ 575 Andre Rison	.15	.07	.01
☐ 576 Darion Conner	.06	.03	.00
☐ 577 Brian Jordan	.20	.10	.02
☐ 578 Michael Haynes	.20	.10	.02
☐ 579 Oliver Barnett	.06	.03	.00
☐ 580 Shawn Collins	.06	.03	.00
☐ 581 Tim Green	.06	.03	.00
☐ 582 Deion Sanders	.20	.10	.02
☐ 583 Mike Kenn	.03	.01	.00
☐ 584 Mike Gann	.03	.01	.00
☐ 585 Chris Miller	.15	.07	.01
☐ 586 Tory Epps	.03	.01	.00
☐ 587 Steve Broussard	.10	.05	.01
☐ 588 Gary Wilkins	.08	.04	.01
☐ 589 Eric Turner	.45	.22	.04
☐ 590 Thane Gash	.03	.01	.00
☐ 591 Clay Matthews	.03	.01	.00
☐ 592 Mike Johnson	.03	.01	.00
☐ 593 Raymond Clayborn	.03	.01	.00
☐ 594 Leroy Hoard	.15	.07	.01
☐ 595 Reggie Langhorne	.03	.01	.00
☐ 596 Mike Baab	.03	.01	.00
☐ 597 Anthony Pleasant	.03	.01	.00

☐ 598 David Grayson	.03	.01	.00
☐ 599 Rob Burnett	.08	.04	.01
☐ 600 Frank Minnifield	.03	.01	.00
☐ 601 Gregg Rakoczy	.06	.03	.00
☐ 602 Eric Metcalf	.06	.03	.00
☐ 603 Paul Farren	.06	.03	.00
☐ 604 Brian Brennan	.03	.01	.00
☐ 605 Tony Jones	.08	.04	.01
☐ 606 Stephen Braggs	.03	.01	.00
☐ 607 Kevin Mack	.06	.03	.00
☐ 608 Pat Harlow	.15	.07	.01
☐ 609 Marv Cook	.10	.05	.01
☐ 610 John Stephens	.08	.04	.01
☐ 611 Ed Reynolds	.06	.03	.00
☐ 612 Tim Goad	.06	.03	.00
☐ 613 Chris Singleton	.06	.03	.00
☐ 614 Bruce Armstrong	.03	.01	.00
☐ 615 Tommy Hodson	.08	.04	.01
☐ 616 Sammy Martin	.06	.03	.00
☐ 617 Andre Tippett	.06	.03	.00
☐ 618 Johnny Rembert	.03	.01	.00
☐ 619 Maurice Hurst	.03	.01	.00
☐ 620 Vincent Brown	.06	.03	.00
☐ 621 Ray Agnew	.03	.01	.00
☐ 622 Ronnie Lippett	.03	.01	.00
☐ 623 Greg McMurtry	.08	.04	.01
☐ 624 Brent Williams	.03	.01	.00
☐ 625 Jason Staurovsky	.06	.03	.00
☐ 626 Marvin Allen	.03	.01	.00
☐ 627 Hart Lee Dykes	.03	.01	.00
☐ 628 Atlanta Falcons Team: (Keith) Jones Jumps for Yardage	.06	.03	.00
☐ 629 Buffalo Bills Team: (Jeff) Wright Goes for a Block	.06	.03	.00
☐ 630 Chicago Bears Team: (Jim) Harbaugh Makes Like a Halfback	.06	.03	.00
☐ 631 Cincinnati Bengals Team: (Stanford) Jennings Cuts Through Hole	.06	.03	.00
☐ 632 Cleveland Browns Team: (Eric) Metcalf Makes a Return	.06	.03	.00
☐ 633 Dallas Cowboys Team: (Kelvin) Martin Makes a Move	.06	.03	.00
☐ 634 Denver Broncos Team: (Shannon) Sharpe Into the Wedge	.06	.03	.00
☐ 635 Detroit Lions Team: (Rodney) Peete Hunted by a Bear (Mike Singletary)	.06	.03	.00
☐ 636 Green Bay Packers Team: (Don) Majkowski	.06	.03	.00

Orchestrates Some Magic			
☐ 637 Houston Oilers 10	.05	.01	
Team: (Warren) Moon			
Monitors the Action			
☐ 638 Indianapolis Colts 12	.06	.01	
Team: (Jeff) George			
Releases Just in Time			
☐ 639 Kansas City Chiefs 06	.03	.00	
Team: (Christian) Okoye			
Powers Ahead			
☐ 640 Los Angeles Raiders 06	.03	.00	
Team: (Marcus) Allen			
Crosses the Plane			
☐ 641 Los Angeles Rams 06	.03	.00	
Team: (Jim) Everett			
Connects With Soft Touch			
☐ 642 Miami Dolphins 06	.03	.00	
Team: (Pete) Stoyanovich			
Kicks It Through			
☐ 643 Minnesota Vikings 06	.03	.00	
Team: (Rich) Gannon			
Loads Cannon			
☐ 644 New Eng. Patriots 06	.03	.00	
Team: (John) Stephens			
Gets Stood Up			
☐ 645 New Orleans Saints 06	.03	.00	
Team: (Gill) Fenerty			
Finds Opening			
☐ 646 New York Giants 06	.03	.00	
Team: (Maurice) Carthon			
Inches Ahead			
☐ 647 New York Jets 06	.03	.00	
Team: (Pat) Leahy			
Perfect on Extra Point			
☐ 648 Philadelphia Eagles 08	.04	.01	
Team: (Randall) Cunningham			
Calls Own Play for TD			
☐ 649 St. Louis Cardinals 06	.03	.00	
Team: (Bill) Lewis			
Provides the Protection			
☐ 650 Pittsburgh Steelers 06	.03	.00	
Team: (Bubby) Brister			
Eyes Downfield Attack			
☐ 651 San Diego Chargers 10	.05	.01	
Team: (John) Friesz			
Finds the Passing Lane			
☐ 652 San Francisco 49ers 06	.03	.00	
Team: (Dexter) Carter			
Follows Rathman's Block			
☐ 653 Seattle Seahawks 06	.03	.00	
Team: (Derrick) Fenner			
With Fancy Footwork			
☐ 654 Tampa Bay Buccaneers ..06	.03	.00	
Team: (Reggie) Cobb			
Hurdles His Way			
to First Down			
☐ 655 Washington Redskins 06	.03	.00	

Team: (Earnest) Byner			
Cuts Back to			
Follow Block			
☐ 656 Checklist 1 06	.01	.00	
☐ 657 Checklist 2 06	.01	.00	
☐ 658 Checklist 3 06	.01	.00	
☐ 659 Checklist 4 06	.01	.00	
☐ 660 Checklist 5 07	.01	.00	

1991 Topps Stadium Club

The 1991 Topps Stadium Club Football set contains 500 cards measuring the standard size (2 1/2" by 3 1/2"). The fronts have full-bleed glossy color action photos. At the bottom, the player's name appears in an aqua stripe that is bordered in gold. On a colorful drawing of a football field and stadium background, the horizontally oriented backs have biography, The Sporting News Football Analysis Report (which consists of strengths and comments), and a miniature replica of the player's Topps rookie cards. The cards are numbered on the back. The key rookies in the set are Nick Bell, Mike Croel, Ricky Ervins, Randal Hill, Todd Marinovich, Dan McGwire, Browning Nagle, Leonard Russell, and Harvey Williams.

	MINT	EXC	G-VG
COMPLETE SET (500)	135.00	60.00	12.00
COMMON PLAYER (1-500)	.20	.10	.02
☐ 1 Pepper Johnson 30	.15	.03	
New York Giants			
☐ 2 Emmitt Smith 18.00	9.00	1.80	

Dallas Cowboys
- ☐ 3 Deion Sanders .... 1.50 .75 .15
  Atlanta Falcons
- ☐ 4 Andre Collins .... .30 .15 .03
  Washington Redskins
- ☐ 5 Eric Metcalf .... .30 .15 .03
  Cleveland Browns
- ☐ 6 Richard Dent .... .30 .15 .03
  Chicago Bears
- ☐ 7 Eric Martin .... .30 .15 .03
  New Orleans Saints
- ☐ 8 Marcus Allen .... .50 .25 .05
  Los Angeles Raiders
- ☐ 9 Gary Anderson .... .20 .10 .02
  Pittsburgh Steelers
- ☐ 10 Joey Browner .... .30 .15 .03
  Minnesota Vikings
- ☐ 11 Lorenzo White .... .30 .15 .03
  Houston Oilers
- ☐ 12 Bruce Smith .... .40 .20 .04
  Buffalo Bills
- ☐ 13 Mark Boyer .... .20 .10 .02
  New York Jets
- ☐ 14 Mike Piel .... .20 .10 .02
  Los Angeles Rams
- ☐ 15 Albert Bentley .... .30 .15 .03
  Indianapolis Colts
- ☐ 16 Bennie Blades .... .30 .15 .03
  Detroit Lions
- ☐ 17 Jason Staurovsky .... .20 .10 .02
  New England Patriots
- ☐ 18 Anthony Toney .... .20 .10 .02
  Philadelphia Eagles
- ☐ 19 Dave Krieg .... .30 .15 .03
  Seattle Seahawks
- ☐ 20 Harvey Williams .... 5.00 2.50 .50
  Kansas City Chiefs
- ☐ 21 Bubba Paris .... .20 .10 .02
  San Francisco 49ers
- ☐ 22 Tim McGee .... .30 .15 .03
  Cincinnati Bengals
- ☐ 23 Brian Noble .... .20 .10 .02
  Green Bay Packers
- ☐ 24 Vinny Testaverde .... .30 .15 .03
  Tampa Bay Buccaneers
- ☐ 25 Doug Widell .... .20 .10 .02
  Denver Broncos
- ☐ 26 John Jackson .... .30 .15 .03
  Phoenix Cardinals
- ☐ 27 Marion Butts .... .50 .25 .05
  San Diego Chargers
- ☐ 28 Deron Cherry .... .30 .15 .03
  Kansas City Chiefs
- ☐ 29 Don Warren .... .30 .15 .03
  Washington Redskins
- ☐ 30 Rod Woodson .... .30 .15 .03
  Pittsburgh Steelers
- ☐ 31 Mike Baab .... .20 .10 .02
  Cleveland Browns
- ☐ 32 Greg Jackson .... .30 .15 .03
  New York Giants
- ☐ 33 Jerry Robinson .... .20 .10 .02
  Los Angeles Raiders
- ☐ 34 Dalton Hilliard .... .30 .15 .03
  New Orleans Saints
- ☐ 35 Brian Jordan .... .60 .30 .06
  Atlanta Falcons
- ☐ 36 James Thornton UER .... .20 .10 .02
  Chicago Bears
  (Misspelled Thorton
  on card back)
- ☐ 37 Michael Irvin .... 2.50 1.25 .25
  Dallas Cowboys
- ☐ 38 Billy Joe Tolliver .... .30 .15 .03
  San Diego Chargers
- ☐ 39 Jeff Herrod .... .20 .10 .02
  Indianapolis Colts
- ☐ 40 Scott Norwood .... .20 .10 .02
  Buffalo Bills
- ☐ 41 Ferrell Edmunds .... .20 .10 .02
  Miami Dolphins
- ☐ 42 Andre Waters .... .20 .10 .02
  Philadelphia Eagles
- ☐ 43 Kevin Glover .... .20 .10 .02
  Detroit Lions
- ☐ 44 Ray Berry .... .20 .10 .02
  Minnesota Vikings
- ☐ 45 Timm Rosenbach .... .30 .15 .03
  Phoenix Cardinals
- ☐ 46 Reuben Davis .... .20 .10 .02
  Tampa Bay Buccaneers
- ☐ 47 Charles Wilson .... .20 .10 .02
  Green Bay Packers
- ☐ 48 Todd Marinovich .... 6.00 3.00 .60
  Los Angeles Raiders
- ☐ 49 Harris Barton .... .20 .10 .02
  San Francisco 49ers
- ☐ 50 Jim Breech .... .20 .10 .02
  Cincinnati Bengals
- ☐ 51 Ron Holmes .... .20 .10 .02
  Denver Broncos
- ☐ 52 Chris Singleton .... .30 .15 .03
  New England Patriots
- ☐ 53 Pat Leahy .... .30 .15 .03
  New York Jets
- ☐ 54 Tom Newberry .... .20 .10 .02
  Los Angeles Rams
- ☐ 55 Greg Montgomery .... .20 .10 .02
  Houston Oilers
- ☐ 56 Robert Blackmon .... .20 .10 .02
  Seattle Seahawks
- ☐ 57 Jay Hilgenberg .... .30 .15 .03
  Chicago Bears
- ☐ 58 Rodney Hampton .... 2.00 1.00 .20

New York Giants
☐ 59 Brett Perriman .... .30 .15 .03
New Orleans Saints
☐ 60 Ricky Watters .... 1.00 .50 .10
San Francisco 49ers
☐ 61 Howie Long .... .30 .15 .03
Los Angeles Raiders
☐ 62 Frank Cornish .... .20 .10 .02
San Diego Chargers
☐ 63 Chris Miller .... 1.00 .50 .10
Atlanta Falcons
☐ 64 Keith Taylor .... .20 .10 .02
Indianapolis Colts
☐ 65 Tony Paige .... .20 .10 .02
Miami Dolphins
☐ 66 Gary Zimmerman .... .20 .10 .02
Minnesota Vikings
☐ 67 Mark Royals .... .30 .15 .03
Tampa Bay Buccaneers
☐ 68 Ernie Jones .... .30 .15 .03
Phoenix Cardinals
☐ 69 David Grant .... .20 .10 .02
Cincinnati Bengals
☐ 70 Shane Conlan .... .30 .15 .03
Buffalo Bills
☐ 71 Jerry Rice .... 2.00 1.00 .20
San Francisco 49ers
☐ 72 Christian Okoye .... .60 .30 .06
Kansas City Chiefs
☐ 73 Eddie Murray .... .20 .10 .02
Detroit Lions
☐ 74 Reggie White .... .50 .25 .05
Philadelphia Eagles
☐ 75 Jeff Graham .... .60 .30 .06
Pittsburgh Steelers
☐ 76 Mark Jackson .... .30 .15 .03
Denver Broncos
☐ 77 David Grayson .... .20 .10 .02
Cleveland Browns
☐ 78 Dan Stryzinski .... .20 .10 .02
Pittsburgh Steelers
☐ 79 Sterling Sharpe .... .60 .30 .06
Green Bay Packers
☐ 80 Cleveland Gary .... .30 .15 .03
Los Angeles Rams
☐ 81 Johnny Meads .... .20 .10 .02
Houston Oilers
☐ 82 Howard Cross .... .20 .10 .02
New York Giants
☐ 83 Ken O'Brien .... .30 .15 .03
New York Jets
☐ 84 Brian Blades .... .30 .15 .03
Seattle Seahawks
☐ 85 Ethan Horton .... .30 .15 .03
Los Angeles Raiders
☐ 86 Bruce Armstrong .... .20 .10 .02
New England Patriots

☐ 87 James Washington .... .30 .15 .03
Dallas Cowboys
☐ 88 Eugene Daniel .... .20 .10 .02
Indianapolis Colts
☐ 89 James Lofton .... .60 .30 .06
Buffalo Bills
☐ 90 Louis Oliver .... .30 .15 .03
Miami Dolphins
☐ 91 Boomer Esiason .... .50 .25 .05
Cincinnati Bengals
☐ 92 Seth Joyner .... .30 .15 .03
Philadelphia Eagles
☐ 93 Mark Carrier .... .30 .15 .03
Tampa Bay Buccaneers
☐ 94 Brett Favre UER .... 2.00 1.00 .20
Atlanta Falcons
(Favre misspelled
as Farve)
☐ 95 Lee Williams .... .30 .15 .03
San Diego Chargers
☐ 96 Neal Anderson .... .60 .30 .06
Chicago Bears
☐ 97 Brent Jones .... .30 .15 .03
San Francisco 49ers
☐ 98 John Alt .... .20 .10 .02
Kansas City Chiefs
☐ 99 Rodney Peete .... .30 .15 .03
Detroit Lions
☐ 100 Steve Broussard .... .40 .20 .04
Atlanta Falcons
☐ 101 Cedric Mack .... .20 .10 .02
Phoenix Cardinals
☐ 102 Pat Swilling .... .30 .15 .03
New Orleans Saints
☐ 103 Stan Humphries .... .30 .15 .03
Washington Redskins
☐ 104 Darrell Thompson .... .60 .30 .06
Green Bay Packers
☐ 105 Reggie Langhorne .... .20 .10 .02
Cleveland Browns
☐ 106 Kenny Davidson .... .20 .10 .02
Pittsburgh Steelers
☐ 107 Jim Everett .... .50 .25 .05
Los Angeles Rams
☐ 108 Keith Millard .... .30 .15 .03
Minnesota Vikings
☐ 109 Garry Lewis .... .20 .10 .02
Los Angeles Raiders
☐ 110 Jeff Hostetler .... .75 .35 .07
New York Giants
☐ 111 Lamar Lathon .... .30 .15 .03
Houston Oilers
☐ 112 Johnny Bailey .... .30 .15 .03
Chicago Bears
☐ 113 Cornelius Bennett .... .40 .20 .04
Buffalo Bills
☐ 114 Travis McNeal .... .20 .10 .02

Seattle Seahawks
☐ 115 Jeff Lageman ....30 .15 .03
New York Jets
☐ 116 Nick Bell ....4.00 2.00 .40
Los Angeles Raiders
☐ 117 Calvin Williams ....30 .15 .03
Philadelphia Eagles
☐ 118 Shawn Lee ....30 .15 .03
Miami Dolphins
☐ 119 Anthony Munoz ....30 .15 .03
Cincinnati Bengals
☐ 120 Jay Novacek ....50 .25 .05
Dallas Cowboys
☐ 121 Kevin Fagan ....20 .10 .02
San Francisco 49ers
☐ 122 Leo Goeas ....20 .10 .02
San Diego Chargers
☐ 123 Vance Johnson ....30 .15 .03
Denver Broncos
☐ 124 Brent Williams ....20 .10 .02
New England Patriots
☐ 125 Clarence Verdin ....20 .10 .02
Indianapolis Colts
☐ 126 Luis Sharpe ....20 .10 .02
Phoenix Cardinals
☐ 127 Darrell Green ....40 .20 .04
Washington Redskins
☐ 128 Barry Word ....1.25 .60 .12
Kansas City Chiefs
☐ 129 Steve Walsh ....40 .20 .04
New Orleans Saints
☐ 130 Bryan Hinkle ....20 .10 .02
Pittsburgh Steelers
☐ 131 Ed West ....20 .10 .02
Green Bay Packers
☐ 132 Jeff Campbell ....20 .10 .02
Detroit Lions
☐ 133 Dennis Byrd ....30 .15 .03
New York Jets
☐ 134 Nate Odomes ....20 .10 .02
Buffalo Bills
☐ 135 Trace Armstrong ....20 .10 .02
Chicago Bears
☐ 136 Jarvis Williams ....20 .10 .02
Miami Dolphins
☐ 137 Warren Moon ....1.50 .75 .15
Houston Oilers
☐ 138 Eric Moten ....50 .25 .05
San Diego Chargers
☐ 139 Tony Woods ....30 .15 .03
Seattle Seahawks
☐ 140 Phil Simms ....40 .20 .04
New York Giants
☐ 141 Ricky Reynolds ....20 .10 .02
Tampa Bay Buccaneers
☐ 142 Frank Stams ....20 .10 .02
Los Angeles Rams

☐ 143 Kevin Mack ....30 .15 .03
Cleveland Browns
☐ 144 Wade Wilson ....30 .15 .03
Minnesota Vikings
☐ 145 Shawn Collins ....30 .15 .03
Atlanta Falcons
☐ 146 Roger Craig ....40 .20 .04
Los Angeles Raiders
☐ 147 Jeff Feagles ....30 .15 .03
Philadelphia Eagles
☐ 148 Norm Johnson ....20 .10 .02
Seattle Seahawks
☐ 149 Terance Mathis ....40 .20 .04
New York Jets
☐ 150 Reggie Cobb ....60 .30 .06
Tampa Bay Buccaneers
☐ 151 Chip Banks ....20 .10 .02
Indianapolis Colts
☐ 152 Darryl Pollard ....20 .10 .02
San Francisco 49ers
☐ 153 Karl Mecklenburg ....30 .15 .03
Denver Broncos
☐ 154 Ricky Proehl ....50 .25 .05
Phoenix Cardinals
☐ 155 Pete Stoyanovich ....20 .10 .02
Miami Dolphins
☐ 156 John Stephens ....30 .15 .03
New England Patriots
☐ 157 Ron Morris ....20 .10 .02
Chicago Bears
☐ 158 Steve DeBerg ....30 .15 .03
Kansas City Chiefs
☐ 159 Mike Munchak ....30 .15 .03
Houston Oilers
☐ 160 Brett Maxie ....30 .15 .03
New Orleans Saints
☐ 161 Don Beebe ....30 .15 .03
Buffalo Bills
☐ 162 Martin Mayhew ....20 .10 .02
Washington Redskins
☐ 163 Merril Hoge ....30 .15 .03
Pittsburgh Steelers
☐ 164 Kelvin Pritchett ....30 .15 .03
Detroit Lions
☐ 165 Jim Jeffcoat ....20 .10 .02
Dallas Cowboys
☐ 166 Myron Guyton ....20 .10 .02
New York Giants
☐ 167 Ickey Woods ....30 .15 .03
Cincinnati Bengals
☐ 168 Andre Ware ....50 .25 .05
Detroit Lions
☐ 169 Gary Plummer ....20 .10 .02
San Diego Chargers
☐ 170 Henry Ellard ....30 .15 .03
Los Angeles Rams
☐ 171 Scott Davis ....20 .10 .02

Los Angeles Raiders
☐ 172 Randall McDaniel .....20 .10 .02
Minnesota Vikings
☐ 173 Randal Hill ....2.00 1.00 .20
Miami Dolphins
☐ 174 Anthony Bell ....20 .10 .02
Phoenix Cardinals
☐ 175 Gary Anderson ....30 .15 .03
Tampa Bay Buccaneers
☐ 176 Byron Evans ....20 .10 .02
Philadelphia Eagles
☐ 177 Tony Mandarich ....30 .15 .03
Green Bay Packers
☐ 178 Jeff George ....1.50 .75 .15
Indianapolis Colts
☐ 179 Art Monk ....75 .35 .07
Washington Redskins
☐ 180 Mike Kenn ....20 .10 .02
Atlanta Falcons
☐ 181 Sean Landeta ....20 .10 .02
New York Giants
☐ 182 Shaun Gayle ....20 .10 .02
Chicago Bears
☐ 183 Michael Carter ....30 .15 .03
San Francisco 49ers
☐ 184 Robb Thomas ....30 .15 .03
Kansas City Chiefs
☐ 185 Richmond Webb ....30 .15 .03
Miami Dolphins
☐ 186 Carnell Lake ....20 .10 .02
Pittsburgh Steelers
☐ 187 Rueben Mayes ....30 .15 .03
New Orleans Saints
☐ 188 Issiac Holt ....20 .10 .02
Dallas Cowboys
☐ 189 Leon Seals ....20 .10 .02
Buffalo Bills
☐ 190 Al Smith ....20 .10 .02
Houston Oilers
☐ 191 Steve Atwater ....30 .15 .03
Denver Broncos
☐ 192 Greg McMurtry ....30 .15 .03
New England Patriots
☐ 193 Al Toon ....30 .15 .03
New York Jets
☐ 194 Cortez Kennedy ....40 .20 .04
Seattle Seahawks
☐ 195 Gill Byrd ....30 .15 .03
San Diego Chargers
☐ 196 Carl Zander ....20 .10 .02
Cincinnati Bengals
☐ 197 Robert Brown ....20 .10 .02
Green Bay Packers
☐ 198 Buford McGee ....20 .10 .02
Los Angeles Rams
☐ 199 Mervyn Fernandez ....30 .15 .03
Los Angeles Raiders

☐ 200 Mike Dumas ....50 .25 .05
Houston Oilers
☐ 201 Rob Burnett ....50 .25 .05
Cleveland Browns
☐ 202 Brian Mitchell ....40 .20 .04
Washington Redskins
☐ 203 Randall Cunningham .....60 .30 .06
Philadelphia Eagles
☐ 204 Sammie Smith ....30 .15 .03
Miami Dolphins
☐ 205 Ken Clarke ....20 .10 .02
Minnesota Vikings
☐ 206 Floyd Dixon ....20 .10 .02
Atlanta Falcons
☐ 207 Ken Norton ....20 .10 .02
Dallas Cowboys
☐ 208 Tony Siragusa ....30 .15 .03
Indianapolis Colts
☐ 209 Louis Lipps ....30 .15 .03
Pittsburgh Steelers
☐ 210 Chris Martin ....20 .10 .02
Kansas City Chiefs
☐ 211 Jamie Mueller ....20 .10 .02
Buffalo Bills
☐ 212 Dave Waymer ....20 .10 .02
San Francisco 49ers
☐ 213 Donnell Woolford ....20 .10 .02
Chicago Bears
☐ 214 Paul Gruber ....30 .15 .03
Tampa Bay Buccaneers
☐ 215 Ken Harvey ....20 .10 .02
Phoenix Cardinals
☐ 216 Henry Jones ....30 .15 .03
Buffalo Bills
☐ 217 Tommy Barnhardt ....30 .15 .03
New Orleans Saints
☐ 218 Arthur Cox ....20 .10 .02
San Diego Chargers
☐ 219 Pat Terrell ....20 .10 .02
Los Angeles Rams
☐ 220 Curtis Duncan ....30 .15 .03
Houston Oilers
☐ 221 Jeff Jaeger ....20 .10 .02
Los Angeles Raiders
☐ 222 Scott Stephen ....30 .15 .03
Green Bay Packers
☐ 223 Rob Moore ....2.00 1.00 .20
New York Jets
☐ 224 Chris Hinton ....30 .15 .03
Atlanta Falcons
☐ 225 Marv Cook ....40 .20 .04
New England Patriots
☐ 226 Patrick Hunter ....30 .15 .03
Seattle Seahawks
☐ 227 Earnest Byner ....30 .15 .03
Washington Redskins
☐ 228 Troy Aikman ....4.50 2.25 .45

Dallas Cowboys
- [ ] 229 Kevin Walker ....35 .17 .03
Cincinnati Bengals
- [ ] 230 Keith Jackson ....30 .15 .03
Philadelphia Eagles
- [ ] 231 Russell Maryland ....2.00 1.00 .20
Dallas Cowboys
- [ ] 232 Charles Haley ....30 .15 .03
San Francisco 49ers
- [ ] 233 Nick Lowery ....20 .10 .02
Kansas City Chiefs
- [ ] 234 Erik Howard ....20 .10 .02
New York Giants
- [ ] 235 Leonard Smith ....20 .10 .02
Buffalo Bills
- [ ] 236 Tim Irwin ....20 .10 .02
Minnesota Vikings
- [ ] 237 Simon Fletcher ....30 .15 .03
Denver Broncos
- [ ] 238 Thomas Everett ....20 .10 .02
Pittsburgh Steelers
- [ ] 239 Reggie Roby ....20 .10 .02
Miami Dolphins
- [ ] 240 Leroy Hoard ....50 .25 .05
Cleveland Browns
- [ ] 241 Wayne Haddix ....30 .15 .03
Tampa Bay Buccaneers
- [ ] 242 Gary Clark ....75 .35 .07
Washington Redskins
- [ ] 243 Eric Andolsek ....20 .10 .02
Detroit Lions
- [ ] 244 Jim Wahler ....30 .15 .03
Phoenix Cardinals
- [ ] 245 Vaughan Johnson ....30 .15 .03
New Orleans Saints
- [ ] 246 Kevin Butler ....20 .10 .02
Chicago Bears
- [ ] 247 Steve Tasker ....20 .10 .02
Buffalo Bills
- [ ] 248 LeRoy Butler ....20 .10 .02
Green Bay Packers
- [ ] 249 Darion Conner ....30 .15 .03
Atlanta Falcons
- [ ] 250 Eric Turner ....2.50 1.25 .25
Cleveland Browns
- [ ] 251 Kevin Ross ....20 .10 .02
Kansas City Chiefs
- [ ] 252 Stephen Baker ....30 .15 .03
New York Giants
- [ ] 253 Harold Green ....75 .35 .07
Cincinnati Bengals
- [ ] 254 Rohn Stark ....20 .10 .02
Indianapolis Colts
- [ ] 255 Joe Nash ....20 .10 .02
Seattle Seahawks
- [ ] 256 Jesse Sapolu ....20 .10 .02
San Francisco 49ers

- [ ] 257 Willie Gault ....30 .15 .03
Los Angeles Raiders
- [ ] 258 Jerome Brown ....30 .15 .03
Philadelphia Eagles
- [ ] 259 Ken Willis ....20 .10 .02
Dallas Cowboys
- [ ] 260 Courtney Hall ....20 .10 .02
San Diego Chargers
- [ ] 261 Hart Lee Dykes ....20 .10 .02
New England Patriots
- [ ] 262 William Fuller ....20 .10 .02
Houston Oilers
- [ ] 263 Stan Thomas ....30 .15 .03
Chicago Bears
- [ ] 264 Dan Marino ....1.50 .75 .15
Miami Dolphins
- [ ] 265 Ron Cox ....20 .10 .02
Chicago Bears
- [ ] 266 Eric Green ....75 .35 .07
Pittsburgh Steelers
- [ ] 267 Anthony Carter ....30 .15 .03
Minnesota Vikings
- [ ] 268 Jerry Ball ....20 .10 .02
Detroit Lions
- [ ] 269 Ron Hall ....20 .10 .02
Tampa Bay Buccaneers
- [ ] 270 Dennis Smith ....20 .10 .02
Denver Broncos
- [ ] 271 Eric Hill ....20 .10 .02
Phoenix Cardinals
- [ ] 272 Dan McGwire ....5.00 2.50 .50
Seattle Seahawks
- [ ] 273 Lewis Billups ....20 .10 .02
Cincinnati Bengals
- [ ] 274 Rickey Jackson ....30 .15 .03
New Orleans Saints
- [ ] 275 Jim Sweeney ....20 .10 .02
New York Jets
- [ ] 276 Pat Beach ....20 .10 .02
Indianapolis Colts
- [ ] 277 Kevin Porter ....20 .10 .02
Kansas City Chiefs
- [ ] 278 Mike Sherrard ....30 .15 .03
San Francisco 49ers
- [ ] 279 Andy Heck ....20 .10 .02
Seattle Seahawks
- [ ] 280 Ron Brown ....20 .10 .02
Los Angeles Raiders
- [ ] 281 Lawrence Taylor ....60 .30 .06
New York Giants
- [ ] 282 Anthony Pleasant ....20 .10 .02
Cleveland Browns
- [ ] 283 Wes Hopkins ....20 .10 .02
Philadelphia Eagles
- [ ] 284 Jim Lachey ....30 .15 .03
Washington Redskins
- [ ] 285 Tim Harris ....30 .15 .03

Green Bay Packers
- [ ] 286 Tory Epps .... .20 .10 .02
Atlanta Falcons
- [ ] 287 Wendell Davis .... .75 .35 .07
Chicago Bears
- [ ] 288 Bubba McDowell .... .20 .10 .02
Houston Oilers
- [ ] 289 Bubby Brister .... .30 .15 .03
Pittsburgh Steelers
- [ ] 290 Chris Zorich .... .75 .35 .07
Chicago Bears
- [ ] 291 Mike Merriweather ...... .20 .10 .02
Minnesota Vikings
- [ ] 292 Burt Grossman .... .20 .10 .02
San Diego Chargers
- [ ] 293 Erik McMillan .... .20 .10 .02
New York Jets
- [ ] 294 John Elway .... 1.00 .50 .10
Denver Broncos
- [ ] 295 Toi Cook .... .30 .15 .03
New Orleans Saints
- [ ] 296 Tom Rathman .... .30 .15 .03
San Francisco 49ers
- [ ] 297 Matt Bahr .... .20 .10 .02
New York Giants
- [ ] 298 Chris Spielman .... .30 .15 .03
Detroit Lions
- [ ] 299 Freddie Joe Nunn .... .30 .15 .03
Phoenix Cardinals
(Troy Aikman and
Emmitt Smith shown
in background)
- [ ] 300 Jim C. Jensen .... .20 .10 .02
Miami Dolphins
- [ ] 301 David Fulcher UER .... .20 .10 .02
Cincinnati Bengals
(Rookie card should
be '88, not '89)
- [ ] 302 Tommy Hodson .... .30 .15 .03
New England Patriots
- [ ] 303 Stephone Paige .... .30 .15 .03
Kansas City Chiefs
- [ ] 304 Greg Townsend .... .20 .10 .02
Los Angeles Raiders
- [ ] 305 Dean Biasucci .... .20 .10 .02
Indianapolis Colts
- [ ] 306 Jimmie Jones .... .20 .10 .02
Dallas Cowboys
- [ ] 307 Eugene Marve .... .20 .10 .02
Tampa Bay Buccaneers
- [ ] 308 Flipper Anderson .... .30 .15 .03
Los Angeles Rams
- [ ] 309 Darryl Talley .... .30 .15 .03
Buffalo Bills
- [ ] 310 Mike Croel .... 2.50 1.25 .25
Denver Broncos
- [ ] 311 Thane Gash .... .20 .10 .02

Cleveland Browns
- [ ] 312 Perry Kemp .... .20 .10 .02
Green Bay Packers
- [ ] 313 Heath Sherman .... .30 .15 .03
Philadelphia Eagles
- [ ] 314 Mike Singletary .... .30 .15 .03
Chicago Bears
- [ ] 315 Chip Lohmiller .... .20 .10 .02
Washington Redskins
- [ ] 316 Tunch Ilkin .... .20 .10 .02
Pittsburgh Steelers
- [ ] 317 Junior Seau .... .30 .15 .03
San Diego Chargers
- [ ] 318 Mike Gann .... .20 .10 .02
Atlanta Falcons
- [ ] 319 Tim McDonald .... .20 .10 .02
Phoenix Cardinals
- [ ] 320 Kyle Clifton .... .20 .10 .02
New York Jets
- [ ] 321 Dan Owens .... .20 .10 .02
Detroit Lions
- [ ] 322 Tim Grunhard .... .20 .10 .02
Kansas City Chiefs
- [ ] 323 Stan Brock .... .20 .10 .02
New Orleans Saints
- [ ] 324 Rodney Holman .... .20 .10 .02
Cincinnati Bengals
- [ ] 325 Mark Ingram .... .20 .10 .02
New York Giants
- [ ] 326 Browning Nagle .... 4.50 2.25 .45
New York Jets
- [ ] 327 Joe Montana .... 2.00 1.00 .20
San Francisco 49ers
- [ ] 328 Carl Lee .... .20 .10 .02
Minnesota Vikings
- [ ] 329 John L. Williams .... .30 .15 .03
Seattle Seahawks
- [ ] 330 David Griggs .... .20 .10 .02
Miami Dolphins
- [ ] 331 Clarence Kay .... .20 .10 .02
Denver Broncos
- [ ] 332 Irving Fryar .... .30 .15 .03
New England Patriots
- [ ] 333 Doug Smith .... .30 .15 .03
Houston Oilers
- [ ] 334 Kent Hull .... .20 .10 .02
Buffalo Bills
- [ ] 335 Mike Wilcher .... .20 .10 .02
Los Angeles Rams
- [ ] 336 Ray Donaldson .... .20 .10 .02
Indianapolis Colts
- [ ] 337 Mark Carrier USC UER .. .50 .25 .05
Chicago Bears
(Rookie card should
be '90, not '89)
- [ ] 338 Kelvin Martin .... .30 .15 .03
Dallas Cowboys

☐ 339 Keith Byars 30	.15	.03
Philadelphia Eagles		
☐ 340 Wilber Marshall 30	.15	.03
Washington Redskins		
☐ 341 Ronnie Lott 50	.25	.05
Los Angeles Raiders		
☐ 342 Blair Thomas 2.00	1.00	.20
New York Jets		
☐ 343 Ronnie Harmon 20	.10	.02
San Diego Chargers		
☐ 344 Brian Brennan 20	.10	.02
Cleveland Browns		
☐ 345 Charles McRae 60	.30	.06
Tampa Bay Buccaneers		
☐ 346 Michael Cofer 20	.10	.02
Detroit Lions		
☐ 347 Keith Willis 20	.10	.02
Pittsburgh Steelers		
☐ 348 Bruce Kozerski 20	.10	.02
Cincinnati Bengals		
☐ 349 Dave Meggett 60	.30	.06
New York Giants		
☐ 350 John Taylor 60	.30	.06
San Francisco 49ers		
☐ 351 Johnny Holland 20	.10	.02
Green Bay Packers		
☐ 352 Steve Christie 20	.10	.02
Tampa Bay Buccaneers		
☐ 353 Ricky Ervins 12.00	6.00	1.20
Washington Redskins		
☐ 354 Robert Massey 20	.10	.02
New Orleans Saints		
☐ 355 Derrick Thomas 1.00	.50	.10
Kansas City Chiefs		
☐ 356 Tommy Kane 50	.25	.05
Seattle Seahawks		
☐ 357 Melvin Bratton 20	.10	.02
Denver Broncos		
☐ 358 Bruce Matthews 20	.10	.02
Houston Oilers		
☐ 359 Mark Duper 30	.15	.03
Miami Dolphins		
☐ 360 Jeff Wright 30	.15	.03
Buffalo Bills		
☐ 361 Barry Sanders 9.00	4.50	.90
Detroit Lions		
☐ 362 Chuck Webb 75	.35	.07
Green Bay Packers		
☐ 363 Darryl Grant 20	.10	.02
Washington Redskins		
☐ 364 William Roberts 20	.10	.02
New York Giants		
☐ 365 Reggie Rutland 20	.10	.02
Minnesota Vikings		
☐ 366 Clay Matthews 20	.10	.02
Cleveland Browns		
☐ 367 Anthony Miller 30	.15	.03
San Diego Chargers		
☐ 368 Mike Prior 20	.10	.02
Indianapolis Colts		
☐ 369 Jessie Tuggle 20	.10	.02
Atlanta Falcons		
☐ 370 Brad Muster 30	.15	.03
Chicago Bears		
☐ 371 Jay Schroeder 30	.15	.03
Los Angeles Raiders		
☐ 372 Greg Lloyd 20	.10	.02
Pittsburgh Steelers		
☐ 373 Mike Cofer 20	.10	.02
San Francisco 49ers		
☐ 374 James Brooks 30	.15	.03
Cincinnati Bengals		
☐ 375 Danny Noonan UER 20	.10	.02
Dallas Cowboys		
(Misspelled Noonen		
on card back)		
☐ 376 Latin Berry 30	.15	.03
Los Angeles Rams		
☐ 377 Brad Baxter 50	.25	.05
New York Jets		
☐ 378 Godfrey Myles 30	.15	.03
Dallas Cowboys		
☐ 379 Morten Andersen 30	.15	.03
New Orleans Saints		
☐ 380 Keith Woodside 30	.15	.03
Green Bay Packers		
☐ 381 Bobby Humphrey 50	.25	.05
Denver Broncos		
☐ 382 Mike Golic 20	.10	.02
Philadelphia Eagles		
☐ 383 Keith McCants 30	.15	.03
Tampa Bay Buccaneers		
☐ 384 Anthony Thompson 50	.25	.05
Phoenix Cardinals		
☐ 385 Mark Clayton 30	.15	.03
Miami Dolphins		
☐ 386 Neil Smith 30	.15	.03
Kansas City Chiefs		
☐ 387 Bryan Millard 20	.10	.02
Seattle Seahawks		
☐ 388 Mel Gray UER 20	.10	.02
Detroit Lions		
(Wrong Mel Gray		
pictured on card back)		
☐ 389 Ernest Givins 40	.20	.04
Houston Oilers		
☐ 390 Reyna Thompson 20	.10	.02
New York Giants		
☐ 391 Eric Bieniemy 1.00	.50	.10
San Diego Chargers		
☐ 392 Jon Hand 20	.10	.02
Indianapolis Colts		
☐ 393 Mark Rypien 2.50	1.25	.25
Washington Redskins		

☐ 394	Bill Romanowski ....20 San Francisco 49ers	.10	.02
☐ 395	Thurman Thomas ...... 6.00 Buffalo Bills	3.00	.60
☐ 396	Jim Harbaugh ....60 Chicago Bears	.30	.06
☐ 397	Don Mosebar ....20 Los Angeles Raiders	.10	.02
☐ 398	Andre Rison ....75 Atlanta Falcons	.35	.07
☐ 399	Mike Johnson ....20 Cleveland Browns	.10	.02
☐ 400	Dermontti Dawson ....20 Pittsburgh Steelers	.10	.02
☐ 401	Herschel Walker ....50 Minnesota Vikings	.25	.05
☐ 402	Joe Prokop ....20 New York Jets	.10	.02
☐ 403	Eddie Brown ....30 Cincinnati Bengals	.15	.03
☐ 404	Nate Newton ....20 Dallas Cowboys	.10	.02
☐ 405	Damone Johnson ....30 Los Angeles Rams	.15	.03
☐ 406	Jessie Hester ....30 Indianapolis Colts	.15	.03
☐ 407	Jim Arnold ....20 Detroit Lions	.10	.02
☐ 408	Ray Agnew ....20 New England Patriots	.10	.02
☐ 409	Michael Brooks ....20 Denver Broncos	.10	.02
☐ 410	Keith Sims ....20 Miami Dolphins	.10	.02
☐ 411	Carl Banks ....30 New York Giants	.15	.03
☐ 412	Jonathan Hayes ....20 Kansas City Chiefs	.10	.02
☐ 413	Richard Johnson ....30 Houston Oilers	.15	.03
☐ 414	Darryll Lewis ....50 Houston Oilers	.25	.05
☐ 415	Jeff Bryant ....20 Seattle Seahawks	.10	.02
☐ 416	Leslie O'Neal ....30 San Diego Chargers	.15	.03
☐ 417	Andre Reed ....75 Buffalo Bills	.35	.07
☐ 418	Charles Mann ....30 Washington Redskins	.15	.03
☐ 419	Keith DeLong ....20 San Francisco 49ers	.10	.02
☐ 420	Bruce Hill ....20 Tampa Bay Buccaneers	.10	.02
☐ 421	Matt Brock ....40 Green Bay Packers	.20	.04
☐ 422	Johnny Johnson .... 1.25 Phoenix Cardinals	.60	.12
☐ 423	Mark Bortz ....20 Chicago Bears	.10	.02
☐ 424	Ben Smith ....20 Philadelphia Eagles	.10	.02
☐ 425	Jeff Cross ....20 Miami Dolphins	.10	.02
☐ 426	Irv Pankey ....20 Los Angeles Rams	.10	.02
☐ 427	Hassan Jones ....20 Minnesota Vikings	.10	.02
☐ 428	Andre Tippett ....30 New England Patriots	.15	.03
☐ 429	Tim Worley ....30 Pittsburgh Steelers	.15	.03
☐ 430	Daniel Stubbs ....20 Dallas Cowboys	.10	.02
☐ 431	Max Montoya ....20 Los Angeles Rams	.10	.02
☐ 432	Jumbo Elliott ....20 New York Giants	.10	.02
☐ 433	Duane Bickett ....20 Indianapolis Colts	.10	.02
☐ 434	Nate Lewis ....40 San Diego Chargers	.20	.04
☐ 435	Leonard Russell .... 4.50 New England Patriots	2.25	.45
☐ 436	Hoby Brenner ....20 New Orleans Saints	.10	.02
☐ 437	Ricky Sanders ....30 Washington Redskins	.15	.03
☐ 438	Pierce Holt ....20 San Francisco 49ers	.10	.02
☐ 439	Derrick Fenner ....50 Seattle Seahawks	.25	.05
☐ 440	Drew Hill ....30 Houston Oilers	.15	.03
☐ 441	Will Wolford ....20 Buffalo Bills	.10	.02
☐ 442	Albert Lewis ....30 Kansas City Chiefs	.15	.03
☐ 443	James Francis ....30 Cincinnati Bengals	.15	.03
☐ 444	Chris Jacke ....20 Green Bay Packers	.10	.02
☐ 445	Mike Farr ....20 Detroit Lions	.10	.02
☐ 446	Stephen Braggs ....20 Cleveland Browns	.10	.02
☐ 447	Michael Haynes .... 1.50 Atlanta Falcons	.75	.15
☐ 448	Freeman McNeil UER ....30 New York Jets (2008 pounds, sic)	.15	.03
☐ 449	Kevin Donnalley ....30 Houston Oilers	.15	.03
☐ 450	John Offerdahl 30	.15	.03

Miami Dolphins
- [ ] 451 Eric Allen ....20 .10 .02
  Philadelphia Eagles
- [ ] 452 Keith McKeller ....30 .15 .03
  Buffalo Bills
- [ ] 453 Kevin Greene ....30 .15 .03
  Los Angeles Rams
- [ ] 454 Ronnie Lippett ....20 .10 .02
  New England Patriots
- [ ] 455 Ray Childress ....30 .15 .03
  Houston Oilers
- [ ] 456 Mike Saxon ....20 .10 .02
  Dallas Cowboys
- [ ] 457 Mark Robinson ....20 .10 .02
  Tampa Bay Buccaneers
- [ ] 458 Greg Kragen ....20 .10 .02
  Denver Broncos
- [ ] 459 Steve Jordan ....30 .15 .03
  Minnesota Vikings
- [ ] 460 John Johnson ....30 .15 .03
  San Francisco 49ers
- [ ] 461 Sam Mills ....30 .15 .03
  New Orleans Saints
- [ ] 462 Bo Jackson ....1.50 .75 .15
  Los Angeles Raiders
- [ ] 463 Mark Collins ....20 .10 .02
  New York Giants
- [ ] 464 Percy Snow ....30 .15 .03
  Kansas City Chiefs
- [ ] 465 Jeff Bostic ....20 .10 .02
  Washington Redskins
- [ ] 466 Jacob Green ....20 .10 .02
  Seattle Seahawks
- [ ] 467 Dexter Carter ....30 .15 .03
  San Francisco 49ers
- [ ] 468 Rich Camarillo ....20 .10 .02
  Phoenix Cardinals
- [ ] 469 Bill Brooks ....20 .10 .02
  Indianapolis Colts
- [ ] 470 John Carney ....20 .10 .02
  San Diego Chargers
- [ ] 471 Don Majkowski ....30 .15 .03
  Green Bay Packers
- [ ] 472 Ralph Tamm ....30 .15 .03
  Cleveland Browns
- [ ] 473 Fred Barnett ....1.50 .75 .15
  Philadelphia Eagles
- [ ] 474 Jim Covert ....30 .15 .03
  Chicago Bears
- [ ] 475 Kenneth Davis ....30 .15 .03
  Buffalo Bills
- [ ] 476 Jerry Gray ....30 .15 .03
  Los Angeles Rams
- [ ] 477 Broderick Thomas ....30 .15 .03
  Tampa Bay Buccaneers
- [ ] 478 Chris Doleman ....30 .15 .03
  Minnesota Vikings

- [ ] 479 Haywood Jeffires ....1.50 .75 .15
  Houston Oilers
- [ ] 480 Craig Heyward ....30 .15 .03
  New Orleans Saints
- [ ] 481 Markus Koch ....30 .15 .03
  Washington Redskins
- [ ] 482 Tim Krumrie ....20 .10 .02
  Cincinnati Bengals
- [ ] 483 Robert Clark ....20 .10 .02
  Detroit Lions
- [ ] 484 Mike Rozier ....30 .15 .03
  Atlanta Falcons
- [ ] 485 Danny Villa ....20 .10 .02
  New England Patriots
- [ ] 486 Gerald Williams ....20 .10 .02
  Pittsburgh Steelers
- [ ] 487 Steve Wisniewski ....20 .10 .02
  Los Angeles Raiders
- [ ] 488 J.B. Brown ....20 .10 .02
  Miami Dolphins
- [ ] 489 Eugene Robinson ....20 .10 .02
  Seattle Seahawks
- [ ] 490 Ottis Anderson ....30 .15 .03
  New York Giants
- [ ] 491 Tony Stargell ....20 .10 .02
  New York Jets
- [ ] 492 Jack Del Rio ....20 .10 .02
  Dallas Cowboys
- [ ] 493 Lamar Rogers ....30 .15 .03
  Cincinnati Bengals
- [ ] 494 Ricky Nattiel ....30 .15 .03
  Denver Broncos
- [ ] 495 Dan Saleaumua ....20 .10 .02
  Kansas City Chiefs
- [ ] 496 Checklist Card ....20 .03 .01
- [ ] 497 Checklist Card ....20 .03 .01
- [ ] 498 Checklist Card ....20 .03 .01
- [ ] 499 Checklist Card ....20 .03 .01
- [ ] 500 Checklist Card ....20 .03 .01

1991 Upper Deck I

This 500-card standard size set is the first set produced by Upper Deck. The cards have the typical Upper Deck look to them with attractive color photos on both sides of the card and stats and a brief biography on the back. Cards 72-99 feature team checklists with Vernon Wells drawings. Other special subsets included

are Star Rookies (1-29), Aerial Threats (30-35), Season Leaders (401-406), and Team MVP's (450-487). The key Rookie Cards in this set are Todd Marinovich, Dan McGwire, Browning Nagle, and Harvey Williams.

	MINT	EXC	G-VG
COMPLETE SET (500)	24.00	10.00	2.00
COMMON PLAYER (1-500)	.03	.01	.00

		MINT	EXC	G-VG
☐ 1	Star Rookie Checklist	.50	.15	.03
	Dan McGwire			
☐ 2	Eric Bieniemy	.30	.15	.03
	San Diego Chargers			
☐ 3	Mike Dumas	.15	.07	.01
	Houston Oilers			
☐ 4	Mike Croel	.75	.35	.07
	Denver Broncos			
☐ 5	Russell Maryland	.45	.22	.04
	Dallas Cowboys			
☐ 6	Charles McRae	.15	.07	.01
	Tampa Bay Buccaneers			
☐ 7	Dan McGwire	1.25	.60	.12
	Seattle Seahawks			
☐ 8	Mike Pritchard	.60	.30	.06
	Atlanta Falcons			
☐ 9	Ricky Watters	.35	.17	.03
	San Francisco 49ers			
☐ 10	Chris Zorich	.25	.12	.02
	Chicago Bears			
☐ 11	Browning Nagle	1.00	.50	.10
	New York Jets			
☐ 12	Wesley Carroll	.40	.20	.04
	New Orleans Saints			
☐ 13	Brett Favre	.75	.35	.07
	Atlanta Falcons			
☐ 14	Rob Carpenter	.12	.06	.01
	Cincinnati Bengals			
☐ 15	Eric Swann	.20	.10	.02
	Phoenix Cardinals			
☐ 16	Stanley Richard	.25	.12	.02
	San Diego Chargers			
☐ 17	Herman Moore	.60	.30	.06
	Detroit Lions			
☐ 18	Todd Marinovich	1.50	.75	.15
	Los Angeles Raiders			
☐ 19	Aaron Craver	.30	.15	.03
	Miami Dolphins			
☐ 20	Chuck Webb	.25	.12	.02
	Green Bay Packers			
☐ 21	Todd Lyght	.40	.20	.04
	Los Angeles Rams			
☐ 22	Greg Lewis	.35	.17	.03
	Denver Broncos			
☐ 23	Eric Turner	.50	.25	.05
	Cleveland Browns			
☐ 24	Alvin Harper	.75	.35	.07
	Dallas Cowboys			
☐ 25	Jarrod Bunch	.15	.07	.01
	New York Giants			
☐ 26	Bruce Pickens	.20	.10	.02
	Atlanta Falcons			
☐ 27	Harvey Williams	1.00	.50	.10
	Kansas City Chiefs			
☐ 28	Randal Hill	.60	.30	.06
	Miami Dolphins			
☐ 29	Nick Bell	.75	.35	.07
	Los Angeles Raiders			
☐ 30	Jim Everett AT	.08	.04	.01
	Henry Ellard			
	Los Angeles Rams			
☐ 31	Randall Cunningham AT	.10	.05	.01
	Keith Jackson			
	Philadelphia Eagles			
☐ 32	Steve DeBerg AT	.08	.04	.01
	Stephone Paige			
	Kansas City Chiefs			
☐ 33	Warren Moon AT	.10	.05	.01
	Drew Hill			
	Houston Oilers			
☐ 34	Dan Marino AT	.15	.07	.01
	Mark Clayton			
	Miami Dolphins			
☐ 35	Joe Montana AT	.20	.10	.02
	Jerry Rice			
	San Francisco 49ers			
☐ 36	Percy Snow	.08	.04	.01
	Kansas City Chiefs			
☐ 37	Kelvin Martin	.06	.03	.00
	Dallas Cowboys			
☐ 38	Scott Case	.03	.01	.00
	Atlanta Falcons			
☐ 39	John Gesek	.08	.04	.01
	Dallas Cowboys			
☐ 40	Barry Word	.25	.12	.02
	Kansas City Chiefs			
☐ 41	Cornelius Bennett	.08	.04	.01
	Buffalo Bills			

☐ 42	Mike Kenn 03	.01	.00	
	Atlanta Falcons			
☐ 43	Andre Reed 10	.05	.01	
	Buffalo Bills			
☐ 44	Bobby Hebert 08	.04	.01	
	New Orleans Saints			
☐ 45	William Perry 08	.04	.01	
	Chicago Bears			
☐ 46	Dennis Byrd 03	.01	.00	
	New York Jets			
☐ 47	Martin Mayhew 03	.01	.00	
	Washington Redskins			
☐ 48	Issaic Holt 03	.01	.00	
	Dallas Cowboys			
☐ 49	William White 03	.01	.00	
	Detroit Lions			
☐ 50	JoJo Townsell 03	.01	.00	
	New York Jets			
☐ 51	Jarvis Williams 03	.01	.00	
	Miami Dolphins			
☐ 52	Joey Browner 06	.03	.00	
	Minnesota Vikings			
☐ 53	Pat Terrell 03	.01	.00	
	Los Angeles Rams			
☐ 54	Joe Montana UER 60	.30	.06	
	San Francisco 49ers			
	(Born Monongahela,			
	not New Eagle)			
☐ 55	Jeff Herrod 03	.01	.00	
	Indianapolis Colts			
☐ 56	Cris Carter 06	.03	.00	
	Minnesota Vikings			
☐ 57	Jerry Rice 35	.17	.03	
	San Francisco 49ers			
☐ 58	Brett Perriman 06	.03	.00	
	New Orleans Saints			
☐ 59	Kevin Fagen 03	.01	.00	
	San Francisco 49ers			
☐ 60	Wayne Haddix 06	.03	.00	
	Tampa Bay Buccaneers			
☐ 61	Tommy Kane 15	.07	.01	
	Seattle Seahawks			
☐ 62	Pat Beach 03	.01	.00	
	Indianapolis Colts			
☐ 63	Jeff Lageman 06	.03	.00	
	New York Jets			
☐ 64	Hassan Jones 06	.03	.00	
	Minnesota Vikings			
☐ 65	Bennie Blades 06	.03	.00	
	Detroit Lions			
☐ 66	Tim McGee 06	.03	.00	
	Cincinnati Bengals			
☐ 67	Robert Blackmon 03	.01	.00	
	Seattle Seahawks			
☐ 68	Fred Stokes 12	.06	.01	
	Washington Redskins			
☐ 69	Barney Bussey 08	.04	.01	

	Cincinnati Bengals			
☐ 70	Eric Metcalf 06	.03	.00	
	Cleveland Browns			
☐ 71	Mark Kelso 03	.01	.00	
	Buffalo Bills			
☐ 72	Neal Anderson TC 08	.04	.01	
	Chicago Bears			
☐ 73	Boomer Esiason TC 08	.04	.01	
	Cincinnati Bengals			
☐ 74	Thurman Thomas TC 20	.10	.02	
	Buffalo Bills			
☐ 75	John Elway TC 10	.05	.01	
	Denver Broncos			
☐ 76	Eric Metcalf TC 06	.03	.00	
	Cleveland Browns			
☐ 77	Vinny Testaverde TC 06	.03	.00	
	Tampa Bay Buccaneers			
☐ 78	Johnny Johnson TC 15	.07	.01	
	Phoenix Cardinals			
☐ 79	Anthony Miller TC 06	.03	.00	
	San Diego Chargers			
☐ 80	Derrick Thomas TC 08	.04	.01	
	Kansas City Chiefs			
☐ 81	Jeff George TC 15	.07	.01	
	Indianapolis Colts			
☐ 82	Troy Aikman TC 15	.07	.01	
	Dallas Cowboys			
☐ 83	Dan Marino TC 15	.07	.01	
	Miami Dolphins			
☐ 84	Randall Cunningham TC ..08	.04	.01	
	Philadelphia Eagles			
☐ 85	Deion Sanders TC 12	.06	.01	
	Atlanta Falcons			
☐ 86	Jerry Rice TC 15	.07	.01	
	San Francisco 49ers			
☐ 87	Lawrence Taylor TC 08	.04	.01	
	New York Giants			
☐ 88	Al Toon TC 06	.03	.00	
	New York Jets			
☐ 89	Barry Sanders TC 25	.12	.02	
	Detroit Lions			
☐ 90	Warren Moon TC 10	.05	.01	
	Houston Oilers			
☐ 91	Sterling Sharpe TC 06	.03	.00	
	Green Bay Packers			
☐ 92	Andre Tippett TC 06	.03	.00	
	New England Patriots			
☐ 93	Bo Jackson TC 15	.07	.01	
	Los Angeles Raiders			
☐ 94	Jim Everett TC 08	.04	.01	
	Los Angeles Rams			
☐ 95	Art Monk TC 08	.04	.01	
	Washington Redskins			
☐ 96	Morten Andersen TC 06	.03	.00	
	New Orleans Saints			
☐ 97	John L. Williams TC 06	.03	.00	
	Seattle Seahawks			

☐ 98 Rod Woodson TC	.06	.03	.00
Pittsburgh Steelers			
☐ 99 Herschel Walker TC	.08	.04	.01
Minnesota Vikings			
☐ 100 Checklist	.06	.01	.00
☐ 101 Steve Young	.12	.06	.01
San Francisco 49ers			
☐ 102 Jim Lachey	.06	.03	.00
Washington Redskins			
☐ 103 Tom Rathman	.06	.03	.00
San Francisco 49ers			
☐ 104 Earnest Byner	.08	.04	.01
Washington Redskins			
☐ 105 Karl Mecklenburg	.06	.03	.00
Denver Broncos			
☐ 106 Wes Hopkins	.03	.01	.00
Philadelphia Eagles			
☐ 107 Michael Irvin	.20	.10	.02
Dallas Cowboys			
☐ 108 Burt Grossman	.06	.03	.00
San Diego Chargers			
☐ 109 Jay Novacek UER	.12	.06	.01
Dallas Cowboys			
(Wearing 82, but card			
says he wears 84)			
☐ 110 Ben Smith	.03	.01	.00
Philadelphia Eagles			
☐ 111 Rod Woodson	.08	.04	.01
Pittsburgh Steelers			
☐ 112 Ernie Jones	.06	.03	.00
Phoenix Cardinals			
☐ 113 Bryan Hinkle	.03	.01	.00
Pittsburgh Steelers			
☐ 114 Vai Sikahema	.03	.01	.00
Phoenix Cardinals			
☐ 115 Bubby Brister	.08	.04	.01
Pittsburgh Steelers			
☐ 116 Brian Blades	.08	.04	.01
Seattle Seahawks			
☐ 117 Don Majkowski	.08	.04	.01
Green Bay Packers			
☐ 118 Rod Bernstine	.06	.03	.00
Green Bay Packers			
☐ 119 Brian Noble	.03	.01	.00
Green Bay Packers			
☐ 120 Eugene Robinson	.03	.01	.00
Seattle Seahawks			
☐ 121 John Taylor	.12	.06	.01
San Francisco 49ers			
☐ 122 Vance Johnson	.06	.03	.00
Denver Broncos			
☐ 123 Art Monk	.12	.06	.01
Washington Redskins			
☐ 124 John Elway	.15	.07	.01
Denver Broncos			
☐ 125 Dexter Carter	.08	.04	.01
San Francisco 49ers			
☐ 126 Anthony Miller	.08	.04	.01
San Diego Chargers			
☐ 127 Keith Jackson	.08	.04	.01
Philadelphia Eagles			
☐ 128 Albert Lewis	.06	.03	.00
Kansas City Chiefs			
☐ 129 Billy Ray Smith	.06	.03	.00
San Diego Chargers			
☐ 130 Clyde Simmons	.06	.03	.00
Philadelphia Eagles			
☐ 131 Merril Hoge	.06	.03	.00
Pittsburgh Steelers			
☐ 132 Ricky Proehl	.10	.05	.01
Phoenix Cardinals			
☐ 133 Tim McDonald	.06	.03	.00
Phoenix Cardinals			
☐ 134 Louis Lipps	.06	.03	.00
Pittsburgh Steelers			
☐ 135 Ken Harvey	.03	.01	.00
Phoenix Cardinals			
☐ 136 Sterling Sharpe	.10	.05	.01
Green Bay Packers			
☐ 137 Gill Byrd	.06	.03	.00
San Diego Chargers			
☐ 138 Tim Harris	.06	.03	.00
Green Bay Packers			
☐ 139 Derrick Fenner	.12	.06	.01
Seattle Seahawks			
☐ 140 Johnny Holland	.03	.01	.00
Green Bay Packers			
☐ 141 Ricky Sanders	.08	.04	.01
Washington Redskins			
☐ 142 Bobby Humphrey	.10	.05	.01
Denver Broncos			
☐ 143 Roger Craig	.10	.05	.01
San Francisco 49ers			
☐ 144 Steve Atwater	.06	.03	.00
Denver Broncos			
☐ 145 Ickey Woods	.06	.03	.00
Cincinnati Bengals			
☐ 146 Randall Cunningham	.15	.07	.01
Philadelphia Eagles			
☐ 147 Marion Butts	.10	.05	.01
San Diego Chargers			
☐ 148 Reggie White	.08	.04	.01
Philadelphia Eagles			
☐ 149 Ronnie Harmon	.03	.01	.00
San Diego Chargers			
☐ 150 Mike Saxon	.03	.01	.00
Dallas Cowboys			
☐ 151 Greg Townsend	.03	.01	.00
Los Angeles Raiders			
☐ 152 Troy Aikman	.40	.20	.04
Dallas Cowboys			
☐ 153 Shane Conlan	.06	.03	.00
Buffalo Bills			
☐ 154 Deion Sanders	.20	.10	.02

	Atlanta Falcons			
☐ 155	Bo Jackson	.35	.17	.03
	Los Angeles Raiders			
☐ 156	Jeff Hostetler	.20	.10	.02
	New York Giants			
☐ 157	Albert Bentley	.06	.03	.00
	Indianapolis Colts			
☐ 158	James Williams	.03	.01	.00
	Buffalo Bills			
☐ 159	Bill Brooks	.03	.01	.00
	Indianapolis Colts			
☐ 160	Nick Lowery	.03	.01	.00
	Kansas City Chiefs			
☐ 161	Ottis Anderson	.08	.04	.01
	New York Giants			
☐ 162	Kevin Greene	.06	.03	.00
	Los Angeles Rams			
☐ 163	Neil Smith	.06	.03	.00
	Kansas City Chiefs			
☐ 164	Jim Everett	.10	.05	.01
	Los Angeles Rams			
☐ 165	Derrick Thomas	.15	.07	.01
	Kansas City Chiefs			
☐ 166	John L. Williams	.08	.04	.01
	Seattle Seahawks			
☐ 167	Timm Rosenbach	.10	.05	.01
	Atlanta Falcons			
☐ 168	Leslie O'Neal	.06	.03	.00
	San Diego Chargers			
☐ 169	Clarence Verdin	.06	.03	.00
	Indianapolis Colts			
☐ 170	Dave Krieg	.08	.04	.01
	Seattle Seahawks			
☐ 171	Steve Broussard	.10	.05	.01
	Atlanta Falcons			
☐ 172	Emmitt Smith	2.00	1.00	.20
	Dallas Cowboys			
☐ 173	Andre Rison	.15	.07	.01
	Atlanta Falcons			
☐ 174	Bruce Smith	.08	.04	.01
	Buffalo Bills			
☐ 175	Mark Clayton	.08	.04	.01
	Miami Dolphins			
☐ 176	Christian Okoye	.08	.04	.01
	Kansas City Chiefs			
☐ 177	Duane Bickett	.03	.01	.00
	Indianapolis Colts			
☐ 178	Stephone Paige	.06	.03	.00
	Kansas City Chiefs			
☐ 179	Fredd Young	.03	.01	.00
	Los Angeles Raiders			
☐ 180	Mervyn Fernandez	.06	.03	.00
	Los Angeles Raiders			
☐ 181	Phil Simms	.08	.04	.01
	New York Giants			
☐ 182	Pete Holohan	.03	.01	.00
	Los Angeles Rams			

☐ 183	Pepper Johnson	.06	.03	.00
	New York Giants			
☐ 184	Jackie Slater	.06	.03	.00
	Los Angeles Rams			
☐ 185	Stephen Baker	.06	.03	.00
	New York Giants			
☐ 186	Frank Cornish	.03	.01	.00
	San Diego Chargers			
☐ 187	Dave Waymer	.03	.01	.00
	San Francisco 49ers			
☐ 188	Terance Mathis	.15	.07	.01
	New York Jets			
☐ 189	Darryl Talley	.06	.03	.00
	Buffalo Bills			
☐ 190	James Hasty	.03	.01	.00
	New York Jets			
☐ 191	Jay Schroeder	.08	.04	.01
	Los Angeles Raiders			
☐ 192	Kenneth Davis	.06	.03	.00
	Buffalo Bills			
☐ 193	Chris Miller	.15	.07	.01
	Atlanta Falcons			
☐ 194	Scott Davis	.06	.03	.00
	Los Angeles Raiders			
☐ 195	Tim Green	.03	.01	.00
	Atlanta Falcons			
☐ 196	Dan Saleaumua	.03	.01	.00
	Kansas City Chiefs			
☐ 197	Rohn Stark	.03	.01	.00
	Indianapolis Colts			
☐ 198	John Alt	.03	.01	.00
	Kansas City Chiefs			
☐ 199	Steve Tasker	.03	.01	.00
	Buffalo Bills			
☐ 200	Checklist 101-200	.06	.01	.00
☐ 201	Freddie Joe Nunn	.03	.01	.00
	Phoenix Cardinals			
☐ 202	Jim Breech	.03	.01	.00
	Cincinnati Bengals			
☐ 203	Roy Green	.06	.03	.00
	Phoenix Cardinals			
☐ 204	Gary Anderson	.08	.04	.01
	Tampa Bay Buccaneers			
☐ 205	Rich Camarillo	.03	.01	.00
	Phoenix Cardinals			
☐ 206	Mark Bortz	.03	.01	.00
	Chicago Bears			
☐ 207	Eddie Brown	.06	.03	.00
	Cincinnati Bengals			
☐ 208	Brad Muster	.06	.03	.00
	Chicago Bears			
☐ 209	Anthony Munoz	.08	.04	.01
	Cincinnati Bengals			
☐ 210	Dalton Hilliard	.06	.03	.00
	New Orleans Saints			
☐ 211	Erik McMillan	.06	.03	.00
	New York Jets			

☐ 212	Perry Kemp .... .03 Green Bay Packers	.01	.00	
☐ 213	Jim Thornton .... .03 Chicago Bears	.01	.00	
☐ 214	Anthony Dilweg .... .08 Green Bay Packers	.04	.01	
☐ 215	Cleveland Gary .... .06 Los Angeles Rams	.03	.00	
☐ 216	Leo Goeas .... .03 San Diego Chargers	.01	.00	
☐ 217	Mike Merriweather .... .03 Minnesota Vikings	.01	.00	
☐ 218	Courtney Hall .... .03 San Diego Chargers	.01	.00	
☐ 219	Wade Wilson .... .08 Minnesota Vikings	.04	.01	
☐ 220	Billy Joe Tolliver .... .08 San Diego Chargers	.04	.01	
☐ 221	Harold Green .... .15 Cincinnati Bengals	.07	.01	
☐ 222	Al(Bubba) Baker .... .03 Cleveland Browns	.01	.00	
☐ 223	Carl Zander .... .03 Cincinnati Bengals	.01	.00	
☐ 224	Thane Gash .... .03 Cleveland Browns	.01	.00	
☐ 225	Kevin Mack .... .06 Cleveland Browns	.03	.00	
☐ 226	Morten Andersen .... .06 New Orleans Saints	.03	.00	
☐ 227	Dennis Gentry .... .03 Chicago Bears	.01	.00	
☐ 228	Vince Buck .... .08 New Orleans Saints	.04	.01	
☐ 229	Mike Singletary .... .08 Chicago Bears	.04	.01	
☐ 230	Rueben Mayes .... .06 New Orleans Saints	.03	.00	
☐ 231	Mark Carrier .... .08 Tampa Bay Buccaneers	.04	.01	
☐ 232	Tony Mandarich .... .06 Green Bay Packers	.03	.00	
☐ 233	Al Toon .... .08 New York Jets	.04	.01	
☐ 234	Renaldo Turnbull .... .06 New Orleans Saints	.03	.00	
☐ 235	Broderick Thomas .... .06 Tampa Bay Buccaneers	.03	.00	
☐ 236	Anthony Carter .... .08 Minnesota Vikings	.04	.01	
☐ 237	Flipper Anderson .... .06 Los Angeles Rams	.03	.00	
☐ 238	Jerry Robinson .... .03 Los Angeles Raiders	.01	.00	
☐ 239	Vince Newsome .... .03 Los Angeles Rams	.01	.00	
☐ 240	Keith Millard .... .06 Minnesota Vikings	.03	.00	
☐ 241	Reggie Langhorne .... .03 Cleveland Browns	.01	.00	
☐ 242	James Francis .... .08 Cincinnati Bengals	.04	.01	
☐ 243	Felix Wright .... .03 Cleveland Browns	.01	.00	
☐ 244	Neal Anderson .... .15 Chicago Bears	.07	.01	
☐ 245	Boomer Esiason .... .10 Cincinnati Bengals	.05	.01	
☐ 246	Pat Swilling .... .10 New Orleans Saints	.05	.01	
☐ 247	Richard Dent .... .08 Chicago Bears	.04	.01	
☐ 248	Craig Heyward .... .08 New Orleans Saints	.04	.01	
☐ 249	Ron Morris .... .03 Chicago Bears	.01	.00	
☐ 250	Eric Martin .... .06 New Orleans Saints	.03	.00	
☐ 251	Jim C. Jensen .... .03 Miami Dolphins	.01	.00	
☐ 252	Anthony Toney .... .03 Philadelphia Eagles	.01	.00	
☐ 253	Sammie Smith .... .08 Miami Dolphins	.04	.01	
☐ 254	Calvin Williams .... .08 Philadelphia Eagles	.04	.01	
☐ 255	Dan Marino .... .25 Miami Dolphins	.12	.02	
☐ 256	Warren Moon .... .20 Houston Oilers	.10	.02	
☐ 257	Tommie Agee .... .03 Dallas Cowboys	.01	.00	
☐ 258	Haywood Jeffires .... .20 Houston Oilers	.10	.02	
☐ 259	Eugene Lockhart .... .03 Dallas Cowboys	.01	.00	
☐ 260	Drew Hill .... .08 Houston Oilers	.04	.01	
☐ 261	Vinny Testaverde .... .08 Tampa Bay Buccaneers	.04	.01	
☐ 262	Jim Arnold .... .03 Detroit Lions	.01	.00	
☐ 263	Steve Christie .... .03 Tampa Bay Buccaneers	.01	.00	
☐ 264	Chris Spielman .... .06 Detroit Lions	.03	.00	
☐ 265	Reggie Cobb .... .15 Tampa Bay Buccaneers	.07	.01	
☐ 266	John Stephens .... .08 New England Patriots	.04	.01	
☐ 267	Jay Hilgenberg .... .06 Chicago Bears	.03	.00	
☐ 268	Brent Williams .... .03 New England Patriots	.01	.00	

□ 269	Rodney Hampton 40	.20	.04	
	New York Giants			
□ 270	Irving Fryar 06	.03	.00	
	New England Patriots			
□ 271	Terry McDaniel 03	.01	.00	
	Los Angeles Raiders			
□ 272	Reggie Roby 03	.01	.00	
	Miami Dolphins			
□ 273	Allen Pinkett 06	.03	.00	
	Houston Oilers			
□ 274	Tim McKyer 03	.01	.00	
	Miami Dolphins			
□ 275	Bob Golic 03	.01	.00	
	Los Angeles Raiders			
□ 276	Wilber Marshall 06	.03	.00	
	Washington Redskins			
□ 277	Ray Childress 06	.03	.00	
	Houston Oilers			
□ 278	Charles Mann 06	.03	.00	
	Washington Redskins			
□ 279	Cris Dishman 20	.10	.02	
	Houston Oilers			
□ 280	Mark Rypien 20	.10	.02	
	Washington Redskins			
□ 281	Michael Cofer 03	.01	.00	
	Cleveland Browns			
□ 282	Keith Byars 06	.03	.00	
	Philadelphia Eagles			
□ 283	Mike Rozier 06	.03	.00	
	Atlanta Falcons			
□ 284	Seth Joyner 06	.03	.00	
	Philadelphia Eagles			
□ 285	Jessie Tuggle 03	.01	.00	
	Atlanta Falcons			
□ 286	Mark Bavaro 06	.03	.00	
	New York Giants			
□ 287	Eddie Anderson 03	.01	.00	
	Los Angeles Raiders			
□ 288	Sean Landeta 03	.01	.00	
	New York Giants			
□ 289	Howie Long 12	.06	.01	
	(With George Brett)			
	Los Angeles Raiders			
□ 290	Reyna Thompson 03	.01	.00	
	New York Giants			
□ 291	Ferrell Edmunds 03	.01	.00	
	Miami Dolphins			
□ 292	Willie Gault 06	.03	.00	
	Los Angeles Raiders			
□ 293	John Offerdahl 06	.03	.00	
	Miami Dolphins			
□ 294	Tim Brown 10	.05	.01	
	Los Angeles Raiders			
□ 295	Bruce Matthews 03	.01	.00	
	Houston Oilers			
□ 296	Kevin Ross 03	.01	.00	
	Kansas City Chiefs			
□ 297	Lorenzo White 06	.03	.00	
	Houston Oilers			
□ 298	Dino Hackett 03	.01	.00	
	Kansas City Chiefs			
□ 299	Curtis Duncan 06	.03	.00	
	Houston Oilers			
□ 300	Checklist 201-300 06	.01	.00	
□ 301	Andre Ware 12	.06	.01	
	Detroit Lions			
□ 302	David Little 03	.01	.00	
	Pittsburgh Steelers			
□ 303	Jerry Ball 03	.01	.00	
	Detroit Lions			
□ 304	Dwight Stone 03	.01	.00	
	Pittsburgh Steelers			
□ 305	Rodney Peete 08	.04	.01	
	Detroit Lions			
□ 306	Mike Baab 03	.01	.00	
	Cleveland Browns			
□ 307	Tim Worley 06	.03	.00	
	Pittsburgh Steelers			
□ 308	Paul Farren 03	.01	.00	
	Cleveland Browns			
□ 309	Carnell Lake 03	.01	.00	
	Pittsburgh Steelers			
□ 310	Clay Matthews 03	.01	.00	
	Cleveland Browns			
□ 311	Alton Montgomery 03	.01	.00	
	Denver Broncos			
□ 312	Ernest Givins 10	.05	.01	
	Houston Oilers			
□ 313	Mike Horan 03	.01	.00	
	Denver Broncos			
□ 314	Sean Jones 03	.01	.00	
	Houston Oilers			
□ 315	Leonard Smith 03	.01	.00	
	Buffalo Bills			
□ 316	Carl Banks 06	.03	.00	
	New York Giants			
□ 317	Jerome Brown 06	.03	.00	
	Philadelphia Eagles			
□ 318	Everson Walls 03	.01	.00	
	New York Giants			
□ 319	Ron Heller 03	.01	.00	
	Philadelphia Eagles			
□ 320	Mark Collins 03	.01	.00	
	New York Giants			
□ 321	Eddie Murray 03	.01	.00	
	Detroit Lions			
□ 322	Jim Harbaugh 10	.05	.01	
	Chicago Bears			
□ 323	Mel Gray 03	.01	.00	
	Detroit Lions			
□ 324	Keith Van Horne 03	.01	.00	
	Chicago Bears			
□ 325	Lomas Brown 03	.01	.00	
	Detroit Lions			

☐ 326	Carl Lee 03	.01	.00
	Minnesota Vikings		
☐ 327	Ken O'Brien 08	.04	.01
	New York Jets		
☐ 328	Dermontti Dawson 03	.01	.00
	Pittsburgh Steelers		
☐ 329	Brad Baxter 12	.06	.01
	New York Jets		
☐ 330	Chris Doleman 06	.03	.00
	Minnesota Vikings		
☐ 331	Louis Oliver 03	.01	.00
	Miami Dolphins		
☐ 332	Frank Stams 03	.01	.00
	Los Angeles Rams		
☐ 333	Mike Munchak 06	.03	.00
	Houston Oilers		
☐ 334	Fred Strickland 03	.01	.00
	Los Angeles Rams		
☐ 335	Mark Duper 06	.03	.00
	Miami Dolphins		
☐ 336	Jacob Green 06	.03	.00
	Seattle Seahawks		
☐ 337	Tony Paige 03	.01	.00
	Miami Dolphins		
☐ 338	Jeff Bryant 03	.01	.00
	Seattle Seahawks		
☐ 339	Lemuel Stinson 03	.01	.00
	Chicago Bears		
☐ 340	David Wyman 03	.01	.00
	Seattle Seahawks		
☐ 341	Lee Williams 06	.03	.00
	San Diego Chargers		
☐ 342	Trace Armstrong 03	.01	.00
	Chicago Bears		
☐ 343	Junior Seau 08	.04	.01
	San Diego Chargers		
☐ 344	John Roper 06	.03	.00
	Chicago Bears		
☐ 345	Jeff George 35	.17	.03
	Indianapolis Colts		
☐ 346	Herschel Walker 10	.05	.01
	Minnesota Vikings		
☐ 347	Sam Clancy 03	.01	.00
	Indianapolis Colts		
☐ 348	Steve Jordan 06	.03	.00
	Minnesota Vikings		
☐ 349	Nate Odomes 03	.01	.00
	Buffalo Bills		
☐ 350	Martin Bayless 03	.01	.00
	San Diego Chargers		
☐ 351	Brent Jones 06	.03	.00
	San Francisco 49ers		
☐ 352	Ray Agnew 03	.01	.00
	New England Patriots		
☐ 353	Charles Haley 06	.03	.00
	San Francisco 49ers		
☐ 354	Andre Tippett 06	.03	.00
	New England Patriots		
☐ 355	Ronnie Lott 10	.05	.01
	San Francisco 49ers		
☐ 356	Thurman Thomas 50	.25	.05
	Buffalo Bills		
☐ 357	Fred Barnett 15	.07	.01
	Philadelphia Eagles		
☐ 358	James Lofton 15	.07	.01
	Buffalo Bills		
☐ 359	William Frizzell 15	.07	.01
	Philadelphia Eagles		
☐ 360	Keith McKeller 08	.04	.01
	Buffalo Bills		
☐ 361	Rodney Holman 03	.01	.00
	Cincinnati Bengals		
☐ 362	Henry Ellard 08	.04	.01
	Los Angeles Rams		
☐ 363	David Fulcher 03	.01	.00
	Cincinnati Bengals		
☐ 364	Jerry Gray 03	.01	.00
	Los Angeles Rams		
☐ 365	James Brooks 08	.04	.01
	Cincinnati Bengals		
☐ 366	Tony Stargell 03	.01	.00
	New York Jets		
☐ 367	Keith McCants 08	.04	.01
	Tampa Bay Buccaneers		
☐ 368	Lewis Billups 03	.01	.00
	Cincinnati Bengals		
☐ 369	Ervin Randle 03	.01	.00
	Tampa Bay Buccaneers		
☐ 370	Pat Leahy 03	.01	.00
	New York Jets		
☐ 371	Bruce Armstrong 03	.01	.00
	New England Patriots		
☐ 372	Steve DeBerg 08	.04	.01
	Kansas City Chiefs		
☐ 373	Guy McIntyre 03	.01	.00
	San Francisco 49ers		
☐ 374	Deron Cherry 06	.03	.00
	Kansas City Chiefs		
☐ 375	Fred Marion 03	.01	.00
	New England Patriots		
☐ 376	Michael Haddix 06	.03	.00
	Green Bay Packers		
☐ 377	Kent Hull 03	.01	.00
	Buffalo Bills		
☐ 378	Jerry Holmes 03	.01	.00
	Green Bay Packers		
☐ 379	Jim Richter 03	.01	.00
	Buffalo Bills		
☐ 380	Ed West 03	.01	.00
	Green Bay Packers		
☐ 381	Richmond Webb 06	.03	.00
	Miami Dolphins		
☐ 382	Mark Jackson 06	.03	.00
	Denver Broncos		

☐ 383 Tom Newberry ....03 Los Angeles Rams	.01	.00
☐ 384 Ricky Nattiel ....06 Denver Broncos	.03	.00
☐ 385 Keith Sims ....03 Miami Dolphins	.01	.00
☐ 386 Ron Hall ....03 Tampa Bay Buccaneers	.01	.00
☐ 387 Ken Norton ....03 Dallas Cowboys	.01	.00
☐ 388 Paul Gruber ....06 Tampa Bay Buccaneers	.03	.00
☐ 389 Danny Stubbs ....03 Dallas Cowboys	.01	.00
☐ 390 Ian Beckles ....03 Tampa Bay Buccaneers	.01	.00
☐ 391 Hoby Brenner ....03 New Orleans Saints	.01	.00
☐ 392 Tory Epps ....03 Atlanta Falcons	.01	.00
☐ 393 Sam Mills ....06 New Orleans Saints	.03	.00
☐ 394 Chris Hinton ....06 Atlanta Falcons	.03	.00
☐ 395 Steve Walsh ....08 New Orleans Saints	.04	.01
☐ 396 Simon Fletcher ....06 Denver Broncos	.03	.00
☐ 397 Tony Bennett ....06 Green Bay Packers	.03	.00
☐ 398 Aundray Bruce ....06 Atlanta Falcons	.03	.00
☐ 399 Mark Murphy ....03 Green Bay Packers	.01	.00
☐ 400 Checklist 301-400 ....06 Detroit Lions	.01	.00
☐ 401 Barry Sanders LL ....30 Detroit Lions	.15	.03
☐ 402 Jerry Rice LL ....15 San Francisco 49ers	.07	.01
☐ 403 Warren Moon LL ....10 Houston Oilers	.05	.01
☐ 404 Derrick Thomas LL ....08 Kansas City Chiefs	.04	.01
☐ 405 Nick Lowery LL ....03 Kansas City Chiefs	.01	.00
☐ 406 Mark Carrier LL ....06 Chicago Bears	.03	.00
☐ 407 Michael Carter ....06 San Francisco 49ers	.03	.00
☐ 408 Chris Singleton ....06 New England Patriots	.03	.00
☐ 409 Matt Millen ....03 San Francisco 49ers	.01	.00
☐ 410 Ronnie Lippett ....03 New England Patriots	.01	.00
☐ 411 E.J. Junior ....03 Miami Dolphins	.01	.00

☐ 412 Ray Donaldson ....03 Indianapolis Colts	.01	.00
☐ 413 Keith Willis ....03 Pittsburgh Steelers	.01	.00
☐ 414 Jessie Hester ....08 Indianapolis Colts	.04	.01
☐ 415 Jeff Cross ....03 Miami Dolphins	.01	.00
☐ 416 Greg Jackson ....08 New York Giants	.04	.01
☐ 417 Alvin Walton ....03 Washington Redskins	.01	.00
☐ 418 Bart Oates ....03 New York Giants	.01	.00
☐ 419 Chip Lohmiller ....03 Washington Redskins	.01	.00
☐ 420 John Elliott ....03 New York Giants	.01	.00
☐ 421 Randall McDaniel ....03 Minnesota Vikings	.01	.00
☐ 422 Richard Johnson ....08 Houston Oilers	.04	.01
☐ 423 Al Noga ....03 Minnesota Vikings	.01	.00
☐ 424 Lamar Lathon ....06 Houston Oilers	.03	.00
☐ 425 Rick Fenney ....06 Minnesota Vikings	.03	.00
☐ 426 Jack Del Rio ....03 Dallas Cowboys	.01	.00
☐ 427 Don Mosebar ....03 Los Angeles Raiders	.01	.00
☐ 428 Luis Sharpe ....03 Phoenix Cardinals	.01	.00
☐ 429 Steve Wisniewski ....03 Los Angeles Raiders	.01	.00
☐ 430 Jimmie Jones ....03 Dallas Cowboys	.01	.00
☐ 431 Freeman McNeil ....08 New York Jets	.04	.01
☐ 432 Ron Rivera ....03 Chicago Bears	.01	.00
☐ 433 Hart Lee Dykes ....03 New England Patriots	.01	.00
☐ 434 Mark Carrier ....08 Chicago Bears	.04	.01
☐ 435 Rob Moore ....50 New York Jets	.25	.05
☐ 436 Gary Clark ....15 Washington Redskins	.07	.01
☐ 437 Heath Sherman ....08 Philadelphia Eagles	.04	.01
☐ 438 Darrell Green ....10 Washington Redskins	.05	.01
☐ 439 Jessie Small ....03 Philadelphia Eagles	.01	.00
☐ 440 Monte Coleman 03	.01	.00

Washington Redskins					
☐ 441 Leonard Marshall	.06	.03	.00		
New York Giants					
☐ 442 Richard Johnson	.03	.01	.00		
Detroit Lions					
☐ 443 Dave Meggett	.10	.05	.01		
New York Giants					
☐ 444 Barry Sanders	1.00	.50	.10		
Detroit Lions					
☐ 445 Lawrence Taylor	.10	.05	.01		
New York Giants					
☐ 446 Marcus Allen	.10	.05	.01		
Los Angeles Raiders					
☐ 447 Johnny Johnson	.25	.12	.02		
Phoenix Cardinals					
☐ 448 Aaron Wallace	.08	.04	.01		
Los Angeles Raiders					
☐ 449 Anthony Thompson	.10	.05	.01		
Phoenix Cardinals					
☐ 450 Steve DeBerg	.15	.04	.01		
Kansas City Chiefs					
and Dan Marino					
Miami Dolphins					
Team MVP CL 453-473					
☐ 451 Andre Rison MVP	.08	.04	.01		
Atlanta Falcons					
☐ 452 Thurman Thomas MVP	.20	.10	.02		
Buffalo Bills					
☐ 453 Neal Anderson MVP	.08	.04	.01		
Chicago Bears					
☐ 454 Boomer Esiason MVP	.08	.04	.01		
Cincinnati Bengals					
☐ 455 Eric Metcalf MVP	.06	.03	.00		
Cleveland Browns					
☐ 456 Emmitt Smith MVP	.75	.35	.07		
Dallas Cowboys					
☐ 457 Bobby Humphrey MVP	.08	.04	.01		
Denver Broncos					
☐ 458 Barry Sanders MVP	.50	.25	.05		
Detroit Lions					
☐ 459 Sterling Sharpe MVP	.08	.04	.01		
Green Bay Packers					
☐ 460 Warren Moon MVP	.10	.05	.01		
Houston Oilers					
☐ 461 Albert Bentley MVP	.06	.03	.00		
Indianapolis Colts					
☐ 462 Steve DeBerg MVP	.06	.03	.00		
Kansas City Chiefs					
☐ 463 Greg Townsend MVP	.06	.03	.00		
Los Angeles Raiders					
☐ 464 Henry Ellard MVP	.06	.03	.00		
Los Angeles Rams					
☐ 465 Dan Marino MVP	.15	.07	.01		
Miami Dolphins					
☐ 466 Anthony Carter MVP	.06	.03	.00		
Minnesota Vikings					
☐ 467 John Stephens MVP	.06	.03	.00		

New England Patriots					
☐ 468 Pat Swilling MVP	.06	.03	.00		
New Orleans Saints					
☐ 469 Ottis Anderson MVP	.06	.03	.00		
New York Giants					
☐ 470 Dennis Byrd MVP	.06	.03	.00		
New York Jets					
☐ 471 Randall Cunningham MVP	.08	.04	.01		
Philadelphia Eagles					
☐ 472 Johnny Johnson MVP	.15	.07	.01		
Phoenix Cardinals					
☐ 473 Rod Woodson MVP	.06	.03	.00		
Pittsburgh Steelers					
☐ 474 Anthony Miller MVP	.06	.03	.00		
San Diego Chargers					
☐ 475 Jerry Rice MVP	.15	.07	.01		
San Francisco 49ers					
☐ 476 John L.Williams MVP	.06	.03	.00		
Seattle Seahawks					
☐ 477 Wayne Haddix MVP	.06	.03	.00		
Tampa Bay Buccaneers					
☐ 478 Earnest Byner MVP	.06	.03	.00		
Washington Redskins					
☐ 479 Doug Widell	.03	.01	.00		
Denver Broncos					
☐ 480 Tommy Hodson	.08	.04	.01		
New England Patriots					
☐ 481 Shawn Collins	.03	.01	.00		
Atlanta Falcons					
☐ 482 Rickey Jackson	.06	.03	.00		
New Orleans Saints					
☐ 483 Tony Casillas	.06	.03	.00		
Atlanta Falcons					
☐ 484 Vaughan Johnson	.06	.03	.00		
New Orleans Saints					
☐ 485 Floyd Dixon	.03	.01	.00		
Atlanta Falcons					
☐ 486 Eric Green	.15	.07	.01		
Pittsburgh Steelers					
☐ 487 Harry Hamilton	.03	.01	.00		
Tampa Bay Buccaneers					
☐ 488 Gary Anderson	.03	.01	.00		
Pittsburgh Steelers					
☐ 489 Bruce Hill	.03	.01	.00		
Tampa Bay Buccaneers					
☐ 490 Gerald Williams	.03	.01	.00		
Pittsburgh Steelers					
☐ 491 Cortez Kennedy	.10	.05	.01		
Seattle Seahawks					
☐ 492 Chet Brooks	.03	.01	.00		
San Francisco 49ers					
☐ 493 Dwayne Harper	.12	.06	.01		
Seattle Seahawks					
☐ 494 Don Griffin	.03	.01	.00		
San Francisco 49ers					
☐ 495 Andy Heck	.03	.01	.00		
Seattle Seahawks					

☐ 496	David Treadwell 03	.01	.00
	Denver Broncos		
☐ 497	Irv Pankey 03	.01	.00
	Los Angeles Rams		
☐ 498	Dennis Smith 03	.01	.00
	Denver Broncos		
☐ 499	Marcus Dupree 06	.03	.00
	Los Angeles Rams		
☐ 500	Checklist 401-500 06	.01	.00
☐ SP1	Darrell Green SP 9.00	4.50	.90
	NFL's Fastest Man		

	MINT	EXC	G-VG
COMPLETE SET (10) 28.00	14.00	2.80
COMMON PLAYER (1-9) 2.00	1.00	.20

		MINT	EXC	G-VG
☐ 1	1974-78 College Years 2.00	1.00	.20
☐ 2	1981 A Star is Born 2.00	1.00	.20
☐ 3	1984 Super Bowl MVP 2.00	1.00	.20
☐ 4	1987 1st Passing Title 2.00	1.00	.20
☐ 5	1988 Rematch 2.00	1.00	.20
☐ 6	1989 NFL's MVP 2.00	1.00	.20
☐ 7	1989 Back-to-Back 2.00	1.00	.20
☐ 8	1990 Career Highs 2.00	1.00	.20
☐ 9	Checklist Heroes 1-9 ...... 2.00	1.00	.20
	(Vernon Wells portrait			
	of Joe Montana)			
☐ xx	Title/Header card SP 15.00	7.50	1.50
	(Unnumbered)			

1991 Upper Deck Heroes Joe Montana

This ten-card Joe Montana set introduces Upper Deck's "Football Heroes" series, which were randomly inserted into 1991 Upper Deck first series foil packs. The cards were inserted in its low number series packs. Montana personally autographed 2,500 of these cards, which feature a diamond hologram as a sign of authenticity. The cards measure the standard size (2 1/2" by 3 1/2"). The front design has color player photos in an oval frame with white and blue borders, on a card face that shades from mustard to brown as one moves from top to bottom. The Upper Deck Football Heroes logo is superimposed at the lower left corner. The backs have a green football field design and summarize various high points in his career. Card number 9 features a portrait of Montana by noted sports artist Vernon Wells. The cards are numbered on the back.

1991 Upper Deck Game Breaker Holograms

This nine-card hologram set spotlights outstanding NFL running backs. Holograms 1-6 were randomly inserted in Upper Deck low series wax packs, and holograms 7-9 were inserted in the high series. The standard-size (2 1/2" by 3 1/2") holograms feature a player action shot against the background of a football play diagram with X's and O's. The player's name appears in a stripe toward the bottom, with the words "Game Breakers" in the lower right corner. The backs have the team logo and career summary. The cards are numbered on the back.

	MINT	EXC	G-VG
COMPLETE SET (9)	18.00	9.00	1.80
COMMON PLAYER (1-9)	1.25	.60	.12

		MINT	EXC	G-VG
☐ GB1	Barry Sanders Detroit Lions	4.50	2.25	.45
☐ GB2	Thurman Thomas Buffalo Bills	4.00	2.00	.40
☐ GB3	Bobby Humphrey Denver Broncos	1.25	.60	.12
☐ GB4	Earnest Byner Washington Redskins	1.25	.60	.12
☐ GB5	Emmitt Smith Dallas Cowboys	5.00	2.50	.50
☐ GB6	Neal Anderson Chicago Bears	1.75	.85	.17
☐ GB7	Marion Butts San Diego Chargers	1.75	.85	.17
☐ GB8	James Brooks Cincinnati Bengals	1.25	.60	.12
☐ GB9	Marcus Allen Los Angeles Raiders	1.75	.85	.17

1991 Upper Deck II

The high-number series of the 1991 Upper Deck set contains 200 standard-size (2 1/2" by 3 1/2") cards numbered in continuation of the low series. The cards have the same design as the first series, with attractive color photos on both sides and biographical and statistical information on the backs. The front photos are accented by two color border stripes reflecting the team's colors, and the team's emblem appears in the lower right corner. The set includes a Rookie Force subset depicting 50 top rookies in their NFL uniforms (AFC 601-

626 and NFC 627-652) and an Arch Rivals subset with split-photo cards presenting one-on-one rivalries (653-658). The nine "Football Heroes" insert cards spotlight Hall of Famer Joe Namath and 2,500 of his autographed cards were randomly inserted in high series 12-card foil packs. The final three Game Breaker hologram insert cards were included with this series only and round out the nine-card hologram set. A special insert card (SP2) commemorating Don Shula's historic 300th NFL victory was also randomly inserted in these Upper Deck high series foil packs. The key Rookie Cards in this series are Ricky Ervins and Leonard Russell.

		MINT	EXC	G-VG
COMPLETE SET (200)		12.00	6.00	1.20
COMMON PLAYER (501-700)		.03	.01	.00
☐ 501	Wendell Davis Chicago Bears	.15	.07	.01
☐ 502	Matt Bahr New York Giants	.03	.01	.00
☐ 503	Rob Burnett Cleveland Browns	.08	.04	.01
☐ 504	Maurice Carthon New York Giants	.03	.01	.00
☐ 505	Donnell Woolford Chicago Bears	.03	.01	.00
☐ 506	Howard Ballard Buffalo Bills	.03	.01	.00
☐ 507	Mark Boyer New York Jets	.03	.01	.00
☐ 508	Eugene Marve Tampa Bay Buccaneers	.03	.01	.00
☐ 509	Joe Kelly New York Jets	.03	.01	.00
☐ 510	Will Wolford Buffalo Bills	.03	.01	.00
☐ 511	Robert Clark Detroit Lions	.03	.01	.00
☐ 512	Matt Brock Green Bay Packers	.12	.06	.01
☐ 513	Chris Warren Seattle Seahawks	.06	.03	.01
☐ 514	Ken Willis Dallas Cowboys	.03	.01	.00
☐ 515	George Jamison Detroit Lions	.08	.04	.01
☐ 516	Rufus Porter Seattle Seahawks	.03	.01	.00
☐ 517	Mark Higgs Miami Dolphins	.60	.30	.06
☐ 518	Thomas Everett Pittsburgh Steelers	.03	.01	.00
☐ 519	Robert Brown	.03	.01	.00

	Green Bay Packers		
☐ 520	Gene Atkins 03	.01	.00
	New Orleans Saints		
☐ 521	Hardy Nickerson 03	.01	.00
	Pittsburgh Steelers		
☐ 522	Johnny Bailey 08	.04	.01
	Chicago Bears		
☐ 523	William Frizzell 08	.04	.01
	Tampa Bay Buccaneers		
☐ 524	Steve McMichael 06	.03	.01
	Chicago Bears		
☐ 525	Kevin Porter 03	.01	.00
	Kansas City Chiefs		
☐ 526	Carwell Gardner 08	.04	.01
	Buffalo Bills		
☐ 527	Eugene Daniel 03	.01	.00
	Indianapolis Colts		
☐ 528	Vestee Jackson 03	.01	.00
	Miami Dolphins		
☐ 529	Chris Goode 03	.01	.00
	Indianapolis Colts		
☐ 530	Leon Seals 03	.01	.00
	Buffalo Bills		
☐ 531	Darion Conner 06	.03	.00
	Atlanta Falcons		
☐ 532	Stan Brock 03	.01	.00
	New Orleans Saints		
☐ 533	Kirby Jackson 08	.04	.01
	Buffalo Bills		
☐ 534	Marv Cook 10	.05	.01
	New England Patriots		
☐ 535	Bill Fralic 06	.03	.00
	Atlanta Falcons		
☐ 536	Keith Woodside 06	.03	.00
	Green Bay Packers		
☐ 537	Hugh Green 06	.03	.00
	Miami Dolphins		
☐ 538	Grant Feasel 03	.01	.00
	Seattle Seahawks		
☐ 539	Bubba McDowell 03	.01	.00
	Houston Oilers		
☐ 540	Vai Sikahema 03	.01	.00
	Green Bay Packers		
☐ 541	Aaron Cox 03	.01	.00
	Los Angeles Rams		
☐ 542	Roger Craig 10	.05	.01
	Los Angeles Raiders		
☐ 543	Robb Thomas 08	.04	.01
	Kansas City Chiefs		
☐ 544	Ronnie Lott 10	.05	.01
	Los Angeles Raiders		
☐ 545	Robert Delpino 06	.03	.00
	Los Angeles Rams		
☐ 546	Greg McMurtry 08	.04	.01
	New England Patriots		
☐ 547	Jim Morrissey 12	.06	.01
	Chicago Bears		
☐ 548	Johnny Rembert 03	.01	.00
	New England Patriots		
☐ 549	Markus Paul 15	.07	.01
	Chicago Bears		
☐ 550	Karl Wilson 15	.07	.01
	Los Angeles Rams		
☐ 551	Gaston Green 30	.15	.03
	Denver Broncos		
☐ 552	Willie Drewrey 03	.01	.00
	Tampa Bay Buccaneers		
☐ 553	Michael Young 06	.03	.00
	Denver Broncos		
☐ 554	Tom Tupa 10	.05	.01
	Phoenix Cardinals		
☐ 555	John Friesz 35	.17	.03
	San Diego Chargers		
☐ 556	Cody Carlson 15	.07	.01
	Houston Oilers		
☐ 557	Eric Allen 03	.01	.00
	Philadelphia Eagles		
☐ 558	Tom Bensen 03	.01	.00
	Los Angeles Raiders		
☐ 559	Scott Mersereau 08	.04	.01
	New York Jets		
☐ 560	Lionel Washington 03	.01	.00
	Los Angeles Raiders		
☐ 561	Brian Brennan 03	.01	.00
	Cleveland Browns		
☐ 562	Jim Jeffcoat 03	.01	.00
	Dallas Cowboys		
☐ 563	Jeff Jaeger 03	.01	.00
	Los Angeles Raiders		
☐ 564	David Johnson 08	.04	.01
	Pittsburgh Steelers		
☐ 565	Danny Villa 03	.01	.00
	New England Patriots		
☐ 566	Don Beebe 10	.05	.01
	Buffalo Bills		
☐ 567	Michael Haynes 25	.12	.02
	Atlanta Falcons		
☐ 568	Brett Faryniarz 10	.05	.01
	Los Angeles Rams		
☐ 569	Mike Prior 03	.01	.00
	Indianapolis Colts		
☐ 570	John Davis 12	.06	.01
	Buffalo Bills		
☐ 571	Vernon Turner 15	.07	.01
	Los Angeles Rams		
☐ 572	Michael Brooks 03	.01	.00
	Denver Broncos		
☐ 573	Mike Gann 03	.01	.00
	Atlanta Falcons		
☐ 574	Ron Holmes 03	.01	.00
	Denver Broncos		
☐ 575	Gary Plummer 03	.01	.00
	San Diego Chargers		
☐ 576	Bill Romanowski .... .03	.01	.00

	San Francisco 49ers					Kansas City Chiefs		
☐ 577	Chris Jacke	.03	.01	.00	☐ 604	Ed King RF	.15	.07	.01
	Green Bay Packers					Cleveland Browns		
☐ 578	Gary Reasons	.03	.01	.00	☐ 605	Shane Curry RF	.08	.04	.01
	New York Giants					Indianapolis Colts		
☐ 579	Tim Jorden	.08	.04	.01	☐ 606	Mike Croel RF	.60	.30	.06
	Phoenix Cardinals					Denver Broncos		
☐ 580	Tim McKyer	.03	.01	.00	☐ 607	Bryan Cox RF	.15	.07	.01
	Atlanta Falcons					Miami Dolphins		
☐ 581	Johnny Jackson	.12	.06	.01	☐ 608	Shawn Jefferson RF	.20	.10	.02
	San Francisco 49ers					San Diego Chargers		
☐ 582	Ethan Horton	.10	.05	.01	☐ 609	Kenny Walker RF	.45	.22	.04
	Los Angeles Raiders					Denver Broncos		
☐ 583	Pete Stoyanovich	.03	.01	.00	☐ 610	Michael Jackson RF	.35	.17	.03
	Miami Dolphins					Cleveland Browns		
☐ 584	Jeff Query	.06	.03	.00	☐ 611	Jon Vaughn RF	.60	.30	.06
	Green Bay Packers					New England Patriots		
☐ 585	Frank Reich	.08	.04	.01	☐ 612	Greg Lewis RF	.20	.10	.02
	Buffalo Bills					Denver Broncos		
☐ 586	Riki Ellison	.03	.01	.00	☐ 613	Joe Valerio RF	.10	.05	.01
	Los Angeles Raiders					Kansas City Chiefs		
☐ 587	Eric Hill	.03	.01	.00	☐ 614	Pat Harlow RF	.15	.07	.01
	Phoenix Cardinals					New England Patriots		
☐ 588	Anthony Shelton	.15	.07	.01	☐ 615	Henry Jones RF	.15	.07	.01
	San Diego Chargers					Buffalo Bills		
☐ 589	Steve Smith	.03	.01	.00	☐ 616	Jeff Graham RF	.20	.10	.02
	Los Angeles Raiders					Pittsburgh Steelers		
☐ 590	Garth Jax	.08	.04	.01	☐ 617	Darryll Lewis RF	.15	.07	.01
	Phoenix Cardinals					Houston Oilers		
☐ 591	Greg Davis	.08	.04	.01	☐ 618	Keith Traylor RF	.12	.06	.01
	Phoenix Cardinals					Denver Broncos		
☐ 592	Bill Maas	.03	.01	.00	☐ 619	Scott Miller RF	.10	.05	.01
	Kansas City Chiefs					Miami Dolphins		
☐ 593	Henry Rolling	.08	.04	.01	☐ 620	Nick Bell RF	.40	.20	.04
	San Diego Chargers					Los Angeles Raiders		
☐ 594	Keith Jones	.06	.03	.00	☐ 621	John Flannery RF	.15	.07	.01
	Atlanta Falcons					Houston Oilers		
☐ 595	Tootie Robbins	.03	.01	.00	☐ 622	Leonard Russell RF	1.25	.60	.12
	Phoenix Cardinals					New England Patriots		
☐ 596	Brian Jordan	.20	.10	.02	☐ 623	Alfred Williams RF	.15	.07	.01
	Atlanta Falcons					Cincinnati Bengals		
☐ 597	Derrick Walker	.10	.05	.01	☐ 624	Browning Nagle RF	.40	.20	.04
	San Diego Chargers					New York Jets		
☐ 598	Jonathan Hayes	.03	.01	.00	☐ 625	Harvey Williams RF	.75	.35	.07
	Kansas City Chiefs					Kansas City Chiefs		
☐ 599	Nate Lewis	.15	.07	.01	☐ 626	Dan McGwire RF	.75	.35	.07
	San Diego Chargers					Seattle Seahawks		
☐ 600	Checklist 501-600	.06	.01	.00	☐ 627	NFC Checklist RF	.15	.04	.01
☐ 601	AFC Checklist RF	.15	.04	.01		Brett Favre		
	Mike Croel					Moe Gardner		
	Greg Lewis					Erric Pegram		
	Keith Traylor					Bruce Pickens		
	Kenny Walker					Mike Pritchard		
	Denver Broncos					Atlanta Falcons		
☐ 602	James Jones RF	.10	.05	.01	☐ 628	William Thomas RF	.10	.05	.01
	Cleveland Browns					Philadelphia Eagles		
☐ 603	Tim Barnett RF	.30	.15	.03	☐ 629	Lawrence Dawsey RF	.45	.22	.04

	Tampa Bay Buccaneers			
☐ 630	Aeneas Williams RF	.15	.07	.01
	Phoenix Cardinals			
☐ 631	Stan Thomas RF	.10	.05	.01
	Chicago Bears			
☐ 632	Randal Hill RF	.30	.15	.03
	Phoenix Cardinals			
☐ 633	Moe Gardner RF	.20	.10	.02
	Atlanta Falcons			
☐ 634	Alvin Harper RF	.35	.17	.03
	Dallas Cowboys			
☐ 635	Esera Tuaolo RF	.10	.05	.01
	Green Bay Packers			
☐ 636	Russell Maryland RF	.25	.12	.02
	Dallas Cowboys			
☐ 637	Anthony Morgan RF	.25	.12	.02
	Chicago Bears			
☐ 638	Erric Pegram RF	.25	.12	.02
	Atlanta Falcons			
☐ 639	Herman Moore RF	.50	.25	.05
	Detroit Lions			
☐ 640	Ricky Ervins RF	2.50	1.25	.25
	Washington Redskins			
☐ 641	Kelvin Pritchett RF	.15	.07	.01
	Detroit Lions			
☐ 642	Roman Phifer RF	.15	.07	.01
	Los Angeles Rams			
☐ 643	Antone Davis RF	.12	.06	.01
	Philadelphia Eagles			
☐ 644	Mike Pritchard RF	.35	.17	.03
	Atlanta Falcons			
☐ 645	Vinnie Clark RF	.12	.06	.01
	Green Bay Packers			
☐ 646	Jake Reed RF	.15	.07	.01
	Minnesota Vikings			
☐ 647	Brett Favre RF	.40	.20	.04
	Atlanta Falcons			
☐ 648	Todd Lyght RF	.20	.10	.02
	Los Angeles Raiders			
☐ 649	Bruce Pickens RF	.15	.07	.01
	Atlanta Falcons			
☐ 650	Darren Lewis RF	.35	.17	.03
	Chicago Bears			
☐ 651	Wesley Carroll RF	.30	.15	.03
	New Orleans Saints			
☐ 652	James Joseph RF	.50	.25	.05
	Philadelphia Eagles			
☐ 653	Robert Delpino AR	.06	.03	.00
	Los Angeles Rams			
	Tim McDonald			
	Phoenix Cardinals			
☐ 654	Vencie Glenn AR	.12	.06	.01
	New Orleans Saints			
	Deion Sanders			
	Atlanta Falcons			
☐ 655	Jerry Rice AR	.15	.07	.01
	San Francisco 49ers			
	Terry McDaniels			
	Los Angeles Rams			
☐ 656	Barry Sanders AR	.25	.12	.02
	Detroit Lions			
	Derrick Thomas			
	Kansas City Chiefs			
☐ 657	Ken Tippins AR	.06	.03	.00
	Atlanta Falcons			
	Lorenzo White			
	Houston Oilers			
☐ 658	Christian Okoye AR	.06	.03	.00
	Kansas City Chiefs			
	Jacob Green			
	Seattle Seahawks			
☐ 659	Rich Gannon	.08	.04	.01
	Minnesota Vikings			
☐ 660	Johnny Meads	.03	.01	.00
	Houston Oilers			
☐ 661	J.J. Birden	.15	.07	.01
	Kansas City Chiefs			
☐ 662	Bruce Kozerski	.03	.01	.00
	Cincinnati Bengals			
☐ 663	Felix Wright	.03	.01	.00
	Minnesota Vikings			
☐ 664	Al Smith	.03	.01	.00
	Houston Oilers			
☐ 665	Stan Humphries	.08	.04	.01
	Washington Redskins			
☐ 666	Alfred Anderson	.03	.01	.00
	Minnesota Vikings			
☐ 667	Nate Newton	.03	.01	.00
	Dallas Cowboys			
☐ 668	Vince Workman	.25	.12	.02
	Green Bay Packers			
☐ 669	Ricky Reynolds	.03	.01	.00
	Tampa Bay Buccaneers			
☐ 670	Bryce Paup	.20	.10	.02
	Green Bay Packers			
☐ 671	Gill Fenerty	.10	.05	.01
	New Orleans Saints			
☐ 672	Darrell Thompson	.12	.06	.01
	Green Bay Packers			
☐ 673	Anthony Smith	.06	.03	.00
	Los Angeles Raiders			
☐ 674	Darryl Henley	.15	.07	.01
	Los Angeles Rams			
☐ 675	Brett Maxie	.08	.04	.01
	New Orleans Saints			
☐ 676	Craig Taylor	.15	.07	.01
	Cincinnati Bengals			
☐ 677	Steve Wallace	.06	.03	.00
	San Francisco 49ers			
☐ 678	Jeff Feagles	.08	.04	.01
	Philadelphia Eagles			
☐ 679	James Washington	.08	.04	.01
	Dallas Cowboys			
☐ 680	Tim Harris	.06	.03	.00

	San Francisco 49ers			
☐ 681	Dennis Gibson	.03	.01	.00
	Detroit Lions			
☐ 682	Toi Cook	.08	.04	.01
	New Orleans Saints			
☐ 683	Lorenzo Lynch	.06	.03	.00
	Phoenix Cardinals			
☐ 684	Brad Edwards	.12	.06	.01
	Washington Redskins			
☐ 685	Ray Crockett	.10	.05	.01
	Detroit Lions			
☐ 686	Harris Barton	.03	.01	.00
	San Francisco 49ers			
☐ 687	Byron Evans	.03	.01	.00
	Philadelphia Eagles			
☐ 688	Eric Thomas	.03	.01	.00
	Cincinnati Bengals			
☐ 689	Jeff Criswell	.03	.01	.00
	New York Jets			
☐ 690	Eric Ball	.03	.01	.02
	Cincinnati Bengals			
☐ 691	Brian Mitchell	.20	.10	.02
	Washington Redskins			
☐ 692	Quinn Early	.03	.01	.00
	New Orleans Saints			
☐ 693	Aaron Jones	.06	.03	.00
	Philadelphia Eagles			
☐ 694	Jim Dombrowski	.03	.01	.00
	New Orleans Saints			
☐ 695	Jeff Bostic	.03	.01	.00
	Washington Redskins			
☐ 696	Tony Casillas	.06	.03	.00
	Dallas Cowboys			
☐ 697	Ken Lanier	.03	.01	.00
	Denver Broncos			
☐ 698	Henry Thomas	.03	.01	.00
	Minnesota Vikings			
☐ 699	Steve Beuerlein	.12	.06	.01
	Dallas Cowboys			
☐ 700	Checklist 601-700	.06	.01	.00
☐ SP2	Don Shula CO SP	8.00	4.00	.80
	300th Victory			

1991 Upper Deck Heroes Joe Namath

This ten-card Joe Namath set is part of Upper Deck's "Football Heroes" series, which were inserted in its High Number Series packs. Namath personally autographed 2,500 of these

cards, and every 100th card was signed "Broadway Joe." The cards measure the standard size (2 1/2" by 3 1/2"). The front design has color player photos in an oval frame with white and blue borders, on a card face that shades from mustard to brown as one moves from top to bottom. The Upper Deck Football Heroes logo is superimposed at the lower left corner. The backs have a green football field design and summarize various high points in his career. Card number 18 features a portrait of Namath by noted sports artist Vernon Wells. The cards are numbered on the back.

	MINT	EXC	G-VG
COMPLETE SET (10)	28.00	14.00	2.50
COMMON PLAYER (10-18)	2.00	1.00	2.00
☐ 10 1962-65 Crimson Tide	2.00	1.00	.20
☐ 11 1965 Broadway Joe	2.00	1.00	.20
☐ 12 1967 4,000 Yards Passing	2.00	1.00	.20
☐ 13 1968 AFL MVP	2.00	1.00	.20
☐ 14 1969 Super Bowl III	2.00	1.00	.20
☐ 15 1969 All-Pro	2.00	1.00	.20
☐ 16 1972 400 Yards	2.00	1.00	.20
☐ 17 1985 Hall of Fame	2.00	1.00	.20
☐ 18 Checklist Heroes 10-18 (Vernon Wells portrait of Joe Namath)	2.00	1.00	.20
☐ xx Title/Header Card SP (Unnumbered)	15.00	7.50	1.50

1991 Wild Card College Draft Picks

The Wild Card College Football Draft Picks set contains 160 cards measuring the standard size (2 1/2" by 3 1/2"). Supposedly, production quantities were limited to 20,000 numbered cases (or 630,000 sets). The front design features glossy color action player photos, on a black card face with an orange frame around the picture and different color numbers appearing in the top and right borders. The words "1st edition" in a circular emblem overlay the lower left corner of the picture. The backs have different shades of purple and a color headshot, biography, and complete college statistics (1987-90). One of out every 100 cards is "wild," with a numbered stripe to indicate how many cards it can be redeemed for. There are 5, 10, 20, 50, 100, and 1,000 denominations, with the highest numbers the scarcest. Whatever the number, the card can be redeemed for that number of regular cards of the same player, after paying a redemption fee of 4.95 per order. The secondary market value of the striped cards has not proven to be as strong as Wild Card may have anticipated. There have been numerous examples available at card shows and stores of higher stripe cards being offered at 50 percent of their theoretical value based on multiplying the stripe number times the single card value. The set included three surprise wild cards (1, 15, and 22). If these cards were redeemed before April 30, 1992, the collector received three cards to complete the set and a bonus set of six 1992 collegiate football prototype cards. Collectors who redeemed their cards after April 30 did not receive the prototype cards. Also, Kenny

Anderson and Larry Johnson promo cards, numbers P2 and P1 respectively, were randomly inserted, and they may be redeemed after January 2, 1992 for then-unknown player cards. The cards are numbered on the back.

	MINT	EXC	G-VG
COMPLETE SET (160)	15.00	7.50	1.50
COMMON PLAYER (1-160)	.05	.02	.00
☐ 1 Wild Card 1 Todd Lyght Notre Dame	.60	.30	.06
☐ 2 Kelvin Pritchett Mississippi	.20	.10	.02
☐ 3 Robert Young Mississippi State	.05	.02	.00
☐ 4 Reggie Johnson Arizona	.05	.02	.00
☐ 5 Eric Turner UCLA	.50	.25	.05
☐ 6 Pat Tyrance Nebraska	.10	.05	.01
☐ 7 Curvin Richards Pittsburgh	.20	.10	.02
☐ 8 Calvin Stephens South Carolina	.10	.05	.01
☐ 9 Corey Miller South Carolina	.05	.02	.00
☐ 10 Michael Jackson Southern Mississippi	.30	.15	.03
☐ 11 Simmie Carter Southern Mississippi	.05	.02	.00
☐ 12 Roland Smith Miami Florida	.10	.05	.01
☐ 13 Pat O'Hara Southern California	.20	.10	.02
☐ 14 Scott Conover Purdue	.05	.02	.00
☐ 15 Wild Card 2 Russell Maryland Miami	.75	.35	.07
☐ 16 Greg Amsler Tennessee	.10	.05	.01
☐ 17 Moe Gardner Illinois	.30	.15	.03
☐ 18 Howard Griffith Illinois	.20	.10	.02
☐ 19 David Daniels Penn State	.10	.05	.01
☐ 20 Henry Jones Illinois	.10	.05	.01
☐ 21 Don Davey Wisconsin	.10	.05	.01
☐ 22 Wild Card 3 Raghib(Rocket) Ismail Notre Dame	1.00	.50	.10

☐ 23 Richie Andrews 05	.02	.00
Florida State		
☐ 24 Shawn Moore 25	.12	.02
Virginia		
☐ 25 Anthony Moss 10	.05	.01
Florida State		
☐ 26 Vince Moore 05	.02	.00
Tennessee		
☐ 27 Leroy Thompson 15	.07	.01
Penn State		
☐ 28 Darrick Brownlow 20	.10	.02
Illinois		
☐ 29 Mel Agee 10	.05	.01
Illinois		
☐ 30 Darryll Lewis UER 25	.12	.02
Arizona		
(Misspelled Darryl		
on both sides)		
☐ 31 Hyland Hickson 05	.02	.00
Michigan State		
☐ 32 Leonard Russell 1.00	.50	.10
Arizona State		
☐ 33 Floyd Fields 05	.02	.00
Arizona State		
☐ 34 Esera Tuaolo 15	.07	.01
Oregon State		
☐ 35 Todd Marinovich 1.25	.60	.12
Southern California		
☐ 36 Gary Wellman 10	.05	.01
Southern California		
☐ 37 Ricky Ervins 2.50	1.25	.25
Southern California		
☐ 38 Pat Harlow 20	.10	.02
Southern California		
☐ 39 Mo Lewis 25	.12	.02
Georgia		
☐ 40 John Kasay 30	.15	.03
Georgia		
☐ 41 Phil Hansen 10	.05	.01
North Dakota		
☐ 42 Kevin Donnalley 10	.05	.01
North Carolina		
☐ 43 Dexter Davis 10	.05	.01
Clemson		
☐ 44 Vance Hammond 05	.02	.00
Clemson		
☐ 45 Chris Gardocki 10	.05	.01
Clemson		
☐ 46 Bruce Pickens 20	.10	.02
Nebraska		
☐ 47 Godfrey Myles 15	.07	.01
Florida		
☐ 48 Ernie Mills 25	.12	.02
Florida		
☐ 49 Derek Russell 35	.17	.03
Arkansas		
☐ 50 Chris Zorich 50	.25	.05
Notre Dame		
☐ 51 Alfred Williams 25	.12	.02
Colorado		
☐ 52 Jon Vaughn 45	.22	.04
Michigan		
☐ 53 Adrian Cooper 25	.12	.02
Oklahoma		
☐ 54 Eric Bieniemy 35	.17	.03
Colorado		
☐ 55 Robert Bailey 05	.02	.00
Miami Florida		
☐ 56 Ricky Watters 25	.12	.02
Notre Dame		
☐ 57 Mark Vander Poel 10	.05	.01
Colorado		
☐ 58 James Joseph 50	.25	.05
Auburn		
☐ 59 Darren Lewis 45	.22	.04
Texas A and M		
☐ 60 Wesley Carroll 40	.20	.04
Miami Florida		
☐ 61 Dave Key 10	.05	.01
Michigan		
☐ 62 Mike Pritchard 75	.35	.07
Colorado		
☐ 63 Craig Erickson 40	.20	.04
Miami Florida		
☐ 64 Browning Nagle 75	.35	.07
Louisville		
☐ 65 Mike Dumas 20	.10	.02
Indiana		
☐ 66 Andre Jones 05	.02	.00
Notre Dame		
☐ 67 Herman Moore 75	.35	.07
Virginia		
☐ 68 Greg Lewis 60	.30	.06
Washington		
☐ 69 James Goode 05	.02	.00
Oklahoma		
☐ 70 Stan Thomas 10	.05	.01
Texas		
☐ 71 Jerome Henderson 10	.05	.01
Clemson		
☐ 72 Doug Thomas 10	.05	.01
Clemson		
☐ 73 Tony Covington 10	.05	.01
Virginia		
☐ 74 Charles Mincy 05	.02	.00
Washington		
☐ 75 Kanavis McGhee 20	.10	.02
Colorado		
☐ 76 Tom Backes 05	.02	.00
Oklahoma		
☐ 77 Fernandus Vinson 05	.02	.00
North Carolina State		
☐ 78 Marcus Robertson 05	.02	.00
Iowa State		

☐ 79 Eric Harmon .... .05 Clemson	.02	.00	
☐ 80 Rob Selby .... .10 Auburn	.05	.01	
☐ 81 Ed King .... .20 Auburn	.10	.02	
☐ 82 William Thomas .... .10 Texas A and M	.05	.01	
☐ 83 Mike Jones .... .10 North Carolina State	.05	.01	
☐ 84 Paul Justin .... .20 Arizona State	.10	.02	
☐ 85 Robert Wilson .... .20 Texas A and M	.10	.02	
☐ 86 Jesse Campbell .... .10 North Carolina State	.05	.01	
☐ 87 Hayward Haynes .... .05 Florida State	.02	.00	
☐ 88 Mike Croel .... .75 Nebraska	.35	.07	
☐ 89 Jeff Graham .... .20 Ohio State	.10	.02	
☐ 90 Vinnie Clark .... .25 Ohio State	.12	.02	
☐ 91 Keith Cash .... .20 Texas	.10	.02	
☐ 92 Tim Ryan .... .10 Notre Dame	.05	.01	
☐ 93 Jarrod Bunch .... .20 Michigan	.10	.02	
☐ 94 Stanley Richard .... .30 Texas	.15	.03	
☐ 95 Alvin Harper .... .60 Tennessee	.30	.06	
☐ 96 Bob Dahl .... .10 Notre Dame	.05	.01	
☐ 97 Mark Gunn .... .05 Pittsburgh	.02	.00	
☐ 98 Frank Blevins .... .05 Oklahoma	.02	.00	
☐ 99 Harvey Williams .... 1.00 LSU	.50	.10	
☐ 100 Dixon Edwards ..... .20 Michigan State	.10	.02	
☐ 101 Blake Miller .... .05 LSU	.02	.00	
☐ 102 Bobby Wilson .... .25 Michigan State	.12	.02	
☐ 103 Chuck Webb .... .25 Tennessee	.12	.02	
☐ 104 Randal Hill .... .75 Miami Florida	.35	.07	
☐ 105 Shane Curry .... .05 Miami Florida	.02	.00	
☐ 106 Barry Sanders ..... .75 Oklahoma State	.35	.07	
☐ 107 Richard Fain .... .15 Florida	.07	.01	
☐ 108 Joe Garten .... .05 Colorado	.02	.00	
☐ 109 Dean Dingman ..... .05 Michigan	.02	.00	
☐ 110 Mark Tucker .... .05 Southern California	.02	.00	
☐ 111 Dan McGwire ...... 1.00 San Diego State	.50	.10	
☐ 112 Paul Glonek .... .05 Arizona	.02	.00	
☐ 113 Tom Dohring .... .05 Michigan	.02	.00	
☐ 114 Joe Sims .... .05 Nebraska	.02	.00	
☐ 115 Bryan Cox .... .30 Western Illinois	.15	.03	
☐ 116 Bobby Olive .... .05 Ohio State	.02	.00	
☐ 117 Blaise Bryant ...... .15 Iowa State	.07	.01	
☐ 118 Charles Johnson .. .15 Colorado	.07	.01	
☐ 119 Brett Favre .... .60 Southern Mississippi	.30	.06	
☐ 120 Luis Cristobal ...... .05 Miami Florida	.02	.00	
☐ 121 Don Gibson .... .05 Southern California	.02	.00	
☐ 122 Scott Ross .... .05 Southern California	.02	.00	
☐ 123 Huey Richardson .. .15 Florida	.07	.01	
☐ 124 Chris Smith .... .10 Brigham Young	.05	.01	
☐ 125 Duane Young .... .05 Michigan State	.02	.00	
☐ 126 Eric Swann .... .30 (No College)	.15	.03	
☐ 127 Jeff Fite .... .05 Memphis State	.02	.00	
☐ 128 Eugene Williams .. .05 Iowa State	.02	.00	
☐ 129 Harlan Davis .... .05 Tennessee	.02	.00	
☐ 130 James Bradley ..... .05 Michigan State	.02	.00	
☐ 131 Rob Carpenter .... .20 Syracuse	.10	.02	
☐ 132 Dennis Ransom ... .05 Texas A and M	.02	.00	
☐ 133 Mike Arthur .... .05 Texas A and M	.02	.00	
☐ 134 Chuck Weatherspoon .30 Houston	.15	.03	
☐ 135 Darrell Malone ..... .05 Jacksonville State	.02	.00	

☐ 136	George Thornton 10	.05	.01	
	Alabama			
☐ 137	Lamar McGriggs 05	.02	.00	
	Western Illinois			
☐ 138	Alex Johnson 05	.02	.00	
	Miami Florida			
☐ 139	Eric Moten 10	.05	.01	
	Michigan State			
☐ 140	Joe Valerio 10	.05	.01	
	Pennsylvania			
☐ 141	Jake Reed 20	.10	.02	
	Grambling			
☐ 142	Ernie Thompson 10	.05	.01	
	Indiana			
☐ 143	Roland Poles 05	.02	.00	
	Tennessee			
☐ 144	Randy Bethel 05	.02	.00	
	Miami Florida			
☐ 145	Terry Bagsby 05	.02	.00	
	East Texas State			
☐ 146	Tim James 05	.02	.00	
	Colorado			
☐ 147	Kenny Walker 60	.30	.06	
	Nebraska			
☐ 148	Nolan Harrison 05	.02	.00	
	Indiana			
☐ 149	Keith Traylor 20	.10	.02	
	Central Oklahoma			
☐ 150	Nick Subis 05	.02	.00	
	San Diego State			
☐ 151	Scott Zolak 25	.12	.02	
	Maryland			
☐ 152	Pio Sagapolutele 15	.07	.01	
	San Diego State			
☐ 153	James Jones 10	.05	.01	
	Northern Iowa			
☐ 154	Mike Sullivan 05	.02	.00	
	Miami Florida			
☐ 155	Joe Johnson 05	.02	.00	
	North Carolina State			
☐ 156	Todd Scott 10	.05	.01	
	Southwest Louisiana			
☐ 157	Checklist 1 05	.02	.00	
☐ 158	Checklist 2 05	.02	.00	
☐ 159	Checklist 3 05	.02	.00	
☐ 160	Checklist 4 05	.02	.00	

1991 Wild Card NFL

The Wild Card NFL Football set contains 160 cards measuring the standard size (2 1/2" by

3 1/2"). Supposedly production quantities were limited to 30,000 numbered ten-box cases. The series included three bonus cards (Wild Card Case Card, Wild Card Box Card, and Wild Card Hat Card) that were redeemable for the item pictured. Surprise wild card number 126 could be exchanged for a ten-card NFL Experience set, featuring five players each from the Washington Redskins and the Buffalo Bills. This set resembles that given away at the Super Bowl Show, except that the cards bear no date. The front design features glossy color action player photos, highlighted in mustard on a black card face. Different color numbers appear in the top and right borders. The words "NFL Premier Edition" in a football icon overlay the lower left corner of the picture. The backs shade from black to mustard and carry a color headshot, biography, statistics, and card number. The secondary market value of the striped cards has not proven to be as strong as Wild Card may have anticipated. There have been numerous examples available at card shows and stores of higher stripe cards being offered at 50 percent of their theoretical value based on multiplying the stripe number times the single card value. The key rookie cards in this set are Ricky Ervins, Todd Marinovich, Dan McGwire, Neil O'Donnell, and Leonard Russell.

	MINT	EXC	G-VG
COMPLETE SET (160) 15.00	15.00	7.50	1.50
COMMON PLAYER (1-160) 03	.03	.01	.00
☐ 1 Jeff George 35	.35	.17	.03
Indianapolis Colts			
☐ 2 Sean Jones 03	.03	.01	.00
Houston Oilers			
☐ 3 Duane Bickett 03	.03	.01	.00
Indianapolis Colts			

☐ 4 John Elway 15	.07	.01	
Denver Broncos			
☐ 5 Christian Okoye 08	.04	.01	
Kansas City Chiefs			
☐ 6 Steve Atwater 06	.03	.00	
Denver Broncos			
☐ 7 Anthony Munoz 08	.04	.01	
Cincinnati Bengals			
☐ 8 Dave Krieg 08	.04	.01	
Seattle Seahawks			
☐ 9 Nick Lowery 06	.03	.00	
Kansas City Chiefs			
☐ 10 Albert Bentley 06	.03	.00	
Indianapolis Colts			
☐ 11 Mark Jackson 06	.03	.00	
Denver Broncos			
☐ 12 Jeff Bryant 03	.01	.00	
Seattle Seahawks			
☐ 13 Johnny Hector 03	.01	.00	
New York Jets			
☐ 14 John L. Williams 08	.04	.01	
Seattle Seahawks			
☐ 15 Jim Everett 15	.07	.01	
Los Angeles Rams			
☐ 16 Mark Duper 06	.03	.00	
Miami Dolphins			
☐ 17 Drew Hill UER 08	.04	.01	
(Reversed negative			
on card front)			
Houston Oilers			
☐ 18 Randal Hill 60	.30	.06	
Phoenix Cardinals			
☐ 19 Ernest Givins 10	.05	.01	
Houston Oilers			
☐ 20 Ken O'Brien 08	.04	.01	
New York Jets			
☐ 21 Blair Thomas 40	.20	.04	
New York Jets			
☐ 22 Derrick Thomas 15	.07	.01	
Kansas City Chiefs			
☐ 23 Harvey Williams 75	.35	.07	
Kansas City Chiefs			
☐ 24 Simon Fletcher 03	.01	.00	
Denver Broncos			
☐ 25 Stephone Paige 06	.03	.00	
Kansas City Chiefs			
☐ 26 Barry Word 25	.12	.02	
Kansas City Chiefs			
☐ 27 Warren Moon 20	.10	.02	
Houston Oilers			
☐ 28 Derrick Fenner 12	.06	.01	
Seattle Seahawks			
☐ 29 Shane Conlan 06	.03	.00	
Buffalo Bills			
☐ 30 Karl Mecklenburg 06	.03	.00	
Denver Broncos			
☐ 31 Gary Anderson 06	.03	.00	

Tampa Bay Buccaneers			
☐ 32 Sammie Smith 08	.04	.01	
Miami Dolphins			
☐ 33 Steve DeBerg 08	.04	.01	
Kansas City Chiefs			
☐ 34 Dan McGwire 1.25	.60	.12	
Seattle Seahawks			
☐ 35 Roger Craig 10	.05	.01	
Los Angeles Raiders			
☐ 36 Tom Tupa 10	.05	.01	
Phoenix Cardinals			
☐ 37 Rod Woodson 08	.04	.01	
Pittsburgh Steelers			
☐ 38 Junior Seau 08	.04	.01	
San Diego Chargers			
☐ 39 Bruce Pickens 20	.10	.02	
Atlanta Falcons			
☐ 40 Greg Townsend 03	.01	.00	
Los Angeles Raiders			
☐ 41 Gary Clark 12	.06	.01	
Washington Redskins			
☐ 42 Broderick Thomas 06	.03	.00	
Tampa Bay Buccaneers			
☐ 43 Charles Mann 06	.03	.00	
Washington Redskins			
☐ 44 Browning Nagle 75	.35	.07	
New York Jets			
☐ 45 James Joseph 45	.22	.04	
Philadelphia Eagles			
☐ 46 Emmitt Smith UER 1.25	.60	.12	
Dallas Cowboys			
(Scoring 1 TD,			
should be 11)			
☐ 47 Cornelius Bennett 08	.04	.01	
Buffalo Bills			
☐ 48 Maurice Hurst 03	.01	.00	
New England Patriots			
☐ 49 Art Monk 10	.05	.01	
Washington Redskins			
☐ 50 Louis Lipps 06	.03	.00	
Pittsburgh Steelers			
☐ 51 Mark Rypien 20	.10	.02	
Washington Redskins			
☐ 52 Bubby Brister 08	.04	.01	
Pittsburgh Steelers			
☐ 53 John Stephens 06	.03	.00	
New England Patriots			
☐ 54 Merril Hoge 03	.01	.00	
Pittsburgh Steelers			
☐ 55 Kevin Mack 06	.03	.00	
Cleveland Browns			
☐ 56 Al Toon 08	.04	.01	
New York Jets			
☐ 57 Ronnie Lott 10	.05	.01	
Los Angeles Raiders			
☐ 58 Eric Metcalf 06	.03	.00	
Cleveland Browns			

☐ 59 Vinny Testaverde	.08	.04	.01
Tampa Bay Buccaneers			
☐ 60 Darrell Green	.10	.05	.01
Washington Redskins			
☐ 61 Randall Cunningham	.15	.07	.01
Philadelphia Eagles			
☐ 62 Charles Haley	.06	.03	.00
San Francisco 49ers			
☐ 63 Mark Carrier	.08	.04	.01
Chicago Bears			
☐ 64 Jim Harbaugh	.10	.05	.01
Chicago Bears			
☐ 65 Richard Dent	.08	.04	.01
Chicago Bears			
☐ 66 Stan Thomas	.08	.04	.01
Chicago Bears			
☐ 67 Neal Anderson	.15	.07	.01
Chicago Bears			
☐ 68 Troy Aikman	.35	.17	.03
Dallas Cowboys			
☐ 69 Mike Pritchard	.60	.30	.06
Atlanta Falcons			
☐ 70 Deion Sanders	.20	.10	.02
Atlanta Falcons			
☐ 71 Andre Rison	.15	.07	.01
Atlanta Falcons			
☐ 72 Keith Millard	.06	.03	.00
Minnesota Vikings			
☐ 73 Jerry Rice	.35	.17	.03
San Francisco 49ers			
☐ 74 Johnny Johnson	.25	.12	.02
Phoenix Cardinals			
☐ 75 Tim McDonald	.06	.03	.00
Phoenix Cardinals			
☐ 76 Leonard Russell	1.25	.60	.12
New England Patriots			
☐ 77 Keith Jackson	.08	.04	.01
Philadelphia Eagles			
☐ 78 Keith Byars	.06	.03	.00
Philadelphia Eagles			
☐ 79 Ricky Proehl	.10	.05	.01
Phoenix Cardinals			
☐ 80 Dexter Carter	.08	.04	.01
San Francisco 49ers			
☐ 81 Alvin Harper	.50	.25	.05
Dallas Cowboys			
☐ 82 Irving Fryar	.06	.03	.00
New England Patriots			
☐ 83 Marion Butts	.10	.05	.01
San Diego Chargers			
☐ 84 Alfred Williams	.15	.07	.01
Cincinnati Bengals			
☐ 85 Timm Rosenbach	.10	.05	.01
Phoenix Cardinals			
☐ 86 Steve Young	.10	.05	.01
San Francisco 49ers			
☐ 87 Albert Lewis	.06	.03	.00
Kansas City Chiefs			
☐ 88 Rodney Peete	.08	.04	.01
Detroit Lions			
☐ 89 Barry Sanders	.75	.35	.07
Detroit Lions			
☐ 90 Bennie Blades	.06	.03	.00
Detroit Lions			
☐ 91 Chris Spielman	.06	.03	.00
Detroit Lions			
☐ 92 John Friesz	.35	.17	.03
San Diego Chargers			
☐ 93 Jerome Brown	.06	.03	.00
Philadelphia Eagles			
☐ 94 Reggie White	.08	.04	.01
Philadelphia Eagles			
☐ 95 Michael Irvin	.20	.10	.02
Dallas Cowboys			
☐ 96 Keith McCants	.08	.04	.01
Tampa Bay Buccaneers			
☐ 97 Vinnie Clark	.10	.05	.01
Green Bay Packers			
☐ 98 Louis Oliver	.03	.01	.00
Miami Dolphins			
☐ 99 Mark Clayton	.08	.04	.01
Miami Dolphins			
☐ 100 John Offerdahl	.03	.01	.00
Miami Dolphins			
☐ 101 Michael Carter	.06	.03	.00
San Francisco 49ers			
☐ 102 John Taylor	.12	.06	.01
San Francisco 49ers			
☐ 103 William Perry	.08	.04	.01
Chicago Bears			
☐ 104 Gill Byrd	.06	.03	.00
San Diego Chargers			
☐ 105 Burt Grossman	.03	.01	.00
San Diego Chargers			
☐ 106 Herman Moore	.60	.30	.06
Detroit Lions			
☐ 107 Howie Long	.06	.03	.00
Los Angeles Raiders			
☐ 108 Bo Jackson	.35	.17	.03
Los Angeles Raiders			
☐ 109 Kelvin Pritchett	.12	.06	.01
Detroit Lions			
☐ 110 Jacob Green	.06	.03	.00
Seattle Seahawks			
☐ 111 Chris Doleman	.06	.03	.00
Minnesota Vikings			
☐ 112 Herschel Walker	.12	.06	.01
Minnesota Vikings			
☐ 113 Russell Maryland	.45	.22	.04
Dallas Cowboys			
☐ 114 Anthony Carter	.08	.04	.01
Minnesota Vikings			
☐ 115 Joey Browner	.06	.03	.00
Minnesota Vikings			

☐ 116	Tony Mandarich 06	.03	.00
	Green Bay Packers		
☐ 117	Don Majkowski 08	.04	.01
	Green Bay Packers		
☐ 118	Ricky Ervins 1.50	.75	.15
	Washington Redskins		
☐ 119	Sterling Sharpe 10	.05	.01
	Green Bay Packers		
☐ 120	Tim Harris 06	.03	.00
	San Francisco 49ers		
☐ 121	Hugh Millen 75	.35	.07
	New England Patriots		
☐ 122	Mike Rozier 06	.03	.00
	Atlanta Falcons		
☐ 123	Chris Miller 15	.07	.01
	Atlanta Falcons		
☐ 124	Morten Andersen 06	.03	.00
	New Orleans Saints		
☐ 125	Neil O'Donnell 90	.45	.09
	Pittsburgh Steelers		
☐ 126	Surprise Wild Card 2.50	1.25	.25
	(Exchangeable for		
	ten-card NFL		
	Experience set)		
☐ 127	Eddie Brown 06	.03	.00
	Cincinnati Bengals		
☐ 128	James Francis 08	.04	.01
	Cincinnati Bengals		
☐ 129	James Brooks 08	.04	.01
	Cincinnati Bengals		
☐ 130	David Fulcher 03	.01	.00
	Cincinnati Bengals		
☐ 131	Michael Jackson 35	.17	.03
	Cleveland Browns		
☐ 132	Clay Matthews 03	.01	.00
	Cleveland Browns		
☐ 133	Scott Norwood 03	.01	.00
	Buffalo Bills		
☐ 134	Wesley Carroll 40	.20	.04
	New Orleans Saints		
☐ 135	Thurman Thomas 45	.22	.04
	Buffalo Bills		
☐ 136	Mark Ingram 03	.01	.00
	New York Giants		
☐ 137	Bobby Hebert 08	.04	.01
	New Orleans Saints		
☐ 138	Bobby Wilson 08	.04	.01
	Washington Redskins		
☐ 139	Craig Heyward 08	.04	.01
	New Orleans Saints		
☐ 140	Dalton Hilliard 06	.03	.00
	New Orleans Saints		
☐ 141	Jeff Hostetler 20	.10	.02
	New York Giants		
☐ 142	Dave Meggett 10	.05	.01
	New York Giants		
☐ 143	Cris Dishman 20	.10	.02
	Houston Oilers		
☐ 144	Lawrence Taylor 10	.05	.01
	New York Giants		
☐ 145	Leonard Marshall 06	.03	.00
	New York Giants		
☐ 146	Pepper Johnson 06	.03	.00
	New York Giants		
☐ 147	Todd Marinovich 1.25	.60	.12
	Los Angeles Raiders		
☐ 148	Mike Croel 75	.35	.07
	Denver Broncos		
☐ 149	Erik McMillan 06	.03	.00
	New York Jets		
☐ 150	Flipper Anderson 06	.03	.00
	Los Angeles Rams		
☐ 151	Cleveland Gary 06	.03	.00
	Los Angeles Rams		
☐ 152	Henry Ellard 08	.04	.01
	Los Angeles Rams		
☐ 153	Kevin Greene 06	.03	.00
	Los Angeles Rams		
☐ 154	Michael Cofer 03	.01	.00
	Detroit Lions		
☐ 155	Todd Lyght 40	.20	.04
	Los Angeles Rams		
☐ 156	Bruce Smith 08	.04	.01
	Buffalo Bills		
☐ 157	Checklist 1 06	.01	.00
☐ 158	Checklist 2 06	.01	.00
☐ 159	Checklist 3 06	.01	.00
☐ 160	Checklist 4 06	.01	.00

1991 Wild Card NFL Redemption Cards

This ten-card standard-size (2 1/2" by 3 1/2") set commemorates Super Bowl XXVI and features five players from each team. These cards were exchanged for Wild Card surprise card number 126, and thus they are numbered 126A-J. In design, they are identical to the 1991 Wild Card NFL Super Bowl Promos/NFL Experience set. The only detectible difference is that the Super Bowl promos have the date and location of the Super Bowl Card Show III on the back, while these redemption cards do not carry that information and are numbered differently.

packs. The cards are numbered on the back and checklisted below alphabetically according to teams as follows: Atlanta Falcons (331-341), Buffalo Bills (342-352), Chicago Bears (353-363), Cincinnati Bengals (364-374), Cleveland Browns (375-385), Dallas Cowboys (386-396), Denver Broncos (397-407), Detroit Lions (408-418), Green Bay Packers (419-429), Houston Oilers (430-440), Indianapolis Colts (441-451), Kansas City Chiefs (452-463), Los Angeles Raiders (464-474), Los Angeles Rams (475-487), Miami Dolphins (488-498), Minnesota Vikings (499-509), New England Patriots (510-522), New Orleans Saints (523-535), New York Giants (536-547), New York Jets (548-558), Philadelphia Eagles (559-570), Phoenix Cardinals (571-582), Pittsburgh Steelers (583-593), San Diego Chargers (594-604), San Francisco 49ers (605-615), Seattle Seahawks (616-626), Tampa Bay Buccaneers (627-637), and Washington Redskins (638-648). The set closes with a Rookies subset (649-660).

	MINT	EXC	G-VG
COMPLETE SET (10)	3.50	1.50	.30
COMMON PLAYER (126A-J)	.12	.05	.01
☐ 126A Mark Rypien	.60	.25	.05
☐ 126B Ricky Ervins	1.50	.60	.12
☐ 126C Darrell Green	.25	.10	.02
☐ 126D Charles Mann	.12	.05	.01
☐ 126E Art Monk	.30	.12	.02
☐ 126F Thurman Thomas	.90	.35	.07
☐ 126G Bruce Smith	.30	.12	.02
☐ 126H Cornelius Bennett	.25	.10	.02
☐ 126I Scott Norwood	.12	.05	.01
☐ 126J Shane Conlan	.18	.07	.01

Late Breaking 1992 Sets

1992 Pacific Plus II

The 1992 Pacific Plus II series contains 330 standard-size (2 1/2" by 3 1/2") cards. They display the same design as the first series, with glossy color action photos bordered on the left by a color stripe. Series II highlights include a nine-card Legends of the Game subset featuring Hall of Famer Bob Griese, with 1,000 numbered cards bearing his autograph. In addition, "Pacific Picks the Pros" gold-foil cards were randomly inserted in 14-card foil packs, while silver-foil versions of the same subset were inserted in 24-card foil

	MINT	EXC	G-VG
COMPLETE SET (330)	12.00	6.00	1.20
COMMON PLAYER (331-660)	.03	.01	.00
☐ 331 Oliver Barnett	.03	.01	.00
☐ 332 Aundray Bruce	.03	.01	.00
☐ 333 Ken Tippins	.10	.05	.01
☐ 334 Jessie Tuggle	.03	.01	.00
☐ 335 Brian Jordan	.12	.06	.01
☐ 336 Andre Rison	.15	.07	.01
☐ 337 Houston Hoover	.03	.01	.00
☐ 338 Bill Fralic	.06	.03	.00
☐ 339 Pat Chaffey	.10	.05	.01
☐ 340 Keith Jones	.03	.01	.00
☐ 341 Jamie Dukes	.12	.06	.01
☐ 342 Chris Mohr	.03	.01	.00
☐ 343 John Davis	.03	.01	.00
☐ 344 Ray Bentley	.03	.01	.00
☐ 345 Scott Norwood	.03	.01	.00
☐ 346 Shane Conlan	.06	.03	.00
☐ 347 Steve Tasker	.03	.01	.00
☐ 348 Will Wolford	.03	.01	.00
☐ 349 Gary Baldinger	.10	.05	.01
☐ 350 Kirby Jackson	.03	.01	.00
☐ 351 Jamie Mueller	.03	.01	.00
☐ 352 Pete Metzelaars	.03	.01	.00
☐ 353 Richard Dent	.06	.03	.00
☐ 354 Ron Rivera	.03	.01	.00
☐ 355 Jim Morrissey	.03	.01	.00
☐ 356 John Roper	.03	.01	.00
☐ 357 Steve McMichael	.03	.01	.00
☐ 358 Ron Morris	.03	.01	.00
☐ 359 Darren Lewis	.15	.07	.01

☐ 360 Anthony Morgan	.12	.06	.01
☐ 361 Stan Thomas	.03	.01	.00
☐ 362 James Thornton	.03	.01	.00
☐ 363 Brad Muster	.06	.03	.00
☐ 364 Tim Krumrie	.03	.01	.00
☐ 365 Lee Johnson	.03	.01	.00
☐ 366 Eric Ball	.03	.01	.00
☐ 367 Alonzo Mitz	.10	.05	.01
☐ 368 David Grant	.03	.01	.00
☐ 369 Lynn James	.06	.03	.00
☐ 370 Lewis Billups	.03	.01	.00
☐ 371 Jim Breech	.03	.01	.00
☐ 372 Alfred Williams	.06	.03	.00
☐ 373 Wayne Haddix	.03	.01	.00
☐ 374 Tim McGee	.06	.03	.00
☐ 375 Michael Jackson	.12	.06	.01
☐ 376 Leroy Hoard	.08	.04	.01
☐ 377 Tony Jones	.06	.03	.00
☐ 378 Vince Newsome	.03	.01	.00
☐ 379 Todd Philcox	.15	.07	.01
☐ 380 Eric Metcalf	.06	.03	.00
☐ 381 John Rienstra	.03	.01	.00
☐ 382 Matt Stover	.03	.01	.00
☐ 383 Brian Hansen	.03	.01	.00
☐ 384 Joe Morris	.06	.03	.00
☐ 385 Anthony Pleasant	.03	.01	.00
☐ 386 Mark Stepnoski	.03	.01	.00
☐ 387 Erik Williams	.03	.01	.00
☐ 388 Jimmie Jones	.03	.01	.00
☐ 389 Kevin Gogan	.03	.01	.00
☐ 390 Manny Hendrix	.08	.04	.01
☐ 391 Issiac Holt	.03	.01	.00
☐ 392 Ken Norton	.03	.01	.00
☐ 393 Tommie Agee	.03	.01	.00
☐ 394 Alvin Harper	.20	.10	.02
☐ 395 Alexander Wright	.06	.03	.00
☐ 396 Mike Saxon	.03	.01	.00
☐ 397 Michael Brooks	.03	.01	.00
☐ 398 Bobby Humphrey	.10	.05	.01
☐ 399 Ken Lanier	.03	.01	.00
☐ 400 Steve Sewell	.06	.03	.00
☐ 401 Robert Perryman	.03	.01	.00
☐ 402 Wymon Henderson	.03	.01	.00
☐ 403 Keith Kartz	.03	.01	.00
☐ 404 Clarence Kay	.03	.01	.00
☐ 405 Keith Traylor	.03	.01	.00
☐ 406 Doug Widell	.03	.01	.00
☐ 407 Dennis Smith	.03	.01	.00
☐ 408 Marc Spindler	.03	.01	.00
☐ 409 Lomas Brown	.03	.01	.00
☐ 410 Robert Clark	.03	.01	.00
☐ 411 Eric Andolsek	.03	.01	.00
☐ 412 Mike Farr	.03	.01	.00
☐ 413 Ray Crockett	.03	.01	.00
☐ 414 Jeff Campbell	.03	.01	.00
☐ 415 Dan Owens	.03	.01	.00
☐ 416 Jim Arnold	.03	.01	.00
☐ 417 Barry Sanders	.75	.35	.07
☐ 418 Eddie Murray	.03	.01	.00
☐ 419 Vince Workman	.10	.05	.01
☐ 420 Ed West	.03	.01	.00
☐ 421 Charles Wilson	.03	.01	.00
☐ 422 Perry Kemp	.03	.01	.00
☐ 423 Chuck Cecil	.03	.01	.00
☐ 424 James Campen	.03	.01	.00
☐ 425 Robert Brown	.03	.01	.00
☐ 426 Brian Noble	.03	.01	.00
☐ 427 Rich Moran	.03	.01	.00
☐ 428 Vai Sikahema	.03	.01	.00
☐ 429 Allen Rice	.03	.01	.00
☐ 430 Haywood Jeffires	.15	.07	.01
☐ 431 Warren Moon	.20	.10	.02
☐ 432 Greg Montgomery	.03	.01	.00
☐ 433 Sean Jones	.03	.01	.00
☐ 434 Richard Johnson	.03	.01	.00
☐ 435 Al Smith	.03	.01	.00
☐ 436 Johnny Meads	.03	.01	.00
☐ 437 William Fuller	.03	.01	.00
☐ 438 Mike Munchak	.06	.03	.00
☐ 439 Ray Childress	.06	.03	.00
☐ 440 Cody Carlson	.06	.03	.00
☐ 441 Scott Radecic	.03	.01	.00
☐ 442 Quintus McDonald	.12	.06	.01
☐ 443 Eugene Daniel	.03	.01	.00
☐ 444 Mark Herrmann	.15	.07	.01
☐ 445 John Baylor	.12	.06	.01
☐ 446 Dave McCloughan	.06	.03	.00
☐ 447 Mark Vander Poel	.03	.01	.00
☐ 448 Randy Dixon	.03	.01	.00
☐ 449 Keith Taylor	.03	.01	.00
☐ 450 Alan Grant	.03	.01	.00
☐ 451 Tony Siragusa	.03	.01	.00
☐ 452 Rich Baldinger	.03	.01	.00
☐ 453 Derrick Thomas	.17	.08	.01
☐ 454 Bill Jones	.20	.10	.02
☐ 455 Troy Stradford	.03	.01	.00
☐ 456 Barry Word	.17	.08	.01
☐ 457 Tim Grunhard	.03	.01	.00
☐ 458 Chris Martin	.03	.01	.00
☐ 459 Jayice Pearson	.12	.06	.01
☐ 460 Dino Hackett	.03	.01	.00
☐ 461 David Lutz	.03	.01	.00
☐ 462 Albert Lewis	.06	.03	.00
☐ 463 Fred Jones	.17	.08	.01
☐ 464 Winston Moss	.03	.01	.00
☐ 465 Sam Graddy	.20	.10	.02
☐ 466 Steve Wisniewski	.03	.01	.00
☐ 467 Jay Schroeder	.08	.04	.01
☐ 468 Ronnie Lott	.10	.05	.01
☐ 469 Willie Gault	.06	.03	.00
☐ 470 Greg Townsend	.03	.01	.00
☐ 471 Max Montoya	.03	.01	.00
☐ 472 Howie Long	.06	.03	.00
☐ 473 Lionel Washington	.03	.01	.00

☐ 474	Riki Ellison	.03	.01	.00
☐ 475	Tom Newberry	.03	.01	.00
☐ 476	Damone Johnson	.03	.01	.00
☐ 477	Pat Terrell	.03	.01	.00
☐ 478	Marcus Dupree	.06	.03	.00
☐ 479	Todd Lyght	.12	.06	.01
☐ 480	Buford McGee	.03	.01	.00
☐ 481	Bern Brostek	.03	.01	.00
☐ 482	Jim Price	.03	.01	.00
☐ 483	Robert Young	.03	.01	.00
☐ 484	Tony Zendejas	.03	.01	.00
☐ 485	Robert Bailey	.10	.05	.01
☐ 486	Alvin Wright	.06	.03	.00
☐ 487	Pat Carter	.03	.01	.00
☐ 488	Pete Stoyanovich	.03	.01	.00
☐ 489	Reggie Roby	.03	.01	.00
☐ 490	Harry Galbreath	.03	.01	.00
☐ 491	Michael McGruder	.12	.06	.01
☐ 492	J.B. Brown	.03	.01	.00
☐ 493	E.J. Junior	.03	.01	.00
☐ 494	Ferrell Edmunds	.03	.01	.00
☐ 495	Scott Secules	.03	.01	.00
☐ 496	Greg Baty	.10	.05	.01
☐ 497	Mike Iaquaniello	.03	.01	.00
☐ 498	Keith Sims	.03	.01	.00
☐ 499	John Randle	.03	.01	.00
☐ 500	Joey Browner	.06	.03	.00
☐ 501	Steve Jordan	.06	.03	.00
☐ 502	Darrin Nelson	.06	.03	.00
☐ 503	Audray McMillian	.03	.01	.00
☐ 504	Harry Newsome	.03	.01	.00
☐ 505	Hassan Jones	.03	.01	.00
☐ 506	Ray Berry	.03	.01	.00
☐ 507	Mike Merriweather	.03	.01	.00
☐ 508	Leo Lewis	.03	.01	.00
☐ 509	Tim Irwin	.03	.01	.00
☐ 510	Kirk Lowdermilk	.03	.01	.00
☐ 511	Alfred Anderson	.03	.01	.00
☐ 512	Michael Timpson	.10	.05	.01
☐ 513	Jerome Henderson	.06	.03	.00
☐ 514	Andre Tippett	.06	.03	.00
☐ 515	Chris Singleton	.06	.03	.00
☐ 516	John Stephens	.06	.03	.00
☐ 517	Ronnie Lippett	.03	.01	.00
☐ 518	Bruce Armstrong	.03	.01	.00
☐ 519	Marion Hobby	.12	.06	.01
☐ 520	Tim Goad	.03	.01	.00
☐ 521	Mickey Washington	.10	.05	.01
☐ 522	Fred Smerlas	.03	.01	.00
☐ 523	Wayne Martin	.03	.01	.00
☐ 524	Frank Warren	.03	.01	.00
☐ 525	Floyd Turner	.03	.01	.00
☐ 526	Wesley Carroll	.20	.10	.02
☐ 527	Gene Atkins	.03	.01	.00
☐ 528	Vaughan Johnson	.03	.01	.00
☐ 529	Hoby Brenner	.03	.01	.00
☐ 530	Renaldo Turnbull	.03	.01	.00
☐ 531	Joel Hilgenberg	.03	.01	.00
☐ 532	Craig Heyward	.06	.03	.00
☐ 533	Vince Buck	.03	.01	.00
☐ 534	Jim Dombrowski	.03	.01	.00
☐ 535	Fred McAfee	.20	.10	.02
☐ 536	Phil Simms	.10	.05	.01
☐ 537	Lewis Tillman	.03	.01	.00
☐ 538	John Elliott	.03	.01	.00
☐ 539	Dave Meggett	.08	.04	.01
☐ 540	Mark Collins	.03	.01	.00
☐ 541	Ottis Anderson	.06	.03	.00
☐ 542	Bobby Abrams	.12	.06	.01
☐ 543	Sean Landeta	.03	.01	.00
☐ 544	Brian Williams	.03	.01	.00
☐ 545	Erik Howard	.03	.01	.00
☐ 546	Mark Ingram	.03	.01	.00
☐ 547	Kanavis McGhee	.06	.03	.00
☐ 548	Kyle Clifton	.03	.01	.00
☐ 549	Marvin Washington	.03	.01	.00
☐ 550	Jeff Criswell	.03	.01	.00
☐ 551	Dave Cadigan	.03	.01	.00
☐ 552	Chris Burkett	.03	.01	.00
☐ 553	Erik McMillin	.03	.01	.00
☐ 554	James Hasty	.03	.01	.00
☐ 555	Louie Aguiar	.10	.05	.01
☐ 556	Troy Johnson	.10	.05	.01
☐ 557	Troy Taylor	.20	.10	.02
☐ 558	Pat Kelly	.10	.05	.01
☐ 559	Heath Sherman	.06	.03	.00
☐ 560	Roger Ruzek	.03	.01	.00
☐ 561	Andre Waters	.03	.01	.00
☐ 562	Izel Jenkins	.03	.01	.00
☐ 563	Keith Jackson	.06	.03	.00
☐ 564	Byron Evans	.03	.01	.00
☐ 565	Wes Hopkins	.03	.01	.00
☐ 566	Rich Miano	.03	.01	.00
☐ 567	Seth Joyner	.06	.03	.00
☐ 568	Thomas Sanders	.03	.01	.00
☐ 569	David Alexander	.03	.01	.00
☐ 570	Jeff Kemp	.06	.03	.00
☐ 571	Jock Jones	.12	.06	.01
☐ 572	Craig Patterson	.12	.06	.01
☐ 573	Robert Massey	.03	.01	.00
☐ 574	Bill Lewis	.03	.01	.00
☐ 575	Freddie Joe Nunn	.03	.01	.00
☐ 576	Aeneas Williams	.03	.01	.00
☐ 577	John Jackson	.03	.01	.00
☐ 578	Tim McDonald	.03	.01	.00
☐ 579	Michael Zordich	.10	.05	.01
☐ 580	Eric Hill	.03	.01	.00
☐ 581	Lorenzo Lynch	.03	.01	.00
☐ 582	Vernice Smith	.10	.05	.01
☐ 583	Greg Lloyd	.03	.01	.00
☐ 584	Carnell Lake	.03	.01	.00
☐ 585	Hardy Nickerson	.03	.01	.00
☐ 586	Delton Hall	.03	.01	.00
☐ 587	Gerald Williams	.03	.01	.00

☐ 588 Bryan Hinkle ..... .03	.01	.00
☐ 589 Barry Foster ..... .08	.04	.01
☐ 590 Bubby Brister ..... .08	.04	.01
☐ 591 Rick Strom ..... .15	.07	.01
☐ 592 David Little ..... .03	.01	.00
☐ 593 Leroy Thompson ..... .03	.01	.00
☐ 594 Eric Bieniemy ..... .12	.06	.01
☐ 595 Courtney Hall ..... .03	.01	.00
☐ 596 George Thornton ..... .03	.01	.00
☐ 597 Donnie Elder ..... .03	.01	.00
☐ 598 Billy Ray Smith ..... .03	.01	.00
☐ 599 Gill Byrd ..... .03	.01	.00
☐ 600 Marion Butts ..... .10	.05	.01
☐ 601 Ronnie Harmon ..... .03	.01	.00
☐ 602 Anthony Shelton ..... .03	.01	.00
☐ 603 Mark May ..... .03	.01	.00
☐ 604 Craig McEwen ..... .15	.07	.01
☐ 605 Steve Young ..... .10	.05	.01
☐ 606 Keith Henderson ..... .10	.05	.01
☐ 607 Pierce Holt ..... .03	.01	.00
☐ 608 Roy Foster ..... .03	.01	.00
☐ 609 Don Griffin ..... .03	.01	.00
☐ 610 Harry Sydney ..... .03	.01	.00
☐ 611 Todd Bowles ..... .03	.01	.00
☐ 612 Ted Washington ..... .03	.01	.00
☐ 613 Johnny Jackson ..... .03	.01	.00
☐ 614 Jesse Sapolu ..... .03	.01	.00
☐ 615 Brent Jones ..... .06	.03	.00
☐ 616 Travis McNeal ..... .03	.01	.00
☐ 617 Darrick Brilz ..... .03	.01	.00
☐ 618 Terry Wooden ..... .03	.01	.00
☐ 619 Tommy Kane ..... .10	.05	.01
☐ 620 Nesby Glasgow ..... .03	.01	.00
☐ 621 Dwayne Harper ..... .08	.04	.01
☐ 622 Rick Tuten ..... .03	.01	.00
☐ 623 Chris Warren ..... .06	.03	.00
☐ 624 John L. Williams ..... .06	.03	.00
☐ 625 Rufus Porter ..... .03	.01	.00
☐ 626 David Daniels ..... .03	.01	.00
☐ 627 Keith McCants ..... .06	.03	.00
☐ 628 Reuben Davis ..... .03	.01	.00
☐ 629 Mark Royals ..... .03	.01	.00
☐ 630 Marty Carter ..... .10	.05	.01
☐ 631 Ian Beckles ..... .03	.01	.00
☐ 632 Ron Hall ..... .03	.01	.00
☐ 633 Eugene Marve ..... .03	.01	.00
☐ 634 Willie Drewrey ..... .03	.01	.00
☐ 635 Tom McHale ..... .10	.05	.01
☐ 636 Kevin Murphy ..... .03	.01	.00
☐ 637 Robert Hardy ..... .15	.07	.01
☐ 638 Ricky Sanders ..... .06	.03	.00
☐ 639 Gary Clark ..... .12	.06	.01
☐ 640 Andre Collins ..... .06	.03	.00
☐ 641 Brad Edwards ..... .03	.01	.00
☐ 642 Monte Coleman ..... .03	.01	.00
☐ 643 Clarence Vaughn ..... .10	.05	.01
☐ 644 Fred Stokes ..... .03	.01	.00
☐ 645 Charles Mann ..... .06	.03	.00

☐ 646 Earnest Byner ..... .06	.03	.00
☐ 647 Jim Lachey ..... .06	.03	.00
☐ 648 Jeff Bostic ..... .03	.01	.00
☐ 649 Chris Mims ..... .15	.07	.01
☐ 650 George Williams ..... .12	.06	.01
☐ 651 Ed Cunningham ..... .10	.05	.01
☐ 652 Tony Smith ..... .25	.12	.02
☐ 653 Will Furrer ..... .15	.07	.01
☐ 654 Matt Elliott ..... .10	.05	.01
☐ 655 Mike Mooney ..... .12	.06	.01
☐ 656 Eddie Blake ..... .15	.07	.01
☐ 657 Leon Searcy ..... .15	.07	.01
☐ 658 Kevin Turner ..... .15	.07	.01
☐ 659 Keith Hamilton ..... .10	.05	.01
☐ 660 Alan Haller ..... .20	.10	.02

1992 Topps I

The first series of the 1992 Topps football set contains 330 standard-size (2 1/2" by 3 1/2") cards. Gold-foil versions of each card were also produced, and these were inserted one per foil pack. The fronts feature color action player photos while the backs carry biographical and statistical information. The cards are numbered on the back.

	MINT	EXC	G-VG
COMPLETE SET (330)	14.00	7.00	1.40
COMMON PLAYER (1-330)	.03	.01	.00
☐ 1 Tim McGee	.06	.03	.00
Atlanta Falcons			
☐ 2 Rich Camarillo	.03	.01	.00
Phoenix Cardinals			
☐ 3 Anthony Johnson	.03	.01	.00
Atlanta Falcons			
☐ 4 Larry Kelm	.03	.01	.00
Los Angeles Rams			
☐ 5 Irving Fryar	.06	.03	.00
New England Patriots			
☐ 6 Joey Browner	.06	.03	.00
Minnesota Vikings			
☐ 7 Michael Walter	.03	.01	.00
San Francisco 49ers			
☐ 8 Cortez Kennedy	.06	.03	.00
Seattle Seahawks			
☐ 9 Reyna Thompson	.03	.01	.00
New York Giants			
☐ 10 John Friesz	.15	.07	.01
San Diego Chargers			
☐ 11 Leroy Hoard	.08	.04	.01

Cleveland Browns			
☐ 12 Steve McMichael	.03	.01	.00
Chicago Bears			
☐ 13 Marvin Washington	.03	.01	.00
New York Jets			
☐ 14 Clyde Simmons	.03	.01	.00
Philadelphia Eagles			
☐ 15 Stephone Paige	.06	.03	.00
Kansas City Chiefs			
☐ 16 Mike Utley	.15	.07	.01
Detroit Lions			
☐ 17 Tunch Ilkin	.03	.01	.00
Pittsburgh Steelers			
☐ 18 Lawrence Dawsey	.12	.06	.01
Tampa Bay Buccaneers			
☐ 19 Vance Johnson	.06	.03	.00
Denver Broncos			
☐ 20 Bryce Paup	.03	.01	.00
Green Bay Packers			
☐ 21 Jeff Wright	.03	.01	.00
Buffalo Bills			
☐ 22 Gill Fenerty	.06	.03	.00
New Orleans Saints			
☐ 23 Lamar Lathon	.06	.03	.00
Houston Oilers			
☐ 24 Danny Copeland	.03	.01	.00
Washington Redskins			
☐ 25 Marcus Allen	.08	.04	.01
Los Angeles Raiders			
☐ 26 Tim Green	.03	.01	.00
Atlanta Falcons			
☐ 27 Pete Stoyanovich	.03	.01	.00
Miami Dolphins			
☐ 28 Alvin Harper	.20	.10	.02
Dallas Cowboys			
☐ 29 Roy Foster	.03	.01	.00
San Francisco 49ers			
☐ 30 Eugene Daniel	.03	.01	.00
Indianapolis Colts			
☐ 31 Luis Sharpe	.03	.01	.00
Phoenix Cardinals			
☐ 32 Terry Wooden	.03	.01	.00
Seattle Seahawks			
☐ 33 Jim Breech	.03	.01	.00
Cincinnati Bengals			
☐ 34 Randy Hilliard	.10	.05	.01
Cleveland Browns			
☐ 35 Roman Phifer	.03	.01	.00
Los Angeles Rams			
☐ 36 Erik Howard	.03	.01	.00
New York Giants			
☐ 37 Chris Singleton	.06	.03	.00
Indianapolis Colts			
☐ 38 Matt Stover	.03	.01	.00
Cleveland Browns			
☐ 39 Tim Irwin	.03	.01	.00
Minnesota Vikings			
☐ 40 Karl Mecklenburg	.06	.03	.00

Denver Broncos			
☐ 41 Joe Phillips	.03	.01	.00
San Diego Chargers			
☐ 42 Bill Jones	.12	.06	.01
Kansas City Chiefs			
☐ 43 Mark Carrier	.06	.03	.00
Chicago Bears			
☐ 44 George Jamison	.03	.01	.00
Detroit Lions			
☐ 45 Rob Taylor	.03	.01	.00
Tampa Bay Buccaneers			
☐ 46 Jeff Jaeger	.03	.01	.00
Los Angeles Raiders			
☐ 47 Don Majkowski	.08	.04	.01
Green Bay Packers			
☐ 48 Al Edwards	.03	.01	.00
Buffalo Bills			
☐ 49 Curtis Duncan	.03	.01	.00
Houston Oilers			
☐ 50 Sam Mills	.03	.01	.00
New Orleans Saints			
☐ 51 Terance Mathis	.06	.03	.00
New York Jets			
☐ 52 Brian Mitchell	.10	.05	.01
Washington Redskins			
☐ 53 Mike Pritchard	.30	.15	.03
Atlanta Falcons			
☐ 54 Calvin Williams	.06	.03	.00
Philadelphia Eagles			
☐ 55 Hardy Nickerson	.03	.01	.00
Pittsburgh Steelers			
☐ 56 Nate Newton	.03	.01	.00
Dallas Cowboys			
☐ 57 Steve Wallace	.03	.01	.00
San Francisco 49ers			
☐ 58 John Offerdahl	.06	.03	.00
Denver Broncos			
☐ 59 Aeneas Williams	.03	.01	.00
Phoenix Cardinals			
☐ 60 Lee Johnson	.03	.01	.00
San Diego Chargers			
☐ 61 Ricardo McDonald	.10	.05	.01
Cincinnati Bengals			
☐ 62 David Richards	.03	.01	.00
San Diego Chargers			
☐ 63 Paul Gruber	.03	.01	.00
Tampa Bay Buccaneers			
☐ 64 Greg McMurtry	.06	.03	.00
New England Patriots			
☐ 65 Jay Hilgenberg	.06	.03	.00
Chicago Bears			
☐ 66 Tim Grunhard	.03	.01	.00
Kansas City Chiefs			
☐ 67 Dwayne White	.08	.04	.01
New York Jets			
☐ 68 Don Beebe	.06	.03	.00
Buffalo Bills			
☐ 69 Simon Fletcher	.03	.01	.00

☐ 70	Warren Moon 20	.10	.02	
	Houston Oilers			
☐ 71	Chris Jacke 03	.01	.00	
	Green Bay Packers			
☐ 72	Steve Wisniewski 03	.01	.00	
	Los Angeles Raiders			
☐ 73	Mike Cofer 03	.01	.00	
	San Francisco 49ers			
☐ 74	Tim Johnson 03	.01	.00	
	Washington Redskins			
☐ 75	T.J. Turner 03	.01	.00	
	Miami Dolphins			
☐ 76	Scott Case 03	.01	.00	
	Atlanta Falcons			
☐ 77	Michael Jackson 12	.06	.01	
	Cleveland Browns			
☐ 78	Jon Hand 03	.01	.00	
	Indianapolis Colts			
☐ 79	Stan Brock 03	.01	.00	
	New Orleans Saints			
☐ 80	Robert Blackmon 03	.01	.00	
	Seattle Seahawks			
☐ 81	David Johnson 03	.01	.00	
	Pittsburgh Steelers			
☐ 82	Damone Johnson 03	.01	.00	
	Los Angeles Rams			
☐ 83	Marc Spindler 03	.01	.00	
	Detroit Lions			
☐ 84	Larry Brown 03	.01	.00	
	Dallas Cowboys			
☐ 85	Ray Berry 03	.01	.00	
	Minnesota Vikings			
☐ 86	Andre Waters 03	.01	.00	
	Philadelphia Eagles			
☐ 87	Carlos Huerta 10	.05	.01	
	San Diego Chargers			
☐ 88	Brad Muster 06	.03	.00	
	Chicago Bears			
☐ 89	Chuck Cecil 03	.01	.00	
	Green Bay Packers			
☐ 90	Nick Lowery 03	.01	.00	
	Kansas City Chiefs			
☐ 91	Cornelius Bennett 08	.04	.01	
	Buffalo Bills			
☐ 92	Jessie Tuggle 03	.01	.00	
	Atlanta Falcons			
☐ 93	Mark Schlereth 10	.05	.01	
	Washington Redskins			
☐ 94	Vestee Jackson 03	.01	.00	
	Chicago Bears			
☐ 95	Eric Bieniemy 12	.06	.01	
	San Diego Chargers			
☐ 96	Jeff Hostetler 15	.07	.01	
	New York Giants			
☐ 97	Ken Lanier 03	.01	.00	
	Denver Broncos			
☐ 98	Wayne Haddix 03	.01	.00	
	Atlanta Falcons			
☐ 99	Lorenzo White 03	.01	.00	
	Houston Oilers			
☐ 100	Mervyn Fernandez 06	.03	.00	
	Los Angeles Raiders			
☐ 101	Brent Williams 03	.01	.00	
	New England Patriots			
☐ 102	Ian Beckles 03	.01	.00	
	Tampa Bay Buccaneers			
☐ 103	Harris Barton 03	.01	.00	
	San Francisco 49ers			
☐ 104	Edgar Bennett 35	.17	.03	
	Green Bay Packers			
☐ 105	Mike Pitts 03	.01	.00	
	Philadelphia Eagles			
☐ 106	Fuad Reveiz 03	.01	.00	
	Minnesota Vikings			
☐ 107	Vernon Turner 03	.01	.00	
	Buffalo Bills			
☐ 108	Tracy Hayworth 10	.05	.01	
	Detroit Lions			
☐ 109	Checklist 1-110 06	.03	.00	
☐ 110	Tom Waddle 15	.07	.01	
	Chicago Bears			
☐ 111	Fred Stokes 03	.01	.00	
	Washington Redskins			
☐ 112	Howard Ballard 03	.01	.00	
	Buffalo Bills			
☐ 113	David Szott 03	.01	.00	
	Kansas City Chiefs			
☐ 114	Tim McKyer 03	.01	.00	
	Atlanta Falcons			
☐ 115	Kyle Clifton 03	.01	.00	
	New York Jets			
☐ 116	Tony Bennett 03	.01	.00	
	Green Bay Packers			
☐ 117	Joel Hilgenberg 03	.01	.00	
	New Orleans Saints			
☐ 118	Dwayne Harper 08	.04	.01	
	Seattle Seahawks			
☐ 119	Mike Baab 03	.01	.00	
	Cleveland Browns			
☐ 120	Mark Clayton 08	.04	.01	
	Miami Dolphins			
☐ 121	Eric Swann 06	.03	.00	
	Phoenix Cardinals			
☐ 122	Neil O'Donnell 40	.20	.04	
	Pittsburgh Steelers			
☐ 123	Mike Munchak 06	.03	.00	
	Houston Oilers			
☐ 124	Howie Long 06	.03	.00	
	Los Angeles Raiders			
☐ 125	John Elway 15	.07	.01	
	Denver Broncos			
☐ 126	Joe Prokop 03	.01	.00	
	New York Jets			
☐ 127	Pepper Johnson 03	.01	.00	
	New York Giants			

☐ 128 Richard Dent 06	.03	.00	☐ 157 Darren Comeaux 03	.01	.00
Chicago Bears			Seattle Seahawks		
☐ 129 Robert Porcher 20	.10	.02	☐ 158 David Williams 03	.01	.00
Detroit Lions			Houston Oilers		
☐ 130 Earnest Byner 06	.03	.00	☐ 159 Rich Gannon 06	.03	.00
Washington Redskins			Minnesota Vikings		
☐ 131 Kent Hull 03	.01	.00	☐ 160 Kevin Mack 03	.01	.00
Buffalo Bills			Cleveland Browns		
☐ 132 Mike Merriweather 03	.01	.00	☐ 161 Jim Arnold 03	.01	.00
Minnesota Vikings			Detroit Lions		
☐ 133 Scott Fulhage 03	.01	.00	☐ 162 Reggie White 08	.04	.01
Atlanta Falcons			Philadelphia Eagles		
☐ 134 Kevin Porter 03	.01	.00	☐ 163 Leonard Russell 60	.30	.06
Kansas City Chiefs			New England Patriots		
☐ 135 Tony Casillas 03	.01	.00	☐ 164 Doug Smith 03	.01	.00
Dallas Cowboys			Los Angeles Rams		
☐ 136 Dean Biasucci 03	.01	.00	☐ 165 Tony Mandarich 06	.03	.00
Indianapolis Colts			Green Bay Packers		
☐ 137 Ben Smith 03	.01	.00	☐ 166 Greg Lloyd 03	.01	.00
Philadelphia Eagles			Pittsburgh Steelers		
☐ 138 Bruce Kozerski 03	.01	.00	☐ 167 Jumbo Elliott 03	.01	.00
Cincinnati Bengals			New York Giants		
☐ 139 Jeff Campbell 03	.01	.00	☐ 168 Jonathan Hayes 03	.01	.00
Detroit Lions			Kansas City Chiefs		
☐ 140 Kevin Greene 06	.03	.00	☐ 169 Jim Ritcher 03	.01	.00
Los Angeles Rams			Buffalo Bills		
☐ 141 Gary Plummer 03	.01	.00	☐ 170 Mike Kenn 03	.01	.00
Chicago Bears			Atlanta Falcons		
☐ 142 Vincent Brown 03	.01	.00	☐ 171 James Washington 03	.01	.00
New England Patriots			Dallas Cowboys		
☐ 143 Ron Hall 03	.01	.00	☐ 172 Tim Harris 06	.03	.00
Tampa Bay Buccaneers			San Francisco 49ers		
☐ 144 Louie Aguiar 10	.05	.01	☐ 173 James Thornton 03	.01	.00
New York Jets			Chicago Bears		
☐ 145 Mark Duper 06	.03	.00	☐ 174 John Brandes 10	.05	.01
Miami Dolphins			Washington Redskins		
☐ 146 Jesse Sapolu 03	.01	.00	☐ 175 Fred McAfee 20	.10	.02
San Francisco 49ers			New Orleans Saints		
☐ 147 Jeff Gossett 03	.01	.00	☐ 176 Henry Rolling 03	.01	.00
Los Angeles Raiders			San Diego Chargers		
☐ 148 Brian Noble 03	.01	.00	☐ 177 Tony Paige 03	.01	.00
Green Bay Packers			Miami Dolphins		
☐ 149 Derek Russell 10	.05	.01	☐ 178 Jay Schroeder 08	.04	.01
Denver Broncos			Los Angeles Raiders		
☐ 150 Carlton Bailey 12	.06	.01	☐ 179 Jeff Herrod 03	.01	.00
Buffalo Bills			Indianapolis Colts		
☐ 151 Kelly Goodburn 03	.01	.00	☐ 180 Emmitt Smith 1.00	.50	.10
Washington Redskins			Dallas Cowboys		
☐ 152 Audray McMillian 03	.01	.00	☐ 181 Wymon Henderson 03	.01	.00
Minnesota Vikings			San Francisco 49ers		
☐ 153 Neal Anderson 12	.06	.01	☐ 182 Rob Moore 25	.12	.02
Chicago Bears			New York Jets		
☐ 154 Bill Maas 03	.01	.00	☐ 183 Robert Wilson 08	.04	.01
Kansas City Chiefs			Tampa Bay Buccaneers		
☐ 155 Rickey Jackson 03	.01	.00	☐ 184 Michael Zordich 10	.05	.01
Denver Broncos			Phoenix Cardinals		
☐ 156 Chris Miller 15	.07	.01	☐ 185 Jim Harbaugh 08	.04	.01
Atlanta Falcons			Chicago Bears		

☐ 186	Vince Workman 10	.05	.01	
	Green Bay Packers			
☐ 187	Ernest Givins 10	.05	.01	
	Houston Oilers			
☐ 188	Herschel Walker 12	.06	.01	
	Minnesota Vikings			
☐ 189	Dan Fike 03	.01	.00	
	Cleveland Browns			
☐ 190	Seth Joyner 06	.03	.00	
	Philadelphia Eagles			
☐ 191	Steve Young 10	.05	.01	
	San Francisco 49ers			
☐ 192	Dennis Gibson 03	.01	.00	
	Detroit Lions			
☐ 193	Darryl Talley 06	.03	.00	
	Buffalo Bills			
☐ 194	Emile Harry 03	.01	.00	
	Kansas City Chiefs			
☐ 195	Bill Fralic 06	.03	.00	
	Atlanta Falcons			
☐ 196	Michael Stewart 03	.01	.00	
	Los Angeles Rams			
☐ 197	James Francis 06	.03	.00	
	Cincinnati Bengals			
☐ 198	Jerome Henderson 03	.01	.00	
	New England Patriots			
☐ 199	John L. Williams 06	.03	.00	
	Seattle Seahawks			
☐ 200	Rod Woodson 06	.03	.00	
	Pittsburgh Steelers			
☐ 201	Mike Farr 03	.01	.00	
	Detroit Lions			
☐ 202	Greg Montgomery 03	.01	.00	
	Houston Oilers			
☐ 203	Andre Collins 03	.01	.00	
	Washington Redskins			
☐ 204	Scott Miller 03	.01	.00	
	Miami Dolphins			
☐ 205	Clay Matthews 03	.01	.00	
	Cleveland Browns			
☐ 206	Ethan Horton 06	.03	.00	
	Los Angeles Raiders			
☐ 207	Rich Miano 03	.01	.00	
	Philadelphia Eagles			
☐ 208	Chris Mims 15	.07	.01	
	San Diego Chargers			
☐ 209	Anthony Morgan 12	.06	.01	
	Chicago Bears			
☐ 210	Rodney Hampton 20	.10	.02	
	New York Giants			
☐ 211	Chris Hinton 06	.03	.00	
	Indianapolis Colts			
☐ 212	Esera Tuaolo 03	.01	.00	
	Green Bay Packers			
☐ 213	Shane Conlan 06	.03	.00	
	Buffalo Bills			
☐ 214	John Carney 03	.01	.00	
	San Diego Chargers			
☐ 215	Kenny Walker 25	.12	.02	
	Denver Broncos			
☐ 216	Scott Radecic 03	.01	.00	
	Indianapolis Colts			
☐ 217	Chris Martin 03	.01	.00	
	Kansas City Chiefs			
☐ 218	Checklist 111-220 06	.03	.00	
☐ 219	Wesley Carroll 20	.10	.02	
	New Orleans Saints			
☐ 220	Bill Romanowski 03	.01	.00	
	San Francisco 49ers			
☐ 221	Reggie Cobb 12	.06	.01	
	Tampa Bay Buccaneers			
☐ 222	Alfred Anderson 03	.01	.00	
	Minnesota Vikings			
☐ 223	Cleveland Gary 06	.03	.00	
	Los Angeles Rams			
☐ 224	Eddie Blake 15	.07	.01	
	Miami Dolphins			
☐ 225	Chris Spielman 06	.03	.00	
	Detroit Lions			
☐ 226	John Roper 03	.01	.00	
	Chicago Bears			
☐ 227	George Thomas 12	.06	.01	
	Atlanta Falcons			
☐ 228	Jeff Faulkner 03	.01	.00	
	Phoenix Cardinals			
☐ 229	Chip Lohmiller 03	.01	.00	
	Washington Redskins			
☐ 230	Hugh Millen 40	.20	.04	
	New England Patriots			
☐ 231	Ray Horton 03	.01	.00	
	Dallas Cowboys			
☐ 232	James Campen 03	.01	.00	
	Green Bay Packers			
☐ 233	Howard Cross 03	.01	.00	
	New York Giants			
☐ 234	Keith McKeller 06	.03	.00	
	Buffalo Bills			
☐ 235	Dino Hackett 03	.01	.00	
	Kansas City Chiefs			
☐ 236	Jerome Brown 03	.01	.00	
	Philadelphia Eagles			
☐ 237	Andy Heck 03	.01	.00	
	Seattle Seahawks			
☐ 238	Rodney Holman 03	.01	.00	
	Cincinnati Bengals			
☐ 239	Bruce Matthews 03	.01	.00	
	Houston Oilers			
☐ 240	Jeff Lageman 03	.01	.00	
	New York Jets			
☐ 241	Bobby Hebert 08	.04	.01	
	New Orleans Saints			
☐ 242	Gary Anderson 03	.01	.00	
	Pittsburgh Steelers			
☐ 243	Mark Bortz 03	.01	.00	
	Chicago Bears			
☐ 244	Rich Moran 03	.01	.00	

Green Bay Packers				New York Jets			
☐ 245 Jeff Uhlenhake	.03	.01	.00	☐ 274 Roger Ruzek	.03	.01	.00
Miami Dolphins				Philadelphia Eagles			
☐ 246 Ricky Sanders	.06	.03	.00	☐ 275 Steve Smith	.03	.01	.00
Washington Redskins				Los Angeles Raiders			
☐ 247 Clarence Kay	.03	.01	.00	☐ 276 Bo Orlando	.20	.10	.02
Denver Broncos				Houston Oilers			
☐ 248 Ed King	.03	.01	.00	☐ 277 Louis Oliver	.03	.01	.00
Cleveland Browns				Miami Dolphins			
☐ 249 Eddie Anderson	.03	.01	.00	☐ 278 Toi Cook	.03	.01	.00
Los Angeles Raiders				New Orleans Saints			
☐ 250 Amp Lee	.35	.17	.03	☐ 279 Eddie Brown	.06	.03	.00
San Francisco 49ers				Cincinnati Bengals			
☐ 251 Norm Johnson	.03	.01	.00	☐ 280 Keith McCants	.06	.03	.00
Atlanta Falcons				Tampa Bay Buccaneers			
☐ 252 Michael Carter	.03	.01	.00	☐ 281 Rob Burnett	.03	.01	.00
San Francisco 49ers				Cleveland Browns			
☐ 253 Felix Wright	.03	.01	.00	☐ 282 Keith DeLong	.03	.01	.00
Minnesota Vikings				San Francisco 49ers			
☐ 254 Leon Seals	.03	.01	.00	☐ 283 Stan Thomas	.03	.01	.00
Buffalo Bills				Chicago Bears			
☐ 255 Nate Lewis	.03	.01	.00	☐ 284 Robert Brown	.03	.01	.00
San Diego Chargers				Green Bay Packers			
☐ 256 Kevin Call	.03	.01	.00	☐ 285 John Alt	.03	.01	.00
Indianapolis Colts				Kansas City Chiefs			
☐ 257 Darryl Henley	.06	.03	.00	☐ 286 Randy Dixon	.03	.01	.00
Los Angeles Rams				Indianapolis Colts			
☐ 258 Jon Vaughn	.30	.15	.03	☐ 287 Siran Stacy	.35	.17	.03
New England Patriots				Philadelphia Eagles			
☐ 259 Matt Bahr	.03	.01	.00	☐ 288 Ray Agnew	.03	.01	.00
New York Giants				New England Patriots			
☐ 260 Johnny Johnson	.15	.07	.01	☐ 289 Darion Conner	.06	.03	.00
Phoenix Cardinals				Atlanta Falcons			
☐ 261 Ken Norton	.03	.01	.00	☐ 290 Kirk Lowdermilk	.03	.01	.00
Dallas Cowboys				Minnesota Vikings			
☐ 262 Wendell Davis	.12	.06	.01	☐ 291 Greg Jackson	.03	.01	.00
Chicago Bears				New York Giants			
☐ 263 Eugene Robinson	.03	.01	.00	☐ 292 Ken Harvey	.03	.01	.00
Seattle Seahawks				Phoenix Cardinals			
☐ 264 David Treadwell	.03	.01	.00	☐ 293 Jacob Green	.03	.01	.00
Denver Broncos				Seattle Seahawks			
☐ 265 Michael Haynes	.20	.10	.02	☐ 294 Mark Tuinei	.03	.01	.00
Atlanta Falcons				Dallas Cowboys			
☐ 266 Robb Thomas	.06	.03	.00	☐ 295 Mark Rypien	.20	.10	.02
Kansas City Chiefs				Washington Redskins			
☐ 267 Nate Odomes	.03	.01	.00	☐ 296 Gerald Robinson	.08	.04	.01
Buffalo Bills				Los Angeles Rams			
☐ 268 Martin Mayhew	.03	.01	.00	☐ 297 Broderick Thompson	.03	.01	.00
Washington Redskins				San Diego Chargers			
☐ 269 Perry Kemp	.03	.01	.00	☐ 298 Doug Widell	.03	.01	.00
Green Bay Packers				Denver Broncos			
☐ 270 Jerry Ball	.03	.01	.00	☐ 299 Carwell Gardner	.03	.01	.00
Detroit Lions				Buffalo Bills			
☐ 271 Tommy Vardell	.60	.30	.06	☐ 300 Barry Sanders	.75	.35	.07
Cleveland Browns				Detroit Lions			
☐ 272 Ernie Mills	.08	.04	.01	☐ 301 Eric Metcalf	.06	.03	.00
Pittsburgh Steelers				Cleveland Browns			
☐ 273 Mo Lewis	.06	.03	.00	☐ 302 Eric Thomas	.03	.01	.00

	Cleveland Browns			
☐ 303	Terrell Buckley	.75	.35	.07
	Green Bay Packers			
☐ 304	Byron Evans	.03	.01	.00
	Philadelphia Eagles			
☐ 305	Johnny Hector	.03	.01	.00
	New York Jets			
☐ 306	Steve Broussard	.10	.05	.01
	Atlanta Falcons			
☐ 307	Gene Atkins	.03	.01	.00
	New Orleans Saints			
☐ 308	Terry McDaniel	.03	.01	.00
	Los Angeles Raiders			
☐ 309	Charles McRae	.03	.01	.00
	Tampa Bay Buccaneers			
☐ 310	Jim Lachey	.06	.03	.00
	Washington Redskins			
☐ 311	Pat Harlow	.06	.03	.00
	New England Patriots			
☐ 312	Kevin Butler	.03	.01	.00
	Chicago Bears			
☐ 313	Scott Stephen	.03	.01	.00
	Green Bay Packers			
☐ 314	Dermontti Dawson	.03	.01	.00
	Pittsburgh Steelers			
☐ 315	Johnny Meads	.03	.01	.00
	Houston Oilers			
☐ 316	Checklist 221-330	.06	.03	.00
☐ 317	Aaron Craver	.06	.03	.00
	Miami Dolphins			
☐ 318	Michael Brooks	.03	.01	.00
	Denver Broncos			
☐ 319	Guy McIntyre	.03	.01	.00
	San Francisco 49ers			
☐ 320	Thurman Thomas	.40	.20	.04
	Buffalo Bills			
☐ 321	Courtney Hall	.03	.01	.00
	San Diego Chargers			
☐ 322	Dan Saleaumua	.03	.01	.00
	Kansas City Chiefs			
☐ 323	Vinson Smith	.10	.05	.01
	Dallas Cowboys			
☐ 324	Steve Jordan	.06	.03	.00
	Minnesota Vikings			
☐ 325	Walter Reeves	.03	.01	.00
	Phoenix Cardinals			
☐ 326	Erik Kramer	.40	.20	.04
	Detroit Lions			
☐ 327	Duane Bickett	.03	.01	.00
	Indianapolis Colts			
☐ 328	Tom Newberry	.03	.01	.00
	Los Angeles Rams			
☐ 329	John Kasay	.03	.01	.00
	Seattle Seahawks			
☐ 330	Dave Meggett	.08	.04	.01
	New York Giants